DEVELOPMENTAL PSYCHOLOGY

THEORY, RESEARCH, AND APPLICATIONS

BROOKS/COLE PUBLISHING COMPANY
MONTEREY, CALIFORNIA

DEVELOPMENTAL PSYCHOLOGY

THEORY, RESEARCH, AND APPLICATIONS

DAVID R. SHAFFER ∎

UNIVERSITY OF GEORGIA

Brooks/Cole Publishing Company
A Division of Wadsworth, Inc.

Printed in the United States of America
10 9 8 7 6 5 4 3

Library of Congress Cataloging in Publication Data

Shaffer, David R.
   Developmental psychology

   Bibliography: p.
   Includes index.
   1. Child psychology. I. Title.
BF721.S4688   1985   155.4   84-12658
ISBN 0-534-02756-3

Sponsoring Editor: *C. Deborah Laughton*
Editorial Assistant: *Mary Tudor*
Project Development Editor: *John Bergez*
Production Coordinator: *Fiorella Ljunggren*
Manuscript Editor: *Rephah Berg*
Permissions Editor: *Carline Haga*
Interior and Cover Design: *Katherine Minerva*
Cover Art: Maypole, Central Park, *by William Glackens.*
   Permission of the Fine Arts Museum of San Francisco,
   Gift of the Charles E. Merrill Trust with matching
   funds from The de Young Museum Society.
Art Coordinator: *Judith Macdonald*
Interior Illustrations: *Wayne Clark and Cyndie Clark-Heugel*
Cartoons: *Ryan Cooper*
Photo Editor: *Judy K. Blamer*
Photo Researcher: *Judith Mason*
Typesetting: *Jonathan Peck Typographers, Ltd.,*
   Santa Cruz, California
Cover Printing: *Phoenix Color Corporation,*
   Long Island City, New York
Printing and Binding: *R. R. Donnelley & Sons Company,*
   Crawfordsville, Indiana
Photographs by Frank Keillor were created for this book.
(Credits continue on p. C1 following Subject Index)

PREFACE

My purpose in writing this book has been to produce a current and comprehensive overview of developmental psychology that reflects the best theories, research, and practical advice that developmentalists have to offer. Throughout my 12 years of teaching, I have longed for a substantive introductory text that is also interesting, accurate, up to date, and written in clear, concise language that an introductory student can easily understand. At this level, a good text should talk "to" rather than "at" its readers, anticipating their interests, questions, and concerns and treating them as active participants in the learning process. In the field of developmental psychology, a good text should also stress the processes that underlie developmental change, so that students come away from the course with a firm understanding of the causes and complexities of human development. Last but not least, a good text is a relevant text—one that shows how the theory and research that students are asked to digest can be applied to a number of real-life settings. The present volume represents my attempt to accomplish all of these objectives.

Although this book is a rigorous and research-oriented portrayal of developmental psychology, the word *applications* in the title is not a misnomer. Throughout the text, I have illustrated how information gleaned from theory and basic research has helped us to understand and, in many cases, to solve a variety of real-life problems. For example, the laws of genetics are discussed in terms of both their broad implications for human development and their contributions to the treatment and prevention of hereditary disorders. I've shown how basic research on observational-learning processes has furthered our understanding of personality development, while also suggesting a number of very useful strategies for treating phobic reactions, reducing racial and ethnic prejudices, and promoting children's intellectual development. Theory and research on parent/infant attachment are discussed in terms of their relevance to emotional development as well

as of their implications for the structuring of orphanages, nursery schools, and day-care centers. Many other contemporary issues and practices such as home birthing, maternal employment, mainstreaming, compensatory education, grade retention, single parenting, stepparenting, and child abuse are examined from both a theoretical and a practical perspective. In summary, I have tried to write a book that is both rigorous and applied, one that challenges students to think about the fascinating process of human development, to share in the excitement of our young and dynamic discipline, and to acquire a knowledge of developmental principles that will serve them well in their roles as parents, teachers, nurses, day-care workers, pediatricians, psychologists, or in any other capacity by which they may one day influence the lives of developing persons.

Philosophy

Certain philosophical views are inherent in any systematic treatment of a field as broad as developmental psychology. My philosophy can be summarized as follows:

• *I believe in theoretical eclecticism.* This book will not attempt to convince its readers that any one theoretical viewpoint is "best." The psychoanalytic, behavioristic, cognitive-developmental, and ethological viewpoints (as well as several less-encompassing theories that address selected aspects of development) are all treated with respect.

• *The best information about human development comes from systematic research.* To teach this course effectively, I believe that one must convince students of the value of theory and systematic research. Although there are many ways to achieve these objectives, I have chosen to contrast modern developmental psychology with its "prescientific" origins and then to discuss and illustrate the many methodological approaches that researchers use to test their theories and answer important questions about developing children and adolescents. I've taken care to explain why there is no one "best method" for studying human development, and I've repeatedly stressed that our most reliable findings are those that can be replicated using a variety of methods.

• *I favor a strong process orientation.* A major complaint with many developmental texts (including some best sellers) is that they describe human development without explaining why it occurs. My own process orientation is based on the belief that students are more likely to remember what develops and when if they know and understand the reasons that these developments take place.

• *Human development is a holistic process.* Although individual researchers may concentrate on particular topics such as physical development, cognitive development, or the development of moral reasoning, development is not piecemeal but *holistic:* human beings are at once physical, cognitive, and social creatures, and each of these components of "self" depends, in part, on the changes that are taking place in other areas of development. This holistic perspective is a central theme of modern developmental psychology—and one that is emphasized throughout the text.

• *A developmental psychology text should be a resource book for students—one that reflects current knowledge.* I have chosen to cite a fair number of very recent studies and reviews to ensure that my coverage (and any outside reading that students may undertake) will represent our current understanding of a topic or topics. However, I have tried to avoid the tendency, common in textbooks, to ignore older research simply because it is older. In fact, many of the "classics" of developmental psychology are prominently displayed throughout the text to illustrate important breakthroughs and to show how our knowledge about developing persons gradually builds on these earlier findings and insights.

Organization and Content

There are two traditional ways of presenting human development. In the *chronological*, or "ages and stages," approach, the coverage begins at conception and proceeds through the life cycle, using ages or chronological periods as the organizing principle. By contrast, the topical approach is organized around areas of development and follows each from its origins to its most mature forms. Each of these presentations has its advantages and disadvantages. On the one hand, a chronological focus highlights the holistic character of development but may obscure the links between early and later events within each developmental domain. On the other hand, a topical approach highlights developmental sequences and processes but at the risk of failing to convey that development is a holistic enterprise.

I've chosen to organize this book topically to focus intently on developmental processes and to provide the student with an uninterrupted view of the sequences of change that children experience within each developmental domain. At the same time, I consider it essential to paint a holistic portrait of the developing person. To accomplish this objective, I've stressed the fundamental interplay among biological, cognitive, social, and ecological influences in my coverage of *each and every facet of development.* So even though this text is topically organized, students will not lose sight of the whole person and the holistic character of human development.

Content. The book is divided into five major parts, each of which is introduced by a brief opener. Part One presents an orientation to the discipline and the tools of the trade, including a thorough discussion and illustration of research methodologies (Chapter One) and a succinct review of psychoanalytic, behavioristic, cognitive-developmental, and ethological theories of development (Chapter Two). An important feature of this coverage is my analysis of the contributions and the limitations of each research method and each of the major developmental theories.

Parts Two through Five focus on the major themes, processes, and products of development, including Biological Foundations of Development (Part Two), Language, Learning, and Cognitive Development (Part Three), Social and Personality Development (Part Four), and The Ecology of Human Development (Part Five). A few of the highlights that distinguish my coverage from that found in other texts are:

• A contemporary treatment of theory and research in behavior genetics in Chapter Three.
• A thorough consideration of social and environmental influences on physical development in Chapter Five.

- An entire chapter (Chapter Six) on perceptual development that traces the growth of perceptual abilities *throughout childhood and early adolescence* and discusses the many social and ecological influences on this important cognitive process.
- A truly developmental perspective on learning in Chapter Seven.
- Piaget's theory of language acquisition in Chapter Eight.
- An even-handed critique of both the Piagetian and the information-processing approaches to cognitive development in Chapter Nine.
- An updated analysis and evaluation of compensatory education in Chapter Ten.
- A new look at parent/infant bonding in Chapter Eleven.
- Extensive coverage of the development of self-knowledge and its relation to social cognition and personality development in Chapter Twelve.
- A contemporary view of psychological androgyny in Chapter Thirteen.
- A thorough coverage of moral development in Chapter Fourteen that includes Gilligan's theory of sex differences in moral reasoning and an in-depth analysis of the development of patience and self-control.
- Treatment of the family as a *social system* in Chapter Fifteen, including father and sibling influences as well as the impact of ecological variables (for example, subculture and neighborhood) and important events such as divorce and remarriage.
- A current assessment of the developmental implications of schooling, covering practices such as ability grouping, peer tutoring, and grade retention in Chapter Sixteen.
- Consistent attention to cross-cultural research. Not only do students enjoy learning about the development of people in other cultures, but the cross-cultural literature also helps them to see how human beings can be so much alike and, at the same time, so different from one another.
- Discussions throughout the text, at the most relevant junctures, of the various abnormalities and behavior problems in order to illustrate the relations between normal and atypical patterns of development.

In my experience, such a presentation leads to less "stigmatizing" of those individuals who are in some way atypical, without compromising the amount of material that one can present on the causes, consequences, and treatment of developmental problems and disorders.

Writing Style

My goal has been to write a book that talks directly to its readers and treats them as active participants in an ongoing discussion. I have tried to be relatively informal and down to earth in my writing style and to rely heavily on questions, thought problems, and a number of other exercises to stimulate student interest and involvement. Most of the chapters were "pretested" on my own students, who red-penciled whatever wasn't clear to them and suggested several of the concrete examples, analogies, and occasional anecdotes that I've used when introducing and explaining complex ideas. So, with the valuable assistance of my student-critics, I have attempted to prepare a manuscript that is substantive and challenging but that reads more like a story than like an encyclopedia.

Special Features

Among the features I've included to make the book more interesting and the material easier to learn are the following:

- *Boxes.* Each chapter contains a number of boxes, done in a second color, that call attention to important issues, ideas, or applications. The aim of these boxes is to permit a closer and more personal examination of selected topics while stimulating the reader to think about the questions, controversies, practices, and policies under scrutiny. Some of the boxes address methodological issues (e.g., research ethics), whereas others focus on theoretical and empirical controversies (e.g., Can apes acquire language?), practical concerns (e.g., fathers as custodial parents), applications (e.g., improving children's social skills), and policy decisions (e.g., mainstreaming). All the boxes were carefully selected to reinforce central themes in the text.
- *Outlines and chapter summaries.* Outlines at the beginning of each chapter provide the student with a preview of what will be covered. Each chapter concludes with a succinct sum-

mary that allows the student to quickly review the chapter's major points.

- **Subtitles.** Subtitles are employed *very* frequently to keep the material well organized and to divide the coverage into manageable bites.
- **Vocabulary.** Key terms appear in boldface type to alert the student that these are important concepts to learn.
- **Running glossary.** At the bottom of each right-hand page a running glossary provides on-the-spot definitions for boldface vocabulary items as they appear in the text for the first time (and occasionally a second time if a term reappears in a later chapter and is critical at that point). These glossary items are boxed and done in a second color to command attention.
- **Glossary indexing.** Page references for running-glossary items appear at the end of the book in the subject index. So if students forget a definition, they don't have to search frantically for the page where it originally appeared.
- **Italics.** Italics are used liberally throughout the text to emphasize important points.
- **Illustrations.** Photographs, tables, and figures are used extensively. Although these features are designed, in part, to provide visual relief and to maintain student interest, they are not merely decorations. All visual aids, including the occasional cartoons, were selected to illustrate important principles and outcomes and thereby enhance the educational goals of the text.

Supplementary Aids

■ Instructor's Resource Manual
For the instructor, there is a comprehensive *Instructor's Resource Manual* that represents far more than a rehash of the text. The manual contains new ideas for lectures, research highlights, questions for class discussion and/or essay exams, suggestions for research projects, and a list of films suitable for class use.

■ Test-item bank and testing file
An extensive testing file is available to all instructors who adopt *Developmental Psychology*. The test file for each chapter consists of two different sets of multiple-choice items, five to ten short-answer questions, three to five essay questions, and answers for *all* test items. For those instruc-

tors with access to microcomputers, the test file is also available on floppy disk with some special features that the Brooks/Cole sales representative will describe to the instructor in detail.

■ Student Study Guide
A very thorough study guide is also available to help students master the information in the text. The study materials for each chapter include a detailed summary that highlights all important principles and concepts, a programmed Personalized System of Instruction (PSI) review, a preliminary multiple-choice self-test emphasizing concepts, a research digest and drill, and a comprehensive multiple-choice self-test covering concepts, theory, research, and applications. In addition to these more traditional review materials, there are also a number of probing "applications" exercises and conceptual vignettes that challenge students to think about and to apply what they have learned. This study guide should be a particularly helpful learning aid for the students, and I urge the instructor to take a good look at it.

Acknowledgments

So many individuals have assisted me with the planning and production of this text that I could never adequately thank them all. I am especially grateful to my wife, Garnett, who not only tolerated the presence of a cranky author for the first two and a half years of our marriage, while she was completing her doctoral degree, but also contributed substantially to the project by co-authoring Chapter Ten. Without her support and encouragement, this book could not be.

Ignatius J. Toner of the University of North Carolina at Charlotte is more responsible for the appearance of this volume than he realizes. Not only did this trusted friend and colleague convince me that I could produce a developmental text, but he and his wife, Fiona Ritchie, then helped me along by writing a very fine first draft of Chapter Fourteen.

Several other people have prepared helpful materials for use both within and outside the text. I wish to thank Don Baucum of the University of Alabama, who wrote an excellent study guide; Rob Woodson of the University of Texas, who compiled the Test File; Dana Birnbaum of the

University of Maine, who prepared an innovative instructor's manual; Wayne Clark and Cyndie Clark-Heugel, who illustrated the book; Judy Mason, who diligently searched for and found photographs that capture the essence of development; and Frank Keillor, who took most of the part- and chapter-opening photographs.

The quality of any developmental text depends to a large extent on the quality of the pre-publication reviews from developmentalists around the country. Many of my colleagues have influenced this book by contributing detailed and constructive criticisms, as well as useful suggestions, references, and a lot of encouragement. Each of these experts has helped to make the final product a better one, and I thank them all: Martin Banks, University of Texas; Don Baucum, University of Alabama; Jay Belsky, Pennsylvania State University; Keith Berg, University of Florida; Marvin Berkowitz, Marquette University; Dana Birnbaum, University of Maine at Orono; Kathryn Black, Purdue University; Robert Bohlander, Wilkes College; Cathryn Booth, University of Washington; Yvonne Brackbill, University of Florida; Cheryl Bradley, Central Virginia Community College; John Condry, Cornell University; David Crowell, University of Hawaii; Connie Hamm Duncanson, Northern Michigan University; Mary Ellen Durrett, University of Texas at Austin; Beverly Eubank, Lansing Community College; Beverly Fagot, University of Oregon; Larry Fenson, San Diego State University; Harold Goldsmith, University of Texas at Austin; Charles Halverson, University of Georgia; Lillian Hix, Houston Community College; Patricia Leonhard, University of Illinois at Champaign-Urbana; Frank Laycock, Oberlin College; Mark Lepper, Stanford University; John Ludeman, Stephens College; Phil Mohan, University of Idaho; Robert Plomin, University of Colorado; Judith Powell, University of Wyoming; Daniel Richards, Houston Community College; Peter Scharf, University of Seattle; and Rob Woodson, University of Texas at Austin.

I am also indebted to my friend and colleague William G. Graziano, who critiqued Chapters One through Four, and to the many students who so generously volunteered to read and comment on various portions of the manuscript. Their collective contribution to the book's readability has been substantial.

Special thanks go to Geraldine Moon, who coordinated the efforts of the project's clerical staff, and to Anita Barron, Melanie Colegrove, and Kay Moore, who never ceased to amaze me with their ability to transform my microscopic scrawl into polished manuscript. It is difficult to express in words just how much their contributions have meant to me.

Finally, I cannot say enough about the people from Brooks/Cole, a staff dedicated to producing excellent textbooks. John Bergez provided a line-by-line review of the entire manuscript, offering many useful suggestions for tightening the presentation without deleting information. As the project neared completion and was ready to become a book, Fiorella Ljunggren took charge, imposing impossible deadlines along with the support and encouragement required to meet them. The copy editing of Rephah Berg was exceptional; her command of the English language and attention to detail added immeasurably to the quality of the book. Carline Haga has been very helpful in securing permissions, and the art department has devoted countless hours to the project. I am grateful to all of them, especially Senior Designer Katherine Minerva, Photo Editor Judy Blamer, and Art Coordinator Judy Macdonald.

Last, but certainly not least, I owe an especially important debt of gratitude to C. Deborah Laughton, my project editor (and major link with the outside world), who persuaded me to sign with Brooks/Cole, and was there throughout the project to answer questions, offer suggestions, solve problems, and gently prod this recalcitrant author to keep working during important historical events (such as the World Series). C. Deborah's advice and counsel were simply invaluable, although she never could convince me that I'd easily make impending deadlines if only I'd stop being stubborn and begin to write with both hands.

David R. Shaffer

BRIEF CONTENTS

PART ONE   AN OVERVIEW OF DEVELOPMENTAL PSYCHOLOGY 2

Chapter One   Introduction 4

Chapter Two   Theories of Human Development 38

PART TWO   BIOLOGICAL FOUNDATIONS OF DEVELOPMENT 72

Chapter Three   Hereditary Influences on Human Development 74

Chapter Four   Prenatal Development and Birth 116

Chapter Five   The Physical Child: Sensory Capabilities, Motor Development, and Growth 156

PART THREE   LANGUAGE, LEARNING, AND COGNITIVE DEVELOPMENT 200

Chapter Six   Perceptual Development 202

Chapter Seven   Learning and Development 242

Chapter Eight   Development of Language and Communication Skills 284

Chapter Nine   Cognitive Development 332

Chapter Ten   Intelligence: Measuring Mental Performance 380

PART FOUR   SOCIAL AND PERSONALITY DEVELOPMENT 422

Chapter Eleven   Attachment: The Development of Intimate Relationships 424

Chapter Twelve   The Self and Social Development 466

Chapter Thirteen   Sex Differences and Sex-Role Development 514

Chapter Fourteen   Moral Development and Self-Control 554

PART FIVE   THE ECOLOGY OF DEVELOPMENT 598

Chapter Fifteen   The Family 600

Chapter Sixteen   Beyond the Home Setting: Extrafamilial Influences 644

CONTENTS

PART ONE   AN OVERVIEW OF DEVELOPMENTAL PSYCHOLOGY   2

CHAPTER ONE   INTRODUCTION   4

THE CONCEPT OF DEVELOPMENT   6

Human Development as a Continual and Cumulative Process   6

Human Development as a Holistic Process   7

A Brief Overview of the Text   8

HUMAN DEVELOPMENT IN HISTORICAL PERSPECTIVE   9

Childhood in Premodern Times   9

BOX 1-1   A PROPOSED BILL OF RIGHTS FOR CHILDREN   10

Origins of Modern-Day Views on Childhood   10

Emergence of a Psychology of Childhood   13

RESEARCH METHODS IN DEVELOPMENTAL PSYCHOLOGY   14

The Scientific Method   14

Applying the Scientific Method to the Study of Children and Adolescents   15

BOX 1-2   CONVERGING EVIDENCE FOR THE ADAGE "PRACTICE WHAT YOU PREACH"   16

BOX 1-3   THE DIFFERENCE BETWEEN CORRELATION AND CAUSATION   24

Designing Research to Measure Developmental Change   26

The Cross-Cultural Comparison   31

ETHICAL CONSIDERATIONS IN DEVELOPMENTAL RESEARCH   32

BOX 1-4   TO PROCEED OR NOT TO PROCEED—THAT IS THE QUESTION   34

SUMMARY   36

CHAPTER TWO   THEORIES OF HUMAN DEVELOPMENT   38

QUESTIONS AND CONTROVERSIES ABOUT HUMAN DEVELOPMENT   40

THE PSYCHOANALYTIC VIEWPOINT   42

BOX 2-1   MATCH WITS WITH THE THEORISTS   43

Overview of Freud's Psychoanalytic Theory   44

BOX 2-2   EARLY EXPERIENCES MAY AFFECT THE ADULT PERSONALITY   48

Erik Erikson's Theory of Psychosocial Development   50

Psychoanalytic Theory Today   52

THE LEARNING VIEWPOINT (BEHAVIORISM)   53

What Is Learning?   54

Theories of Social Learning   56

Social Learning as a Reciprocal Process   59

Contributions and Criticisms of Learning Theory   60

THE COGNITIVE-DEVELOPMENTAL VIEWPOINT   60

Origins of Piaget's Cognitive Theory   61

Piaget's View of Intelligence   62

Stages of Cognitive Development   64

Piaget on Social Learning   64

Contributions and Criticisms of the Cognitive-Developmental Viewpoint   65

BOX 2-3   CHARACTERISTICS OF CHILDREN'S RULE-BOUND PLAY: CONCRETE OPERATIONS IMPLY CONCRETE INTERPRETATIONS   66

THE ETHOLOGICAL VIEWPOINT 67

Contributions of the Ethological
Viewpoint 68

Criticisms of Ethology 68

BOX 2-4 IS ALTRUISM PART OF HUMAN
NATURE? 69

A FINAL COMMENT ON DEVELOPMENTAL
THEORIES 70

SUMMARY 70

PART TWO BIOLOGICAL
FOUNDATIONS OF HUMAN
DEVELOPMENT 72

CHAPTER THREE HEREDITARY
INFLUENCES ON HUMAN
DEVELOPMENT 74

HEREDITY IN HISTORICAL
PERSPECTIVE 75

The Doctrine of Preformationism 76

Modern Genetic Theories 76

PRINCIPLES OF HEREDITARY
TRANSMISSION 78

Conception 78

Growth of the Zygote and Production of Body
Cells 79

Germ Cells and Hereditary Transmission 80

BOX 3-1 TWINNING, SIBSHIP, AND OTHER
KINSHIP RELATIONS 82

Patterns of Genetic Expression 84

BOX 3-2 EXAMPLES OF DOMINANT AND
RECESSIVE TRAITS IN HUMAN HEREDITY 86

CHROMOSOMAL AND GENETIC
ABNORMALITIES 89

Chromosomal Abnormalities 89

Genetic Abnormalities 93

BOX 3-3 THE GENETIC BASIS FOR LAWS
PROHIBITING MARRIAGES BETWEEN CLOSE
RELATIVES 96

HEREDITARY INFLUENCES ON ABILITY,
PERSONALITY, AND BEHAVIOR 98

Methods of Assessing Hereditary
Influences 99

BOX 3-4 CORRELATIONS, CORRELATION
COEFFICIENTS, AND ESTIMATES OF
HERITABILITY 100

Hereditary Contributions to Intelligence 101

Hereditary Contributions to Temperament and
Personality 104

BOX 3-5 IMPORTANCE OF NONSHARED
ENVIRONMENTAL INFLUENCES IN PERSONALITY
DEVELOPMENT 106

Hereditary Contributions to Mental
Illness 108

ANOTHER LOOK AT THE NATURE/
NURTURE CONTROVERSY 109

The Rubber-Band Hypothesis 109

BOX 3-6 ENVIRONMENTAL TRIGGERS FOR
HERITABLE DISORDERS 110

Canalization 111

Can We Create Optimal Environments? 111

SUMMARY 112

CHAPTER FOUR PRENATAL
DEVELOPMENT AND BIRTH 116

FROM CONCEPTION TO BIRTH 118

The Germinal Period 118

The Period of the Embryo 119

The Period of the Fetus 122

ENVIRONMENTAL INFLUENCES ON
PRENATAL DEVELOPMENT 125

Maternal Characteristics 125

Nutrition 127

BOX 4-1   THE EFFECTS OF FAMINE ON INFANT MORTALITY AND INTELLECTUAL DEVELOPMENT   128

Teratogens   129

BOX 4-2   HOW TO PREVENT BIRTH DEFECTS: A CHECKLIST FOR PROSPECTIVE PARENTS   140

On the Prevention of Birth Defects   141

THE BIRTH PROCESS   141

The Normal Birth   141

Complications of Birth   145

BOX 4-3   MEDICAL PROCEDURES THAT HELP TO UNCOMPLICATE THE COMPLICATED BIRTH   146

Complications of Low Birth Weight   148

Postmaturity   150

Should You Have Your Baby at Home?   150

SUMMARY   152

CHAPTER FIVE   THE PHYSICAL CHILD: SENSORY CAPABILITIES, MOTOR DEVELOPMENT, AND GROWTH   156

THE NEONATE   157

BOX 5-1   SOME BASIC QUESTIONS ABOUT PHYSICAL GROWTH AND DEVELOPMENT   158

Is My Baby Normal?   158

BOX 5-2   BRAZELTON TRAINING: EFFECTS ON PARENTS AND INFANTS   160

Capabilities of the Newborn Infant   160

Living with an Infant   165

MATURATION AND GROWTH   170

Changes in Height and Weight   170

Changes in Body Proportions   171

Skeletal Development   172

Muscular Development   172

Development of the Brain and Nervous System   173

MOTOR DEVELOPMENT   176

Basic Trends in Locomotor Development   176

Other Motor Milestones   176

Beyond Infancy—Motor Development in Childhood   178

PUBERTY—THE PHYSICAL TRANSITION FROM CHILD TO ADULT   179

The Adolescent Growth Spurt   180

Sexual Maturation   181

Psychological Impact of Adolescent Growth and Development   184

BOX 5-3   ON FEELING OBESE AT 60 POUNDS— ANOREXIA NERVOSA   184

CAUSES AND CORRELATES OF PHYSICAL GROWTH AND DEVELOPMENT   187

Biological Mechanisms   187

Environmental Influences   189

BOX 5-4   WHO BECOMES OBESE—AND WHY?   192

SUMMARY   195

PART THREE   LANGUAGE, LEARNING, AND COGNITIVE DEVELOPMENT   200

CHAPTER SIX   PERCEPTUAL DEVELOPMENT   202

THE NATIVIST/EMPIRICIST CONTROVERSY   204

VISUAL PERCEPTION IN INFANCY   204

Pattern Perception   204

Perception of Faces   207

BOX 6-1   VISUAL SCANNING IN NEONATES AND OLDER INFANTS   208

BOX 6-2   DO YOUNG INFANTS REALLY PERCEIVE "FORMS"?   209

Spatial Perception   210

AUDITORY PERCEPTION IN INFANCY   214

Voice Recognition   214

Reactions to Speech and Language   214

The Sound of Music   215

INTERSENSORY PERCEPTION   215

Theories of Intersensory Integration   216

Research on Intersensory Perception   217

Another Look at the Enrichment/
Differentiation Controversy   220

Sensory Dominance   220

**PERCEPTUAL LEARNING AND
DEVELOPMENT IN CHILDHOOD   221**

Development of Attention   221

Development of Form Perception   224

BOX 6-3   HOW DO WE LEARN TO READ?   228

**ENVIRONMENTAL INFLUENCES ON
PERCEPTION   229**

What Kinds of Experiences Are
Important?   230

Social and Cultural Influences   233

*BOX 6-4   SOCIOCULTURAL INFLUENCES ON
PICTURE PERCEPTION   236*

**WHAT IS PERCEPTUAL
DEVELOPMENT?   237**

SUMMARY   238

*CHAPTER SEVEN   LEARNING AND
DEVELOPMENT   242*

WHAT IS LEARNING?   243

**HABITUATION AND MERE EXPOSURE
EFFECTS   244**

Developmental Trends   244

Mere Exposure and the Development of
Positive Attitudes   244

CLASSICAL CONDITIONING   244

The Classical Conditioning of Emotions and
Attitudes   246

Can Neonates Be Classically
Conditioned?   247

**OPERANT (INSTRUMENTAL)
CONDITIONING   247**

*BOX 7-1   CLASSICAL CONDITIONING AS
THERAPEUTIC TECHNIQUE   248*

Reinforcement and Punishment   249

*BOX 7-2   DISTINCTIONS AMONG POSITIVE
REINFORCEMENT, NEGATIVE REINFORCEMENT,
AND TWO KINDS OF PUNISHMENT   250*

Operant Conditioning in Infancy   251

Shaping of Complex Behaviors   252

Factors That Affect Operant
Conditioning   253

*BOX 7-3   SHAPING IN THE CLINIC: TEACHING
LANGUAGE AND SOCIAL SKILLS TO AUTISTIC
CHILDREN   254*

Why Do Reinforcers Reinforce?   256

*BOX 7-4   A CREATIVE APPLICATION OF THE
PREMACK PRINCIPLE IN A NURSERY SCHOOL
CLASSROOM   258*

Punishment: The Aversive Control of
Behavior   260

OBSERVATIONAL LEARNING   264

How Do We "Learn" by Observation?   265

Developmental Trends in Imitation and
Observational Learning   268

Television as a Modeling Influence   269

*BOX 7-5   MEDIA MODELS AS
THERAPISTS   272*

COMPLEX PROCESSES IN LEARNING   273

Later Developments in Concept Learning:
The "5 to 7 Shift"   274

SUMMARY   278

CHAPTER EIGHT DEVELOPMENT OF LANGUAGE AND COMMUNICATION SKILLS 284

TWO BASIC QUESTIONS ABOUT LANGUAGE DEVELOPMENT 286

The "What" Question 286

The "How" Question 288

BEFORE LANGUAGE: THE PRELINGUISTIC STAGE 289

The Infant's Reactions to Language 289

Producing Sounds: The Infant's Prelinguistic Vocalizations 290

Are Prelinguistic Vocalizations Related to Meaningful Speech? 291

What Do Prelinguistic Infants Know about Language? 292

BOX 8-1 *WHAT MOTHERS COMMUNICATE BY THEIR TONE OF VOICE 292*

ONE WORD AT A TIME: THE HOLOPHRASTIC STAGE 294

The Infant's Choice of Words 294

Individual Differences in Language Production 295

Early Semantics: The Development of Word Meanings 296

FROM HOLOPHRASES TO SIMPLE SENTENCES: THE TELEGRAPHIC STAGE 298

Characteristics of Telegraphic Speech 299

Grammatical Analyses of Early Speech 300

The Pragmatics of Early Speech 301

BOX 8-2 *LEARNING A GESTURAL LANGUAGE 302*

LANGUAGE LEARNING DURING THE PRESCHOOL PERIOD 304

Acquiring Grammatical Morphemes 304

Mastering Transformational Rules 306

Semantic Development 308

Pragmatics and Communication Skills 309

REFINEMENT OF LANGUAGE SKILLS 310

Later Syntactic Development 310

Semantics and Metalinguistic Awareness 311

BOX 8-3 *HAVE YOU HEARD THE ONE ABOUT . . . ? CHILDREN'S APPRECIATION OF LINGUISTIC HUMOR 312*

Growth of Communication Skills 312

THEORIES OF LANGUAGE DEVELOPMENT 314

Learning Theories 314

The Nativist Perspective 318

BOX 8-4 *LANGUAGE LEARNING IN CHIMPANZEES 320*

BOX 8-5 *A CHILDHOOD WITHOUT LANGUAGE: THE CURIOUS CASE OF GENIE 324*

The Interactionist Perspective 325

SUMMARY 326

CHAPTER NINE COGNITIVE DEVELOPMENT 332

WHAT ARE COGNITION AND COGNITIVE DEVELOPMENT? 333

PIAGET'S BASIC IDEAS ABOUT COGNITION 334

What Is Intelligence? 334

Cognitive Schemata: The Structural Aspects of Intelligence 335

BOX 9-1 *PIAGET'S CLINICAL METHOD: A CLOSER LOOK 336*

How Is Knowledge Gained? The Functional Basis of Intelligence 337

PIAGET'S STAGES OF COGNITIVE DEVELOPMENT 338

The Sensorimotor Stage (Birth to 2 Years) 338

*BOX 9-2   DO INFANTS KNOW MORE
ABOUT OBJECTS THAN PIAGET
ASSUMES?   343*

The Preoperational Stage (2 to 7 Years)   344

*BOX 9-3   PLAY IS SERIOUS
BUSINESS   346*

The Concrete-Operational Stage (7 to 11
Years)   351

The Formal-Operational Stage (Age 11–12 and
Beyond)   354

*BOX 9-4   CHILDREN'S RESPONSES TO A
HYPOTHETICAL PROPOSITION   356*

**AN EVALUATION OF PIAGET'S
THEORY   358**

The Issue of Timing   358

Does Cognitive Development Occur in
Stages?   359

Does Piaget's Theory "Explain" Cognitive
Development?   359

Present and Future Directions   360

**THE INFORMATION-PROCESSING
APPROACH   360**

Attentional Processes: Getting Information into
the System   361

Memory Processes: Retaining What One Has
Experienced   363

Hypothesis Testing and Problem Solving:
Using Information One Has Retained   371

The Current Status of Information-Processing
Theory   373

**INDIVIDUAL DIFFERENCES IN COGNITIVE
STYLE   373**

Implications of Reflective and Impulsive
Styles   374

Can Conceptual Tempo Be Modified?   374

SUMMARY   375

*CHAPTER TEN   INTELLIGENCE:
MEASURING MENTAL
PERFORMANCE   380*

WHAT IS INTELLIGENCE?   382

The Nature/Nurture Controversy   382

Is Intelligence a Single Attribute or Many
Attributes?   383

HOW IS INTELLIGENCE MEASURED?   386

The First Intelligence Tests   386

Modern IQ Tests   388

**WHAT DO INTELLIGENCE TESTS
PREDICT?   393**

IQ as a Predictor of Scholastic
Achievement   393

*BOX 10-1   PRINCIPLES OF TEST
CONSTRUCTION   394*

IQ as a Predictor of Occupational Status   394

IQ as a Predictor of Health, Adjustment, and
Life Satisfaction   396

**FACTORS THAT INFLUENCE IQ
SCORES   397**

The Evidence for Heredity   398

Environmental Influences   398

*BOX 10-2   IS INTELLIGENCE REALLY HERITABLE?
AN ENVIRONMENTALIST'S PERSPECTIVE   400*

**SOCIOCULTURAL CORRELATES OF
INTELLECTUAL PERFORMANCE   400**

The Home Environment as a Determinant of
Intellectual Growth   400

Effects of Birth Order and the Family
Configuration   404

Social-Class, Racial, and Ethnic Differences
in IQ   406

Why Do Groups Differ in Intellectual
Performance?   407

*BOX 10-3   WHY HERITABILITY ESTIMATES DO
NOT EXPLAIN GROUP DIFFERENCES IN IQ   410*

**IMPROVING INTELLECTUAL PERFORMANCE
THROUGH COMPENSATORY
EDUCATION   413**

Long-Term Follow-Ups   413

Home-Based Interventions   414

Limitations of Compensatory Education   415

SOME COMMON USES (AND ABUSES) OF IQ TESTS   416

SUMMARY   417

PART FOUR   SOCIAL AND PERSONALITY DEVELOPMENT   422

CHAPTER ELEVEN   ATTACHMENT: THE DEVELOPMENT OF INTIMATE RELATIONSHIPS   424

A DEFINITION OF ATTACHMENT   426

THE CAREGIVER'S ATTACHMENT TO THE INFANT   427

Early Emotional Bonding   427

Infant Characteristics That Promote Caregiver-to-Infant Attachments   429

BOX 11-1   THE ASOCIAL SMILE BECOMES A SOCIAL SMILE   430

Problems in Establishing Caregiver-to-Infant Attachments   432

THE INFANT'S ATTACHMENT TO CAREGIVERS   434

Development of Primary Social Attachments   434

Theories of Attachment   435

DEVELOPMENT OF FEARFUL REACTIONS   440

Stranger Anxiety   440

Separation Anxiety   444

LONG-TERM EFFECTS OF EARLY SOCIAL AND EMOTIONAL DEVELOPMENT   447

Individual Differences in the Quality of Attachments   448

BOX 11-2   FATHERS AS ATTACHMENT OBJECTS   450

The Unattached Infant: Effects of Restricted Social Contacts during Infancy   453

BOX 11-3   MATERNAL EMPLOYMENT AND ALTERNATIVE CAREGIVING: DO THEY HINDER CHILDREN'S EMOTIONAL DEVELOPMENT?   454

SUMMARY   461

CHAPTER TWELVE   THE SELF AND SOCIAL DEVELOPMENT   466

DEVELOPMENT OF THE SELF-CONCEPT   468

The Self as Separate from Others   468

When Do Children Recognize Themselves?   469

The Preschooler's Conceptions of Self   469

Conceptions of Self in Middle Childhood and Adolescence   472

Self-Esteem: The Affective Component of Self   473

KNOWING ABOUT OTHERS   475

BOX 12-1   WHO AM I TO BE? A CLOSER LOOK AT THE ADOLESCENT IDENTITY CRISIS   476

Age Trends in Impression Formation   476

Role Taking as a Determinant of Social Cognition   479

SOCIABILITY: DEVELOPMENT OF THE SOCIAL SELF   482

Sociability during the First Three Years   482

Individual Differences in Sociability   483

Sociability during the Preschool Period   484

Is Sociability a Stable Attribute?   485

BOX 12-2   IMPROVING THE SOCIAL SKILLS OF UNSOCIABLE CHILDREN   486

ALTRUISM: DEVELOPMENT OF THE PROSOCIAL SELF   486

Developmental Trends in Altruism   486

Training Altruism: Cultural and Social Influences   489

BOX 12-3   PROMOTING ALTRUISM THROUGH COOPERATIVE GAMES   490

Cognitive and Affective Contributors to
Altruism   492

Who Raises Altruistic Children?   493

THE DEVELOPMENT OF AGGRESSION   494

What Is Aggression?   494

Origins of Aggression   495

Age-Related Changes in the Nature of
Aggression   495

Is Aggression a Stable Attribute?   497

Sex Differences in Aggression   497

Cultural Influences   497

Familial Influences   498

Methods of Controlling Aggression 499

*BOX 12-4   HELPING CHILDREN (AND PARENTS)
WHO ARE "OUT OF CONTROL"   500*

**ACHIEVEMENT: DEVELOPMENT OF THE
COMPETENT SELF   502**

What Is Achievement Motivation?   502

Home and Family Influences on
Achievement   503

Can I Achieve? The Role of Expectancies in
Children's Achievement Behavior   504

Why Do I Succeed (or Fail)? Locus of Control
and Children's Achievement Behavior   504

*BOX 12-5   CHILD-REARING PRACTICES AND
CHILDREN'S ACHIEVEMENT MOTIVATION   505*

SUMMARY   507

*CHAPTER THIRTEEN   SEX DIFFERENCES
AND SEX-ROLE DEVELOPMENT   514*

**CATEGORIZING MALES AND FEMALES:
SEX-ROLE STANDARDS   516**

**SOME FACTS AND FICTIONS ABOUT SEX
DIFFERENCES   518**

Sex Differences That Appear to Be Real   519

Attributes That May Differentiate the
Sexes   520

Cultural Myths   520

Evaluating the Accomplishments of Males and
Females   520

**DEVELOPMENTAL TRENDS IN SEX
TYPING   522**

Development of the Gender Concept   522

Acquiring Sex-Role Stereotypes   523

Development of Sex-Typed Behavior   523

**THEORIES OF SEX TYPING AND SEX-ROLE
DEVELOPMENT   526**

The Biological Approach   526

*BOX 13-1   A CASE STUDY IN SEXUAL
REASSIGNMENT   531*

Freud's Psychoanalytic Theory   532

Social-Learning Theory   534

Kohlberg's Cognitive-Developmental
Theory   536

*BOX 13-2   CHILDREN'S CONCEPTIONS OF SEX-
ROLE STEREOTYPES   538*

An Attempt at Integration   538

**SEX TYPING IN THE NONTRADITIONAL
FAMILY   540**

Effects of Maternal Dominance   541

Effects of Father Absence   542

Effects of Maternal Employment   545

**PSYCHOLOGICAL ANDROGYNY: A NEW
LOOK AT SEX ROLES   545**

Is Androgyny a Desirable Attribute?   546

Who Raises Androgynous Offspring?   547

Implications and Prescriptions for the
Future   548

SUMMARY   548

*CHAPTER FOURTEEN   MORAL
DEVELOPMENT AND SELF-CONTROL   554*

A DEFINITION OF MORALITY   556

**PSYCHOANALYTIC EXPLANATIONS OF
MORAL DEVELOPMENT   557**

Freud's Theory of Oedipal Morality   557

Erikson's Views on Moral Development   558

COGNITIVE-DEVELOPMENTAL THEORY: THE CHILD AS A MORAL PHILOSOPHER 558

Piaget's Theory of Moral Development 558

Tests of Piaget's Theory 561

Kohlberg's Theory of Moral Development 563

Tests of Kohlberg's Theory 565

BOX 14-1 EXAMPLES OF HOW SUBJECTS AT EACH OF KOHLBERG'S SIX MORAL STAGES MIGHT RESPOND TO THE HEINZ DILEMMA 566

MORALITY AS A PRODUCT OF SOCIAL LEARNING 571

How Consistent Is Moral Behavior? 571

BOX 14-2 GILLIGAN'S THEORY OF FEMALE MORAL DEVELOPMENT 572

Determinants of Children's Resistance to Temptation 573

Is Morality a Stable and Unitary Attribute? 578

WHO RAISES CHILDREN WHO ARE MORALLY MATURE? 578

THE DEVELOPMENT OF SELF-CONTROL 580

Motor Inhibition 581

BOX 14-3 AN EXPERIMENTAL DEMONSTRATION OF THE EFFECTIVENESS OF INDUCTIVE DISCIPLINE 582

Delay of Gratification 582

BOX 14-4 ME SACRIFICE FOR SOMEONE ELSE! WELL . . . THAT DEPENDS 586

A Final Note on Self-Control 592

SUMMARY 592

PART FIVE   THE ECOLOGY OF DEVELOPMENT 598

CHAPTER FIFTEEN   THE FAMILY 600

BASIC FEATURES AND FUNCTIONS OF THE FAMILY 602

The Functions of a Family 602

The Goals of Parenting 602

BOX 15-1   METHODS OF STUDYING THE FAMILY 604

SOME CAUTIONARY COMMENTS ABOUT THE STUDY OF FAMILIES 605

The Middle-Class Bias 606

The Directionality Issue 606

Reconceptualizing Family Effects: The Family as a Social System 608

The Changing American Family 608

INTERACTIONS BETWEEN PARENTS AND THEIR INFANTS 609

The Transition to Parenthood 610

The Effects of Parents on Their Infants 610

PARENTAL EFFECTS ON PRESCHOOL AND SCHOOL-AGE CHILDREN 613

Two Major Dimensions of Child Rearing 613

Patterns of Parental Control 614

Parental Warmth/Hostility 616

BOX 15-2   PARENT/CHILD RELATIONSHIPS AS A CONTRIBUTOR TO ADULT DEPRESSION 617

Patterns of Parental Discipline 618

BOX 15-3   WHY "MOM IS THE GREATEST" 619

Social-Class Differences in Parenting 619

EFFECTS OF SIBLINGS AND THE FAMILY CONFIGURATION 623

The Nature of Sibling Interactions 623

Origins and Determinants of Sibling Rivalry 623

Positive Effects of Sibling Interaction 624

Characteristics of First-Born and Later-Born Children 626

THE IMPACT OF DIVORCE   627

The Immediate Effects   627

The Crisis Phase   628

BOX 15-4   THE FATHER AS A CUSTODIAL
PARENT   630

Long-Term Reactions to Divorce   630

Children in Reconstituted Families   631

EFFECTS OF MATERNAL
EMPLOYMENT   631

WHEN PARENTING BREAKS DOWN: THE
PROBLEM OF CHILD ABUSE   632

Who Is Abused?   633

Who Are the Abusers?   633

Social-Situational Triggers: The Ecology of
Child Abuse   634

SUMMARY   637

CHAPTER SIXTEEN   BEYOND THE HOME
SETTING: EXTRAFAMILIAL
INFLUENCES   644

THE EARLY WINDOW: EFFECTS OF
TELEVISION ON CHILDREN AND
YOUTH   646

Children's Use of Television   646

Effects of Televised Violence   647

Television as a Source of Social
Stereotypes   651

Children's Reactions to Commercial
Messages   652

Television as a Prosocial Instrument   653

Television as a Contributor to Cognitive
Development   654

Should Television Be Used to Socialize
Children?   657

THE SCHOOL AS A SOCIALIZATION
AGENT   657

Does Schooling Promote Cognitive
Development?   658

Determinants of Effective and Ineffective
Schooling   659

BOX 16-1   EDUCATING THE HANDICAPPED—IS
"MAINSTREAMING" THE ANSWER?   662

The Teacher's Influence   666

The School as a Middle-Class Institution:
Effects on Disadvantaged Youth   668

BOX 16-2   REPEATING A GRADE: PERSONAL,
SOCIAL, AND ACADEMIC CONSEQUENCES   670

THE SECOND WORLD OF CHILDHOOD:
PEERS AS SOCIALIZATION AGENTS   672

Who or What Is a Peer?   673

The Role of Peers in the Socialization
Process   675

BOX 16-3   SOME DETERMINANTS OF STATUS
AND POPULARITY IN THE PEER GROUP   678

BOX 16-4   CHILDREN AS TEACHERS—A SPECIAL
KIND OF PEER INFLUENCE   682

Peer versus Adult Influence: The Question of
Cross-Pressures   683

The Role of the Peer Group in Other
Societies   685

SUMMARY   687

DEVELOPMENTAL PSYCHOLOGY

THEORY, RESEARCH, AND APPLICATIONS

PART ONE

This is a book about children and adolescents—a description and explanation of their behaviors, thoughts, perceptions, emotions, and abilities. At the same time, this is a book about developmental psychology—the study of how individuals develop and change over the course of their lives.

Part One consists of two chapters designed to orient you to the field of developmental psychology. Chapter One sets the stage. We will

AN OVERVIEW OF DEVELOPMENTAL PSYCHOLOGY

first discuss the meaning of development and see just how recent this concept really is. After considering how the scientific community gradually became interested in developing children, we will focus on the methods and strategies that researchers have used to detect and explain developmental change.

Perhaps the most useful tools that developmental researchers have at their disposal are the many theories that have been proposed to account for human development. In Chapter Two we will take a closer look at the role of theory in developmental psychology as we examine several of the more influential theories of child and adolescent development.

Taken together, these opening chapters provide an orientation and some important background for the material presented throughout the text. They will help you understand what developmental psychology is and how researchers go about answering questions they may have about developing children and adolescents.

CHAPTER ONE ■

INTRODUCTION

■ *The concept of development*
Human development as a continual and
cumulative process
Human development as a holistic process
A brief overview of the text

■ *Human development in historical
perspective*
Childhood in premodern times
Origins of modern-day views on childhood
Emergence of a psychology of childhood

■ *Research methods in developmental
psychology*
The scientific method
Applying the scientific method to the study of
children and adolescents
Designing research to measure developmental
change
The cross-cultural comparison

■ *Ethical considerations in developmental
research*

■ *Summary*

There may be several reasons that you have chosen to enroll in a child development course. For many students majoring in psychology, home economics, elementary education, or nursing, the class is required and there is no way around it. Expectant parents sometimes take the course in order to learn more about babies as part of their preparation for parenthood. Occasionally students will elect the course seeking to answer specific questions about their own behavior or that of a friend or a family member. For example, a college roommate of mine, who happened to be a fisheries major, dabbled in child development hoping to discover why he and his identical twin often seemed to be thinking the same things in similar situations. Another classmate, who was Chinese, was forever asking questions about American family life. He had taken the course thinking he might acquire a better understanding of Western culture by learning how American children are raised. As our friendship blossomed, he ended up learning a lot about one grand old Western institution—poker—and we both learned a fair number of things about developing children as well.

Whatever your reasons for taking this course, at one time or another you have probably been curious about one or more aspects of human development. For example:

· Have you ever wondered what the world looks like to newborn infants? Do you suppose they can make any sense of their new surroundings?
· When do you think infants will first recognize their mothers? their fathers? themselves (in a mirror)?
· Why do many 1-year-olds seem so attached to their mothers and so fearful of strangers?
· Foreign languages are difficult for us to follow if we merely listen to conversations among people who speak these tongues. Yet infants and toddlers pay close attention to conversations and will acquire their native language in the absence of formal instruction. How is this possible? Is language learning easier for children than for adults?
· Why do many young children think that things that move, like the sun and the wind, are alive?
· Do you suppose we could teach algebra to a

fourth-grader who had learned to multiply and divide?

• Why are some people friendly and outgoing while others are shy and reserved? Does the quality of family life determine one's personality? If so, then why are children from the same family often so different from one another?

These are just a few of the issues that students say they wish to learn more about in electing a course in human development. As one perceptive sophomore recently remarked, "I want to know why all of us turn out so much alike and, at the same time, so different from one another." As we will see, her interests are shared by all developmental researchers.

THE CONCEPT OF DEVELOPMENT

Simply stated, **development** refers to the process by which organisms grow and change over the course of their lives. The study of child development is but one part of a larger discipline called **developmental psychology**—a discipline that seeks to identify and explain the changes that individuals undergo from the moment of conception (when the father's sperm penetrates the mother's ovum, creating a new organism) until the day they die. Of primary interest are the changes that occur in physical growth and motor skills, mental or reasoning abilities, emotional expression, and patterns of social behavior.

The child developmentalist focuses on one particular segment of the life span: the period between conception and *puberty*—an event (or series of events) that typically occurs at 11 to 14 years of age and marks the passage from childhood into adolescence. Those who are interested in adolescent development concentrate on the changes that occur between puberty and young adulthood, when the individual leaves home to work or to study and is now reasonably independent of parental sanctions. In this text, we will consider the major developments of both these phases of life. Our two major concerns in studying child and adolescent development will be to specify *how* children and adolescents change over time and *why* these developments take place.

When social scientists began to chart the course of human development over the first several years

of life, they soon discovered that no two children are exactly alike. Even newborn infants vary considerably in their alertness, their activity levels, and their responsiveness to other people. During the first year, some infants develop an intense fear of strangers and others do not. As they continue to mature, children clearly differ in the ages at which they reach important milestones such as walking, talking, learning to count, or riding a bicycle. Youngsters raised within a particular culture, a neighborhood, or even the same household often display very different interests, values, mental abilities, and patterns of social behavior. So even though some features of human development may be universal, each of us is in many ways a unique individual. Therefore, a third major concern of the child developmentalist is to identify the important ways in which children differ from one another and to explain why these developmental variations might occur.

Human Development as a Continual and Cumulative Process

In his famous poem *Paradise Lost,* John Milton wrote: "Childhood shows the man as morning shows the day." This interesting analogy can be interpreted in at least two ways. It could be translated to mean that the events of childhood have little or no real impact on one's adult life, just as a sunny summer morning often fails to forecast an impending afternoon thundershower. Yet most people do not interpret Milton's statement that way. Most take it to mean that the events of childhood play a very meaningful role in forecasting the future. Child developmentalists clearly favor this latter interpretation.

Although no one can specify precisely what adulthood holds in store from even the most meticulous examination of a person's childhood, developmentalists have learned that the first 12 to 15 years are an extremely important segment of the life span—one that sets the stage for adolescence and adulthood. And yet how we perform on that stage will also depend on the experiences we have as adolescents and adults. Obviously, you are not the same person you were at age 10 or even at age 15. You have probably grown somewhat (either up or out), acquired new academic skills, and developed very different interests and aspirations from those you had as a fifth-grader or a high school sophomore. And the path of such developmental change stretches ever onward, through middle age and beyond, culminating, of course, in the final change that occurs when we die. In sum, human development is best described as a *continual* and cumulative process. The only thing that is constant is change, and the changes that occur at each major phase of life have important implications for the future.

Table 1-1 presents a chronological overview of the life span as the developmental psychologist sees it. Our focus in this text is on development during the first six periods of life—the epochs known as childhood and adolescence. By examining how children develop from the moment they are conceived until they reach young adulthood, each of us will undoubtedly learn a little more about ourselves and the determinants of our behavior. Our review of the many factors that in-

fluence human development should also provide some insight into why no two children are ever exactly alike, even when they are raised together in the same home. Before we begin our journey through the world of childhood, let's note that we do not yet have answers for all the important questions you may have about developing children. Quite the contrary—developmental psychology is a young discipline with many unresolved issues. But as we proceed through the text, it should become quite clear that the developmentalists of the past half century have provided an enormous amount of very practical information about the younger set—information that can help us to become better educators, better child practitioners, and better-informed parents.

Human Development as a Holistic Process

In years gone by, it was fashionable to divide developmental psychologists into three camps: (1) those who studied physical growth and development, including bodily changes and the sequencing of motor skills, (2) those who studied the cognitive aspects of development, including perception, language, learning, and thinking, and (3) those who concentrated on the psychosocial aspects of development, including emotions, personality, and the growth of interpersonal relationships. Today we know that this classification is somewhat artificial and misleading. Researchers who work in any of these three areas can't help noticing that changes in one aspect of development have important implications for other aspects. Let's consider an example.

What determines a person's popularity with peers? If you were to say that the person's social skills are important, you would be right. Social skills such as warmth, friendliness, and willingness to cooperate are characteristics that popular children typically display. However, there is much more to popularity (or peer acceptance) than meets the eye. We now have some indication

TABLE 1-1. A chronological overview of human development

Period of life	Chronological time frame
1. Prenatal period	Conception to birth
2. Infancy	First two years of life
3. Toddler period	2 to 3 years of age
4. Preschool period	3 to 6 years of age
5. Middle childhood	6 to 13 or 14 years of age (onset of puberty marks the end of this period)
6. Adolescence	13 or 14 to 20 years of age (many developmental psychologists define the end of adolescence as the point at which the individual begins to work and is reasonably independent of parental sanctions)
7. Young adulthood	20 to 40 years of age
8. Middle age	40 to 65 years of age
9. Old age	65 years of age and older (postretirement)

Note: The age ranges listed here are approximate and may not apply to any particular individual. For example, a few 10-year-olds have experienced puberty and are properly classified as adolescents. Some teenagers are fully self-supporting with children of their own and are best classified as young adults.

development: *the process by which organisms grow and change over the course of their lives.*
developmental psychology: *the scientific study of how individuals change over time and the factors that produce these changes.*

that the age at which a child reaches puberty (an important milestone in physical development) has a very real effect on social life. For example, boys who reach puberty early enjoy better subsequent relations with their peers than boys who reach puberty later. Let's also note that bright children who do well in school tend to be more popular with their peers than children of average intelligence or below who perform somewhat less admirably in the classroom.

We see, then, that one's "popularity" depends not only on social skills but also on cognitive prowess and physical characteristics. As this example illustrates, development is not piecemeal but **holistic**—human beings are physical, cognitive, and social creatures, and each of these components of "self" depends, in part, on changes that are taking place in other areas of development. This holistic perspective is perhaps the dominant theme of human development in the 1980s—and the theme around which our book is organized.

A Brief Overview of the Text

To this point, we have suggested that development is a cumulative process and that the many changes that each person experiences are meaningfully related to one another. How did developmentalists make these important discoveries? What methods do they use to chart the course of development? How do they decide what to study and why it may be important to look at these phenomena?

The aim of this book is to answer each of these questions by introducing you to the goals, methods, theories, findings, and practical accomplishments of modern developmental psychology. Part One sets the stage. In the remainder of this first chapter, we will see how the scientific community gradually became interested in developing children and then devised a number of strategies for detecting and explaining developmental change. In Chapter Two we take a closer look at the role of theory in developmental psychology as we examine four major theories of human development and see that the assumptions made by developmental theorists largely determine the phenomena that they choose to study.

The rest of the text is organized around broad areas of study and research. Human beings are biological creatures, and our emphasis in Part Two is on physical changes and the biological bases of development. Among the more remarkable developments of childhood and adolescence are the changes that occur in perceiving, thinking, reasoning, and remembering. These cognitive, or intellectual, developments are examined in detail in Part Three. Of course, humans are also social animals, and our focus in Part Four shifts to social and personality development. And in Part Five, we will go beyond the individual child to consider the influence of the family and society on the development of children and adolescents.

The organization of this text around particular topics and processes reflects the specialization of modern developmental psychology: each major developmental theory emphasizes different aspects of development, and investigators typically concentrate on specific topics and processes when conducting research. Yet a division of the field into areas and topics is merely a convenient way of organizing a vast amount of information about developing persons, and it is important to remember that human development is a *holistic* process. For example, one cannot hope to understand a topic such as sex-role development without knowing how biology, learning, cognition, and important social forces combine to influence a person's perception of self as a male or a female who is expected to behave like other males or females in his or her culture. So even though this text is topically organized, we will not lose sight of the whole person or the holistic nature of human development.

The reason we concentrate on research and its application in this text is that most of what we know about developmental processes comes from the results of empirical research. Today there are many excellent methods for studying human development—a variety of techniques that we are about ready to discuss in some detail. But before we do, it is necessary to take a brief look at the history of developmental psychology in order to understand and appreciate why this field has become an empirical science.

HUMAN DEVELOPMENT IN HISTORICAL PERSPECTIVE

Childhood and adolescence were not always regarded as the very special and sensitive periods that we know them to be today (see Box 1-1). To understand how developmentalists think about and approach the study of children, it is necessary to see how the concept of childhood developed over time. You may be surprised to learn just how recent this concept really is. Of course, only after people came to view childhood as a very special period did they begin to study children and the developmental process.

Childhood in Premodern Times

For a glimpse of childhood in the ancient past, imagine that you have just become a parent in the ninth century B.C. in the warlike city-state of Sparta. Chances are you feel relieved that the birth is over and has gone well but, at the same time, very anxious, for a moment of truth is rapidly approaching. In a few short hours, your infant will undergo a rigorous examination by the Spartan Council of Elders. The job of the elders is to inspect all newborns to determine whether the infants are sufficiently strong and healthy that they may be allowed to live. If your infant is judged weak or defective, he or she will be taken into the wilderness and left alone to die (Despert, 1965). The "lucky" infants who are pronounced healthy will soon be exposed to a strict training regimen designed to "harden" them for the grim task of serving a military state. For example, Spartan children are not permitted to display weakness of character by crying, and even very young infants are to be "toughened" by growing accustomed to cold-water baths (Despert, 1965). At 7 years of age, when American children of a future era are entering the second grade, your sons will be taken from your home and raised in a public barracks. While living in the barracks, they will very likely be beaten often or go for days at a time without food, for these are the methods used by the barracks masters to instill the discipline and mental toughness that your sons will require to become admirable warriors and credits to the Spartan nation (deMause, 1974; Despert, 1965).

PHOTO 1-1. *The concept of childhood is a recent one. In the past, children were treated as miniature adults.*

Not all early societies treated their children as harshly as the citizens of Sparta. Yet, for several centuries after the birth of Christ, children were viewed as family "possessions" or resources that parents were free to use as they saw fit. In fact, it wasn't until the 12th century A.D. in Christian Europe that secular legislation equated infanticide—the killing of children—with murder (deMause, 1974)!

Historical records and paintings from medieval Europe provide some clues about what your childhood would have been like had you lived during that era (see Aries, 1962; deMause, 1974). Although you might not have received the extensive attention and coddling that infants and tod-

---

holistic perspective: *a unified view of the developmental process that emphasizes the important interrelationships among the physical, mental, social, and emotional aspects of human development.*

BOX 1-1
*A PROPOSED BILL OF RIGHTS
FOR CHILDREN*

You may have heard it said that contemporary Western societies, particularly the United States, are "child-centered." Does the argument have any merit? Well, consider that people in the United States often call births "blessed events" and refer to infants as "bundles of joy" who are considered worthy of extensive care and protection. A child's world is filled with toys, activities, and organizations (including commercial institutions) designed exclusively to serve children. Western societies spend billions of dollars annually to educate their young and do not require children to shoulder the full responsibilities of citizenship until they have attained the legal age of 14–21 (depending on the society), when they have presumably acquired the wisdom and skills to "pull their own weight." So perhaps it can be argued that modern societies are child-centered and that children and adolescents are privileged characters.

Of course, some parents continue to treat their young as personal possessions, and many youngsters, even in today's enlightened era, will suffer and die from parental abuse or neglect. In 1970 a group of child-care professionals who participated in a White House Conference on Children took the position that children are a unique class of human beings who must be afforded the following rights:

1. The right to grow in a society that represents the dignity of life and is free of poverty, discrimination, and any other forms of degradation.
2. The right to be born and be healthy and wanted throughout childhood.

3. The right to grow up nurtured by affectionate parents.
4. The right to be a child during childhood, to have meaningful choices in the processes of maturation and development, and to have a meaningful voice in the community.
5. The right to have social mechanisms to enforce the foregoing rights.

Of course, this Bill of Rights for Children is a recommendation rather than law, and we are a long way from accomplishing any of these objectives at this point in history. However, it is important to recognize that in the 1980s our society clearly acknowledges that children are a special class of human beings who have special needs that we must guarantee if we wish them to develop into healthy, happy, and productive adults.

---

dlers receive today, you would definitely have been cared for until you could dress, feed, and bathe yourself. At about age 6, you would have begun to wear downsized versions of adult clothing. You would also have begun a career by working with adults (often a parent or relative) at home, at the shop, or in the fields. You would have had the opportunity or privilege of partying with adults and partaking in the same social and sexual practices that adults favored. Lest the life sound like a pleasant one, you would soon have learned that the laws of the day made no distinction between children and adults. Had you, as a 10-year-old, been convicted of stealing, you would have been treated as a common thief and

perhaps hanged for your offense (Kean, 1937). Historian Philippe Aries (1962) concludes from the record that European societies had no concept of "childhood" as we know it before 1600. Medieval children were treated as miniature adults.

Origins of Modern-Day Views on Childhood

During the 17th and 18th centuries, attitudes toward children and child rearing began to change. Religious leaders of that era stressed that children were innocent and helpless souls who should be shielded from the wild and wanton behavior of adults and adolescents. One method of accomplishing this objective was to send children to school. Although the primary purpose of schooling was to provide a proper moral and religious education, it was now recognized that important subsidiary skills such as reading and writing must be taught in order to transform the innocents into "servants and workers" who would provide society "with a good labor force" (Aries, 1962, p. 10). Despite the fact that children were still considered family possessions, parents were now discouraged from beating their sons and daughters and were urged to treat them with more warmth and affection (Aries, 1962; Despert, 1965).

■ *Early philosophical perspectives on childhood*

Why did attitudes toward children change so drastically in the 17th and 18th centuries? Although the historical record is hazy on this point, it is likely that the thinking of influential social philosophers contributed in a meaningful way to the "new look" at children and child care. Lively speculation about human nature led these philosophers to carefully consider each of the following issues:

1. Are children inherently good or inherently bad?
2. Are children driven by inborn motives and instincts; or, rather, are they products of their environments?
3. Are children actively involved in determining their characters; or, rather, are they passive creatures molded by parents, teachers, and other agents of society?

Debates about these philosophical questions produced quite different perspectives on children and child rearing, ranging from Thomas Hobbes's (1651/1904) doctrine of **original sin,** which held

ORIGINAL SIN

INNATE PURITY

that children are inherently selfish egoists who must be controlled by society, to Jean Jacques Rousseau's doctrine of **innate purity**—the notion that children are born with an intuitive sense of right and wrong that is often misdirected by society. These two viewpoints clearly differ in their implications for child rearing. Proponents of original sin argued that parents must actively restrain their egoistic offspring, while the innate purists viewed children as "noble savages" who should be given the freedom to follow their inherently positive inclinations.

Another view on children and child rearing was suggested by John Locke, who believed that the mind of an infant is a **tabula rasa,** or "blank slate," and that children have no inborn tendencies. In other words, children are neither inherently good nor inherently bad, and how they turn out will depend entirely on their worldly experiences. Like Hobbes, Locke argued in favor of disciplined

---

original sin: *the idea that children are inherently negative creatures who must be taught to rechannel their selfish interests into socially acceptable outlets.*

innate purity: *the idea that infants are born with an intuitive sense of right and wrong that is often misdirected by the demands and restrictions of society.*

tabula rasa: *the idea that the mind of an infant is a "blank slate" and that all knowledge, abilities, behaviors, and motives are acquired through experience.*

TABULA RASA

child rearing to ensure that children develop good habits and acquire few if any unacceptable impulses.

These philosophers also differed on the question of children's participation in their own development. Hobbes maintained that children must learn to rechannel their naturally selfish interests into socially acceptable outlets; in this sense, they are passive subjects to be molded by the more powerful elements of society—namely, parents. Locke too believed that the child's role is passive, since the mind of an infant is a blank slate on which experience writes its lessons. But a strikingly different view was proposed by Rousseau, who believed that children are actively involved in the shaping of their intellects and personalities. In Rousseau's words, the child is not a "passive recipient of the tutor's instruction" but a "busy, testing, motivated explorer. The active searching child, setting his own problems, stands in marked contrast to the receptive one . . . on whom society fixes its stamp" (as cited in Kessen, 1965, p. 75).

Clearly these philosophers had some interesting ideas about children and how they should be raised. But how could anyone decide whether their views were correct? Unfortunately, the philosophers collected no objective data to back their contentions, and the few observations they did make were limited and unsystematic. Can you anticipate the next step in the evolution of developmental psychology?

■ *Children as subjects: The baby biographies*

As children became a proper topic for philosophical debate, the child's world began to change. The English formed societies for the prevention of cruelty to children. Education became increasingly widespread, and teachers began to use toys and picture books to facilitate the learning of their very young pupils (Despert, 1965). Pediatrics— the branch of medicine focusing on the care of infants and children—was recognized as a worthy medical specialty (deMause, 1974). Finally, philosophers, educators, and scientists from a variety of academic backgrounds began to observe the growth and development of their own children and to publish these data in works known as **baby biographies.**

Perhaps the most influential of the baby biographers was Charles Darwin, who made daily records of the early development of his own son (Darwin, 1877). Darwin's curiosity about child development stemmed from his earlier theory of evolution, which had appeared in his book *The Origin of Species.* Most of us are familiar with Darwin's ideas that human beings gradually evolved from lower species. But how did this theory lead him to study children? On this point Darwin was clear. He believed that young, untrained infants shared many characteristics with their subhuman ancestors. For example, he described both babies and beasts as amoral creatures who must be disciplined before they would acquire any desirable habits. Furthermore, Darwin proposed that careful observation of the developing child should retrace the evolutionary history of the species and thereby illustrate the "descent of man." In sum, Darwin believed that the way to approach thorny philosophical questions about human nature was to study the origins of humanity—both in nature and in developing children (Kessen, 1965).

One might suspect that the data recorded in the numerous baby biographies of the 18th and 19th centuries would have led to a comprehensive theory of child development (or, at least, to a theory of infant development). Unfortunately, this proved not to be the case. Observations for many of the baby biographies were made at irregular intervals, and different biographers emphasized very different aspects of their children's behavior. Consequently, the data provided by various biographers were often not comparable. We might also note that the persons making observations in these biographical studies were generally the child's parents. This presents a problem because observers who are also kin may selectively record pleasant or positive incidents while paying much less attention to unpleasant or negative episodes. Yet another type of observer bias may result if the investigator has a number of "pet" assumptions about the nature of development and then notices or records only those observations that appear consistent with his or her point of view. Perhaps you can see how that could have been a problem in the baby biography reported by Charles Darwin. Finally, almost every baby biography was based on observations of a single child, and it is difficult to know whether conclusions based on a single case would hold for other children.

Although the baby biographies were not very useful as a source of scientific information, they were a step in the right direction. Indeed, the fact that eminent scientists such as Charles Darwin were now writing about developing children implied that human development was a topic worthy of careful scientific scrutiny.

Emergence of a Psychology of Childhood

Introductory textbooks in virtually all academic areas typically credit someone as the "founder" of the discipline. In developmental psychology there are at least two viable candidates for this honor. One is an American psychologist, G. Stanley Hall, whose most influential work was published in 1891.

Well aware of the shortcomings of baby biographies based on single children, Hall set out to collect more objective data on larger samples. Specifically, he was interested in the character of children's thinking, and he developed a familiar research tool—the **questionnaire**—to "discover the contents of children's minds" (Hall, 1891). What he found was that children's understanding of worldly events increases rapidly over the course of childhood. Hall also discovered that the reasoning of young children is rather curious at times, deviating radically from that dictated by formal logic. Here, then, was the first large-scale scientific investigation of developing children, and it is on this basis that G. Stanley Hall merits consideration as the founder of developmental psychology.

At about the same time that Hall was using questionnaires to study children's thinking, a young European neurologist was trying a very different method of probing the mind and revealing its contents. The neurologist's approach was extremely fruitful, providing information that led him to propose a theory that revolutionized thinking about children and childhood. This neurologist was Sigmund Freud. His ideas came to be known as *psychoanalytic theory.*

In many areas of science, psychology included, new theories are often revisions or modifications of old theories. However, in Freud's day, there were few "old" theories of human behavior to modify. Freud was truly a pioneer, formulating his psychoanalytic theory from the thousands of notes he took and observations he made while treating patients for various kinds of "nervous" (emotional) disturbances.

Ever the astute observer, Freud happened to notice that patients would often describe very similar experiences or events that had been noteworthy to them while they were growing up. He then inferred that there must be important milestones in human development that all people share. As he continued to observe his patients and listen to their accounts of their lives, Freud concluded that each milestone in the life history of a patient was related in some meaningful way to earlier events. At this point, he recognized that he had the data—the pieces of the puzzle—from which to construct a comprehensive theory of human development.

The genius of Freud soon attracted many followers. Shortly after the publication of Freud's earliest theoretical monographs, the *International Journal of Psychoanalysis* was founded, and other researchers began to report their tests of Freud's thinking. By the mid-1930s much of Freud's work had been translated into other languages, and the impact of psychoanalytic theory was felt around the world. Over the years, Freud's theory proved to be quite *heuristic*—meaning that it continued to generate new research and to prompt other researchers to extend Freud's thinking. Clearly, the field of child development was itself a healthy,

---

baby biography: *a detailed record of an infant's behavior over a period of time.*

questionnaire: *a research instrument that asks the persons being studied to respond to a number of written questions.*

thriving infant by the time Freud died, in 1939.

Freud's work illustrates the role that theories play in the scientific study of human development. Although the word *theory* is an imposing term, it so happens that theories are something that everybody has. If someone were to ask you why males and females appear so very different as adults when they seem so very similar as infants, you would undoubtedly have something to say on the issue. In answering, you would be stating or at least reflecting your own underlying theory of sex differences. So a **theory** is really nothing more than a set of concepts and propositions that allow the theorist to describe and explain some aspect of experience. In the field of psychology, theories help us to describe various patterns of behavior and to explain why those behaviors occur.

Good theories have another important feature: the ability to predict future events. These theoretical predictions, or **hypotheses**, are then tested by collecting additional data. The information that we obtain when testing hypotheses not only provides some clues about the theory's ability to explain new observations but may also lead to new theoretical insights that extend our knowledge even further.

Today there are many theories that contribute to our understanding of developing children, and in Chapter Two we will examine several of the more influential of these viewpoints. Although it is quite natural for people reading about these theories to pick a favorite, the scientist uses a rather stringent yardstick to evaluate theories: he or she will formulate hypotheses and conduct research to see whether the theory can adequately predict and explain new observations. Thus, there is no room for subjective bias when evaluating a theory. Theories in developmental psychology are only as good as their ability to predict and explain important aspects of human growth and development.

In the next section of the chapter, we will focus on the "tools of the trade"—that is, the research methods that developmentalists use to test their theories and gain a better understanding of the child's world.

RESEARCH METHODS IN DEVELOPMENTAL PSYCHOLOGY

When detectives are assigned cases to solve, they first gather the facts, formulate hunches, and then

sift through the clues or collect additional information until one of their hunches proves correct. Unraveling the mysteries of development is in many ways a similar endeavor. Investigators must carefully observe their subjects, study the information they have collected, and then use these data to draw conclusions about the ways people develop.

The focus in this section is on the methods that researchers use to gather information about developing children and adolescents. Our first task is to understand why developmentalists consider it absolutely essential to collect all these facts. We will then discuss the advantages and disadvantages of six basic factfinding strategies: naturalistic observation, interviews, case studies, clinical methods, experiments, and quasi-experiments. Finally, we will consider the ways that developmentalists use these strategies to detect and explain age-related changes in children's feelings, thoughts, and behaviors.

The Scientific Method

Modern developmental psychology is appropriately labeled a scientific enterprise because those who study developing organisms have adopted a value system we call the **scientific method** that guides their attempts at understanding. There is nothing mysterious about the scientific method. It is really more of an *attitude* or *value* than a method; the attitude dictates that, above all, investigators must be *objective* and must allow their observations (or data) to decide the merits of their thinking.

In the 17th and 18th centuries, when social philosophers were presenting their views on children and child rearing, their ideas were often interpreted as fact. It was as if people assumed that great minds always had great insights. Very few individuals questioned the word of these well-known scholars, because the scientific method was not yet an important criterion for evaluating wisdom or knowledge.

The intent here is not to criticize the early social philosophers. In fact, contemporary developmentalists (and today's children) are indebted to these men for helping to modify the ways in which society thought about and treated its young. However, so-called great minds may produce miserable ideas on occasion, and if poorly conceived notions have implications for the way human beings are to be treated, it behooves us to discover these erroneous assumptions before they harm anyone. The scientific method, then, is a value that helps to protect the scientific community and society at large against flawed reasoning. The protection comes from the practice of evaluating the merits of various theoretical pronouncements against the objective record, rather than simply relying on the academic, political, or social credibility of the theorist. Of course, this means that the theorist whose ideas are being evaluated must be equally objective and, thus, willing to discard pet notions when there is evidence that they have outlived their usefulness.

Applying the Scientific Method to the Study of Children and Adolescents

Today researchers are rather fortunate in having many methods that they can use to test their hypotheses about human development. This diversity of available research techniques is a strength because discoveries produced by one technique can be verified by other methods. Such *converging evidence* is extremely important, for it demonstrates that the "discovery" one has made is truly a discovery and not merely an artifact of the method used to collect the original data (see Box 1-2).

In the pages that follow, we will consider several of the methods that investigators use when trying to unravel the mysteries of development. Before we begin, here is an exercise, or "thought problem," that you may find interesting: In re-

PHOTO 1-2. *Children's tendency to perform for an observer is one of the problems researchers must overcome when using the method of naturalistic observation.*

viewing each method, we will consider an example of the kind of research that this approach has generated. Look carefully at these examples and select the study that you find most interesting. Then see whether you can think of a way that one or more of the other research methods might be used to provide converging evidence for the results of that study.

■ *Naturalistic observation*

A research method that many psychologists favor is **naturalistic observation**—observing people in their common, everyday (that is, natural) sur-

---

theory: *a set of concepts and propositions designed to organize, describe, and explain an existing set of observations.*
hypothesis: *a theoretical prediction about some aspect of experience.*
scientific method: *an attitude or value about the pursuit of knowledge that dictates that investigators must be objective and must allow their data to decide the merits of their theorizing.*
naturalistic observation: *a method in which the scientist tests hypotheses by observing people as they engage in everyday activities in their natural habitats (for example, at home, at school, or on the playground).*

We all know that parents are quick to provide us with lists of do's and don't's—words of wisdom that, if heeded, will presumably make us healthier, wealthier(?), and wiser. One value that many parents stress is *altruism*—the willingness to share with others who are less fortunate than ourselves and to help those who need our assistance. Are some child-rearing techniques more effective than others at persuading children to be altruistic? Developmental psychologists think so.

In 1970 David Rosenhan interviewed a number of people whom he believed to be rather altruistic. These people were "freedom riders" who had participated in the civil rights movement in the Southern part of the United States during the early 1960s. Rosenhan's interviews suggested that the freedom riders could be classified into two groups: (1) *fully committed* activists who had made great sacrifices such as giving up their homes, jobs, or education to participate extensively for the cause of civil rights and (2) *partially committed* activists who had limited their involvement to one or two freedom rides without altering their lifestyle in any meaningful way.

If we can agree with Rosenhan that the fully committed activists were the more altruistic of the two groups, we might wonder why these people were more helpful than the partially committed activists. Rosenhan quickly ruled out one possible explanation when his interviews revealed that attitudes toward racial equality and civil rights were equally (and extremely) favorable among members of both groups. But as the interviews progressed, Rosenhan noticed some very real differences in the ways that fully and partially committed activists described their previous family lives. For example, fully committed activists portrayed their parents as people who had preached altruism and who themselves had strived to help those who needed their assistance. In contrast, partially committed activists had parents who had often preached but rarely practiced altruism. Rosenhan concluded that children are most likely to heed their parents' urgings to be altruistic when parents have practiced what they preach.

Unfortunately, one disadvantage of interview data is that people may not answer questions truthfully and accurately. For example, were the parents of fully committed activists really that altruistic; or, rather, were these altruistic activists simply being charitable in their memories of their parents? The second interpretation seems quite reasonable in view of the fact that fully committed activists reported having *warmer* relations with their parents than did partially committed activists and, therefore, may have had more reason than the partially committed activists to portray their parents in a positive light. However, it is impossible to tell which of these interpretations of Rosenhan's data is correct without conducting additional research. Perhaps the best way to

roundings. To observe children, this would usually mean going into homes, schools, or public parks and playgrounds and carefully recording what happens. Rarely will the observer try to record every event that occurs. Generally speaking, the researcher will be testing a specific hypothesis about one particular class of behavior, such as cooperation or aggression. He or she will then focus exclusively on this type of behavior and perhaps its causes and consequences (if they can be determined from the observational record).

Naturalistic observation is not as simple as it at first appears. It is difficult to observe a single child continuously and to record all the behaviors of interest; fatigue and the necessity to look away to tabulate what one has observed make continuous observation almost impossible. The problem is compounded, of course, if you are observing many children at the same time. As a result, observational researchers have devised *time-sampling*

techniques in which each child in the sample is observed for several short periods to see whether he or she is involved in one or more of the behaviors under investigation. For example, an observer interested in the amount of altruistic behavior that occurs among six children during a 60-minute play period might carefully observe each of the six children for four two-minute periods during the hour, recording any instances of sharing, helpfulness, or emotional support that the child provides during those observation periods.

A researcher using the observational method must be extremely careful to guard against **observer bias**—the tendency to confirm one's hypothesis by reading too much (or too little) into naturally occurring events. In other words, the observational record must be as objective as possible, calling for a minimum of interpretation by the observer. One way to increase objectivity is to

approach the problem is to test Rosenhan's conclusion using a method that does not rely on interview data, which may be biased or inaccurate.

Two years later, Elizabeth Midlarsky and James Bryan designed a laboratory experiment to test the proposition that parents should practice what they preach. In this study, children watched as an adult made ten attempts at a game of skill, winning five times and losing five times. On all winning attempts, the adult behaved either *charitably,* by donating some of his winnings to a needy children's fund, or *selfishly,* by keeping all winnings for himself. On all losing attempts, the adult preached either *charity* ("I know I don't have to give, but it would make some children very happy") or *self-interest* ("I could really use some spending money this week"). After watching the adult, the child played the game, won five times, and thus had five opportunities to share money with needy children.

The results of this experiment are summarized in the table at the right.

To interpret the results, let's first consider the average donations that children made after listening to an adult who *preached* either charity or self-interest. Looking down the columns, we see that the adult who preached charity elicited larger donations from the children (30.8%) than the adult who preached self-interest (19%). This finding perhaps explains why Rosenhan's partially committed activists, whose parents often encouraged them to be helpful, were willing to provide at least some assistance in promoting civil rights. However, the most

Average percentage of winnings donated by children exposed to charitable or selfish adults who preached either charity or self-interest

Adult's behavior	Adult's verbal encouragement		Average percentage
	Charity	Self-interest	
Charitable	44.0	27.5	35.8
Selfish	17.5	10.5	14.0
Average percentage	30.8	19	

dramatic finding in Midlarsky and Bryan's experiment was that the children who were most charitable of all (giving 44% of their winnings) were those who had heard an adult describe the virtues of altruism and then *practice* what he preached.

Here, then, is converging evidence for Rosenhan's original contention that parents who hope to influence their children should practice what they preach. Our confidence in the conclusion is strengthened by the fact that the data from Midlarsky and Bryan's experiment are objective behavioral responses (donations) elicited by adults who actually did (in some cases) practice what they preached. Whenever we can successfully replicate a finding using a variety of research techniques, we become much more confident that the finding is valid and is not merely an artifact of the method we originally used to conduct our research.

specify in advance precisely what kinds of activity qualify as examples of the behavior that you wish to study. You must also assess the **reliability** of your observations as a check on the objectivity of the procedure. Reliability is most often measured by asking a second person to observe the same events that the first observer witnesses and then comparing the observational records of the two observers. If independent observers largely agree on what occurred, the observational records are reliable. A lack of agreement indicates that the observational scheme is unreliable and needs to be revised.

Finally, the mere presence of an unfamiliar adult observer is itself an unusual event that may make children behave rather atypically. Consider the experiences of one graduate student who attempted to take pictures of children's playground antics. What he recorded in many of his photos was somewhat less than spontaneous play. For

example, one child who was playing alone with a doll jumped up when the student approached with the camera and informed him that he should take a picture of her "new trick" on the monkey bars. Another child who was playing kickball said "Get this" as he broke away from the kickball game and laid a blindside tackle on an unsuspecting onlooker. Clearly, observers should do what they can to minimize the influence they are likely to have on the behavior of their subjects.

> **observer bias:** *a tendency of an observer to over- or underinterpret naturally occurring experiences rather than simply recording the events that take place.*
>
> **observer reliability:** *the degree of agreement between independent observers on what they have witnessed in an observational study.*

One way to approach the problem is to videotape the behavioral record for later viewing by members of the research team.[1] If this is not feasible, observers can minimize their influence by mingling with the children in their natural habitats before the actual conduct of the study. In this way, children become accustomed to the observers' presence and therefore are less likely to "perform" for them or alter their behavior in any significant way.

An example of naturalistic observation.   Several years ago, Rosalind Charlesworth and Willard Hartup (1967) used naturalistic observation to see whether nursery school children become more pleasant to one another as they grow older. Before any data were collected, the observers spent time at the nursery school improving the reliability of their observational scheme, learning the children's names, and allowing these preschoolers to become accustomed to their presence. Then, over a five-week period, they used a time-sampling procedure to observe the children at play, recording those instances in which each child dispensed positive social reinforcement to a classmate. Examples of positive social reinforcement were specified in advance and included such behaviors as showing affection or approval, cooperating, sharing, and giving another child tangible objects such as toys or snacks.

If you have ever worked with preschool children in a group setting, you may be able to anticipate some of the findings of this study. First, there were age differences in the distribution of positive social reinforcers: the 4-year-olds gave more reinforcers to peers and distributed these reinforcers to a larger number of classmates than did the 3-year-olds. This finding suggests that children may become more responsive to peers as they grow older. Second, children did not distribute their reinforcements indiscriminately. Boys generally reinforced boys, and girls reinforced girls. Finally, there was a strong relationship between giving and receiving positive social reinforcers: children who gave the most got the most, and children who infrequently reinforced their peers received few niceties in return. In other words, these children appeared to engage in a *reciprocal exchange* of positive reinforcers. Many theorists have argued that a kind of reciprocal exchange, or "equity," underlies most social encounters between adults (see, for example, Walster, Walster, & Berscheid, 1978). Charlesworth and Hartup's observations suggest that we may learn a great deal about the origins of social equity by observing the mutual give and take among young children at play in their peer groups.

A limitation of naturalistic observation.   From a procedural standpoint, Charlesworth and Hartup's study is an excellent piece of naturalistic observation. The investigators had rather precise definitions of the behaviors they wished to record, and they took care to ensure that their measures were reliable. They also tried to minimize their own influence on the children's behavior by allowing their subjects to get to know them and to grow accustomed to their presence. Yet it can be argued that the knowledge we gain from any observational study is somewhat limited, no matter how carefully the investigator has designed the project.

The major limitation of observational research is its inability to differentiate among several possible causes for the observations made. Let's reconsider a major result of Charlesworth and Hartup's study: Do 4-year-olds reinforce peers more than 3-year-olds do *because* the older children have learned that peers will return their acts of kindness? Or, rather, do 4-year-olds simply favor *group* play activities that just happen to provide more opportunities to give and receive social reinforcers? The latter explanation is not at all farfetched if the nursery school setting has few solitary (that is, one-person) toys that are sufficiently interesting to capture the imagination of the typical 4-year-old. In sum, there are many variables in the natural setting that may affect children's behavior, and it is often difficult to

---

[1]Videotaping is particularly effective at minimizing the influence of an observer if the taping is done from a concealed location or if the videotape equipment is in place for a long period so that children become less intrigued by this unusual machinery.

specify which of these variables or what combination of them is responsible for an observation or pattern of observations. But please note that this is merely a limitation of observational research, not a devastating critique. Naturalistic observation is an excellent procedure for detecting developmental trends or changes in behavior, which, once observed, may then be subjected to intensive causal analyses in later research.

■ *Interviews, case studies, and the clinical method*

Three common methods that developmental psychologists use to gather information and test hypotheses are the interview technique, the case study, and the clinical method. Although these approaches are similar in many respects, they differ in the extent to which the individuals who participate in the research are treated alike by the investigator.

The interview method. A researcher who opts for the interview method will ask the child (or the parents) a series of questions about one or more aspects of the child's life. If the session is a **structured interview,** all who participate in the study are asked exactly the same questions in the same order. The purpose of this standardized, or structured, format is to treat each person alike so that the responses of different participants can be compared.

We have already discussed one project that made good use of the interview method—Rosenhan's (1970) study of civil rights activists (see Box 1-2). Another interesting application of this technique is a project in which kindergarten, second-grade, and fourth-grade children responded to 24 questions designed to assess their knowledge of social stereotypes about males and females (Williams, Bennett, & Best, 1975). Each question came in response to a different short story in which the central character was described by either stereotypically masculine adjectives (for example, *aggressive, forceful, tough*) or stereotypically feminine adjectives (for example, *emotional, excitable*). The child's task was to indicate whether the character in each story was a male or a female. Williams and her associates found that even kindergartners were quite knowledgeable about gender stereotypes, although children's thinking became much more stereotyped between kindergarten and the second grade. One implication of these results is that stereotyping of the sexes must begin very early if 5-year-old kindergartners are already thinking along stereotyped lines.

The interview method has some very real shortcomings. Investigators must hope that the answers they receive are honest and accurate and that they are not merely attempts by respondents to present themselves in a favorable or socially desirable manner. Clearly, inaccurate responses will lead to erroneous conclusions. When interviewing children of different ages, the investigator must also ensure that all questions are clearly understood by even the youngest respondents; otherwise, the age trends observed in one's study may represent differences in children's ability to comprehend and communicate rather than real underlying changes in children's feelings, thoughts, or behaviors.

In spite of these potential shortcomings, the structured interview can be an excellent research tool. Interviews are particularly useful when the interviewer *challenges* children to display what they know about an issue, for the socially desirable response to such a challenge is likely to be a truthful or accurate answer. In the gender stereotyping study, for example, the investigators wished to determine whether children of different ages had an understanding of common stereotypes about men and women. The participants probably considered each question a personal challenge or a puzzle to be solved and therefore were motivated to answer accurately and to display exactly what they knew about males and females. Under the circumstances, then, the structured interview was an excellent method of assessing children's perceptions of the sexes.

---

structured interview: *a technique in which all interviewees are asked the same questions in precisely the same order so that the responses of different participants can be compared.*

The case study. Yet another method of researching human development is the **case-study** approach. An investigator who uses this method prepares detailed descriptions of one or more individuals and then attempts to draw conclusions by analyzing these "cases." In preparing an individualized record, or "case," the psychologist will typically include many sources of information about the individual, such as his or her family background, socioeconomic status, education and work history, health record, self-descriptions of significant life events, and performance on psychological tests. Much of the information included in any case history comes from interviews with the individual, although the questions asked are typically not standardized and may vary considerably from case to case.

The baby biographies of the 18th and 19th centuries are examples of case studies, each of which was based on a single subject. But perhaps the best known of the case-study researchers is Sigmund Freud, who prepared and analyzed dozens of cases and, from these records, formulated a comprehensive theory of human development—psychoanalytic theory.

Although Freud was a strong proponent of the case study and used it to great advantage, this method has three major shortcomings that seriously limit its usefulness. First, the validity of an investigator's conclusions will obviously depend on the accuracy of the information received from the "cases." Unfortunately, the potential for inaccuracy is great in a method in which adult subjects try to recall the causes and consequences of important events that happened years ago in childhood. Second, the data on any two (or more) individuals may not be directly comparable if the investigator has asked each participant different questions rather than posing a standard set of questions to all. Finally, the case study may lack *generalizability*—that is, conclusions drawn from the experiences of the particular individuals who were studied may not apply to most people. In fact, one recurring criticism of Freud's psychoanalytic theory is that it was formulated from the experiences and recollections of emotionally disturbed patients who were hardly typical of the general population. In sum, the case study can serve as a rich source of ideas about human development. However, its limitations are many, and any conclusions drawn from case studies should be verified through the use of other research techniques.

The clinical method. The **clinical method** is a close relative of the case-study approach. The investigator is usually interested in testing a particular hypothesis by presenting the research participant with a task or stimulus of some sort and then inviting a response. When the participant has responded, the investigator will typically ask a second question or introduce a new task in the hope of clarifying the participant's original answer. The questioning continues until the investigator has the information needed to evaluate his or her hypothesis. Although participants are often asked the same questions in the initial stages of the research, their answers to each question determine what the investigator asks next. Since participants' answers often differ, it is possible that no two participants will ever receive exactly the same treatment. In other words, the clinical method considers each subject to be unique.

Jean Piaget, a famous Swiss psychologist, has relied extensively on the clinical method to study children's intellectual development. The data from Piaget's research are largely protocol records of his interactions with individual children. The following is a sample protocol that describes the interaction between the investigator and a 6-year-old named Lau, who participated in a study designed to test children's understanding of the concept of number. Lau first lined up six glasses with six bottles to form two rows of equal length. The investigator then grouped the glasses together and asked: "Are they still the same?"

Lau: Yes, it's the same number of glasses. You've only put them closer together, but it's still the same number.
Investigator (grouping the bottles and spacing the glasses): And now, are there more bottles [grouped] or more glasses [spaced out]?
Lau: They are still the same. You've only put the bottles close together [Piaget, 1965, p. 47].

Most of Piaget's published studies contain several such protocols, which are normally preceded, accompanied, and followed by a fair amount of theoretical interpretation. This protocol suggested to Piaget that 6-year-old Lau had acquired the concept of number, for Lau recognized that the number of bottles (and glasses) remains constant regardless of whether they are spaced out or placed together. In contrast, many 4-year-olds are fooled by appearances and will say that there are more bottles than glasses if the bottles are spaced in a long row and the glasses are bunched together. Piaget interprets this confusion as evidence that these 4-year-olds do not truly understand the concept of number.

We need only examine the richness of Piaget's thinking (as we will in Chapters Two and Nine) to see that the clinical method can provide a wealth of information about developing children. However, the clinical approach is a controversial technique that presents some thorny interpretive problems. We have already noted the difficulties in comparing cases or protocols generated by a procedure that treats each participant differently. Furthermore, the nonstandardized treatment of participants raises the possibility that the examiner's preexisting theoretical biases may affect the questions asked and the interpretations provided. Since conclusions drawn from the clinical method depend, in part, on the investigator's *subjective* assessments and interpretations, it is desirable to provide converging evidence for clinical insights by verifying them with other research techniques.

■ *The experimental method*

The laboratory experiment is perhaps the most popular method of studying children because it permits the researcher to conduct reasonably unambiguous tests of his or her hypothesis. To introduce the essential features of this important technique, let's consider a problem that seems well suited for the **experimental method.**

Suppose we believe that children learn a lot from watching television and that they are likely to imitate the behavior of the television characters to whom they are exposed. One hypothesis we might derive from this line of reasoning is that children who watch "helpful" television characters are likely to become more helpful themselves when they have opportunities to provide assistance to others in the near future. If we analyze our hypothesis, what we are saying is that a change in one variable (the kind of television program that children watch) will produce changes in a second variable (helpfulness).

In conducting a laboratory experiment to test this (or any) hypothesis, we would bring our participants together in a controlled environment, expose them to different treatments, and record as data their responses to the treatments. The different treatments to which we expose our participants represent the **independent variable** of our experiment. To test the hypothesis that we have proposed, our independent variable (or treatments) would be the type of television program that we show to our participants. Half of our children might view a program in which one or more characters were helpful to others, and the other half would watch a program in which the characters were not especially helpful. Children's reactions to the television shows would become the data, or **dependent variable,** in our experiment. Since our hypothesis involves helpgiving, we would want to measure (as our dependent variable) how helpful children are after watching each type of television show. A dependent variable is called "dependent" because its value presumably "depends" on the independent variable. In the present case, we are hypothesizing that future helpgiving (our dependent variable) will be greater for those children who watch programs that demonstrate helpgiving (one level of the independent variable) than for children who watch programs that show little or no helpgiving (the

---

case study: *a research method in which the investigator gathers extensive information about the life of an individual and then tests developmental hypotheses by analyzing the events of the person's life history.*

clinical method: *a type of interview in which a child's response to each successive question (or problem) determines what the investigator will ask next.*

experimental method: *a research strategy in which the investigator introduces some change in the child's environment and then measures the effect of that change on the child's behavior.*

independent variable: *the aspect of a child's environment that an experimenter modifies or manipulates in order to measure its impact on the child's behavior.*

dependent variable: *the aspect of a child's behavior that is measured in an experiment and assumed to be under the control of the independent variable.*

second level of the independent variable). If we are careful experimenters and exercise precise control over *all* other factors that may affect children's helpgiving, then the pattern of results that we have anticipated would allow us to draw a strong conclusion: watching television programs that demonstrate helpgiving *causes* children to become more helpful in the near future. Indeed, the most important advantage of the experimental method is that it permits a precise assessment of the cause-and-effect relationship that may exist between two variables.

Several years ago, the experiment we have discussed was actually conducted (Sprafkin, Liebert, & Poulous, 1975). The 6-year-olds who participated in this study watched one of two programs: an episode from the popular *Lassie* series that contained a dramatic rescue scene or a *Lassie* episode that contained no outstanding acts of helpgiving. Thus, the independent variable was the type of program the children watched. After watching one or the other show, each child began to play a game in an attempt to win a prize. While playing, he or she could hear some puppies in an adjacent area that were apparently discomforted. The dependent variable in this experiment was the amount of time children would spend away from the game giving help or comfort to the crying puppies. Note that, to help, the children had to leave the game and thereby decrease their chances of winning a prize.

Was helpgiving at all influenced by the type of program the children had watched? Indeed it was, for the children who had watched the episode in which helpgiving was emphasized spent considerably more time comforting the distressed pups than did the children who had watched the other episode. So it appears that examples of helpgiving on television can have a positive *effect* on the behavior of young children.

When students discuss this experiment in class, someone invariably challenges this interpretation of the results. For example, one perceptive young woman advanced the alternative explanation that "maybe the kids who watched helpgiving on TV simply liked dogs better than kids who saw a TV program with no helpgiving." In other words, she was suggesting that children's "liking for dogs" had determined the amount of help they gave and that the independent variable (type of television program) had had no effect at all! Could she have

been correct? How do we know that the children in the two experimental conditions really didn't differ in some important way (such as their liking for dogs) that may have affected their willingness to help the puppies?

This question brings us to the crucial issue of **experimental control.** In order to conclude that the independent variable is causally related to the dependent variable, the experimenter must ensure that all other factors that could affect the dependent variable are *controlled*—that is, equivalent in each experimental condition. One way to equalize these extraneous factors is to do what Sprafkin et al. (1975) did: randomly assign children to their experimental treatments. The concept of *randomization*, or **random assignment,** means that each research participant has an equal probability of being exposed to each experimental treatment or condition. Assignment of individual participants to a particular treatment is accomplished by an unbiased procedure such as the flip of a coin. If the assignment is truly random, there is only a very slim chance that participants in the two (or more) experimental conditions will differ on any characteristic that might affect their performance on the dependent variable: all of these "extraneous" characteristics will have been randomly distributed within each condition and equalized across the different conditions. Since Sprafkin et al. randomly assigned children to experimental conditions, they could be reasonably certain that the group of children who watched the "helpful" TV program had no greater "liking for dogs" than children who watched the "nonhelpful" TV program. So it was reasonable for them to conclude that the former group of children were the more helpful group *because* they had watched a TV program in which helpgiving was a central theme (see also Box 1-3 on p. 24).

A possible limitation of laboratory experiments. Critics of laboratory experimentation have argued that the tightly controlled laboratory "environment" is highly artificial and that children are likely to behave very differently in these surroundings than they would in a natural setting. Consequently, it is quite possible that conclusions drawn from laboratory experiments will not always apply in the real world.

One way around this criticism is to design experiments that seem quite natural to children—experiments that take place in familiar surroundings and require children to perform highly typical or familiar activities. Urie Bronfenbrenner (1977) has suggested several ways to make the experimental setting seem more natural to children. For example, the study might take place in comfortable settings such as the home or school. Furthermore, children may behave more naturally as participants if their teachers or parents serve as the experimenter rather than a strange adult. Finally, we might urge investigators to make their procedures seem more typical or familiar to children. Researchers who study intellectual development, for example, might present their questions as a game or as a puzzle to be solved, rather than simply asking the child to take a test.

The field experiment.   Perhaps the best way of determining whether a conclusion drawn from a laboratory experiment applies in the real world is to seek converging evidence by conducting an experiment in the natural environment—that is, a **field experiment.** This approach combines the advantages of naturalistic observation with the more rigorous control of an experiment. In addition, children are typically not apprehensive about participating in a "strange" experiment, because all the activities that they undertake are everyday activities, and they may not even be aware that they are being observed.

Let's consider an example of a field experiment that provides converging evidence for the hypothesis that children who watch **prosocial** television programs that display helpfulness, cooperation, and affection will themselves become more prosocially inclined. Lynette Friedrich and Aletha Stein (1973) went into a nursery school, became acquainted with the children there, and then observed how often each child was helpful, cooperative, or affectionate toward other children. This initial measure of the child's prosocial behavior provided a *baseline* against which future increases in helpfulness or cooperation could be measured. After the baseline data were collected, the children were randomly assigned to different experimental conditions. Some of the children watched prosocial television programming (*Mister Rogers' Neighborhood*) at school, three days a week for a month. Other children spent an equal amount of time at school watching neutral films featuring circuses and farm scenes. At the end of this month-long treatment phase, each child was observed daily in the nursery school setting for two additional weeks to determine

PHOTO 1-3. In a field experiment, the investigator manipulates some aspect of children's experience and then observes their behavior as they take part in everyday activities.

experimental control: *steps taken by an experimenter to ensure that all extraneous factors that could influence the dependent variable are roughly equivalent in each experimental condition; these precautions must be taken before an experimenter can be reasonably certain that observed changes in the dependent variable were caused by the manipulation of the independent variable.*

random assignment: *a control technique in which participants are assigned to experimental conditions through an unbiased procedure so that the members of the groups are not systematically different from one another.*

field experiment: *an experiment that takes place in a naturalistic setting such as the home, the school, or a playground.*

prosocial responses: *behaviors such as cooperation, helping, sharing, or comfort giving that benefit other people.*

BOX 1-3
THE DIFFERENCE BETWEEN
CORRELATION AND CAUSATION

There are many strategies that one can use to study the relationship between variables such as children's exposure to prosocial television and their helpgiving. Suppose, for example, that we had *interviewed* several dozen youngsters to determine each child's favorite TV shows and then *observed* the children at play, noting that those who preferred prosocial programming were much more helpful than those who favored other kinds of televised entertainment. What these data would show is that there is a meaningful relationship, or *correlation,* between children's television preferences and their helpfulness during free play. But would this correlation imply that watching prosocial television causes children to become more helpful?

No, it would not! Although we would have detected a relationship between children's preferences for prosocial programming and their helpgiving, the direction of this relationship is not at all clear. An equally plausible interpretation for our correlational finding is that helpful children are the ones who prefer prosocial programs! Another possibility is that neither of these variables causes the other and that

both are actually caused by a third variable that we have not measured. For example, if parental encouragement of helpgiving causes children to become more helpful *and* to prefer prosocial TV programs, then the latter two variables may be correlated, even though their relationship is not one of cause and effect. So correlational findings point to systematic relationships between variables, but they do not establish causality.

Naturalistic observation, interviews, case studies, and the clinical method are all excellent strategies for determining whether two or more variables are correlated. But since correlations do not imply causation, these methods cannot be used to establish the underlying causes of any aspect of human development. By contrast, the experimental method allows an investigator to determine whether two variables are causally related by systematically manipulating one of these variables to observe its *effect* (if any) on the other. So when Joyce Sprafkin and her colleagues manipulated children's exposure to different kinds of television programming and found that those who had watched prosocial programs became more helpful than those who had watched other programs, they were able to conclude that exposure to prosocial programming *causes* children to become more helpful, at least in the short run.

---

whether the television programming had had any effects on their willingness to cooperate with others or to give help and affection.

The results of this field experiment clearly indicated that children who had watched the prosocial programming did, indeed, become more cooperative and affectionate toward their peers than they had been during the initial baseline period. Not only are the results of this field experiment consistent with those reported by Sprafkin et al. (1975), but they also demonstrate that the conclusions drawn from that laboratory experiment are definitely applicable to the real world.

■ *The quasi-experiment*

There are many developmental issues to which the experimental method is not easily applied. Suppose, for example, that a developmental psychologist wanted to study the effects of school desegregation on the academic performance of Black children in Macon, Georgia. If it were pos-

sible to apply the experimental method, the psychologist might randomly assign half the Black students in Macon to integrated schools, while the other half would remain in segregated schools. After a year or so, the scholastic performance of these two groups could be compared to assess the academic effects of desegregation on Black schoolchildren. However, school desegregation generally takes place at roughly the same time for everyone within a given school district. Therefore, public policy makes the researcher's proposed experiment impossible. In cases such as this one, the psychologist would attempt to study the issue in question by conducting a quasi-experiment.

The **quasi-experiment** is a study in which the investigator observes the consequences of some natural event or policy decision that he or she assumes will have an impact on people's lives. The "independent variable" in a quasi-experiment is the event or "happening," which presumably will have consequences for those who experience it. But unlike experimental research, in which the investigator controls the independent variable and the assignment of participants to treatments, the quasi-experiment does not allow for such tight controls. Indeed, the quasi-experimenter must study the effects of natural events whenever, wherever, and however they may occur.

Thomas Cook and Donald Campbell (1979) describe an interesting quasi-experiment centered in Winston-Salem, North Carolina. The event that took place (that is, the "treatment") was a campaign in which a large group of young children were encouraged to watch the educational television program *Sesame Street* on a regular basis. Other children, whom the campaign would not reach, served as a no-treatment control group. The dependent variable was a test of children's general knowledge. Both groups were given the test before the campaign and again, well after the treatment group had been encouraged to become regular viewers of *Sesame Street*. At the time of the pretest, children in the treatment group knew significantly *less* general information than children in the control group. At the later testing, however, children in the treatment group knew significantly *more* than children in the control group. These findings, illustrated in Figure 1-1, suggest that

Sesame Street is rather effective at furthering the general knowledge of young children.

The major limitation of a quasi-experiment is that the investigator often has too little information about research participants and too little control over natural events to draw firm conclusions about cause and effect. For example, in the quasi-experiment described by Cook and Campbell (1979), the nature of the campaign was such that children were not randomly assigned to the treatment and no-treatment groups. And as is often the case in nonrandom assignment, the children did differ—those in the treatment group know *less* initially than those in the control group. Unfortunately, this initial difference between the groups suggests an alternative interpretation for the results. Suppose that children in the treatment condition were both *younger* and *smarter* than children in the control group. If this were true, it might be that children in the treatment group knew less on the initial test *because they were younger* but that their knowledge increased faster over time *because they were brighter*. The implication, then, is that encouraging children in the treatment group to watch *Sesame Street* may have had little if any effect on their general knowledge. Clearly, the investigators' lack of control over important aspects of the research makes the results of quasi-experiments vulnerable to alternative interpretations.

Despite its inability to make *strong* statements about cause and effect, the quasi-experiment is nevertheless useful in determining whether a natural event could *possibly* have had an effect on those who experience it. For example, the fact that those children who were encouraged to watch *Sesame Street* showed the greater increases in knowledge at least suggests that *Sesame Street* may have contributed to their relatively large gains. So quasi-experiments often provide meaningful *clues* about cause and effect. However, their results always remain open to alternative interpretations.

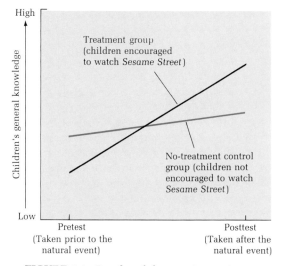

FIGURE 1-1. *Results of the quasi-experiment described by Cook and Campbell (1979).*

quasi-experiment: *a study in which the investigator measures the impact of some naturally occurring event that is assumed to affect people's lives.*

Designing Research to Measure Developmental Change

To this point, we have reviewed many of the techniques that developmentalists use to gather information about their research participants. However, these researchers are not merely interested in looking at children's behavior at any one moment; generally, they hope to determine how children's feelings, thoughts, and behaviors *develop* or *change* over time. How do they design their research to chart these developmental trends? Let's briefly consider three methods: the cross-sectional comparison, the longitudinal comparison, and the cross-sectional/short-term longitudinal comparison.

■ *Cross-sectional comparisons*

The **cross-sectional comparison** is a method in which groups of children who *differ in age* are studied at the *same point in time*. By comparing the responses of children in the different age groups, investigators can identify and often explain age-related changes in whatever aspect of development they are studying.

An experiment by Brian Coates and Willard Hartup (1969) is an excellent example of a cross-sectional comparison. Coates and Hartup were interested in determining why preschool children are less proficient than first- or second-graders at learning new responses displayed by an adult model. Their hypothesis was that younger children do not spontaneously *describe* what they are observing, whereas older children will produce verbal descriptions of the modeled sequence. When asked to perform the actions they have witnessed, the preschoolers are at a distinct disadvantage because they have no verbal "learning aids" that would help them to recall and reproduce the model's behavior.

To test these hypotheses, Coates and Hartup designed an interesting cross-sectional experiment. Children from two age groups—4- to 5-year-olds and 7- to 8-year-olds—watched a short film in which an adult model displayed 20 novel responses, such as shooting at a tower of blocks with a pop gun, throwing a beanbag between his legs, and lassoing an inflatable toy with a Hula Hoop. Some of the children from each age group were instructed to describe the model's actions, and they did so as they watched the film (induced-

verbalization condition). Other children were not required to describe the model's actions as they observed them (passive-observation condition). When the show ended, each child was taken to a room that contained the same toys seen in the film and was asked to demonstrate what the model had done with these toys.

Three interesting findings emerged from this experiment (the data appear in Figure 1-2). First, the 4–5-year-olds who were *not* told to describe what they had seen (that is, the passive observers) reproduced *fewer* of the model's responses than the 4–5-year-olds who described the model's behavior (the induced verbalizers) or the 7–8-year-olds in either experimental condition. This finding suggests that 4–5-year-old children may not produce the verbal descriptions that would help them to learn unless they are explicitly instructed to do so. Second, the performance of younger and older children in the induced-verbalization condition was comparable. So younger children can learn just as much as older children by observing a social model *if the*

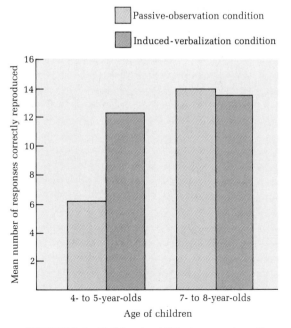

FIGURE 1-2. *Children's ability to reproduce the behavior of a social model as a function of age and verbalization instructions.*

younger children are told to describe what they are seeing. Finally, 7–8-year-olds in the passive-observation condition reproduced about the same number of behaviors as 7–8-year-olds in the induced-verbalization condition. This finding suggests that instructions to describe the model's actions had little effect on 7–8-year-olds, who will apparently describe what they have seen even when not explicitly told to. Taken together, the results imply that 4–5-year-olds in the natural setting may learn less from social models because they, unlike older children, do not spontaneously produce the verbal descriptions that would help them to remember what they have observed.

An important advantage of the cross-sectional method is that the investigator can collect data from children of different ages over a short time. For example, Coates and Hartup did not have to wait three years for their 4–5-year-olds to become 7–8-year-olds in order to test their developmental hypotheses. They merely sampled from two age groups and tested both samples simultaneously.

Notice that, in cross-sectional research, participants at each age level are *different* people. Hence, any "age-related" effects that are found in a cross-sectional study may not always be due to age or development but, rather, to some other feature that distinguishes participants at different age levels. An example may clarify the issue. For years, cross-sectional research had consistently indicated that young adults score higher on intelligence tests than middle-aged adults, who, in turn, score higher than the elderly. But does intelligence decline with age, as these findings would seem to indicate? Not necessarily! More recent research (Baltes, 1968) reveals that individuals' intelligence-test scores remain stable over the years and that the earlier studies were really measuring something quite different: age differences in education. The older adults in the cross-sectional studies had had less schooling and, therefore, scored lower on intelligence tests than the middle-aged or young adult samples. Their test scores had not declined but, rather, had always been lower than those of the younger adults with whom they were compared.

This example points directly to a second problem with the cross-sectional method: it tells us nothing about the development of *individuals* because each person is observed *at only one point in time.* So cross-sectional comparisons cannot pro- vide answers to questions such as "When will my child become more independent?" or "Will aggressive 2-year-olds become aggressive 5-year-olds?" To address issues like these, the investigator often turns to a second kind of developmental comparison, the longitudinal method.

■ *Longitudinal comparisons*

The **longitudinal comparison** is a method whereby the same children are observed repeatedly over a period of time. The time period may be very long or reasonably short. The investigators may be looking at one particular aspect of development, such as intelligence, or at many. By repeatedly testing the same children, investigators can assess the stability of various attributes and the patterns of developmental change for *each* child in the sample. In addition, they can identify general developmental trends and processes by looking for commonalities, such as the point(s) at which most children undergo various changes and the experiences, if any, that children seem to share prior to reaching these milestones. Finally, the tracking of several children over time will help investigators to understand *individual differences* in development, particularly if they are able to establish that different kinds of earlier experiences lead to very different outcomes.

One of the most famous longitudinal projects in the history of developmental psychology began in 1929 at the Fels Research Institute in Yellow Springs, Ohio. Imagine that you had been a new parent in 1929 and had responded to an ad requesting that you bring your newborn infant to the Fels Institute. The purpose of your visit: so that you and your child might participate together in an exciting new research project. When you arrive, a member of the Fels staff explains that this project is an ambitious one that will teach us a great deal about the child's world and the ways children develop. As he describes the project fur-

---

cross-sectional comparison: *a research design in which subjects from different age groups are studied at the same point in time.*
longitudinal comparison: *a research design in which one group of subjects is studied repeatedly over a period of months or years.*

ther, you suddenly realize that he is asking you to submit to at least one interview a year and to have your child weighed, measured, tested, and observed *for the next 18 years!* Would you volunteer? Many mothers did, for the Fels researchers began their longitudinal study with a total of 89 children, 45 males and 44 females.

Over the course of this project, the amount of information collected from each child (and from his or her mother) was simply staggering. For the first six years of the child's life, a professional interviewer made half-day, semiannual visits to the home, interviewing the mother and watching her interact with her child. These visits continued on an annual basis when the child was between 6 and 12 years of age. In addition, each child was repeatedly observed interacting with peers in a nursery school setting between the ages of 2½ and 5 and in a day camp between the ages of 6 and 10. In each of these settings, children were rated on traits such as aggression, achievement, conformity, dependency, sex-typed play, and verbal fluency. At three-year intervals between the ages of 8 and 17, each of the Fels children took an extensive battery of personality tests. Finally, 71 of the participants were located, tested, and interviewed when they were young adults between the ages of 20 and 29.

Can you imagine the work involved in analyzing all this information? Indeed, the data were analyzed, and they allowed members of the research team to draw important conclusions about the long-term stability or instability of behaviors such as aggression, achievement, and dependency. The investigators were also able to make inferences about the effects of various methods of parenting on the child's later feelings, aspirations, and behavior. Clearly, the Fels project was an undertaking of monumental proportions. We will return to this important study on several occasions as we continue along our journey through the child's world.

Although we have portrayed the longitudinal comparison in a very favorable manner, this procedure does have several drawbacks of which you should be aware. For example, longitudinal projects can be very *costly* (imagine the bill for 18 years of research in the Fels study) and *time-consuming.* The latter point is more important than it may first appear, for the focus of theory and

research in developmental psychology is constantly changing, and longitudinal questions that seem very exciting at the beginning of a long-term project may seem rather trivial by the time the project ends. As longitudinal researchers, we may also have a problem with *subject loss;* children may move away, get sick, or become bored with repeated testing, and they occasionally have parents who, for one reason or another, will not allow them to continue in the study. The result is a smaller and potentially **nonrepresentative sample** that not only provides less information about the developmental issues in question but also may limit the conclusions of the study to those healthy children who do not move away and who remain cooperative over the long run.

There is another shortcoming of longitudinal research that students often see right away—the **cross-generational problem.** Children growing up in one era may be exposed to very different kinds of experiences than children from another era. As a consequence, the patterns of development that characterize one generation of children may not always apply to other generations.

To clarify the issue, we need only note how times have changed since the 1930s and '40s, when the Fels children were growing up. In this age of working mothers, more youngsters are attending day-care centers and nursery schools than ever before. Modern families are smaller than those of years past, meaning that children now have fewer brothers and sisters. Families also move more frequently than they did in the 1930s and '40s, so that many children from the modern era are exposed to a wider variety of people and places than was typical in years gone by. And no matter where they may be living, today's youngsters grow up in front of television sets, an influence that was not widely available until the mid-1950s. So children of the 1930s and 1940s lived in a very different world, and we cannot be certain that these youngsters developed in precisely the same way as today's children. In other words, cross-generational changes in the environment may limit the conclusions of a longitudinal project to those children who were growing up while the study was in progress.

We have seen that the cross-sectional and the longitudinal methods each have distinct advantages and disadvantages. Might it be possible to

PHOTO 1-4. *Leisure activities of the 1930s (left) and the 1980s (right). As these photos illustrate, children growing up in the 1930s had very different kinds of experiences from those of today's youth. Many believe that cross-generational changes in the environment may limit the results of a longitudinal study to the youngsters who were growing up while that research was in progress.*

combine the best features of both approaches? A third kind of developmental comparison—the cross-sectional/short-term longitudinal method—tries to do just that.

■ *The cross-sectional/short-term longitudinal comparison*

Suppose that we have developed a training program designed to reduce racial prejudice among 6- to 10-year-olds. Before administering our program on a large scale, we will want to try it out on a smaller number of children to see whether it works. However, there are a number of additional questions that others may have about our program, such as "When can children first understand it?" or "At what age will children respond most favorably to the technique?" Finally, educators and child-care personnel would want to know whether any immediate reductions in prejudice produced by our program will persist over time. In order to address all these issues in our research, we will need a design that measures *both* the short-term and the long-term effects of our program on children of *different ages.*

Clearly, the cross-sectional comparison cannot answer all our questions. The cross-sectional design, which employs different children at each age level, cannot tell us anything about the long-term effects of our program on an individual child. The longitudinal method can tell us about long-term effects. But since all the participants would be exposed to the program at the same age (say, age 6), a longitudinal study would not tell us whether this training would be any more (or less) effective if it were first administered when children were a little older.

The only design that allows us to answer all our questions is the **cross-sectional/short-term longitudinal comparison.** This procedure combines the best features of the cross-sectional and the longitudinal approaches by selecting children of different ages and then studying each of these age

---

nonrepresentative sample: *a subgroup that differs in important ways from the larger group (or population) to which it belongs.*

cross-generational problem: *the fact that long-term changes in the environment may limit conclusions of a longitudinal project to that generation of children who were growing up while the study was in progress.*

cross-sectional/short-term longitudinal comparison: *a complex research design in which subjects from different age groups are studied repeatedly over a period of months or years.*

groups over time. For purposes of our proposed research, we might begin by administering our training program to a group of 6-year-olds, a group of 8-year-olds, and a group of 10-year-olds. Of course, we would want to randomly assign other 6-, 8-, and 10-year-olds to control groups that were not to be exposed to the training program. The children who were "trained" would then be observed and compared with their age mates in the control group to determine (1) whether the pro-

gram was immediately effective at reducing racial prejudice and (2) if so, the age at which the program had its largest immediate impact. This is the information that we would obtain had we conducted a standard cross-sectional experiment.

However, our choice of the cross-sectional/short-term longitudinal method allows us to measure the enduring effects of our program by simply retesting our samples of 6- and 8-year-olds two years later. This approach has several advantages

TABLE 1-2. Three methods of detecting developmental trends

	Cross-sectional method	Longitudinal method	Cross-sectional/short-term longitudinal method
Procedure	Observe children of different ages at one point in time	Observe children of one age on more than one occasion over time	Observe children of different ages on more than one occasion over time
Information gained	Differences in the behavior of older and younger children (children in each age group are different people)	Changes in the behavior of individual children over time	Changes over time in the behavior of children of different ages
Implications of information gained	Hints at developmental trends	Reflects developmental trends for individual children from one age group	Reflects developmental trends for individual children from several age groups
Advantages	1. Demonstrates age differences in behavior 2. Relatively inexpensive 3. Takes little time to conduct	Provides data on the development of individual children	1. Provides data on the development of individual children of different ages 2. Less time-consuming than longitudinal research 3. May be less costly and more informative than longitudinal research
Disadvantages	1. Age trends may reflect extraneous differences between older and younger children rather than true developmental change 2. Provides no data on the development of individuals because each participant is observed at only one point in time	1. Relatively expensive 2. Extremely time-consuming 3. Participants may drop out of the project 4. Cross-generational problems	1. More costly than cross-sectional research 2. More time-consuming than cross-sectional research

PHOTO 1-5. *Cross-cultural comparisons allow us to identify similarities and differences in the development of children from different cultures.*

over the standard longitudinal comparison. The first is a *time saving:* in only two years, we have learned about the long-term effects of the program on those children who are still between the target ages of 6 and 10. A standard longitudinal comparison would require four years to provide similar information. Second, the cross-sectional/short-term longitudinal design actually yields *more information* about long-term effects than the longitudinal approach does. If we had chosen the longitudinal method, we would have data on the long-term effects of a program administered *only* to 6-year-olds. However, the cross-sectional/short-term longitudinal design allows us to determine whether the program has *comparable* long-term effects when administered to both 6- and 8-year-olds. Clearly, this combination of the cross-sectional and longitudinal methods provides a rather versatile alternative to either of these approaches (see Table 1-2 for a brief summary of the aims, implications, advantages, and disadvantages of each type of developmental comparison).

The Cross-Cultural Comparison

Developmental researchers are normally hesitant to publish a new finding or conclusion until they have studied enough children to determine that their "discovery" is reliable. However, their conclusions are frequently based on children living at one point in time within one particular culture, and it is often difficult to know whether these conclusions will apply to future generations or even to children who are currently growing up in other areas around the world. Today, the generalizability of findings across samples and settings has become an important issue, for many theorists have implied that there are "universals" in human development—events and outcomes that all children share as they progress from infancy to adulthood.

Cross-cultural studies are those in which participants from different cultural backgrounds are observed, tested, and compared on some aspect of their psychological functioning. Studies of this kind serve many purposes. For example, they allow the investigator to determine whether conclusions drawn about the development of children from one society apply to children growing up in other societies. So the **cross-cultural comparison** guards against the overgeneralization of research findings and, indeed, is the only way to determine whether there are truly "universals" in human development.

Although cross-cultural research has led to the discovery of several apparent "universals" in human development, many investigators who favor and use this approach are looking for *differences* rather than similarities. They recognize that human beings develop in societies that have very different ideas about issues such as the age at which mothers should wean their infants, when and how children should be punished, the activities that are most appropriate for boys and girls, the time at which childhood ends and adulthood begins, the treatment of the aged, and countless other aspects of life. They have also learned that people from various cultures differ in the ways they perceive the world, express their emotions, think, and solve problems. Ruth Benedict (1934) used the term *cultural relativity* to express her belief that a person's behavior can be understood only within the context of his or her cultural environment. Child development in cross-cultural perspective is, in part, an attempt to discover how societies differ in the ways they raise their children and how these differences may then contribute to the development of culture-specific patterns of behavior, or distinct "cultural personalities."

We have now reviewed a variety of research designs and techniques, each of which has definite strengths and weaknesses. Perhaps this is the time to say that there is no "best method" for studying children; each of the methods we have considered has contributed in a meaningful way to the science of developmental psychology. When planning a research project, developmentalists will select a method only after carefully considering what it will take to answer the questions they are asking and then comparing these needs against available resources, such as the size of their research budget, the amount of time that they have to conduct the research, and the availability of research participants.

There is yet another important concern that investigators must consider—the impact of their research on the child. In Box 1-1 we referred to a Bill of Rights for Children as a reflection of just how far Western cultures have progressed in their regard for and treatment of the young. Children serving as participants in psychological experiments have important rights as well—rights that the investigator is ethically bound to protect.

ETHICAL CONSIDERATIONS IN DEVELOPMENTAL RESEARCH

Many years ago, Sigmund Freud proposed that children must establish a close emotional relationship with a mother figure during the first year or two of life, or they would remain forever cold and emotionally unresponsive to other people. There is a very simple experiment that one could conduct to test this hypothesis: Randomly assign one group of infants to an experimental condition in which they are locked in an attic and receive only the most basic care for the first two years of their lives. The remaining infants would be reared in their normal home environments for the same length of time. If Freud was correct, we should find that our socially isolated group would remain wary of people and unable to form close emotional attachments to others for as long as we might care to observe them. In contrast, children reared at home should show a normal pattern of emotional responsiveness.

Now you may be thinking "Heaven forbid! Only a barbarian would propose such an experiment!" This example is admittedly extreme, but purposefully so to make a point: a researcher is never justified in exposing children to any situation or experimental procedure that is likely to seriously harm them. In the case of our hypothetical experiment, we have reason to believe that social isolation will have harmful and possibly even pathological consequences for research participants. Thus, the project represents a gross violation of **research ethics**, and it is unlikely that any developmental researcher would even contemplate such a course of action (except, of course, to make a point about ethical guidelines in research with children).

The ethical issues encountered in most research are far more subtle. Here are some of the dilemmas

TABLE 1-3. The rights of children and responsibilities of investigators involved in psychological research

In order to protect children who participate in psychological research and to clarify the responsibilities of researchers who work with children, the American Psychological Association (1973) has endorsed the following ethical guidelines:

1. No matter how young the child he has rights that supersede the rights of the investigator. The investigator should measure each operation he proposes in terms of the child's rights, and before proceeding, he should obtain the approval of a committee of [the investigator's fellow scientists].

2. The final responsibility to establish and maintain ethical practices in research remains with the individual investigator. He is also responsible for the ethical practices of all [research collaborators who, in turn] incur parallel obligations.

4. The investigator should inform the child of all features of the research that may affect his willingness to participate.

5. The investigator should respect the child's freedom to refuse to participate in research . . . as well as to discontinue participation at any time.

6. The informed consent of parents or of those who act [in the child's behalf—teachers, superintendents of institutions] should be obtained, preferably in writing. Informed consent requires that the parent or other responsible adult be told all features of the research that may affect his willingness to allow the child to participate.

9. The investigator uses no research operation that may harm the child either physically or psychologically. Psychological harm, to be sure, is difficult to define; nevertheless, its definition remains the responsibility of the investigator. When the investigator is in doubt about the possible harmful effects of the research operations, he seeks consultation from others. When harm seems possible, he is obligated to find other means of obtaining the information or to abandon the research.

10. Although we accept the ethical ideal of full disclosure of information, a particular study may necessitate concealment or deception. Whenever concealment or deception is thought to be essential to the conduct of the study, the investigator should satisfy a committee of his peers that his judgment is correct. If concealment or deception is practiced, adequate measures should be taken after the study to ensure the participant's understanding of the reasons for the concealment or deception.

11. The investigator should keep in confidence all information obtained about research participants.

that developmental psychologists may have to resolve during their careers as researchers:

1. Is it appropriate to expose children to situations that virtually guarantee that they will violate certain prohibitions or behave in some other socially undesirable manner?

2. Can I ask children or adolescents about the ways their parents punish them, or is this line of questioning an invasion of the children's (or parents') privacy?

3. Am I ever justified in deceiving children in some way, either by misinforming them about the purpose of my study or by telling them something untrue about themselves (for example, "You did poorly on this test")?

4. Can I observe my participants in the natural setting without informing them that they are the subjects of a scientific investigation?

5. Is it acceptable to tell children that their classmates think that an obviously incorrect answer is "correct" in order to see whether participants will conform to the judgments of their peers?

6. Am I justified in using verbal punishment (disapproval) as part of my research procedure?

Before reading further, you may wish to think about these issues and formulate your own opinions. Then read Table 1-3 and reconsider each of your points of view.

cross-cultural comparison: *a study that compares the behavior and/or development of people from different cultural backgrounds.*

research ethics: *standards of conduct that investigators are ethically bound to honor in order to protect their research participants from physical or psychological harm.*

BOX 1-4
TO PROCEED OR NOT TO PROCEED—
THAT IS THE QUESTION

This box illustrates how one child developmentalist grappled with a number of ethical issues while attempting to investigate a possible contributing factor to children's aggressive behavior. Let's first consider the nature of the research and how it was conceived.

The investigator had read a report (Straus, Gelles, & Steinmetz, 1980) suggesting that victims of child abuse often become child abusers if they later have children of their own. Why? One possibility is that an abused child may infer from his or her own horrible experiences that the way people treat irritating children is to abuse them. Consequently, the abused may later become an abuser when his or her own children are demanding, fussy, or otherwise irritating.

This line of reasoning made sense to the investigator. However, he couldn't help wondering whether abused children might not also learn to assault *anyone* who irritates them, including their childhood friends and playmates. He then set out to test this hypothesis by proposing to question children about the methods that their parents used to punish them. The plan was to examine the children's responses to a structured interview and then to divide the children into (1) an "abused" group who reported that their parents were often violent and used very intense forms of physical punishment and (2) a "control" group whose parents were not described as violent or intense in their disciplinary practices. He then proposed to observe these children during their school recess periods in order to determine whether youngsters in the "abused" group were any more physically aggressive toward their playmates than were children in the "control" group.

Now let's consider the potential *risks* to research participants. Clearly, the investigator was asking them questions about members of their families and perhaps invading their privacy (or that of their parents). How could this risk be minimized? The investigator's strategy was to tell the children that (1) no one other than he would ever know how they had answered any question and (2) that they didn't have to answer any question that they didn't feel like answering. The investigator also promised to destroy his notes of each interview after the data were analyzed. Finally, he proposed to obtain the *informed consent* (see Table 1-3, guideline 6) of the children's teachers and the school's head administrator.

A second concern with this project was that the investigator would be observing the children without telling them he was interested in aggressive behavior (or even that their play activities were the subject of scientific investigation). He was hesitant to provide children with this knowledge in advance for fear that some of them might begin to punch, kick, or bite their playmates in order to attract his attention (both the review committee and the school's head administrator agreed that this was a possibility). However, he did plan to tell the children what he had been observing when the study was over. He also intended to inform them that no one would ever know how they had behaved and to allow each child to decide whether he or she wished to be a part of this project. Data from any child who did not wish to

Have any of your opinions changed? It would not be terribly surprising if they hadn't. As you can see, the guidelines in Table 1-3 are very general; they do not explicitly permit or prohibit specific operations or practices such as those described in the dilemmas. The responsibility for treating children fairly and protecting them from harm falls squarely on the shoulders of the investigator.

How, then, do investigators decide whether to use a procedure that some may consider questionable on ethical grounds? They generally weigh the advantages and disadvantages of the research by carefully calculating its possible *benefits* (to humanity or to the participants) and comparing them against the potential *risks* that participants may face. If the potential benefits greatly outweigh the potential risks, and if there are no other less risky procedures that could be used to produce these same benefits, the investigator will generally proceed. However, there are safeguards against overzealous researchers who underestimate the riskiness of their procedures. In the United States, for example, universities, research foundations, and government agencies that fund research with children have set up "human-subjects review committees" to provide second (and sometimes third) opinions on the ethical standards and considerations of all proposed research. The function of these review committees is to reconsider the potential risks and benefits of the proposed research and, more important, to help ensure that all

participate were to be destroyed immediately and hence would not be tabulated, analyzed, and included in any forthcoming report of the results.

What were the potential *benefits* of this line of research? The investigator felt there were many. First, he hoped to determine whether a structured interview might reliably identify current or potential victims of child abuse. True, he had promised to keep all interview responses confidential and would not be following up on his "abused" group. However, he believed that social service agencies that handle child abuse cases might be able to use his interview technique if it looked promising. Of course, a successful method of identifying victims of child abuse would be of obvious benefit to any victim who was then identified as a victim and who subsequently became an ex-victim. In addition, the research promised to increase our knowledge about the consequences of child abuse if it could be demonstrated that abused children become abusive playmates. In sum, the investigator concluded that the potential benefits of his research far outweighed the risks to participants. He then submitted his research proposal to the university's human-subjects review committee.

The committee members agreed with his assessments of the benefits and risks involved in this research. But in their view, the proposal had not gone far enough in minimizing the risks that children might face by responding to the structured interview. The committee suggested that the investigator should *not* reveal the identities of children in the "abused" group to teachers or to school administrators. This was clearly a sticky point, for the investigator felt that he had a responsibility to inform officials that certain children were worth observing if they told him that they were often beaten or otherwise mistreated at home. But there was another side to this issue. The committee noted that children have active imaginations and that the interview method may be imperfect. In other words, parents described as "abusers" by their children may not be abusers at all. Second, and of greater importance: if parents described as abusers really were abusive, they might abuse their children further if an indignant teacher were to state that their children had labeled them as abusive. The investigator concluded that the committee had a point, and he agreed *not* to reveal the identities of children classified as "abused" on the basis of their responses to his structured interview.*

This case study illustrates that researchers and the institutions that oversee research are genuinely concerned about the welfare of children who participate in psychological research. Research can be a valuable tool for increasing our knowledge of children— knowledge that should benefit us all. However, we must guarantee that the knowledge we gain in conducting this research does not come at the expense of those youngsters who so generously provide it.

*Many states now have laws that would prohibit an investigator from withholding the names of children who might be the victims of child abuse. Lawmakers in these states have decided that the rights of the young must always be protected and that it is the responsibility of social service agencies (rather than researchers or review committees) to determine whether children are fabricating stories about parental abuse.

possible steps are taken to protect the welfare and maintain the integrity of those who may choose to participate in the project.

Although it is your right and privilege to disagree, any of the dilemmas outlined above can be resolved in ways that permit the investigator to use the procedures in question and still remain well within current ethical guidelines. One investigator's resolution of dilemmas 2 and 4, which is described in Box 1-4, illustrates how researchers approach ethical issues and how these issues are subsequently weighed and evaluated by a human-subjects review committee.

Of course, final approval by a review committee does not absolve the investigator of the need to reevaluate the benefits and costs of his project, even while the research is in progress. Suppose, for example, that the children who participated in the project described in Box 1-4 had discovered the investigator's fascination with aggressive behavior and then begun to beat on one another in order to attract his attention. At that point, the risks to participants would have escalated far beyond the researcher's initial estimates, and he would have been ethically bound (in my opinion) to discontinue the research immediately.

In the final analysis, guidelines and review committees do not guarantee that research participants will be treated responsibly; only investigators can do that, by constantly reevaluating the consequences of their operations and by modifying or abandoning any procedure that may compromise the welfare or the dignity of those who have volunteered to participate.

SUMMARY

Developmental psychology is the study of changes that people experience from the day they are conceived until the day they die. Developmentalists are particularly concerned with identifying significant changes in physical growth, mental abilities, emotional expression, and social behaviors and with explaining why these changes occur. Human development continues throughout the life span and is holistic—meaning that changes in one aspect of development often have implications for other, seemingly unrelated aspects.

Until the recent past, children were treated harshly and considered little more than miniature adults. The viewpoints of important social philosophers of the 17th and 18th centuries contributed to a more humane outlook on children and child rearing, and shortly thereafter, people began to study their sons and daughters and to report their findings in baby biographies. The scientific study of children did not emerge until about 1900 as G. Stanley Hall, in the United States, and Sigmund Freud, in Europe, began to collect objective data and to formulate theories about human growth and development. Soon other investigators were conducting research to evaluate and extend these theories, and the study of developmental psychology began to thrive.

Developmental psychology in the 1980s is a truly objective science. Gone forever are the days when the merits of a theory depended on the social or academic prestige of the theorist. Today a child developmentalist determines the adequacy of a theory by deriving hypotheses and conducting research to see whether the theory can predict and explain the new observations that he or she has made. There is no room for subjective bias in evaluating ideas; theories in developmental psychology are only as good as their ability to account for the important aspects of children's growth and development.

Developmentalists are fortunate to have available a variety of useful methods for studying children and detecting developmental changes. The major methods for conducting research with children include naturalistic observation, interviews, case studies, clinical approaches, experiments, and quasi-experiments. Developmental trends are detected by adapting one or more of these techniques to provide cross-sectional or longitudinal comparisons. The cross-sectional comparison assesses developmental change by studying children of different ages at the same point in time. The longitudinal approach detects developmental trends by repeatedly examining the same children as they grow older. A combination of the cross-sectional and the longitudinal approaches is also available to the investigator who wishes to take advantage of the best features of both strategies. Each of these research techniques and designs has advantages and disadvantages, and there is no "best method" for studying children. When planning a research project, the developmental psychologist selects a particular technique and research design only after considering the nature of the problem under investigation, the costs involved, and the availability of research participants.

Developmentalists may face difficult ethical dilemmas when conducting research with children. No matter how important the knowledge that might be gained, a researcher is never justified in harming children or in undermining their dignity. The knowledge gained from research with children should benefit us all, but it is the responsibility of the investigator to guarantee that this knowledge does not come at the expense of the participants who so generously provide it.

REFERENCES

American Psychological Association. (1973). Ethical principles in the conduct of research with human participants. Washington, DC: Author.

Aries, P. (1962). Centuries of childhood. New York: Knopf.

Baltes, P. B. (1968). Longitudinal and cross-sectional sequences in the study of age and generation effects. Human Development, 11, 145–171.

Benedict, R. (1934). Patterns of culture. Boston: Houghton Mifflin.

Bronfenbrenner, U. (1977). Toward an experimental ecology of human development. American Psychologist, 32, 513–531.

Charlesworth, R., & Hartup, W. W. (1967). Positive social reinforcement in the nursery school peer group. Child Development, 38, 993–1002.

Coates B., and Hartup, W. W. (1969). Age and verbalization in observational learning. *Developmental Psychology, 1,* 556–562.

Cook, T. D. & Campbell, D. T. (1979). *Quasi-experimentation: Design and analysis issues for field settings.* Chicago: Rand McNally.

Darwin, C. A. (1877). A biographical sketch of an infant. *Mind, 2,* 285-294.

deMause, L. (1974). The evolution of childhood. In L. deMause (Ed.), *The history of childhood.* New York: Harper & Row.

Despert, J. L. (1965). *The emotionally disturbed child: Then and now.* New York: Brunner/Mazel.

Friedrich, L. K. & Stein, A. H. (1973). Aggressive and prosocial television programs and the natural behavior of preschool children. *Monographs of the Society for Research in Child Development, 38* (4, Serial No. 51).

Hall, G. S. (1891). The contents of children's minds on entering school. *Pedagogical Seminary, 1,* 139–173.

Hobbes, T. (1904). *Leviathan.* Cambridge: Cambridge University Press. (Original work published 1651)

Kean, A. W. G. (1937). The history of the criminal liability of children. *Law Quarterly Review, 3,* 364–370.

Kessen, W. (1965). *The child.* New York: Wiley.

Midlarsky, E., & Bryan, J. H. (1972). Affect expressions and children's imitative altruism. *Journal of Experimental Research in Personality, 6,* 195–203.

Piaget, J. (1965). *The child's conception of number.* New York: Norton.

Rosenhan, D. L. (1970). The natural socialization of altruistic autonomy. In J. L. Macaulay & L. Berkowitz (Eds.), *Altruism and helping behavior.* New York: Academic Press.

Sprafkin, J. L., Liebert, R. M., & Poulous, R. W. (1975). Effects of a prosocial televised example on children's helping. *Journal of Experimental Child Psychology, 20,* 119–126.

Straus, M. A., Gelles, R. J., & Steinmetz, S. K. (1980). *Behind closed doors.* New York: Anchor Books.

Walster, E., Walster, G. W., & Berscheid, E. (1978). *Equity: Theory and research.* Boston: Allyn & Bacon.

Williams, J. E., Bennett, S. M., & Best, D. L. (1975). Awareness and expression of sex stereotypes in young children. *Developmental Psychology, 11,* 635–642.

CHAPTER TWO ■

THEORIES OF HUMAN DEVELOPMENT

■ *Questions and controversies about human development*

■ *The psychoanalytic viewpoint*
Overview of Freud's psychoanalytic theory
Erik Erikson's theory of psychosocial development
Psychoanalytic theory today

■ *The learning viewpoint (behaviorism)*
What is learning?
Theories of social learning
Social learning as a reciprocal process
Contributions and criticisms of learning theory

■ *The cognitive-developmental viewpoint*
Origins of Piaget's cognitive theory
Piaget's view of intelligence
Stages of cognitive development
Piaget on social learning
Contributions and criticisms of the cognitive-developmental viewpoint

■ *The ethological viewpoint*
Contributions of the ethological viewpoint
Criticisms of ethology

■ *A final comment on developmental theories*

■ *Summary*

*T*hat's only true in theory, not in practice!

ANONYMOUS

There is nothing as practical as a good theory.

KURT LEWIN

In our introductory chapter, we talked only briefly about theories, portraying them as sets of concepts and propositions that describe and explain certain aspects of our experience. We also noted that everyone is a "theorist" in one sense of the term, for each of us has a definite point of view reflecting what he or she believes to be true about many issues, observations, and events.

A *scientific* theory is a public pronouncement that indicates what a scientist believes to be true about his or her specific area of investigation. Ideally, a theory is concise and yet can describe and explain a wide range of phenomena. A theory should also be *precise*—that is, capable of making explicit predictions about future events so that the theory can be either supported or disconfirmed by later research.

If subsequent research should indicate that a theory cannot adequately predict and explain new findings, the theory may have to be revised extensively or discarded altogether. Thus, it may seem at times that some theoretical pronouncements *are* true only in theory, not in practice. However, there is clearly another side to this issue. Couldn't we argue that even "bad" theories that are later abandoned have served a useful purpose by stimulating the new knowledge that led to their ultimate demise? We might also note that good theories survive because they continue to generate new knowledge, much of which may have practical implications that truly benefit humanity. In this sense, there is nothing quite so practical as a *good* theory.

In this chapter we will consider the four theoretical viewpoints that have had the greatest impact on developmental psychology: the *psychoanalytic* viewpoint, the *learning* viewpoint, the *cognitive-developmental* viewpoint, and the *etho-*

logical viewpoint.[1] We will see that each of these theories emphasizes different areas or aspects of human behavior. In addition, each theory makes different assumptions about human nature and the causes of development. Before reviewing the content of these theories, it may be helpful to consider some of the more basic issues or points of contention on which they differ.

QUESTIONS AND CONTROVERSIES ABOUT HUMAN DEVELOPMENT

Developmental theorists have different points of view on at least four basic issues:

1. Are children inherently good or inherently bad?
2. Is nature (biological forces) or nurture (environmental forces) the primary influence on human development?
3. Are children actively involved in the developmental process, or rather, are they passive recipients of social and biological influences?
4. Is development continuous or discontinuous?

1. *Assumptions about human nature.* We learned in Chapter One that social philosophers of the 17th and 18th centuries portrayed children as inherently bad (doctrine of original sin), as inherently good (doctrine of innate purity), or as neither bad nor good (doctrine of *tabula rasa*). As it turns out, each of these ideas remains with us today in one or more contemporary theories of human development. Although one may search a theory in vain for explicit statements about human nature, the theorist will typically emphasize either the positive or negative aspects of children's character or perhaps will note that positivity or negativity of character depends on the child's experiences. These assumptions about human nature are important, for they influence the content of each developmental theory—

particularly what the theory has to say about child rearing.

2. *Nature versus nurture.* One of the oldest controversies among developmental theorists is the "nature versus nurture" issue: Are human beings a product of their heredity and other biological predispositions, or are they shaped by the environment in which they are raised? Here are two opposing viewpoints:

> Heredity and not environment is the chief maker of man. . . . Nearly all of the misery and nearly all of the happiness in the world are due not to environment. . . . The differences among men are due to differences in the germ cells with which they were born [Wiggam, 1923, p. 42].

> Give me a dozen healthy infants, well formed, and my own specified world to bring them up in and I'll guarantee to take any one at random and train him to become any type of specialist I might select—doctor, lawyer, artist, merchant, chief, and yes, even beggar-man and thief, regardless of his talents, penchants, tendencies, abilities, vocations, and race of his ancestors. There is no such thing as an inheritance of capacity, talent, temperament, mental constitution, and behavioral characteristics [Watson, 1925, p. 82].

Although few contemporary psychologists would endorse either of these radical points of view, the **nature/nurture controversy** rages on. For example, Arthur Jensen (1969) has argued that heredity accounts for 80% of the variability in human intelligence; most developmental researchers, however, consider this an overestimate. Toward the other end of the continuum, B. F. Skinner (1971) believes that many human attributes are determined largely by environment, biology playing only a minor role.

Of course, there is a middle ground. The majority of child developmentalists now believe that the relative contributions of nature and nurture depend on the aspect of development in question. However, they stress that complex human attributes such as temperament, intelligence, and personality are the end products of a long and involved interplay between biological predispositions and environmental forces. Their advice to us, then, is to think less about nature *versus* nurture and more about how these two sets of influences combine or *interact* to produce developmental change.

[1]Many other theories have been proposed to account for particular developmental phenomena such as physical growth and various aspects of social, personality, and intellectual development. Although we focus on the four grand theories of human development in this chapter, the strengths and weaknesses of these other "mini-theories" will be considered when we discuss the topics to which they apply.

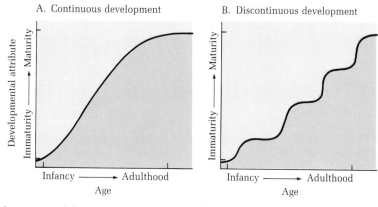

FIGURE 2-1. *The course of development as described by continuity and discontinuity (stage) theorists.*

3. *Activity versus passivity.* Another topic of theoretical debate is the **activity/passivity** issue. Are children curious, active creatures who largely determine how agents of society treat them? Or are they passive souls on whom society fixes its stamp? Consider the implications of these opposing viewpoints. If it could be shown that children are extremely malleable—literally at the mercy of those who raise them—then perhaps individuals who turned out to be less than productive would be justified in suing their overseers for malfeasance. Indeed, one young man in the United States recently used this logic to bring a malfeasance suit against his parents. Perhaps you can anticipate the defense that the parents' lawyer would offer. Counsel would surely argue that the parents tried many strategies in an attempt to raise their child right but that he responded favorably to none of them. The implication is that this young man played an active role in determining how his parents treated him and therefore is largely responsible for creating the climate in which he was raised.

Which of these points of view do you consider the more reasonable? In a moment, you will have an opportunity to compare your answer against those offered by several well-known developmental theorists.

4. *Continuity versus discontinuity.* Think for a moment about the concept of developmental change. Do you think that the changes we experience along the road to maturity occur very gradually? Or would you say that these changes are rather abrupt?

Continuity theorists view human development as an additive process that occurs in small steps, without sudden changes. They might represent the course of developmental change with a relatively smooth growth curve like the one in Figure 2-1A. In contrast, **discontinuity**, or "stage," theorists believe that the developing child proceeds through a series of abrupt changes, each of which elevates the child to a new and presumably more advanced *stage* of development. These stages are represented by the plateaus in the discontinuous growth curve in Figure 2-1B.

A **developmental stage** is a period of the life cycle characterized by a particular set of abilities, motives, behaviors, or emotions that occur

nature/nurture controversy: *the debate within developmental psychology over the relative importance of biological predispositions (nature) and environmental influences (nurture) as determinants of human development.*

activity/passivity issue: *a debate among developmental theorists about whether children are active contributors to their own development or, rather, passive recipients of environmental influence.*

continuity/discontinuity issue: *an argument among theorists about whether human development is best characterized as gradual and continuous or abrupt and stagelike.*

developmental stage: *a distinct phase within a larger sequence of development; a period characterized by a particular set of abilities, motives, behaviors, or emotions that occur together and form a coherent pattern.*

together and form a coherent pattern. However, it is important to note that a stage is merely a *description* of the attributes that appear at one point in the life cycle: A theorist who summarizes the course of development with a series of stages has not necessarily explained why that development occurred. To qualify as an *explanation* of development, a stage theory must tell (1) how or why components of each stage "hang together" as an organized whole and (2) how or why children progress from stage to stage.

The continuity/discontinuity controversy is not easily resolved. Consider the following example. One teenager thought he would never grow. Although his height had been increasing at about one inch per year for several years, he was only 5′2″ at the beginning of his third year of high school. His friends (and some prospective dates) called him "shrimpie." Ah, but that glorious junior year! He grew nine inches, gained 45 pounds, and suddenly found himself being "drafted" in the earlier rounds when team captains chose players for football games in gym class.

Isn't this discontinuous development—a spurt of nine inches in one year after growing but five inches over the past five years? Stage theorists would certainly say it is. Continuity theorists, however, might argue that the boy's growth had been very steady during the previous five years. They would also note that he didn't grow nine inches overnight—it took a year to do so. What was happening, in their view, was that the boy was experiencing an event, puberty, that caused his rate of physical development to accelerate. But even though he was growing faster during his one-year "growth spurt," this growth remained gradual, or continuous, over that year.

One reason for the continuity/discontinuity debate is that discontinuity theorists tend to focus on the visible results of development—the obvious changes in the child with age—whereas continuity theorists are looking at the processes that give rise to these changes. Research in developmental psychology shows that different types of development are important at different periods of the life cycle. For example, physical growth is most rapid during infancy and early adolescence; language emerges during the preschool period; logical thinking appears during middle childhood; and abstract reasoning develops during preadolescence (that is, ages 11 to 13). If we con-

centrate on *what it is that is developing* (for example, intelligence, language, or moral reasoning), human development may often appear to be rather discontinuous—that is, stagelike. However, if we focus on the *processes that underlie these developments* (for example, learning and biological maturation), then development may seem rather gradual, or continuous. As we review the leading theories of child development, we will see that continuity theorists do tend to concentrate on the *processes* that underlie developmental change, whereas stage theorists are concerned mainly with the nature or *content* of these changes.

In Chapter One we noted that many people find it exceedingly difficult *not* to select a "favorite" theory of human development after scanning several of these approaches for the first time. The reason that we tend to "play favorites" may be quite simple: we all make assumptions about children and the ways they develop, and perhaps we tend to favor theories that make assumptions similar to our own. See whether you find this true of yourself. Take the short quiz in Box 2-1 and compare the overall pattern of your five responses against the several patterns that appear in the key. Then, after completing this chapter, see whether the theory you prefer is the one that most closely matches the pattern of responses you favored when completing this exercise. (Let's note, however, that the best way to evaluate these theories is on the demonstrated ability of each to predict and explain significant aspects of human development, not on the basis of our first impressions or preferences.)

THE PSYCHOANALYTIC VIEWPOINT

With the possible exception of Charles Darwin's theory of evolution, no scientific theory has had a greater impact on Western thought than Sigmund Freud's psychoanalytic theory. One professor claimed that Freud's name was recognized by a larger percentage of the American people than that of any other scientific personality. And he may have been correct. Many laypersons have been exposed to at least some of Freud's ideas, and it would not be surprising if friends and rela-

BOX 2-1
MATCH WITS WITH THE THEORISTS

All of us have made certain assumptions about children and child rearing. Developmental theorists make assumptions too, and their assumptions largely determine what they may propose in the way of a theory. You may find it interesting to match wits with these influential scholars to see with whom you most agree (initially, at least). Answer the five questions that follow. Then compare the patterning of your five responses against the patterns that appear in the "key" at the end of this exercise. The pattern that comes closest to your own will tell you with which group of theorists you are most philosophically consistent.

1. Biological factors (for example, heredity, maturation) and social forces (for example, culture, methods of parenting) are thought to contribute to human development. All things considered, which set of forces contributes more heavily in this regard?
   a. Biological factors contribute more than 70% to developmental outcomes.
   b. Biological factors contribute 60–70%; social forces contribute 30–40%.
   c. Biological factors and social forces are equally important.
   d. Social forces contribute 60–70%; biological factors contribute 30–40%.
   e. Social forces contribute more than 70% to developmental outcomes.
2. Children are—
   a. "Seething cauldrons"—creatures whose basically negative impulses must be controlled.
   b. Neither inherently good nor inherently bad.
   c. Noble savages—creatures who are born with many positive and few negative tendencies.
3. Development proceeds—
   a. In stages—that is, through a series of fairly abrupt changes.
   b. Continuously—in small increments without abrupt changes.
4. Children are basically—
   a. Active creatures who play a major role in determining their own character.
   b. Passive creatures whose characters are molded by parents, teachers, and other agents of society.

5. Character attributes such as aggressiveness or dependency—
   a. First appear in childhood and remain relatively stable over time.
   b. First appear in childhood but may change rapidly at some later time.

Now transcribe your answers in the space marked "Your Pattern." Then invert the page and compare your pattern with the patterns that appear in the key. On the basis of the five assumptions you have made, are you a budding psychoanalyst, learning theorist, cognitive-developmentalist, or ethologist?

Question

Your pattern: 1 2 3 4 5

— — — — —

Key

*Some ethologists stress biology more than others.

Note the similarities here. These patterns describe the assumptions made by learning theorists. Different learning theorists make slightly different assumptions, but if your pattern closely approximates one of these, you are most philosophically consistent with the learning viewpoint.

Theory and/or theorist	1	2	3	4	5
Sigmund Freud's psychoanalytic theory.	c	a	b	a	a
Erik Erikson's psychosocial theory (a revision and extension of Freud's thinking).	d	a	a	a	a
	d	b	b	b	e
	b	b	b	b	e
	b	a	b	b	e
Jean Piaget's cognitive-developmental theory.	b	c	a	a	b
The ethological perspective.	a or b*	b	a	a	b

Pattern of answers

PHOTO 2-1. *The psychoanalytic theory of Sigmund Freud (1856–1939) changed our thinking about developing children.*

tives were to ask your opinion of Freud (and his theory) when they learn that you are taking a psychology course.

Almost no one is neutral about Sigmund Freud. His followers thought him a genius even though they didn't agree with all his ideas. Yet many of his contemporaries in the medical profession ridiculed Freud, calling him a quack, a crackpot, and other less complimentary names. What was it about this man and his theory that made him so controversial? For one thing, he emphasized the importance of sexual urges as determinants of behavior, for children as well as for adults! In this section of the chapter, we will first consider Freud's interesting perspective on human development and then compare Freud's theory with that of his best-known follower, Erik Erikson.

Overview of Freud's Psychoanalytic Theory

In Chapter One we saw that Freud formulated his psychoanalytic theory from the observations and notes that he made about the life histories of his mentally disturbed patients. Freud assumed that people are often reluctant to discuss very personal matters with a stranger, even if the stranger is a therapist. For this reason, he favored non-traditional methods of interviewing patients—methods such as hypnosis, free association (in which the patient discusses anything that comes to mind), and *dream analysis*. While reclining on the couch, the patient would relax and talk about anything and everything that popped into his or her head. Dreams were thought to be a particularly rich source of information, for they gave some indication of a patient's **unconscious motivations.** Freud assumed that we all dream about what we really want—for example, sex and power—unhindered by social prohibitions that tend to suppress these desires when we are awake.

From his analyses of patients' dreams, slips of the tongue, unexpected free associations, and childhood memories, Freud was able to infer that all of us experience intense conflicts that influence our behavior. As biological creatures, we have goals or motives that must be satisfied. Yet society dictates that many of these basic urges are undesirable and must be suppressed or controlled. According to Freud, these conflicts emerge at several points during childhood and play a major role in determining the course and character of one's social and personality development.

■ *Instincts, goals, and motives*

Freud believed that all human behavior is energized by *psychodynamic* forces. Presumably each individual has a fixed amount of *psychic* (or mental) energy that he or she uses to think, to learn, and to perform other mental functions.

According to Freud, a child needs psychic energy in order to satisfy basic urges. And what kind of urges are children born with? Bad ones! Freud viewed the newborn as a "seething cauldron"—that is, an inherently negative creature who is relentlessly "driven" by two kinds of biological **instincts** (or motives), which he called **Eros** and **Thanatos**. Eros, or the life instincts, helps the child (and the species) to survive; it directs life-sustaining activities such as respiration, eating, sex, and the fulfillment of all other bodily needs. In contrast, Thanatos—the death instincts—was viewed as a set of destructive forces present in all human beings. Freud believed that Eros is stronger than Thanatos, thus enabling us to survive rather than self-destruct. But he argued that if the psychic energy of Thanatos reached a critical point, the death instincts would be expressed in some way. For example, Freud thought that destructive acts such as arson, fist fights, murder, war, and even masochism (physical harm directed against the self) were outward expressions of the death instincts.

■ Three components of personality: Id, ego, and superego

According to Freud (1933), the psychic energy that serves the instincts is eventually divided among three components of personality—the id, ego, and superego.

The id: Legislator of the personality. At birth, the personality is all **id**. The major function of the id is to serve the instincts by seeking objects that will satisfy them.

Have you ever heard a hungry baby cry until someone comes to feed him or her? A Freudian would say that the baby's cries and agitated limb movements are energized by the hunger instinct. Presumably the id directs these actions as a means of attracting the mother or another adult and thereby producing the object (food—or, literally, the mother's breast) that reduces hunger.

According to Freud, the id obeys the **pleasure principle** by seeking immediate gratification for instinctual needs. This impulsive thinking (also called "primary-process thinking") is rather unrealistic, however, for the id will invest psychic energy in any object that seems as if it will gratify the instincts, regardless of whether the object can actually do so. If we had never progressed beyond this earliest type of thinking, we might gleefully ingest wax fruit to satisfy hunger, reach for an empty pop bottle when thirsty, or direct our sexual energies at racy magazines and inflatable love dolls. Perhaps you can see the problem: we would have a difficult time satisfying our needs by relying on our irrational ids. Freud believed that these very difficulties lead to the development of the second major component of personality—the ego.

The ego: Executive of the personality. According to Freud (1933), the **ego** emerges when psychic energy is diverted from the id to energize important cognitive processes such as perception, learning, and logical reasoning. The goal of the rational ego is to serve the **reality principle**—that is, to find realistic ways of gratifying the instincts.

At the same time, the ego must invest some of its available psychic energy to block the id's irrational thinking.

Freud stressed that the ego is both servant and master to the id. The ego's mastery is reflected by its ability to delay gratification until reality is served. But the ego continues to serve the id as an executive serves subordinates, pondering several alternative courses of action and selecting a plan that will best satisfy the id's basic needs.

The superego: Judicial branch of the personality. The **superego** is the person's moral arbiter. It develops from the ego, represents the ideal, and strives for *perfection* rather than for pleasure or reality (Freud, 1933).

Freud believed that 3–6-year-old children are gradually internalizing the moral standards of their parents, eventually adopting these guidelines as their own. These *internalized* "codes of conduct" form the child's superego. At this point, children do not need an adult to tell them when

---

unconscious motivation: *Freud's term for feelings, experiences, and conflicts that influence a person's thinking and behavior, even though they cannot be recalled.*

instinct: *an inborn biological force that motivates a particular response or class of responses.*

Eros: *Freud's name for instincts such as respiration, hunger, and sex that help the individual (and the species) to survive.*

Thanatos: *Freud's name for inborn, self-destructive instincts that were said to characterize all human beings.*

id: *psychoanalytic term for the inborn component of the personality that is driven by the instincts.*

pleasure principle: *tendency of the id to seek immediate gratification for instinctual needs, even when realistic methods for satisfying these needs are unavailable.*

ego: *psychoanalytic term for the rational component of the personality.*

reality principle: *tendency of the ego to defer immediate gratification in order to find rational and realistic methods for satisfying the instincts.*

superego: *psychoanalytic term for the component of the personality that consists of one's internalized moral standards.*

they have been bad; they are now aware of their transgressions and will feel guilty or ashamed of what they have done. Freud argued that the biggest task faced by parents when raising a child is to ensure that the child develops a stable superego. This internal censor is presumably *the* mechanism that prevents human beings from expressing undesirable sexual and aggressive instincts in ways that could threaten society and the social order.

Dynamics of the personality.   We see, then, that the superego's main function is to monitor the ego—that is, to ensure that the ego violates no moral principles. Note, however, that since the ego serves the id, the superego's major adversary is really the id. In other words, the superego attempts to persuade the ego to find socially acceptable outlets for the id's undesirable impulses—a process called **sublimation.** Sublimation might be illustrated by a person who decides to exercise vigorously or to take a cold shower in order to "drain away" unacceptable sexual urges.

Although the three components of personality may have conflicting goals or purposes, they normally do not incapacitate one another. The mature, healthy personality is best described as a dynamic set of checks and balances: The id communicates basic needs, the ego restrains the impulsive id long enough to find realistic methods of satisfying these needs, and the superego decides whether the ego's problem-solving strategies are

morally acceptable. The ego is clearly "in the middle" and must serve two harsh masters by striking a balance between the opposing demands of the id and the superego.

Of course, not everyone is perfectly normal or healthy. Abnormalities or unusual quirks may arise if psychic energy is unequally distributed across the id, ego, and superego. For example, a sociopath might have a very strong id, a normal ego, and a very weak superego. In contrast, the righteous moralist may have a personality in which the majority of psychic energy is controlled by a very strong superego. These are but two of the many abnormal personalities that could result from uneven distributions of psychic energy among the id, ego, and superego.

■ *Freud's stages of psychosexual development*

Freud viewed the sex instinct as the most important of the life forces because he often discovered that the mental disturbances of his patients revolved around earlier sexual conflicts that they had **repressed**—that is, forced out of conscious awareness. Yet Freud's use of the term *sex* refers to much more than the need to copulate. Many simple bodily functions that most of us would consider rather asexual were viewed by Freud as "erotic" activities, motivated by this general life force that he called the sex instinct.

Although the sex instinct is presumably inborn, Freud (1940/1964) felt that the character of this life force changes over time, as dictated by biological maturation. **Maturation** refers to changes that result from the aging process (for example, teething in infants; the growth spurt of puberty), rather than from learning, injury, or other life experiences. As the sex instinct matures, its energy, or **libido,** gradually shifts from one part of the body to another, and the child enters a new stage of *psychosexual* development. Freud called these stages "psychosexual" to underscore his view that the maturation of the sex instinct leaves distinct imprints on the developing psyche (that is, the mind, or personality).

The oral stage (birth to 1 year).   Freud was struck by the fact that infants spend much of the first year spitting, chewing, sucking, and biting on objects, and he concluded that the sex instinct must be centered on the mouth during this "oral"

PHOTO 2-2. In the oral stage, children derive pleasure from sucking on, chewing, or biting objects.

period. Indeed, he believed that oral activities are methods of gratifying the sex instinct, because children will suck, bite, or chew just about anything that comes into contact with their mouths—their thumbs, lips, toys, and parts of their mother's body—even when they are not particularly hungry or thirsty.

Freud argued that infants in the **oral stage** may adopt any of several basic methods—for example, sucking, biting, or spitting—to gratify the sex instinct. Presumably, the child will prefer one (or some combination) of these techniques over all others. This choice is thought to be important, for the child's preferred method of oral gratification may give some indication of the kind of personality that he or she will have later in life. Note the implication here: Freud is saying that *early experiences may have a long-term effect on social and personality development.* In Box 2-2 we will see why Freud believed that earlier modes of functioning are likely to surface in the adult personality.

The anal stage (1 to 3 years).

In the second year of life, libido concentrates in the anal region as the sphincter muscles begin to mature. For the first time, the child has the ability to withhold or expel fecal material at will, and Freud believed that voluntary defecation becomes the primary method of gratifying the sex instinct.

During the **anal stage,** children must endure the demands of toilet training. For the first time, outside agents are interfering with instinctual impulses by insisting that the child inhibit the urge

to defecate until he or she has reached a designated locale. There are, of course, many strategies that parents might adopt when seeing their child through this first "social" conflict. Freud believed that the emotional climate created by parents in their attempts at toilet training is very important, for it may have a lasting effect on the child's personality.

The phallic stage (3 to 6 years).

We now come to the aspect of Freudian theory that many people find so controversial. Freud's view was that 4-year-old children have matured to the point that their genitals have become an interesting and sensitive area of the body. Libido presumably flows to this area as children derive pleasure from stroking and fondling their genitals. What is so controversial? According to Freud, all children at this age develop a strong incestuous desire for the parent of the other sex. He called this period the **phallic stage** because he believed that the phallus (penis) assumes a critically important role in the psychosexual development of both boys and girls.

---

sublimation: *the mechanism by which the ego finds socially acceptable outlets for the id's undesirable impulses.*

repression: *a type of motivated forgetting in which anxiety-provoking thoughts and conflicts are forced out of conscious awareness.*

maturation: *developmental changes in the body or behavior that result from the aging process rather than from learning, injury, illness, or some other life experience.*

libido: *Freud's term for the biological energy of the sex instinct.*

oral stage: *Freud's first stage of psychosexual development (from birth to 1 year), in which children gratify the sex instinct by stimulating the mouth, lips, teeth, and gums.*

anal stage: *Freud's second stage of psychosexual development (from 1 to 3 years of age), in which anal activities such as defecation become the primary methods of gratifying the sex instinct.*

phallic stage: *Freud's third stage of psychosexual development (from 3 to 6 years of age), in which children gratify the sex instinct by fondling their genitals and developing an incestuous desire for the parent of the other sex.*

BOX 2-2
*EARLY EXPERIENCES MAY AFFECT THE
ADULT PERSONALITY*

Freud (1940–1964) described several mechanisms that children may use to defend themselves (literally, their egos) against the anxieties or uncertainties of growing up. We have already discussed one such "defense" mechanism—sublimation—in which the child finds socially acceptable outlets for unacceptable motives. Freud believed that frequent use of these defense mechanisms may have long-term effects on the personality. For example, a teenaged girl who habitually sublimates her sexual desires by taking cold showers may become a "cleanliness nut" as an adult.

Another important ego defense mechanism is *fixation,* or arrested development. According to Freud, the child who experiences severe conflicts at any particular stage of development may be reluctant to move or incapable of moving to the next stage, where the uncertainties are even greater. The child may then fixate at the earlier stage, and further development will be arrested or at least impaired. Freud be-

lieved that some people become fixated at the level of primary-process thinking and consequently remain "dreamers" or "unrealistic optimists" throughout their lives. Others fixate on particular behaviors. An example is the chronic thumbsucker whose oral fixation is expressed later in life in substitute activities such as smoking or oral sex. In sum, Freud was convinced that childhood fixations were important determinants of many personality characteristics.

A person who experiences too much anxiety or too many conflicts at any stage of development may retreat to an earlier, less traumatic stage. Such developmental reversals are examples of an ego-defense mechanism that Freud called *regression.* Even a well-adjusted adult may regress from time to time in order to forget problems or reduce anxiety. For example, masturbation is one earlier mode of sexual functioning that a person may undertake to reduce sexual conflicts or frustrations. Dreaming is a regressive activity that enables a person to resolve conflicts and obtain pleasure through the magic of wishful thinking. Thus, regression is a third way in which earlier events, activities, and thought processes may affect the behavior of adults.

Let's examine this stage for boys. According to Freud, 4-year-old boys develop an intense sexual longing for their mothers. At the same time, they become jealous: if they could have their way, they would destroy their chief rivals for maternal affection, their fathers. Freud called this state of affairs the **Oedipus complex** after the legendary Oedipus, king of Thebes, who unwittingly killed his father and married his mother.

Now 3–5-year-old boys are not as powerful as King Oedipus, and they face certain defeat in their quest to win the sexual favors of their mothers. In fact, Freud suggests that a jealous young son will have many conflicts with his paternal rival and will eventually fear that his father might castrate him for this rivaling conduct. When this *castration anxiety* becomes sufficiently intense, the boy (if development is normal) will then resolve his Oedipus complex by repressing his incestuous desire for the mother and identifying with the father. This *"indentification with the aggressor"* lessens the chances of castration, for the boy is no longer a rival. He will try to emulate the father, incorporating all the father's attitudes, attributes, and behaviors. In so doing, the son is likely to adopt a distinct preference for the masculine sex

role and become a "male" psychologically. Identification with the aggressor should also place the crowning touch on the boy's superego, for he will repress two of the most taboo of motives—incest and murder—and internalize the moral standards of his feared and respected rival. In short, the boy has become a well-behaved youngster—daddy's "little man."

And what about girls? Freud contends that, before age 4, girls prefer their mothers to their fathers. But once the girl discovers that she lacks a penis, she is thought to blame her closest companion, the mother, for this "castrated" condition. This traumatic discovery results in a transfer of affection from the mother to the father. Freud believed that a girl of this age envies her father for possessing a penis and that she will choose him as a sex object in the hope that he will share with her the valued organ that she lacks (Freud assumed that the girl's *real* underlying motive was to bear her father's child, an event that would compensate for her lack of a penis, especially if the child was a male).

The female Oedipus complex (known as the **Electra complex**) bears some obvious similarities to that of the male. Children of each sex value the

"It's from Oedipus. He says he's found a girl just like the girl who married dear old dad."

male phallus; girls hope to gain one, and boys hope to keep theirs. Furthermore, both boys and girls perceive the parent of the same sex as their major rival for the affection of the other parent. However, Freud was uncertain just how (or why) girls ever resolved their Electra complexes. Boys fear castration, and this intense fear forces them to renounce their Oedipus complexes by identifying with their fathers. But what do girls fear? After all, they supposedly believe that they have already been castrated, and they attribute this act of brutality to their mothers. To Freud's way of thinking, they no longer have any reason to fear the mother.

Why, then, does the Electra complex subside? Freud (1924/1961) assumed that it may simply fade away as the girl faces reality and recognizes the impossibility of possessing her father. However, he suggested that girls will develop weaker superegos than boys because their resolution of the Electra complex is *not* based on a fear of retaliation (castration anxiety) that would force them to internalize the ethical standards of their mothers (or their fathers).

The latency period (ages 6–12).   Between ages 6 and 12, the child's sex instincts are relatively quiet. The sexual traumas of the phallic stage are forgotten, and all available libido is channeled into some socially acceptable activity, such as schoolwork or vigorous play, that consume most of the child's physical and psychic energy. The **latency period** continues until puberty, when the child suddenly experiences a number of biological changes that mark the beginning of Freud's final psychosexual stage.

The genital stage (age 12 onward).   With the onset of puberty come maturation of the reproductive system, production of sex hormones, and, according to Freud, a reactivation of the genital zone as an area of sensual pleasure. The adolescent may openly express libido toward members of the other sex, but for the first time, the underlying aim of the sex instincts is reproduction. Throughout adolescence and young adulthood, libido is invested in activities— forming friendships, preparing for a career, courting, marriage—that prepare the individual to satisfy the fully mature sex instinct by having children. The **genital period** is the longest of Freud's psychosexual stages. It lasts from puberty to old age, when the individual may regress to an earlier stage and begin a "second childhood."

■ *Evaluation of Freud's theory*
How plausible do you think Freud's ideas are? Do you think that we are all relentlessly driven by sexual and aggressive instincts? Could we have

---

Oedipus complex: *Freud's term for the conflict that 4- to 6-year-old boys experience when they develop an incestuous desire for their mothers and, at the same time, a jealous and hostile rivalry with their fathers.*

Electra complex: *female version of the Oedipus complex, in which a 4- to 6-year-old girl was said to envy her father for possessing a penis and would choose him as a sex object in the hope of sharing this valuable organ that she lacks.*

latency period: *Freud's fourth stage of psychosexual development (age 6 to puberty), in which sexual desires are repressed and all the child's available libido is channeled into socially acceptable outlets such as schoolwork or vigorous play.*

genital stage: *Freud's final stage of psychosexual development (from puberty onward), in which the underlying aim of the sex instinct is to establish an erotic relationship with another adult and to have children.*

really experienced Oedipus or Electra complexes and simply repressed these traumatic events? And what about the role of culture in human development? In 19th- and early 20th-century Europe, there were no clinical psychologists or sex therapists, and the topic of sex was not discussed publicly in this outwardly prudish Victorian era. Could the sexual conflicts that Freud thought so important have merely been reflections of the sexually repressive culture in which his patients lived?

Few contemporary psychologists accept all of Freud's major premises and propositions. For example, there is not much evidence for the notion that the oral and anal activities of childhood predict one's later personality. Nor is there reason to believe that all children experience Oedipus and Electra complexes. To experience these conflicts, 4- to 6-year-old children would have to recognize the anatomical differences between the sexes, and there is little evidence that they do. In fact, Alan Katcher (1955) found that the majority of 4- to 5-year-olds are inept at assembling a doll so that its genitals match other parts of its body. Even 6-year-olds often made mistakes such as attaching a lower torso containing a penis to an upper body with breasts. Clearly, these "oedipal-aged" children were confused or ignorant about sex differences in genital anatomy, and it seems highly unlikely that they could be experiencing any castration anxiety or penis envy.

But we cannot reject all of Freud's ideas simply because some of them may seem a bit outlandish. Indeed, there are several reasons that Sigmund Freud will always remain an important figure in the history of the behavioral sciences. For one thing, his theory was the first systematic explanation of human behavior, and it revolutionized the study of psychology. When psychology came into being, in the middle of the 19th century, investigators were concerned with understanding isolated aspects of conscious experience, such as sensory processes and perceptual illusions. It was Freud who first noted that these scientists were studying the tip of an iceberg when he proclaimed that the vast majority of psychic experience lay below the level of conscious awareness. Perhaps Freud's most important contribution was his concept of *unconscious motivation,* the idea that much of our behavior is caused by forces or repressed conflicts of which we are not consciously

aware. Freud also convinced many scientists that development occurs in stages and that childhood is the foundation from which the adult character arises. In sum, psychoanalysis was a new look at human behavior that explained a wide range of phenomena that Freud's predecessors had not even considered. Freud was truly a great explorer who dared to navigate murky, uncharted waters. In the process, he changed our view of humankind.

Erik Erikson's Theory of Psychosocial Development

As Freud became widely read, he attracted many followers. However, Freud's pupils did not always agree with the master, and eventually they began to modify some of Freud's ideas and became important theorists in their own right. Among the best known of these *neo-Freudian* scholars is Erik Erikson.

Erikson accepts many of Freud's ideas. He agrees that people are born with a number of basic instincts and that the personality has three components: the id, ego, and superego. Erikson also assumes that development occurs in stages and that the child must successfully resolve some crisis or conflict at each stage in order to be prepared for the crises that will emerge later in life.

However, Erikson is truly a revisionist, for his theory differs from Freud's in several important respects. First, Erikson (1963, 1972) stresses that children are *active, adaptive* explorers who seek to control their environment rather than passive creatures who are molded by their parents. He has also been labeled an *ego* psychologist because he believes that an individual must first understand the *realities* of the social world (an ego function) in order to adapt successfully and show a normal pattern of personal growth. This is perhaps the major difference between Freud and Erikson. Unlike Freud, who felt that the most interesting aspects of behavior stemmed from conflicts between the id and the superego, Erikson assumes that human beings are basically rational creatures whose thoughts, feelings, and actions are largely controlled by the ego.

Clearly, Erikson's thinking was shaped by his own interesting experiences. He was born in Denmark, was raised in Germany, and spent much of his adolescence wandering throughout Europe. After receiving his professional training, Erikson emigrated to the United States, where he studied college students, victims of combat fatigue during World War II, civil rights workers in the South, and American Indians. With this kind of cross-cultural background, it is hardly surprising that Erikson would emphasize social and cultural aspects of development in his own theory. Henry Maier (1969, p. 23) used these words to reflect Erikson's point of view:

> Culture adds the human aspect of living. Man lives by instinctual forces, and culture insists upon the "proper" use of these forces. [But] it is the cultural environment . . . which determines the nature of each individual's experience. The child and his parents are never alone; through the parent's conscience [many past] generations are looking upon a child's actions, helping him to integrate his relationships with their approval. . . . A culture, class, or ethnic group's basic ways of [viewing the world] are transmitted to the [child] . . . and tie the child forever to his original milieu.

In sum, Erikson believes that we are largely products of our *society* rather than our sex instincts. For this reason, his approach should be labeled a theory of *psychosocial* development.

■ *Eight life crises*

Erikson believes that all human beings face a minimum of eight major crises, or conflicts, during the course of their lives. Each crisis is primarily "social" in character and has very real implications for the future. Table 2-1 compares Freud's psychosexual and Erikson's psychosocial stages. Note that Erikson's developmental stages do not end at adolescence or young adulthood. Erikson believes that the problems of adolescents and young adults are very different from those faced by parents who are raising children or by the aged who must grapple with the specter of retirement, a sense of uselessness, and death. Most contemporary psychologists would definitely agree.

As we have seen, Erikson feels that the successful resolution of each life crisis prepares the person for the next of life's conflicts. By contrast, the individual who fails to resolve one or more of the life crises is almost certain to encounter problems in the future. For example, a child who learns to mistrust other human beings in infancy may find it exceedingly difficult to trust a prospective friend or lover later in life. An adolescent who fails to establish a strong personal identity may be reluctant to commit his or her fragile sense of "self" to a "shared identity" with a prospective spouse. We see, then, that later crises may become very formidable hurdles for the individual who stumbles early.

Although Erikson believes that the crises of childhood set the stage for our adult lives, we must remember that he views human beings as rational, adaptive creatures who struggle to the very end in their attempts to cope successfully with their social environment. Charles Dickens' Scrooge, a fictional character from *A Christmas Carol*, aptly illustrates the self-centered, "stagnated" adult—one who is failing at Erikson's seventh life crisis (and who has been unsuccessful at establishing a sense of intimacy as well). You may remember that old Scrooge was so absorbed in his own interests (making money) that he completely ignored the needs and wishes of his young storekeeper, Bob Cratchit. Scrooge's tale had a happy ending, however. By the end of the story, he had acquired a sense of intimacy and generativity that had eluded him earlier, and he was now ready to face life's final crisis in a positive frame of mind. An unlikely reversal? Not necessarily! Erikson is quite the optimist; he maintains that "there is little that cannot be remedied later, there is much [in the way of harm] that can be prevented from happening at all" (1950, p. 104).

■ *Evaluation of Erikson's theory*

Many people prefer Erikson's theory to Freud's because they simply refuse to believe that human beings are dominated by sexual instincts. An analyst like Erikson, who stresses our rational, adaptive nature, is so much easier to accept. In addition, Erikson emphasizes many of the social conflicts and personal dilemmas that people may remember, are currently experiencing, or can easily anticipate. In the words of one student, "Erikson's theory is so relevant . . . Freud's is a figment of his *wild* imagination."

One major shortcoming of Erikson's theory is that it does not clearly specify the kinds of experiences that people must have in order to cope with and resolve various psychosocial crises. For exam-

TABLE 2-1. Erikson's and Freud's stages of development

Approximate age	Erikson's stage or "psychosocial" crisis	Erikson's viewpoint: Significant events and social influences	Corresponding Freudian stage
Birth to 1 year	Basic trust versus mistrust	Infants must learn to trust others to care for their basic needs. If caregivers are rejecting or inconsistent in their care, the infant may view the world as a dangerous place filled with untrustworthy or unreliable people. The mother or primary caretaker is the key social agent.	Oral
1 to 3 years	Autonomy versus shame and doubt	Children must learn to be "autonomous"—to feed and dress themselves, to look after their own hygiene, and so on. Failure to achieve this independence may force the child to doubt his or her own abilities and feel shameful. Parents are the key social agents.	Anal
3 to 6 years	Initiative versus guilt	Children attempt to act grown up and will try to accept responsibilities that are beyond their capacity to handle. They sometimes undertake goals or activities that conflict with those of parents and other family members, and these conflicts may make them feel guilty. Successful resolution of this crisis requires a balance: the child must retain a sense of initiative and yet learn not to impinge on the rights, privileges, or goals of others. The family is the key social agent.	Phallic
6 to 12 years	Industry versus inferiority	Children must master important social and academic skills. This is a period when the child compares the self with peers. If sufficiently industrious, children will acquire the social and academic skills to feel self-assured. Failure to acquire these important attributes leads to feelings of inferiority. Significant social agents are teachers and peers.	Latency

ple, what kinds of caregiving might lead an infant to trust (or mistrust) other people? Why is trust important for the child's developing sense of autonomy, initiative, or industry? Exactly how do adolescents formulate stable identities with which to face the tasks of young adulthood? Erikson is simply not very explicit about any of these important issues. His theory is a *descriptive* overview of human social and emotional development that does not do a very good job of explaining how or why this development takes place.

Researchers who study such topics as the emotional development of infants or the growth of the adolescent self-concept are beginning to pay more attention to Erikson, for they often find that their results are consistent with his descriptive framework. Many of these investigators are now using Erikson's description of psychosocial development as a general starting point and then trying to *explain* how children are able to develop a sense of trust, autonomy, initiative, industry, or a personal identity. So Erikson's theory is having an impact, and we will look at some of the more encouraging of the early returns as we proceed through the text.

Psychoanalytic Theory Today

Today psychoanalysts represent a small minority within the community of child developmentalists. Many researchers have abandoned the psychoanalytic approach (particularly Freud's theory)

TABLE 2-1. Erikson's and Freud's stages of development *(continued)*

Approximate age	Erikson's stage or "psychosocial" crisis	Erikson's viewpoint: Significant events and social influences	Corresponding Freudian stage
12 to 20 years	Identity versus role confusion	This is the crossroad between childhood and maturity. The adolescent grapples with the question "Who am I?" Adolescents must establish basic social and occupational identities, or they will remain confused about the roles they should play as adults. The key social agent is the society of peers.	Early genital (adolescence)
20 to 40 years (young adulthood)	Intimacy versus isolation	The primary task at this stage is to form strong friendships and to achieve a sense of love and companionship (or a shared identity) with another person. Feelings of loneliness or isolation are likely to result from an inability to form friendships or an intimate relationship. Key social agents are lovers, spouses, and close friends (of both sexes).	Genital
40 to 65 years (middle adulthood)	Generativity versus stagnation	At this stage, adults face the tasks of becoming productive in their work and raising their families or otherwise looking after the needs of young people. These standards of "generativity" are defined by one's culture. Those who are unable or unwilling to assume these responsibilities will become stagnant and/or self-centered. Significant social agents are the spouse, children, and cultural norms.	Genital
Old age	Ego integrity versus despair	The older adult will look back at life, viewing it as either a meaningful, productive, and happy experience or as a major disappointment full of unfulfilled promises and unrealized goals. One's life experiences, particularly social experiences, will determine the outcome of this final life crisis.	Genital

because it is difficult to verify or disconfirm. Suppose, for example, that we wanted to test the basic Freudian proposition that the "healthy" personality is one in which psychic energy is evenly distributed among the id, ego, and superego. How could we do it? There are objective tests that we could use to select "mentally healthy" subjects, but we have no instrument that measures psychic energy or the relative strengths of the id, ego, and superego. The point is that many psychoanalytic assertions are untestable by any method other than the interview or a clinical approach, and unfortunately, these techniques are time-consuming, expensive, and among the least objective of all methods used to study developing children.

Of course, the main reason that developmental researchers have abandoned the psychoanalytic perspective is that other theories seem more compelling to them. One theory favored by many is the learning approach, to which we now turn.

THE LEARNING VIEWPOINT (BEHAVIORISM)

John B. Watson was a radical in his own time. He was the person who proclaimed that he could take a dozen healthy infants and train them to be whatever he chose—doctor, lawyer, beggar, and so on, regardless of their backgrounds or ancestry. This statement alone was sufficient to raise more than a few eyebrows. Watson (1913) also believed that the psychologists of his day were wasting their time studying subjective, "mentalistic" concepts such as sensation, volition, and emotion. On many occasions he argued that subjective, nonobservable phenomena are best left to philosophy; surely they have no place in a *science* of psychology. Watson's point was that the larger community of scientists would never take psychology seriously unless psychologists began to study what they could see—overt behavioral responses.

A basic premise of Watson's "**behaviorism**" is that the mind of an infant is a *tabula rasa* and that *learned* associations between stimuli and responses are the building blocks of human development. According to Watson, development does not proceed through a series of stages; it is a continuous process marked by the gradual acquisition of new and more sophisticated behavioral patterns, or habits. Watson believed that

PHOTO 2-3. John B. Watson (1878–1958) was the father of behaviorism and the first social-learning theorist.

only the simplest of human reflexes (for example, the sucking reflex) are inborn and that all important behavioral tendencies, including traits, talents, values, and aspirations, are learned.

The behaviorists of the 1980s are more moderate in their views. They recognize that heredity and maturation play meaningful roles in human development and that no amount of prompting or environmental enrichment could transform a severely retarded person into a lawyer or a brain surgeon. However, these contemporary learning theorists believe that biological factors merely place limits on what children are capable of learning. And to this day, theorists who favor the learning approach feel that the most significant aspects of human behavior—those habits and qualities that make us "human"—are learned.

What Is Learning?

Simply stated, **learning** is a process that produces relatively *permanent* changes in behavior or behavioral potential. These behavioral changes are the result of one's *experiences* or *practice,* as opposed to natural causes such as maturation, fatigue, injury, or illness.

Learned responses or habits may be acquired in several ways. **Classical conditioning** is a type of learning in which a person comes to associate a neutral stimulus with a second, nonneutral stimulus that always elicits a particular response. After this association has been made, the formerly neutral stimulus will have acquired the capacity to evoke the response in question. For example, very young children are unlikely to lick their lips the first two or three times they hear the jingling of an ice-cream truck as it passes before their house. But this initially neutral jingling sound may soon begin to elicit lip licking (and perhaps a host of other behaviors as well) as soon as children associate it with ice cream, a nonneutral stimulus that does produce lip licking (see Figure 2-2). In Chapter Seven we will see that classical conditioning is a common occurrence in everyday life and may be the basis for many of our fears, attitudes, and prejudices.

Operant (or *instrumental*) **conditioning** is a second type of learning, in which a child first emits a response and then comes to associate it

INITIALLY:

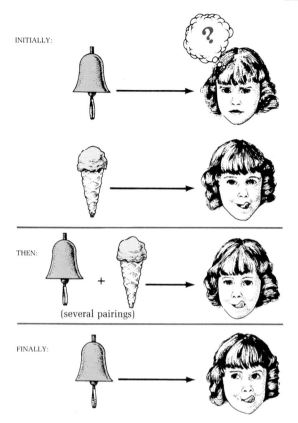

THEN:

+

(several pairings)

FINALLY:

FIGURE 2-2. In classical conditioning, an initially neutral stimulus (such as a bell) acquires the ability to elicit a response (such as lip licking) by virtue of its repeated association with a second, nonneutral stimulus (ice cream) that always elicits the response.

with a particular outcome, or consequence. Two kinds of consequences are significant in operant conditioning—reinforcers and punishments. **Reinforcers** are consequences that promote operant learning by increasing the probability that a response will occur in the future. For example, a mother who praises her son for sharing a cookie with a playmate is using praise as a reinforcer. And if the boy recognizes that sharing is what produced this pleasant outcome, he is likely to share again with his friend when the opportunity presents itself. **Punishments** are consequences that suppress a response and may decrease the likelihood that it will occur in the future. For ex-

ample, an infant whose hands are slapped every time she reaches for her mother's glasses may soon refrain from reaching for people's glasses, at least her mother's. An adolescent who is grounded for sassing his father will probably think twice before repeating this "mistake." In sum, operant conditioning is a very common form of learning in which various acts become either more or less probable, depending on the consequences they produce.

Observational learning is a third process by which we acquire new feelings, attitudes, and behaviors. If a child watches someone do something or listens attentively to that person's reasoning, then the child may learn to do, think, or feel as the person did. Even toddlers can learn by observing other people. A 2-year-old boy may discover how to approach and pet the family dog simply by noting how his older sister does it. A young girl may acquire a negative attitude toward a minority

---

behaviorism: *a school of thinking in psychology that holds that conclusions about human development should be based on controlled observations of overt behavior rather than speculation about unconscious motives or other unobservable phenomena; the philosophical underpinning for the early theories of learning.*

learning: *a process that produces relatively permanent changes in behavior (or behavioral potential) that are the result of experience or practice.*

classical conditioning: *a form of learning in which an initially neutral stimulus is repeatedly paired with a meaningful stimulus so that the neutral stimulus eventually elicits the response originally made only to the meaningful stimulus.*

operant conditioning: *a form of learning in which freely emitted acts (or operants) become either more or less probable, depending on the consequences they produce.*

reinforcer: *any consequence of an act that increases the probability that the act will recur.*

punishment: *any consequence of an act that suppresses that act and/or decreases the probability that it will recur.*

observational learning: *learning that results from observing the behavior of others.*

group after hearing her parents talk about those people in a disparaging way. In the language of observational learning, the individual who is observed and imitated is called a social *model.* Over the years, children are exposed to hundreds of social models and have the opportunity to learn literally thousands of responses (some good, some bad) simply by observing others perform them.

Theories of Social Learning

Although Watson argued that learned associations between stimuli and responses are the "bricks" in the "edifice of human development," he really did not have a developmental theory to work with. Since Watson's day, three major theories have been proposed to explain social learning and the process of human development: the drive theory of Clark Hull, the operant-learning theory of B. F. Skinner, and the cognitive social-learning theory of Albert Bandura.

■ *Neo-Hullian theory*

The origins of the first major social-learning theory can be traced to 1936, the year that a group of anthropologists, psychologists, and sociologists began an interdisciplinary seminar at Yale University. The goal of the Yale group was rather ambitious: these scientists hoped to construct a theory of human development based on principles of learning outlined earlier by Clark Hull, a famous experimental psychologist who worked with animals. At that time Freud's psychoanalytic viewpoint was the dominant theory of human development. Several of the Yale theorists were well versed in psychoanalytic principles, and they believed that any theory they might construct must be able to explain all the developmental phenomena that Freud had described.

The theory that evolved from the Yale seminar differed from the psychoanalytic approach in four important respects. First, instincts played virtually no role in this neo-Hullian theory. Second, the personality was no longer described as a system composed of an id, ego, and superego. Instead, the neo-Hullians used the term **habit** to describe the relatively stable aspects of one's character, where a habit was defined as a well-learned association between a stimulus and a response. Presumably, our interactions with other people will lead to the development of many

habits, which collectively make up our personalities. Third, members of the Yale group assumed that development occurs continuously and is not at all stagelike. Neo-Hullians John Dollard and Neil Miller (1950) described the personality as a system in transition: people will interact with one another until the day they die, and these new social encounters are continually modifying their existing habits. Finally, each individual was said to develop a unique habit structure (or personality), because no two persons are ever exposed to precisely the same set of social-learning experiences.

According to the neo-Hullians, most human behavior is motivated by **primary** and **secondary drives.** Primary drives are unlearned motives, such as hunger, thirst, or the need for sexual gratification, that impel the organism into action. Secondary drives are all motives that are not present at birth and must be acquired as a result of experience (for example, the need for social approval). Dollard and Miller (1950) propose that the goal of a drive-ridden organism is to reduce whatever drive the organism is experiencing. In fact, they defined *learning* as the development of a response (or habit) that proves to be a reliable method of reducing a drive.

Responses that reduce one or more drives were said to be reinforcing. When a child is reinforced for responding in a particular way to a stimulus—that is, when the response reduces a drive—the act that the child has performed will become conditioned to that stimulus, and a habit is formed. Dollard and Miller argue that there are two kinds of reinforcers: **primary reinforcers** and **secondary reinforcers**. Primary reinforcers are substances or activities, such as food, water, and sex, that reduce primary drives. Secondary reinforcers are initially neutral objects, events, or activities that gradually acquire some value by virtue of their association with one or more primary reinforcers. Take money, for example. Young children do not value money until they learn that coins and currency can be used to purchase goods such as candy or soda that reduce primary drives. But once money becomes a valuable commodity (that is, a secondary reinforcer), the child acquires a motive (or secondary drive) to obtain money, and any response that "earns" money will be reinforced.

The neo-Hullians proposed that most of our

everyday behaviors are motivated by secondary (or acquired) drives and sustained by secondary reinforcers. For example, human beings are said to develop a "need for social approval," which motivates any behavior that is likely to be reinforced by a smile, a pat on the back, or some other sign of acceptance or approval. Other complex human motives that are said to evolve from primary drives include the needs for affiliation, love, competence, achievement, power, status, and security. Each of these "acquired drives" is thought to motivate a variety of behaviors that can be "strengthened" by one or more secondary reinforcers.

When parents attempt to train, or "socialize," a child, they are trying to induce their youngster to make "socially appropriate" responses to a variety of cues. Dollard and Miller assumed that often the child's most probable responses to a stimulus or situation may be quite effective at reducing a drive but are not the kinds of acts that parents are likely to condone. For example, masturbation may reduce the sex drive but also elicit negative reactions from others. But will a young boy quit fondling his genitals because he struggles through an Oedipus complex and fears that he may be castrated (as Freud had assumed)? Dollard and Miller considered this scenario highly improbable. Instead, they argue that masturbation will eventually wane as parents discourage this activity while encouraging socially desirable alternative responses (for example, vigorous play) that will satisfy one or more acquired drives, such as the need for approval, competence, or exploration.

In sum, Dollard and Miller (1950) view development as the changes that occur in a child's behavior as a result of his or her experiences. The ideal outcome of these learning experiences is a collection of habits (or a personality) that is structured so that the most probable responses to any given stimulus are both socially desirable and effective at reducing a primary or secondary drive.

■ *Skinner's operant-learning approach (radical behaviorism)*

While the neo-Hullians were formulating their theory of human development, psychologist B. F. Skinner was conducting research with animals and discovering important principles that would eventually lead to a second social-learning the-

PHOTO 2-4. *B. F. Skinner (1904–   ) proposed a social-learning theory that emphasizes the role of external stimuli in controlling human behavior.*

ory—one very different from the neo-Hullian approach. For example, Skinner (1953) clearly rejects the notion that most human behavior is motivated by primary and secondary drives. In fact, he considers the term *drive* a circular motivational label that has little or no explanatory value, a sentiment shared by many contemporary researchers:

It is not the existence of motivated behavior that is being questioned, but whether such behavior [can be] explained by ascribing it to the action of drives. The limitations of this type of analysis can

habits: *the neo-Hullian term for the well-learned associations between various stimuli and responses that represent the stable aspects of one's personality.*

primary drives: *innate (nonlearned) motives such as hunger and sex that impel the organism into action.*

secondary drives: *all motives that are not present at birth and must be acquired as a result of experience.*

primary reinforcer: *a substance or activity that reduces (that is, satisfies) a primary drive.*

secondary reinforcer: *an initially neutral stimulus or activity that acquires some value by virtue of its repeated association with one or more primary reinforcers.*

be illustrated by considering a common activity such as reading . . . people spend large sums . . . purchasing reading material; . . . they [read] for hours on end; and they can become emotionally upset when deprived of reading material [such as a missed newspaper]. . . .

One could ascribe [reading behavior] to the force of a "reading drive." . . . However, if one wanted to *predict* what people read, when, how long, and the order in which they choose to read different material, one would look not for drives, but for preceding inducements and expected benefits derived from reading [Bandura, 1977, p. 3; italics added].

Why, then, do people read? For any number of reasons. One person may be reading because she finds the activity pleasurable; another reader may be studying for an exam; a third may be trying to understand his income-tax form; a fourth reader may be planning a vacation. To attribute the behavior of these four individuals to a "reading drive" is surely a grossly oversimplified analysis.

According to Skinner (1953), the majority of habits that children acquire are freely emitted responses (or operants) that become either more or less probable as a function of their consequences. In other words, Skinner proposes that behavior is motivated by *external* stimuli—reinforcers or punitive events—rather than by internal forces, or drives.

In Chapter Seven we will take a closer look at the process of operant learning and its contribution to human development. For now, let's simply note that even young infants can learn to alter their behavior (that is, form new habits) in order to obtain reinforcement or to avoid punitive consequences. Consider the following demonstration. Paul Weisberg (1963) exposed 3-month-old infants to four experimental treatments to see whether he could teach some of them to babble to a caregiver. One group of infants received social stimulation in the form of smiles and gentle rubs of the chin whenever they happened to babble (*contingent* social stimulation). A second group were given the same kinds of social stimulation, but these gestures were *noncontingent;* that is, they were presented at random and did not depend on the infant's babbling behavior. Two other groups received nonsocial stimulation (the sound of chimes) that was either contingent or non-

contingent on their babbling responses. Weisberg found that neither noncontingent social stimulation nor the sound of chimes was sufficient to reinforce babbling behavior. Babbling became more frequent only when it was accompanied by contingent social stimulation.

Skinner would argue that it makes little sense to attribute the babbling of these infants to a "babbling drive." Instead, the infants appear to have learned to babble because this act produced *external* stimuli (smiles and pats) that they found satisfying.

Recently a number of learning theorists have noted some serious deficiencies in Skinner's operant analysis of human behavior. For example, Albert Bandura (1977) calls Skinner's theory "radical behaviorism" because it focuses exclusively on the *external* stimuli (rewards and punishments) that influence our behavior and ignores all *cognitive* determinants of social learning. Unlike Skinner, Bandura proposes that much of what we "learn" over the course of a lifetime is acquired long before we are ever reinforced for performing these acts. He makes this claim because children are quite proficient at a form of cognitive learning in which they acquire new responses by observing other people performing them.

■ *Bandura's cognitive social-learning theory*

According to Bandura, children can learn novel responses by merely observing the behavior of a model, making mental notes on what they have seen, and then using these mental representations to reproduce the model's behavior at some future time. This is clearly a form of *cognitive* learning, for as we will see in Chapter Seven, children need not be reinforced or even respond in order to learn by observing others. All that is required for observational learning is that the observer pay close attention to the model's behavior and then store this information in memory so that it can be retrieved for use at a later date (Bandura, 1977).

Bandura suggests that observational learning permits young children to acquire any number of new responses in a variety of settings where their "models" are simply pursuing their own interests and are not trying to teach them anything in particular. In fact, many of the behaviors to which children attend (and which they may imitate) are

PHOTO 2-5. *In his theory of human development, Albert Bandura (1925–) emphasizes the cognitive aspects of social learning.*

actions that models display but would like to discourage—practices such as swearing, smoking, or eating between meals. Bandura's point is that children are continually learning both desirable and undesirable responses by "keeping their eyes (and ears) open," and he is not at all surprised that human development proceeds so very rapidly along so many paths.

Social Learning as a Reciprocal Process

Compared with psychoanalytic theory, early versions of learning theory seem rather bleak and barren. Nowhere does one find lists of habits or traits that describe the healthy or the abnormal personality. There are no "stages" in learning theory. Presumably, development proceeds in small steps without sudden changes, and this gradual learning process occurs over the entire life span. In addition, early versions of learning theory were largely tributes to Watson's doctrine of **environmental determinism**: young, unknowing children were viewed as passive recipients of environmental influence—they would become whatever parents, teachers, and other agents of society groomed them to be. In fact, B. F. Skinner, the famous "radical behaviorist" of recent times, has

taken a position that many students find difficult to accept: not only are we products of our experiences, we have little say in determining the character of those experiences. In other words, Skinner (1971) is arguing that "free will," or the concept of conscious choice, is merely an illusion.

Students are not the only ones who object to Skinner's statements or to a strict interpretation of environmental determinism. In recent years, cognitive social-learning theorists have argued that children are active, thinking creatures who contribute in meaningful ways to their own development. For example, observational learning requires the child to *actively* observe and encode into memory the behaviors displayed by social models. Moreover, the child must later *decide* whether and when he or she will perform these learned responses.

Children are also active in another important respect—they are often responsible for creating the very reinforcers that strengthen new habits. Suppose that a little boy discovers he can gain control over desirable toys by assaulting his playmates. In this case, control over the desired toy is a pleasant outcome that reinforces the child's aggressive behavior. But note that the reinforcer here is produced by the child himself— through his aggressive actions. Not only has bullying behavior been reinforced (by obtaining the toy), but the character of the play environment has changed. Our bully becomes more likely to assault his playmates in the future. And the playmates may become more likely to "give in" to the bully.

In sum, cognitive learning theorists such as Albert Bandura (1977) and Richard Bell (1979) believe that human development is best described as a continuous *reciprocal interaction* between children and their environments (**reciprocal determinism**): the environment clearly affects the

---

environmental determinism: *the notion that children are passive creatures who are molded by their environments.*

reciprocal determinism: *the notion that the flow of influence between children and their environments is a two-way street; the environment may affect the child, but the child's behavior will also influence the environment.*

child, but the child's behavior is thought to affect the environment as well. The implication is that children are *actively involved* in creating the very environments that will influence their growth and development.

Contributions and Criticisms of Learning Theory

Child developmentalists have benefited from the learning viewpoint in many ways. For example, the learning theorist's emphasis on overt behavior and its immediate causes has produced important clinical insights. Many problem behaviors can now be treated rapidly by a method called *counterconditioning* in which the therapist (1) identifies the reinforcers that sustain undesirable habits and eliminates them while (2) reinforcing alternative behaviors that are more desirable. Thus, childhood phobias such as a fear of school may be eliminated in a matter of weeks, rather than the months (or years) that a psychoanalyst might take probing the child's unconscious, trying to find the underlying conflict that is producing the phobic reaction.

Perhaps the major contribution of the learning viewpoint is the wealth of information it has provided about developing children. By observing how children react to various environmental influences, learning theorists have begun to understand how and why children form emotional attachments to others, adopt sex roles, become interested in doing well at school, learn to abide by moral rules, form friendships, and so on. Much of what we know about child development stems from the research of "behavioral," or learning, theorists.

Finally, behaviorists stress *objectivity* in all phases of their work. Their units of analysis are objective behavioral responses, rather than subjective phenomena that are difficult to observe or measure. Behaviorists carefully define their concepts, test hypotheses, and conduct tightly controlled experiments to provide objective evidence for the suspected causes of developmental change. The demonstrated success of their approach has encouraged researchers from all theoretical backgrounds to become more objective when studying developing children.

In spite of its strengths, however, many view the learning approach as an oversimplified account of human development. Consider its explanation of individual differences: presumably, individuals follow different developmental paths because no two persons grow up in exactly the same environment. Yet critics are quick to note that each of us comes into the world with a unique genetic inheritance. Also, children mature at different rates, a factor that affects how other people respond to them and how they will react to the behavior of others. One's genetic inheritance and maturational timetable may have direct effects on development, or they may have indirect effects by determining what a person is capable of learning (or would find reinforcing) at any given point in the life cycle. Thus, learning theorists may have oversimplified the issue of individual differences in human development by downplaying the contribution of important biological factors.

Despite the popularity of recent cognitively oriented learning theories that stress the child's active role in the developmental process, some critics maintain that *no* learning theorist pays enough attention to the *cognitive* determinants of human development. Proponents of this third, or "cognitive," viewpoint believe that the child's mental abilities undergo a series of qualitative changes (or stages) that the behaviorists completely ignore. Further, they argue, a child's impressions of and reactions to the environment depend largely on his or her level of **cognitive development.** Recently, this "cognitive-developmental" perspective has begun to attract many followers.

THE COGNITIVE-DEVELOPMENTAL VIEWPOINT

The major contributor to the cognitive viewpoint is unquestionably Jean Piaget, a Swiss scholar who began to study children's intellectual development during the 1920s. According to Piaget, children are neither driven by undesirable instincts nor "molded" by environmental influences. Piaget and his followers view children as *constructivists*—that is, as curious, active explorers who respond to the environment according to their *understanding* of its essential features. Presumably, any two children might react very differently to some aspect of the environment if

PHOTO 2-6. *In his cognitive-developmental theory, Swiss scholar Jean Piaget (1896–1980) focused on the growth of children's knowledge and reasoning skills.*

they interpret it differently. To predict how a child will respond to a praising mother, a scolding father, or a bossy playmate, one has to know how the child perceives, or construes, that event.

Piaget adds that a child's constructions of reality (interpretations of the environment) depend on his or her level of cognitive development. If he is correct, it follows that a child's cognitive abilities largely determine (1) how the child will respond to environmental events and thus (2) what effect these events will have on the child's development.

Origins of Piaget's Cognitive Theory

Jean Piaget was an unusual young man. At the age of 10 he published his first scientific article, about a rare albino sparrow. Shortly thereafter he began an after-school job assisting the director of the local museum of natural history. By age 15, Piaget was publishing zoological articles about shellfish. One of these papers resulted in a job offer as curator of the Geneva Museum of Natural History. Piaget regretfully declined the position in order to finish high school.

Piaget completed a Ph.D. in zoology in 1918. His secondary interest was epistemology (the branch of philosophy concerned with the origins of knowledge), and he hoped desperately to be able to integrate his two interests. At that point, he felt psychology was the answer. He journeyed to Paris, spending two years at the Sorbonne studying clinical psychology, logic, and philosophy of science. During his stay in Paris, Piaget was offered a position standardizing intelligence tests at the Alfred Binet laboratories. His decision to accept this position had a profound influence on the direction of his career.

Many of us would find the task of standardizing an intelligence test rather tedious. The examiner must administer a preestablished sequence of precisely worded questions to the test taker according to a set procedure. This standardized format ensures that variations in test performance reflect individual differences in intelligence rather than variations in the examiner's methods or the questions asked of the examinee. The person's intellectual ability is then estimated from the number and types of questions that he or she answers correctly.

However, Piaget soon discovered that he was more interested in test takers' *incorrect* answers. It seemed to him that children of about the same age were producing the same kinds of "wrong answers" for certain questions. But why? Piaget then proceeded to question children about their misconceptions, using the clinical method he had learned earlier while working in a psychiatric clinic. He soon discovered that children of *different* ages produced *different* kinds of wrong answers, and he concluded from these observations that intelligence must be a multidimensional attribute. Older children are not simply "more intelligent" than younger children; their thought processes are completely different. Piaget then set up his own laboratory and attempted to determine how children progress from one mode (or stage) of thinking to another. The work of this remarkable man continued for some 60 years, until he died in

---

cognitive development: *age-related changes that occur in mental activities such as attending, perceiving, learning, thinking, and remembering.*

1980. We now consider some of Piaget's basic ideas about intelligence and its impact on human development.

Piaget's View of Intelligence

Many psychologists define intelligence as a person's mental capacity or ability to profit from experience. They measure intelligence by asking each child a series of questions and totaling the number of correct answers, which is then compared against the child's chronological age to yield an *intelligence quotient,* or *IQ.* Piaget became dissatisfied with this approach because he felt that IQ tests overemphasize intellectual content, or *what* the child thinks, while ignoring the question *how* or *why* the child thinks these things. As a result, he turned away from the study of intellectual performance and began to investigate the *process* of thinking.

Piaget's definition of intelligence reflects his background in biology. He viewed intelligence as a basic life function that helps the organism adapt to its environment. He added that intelligence is "a form of **equilibrium** toward which all [cognitive structures] tend" (1950, p. 6; boldface added). So, according to Piaget, intellectual activity is undertaken with one goal in mind: to produce a balanced or harmonious relationship between one's thought processes and the environment. Piaget believed that the environment is an exciting place full of many new stimuli that are not immediately understood by the curious, active child. Any "disequilibrium" between the environment and the child's modes of thinking should prompt the child to make mental adjustments in an attempt to cope with puzzling new experiences. In sum, the Piagetian approach to intelligence is a "biologically oriented" viewpoint which implies that imbalances between one's mental abilities and the environment stimulate cognitive activity and intellectual growth.

At this point, you may be thinking that intelligence is a very complex attribute. Piaget agrees. He states that intellect consists of no fewer than three interrelated components: *content, structure,* and *function.*

■ *Intellectual content*

When Piaget speaks of intellectual content, he is referring to "what" the child thinks. For example, when a 4-year-old girl says that the sun is alive because it moves across the sky or that rules made by her parents apply to all children, we have some indication of the content of her thinking. According to Piaget, content (or intellectual performance) is determined by an underlying *structure* (or concept). Although Piaget's main interest during the early stages of his career was the content of children's thinking, he soon realized that studies of intellectual content cannot explain why children think the way they do or how they progress from one type of thinking to another. For these reasons, Piaget devoted most of his career to the study of intellectual structure and function.

■ *Cognitive structures*

A cognitive structure, or **schema,** is an organized pattern of thought or action that is used to interpret some aspect of one's experience. For example, the 4-year-old who says the sun is alive because it moves is operating on the basis of a simple cognitive schema—things that move are alive. The same child might say that a tree is dead, simply because it does not move (or because its limited movement is attributable to the wind).

According to Piaget, neonates enter the world without any cognitive structures, although they

PHOTO 2-7. *Piaget believed that children are naturally curious explorers who try to make sense of their surroundings.*

do come equipped with a number of inborn reflexes, such as sucking or grasping, that help them to adapt to the environment. But aside from their adaptive significance, these innate reflexes serve another important function: they are soon modified by experience to become the child's first true schemata. For example, true reflexive sucking occurs only if an object comes into contact with the infant's lips. Yet, Piaget (1952), carefully observing his own son, noted:

> During the second day . . . Laurent begins to make sucking movements between meals. . . . His lips open and close as if to receive a real nippleful but without having an object [to suck]. This behavior became more frequent [with the passage of time] [pp. 25–26].

Soon Laurent began to further modify his sucking response by taking many objects into his mouth. Shortly after he was a month old, he had developed a coordinated motor habit, or *behavioral* schema:

> After a meal . . . his arms . . . instead of gesticulating aimlessly, constantly move toward his mouth. . . . Thirteen times in succession I have been able to observe the hand go back into the mouth. There is no longer any doubt that coordination exists. . . . I remove the hand and place it near his waist. After a few minutes the lips move and the hand approaches them again. . . . [Finally] the hand enters the mouth, the thumb alone is retained, and sucking continues [1952, pp. 51–53].

This thumbsucking schema is only one of many that evolve from basic reflexes. Now you may be thinking, So what? How are these simple behavioral schemata related to what we think of as "thinking," or mental schemata? Piaget would answer that *mental schemata evolve from behavioral schemata.* We shall examine this transformation in some detail when we consider the topic of cognitive development in Chapter Nine.

■ *Intellectual functions—Piaget's mechanisms for change*

Piaget believed that human beings inherit two important intellectual functions that he called "organization" and "adaptation." **Organization** refers to the child's tendency to arrange available schemata into coherent systems, or bodies of knowledge. For example, a boy may initially believe that anything that flies is a "bird." When he discovers that many things that are not birds can also fly, he may organize this new knowledge into a new, more complex mental structure such as this one:

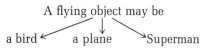

Organization is inborn and automatic; children are constantly rearranging their existing knowledge to produce new and more complex mental structures.

The goal of organization is to further the process of **adaptation.** The adaptive function is the child's tendency to adjust to the demands of the environment. According to Piaget, adaptation occurs in two ways: **assimilation** and **accommodation.**

Assimilation is a process in which children seek to incorporate some new experience into schemata that they already have. Imagine the reaction of an infant who is exposed for the first time to a beach ball. She may first try to grasp it with one hand and thus assimilate it into her "grasping" schema in much the same way that rattles,

---

equilibrium: *Piaget's term for the state of affairs in which there is a balanced or harmonious relationship between one's thought processes and environmental events.*

schema (plural, **schemata**): *an organized pattern of thought or action that a child develops to make sense of some aspect of his or her experience; Piaget sometimes uses the term* cognitive structures *as a synonym for* schemata.

organization: *Piaget's name for the child's inborn tendency to combine and integrate available schemata into coherent systems, or bodies of knowledge.*

adaptation: *Piaget's name for the child's inborn tendency to adjust to the demands of the environment.*

assimilation: *Piaget's term for the process by which children interpret new experiences by incorporating them into their existing schemata.*

accommodation: *Piaget's term for the process by which children modify their existing schemata in order to incorporate or adapt to new experiences.*

rubber animals, and other crib toys have been assimilated in the past. In other words, this infant is trying to adapt to a novel stimulus by construing it as something familiar—namely, something to be grasped.

By itself, assimilation would rarely allow one to adapt successfully to new experiences. Piaget (1952) believed that persons who assimilate novel aspects of the environment will also *accommodate* to that experience—that is, alter their existing schemata in response to environmental demands. For example, the infant may have to alter her grasping structure (accommodate) by using two hands instead of one in order to assimilate a beach ball into that particular schema. Assimilation and accommodation are complementary aspects of all adaptive acts. They are inborn processes that come into play whenever the child encounters new and interesting objects, events, or situations.

We can compare the activity of cognitive schemata to the behavior of an amoeba. This one-celled animal is a perpetual "eating machine" that engulfs food particles, changes shape, and grows. Cognitive growth occurs in a somewhat similar fashion. Children extend their schemata to novel aspects of the environment, and in the process of ingesting (assimilating) this environmental "nutriment," their schemata are changed (accommodated). The product of this intellectual functioning is adaptation—a state of equilibrium between the child's cognitive schemata and the environment.

But equilibrium is short-lived, according to Piaget. Just as an amoeba repeatedly changes shape by ingesting more food, one's cognitive structures are repeatedly changing (accommodating) as new

AN INFANT ACCOMMODATING HIS MOUTH TO THE SHAPE OF AN OBJECT

experiences are assimilated. And even during periods when they are not experiencing anything new, children are actively organizing their existing knowledge into higher-order schemata. So two kinds of activity—organization and adaptation—make possible a progressively greater understanding of the world. Piaget stressed that these intellectual functions operate in a reciprocal fashion: assimilations bring about new accommodations, which stimulate reorganizations, which, in turn, allow further assimilations, and so on. In the long run, the child's cognitive abilities will eventually mature to an extent that he or she becomes capable of thinking about old issues in a completely new way and will pass from one stage of intellectual development to the next.

Stages of Cognitive Development

Piaget divided intellectual development into four major periods: the *sensorimotor* stage (birth to age 2), the *preoperational* stage (ages 2 to 7), the *concrete-operational* stage (ages 7 to 11), and the *formal-operational* stage (ages 11–12 and beyond). These stages are increasingly complex. They form what Piaget called an *invariant developmental sequence*—that is, children progress through the stages in exactly the order in which they are listed. There is no skipping of stages, because each successive stage builds on previous ones. For example, formal operations, Piaget's highest stage, includes all the aspects of its predecessor, concrete operations, with the difference that the mental abilities that characterize concrete operations are now reorganized in a way that permits the child to reason at a higher level.

Table 2-2 describes some of the basic features of Piaget's four cognitive stages. Each of these periods of intellectual growth will be discussed in much greater detail when we return to the topic of cognitive development in Chapter Nine.

Piaget on Social Learning

Piaget adopted a holistic perspective on human development: he believed that physical growth and maturation, cognitive development, and social and personality development are interrelated. But unlike the learning theorists, who view development as the product of social learning, cognitive theorists argue just the opposite:

TABLE 2-2. Piaget's stages of cognitive development

Approximate age	Stage	Primary schemata or methods of representing experience	Major developments
Birth to 2 years	Sensorimotor	Infants use sensory and motor capabilities to explore and gain a basic understanding of the environment. At birth, they have only innate reflexes with which to engage the world. By the end of the sensorimotor period, they are capable of complex sensorimotor coordinations.	Infants acquire a primitive sense of "self" and "others," learn that objects continue to exist when they are out of sight (object permanence), and begin to internalize behavioral schemata to produce images, or mental schemata.
2 to 7 years	Preoperational	Children use symbolism (images and language) to represent and understand various aspects of the environment. They respond to objects and events according to the way things appear to be. Thought is egocentric, meaning that children think everyone sees the world in much the same way that they do.	Children become imaginative in their play activities. They gradually begin to recognize that other people may not always perceive the world as they do.
7 to 11 years	Concrete operations	Children acquire and use cognitive operations (mental activities that are components of logical thought).	Children are no longer fooled by appearances. By relying on cognitive operations, they understand the basic properties of and relations among objects and events in the everyday world. They are becoming much more proficient at inferring motives by observing others' behavior and the circumstances in which it occurs.
11 years and beyond		Children's cognitive operations are reorganized in a way that permits them to operate on operations (think about thinking). Thought is now systematic and abstract.	No longer is logical thinking limited to the concrete or the observable. Children enjoy pondering hypothetical issues and, as a result, may become rather idealistic. They are capable of systematic, deductive reasoning that permits them to consider many possible solutions to a problem and pick the correct answer.

social learning is a product of development. In other words, cognitive theorists assume that a child's level (or stage) of intellectual growth largely determines *what* the child will learn by interacting with other people and thus *how* he or she will behave toward others. Box 2-3 describes how cognitive development may affect one important aspect of social life—the child's reactions to socially transmitted rules, norms, or laws that are designed to sanction certain behaviors while prohibiting others.

Contributions and Criticisms of the Cognitive-Developmental Viewpoint

Like Watson and Freud, Piaget was an innovative renegade. He believed that people who studied intelligence largely ignored its most interesting features—intellectual structure and function. Of course, this view made Piaget quite unpopular among the psychometricians who were presumably measuring the least interesting aspect of intelligence, intellectual content, with their IQ

BOX 2-3
CHARACTERISTICS OF CHILDREN'S RULE-BOUND PLAY: CONCRETE OPERATIONS IMPLY CONCRETE INTERPRETATIONS

Children in middle childhood (ages 7 to 11, or Piaget's stage of concrete operations) spend much of their day playing together at games governed by explicit rules. Piaget (1965) suspected that the ways children interpret these rules would depend on their levels of cognitive development. He set out to test his hypothesis by getting down on his hands and knees and playing a rule-bound game, marbles, with children of different ages.

The fruits of Piaget's labors will be described in more detail when we take up the topic of moral development in Chapter Fourteen. Briefly, Piaget found that many 7-to-11-year-olds have a very rigid conception of the rules of a game, generally viewing them as *moral absolutes* that are not to be challenged. A child who breaks the rules or who tries to persuade the group to change them risks being called "cheater" by playmates.

By the time children have reached age 11 to 12 and approach Piaget's stage of formal operations, their impressions of rules are changing. The older child now recognizes that social rules and regulations are not absolute; they are arbitrary agreements that can be challenged and even changed as long as everybody concerned (or at least the majority) agrees to the changes. In other words, cognitive development affects social development. The child may have a rather rigid, or concrete, impression of rules and other moral dictates during the stage of concrete operations. However, this general impression and the behaviors it would dictate gradually give way to a more relativistic conception of rules as the child's thinking becomes more abstract during the stage of formal operations.

Now let's look more closely at this issue. Just because older children are capable of thinking of rules and regulations in a less rigid fashion does not mean they always will. You have probably heard adults say things like "Drivers who exceed 55 miles an hour should be punished" or "I don't make the laws, Bud—I only enforce them." In these instances, people may be treating certain rules as moral absolutes because they (1) fear punishment for violating them, (2) believe the laws are sound ones, or (3) are required to by virtue of their role in society. Thus, the moral judgments (and behavior) of adults depend, in part, on factors other than their level of cognitive development. In Chapter Fourteen we shall see that cognitive development may be necessary for "mature" forms of moral reasoning but is not sufficient, by itself, to guarantee that people will always favor the highest ethical standards.

---

tests. In addition, Piaget stressed a mentalistic concept, "cognition," that had fallen from favor among psychologists from the behaviorist tradition. So in the beginning, Piaget and his closest associates stood alone, receiving little if any encouragement from other members of the psychological community.

Clearly, the times have changed. By demonstrating the relation of cognitive abilities to learning and human development, Piaget was largely responsible for the emergence of a contemporary subdiscipline known as "cognitive psychology." Today many researchers who were trained in the rigid behavioral mold spend much of their time applying experimental methods to the study of cognition and its effects on behavior.

Piaget's notion that social development depends on cognitive development has spawned a whole new area of developmental research—the study of **social cognition**. Students of social cognition seek to determine how children come to understand the thoughts, emotions, and behavior of other people and how this knowledge then affects their own social behavior. Social cognition and its effects on social and personality development will be discussed throughout the text.

Finally, Piaget was the first major developmental theorist to stress that children are active, adaptive creatures whose thought processes are very different from those of adults. Educators soon recognized the implications of this line of reasoning for their own field as they began to treat children less like little adults and more like curious explorers who should be given educational experiences that they are capable of understanding. For example, many teachers now introduce the difficult concept of number by presenting young children with different numbers of objects to stack, color, or arrange. Presumably, new concepts like number are best taught by a method in which active children can apply their existing schemata and make the critical "discoveries" for themselves.

In spite of these many contributions, Piaget and his theory have been severely criticized. Psychoanalysts, not surprisingly, argue that Piaget ignores the most important of all "mentalistic" phenomena—unconscious motivation and its impact on behavior. In addition, learning theorists have found that not all children enter Piaget's stages when he says they should. Nor do children always act as if they were at only one particular stage. Consequently, those who favor the learning viewpoint have challenged the notion that Piaget's periods of cognitive development are true "stages" that unfold in a prescribed (invariant) sequence. They also believe that Piaget, the trained zoologist, overemphasized the role of biological factors in human development. This is an interesting critique because there are those who feel that Piaget paid insufficient attention to biological factors. Who would make such a claim? The ethologists.

THE ETHOLOGICAL VIEWPOINT

Ethology is the study of the biological bases of behavior, including its evolution, causation, and development (Cairns, 1979). This theoretical approach arose from the efforts of several European zoologists who argued that other theorists had overlooked or ignored important biological contributions to human and animal behavior.

According to ethologists, members of each species are born with a number of innate responses that are products of evolution. These "biologically programmed" behaviors are thought to have evolved as a result of the Darwinian process of **natural selection**. Presumably, environmental stresses or demands impinge on members of all species, ensuring that only those individuals with the most adaptive characteristics will survive to pass these attributes along to their offspring. Thus, each "species-specific" behavior is "preselected"—meaning that it has persisted because it serves some function that increases the chances of survival for the individual and the species (Blurton-Jones, 1972). Examples of preselected characteristics are the nest-building behavior of lovebirds, nut cracking by red squirrels, and crying to communicate discomfort by human infants.

When conducting research, ethologists prefer the method of naturalistic observation because they believe that "biologically programmed" behaviors that affect human (or animal) development are best identified and understood if they are observed in a setting in which they have adaptive significance (Charlesworth, 1980). Stated another way, it makes little sense to look for innate responses to the natural environment in the highly artificial context of the laboratory. (Ethologists do occasionally conduct laboratory experiments, but usually only to confirm or clarify observations made in the natural environment.)

When testing a hypothesis in the field, a human ethologist makes detailed records of children's interactions, noting when the critical behavior occurred and what happened before and after the critical event. Of particular interest are any possible innate responses (for example, facial features or postural cues) that may have elicited or terminated the behavior in question. Ethologists believe that all our innate responses have the function of promoting particular kinds of experiences that will affect our development. For example, the cry of a human infant is thought to be a biologically programmed "distress signal" that brings caretakers running. Its adaptive significance is to ensure (1) that the infant's basic needs (hunger, thirst, safety) will be satisfied and (2) that the infant will have sufficient contact with other human beings to form primary social and emotional relationships (Bowlby, 1973).

Although ethologists are critical of learning theorists for largely ignoring the biological bases of human development, they are well aware that development could not progress very far without learning. For example, the cry of an infant may be an innate signal that promotes the human contact from which emotional attachments emerge. However, these emotional attachments do not simply

---

social cognition: *the study of children's thinking about the thoughts, motives, intentions, and behaviors of themselves and other people.*

ethology: *the study of the bioevolutionary bases of behavior.*

natural selection: *the evolutionary principle that individuals who have characteristics advantageous for survival in a particular environment are the ones who are most likely to survive and reproduce. Over many generations, this process of "survival of the fittest" will lead to development of new species.*

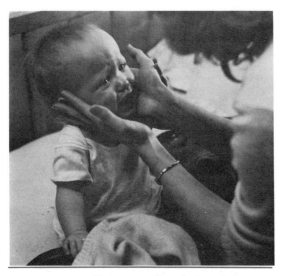

PHOTO 2-8. *The cry is a distress signal that attracts the attention of caregivers.*

"happen" automatically. The infant must first *learn* to discriminate familiar faces from those of strangers before he or she will show any evidence of being emotionally attached to a regular companion. Presumably, the adaptive significance of this kind of discriminatory learning goes back to that period in evolutionary history when humans traveled in nomadic tribes and lived in the great outdoors. In those days, it was crucial that an infant become attached to familiar companions and fearful of strangers, for failure to cry in response to a strange face might make the infant "easy pickings" for a predatory animal.

Now consider the opposite side of the coin. Caretakers may be inattentive or neglectful, so that the infant's cries rarely promote any contact with them. Such an infant will probably not form strong emotional attachments and may remain shy or emotionally unresponsive to others throughout life. What this infant has learned from these early experiences is that close companions are unreliable and not to be trusted. Consequently, the child becomes ambivalent or wary around caretakers and may generalize these feelings to other people (Ainsworth, 1973; Bowlby, 1973).

In sum, ethologists clearly acknowledge that we are largely a product of our experiences. Yet they are quick to remind us that we are inherently biological creatures who have inborn characteristics

that affect the kinds of learning experiences we are likely to have.

Contributions of the Ethological Viewpoint

If this chapter had been written in 1970, it would not have included a section on ethological theory. Although ethology came into being more than 30 years ago, the early ethologists studied animal behavior; only within the past 10–15 years have proponents of ethology made a serious attempt to specify the biological bases of human development. Yet in that short time they have made developmental researchers increasingly aware that every child has a bioevolutionary heritage that affects his or her own behavior and the reactions of others to the child.

One interesting ethological idea is that infants are sociable creatures who are quite capable of promoting and maintaining social encounters from the day they are born. This viewpoint contrasts sharply with that of the behaviorists, who portray the neonate as a *tabula rasa,* or with Piaget's "asocial" infant, who comes into the world equipped with only a few basic reflexes. Ethologists also believe that our evolutionary history provides us with inborn motives that affect our behavior in important ways (shades of Freud and the concept of instincts). For example, the motive of altruism presumably has evolved because it promotes survival of the species (though not necessarily survival of the altruistic individual). Box 2-4 describes some recent observations that are consistent with this point of view.

In the 1980s, the ethological viewpoint is itself a thriving infant—one that should continue to develop and perhaps have an even stronger impact on the field of developmental psychology in the years ahead.

Criticisms of Ethology

Recall that Freudian psychoanalysis is often criticized as being *untestable:* how, for example, does one measure instincts or components of the personality such as the id, ego, and superego? The same criticism can be aimed at the ethologists: how does one prove that certain motives or behaviors are (1) inborn or (2) products of evolutionary history? These claims are difficult if not impossible to confirm. In addition, ethological

BOX 2-4
IS ALTRUISM PART OF HUMAN NATURE?

Darwin's notion of "survival of the fittest" seems to argue against altruism as an inborn motive. Many have interpreted Darwin's idea to mean that powerful, self-serving individuals who place their own needs ahead of others' are the ones who are most likely to survive. If this were so, evolution would favor the development of selfish, egoistic motives—not altruism—as basic components of human nature.

Martin Hoffman (1981) has recently challenged this point of view, listing several reasons that the concept of "survival of the fittest" actually implies altruism. His arguments hinge on the assumption that human beings are more likely to receive protection from natural enemies, satisfy all their basic needs, and successfully reproduce if they live together in cooperative social units. If this assumption is correct, cooperative, altruistic individuals would be the ones who are most likely to survive long enough to pass along their "altruistic genes" to their offspring; individualists who "go it alone" would probably succumb to famine, predators, or some other natural disaster that they could not cope with by themselves. So over thousands of generations, natural selection would favor the development of innate social motives such as altruism. Presumably, the tremendous survival value of being "social" makes altruism, cooperation, and other social motives much more plausible as components of human nature than competition, selfishness, and the like.

It is obviously absurd to argue that infants routinely help other people. However, Hoffman believes that even newborn babies are capable of recognizing and experiencing the emotions of others. This ability, known as *empathy,* is thought to be an important contributor to altruism, for a person must recognize that others are distressed in some way before he or she is likely to help. So Hoffman is suggesting that at least one aspect of altruism—empathy—is present at birth.

Hoffman's claim is based on an experiment (Sagi & Hoffman, 1976) in which infants less than 36 hours old listened to (1) another infant's cries, (2) an equally loud computer simulation of a crying infant, or (3) no sounds at all (silence). The infants who heard a real infant crying soon began to cry themselves, to display physical signs of agitation such as kicking, and to grimace. Infants exposed to the simulated cry or to silence cried much less and seemed not to be very discomforted. (A recent study by Martin & Clark, 1982, has confirmed these observations.)

Hoffman argues that there is something quite distinctive about the human cry. His contention is that infants listen to and experience the distress of (that is, empathize with) another crying infant and become distressed themselves. Of course, this finding does not conclusively demonstrate that humans are altruistic by nature. But it does imply that empathy may be present at birth and thus serve as a biological basis for the eventual development of altruistic behavior.

theory is often criticized as being a *retrospective*, or "post hoc," explanation of development. One can easily apply evolutionary concepts to explain what has already happened, but can the theory predict what is likely to happen in the future? Many developmentalists believe that it cannot.

Finally, proponents of learning theory have an interesting viewpoint on ethology. They argue that even if the bases for certain motives or behaviors are biologically programmed, these innate responses are so modified by learning that it may not be helpful to spend much time wondering about their prior evolutionary significance. Albert Bandura (1973), for example, makes the following observation when comparing the aggressive behaviors of humans and animals:

[Unlike animals], man does not rely heavily on auditory, postural and olfactory signals for conveying aggressive intent or appeasement. He has [developed] a much more intricate system of communication—namely language—for controlling aggression. National leaders can . . . better safeguard against catastrophic violence by verbal communiques than by snapping their teeth or erecting their hair, especially in view of the prevalence of baldness among the higher echelons [p. 16].

In spite of these criticisms, the ethological perspective is a valuable addition to the field of developmental psychology. It has made us aware of important biological contributors to human development and has led to several discoveries that were neither anticipated nor easily explained by other theoretical approaches.

A FINAL COMMENT ON DEVELOPMENTAL THEORIES

The four broad theoretical perspectives that we have reviewed differ in many respects. They make different assumptions about children and the developmental process; they rely on different research methods to test assumptions and hypotheses; and last but not least, *they emphasize different aspects of development.* Psychoanalytic theorists focus on social and emotional development. They have made us aware that early experiences and unconscious emotional conflicts can have a dramatic effect on the developing personality. Learning theorists are concerned mainly with the *process* of development itself. They have helped us to understand how children are influenced by their environment and how interactions between person and environment lead to the development of stable habits, traits, talents, and peculiarities. Cognitive theorists concentrate on the intellectual aspects of human development. They remind us that children are active and curious "thinkers" whose interpretations of the environment determine what kinds of learning experiences they are likely to have. Ethologists can agree, in part, with each of these arguments. But they would also emphasize that human beings are biological creatures who inherit various mannerisms, behaviors, and motives that help to steer them along particular developmental paths.

We have seen that each of these theories has definite strengths and that each is subject to criticism. Today many developmentalists can be described as *theoretical eclectics*—those who recognize that none of these theories can explain all aspects of human development but that each has contributed in important ways to what we know about developing children. The plan for the remainder of this book is to take an eclectic approach, borrowing from many theories to integrate their contributions into a unified, holistic portrait of the developing child. However, we will not shy away from theoretical controversies, for these squabbles often produce some of the most exciting breakthroughs in the field. The next chapter, for example, will show how the "nature versus nurture" controversy has helped us to understand

how heredity and environment interact to affect intelligence, personality, and mental health.

SUMMARY

A theory is a set of concepts and propositions that help to describe and explain observations that one has made. Theories are particularly useful if they are *concise* and yet applicable to a wide range of phenomena. Good theories are also *precise*—that is, capable of making explicit predictions that can be evaluated in later research. There are four major theoretical perspectives on human development: psychoanalytic theory, learning theory (behaviorism), cognitive-developmental theory, and ethological theory.

The psychoanalytic perspective originated from the work of Sigmund Freud, who depicted children as "seething cauldrons" driven by inborn erotic and destructive instincts. At birth, the child's personality consists only of these instinctual forces (called the "id"). However, these id forces are gradually diverted into a system of rational thought, the "ego," and an irrational but ethical component of personality, the "superego." The child is thought to pass through five psychosexual stages—oral, anal, phallic, latency, and genital—that parallel the maturation of the sex instinct. Freud assumed that the activities and conflicts that emerge at each psychosexual stage would have lasting effects on the developing personality.

Erik Erikson has extended Freud's theory by concentrating less on the sex instinct and more on important sociocultural determinants of human development. According to Erikson, people progress through a series of eight psychosocial stages. Each stage is characterized by a conflict, or "crisis," that the individual must successfully resolve in order to develop in a healthy direction.

The learning, or behaviorist, viewpoint originated with John B. Watson, who argued that newborn infants are *tabulae rasae* who are gradually conditioned by their experiences to feel, think, and act in certain ways. Learning theorists believe that learned associations between stimuli and responses (habits) are the building blocks of human development. Presumably, development is a continuous process marked by gradual acquisition of new and more sophisticated habits. These habits may be acquired by classical conditioning, operant conditioning, or observational learning.

The cognitive-developmental viewpoint of Jean Piaget stresses that children are active explorers who have an intrinsic need to adapt to their environments. Piaget described the course of intellectual development as an invariant sequence of four stages, each of which evolves from its predecessors. According to Piaget, the child's stage of cognitive development determines how he or she will interpret various events and, thus, what the child will learn from interacting with others. The implication is that cognitive abilities play a central role in children's overall development, particularly their social and personality development.

The ethological viewpoint is that children are born with a number of adaptive responses that evolved over the course of human history and serve to channel development along particular paths. Ethologists recognize that human beings are largely products of their experiences (learning). However, they remind us that we are biological creatures whose innate characteristics affect the kind of learning experiences we are likely to have.

Although no single theoretical viewpoint offers a totally satisfactory explanation of human development, each of the four reviewed in this chapter has contributed in important ways to our understanding of developing children. Most contemporary developmentalists are eclectic, meaning that they borrow from many theories, attempting to integrate these contributions into a holistic portrait of the developing child.

REFERENCES

Ainsworth, M. D. S. (1973). The development of infant-mother attachment. In B. Caldwell & H. Ricciuti (Eds.), *Review of child development research* (Vol. 3). Chicago: University of Chicago Press.

Bandura, A. (1973). *Aggression: A social learning analysis.* Englewood Cliffs, NJ: Prentice-Hall.

Bandura, A. (1977). *Social learning theory.* Englewood Cliffs, NJ: Prentice-Hall.

Bell, R. Q. (1979). Parent, child, and reciprocal influences. *American Psychologist, 34,* 821–826.

Blurton-Jones, N. (1972). Characteristics of ethological studies of human behavior. In N. Blurton-Jones (Ed.), *Ethological studies of child behavior.* London: Cambridge University Press.

Bowlby, J. (1973). *Attachment and loss.* Vol. 2: *Separation.* London: Hogarth Press.

Cairns, R. B. (1979). *Social development: The origins and plasticity of interchanges.* San Francisco: W. H. Freeman.

Charlesworth, W. R. (1980). Teaching ethology of human behavior. *Human Ethology Newsletter, 28,* 7–9.

Dollard J., & Miller, N. E. (1950). *Personality and psychotherapy: An analysis in terms of language, thinking, and culture.* New York: McGraw-Hill.

Erikson, E. H. (1950). In M. J. E. Senn (Ed.), *Symposium on the healthy personality.* New York: Josiah Macy, Jr., Foundation.

Erikson, E. H. (1963). *Childhood and society* (2nd ed.). New York: Norton.

Erikson, E. H. (1972). Eight ages of man. In C. S. Lavatelli & F. Stendler (Eds.), *Readings in child behavior and child development.* New York: Harcourt Brace Jovanovich.

Freud, S. (1933). *New introductory lectures in psychoanalysis.* New York: Norton.

Freud, S. (1947). *The ego and the id.* London: Hogarth Press. (Original work published 1923)

Freud, S. (1961). The dissolution of the Oedipus complex. In J. Strachey (Ed.), *The standard edition of the complete psychological works of Sigmund Freud* (Vol. 19). London: Hogarth Press. (Original work published 1924)

Freud, S. (1964). An outline of psychoanalysis. In J. Strachey (Ed.), *The standard edition of the complete psychological works of Sigmund Freud* (Vol. 23). London: Hogarth Press. (Original work published 1940)

Hoffman, M. L. (1981). Is altruism part of human nature? *Journal of Personality and Social Psychology, 40,* 121–137.

Jensen, A. R. (1969). How much can we boost I.Q. and scholastic achievement? *Harvard Educational Review, 39,* 1–123.

Katcher, A. (1955). The discrimination of sex differences by young children. *Journal of Genetic Psychology, 87,* 131–143.

Maier, H. W. (1969). *Three theories of child development.* New York: Harper & Row.

Martin, G. B., & Clark, R. D., III. (1982). Distress crying in neonates: Species and peer specificity. *Developmental Psychology, 18,* 3–9.

Piaget, J. (1950). *The psychology of intelligence.* New York: Harcourt Brace Jovanovich.

Piaget, J. (1952). *The origins of intelligence in children.* New York: International Universities Press.

Piaget, J. (1965). *The moral judgment of the child.* New York: Free Press. (Original work published 1932)

Sagi, A., & Hoffman, M. L. (1976). Empathic distress in newborns. *Developmental Psychology, 12,* 175–176.

Skinner, B. F. (1953). *Science and human behavior.* New York: Macmillan.

Skinner, B. F. (1971). *Beyond freedom and dignity.* New York: Knopf.

Watson, J. B. (1913). Psychology as the behaviorist views it. *Psychological Review, 20,* 158–177.

Watson, J. B. (1925). *Behaviorism.* New York: Norton.

Weisberg, P. (1963). Social and nonsocial conditioning of infant vocalization. *Child Development, 34,* 377–388.

Wiggam, A. E. (1923). *The new decalogue of science.* Indianapolis: Bobbs-Merrill.

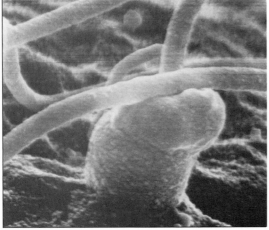

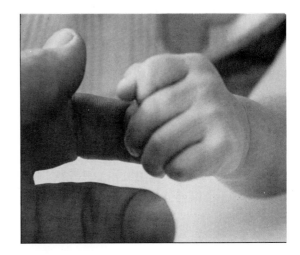

PART TWO

Human beings are biological creatures, and our emphasis in Part Two is on the biological bases of development. In Chapter Three we will discuss the concept of heredity and see that hereditary processes contribute in important ways to our physical, social, and intellectual development. We will also learn how our knowledge of genetic transmission has helped to promote healthy development by allowing us to prevent or minimize the effects of many hereditary abnormalities.

BIOLOGICAL FOUNDATIONS OF DEVELOPMENT

Our focus in Chapter Four shifts to the remarkable developments that take place during the prenatal period—the nine months between conception and birth during which a single cell evolves into a recognizable human being. Although prenatal development unfolds in an orderly sequence and follows a distinct biological timetable, we will see that the 266 days before birth are truly a sensitive period in which a variety of environmental influences can interfere with nature's grand plan and produce any number of harmful consequences.

Psychological development depends to a large extent on physical development: our size, shape, strength, sensory capabilities, and muscle coordination clearly affect how we feel, think, and act. Chapter Five describes the characteristics and capabilities of newborns and

then traces their physical development from infancy through adolescence as they grow, acquire important motor skills, and become more and more like adults, both in appearance and in physical prowess.

Although in this section we concentrate on aspects of development that are heavily influenced by our biological heritage, each of the areas we will consider is subject to a variety of social and environmental influences. Thus, the three chapters in Part Two also illustrate how the forces of nature and nurture combine (or interact) to determine developmental outcomes.

CHAPTER THREE ■

HEREDITARY INFLUENCES ON HUMAN DEVELOPMENT

■ *Heredity in historical perspective*
The doctrine of preformationism
Modern genetic theories

■ *Principles of hereditary transmission*
Conception
Growth of the zygote and production of body
 cells
Germ cells and hereditary transmission
Patterns of genetic expression

■ *Chromosomal and genetic abnormalities*
Chromosomal abnormalities
Genetic abnormalities

■ *Hereditary influences on ability,*
 personality, and behavior
Methods of assessing hereditary influences
Hereditary contributions to intelligence
Hereditary contributions to temperament and
 personality
Hereditary contributions to mental illness

■ *Another look at the nature/nurture*
 controversy
The rubber-band hypothesis
Canalization
Can we create optimal environments?

■ *Summary*

Can you remember when you were first introduced to the concept of heredity? You may find it amusing to consider the experience of one first-grader at a parent/teacher conference. The teacher asked the boy whether he knew in which country his ancestors had lived before coming to the United States. He proudly proclaimed "The Old West" because he was "half cowboy and half Negro." Everyone present had a good laugh and then tried to convince the boy that he couldn't be of Afro-American ancestry because his parents were not—that he could only become what mom and dad already were. Evidently, the constraints of heredity did not go over too well. The child became rather distressed and asked "You mean I can't be a fireman?"

In this chapter we will consider the "constraints of heredity" in the light of what we have learned about the biological bases of development over the past 300 years. In so doing, we'll see that our understanding of the fundamentals of hereditary transmission is itself a recent development and that many thorny issues remain to be resolved. After considering how hereditary information is passed from parents to children, we will explore the hereditary basis for important psychological characteristics such as intelligence, personality, and mental health. Finally, we will see that the expression "hereditary constraint" is something of a misnomer, for most complex human attributes are the result of a long and involved interplay between the forces of nature (heredity) and nurture (the environment).

HEREDITY IN HISTORICAL PERSPECTIVE

The concept of heredity dates back to at least 6000 years ago, when historical records describe farmers' attempts to produce better crops and hardier livestock by selective breeding (Burns, 1976). Before the 17th century, it was commonly assumed that children inherited their traits, talents, and peculiarities from their fathers. For example, Aristotle, writing in the fourth century B.C., argued that "nature seeks to reproduce the father exactly in the offspring but fails in different degrees. The ideal would be for male to produce male only; the first fall from this is the production of females, and thence we can proceed by gentle gradations to freaks" (1912, p. 767). According to Aristotle, fathers would fail to produce male offspring if they married too young or chose the wrong time of year for procreation. Ideally, men should be at least 37 and women 18 before they began to reproduce. Presumably, winter was the season when men would have the time and energy to reproduce themselves without generating "accidents of nature" such as daughters or small and defective sons.

The Doctrine of Preformationism

In the 17th century, the invention of the compound microscope led to the discovery of sperm and ova. Dutch scientist Anton van Leeuwenhoek (1677) observed the movement of sperm cells under a microscope and concluded that sperm were alive. His countryman Jan Swammerdam soon proposed a *preformationist* theory, which stated that each sperm cell contains a tiny "preformed" embryo, or **homunculus,** that was nourished by the female ovum (egg) and would grow only if deposited in the womb (see Figure 3-1). Clearly, Leeuwenhoek and Swammerdam agreed with Aristotle on one important point—inheritance flowed from father to offspring, the mother serving as an incubator.

However, Swammerdam's "homunculus" theory was soon challenged by other scientists, who noted that many children resemble their mothers much more than their fathers. One group of biologists (the *ovists*) argued that preformed human embryos appeared not in the father's sperm but in the mother's ova. Presumably, sperm was little more than a "fertilizer" that triggered the growth of an embryo. The ovist viewpoint was popular in its day because it seemed to legitimize the tendency of many to blame mothers for producing deformed babies or for failing to produce male heirs.

In 1759 Kaspar Wolff, a German-born anatomist, reported a set of observations that forever changed our thinking about hereditary processes (Wolff, 1759/1959). Wolff suspected that sperm and ovum unite to form a single cell that soon begins to divide. As this process of cell division was re-

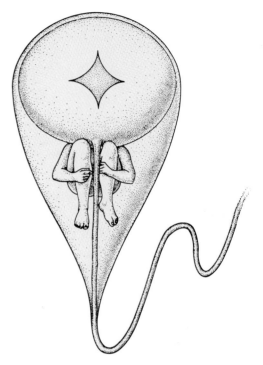

FIGURE 3-1. *The homunculus. Leeuwenhoek believed that each sperm cell contained a preformed embryo, or "homunculus," that would grow if deposited in the womb of an adult female.*

peated thousands of times, Wolff was able to observe the gradual development of recognizable organs and body parts. This remarkable discovery implied that neither the sperm nor the ovum contained a preformed embryo. Clearly, Wolff had witnessed the evolution, or "epigenesis," of an embryo from a single fertilized ovum (or zygote) to which both parents had contributed.

Modern Genetic Theories

Although Wolff's observations were hailed as a major advance in knowledge, several puzzles remained to be solved. For example, if each parent makes a roughly equivalent hereditary contribution to the offspring, why do some children resemble one parent more than the other? The answer was more than 100 years in coming.

■ *The work of Gregor Mendel*

In 1865 Gregor Mendel reported an extensive program of research on the inheritance of color and other attributes in flowering sweet peas. During eight years of work, Mendel cross-fertilized 22 varieties of garden peas and carefully recorded the characteristics of the hybrid offspring. Fertile hybrids were then crossed to see what kinds of offspring they would produce. From his many observations, Mendel inferred the following:

1. Inherited attributes such as color in the flowers of sweet peas are produced by "characters" (later to be labeled **genes**) that are transmitted unchanged from generation to generation.
2. Each inherited attribute is determined by a pair of genes, *one of which is inherited from each parent.*
3. When an individual inherits a pair of genes that differ in their effects, one of these genes will *dominate* the other, and the characteristic of *only the dominant gene* will be expressed.
4. When a parent produces *gametes* (sperm for males and ova for females), the gene pair for each attribute divides so that each gamete contains but one member of the pair (law of segregation).

Mendel's early conclusions were brilliant insights that provided the foundation for modern genetics. Perhaps his most notable of many important contributions is the concept of genetic dominance —the principle that explains why a child may resemble one parent more than the other. According to the dominance principle, a child who inherits a different form of a particular gene from each parent will not be a "blend" of the parents' attributes. Instead, one of the parental genes will completely dominate the other, and the child will resemble the parent who contributed the dominant gene.

■ *The work of Thomas Scott Morgan*

In 1933 the zoologist Thomas Scott Morgan won the Nobel Prize in medicine for discovering that Mendel's "characters," or genes, are actual structures that are components of larger bodies, called **chromosomes,** that appear within the nuclei of all cells. Although they are not visible as separate entities, as many as 10,000–20,000 genes are said to lie like "beads on a string" along each chromosome (see Photo 3-1).

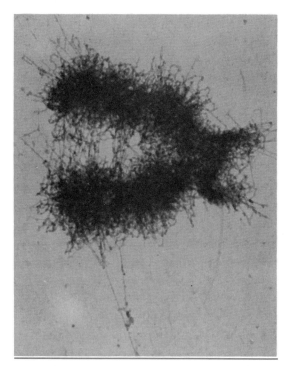

PHOTO 3-1. *A pair of human chromosomes. Although not visible as separate entities, as many as 10,000–20,000 genes lie like "beads on a string" along each chromosome.*

Morgan's discoveries were based on his study of a relatively simple species, the vinegar fly. However, other researchers soon discovered that members of each species have a set number of chromosomes within the nucleus of each body cell. For example, normal human beings have 46 chromosomes per cell; other species have larger or smaller numbers.

The field of genetics flourished after Morgan reported that genes are located within the chromo-

---

homunculus: *a preformed human embryo that biologists once believed to be present in each sperm cell.*

genes: *hereditary blueprints for development that are transmitted unchanged from generation to generation.*

chromosome: *a threadlike structure made up of genes; in humans there are 46 chromosomes in the nucleus of each cell.*

somes of cell nuclei. Today we have a reasonably good understanding of how genes (and chromosomes) replicate themselves, thus allowing the human to evolve from a simple one-celled organism at conception to a complex being who enters the world with many interrelated systems, organs, and body parts. In Chapter Four we will focus on the remarkable developments that occur during the nine-month *prenatal* period between conception and birth. However, our immediate concern is heredity—that is, what the child inherits from his or her parents and how this genetic inheritance affects the course of development.

PRINCIPLES OF HEREDITARY TRANSMISSION

At puberty or shortly thereafter, human females begin a process known as **ovulation:** approximately once every 28 days, an ovum ripens, leaves the ovary, and enters the fallopian tube. The average woman will ovulate some 300–500 times over the 30–40 years that she remains fertile. The vast majority of these ovulations are rather uneventful:

the ripened ovum simply disintegrates when it reaches the uterus, and it leaves the body about seven to ten days later as part of the woman's menstrual flow.

Conception

Suppose, however, that a woman has sexual intercourse with a fertile male a few days before or after ovulation. When the male ejaculates, his seminal fluid may contain half again as many sperm cells (300–450 million) as there are people in the United States. These tiny, tadpole-like sperm immediately begin to swim in all directions. Perhaps as many as 5000–20,000 of them will survive the long journey from the vagina through the uterus and into the fallopian tubes, where one may meet and penetrate the shell of a ripened ovum that is beginning its descent from the ovary (see Figure 3-2). This is **conception**—the beginning of a long developmental process.

The very first development that occurs is protective: when a sperm cell penetrates the lining of the ovum, a biochemical reaction repels other sperm, thus preventing them from repeating the fertilization process. Within a few hours, the

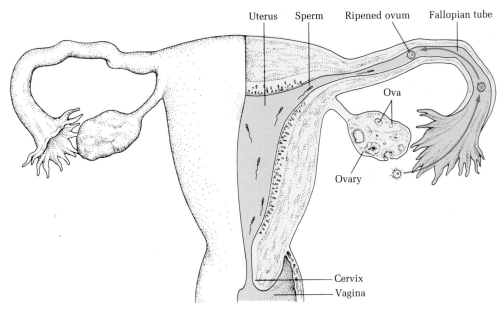

FIGURE 3-2. *The anatomy of conception. Conception occurs in the fallopian tube as a sperm penetrates a ripened ovum that is descending from the ovary to the uterus.*

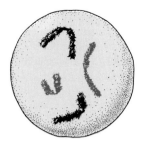

STEP 1
Original parent cell (for illustrative purposes this cell contains but four chromosomes).

STEP 2
Each chromosome splits lengthwise, producing a duplicate.

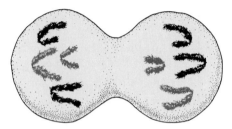

STEP 3
The duplicate sets of chromosomes move to opposite ends of the parent cell, which then begins to divide.

STEP 4
The cell completes its division, producing two daughter cells that have identical sets of chromosomes.

FIGURE 3-3. Mitosis—the way cells reproduce themselves.

sperm cell begins to disintegrate, releasing its 23 chromosomes. At about the same time, the nucleus of the ovum releases 23 chromosomes of its own. As a new cell nucleus forms around these 23 pairs of chromosomes, the sperm and ovum become one cell—a **zygote**—that is only 1/20th the size of the head of a pin. Yet this tiny cell may contain as many as 500,000 pairs of genes—one member of each pair coming from each parent—that provide the code, or biochemical recipe, for the zygote's development from a single cell into a recognizable human being.

Growth of the Zygote and Production of Body Cells

As the zygote moves through the fallopian tube toward its prenatal home in the uterus, it begins to reproduce itself through the process of **mitosis**. At first the zygote divides into two cells, but the two soon become four, four become eight, eight become sixteen, and so on. Just before each division,

the cell duplicates its 46 chromosomes, and these duplicate sets move in opposite directions. The division of the cell then proceeds, resulting in two "daughter" cells, each of which has the identical 23 pairs of chromosomes (46 in all) and thus the same genetic code as the original parent cell. This remarkable process is illustrated in Figure 3-3.

By the time a child is born, he or she consists of billions of cells, each of which has been created through mitosis. Indeed, all the *somatic* (body)

ovulation: *the process in which a female gamete (or ovum) matures in one of the ovaries and is released into the fallopian tube.*
conception: *the moment of fertilization, when a sperm penetrates an ovum, forming a zygote.*
zygote: *a single cell formed at conception from the union of a sperm and an ovum.*
mitosis: *the process in which a cell duplicates its chromosomes and then divides into two genetically identical daughter cells.*

cells that make up our muscles, bones, organs, and other bodily structures are products of mitosis. Mitosis continues throughout life, creating new cells that enable us to grow and replacing old ones that are damaged. With each division, the hereditary blueprint is duplicated, so that every new cell contains an exact copy of the 46 chromosomes that we inherited at conception.

Germ Cells and Hereditary Transmission

We have learned that sperm and egg combine to form a zygote that has 46 chromosomes (23 of which come from each parent). But if cells normally contain 46 chromosomes apiece, why doesn't a person start life with 92 chromosomes, 46 coming from the father's sperm cell and 46 from the mother's ovum?

The answer is relatively simple. In addition to body cells, mature human beings have *germ* cells that serve one particular hereditary function—to produce *gametes* (sperm in males and ova in females). When male germ cells in the testes and female germ cells in the ovaries produce sperm and ova, they do so by a process called **meiosis**. In meiosis, the 23 pairs of chromosomes in the parent cell divide so that each daughter cell contains 23 single, or *unpaired,* chromosomes (see Figure 3-4). Thus, a sperm with 23 chromosomes unites with an ovum with 23 chromosomes, producing a zygote that has a full complement of 46 chromosomes (23 pairs).

Hereditary uniqueness.   Full brothers and sisters have the same mother and father and have inherited 23 chromosomes from each of these par-

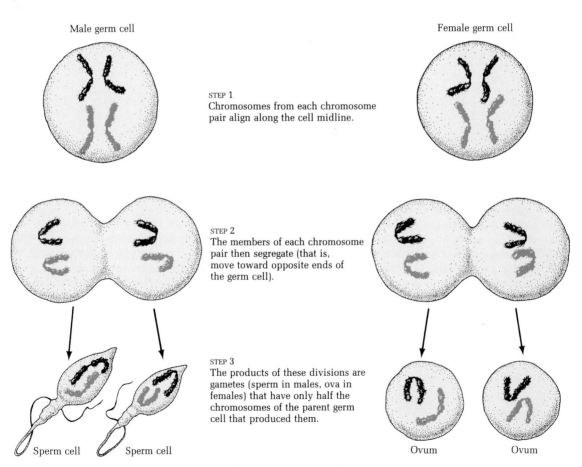

Male germ cell

Female germ cell

STEP 1
Chromosomes from each chromosome pair align along the cell midline.

STEP 2
The members of each chromosome pair then segregate (that is, move toward opposite ends of the germ cell).

STEP 3
The products of these divisions are gametes (sperm in males, ova in females) that have only half the chromosomes of the parent germ cell that produced them.

Sperm cell   Sperm cell

Ovum   Ovum

FIGURE 3-4. *Meiosis—the way germ cells produce sperm and ova.*

ents. In view of this common heritage, why do you suppose that children from the same family do not look more alike?

Again the answer is relatively simple. When a pair of chromosomes segregates during meiosis, it is a matter of chance which of the two chromosomes will end up in a particular gamete. And because each chromosome pair segregates independently of all other pairs, there are many different combinations of chromosomes that could result from the meiosis of a single germ cell. Since human germ cells contain 23 chromosome pairs, each of which is segregating independently of the others, the laws of probability tell us that there are 2^{23} possible outcomes of a meiotic division. In other words, a mature human being is capable of producing more than 8 million *different* gametes–different in that no two will carry exactly the same hereditary instructions. Because the 8 million combinations a father is capable of producing are independent of the mother's 8 million possible combinations, any couple could theoretically have 64 trillion babies without producing two children who inherited precisely the same set of genes.

In fact, the odds of exact genetic replication in two siblings born at different times is even less than 1 in 64 trillion, because of a quirk of meiosis known as the **crossing over** phenomenon. When pairs of chromosomes line up just before segregating, parts of them cross, break at the point of crossing, and exchange equivalent amounts of genetic material, much as if you were to exchange hands with a friend after a handshake. This process is illustrated in Figure 3-5. So the crossing-over phenomenon actually alters the genetic composition of a chromosome and thereby increases the number of gametes that an individual is capable of producing far beyond the figure of 8 million that would be possible if chromosomes segregated cleanly during meiosis, without exchanging genetic information.

Of course, brothers and sisters will resemble one another to some extent because their genes are drawn from a gene pool provided by the same two parents. Each brother or sister inherits half of each parent's genes, although two siblings never inherit the same half, owing to the random methods by which parental chromosomes (and genes) segregate into the sperm and ovum that combine to produce each offspring. Thus, each individual is

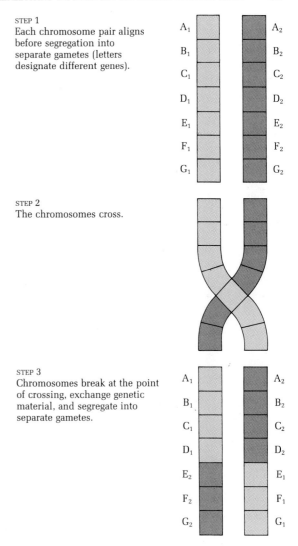

STEP 1
Each chromosome pair aligns before segregation into separate gametes (letters designate different genes).

STEP 2
The chromosomes cross.

STEP 3
Chromosomes break at the point of crossing, exchange genetic material, and segregate into separate gametes.

FIGURE 3-5. *The crossing-over phenomenon.*

---

meiosis: *the process in which a germ cell divides, producing gametes (sperm or ova) that each contain half of the parent cell's original complement of chromosomes; in humans, the products of meiosis contain 23 chromosomes.*

crossing over: *a process in which genetic material is exchanged between pairs of chromosomes.*

BOX 3-1
TWINNING, SIBSHIP, AND
OTHER KINSHIP RELATIONS

Although individuals are genetically unique, each child is biologically related to his or her parents by virtue of having inherited exactly half of their genes. The term *kinship* refers to the extent to which any two individuals inherit overlapping genes from their ancestors. Since each child inherits half the genes of each parent, the child's degree of kinship with each parent (or kinship quotient) is .50. Because chromosomes segregate randomly and independently during meiosis, the laws of probability also imply that siblings (that is, brothers and sisters) having the same parents will have 50% of their genes in common. Hence, their degree of kinship is also .50. Half brothers and sisters, who have only one parent in common, share 25% of their genes, for a kinship quotient of .25. Finally, children who have no common ancestors are said to be genetically unrelated, with a kinship of .00.

The principle of kinship is an important one for scientists who are interested in determining whether genetic inheritance, or *genotype,* affects the course of human development. If genotype has a direct effect on development, then people with a high degree of kinship (who share many genes) should be more alike than people with a low degree of kinship (who share few). For example, if heredity affects intelligence, then siblings should be more similar to each other in intellectual abilities than would pairs of unrelated children selected at random.

There is one exception to the rule of genetic uniqueness. About 1 of every 270 zygotes will divide in two, segregate, and develop as two separate individuals, or *identical* twins (Scheinfeld, 1967). These individuals are called *monozygotic (MZ)* twins because they develop from a single ("mono-") zygote. Since they have exactly the same hereditary blueprint, MZ twins will look alike, will be of the same sex, and will have a kinship quotient of 1.00. In other words, they are genetically identical and should exhibit very similar developmental progress if genotype has much effect on human development.

Most twins are not identical. At least two-thirds of the twin pairs born in the United States are *dizygotic (DZ),* or *fraternal* twins. Fraternals result when a mother releases two ova at roughly the same time and each is fertilized by a different sperm. Dizygotic twins thus develop from separate zygotes that have separate hereditary blueprints. As a result, DZ twins may differ considerably in appearance and may even be of different sexes. Although they are born at the same time and have had the same prenatal environment, DZ twins have no more genes in common than any other pair of siblings.

Developmental psychologists think of twins as fascinating research subjects. Here are pairs of indi-

genetically unique. (The one exception to this rule is identical twinning, which results from the splitting of a zygote into two identical cells that develop independently.) From an evolutionary perspective, we are probably rather fortunate to be genetically unique, for species that produce many variations of their own kind are more likely to survive drastic changes in the environment.

Determination of gender. A hereditary basis for sex differences becomes apparent if we examine the chromosomes of typical men and women. These chromosomal portraits, or **karyotypes,** reveal that 22 of 23 pairs of chromosomes found in human beings are similar in males and females. Gender is determined by the 23rd pair. In a normal male, the 23rd pair consists of one elongated body known as an **X chromosome** (from its shape) and a short, stubby companion called a **Y chromosome**. In the female, both these "sex" chromosomes are Xs (see Photo 3-2 on p. 84). Thus, the presence of a Y chromosome in one's hereditary blueprint means that one is a genetic male, while the absence of a Y chromosome defines a genetic female.

Pity the hundreds of thousands of women who throughout history have been belittled, tortured, divorced, or even beheaded for failing to bear their husbands a male heir! Since the father is the only parent who can provide the offspring with a Y chromosome, it is he who determines a child's gender. When the sex chromosomes segregate into gametes during meiosis, half the sperm of a genetic (XY) male will contain an X chromosome and half will contain a Y chromosome. In contrast, the ova produced by a genetic (XX) female will normally contain a single X chromosome. Thus, the determination of gender is straightforward: If an ovum is fertilized by a sperm bearing a Y chromosome, the product is an XY zygote, which

Identical, or monozygotic, twins (left) develop from a single zygote. Because they have inherited identical sets of genes, they will look alike, be of the same sex, and share all other inherited characteristics.

Fraternal, or dizygotic, twins (right) develop from separate zygotes and have no more genes in common than siblings born at different times. Consequently, they may not look alike (as we see in this photo) or even be of the same sex.

viduals who are born together, live in the same household, and may have a highly similar environment throughout childhood. By studying children with the same genes in a similar environment (identical twins) and comparing them with children with different genes in a similar environment (fraternal twins), one can estimate the contribution of genetic factors to almost any attribute or developmental index. Later in the chapter, we will see what twin studies can tell us about hereditary contributions to intelligence, temperament, personality, and mental illness.

will become a male. However, if a sperm carrying an X chromosome reaches the ovum first, the result is an XX zygote, or a female.

Since half the father's sperm contain Y chromosomes, the probability of conceiving a male child should be exactly 50/50. However, this is one case in which biology appears to defy the laws of probability. It has been estimated that as many as 150 males are conceived for every 100 females (a 60/40 ratio). And even though males are more likely to be miscarried (spontaneously aborted) during the prenatal period, they continue to outnumber females (by 106 to 100) at birth (McMillen, 1979; Stern, 1973).

Although we are not sure why sperm bearing Y chromosomes are more likely to reach and penetrate the ovum, both geneticists and students love to speculate about this issue. The most popular hypothesis is that sperm bearing a smaller Y chromosome can swim faster than those bearing a larger (and presumably heavier) X chromosome. Others wonder whether Y-bearing sperm might not be more resistant to adverse biochemical conditions present in the intrauterine environment.

The latter hypothesis receives some support from the work of Rorvik and Shettles (1970), who claim they have increased the odds that couples will conceive a child of the desired sex by al-

> **karyotype:** *a chromosomal portrait created by staining chromosomes and then photographing them under a high-power microscope.*
> **X chromosome:** *the longer of the two sex chromosomes; normal females have two X chromosomes, whereas normal males have but one.*
> **Y chromosome:** *the shorter of the two sex chromosomes; normal males have one Y chromosome, whereas females have none.*

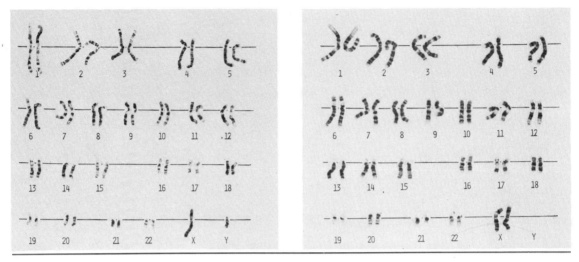

PHOTO 3-2. *These karyotypes of a male (left) and a female (right) have been arranged so that the chromosomes could be displayed in pairs. Note that the 23rd pair of chromosomes for the male consists of one elongated X chromosome and a Y chromosome that is noticeably smaller, whereas the 23rd pair for the female consists of two X chromosomes.*

tering the acidity of the woman's reproductive tract (a less acidic environment presumably favors conception of a male). However, other scientists have severely criticized this research, and perhaps we should consider it suggestive at best.

Patterns of Genetic Expression

To this point, we have learned that children inherit about half a million pairs of genes and that one member of each gene pair comes from each parent. The question that can now be asked is how one's genetic inheritance or **genotype,** affects one's **phenotype**—the way one looks, feels, thinks, and behaves. Let's begin our discussion of genetic influences by returning to an important principle discovered by Gregor Mendel more than 100 years ago—the principle of genetic dominance.

■ *Dominant and recessive alleles*
Many characteristics are determined by the interaction of a single pair of genes, or **alleles.** In human beings, eye color is a classic example. We receive one allele for eye color from each parent, and the particular combination of alleles that we have inherited determines what color our eyes will be.

Of course, the alleles that determine a characteristic like eye color may be of different kinds, as illustrated by the fact that not all people have eyes of the same color. Now suppose that you had inherited the following genotype for eye color: an allele for blue eyes from your father and an allele for brown eyes from your mother. What color eyes would you have? If you looked in the mirror, you would immediately discover that you did *not* have one blue eye and one brown eye, and you could then infer that your alleles did not express themselves independently. In fact, when a person inherits alternative forms of a gene, one allele will often dominate the other, so that only the characteristic associated with the dominant form of the gene will be expressed. It happens that the allele for brown eyes is **dominant** and the weaker blue-eyed allele is said to be **recessive.** Thus, a person who inherited a brown-eyed allele and a blue-eyed allele would have a "phenotype" of brown eyes.

Since a brown-eyed allele dominates a blue-eyed allele, we represent the brown-eyed gene with a capital *B* and the blue-eyed gene with a lower-case *b*. Clearly, human beings can have one of three genotypes for eye color: (1) two brown-eyed alleles (BB), (2) two blue-eyed alleles (bb), or (3) one of each (Bb). People whose genotype for an attribute consists of two genes of the same kind are said to be **homozygous** for that attribute. A person who is BB for eye color is homozygous brown and will pass only brown-eyed genes to his or her offspring. The person who is bb is homozygous blue (the only way one can have blue eyes is to inherit two recessive blue-eyed alleles) and will pass blue-eyed genes to his or her offspring. Finally, a person who is Bb is said to be **heterozygous** for eye color because he or she has two different alleles for this attribute. As we have seen, this individual will have brown eyes, because the B allele is dominant. And what kind of alleles will the heterozygous person pass along to offspring? Either a blue-eyed gene or a brown-eyed gene. Even though a heterozygous person has brown eyes, he or she can transmit a blue-eyed gene to children. Half the gametes produced by this individual will carry a gene for blue eyes, and half will carry a gene for brown eyes. Therefore, *phenotype does not alter genotype.* This is what Mendel (1865/1959) had in mind when he proclaimed that genes are transmitted unchanged from one generation to another.

Now consider a sample problem. Can two brown-eyed individuals ever produce a blue-eyed child? The answer is yes—as long as the genotype of each parent is heterozygous for eye color (that is, Bb). In Figure 3-6 the genotype of a heterozygous brown-eyed father appears at the head of the columns, and that of a heterozygous brown-eyed mother appears at the left of the rows. When the germ cells of each parent undergo meiosis, the resulting gametes will each contain only one allele for eye color—in this case, either a blue-eyed allele or a brown-eyed allele. What color eyes will the children have? The various possibilities appear in the four quadrants of the chart. If a sperm bearing a brown-eyed (B) gene unites with an ovum carrying a brown-eyed (B) gene, the result is a BB, or homozygous brown-eyed child. If a sperm containing a B gene fertilizes an ovum carrying a b gene, or if a b sperm fertilizes a B ovum, the result

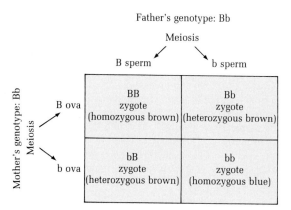

FIGURE 3-6. Possible genotypes and phenotypes resulting from a mating of two heterozygotes for eye color.

is a heterozygous brown-eyed (Bb) child. Finally, if both sperm and ovum carry a blue-eyed gene, the child will have blue eyes. Since each of these four combinations is equally likely to occur on any given mating, the odds are 1 in 4 that a child of two heterozygous brown-eyed parents will have blue eyes.

Eye color is but one of the many human attributes that are determined by a single gene pair in which one particular allele will dominate

---

genotype: *the genetic endowment that an individual inherits.*

phenotype: *the ways in which a person's genotype is expressed in observable or measurable characteristics.*

alleles: *alternative forms of a gene that is coded for a particular trait.*

dominant allele: *a relatively powerful gene that is expressed phenotypically and masks the effect of a less powerful gene.*

recessive allele: *a less powerful gene that is not expressed phenotypically when paired with a dominant allele.*

homozygous: *having inherited two alleles for an attribute that are identical in their effects.*

heterozygous: *having inherited two alleles for an attribute that have different effects.*

Our discussion of dominant and recessive genes has centered on two particular alleles, a gene for brown eyes and a gene for blue eyes. Yet eye coloring in human beings is more complex than our examples would indicate, for there are also genes for green, hazel, and gray eyes (all of which dominate a blue-eyed allele and are dominated by a gene for brown eyes). Listed below are other examples of dominant and recessive characteristics in human heredity.

Dominant traits	Recessive traits
Brown eyes	Gray, green, hazel, or blue eyes
Dark hair	Blond hair
Non-red hair (blond, brunette)	Red hair
Full head of hair	Pattern baldness*
Curly hair	Straight hair
Normal vision	Nearsightedness
Farsightedness	Normal vision
Normal vision	Color blindness
Roman nose	Straight nose
Broad lips	Thin lips
Short digits	Normal digits
Extra digits	Five digits
Double-jointedness	Normal joints

Dominant traits	Recessive traits
Immunity to poison ivy	Susceptibility to poison ivy
Pigmented skin	Albinism
Type A blood	Type O blood
Type B blood	Type O blood
Normal blood clotting	Hemophilia*
Normal hearing	Congenital deafness
Normal blood cells	Sickle-cell anemia*
Huntington's chorea	Normal brain and body maturation
Normal physiology	Phenylketonuria*
Normal physiology	Tay-Sachs disease*

A quick glance through the list reveals that most of the undesirable or maladaptive attributes are recessive. For that we can be thankful; otherwise genetically linked diseases and defects might soon destroy the species.

One important genetic disease produced by a *dominant* gene is Huntington's chorea, a condition that causes a gradual deterioration of the nervous system, leading to a progressive decline in one's physical and mental abilities and ultimately to death. Although some victims of Huntington's chorea die in young adulthood, normally the disease appears much later, usually after age 40. Fortunately, the dominant allele that is responsible for this lethal condition is very rare.

*This condition will be discussed elsewhere in the chapter.

another.[1] Box 3-2 lists a number of other common dominant and recessive characteristics that people may inherit.

■ Incomplete dominance

Alternative forms of a gene do not always follow the simple dominant/recessive pattern described by Gregor Mendel. For example, some "dominant" alleles fail to mask all the effects of a "recessive"

[1]We have talked as if each pair of alleles were responsible for determining only one characteristic. Yet geneticists have discovered that some genes are *pleiotropic*—that is, they influence many characteristics. For example, a single pair of alleles is responsible for the appearance of Marfan's syndrome, a rare disorder that Abraham Lincoln may have inherited. Marfan's syndrome includes characteristics such as long, bony limbs, eye problems, a loss of hearing, and heart defects—all determined by a single pair of pleiotropic alleles.

gene—that is, theirs is an **incomplete dominance**. A child who inherits heterozygous alleles of this type will have a phenotype that represents a "blending" of the two genes, although the stronger (or incompletely dominant) gene plays the major role in determining the child's phenotype.

The *sickle cell* trait provides an example of incomplete dominance in human heredity. About 9% of all Blacks in the United States (and relatively few Whites) are heterozygous for this attribute, carrying a recessive "sickle cell" allele (Thompson, 1975). The presence of this one recessive gene causes a substantial percentage of the person's red blood cells to assume an unusual crescent, or sickle, shape (see Photo 3-3). Sickled cells are a problem because they tend to cluster together, distributing less oxygen throughout the circulatory system. At high altitudes, even minimal stress or physical exertion can trigger a cir-

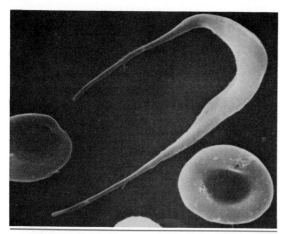

PHOTO 3-3. *Normal (left and right) and "sickled" (center) red blood cell from a person with sickle-cell anemia.*

culatory crisis in sickle-cell "carriers," resulting in a very painful swelling of the joints and severe fatigue (Wilson, 1982).

For those individuals who inherit *two* recessive sickle-cell genes (approximately 1 of every 400 Blacks in the United States), the consequences are much more severe. These people inherit a disease called **sickle-cell anemia,** which causes massive sickling of the red blood cells and inefficient distribution of oxygen at all times. Many who suffer from sickle-cell anemia will die from heart and/or kidney failure by adolescence. In contrast, heterozygous individuals who carry but one recessive sickle-cell gene are more phenotypically similar to the person who inherits two "normal" genes—their blood cells sickle to some extent, but they remain unaffected unless they are exposed to high altitudes or extreme emotional distress or unless they deprive themselves of oxygen through heavy physical exertion.

We see, then, that the "dominant" allele that produces normal red blood cells does not completely suppress the effects of a sickle-cell gene. If the dominance were complete, those who inherited a single recessive gene would not produce any sickled red blood cells.

■ *Codominance*

Some heterozygous alleles are equally strong or expressive, meaning that neither form of the gene is able to dominate the other. This type of genetic interaction is called **codominance** because the

phenotype of the heterozygous individual represents an exact compromise, or combination, of the two genes that he or she has inherited.

The genes for the human blood types A and B are equally expressive. Each of these alleles dominates the gene for blood type O, but neither of the two alleles dominates the other. A heterozygous person who inherits an allele for blood type A from one parent and an allele for blood type B from the other has both A antigens and B antigens in his or her blood—a phenotype that represents an exact compromise between blood types A and B. If you have inherited the blood type known as AB, you illustrate this principle of genetic codominance.

■ *Sex-linked characteristics*

Some characteristics are called **sex-linked** because they are determined by genes located on the sex chromosomes. In fact, the vast majority of these sex-linked attributes are produced by recessive genes that are found only on X chromosomes. Who do you suppose is more likely to inherit these X-linked traits, males or females?

The answer is males, a point we can easily illustrate with a common sex-linked characteristic, *red/green color blindness.* Many people cannot distinguish red from green, an inability caused by a recessive gene that appears only on X chromosomes. Now recall that a normal (XY) male has but one X chromosome—the one he inherited

incomplete dominance: *condition in which a stronger allele fails to mask all the effects of a weaker allele; a phenotype results that is similar but not identical to the effect of the stronger gene.*

sickle-cell anemia: *a genetic blood disease that causes red blood cells to assume an unusual sickled shape and to become inefficient at distributing oxygen throughout the body.*

codominance: *condition in which two heterozygous but equally powerful alleles produce a phenotype in which both genes are fully and equally expressed.*

sex-linked characteristic: *an attribute determined by a gene that appears on only one of the two types of sex chromosomes, usually the X chromosome.*

from his mother. If this X chromosome carries a recessive gene for color blindness, the male will be color-blind. Why? Because there is no corresponding gene on his Y chromosome that might counteract the effect of this "color blind" allele. In contrast, a genetic (XX) female who inherits a single gene for color blindness will not be color-blind, for the "color normal" gene on her second X chromosome will dominate the "color blind" gene, thereby enabling her to distinguish red from green. Thus, a female cannot be color-blind unless *both* her X chromosomes contain a recessive gene for color blindness.

So immediately we have reason to suspect that more males than females will be color-blind. Among White males in the United States, approximately 8 in 100 cannot distinguish red from green. This finding suggests that the ratio of "color blind" to "color normal" genes in the gene pool is approximately 1:12 (Burns, 1976). Since the odds are only 1 in 12 that any single X chromosome will contain a gene for color blindness, the likelihood that a female will inherit two of these genes (and be color-blind) is $1/12 \times 1/12$, or only 1 in 144.

Geneticists have now identified at least 93 sex-linked traits, most of which are disabling in some way (see Table 3-1 for some examples). Since these characteristics are typically produced by recessive genes on X chromosomes, males are more likely than females to suffer the consequences of sex-linked genetic disorders.

■ *Modifier genes and polygenic inheritance*

To this point, we have considered the simplest form of genetic transmission, in which a characteristic is determined by a single pair of genes. Yet alleles may also act as **modifier genes** by influencing the action or expression of other genes. An attribute that characterizes many adult males—

TABLE 3-1. Examples of sex-linked characteristics in human heredity

Attribute	Linkage	Gender most commonly affected
Color blindness (inability to distinguish reds and greens)	X chromosome (recessive)	Males
Hemophilia, or "bleeder's disease" (deficiency in the clotting of blood)	X chromosome (recessive)	Males
Muscular dystrophy (MD) (actually, there are 13 forms of MD; one form—Duchenne's—is sex-linked)	X chromosome (recessive)	Males
Diabetes (two forms)	X chromosome (recessive)	Males
Anhidrotic ectodermal dysplasia (absence of sweat glands and teeth)	X chromosome (recessive)	Males
Certain forms of night blindness	X chromosome (recessive)	Males
Certain forms of deafness	X chromosome (recessive)	Males
Atrophy of optic nerve	X chromosome (recessive)	Males
White forelock (a patch of light frontal hair on the head)	X chromosome (recessive)	Males
Hereditary enamel hypoplasia (tooth enamel is abnormally thin; teeth are small and soon wear down to the gums)	X chromosome (dominant)	Females
Hypertrichosis (excessive hair growing on and from the ears)	Y chromosome	Males

pattern baldness—is a particularly interesting hereditary phenomenon because the gene that produces it is dominant to the gene for normal hair in males but is recessive to the gene for normal hair in females. Therefore, a man who is heterozygous for pattern baldness will eventually lose some of his hair, whereas a heterozygous female will keep all of hers.

This sex difference is attributable to a modifier gene present in males. The gene(s) responsible for production of the male hormone androgen modify the gene for pattern baldness, making it dominant over the gene for normal hair. As a result, males who inherit but one gene for pattern baldness will show some degree of balding as they mature (the degree may well depend on the presence of yet other modifier genes). In contrast, females inherit a different set of genes that inhibit the production of androgen and do not alter the normally recessive nature of the gene for pattern baldness. So women must ordinarily inherit two genes for pattern baldness before they will experience a genetically based thinning of the hair (Burns, 1976).

Most complex human attributes are **polygenic**—that is, influenced by many genes rather than a single pair. One notable example is human intelligence. People are not merely bright or dull; their intellectual performances are distributed at all levels between these two extremes. The current thinking is that many continuous attributes such as intelligence, height, weight, skin color, and temperament are influenced by a large number of genes, each of which contributes in a small way to one's phenotype.

■ *A final note on genetic transmission*

Our discussion so far has implied that characteristics are *determined* by the genes that people inherit. Yet as we will see later in the chapter and throughout the text, behavioral attributes such as intelligence, temperament, and sociability are strongly influenced by environmental factors. Even physical characteristics such as height and weight depend to some extent on one's medical history and the adequacy of one's diet. In sum, the genes a child inherits may be an important contributor to his or her phenotype—but hardly the sole contributor. Most human attributes are the product of a long and involved interplay between the forces of nature and nurture.

Now let's consider the exceptions to this general rule. There are a number of hereditary quirks, or aberrations, that exert a powerful (and in some cases prepotent) influence on the development of children who inherit them. In the following section we will consider the causes and consequences of some of the more common of these hereditary abnormalities.

CHROMOSOMAL AND GENETIC ABNORMALITIES

Although the vast majority of newborn infants are pronounced healthy at birth, approximately 1 of every 7 has a congenital problem of some kind (Apgar & Beck, 1974). By definition, **congenital defects** are those that are present at birth, although many of these afflictions are not detectable when the child is born. For example, Huntington's chorea is a congenital problem because the gene that produces this disease is present from the moment of conception. But as we learned in Box 3-2, the gradual deterioration of the nervous system associated with this condition is not apparent at birth and will not ordinarily appear until much later—usually after age 40.

In Chapter Four we will consider a variety of congenital defects that are likely to result from abnormalities in the birth process or from harmful conditions to which children are exposed while developing within the womb. Here we will look only at those problems that are caused by abnormal genes and chromosomes.

Chromosomal Abnormalities

When a germ cell divides during meiosis, the distribution of its 46 chromosomes into pairs of

---

modifier gene: *a gene that influences the expression of other alleles.*

polygenic trait: *a characteristic that is influenced by the action of many genes rather than a single pair.*

congenital defect: *a problem that is present (though not necessarily apparent) at birth; such defects may stem from genetic and prenatal influences or from complications of the birth process.*

sperm or ova is sometimes uneven. In other words, one of the resulting gametes may have too many chromosomes, while the other has too few. The vast majority of these chromosomal abnormalities are *lethal*, meaning that a zygote formed from the union of an abnormal and a normal gamete will fail to develop or will be spontaneously aborted. However, some chromosomal aberrations are not lethal, as illustrated by the finding that approximately 1 child in 100 is born with either one chromosome too many (47) or one too few (45).

■ *Abnormalities of the sex chromosomes*

Many chromosomal abnormalities involve the 23rd pair—the sex chromosomes. Occasionally males are born with an extra X or Y chromosome, producing the genotype XXY or XYY, and females will often survive if they inherit a single X chromosome (XO) or even three (XXX), four (XXXX), or five (XXXXX) X chromosomes. Each of these conditions has somewhat different implications for the child's development, as we will see in examining a few of the more common sex chromosome abnormalities.

Turner's syndrome.   About 1 in 3000 females is born with a single X chromosome (XO, or **Turner's syndrome**) rather than two. These children are phenotypically female, although they differ from normal (XX) females in that they remain small in stature and often have stubby fingers and toes, a "webbed" neck, a broad chest, and small, underdeveloped breasts (see Photo 3-4). At puberty, girls with Turner's syndrome fail to produce the female hormone estrogen, which would lead to normal sexual development. Although administration of estrogen will give a Turner female a more "womanly" appearance, she will remain sterile. Turner females are typically rather quiet and cheerful, and they favor traditionally feminine interests and activities. As a group, they are about average on tests of verbal intelligence, although they frequently score below average on tests of spatial abilities such as maze learning and the mental rotation of figures (Rovet & Netley, 1982).

The "super female" syndrome.   About 1 female in 1000 inherits three or more X chromosomes rather than the customary two (Jacobs, 1979). As a

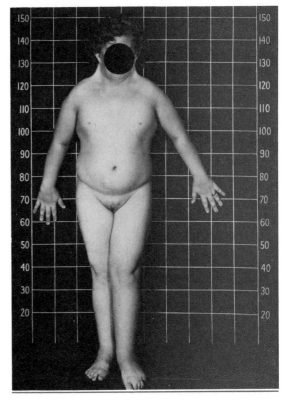

PHOTO 3-4. This girl's short stature, webbed neck, and lack of secondary sex characteristics are physical signs of Turner's syndrome.

group, these females with **poly-X syndrome** are quite normal in appearance, and they remain fertile. Moreover, they produce children who have the usual number of sex chromosomes—XX for daughters, XY for sons (Stern, 1973).

Most poly-X females perform below average on intelligence tests, and their intellectual deficits are detectable as early as age 2. For example, XXX females tend to lag behind on important developmental milestones such as the onset of walking and talking, and these early indicators predict later deficits in their intellectual functioning (Pennington, Puck, & Robinson, 1980).

Klinefelter's syndrome.   Since 1968, members of women's Olympic teams have been required to demonstrate that they are indeed female by submitting to a simple medical test. One famous shotputter, a previous women's Olympic champion from an Eastern European country, refused to take the test and was not allowed to compete in the 1968 Olympic games. Speculation has it that this individual would not have "passed" the sex test because "she" was actually a Klinefelter male.

Perhaps as many as 1 male in 200 is born with one or more extra X chromosomes (for example, XXY or XXXY), a condition known as **Klinefelter's syndrome.** Klinefelter males appear normal until puberty, when they frequently begin to exhibit female sex characteristics such as enlarging of the breasts and broadening of the hips. These individuals often retain a high-pitched, boyish voice, and they remain sterile because their male sex organs (penis and testes) fail to mature. However, the overall body type of XXY individuals is basically male: they tend to be rather tall, even compared with normal (XY) males, and their musculature closely resembles that of XY males. From this "mixed" physical profile, it is perhaps understandable how a Klinefelter male might "pass" as a female and yet become a championship-caliber athlete when competing against women in events that place a premium on physical strength.

About 20–30% of Klinefelter males are mentally deficient (particularly in verbal intelligence), and the extent of their retardation becomes more pronounced with an increase in the number of extra X chromosomes that they have inherited (Burns, 1976; Pennington & Smith, 1983).

The "supermale" syndrome. About 1 male in 300 inherits an extra Y chromosome from his father (XYY), a condition that is sometimes called the **supermale syndrome.** Supermales tend to be taller than normal males (averaging 72 inches, compared with 69 inches). They also tend to have severe cases of acne during adolescence, and many of them score below average on intelligence tests, although their mental deficiencies are typically not profound.

In the mid-1960s, an interesting finding emerged: men having an extra Y chromosome were far more common among populations of prisoners than among the male population as a whole (Jacobs, Brunton, & Melville, 1965). When other investigators began to make the same observation, it was thought that the extra Y chromosome inherited by supermales might make them rather aggressive and criminally inclined (Jarvik, Kodin, & Matsuyama, 1973). Although

this conclusion seemed warranted at the time, later research shows that one should always be cautious when drawing conclusions about the genetic bases of behavior. In a study of 4139 Danish males, Herman Witkin and associates (1976) found XYYs to have a higher rate of criminal conviction than normal (XY) males. However, the crimes committed by supermales were typically nonviolent property offenses, such as theft, rather than violent or aggressive acts. Moreover, careful inspection of the records revealed that these relatively dull supermales were no more likely to be convicted of a crime than equally dull XY males— suggesting that subnormal intelligence, not an extra Y chromosome, is the factor that contributes most to criminality among supermales.

■ *Other chromosomal abnormalities*

Many hereditary abnormalities are attributable to the autosomes—that is, the 22 pairs of chromosomes that are similar in males and females. The most common type of autosomal abnormalities occurs when an abnormal sperm or ovum carrying an extra autosome combines with a normal gamete to form a zygote that has 47 chro-

---

Turner's syndrome: *a sex chromosome abnormality in which females inherit only one X chromosome (XO); they remain small in stature, fail to develop secondary sex characteristics, and may show some mental deficiencies.*

poly-X syndrome: *a sex chromosome abnormality involving females who inherit three or more X chromosomes; these females are normal in appearance, remain fertile, and tend to score substantially below average on intelligence tests.*

Klinefelter's syndrome: *a sex chromosome abnormality involving males who inherit two or more X chromosomes (XXY or XXXY); these males fail to develop secondary sex characteristics and often show deficiencies on tests of verbal ability.*

supermale syndrome: *a sex chromosome abnormality involving males who have inherited an extra Y chromosome (XYY); supermales are taller than average and tend to score below average on intelligence tests.*

mosomes (2 sex chromosomes and 45 autosomes). In these cases the extra chromosome appears along with one of the 22 pairs of autosomes to yield three chromosomes of that type, or a *trisomy*.

By far the most frequent of all autosomal abnormalities (occurring once in every 600 births) is **Down's syndrome,** or *trisomy-21,* a condition in which the child has inherited an extra 21st chromosome (hence the name "trisomy-21"). Children with Down's syndrome are mentally retarded, with IQs that average 50 (the average IQ among normal children is 100). They may also have congenital eye, ear, and heart defects and are usually characterized by a number of distinctive physical features, including a sloping forehead, a protruding tongue, short stubby limbs, a slightly flattened nose, and a peculiar fold to the eyelids that gives their eyes an Oriental appearance (see Photo 3-5). In years gone by, researchers often called

PHOTO 3-5. *Children with Down's syndrome can live happy lives if they receive affection and encouragement from their companions.*

these children "Mongoloid idiots" and believed that they were largely incapable of learning. This was an unfortunate assumption, for recent research indicates that these so-called idiots can be taught to care for many of their basic needs, and some have even learned to read (Hayden & Haring, 1976; Reed, 1975). Moreover, children with Down's syndrome tend to be cheerful and affectionate and may live a happy life if they receive adequate emotional support and attention from their families or caretakers.

■ Causes of chromosomal abnormalities

Perhaps the most basic cause of chromosomal abnormalities is *uneven segregation of chromosomes* into daughter cells during mitosis and meiosis. Sometimes, for example, the meiosis of a female germ cell produces one ovum containing two X chromosomes and a second ovum with no X chromosome. Such an imbalance in the distribution of X chromosomes allows several interesting possibilities. If the first (XX) ovum is fertilized by a sperm bearing an X chromosome, the result is a poly-X (XXX) female. However, if a sperm bearing a Y chromosome reaches that ovum first, the zygote will become a Klinefelter male (XXY). And if the ovum containing no X chromosome is fertilized by an X-bearing sperm, the child will be an XO female who has Turner's syndrome. Of course, some of these abnormalities can also result from the uneven meiosis of a male germ cell.

The probability that a child will inherit Down's syndrome, Klinefelter's syndrome, or the poly-X syndrome increases dramatically if the mother is over 35. Table 3-2 illustrates the relationship of Down's syndrome to the age of the mother. Note in examining the table that mothers who have already given birth to a child with Down's syndrome are much more likely to have another child with Down's syndrome, should they give birth again, than are other women of the same age.

Why are children of older mothers more likely to inherit chromosomal abnormalities? One possible explanation is the **"aging ova" hypothesis**. Ova are formed only once, during prenatal development, so that a 45-year-old woman has ova that are more than 45 years old. The aging-ova hypothesis implies that a woman's ova may simply degenerate and become abnormal as she matures and nears the end of her reproductive years.

TABLE 3-2. Risk of Down's syndrome as a function of mother's age

| | Probability that the child will have Down's syndrome | |
| | | |
Age of mother	At any pregnancy	After the birth of a child with Down's syndrome
−29	1 in 1000	1 in 100
30–34	1 in 600	1 in 100
35–39	1 in 200	1 in 100
40–44	1 in 65	1 in 25
45–49	1 in 25	1 in 15

Of course, an alternative explanation is that older women have had more opportunities to become exposed to *environmental hazards* (such as radiation, drugs, chemicals, and viruses) that could lead to the production of abnormal ova.

A final point: It is clearly inappropriate to blame mothers for all chromosomal abnormalities. The geneticist George Burns (1976) reports that the majority of children with Turner's syndrome originate from a normal (X) ovum that is fertilized by an abnormal *sperm*—that is, one that contains neither an X nor a Y chromosome. In addition, R. E. Magenis and his associates (1977) found that 25% of children with Down's syndrome received their "extra" chromosome from their fathers rather than their mothers. The only chromosomal abnormality that is always attributable to one particular parent is the XYY, or "supermale," syndrome. In this case, the child had to receive the extra Y chromosome from the father, for the mother has no Y chromosomes to transmit to her offspring.

Genetic Abnormalities

Parents who are themselves healthy are often amazed to learn that a child of theirs could have a hereditary defect. Their surprise is certainly understandable, for most genetic problems are recessive traits that few if any close relatives have had. In addition, these problems simply will not appear unless both parents carry the harmful allele *and* the child inherits this particular gene from each parent. The exceptions to this rule are recessive defects that are sex-linked. In these cases, a male child will inherit the problem if a recessive allele should appear on the X chromosome that he inherits from his mother (recall

that because a boy has only one X chromosome, he has no corresponding gene that might counteract the effect of an X-linked recessive allele).

Earlier in the chapter, we discussed two recessive hereditary defects, one that is sex-linked (color blindness) and one that is not (sickle-cell anemia). Table 3-3 describes a number of additional crippling or fatal diseases that are attributable to a single pair of recessive alleles.

■ *Mutations*

Genetic abnormalities may also result from the development of mutations. A **mutation** is a change in the chemical structure or arrangement of one or more genes that has the effect of producing a new phenotype. Many mutations such as the recessive gene for hemophilia (see Table 3-3) are harmful or even fatal, and geneticists are uncertain exactly how or why these mutations might occur. However, recent research indicates that environmental hazards such as high temperatures,

> **Down's syndrome:** *a chromosomal abnormality (also known as trisomy-21) caused by the presence of an extra 21st chromosome; people with this syndrome have a distinct physical appearance and are moderately to severely retarded.*
>
> **aging-ova hypothesis:** *the hypothesis that an older mother is more likely to have children with chromosomal abnormalities because her ova are degenerating as she nears the end of her reproductive years.*
>
> **mutation:** *a change in the chemical structure or arrangement of one or more genes that has the effect of producing a new phenotype.*

TABLE 3-3. Brief descriptions of some major recessive hereditary defects

Defect	Description
Cystic fibrosis	A fatal disease that occurs in about 1 in 1000 births. The child lacks an enzyme that prevents mucus from obstructing the lungs and digestive tract. Only a few who inherit this condition survive beyond adolescence. Over 10 million Americans are carriers who can transmit the gene for cystic fibrosis to their offspring.
Muscular dystrophy (MD)	There are more than ten forms of this genetic disease, which attacks the muscles. As the disease progresses, the individual often begins to show slurred speech, becomes unable to walk, and may gradually lose most or all motor capabilities. Occasionally MD causes death. One form, Duchenne's muscular dystrophy, is sex-linked. About 1 in 4000 males will develop Duchenne's disease; more than 100,000 Americans have inherited some form of MD.
Phenylketonuria (PKU)	The child lacks an enzyme necessary to digest foods (including milk) that contain the amino acid phenylalanine. If this condition is not detected and the child placed on a diet of milk substitutes, phenylpyruvic acid will accumulate in the body and attack the developing nervous system. Long-term effects of untreated PKU are hyperactivity and severe mental retardation. Occurs in 1 of every 10,000 Caucasian births and is much less frequent among Blacks and Orientals.
Tay-Sachs disease (infantile amaurotic idiocy)	A degenerative disease of the nervous system that will kill its victims, usually by their third birthday. Primarily affects Jewish children of Eastern European ancestry. Approximately 1 in 30 American Jews is a carrier.
Hemophilia	A sex-linked condition sometimes called "bleeder's disease." The child lacks a substance that causes the blood to clot and could bleed to death if scraped, bruised, or cut. Hemophilia was well known among the royal families of Europe and can be traced to Queen Victoria of England. Since no hemophilia is known in Victoria's ancestry, it appears that the recessive gene for hemophilia may have been a mutation that Queen Victoria then passed to her offspring.[a] Though quite rare in females, hemophilia may occur as often as once in every 1000 male births.
Diabetes	An inherited condition in which the individual is unable to metabolize sugar properly because the body does not produce enough insulin. Two of the many forms of this disease are sex-linked. If untreated, diabetes is usually fatal. However, the disease can be controlled by taking insulin and restricting one's diet. Diabetes usually appears in late adulthood, although as many as 1 child in 2500 is diabetic.

[a]Of course, this does not mean that everyone who has hemophilia is related to Queen Victoria. A mutation, such as that producing the recessive allele for hemophilia, may occur spontaneously at any time. In at least 30% of cases of hemophilia, there is no family history of the disease. These new cases probably arise from spontaneous mutations (Apgar & Beck, 1974).

toxic chemicals, and radiation can increase the rate of mutations in animals (Burns, 1976).

Evolutionary theorists believe that some mutations are beneficial. Presumably, any mutation that is stimulated by harmful conditions present in the environment can provide an "adaptive" advantage to those who inherit the mutant genes, thus enabling these individuals to survive. For example, the sickle-cell gene is a mutation that originated in Africa, Central America, and other tropical areas where malaria is widespread. Heterozygous children who inherit a single sickle-cell allele are well adapted to these environments because the mutant gene makes them more resistant to malarial infection and thus more likely to survive. Of course, the mutant sickle-cell gene is not advantageous (and can be harmful) in environments where malaria is not a problem.

■ *Prevention and treatment
of genetic abnormalities*

Now try to imagine that someone in your family has a recessive genetic defect such as sickle-cell anemia and you suspect you might be a carrier. You then meet and marry a person who also believes he or she might be a carrier of this same defect. Assuming that both of you want to have children, should you now decide against it? Can you tell whether your child will be defective before birth? Is all hope lost if you produce a child who has a hereditary disease? These are issues that you and your spouse would probably wish to explore with a genetic counselor.

In recent years, a service called **genetic counseling** has been developed to help prospective parents assess the likelihood that their children will be free of hereditary defects. Although any couple who hope to have children might wish to talk with a genetic counselor about the hereditary risks their children may encounter, genetic counseling is particularly helpful for couples who have relatives with hereditary disorders or for parents who have already borne a defective child.

A genetic counselor may be a medical researcher, a geneticist, or a practitioner such as a pediatrician, obstetrician, or family doctor. He or she will usually begin by asking prospective parents why they have sought genetic counseling, thus seeking to determine whether the defect(s) that concern the couple are really hereditary in origin. If they are hereditary, the counselor will take a complete family history from each prospective parent—one that includes information about the diseases and causes of death of siblings, parents, and other blood relatives; the ethnicity and countries of origin of blood relatives who were immigrants; intermarriages that may have occurred in the past between close relatives (such as cousins); and previous problems in the child-bearing process, such as miscarriages or still-births. The couple will also take a complete physical examination. If specific tests are available, prospective parents will be screened to determine whether they carry the genes that are responsible for producing the hereditary defect(s) that prompted them to seek counseling. From the overall profile, the genetic counselor will determine the mathematical odds that a child of the couple could inherit the defect in question and then tell the prospective parents whether there is anything they can do to reduce these odds.

Methods of detecting carriers.   Fortunately, several recessive genes that produce hereditary defects can be detected by simple laboratory tests. For example, blood tests can determine whether a prospective parent carries the recessive allele for Tay-Sachs disease, sickle-cell anemia, hemophilia, or phenylketonuria (Apgar & Beck, 1974; Milunsky, 1973). In addition, chromosomal abnormalities can be detected by taking a small sample of each parent's skin (a few cells will do) and preparing karyotypes. Recent advances in the preparation of karyotypes make it possible, in some cases, to determine whether a seemingly normal individual might transmit hereditary defects to his or her children. Finally, couples who have already borne a child with a recessive hereditary defect have already shown themselves to be carriers for that attribute.

Unfortunately, an adult may carry harmful recessive genes that are undetectable by medical tests. **Cystic fibrosis** is one example. If prospective parents are concerned about the possibility of transmitting cystic fibrosis to their children, the genetic counselor will carefully analyze their family histories and note whether any close blood relatives in either of their families have had the disease. If a client's family history reveals several cases of cystic fibrosis, there is a good possibility that he or she carries the recessive gene for this hereditary defect. However, the likelihood that the client's child will inherit cystic fibrosis is very small unless cystic fibrosis has also occurred among the spouse's blood relatives.

An example will help to illustrate how genetic counseling works. One married couple recently requested genetic counseling and learned that

> **genetic counseling:** *a service designed to inform prospective parents about genetic diseases and to help them determine the likelihood that they would transmit such disorders to their children.*
> **cystic fibrosis:** *a genetic disease in which an enzyme is lacking that would prevent mucus from obstructing the lungs and digestive tract (see Table 3-3).*

Genetic counselors are often asked whether a marriage between blood relatives would affect any children who might result. The answer depends on the exact degree of relationship between the couple and on the defective genes that they may carry (Apgar & Beck, 1974).

First cousins share one pair of grandparents and, therefore, have approximately one-eighth of their genes in common. If it can be assumed that every individual carries several harmful recessive alleles, then it is likely that pairs of first cousins will share one or more of these defective genes. Perhaps you can see the problem. If two cousins have a defective gene in common, the chances are 1 in 4 that a child of theirs will inherit this gene from both of them and, thus enter the world with a serious genetic disorder.

Another way to make this point is to compare the likelihood that children of cousins and children of unrelated couples will inherit the same genetic disease. About 1 person in 20 carries the recessive allele for cystic fibrosis (Apgar & Beck, 1974). This means that the probability that genetically unrelated parents will both carry this recessive allele is $1/20 \times 1/20$, or 1 in 400, and the likelihood that a child of theirs will inherit cystic fibrosis is $1/400 \times 1/4$, or *1 in 1600.* Now suppose that first cousins, who share one-eighth of

their genes, should marry and have a child. If one cousin carries the recessive allele for cystic fibrosis, the chances are 1 in 8 that the other shares this gene. Therefore, the likelihood that their child will inherit cystic fibrosis is $1/8 \times 1/4$, or *1 in 32!* No matter how rare an abnormal recessive allele may be in the general population, a carrier of this gene will have at least 1 chance in 8 of marrying another carrier if he or she marries a first cousin, and each of their children will have at least 1 chance in 32 of inheriting the condition caused by this gene (Apgar & Beck, 1974). This is one of the major reasons that many governments do not permit first cousins to marry.

As you might imagine, the probability of birth defects is even greater if the genetic relationship between a mother and a father is closer than cousinhood. You may recall the recent incident in which a brother and sister, separated since early childhood, fell in love and married when they found each other as adults. When the authorities discovered that this marriage had taken place, they immediately declared it illegal—a clear case of incest. And from a genetic perspective this marriage is as risky as one can be. Since the couple had common parents, they share one-half of their genes. If one of them carries a harmful recessive allele, the odds are 1 in 2 that the other carries this same gene. Thus, each of their children will have *1 chance in 8* of inheriting that particular genetic defect. Since every individual may carry *several* harmful alleles, it is quite likely that children resulting from marriages of siblings will inherit some kind of genetic abnormality.

they were both carriers for **Tay-Sachs disease**, a condition that normally kills an affected child within the first three years of life (see Table 3-3). The genetic counselor explained to this couple that there was 1 chance in 4 that *any* child they conceived would inherit a recessive allele from each of them and have Tay-Sachs disease. However, there was also 1 chance in 4 that the child would inherit the dominant gene from each parent, and there were 2 chances in 4 that the child would be just like its parents—phenotypically normal but a carrier of the recessive Tay-Sachs allele. After receiving this information, the young woman expressed strong reservations about having children. To her way of thinking, the 1 chance in 4 that each of her children would inherit a disease that medical science cannot treat was simply too high for her to want to take *any* chances.

At this point the genetic counselor informed the young woman that before she made a firm decision against having children, she ought to be aware of procedures that can detect many genetic abnormalities, including Tay-Sachs disease, long before her child would be born. He then told the couple that these screening procedures cannot reverse any abnormalities that are found. However, they allow expectant parents to decide whether to terminate a pregnancy rather than give birth to a defective child.

Prenatal detection of hereditary abnormalities. A common method of detecting abnormalities during the prenatal period is **amniocentesis.** A large, hollow needle is inserted into the abdomen of a pregnant woman in order to withdraw a sample of the amniotic fluid that surrounds the fetus. This fluid contains fetal body cells that can by karyotyped to determine the sex of the fetus and the presence of chromosomal abnormalities such as Down's syndrome. In addition, more than 75 genetic disorders—including Tay-Sachs disease, sickle-cell anemia, hemophilia, and Marfan's syndrome—can now be diagnosed by analyzing fetal cells taken from the amniotic fluid or from the placenta that bonds the mother and the fetus (Fuchs & Cederquist, 1978; Golbus, 1978). Amniocentesis is not very painful, and it presents only a minimal risk to the woman and the fetus (Fairweather, 1978).[2]

One serious disadvantage of amniocentesis is that the procedure cannot be performed before the 14–16th week of pregnancy, when amniotic fluid becomes sufficiently plentiful to withdraw for analysis. The results of the tests will not come back for another two weeks, leaving parents little time to consider a second-trimester abortion if the fetus is abnormal. But there is a new technique, now being tested in the United States, that looks promising as an alternative to amniocentesis. This procedure, called **chorionic villus biopsy,** collects tissue for the same tests as amniocentesis does—and can be performed during the 10th week of pregnancy (Begley, Carey, & Katz, 1984). As illustrated in Figure 3-7, a catheter is inserted through the mother's cervix, into the chorion, to extract fetal cells, which are then tested for hereditary abnormalities. This technique would allow parents to know whether their fetus is abnormal by as early as the 12th week of pregnancy, leaving them more time to carefully consider the pros and cons of a therapeutic abortion in the event the fetus has inherited a serious defect.

Another prenatal diagnostic technique is **ultrasound** (sonar), a method of scanning the womb with sound waves. Ultrasound provides the attending physician with an outline of the fetus in much the same way that sonar reveals outlines of the fish beneath a fishing boat. Like amniocentesis, ultrasound presents only a minimal risk to the developing fetus. It is particularly useful for

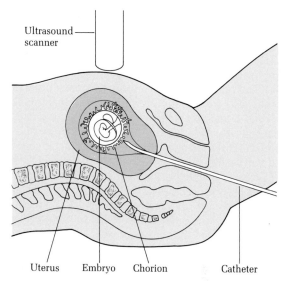

Ultrasound scanner

Uterus   Embryo   Chorion   Catheter

FIGURE 3-7. *In a chorionic villus biopsy, a catheter is inserted through the mother's cervix to collect fetal cells for prenatal tests.*

detecting genetic defects that produce gross physical abnormalities.

Treatment of hereditary disorders.   Prenatal detection of a hereditary disorder leaves many couples in a quandary, particularly if their religious background or personal beliefs argue against the option of a therapeutic abortion. If the disease in question is invariably fatal, like Tay-Sachs, the

---

Tay-Sachs disease: *a genetic disease that attacks the nervous system, causing it to degenerate (see Table 3-3).*

amniocentesis: *a method of extracting amniotic fluid from a pregnant woman so that fetal body cells within the fluid can be tested for chromosomal abnormalities and other genetic defects*

chorionic villus biopsy: *an alternative to amniocentesis in which a catheter is inserted through the cervix to withdraw fetal cells for prenatal tests.*

ultrasound: *method of detecting gross physical abnormalities by scanning the womb with sound waves, thereby producing a visual outline of the fetus.*

---

[2]Although amniocentesis is considered a very safe procedure, it can trigger a miscarriage in a very small percentage of cases. In fact, it has been argued that the risks of miscarriage (though very small) are actually greater than the risks of a birth defect if the mother is under age 35.

couple must decide either to violate their moral principles and terminate the pregnancy or to have a baby who will appear normal and healthy but who will show a progressive decline in all of his or her functions and die young.

This quandary may someday become a thing of the past, for geneticists are hopeful that many lethal hereditary diseases will become "curable" in the near future. And there is reason for optimism. Only 35 years ago, medical science could do little for children with another degenerative disease of the nervous system—**phenylketonuria, or PKU.** Like Tay-Sachs disease, PKU is a metabolic disorder. Affected children lack a critical enzyme that would allow them to metabolize phenylalanine, a component of many foods, including milk. As phenylalanine gradually accumulates in the body, it is converted to a harmful substance, phenylpyruvic acid, that attacks the nervous system. In years gone by, the majority of children who inherited this disorder soon became hyperactive and severely retarded.

A major breakthrough came in the mid-1950s when scientists developed a diet low in phenylalanine that minimized the degenerative effects of PKU: children who adhered to this special diet showed much less damage to their nervous systems than they would otherwise have suffered. However, doctors could detect PKU only from its harmful effects, and unfortunately the special diet could not reverse damage already done.

In 1961 researchers discovered that the degenerative effect of PKU could be detected in its earliest stages by analyzing a blood sample taken only a few days after birth. Infants are now routinely screened for PKU, and those affected are immediately placed on the low-phenylalanine diet. The outcome of this therapeutic intervention is a happy one: children who remain on the special diet for the next several years suffer virtually none of the harmful complications of what only a short time ago was considered an incurable disease.

Today the potentially devastating effects of many hereditary abnormalities can be minimized or controlled. For example, children who inherit either Turner's syndrome or Klinefelter's syndrome can be given hormones to make them more normal in appearance. Those who have blood disorders such as hemophilia or sickle-cell anemia now receive periodic transfusions that provide these patients with the clotting agents or the normal red blood cells that they lack. The discomfort experienced by children with cystic fibrosis can be lessened by antibiotics. Diabetes can be controlled by a low-sugar diet and by periodic injections of insulin, which help the patient to metabolize sugar. In sum, many abnormal children can lead approximately normal lives if their hereditary disorders are detected and treated before serious harm has been done.

How to obtain more information about genetic counseling services. Your local library may carry the *International Directory of Genetic Services,* published by the National Foundation/ March of Dimes. This volume lists some 400 centers in the United States that offer genetic counseling services. For information about the services offered by centers nearest you, write to the National Foundation/March of Dimes, 1275 Mamaroneck Ave., White Plains, New York 10605.

HEREDITARY INFLUENCES ON ABILITY, PERSONALITY, AND BEHAVIOR

We have seen that genes play a major role in determining our physical appearance and many of our metabolic characteristics. But to what extent does heredity affect such characteristics as intelligence? Can a strong case be made for genetic contributions to personality, temperament, and mental health?

In recent years, investigators from the fields of genetics, embryology, population biology, and psychology have asked the question "Are there certain abilities, traits, and patterns of behavior that are inherited, and if so, are these attributes likely to be modified by experience?" Those who focus on these issues in their research are known as behavior geneticists.

Before we take a closer look at the field of **behavior genetics,** it is necessary to dispel a common myth. Behavior geneticists are not strict hereditarians. They recognize, for example, that even physical characteristics such as height and weight depend to some extent on environmental variables, such as diet (Fuller & Thompson, 1978). They clearly acknowledge that the long-term effects of inherited metabolic disorders such as PKU or diabetes also depend on one's environment—namely, the availability of personnel to detect and to treat these conditions. In other words, the behavior geneticist is well aware that even attributes that have a strong hereditary component are often modified in important ways by environmental influences. This is a point to keep in mind as we discuss the implications of behavior genetics research in the pages that follow.

Methods of Assessing Hereditary Influences

Behavior geneticists use three basic strategies to study hereditary contributions to behavior: *within-species comparisons, selective breeding,* and *family studies.* Each of these approaches attempts to specify the **heritability** of various behavioral characteristics—that is, the extent to which the attributes in question result from hereditary factors.

■ *Within-species comparisons*

One method of assessing the effects of heredity on behavior is to look for behavioral similarities among members of a species. Suppose, for example, that all dogs are observed to chase cats without having to learn to do so. A behavior geneticist would interpret this finding as an indication that cat chasing by dogs is an inherited pattern of behavior.

Studies of human infants suggest that many behaviors are inherited. All normal children will suck on objects that touch their lips, will cry when discomforted, and will smile or laugh in response to a variety of stimuli. According to behavior geneticists, smiling must be inherited, because even blind and deaf children, who have little opportunity to learn this response, have been observed to smile soon after birth (Eibl-Eibesfeldt, 1975).

■ *Selective breeding*

Of course, the members of any species, particularly human beings, differ considerably in their basic abilities, peculiarities, and patterns of behavior. Could these individual differences be hereditary? Do they simply reflect the fact that no

two individuals (except identical twins) inherit the same pattern of genes?

Many investigators have tried to answer this question by seeing whether they could selectively breed particular attributes in animals. A famous example of a selective breeding experiment is R. C. Tryon's (1940) attempt to show that maze-learning ability is a heritable attribute in rats. Tryon started by testing a large number of rats for ability to run a complex maze. Rats that made few errors were labeled "maze-bright"; those that made many errors were termed "maze-dull." Then, across several successive generations, Tryon mated the brightest of the maze-bright rats together, while also inbreeding the dullest of the maze-dull group. This was a well-controlled experiment in that Tryon occasionally took offspring from each group and had them raised by mothers from the other group. This *cross-fostering* procedure helps to ensure that any difference in maze-learning ability between the offspring of the two strains is due to selective breeding (heredity), rather than the type of early stimulation that the young animals received from their mother figure (environment).

Figure 3-8 shows the results of Tryon's selective breeding experiment. Note that across generations the differences in maze-running performance between the maze-bright and the maze-dull groups became increasingly apparent. By the 18th generation, the worst performer among the maze-bright group was better at running mazes than the best performer from the maze-dull group. Clearly, Tryon had shown that maze-learning ability in rats is influenced by hereditary factors. Other investigators have used the selective breeding technique to demonstrate genetic contributions to

---

phenylketonuria (PKU): *a genetic disease in which the child is unable to metabolize phenylalanine; if left untreated, it soon causes hyperactivity and mental retardation.*

behavior genetics: *the scientific study of how genotype interacts with environment to determine behavioral attributes such as intelligence, temperament, and personality.*

heritability: *the amount of variability in a trait that is attributable to hereditary factors.*

Simply stated, a correlation indicates whether two variables are related. In other words, if one asks whether two attributes are correlated, one wants to know whether those attributes "go together" in some meaningful way. An agricultural scientist might wish to know whether crop yield is related to rainfall. A medical researcher may seek to determine whether physical exercise is related to the incidence of heart disease. A behavior geneticist conducting a family study may wish to determine whether the IQ scores of twins are related to the IQ scores of their cotwins.

Any two variables may be *positively correlated, negatively correlated,* or *uncorrelated.* A positive correlation indicates that high scores on variable X are associated with high scores on variable Y and that low scores on X are associated with low scores on Y. For example, height and weight are positively correlated: children who are *taller* also tend to be *heavier.* A negative correlation means that high scores on variable X are associated with low scores on variable Y and vice versa. For example, exercise is negatively correlated with the incidence of heart disease: people who exercise *more* are *less* likely to have heart at-

tacks. Finally, if scores on variable X are not at all associated with scores on variable Y, the two factors are said to be uncorrelated, or unrelated.

The strength, or magnitude, of a correlation can be determined statistically and is represented as a *correlation coefficient* (symbolized r) with a value between −1.00 and +1.00. Positive correlations range from .01 to 1.00; negative correlations range from −.01 to −1.00. The absolute size of a correlation coefficient (disregarding its sign) provides information about the strength of the relationship between the variables. For example, the correlation coefficients −.70 and +.70 are equal in magnitude but opposite in direction. Both are stronger relationships than a correlation of .50. A correlation coefficient of .00 indicates that the variables under consideration are unrelated.

There are two common misconceptions about correlation coefficients. First, the fact that two variables are correlated does not necessarily mean that one causes the other. For example, the positive correlation between the number of crimes reported in cities and the number of churches in those cities does not mean that churches cause crime. In this case, a third variable, population, determines both the number of crimes in a city and the number of churches built there. Although the latter two variables are correlated, the relationship between them is not one of cause and effect.

such attributes as activity level, emotionality, aggressiveness, and sex drive in rats, mice, and chickens (Plomin, DeFries, & McClearn, 1980).

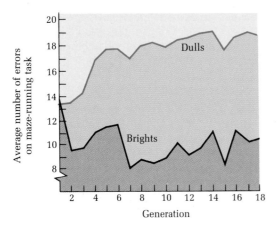

FIGURE 3-8. *Maze-running performance by inbred maze-bright and maze-dull rats over 18 generations.*

■ Family studies

The field of human behavior genetics relies heavily on a method known as the family study. In a typical family study, persons who live in the same household are compared to see how similar they are on one or more attributes. If the attribute in question is heritable, then the similarity between any two pairs of individuals who live in the same environment should increase as a function of their **kinship**—that is, the extent to which they have the same genes. For example, pairs of identical twins who have the same genotype (kinship = 1.00) should be more similar on a heritable attribute than either fraternal twins or ordinary siblings, who have only half their genes in common (kinship = .50). And fraternal twins and siblings should be more similar than either half-siblings (kinship = .25) or pairs of genetically unrelated children who live in the same household (kinship = .00).

The family study can also help us to determine the extent to which various abilities and behaviors

Second, people often assume that a correlation (r) of .70 is twice as large as a correlation of .35, for example, or that a correlation of .50 is twice as large as a correlation of .25. This is incorrect. To determine the relative magnitude of any two correlations, we must compare the squared correlation coefficients. Thus, an r of .70 is roughly 4 times as strong as an r of .35 (because $.70^2 = .49$ and $.35^2 = .12$).

How can the heritability of an attribute be estimated from correlations? Suppose that we had just conducted a study of 50 families, 25 that have a pair of identical twins and 25 that have a pair of fraternal twins. While conducting the study, we measured some aspect of personality in each twin and found that the correlation between identical twins on this trait was +.50 while the correlation between fraternal twins was +.30. Since members of each twin pair live in the same household, we might assume that they have had highly similar environments. Thus, the fact that identical twins are more alike on this personality dimension than fraternal twins suggests that the trait in question is affected by heredity. Now we may wonder, just how strong is the hereditary contribution?

In recent years, behavior geneticists have proposed a statistical technique to estimate the amount of variation in a characteristic that is attributable to hereditary factors. This index, called a *heritability quotient,* is calculated as follows:

$$H = (r \text{ identical twins} - r \text{ fraternal twins}) \times 2$$

In words, the equation reads: Heritability of an attribute equals the correlation between identical twins minus the correlation between fraternal twins, all multiplied by a factor of 2 (Plomin, DeFries, & McClearn, 1980).

Now we can estimate the contribution that heredity makes to the aspect of personality that we measured in our hypothetical study. Recall that the correlation between identical twins on the attribute was +.50 and the correlation between fraternal twins was +.30. Plugging these values into the formula yields the following heritability quotient (H):

$$H = (.50 - .30) \times 2 = .20 \times 2 = .40$$

The heritability quotient is about .40, which, on a scale ranging from 0 (not at all heritable) to 1.00 (totally heritable), is moderate at best. We might conclude that, within the population from which our subjects were selected, this aspect of personality is influenced to some extent by hereditary factors. However, it appears that much of the variability among people on this trait is attributable to non-hereditary factors—that is, to environmental influences and to errors we may have made in measuring the trait (no measure is perfect).

are affected by the environment. Consider genetically unrelated adopted children living in the same household. Their degree of kinship with one another and with their adoptive parents is .00. Consequently, there is no reason to suspect that these children will resemble one another or their adoptive parents unless their common environment plays some part in determining their standing on the ability or behavior in question. Another way the effects of environment can be inferred is to compare identical twins raised in the same environment with identical twins raised in different environments. The kinship of all pairs of identical twins, reared together or apart, is 1.00. So if identical twins reared together are more alike on an attribute than identical twins reared apart, we can infer that the environment plays a role in determining that attribute.

We are now almost ready to examine the results of several family studies in order to gauge the impact of heredity and environment on complex attributes such as intelligence, temperament, personality, and mental illness. To evaluate this research, however, one needs to know what a correlation is and how correlations can help us to determine whether an attribute is affected by hereditary factors. At this point, you may find it helpful to turn to Box 3-4, which discusses the concept of correlation and the role that correlations play in behavior genetics research.

Hereditary Contributions to Intelligence

Earlier in the chapter, we learned that many forms of mental retardation may result should one inherit abnormal genes and chromosomes. Although most children are not mentally retarded, they do

---

kinship: *the extent to which two individuals have genes in common.*

TABLE 3-4. Average correlation coefficients for intelligence test scores from 52 family studies involving persons at three levels of kinship (genetic similarity)

Genetic relationship (kinship)	Reared together (in same household)	Reared apart (in different households)
Unrelated persons (kinship = .00)	+.23	−.01
Foster parent/child (kinship = .00)	+.20	—
Biological parent/child (kinship = .50)	+.50	—
Siblings (kinship = .50)	+.49	+.40
Twins		
Fraternal—like sex (kinship = .50)	+.53	—
Fraternal—different sex (kinship = .50)	+.53	—
Identical (kinship = 1.00)	+.87	+.75

vary considerably in their performance on intelligence (IQ) tests. Could it be that children make widely varying scores on tests of mental ability because they have each inherited a different set of genes?

Over the past 60 years, more than 80 family studies have been conducted to measure the effects of heredity on intellectual performance. Table 3-4 summarizes the findings of 52 of the more ambitious of these projects. From the data in the "Reared together" column, it is clear that the intellectual resemblance between pairs of individuals living in the same household increases as a function of their degree of kinship (that is, genetic similarity). In addition, we see that identical twins reared apart are more similar in IQ than fraternal twins reared together. Both these findings imply that heredity contributes in a meaningful way to IQ. In fact, the heritability quotient for IQ that can be calculated from the data on twins living together is .68, a figure that suggests that abilities measured by intelligence tests are highly heritable.

Further evidence for the heritability of intelligence comes from studies of young children. As early as 3 to 6 months of age, identical twins are already more similar than fraternal twins on tests of infant intelligence (Nichols & Broman, 1974; Wilson, 1972). And follow-up data collected on these children over the next 15 years indicate that identical twins are more similar than fraternal twins both in the age at which they reach various intellectual milestones and in the patterning of their performances across many different tests of intellectual ability (Wilson, 1975, 1978, 1983).

■ Do family studies overestimate the heritability of intelligence?

Those who conduct family studies assume that the environments of identical twins in the same household are no more similar than the environments of fraternal twins, siblings, or pairs of foster children. Many critics have argued otherwise. Identical twins are often dressed alike, given duplicate sets of toys, and treated alike by parents, siblings, teachers, and anyone else who has a difficult time telling them apart. Thus, the home environments of identical twins may be more similar than those of fraternal twins—who, incidentally, are often not even the same sex. The implication of this line of reasoning is that estimates of the heritability of IQ that come from twin studies may be artificially high. If identical twins experience more similar environments than fraternal twins, then perhaps it is their "identical environments" rather than their "identical genes" that make identical twins so similar in intelligence.

Hugh Lytton (1977) has found that parents do respond in a more similar fashion to identical twins than to fraternal twins. However, he also notes that identical twins elicit highly similar responses from their parents because they behave more alike than fraternal twins do. Lytton suggests that *identical genotypes* of identical twins may predispose these children to similar patterns of behavior, which, in turn, produce similar responses from parents. So perhaps heredity, not environment, is ultimately responsible for the many behavioral similarities observed among identical twins.

Sandra Scarr is another researcher who believes that the remarkable intellectual similarities of identical twins stem mainly from the twins' identical genotypes. Scarr and Carter-Saltzman (1979) tested the intellectual ability of 400 pairs of same-sex twins, who were then classified into the following four groups:

1. Identical twins who believed that they were identicals.
2. Fraternal twins who believed that they were fraternals.
3. Identical twins who believed that they were fraternals (mistaken identity).
4. Fraternal twins who believed that they were identicals (mistaken identity).

The latter two groups are particularly interesting. Assuming that the children's mistaken identities stem from their parents' beliefs, one might predict that fraternal twins who believed themselves to be identicals would be treated very similarly by their parents and that identical twins who thought they were fraternals would be treated less similarly. Therefore, if the intellectual similarities between twins result from the similarity of their environments, one would predict that fraternal twins raised as identicals would be as similar intellectually as identicals raised as identicals. Furthermore, identical twins raised as fraternals should be no more similar intellectually than fraternals raised as fraternals.

The results of this study were revealing. On all intellectual measures, identical twins who believed they were fraternals were as similar to each other as identical twins who correctly labeled themselves as identicals. In contrast, fraternal twins who believed they were identicals were no more alike intellectually than fraternal twins who knew they were fraternals. In sum, the intellectual resemblance of twins depended not on the probable similarity of their environments but, rather, on their degree of kinship (that is, their actual genetic similarity).

We can conclude from these findings that intelligence is a heritable attribute and that family studies provide a reasonable (though hardly perfect) estimate of its heritability. Does this mean that the environment plays little or no role in determining intellectual ability? No, it does not! In fact, we need look no further than the family studies that we have already reviewed to find evidence of environmental effects on intelligence. Can you find such evidence in Table 3-4?

■ *Evidence for environmental influences*

If we reexamine Table 3-4, we will see that at each level of kinship where data are available, individuals living together are more intellectually similar than individuals living apart. This finding clearly indicates that the environment affects intelligence. Perhaps the most striking data are those provided by individuals who are not biologically related. As expected, children who have no genes in common and who live in different environments do not resemble each other intellectually ($r = -.01$). In contrast, biologically unrelated children who live in the same household show a definite intellectual resemblance ($r = .23$), which can only be attributed to the similarity of their environments.

Recent studies of adopted children clearly indicate that intelligence is a product of both hereditary and environmental influences. Consider first the evidence for heredity. Several investigators have found that adopted children are more similar intellectually to their biological parents than to their adoptive parents (Horn, 1983; Plomin & DeFries, 1983). This finding can be interpreted as evidence for a genetic influence on intelligence, for adoptees share genes with their biological parents but not with adoptive caregivers.

The environmental contribution to intelligence is illustrated in a recent adoption study by Sandra Scarr and Richard Weinberg (1977, 1983). Several of Scarr and Weinberg's adoptees were Black children who had been placed into White homes where the adoptive parents had one or more biological children. Did the interracial (that is, Black and White) siblings resemble each other intellectually? Indeed they did ($r = .30$). Since interracial siblings have no genes in common, their intellectual similarities must be attributable to their common environment. Furthermore, the intellectual resemblance between pairs of genetically unrelated Black adoptees who lived in the same home was substantial ($r = .49$), indicating that their common environment was having a strong impact on their intellectual development. Finally, Scarr and Weinberg (1983) report that their sample of Black adoptees averaged about 20 points higher on IQ tests than comparable children who are raised in the Black community.

Since the adopting parents in this study were from middle-class backgrounds and highly educated, they may have provided very stimulating home environments for their interracial adoptees— environments that enabled these youngsters to flourish intellectually and outperform their less advantaged Black age mates on intelligence tests.

Perhaps you can see why investigators often disagree about whether heredity or environment is more important in determining human intelligence. An investigator who focuses on the twin data will undoubtedly conclude that intelligence is highly heritable. However, one who concentrates on the similarities between unrelated children raised in the same environment will conclude that environmental factors play a prominent role in determining intellectual capabilities.

Although behavior geneticists believe that human intelligence is unquestionably a heritable attribute, they stress that even highly heritable characteristics are subject to environmental influence (Plomin, DeFries, & McClearn, 1980). In the final section of this chapter, we will review some of the theories that have been proposed to explain how heredity and environment may combine or interact to affect our abilities, talents, temperaments, and peculiarities. But, first, let's review the evidence that suggests that our temperaments and personalities do depend, in part, on the genes that we have inherited from our parents.

Hereditary Contributions to Temperament and Personality

When psychologists speak of "personality," they are referring to a broad collection of attributes— including **temperament,** attitudes, values, and distinctive behavioral patterns (or habits)—that seem to characterize an individual. Unfortunately, the personality consists of so many characteristics that it is virtually impossible to measure them all with any single test. However, it is possible to focus on specific aspects of personality to see whether there is any hereditary basis for the ways we behave.

■ *Inheritance of temperament*

Selective breeding experiments conducted with various animal species reveal that temperamental characteristics such as activity level, fearfulness, and sociability seem to have a strong hereditary component (McClearn, 1970; Scott & Fuller, 1965). Could the same be true of human beings? Daniel Freedman (1965, 1974) tried to answer this question by observing the social responsiveness of 20 pairs of infant twins. At monthly intervals over the first year of life, the twins in each pair were tested to determine their frequency of social smiling and their fear of strangers. Neither the investigators nor the twins' parents knew whether the twin pairs were identical or fraternal until the end of the study, when blood serum analyses revealed 11 fraternal and 9 identical twin pairs. Freedman found that pairs of identical twins were more similar than fraternal twins in the frequency, intensity, and time of appearance of both social smiling and fear of strangers. Since neither the investigators nor the twins' parents knew the twins' actual zygosity, it cannot be argued that the greater similarities between identical twins resulted from either a rating bias on the part of the investigators or the differential treatment of identical and fraternal twins by their parents. Clearly, Freedman's data suggest that one's social responsiveness, or "sociability," is partly determined by hereditary factors.

Other studies of young children show that identical twins are more alike than fraternal twins in temperamental attributes such as activity level, displays of temper, demands for attention, and irritability (Goldsmith & Gottesman, 1981; Matheny, 1980; Wilson, 1972). In addition, babies from different ethnic backgrounds show distinct temperamental characteristics as early as the first few days of life. In one study, Freedman (1979) compared the temperaments of newborn Caucasian and Chinese-American infants. The ethnic differences were clear: Caucasian babies were more irritable and harder to comfort than Chinese-American babies. Since the Caucasian and the Chinese-American mothers had received the same prenatal care, it appears that the temperamental differences between their infants may well have been hereditary.

Alexander Thomas, Stella Chess, and Herbert Birch (1970) have noted that certain temperamental attributes tend to cluster together. For example, highly active children are often irritable and irregular in their feeding, sleeping, and bowel habits, whereas passive babies tend to be good-

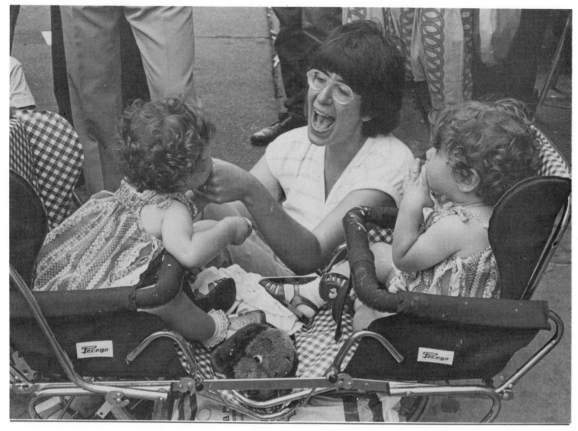

PHOTO 3-6. *Identical twins are more alike than fraternal twins in temperamental attributes such as activity level, irritability, and demands for attention.*

natured and regular in their habits. Thomas and Chess (1977) believe that most infants can be placed into one of three categories based on their overall pattern of temperamental characteristics:

1. *The easy child.* Easygoing children are even-tempered, are typically in a positive mood, and are quite open and adaptable to new experiences. Their habits are regular and predictable.
2. *The difficult child.* Difficult children are active, irritable, and irregular in their habits. They often react very negatively (and vigorously) to changes in routine and are slow to adapt to new persons or situations.
3. *The slow-to-warm-up child.* These children are quite inactive and moody. They, too, are slow to adapt to new persons and situations, but unlike the difficult child, they typically re-

spond to novelty or to changes in routine with mild forms of passive resistance. For example, they may resist cuddling by directing their attention elsewhere rather than by crying or kicking.

These early temperamental patterns may persist over time and affect the child's adjustment to a variety of settings and situations later in life. For example, children with difficult temperaments are more likely than other children to have problems adjusting to school activities (Thomas & Chess,

---

temperament: *such components of behavior as activity level, emotionality, irritability, behavioral tempo, and social responsivity.*

As noted in the text, heredity and environment interact to determine our adult personalities. At this point, it is certainly legitimate to ask "What environmental influences contribute most to the shaping of personality?"

Developmental psychologists have traditionally assumed that the home environment is especially important. Yet as we will see in Table 3-5 (p. 108), the personality resemblances of fraternal twins are very modest ($r = +.25$). In fact, the personalities of genetically unrelated individuals who live in the same household barely resemble one another ($r = +.07$). Therefore, those aspects of the home environment that all family members *share* must not contribute much to the development of personality. Otherwise, the personalities of children who live in the same home should be much more similar than the family studies have indicated. How, then, does the environment affect personality? Precisely what environmental influences are important?

David Rowe and Robert Plomin (1981) have recently argued that the environmental influences that contribute most heavily to personality are those that make individuals *different* from one another—that is, situations, events, and experiences that children within any family do *not* share. An example of a "nonshared" environmental influence within the home is a tendency of one or both parents to respond differently to sons and daughters, to first-born and later-born children, and so on. To the extent that two siblings are treated differently by parents, they will experience different environments, which will increase the likelihood that their personalities will differ in important ways. Interactions among siblings provide another source of "nonshared" environmental influence on the developing personalities of children within a family. For example, an older sibling who successfully dominates a younger one may become generally assertive and dominant as a

result of these home experiences. However, the influence of such a family environment on the younger sibling may be very different. For the younger child, the home environment is a dominating environment that may foster the development of such personality traits as passivity, tolerance, and cooperation.

Of course, many sources of nonshared environmental influence exist outside the home. For example, siblings are likely to have different playmates, friends, and teachers. They may belong to different clubs and organizations and develop different interests. Even identical twins are likely to have a number of important nonshared experiences should one member of the pair have a serious accident or illness or if the twins should consciously attempt to establish separate personal identities by selecting different "best friends" and pursuing different interests, goals, and so on.

Rowe and Plomin (1981) suggest the following formula as an estimate of the effect of nonshared environmental influences on the adult personality (or any other attribute):

$$\text{Nonshared environmental effects} = 1 - r \text{ identical twins}$$

In words, the equation reads: The effect of nonshared environmental influences on an attribute equals one minus the correlation between identical twins for that attribute. Rowe and Plomin justify the use of this estimate in these words:

> Because [identical] twins are perfectly matched from a genetic standpoint, any differences of pair members must arise, for pairs reared together, from [nonshared] environmental influences. . . . One minus the correlation for identical twins is therefore an estimate of the [contribution] of all [nonshared] environmental causes that make identical twins different from one another [p. 521].

Table 3-5 shows that the median correlation for identical twins across several personality attributes is $+.52$. Thus, it appears that nonshared environmental influences (that is, $1 - .52 = .48$) are, indeed, important contributors to the adult personality.

1977), and they are often irritable and aggressive in their interactions with peers (Rutter, 1978). Yet Thomas and Chess (1977) point out that temperament can be modified by environmental factors—particularly the patterns of child-rearing used by parents. For example, a difficult infant who has problems adapting to new routines may become more adaptable if parents exercise restraint by allowing the infant to respond to novelty at a leisurely pace.

In sum, the evidence we have reviewed suggests that temperamental characteristics such as social responsiveness, activity, and emotionality do have a hereditary component. However, we should keep in mind that early temperamental patterns can be altered and that the changes in temperament that are commonly observed over the course of childhood suggest that this aspect of personality is highly susceptible to environmental influence.

■ *Hereditary contributions to the adult personality*

Psychologists have often assumed that the relatively stable traits and habits that make up our adult personalities are determined by the environment. Presumably, our feelings, attitudes, values, and characteristic patterns of behavior have been shaped by the familial and cultural contexts in which we live. Ruth Benedict (1934) put it this way: "The life-history of an individual is first and foremost an accommodation to the patterns and standards traditionally handed down in his community. From the moment of birth, the customs into which he is born shape his experience and behavior." Behavior geneticists can certainly agree with Benedict's conclusions. However, they believe that psychologists may overestimate the impact of the environment on the developing personality and underestimate the importance of hereditary factors (Goldsmith, 1983).

Family studies of personality suggest that many attributes have a hereditary component. One example of a heritable trait is **introversion/ extraversion**. Introverts are people who are generally quiet, anxious, and uncomfortable around others. As a result, they often shun social contact. Extraverts are highly sociable people who enjoy being with others. Identical twins are moderately similar on this attribute, and their resemblance is greater than that of fraternal twins, ordinary siblings, or pairs of genetically unrelated children raised in the same household (Nichols, 1978; Scarr, Webber, Weinberg, & Wittig, 1981).

Another interesting attribute that may be influenced by heredity is **empathic concern**. A person high in empathy is a compassionate soul who recognizes the needs of others and is concerned about their welfare. In Box 2-4 we saw that newborn infants will react to the distress of another infant by becoming distressed themselves—a finding that implies that empathy may be innate. If it is, identical twins should be more similar in empathic concern than fraternal twins.

Karen Matthews, Daniel Batson, Joseph Horn, and Ray Rosenman (1981) administered a test of empathic concern to 114 pairs of identical twins and 116 pairs of fraternal twins who ranged in age from 42 to 57 years. These twins were all males who had been raised in the same household, but most had not lived together for many years. Even though the vast majority of the twins had lived apart in different environments for long periods, the identical twins were still more alike in empathic concern ($r = .41$) than the fraternal twins ($r = .05$), suggesting that empathy is a reasonably heritable attribute. The implications of these results are interesting. In the words of the authors, "If empathic concern for others leads to altruistic motivation, the present study provides evidence for a genetic basis for individual differences in altruistic behavior" (p. 246).

■ *Just how heritable is personality?*

Table 3-5 shows that resemblances among pairs of family members at each level of kinship are greater for intelligence than for personality. If we were to use the twin data to estimate the genetic contribution to personality, we might conclude that many personality traits are moderately heritable. Of course, one implication of a moderate heritability quotient is that personality is strongly influenced by environmental factors.

How do heredity and environment interact to affect the developing personality? One possibility is that a child's heritable attributes will influence the reactions of others to the child. For example, smiley, active babies may receive more social stimulation than moody and passive ones. In turn, the reactions of others to the child (and the child's behavior) are environmental influences that may play an important role in shaping the child's personality (see also Box 3-5). So it appears that one way in which heredity contributes to the adult personality is by influencing the character of the social environment in which the personality develops.

---

introversion/extraversion: *the opposite poles of a personality dimension: introverts are shy, anxious around others, and ready to withdraw from social situations; extraverts are highly sociable and enjoy being with others.*

empathic concern: *a measure of the extent to which an individual recognizes the needs of others and is concerned about their welfare.*

TABLE 3-5. Correlation coefficients for IQ test scores and personality attributes for family members at three levels of kinship

	Kinship			
Measure	1.00 (identical twins)	.50 (fraternal twins)	.50 (nontwin siblings)	.00 (unrelated children raised in the same household)
IQ test scores	.87	.53	.49	.23
Personality attributes (average correlations across several personality traits)	.52	.25	.20	.07

Hereditary Contributions to Mental Illness

Is there a hereditary basis for mental illness? Might some among us be genetically predisposed to commit deviant or antisocial acts? It now appears that the answer to both questions is a qualified yes.

The evidence for hereditary contributions to abnormal behavior comes from family studies in which investigators calculate **concordance rates** for various disorders. In a twin study, for example, the concordance rate for a disorder is a measure of the likelihood that the second twin will exhibit that problem, given that the first twin does. If concordance rates are higher for identical twins than for fraternal twins, one can conclude that the disorder is influenced by heredity.

Schizophrenia is a serious form of mental illness characterized by disturbances in thinking, emotional expression, and behavior. Schizophrenics are often so deficient at forming simple concepts and making logical connections between everyday events that they are unable to distinguish fantasy from reality. As a consequence, they may experience delusions or vivid hallucinations that contribute to their apparently irrational and inappropriate behavior. A survey of 11 twin studies of schizophrenia suggests an average concordance rate of .57 for identical twins but only .13 for fraternal twins (Gottesman & Shields, 1973). This is a strong indication that schizophrenia is a heritable disorder. In addition, studies of adults who grew up in adoptive homes reveal that the incidence of schizophrenia (and other disorders) among these adoptees is more closely related to the incidence of schizophrenia

among their biological relatives than among members of their adoptive families (DeFries & Plomin, 1978; Heston & Denny, 1968).

In recent years it has become increasingly apparent that heredity also contributes to abnormal behaviors and conditions such as alcoholism, criminality, depression, hyperactivity, **manic-depressive** psychosis, and a number of **neurotic disorders** (Fuller & Thompson, 1978; Schwarz, 1979). Now, it is possible that you have or have had close relatives who were diagnosed as alcoholic, neurotic, manic-depressive, or schizophrenic. Rest assured that this does *not* mean that you or your children will develop these problems. Only 10–14% of children who have one schizophrenic parent ever develop any symptoms that might be labeled "schizophrenic" (Kessler, 1975). Even if you are an identical twin whose cotwin has a serious psychiatric disorder, the odds are only between 1 in 2 and 1 in 10 (depending on the disorder) that you would ever experience anything that even approaches the problem that affects your twin.

Since identical twins are often *discordant* (that is, not alike) with respect to illnesses such as schizophrenia, it is obvious that environment must be a very important contributor to behavioral abnormalities and mental illness. In other words, people do not inherit particular disorders—they inherit genetic predispositions to develop certain illnesses or deviant patterns of behavior. But even when such a genetic predisposition has been inherited, it may take one or more stressful experiences (for example, rejecting parents, a failure at school, or a crumbling marriage) to trigger the illness in question.

At present, we can identify high-risk children who may have a genetic predisposition for emotional problems. This is done by examining the child's family history for evidence of emotional disturbances among close blood relatives, such as parents or siblings. What we lack in order to prevent the occurrence of many heritable childhood disorders is precise knowledge of the kinds of environmental experiences that are likely to trigger these problems. Researchers are currently trying to determine what these experiences may be, and they are meeting with some success (see Box 3-6). If this research continues to be fruitful, it should eventually provide child-care professionals with the knowledge they need to shield high-risk children from the adverse events that contribute to severe emotional distress and mental illness.

ANOTHER LOOK AT THE NATURE/NURTURE CONTROVERSY

Thirty years ago, developmental psychologists were embroiled in the nature/nurture controversy: Was heredity or environment the primary determinant of human potential? Those who were more biologically oriented believed that the course of development is determined at conception and will follow whatever genetic blueprint the child happens to inherit from his or her parents. The environmentalists, in contrast, argued that all developmental outcomes of any real consequence are largely the product of environmental forces—learning and experience—with biological factors playing a lesser role.

Although this chapter has focused on biological influences, it should now be apparent heredity alone does not determine how intelligent we are, our liking for people, our mental health, or even how tall we become or how much we will weigh. Clearly, the extreme positions taken by the hereditarians and environmentalists of yesteryear are oversimplified. Although many human characteristics are obviously influenced by heredity, the same hereditary predisposition may lead to any of several developmental outcomes, depending on the environment to which the child is exposed. Perhaps we should think less about nature *versus*

nurture and concentrate instead on the ways these two important influences combine or interact to promote developmental change.

The Rubber-Band Hypothesis

One of the more influential statements about the interplay between heredity and environment is Curt Stern's (1956) **"rubber band" hypothesis.** Stern argues:

> The genetic endowment with respect to any one trait can be compared to a rubber band, and the trait itself to the length which the rubber band assumes when it is stretched by [environmental] forces. Different people may initially have been given different lengths of unstretched [genetic] endowment, but the natural forces of the environment may have stretched their expression to equal lengths, or led to differences in attained length sometimes corresponding in their innate differences, and at other times in reverse of [these innate predispositions][p. 56].

In Figure 3-9 we see some of the implications of Stern's point of view. First, note that intellectual performance (that is, IQ score) depends on (1) the person's genetic potential for intellectual development (heredity) and (2) the type of environment in which the person is raised. Now let's make some specific comparisons to explore Stern's ideas further. If we first compare the person with high potential raised in an average envi-

concordance rate: *the percentage of cases in which a particular attribute is present for both members of a twin pair if it is present for one member.*

schizophrenia: *a serious form of mental illness characterized by disturbances in logical thinking, emotional expression, and interpersonal behavior.*

manic-depression: *a psychotic disorder characterized by extreme fluctuations in mood.*

neurotic disorder: *an irrational pattern of thinking or behavior that a person may use to contend with stress or to avoid anxiety.*

rubber-band hypothesis: *the notion that a person's phenotype depends on two factors: (1) his or her genetic potential for development and (2) the extent to which the environment allows the person to reach that potential.*

BOX 3-6
ENVIRONMENTAL TRIGGERS
FOR HERITABLE DISORDERS

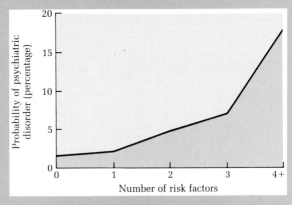

Recently developmental psychologists have begun to identify the kinds of environmental events that are reliably associated with children's psychiatric disorders. Six family characteristics appear to be particularly important:

1. Severe marital disharmony (including divorce)
2. Low social status
3. Large families and/or overcrowding in the home
4. Having a father who is a criminal
5. Having a mother who has a psychiatric disorder
6. Being admitted into the care of the local authorities

Probability of developing psychiatric disorders as a function of the number of environmental stressors the child experiences.

Michael Rutter (1979b) conducted a study of a large number of 10-year-olds, measuring the presence or absence of each of the six risk factors for each child and then noting whether the child had any psychiatric problems. The relationship between the presence of one or more of these risk factors and the incidence of childhood emotional disturbances is shown in the accompanying graph. Note that children who experienced only a single risk factor were no more likely to have psychiatric problems than children with no risk factors. However, when two or more risk factors are present, the probability of psychiatric disturbances increases as a function of the number of risks the child experiences.

In another study, Rutter (1979a) showed that genetic predispositions and environmental events may interact to produce psychiatric disorders. Children in this project were from homes in which parents were highly quarrelsome (a rather potent environmental risk factor). The children themselves were classified as temperamentally unattractive (active, irritable, demanding) or temperamentally attractive (pleasant, good-natured), attributes that are moderately heritable. Rutter found that temperamentally unattractive children drew far more criticism from their quarrelsome parents and were much more likely to develop psychiatric disorders than children who were temperamentally attractive. Perhaps children who are

not genetically at risk for psychiatric disorders or who do not have abrasive personal qualities are able to thrive despite severe environmental stress.

Finally, reexamination of the graph indicates that the vast majority of "high risk" children are able to cope with severe adverse environmental events without developing serious emotional problems. How do they cope? It appears that a positive relationship with a caring adult (for example, a parent, teacher, neighbor, or scout leader) helps to shield high-risk children from psychiatric disorders (Garmezy, Masten, Nordstrom, & Ferrarese, 1979; Rutter, 1979b). In addition, children who have many friends and who are accepted by the peer group are much less likely to develop severe emotional disturbances than children who have no close friends or those who have been rejected by their peers (Cowen, Pederson, Babigan, Izzo, & Trost, 1973; Kent & Rolf, 1979).

The picture that emerges, then, is that heritable psychiatric disorders may be preventable in the vast majority of cases if only we were to learn more about (1) the adverse events that trigger these disturbances and (2) the factors that enable children to maintain their emotional stability in the face of environmental stress.

ronment and the person with low potential raised in an enriched environment, we see a circumstance in which different "amounts" of genetic endowment might be "stretched" to approximately the same level of intellectual performance. Note also that innate predispositions can be reversed.

That is, a person with a lower genetic endowment who is raised in an intellectually stimulating environment might actually outperform a person of higher genetic potential whose endowment remains unstretched because of an intellectually impoverished environment.

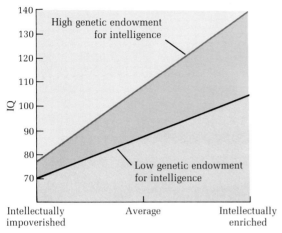

FIGURE 3-9. *The rubber-band hypothesis. Individuals with different genetic potentials for intellectual development may exhibit widely varying levels of intellectual performance depending on the environments to which they are exposed.*

Figure 3-9 also illustrates a second important point about the interaction of heredity and the environment: the **range-of-reaction principle** (Gottesman, 1963)—the idea that genotype sets limits on the *range* of possible phenotypes that a person might display in response to different environmental influences. As the figure shows, individuals with a high genetic endowment may vary in IQ by as much as 60 points, depending on the environment in which they are raised. Their "range of reaction" for intellectual performance is very broad. However, those with lower genetic potentials show less variation in intellectual performance (only 30 IQ points) across these same three environments. In sum, it appears that one's genotype helps to set a range of possible outcomes for any particular attribute but that the environment may determine the point within that range where the individual will fall.

Canalization

The ability of the environment to shape an attribute will also depend on the **canalization** of that attribute (Waddington, 1966). A highly canalized attribute is one that is relatively difficult to

modify; that is, genes channel development along predetermined pathways, and the environment has a much smaller effect on the phenotype that emerges. Characteristics such as eye color and blood type and conditions such as Down's syndrome and Tay-Sachs disease are said to be highly canalized because they are not influenced to any great extent by environmental factors. However, intelligence, temperament, and personality are less highly canalized, since these characteristics can be modified in any of several ways by a variety of life experiences.

Can We Create Optimal Environments?

Some who have read Stern's rubber-band hypothesis have suggested that we might improve on humanity if only we could create "optimal" environments that would "stretch" children's genetic endowments in a positive direction. Isn't it appealing to think that we might expose our children to settings and situations that will make them brighter, more cooperative or altruistic, and less irritable or quarrelsome? Is there any future for environmental engineering of this kind? Will we discover environments that allow all our children to fully realize their genetic potentials and become the best people they can be?

It would be nice to be able to answer these questions with an unqualified yes. However, it may be impossible to create a single environment that is optimal for everyone, for the same environment may have very different effects on individuals with different genotypes. Consider a study by Fuller and Clark (1968), who reared two breeds of puppies—beagles and terriers—in social isolation in order to assess the impact of that experi-

> range-of-reaction principle: *the idea that genotype sets limits on the range of possible phenotypes that a person might display in response to different environmental influences.*
> canalization: *the extent to which genotype limits phenotype to a small number of developmental outcomes; a highly canalized attribute is one for which genes channel development along predetermined pathways, so that the environment has little effect on the phenotype that emerges.*

ence on the puppies' activity levels. The experience had opposite effects on the two breeds: terriers became more active when raised in isolation, beagles less active.

Studies with human beings also reveal that the effectiveness of a particular teaching method or child-rearing strategy may depend on the child's innate characteristics, or genetic potentials. For example, Steven Vandenberg (1965) cites a study in which twins were taught to read using two training techniques. One member of each twin pair was taught by the "sight" method, the other twin by the more traditional "phonics" method. For twins of average intelligence, the phonics method was the superior technique. However, the phonics method was not superior to the sight method for the gifted twins in the sample. So the procedures that were optimal for one group of children were somewhat less than optimal for others. But why?

One possibility is that hereditary factors may help to determine the kinds of experience that people will find most interesting or satisfying. Indeed, Sandra Scarr and Kathleen McCartney (1983) have recently proposed that the environments that children prefer and seek out will depend in part on the children's genetic characteristics. For example, grade-school students who have inherited muscular physiques may be genetically predisposed to prefer sporting activities, whereas their classmates with other physiques may be more inclined to choose other methods of passing their leisure time (for example, reading or playing board games). The implication of Scarr and McCartney's theory is that people with different genotypes will actively select different "environmental niches" for themselves—niches that will then have a profound effect on their future social, emotional, and intellectual development.

Now let's place the question of environmental engineering in proper perspective. Many developmental psychologists believe that it is possible to create environments that will facilitate the development of most children. But in so doing, we must not make the mistake of trying to fit square pegs into round holes. We need to recognize that treatments that are highly beneficial for one child with one set of genes may not be best for other children who have inherited different genetic predispositions. Perhaps the environmental engineers of the future will learn much from the con-

tinuing efforts of behavior geneticists. The more we learn about the hereditary basis of human development and genotype/environment interactions, the better we will become at providing environments that help each individual to reach his or her innate potentials.

SUMMARY

Since the dawn of recorded history, people have tried to understand how characteristics are transmitted from parents to offspring. Early theories of heredity claimed that the germ cells of either the father or the mother contained tiny preformed embryos that would begin to develop after a mating. However, biologists eventually discovered that each parent contributes equally to the creation of a child by passing hereditary "characters," or genes, to the offspring.

Development begins at conception, when a sperm cell from the father penetrates the wall of an ovum from the mother, forming a zygote. A normal zygote contains 46 chromosomes (23 from each parent), each of which consists of approximately 20,000 genes. Thus, each zygote may have as many as 500,000 pairs of genes that provide the hereditary blueprint for the development of this single cell into a recognizable human being.

Human beings consist of two kinds of cells: (1) body cells, which make up our bodies and organs, and (2) germ cells, which produce gametes—sperm in males and ova in females. Our body cells each contain duplicates of the 46 chromosomes (23 pairs) that we inherited at conception. Germ cells, which also have 23 pairs of chromosomes, divide by a process called meiosis to produce gametes that each contain 23 single (unpaired) chromosomes. Since individual gametes do not contain all the parent's chromosomes, the genetic composition of each sperm or ovum will differ. Therefore, each child inherits a unique combination of genes. The one exception is identical twins, who are formed from a single zygote that divides, creating two individuals with identical genes.

There are many ways in which one's genotype may affect phenotype—the way one looks, feels, thinks, or behaves. At least one phenotypic characteristic—gender—is determined by the 23rd pair of chromosomes (that is, the sex chromosomes). Normal females have inherited one relatively large sex chromosome (called an X chromosome) from each parent, whereas males have inherited an X chromosome and a smaller Y chromosome. An adult female (XX) can pass only X chromosomes to her offspring. However, an adult male (XY) can transmit either an X chromosome or a Y chromosome to his offspring. Thus, the father, not the mother, determines the sex of a child.

Some characteristics are determined by a single pair of genes, one of which is inherited from each parent. In dominant/recessive pairs, the individual will exhibit the phenotype of the dominant gene. If a gene pair is codominant or incompletely dominant, the individual will develop a phenotype in between those ordinarily produced by the dominant and the dominated (or recessive) genes. Sex-linked characteristics are caused by recessive genes that appear on only one of the two kinds of sex chromosomes (usually the X chromosome). Females must inherit two of these recessive genes (one on each X chromosome) in order to exhibit a sex-linked characteristic. However, males need only inherit one recessive gene to show the characteristic, because they have only one X chromosome.

Most complex human attributes such as intelligence and personality are polygenic, meaning that they are influenced by several pairs of genes rather than a single pair. In addition, the action or expression of one set of genes may be altered by the presence of modifier genes.

Occasionally children inherit abnormal genes and chromosomes. In most cases of chromosome abnormalities, the child has inherited too few or too many sex chromosomes. In about 1 in 600 births, a child inherits an extra 21st chromosome. The resulting phenotype is known as Down's syndrome, in which the child has a number of distinctive physical features and will be mentally retarded.

There are also a number of genetic diseases that children may inherit from parents who themselves are not affected but who carry the abnormal genes. In recent years, genetic counselors have had some success at using medical tests and family histories to establish the likelihood that prospective parents will have a child with a genetic problem. Many hereditary disorders cannot be detected before the child is born. However, the harmful effects of some of these diseases can be minimized by medical treatment if the condition is discovered soon after birth.

Behavior geneticists have looked for similarities among blood relatives to determine whether heredity contributes to important psychological characteristics. These family studies indicate that genetic factors play a role in the development of intelligence, temperament, personality, and mental illness. However, they also indicate that environmental forces make important contributions to each of these attributes; so it is important to recognize that behavioral attributes that are influenced by heredity can be modified by experience. Heredity may define our capacity or potential for development—but the type of environment we experience may determine how close we come to realizing these genetic potentials.

REFERENCES

Apgar, V., & Beck, J. (1974). *Is my baby all right?* New York: Pocket Books.

Aristotle. (1912). *De generatione animalium* (A. Platt, Trans.). In J. A. Smith & W. D. Ross (Eds.), *The works of Aristotle* (Vol. 5). Oxford: Clarendon Press.

Begley, S., Carey, J., & Katz, S. (1984, March 5). The genetic counselors. *Newsweek*, p. 69.

Benedict, R. (1934). *Patterns of culture*. Boston: Houghton Mifflin.

Burns, G. W. (1976). *The science of genetics*. New York: Macmillan.

Cowen, E. L., Pederson, A., Babigan, H., Izzo, L. D., & Trost, M. A. (1973). Long-term follow up of early detected vulnerable children. *Journal of Consulting and Clinical Psychology, 41,* 438–446.

DeFries, J. C., & Plomin, R. (1978). Behavioral genetics. In M. R. Rosenzweig & L. W. Porter (Eds.), *Annual review of psychology, 29,* 473–515.

Eibl-Eibesfeldt, I. (1975). *Ethology: The biology of behavior*. New York: Holt, Rinehart and Winston.

Fairweather, D. V. I. (1978). Techniques and safety of amniocentesis. In D. V. I. Fairweather & T. K. A. B. Eskes (Eds.), *Amniotic fluid: Research and clinical application*. Amsterdam: Elsevier.

Freedman, D. G. (1965). Hereditary control of early social behavior. In B. M. Foss (Ed.), *Determinants of infant behavior* (Vol. 3). New York: Wiley.

Freedman, D. G. (1974). *Human infancy: An evolutionary perspective*. Hillsdale, NJ: Erlbaum.

Freedman, D. G. (1979). Ethnic differences in babies. *Human Nature, 2,* 36–43.

Fuchs, F., & Cederquist, L. L. (1978). Use of amniotic fluid cells in prenatal diagnosis. In D. V. I. Fairweather and T. K. A. B. Eskes (Eds.), *Amniotic fluid: Research and clinical application.* Amsterdam: Elsevier.

Fuller, J. L., & Clark, L. D. (1968). Genotype and behavioral vulnerability to isolation in dogs. *Journal of Comparative and Physiological Psychology, 66,* 151–156.

Fuller, J. L., & Thompson, W. R. (1978). *Genetic basis of behavior.* St. Louis: Mosby.

Garmezy, N., Masten, A., Nordstrom, L., & Ferrarese, M. (1979). The nature of competence in normal and deviant children. In M. W. Kent & J. E. Rolf (Eds.), *Primary prevention of psychopathology. Vol. 3: Social competence in children.* Hanover, NH: University Press of New England.

Golbus, M.S. (1978). Prenatal diagnosis of genetic defects—where it is and where it is going. In J. W. Littlefield & J. DeGrouchy (Eds.), *Birth defects.* Amsterdam: Excerpta Medica.

Goldsmith, H. H. (1983). Genetic influences on personality from infancy to adulthood. *Child Development, 54,* 331–335.

Goldsmith, H. H., & Gottesman, I. I. (1981). Origins of variation in behavioral style: A longitudinal study of temperament in young twins. *Child Development, 52,* 91–103.

Gottesman, I. I. (1963). Heritability of personality: A demonstration. *Psychological Monographs, 77* (Whole No. 572).

Gottesman, I. I., & Shields, J. (1973). Genetic theorizing and schizophrenia. *British Journal of Psychiatry, 122,* 17–18.

Hayden, A. H., & Haring, N. G. (1976). Early intervention for high risk infants and young children: Programs for Down's syndrome children. In T. D. Tjossem (Ed.), *Intervention strategies for high risk infants and young children.* Baltimore: University Park Press.

Heston, L., & Denny, D. (1968). Interactions between early life experiences and biological factors in schizophrenia. *Journal of Psychiatric Research, 6,* 363–376.

Horn, J. M. (1983). The Texas adoption project: Adopted children and their intellectual resemblance to biological and adoptive parents. *Child Development, 54,* 268–275.

Jacobs, P. A. (1979). The incidence and etiology of sex chromosome abnormalities in man. In A. Robinson, H. Lubs, & D. Bergsma (Eds.), *Sex chromosome aneuploidy: Prospective studies in children.* National Foundation/March of Dimes, Birth Defects, Original Article Series, Vol. 15, No. 1. New York: Alan R. Liss.

Jacobs, P. A., Brunton, M., & Melville, M. M. (1965). Aggressive behavior, mental subnormality, and the XYY male. *Nature, 208,* 1351–1352.

Jarvik, L. F., Kodin, V., & Matsuyama, S. S. (1973). Human aggression and the extra Y chromosome: Fact or fantasy. *American Psychologist, 27,* 674–682.

Kent, M. W., & Rolf, J. E. (1979). *Primary prevention of psychopathology. Vol. 3: Social competence in children.* Hanover, NH: University Press of New England.

Kessler, S. (1975). Psychiatric genetics. In D. A. Hamburg & K. Brodie (Eds.), *American handbook of psychiatry. Vol. 6: New psychiatric frontiers.* New York: Basic Books.

Leeuwenhoek, A. van. (1677). Observations concerning little animals, etc. *Philosophical Transactions* (London), *2,* 82.

Lytton, H. (1977). Do parents create, or respond to, differences in twins? *Developmental Psychology, 13,* 456–459.

Magenis, R. E., Overton, K. M., Chamberlin, J., Brady, T., & Lorrien, E. (1977). Parental origin of the extra chromosome in Down's syndrome. *Human Genetics, 37,* 7–16.

Matheny, A. P. (1980). Bayley's Infant Behavior Record: Behavioral components and twin analysis. *Child Development, 51,* 1157–1167.

Matthews, K. A., Batson, C. D., Horn, J., & Rosenman, R. H. (1981). "Principles in his nature which interest him in the fortune of others . . .": The heritability of empathic concern for others. *Journal of Personality, 49,* 237–247.

McClearn, G. E. (1970). Genetic influences on behavior and development. In P. H. Mussen (Ed.), *Carmichael's manual of child psychology* (Vol. 1). New York: Wiley.

McMillen, M. M. (1979). Differential mortality by sex in fetal and neonatal deaths. *Science, 204,* 89–91.

Mendel, G. (1959). Experiments in plant-hybridization, 1865. Reprinted in J. A. Peters (Ed.), *Classic papers in genetics.* Englewood Cliffs, NJ: Prentice-Hall.

Milunsky, A. (1973). *The prenatal diagnosis of hereditary disorders.* Springfield, IL: Charles C Thomas.

Nichols, P. H., & Broman, S. H. (1974). Familial resemblance in infant mental development. *Developmental Psychology, 10,* 442-446.

Nichols, R. C. (1978). Heredity and environment: Major findings from twin studies of ability, personality, and interests. *Homo, 29,* 158–173.

Pennington, B. F., Puck, M., & Robinson, A. (1980). Language and cognitive development in 47, XXX females followed since birth. *Behavior Genetics, 10,* 31–41.

Pennington, B. F., & Smith, S. D. (1983). Genetic influences on learning disabilities and speech and language disorders. *Child Development, 54,* 369–387.

Plomin, R., & DeFries, J. C. (1983). The Colorado adoption project. *Child Development, 54,* 276–289.

Plomin, R., DeFries, J. C., & McClearn, G. E. (1980). *Behavioral genetics: A primer.* San Francisco: W. H. Freeman.

Reed, E. W. (1975). Genetic anomalies in development. In F. D. Horowitz (Ed.), *Review of child development research* (Vol. 4). Chicago: University of Chicago Press.

Rorvik, D. M., & Shettles, L. B. (1970). *Your baby's sex: Now you can choose.* New York: Dodd, Mead.

Rovet, J., & Netley, C. (1982). Processing deficits in Turner's syndrome. *Developmental Psychology, 18,* 77–94.

Rowe, D. C., & Plomin, R. (1981). The importance of non-shared (E_1) environmental influences in behavioral development. *Developmental Psychology, 17,* 517–531.

Rutter, M. (1978). Family, area, and school influences in the genesis of conduct disorders. In L. Hersov, M. Berber, & D. Shaffer (Eds.), *Aggression and antisocial behavior in childhood and adolescence.* Oxford: Pergamon Press.

Rutter, M. (1979a). Maternal deprivation 1972–1977: New findings, new concepts, new approaches. *Child Development, 50,* 283–305.

Rutter, M. (1979b). Protective factors in children's responses to stress and disadvantage. In M. W. Kent & J. E. Rolf (Eds.), *Primary prevention of psychopathology. Vol. 3: Social competence in children.* Hanover, NH: University Press of New England.

Scarr, S., & Carter-Saltzman, L. (1979). Twin method: Defense of a critical assumption. *Behavior Genetics, 9,* 527–542.

Scarr, S., & McCartney, K. (1983). How people make their own environments: A theory of genotype → environment effects. *Child Development, 54,* 424–435.

Scarr, S., Webber, P. L., Weinberg, R. A., & Wittig, M. A. (1981). Personality resemblance among adolescents and their parents in biologically related and adoptive families. *Journal of Personality and Social Psychology, 40,* 885–898.

Scarr, S., & Weinberg, R. A. (1977). Intellectual similarities within families of both adopted and biological children. *Intelligence, 1977, 32,* 170–191.

Scarr, S., & Weinberg, R. A. (1983). The Minnesota adoption studies: Genetic differences and malleability. *Child Development, 54,* 260–267.

Scheinfeld, A. (1967). *Twins and supertwins.* Philadelphia: Lippincott.

Schwarz, J. C. (1979). Childhood origins of psychopathology. *American Psychologist, 34,* 879–885.

Scott, J. P., & Fuller, J. L. (1965). *Genetics of the social behavior of the dog.* Chicago: University of Chicago Press.

Stern, C. (1956). Hereditary factors affecting adoption. In *A study of adoption practices* (Vol. 2). New York: Child Welfare League of America.

Stern, C. (1973). *Principles of human genetics.* San Francisco: W. H. Freeman.

Thomas, A., & Chess, S. (1977). *Temperament and development.* New York; Brunner/Mazel.

Thomas, A., Chess, S., & Birch, H. G. (1970). The origin of personality. *Scientific American, 223,* 102–109.

Thompson, R. F. (1975). *Introduction to physiological psychology.* New York: Harper & Row.

Tryon, R. C. (1940). Genetic differences in maze learning in rats. *Yearbook of the National Society for Studies in Education, 39,* 111–119.

Vandenberg, S. G. (1965). Multivariate analysis of twin differences. In S. G. Vandenberg (Ed.), *Methods and goals in human behavior genetics.* New York: Academic Press.

Waddington, C. H. (1966). *Principles of development and differentiation.* New York: Macmillan.

Wilson, M. (1982, January 14). Sickle cell carriers at risk at high altitudes. *Athens Banner Herald,* p. 2-B.

Wilson, R. S. (1972). Early mental development. *Science, 175,* 914–917.

Wilson, R. S. (1975). Twins: Patterns of cognitive development as measured on the Wechsler Preschool and Primary Scale of Intelligence. *Developmental Psychology, 11,* 126–134.

Wilson, R. S. (1978). Synchronies in mental development: An epigenetic perspective. *Science, 202,* 939–948.

Wilson, R. S. (1983). The Louisville twin study: Developmental synchronies in behavior. *Child Development, 54,* 298–316.

Witkin, H. A., Mednick, S. A., Schulsinger, F., Bakkestrom, E., Christiansen, K. D., Goodenough, D. R., Hirshhorn, K., Lundsteen, C., Owen, D. R., Philip, J., Rubin, D. B., & Stocking, M. (1976). Criminality in XYY and XXY men. *Science, 196,* 547–555.

Wolff, K. F. (1959). *Theoria generationis.* In J. Needham, *A history of embryology.* New York: Abelard-Schulman. (Original work published 1759)

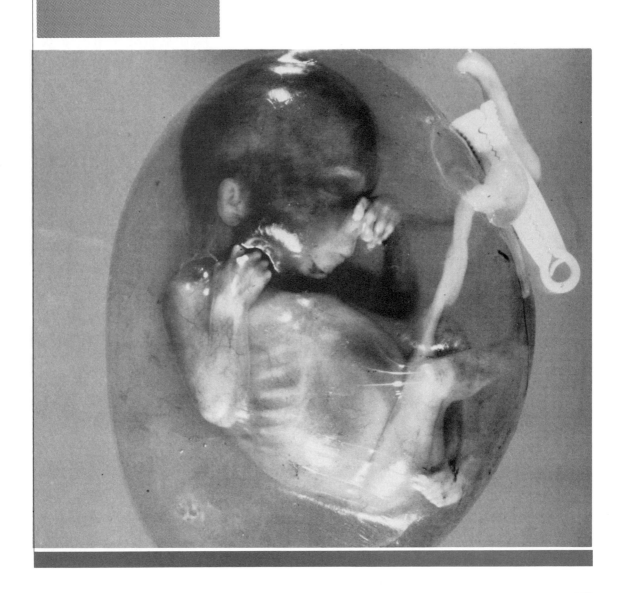

CHAPTER FOUR ■

PRENATAL DEVELOPMENT AND BIRTH

■ *From conception to birth*
The germinal period
The period of the embryo
The period of the fetus

■ *Environmental influences on prenatal development*
Maternal characteristics
Nutrition
Teratogens
On the prevention of birth defects

■ *The birth process*
The normal birth
Complications of birth
Complications of low birth weight
Postmaturity
Should you have your baby at home?

■ *Summary*

*T*rue or false?

1. Human beings develop most rapidly between birth and 2 years of age.

2. The mother's womb is a protective haven that shields an unborn child from external hazards such as pollution and disease.

3. The environment has a meaningful effect on human development from the moment that a child is born.

How old are you? This apparently straightforward question means slightly different things to different people. Many Oriental cultures date children from the moment of conception and consider them to be about 1 year old when they emerge from the womb. In contrast, we Westerners date ourselves from the moment of birth.

From a strict developmental perspective, the Oriental method of reckoning age may be the more realistic. Not only do hundreds of remarkable developments occur before a child is born, but many of these events take place within eight short weeks of conception. As we trace the miraculous evolution of a one-celled zygote into a recognizable human being, it will become apparent that human growth and development occur most rapidly during the *prenatal* period, months before birth.

When might environmental influences first occur? Once again, the answer is long before birth. **Prenatal development** does not take place in a vacuum; it occurs within the mother's uterus—an "environment" that will differ from mother to mother and may well affect the product that emerges in the delivery room. We are quite accustomed to thinking of the intrauterine environment as a safe, protective haven that enables an unborn child to take shape, grow, and become stronger in preparation for birth. This impression was created by influential scientists of the 18th century who described the womb as a kind of vacuum-packed mausoleum that "entombs" a fetus, thereby protecting it from all external hazards (MacFarlane, 1977). Yet we will see that the degree of safety or

---

prenatal development: *development that occurs between the moment of conception and the beginning of the birth process.*

"protection" offered by the womb depends on a variety of factors, including the mother's age, health, and emotional state, the food she eats, the drugs she takes, and the chemicals or levels of radiation to which she is exposed.

In years gone by, people believed that a fetus could be affected by just about any experience that the mother might have. For example, it was once assumed, even by some physicians, that women who "failed" to bear their husbands a male heir were "at fault" because they got insufficient exercise during their pregnancies. Presumably, maternal exercise caused an unborn child to move, thereby stimulating the development of fetal muscle and increasing the probability that the fetus would become a male! Other common beliefs included the notions that a pregnant woman who often listened to music would have a musical child and that mothers who were sexually active while pregnant would produce sexually precocious children. Today we know that these ideas are unfounded, for only those maternal experiences that directly affect the intrauterine environment can influence an embryo or fetus. The reason will become clear as we look at the course of prenatal development and learn more about the interesting relationship that emerges between a mother and the unborn organism in her womb.

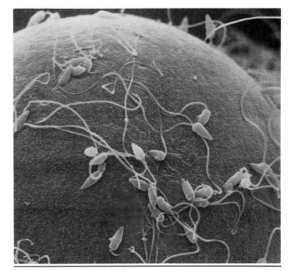

PHOTO 4-1. *Ovum just before conception. Only one of these sperm will penetrate the egg, forming a zygote.*

FROM CONCEPTION TO BIRTH

In Chapter Three we learned that development begins in the fallopian tube when a sperm penetrates the wall of a ripened ovum, forming a zygote (see Photo 4-1). From the moment of conception, it will take approximately 266 days for this tiny, one-celled zygote to become a fetus of some 200 billion cells that is ready to be born.

Prenatal development is often divided into three major phases. The first phase, called the **germinal period,** lasts from conception until implantation—when the developing zygote becomes firmly attached to the wall of the uterus. The germinal period normally lasts about 8–14 days. The second phase of prenatal development, the **period of the embryo,** lasts from the beginning of the third week through the end of the eighth. This is the time when virtually all the major organs are formed and the heart begins to

beat. The third phase, the **period of the fetus,** lasts from the ninth week of pregnancy until the child is born. During this phase, the major organ systems begin to function, and the developing organism grows rapidly.

The Germinal Period

Once conception has occurred, the fertilized ovum, or zygote, continues its journey down the fallopian tube toward the uterus. Within 24–36 hours the zygote divides by mitosis into two cells. These two cells and all their daughter cells continue to divide at periodic intervals, forming a ball-like structure, or **blastula,** that will contain 100–150 cells within seven days of conception (see Figure 4-1). Cell differentiation has already begun. The inner layer of the blastula, called the **blastocyst,** will become the embryo. The outer layer of cells, or **trophoblast,** will develop into tissues that protect and nourish the embryo.

As the blastula approaches the uterus some 6–10 days after conception, small burrlike tendrils have emerged from the outer surface of the trophoblast. As nature would have it, the blastula reaches the uterus at the point in the woman's menstrual cycle when the uterine lining is en-

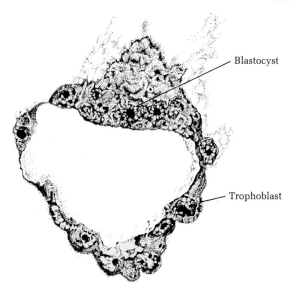

FIGURE 4-1. *A 107-cell blastula, showing the*
trophoblast and blastocyst.

already working to ensure its continued survival. Its first accomplishment is to secrete a hormone that prevents the woman from menstruating and thereby shedding the lining of her uterus, where the blastula is implanted. This hormone circulates throughout the woman's body and is eventually detectable in her urine, where its presence is taken as a positive indication of pregnancy in a common pregnancy test.

During the second and third weeks after conception, further differentiations of the ball-like blastula take place. The outer layer, or trophoblast, forms four membranes that make it possible for the embryo to develop. One membrane, the **amnion,** is a watertight bag that surrounds the embryo, filling with fluid that seeps in from the mother's tissues. The purpose of the amnion and its amniotic fluid is to cushion the developing organism against injuries, to maintain a constant warm temperature, and to provide a weightless

gorged with small blood vessels that can provide nourishment to this primitive little creature. When the blastula comes into contact with the uterine wall, its tendrils burrow inward, tapping into the woman's blood supply. This is **implantation**. Soon cells from the uterus grow around the implanted blastula, providing a rudimentary protective covering. Within 8–14 days after conception, the site of implantation looks like a small, translucent blister on the lining of the uterus (Apgar & Beck, 1974). At this point, the germinal period comes to an end.

Implantation is a critical event in human development. Only about half of all fertilized ova are successfully implanted in the uterus (Roberts & Lowe, 1975), and perhaps as many as half of all implanted embryos are abnormal in some way (or burrow into a site incapable of sustaining them) and will not develop to term (Adler & Carey, 1982). So it appears that approximately 1 zygote in 4 will survive the initial phases of prenatal development.

The Period of the Embryo

From the moment of implantation, the blastula, which is still no bigger than the head of a pin, is

germinal period: *first phase of prenatal development, lasting from conception until the developing organism becomes attached to the wall of the uterus.*

period of the embryo: *second phase of prenatal development, lasting from the third through the eighth prenatal week, during which the major organs and anatomical structures begin to develop.*

period of the fetus: *third phase of prenatal development, lasting from the ninth prenatal week until birth; during this period, the major organ systems begin to function and the fetus grows rapidly.*

blastula: *a hollow sphere of about 100–150 cells that results from the rapid division of the zygote as it moves through the fallopian tube.*

blastocyst: *inner layer of the blastula, which becomes the embryo.*

trophoblast: *outer cells of the blastula, which eventually develop into tissues that serve to protect and nourish the embryo.*

implantation: *the burrowing of the blastula into the lining of the uterus.*

amnion: *a watertight membrane that develops from the trophoblast and surrounds the developing embryo, serving to regulate its temperature and to cushion it against injuries.*

environment that makes it easy for the developing organism to move and to exercise its growing body (Apgar & Beck, 1974). Floating beside the tiny embryo is a balloon-shaped **yolk sac** that produces blood cells until the embryo is capable of producing its own. This yolk sac is attached to a third membrane, the **chorion**, which surrounds the amnion and the embryo. One side of the chorionic sac is covered with rootlike structures, or villi, that gather nourishment from the uterine tissues. This area eventually becomes the lining of the **placenta**—a multipurpose organ that we are about to discuss in detail. A fourth membrane, the **allantosis,** forms the embryo's umbilical cord and the blood vessels in the placenta.

■ Function of the placenta

Once the placenta develops, it is fed by blood vessels from the mother and the embryo, although a membrane called the placental barrier prevents these two bloodstreams from mixing. The placental barrier is semipermeable, meaning that it allows some substances to pass through but not others. Gases such as oxygen and carbon dioxide, salts, and various nutrients such as sugars, proteins, and fats are small enough to permeate the placenta. However, blood cells are too large and, thus, cannot cross the placental barrier.

As maternal blood flows into the placenta, oxygen and nutrients pass through this semipermeable membrane into the embryo's bloodstream. The embryo is connected to the placenta by means of its lifeline, the **umbilical cord,** which contains two arteries and a vein. The vein carries oxygen and foodstuffs to the embryo. The two arteries carry carbon dioxide and metabolic wastes from the embryo. These waste products cross the placental barrier, enter the mother's bloodstream, and are expelled from the mother's body along with her own metabolic wastes. We see, then, that the developing organism is something of a parasite—it is totally dependent on its mother for oxygen, food, and elimination. The placenta plays a crucial role in prenatal development, because this remarkable organ is the site of all metabolic transactions that sustain the embryo.

■ Development of the embryo

As the blastula becomes implanted in the wall of the uterus and as the outer protective membranes are forming, the innermost cells (or blastocyst) are rapidly differentiating into three distinct layers. The outer layer, or *ectoderm,* will eventually become the child's skin, hair, nails, oil and sweat glands, and nervous system. The middle layer, or *mesoderm,* will form muscles, bones, connective tissue, and the circulatory and excretory systems. From the inner layer, or *endoderm,* come the digestive tract, trachea, bronchi, lungs, and other vital organs such as the pancreas and liver.

During the period of the embryo, development proceeds at a breathtaking pace. About 14 days after conception, a portion of the ectoderm folds into a neural tube that soon becomes the head, brain, and spinal cord. By the end of the third week, a primitive heart and blood vessels have formed. In the fourth week, the heart begins to beat, pushing blood through the embryo's tiny arteries and veins. The eyes, ears, nose, and mouth are also taking shape, and buds that will become arms and legs suddenly appear. Thirty days after conception, the embryo is only about 1/4 of an inch long—but 10,000 times the size of the zygote from which it developed. At no time in the future will this organism ever grow as rapidly or change as much as it has during the first prenatal month (Apgar & Beck, 1974).

During the second month, the body becomes much more human in appearance as it grows about 1/30th of an inch per day. A primitive tail appears, but it is soon enclosed by protective tis-

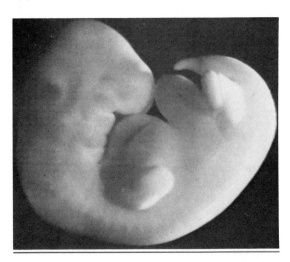

PHOTO 4-2. *A human embryo at 38 days. The heart is now beating, and the limbs are growing rapidly.*

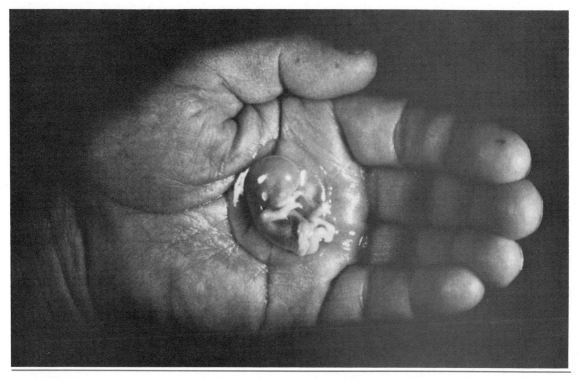

PHOTO 4-3. A human embryo at 60 days. All of the major organs have begun to form, and the embryo is now a fetus.

sue and becomes the tip of the backbone, the coccyx. By the middle of the fifth week, the eyes have corneas and lenses. By the seventh week, the ears are well formed and the embryo has a rudimentary skeleton. Limbs are now developing from the body outward; that is, the upper arms develop first, followed by forearms, hands, and then fingers. The legs follow a similar pattern a few days later. The brain develops rapidly during the second month, and it directs the organism's first muscular contractions by the end of the embryonic period. At 60 days after conception, the organism is slightly more than an inch long and weighs less than 1/10th of an ounce. It appears humanoid (see Photo 4-3), although its head is at least as long as the rest of its body. Apgar and Beck (1974, p. 57) offer the following description of the eight-week-old embryo:

All of the structures which will be present when the baby is born in seven more months have already been formed, at least in beginning stages. . . . Medically, the unborn baby is no longer an

embryo, but a fetus; not an it, but a he or she; not an indistinct cluster of cells, but an increasingly recognizable, unique human being in the making.

> **yolk sac:** *a balloonlike structure that develops from the trophoblast and produces blood cells until the embryo is capable of manufacturing its own.*
>
> **chorion:** *a membrane that develops from the trophoblast and becomes attached to the uterine tissues to gather nourishment for the embryo.*
>
> **placenta:** *an organ, formed from the lining of the uterus and the chorion, that provides for the nourishment of the unborn child and the elimination of its metabolic wastes.*
>
> **allantosis:** *a membrane that develops from the trophoblast and forms the umbilical cord.*
>
> **umbilical cord:** *a soft tube containing blood vessels that connects the embryo to the placenta.*

■ *Sensitive nature of embryonic development*

The first two months of pregnancy are critical in several respects. This is the period when most miscarriages (spontaneous abortions) occur as the embryo becomes detached from the uterine wall and is expelled. Perhaps as many as 30–50% of pregnancies end in spontaneous abortion (Roberts & Lowe, 1975), and many women miscarry before they are even aware that they are pregnant (Browne & Dixon, 1978). Spontaneous abortion may be triggered by a variety of factors: The woman's uterus may be malformed or immature. The blastula may have become implanted at a location incapable of sustaining the embryo. But in the majority of cases aborted embryos are thought to be genetically abnormal (Ash, Vennart, & Carter, 1977). Thus, spontaneous abortions can be adaptive, representing "nature's way of discouraging [harmful] mutations from being incorporated into the hereditary pattern" (Browne & Dixon, 1978, p. 105).

Even genetically normal embryos that are firmly implanted in a healthy uterus are at risk during the first two months of pregnancy. Indeed, the time between two and eight weeks after conception is often labeled the "sensitive period" of pregnancy because the embryo is now particularly susceptible to the influence of **teratogens**— viruses, chemicals, drugs, and radiation—that can interfere with ongoing development and produce birth defects. Although teratogens are capable of damaging organs or body parts that have already formed, they are likely to have a much stronger impact on organs that are currently developing. Thus, the human embryo is especially susceptible to teratogens between two and eight weeks after conception because this is the time when many of its vital structures, organs, and organ systems are beginning to develop.

The Period of the Fetus

In the third prenatal month, bones begin to harden, muscles are rapidly developing, and the embryo, which has become increasingly human in appearance, is called a *fetus.*

Sexual differentiation continues during the third month. In the seventh and eighth prenatal weeks, the embryo's sexual development begins with the appearance of a genital ridge called the **indifferent gonad**. If the embryo is a male, a gene on its Y chromosome triggers a biochemical reaction that instructs the indifferent gonad to produce testes. If the embryo is a female, the indifferent gonad receives no such instructions and will produce ovaries. As the testes mature during the ninth and tenth prenatal weeks, they manufacture male sex hormones, which stimulate the development of a male reproductive system.[1] However, the female fetus will develop a female reproductive system even if its tiny ovaries are damaged or do not function. It appears, then, that nature's first choice is female and that "maleness" requires a "male" gene to (1) trigger the development of testes, which (2) must then function properly in order to produce other male sex organs.

By the end of the third month, the fetus is already performing many interesting maneuvers in its watery environment—moving its arms, kicking its legs, making fists, twisting its body, and even turning somersaults—although these activities are not yet detected by the mother (Apgar & Beck, 1974). The fetus now has eyelids, vocal cords, lips, and a prominent nose. Several organ systems are operational, allowing the fetus to swallow, to digest nutrients, and to urinate. Gender is readily apparent, and the fetal reproductive system already contains immature ova or sperm cells. All this detail is present after 12 weeks even though the fetus is a mere 3 inches long and weighs but 1/2 to 3/4 of an ounce (see Photo 4-4).

■ *The second trimester*

The fourth, fifth, and sixth months of pregnancy, called the "second trimester," are a period of rapid growth and development. During the fourth month, toenails and fingernails appear, and the muscles develop rapidly. At 16 weeks of age, the fetus is 8–10 inches long and weighs about six ounces. Its motor activity may include refined actions such as thumbsucking, as well as vigorous kicks that are strong enough to be felt by the

---

[1]One sex-linked genetic anomaly, the testicular feminization syndrome, makes a genetic male (XY) fetus insensitive to the male hormone androgen. A male fetus that inherits this condition will develop the external genitalia of a female even though testes (which will remain out of sight within the body) have evolved from the indifferent gonad (Money & Ehrhardt, 1972).

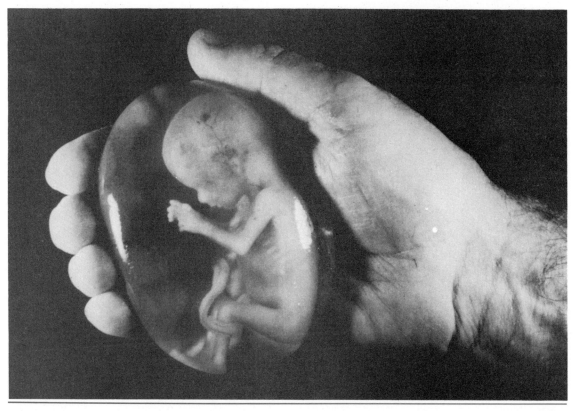

PHOTO 4-4. *A human fetus at 12 weeks. Most organ systems are now functioning, even though the fetus is only 3 inches long and weighs less than an ounce.*

mother. The fetal heartbeat can now be heard with a stethoscope, and the hardening skeleton can be detected by X rays or ultrasound. By the end of the fourth month, the fetus has assumed a distinctly human appearance (see Photo 4-5), even though it stands absolutely no chance of surviving outside the womb.

During the fifth and sixth months, the nails begin to harden, the skin thickens, and eyebrows, eyelashes, and scalp hair suddenly appear. At 20 weeks, the sweat glands are functioning, and the fetal heartbeat is often strong enough to be heard by placing an ear on the mother's abdomen. The fetus is now about 12 inches long and weighs between 12 and 16 ounces. By the end of the 24th week, the fetus can open and close its eyelids at will, although it is doubtful that anything can be seen within the darkness of the womb. However, the fetus can hear! Loud noises may produce a startle response and increase the fetus's motor ac-

tivity, whereas internal noises such as the mother's heartbeat appear to be soothing (Mac-Farlane, 1977). Six months after conception, the fetus is approximately 14–15 inches long and weighs about two pounds.

The end of the second trimester is yet another critical period in human development. At some point between the 24th and the 28th week after conception, the fetal brain and respiratory system have matured to an extent that the fetus attains the

---

teratogens: *external agents such as viruses, drugs, chemicals, and radiation that can cross the placental barrier and harm a developing embryo or fetus.*

indifferent gonad: *undifferentiated tissue that produces testes in males and ovaries in females.*

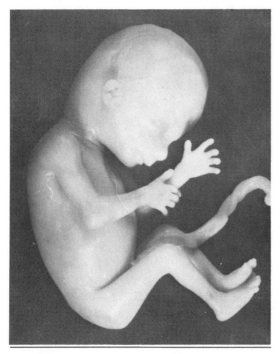

PHOTO 4-5. 120 days after conception, the kicks of a 6-ounce fetus are often strong enough to be felt by the mother.

age of viability—the point at which survival outside the uterus *may* be possible. On March 5, 1982, Daniel Sumi made medical history by becoming the smallest baby ever to be born and subsequently live (Associated Press, 1983). This hardy young man weighed in at 13 ounces (369 grams) when he was delivered in his 27th prenatal week. (Other babies have been born earlier—as early as the 22nd week—and survived, but none of these infants weighed less than Daniel.) Until this birth, only one child weighing less than one pound had ever survived. In fact, the majority of newborns who weigh less than 3¼ pounds (1500 grams) do not survive, even with excellent medical care (Kessner, 1973; Browne & Dixon, 1978).

There is a very definite relationship between the birth weight of a child and the child's probability of surviving: the less a baby weighs at birth, the greater the likelihood that he or she will die during the birth process or soon thereafter (see Table 4-1). Each additional day that a fetus continues to develop within the uterus increases the probability of survival in the outside world.

■ *The third trimester*

The seventh, eighth, and ninth months of pregnancy—the third trimester—are a period of rapid growth. By the end of the seventh month, the fetus weighs about 4 pounds and is about 16–17 inches long. One month later, the fetus has grown to 18 inches and put on another 1 to 2½ pounds. Much of the weight gain during this period comes from a padding fat that is deposited beneath the skin. After birth this fatty layer will help to insulate the child from changes in temperature (Browne & Dixon, 1978). By the time the fetus weighs 3½ to 4 pounds, odds of survival in the event of premature birth are good. A fetus weighing at least 5 pounds at birth may not even require an incubator.

By the second half of the ninth prenatal month, the fetus is so large (19–20 inches long, with an average weight of 7 to 7½ pounds) that its uterine home has become a bit cramped. At this point, it is not at all unusual for a mother to observe the outline of a tiny hand or the bump of a head pressing outward against her midsection. If one presses gently on the mother's abdomen, the firm shape of

TABLE 4-1. Infant mortality as a function of birth weight

	Birth weight		Percentage of babies who die
	In grams	*In pounds*	
Low-birth-weight babies	1000 or less	2 lb, 3 oz. or less	92
	1000–1500	2 lb, 4 oz–3 lb, 4 oz	55
	1501–2500	3 lb, 5 oz–4 lb, 6 oz	21
	2001–2500	4 lb, 7 oz–5 lb, 8 oz	6
Average-birth-weight babies	2501–3000	5 lb, 9 oz–6 lb, 9 oz	2
	3001–4500	6 lb, 10 oz–9 lb, 14 oz	1

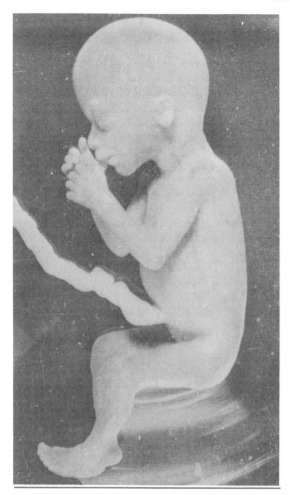

PHOTO 4-6. A human fetus at 210 days. By this age, survival outside the womb may be possible.

the fetus can be felt—and the fetus will probably shift around a bit in response to this mild tactile stimulation (Browne & Dixon, 1978).

As the uterus expands during the third trimester, it assumes the shape of an inverted pear. By the middle of the ninth month, the fetus is so large that the most comfortable lie within its restricted uterine environment is likely to be a head-down posture at the base of the uterus, with the limbs curled up in the so-called fetal position. At irregular intervals over the last month of pregnancy, the mother's uterus will contract and then relax. These contractions serve to tone the uterine muscle, to dilate the cervix, and to help position the head of the now-inverted fetus into the gap between the pelvic bones through which it will soon be pushed. When the uterine contractions become stronger, more frequent, and regular, the prenatal period draws to a close. The mother is now in the first stage of labor, and within a matter of hours she will give birth to her child.

ENVIRONMENTAL INFLUENCES ON PRENATAL DEVELOPMENT

The pattern of prenatal development just described is an overview of what typically occurs between conception and birth. The vast majority of unborn children follow this "normal" pattern—and for that we can be thankful. Nevertheless, there are those who encounter environmental roadblocks during the prenatal period—blocks that may be sufficiently formidable to channel their development along an abnormal path. We will now consider a number of agents and circumstances that can have an adverse effect on the unborn child.

Maternal Characteristics

■ Maternal age
You may recall that Aristotle cautioned women to have their babies early. He believed that women were hardiest at age 18 and that this was the time when they were most likely to bear normal, healthy children. Some 2400 years later, psychologist B. F. Skinner (1971) offered a similar recommendation for young women, but for different reasons. Skinner felt that, in the best of all worlds, women would have their children by age 20, leave their youngsters in the care of professional child rearers, and thus be completely free to pursue a career.

Although many career-oriented mothers might applaud Skinner's suggestion, large-scale implementation of his plan could well result in a dramatic increase in infant mortality. Figure 4-2 illustrates the relationships that emerged in one large

> age of viability: *a point between the 24th and 28th prenatal weeks when a fetus may survive outside the uterus if excellent medical care is available.*

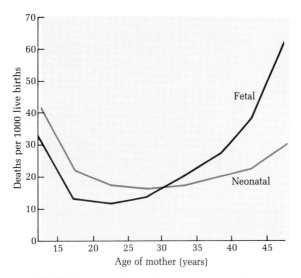

FIGURE 4-2. Relationship between mother's age and risk of death for the fetus or neonate.

study between mother's age and risk of death for a fetus or a **neonate** (newborn). As we see in the figure, younger mothers, particularly those 18 and under, face an added risk of bearing a stillborn fetus or a live child who fails to survive. In addition, mothers under 20 are more likely to experience obstetrical complications and to die during childbirth than those in their twenties (Planned Parenthood Federation of America, 1976). Why are younger mothers and their offspring at risk? Perhaps because many women are not physically mature before age 18–20. As a consequence, a very young mother who is still growing may have an underdeveloped reproductive system or extensive nutritional needs of her own—factors that may limit her capacity to sustain a healthy embryo or fetus.

Figure 4-2 also shows that mothers older than 35 face extra risk of obstetrical problems and infant mortality. At the older end of the age continuum, many of the complications of pregnancy and prenatal development are experienced by women over 35 who are having a *first* child. These older "first-timers" are more likely than women in their twenties to be ill during pregnancy, to have longer and more difficult labors, and to deliver infants who are small, premature, or stillborn or who show any of a variety of congenital defects (Browne & Dixon, 1978; Kessner, 1973). However, we should bear in mind that the vast majority of

older mothers have pregnancies that last the full nine months and produce perfectly normal babies.

■ Parity (number of previous pregnancies)

Many women having a second baby are amazed that their time in labor is so much less than that spent delivering their first child. One might be inclined to liken the female reproductive system to an automobile engine—both are presumably more efficient once they are "broken in." If we pursue this analogy, we will recall that engines are more likely to "wear out" the more they are used. Is the same thing true of a mother's reproductive apparatus?

Unfortunately, there is no clear answer for this question. Kessner (1973) did find a **parity effect:** women who had been pregnant more than four times were more likely to deliver stillborn or low-birth-weight babies than women who had been pregnant on fewer occasions. In addition, Eleanor Maccoby and her associates have recently found that later-born infants have lower concentrations of hormones in their blood than first-born infants, particularly when the pregnancies were closely spaced (Maccoby, Doering, Jacklin, & Kraemer, 1979).

Although these findings suggest that pregnancy and childbirth may somehow "deplete" a mother's reproductive system, other interpretations are possible. For example, the *age* of the mother may account for the "parity effect" if it turns out that women with more than four children are older than those with fewer offspring. This "aging" hypothesis seems all the more reasonable when we recall that older "first-time" mothers, who have not "depleted" their reproductive systems, are also more likely to have difficult pregnancies and small or stillborn babies. So it appears that women who have had many children are at greater risk for various complications of pregnancy; but at present we can only speculate about the cause of this parity effect.

■ Mother's emotional state

Although many women are happy to learn that they are pregnant, the fact remains that about half of all pregnancies are unplanned (Y. Brackbill, personal communication, August 1982) and that single women and those who are unhappily married are often bitter, depressed, or angry about their pregnancies (Browne & Dixon, 1978). Even a woman who is eagerly anticipating the birth of her child may be quite anxious about the welfare of her fetus and generally apprehensive about the birth process, particularly in a first pregnancy. Do these emotional states and attitudes toward pregnancy have any effect on prenatal development? Can they affect the birth process?

Although there are no direct connections between a woman's nervous system and that of her fetus, a mother's emotional state can affect her unborn child. When a mother becomes emotionally aroused, her endocrine glands and autonomic nervous system secrete powerful hormones, such as adrenalin, that may cross the placental barrier and enter the fetal bloodstream. At the very least, the presence of these activating substances can significantly increase the fetus's motor activity (Sontag, 1941). And if emotional stress or anxiety lasts throughout pregnancy, expectant mothers are at risk for complications such as miscarriage, prolonged and painful labor, and premature delivery (Sameroff & Chandler, 1975). Of course, not all women who are anxious or emotionally upset will experience these problems. A mother's emotions are most likely to affect her fetus and the birth process when she is (1) extremely anxious, (2) highly dependent on others, and (3) ambivalent or negative about her pregnancy (McDonald, 1968).

Once they are born, the babies of highly anxious mothers tend to be hyperactive, irritable, and quite irregular in their feeding, sleeping, and bowel habits (Sontag, 1944; Sameroff & Chandler, 1975). It may be that this "difficult" temperamental profile is genetically based or is directly attributable to the mother's heightened emotional state during pregnancy. However, it is possible that mothers who have been anxious or resentful about their pregnancies may retain some of these feelings after giving birth and then respond to their babies in ways that make these children irritable or difficult.

Nutrition

Forty years ago, doctors often advised expectant mothers that they need not eat any more than they cared to in order to have a healthy baby. The rule of thumb in those days was that women should gain no more than two pounds a month while pregnant. The thinking was that excessive weight gains could be harmful for the mother and that a tiny fetus could extract the nutrients it needed even if the mother gained very little weight (15–18 pounds).

Today most obstetricians would be very concerned if a patient of theirs gained too little weight, for they are now well aware of the many harmful complications that can result from inadequate prenatal nutrition. Women are currently advised to gain three to four pounds during the first three months of pregnancy and approximately a pound a week thereafter—a total increase of 24–28 pounds (B. G. Brown, personal communication, March 1982).

Much of what we know about nutrition and prenatal development comes from studies of expectant mothers who were severely malnourished. Severe malnutrition increases the risk of congenital defects, prolonged labor, stillbirth, and infant mortality during the first year. Apparently the harmful consequences of prenatal malnutrition are greatest when the nutritional deficiency occurs later in pregnancy, particularly during the last three months (see Box 4-1). This third trimester is the time when fetal brain cells are rapidly multiplying and the unborn child is gaining most of its eventual birth weight. It should therefore come as no surprise that mothers who are severely malnourished during this period are likely to deliver rather small babies who have fewer brain cells than do children born to women whose nutrition was adequate (Lewin, 1975; Winick, 1976).

The long-term effects of prenatal malnutrition will depend, in part, on the adequacy of the child's diet after birth. A malnourished infant who lives in an economically impoverished environment where nutrition *remains* inadequate is likely to show long-term deficits in physical growth and intellectual performance (Winick, 1976). Fortunately, dietary supplements given to malnourished mothers during the last half of

---

neonate: *a newborn infant from birth to approximately 1 month of age.*

parity effect: *the greater risk for various complications of pregnancy among women who have had several children than among those who have had fewer.*

Between October 1944 and March 1945, a large area of western Holland was subjected to conditions of famine. During this period of World War II, many Dutch citizens were trying to support Allied forces, and the occupying German troops retaliated by closing the roads and the rail system, thereby restricting civilian transport. This "embargo" severely limited the availability of food and other essential supplies to most large cities, and shortage of food soon became serious. Rations dropped from over 2000 calories per person per day before the famine to 500–700 calories (with a severe reduction in protein) by the time conquering Allied troops lifted the blockade.

Some thirty years later, Zela Stein and her associates (Stein & Susser, 1976; Stein, Susser, Saenger, & Marolla, 1975) examined hospital birth and death records from this period to study the effects of famine on infant mortality. And because all Dutch males must take intelligence tests when they undergo compulsory military training at age 19, it was also possible to determine whether the surviving male children born during or shortly after the famine showed any long-term intellectual deficits as a result of their early malnutrition.

The short-term effects were clear. Stein et al. (1975) found that women who were malnourished during the *last three months* of their pregnancies were much more likely to have small, underweight babies than mothers who were malnourished during their first or second trimester. The effects of malnutrition on infant mortality were almost identical, as indicated in the accompanying table.

Stein and her colleagues then compared the later intellectual performance of military inductees from the famine area with that of their peers born in parts of Holland that were not affected by the famine. Once again, the results were clear and somewhat surprising—malnourished males from the famine area scored no lower on the test battery than well-nourished males from nonfamine areas.

Since it is well known that malnourished fetuses often have smaller brains and fewer brain cells (see text for details), why do you suppose the malnourished males in this study showed no long-term cognitive deficits? Stein and her colleagues offer one possible explanation. They note that the mothers of these boys (and the boys themselves) were adequately nourished after the famine. Since the first two years of life is a period of rapid brain growth and development, it is certainly possible that adequate nutrition during this critical phase may compensate for any adverse effects of poor prenatal nutrition. In other words, if the fetally malnourished infant should survive, it appears that a good *postnatal* diet may help to prevent long-term deficits in neurological development and intellectual performance.

Condition	Infant mortality in first 12 months (deaths per 1000 births)
Child born before famine (mother not malnourished)	9
Mother malnourished—last 3 months of pregnancy	30
Mother malnourished—first 6 months	18
Mother malnourished—first 3 months	6
Child conceived and born after famine (mother not malnourished)	6

pregnancy or to their infants soon after birth can help to reduce the chances that early malnutrition will have harmful consequences that persist over time (Barrett, Radke-Yarrow, & Klein, 1982; Habicht, Yarbrough, Lectig, & Klein, 1974).

However, dietary supplements by themselves may not be sufficient to shield the fetally malnourished child from all long-term deficits in intellectual functioning. Philip Zeskind and Craig Ramey (1978, 1981) have noted that fetally malnourished infants are often unresponsive, apathetic children who become irritable when aroused—qualities that may make them unpleasant to deal with. As a result, these children may not receive the emotional support or playful stimulation from caretakers that would facilitate their social and intellectual development. Zeskind and Ramey believe that fetally malnourished infants must have both adequate nutrition and a supportive environment in which to grow if they are to develop normally and show no long-term effects of their earlier malnutrition.

This hypothesis was tested in a recent longitudinal experiment (Zeskind & Ramey, 1978, 1981). At age 3 months, fetally malnourished infants were randomly assigned to two conditions.

Children assigned to an *early intervention* condition participated eight hours a day, 50 weeks a year, in a day-care program designed to teach basic language, cognitive, and social skills. These children received proper nutritional care and medical attention. Children assigned to the *nonintervention* condition received similar medical and nutritional services but did not attend the day-care program. At regular intervals over the first three years of life, the children in each condition took an IQ test, as well as a test of their social responsiveness, and they were observed at home with their mothers to determine how involved the mothers were with them (that is, how much each mother attended to or played with her child).

The results were dramatic. Even though these two groups of fetally malnourished infants had received the same nutritional services from the age of 3 months, their intellectual development over the first three years took very different paths (see Figure 4-3). At the beginning of the program, children assigned to the intervention condition performed no better on a test of infant intelligence than children in the nonintervention condition. But as time passed, children exposed to the supportive environment of the day-care center showed an approximately normal pattern of intellectual growth, while those who did not attend the day-care program showed a progressive decline in intellectual functioning. In addition, mothers of children in the intervention group became more responsive as their children progressed in the day-care program, while mothers of children in the nonintervention condition became less responsive. Finally, children who attended the day-care program were friendlier, more self-assured, and less anxious at 3 years of age than their counterparts who had remained at home. Zeskind and Ramey concluded that the behavioral improvement of children in the program had resulted from "the supportive qualities of the caregiving environment" and from a "maternal environment" that changed for the better as the children improved (1981, p. 216).

At this point, we know that severe fetal malnutrition can have harmful long-term effects, particularly if the child's diet remains inadequate after birth. However, Zeskind and Ramey's study should remind us that merely supplementing the child's diet is not enough. The fetally malnourished child will also require a supportive

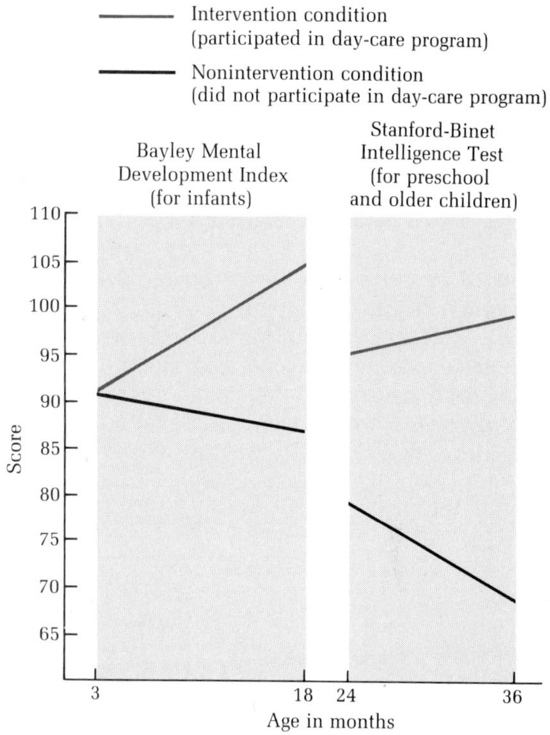

FIGURE 4-3. Intellectual development of fetally malnourished infants between 3 months and 3 years of age.

home and school environment in order to completely overcome the cognitive and social deficits often associated with prenatal malnutrition.

Teratogens

Teratology, the study of prenatal malformations and birth defects, is a young science with many unresolved issues. Not all the diseases, drugs, chemicals, and other environmental hazards that can harm a developing fetus have yet been identified. Moreover, the study of teratology is complicated by the findings that (1) few if any of the known teratogens will affect all unborn children who are exposed to these agents, (2) a single teratogen may have more than one harmful effect,

---

teratology: *the scientific study of birth defects caused by genetic and prenatal influences or by complications of the birth process.*

and (3) a particular birth defect may be caused by any of several teratogens (Abel, 1981; Browne & Dixon, 1978; Tuchmann-Duplessis, 1975).

We do know that some unborn children are more vulnerable than others to teratogenic agents. For example, a particular teratogen is more likely to produce a congenital problem of some kind if the embryo or fetus is a later-born or a male and if the mother is poor, undernourished, and younger than 20 or older than 40 (Apgar & Beck, 1974; Browne & Dixon, 1978).

The effects of a teratogen will also depend on the developmental stage of the embryo or the fetus. Each major organ system or body part has a critical period when it is most sensitive to teratogenic agents—namely, the time when that par-

ticular part of the body is evolving and taking shape. As we see in Figure 4-4, the most sensitive period for gross physical defects of the head and spinal column is the third through the fifth prenatal weeks. The heart is particularly vulnerable from the middle of the third through the middle of the sixth prenatal week; the most sensitive period for many other organs and body parts is the second prenatal month. Is it any wonder, then, that the period of the embryo—when the body and organs are rapidly forming—is often called the critical (or sensitive) phase of pregnancy?

Once an organ or body part is fully formed, it becomes somewhat less susceptible to the influence of most teratogens. However, this does not mean that the structure in question is now in-

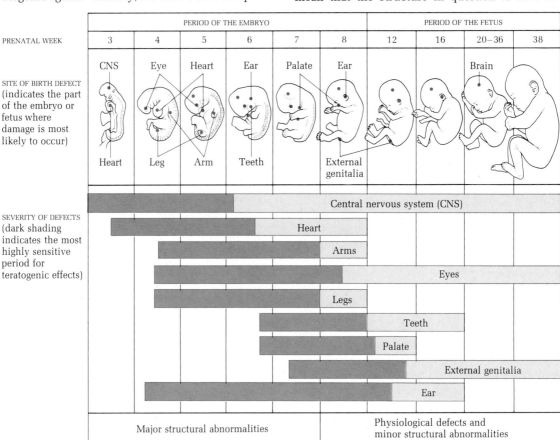

FIGURE 4-4. *The critical periods of prenatal development. Teratogens are more likely to produce major structural abnormalities during the third through the eighth prenatal week. Note, however, that many organs and body parts remain sensitive to teratogenic agents throughout the nine-month prenatal period.*

vulnerable. Recently, Olli Heinonin and his associates (Heinonin, Slone, & Shapiro, 1977) concluded that many of the birth defects found among the 50,282 children in their sample were **anytime malformations**—problems that could have been caused by teratogens at any point during the nine-month prenatal period. Among the more common of these "anytime malformations" were defects of the central nervous system, such as microcephaly (an unusually small head often associated with mental retardation), dislocations of the hip, hernias, genital abnormalities, cataracts, and benign tumors.

We will now consider some of the more common diseases, drugs, chemicals, and other environmental teratogens that can disrupt prenatal development and produce serious birth defects.

■ *Maternal diseases*

Until the early 1940s, it was assumed that the placenta was a marvelous screening device that prevented viruses and other infectious organisms from reaching the developing embryo or fetus. Today we know that this is false. Many disease agents are capable of crossing the placental barrier and doing much more damage to a developing embryo or fetus than to the mother herself. This makes sense when we remember that an unborn child has an immature immune system that cannot produce enough antibodies to combat the disease agent effectively.

Rubella.   The medical community became aware of the teratogenic effect of diseases in 1941 when an Australian physician, McAllister Gregg, noticed that many mothers who had had **rubella (German measles)** early in pregnancy were delivering babies who were congenitally blind. After Gregg alerted the medical community, doctors began to notice that pregnant rubella patients were regularly bearing children with a variety of defects, including blindness, deafness, cardiac abnormalities, and mental retardation. Rubella is most dangerous during the first trimester. Studies have shown that 50–80% of babies whose mothers had rubella in the first month will have birth defects, compared with about 25% of those infected in the second month and 6% of those infected in the third month (Browne & Dixon, 1978; Fuhrmann & Vogel, 1976). Rubella is less teratogenic in the fourth prenatal month, although unborn chil-

dren infected at this time may later show some speech or hearing difficulties and slight mental retardation (Browne & Dixon, 1978). Today doctors stress that no woman should try to become pregnant unless she has been immunized against rubella or has already had the disease. Ideally, women should wait two to three months after a rubella vaccination before becoming pregnant, for the vaccine (which contains a weakened form of the rubella virus) is itself a teratogen that may harm an unborn child.

Other infectious diseases.   Many diseases other than rubella are known teratogens (see Table 4-2 for several examples). One of the more common of these diseases, congenital **syphilis,** is most harmful in the middle and later stages of pregnancy since syphilitic spirochetes (the microscopic organisms that transmit the disease) cannot cross the placental barrier until the 18th prenatal week. This is fortunate in one sense, for the disease can be diagnosed with a blood test and treated with antibiotics long before it could harm the fetus. However, the mother who receives no treatment runs the risk of miscarrying or of giving birth to a child who has serious eye, ear, bone, or brain damage (Miller, 1976; see also Table 4-2).

Rh disease.   Rh disease is not really a disease but, rather, a complication that can result when there is an incompatibility of blood type between a mother and her fetus. The term *Rh* stands for a protein substance that is produced by a dominant gene and is present in the blood of 86% of all human beings (although there are some ethnic and racial variations). The **Rh factor** becomes a problem in the 10–12% of all marriages in which the

---

anytime malformations: *congenital defects that could have been caused by teratogens at any point during the prenatal period.*

rubella (German measles): *a disease that has little effect on a mother but may cause a number of serious birth defects in unborn children who are exposed in the first 3–4 months of pregnancy.*

syphilis: *a common venereal disease that may cross the placental barrier in the middle and later stages of pregnancy, causing miscarriage or serious birth defects.*

TABLE 4-2. Some diseases that may affect an embryo, fetus, or newborn

Sexually transmitted diseases	Effects on the fetus or newborn
Gonorrhea	Major hazard is that the gonococcus organism may attack the eyes of a child passing through an infected birth canal. Infections are treated with silver nitrate eyedrops immediately after birth. If left untreated, gonorrhea can blind the child within two days.
Herpes simplex (genital herpes)	Although the herpes virus may cross the placental barrier, most infections occur at birth as the newborn comes in contact with herpes lesions on the mother's genitals. The infection can cause eye damage and serious brain damage. There is no cure for this disease. Mothers with active genital herpes often undergo a Cesarean delivery (see Box 4-3) to avoid infecting their babies.
Syphilis	Untreated syphilis may cause miscarriage or several serious birth defects (see text). Occasionally babies of untreated mothers are born without showing any syphilitic symptoms. If this "latent" syphilis is not detected and treated, it will produce severe consequences 5 to 15 years later. The most common problems include blindness, deterioration of the central nervous system, and congestive heart failure. The vast majority of children who have long-term (tertiary) syphilis will die from its complications.

Other maternal conditions or diseases	Effects on the fetus or newborn
Chicken pox	Does not produce fetal malformations but may lead to spontaneous abortion or premature delivery. A premature infant who has chicken pox is usually very weak and likely to die.
Cholera	Interferes with the transfer of oxygen from mother to fetus. Infection during the third trimester is likely to kill the fetus (resulting in a stillbirth).
Cytomegalovirus	Produces no symptoms in adults but may produce microcephaly (small head), brain damage, and blindness in the embryo or fetus. May also induce miscarriages.
Diabetes	Diabetics face a greater risk of delivering a stillborn fetus or a child who will die in the first few days after birth. Babies of diabetics may have any of a number of malformations. They are often very large because they have accumulated a large amount of fat during the third trimester. Although a diabetic mother requires special care to prevent the death of her child, more than 85% of these children currently survive.

man is Rh positive and the woman Rh negative— that is, she has no Rh factor in her blood.

The problem is this: When an Rh-positive baby is about to be born to an Rh-negative mother, fetal blood cells containing the Rh factor may cross the deteriorating placental barrier and enter the mother's bloodstream. The Rh-negative mother then produces Rh antibodies, which remain permanently within her body. In any later pregnancy, these Rh antibodies may then cross the placental barrier, where they enter the fetal bloodstream and begin to attack and destroy the fetus's red blood cells. This results in **erythroblastosis,** or Rh disease, a complication that can produce serious birth defects such as deafness, cerebral palsy, mental retardation, or even death. A first child will ordinarily not be affected, because the Rh-negative mother will not come into contact with Rh-positive blood (and produce antibodies) until she gives birth to her first baby.

Fortunately, Rh disease can now be controlled. When an Rh-negative mother gives birth to an Rh-positive child, she is now given a vaccine called **Rhogam** within 72 hours after delivering. Rhogam prevents the mother from forming Rh antibodies and thereby protects her future children against Rh disease.

Of course, it is likely that some Rh-negative mothers will not be identified as Rh negative (or will not receive Rhogam) after delivering a child.

TABLE 4-2. Some diseases that may affect an embryo, fetus, or newborn *(continued)*

Other maternal conditions or diseases	*Effects on the fetus or newborn*
Hepatitis	A child born to a mother with hepatitis is likely to have this disease. The infection is thought to occur during the birth process when the fetus swallows infected maternal blood that may be present as the umbilical cord separates from the placenta.
Hypertension (chronic high blood pressure)	Increases the probability of miscarriage and infant death. The higher a woman's blood pressure, the greater the likelihood of prenatal complications.
Influenza	The more powerful strains can induce spontaneous abortion or produce a number of abnormalities during the early stages of pregnancy.
Mumps	Although this is a relatively mild disease, even in adults, perhaps as many as 27% of affected fetuses will die within the womb and be spontaneously aborted or stillborn.
Rubella	See text.
Smallpox	This disease is particularly troublesome because the mother's immunity (by vaccination) does nothing to protect her embryo or fetus. Although smallpox does not induce malformations, it does increase the risk of spontaneous abortion and stillbirth.
Toxemia (eclampsia)	Toxemia of pregnancy is a disorder of unknown origin that affects about 5% of pregnant women in the United States during the third trimester. Its mildest form, called *preeclampsia,* mainly affects the mother and includes symptoms such as high blood pressure, rapid weight gain, and protein in the urine. Untreated preeclampsia may worsen and become *eclampsia,* a condition that may cause maternal convulsions and coma. About half the unborn children and 10–15% of affected mothers will die from eclampsia; surviving infants are likely to suffer brain damage.
Toxoplasmosis	About one-fourth of adults have had this mild disease, which produces symptoms similar to a common cold. The agent responsible is a parasite present in raw meat and cat feces. If a medical exam reveals that a woman has no antibodies against toxoplasmosis, she should avoid undercooked meat and locations where cat feces are likely to be present (for example, garden, pet's litter box) during her pregnancy. Toxoplasmosis is a powerful teratogen that can produce serious eye or brain damage and possibly even kill an unborn child.

However, the later-born children of these women are not doomed by any means; Rh disease can be detected through amniocentesis, and the prognosis for an affected child is excellent. The child will ordinarily receive periodic transfusions of new blood—a lifesaving strategy that can be administered even before birth (Browne & Dixon, 1978).

■ *Drugs*

People have long suspected that drugs taken by pregnant women could have any number of harmful effects on unborn children. Even Aristotle thought as much when he noted that many drunken mothers have feeble-minded babies

Rh factor: *a protein in the blood of about 86% of the general population; people who have this substance in their blood are Rh positive; those who lack it are Rh negative.*

erythroblastosis: *a condition (also called Rh disease) in which antibodies produced by an Rh-negative mother attack the red blood cells of an Rh-positive fetus; if untreated, Rh disease can kill a fetus or cause serious birth defects.*

Rhogam: *a vaccine given to Rh-negative mothers that prevents the formation of Rh antibodies and protects Rh-positive children from erythroblastosis.*

TABLE 4-3. Partial list of drugs that affect (or are thought to affect) the fetus or the newborn

Drug	Effect on the fetus or newborn

Antibiotics
  Streptomycin
  Terramycin
  Tetracycline
	Heavy use of streptomycin by mothers can produce hearing loss. Terramycin and tetracycline may be associated with premature delivery, retarded skeletal growth, cataracts, and a staining of the baby's teeth.

Anticoagulants	These agents increase the risk of fetal hemorrhage or death if the mother receives heavy doses.

Anticancer agents
  Amniopterin
  Amethopterin
	A number of congenital anomalies have been reported.

Alcohol	Small head, facial abnormalities, heart defects, low birth weight, and intellectual retardation (see text).
Aspirin and other salicylates	If used in large quantities, these drugs may cause neonatal bleeding and gastrointestinal discomfort. (Other defects have been reported in studies with animals.)
Anticonvulsants	May produce heart defects and anomalies such as cleft lip (failure of the two sides of the upper lip to grow together).
Barbiturates	All barbiturates cross the placental barrier. In clinical doses they cause the fetus or newborn to be lethargic. In large doses they may cause anoxia (oxygen starvation) or interfere with the baby's breathing.

Hallucinogens
  LSD
  Marijuana
  Mescaline
	Suspected to cause chromosome damage, spontaneous abortion, and behavioral abnormalities among newborn infants (see text).

Narcotics
  Codeine
  Heroin
  Methadone
  Morphine
	Addiction increases the risk of premature delivery. Moreover, the fetus is often addicted to the narcotic agent, and this addiction results in a number of complications (see text).

Sex hormones
  Androgens,
  progestogens, estrogens,
  DES (diethylstilbestrol)
	Sex hormones contained in birth control pills and drugs to prevent miscarriages can have a number of harmful effects, including heart malformations, cervical cancer (in female offspring), masculinization of the fetus, and other anomalies (see text).

Tranquilizers (other than thalidomide)
  Chlorpromazine
  Reserpine
	May produce respiratory distress in newborns.

Tobacco	Cigarette smoking may increase the risk of spontaneous abortion, stillbirth, and infant mortality. Smokers also tend to have small babies (see text).
Vaccines	Routine immunization of the mother with live-virus vaccines should be avoided during pregnancy, except when required for rabies and cholera. The viruses in many vaccines (for example, mumps, measles, rubella, smallpox, polio) are powerful teratogens that are likely to harm the developing embryo or fetus.
Vitamins	Excessive amounts of vitamins A, B6, C, D, and K cause prenatal deformities in many animal species and could conceivably have similar effects on human beings.

(Abel, 1981). Today we know that these suspicions were often correct. Consider what Virginia Apgar has to say about drug use during pregnancy:

"A woman who is pregnant, or thinks she could possibly be pregnant, should not take any drugs whatsoever unless absolutely essential—and then only when prescribed by a physician who is aware of the pregnancy" (Apgar & Beck, 1974, p. 445). Dr. Apgar is very cautious in her recommendation because even mild drugs that have few if any lasting effects on a mother may prove extremely hazardous to a developing embryo or fetus. Unfortunately, the medical community learned this lesson the hard way, as we will see in the pages that follow.

The thalidomide tragedy.   In 1960 a West German drug company began to market a mild tranquilizer, sold over the counter, that was said to alleviate the periodic nausea (morning sickness) that many women experience during the first trimester of pregnancy. Presumably, the drug was perfectly safe; in tests on pregnant rats it had had no ill effects on mothers or offspring. The drug was **thalidomide.**

What came to pass quickly illustrated that drugs that appear harmless in tests with laboratory animals may turn out to be violent teratogens for human beings. Thousands of women who had used thalidomide during the first two months of pregnancy were suddenly giving birth to defective children. And the birth defects were horrible: thalidomide babies often had badly deformed eyes, ears, noses, and hearts and a variety of lesser malformations, such as fusing of the fingers and toes. But perhaps the most striking of all birth defects produced by this powerful teratogen was **phocomelia**—a structural abnormality in which all or parts of the limbs are missing and the feet or hands may be attached directly to the torso like flippers.

Doctors soon discovered that the kinds of birth defects produced by thalidomide depended on when the drug was taken. Babies of mothers who had taken the drug on or around the 35th day after their last menstrual period were likely to be born without ears. Those whose mothers had used thalidomide on the 39th through the 41st day after last menstruation often had grossly deformed arms or no arms at all. If the mother had taken the drug between the 40th and the 46th day, her child might have deformed legs or no legs. However, if she had waited until the 52nd day before using thalidomide, her baby was usually not affected (Apgar & Beck, 1974).

So it took a major tragedy to establish that seemingly harmless prescription and nonprescription drugs could be powerful teratogens. Table 4-3 lists

PHOTO 4-7. *This boy has deformed arms and hands, as well as one deformed leg—three of the birth defects produced by thalidomide.*

a number of commonly used medications and other substances that are either known or suspected causes of birth defects in human beings.

Sex hormones.   In recent years it has become apparent that medications containing sex hormones (or their active biochemical ingredients) can affect a developing embryo or fetus. For example, oral contraceptives contain female sex hormones, and if a woman takes the pill, not knowing that she is pregnant, her unborn child faces a slightly increased risk of heart defects and other cardiovascular problems (Heinonen et al., 1977).

Sex hormones are also components of drugs used to prevent miscarriage. One such hormone,

---

thalidomide: *a mild tranquilizer that, taken early in pregnancy, can produce a variety of malformations of the limbs, eyes, ears, and heart.*
phocomelia: *a prenatal malformation in which all or parts of the limbs are missing.*

progesterone, tends to masculinize the fetus (Browne & Dixon, 1978). The effects are most dramatic in females, who may be born with an enlarged clitoris, fused labia that resemble a scrotum, and increased neuromuscular development. Males exposed to progesterone tend to be active, irritable infants who are quite muscular in appearance. They may also show hypertrophy (overdevelopment) of the penis and scrotum.

One synthetic hormone that can have a tragic long-term effect on daughters is **DES (diethylstilbestrol).** From the mid-1940s through 1965, as many as 2 million women may have taken this drug to prevent miscarriages. The drug seemed safe enough—newborns whose mothers had used DES appeared to be normal in every respect. But in 1971 physicians clearly established that 17- to 21-year-old females whose mothers had used DES while pregnant were at risk for developing several abnormalities of the reproductive organs, including a rare form of cervical cancer (Hamm, 1981). The risk of cancer is not very great—fewer than 1% of DES daughters have developed the disease thus far. However, the oldest women who were exposed to DES before birth are now only 40, and we do not yet know whether they will develop cancer or other problems later in life.

Although it appears that prenatal exposure to DES does not cause cancer in males, a number of DES sons have developed abnormalities of the genital tract, and some of these men are sterile (Cosgrove & Henderson, 1977). The U.S. Department of Health and Human Services now recommends a visit to the doctor for all individuals (male or female) who know that they were exposed to DES before birth. The affected patient should describe what is known about his or her exposure and ask the physician to record this information for future reference and consideration (Hamm, 1981).

Alcohol. In 1973 Kenneth Jones and his colleagues described a **fetal alcohol syndrome (FAS)** that affects many children of alcoholic mothers (Jones, Smith, Ulleland, & Streissguth, 1973). The most noticeable characteristics of fetal alcohol syndrome are defects such as microcephaly (small head) and malformations of the heart, limbs, joints, and face. An affected baby is likely to exhibit abnormal behaviors such as excessive irritability, hyperactivity, seizures, and tremors. At

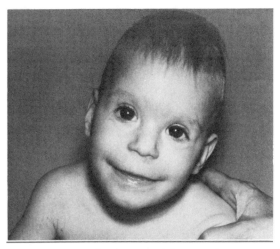

PHOTO 4-8. *This boy's widely spaced eyes, flattened nose, and underdeveloped upper lip are three of the common physical symptoms of fetal alcohol syndrome.*

birth FAS children are smaller and lighter than normal, and their physical growth will lag behind that of normal age mates throughout childhood and adolescence. Moreover, the majority of these children score well below average in intelligence, and many are mentally retarded (Abel, 1981; Streissguth, Herman, & Smith, 1978).

How much alcohol does it take to harm an embryo or fetus? Perhaps a lot less than you might imagine. Recent research indicates that even moderate alcohol consumption (that is, 1–3 ounces a day) by expectant mothers can retard prenatal growth and produce minor physical anomalies or abnormal behavior in newborns (see Abel, 1980; Streissguth, Barr, & Martin, 1983). Even an occasional "drinking binge" could have adverse effects on an unborn child, particularly during the first trimester. Today many doctors are so wary of the potentially harmful consequences of alcohol that they advise pregnant women not to drink at all (B. G. Brown, personal communication, March 1982).

Cigarette smoking. Until recently, neither doctors nor pregnant women had any reason to suspect that an after-dinner cigarette might affect an unborn child. Now we know otherwise. A recent report of the Surgeon General of the United States reviewed more than 200 studies and concluded:

maternal smoking directly retards the rate of fetal growth and increases the risk of spontaneous abortion, of fetal death, and of neonatal death in otherwise normal infants. More important, there is growing evidence that children of smoking mothers [particularly mothers who smoke heavily] *may* have measurable deficiencies in physical growth, intellectual development, and emotional development [U.S. Department of Health, Education and Welfare, 1979, p. ix].

Some researchers have reported that children of smokers show long-term deficits in physical growth and are more likely than children of nonsmokers to experience learning difficulties at school (see Butler & Goldstein, 1973; U.S. Department of Health, Education and Welfare, 1979). Yet it is possible that some factor common to women who smoke other than smoking itself is responsible for these long-term effects. For example, if women who smoke have poorer diets or drink more alcohol than nonsmokers, their dietary inadequacies or alcohol consumption could be responsible for long-term consequences that researchers may have erroneously attributed to smoking.

In one recent study, Monroe Lefkowitz (1981)

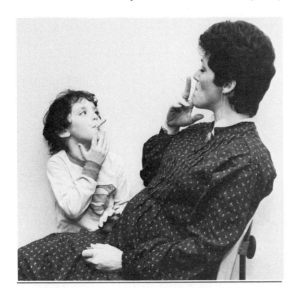

PHOTO 4-9. *A woman who smokes while pregnant may be retarding the growth of her fetus and increasing the risk of birth complications while encouraging her older children to smoke.*

looked at the long-term effects of maternal smoking on 9–11-year-old children. This study was carefully controlled in that mothers who had smoked during pregnancy were comparable to those who did not smoke in age, parity, education, income, and family size—factors known to affect physical growth and intellectual development. Data available on each child in the sample included measures of height, weight, reading ability, classroom achievements, IQ, popularity, and conduct at school. The findings were clear: 9 to 11 years after birth, the children of smokers were no smaller, no less intelligent, and no less achievement oriented, nor were they less well behaved or popular, than the children of nonsmokers.

So the long-term effects of maternal smoking on the developing child are unclear at this time. However, we do know that smoking can have a number of harmful effects on both the smoker and her *unborn* child and that it is a habit that pregnant women (and anyone else who is concerned about his or her health) should undoubtedly avoid (U.S. Department of Health, Education and Welfare, 1979).

Hallucinogens. In view of their popularity as recreational drugs, it is indeed unfortunate that we do not know more about the possible teratogenic effects of marijuana, LSD, mescaline, and other psychoactive agents. Although the evidence is not conclusive, some researchers believe that heavy use of marijuana by pregnant women can inhibit prenatal growth and produce behavioral abnormalities in newborn infants (Fried, 1980;

progesterone: *a female sex hormone that is a component of some drugs used to prevent miscarriage; ironically, this substance appears to masculinize a developing fetus.*

DES (diethylstilbestrol): *a synthetic hormone, prescribed to prevent miscarriage, that can produce cervical cancer in adolescent female offspring and genital-tract abnormalities (and sterility) in males.*

fetal alcohol syndrome (FAS): *a group of congenital problems commonly observed in the offspring of mothers who abuse alcohol during pregnancy.*

Tinklenberg, 1975). Research on the teratogenic effects of LSD are also inconclusive: Some studies have found that women who used LSD before or during pregnancy faced an increased risk of miscarriage, stillbirth, or having babies with a variety of congenital defects, including chromosomal abnormalities (for example, Jacobson & Berlin, 1972). However, it is difficult to tell whether LSD is responsible for these complications, because mothers who use this drug are frequently sick, undernourished, or using other known or suspected teratogens (such as alcohol and narcotic agents).

Narcotic agents: Heroin and methadone.

Although addicting drugs such as codeine, heroin, methadone, and morphine do not appear to produce gross structural abnormalities, they are responsible for other potentially serious complications. For example, the babies of narcotics addicts become addicted in the womb, and about 50% of these children are undersized (Brown, 1979). When deprived of the drug after birth, the addicted infant will experience withdrawal symptoms such as vomiting, dehydration, and convulsions that could prove fatal if not controlled. These unfortunate young addicts will normally continue to receive the addicting agent, but in progressively smaller doses. This treatment prevents severe withdrawal symptoms and allows the child to gradually overcome the addiction.

Methadone is a synthetic opiate often prescribed for addicts as an alternative to heroin. Babies born addicted to this drug are about five times as likely as nonaddicted infants to fall victim to **sudden infant death syndrome** (SIDS), a complication in which apparently healthy infants suddenly stop breathing and die in their sleep (Chavez, Ostrea, Stryker, & Smialek, 1979).

Finally, the behavior of addicted infants is abnormal in several respects. These babies tend to be sluggish, irritable, and inattentive to the environment. In addition, they cry more often than nonaddicted infants and are less likely to cuddle when a caretaker picks them up (Strauss, Lessen-Firestone, Starr, & Ostrea, 1975). Unfortunately, these unpleasant temperamental characteristics may interfere with the emotional bonding that normally occurs between infant and parents and thus may impair the child's later social and emotional development.

■ Environmental hazards

Radiation. Soon after the atomic blasts of 1945 in Hiroshima and Nagasaki, scientists became painfully aware of the teratogenic effects of radiation. Not one pregnant woman who was within one-half mile of these explosions gave birth to a live child. In addition, 75% of the pregnant women who were within a mile and a quarter of the blasts had stillborn infants or seriously handicapped children who died soon after birth (Apgar & Beck, 1974). Even clinical doses of radiation such as those used in diagnostic X rays and cancer treatments can cause mutations, spontaneous abortions, or a variety of serious birth defects—particularly if the mother is exposed during the first trimester of pregnancy.

Unfortunately, no one knows just how much radiation it takes to harm an embryo or a fetus. Today expectant mothers are routinely advised to avoid exposure to X rays unless such treatment is absolutely necessary for their own survival (in these cases, it is assumed that the unborn child may be miscarried, stillborn, or seriously handicapped at birth). In addition, doctors are taught to exercise extreme caution when using radiation on women of childbearing age. Apgar and Beck (1974) recommend that X rays of a woman's pelvis or abdominal region be taken "only during the first two weeks following a menstrual period, so that there is no possibility she could be pregnant without realizing it" (p. 110).

Chemicals and pollutants. In years gone by, a major chemical company in the United States used the advertising slogan "Better things for better living—through chemistry" to extol the virtues of this corporation and its contributions to modern life. Indeed, the benefits of applied chemistry are many. However, we know little about its costs, particularly those affecting unborn children, for very few of the chemicals found in food, cosmetics, and other common household products have been tested for teratogenic effects (Miller, 1976; Streitfeld, 1978).

We do know that heavy or prolonged exposure to many common pesticides can make people sick and produce birth defects in animals. Organic dyes or coloring agents such as Red Dye No. 2, as well as some artificial sweeteners, are suspected carcinogens that may also have teratogenic effects on unborn children (Streitfeld, 1978). Mono-sodium glutamate (MSG), a common additive in processed foods, is known to destroy cultures of cells taken from the central nervous system (Miller, 1976) and could well be a powerful teratogen. Finally, cosmetic products injure as many as 60,000 persons a year in the United States—but the agents responsible for these injuries have not been tested for teratogenic effects.

The air we breathe and the water we drink may contain substances that are potentially harmful to a developing embryo or fetus. In Chicago, for example, 60 tons of industrial dust per square mile are poured into the air every day; in Seattle, automobiles alone saturate the air with more than 1200 tons of hydrocarbons and nitrogen dioxide a week (Miller, 1976). Rural communities are certainly not immune to industrial pollution; some areas may be particularly dangerous to an unborn child (not to mention the mother and anyone else) if mining, chemical, smelting, or cement operations nearby discharge lead, zinc, mercury, or antimony into the air or water. These "heavy metals" are known to impair the physical health and mental abilities of adults and children and to have teratogenic effects (producing physical deformities and mental retardation) on developing embryos and fetuses (Miller, 1976).

It is obviously impractical to advise all pregnant women living in areas of environmental pollution to take up residence elsewhere for the duration of their pregnancies. Such advice, if heeded, would create logistical nightmares and is not warranted on the basis of our current knowledge. But our lack of knowledge is itself a problem. There is a critical need for additional research on the effects of chemicals, additives, wastes, and other environmental hazards on unborn children—research that would permit us to inform an expectant mother of the risks her child would face if she were to carry her pregnancy to term in her normal habitat.

High altitude. Many obstetricians believe that women should not travel by air during the last month of pregnancy. The complication that doctors fear is **anoxia,** or oxygen starvation, a condition that can harm or even kill a fetus, particularly if the mother's placenta is abnormal or is not functioning efficiently. Obstetricians McClure Browne and Geoffrey Dixon (1978) caution women *at all stages of pregnancy* to protect their unborn child against anoxia by avoiding altitudes above 9000 feet. If travel to high altitudes is necessary, the mother should do so before the last month of pregnancy, and then only if she has first undergone a period of altitude acclimatization at elevations of 5000–6000 feet.

Children whose mothers live at high altitudes show the effects of chronic anoxia at birth. In one study (Saco-Pollitt, 1981), babies born at elevations of 14,000 feet in the Peruvian Andes were found to be lighter, shorter, and less active, alert, and cuddly than babies born at sea level. In addition, the "high altitude" infants were also somewhat retarded in their neuromuscular capabilities, although these deficiencies are no longer apparent two months after birth (Haas, 1976). Why were these high-altitude children not seriously harmed by their chronic anoxia? One reason is that the placentas of high-altitude mothers are bigger and have developed more capillaries for efficient distribution of oxygen than those of mothers at sea level. In addition, children born at high altitudes develop larger lungs than their counterparts at sea level. This enlarged lung volume may be an adaptation to high-altitude anoxia that helps to protect the child against long-term deficits in physical growth and neuromuscular development (Saco-Pollitt, 1981).

Sexual intercourse. This is perhaps as good a place as any to dispel the myth that pregnant women should not risk harming their unborn child by having sexual intercourse. Browne and Dixon (1978, p. 52) note that "there is little . . . evidence that intercourse at any time during a normal pregnancy is harmful. However, if bleeding should occur, intercourse is unwise, . . . intercourse should be avoided during the last three weeks of pregnancy [to prevent any possibility of infection] which may complicate labor."

It is important to address this issue because an

---

sudden infant death syndrome: *the unexplained death of a sleeping infant who suddenly stops breathing (also called crib death).*
anoxia: *a lack of sufficient oxygen to the brain; may result in neurological damage or death.*

In their excellent book *Is My Baby All Right?* (1974), Dr. Virginia Apgar and Joan Beck suggest several ways that prospective parents may significantly reduce the likelihood of bearing a defective child. As you read through the list, see whether you can recall why each recommendation makes good sense. In so doing, you will have reviewed much of the material on congenital defects presented in this chapter (as well as Chapter Three).

1. *If you think a close relative has a disorder that might be hereditary, you should take advantage of genetic counseling.* (Do you remember what kinds of services a genetic counselor may offer or suggest? If not, you may wish to review "Prevention and Treatment of Genetic Abnormalities" in Chapter Three.)

2. *The ideal age for a woman to have children is between 20 and 35.* (What complications do older and younger mothers face?)

3. *With every subsequent child, beginning with the third,* * *there is increasing hazard of stillbirth, congenital malformation, and prematurity.* (Do you recall why this is true? If not, you may wish to review the section "Parity" in this chapter.)

4. *Every pregnant woman needs good prenatal care supervised by a physician who keeps current on medical research in the field of teratology and who will help her deliver her baby in a reputable, modern hospital.* (We have not yet examined the birth process and its complications. When we review the pros and cons of "home births," we will see that not everyone agrees that a woman should always give birth in a hospital.)

5. *No woman should become pregnant unless she is sure that she has either had rubella or been effectively immunized against it.* (What defects can rubella cause? When during pregnancy is the disease particularly dangerous?)

6. *From the very beginning of pregnancy, a woman should do everything possible to avoid exposure to contagious diseases.* (Do you remember the teratogenic effects of congenital syphilis, gonorrhea, herpes, and other infectious agents? If not, you may wish to review Table 4-2 and the section of this chapter entitled "Maternal Diseases.")

7. *Pregnant women should avoid eating undercooked red meat or contact with any cat (or cat feces) that may carry toxoplasmosis infection.* (What are the possible consequences of toxoplasmosis for the mother? For her unborn child?)

8. *A pregnant woman should not take any drugs unless absolutely essential—and then only when prescribed by a physician who is aware of the pregnancy.* (Do you remember the effects of DES, alcohol, the hallucinogens, narcotics, and other commonly used substances? If not, you may wish to review Table 4-3 and the section of this chapter entitled "Drugs.")

9. *Unless it is absolutely essential for her own well-being, a pregnant woman should avoid radiation treatments and X-ray examinations.* (What are the possible consequences of such examinations or treatments for the unborn child? How did scientists become aware of the teratogenic effects of radiation?)

10. *Cigarettes should not be smoked during pregnancy.* (Why not? Does a mother's cigarette smoking during pregnancy have long-term effects on her children?)

11. *A prospective mother who is Rh negative should make sure her physician takes the necessary steps to protect her unborn baby and all subsequent children from Rh disease.* (How are subsequent children protected? How do doctors treat a baby who is suffering from Rh disease?)

12. *A nourishing diet, rich in proteins and adequate in total calories, is essential during pregnancy.* (What are the short-term effects of maternal malnutrition on the developing child? Other than adequate nourishment, what else might the fetally malnourished child require in order to develop normally after birth? Should a pregnant woman take large amounts of extra vitamins in order to ensure that her fetus is healthy?)

---

*As noted earlier in the chapter, some experts believe that complications associated with parity are unlikely unless a woman has had more than four children.

---

expectant parent who refrains from sex thinking it harmful may cause arguments or other forms of marital discord that can upset the mother (and her fetus), thereby increasing the probability of obstetrical complications. In addition, wife beating during pregnancy is more common than you might imagine, and one of the major reasons is sexual frustration—either the man or the woman won't engage in sex because he or she thinks it is harmful (Gelles, 1975). So it appears that the "no sex" myth may cause infinitely more harm than the sexual act itself. In fact, we might argue that parents who continue to enjoy sex during pregnancy may ultimately be doing their unborn child a favor—assuming, of course, that they follow established medical guidelines.

On the Prevention of Birth Defects

Reading a chapter such as this one can be frightening to anyone who wishes to have a child. It is easy to come away with the impression that "life before birth" is a veritable minefield: after all, so many hereditary accidents are possible, and even a genetically normal embryo or fetus may encounter a large number of potential hazards while developing within the womb.

But clearly there is another side to this story. Recall that the majority of genetically abnormal embryos do not develop to term. And it appears that the prenatal environment is not so hazardous when we note that more than 90% of newborn babies are perfectly normal and that many of the remaining 7–10% have minor congenital problems that are only temporary or correctable (Heinonen et al., 1977). It is true that there *is* reason for concern. However, concerned parents can significantly reduce the odds that their baby will be abnormal if they follow the simple recommendations in Box 4-2. Failure to abide by one or more of the guidelines will not necessarily mean that your child will be defective. Nor will exact compliance guarantee that the child will be healthy—accidents do happen. Following these recommendations may seem rather tedious at times and perhaps unnecessary to women who have already given birth to healthy children. However, Apgar and Beck (1974, p. 452) remind us that "each pregnancy is different. Each unborn child has a unique genetic make-up. The prenatal environment a mother provides is never quite the same for another baby. Thus, we believe no amount of effort is too great to increase the chances that a baby will be born normal, healthy, and without a handicapping birth defect."

THE BIRTH PROCESS

The birth of a child is a dramatic and emotional event for all parties involved. During the last few weeks of pregnancy, it is natural for parents to be apprehensive about labor and childbirth, particularly if this is their first child. In fact, it is not at all uncommon for primiparous (first-time) mothers to fear that they will be "out of control" in the delivery room, thinking that they may be damaged or disfigured by the delivery (Grossman,

Eichler, & Winickoff, 1980). Once the child is born, mothers (and fathers if they are present) almost always report feeling physically exhausted and relieved that the negative aspects of labor and delivery are things of the past. As they hold their newborn baby, many parents seem awestruck by the realization that *they* have actually created life.

Now let's consider the baby. In its waning hours as a fetus, a relatively carefree existence is coming to an end. Suddenly, a force stronger than the fetus is thrusting it from its comfortable lie within the uterus through a passageway that is smaller and tighter than anything it has ever experienced. After several hours of this, the child emerges into the light, draws a breath, and takes up residence in a strange new world.

Do you think babies are traumatized by the events of birth? Or are they "numb," indifferent, or awestruck? Think about this issue as we take a look at the normal birth and the typical reactions of parents to this event.

The Normal Birth

Childbirth is a three-stage process (see Figure 4-5). The **first stage of labor** begins as the mother experiences uterine contractions spaced at 10–15-minute intervals, and it ends when her cervix has fully dilated so that the fetus's head can pass through. This phase lasts an average of 8–14 hours for first-born children and 3–8 hours for later-borns. As labor proceeds, the uterus contracts more frequently and the contractions become more intense. When the head of the fetus is positioned at the cervical opening, the second phase of labor is about to begin.

The **second stage of labor,** delivery, begins as the fetus's head passes through the cervix into the vagina and ends when the baby emerges from the mother's body. This is the time when the mother may be told to bear down (push) with each con-

---

first stage of labor: *the period of the birth process lasting from the first regular uterine contraction until the cervix is fully dilated.*
second stage of labor: *the period of the birth process during which the fetus moves through the vaginal canal and emerges from the mother's body (also called the delivery).*

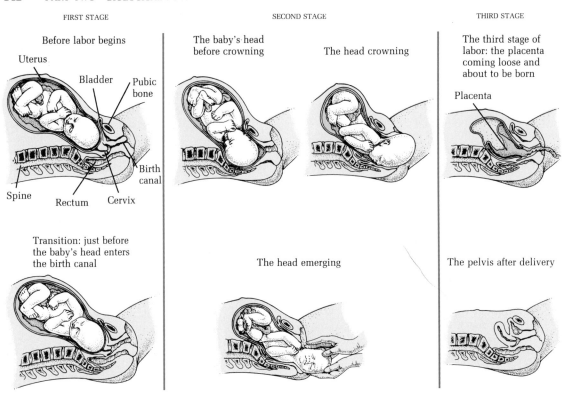

FIRST STAGE   SECOND STAGE   THIRD STAGE

Before labor begins

Uterus

Bladder   Pubic bone

Birth canal

Spine   Rectum   Cervix

The baby's head before crowning

The head crowning

The third stage of labor: the placenta coming loose and about to be born

Placenta

Transition: just before the baby's head enters the birth canal

The head emerging

The pelvis after delivery

FIGURE 4-5. The three phases of childbirth.

traction to assist her child through the birth canal. A quick delivery may take a half hour, whereas a long one may last more than an hour and a half.

The **third stage of labor** takes only a few minutes as the uterus once again contracts and expels the placenta from the mother's body.

■ *The parents' experience*

Although many women are exhilarated by the product of their labor, few enjoy the process; childbirth is an exhausting ordeal that can be rather painful. Obviously, physical factors such as the relative size of the mother's pelvis and the baby's head will affect the length of labor and the amount of discomfort a woman experiences. However, psychological factors such as the mother's attitude toward her pregnancy, her knowledge about the birth process, and even the presence of the father are important determinants of her reactions to childbirth.

In many Western societies, expectant mothers are advised to prepare for their day in the delivery room by attending childbirth classes. Almost all these classes inform the mother (and, ideally, her mate) what to expect during labor. They also teach breathing patterns and methods of relaxation that are thought to make the process of giving birth a little easier. The childbirth class may also give a woman the impression that she has the support of others and will not be undertaking the rigors of childbirth on her own. Apparently this prenatal training does affect the mother's experience: women who regularly attend childbirth classes are more relaxed during labor and view the process as "easier" than those who do not receive instruction (Klusman, 1975; Shereshefsky & Yarrow, 1973).

Effects of father's involvement. The father's participation is also important. When fathers are present in the delivery room, women experience less pain, use less medication, and are likely to feel much more positive about the whole birth process (Grossman et al., 1980; Henneborn &

Cogan, 1975). In addition, fathers who are present or nearby at birth often become fascinated with their neonate, wishing to touch, hold, and caress the baby (Greenberg & Morris, 1974; Peterson, Mehl, & Liederman, 1979). Consider the reaction of one young father: "When I come up to see [my] wife . . . I go look at the kid and then I pick her up and then I put her down . . . I keep going back to the kid. It's like a magnet. That's what I can't get over, the fact that I feel like that" (Greenberg & Morris, 1974, p. 524).

This **"engrossment"** with the newborn is thought to be a form of emotional bonding that increases the father's sense of involvement with his child. Indeed, Greenberg and Morris (1974) found that fathers who had handled and helped care for their babies in the hospital subsequently spent more time with them at home than other fathers who had not had these early interactions with their newborns.

Natural childbirth.   Some obstetricians believe that childbirth is a perfectly natural process that should cause little if any discomfort to women who are both physically and psychologically prepared for the event. The **natural childbirth** movement arose from the work of Grantly Dick-Read, in England, and Fernand Lamaze, in France. These two obstetricians were surprised to find that many women were giving birth painlessly, without medication, if they had been taught to associate childbirth with pleasant feelings and to ready themselves for the process by learning exercises, breathing methods, and relaxation techniques that we now know make childbirth easier (Dick-Read, 1933/1972; Lamaze, 1958). In recent years many women have opted for natural childbirth as scientists began to report that the pain-killing drugs often given during labor could have adverse effects on a baby.

Couples who decide on a natural childbirth will typically attend classes for 8 to 12 weeks before the delivery. They will learn a set of prescribed exercises and relaxation techniques, and the father will become a coach who assists the mother to train her muscles and perfect her breathing for the event that lies ahead. The couple may also visit a delivery room and become familiar with the procedures used there so that they will be less apprehensive when the big day arrives. Although natural childbirth classes do make the childbirth

process easier for couples who diligently apply themselves to the training, many women will still experience discomfort during labor—particularly those who have small pelvic openings or who are delivering large babies. Today most obstetricians tell their natural childbirth patients that they should not hesitate to authorize a physician's assistance (including anesthesia) if they are experiencing a lot of pain. A natural childbirth patient who must resort to drugs to ease her discomfort should not feel discouraged, for her prior training may have enabled her to use less of these potentially harmful substances than she would otherwise have needed.

Postpartum depression.   About 3–8 days after giving birth, many new mothers find that they are depressed, irritable, easily upset, and possibly even resentful of their babies. Ironically, the mothers who are happiest during the last months of pregnancy are the most likely to suffer these "baby blues" (Dalton, 1980). Most women overcome their **postpartum depression** within days or weeks, but as many as 10–15% experience clinical signs of hopelessness or despair that may last for months. Surprisingly, mothers of healthy infants are just as likely to experience postpartum depression as mothers whose babies died or were abnormal (Dalton, 1980).

Any of several factors may contribute to the baby blues. Analgesic and sedative drugs taken during childbirth are known to have a depressive effect on mood. A young mother may also feel depressed and resentful because friends and family are showering the baby with attention while ignoring her own emotional needs. Finally, endo-

---

third stage of labor: *expulsion of the placenta (afterbirth).*

engrossment: *parents' fascination with their neonate; a desire to touch, hold, caress, and talk to the newborn baby.*

natural childbirth: *a delivery in which physical and psychological preparations for the birth are stressed and medical assistance is minimized.*

postpartum depression: *feelings of sadness, resentment, and depression that mothers may experience following a birth (also called the "baby blues").*

crinologists have suggested that postpartum depression may be a psychological reaction to hormonal changes that occur as the mother's body returns from the pregnant state to a normal menstrual cycle (Dalton, 1980). Whatever the cause, it appears that a victim of the baby blues needs the support and attention of her close companions during this difficult time. Katharina Dalton (1980) finds that women who are encouraged to discuss their negative feelings freely with a sympathetic listener are often successful at overcoming them. In England, the Meet-A-Mum-Association (MAMA) has been established to provide depressed young mothers with precisely this kind of emotional support and encouragement.

■ *The baby's experience*
Is birth an unpleasant experience for a baby? Psychoanalyst Otto Rank (1929) believed that it is. After all, a perfectly contented fetus is being expelled from a soft, warm uterus where all its needs are met into a cold, bright world where, for the first time, it will experience chills, pain, hunger, and the startling rush of oxygen into the lungs. According to Rank, babies delivered after a long and complicated labor were especially traumatized by their births and were likely to remain highly anxious and neurotic throughout life.

In 1975 a French obstetrician named Frederick Leboyer attracted a lot of attention by reviving many of Rank's ideas (ideas that had even been dismissed by Rank's mentor, Sigmund Freud). In his popular book *Birth without Violence* (1975), Leboyer objects to common obstetrical practices such as a hasty severing of the umbilical cord, striking the infant to stimulate breathing, weighing the infant on cold metal scales, startling the baby by placing silver nitrate in his or her eyes, and separating the baby from the mother soon after birth—procedures that he describes as the "torture of the innocents." Leboyer believes that birth can be made much less traumatic for a child through his method of **gentle birthing.**

In a gentle birth, the delivery room is quiet and the bright lights are dimmed as the baby emerges. The infant is then placed on the mother's stomach and is caressed or massaged until the umbilical cord stops pulsating and the child is breathing freely on his or her own. After the umbilical cord is severed, the child is placed in a warm bath to simulate the conditions experienced in the womb.

Every attempt is made to eliminate all possible sources of discomfort and to make the child's first several minutes as pleasant as possible. Leboyer (1975) contends that babies who experience gentle births are happy little people who are likely to elicit highly favorable, loving reactions from their parents.

The Leboyer method of gentle birthing is highly controversial. Many obstetricians fear that potentially harmful complications may pass undetected and remain untreated if neonates are examined in dimly lit rooms (B. G. Brown, 1982). In addition, there is no solid evidence that infants who experience gentle birthing are any more calm or blissful than those who undergo standard obstetrical procedures (Hamilton, 1979). Finally, there is reason to believe that birth is not especially traumatic for a neonate. Aidan MacFarlane (1977) has carefully observed newborn babies and noted that most of them quiet down rapidly and begin to cope with their new surroundings soon after that first loud cry. Nevertheless, Leboyer and his followers have had an impact on obstetrical practices. Although newborn babies are rarely given warm baths in dim rooms, they are now routinely handed to their mothers for soothing and comforting soon after they are born.

■ *The older child's experience*
The birth of a child is a mixed blessing for other children in the family, who may feel deserted when the mother leaves for the hospital and neglected after she returns. Recently, Carol Kendrick and Judy Dunn (1980) found that older children are likely to seek attention by doing something naughty while the mother is feeding or caring for a new baby. These actions may well arise from jealousy, for mothers were found to pay less attention to their older children after the birth of a baby.

One implication of these findings is that parents should set time aside for their older children to let them know that they are still loved and considered important members of the family. However, this can be overdone. When Dunn and Kendrick (1981) followed up on their original sample, they found that older children (particularly girls) who were showered with attention during the weeks after the baby was born were the ones who played *least* with their baby brothers and sisters 14 months later. Surprisingly, the older children who were more positive toward

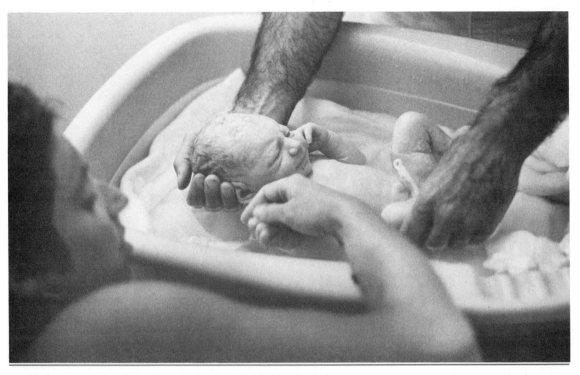

PHOTO 4-10. The Leboyer method of gentle birthing includes immersing the infant in a warm bath soon after birth to simulate the conditions the baby experienced in the womb.

their younger brothers or sisters were those whose mothers had not permitted them to brood or act naughty during the first few weeks after the birth of the baby. The challenge for parents, then, is to control the jealous reactions of the older child while making him or her feel important and wanted. Both the father and the mother can help by taking turns tending to the baby so that the other parent can spend more time with the older children. Parents might also make it easier on older children by stressing their competencies and inviting them to lend a hand in feeding, bathing, or changing the baby.

Complications of Birth

Occasionally a childbirth will not proceed as smoothly as indicated in the earlier account of the "normal" delivery. A number of factors can complicate the process, and some of these complications may have harmful long-term effects on the child.

■ *Anoxia*

Babies who are deprived of oxygen during or just after birth are said to be suffering from anoxia. In many cases of anoxia, the child's supply of oxygen is interrupted because the umbilical cord has become pinched or tangled during childbirth. However, anoxia may also occur after birth if sedatives given to the mother should cross the placental barrier and interfere with the baby's breathing or if mucus ingested during childbirth becomes lodged in the baby's throat. The birth of an anoxic child is a medical emergency: if a baby's brain is deprived of oxygen for more than a few minutes, the infant may suffer serious brain damage and possibly even die. The areas of the brain most noticeably

> **gentle birthing:** *Leboyer's method of childbirth, in which the neonate is comforted, massaged, shielded from unpleasant sensory stimulation, and bathed in warm water in an attempt to reduce any traumas associated with birth.*

Thousands of infants are saved each year because the medical profession has devised reasonably effective ways of anticipating and handling various complications of birth. Some of these lifesaving practices and procedures are as follows.

In utero monitoring. Doctors can now determine the size and positioning of a fetus with *ultrasound.* The attendant uses a hand-held transmitter to scan the mother's abdomen, and deflected sound waves are then converted to a visual image of the fetus on a TV monitor. Use of ultrasound permits the attending physician to anticipate birth complications long before the mother reaches the critical second stage of labor, when a doctor's indecision could cost the baby its life. If the ultrasonic image (called a *sonogram*) reveals that the fetus is extremely large or that its position in the womb would suggest a difficult delivery, the obstetrician may decide to deliver the child by Cesarean section.

Once the amniotic sac has broken and the fetus assumes a normal head-first position at the cervical opening, a second method of fetal monitoring is possible. Doctors can place an electrode in the scalp of the unborn child to monitor its heartbeat and the amount of oxygen in its blood. This procedure is likely to be used if the mother has had a long and complicated first stage of labor, which increases the likelihood of fetal anoxia (Apgar & Beck, 1974). If the fetus's heartbeat slows or its oxygen supply is diminished, the obstetrician may then accelerate the birth process in order to prevent severe anoxia.

Use of obstetrical forceps. One way to hasten the birth process is to perform a *forceps delivery.* An obstetrical forceps is an instrument resembling an oversized pair of salad tongs that is used to grasp the baby's head in order to pull it through the pelvis and the birth canal. This procedure is particularly useful if the child is suffering from anoxia or experiencing considerable pressure to the skull that could cause cranial hemorrhage (and brain damage). However, forceps must be used with extreme caution: the skull of a fetus is very soft, and overzealous use of this instrument (applying too much pressure) may cause the very problems that it is designed to prevent—that is, cranial bleeding and brain damage.

Cesarean section. A Cesarean section, or delivery through an incision in the mother's abdominal wall and uterus, may be necessary under any of the following conditions: (1) if the mother's pelvis is very small or if her baby is quite large, (2) if the baby is in the breech or transverse (crosswise) position and re-

affected are those that control motor activities. Severe anoxia is one of the major causes of *cerebral palsy,* a motor disability in which the affected individual has difficulties controlling muscles of the arms, legs, or head (Apgar & Beck, 1974).

Children suffering from mild anoxia are often irritable at birth and may score below average on tests of motor development and concept formation during the first three years of life (Sameroff & Chandler, 1975). However, these differences between mildly anoxic and normal children eventually lessen to the point that they are no longer apparent by age 7 (Corah, Anthony, Painter, Stern, & Thurston, 1965). So at present there is no compelling evidence that *mild* anoxia has any detrimental long-term effects on children's motor abilities or intellectual development.

■ *Abnormal positioning of the fetus*
Nine times out of ten, a fetus will be born head first. Some, however, are born feet or buttocks first—a condition known as a **breech birth.** The breech presentation is hazardous because the birth process takes longer, increasing the likelihood of anoxia and its complications. Although the majority of breech babies are perfectly normal and healthy at birth, about 2% of children delivered this way will have cerebral palsy (Apgar & Beck, 1974).

Perhaps one fetus in a hundred will be lying sideways in the uterus, a position that makes normal vaginal delivery nearly impossible. The fetus must either be turned so that it assumes a head-first position or else be born by *Cesarean section*, a surgical procedure in which an incision is made in the mother's abdomen and uterus.

■ *Obstetric medications*
In the United States, as many as 95% of mothers receive some kind of drug (and often several) while giving birth (Brackbill, 1979). These drugs may include analgesics and anesthetics to reduce pain, sedatives to relax the mother, and stimulants

sists all attempts at repositioning, (3) if fetal monitoring reveals that the baby is distressed or anoxic during the first stage of labor, or (4) if the placenta is obstructing the cervical opening.

Medical advances of the past 20 years have made Cesarean sections almost as safe as vaginal deliveries. Indeed, Cesarean deliveries have tripled since 1970 and now account for 10–15% of births at many hospitals (Brackbill, 1979).* One advantage of the surgical birth is that doctors can often deliver a baby within 5–10 minutes after anesthetizing the mother and thereby avoid exposing the infant to heavy doses of obstetric medication. But there are disadvantages as well. In a vaginal delivery, mucus is forced from the child's lungs as the baby is pushed through the cervix and the birth canal. In contrast, Cesarean babies will be born with more mucus in their lungs—a complication that can cause respiratory problems. And should a Cesarean baby have difficulty breathing and require immediate medical attention, the resulting separation from parents may hinder the emotional bonding that might otherwise begin to develop in the first few minutes after birth.

The isolette, or "incubator." Babies who are born before the 36th week of pregnancy are immature in many ways. For example, they have not developed the layer of subcutaneous fat that helps to protect full-term babies against fluctuations in temperature.

They are also sensitive to infection, and their lungs may not have enough surfactin, a substance that helps full-term infants to breathe. As a result, many premature infants are unprepared for life outside the womb and require some help in order to survive. The standard procedure in most hospitals is to take preterm babies from their parents and place them in a transparent compartment known as an isolette, where they will often remain for several weeks. The isolette saves young, delicate lives by maintaining the infant's body temperature at a safe level and shielding the child from infection. However, isolette rearing makes close contact with others difficult at best and thus may hinder the development of affectionate emotional bonds between infants and their parents.

*The increase in Cesarean deliveries is, in part, attributable to the more sophisticated techniques that are available for detecting fetal distress. But it has also been argued that some doctors may rely too heavily on Cesarean sections because this technique is convenient, more easily scheduled, and (compared with a complicated vaginal delivery) less likely to result in a malpractice suit (B. G. Brown, personal communication, March 1982). The critics point out that a Cesarean section is a form of major abdominal surgery, which always carries some risk to the patient. Consequently, they believe that it should never be used when a vaginal delivery is possible without undue risk.

to induce or intensify uterine contractions. Obviously, these agents are administered in the hope of making the birth process easier for the mother. But we now know that birth medications may have undesirable consequences for the child and that some of these effects may linger as long as one year after birth (and possibly much longer).

Yvonne Brackbill and her associates (Brackbill, 1979; Brackbill & Broman, cited in Kolata, 1979) have found that babies whose mothers received relatively large doses of obstetrical medication were atypical in several respects: they smiled infrequently, were generally sluggish and irritable, and were difficult to feed or cuddle during the first few weeks of life. Unfortunately, these undesirable characteristics may make it difficult for parents to become highly involved with or emotionally attached to their infant (Murray, Dolby, Nation, & Thomas, 1981). To make matters worse, Brackbill and Broman (cited in Kolata, 1979) found, babies of heavily medicated mothers continued to show deficits in physical and mental

development for at least one year after birth. The children most affected by obstetric medication were those whose mothers had inhaled anesthetics, such as nitrous oxide, while giving birth.

Why do children show any long-term effects from a single brief exposure to birth medications? There may be several reasons. First, a dose of medication sufficient to calm or anesthetize a 140-pound woman is likely to have a much greater impact on a 7-pound baby. Second, newborn children have immature circulatory and excretory systems that may take days or even weeks to purge the body of powerful drugs. Finally, heavily medicated children get a very slow start. They are initially sluggish and unresponsive to the envi-

> breech birth: *a delivery in which the fetus emerges feet first or buttocks first rather than head first.*

ronment, and it may take them months or even years to catch up with their age mates who were not so heavily medicated at birth.

In view of what we know, should we advise *all* mothers against the use of *all* obstetric medication? Probably not, for these drugs are sometimes beneficial to both mother and child. For example, sedatives given to mothers who are "at risk" (that is, those who are small, oddly built, or delivering large babies) may make labor proceed more smoothly and actually decrease the probability of such complications as severe anoxia (Myers, 1980; Myers & Myers, 1979).[2] We might also note that the majority of mothers receive light to moderate doses of medication that do not seriously affect their babies. To draw firm conclusions about the use of obstetric medication, we must seek to determine what drugs in what doses are likely to harm a child. In the meantime, we might advise medical personnel to use medication sparingly, while encouraging expectant mothers to attend childbirth classes and to perfect the techniques taught there so that they will possibly require less medication when they deliver their babies.

Complications of Low Birth Weight

About 90% of babies in the United States are born between the 37th and 43rd weeks of pregnancy and are considered "timely" (Guttmacher, 1973). The average full-term, or "timely," infant is 19–21 inches long and weighs about 3500 grams.

Until recently, the 8–9% of infants who weighed less than 2500 grams (5 1/2 pounds) at birth were simply labeled "premature." Yet there are actually two kinds of low-birth-weight babies. Some infants are small at birth even though they are born very close to their due dates; these babies are called **small for date** (Kopp & Parmelee, 1979). However, the majority of undersized babies are born more than three weeks before their due dates and are called "preterm," or **short gestation**, in-

[2]Myers (1980; Myers & Myers, 1979) points out that barbiturates, in appropriate doses, will depress fetal metabolism and prolong the brain's tolerance for oxygen deprivation. These drugs also reduce the activity of the mother's sympathetic nervous system and thereby increase uterine blood flow and the supply of oxygen to the fetus. Excessively high doses, however, can slow fetal metabolism to a point that anoxia is likely.

fants. Both low birth weight and short gestation are factors that affect the child's ability to survive and to develop normally outside the womb (Kopp & Parmelee, 1979).

What are the causes of low birth weight? We have already seen that mothers who smoke and drink heavily, who are malnourished, or who are in their teens are likely to deliver low-birth-weight babies. Moreover, some illnesses, such as preeclampsia (see Table 4-2), or any accident that impairs the functioning of the placenta can retard fetal growth and result in a baby who is premature or small for date (Browne & Dixon, 1978). Yet another frequent contributor to undersized babies is multiple births. One set of quadruplets recently born in Macon, Georgia, for example, weighed between 499 and 1089 grams each (1.1–2.4 pounds). Multiple fetuses generally gain much less weight than a singleton after the 27th week of pregnancy. And in addition to being small for date, triplets and quadruplets rarely develop to term in the uterus; in fact, they are likely to be born 5 to 12 weeks early (B. G. Brown, personal communication, March 1982; Browne & Dixon, 1978).

■ Short-term consequences of low birth weight

The most trying task for the low-birth-weight child is simply surviving the first few days of life. Although more and more of these infants are surviving each year, better than 50% of those who weigh less than 1500 grams (3 1/4 pounds) die at birth or shortly thereafter (Kessner, 1973). Small-for-date children are often malformed, undernourished, or genetically abnormal—factors that will obviously hinder them as they struggle to survive. Moreover, short-gestation infants are likely to experience a number of additional problems as a consequence of their general immaturity (see Box 4-3). Their most serious difficulty is breathing. A preterm infant often has very little *surfactin*, a substance that normally coats the lungs during the last three to four weeks of pregnancy to prevent them from collapsing. A deficiency of surfactin may result in **hyaline membrane disease** (respiratory distress syndrome). Children who develop this serious respiratory ailment will breath very irregularly, and they may stop breathing altogether.

Short-gestation infants often spend their first few weeks of life in heated isolettes that maintain

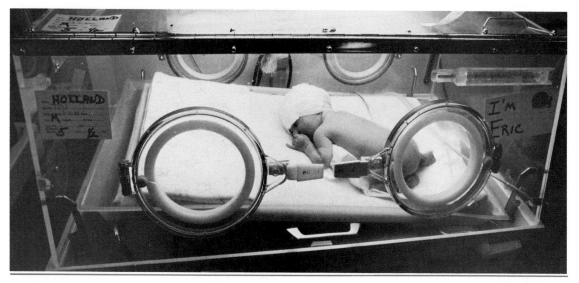

PHOTO 4-11. *Isolettes do isolate. The holes in the apparatus allow parents and hospital staff to care for, talk to, and touch the baby, but close, tender cuddling is nearly impossible.*

their body temperature and protect them from infection. Isolettes are aptly named because they do isolate: the infant is fed, cleaned, and changed through a hole in the device that is much too small to allow the visiting parents to cuddle and love their baby in the usual way (see Photo 4-11). But there are also other reasons preterm infants may be difficult to love: they are likely to be tiny, wrinkled, and fragile in appearance, as well as irritable and unresponsive—in short, a far cry from the smiling, animated creatures that appear in ads for baby products. At home, mothers of preterm infants spend as much time (or more) with their babies as mothers of full-term infants but seem more emotionally detached (Brown & Bakeman, 1980; Crnic, Ragozin, Greenberg, Robinson, & Basham, 1983). In addition, a disproportionate number of short-gestation babies are later abused by their parents (Stern, 1973). Perhaps the preterm child's early isolation, forlorn, fragile appearance, and irritable and irregular behavior can disrupt the formation of a positive emotional bond with parents—sometimes to the point that the child elicits abusive rather than affectionate responses.

Ten years ago, hospitals permitted little if any contact with low-birth-weight babies for fear of harming these fragile little creatures. Today parents are encouraged to visit their child often in the hospital and to become emotionally involved dur-

ing their visits by touching, caressing, and talking to their baby. The objective of these early intervention programs is to allow parents to get to know their child and to foster the development of affectionate emotional bonds between all parties involved. But there may be important additional benefits, for babies in intensive care often become less irritable and more responsive and show quicker neurological and mental development if they are periodically rocked, handled, or soothed by the sound of a mother's voice (Rice, 1977; Rose, 1980; Schaefer, Hatcher, & Barglow, 1980).

■ *Long-term consequences of low birth weight.*

Before 1975 many researchers had found that low-birth-weight infants were likely to experience more learning difficulties later in childhood and

small-for-date babies: *babies born close to their due dates but weighing less than 2500 grams.*
short-gestation (preterm) babies: *babies born more than three weeks before their due dates.*
hyaline membrane disease: *a serious respiratory ailment in which the neonate breathes very irregularly and is at risk of dying (also called respiratory distress syndrome).*

to score lower on IQ tests than full-term infants (Caputo & Mandell, 1970; Drillien, 1969). Today we know that the long-term prognosis for these children depends largely on the environment in which they are raised. Most preterm or small-for-date infants who are raised in stable, supportive homes become emotionally attached to their mothers by 12–15 months of age (Rode, Chang, Fisch, & Sroufe, 1981) and show little evidence of serious intellectual impairment or learning difficulties later in life (Cohen & Parmelee, 1983; Sameroff, 1981). However, low-birth-weight children from unstable and economically disadvantaged backgrounds are likely to remain smaller than full-term children and to show long-term deficits in intellectual growth and academic achievement (Drillien, 1969; Kopp & Parmelee, 1979).

Postmaturity

Occasionally a baby is born two or more weeks beyond the expected due date and is labeled **postmature.** Although the vast majority of postmature babies are delivered routinely and will develop normally, they are sometimes smaller than timely babies, and they face a slightly greater risk of anoxia and its complications—perhaps because an aging placenta becomes less efficient at distributing food and oxygen to the fetus (Browne & Dixon, 1978). Should amniocentesis indicate that a postmature fetus is showing signs of malnutrition or anoxic distress, the attending physician may decide to perform a Cesarean section or to **induce labor** by surgically rupturing the amniotic sac, carefully separating the membranes from the wall of the uterus, and/or administering a drug that causes the uterus to contract (B. G. Brown, personal communication, March 1982; MacFarlane, 1977).[3]

Should You Have Your Baby at Home?

Now that natural childbirth has become so popular, more and more couples are deciding to have

[3]Induction of labor is a controversial practice. Mothers who are "induced" experience more discomfort and require more painkilling drugs (MacFarlane, 1977), and their babies run a greater risk of physical injury and other medical complications. For these reasons, many physicians will not induce labor unless it is absolutely necessary.

their babies at home. Proponents of home deliveries argue that the relaxed atmosphere of the home setting has a calming effect on the mother, making her labor quicker and easier. G. J. Kloosterman, professor of obstetrics at the University of Amsterdam, suggests that "childbirth is itself a natural phenomenon [that] in the large majority of cases needs no interference whatsoever—only close observation, moral support, and protection against human meddling" (cited in MacFarlane, 1977, p. 29). Aidan MacFarlane adds: "A healthy woman who delivers spontaneously performs a job that cannot be improved upon. The job can be done in the best way if the woman is self-confident and stays in surroundings where she is the real center as in her own home" (p. 29).

Those who favor the home delivery back their arguments by citing childbirth statistics from Holland, where about half of all babies are born at home with the assistance of a nurse or midwife. In 1973 the mortality rates for Dutch infants were 16.3 per 1000 births for babies delivered in hospitals but only 4.5 per 1000 for babies delivered at home (MacFarlane, 1977). In addition, 60% of mothers who gave birth in hospitals experienced some postpartum depression, compared with 16% for home births. Of course, the infant mortality rate in hospitals may be artificially high in Holland because all mothers who have already experienced (or are likely to experience) prenatal distress or birth complications are instructed to give birth in a hospital. Nevertheless, the low mortality rate for infants born at home suggests that the physical risks of home deliveries are not great for healthy mothers who have received excellent prenatal care.

In spite of the Dutch experience, obstetricians in England and the United States generally advise their patients to forgo home delivery in favor of a well-equipped hospital setting (MacFarlane, 1977; *60 Minutes,* 1982). Last-minute complications can happen to anyone—even to a healthy mother who has previously given birth without incident. Therefore, most doctors believe that it is in the best interests of both mother and infant to treat all deliveries as "high risk" endeavors that may require medical intervention and the use of facilities available only at a hospital.

People in the United States who would like to have a child at home may have trouble finding an obstetrician who will take them as patients (*60*

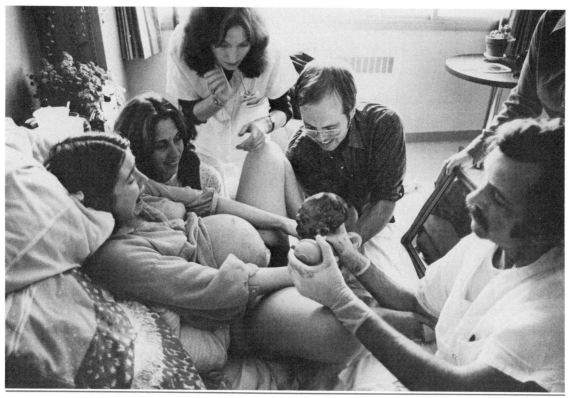

PHOTO 4-12. *Birthing rooms provide many of the comforts of a home delivery within the protective confines of a hospital.*

Minutes, 1982).[4] However, it is now possible to gain many of the advantages of a home delivery in a hospital setting if the hospital maintains birthing rooms. A **birthing room** is a delivery area that is furnished like a typical bedroom (see Photo 4-12). Women who give birth there are permitted (and even encouraged) to have their mates or other close companions present to provide emotional support and perhaps assist with the delivery. And infants who are healthy are often allowed to remain in the same room with their mothers ("rooming in") rather than spending their first few days in the hospital nursery. So the birthing room provides a mother and her infant with many of the comforts of home in a setting that contains all the modern facilities necessary to handle serious complications of birth.

[4]As an alternative, there are a number of certified midwives in the United States who specialize in home deliveries. A certified midwife is usually a registered nurse who has taken an additional one to two years of full-time training in nonsurgical obstetrics at an accredited college. A midwife will typically spend much more time with an expectant mother, use fewer drugs, and rely more on physical and psychological preparations for childbirth than most obstetricians do. To obtain a free list of certified midwives and the cities in which they practice, write to the American College of Nurse-Midwives, 1522 K Street NW, Suite 1120, Washington, D.C. 20005.

---

postmature babies: *babies born two or more weeks beyond their due dates.*
induced labor: *the artificial initiation of uterine contractions by drugs and surgical procedures.*
birthing room: *a hospital delivery area that is furnished like a typical bedroom to provide a homelike atmosphere for childbirth.*

SUMMARY

During the 266 days between conception and birth, the unborn child passes through three successive phases. Within the first two weeks, or germinal period, the single-celled zygote becomes a multicelled blastula that travels down the fallopian tube, implants itself in the uterine lining, and begins to grow.

The second phase of prenatal development lasts from the third through the eighth week of pregnancy and is called the period of the embryo. By the end of this phase, the unborn child is only about an inch long and weighs about 1/10th of an ounce. However, it already bears some resemblance to a human being because most of its organs and body parts have formed or begun to take shape. This is a sensitive period when the organism is particularly susceptible to drugs, diseases, radiation, and other environmental hazards.

From the end of the eighth week until birth is the period of the fetus. As the fetus rapidly grows, the genitals appear, the muscles and bones develop, and all organ systems become integrated in preparation for birth. Between the 24th and 28th weeks, the brain and respiratory system mature to an extent that the fetus attains the age of viability—the point at which survival outside the uterus *may* be possible. At the beginning of the seventh month, the fetus weighs two pounds and is 14–15 inches long. By the end of the ninth month, the full-term fetus will have grown to 19 or 20 inches and will weigh about 7–7½ pounds.

Many environmental influences can complicate prenatal development and the birth process. Among these influences are characteristics of the mother such as her age, emotional state, and number of previous pregnancies. If a mother is malnourished, particularly during the last three months of pregnancy, she runs an increased risk of having a stillborn infant or a premature baby who may fail to survive. In addition, the fetally malnourished child may have fewer brain cells than a well-nourished baby, a liability that could contribute to long-term deficits in intellectual development.

Prenatal development may also be disrupted by teratogens—drugs, diseases, chemicals, and radiation—that can attack the developing embryo or fetus and produce serious birth defects. Teratogens are dangerous throughout pregnancy; however, many of these agents are especially troublesome during the first eight weeks, when the major organs and body parts are developing. Many diseases may produce birth defects; rubella, syphilis, smallpox, and toxoplasmosis are particularly harmful. A large number of drugs, including thalidomide, alcohol, tobacco, hormones, narcotics, and even some antibiotics, are known to cause congenital malformations and complications at birth. In addition, radiation and chemical pollutants such as mercury, lead, and pesticides may have adverse effects on an unborn child.

Childbirth is a three-step process that begins when the uterus contracts and prepares to push the fetus through the cervical opening and ends a few minutes after birth of the baby, when the placenta is expelled from the body. Many women feel exhilarated after giving birth, particularly if the baby's father is present or nearby to provide emotional support. Fathers who watch or participate in the birth process are apt to feel more positive about childbirth and to be more involved with their babies.

Many psychologists believe that babies are insensitive creatures who experience little if any discomfort when they are born. Others believe that birth is extremely traumatic, and they suggest "gentle birthing" as a way of making the process less terrifying.

A new baby is a mixed blessing for an older child, who may feel neglected. Parents can make this period easier by spending time with the older child and inviting him or her to help in caring for the baby.

Complications of birth such as anoxia, breech deliveries, overuse of obstetric medication, and low birth weight may make a baby irritable and unresponsive and may contribute to problems later in childhood, particularly if the child is raised in an unstable or disadvantaged home environment. Fortunately, the problems arising from birth complications are often short-lived.

Some obstetricians believe that mothers should give birth in the familiar surroundings of their own homes; others argue that home deliveries may jeopardize the mother and her infant should complications arise. Today many hospitals maintain birthing rooms—delivery areas furnished like typical bedrooms that provide many of the comforts of home within the protective confines of a hospital.

REFERENCES

Abel, E. L. (1980). Fetal alcohol syndrome: Behavioral teratology. *Psychological Bulletin, 87,* 29–50.

Abel, E. L. (1981). Behavioral teratology of alcohol. *Psychological Bulletin, 90,* 564–581.

Adler, J., & Carey, J. (1982, January 11). But is it a person? *Newsweek,* p. 44.

Apgar, V., & Beck, J. (1974). *Is my baby all right?* New York: Pocket Books.

Ash, P., Vennart, J., & Carter, C. (1977). The incidence of hereditary disease in man. *Lancet, 1,* 849–851.

Associated Press. (1983, April 30). 13 ounces at birth, boy now at 6 lbs. *Atlanta Journal.*

Barrett, D. E., Radke-Yarrow, M., & Klein, R. E. (1982). Chronic malnutrition and child behavior: Effects of early calorie supplementation on socio-emotional functioning at school age. *Developmental Psychology, 18,* 541–556.

Brackbill, Y. (1979). Obstetrical medication and infant behavior. In J. D. Osofsky (Ed.), *Handbook of infant development.* New York: Wiley.

Brown, J. V., & Bakeman, R. (1980). Relationships of human mothers with their infants during the first year of life: Effects of prematurity. In R. W. Bell & W. P. Smotherman (Eds.), *Maternal influence and early behavior.* Jamaica, NY: Spectrum.

Brown, W. A. (1979). *Psychological care during pregnancy and the postpartum period.* New York: Raven Press.

Browne, J. C. M., & Dixon, G. (1978). *Antenatal care.* Edinburgh: Churchill Livingstone.

Butler, N. R., & Goldstein, H. (1973). Smoking in pregnancy and subsequent child development. *British Medical Journal, 4,* 573–575.

Caputo, D. V., & Mandell, W. (1970). Consequences of low birth weight. *Developmental Psychology, 3,* 363–383.

Chavez, C. J., Ostrea, E. M., Stryker, J. C., & Smialek, Z. (1979). Sudden infant death syndrome among infants of drug-dependent mothers. *Journal of Pediatrics, 95,* 407–409.

Cohen, J. E., & Parmelee, A. H. (1983). Prediction of five-year Stanford-Binet scores in preterm infants. *Child Development, 54,* 1242–1253.

Corah, N. L., Anthony, E. J., Painter, P., Stern, J. A., & Thurston, D. (1965). Effects of perinatal anoxia after seven years. *Psychological Monographs, 79* (3, Whole No. 596).

Cosgrove, B. B., & Henderson, B. E. (1977). Male genitourinary abnormalities and maternal diethylstilbestrol. *Journal of Urology, 17,* 220–222.

Crnic, K. A., Ragozin, A. S., Greenberg, M. T., Robinson, N. M., & Basham, R. B. (1983). Social interaction and developmental competence of preterm and full-term infants in the first year of life. *Child Development, 54,* 1199–1210.

Dalton, K. (1980). *Depression after childbirth.* Oxford: Oxford University Press.

Dick-Read, G. (1972). *Childbirth without fear: The original approach to natural childbirth* (Rev. ed.). New York: Harper & Row. (Original work published 1933)

Drillien, C. M. (1969). School disposal and performance for children of different birthweight born 1953-1960. *Archives of Diseases in Childhood, 44,* 562–570.

Dunn, J., & Kendrick, C. (1981). Interaction between young siblings: Association with the interaction between mother and firstborn child. *Developmental Psychology, 17,* 336–343.

Fried, P. A. (1980). Marijuana use by pregnant women: Neurobehavioral effects on neonates. *Drug and Alcohol Dependence, 6,* 415–424.

Fuhrmann, W., & Vogel, F. (1976). *Genetic counseling.* New York: Springer-Verlag.

Gelles, R. J. (1975). Violence and pregnancy: A note on the extent of the problem and needed services. *Family Coordinator, 24,* 81–86.

Greenberg, M., & Morris, N. (1974). Engrossment: The newborn's impact upon the father. *American Journal of Orthopsychiatry, 44,* 520–531.

Grossman, F. K., Eichler, L. S., Winickoff, S. A., & Associates. (1980). *Pregnancy, birth, and parenthood: Adaptations of mothers, fathers, and infants.* San Francisco: Jossey-Bass.

Guttmacher, A. F. (1973). *Pregnancy, birth, and family planning: A guide for expectant parents in the 1970's.* New York: Viking Press.

Haas, J. (1976). Prenatal and infant growth and development. In P. T. Barker & M. A. Little (Eds.), *Man in the Andes.* Stroudsburg, PA: Dowden, Hutchinson, & Ross.

Habicht, J., Yarbrough, C., Lectig, A., & Klein, R. (1974). Relation of maternal supplementary feeding during pregnancy to birth weight and other sociobiological factors. In M. Winick (Ed.), *Nutrition and fetal development.* New York: Wiley.

Hamilton, J. S. (1979). *Crying behavior and the "nonviolent" Leboyer method of delivery.* Paper presented at biennial meeting of the Society for Research in Child Development, San Francisco.

Hamm, A. C. (1981). *Questions and answers about DES exposure during pregnancy and after birth.* NIH Pub. No. 81-1118. Washington, DC: National Institutes of Health, U. S. Department of Health and Human Services.

Heinonen, O. P., Slone, D., & Shapiro, S. (1977). *Birth defects and drugs in pregnancy.* Littleton, MA: Publishing Sciences Group.

Henneborn, W. J., & Cogan, R. (1975). The effect of husband participation on reported pain and probability of medication during labor and birth. *Journal of Psychosomatic Research, 19,* 215-222.

Jacobson, C. B., & Berlin, C. M. (1972). Possible reproductive detriment in LSD users. *Journal of the American Medical Association, 222,* 1367-1373.

Jones, K. L., Smith, D. W., Ulleland, C. N., & Streissguth, A. P. (1973). Pattern of malformation in offspring of chronic alcoholic mothers. *Lancet, 1,* 1267–1271.

Kendrick, C., & Dunn, J. (1980). Caring for a second baby: Effects on interaction between mother and firstborn. *Developmental Psychology, 16,* 303–311.

Kessner, D. M. (1973). *Infant death: An analysis by maternal risk and health care.* Washington, DC: National Academy of Sciences.

Klusman, L. (1975). Reduction of pain in childbirth by the alleviation of anxiety during pregnancy. *Journal of Consulting and Clinical Psychology, 43,* 162–165.

Kolata, G. B. (1979). Scientists attack report that obstetrical medications endanger children. *Science, 204,* 391–392.

Kopp, C. B., & Parmelee, A. H. (1979). Prenatal and perinatal influences on infant behavior. In J. D. Osofsky (Ed.), *Handbook of infant development.* New York: Wiley.

Lamaze, F. (1958). *Painless childbirth: Psychoprophylactic method.* London: Burke.

Leboyer, F. (1975). *Birth without violence.* New York: Knopf.

Lefkowitz, M. M. (1981). Smoking during pregnancy: Long-term effects on offspring. *Developmental Psychology, 17,* 192–194.

Lewin, R. (1975, September). Starved brains. *Psychology Today,* pp. 29–33.

Maccoby, E. E., Doering, C. H., Jacklin, C. N., & Kraemer, H. (1979). Concentrations of sex hormones in umbilical cord blood: Their relation to sex and birth order of infants. *Child Development, 50,* 632–642.

MacFarlane, A. (1977). *The psychology of childbirth.* Cambridge, MA: Harvard University Press.

McDonald, R. L. (1968). The role of emotional factors in obstetric complications: A review. *Psychosomatic Medicine, 30,* 222–237.

Miller, S. S. (1976). *Symptoms: The complete home medical encyclopedia.* New York: Thomas Y. Crowell.

Money, J., & Ehrhardt, A. (1972). *Man and woman, boy and girl.* Baltimore: Johns Hopkins University Press.

Murray, A. D., Dolby, R. M., Nation, R. L., & Thomas, D. B. (1981). Effects of epidural anesthesia on newborns and their mothers. *Child Development, 52,* 71–82.

Myers, R. E. (1980). Reply to Drs. Kron and Brackbill. *American Journal of Obstetrics and Gynecology, 136,* 819–820.

Myers, R. E., & Myers, S. E. (1979). Use of sedative, analgesic, and anesthetic drugs during labor and delivery: Bane or boon. *American Journal of Obstetrics and Gynecology, 133,* 83–104.

Peterson, G. H., Mehl, L. E., & Liederman, P. H. (1979). The role of some birth-related variables in father attachment. *American Journal of Orthopsychiatry, 49,* 330–338.

Planned Parenthood Federation of America (1976). *11 million teenagers: What can be done about the epidemic of adolescent pregnancies in the United States?* New York: Alan Guttmacher Institute.

Rank, O. (1929). *The trauma of birth.* New York: Harcourt, Brace.

Rice, R. D. (1977). Neurophysiological development in premature infants following stimulation. *Developmental Psychology, 13,* 69–76.

Roberts, C. J., & Lowe, C. R. (1975). Where have all of the conceptions gone? *Lancet, 1,* 498–499.

Rode, S. S., Chang, P., Fisch, R. O., & Sroufe, L. A. (1981). Attachment patterns of infants separated at birth. *Developmental Psychology, 17,* 188–191.

Rose, S. A. (1980). Enhancing visual recognition memory in preterm infants. *Developmental Psychology, 16,* 85–92.

Saco-Pollitt, C. S. (1981). Birth in the Peruvian Andes: Physical and behavioral consequences in the neonate. *Child Development, 52,* 839–846.

Sameroff, A. J. (1981). Longitudinal studies of preterm infants: A review of chapters 17–20. In S. L. Friedman & M. Sigman (Eds.), *Preterm birth and psychological development.* New York: Academic Press.

Sameroff, A. J., & Chandler, M. J. (1975). Reproductive risk and the continuum of caretaking causality. In F. D. Horowitz, M. Hetherington, S. Scarr-Salapatek, & G. Siegel (Eds.), *Review of child development research* (Vol. 4). Chicago: University of Chicago Press.

Schaefer, M., Hatcher, R. P., & Barglow, P. D. (1980). Prematurity and infant stimulation: A review of research. *Child Psychiatry and Human Development, 10,* 199–212.

Shereshefsky, P. M., & Yarrow, L. J. (1973). *Psychological aspects of a first pregnancy and early postnatal adaptation.* New York: Raven Press.

60 minutes—the CBS weekly newsmagazine (1982, March 28).

Skinner, B. F. (1971). *Beyond freedom and dignity.* New York: Knopf.

Sontag, L. W. (1941). The significance of fetal environmental differences. *American Journal of Obstetrics and Gynecology, 42,* 996-1003.

Sontag, L. W. (1944). War and the fetal maternal relationship. *Marriage and Family Living, 6,* 1–5.

Stein, Z. A., & Susser, M. W. (1976). Prenatal nutrition and mental competence. In J. D. Lloyd-Still (Ed.), *Malnutrition and intellectual development.* Littleton, MA: Publishing Sciences Group.

Stein, Z. A., Susser, M. W., Saenger, G., & Marolla, F. (1975). *Famine and human development: The Dutch hunger winter of 1944–1945.* New York: Oxford University Press.

Stern, L. (1973). Prematurity as a factor in child abuse. *Hospital Practices, 8,* 117–123.

Strauss, M. E., Lessen-Firestone, J. K., Starr, R. H., & Ostrea, E. M. (1975). Behavior of narcotics-addicted newborns. *Child Development, 46,* 887–893.

Streissguth, A. P., Barr, H. M., & Martin, D. C. (1983). Maternal alcohol use and neonatal habituation assessed by the Brazelton Scale. *Child Development, 54,* 1109–1118.

Streissguth, A. P., Herman, C. S., & Smith, D. W. (1978). Stability of intelligence in the fetal alcohol syndrome: A preliminary report. *Alcoholism: Clinical and Experimental Research, 2,* 165–170.

Streitfeld, P. P. (1978). Congenital malformation: Teratogenic foods and additives. *Birth and Family Journal, 5,* 7–19.

Tinklenberg, J. R. (1975). *Marijuana and health hazards: Methodological issues in current research.* New York: Academic Press.

Tuchmann-Duplessis, H. (1975) Drug effects on the fetus. *Monographs* (Vol. 2). Sydney: ADIS Press.

U.S. Department of Health, Education and Welfare (1979). *Smoking and health: A report to the Surgeon General.* DHEW Pub. No. PHS 79-50066. Washington, DC: U.S. Government Printing Office.

Winick, M. (1976). *Malnutrition and brain development.* New York: Oxford University Press.

Zeskind, P. S., & Ramey, C. T. (1978). Fetal malnutrition: An experimental study of its consequences in two caregiving environments. *Child Development, 49,* 1155–1162.

Zeskind, P. S., & Ramey, C. T. (1981). Preventing intellectual and interactional sequelae of fetal malnutrition: A longitudinal, transactional, and synergistic approach to development. *Child Development, 52,* 213–218.

CHAPTER FIVE ■

THE PHYSICAL CHILD: SENSORY CAPABILITIES, MOTOR DEVELOPMENT, AND GROWTH

■ *The neonate*
Is my baby normal?
Capabilities of the newborn infant
Living with an infant

■ *Maturation and growth*
Changes in height and weight
Changes in body proportions
Skeletal development
Muscular development
Development of the brain and nervous system

■ *Motor development*
Basic trends in locomotor development
Other motor milestones
Beyond infancy—Motor development in
    childhood

■ *Puberty—The physical transition from child
    to adult*
The adolescent growth spurt
Sexual maturation
Psychological impact of adolescent growth and
    development

■ *Causes and correlates of physical growth
    and development*
Biological mechanisms
Environmental influences

■ *Summary*

During the 266 days since conception, the newborn child has grown from a single cell into a marvelously complex being. Now 19–21 inches long and weighing 7 to 7½ pounds (about the size of a small salmon), the child has entered a whole new world full of bright, colorful sights, interesting sounds, strange odors, and many, many objects to explore. Is the neonate ready for all this? Is his or her world really a "buzzing, blooming confusion," as one famous psychologist, William James, once implied? Well, perhaps it is for the first few moments. However, we will see that the human infant is a remarkably capable organism who is well equipped at birth to attend selectively to certain aspects of this "confusing" environment and to make adaptive responses to these interesting new experiences.

In this leg of our journey through childhood, we will first consider the mannerisms and capabilities of newborn infants during the *neonatal* period—the first month of life. We will then concentrate on an aspect of human development that fascinates so many parents and child psychologists—the transformation of the child from a highly dependent, immobile little creature into a running, jumping bundle of energy who continues to grow and who may even surpass the physical dimensions of his or her parents in what, to parents, may seem like a very short time.

Now for a thought question: What causes a child to grow? What factors are responsible for the development of increasingly precise motor skills that enable a child to reach for and to grasp objects, to crawl, to walk, and to run? If you think you know the answers to these questions, you may find it interesting to apply your theory of physical growth and development to each of the issues in Box 5-1. Jot down your responses, and we will see how well your theory fares as we discuss each of these topics at various points in the chapter.

THE NEONATE

Although many parents might argue the point, newborn infants are not very attractive. Their passage through the narrow cervix and birth canal may leave them with flattened noses, misshapen foreheads, and an assortment of bumps and bruises. As the baby is held upside down and measured, parents are apt to see a wrinkled, red-skinned little creature all covered with sticky fluid that mats its hair (if any) and may ooze from its nose and mouth as it wheezes and belts out its first cry. To make matters worse, the silver nitrate drops administered as a precaution against gonorrhea may cause the infant's eyelids to puff or swell. Although the neonate's appearance will change for the better over the first few weeks of life, it will be some time before the infant resembles the smiling, bouncing little imps who appear in baby-food commercials.

Is My Baby Normal?

The Apgar scale. In the first minute of life a baby takes his or her first test. A nurse or a doctor will check the infant's physical condition by looking at five standard characteristics that are rated from 0 to 2, recorded on a chart, and totaled (see Table 5-1). This **Apgar score** (named for Dr. Virginia Apgar, who developed the test) can range from 0 to 10, higher scores indicating a better condition. Five minutes after birth, the Apgar procedure is repeated in order to check on the first

TABLE 5-1. The Apgar test

	Score		
Characteristic	*0*	*1*	*2*
Heart rate	Absent	Slow (less than 100 beats per minute)	Over 100 beats per minute
Respiratory effort	Absent	Slow or irregular	Good, baby is crying
Muscle tone	Flaccid, limp	Weak, some flexion	Strong, active motion
Color	Blue or pale	Body pink, extremities blue	Completely pink
Reflex irritability	No response	Frown, grimace, or weak cry	Vigorous cry

observation and/or to measure improvements in the infant's physical state.

Infants who score 7 or higher on the five-minute version of the Apgar test are not in any immediate danger—they have a steady heartbeat, well-developed reflexes, and a pinkish tone to their skin and are breathing freely. However, infants scoring 4 or lower are in trouble—their heartbeats are sluggish or nonexistent, their muscles are limp, and their breathing is shallow and irregular, if they are breathing at all. These children will require immediate medical intervention in order to survive.

The Brazelton scale. The Apgar test is an excellent method of detecting severe physical or neurological abnormalities that require immediate attention. A second test, the **Brazelton Neonatal Behavioral Assessment Scale,** is a more subtle measure of an infant's neurological well-being and an indication of his or her reactions to other people. The Brazelton test is typically administered on the third day of life and should be repeated two or three days later (Brazelton, 1979). It assesses the strength of 20 infant reflexes as well as the infant's responses to 26 situations (for example, reactions to cuddling, general irritability, orienting to the examiner's face and voice, responses to a rattle). The value of this test lies in its ability to identify babies who are slow to respond

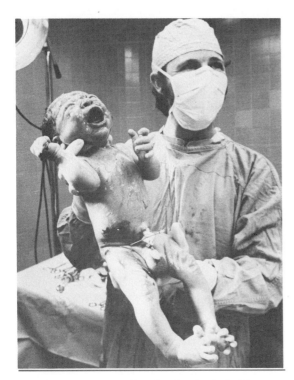

PHOTO 5-1. Immediately after birth, babies are not particularly attractive, but their appearance will improve over the first few weeks of life.

Apgar test: *a quick assessment of the newborn's heart rate, respiration, color, muscle tone, and reflexes; this simple test is performed to determine whether a neonate requires immediate medical assistance.*

Brazelton Neonatal Behavioral Assessment Scale: *an evaluation of an infant's neurological status and responsiveness to other people.*

BOX 5-2
BRAZELTON TRAINING: EFFECTS ON
PARENTS AND INFANTS

Babies who are irritable, unresponsive, and apathetic can be unpleasant companions, and they may not receive enough attention and comforting to promote the development of a warm, loving emotional bond with their parents. As a result, these "high risk" infants often develop feelings of insecurity and any number of other emotional problems. Dr. T. Berry Brazelton (1979) believes that many of these emotional difficulties can be prevented if the parents of sluggish, unresponsive babies learn how to observe, to stimulate, and to comfort their infants.

One method of teaching parents how to interact with their babies is to have them either watch or take part as the Brazelton Neonatal Behavioral Assessment Scale is administered to their child. The Brazelton test is well suited as a teaching device because it is designed to elicit many of the infant's most pleasing characteristics, such as smiling, cooing, and gazing. As the test proceeds, parents will see that their neonate can respond positively to other people, and they will also learn how to elicit these pleasant interactions.

"Brazelton training" has proved to be an effective strategy indeed. Mothers of high-risk children who have had the Brazelton procedure demonstrated to them become more responsive in their face-to-face interactions with their babies. In addition, the infants of these mothers score higher on the Brazelton test

one month later than do high-risk infants whose mothers were not trained (Widmayer & Field, 1980).

Other investigators (Myers, 1982; Worobey & Belsky, 1982) have found that Brazelton training also has positive effects on the parents of healthy, responsive infants. In Barbara Myers's (1982) study, either mothers or fathers in a treatment group were taught to give the Brazelton test to their neonates, while parents in a control group received no such training. When tested four weeks later, parents who had received the Brazelton training were more knowledgeable about infant behavior, more confident in their caretaking abilities, and more satisfied with their infants than control parents. In addition, fathers who had been trained reported that they were much more involved in caring for their infants at home than the fathers who had received no training.

Although many hospitals provide brief instructions on how to diaper and bathe a baby, parents are seldom told anything about the neonate's basic abilities, such as whether newborns can see, hear, or respond to people. Brazelton training clearly illustrates what a new baby is capable of doing, and it appears to have a number of positive effects on both parents and their infants. Barbara Myers (1982), a strong proponent of the Brazelton technique, argues that "the treatment is relatively inexpensive, it only takes about an hour, and the parents reported enjoying it. This type of intervention needs to be tested [further] on other populations . . . for possible consideration as a routine portion of a hospital's postpartum care" (p. 470).

to a variety of everyday experiences. If the infant is extremely unresponsive, the low Brazelton score may indicate brain damage or other neurological dysfunction. If the child is merely sluggish, particularly when responding to social stimulation, it is possible that he or she will not receive enough attention from parents to avoid later feelings of insecurity and other emotional difficulties. So a low Brazelton score is an early indication that problems may arise. Fortunately, parents of these unresponsive babies can be taught how to provide the kinds of attention and comfort that may prevent the emotional difficulties predicted by a low score on the test (see Box 5-2).

Capabilities of the Newborn Infant

In the past, neonates were thought to be fragile, helpless little organisms who were hardly ready

for the cold, cruel world. Indeed, this may have been an adaptive attitude in an era when medical practices and procedures were rather primitive by modern standards and when a substantial percentage of newborns did die. After all, doctors could hardly blame themselves for failing to save a patient who was presumably ill equipped for survival. And parents may have felt pretty much the same way. T. Berry Brazelton (1979, p. 35) notes that "many cultures in which the neonatal death rate is high still institutionalize such practices as not speaking of the newborn as a [human] baby . . . or of not naming him until he is 3 months old and more likely to survive."

Today we know that neonates are much better prepared for life on this earth than many doctors, parents, and developmental psychologists had initially assumed. Not only are babies capable of sensing many of the same events that we adults

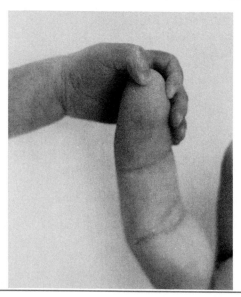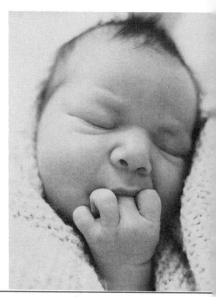

PHOTO 5-2. *Three innate reflexes. The baby in the photograph at the left is displaying the* rooting reflex: *when an object touches the cheek, the infant will turn the head in the direction of the touch, searching for something to suck. In the center is an example of the* grasping reflex—*a curling of the fingers around objects that touch the palm. The infant in the photograph at the right illustrates the rhythmical sucking, or* sucking reflex, *that neonates display when objects are placed into their mouths.*

do, but they even come equipped with a number of inborn **reflexes** that help them to adapt to their new surroundings from the moment of birth.

■ *Innate reflexes*

Many of the neonate's inborn reflexes are reactions that are necessary for survival. Among the more obvious of the **survival reflexes** are the breathing reflex, the eyeblink (which protects the eyes against bright light or foreign particles), and the sucking and swallowing reflexes, by which the infant takes food. Also implicated in feeding is the *rooting* reflex—an infant who is touched on the cheek will turn in that direction and search for something to suck.

In addition to the survival reflexes, the neonate also displays a number of primitive reflexes, which Table 5-2 describes. These reactions can be labeled "primitive" for two reasons: (1) they are controlled by "subcortical" areas of the brain—the areas that develop earliest—and (2) they gradually disappear over the first year of life as the cerebral cortex (a higher brain center) begins to direct and control behavior. Though short-lived, the subcortical reflexes are important in a diagnostic

sense, for the absence or weakness of any of them is an early indication that the child's nervous system may not be functioning properly.

Many ethologists believe that the primitive reflexes listed in Table 5-2 are remnants of our evolutionary history that have adaptive significance to this day. For example, the swimming reflex may help to keep afloat an infant who is accidentally immersed in a body of water. The grasping reflex and the Moro reflex are potentially adaptive in cultures where mothers still carry their newborn infants on their hips or in slings. In fact, ethologist John Bowlby (1973) believes that the major function of the grasping reflex is to promote close contact between the baby and the mother—contact that may help them to become emotionally at-

---

reflex: *an unlearned and automatic response to a stimulus or class of stimuli.*
survival reflexes: *inborn responses such as breathing, sucking, and swallowing that enable the newborn to adapt to the extrauterine environment.*

TABLE 5-2. Major reflexes present in full-term neonates

Name	Response	Developmental course	Significance
I. Survival reflexes			
Breathing reflex	Repetitive inhalation and expiration	Permanent	Provides oxygen and expels carbon dioxide
Eyeblink reflex	Closing or blinking the eyes	Permanent	Protects the eyes from bright aversive stimuli or foreign objects
Pupillary reflex	Constriction of pupils to bright light; dilation to dark or dimly lit surroundings	Permanent	Protects against bright lights; adapts the visual system to low illumination
Rooting reflex	Turning of the cheek in the direction of a tactile (touch) stimulus	Gradually weakens over the first 6 months of life	Orients child to the breast or bottle
Sucking reflex	Sucking on objects placed (or taken) into the mouth	Is gradually modified by experience over the first few months of life	Allows child to take in nutrients
Swallowing reflex	Swallowing	Is permanent but modified by experience	Allows child to take in nutrients
II. Primitive (subcortical) reflexes			
Babinski reflex	Fanning and then curling the toes when the bottom of the foot is stroked	Usually disappears within the first 8 months–1 year of life	Its presence at birth and disappearance in the first year are an indication of normal neurological development
Grasping reflex	Curling of the fingers around objects (such as a finger) that touch the baby's palm	Disappears in first 3–4 months and is then replaced by a voluntary grasp	Its presence at birth and later disappearance are an indication of normal neurological development

tached to each other. We will explore this idea in greater detail when we consider the social world of the human infant in Chapter Eleven.

■ *Sensory capabilities of neonates*

How well do you think infants can see or hear? Do you suppose they can taste, smell, or tell the difference between colors such as red and blue? Assuming that no one knew the answers to these questions, how could we extract such information from a nonverbal creature who cannot easily express what he or she may see, hear, smell, taste, or feel?

To understand the sensory capabilities of neonates, one must devise tests that take advantage of the responses that infants can make. For example, visual preferences can be inferred from the amount of time infants spend looking at different objects. Taste discriminations are apparent if infants suck at different rates in response to sweet, bitter, and sour solutions. The auditory capabilities of newborns can be determined by observing whether infants will turn in the direction of a sound (auditory localization) or whether their heart rate or respiration will change when one sound is substituted for another (auditory discrimination). Through the use of these and other equally creative methods, investigators have been able to determine that all human sensory systems are functional at birth—even though they may be immature by adult standards. Let's now take a closer look at the sensory world of the neonate.

Vision. The eye of the human infant functions reasonably well at birth. Changes in illumination

TABLE 5-2. Major reflexes present in full-term neonates *(continued)*

Name	Response	Developmental course	Significance
Moro reflex	A loud noise or sudden change in the position of the baby's head will cause the baby to throw his or her arms outward, arch the back, and then bring the arms toward each other as if to hold onto something	The arm movements and arching of the back disappear over the first 6–7 months; however, the child continues to react to unexpected noises or a loss of bodily support by showing a startle reflex (which does not disappear)	Its presence at birth and later disappearance (or evolution into the startle reflex) are indications of normal neurological development
Swimming reflex	An infant immersed in water will display active movements of the arms and legs and involuntarily hold his or her breath (thus giving the body buoyancy); this swimming reflex will keep an infant afloat for some time, allowing for the easy rescue of a baby who has fallen into a body of water	Disappears in the first 4–6 months	Its presence at birth and later disappearance are an indication of normal neurological development; on a practical note, some swimming instructors have taught very young infants to adapt the swimming reflex into a primitive type of locomotion in the water (swimming), which is possible long before an infant is capable of walking
Stepping reflex	Infants held upright so that their feet touch a flat surface will step as if to walk	Disappears in the first 8 weeks unless the infant has regular opportunities to practice this response	Its presence at birth and later disappearance are taken as an indication of normal neurological development

Note: Preterm infants may show little or no evidence of subcortical reflexes at birth, and their survival reflexes are likely to be irregular or immature. However, the missing subcortical reflexes will typically appear soon after birth and will disappear a little later than they do among full-term infants.

will elicit a **pupillary reflex**, which indicates that the neonate is sensitive to brightness (Pratt, 1954). Brightness discrimination develops rapidly during the first few weeks, so that by the age of 2 months, infants can discriminate a white bar that differs only 5% in luminance from a solid white background (Peeples & Teller, 1975). In addition, the neonate's world is apparently a colorful place. Even very young infants are capable of discriminating and categorizing colors such as red, blue, green, and yellow (Bornstein, 1979; Werner & Wooten, 1979).

Infants can also detect movement in the visual field. Even neonates can track a moving target with their eyes, although their tracking is imprecise and is unlikely to occur unless the target is moving slowly (Kremenitzer, Vaughn, Kurtzberg, & Dowling, 1979).

By adult standards, the visual acuity of the neonate is poor. At birth, a baby's distance vision is about 20/600, which means that the infant sees at 20 feet what an adult with excellent vision can see at 600 feet. Moreover, the infant's visual images are likely to be blurred because he or she has trouble *accommodating*—that is, changing the shape of the lens of the eye to bring objects into focus. Until recently, investigators believed that neonates could focus reasonably well on objects 7–10 inches from their faces. However, Martin Banks (1980) has found that 1-month-old infants

> **pupillary reflex:** *the reflexive action by which the pupils constrict in bright light and dilate in dark or dimly lit surroundings.*

do not see clearly or produce sharp visual images of targets at any distance. Although visual acuity improves rapidly over the first few months of life, it may take as long as six months to a year before the infant will see as well as an adult (Walk, 1981).

Audition (hearing). Neonates hear fairly well. They are startled by loud, unexpected noises, and they will turn in the direction of a softer sound as if searching for its source (Field, Muir, Pilon, Sinclair, & Dodwell, 1980; Muir & Field, 1979). The fact that babies turn their eyes (and heads) toward a sound implies that they expect to see something making the sound. So the intersensory coordination of vision and audition (that is, the idea that sounds imply sights) may be present at birth (Bower, 1982).

Researchers have used a technique involving **habituation** to learn just how well infants can hear. Habituation is the process whereby a repetitive stimulus becomes so familiar or uninteresting that responses initially associated with it (for example, head or eye movements, changes in respiration or heart rate) are no longer apparent. To test an infant's ability to distinguish two sounds that differ in some way, an investigator will first present one of the sounds until the infant stops responding to it (habituates). Then the second sound is presented. If the infant discriminates the second sound from the first, he or she will indicate as much by orienting to the sound, showing a change in heart rate, or altering his or her behavior in some other meaningful way. Using this habituation technique, researchers have found that neonates are capable of discriminating sounds that differ in loudness, duration, direction, and frequency (Bower, 1982). They hear rather well indeed.

Neonates are particularly responsive to the sound of a human voice. Harriet Rheingold and Judith Adams (1980) found that most caregivers speak to newborn infants and appear to enjoy these "conversations." And what do caregivers find so interesting about a "conversation" with a nonverbal infant? Perhaps it is simply that infants will often stop crying, open their eyes, and begin to look around or to vocalize themselves when they are spoken to (Alegria & Noirot, 1978; Rosenthal, 1982). In fact, there is some evidence that neonates may be programmed to "tune in" to hu-

PHOTO 5-3. *Young infants are particularly responsive to the sound of human voices.*

man speech. William Condon and Lewis Sander (1974) filmed the responses of 2-day-old infants to a variety of sounds, including tapping noises, vowel sounds, and natural speech in English or Chinese. While listening to natural speech, the infants became alert and began to synchronize the movements of their heads, hands, arms, and legs to the starts, pauses, and stops in the sample of speech that they were listening to. Synchrony of movement was observed for both Chinese and English speech but not for tapping noises or vowel sounds. So it is possible that newborn infants are biologically programmed to react to human speech—a characteristic that would help them to elicit the attention and interpersonal contact that will contribute in a positive way to their social and emotional development.

Taste and smell. Neonates are born with some very basic taste preferences. At birth or shortly thereafter, babies will suck faster and longer to sweet (sugary) liquids than to bitter, sour, salty, or neutral (water) solutions (Crook, 1978; Desor, Maller, & Andrews, 1975). Babies are also capable of discriminating between different concentrations of both sugar and salty solutions, preferring the more concentrated of the sweet liquids and sucking less to the saltier of the salty ones (Engen, Lipsitt, & Peck, 1974; Jensen, 1932).

Neonates are also capable of sensing and discriminating a variety of odors, and they react rather vigorously to unpleasant smells such as vinegar or ammonia. The ability to localize odors—that is, to tell which direction they are coming from—is innate (Bower, 1982). We know this to be true because infants only a few hours old will turn their heads away from an unpleasant smell (Rieser, Yonas, & Wilkner, 1976). Within a week, babies who are breast-fed can already discriminate the smell of their mother's feeding pad from that of an unused pad or the pad of another breast-feeding mother (MacFarlane, 1977). This demonstration indicates that babies may use their sense of smell as an early means of "identifying" their closest companions. Ironically, Aidan MacFarlane (1977) reports that the mothers in his study often wanted to rush off and apply their deodorant when he told them he was interested in determining whether their babies could smell them.

Touch, temperature, and pain. The sensitivity of neonates to touch has not been heavily researched. However, we have seen that newborns typically emit reflexive responses if one touches their cheeks (rooting reflex), the palms of their hands (grasping reflex), or the soles of their feet (Babinski reflex). And MacFarlane (1977) reports that a firm touch applied to the chest or stomach of a crying baby is often sufficient to terminate the baby's cries. So it appears that neonates are sensitive to a variety of tactile (touch) stimuli.

Full-term infants are born with a layer of fat under the skin that helps to insulate them against minor variations in temperature. Nevertheless, they are quite sensitive to thermal stimulation (warmth and cold) and will try to maintain their body heat by becoming more active in response to a sudden drop in room temperature (Jensen, 1932; Pratt, 1954).

Do neonates experience much pain? Little research has been done in this area because it is obviously unethical to hurt a baby simply to find out how he or she will react. The research that has been conducted suggests that 1-day-old infants do experience some pain from pin pricks (like those administered in blood tests) or mild electrical shocks. However, sensitivity to pain seems to increase rather dramatically over the first few days of life, for it takes much less aversive stimulation to bother a 5-day-old infant than a 1-day-old infant (Lipsitt & Levy, 1959).

In sum, the sensory equipment of a newborn child is in reasonably good working order. Babies are capable of seeing, hearing, tasting, smelling, and responding to touch, temperature, and pain from the first day of life.

Living with an Infant

Thus far, we have concentrated on the experiences and capabilities of neonates who are wide awake and seemingly willing or even eager to discover what their new world holds in store. Yet almost all parents will tell us that it is often difficult to coax their babies to respond to them, because neonates spend much of their time asleep or in a drowsy, inactive state. Imagine the frustration of a researcher conducting an experiment, or a mother trying to feed her baby, when the infant nods off and falls asleep just as the procedure is about to begin. This scenario is not at all unlikely, for neonates go through many changes in *state* (level of consciousness) every day, and their reactions to the world around them will obviously depend on the state they are in.

■ *A description of infant states*

Peter Wolff (1966) carefully observed the behavior of newborn infants and described several states of consciousness that they experience during a typical day. The six major infant states are as follows:

1. *Regular sleep.* During regular sleep, babies lie still with their eyes closed and unmoving. The child's breathing is regular and the skin is pale. The infant is very passive and does not respond to mild stimuli such as soft voices or flashing lights.
2. *Irregular sleep.* In irregular sleep, the baby's breathing is irregular, and the eyes may move underneath the closed eyelids (a phenomenon known as *rapid eye movements,* or *REMs*). The

---

habituation: *a decrease in one's response to a stimulus that has become familiar through repetition.*

child often grimaces, jerks, and twitches and may stir a bit in response to soft sounds or flashes of light.

3. *Drowsiness.* The drowsy baby who is just waking or falling asleep will intermittently open and close his or her eyes. Drowsy babies are fairly inactive, and their eyes have a glazed appearance when open. Breathing is regular but more rapid than in regular sleep.

4. *Alert inactivity.* The alert, inactive baby has his or her eyes open and scans the environment with interest. Head, trunk, and limb movements may occur, and breathing is fast and irregular. This is the state in which infants are most susceptible to conditioning.

5. *Waking activity.* Hungry or otherwise discomforted babies may awake suddenly and show sudden spurts of vigorous activity in which they twist their torsos and kick their legs. Their eyes are open, but the infants are not actively attending to their surroundings. Breathing is irregular.

6. *Crying.* Waking activity often passes into a crying state in which the infant first whimpers and then bursts forth with loud, agitated cries accompanied by vigorous kicks and arm movements.

During the first few days of life, neonates spend about 70% of their time (16–18 hours a day) sleeping and only 2–3 hours in the alert, inactive (attentive) state (Berg, Adkinson, & Strock, 1973; Hutt, Lenard, & Prechtl, 1969). Sleep cycles are typically brief, lasting from 45 minutes to 2 hours. These seven to ten daily "naps" are separated by periods of waking activity, crying, drowsiness, and alert inactivity.

■ *Developmental changes in state*

Sleep patterns.   As infants develop, they spend less time sleeping and more time awake, alert, and attending to the environment. Four to six weeks after birth, babies are sleeping but 14–15 hours a day, spread over five to seven periods. Somewhere between 3 and 7 months of age, infants reach a milestone that parents appreciate—they begin to sleep through the night and will require but two or three shorter naps during the day (Berg & Berg, 1979; Gesell et al., 1940).

At birth, infants spend approximately half their sleeping hours in a state of active, irregular sleep characterized by rapid eye movements (**REMs**) and brain-wave activity that is more typical of wakefulness than regular (non-REM) sleep. Figure 5-1 shows the average percentage of sleeping time that people of different ages spend in REM and non-REM sleep. Note that the percentage of REM sleep decreases from about 50% of total sleep for newborns to 25–30% of total sleep for infants older than 6 months.

Most adults begin their sleep cycles with a period of regular sleep, followed an hour or two later by REM sleep. When awakened from REM sleep, adults almost always report that they were dreaming. Does this mean that newborn infants are dreaming during their REM sleep? It's possible. However, the sleep cycles of neonates are roughly opposite to those of adults: babies usually drift directly into REM sleep from a drowsy, crying, or alert state, and this REM activity is followed later by periods of regular sleep. Thus, REM sleep may serve a very different function for infants than for adults.

Some psychologists believe that the purpose of REM sleep during the first few months of life is to provide the central nervous system with a source of stimulation that enables the higher brain centers to mature (Roffwarg, Muzio, & Dement, 1966). One implication of this **autostimulation theory** is that infants who are stimulated by many sights and sounds when they are awake will require less REM stimulation while they sleep. J. D. Boismier (1977) tested this hypothesis by showing one group of neonates a number of interesting visual stimuli that increased their alert inactivity. Control infants who did not attend to the stimuli were simply permitted to sleep. Boismier found that infants who received visual stimulation spent less time later in REM sleep than infants in the control group—a finding that is consistent with the autostimulation theory. Perhaps the reason REM sleep declines so dramatically at 4–6 months of age (see Figure 5-1) is that the brain is rapidly maturing, the infant is becoming more alert, and there is simply less need for the stimulation provided by REM activity.

Crib death.   Infants rarely have problems establishing regular sleeping cycles unless their central

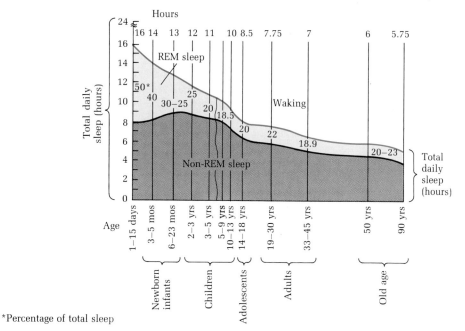

FIGURE 5-1. *Developmental changes in total amounts of REM and non-REM sleep. The amount of REM sleep is shown in the medium-toned portion of the figure. The incidence of REM sleep decreases from 50% of total sleep for neonates to 25–30% of total sleep for infants aged 6–23 months. From age 2 on, REM activity occurs between 18.5 and 25% of the time that people are sleeping.*

nervous system is abnormal in some way (Willemsen, 1979). Yet every year in the United States, as many as 7000–10,000 seemingly healthy infants suddenly stop breathing and die in their sleep.

The exact cause of this *sudden infant death syndrome* (SIDS) is unknown. We do know that later-born males who weigh less than 2500 grams at birth and who score below 7 on the Apgar test are most susceptible. SIDS is most likely to occur during the winter, among infants who are 2–4 months of age and who have a respiratory infection, such as a cold. Some investigators think that a virus is responsible for these "crib deaths." Others point to the fact that victims of SIDS usually have irregular respiratory patterns characterized by periods of *apnea* (spontaneous interruptions in breathing) that occur very frequently and are unusually long (Shannon, 1980; Steinschneider, 1975). Lewis Lipsitt (1979) believes that SIDS occurs most often at 2–4 months

of age because this is the time when subcortical reflexes are diminishing in strength and voluntary cortical responses are not yet well established. Consequently, if mucus should block the nasal passages, a 2–4-month-old infant may not struggle for a breath because his or her innate survival reflexes are waning and learned, protective responses to discomfort are weak or nonexistent.

Unfortunately, many parents blame themselves for crib deaths: they feel that their baby would not

---

REM sleep: *a state of active or irregular sleep in which the eyes move rapidly beneath the eyelids and the person's brain-wave activity is similar to the pattern displayed when awake.*

autostimulation theory: *a theory proposing that REM sleep in infancy is a form of self-stimulation that contributes to the development of the central nervous system.*

have died if only they had been more attentive. What, if anything, can parents do to help prevent SIDS? Proponents of the virus theory would advise them to avoid taking their young infants into crowded public places where contact with viruses is likely. Should the infant catch a virus, parents might periodically check their sleeping baby for respiratory distress. If breathing irregularities are noted, doctors may recommend installation of an **apnea monitor** in the home. An apnea monitor is a device that detects respiratory interruptions and sounds an alarm if the baby stops breathing for more than 20–30 seconds. When they hear the alarm, parents can then wake the baby, thereby coaxing him or her to resume normal breathing.

The course and functions of crying. Neonates spend about 6–7% of their time crying, although there are large individual differences in crying behavior, and the amount that any one child cries may vary considerably from day to day (Korner, Hutchinson, Koperski, Kraemer, & Schneider, 1981).

Pediatricians and nurses are trained to listen to the vocalizations of a newborn infant, for congenital problems are sometimes detectable by the way an infant cries. For example, preterm babies and those who are malnourished or brain-damaged may emit high-pitched, nonrhythmic cries that are perceived as much more aversive than those of healthy, full-term infants (Frodi et al., 1978; Zeskind, 1980). Perhaps this very noxious cry is a factor that contributes to the high incidence of child abuse among preterm infants.

Healthy babies are able to produce at least three cries: (1) a "hunger," or rhythmic, cry that starts with a whimper and becomes louder and more sustained, (2) a "mad," or angry, cry that is also rhythmic but much more intense, and (3) a "pain" cry that begins with a long shriek followed by seconds of silence (as the baby takes a deep breath) and then more vigorous crying. Peter Wolff (1969) conducted an interesting experiment to see whether young, relatively inexperienced mothers could distinguish these three kinds of cries. While he was supposedly observing the neonates in their own rooms, Wolff played a tape recording of the infant crying and waited for the mothers to respond. And respond they did: At the sound of a pain cry, mothers immediately came running to

see what was wrong with their babies. However, mothers responded much more slowly (if at all) to either "hungry" or "mad" cries. So it appears that different cries convey very different messages, even to new mothers who have had little experience with babies.

Although a child's earliest cries are merely reflexive reactions to discomfort, infants as young as 3 weeks of age may begin to emit **"fake cries"** of very low pitch and intensity in an attempt to attract attention (Wolff, 1969). This observation prompts a question: Will parents who quickly respond to their infants' cries produce a spoiled baby who cries a lot and enslaves them with incessant demands for attention? Apparently not! Mary Ainsworth, Sylvia Bell, and Donelda Stayton (1972) observed the reactions of 26 mothers to the cries of their infants over the first year of life. Once every three weeks, a member of the research team made a four-hour visit to each home and recorded how often each baby cried and what the mother did about it. The results were clear: mothers who were quick to respond to their infants' cries had babies who cried very little; children who cried most often at the end of the first year were those whose mothers had not been especially responsive to their cries. Why do babies cry less frequently when their mothers quickly respond to these signals? Ainsworth et al. (1972, p. 131) suggest that

> three interrelated developmental processes are implicated in the reduction of crying: the development in the infant of (1) expectations that his mother will respond to his signals when he gives them, (2) of increasing competence to control what happens to him, and (3) of more varied modes of communication other than crying. . . . An infant whose mother has responded to his cries promptly in the past should develop both trust in her responsiveness and confidence in his increased ability to control what happens to him. In regard to [the development of] more varied communication, we . . . found a significant tendency for infants with more varied, clear, and subtle modes of communication to cry less than those who had a more limited range of communication.

So crying is initially the infant's most effective method of communicating discomforts and seeking others' attention. However, crying usually declines over the first year as infants develop trust or faith in the responsiveness of their caretakers and begin to use other forms of communication to attract attention. Perhaps infants of highly responsive mothers cry infrequently and become rather proficient at the use of alternative social signals such as smiling and babbling because their mothers are also very responsive to these other forms of communication. In other words, mothers who quickly respond to cries are often available to attend to and *reinforce* alternative social gestures, which then replace crying as methods of attracting attention (Gewirtz & Boyd, 1977).

■ *Methods of soothing a fussy baby*

Although babies can be delightful companions when alert and attentive, they may also irritate the most patient of caregivers when they fuss, cry, and are difficult to pacify. Many people think that a crying baby is either hungry, wet, or in pain, and if the infant has not eaten in some time, feeding may be a very effective method of pacification. In fact, pediatricians (and thousands of parents) have discovered that the presentation of a nipplelike pacifier (without food) is often sufficient to coax the baby to suck—an inborn rhythmic activity that apparently reduces stress. But the soothing effect of a pacifier will be short-lived if the baby is really hungry.

A number of researchers have found that rocking, humming, and other forms of continuous, rhythmic stimulation may quiet restless babies. Swaddling (wrapping the child snugly in a blanket) is also comforting because the wraps provide continuous tactile sensation all over the baby's body. Perhaps the infant's nervous system is programmed to respond to soft, rhythmic stimulation, for studies have shown that rocking, swaddling, and continuous rhythmic sounds have the effect of decreasing a baby's muscular activity and lowering heart and respiratory rates (Brackbill, 1975; Lipton, Steinschneider, & Richmond, 1965).

Another method of soothing crying infants is simply to pick them up. Unlike soft, rhythmic stimulation, which may put a baby to sleep, lifting an infant is likely to have the opposite effect (Korner, 1972): When babies are picked up, they become visually alert and begin to look around, particularly if their caregivers place them to the shoulder—an excellent vantage point for visual scanning (see Photo 5-4). Anneliese Korner (1972)

PHOTO 5-4. *A caregiver's shoulder is an excellent vantage point for scanning the environment.*

believes that mothers who soothe their infants by picking them up may be doing them a favor, for the visual exploration that this technique allows will help babies to become familiar with their close companions and to learn more about the environment.

Infants differ in temperament right from birth. Some babies cry a lot, others very little. One baby may sleep 22 hours a day, while another may require but 10–12 hours. Many babies are very active when they are awake; others are generally passive, quiet, and attentive. Babies even differ in their ability to be soothed. In one study (Birns, Blank, & Bridger, 1966), 20 hungry babies 2 to 3 days old were made even more irritable when the experimenters flicked the soles of their feet. Then the investigators tried to soothe the infants by playing soft tones, rocking their bassinettes, offer-

---

apnea monitor: *a device that helps to prevent sudden infant death syndrome by detecting respiratory interruptions and alerting caregivers that their baby has stopped breathing.*

fake cries: *low-pitched vocalizations that young infants emit to attract attention.*

ing them sweetened pacifiers, or immersing their feet in warm water. Some infants were easily irritated and could not be quieted by any of the soothing stimuli. Others became only mildly irritated and were quieted by any (and all) of the soothing techniques. Since these neonates had not yet received much "mothering" from human caregivers, it appears that the differences in their reactions to irritating and pacifying stimuli may be innate.[1]

A baby who is not easily soothed can make a parent feel anxious, irritable, or downright incompetent—reactions that may cause the parent to resent the child and contribute to a poor parent/child relationship. T. Berry Brazelton (1979) believes that parents can come to enjoy even the most active and irritable of infants if they can cast aside any preconceptions they may have about the typical or "perfect" baby and learn how to adjust their parenting techniques to the characteristics of their *own* child. Indeed, the major purpose of Brazelton training (see Box 5-2) is to promote good parent/infant relations by showing parents that their child can respond positively to them and then teaching the parents how to elicit these favorable reactions.

MATURATION AND GROWTH

Adults are often amazed at how quickly children grow. Even tiny babies don't remain tiny for long, for in the first few months of life they are gaining nearly an ounce in weight a day and an inch in length each month. Yet the dramatic increases in height and weight that we can see are accompanied by a number of important *internal* developments in the muscles, bones, and central nervous system—changes that will largely determine the physical feats that children are capable of performing at different ages. In this section of the chapter, we will chart the course of physical

[1]We might also note that male babies are more irritable and difficult to pacify than females (Moss, 1967) and that newborn Caucasian infants are more active, irritable, and difficult to comfort than newborn Chinese-American, Japanese-American, or Navaho infants (Freedman, 1979). Here, then, are two more lines of evidence to suggest that heredity may contribute to neonatal differences in irritability and soothability.

development from birth through childhood and see that there is a clear relationship between those external aspects of growth that are so noticeable and the internal changes that are much harder to detect.

Changes in Height and Weight

Babies grow very rapidly during the first two years, often doubling their birth weight by 4–6 months of age and tripling it (to about 21–22 pounds) by the end of the first year. By 2 years of age, infants are already half their eventual adult height and have quadrupled their birth weight—blossoming to 27–30 pounds. If children continued to grow at this rapid pace until age 18, they would stand about 12'3" and weigh several tons.

From age 2 until puberty, the child's growth is slow and steady, averaging 2–3 inches in height and 6–7 pounds in weight each year (see Figure 5-2). During middle childhood (ages 6–11), children may seem to grow very little—over an entire year, 2 inches and 6 pounds are hard to detect on a child who stands 4 to 4½ feet tall and weighs 60 to

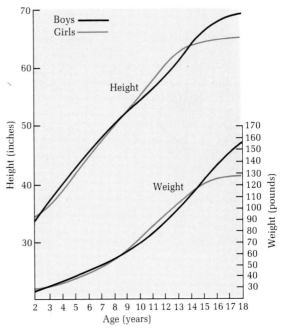

FIGURE 5-2. *Growth in height and weight from 2 to 18 years.*

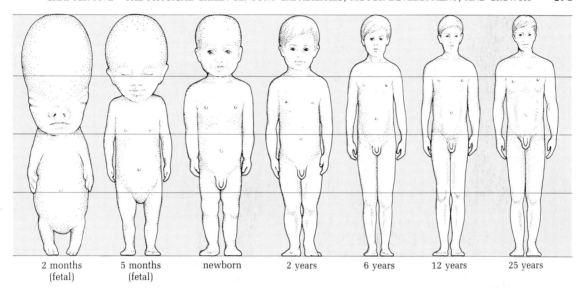

FIGURE 5-3. *Changes in the proportions of the human body from the fetal period through adulthood. The head represents 50% of body length at 2 months after conception but only 12–13% of one's adult stature. In contrast, the legs constitute about 12–13% of the total length of a 2-month-old fetus but 50% of the height of a 25-year-old adult.*

80 pounds (Eichorn, 1979; Lowery, 1978). However, physical growth and development are once again apparent at puberty, when adolescents enter a two- to three-year "growth spurt," during which they may post an annual gain of 10–15 pounds and 3–6 inches in height. After this initial growth spurt, there are typically small increases in height until full adult stature is attained in the mid to late teens.

Changes in Body Proportions

To a casual observer, neonates may appear to be "all head"—and for good reason. The head of a newborn is already 70% of its eventual adult size and constitutes one-quarter of the infant's total body length (the same fraction as the legs). If you asked your friends where you might find a creature whose head was as long as its legs, they might tell you to try science fiction.

As a child grows, body shape rapidly changes. Development proceeds in a **cephalocaudal** (head downward) direction, and it is the trunk that grows fastest during the first year. At 1 year of age, a child's head now accounts for only 20% of total body length. From the child's first birthday until the adolescent growth spurt, the legs are growing

rapidly, accounting for more than 60% of all increases in height (Eichorn, 1979). During adolescence the trunk once again becomes the fastest-growing segment of the body, although the legs are also growing rapidly at this time. When we reach our eventual adult stature, our legs will acount for 50% of total height and our heads only 12% (see Figure 5-3).

While children grow upward, they are also growing outward according to a **proximodistal** (center outward) formula. For example, the chest and internal organs form before the arms, hands, and fingers during prenatal development. The trunk grows faster than the arms and legs during the first year. However, this center-outward se-

> **cephalocaudal development:** *a sequence of physical maturation and growth that proceeds from the head (cephalic region) to the tail (or caudal region).*
>
> **proximodistal development:** *a sequence of physical maturation and development that proceeds from the center of the body (or the proximal region) to the extremities (or distal regions).*

quence reverses just before puberty, when the extremities (hands and feet) begin to grow rapidly and become the first body parts to reach adult proportions, followed by the arms and legs and finally the trunk. One reason teenagers often appear so clumsy or awkward is that their hands and feet (and later their arms and legs) may suddenly seem much too large for the rest of their bodies (Tanner, 1978).

Skeletal Development

The skeletal structures that emerge during the prenatal period are initially formed from soft cartilage tissues that will gradually ossify (harden) into bony material as calcium and other minerals are deposited there. At birth, most of the infant's bones are soft, pliable, and difficult to break. One reason that neonates cannot sit up or balance themselves when pulled to a standing position is that their bones are too small and too flexible to allow these kinds of physical gyrations.

Fortunately for a mother and her baby, the neonate's skull consists of several soft bones that can be compressed to allow the child to pass through the cervix and the birth canal. These skull bones are separated by six soft spots, or **fontanelles**, that are gradually filled in by minerals and will ossify to form a single skull bone by about age 2.

Other parts of the body—namely, the ankles and feet and the wrists and hands—develop *more* (rather than fewer) bones as the child matures. In Figure 5-4 we see that the wrist and hand bones of a 1-year-old infant are both fewer and less well integrated (interconnected) than the corresponding skeletal equipment of an adolescent. As new bones appear, ossify, and grow, children are better able to control the extremities and will become capable of movements that will enable them to tie their shoes, write, jump, climb, ride a bicycle, and perform incredible balancing acts (of the "Look, Ma, no hands" variety) that may occasionally startle or alarm their parents.

Not all parts of the skeleton grow and harden at the same rate. The skull and the hands mature first, whereas the leg bones continue to develop until the mid to late teens. For all practical purposes, skeletal development is complete by age 18, although the width (or thickness) of the skull,

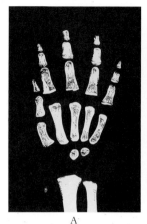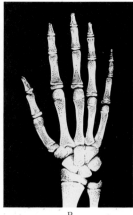

A   B

FIGURE 5-4. *X rays showing the amount of skeletal development seen in (A) the hand of an average male infant at 12 months or an average female infant at 10 months and (B) the hand of an average 13-year-old male or an average 10½-year-old female.*

leg bones, and hands will increase slightly throughout life (Tanner, 1978).

One method of estimating a child's level of physical maturation is to X-ray the wrist and hand (as in Figure 5-4). The X ray indicates the number of bones and the extent of their ossification, which is then interpretable as a **skeletal age**. Using this technique, researchers have found that females mature faster than males. At birth, girls are only four to six weeks ahead of boys in their level of skeletal maturity, but by age 12 the "maturation gap" has widened to two full years (Tanner, 1978).

Muscular Development

Although one might think otherwise after listening to the claims of body builders, neonates are born with all the muscle cells they will ever have (Tanner, 1978). At birth, muscle tissue is 35% water, and it accounts for no more than 18–24% of a baby's body weight (Marshall, 1977). However, muscle fibers soon begin to grow as the cellular fluid in muscle tissue is gradually replaced with protein and salts.

Muscular development proceeds in a cephalocaudal direction; that is, muscles in the head and neck mature earlier than those in the trunk and lower limbs. Like many other aspects of physical development, the maturation of muscle tissue occurs very gradually over childhood and then accelerates during early adolescence. One consequence of this muscular growth spurt is that members of both sexes become noticeably stronger (see Figure 5-5), although increases in both muscle mass and physical strength (as measured in tests of large-muscle activity) are more dramatic for males than for females (Faust, 1977; Tanner, 1978). By the midtwenties, skeletal muscle accounts for 40% of the body weight of an average male, compared with 24% for the average female (Marshall, 1977).

Development of the Brain and Nervous System

At birth, a baby's brain is only 25% of its eventual adult weight. However, this remarkable organ grows rapidly over the first few years of life, increasing to 66% of adult weight by the end of the first year, to 75% of adult weight by age 2, and to fully 90% of its adult weight by the child's fifth birthday (see Table 5-3). In contrast, the weight of

TABLE 5-3. Average weight of the brain at different ages

Age	Weight (in grams)	Percentage of adult weight
2 months after conception	3	Less than 1
5 months after conception	51	4
7 months after conception	138	10
Newborn	350	25
1 year	908	66
2½ years	1050	76
5 years	1242	90
16 years	1330–1380	100

the entire body is only 5% of adult weight at birth, 20% at age 2, and 50% at age 10.

However, an increase in brain weight is a rather gross index that tells us very little about how or when various parts of the brain will mature or how these developments will affect the child's intellectual, perceptual, and motor abilities. Let's take a closer look at the internal organization and development of the central nervous system.

■ Nerve cells

The nervous system consists of two kinds of cells: **neurons,** which receive and transmit neural impulses, and **glia** (or neuroglia), which nourish the neurons and eventually encase them in insulating sheaths of myelin that facilitate the transmission of neural impulses. The brain alone may contain as many as 100 billion neurons, and glia are even more numerous (Tanner, 1978).

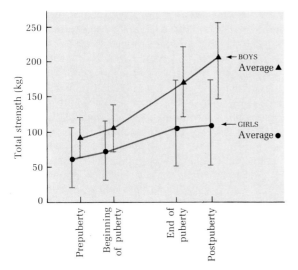

FIGURE 5-5. *Hand and arm strength of males and females at four points during adolescence. The vertical lines at each time period indicate the range of scores obtained by males and females. Before puberty, sex differences in physical strength are not large, but after puberty, the strongest of the females score below the male average.*

fontanelles: *the six soft spots in a baby's skull where the bones are not fully joined.*
skeletal age: *a measure of physical maturation based on the child's level of skeletal development.*
neurons: *nerve cells that receive and transmit neural impulses.*
glia: *nerve cells that nourish neurons and encase them in insulating sheaths of myelin.*

The production of new neurons through mitosis occurs most rapidly during the prenatal period and may continue for several months after birth (Rosenzweig & Leiman, 1982). Glia are also rapidly proliferating during the third trimester of prenatal life, and they continue to form until at least age 2 and possibly longer (Tanner, 1978). If sufficient protein is available from one's diet, new brain cells will immediately begin to increase in size and weight. Indeed, the last three months of prenatal life and the first two years after birth have been termed the period of the **brain growth spurt** because more than half of one's adult brain weight is added at this time (Brierley, 1976). Between the seventh prenatal month and the child's first birthday, the brain is increasing in weight by about 1.7 grams per day—more than a milligram per minute.

■ *Brain differentiation*

Not all parts of the brain develop at the same rate. At birth, the most highly developed areas are the *brain stem* and the *midbrain,* which control the child's states of consciousness, inborn reflexes, and important biological functions such as digestion, respiration, and elimination. Surrounding the midbrain are the cerebrum and cerebral cortex, the areas of the brain that are most directly implicated in bodily movements, perception, and higher intellectual activities such as learning, thinking, and production of language. The first areas of the cerebrum to mature are (1) the *primary motor areas,* which control simple motor activities such as waving the arms, and (2) the *primary sensory areas,* which control sensory processes such as vision, hearing, smelling, or tasting. Within the motor area, the nerve cells controlling the arms and upper trunk develop ahead of those controlling the legs and lower trunk. That is why infants can accomplish many things with their heads, necks, hands, and arms long before they gain enough control over the lower trunk and legs to sit up, crawl, or walk. By 6 months of age, the primary motor areas of the cerebral cortex have developed to the point that they now direct most of the infant's physical activities. At this point, inborn responses such as the palmar grasp and the Babinski reflex should disappear—a positive sign that indicates that the higher cortical centers are assuming proper control over the more primitive "subcortical" areas of the brain.

■ *Myelinization*

As brain cells proliferate and grow, some of the glia begin to produce a waxy substance called *myelin* that forms a sheath around individual neurons. This myelin sheath acts like an insulator to speed the transmission of neural impulses, thus allowing different parts of the body to communicate efficiently with the brain.

Myelinization follows a definite chronological sequence that parallels the maturation of the nervous system. At birth or shortly thereafter, the pathways between the sense organs and the brain are reasonably well myelinated. As a result, the neonate's sensory equipment is in good working order. As neural pathways between the brain and the skeletal muscles myelinate (in a cephalocaudal and proximodistal pattern), the child becomes capable of increasingly complex motor activities such as lifting the head and chest, reaching with the arms and hands, rolling over, sitting, standing, and eventually walking and running. Although myelinization proceeds very rapidly over the first five years of life, some areas of the brain are not completely myelinated until the mid to late teens or early adulthood. For example, the *reticular formation*—a part of the brain that allows us to concentrate on a subject for lengthy periods—is not fully myelinated at puberty (Tanner, 1978). This may be one reason that the attention spans of infants, toddlers, and school-age children are much shorter than those of adolescents and adults.

How important is myelinization? The answer becomes obvious when we consider the plight of those with **multiple sclerosis**, a crippling disease affecting young adults that results when the myelin sheaths surrounding individual neurons begin to disintegrate. The cause of this incurable disease is unknown, and its symptoms vary depending on the part of the nervous system that deteriorates. As the condition worsens, the patient will first lose muscular control over the affected area(s) and may eventually become paralyzed or even die. So the lesson to be learned from the tragedy of multiple sclerosis is that, without myelinization, life as we know it would be difficult if not impossible.

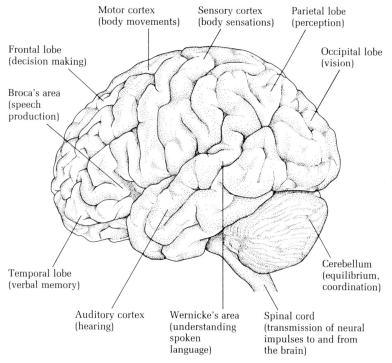

Motor cortex
(body movements)

Sensory cortex
(body sensations)

Parietal lobe
(perception)

Frontal lobe
(decision making)

Occipital lobe
(vision)

Broca's area
(speech
production)

Temporal lobe
(verbal memory)

Cerebellum
(equilibrium,
coordination)

Auditory cortex
(hearing)

Wernicke's area
(understanding
spoken
language)

Spinal cord
(transmission of neural
impulses to and from
the brain)

FIGURE 5-6. *Lateral view of the left cerebral cortex and some of the functions it controls. Although the cerebellum and spinal cord are not part of the cerebral cortex, they serve important functions of their own.*

■ *Specialization of the higher brain centers*

The highest brain center, the *cerebrum*, consists of two halves (or *hemispheres*) connected by a band of fibers called the *corpus callosum*. Each of the hemispheres is covered by a *cerebral cortex*—an outer layer of gray matter that controls sensory and motor processes, perception, and intellectual functioning. Although the left and the right cerebral hemispheres are identical in appearance, they serve different functions and control different areas of the body: the left cerebral hemisphere controls the right side of the body, and the right hemisphere controls the left side. Thus, the brain is a **lateralized** organ.

As the cerebral cortex matures, it becomes even more specialized as certain regions within each hemisphere assume control over particular functions. In Figure 5-6 we see that the cortex of the left cerebral hemisphere contains centers for speech, hearing, motor functions, and processing of verbal information, to name a few. In contrast,

the centers for spatial functions, visual imagery, and tactile sensitivity are located in the cortex of the right cerebral hemisphere. (This lateralization is what we see in right-handed people. Some left-

---

brain growth spurt: *the period between the seventh prenatal month and 2 years of age when more than half of the child's eventual brain weight is added.*

myelinization: *the process by which neurons are encased in waxy myelin sheaths that will facilitate the transmission of neural impulses.*

multiple sclerosis: *a crippling loss of muscular control that occurs when the myelin sheaths surrounding individual neurons begin to disintegrate.*

cerebral lateralization: *the specialization of brain functions in the left and the right cerebral hemispheres.*

handed people show the mirror image of this pattern.) However, this lateralization of function does not mean that each hemisphere is totally independent of the other, for the corpus callosum, which connects the hemispheres, plays an important role in integrating their respective functions.

Although our knowledge is far from complete, it appears that some areas of the cerebral cortex mature much faster than others. The sensory areas may be among the first to specialize, for the sensory capabilities of even a 1-year-old infant are remarkably similar to those of adults. In contrast, specialization of language skills proceeds much more gradually. There is evidence that 3-year-old children who listen to different information in each ear (through stereophonic headphones) are more accurate when reporting the information presented to the right ear (Hiscock & Kinsbourne, 1980). This finding suggests that the left cerebral hemisphere (which receives auditory input from the right ear) is already more responsive to speech than the right hemisphere (which receives input from the left ear). However, clinical evidence indicates that the specialization of language skills is not complete until adolescence. If the language centers of the left hemisphere are severely damaged *after* puberty, most affected individuals will remain mute or only partially recover their linguistic capabilities. But if the damage occurs *before* puberty, affected children are likely to regain much or all of their speech—particularly if the injury takes place early in life. These dramatic age differences suggest that the brain is much more flexible (or less specialized) earlier in development, when areas of the right hemisphere can assume the linguistic functions that would ordinarily be served by the left side of the brain (Lenneberg, 1967).

MOTOR DEVELOPMENT

Perhaps the main reason that neonates seem so helpless is that they are totally incapable of moving about on their own. Oh, it is true that they may turn their heads, flail their arms, and kick their legs a bit; but the human infant is a far cry from the young of many species, who can follow their mothers to food (and then feed themselves) very soon after they are born.

Fortunately, the infant does not remain immobile for long. By the end of the first month, the brain and neck muscles have matured enough to permit most infants to reach the first milestone in motor development—lifting their chins while lying flat on their stomachs. Soon thereafter, children will be lifting their chests as well, reaching for objects, and sitting up if someone is there to support them. Investigators who have charted the motor development of young infants over the first two years of life find that motor skills evolve in a definite sequence, which appears in Table 5-4. Although the ages at which these skills first appear vary considerably from child to child, the developmental norms provide a useful standard that parents can use to gauge the progress of their child as he or she begins to sit, stand, and take those first tentative steps.

Basic Trends in Locomotor Development

There are two fundamental "laws" that describe motor development during the first few years of life. First, development proceeds in a *cephalocaudal* (head to foot) direction: motor activities involving the head, neck, and upper extremities appear before those involving the legs and the lower extremities. At the same time, development advances in a *proximodistal* (center outward) direction: activities involving the trunk and shoulders appear before those involving the hands and fingers. Does this cephalocaudal/proximodistal pattern ring a bell? It should, for we have seen that both the muscles and the myelinization of neural pathways follow the same head-downward, center-outward pattern of development. Mary Shirley (1933) believes that locomotor development is a *maturational* phenomenon: as the nerves and muscles mature in a downward and outward direction, children will gradually gain control over the lower and peripheral parts of their bodies and will come to display locomotor skills in the order shown in Table 5-4.

Other Motor Milestones

The sequence of motor development described in Table 5-4 is concerned with the growth of skills that enable the child to sit, stand, and walk. Two other aspects of motor development also play im-

TABLE 5-4. Age norms (in months) for important motor milestones

Skill	Month when 50% of infants have mastered the skill	Month when 90% of infants have mastered the skill
Lifts head 90° while lying on stomach	2.2	3.2
Rolls over	2.8	4.7
Sits propped up	2.9	4.2
Sits without support	5.5	7.8
Stands holding on	5.8	10.0
Walks holding on	9.2	12.7
Stands alone momentarily	9.8	13.0
Stands well alone	11.5	13.9
Walks well	12.1	14.3
Walks up steps	17.0	22.0
Kicks ball forward	20.0	24.0

portant roles in determining the child's ability to adapt to the environment—manipulation of objects and visual/motor coordination.

■ *Manipulation of objects*

We have learned that newborn babies are already capable of grasping objects with their palms. But as this reflexive "palmar grasp" weakens at 2–4 months of age, an infant's hand skills may seem to deteriorate. At age 3–4 months, infants enjoy slapping at objects but cannot grasp them well: the problem is that they tend to close their hands too early or too late (Bower, 1982). By the middle of the first year, infants can once again grasp small objects, but this **ulnar grasp** is a rather clumsy, clawlike grip involving the palm and outer fingers. Over the next several months, "fingering" skills gradually improve, until at 9–12 months of age the child is capable of using the thumb and forefinger to lift and fondle objects (Halverson, 1931). This **pincer grip** transforms the infant from a little fumbler into a skillful manipulator who may soon begin to corner crawling bugs and to turn knobs, dials, and rheostats, thereby discovering that he can use his newly acquired hand skills to produce any number of interesting results.

As maturation proceeds during the second year, infants become increasingly proficient with their hands. At 16 months of age they can scribble with a crayon, and by the end of the second year, they can copy a simple horizontal or vertical stroke and even build towers of five or more blocks. Yet 2- to 3-year-old children have difficulties catching and throwing a ball, eating with silverware, or drawing within the lines of their coloring books. These skills will emerge later in childhood as the muscles mature and children become more proficient at using visual information to help them coordinate their actions.

■ *Visual/motor coordination*

When we adults see some object that we want, we simply reach out and grab it. In so doing, we use visual information to determine where the object is and therefore where we must guide our arms and hands.

Newborn infants are incapable of this kind of eye/hand coordination. Although neonates do occasionally reach for objects and anticipate contact by opening their hands, their reaching is not very precise. As a result, the neonate hits her target less

---

ulnar grasp: *an early manipulatory skill in which an infant grasps objects by pressing the fingers against the palm.*

pincer grip: *a grasp in which the thumb is used in opposition to the fingers, enabling an infant to become more dexterous at lifting and fondling objects.*

than half the time (Bower, 1982). Before 20 weeks of age, an infant who misses when reaching for an object will retract her hand from the visual field and reach all over again. Early reaching is truly a hit-or-miss proposition. In contrast, infants older than 20 weeks can extend their arms and make in-flight corrections to guide their hands to the target. So the reaching behavior of very young infants is visually *initiated,* while the same behavior in older infants is visually *guided* (Bower, 1982).

Do older infants actually have to watch their hands if they hope to make contact with a desired object? Apparently not. Thomas Bower (1982) describes an experiment in which the lights were extinguished just before 5-month-old infants could reach for attractive objects. Although these infants could no longer rely on visual cues to guide their reaching, they were able to reach out and touch the objects with little or no difficulty. Thus, visual cues help the infant to *locate* an object and tell him where to reach; however, vision is *not* necessary to *direct or control the child's reaching.* It is fortunate that our motor responses do not require visual control; otherwise we would have to watch our feet hit the ground to avoid falling flat on our faces when we walk or run.

The importance of visual/motor coordination can be seen by contrasting the motor development of blind children and "sighted" children. As you might expect, blind infants lag behind sighted infants in the ages at which they sit, stand, and walk (Bower, 1982). And without vision, it is hardly surprising that blind infants are slow to reach for objects. What is surprising is that many blind children fail to develop any reaching ability at all:

> Typically . . . the [blind] child will lie . . . in bed . . . or . . . on the floor, absently mouthing an object. . . . There is no interest in toys that are not stimulating to the mouth [which] remains the primary organ of perception.
> The behavior of the hand is striking. While many [blind] children can use the hand for self-feeding and even use spoons and forks, the hand . . . has no autonomy of its own. It can serve the mouth; . . . but it is not employed for examination or manipulation of objects (Fraiberg & Freedman, 1964).

Blind babies can be taught to reach out and explore the environment through a program that uses sound to guide their reaching and touching activities. Selma Fraiberg (1977) encourages parents to talk to their blind babies as they approach and hold them. Another important aspect of Fraiberg's program involves placing toys that make distinctive sounds within the baby's reach. The goal of the program is to teach the child that sounds signify the presence of an object to be grasped. Presumably, blind infants will associate sounds with touch and will begin to search for and manipulate objects that make interesting sounds.

Fraiberg (1977) found that her program did have some beneficial effects. Blind children who learned to associate sound and touch not only began to seek and to manipulate sound-producing objects, they also stood alone and walked at earlier ages than blind infants who did not participate in the program. Nevertheless, the motor development of blind children who received the special training continued to lag behind that of sighted infants.

In sum, visual/motor coordination is an important milestone that helps the child to locate and explore objects and to perfect motor skills such as crawling, standing, and walking. Nowhere is the interdependence of the visual and motor functions more apparent than in the case of visually handicapped children, who may require special assistance if they are to approximate the motor skills of children who can see.

Beyond Infancy—Motor Development in Childhood

The term *toddler* adequately describes most 2-year-olds, who, like the proverbial drunken sailor, will often fall down or trip over stationary objects when they try to get somewhere in a hurry. But as children mature, their locomotor skills increase by "leaps and bounds." By age 3, children can walk or run in a straight line and leap off the floor with both feet, although they can clear only very small (8–10-inch) objects in a single bound and cannot easily turn or stop while running. Four-year-olds can skip, hop on one foot, catch a large ball with both hands, and run much farther and faster than they could one year earlier (Corbin, 1973). By age 5, children are becoming rather graceful: like adults, they pump their arms when they run, and their balance has improved to the

PHOTO 5-5. *Top-heavy toddlers often lose their balance when they try to move very quickly.*

point that some of them can learn to ride a bicycle. One reason preschool children become more fluid in their large-muscle activities is that they are losing much of their baby fat (including their protruding bellies) as they grow in height. As a result, their centers of gravity move steadily downward, and they become capable of coordinated actions requiring a degree of balance that is quite impossible for a top-heavy infant or toddler (Lowery, 1978).

Eye/hand and small-muscle coordination also improve rather dramatically during the preschool years. Three-year-olds find it difficult to button their clothing, tie a shoe, or copy a figure (other than a circle) on a piece of paper. Two years later, children can accomplish all these objectives and even cut a straight line with scissors, draw a person, and copy letters or numbers with a crayon. About the time children enter the first grade (age 6–7), they can copy complex figures (such as a diamond), cut out angular patterns (paper dolls) with a scissors, and print neatly and accurately (Gesell, Ames, & Ilg, 1977). Further advances in small-muscle coordination will enable the child to take up and enjoy hobbies such as assembling models, painting by the numbers, and sewing. By age 8–9, children can use most household tools (such as screwdrivers and can openers) and have become skillful performers at games such as baseball and jacks that require eye/hand coordination.

With each passing year, school-age children can run a little faster, jump a little higher, and throw a

ball a little farther (Herkowitz, 1978). Boys and girls are nearly equal in physical abilities until puberty, when males continue to post gains on tests of large-muscle activities, while females level off or decline (see Figure 5-7). These sex differences are, in part, attributable to biology: males have more muscle than females and might be expected to outperform them on tests of physical strength. However, the biological explanation does not adequately explain the *declining* performance of females, who continue to grow taller, heavier, and presumably stronger between ages 12 and 17. Jacqueline Herkowitz (1978) has suggested that the apparent physical decline of adolescent females is a product of sex-role socialization: with the widening of the hips and development of breasts, girls are strongly encouraged to become less tomboyish and more interested in traditionally feminine pursuits. The implication is that adolescent females would continue to improve on tests of large-muscle activity if they were more physically active during their teenage years.

PUBERTY—THE PHYSICAL TRANSITION FROM CHILD TO ADULT

The onset of adolescence is heralded by two significant changes in physical development—the **adolescent growth spurt** and **puberty**. The term *puberty* (from the Latin *pubertas,* meaning "age of manhood") refers to that point in life when the individual reaches sexual maturity and becomes capable of producing a child. It is generally assumed that a girl becomes sexually mature at **menarche**—the time of her first menstrual period. However, James Tanner (1978) notes that young girls often menstruate without ovulating, and as a result they *may* remain functionally sterile for 12–18 months after menarche. The timing of pu-

---

adolescent growth spurt: *the rapid increase in physical growth that marks the beginning of adolescence.*

puberty: *the point at which a person reaches sexual maturity and is physically capable of fathering or conceiving a child.*

menarche: *a female's first menstrual period.*

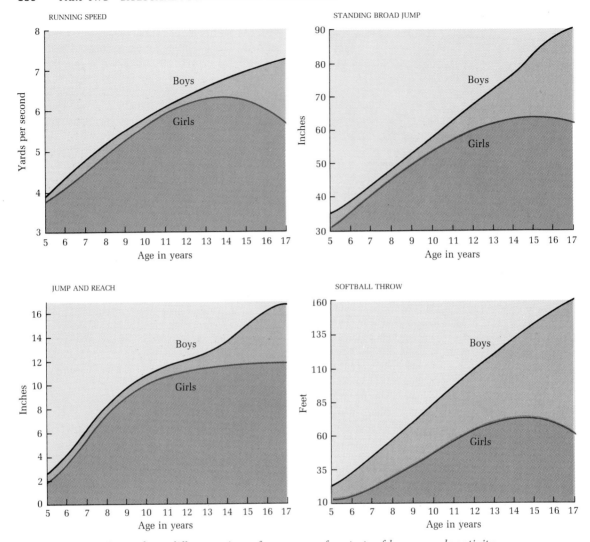

FIGURE 5-7. Age and sex differences in performance on four tests of large-muscle activity.

berty is much harder to pinpoint in males, since production of sperm is not a readily observable phenomenon. The most common index of masculine puberty is the appearance of pigmented pubic hair, an event that may occur well after the boy's penis and testicles have begun to grow (Tanner, 1978).

In this section of the chapter, we will first consider the dramatic physical changes that occur during the first two years of adolescence as the child loses that "boyish" or "girlish" look and begins to resemble an adult. And in considering the physical events of adolescence from the per-

spective of the teenager who experiences them, we will discover that these dramatic biological upheavals play a major role in shaping a teenager's self-concept, which, in turn, may affect the ways he or she relates to other people later in life.

The Adolescent Growth Spurt

The term *growth spurt* describes the rapid acceleration in height and weight that marks the beginning of adolescence. The timing of this event varies considerably from child to child. Girls may begin as early as age 7½ or as late as 12. The typical pattern is for a girl to start her period of rapid growth at age 10½, to reach a peak growth rate at age 12, and to return to a slower, "prespurt" rate of growth by age 13–13½ (Tanner, 1981). Boys lag behind girls by two to three years, entering their period of rapid growth as early as age 10½ or as late as age 16. The typical pattern for males is to begin their growth spurt at age 13, to peak at age 14, and to return to a more gradual rate of growth by age 15½ or 16 (see Figure 5-8). Because girls mature much earlier than boys, it is not at all uncommon for females to be the tallest two or three students in a junior high school classroom.

In addition to growing taller and heavier, the body assumes an adultlike appearance during the adolescent growth spurt. Perhaps the most noticeable changes are a widening of the hips for females and a broadening of the shoulders for males. As the shoulders, hips, chest, and trunk increase rapidly in size, the adolescent's head suddenly seems much smaller relative to the rest of the body. Facial features are also assuming adult proportions as the forehead protrudes, the nose and jaw become more prominent, and the lips enlarge. Gone forever is that soft-featured, innocent look that we associate with childhood.

The adolescent growth spurt is not as uniform as our overview might indicate. Body weight begins to increase first, followed four to six months later by a rapid increase in height (Tanner, 1978). The muscles are growing along with the rest of the body, although the period of greatest muscular development does not occur until a year after the maximum acceleration in height. And because this "muscle spurt" happens earlier for girls than for boys, there is a brief period when the average girl has more muscle than most of her male age mates.

Sexual Maturation

Maturation of the reproductive system occurs at roughly the same time as the adolescent growth spurt and follows a predictable sequence for members of each sex.

■ Sexual development in girls

For most girls, sexual maturation begins at about age 11 as fatty tissue accumulates around their nipples, forming small "breast buds." Usually pubic hair begins to appear a little later, although as many as one-third of all girls develop some pubic hair before the breasts begin to develop (Tanner, 1978).

As a girl enters her height spurt, the breasts grow rapidly and the sex organs begin to mature. Internally, the vagina becomes larger, and the walls of the uterus develop a powerful set of muscles that may one day be used to accommodate a fetus during pregnancy and to push it through the cervix and vagina during the birth process. Externally, the mons pubis (the soft tissue covering the pubic bone), the labia (the fleshy lips surrounding the vaginal opening), and the clitoris all increase in size and become more sensitive to tactile stimulation (Tanner, 1978).

The average female reaches menarche within six months of her 13th birthday—fully two years after the onset of breast development and about the time the height spurt is over (Tanner, 1978).

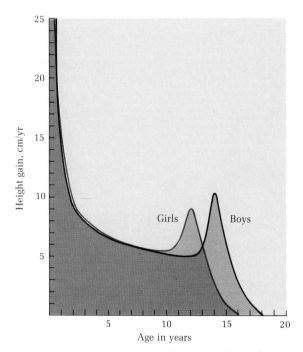

FIGURE 5-8. Gain in height per year by males and females from birth through adolescence. At about age 10½, girls begin their growth spurt. Boys follow some 2½ years later and grow faster than girls once their growth begins.

Within a year of menarche, the young woman's breasts and pubic hair will have fully developed, and she will be grappling with the specter of axillary (armpit) hair—a feature that women in our society have been led to believe they are better off without.

■ Sexual development in boys

For boys, the onset of sexual maturation begins at about 11–11½ with the initial enlargement of the testes and scrotum (the sacklike structure enclosing the testes). The growth of the testes is often accompanied or soon followed by the appearance of unpigmented pubic hair. About six months to a year later, the penis undergoes a period of rapid growth that coincides with the onset of the adolescent growth spurt. By the time the penis is fully developed (typically around age 14½–15), the adolescent male will reach puberty and is now capable of fathering a child.

Facial hair appears somewhat later, as outcroppings first emerge at the corners of the upper lip and then spread to the entire upper lip, to the upper cheeks, and finally to the chin and jawline. Body hair also begins to grow at this time, although that "hoped for" matting of chest hair may

not appear until the late teens or early twenties—if it appears at all.

After reaching sexual maturity, the boy's voice will begin to change from the soprano of childhood to the baritone that characterizes adult males. This turn of events, which may occur gradually or abruptly, is due to growth of the larynx and lengthening of the vocal cords. Voice lowering may have its comical side: almost every man can remember at least one occasion when his voice ranged from squeaky soprano to baritone and back to soprano—sometimes within a single sentence. Although boys are often embarrassed by this "breaking" of the voice, it is a perfectly normal sign of sexual maturity that heralds the coming of manhood.

■ Individual differences in sexual maturation

The sequences of sexual maturation described above are merely norms and averages that will not necessarily characterize the development of an individual child. Figure 5-9 gives us some idea of the wide variation among children in the timing of sexual maturation. Consider, for example, that an early-maturing female who develops breast buds

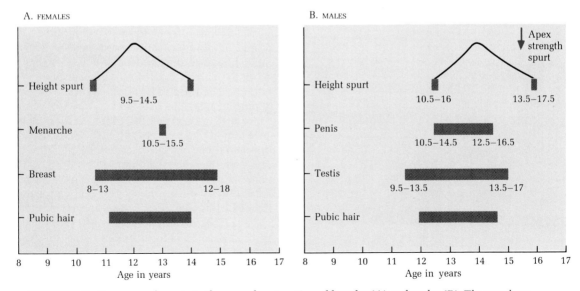

FIGURE 5-9. *Sequence of events in the sexual maturation of females (A) and males (B). The numbers represent the variation among individuals in the ages at which each aspect of sexual maturation begins or ends. For example, we see that the growth of the penis may begin as early as age 10½ or as late as age 14½.*

PHOTO 5-6. *During early adolescence, girls are maturing more rapidly than boys.*

at age 8, has pubic hair at age 11, and experiences menarche at 11½ may nearly complete her sexual maturation before the late developers in her classroom have even begun. Individual variation among males is at least as great: some boys reach sexual maturity as early as age 12½, while others *begin* later than that and do not reach puberty until their mid to late teens. Thus, a 12-year-old girl or a 14-year-old boy might be *prepubertal* (sexually immature), *midpubertal* (rapidly maturing), or *postpubertal* (sexually mature). From a biological perspective, this kind of variation is perfectly normal; and the age at which one attains sexual maturity has no significant effect on one's physical stature (height and weight) as an adult (Faust, 1977).

■ *Secular trends—are we maturing earlier?*

Recently the females in one family were surprised when a member of the younger generation began to menstruate some two months after her 12th birthday. The inevitable comparisons soon began,

as the girl learned that neither of her great-grandmothers had reached this milestone until age 15 and that her grandmother had been nearly 14 and her mother almost 13. At this point, the girl casually replied "Big deal! Lots of girls in my class have got their periods."

As it turns out, this young lady was simply "telling it like it is." In 1900, when her great-grandmother was born, the average age of first menstruation was 14–15. By 1950 most girls were reaching menarche between 13½ and 14, and today's norms have dropped even further, to age 12–12½ (Roche, 1979; Tanner, 1981). This secular trend toward earlier maturation started more than 100 years ago in the industrialized nations of the world, and it is now happening in the more prosperous of the Third World countries as well (Tanner, 1981). In addition, people have been growing taller and heavier over the past century, as we can see in Figure 5-10.

Why are we becoming taller and heavier and reaching puberty earlier than ever before? Robert Malina (1979) believes that these secular trends

BOX 5-3
ON FEELING OBESE AT 60 POUNDS—
ANOREXIA NERVOSA

Anorexia nervosa, or "nervous loss of appetite," is a potentially fatal psychosomatic condition that may affect as many as 1 of every 200 adolescent females (and a much smaller number of males). Typically anorexics are quiet, obedient young ladies who suddenly begin to starve themselves soon after menarche (or after someone happens to mention that they are getting fat). The affected young woman begins by dieting to a desired weight. But once she reaches her target, she simply continues to diet, eating less and less until she is little more than skin and bones. After she loses 20–30% of her body weight, the development of secondary sex characteristics (breasts and hips) may scarcely be noticeable, and menstruation may stop altogether. And even though she may resemble a walking skeleton, the 60–70-pound anorexic will insist she is well-nourished and will feel she could stand to lose a few more pounds (Minuchin, Rosman, & Baker, 1978). Anorexia nervosa is not merely a faddish quirk that is easily overcome; in fact, only 25–30% of anorexics show any improvement without psychological help, and some 5–20% end up starving themselves to death (Schleimer, 1981).

Parents of anorexics are often firm, overprotective guardians who have so controlled their child's activities that she has trouble making decisions and may find it difficult to establish an identity of her own. Psychoanalytic theorists have argued that the purpose of self-starvation is to avoid growing up and having to become independent of one's parents. By remaining childlike in appearance, the anorexic attempts to be a child—someone to be cared for and nurtured. Behaviorists view the condition as a strategy on the part of the child to wrest control of her life from overprotective parents while remaining at the center of their attention.

Although psychoanalysts and behaviorists disagree on the anorexic's underlying motives, members of both groups acknowledge that anorexia nervosa is a family condition that requires family therapy. Treatment may begin by hospitalizing the anorexic and applying operant conditioning techniques to get her to eat. For example, the anorexic may be punished for weight loss by having to stay in bed and rewarded with privileges such as television or visitors on days when she has gained weight. After the patient has begun to eat, the operant therapy is followed by family therapy in which the parents and the affected child are encouraged to view themselves as autonomous individuals who each have their own unique needs, goals, and motives. The purpose of the therapy is to persuade parents to exert less control over the adolescent's activities while convincing the adolescent that she can achieve some autonomy and a personal identity through means other than self-starvation. Although extensive treatment may be called for in some cases, the vast majority of anorexics respond favorably to family therapy, eventually overcoming their condition (Minuchin et al., 1978).

---

are due, in part, to improved medical care and better nutrition. Many crippling or growth-retarding illnesses have been eliminated over the past several decades, and the quality and quantity of nutrition have steadily improved. As a result, today's children are more likely than their parents or grandparents to reach their genetic potentials for maturation and growth.

Psychological Impact of Adolescent Growth and Development

What do adolescents think about the dramatic physical changes they are experiencing? For starters, they become quite concerned about their appearance and spend a great deal of time worrying about how other people will respond to them (Berscheid, Walster, & Bohrnstedt, 1973; Greif & Ulman, 1982). Generally speaking, adolescent females are most concerned about being too tall or too fat, and many well-proportioned young girls may compensate for perceived physical inadequacies by slouching, wearing flats, or trying a seemingly endless number of fad diets (for an example of what can happen if a girl becomes overly preoccupied with her weight, see Box 5-3). Girls are also apt to worry about the condition and texture of their hair and the size of their ears, breasts, noses, and hips. Clearly, adolescent females hope to be attractive to members of the other sex, and their self-concepts depend largely on how attractive they believe themselves to be (Berscheid, Walster, & Bohrnstedt, 1973).

Although adolescent males might have you believe otherwise, they too are very concerned about their body images and masculine prowess. Boys

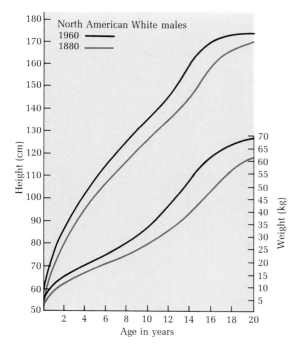

FIGURE 5-10. *Average height and weight of North American White males in 1880 and 1960.*

hope to be tall, muscular, handsome, and hairy, and an obvious deficiency in any of these respects is likely to make the distressed young man the butt of many jokes. (Berscheid, Walster, & Bohrnstedt, 1973).

■ *Effects of body build*

Body build (or physique) is a physical attribute that affects a child's self-concept and popularity with peers. In one study (Staffieri, 1967), children aged 6 to 10 were shown full-length silhouettes of three body types and asked to indicate the physique they preferred. The body types used in this research were **ectomorphs** (thin, linear individuals with underdeveloped muscles), **endomorphs** (individuals with soft, rounded or "chubby" physiques), and **mesomorphs** (individuals with athletic builds—broad shoulders, large muscles, and strong legs). After stating which body type they preferred, the children were given a list of adjectives and asked to select those that applied to each body type. Finally, each child was asked to list the names of five classmates who

could be considered good friends and three classmates whom he or she didn't like very well.

The results of this study were clear: Children preferred to look like the mesomorphic silhouette. Moreover, they assigned positive adjectives—*brave, strong, neat,* and *helpful*—to mesomorphic figures, whereas ectomorphs and endomorphs were described much less favorably. Finally, there was a definite relationship between body build and popularity: the mesomorphs in the class turned out to be the most popular children, while endomorphic classmates were least popular. Later research with adolescents and adults paints a similar picture—mesomorphs are generally popular individuals who rise to positions of leadership, whereas endomorphs and ectomorphs tend to be much less popular with their peers (Clausen, 1975; Lerner, 1969).

Why should body build affect one's popularity? One hypothesis (favored by some behavior geneticists) is that people inherit different patterns or concentrations of hormones, which influence both their body types and their behavior. These behavioral predispositions (or temperament) would then affect the person's standing in the peer group. A second possibility favored by social-learning theorists (Lerner, 1976) is that we have particular expectations about people with different physiques and that we act on those expectations to create a **self-fulfilling prophecy**. For example, we may view mesomorphs as athletes and encourage them along those lines; or we may perceive ectomorphs as intellectually inclined and encourage and reinforce them for solitary activities such as reading or writing poetry. Finally, it is possible that both these theories are partly correct: Children with different body types may be pre-

---

ectomorph: *a person with a thin, linear physique and small or underdeveloped muscles.*
endomorph: *a person with a soft, rounded physique; one who appears chubby and non-muscular.*
mesomorph: *a person with an athletic physique characterized by large bones, broad shoulders, well-developed muscles, and little fat.*
self-fulfilling prophecy: *phenomenon whereby people cause others to act in accordance with the expectations they have about those others.*

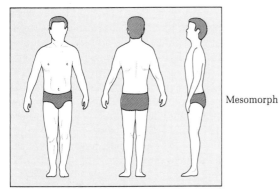

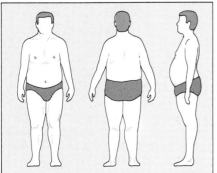

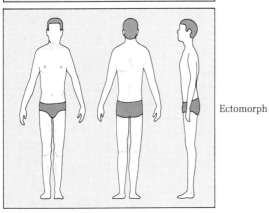

FIGURE 5-11. The three body types used in Staffieri's experiment.

disposed to different patterns of behavior, thus creating stereotyped expectations about their interests and abilities. These stereotypes may then affect the ways other people treat the child, so that the social environment ends up fitting children into distinct personality molds based on their body types.

■ *Does rate of maturation matter?*

Think back for a moment to your own adolescence—to that point when you first realized you were rapidly becoming a man or a woman. Did this happen earlier to you than to your friends, or later? Do you think the timing of these events had any meaningful effects on your personality or your social life?

Longitudinal research conducted at the University of California suggests that boys who mature early enjoy a number of social advantages over boys who mature late. Mary Cover Jones and Nancy Bayley (1950) followed the development of 16 early-maturing and 16 late-maturing male adolescents over a six-year period. They found that late maturers were more eager, anxious, and attention-seeking and were rated as less masculine and less physically attractive than early maturers. Early maturers tended to be poised and confident in social settings, and they were over-represented among those who had won athletic honors or election to student offices. Other researchers have found that late maturers tend to feel unsure of themselves, socially inadequate, and inferior, and they often express a need for encouragement, sympathy, and understanding (Livson & Peskin, 1980; Mussen & Jones, 1957; Weatherley, 1964).

Do boys who mature late eventually overcome the social disadvantages they faced as adolescents? Mary Cover Jones (1957, 1965) tested this hypothesis by following up on the 32 boys from Jones and Bayley's project when these subjects were in their early thirties. Although many of the differences between the two groups had diminished since adolescence, the late maturers were still less sociable, less responsible, less confident, and less popular with peers than members of the early-maturing group. So it seems that the social disadvantages that late-maturing males experience during adolescence sometimes persist well into adulthood.

Why is the early-maturing male in such an advantageous position? Perhaps because adults may react positively to the "adultlike" appearance of an early maturer, affording him privileges and responsibilities normally reserved for older individuals. This kind of treatment may then promote the sense of poise or self-confidence that enables early maturers to become popular and to assume positions of leadership within the peer group

(Eichorn, 1963; Livson & Peskin, 1980). By contrast, if parents, teachers, and peers continue to treat a "boyish-looking" late maturer as if he were somehow less worthy of privileges or responsibility, it is easy to see how he could become unsure of himself and feel rejected.

For girls, the relationship between rate of maturation and social status depends on the age of the peer group. Early maturers among groups of sixth-graders tend to be *less* popular than their prepubertal classmates (Faust, 1960; Jones & Mussen, 1958). However, the early maturer will often rise to a position of prominence in junior high school when the female peer group develops a strong interest in heterosexual relationships and discovers that early-maturing females tend to be popular with males (Faust, 1960).

Now let's speculate a bit. As you can see, most of the research on the effects of early versus late maturing was conducted more than 20 years ago, in the 1950s and early 1960s. Clearly, the times have changed since then. Today adolescents begin to date about three years earlier than they did when the research was conducted, and the time when dating begins now depends more on social factors such as grade in school than on one's level of sexual maturation (Dornbusch et al., 1981). For these reasons, many of today's late maturers have probably already established good relations with members of the other sex *before they begin to mature*—a fact that may make the timing of sexual maturation far less important in the 1980s than it was 25–30 years ago.

CAUSES AND CORRELATES OF PHYSICAL GROWTH AND DEVELOPMENT

At the beginning of the chapter, you were asked to think about *how* and *why* children grow and why they develop increasingly precise motor skills that enable them to crawl, walk, jump, and run. These thought questions normally provoke a lot of discussion in my own classes. Typically, someone will first offer a biological explanation, arguing that our genotypes and maturational timetables determine the rate and extent of physical growth, as well as the sequencing and timing of motor development. But invariably, other students are

quick to point out that environmental factors such as nutrition or opportunities to practice motor skills may also influence the physical aspects of human development. Although these students may not have read the pertinent literature, they are usually able to generate enough anecdotal evidence to conclude that physical growth and development represent a complex interplay between biological predispositions and a variety of environmental influences—with biology assuming the more dominant role. Now let's consider the data that have led many developmental researchers to agree with this conclusion.

Biological Mechanisms

Clearly, biological factors play a major role in the growth process. Although children do not all grow at the same rate, we have seen that the *sequencing* of both physical maturation and motor development are reasonably consistent from child to child. Apparently these regular maturational sequences that all humans share are species-specific attributes—products of our common genetic heritage.

■ Effects of individual genotypes

Aside from our common genetic ties to the human race, we have each inherited a unique combination of genes that will affect our physical growth and development. For example, children of tall parents tend to be taller than children of short parents, a finding that implies that stature is a heritable attribute. The proof comes from family studies: identical twins are much more similar in stature than fraternal twins, regardless of whether the measurements are taken during the first year of life, at 4 years of age, or in early adulthood (Tanner, 1978; Wilson, 1976).

Rate of maturation is also a heritable attribute. James Tanner (1978) reports that female identical twins who live together reach menarche within two months of each other, while fraternal twin sisters are usually 10–12 months apart. Tanner concludes that this genetic control of growth rate "operates throughout the whole process of growth, for skeletal maturity at all ages shows the same type of family correlations as menarche. The age of eruption of the teeth is similarly controlled [by one's genotype]" (p. 126).

Of course, knowing that genotype affects "rate of maturation" and the size or shape that one assumes is only part of the story. The next logical question is "How does genotype influence the growth process?" To be honest, we are not completely certain, although it appears that our genes regulate the production of hormones, which, in turn, have a major effect on physical growth and development.

■ *Hormonal influences—the endocrinology of growth*

In Chapter Four we noted that a male fetus assumes a malelike appearance because (1) a gene on his Y chromosome triggers the development of testes, which (2) secrete a male hormone (testosterone) that is necessary for the development of a male reproductive system. By the fourth prenatal month, the thyroid gland has formed and begins to produce **thyroxine,** a hormone that is essential if the brain and nervous system are to develop properly. Babies who are born with a thyroid deficiency will soon become mentally handicapped if this condition goes undiagnosed and untreated (Tanner, 1978). Those who develop a thyroid deficiency later in childhood will not suffer brain damage, because their brain growth spurt is over. However, they will begin to grow very slowly, a finding that indicates that a certain level of thyroxine is necessary for normal growth and development.

Perhaps the most critical of the *endocrine* (hormone-secreting) glands is the **pituitary,** a "master gland" located at the base of the brain that sends biochemical signals to trigger the release of hormones from all other endocrine glands. For example, the thyroid gland secretes thyroxine only if instructed to do so by a hormone (TSH, or thyroid-stimulating hormone) from the pituitary. In addition to regulating the endocrine system, the pituitary produces a **growth hormone (GH)** that stimulates the rapid growth and development of body cells. Growth hormone is released in small amounts several times a day. When parents tell their children that lots of sleep helps one to grow big and strong, they are right—GH is normally secreted into the bloodstream about 60-90 minutes after a child falls asleep (Tanner, 1978). Although much remains to be learned about how GH stimulates growth, we do know that it is essential for *normal* growth and development. Children who lack this hormone do grow, and they are usually well proportioned as adults. However, they will stand only about 130 cm tall—a little over four feet (Tanner, 1978).

As nearly as we can tell, physical growth in infancy and childhood is regulated by thyroxine and the pituitary growth hormone. However, the picture begins to change as the child approaches adolescence and the body prepares for the growth spurt that is soon to follow.

The dramatic physical changes that occur during adolescence are preceded by more subtle changes in the child's endocrine system. The process begins as the hypothalamus (a part of the brain) instructs the pituitary to activate the **adrenal glands** and the gonads (ovaries or testes). In females, androgenlike hormones secreted by the adrenal cortex trigger the adolescent growth spurt and the development of pubic and axillary hair (Tanner, 1978). At about the same time, the ovaries begin to produce *estrogen* and *progesterone,* female hormones that are responsible for the development of the breasts, uterus, and vagina, the onset of menarche and regulation of the menstrual cycle, and a widening of the hips. For males, the most important hormone is *testosterone,* a substance produced by the testes, which triggers the adolescent growth spurt as well as the growth of the penis and testes, the production of sperm, voice changes, and the development of pubic, axillary, and facial hair (Tanner, 1978). Apparently androgen from the adrenal cortex merely supplements the male growth spurt rather than triggering it. We think this to be true because in the absence of testosterone, no growth spurt takes place at all (Tanner, 1978).

Although levels of the pituitary growth hormone (GH) *do not* increase during adolescence, this substance continues to play an important role in the growth process. Apparently its function is that of a catalyst for the sex hormones, for

> the usual level of GH must be present for testosterone to produce its full growth-effect on the muscles and on the bones of the limbs and shoulders. In the absence of GH the height spurt (in males) is only about two-thirds of normal, and the shoulder width spurt even less. . . . In girls the height spurt is also only about two-thirds of normal in the absence of growth hormone; and the estrogen-induced growth of hip width is likewise reduced [Tanner, 1978, pp. 100–101].

TABLE 5-5. Hormonal influences on growth and development

Endocrine gland	Hormones produced	Effects on growth and development
Pituitary	Activating hormones	Signal other endocrine glands to secrete their hormones
	Growth hormone	Helps to regulate growth from birth through adolescence
Thyroid	Thyroxine	Affects growth and development of the brain and helps to regulate growth of the body during childhood
Adrenal glands	Adrenal androgens	Stimulates the adolescent growth spurt, pubic hair, and axillary hair in females; supplements the adolescent growth spurt in males
Testes	Testosterone	Is responsible for differentiation of the male reproductive system during the prenatal period; triggers the male growth spurt and sexual maturation during adolescence
Ovaries	Estrogen Progesterone	Trigger sexual maturation in females and are responsible for regulating the menstrual cycle

Table 5-5 summarizes the hormonal influences on human growth and development.

Environmental Influences

At least four environmental factors are known to affect physical growth and development: nutrition, illnesses, emotional stress, and practice.

■ Nutrition

Diet is perhaps the most potent of all environmental influences on human growth and development. As you might expect, children who are inadequately nourished will grow very slowly, if they grow at all. The dramatic impact of malnutrition on physical development can be seen by comparing the heights of children before and during wartime periods when food is less readily available. In Figure 5-12 we see that the average heights of schoolchildren in Stuttgart, Germany, increased during the 20 years between the two world wars. However, these secular trends were clearly reversed during the war years, when it was not always possible to satisfy the children's nutritional needs.

Short-term versus prolonged malnutrition. Prolonged malnutrition during the first five years of life may seriously retard brain growth and cause a child to remain smaller than his or her adequately nourished peers throughout the life cycle (Lewin, 1975; Tanner, 1978). These findings make sense when we recall that the first five years is a period

when the brain will normally gain about 65% of its eventual adult weight and the body will grow to nearly two-thirds of its adult height (Tanner, 1978).

If malnutrition is neither prolonged nor especially severe, children will probably recover from any growth deficits by growing much faster than normal once their diet becomes adequate. James Tanner (1978) views this **catch-up growth** as a basic principle of physical development. Presumably children who experience growth deficits because of malnutrition or illness will grow very rapidly in order to regain (or catch up to) the growth trajectory that they are genetically pro-

---

thyroxine: *a hormone produced by the thyroid gland, essential for normal growth of the brain and the body.*

pituitary: *a "master gland" located at the base of the brain that regulates the endocrine glands and produces growth hormone.*

growth hormone (GH): *the pituitary hormone that stimulates the rapid growth and development of body cells.*

adrenal gland: *an endocrine gland that secretes androgen, a hormone that triggers the adolescent growth spurt in females.*

catch-up growth: *a period of accelerated growth in which children who have experienced growth deficits will grow very rapidly to "catch up to" the growth trajectory that they are genetically programmed to follow.*

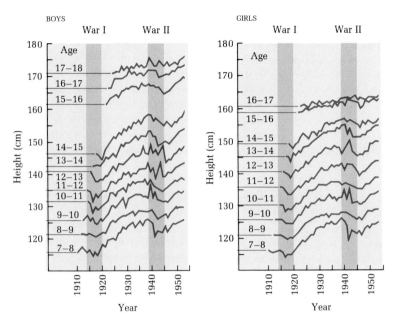

FIGURE 5-12. *The effect of malnutrition on growth. These graphs show the average heights of Stuttgart schoolchildren aged 7–18 between 1910 and the early 1950s. Notice the trend toward increasing height between 1920 and 1940, the period between the two world wars. This secular trend was dramatically reversed during World War II, when nutrition was often inadequate.*

grammed to follow. When growth catches up with its preprogrammed course, it will then slow down and follow the path dictated by heredity.

When is a child malnourished? There are actually two kinds of malnutrition. **Protein/calorie deficiency** occurs when people do not get enough protein and/or total calories to sustain normal growth. The second type of malnutrition is **vitamin/mineral deficiency:** people get enough to eat, but from a diet that is lacking in one or more substances that would help to maintain their health and promote normal growth.

Protein/calorie deficiencies are very common among children living in poor, underdeveloped countries in Africa, Asia, and Latin America (Winick, 1976). When children are severely malnourished, they are likely to suffer from either of two nutritional diseases—**marasmus** and **kwashiorkor**—each of which has a slightly different cause. Marasmus affects babies who get insufficient protein and too few calories—a condition that can easily occur if a mother is malnourished and does not have the resources to

provide her child with a nutritious commercial substitute for mother's milk. A victim of marasmus becomes very frail and wrinkled in appearance as growth stops and the body tissues begin to waste away. If conditions should improve, enabling these children to survive, they will remain smaller than their adequately nourished peers and will probably suffer impaired intellectual development as well (Winick, 1976).

Kwashiorkor affects children who get enough calories but little if any protein. As the disease progresses, the child's hair will thin, the face, legs, and abdomen will swell with water, and severe skin lesions may develop. In many poor countries of the world, about the only high-quality source of protein readily available to children is mother's milk. So breast-fed infants will not ordinarily suffer from marasmus unless their mothers are severely malnourished; however, they may develop kwashiorkor when they are weaned from the breast and thereby denied their primary source of protein.

In the United States, fewer than 2% of preschool children suffer from protein/calorie defi-

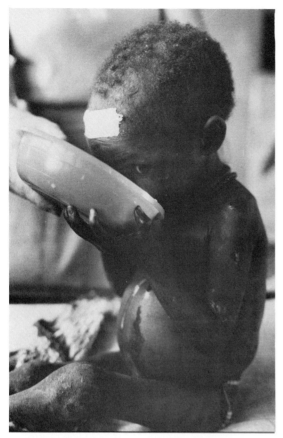

PHOTO 5-7. *The lesions on this little boy's skin and his swollen stomach are symptoms of kwashiorkor. Without adequate protein in his diet, this child will be more susceptible to many diseases and may die from an illness that well-nourished children could easily overcome.*

ciencies, and the few who do are rarely so malnourished that they develop symptoms of marasmus or kwashiorkor. However, vitamin and mineral deficiencies may affect large numbers of children from all social classes in this relatively affluent society. One recent nutritional survey reported that the diets of many preschool children from the lower socioeconomic strata are deficient in vitamins A and C and in riboflavin (Owen, Kram, Garry, Lower, & Lubin, cited in Eichorn, 1979). Another survey conducted in ten states found that over 90% of 1–3-year-olds had diets that were deficient in iron, and 26–48% of these

infants and toddlers (depending on the state) were receiving but one-third of the recommended levels (see Eichorn, 1979). The major effects of these vitamin and mineral deficiencies are to make children irritable and listless and to retard their rate of growth. A malnourished child is also less resistant to other illnesses, which could have their own adverse effects on physical growth and development.

Overnutrition. Dietary excess (eating too much) is yet another form of poor nutrition that may have several long-term consequences for the developing child. The most immediate effect is that the child may become obese and face added risk of serious medical complications such as diabetes or high blood pressure. Obese children may also find it difficult to make friends with age mates, who are apt to tease them about their size and shape. Indeed, we have already seen that endomorphic (chubby to fat) physiques are described in very unfavorable terms (for example, *sloppy, ugly, stupid*) by school-age children and that endomorphic youngsters are among the least popular students in grade-school classrooms (Staffieri, 1967).

Are fat children likely to become fat adults? In Box 5-4 we consider this issue as we take a closer look at some of the causes and consequences of obesity.

■ *Illness*

The very minor illnesses that all children experience have little if any effect on physical growth

---

protein/calorie deficiency: *a form of malnutrition in which children do not receive enough protein or total calories to sustain normal growth.*

vitamin/mineral deficiency: *a form of malnutrition in which the diet provides sufficient calories but is lacking in one or more substances that promote normal growth.*

marasmus: *a growth-retarding disease affecting infants who receive insufficient protein and too few calories.*

kwashiorkor: *a growth-retarding disease affecting children who receive enough calories but little if any protein.*

BOX 5-4
WHO BECOMES OBESE—AND WHY?

Obesity is a medical term describing individuals who are at least 20% above the "ideal" weight for their height, age, and sex. This condition is now rather common in the United States, where as many as 15 million adults and 2–3 million schoolchildren are seriously overweight (National Center for Health Statistics, 1975; Scarrone, 1976). The term "*seriously overweight*" is quite appropriate, for obese people do not live as long as those whose body weight falls within the normal range. Specifically, the obese are prone to a number of serious medical disorders, including heart and kidney disease, high blood pressure, diabetes, liver problems, and crippling arthritis (Scarrone, 1976).

Many factors may contribute to obesity. One is *heredity:* Dr. Jane Mayer (1975) found that 80% of the children of obese parents became obese themselves, compared with only 7% of children whose parents were not overweight.* *Activity level* (which is moderately heritable) is also a contributing factor, or so it seems. Mayer has found that obese children simply do not move as often or burn up as many calories in their day-to-day activities as children of normal weight. Certain *glandular malfunctions,* such as a diminished output of sex hormones or an over-

*Of course, an alternative interpretation is that obese parents tend to have obese children because fat people are likely to (1) overfeed their offspring or (2) serve as models for overeating.

production of insulin, may also contribute to obesity. But the main reason most obese people are overweight is that they simply eat too much. For the obese, "appetite has engulfed hunger—they eat not to satisfy their hunger but to satisfy their appetite" (Scarrone, 1976, p. 496).

Overeating contributes to obesity in two ways: (1) by producing an excess of fat cells and (2) by depositing fatty tissue within these cells, causing them to swell (Eichorn, 1979). Apparently fat cells are most likely to be added during two periods: from the last trimester of pregnancy through age 2 and during the adolescent growth spurt. Once added, a fat cell remains in the body for life. This means that we lose weight by decreasing the *amount of fat* in our fat cells, rather than by ridding the body of these storehouses of fat. So overfeeding during infancy and early adolescence may be particularly harmful. These are periods when overnourished children are likely to develop new fat cells, which may than accumulate fat and swell at any point later in life.

Do chubby babies become fat children? Are fat children likely to become obese adults? The answers are by no means clear at this time, for very little longitudinal research has been conducted. The research that has been done suggests that overweight infants and toddlers tend to be overweight at 6-10 years of age (Neyzi et al., 1976). Moreover, obese schoolchildren are more likely than their thinner peers to be overweight as adolescents and adults (Abraham, Collins, & Nordsieck, 1971; Zack, Harlan, Leaverton, & Cornoni-Huntley, 1979). However, these statistical trends can be deceiving, for many obese children are not obese as adults, and many

and development. Major diseases that keep a child in bed for several months may retard growth; but after recovering, the child will ordinarily show a growth spurt (catch-up growth) that makes up for the progress lost while he or she was sick (Tanner, 1978).

Children with frequently recurring colds, ear problems, sore throats, or skin infections tend to be smaller than their less "sickly" peers (Tanner, 1978). However, these sickly children also tend to come from economically depressed family settings where proper nutrition is lacking. So it is certainly possible that both the slow rates of growth and the recurring illnesses that characterize "sickly" children are attributable, in part, to nutritional deficiencies.

■ *Emotional stress and lack of affection*

Otherwise healthy children who experience too much stress and too little affection are likely to lag far behind their age mates in physical growth and motor development. This **failure to thrive** syndrome may characterize as many as 3% of preschool children in the United States and up to 5% of all patients admitted to pediatric hospitals (Lipsitt, 1979).

Perhaps the most intriguing research on the failure-to-thrive syndrome was reported by Lytt Gardner (1972). Gardner studied the development of healthy, nonabused children who received adequate physical care but little affection from emotionally unresponsive parents. One case involved twins—a boy and a girl—who grew nor-

obese adults were not markedly overweight earlier in life (Roche, 1981).

It is likely that overnourished infants and adolescents do develop extra fat cells that stand ready to soak up excess calories and thereby increase their chances of becoming obese. However, a person's adult weight will also depend on the amount he or she eats and the energy expended in day-to-day activities. In other words, it may be harder for an obese infant or an obese adolescent to keep from being overweight as an adult—but it is by no means impossible. In contrast, even skinny children can become obese adults if they reduce their physical activity and begin to exceed their nutritional requirements, thereby gorging their "normal number" of fat cells with fatty tissue.

How is childhood obesity to be treated? Should parents place their chubby infants and adolescents on crash diets? Probably not, for infancy and adolescence are periods of very rapid growth when a protein/calorie deficiency could seriously hinder the development of the brain, muscles, and bones (Winick, 1975). Besides, once children have become obese, they often eat no more (and sometimes less) than their thinner peers (Mayer, 1975); the reason they stay fat is that they are less active and expend less energy than children of average weight. Today many doctors favor a two-pronged approach to treating childhood obesity. First, the child should be encouraged to burn more calories by getting regular exercise (for example, by walking to school or playing with toys that require large-muscle activity). Second, parents should try to restrict eating to mealtimes and to serve fewer sweets without necessarily alter-

Obese children are more likely than their thinner peers to be overweight as adolescents and adults.

ing the child's intake of calories. The idea is that the child won't feel rejected or mistreated if he can eat as much as he cares to at mealtimes. And if he eats no more than usual, his weight may stabilize, thus allowing him to eventually "outgrow" his endomorphic physique as he becomes taller.

mally for the first four months. Soon thereafter, the twins' father lost his job, their mother became pregnant with an unwanted baby, and the parents blamed each other for the hardships they were experiencing. The father then moved out of the house, and the mother focused her resentment on her infant son, becoming emotionally detached and unresponsive to his bids for affection (she did, however, provide him with adequate nutrition and physical care). Although his sister continued to grow normally, the boy twin at 13 months of age was about the size of an average 7-month-old infant. In other words, his growth was severely retarded, a condition that Gardner called **deprivation dwarfism.**

Gardner believes that deprivation dwarfism is

directly related to the emotional deprivation that the child has experienced at home. He bases his conclusion on the behavior of many deprivation dwarfs who were hospitalized for observation and treatment. The following passage describes a typical case:

---

failure to thrive: *a condition in which seemingly healthy infants fail to grow normally and are much smaller than their age mates.*

deprivation dwarfism: *a retardation in physical growth that is apparently triggered by emotional distress and/or a lack of love and attention.*

The 15-month-old child quickly responded to the attention she received from the hospital staff. She gained weight and made up for lost growth; her emotional state improved strikingly. Moreover, *these changes were . . . unrelated to any changes in food intake.* During her stay in the hospital, she received the same standard nutrient dosage she had received at home. It appears to have been the enrichment of her social environment, not of her diet, that was responsible for the normalization of her growth [Gardner, 1972, p. 78; italics added].

Gardner's deprivation dwarfs (and most children who fail to thrive) are infants and toddlers who have suffered *severe* emotional deprivation. Yet there is evidence that older, school-age children who experience less severe emotional traumas may also grow more slowly than normal. For example, Dr. Elsie Widdowson (1951) found that one group of orphans who were given an enriched diet actually grew *at a slower rate* than a second group of orphans who remained on the standard orphanage fare. The most likely explanation for this puzzling result is that children in the "enriched diet" group were exposed to a strict and emotionally unresponsive teacher/caretaker at precisely the time that their diet changed for the better. Thus, the lack of affection and emotional distress that these children experienced apparently interfered with normal growth even though their diet had actually improved.

Why do you suppose emotional distress inhibits physical growth and development? Apparently the answer is not related to diet, for Gardner's deprivation dwarfs who received attention in the hospital grew rapidly on the same diet on which they had "failed to thrive" and Widdowson's emotionally distressed orphans failed to thrive even though their diets had improved. Current thinking on the subject is that emotional traumas may cause a growth slowdown by inhibiting the production of pituitary growth hormone. Indeed, Gardner (1972) noted that deprivation dwarfs have abnormally low levels of growth hormone in their bloodstreams during periods of subnormal growth. And when these distressed youngsters begin to receive attention, the secretion of growth hormone resumes, enabling them to grow rapidly and make up the ground lost while they were emotionally deprived (Tanner, 1978).

■ *Practice effects*

In 1933 Mary Shirley reported that a typical American infant could sit without support at 7 months, stand while holding a piece of furniture at 9 months, walk when led at 11 months, and walk alone at 15 months. Modern infants develop much faster, reaching each of these important motor milestones some two to four months earlier than the children observed by Shirley in the 1930s (see Table 5-4). How might we explain these discrepant findings?

There are at least two plausible explanations for the precocious motor development of today's children. The most popular explanation is a *secular-trend hypothesis:* children today crawl and walk earlier than children of the 1930s because better nutrition and health care have accelerated the maturation process. Other theorists favor a *practice hypothesis:* modern children are quicker to develop important motor skills because they have more toys to manipulate and are less often confined to cribs and strollers than infants of the 1930s.

Much of the early literature would lead one to believe that practice plays little if any part in the development of basic motor skills. For example, Wayne and Marsena Dennis (1940) found that Hopi Indian infants who had been swaddled and bound to cradleboards for the first nine or ten months of life were no slower to take that first unaided step than Hopi infants whose parents had decided not to follow the tribal custom of tying them down. In addition, Myrtle McGraw (1935) and Arnold Gesell (Gesell & Thompson, 1929) conducted experiments in which one identical twin was allowed to practice motor skills such as climbing stairs or stacking blocks, while the cotwin was denied these experiences. The results of both studies indicated that practice had little effect on motor development: when finally allowed to perform, the unpracticed twin soon matched the skills of the cotwin who had had many opportunities to practice. The investigators concluded that physical maturation is what underlies motor development and that practice merely allows a child to perfect those skills that maturation has made possible.

Proponents of the practice hypothesis believe that this conclusion is much too strong. They note that the Hopi infants who spent their first nine to ten months on cradleboards had several months to move about and practice motor skills before they (and the unbound infants) finally began to walk. Even the "unpracticed" twins of the studies by McGraw (1935) and Gesell and Thompson (1929) were completely free to practice any number of other motor skills (such as grasping objects in their cribs, crawling, walking) that may have enabled them to climb stairs or stack blocks when they were finally given an opportunity to do so. So the critics believe that practice is essential to motor development and that children might never learn to crawl, walk, run, jump, or throw if they are denied all opportunities to rehearse these basic skills.

Evidence for the practice hypothesis. Obviously it would be grossly unethical to tie a child down for five years to see whether he could later crawl or walk without having had an opportunity to practice. However, Wayne Dennis (1960) was able to locate and study two groups of institutionalized orphans in Iran who had had very few opportunities to practice basic motor skills. The orphanages where the children lived were impoverished and understaffed. The children had no toys to play with, and they spent most of their time lying flat on their backs in their cribs. In fact, their mattresses developed hollows that made it nearly impossible for the children to roll over onto their stomachs. These orphans were never placed in a sitting position, were rarely played with, and were even fed in their cribs with their bottles propped on pillows. If a child managed to sit up, he might be taken from his crib and placed on the floor, where he was left alone (without toys) to entertain himself as best he could.

Dennis found that the motor abilities of these institutionalized orphans were severely retarded. Of all infants aged 1–2, only 42% could sit alone, and *none* could walk. In fact, only 8% of the 2–3-year-olds and 15% of the 3–4-year-olds could walk alone! Dennis concluded that maturation is *necessary but not sufficient* for motor development. In other words, children who are physically capable of sitting, crawling, or walking will not be very proficient at these skills unless they have opportunities to practice them.

Importance of an upright posture.   Recently, Esther Thelen and Donna Fisher (1982) have proposed that the age at which infants reach various motor milestones may depend on the amount of time they spend in a vertical posture. Specifically, they believe that an infant who is often placed in an upright posture will develop strength in the legs, neck, and trunk (an acceleration of muscular growth), which, in turn, will promote the development of motor skills such as standing and walking. And they may be correct. Babies from Third World cultures, who are often carried vertically in slings (or held upright on their mothers' laps), do walk earlier than Western infants, who spend much more time in a horizontal posture (Thelen & Fisher, 1982). Moreover, one team of investigators found that 2–8-week-old infants who were held upright and encouraged to practice their "stepping" reflex subsequently walked at an earlier age than infants in a control group who did not receive this early training (Zelazo, Zelazo, & Kolb, 1972).

In sum, it appears that both maturation and experience are important determinants of motor development. Maturation does place limits on the age at which a child will first be *capable* of sitting, standing, or walking. However, it seems that experiences such as upright posturing and various forms of practice may well affect the age at which important physical capabilities are first translated into action.

SUMMARY

Neonates are remarkably capable organisms who come equipped with a number of inborn reflexes (breathing, sucking, swallowing, and so on) that help them to adapt to their new surroundings. In the first five minutes of life, newborns are given the Apgar test to see how well they are breathing and otherwise adjusting to the extrauterine environment. Two to three days later, they often take the Brazelton Neonatal Behavioral Assessment Scale, an instrument designed to measure their reflexes, social responsiveness, and neurological well-being. This scale is particularly useful at identifying infants who are likely to experience later emotional difficulties.

The sensory equipment of newborn children is in reasonably good working order. Neonates can see, hear, smell, taste, and respond to touch, pain, and changes in temperature. Although these senses are not fully developed at birth, they mature rapidly over the course of the first year.

The infant's state (that is, state of consciousness) changes many times during a typical day. Newborns spend nearly 70% of their time asleep; but as they mature, they spend less time sleeping and more time awake, alert, and attending to the environment. Crying is a state that tells us much about the baby. If a neonate's cries are high-pitched and nonrhythmic, he or she may be premature, malnourished, or brain-damaged. Normal, healthy infants emit at least three different cries (hunger, anger, and pain) to communicate their wants and discomforts. However, crying usually diminishes over the first year as parents learn how to soothe their crying infants, and infants learn to use other methods of communicating with their close companions.

The body is constantly changing between infancy and adulthood. Height and weight increase rapidly during the first two years. Growth then becomes more gradual until early adolescence, when there is a rapid "growth spurt." The shape of the body also changes because various body parts grow at different rates and different times. For example, the head and trunk grow rapidly during the prenatal period and infancy, the limbs are growing fastest in late childhood, and the trunk is once again the fastest-growing segment of the body during adolescence.

Skeletal and muscular development parallel the changes occurring in height and weight. The bones become longer and thicker, and they gradually harden, completing their growth and development by the late teens. Muscles increase in density and size, particularly during the growth spurt of early adolescence. The brain develops rapidly over the first five years of life, and nerve cells become encased in myelin—a waxy sheath that acts like an insulator to speed the transmission of neural impulses. Development of the skeletal, muscular, and nervous systems follows a cephalocaudal (head downward) and proximodistal (center outward) pattern: structures in the upper and central regions of the body mature before those in the lower and peripheral regions.

Motor development also proceeds in a cephalocaudal and proximodistal direction. As a result, motor skills evolve in a definite sequence, in which infants gain control over their heads, necks, and upper arms before they become proficient with their legs, feet, and hands. As the nervous system and muscles mature, children gradually acquire more control over their bodies. By age 3 they can run in a straight line, jump, and catch a large ball, although tying their shoes and copying complex figures on paper are impossible tasks. By age 5 the child is quite fluid at large-muscle activities and can draw figures or copy letters with a crayon. By age 8–9 children can easily ride bicycles and use household tools and are becoming skillful performers at games that require eye/hand coordination.

At about age 10½ for females, and age 13 for males, the adolescent growth spurt begins. Weight increases first, followed some four to six months later by a rapid increase in height. The muscles undergo a period of rapid growth about a year after the maximum acceleration in height.

Sexual maturation begins about the same time as the adolescent growth spurt and follows a predictable sequence for members of each sex. For females, the onset of breast and pubic-hair development is followed by a widening of the hips, enlarging of the uterus and vagina, menarche (first menstruation), and completion of breast and pubic-hair growth. For males, development of the testes and scrotum is followed by the emergence of pubic hair, the growth of the penis, the ability to ejaculate, the appearance of facial hair, and a lowering of the voice. Over the past 100 years, males and females have been growing taller and heavier and reaching sexual maturity earlier— possibly because of improved nutrition and health care. Yet there are wide individual variations in the timing of sexual maturation and growth. Early-maturing males experience fewer psychological and social problems than late maturers. Among females, the psychological correlates of early or late maturing are less apparent, although early-maturing girls tend to become quite popular.

Many factors affect physical growth and development. Among the important biological contributors are genotype, maturation, and hormones. Adequate nutrition, good health, and freedom from prolonged emotional traumas are also necessary to ensure normal growth and development. In addition, children must have opportunities to practice important skills such as reaching, grasping, sitting, standing, and walking if motor development is to proceed normally.

REFERENCES

Abraham, S., Collins, G., & Nordsieck, M. (1971). Relationship of childhood weight status to morbidity in adults. *Health Services and Mental Health Administration Health Reports, 86,* 273–284.

Ainsworth, M. D. S., Bell, S. M., & Stayton, D. J. (1972). Individual differences in the development of some attachment behaviors. *Merrill-Palmer Quarterly, 18,* 123–143.

Alegria, J., & Noirot, E. (1978). Neonate orientation behavior towards human voices. *International Journal of Behavioral Development, 1,* 291–312.

Banks, M. S. (1980). The development of visual accommodation during early infancy. *Child Development, 51,* 646–666.

Berg, W. K., Adkinson, C. D., & Strock, B. D. (1973). Duration and frequency of periods of alertness in neonates. *Developmental Psychology, 9,* 434.

Berg, W. K., & Berg, K. M. (1979). Psychological development in infancy: State, sensory function, and attention. In J. D. Osofsky (Ed.), *Handbook of infant development.* New York: Wiley.

Berscheid, E., Walster, E., & Bohrnstedt, G. (1973, June). The happy American body: A survey report. *Psychology Today,* pp. 119–131.

Birns, B., Blank, M., & Bridger, W. H. (1966). The effectiveness of various soothing techniques on human neonates. *Psychosomatic Medicine, 28,* 316–322.

Boismier, J. D. (1977). Visual stimulation and the wake-sleep behavior in human neonates. *Developmental Psychobiology, 10,* 219–227.

Bornstein, M. H. (1979). Perceptual development: Stability and change in feature perception. In M. H. Bornstein & William Kessen (Eds.), *Psychological development from infancy: Image to intention.* Hillsdale, NJ: Erlbaum.

Bower, T. G. R. (1982). *Development in infancy.* San Francisco: W. H. Freeman.

Bowlby, J. (1973). *Attachment and loss.* Vol. 2: *Separation.* London: Hogarth Press.

Brackbill, Y. (1975). Continuous stimulation and arousal level in infancy: Effects of stimulus intensity and stress. *Child Development, 46,* 364–369.

Brazelton, T. B. (1979). Behavioral competence of the newborn infant. *Seminars in Perinatology, 3,* 35–44.

Brierley, J. (1976). *The growing brain.* London: NFER Publishing.

Clausen, J. A. (1975). The social meaning of differential physical maturation. In D. E. Drugastin & G. H. Elder (Eds.), *Adolescence in the life cycle.* New York: Halsted Press.

Condon, W. S., & Sander, L. W. (1974). Neonate movement is synchronized with adult speech: Interactional participation and language acquisition. *Science, 183,* 99–101.

Corbin, C. (1973). *A textbook of motor development.* Dubuque, Iowa: William C. Brown.

Crook, C. K. (1978). Taste perception in the newborn infant. *Infant Behavior and Development, 1,* 52–69.

Dennis, W. (1960). Causes of retardation among institutional children: Iran. *Journal of Genetic Psychology, 96,* 47–59.

Dennis, W., & Dennis, M. G. (1940). The effect of cradling practices upon the onset of walking in Hopi children. *Journal of Genetic Psychology, 56,* 77–86.

Desor, J. A., Maller, O., & Andrews, K. (1975). Ingestive responses of human newborns to salty, sour, and bitter stimuli. *Journal of Comparative and Physiological Psychology, 89,* 966–970.

Dornbusch, S. M., Carlsmith, J. M., Gross, R. T., Martin, J. A., Jennings, D., Rosenberg, A., & Duke, P. (1981). Sexual development, age, and dating: A comparison of biological and social influences upon one set of behaviors. *Child Development, 52,* 179–185.

Eichorn, D. H. (1963). Biological correlates of behavior. In H. W. Stevenson (Ed.), *Child psychology.* Chicago: University of Chicago Press.

Eichorn, D. H. (1979). Physical development: Current foci of research. In J. D. Osofsky (Ed.), *Handbook of infant development.* New York: Wiley.

Engen, T., Lipsitt, L. P., & Peck, M. B. (1974). Ability of newborn infants to discriminate sapid substances. *Developmental Psychology, 10,* 741–744.

Faust, M. S. (1960). Developmental maturity as a determinant of prestige in adolescent girls. *Child Development, 31,* 173–184.

Faust, M. S. (1977). Somatic development of adolescent girls. *Monographs of the Society for Research in Child Development, 42* (Whole No. 169).

Field, J., Muir, D., Pilon, R., Sinclair, M., & Dodwell, P. (1980). Infants' orientation to lateral sounds from birth to three months. *Child Development, 51,* 295–298.

Fraiberg, S. (1977). *Insights from the blind: Comparative studies of blind and sighted infants.* New York: Basic Books.

Fraiberg, S., & Freedman, D. A. (1964). Studies in the ego development of the congenitally blind infant. *Psychoanalytic Study of the Child, 19,* 113–169.

Freedman, D. G. (1979). Ethnic differences in babies. *Human Nature, 2,* 36–43.

Frodi, A. M., Lamb, M. E., Leavitt, L. A., Donovan, W. L., Neff, C., & Sherry, D. (1978). Fathers' and mothers' responses to the faces and cries of normal and premature infants. *Developmental Psychology, 14,* 490–498.

Gardner, L. J. (1972). Deprivation dwarfism. *Scientific American, 227,* 76–82.

Gesell, A., Ames, L. B., & Ilg, F. L. (1977). *The child from five to ten.* New York: Harper & Row.

Gesell, A., Halverson, H. M., Thompson, H., Ilg, F. L., Costner, B. M., Ames, L. B., & Amatruda, C. S. (1940). *The first five years of life: A guide to the study of the preschool child.* New York: Harper & Row.

Gesell, A., & Thompson, H. (1929). Learning and growth in identical twins: An experimental study by the method of co-twin control. *Genetic Psychology Monographs, 6,* 1–123.

Gewirtz, J. L., & Boyd, E. F. (1977). Does maternal responding imply reduced infant crying? A critique of the 1972 Bell and Ainsworth report. *Child Development, 48,* 1200–1207.

Greif, E. B., & Ulman, K. J. (1982). The psychological impact of menarche on early adolescent females: A review of the literature. *Child Development, 53,* 1413–1430.

Halverson, H. M. (1931). An experimental study of prehension in infants by means of systematic cinema records. *Genetic Psychology Monographs, 10,* 107–286.

Herkowitz, J. (1978). Sex-role expectations and motor behavior of the young child. In M. V. Ridenour (Ed.), *Motor development: Issues and applications.* Princeton, NJ: Princeton Book Co.

Hiscock, M., & Kinsbourne, M. (1980). Asymmetries of selective listening and attention switching in children. *Developmental Psychology, 16,* 70–82.

Hutt, S. J., Lenard, H. G., & Prechtl, H. E. R. (1969). Psychophysiology of the newborn. In L. P. Lipsitt & H. W. Reese (Eds.), *Advances in child development and behavior.* New York: Academic Press.

Jensen, K. (1932). Differential reactions to taste and temperature stimuli in newborn infants. *Genetic Psychology Monographs, 12,* 363–479.

Jones, M. C. (1957). The later careers of boys who were early- or late-maturing. *Child Development, 28,* 113–128.

Jones, M. C. (1965). Psychological correlates of somatic development. *Child Development, 36,* 899–911.

Jones, M. C., & Bayley, N. (1950). Physical maturing among boys as related to behavior. *Journal of Educational Psychology, 41,* 129–148.

Jones, M. C., & Mussen, P. H. (1958). Self-conceptions, motivations, and interpersonal attitudes of early- and late-maturing girls. *Child Development, 29,* 491–501.

Kremenitzer, J. P., Vaughn, H. G., Jr., Kurtzberg, D., & Dowling, K. (1979). Smooth-pursuit eye movements in the newborn infant. *Child Development, 50,* 442–448.

Korner, A. F. (1972). State as a variable, as obstacle and as mediator of stimulation in infant research. *Merrill-Palmer Quarterly, 18,* 77–94.

Korner, A. F., Hutchinson, C. A., Koperski, J. A., Kraemer, H. C., & Schneider, P. A. (1981). Stability of individual differences of neonatal motor and crying patterns. *Child Development, 52,* 83–90.

Lenneberg, E. H. (1967). *Biological foundations of language.* New York: Wiley.

Lerner, R. M. (1969). The development of stereotyped expectancies of body build relations. *Child Development, 40,* 137–141.

Lerner, R. M. (1976). *Concepts and theories of development.* Reading, MA: Addison-Wesley.

Lewin, R. (1975, September). Starved brains. *Psychology Today,* pp. 29–33.

Lipsitt, L. P. (1979). Critical conditions in infancy: A psychological perspective. *American Psychologist, 34,* 973–980.

Lipsitt, L. P., & Levy, N. (1959). Electrotactual threshold in the neonate. *Child Development, 30,* 547–554.

Lipton, E. L., Steinschneider, A., & Richmond, J. B. (1965). The autonomic nervous system in early life. *New England Journal of Medicine, 273,* 201–208.

Livson, N., & Peskin, H. (1980). Perspectives on adolescence from longitudinal research. In J. Adelson (Ed.), *Handbook of adolescent psychology.* New York: Wiley.

Lowery, G. H. (1978). *Growth and development of children.* Chicago: Yearbook Medical Publishers.

MacFarlane, A. (1977). *The psychology of childbirth.* Cambridge, MA: Harvard University Press.

Malina, R. M. (1979). Secular changes in size and maturity: Causes and effects. In A. F. Roche (Ed.), Secular trends in human growth, maturation, and development. *Monographs of the Society for Research in Child Development, 44* (Whole No. 179).

Marshall, W. A. (1977). *Human growth and its disorders.* New York: Academic Press.

Mayer, J. (1975). Obesity during childhood. In M. Winick (Ed.), *Childhood obesity.* New York: Wiley.

McGraw, M. B. (1935). *Growth: A study of Johnny and Jimmy.* New York: Appleton-Century-Crofts.

Minuchin, S., Rosman, B. L., & Baker, L. (1978). *Psychosomatic families: Anorexia nervosa in context.* Cambridge, MA: Harvard University Press.

Moss, H. A. (1967). Sex, age, and state as determinants of mother-infant interaction. *Merrill-Palmer Quarterly, 13,* 19–36.

Muir, D., & Field, J. (1979). Newborn infants orient to sounds. *Child Development, 50,* 431–436.

Mussen, P. H., & Jones, M. C. (1957). Self-conceptions, motivations, and interpersonal attitudes of late and early maturing boys. *Child Development, 28,* 243–258.

Myers, B. J. (1982). Early intervention using Brazelton training with middle-class mothers and fathers of newborns. *Child Development, 53,* 462–471.

National Center for Health Statistics. (1975). *Anthropometric and clinical findings: Preliminary findings for the first health and nutrition examination survey, United States, 1971–1972.* DHEW Pub. No. (HRA). Washington, DC: Department of Health, Education and Welfare.

Neyzi, O., Saner, G., Alp, H., Binyildiz, P., Yazicioglu, S., Emre, S., & Gurson, C. T. (1976). Relationships between body weight in infancy and weight in later childhood and adolescence. In Z. Laron (Ed.), *The adipose child.* New York: Karger.

Peeples, D. R., & Teller, D. Y. (1975). Color vision and brightness discrimination in two-month-old human infants. *Science, 189,* 1102–1103.

Pratt, K. C. (1954). The neonate. In L. Carmichael (Ed.), *Manual of child psychology* (2nd ed.). New York: Wiley.

Rheingold, H. L., & Adams, J. L. (1980). The significance of speech to newborns. *Developmental Psychology, 16,* 397–403.

Rieser, J., Yonas, A., & Wilkner, K. (1976). Radial localization of odors by human newborns. *Child Development, 47,* 856–859.

Roche, A. F. (1979). Secular trends in stature, weight, and maturation. In A. F. Roche (Ed.), Secular trends in human growth, maturation, and development. *Monographs of the Society for Research in Child Development, 44,* (Whole No. 179).

Roche, A. F. (1981). The adipocyte-number hypothesis. *Child Development, 52,* 31–43.

Roffwarg, H. P., Muzio, J. W., & Dement, W. C. (1966). Ontogenetic development of the human sleep-dream cycle. *Science, 152,* 604–619.

Rosenthal, M. K. (1982). Vocal dialogues in the neonatal period. *Developmental Psychology, 18,* 17–21.

Rosenzweig, M. R., & Leiman, A. L. (1982). *Physiological psychology.* Lexington, MA: Heath.

Scarrone, L. A. (1976). Nutritional and deficiency disorders. In S. S. Miller (Ed.) *Symptoms: The complete home medical encyclopedia.* New York: Thomas Y. Crowell.

Schleimer, K. (1981). Anorexia nervosa. *Nutrition Review, 38,* 99–103.

Shannon, D. C. (1980). Sudden infant death syndrome and near miss infants. In S. S. Gellis & B. M. Kagan (Eds.), *Current pediatric therapy.* Philadelphia: Saunders.

Shirley, M. M. (1933). *The first two years: A study of 25 babies.* Vol. 1: *Postural and locomotor development.* Minneapolis: University of Minnesota Press.

Staffieri, J. R. (1967). A study of social stereotype of body image in children. *Journal of Personality and Social Psychology, 7,* 101–104.

Steinschneider, A. (1975). Implications of the sudden infant death syndrome for the study of sleep in infancy. In A. D. Pick (Ed.), *Minnesota Symposia on Child Psychology* (Vol. 9). Minneapolis: University of Minnesota Press.

Tanner, J. M. (1978). *Fetus into man: Physical growth from conception to maturity.* Cambridge, MA: Harvard University Press.

Tanner, J. M. (1981). Growth and maturation during adolescence. *Nutrition Review, 39,* 43–55.

Thelen, E., & Fisher, D. M. (1982). Newborn stepping: An explanation for a disappearing reflex. *Developmental Psychology, 18,* 760–775.

Walk, R. D. (1981). *Perceptual development.* Monterey, CA: Brooks/Cole.

Weatherley, D. (1964). Self-perceived rate of physical maturation and personality in late adolescence. *Child Development, 35,* 1197–1210.

Werner, J. S., & Wooten, B. R. (1979). Human infant color vision and color perception. *Infant Behavior and Development, 2,* 241–273.

Widdowson, E. M. (1951). Mental contentment and physical growth. *Lancet, 1,* 1316–1318.

Widmayer, S., & Field, T. (1980). Effects of Brazelton demonstrations on early interactions of preterm infants and their teen-age mothers. *Infant Behavior and Development, 3,* 79–89.

Willemsen, E. (1979). *Understanding infancy.* San Francisco: W. H. Freeman.

Wilson, R. S. (1976). Concordance in physical growth for monozygotic and dizygotic twins. *Annals of Human Biology, 3,* 1–10.

Winick, M. (1975). *Childhood obesity.* New York: Wiley.

Winick, M. (1976). *Malnutrition and brain development.* New York: Oxford University Press.

Wolff, P. H. (1966). The causes, controls, and organization of behavior in the neonate. *Psychological Issues, 5* (1, Whole No. 17).

Wolff, P. H. (1969). The natural history of crying and other vocalizations in early infancy. In B. M. Foss (Ed.), *Determinants of infant behavior* (Vol. 4). London: Methuen.

Worobey, J., & Belsky, J. (1982). Employing the Brazelton Scale to influence mothering: An experimental comparison of three strategies. *Developmental Psychology, 18,* 736–743.

Zack, P. M., Harlan, W. R., Leaverton, P. E., & Cornoni-Huntley, J. (1979). A longitudinal study of body fatness in childhood and adolescence. *Journal of Pediatrics, 95,* 126–130.

Zelazo, P. R., Zelazo, N. A., & Kolb, S. (1972). "Walking" in the newborn. *Science, 176,* 314–315.

Zeskind, P. S. (1980). Adult responses to the cries of low and high risk infants. *Infant Behavior and Development, 3,* 167–177.

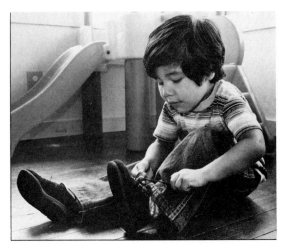

PART THREE

Some of the more remarkable developments of childhood and adolescence are the changes that occur in learning, interpreting, reasoning, remembering, and problem solving. These "cognitive," or intellectual, developments are examined in detail in Part Three.

In Chapter Six we will focus on the growth of perceptual skills and learn how children gradually become more proficient at interpreting information they receive from their sensory receptors. Chapter Seven presents an in-depth

LANGUAGE, LEARNING, AND COGNITIVE DEVELOPMENT

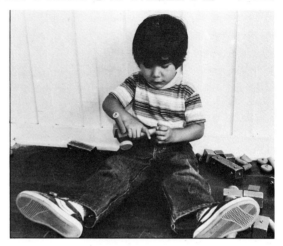

look at the learning process and describes many of the ways in which young people are influenced by their experiences.

One characteristic that distinguishes us humans from other species is our remarkable capacity for language. The development of language and communication skills is the subject of Chapter Eight.

Part Three concludes with an overview of intellectual development. Chapter Nine charts the growth of memory and reasoning skills from birth through adolescence. In Chapter Ten, we turn to the topic of intelligence testing and consider the many factors that contribute to individual differences in intellectual performance.

As you proceed through this section, it will become obvious that all the various cognitive functions are interrelated. For example, infants and toddlers must first perceive the differences among various patterns of sound and then remember these distinctions before they can construct meaningful words and sentences. They must develop an understanding of concepts such as relative size and color before they can use the words *tall* and *green* in the same ways that adults do. So the lines that are drawn between different cognitive operations are somewhat artificial, and we will see that changes in each cognitive process have important implications for all other aspects of cognitive functioning.

CHAPTER SIX

PERCEPTUAL DEVELOPMENT

■ *The nativist/empiricist controversy*

■ *Visual perception in infancy*
Pattern perception
Perception of faces
Spatial perception

■ *Auditory perception in infancy*
Voice recognition
Reactions to speech and language
The sound of music

■ *Intersensory perception*
Theories of intersensory integration
Research on intersensory perception
Another look at the enrichment/differentiation
  controversy
Sensory dominance

■ *Perceptual learning and development in*
  childhood
Development of attention
Development of form perception

■ *Environmental influences on perception*
What kinds of experiences are important?
Social and cultural influences

■ *What is perceptual development?*

■ *Summary*

Beauty is bought by judgment of
   the eye
not utter'd by base sale of chap-
   men's tongues.

SHAKESPEARE, *Love's Labours Lost*

Try to imagine that you are a neonate, only five to ten minutes old, who has just been sponged, swaddled, and handed to your mother. As you stop whimpering, you will probably open your eyes and begin to look around. Your mother or father will undoubtedly say something like "Hello, baby, how are you?" Soon someone might tickle your cheek, causing you to turn in that direction and open your mouth as if to suck (the rooting reflex). What would you make of all this sensory input? How would you interpret these experiences?

Psychologists are careful to distinguish between **sensation** and **perception.** *Sensation* refers to the process by which *information about external events is detected by the sensory receptors and transmitted to the brain.* Clearly, babies can sense the environment: we know that they "see" when light rays strike their retinas; they "hear" when sound waves stimulate the bones of their inner ears; they "smell" when odor-bearing molecules come into contact with the olfactory receptors in their nasal passages. Although these sensory abilities will improve over time, they are present at birth and require only a detectable level of stimulation in order to function.

Perception, however, refers to the *interpretation of sensory input by the brain.* If you or I hear a sound, we are quick to interpret it as a voice, a piece of music, or perhaps the humming of an appliance. When an object of some kind passes into our visual field, we can easily label it as a person, a cat, or an airplane. As adults, we are accomplished perceivers. But what about the neonate? Do you think a newborn can interpret or understand the sights, sounds, tastes, touches, and smells that his or her sensory receptors detect? Can neonates *perceive* anything?

---

sensation: *detection of stimuli by the sensory receptors and transmission of this information to the brain.*
perception: *the process by which we categorize and interpret sensory input.*

THE NATIVIST/EMPIRICIST CONTROVERSY

Long before anyone began to conduct experiments on sensation and perception, philosophers were debating whether neonates could perceive. *Empiricists* such as John Locke (1690/1939) believed that infants were "tabulae rasae" (blank slates) who must learn how to interpret their sensory experiences. Two hundred years later, William James (1890) added that

> *any number of sensory [inputs], falling simultaneously on a mind* WHICH HAS NOT YET EXPERIENCED THEM SEPARATELY, will fuse into a single individual [experience] *for that mind.* The law is that all things fuse that can fuse. . . . To the infant, sounds, sights, touches, and pains, form one unanalyzed [blooming, buzzing] confusion [Vol. 1, pp. 488, 496].

In other words, James believed that the senses are "integrated" at birth and that all sensations combine to produce a global, or holistic, experience. Presumably the child's abilities to discriminate the basic senses and to interpret sensations of a particular kind will gradually develop after a long period of learning.

In contrast, the *nativists* argued that many basic perceptual abilities are already present at birth. For example, René Descartes (1638/1965) and Immanuel Kant (1781/1958) believed that **spatial perception** is innate. Presumably an infant does not have to learn that receding objects will appear smaller or that approaching objects will seem to increase in size; these are spatial inferences (perceptions) that were said to be inborn and attributable to the structural characteristics of the human nervous system.

Perhaps you can see that the major dispute between the nativists and the empiricists is nothing more than the nature/nurture controversy applied to the topic of perceptual development. As we consider the developing perceptual capabilities of the child, it will become obvious that babies can see some order to the universe from the moment of birth. Score one point for the nativists. However, the perceptual world of a neonate is quite primitive by adult standards, and we will see that both maturation and experience (learning) are important contributors to the child's perceptual growth and development.

We will focus mainly on visual perception in this chapter, simply because theorists have often assumed that vision is the dominant sense (for humans, at least). As a result, they have studied vision more than hearing, smell, or taste, and our knowledge about the child's perceptual world is based mostly on the visual modality and its relations to the other senses.

VISUAL PERCEPTION IN INFANCY

Do you think neonates can perceive depth and the third dimension? Can infants see patterns and forms; or, rather, must they learn to construct these visual figures from an assortment of lines, edges, angles, and colors? When do you suppose a child is capable of recognizing a human face and distinguishing the faces of close companions from those of strangers? Could William James have been right when he implied that the senses are integrated at birth and then gradually differentiated after a long period of learning? These are precisely the kinds of questions that have motivated curious investigators to find ways of persuading nonverbal infants to "tell" us what they can see.

Pattern Perception

In the early 1960s, Robert Fantz conducted a number of pioneering experiments to determine

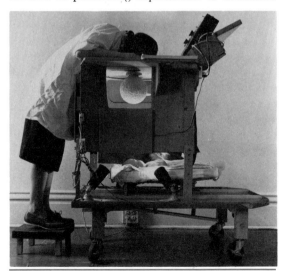

PHOTO 6-1. *The looking chamber that Fantz used to study pattern perception.*

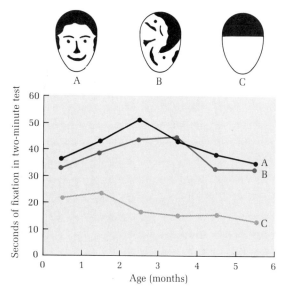

FIGURE 6-1. *Fantz's test of young infants' pattern preferences. Infants aged 4 days to 6 months preferred to look at complex stimuli rather than a simple oval. However, the infants did not prefer a facelike figure to the scrambled face.*

whether infants can discriminate visual forms or patterns. Babies were placed on their backs in a **looking chamber** (see Photo 6-1) and shown two or more stimuli. An observer located above the looking chamber then recorded the amount of time the infant gazed at each of the visual patterns. If the infant looked longer at one target than the other, it was assumed that he or she preferred that pattern.

Fantz's early results were clear. Babies less than 2 days old could easily discriminate visual forms, and they preferred to look at patterned stimuli such as faces or concentric circles rather than at unpatterned disks. Apparently the ability to detect and discriminate patterns is innate (Fantz, 1963).

Fantz also found that infants stared longer at facelike stimuli than at other patterned targets such as a bull's-eye or newsprint. The ethologists became excited about these data. After all, they seemed to imply that a preference for faces may be an innate social attribute that helps infants to recognize and become emotionally attached to their regular companions. However, later research indicates that even 2–3-month-old infants do not necessarily prefer faces to all other patterned stimuli (Haaf & Brown, 1976; Haaf, Smith, &

Smitley, 1983). As we consider what aspects of visual form are likely to capture a baby's attention, we will see why the infants in Fantz's study seemed to be showing a preference for faces when in fact they were not.

■ *Determinants of pattern perception*

One of Fantz's earliest experiments (Fantz, 1961) clearly demonstrates that infants do not prefer faces to all other patterned stimuli. Forty-nine infants were placed in a looking chamber and shown drawings of (1) a face, (2) a stimulus consisting of scrambled facial features, and (3) a simpler stimulus that contained the same amount of light and dark shading that appeared in the "facelike" and "scrambled face" drawings. As we see in Figure 6-1, infants clearly preferred *both* the face and the "scrambled face" to the unpatterned stimulus, but they did not prefer the face to the scrambled face. What, then, made the face and scrambled face equally interesting?

---

spatial perception: *interpretation of relations between objects and space.*

looking chamber: *an enclosed criblike apparatus used to study infants' visual preferences.*

Contour. One possibility is that the face and scrambled face have the same amount of light/dark transition, or **contour**. There is now a good deal of evidence that very young infants scan an object by fixating on its edges and the boundaries between its light and dark areas (see Box 6-1). And the more contour a figure has, the more edges there are for an infant to explore. Marshall Haith (1980) has characterized the very young infant as an information seeker who uses the following strategy to explore the environment:

1. If awake and alert, open the eyes.
2. If the light is dim, scan the surrounding area.
3. If no edges (or contours) are found, continue to search.
4. When edges appear, stop and look carefully at them.
5. Keep looking at and around areas with lots of contour, but scan quickly those areas of low contour.

In sum, the infants in Fantz's (1961) experiment may have preferred to gaze at faces (or scrambled faces) because these were the targets that had the greatest amount of contour.

Complexity. Robert Fantz and Joseph Fagan (1975) have shown that the amount of contour is not the only property that determines what infants will look at. Fantz and Fagan exposed infants to two stimuli: (1) 8 1-inch squares on a homogeneous background and (2) 32 1/4-inch squares on the same kind of background (see Figure 6-2). These two stimuli have the same amount of light/dark contour, but they differ in **complexity**—the number of figures they contain (8 versus 32). Fantz and Fagan discovered that 1-month-old infants preferred to look at the simpler stimulus (the 8 1-inch squares), while infants 2 months of age and older preferred complexity (the 32 smaller squares). Although neonates clearly prefer a patterned stimulus to totally unpatterned visual targets, their preference for visual complexity becomes much stronger over the first two months of life.

Curvature. To this point, we have two clues about why the infants in Fantz's (1961) study preferred a face or a scrambled face to other patterned stimuli: the face had more *contour* and was more *complex* than the other visual patterns. In fact, the reason they did not prefer the real face to the scrambled face is probably that these two stimuli are *equal* in both contour and complexity.

But contour and complexity are not the only determinants of infants' pattern preferences. Robert Fantz, Joseph Fagan, and Simon Miranda (1975) conducted experiments to explore infants' preferences for curved versus straight lines (if neonates have an inborn preference for faces, they ought to prefer curvilinear features, which characterize the human face). Subjects ranging from a few days to several weeks of age were placed in a looking chamber and shown pairs of stimuli such as those in Figure 6-3. Fantz et al. found that babies showed no strong preferences for curvature until they were 2 months old. Perhaps two months of gazing at curvilinear objects such as the mother's face or breasts was sufficient experience for infants to acquire a preference for curvature.

■ *Changes in pattern perception*

If we look carefully at the ground we have covered, it might seem that an infant's pattern preferences begin to change at about 2 months of age. Recall that very young infants pay little atten-

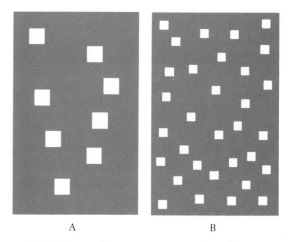

A   B

FIGURE 6-2. These two patterns have the same amount of contour, but pattern B is more complex. One-month-old infants generally prefer to look at the simpler of the two patterns; 2-month-old infants prefer the complex stimulus.

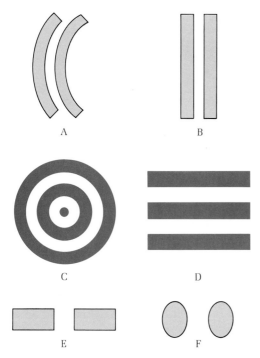

FIGURE 6-3. Testing the infant's preference for curvature. Fantz and his colleagues found that a strong preference for looking at curvilinear patterns (such as A, C, and F) emerges at about 2 months of age.

infants will detect and respond to smaller details located within the boundaries of an object or a pattern (see Banks, 1980).

The child's visual experiences also contribute to changes in pattern perception. As the days pass, an infant will have had many opportunities to gaze at objects and to learn that complex, curvilinear stimuli such as breasts and faces have "meaning" by virtue of their association with food, warmth, and comfort. Indeed, Jerome Kagan (1971) argues that infants are already forming mental representations, or **"schemata,"** for familiar objects during the first few weeks of life.

According to Kagan (1971), infants begin to compare objects against existing schemata at about 2 months of age. If an object is identical to an established schema, the comparison is easy, and the child will scan the object only briefly. If the object is truly novel and unlike any existing schema, the comparison is difficult, and the child will lose interest. However, if the stimulus is *moderately discrepant* from an existing schema (similar but not identical to it), 2-month-olds will scan the new object intently as if trying to interpret it in the light of their current knowledge. If they fail to classify the stimulus as something familiar, they are likely to alter the old schema or form a new one, thereby broadening their perceptual horizons and increasing the range of stimuli that they will try to interpret in the future.

Perception of Faces

Although infants do not have an innate preference for faces, the human face is likely to be one of the more interesting objects that babies encounter on a day-to-day basis. Consider, for example, that faces have moving parts (lips, eyes) and that

tion to detail. Instead, they gaze at contours and edges as if they were concerned mainly with *locating* objects and *defining their boundaries.* Infants older than 2 months use a different strategy: they are captivated by complexity and curvature, and they scan the internal parts of figures as if they were trying to determine *what these objects are.* Perhaps we are not too far off if we characterize the neonate as a form "constructor" (see Box 6-2) and the older infant as a form "interpreter."

How do we explain this shift in pattern perception? One contributing factor is the maturation of the central nervous system. Over the first two months of life, the visual areas of the cerebral cortex are rapidly developing. This means that the baby's **visual acuity** and ability to bring objects into focus (that is, to accommodate) are improving, thereby increasing the likelihood that older

contour: *the amount of light/dark transition in a visual stimulus.*

visual complexity: *the number of elements in a visual stimulus.*

visual acuity: *a measure of the precision with which a person can see small objects and fine detail.*

perceptual schema (*plural* **schemata**): *an internal mental representation of a familiar stimulus.*

BOX 6-1
*VISUAL SCANNING IN NEONATES AND
OLDER INFANTS*

What do neonates and older infants look at when they scan a pattern? To find out, Philip Salapatek (1975) developed a photographic technique to record infants' eye movements as they looked at simple geometric figures such as triangles, stars, and squares. What Salapatek soon discovered is that very young infants tend to scan a small portion of a figure, typically focusing on one angular feature or boundary—for example, one point of the star shown here. In contrast, 2-month-old infants traced a larger portion of the figure and would also examine the figure's center or internal areas. Thus, 2-month-old infants scanned the patterns much more thoroughly than 1-month-olds.

In later research, Daphne Maurer and Philip Salapatek (1976) exposed 1- and 2-month-old infants to human faces and recorded the children's eye movements. In the sample tracings of the infants' visual behavior, note that 1-month-old infants scanned only a small portion of the total facial configuration (its boundaries or contours) and spent very little time examining internal features such as the eyes, nose, and mouth. However, the 2-month-old infants spent considerably more time scanning internal details and paid very little attention to the boundary areas of facial stimuli. We see, then, that very young infants scan faces in much the same way that they scan nonsocial geometric figures—by focusing on edges and angles rather than the internal aspects of the visual target. This is one more line of evidence that the attention of neonates is captured by contour and that infants probably have no innate preference for facial configurations.

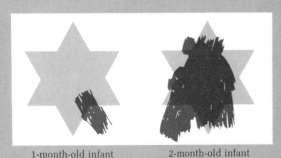

1-month-old infant   2-month-old infant

*Visual scanning of the human face by 1- and
2-month-old infants.*

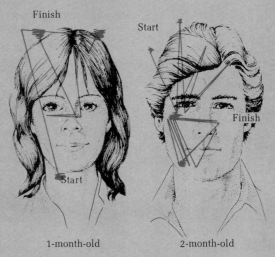

1-month-old   2-month-old

*Visual scanning of a geometric figure by 1- and
2-month-old infants.*

movement attracts immediate attention. Faces are also rich in contour, complexity, and curvature—features that we know will capture infants' attention. Finally, faces are readily available—a baby will be exposed to the faces of caretakers several times each day, whenever he or she is fed, soothed, bathed, or diapered. So we might expect that infants will soon develop a schema for "faceness" and even learn to discriminate the faces of familiar companions from those of strangers.

In Box 6-1 we learned that 4-week-old infants focus almost exclusively on the outer boundaries of facial stimuli, whereas 8-week-olds have at least begun to scan internal features such as the eyes, nose, and mouth. By age 9–11 weeks, infants have become much more interested in the internal features of a face than in its edges (Haith, Bergman, & Moore, 1977). Does this increasing attention to internal detail mean that 2–3-month-olds are developing schemata for human faces? Apparently so. Recently, Maria Barrera and Daphne Maurer (1981b) have shown that 3-month-old infants not only recognize photographs cf their mothers' faces but prefer to look at their

BOX 6-2
DO YOUNG INFANTS REALLY
PERCEIVE "FORMS"?

There is a fundamental problem with the research we have reviewed, and perhaps you have already detected it. Surely the data indicate that even young infants can *discriminate* visual stimuli, for they prefer to look at some patterns more than others. However, a critic could argue that visual preferences do not imply that the infant perceives *form*. For example, we can't tell from visual preference data whether an infant who gazes at a drawing of a triangle sees the geometric triangle that we construct. Perhaps he sees only a line or two and an angle. Do infants really construct, or perceive, forms?

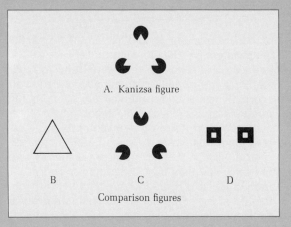

The Kanizsa triangle and the three comparison figures used in Treiber and Wilcox's study.

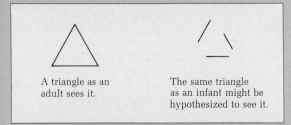

A triangle as an adult sees it.

The same triangle as an infant might be hypothesized to see it.

Yes, they do, or at least they appear to. Recently, Frank Treiber and Steven Wilcox (1980) allowed 1–4-month-old infants to gaze as long as they wished at the Kanizsa stimulus, which consists of three incomplete disks arranged so that adults will perceive the "subjective" contour of a triangle. Would young infants also "construct" this triangle as they gazed at the object?

To find out, Treiber and Wilcox first let the babies habituate to the Kanizsa stimulus. When the children were no longer interested in looking at this object, they were shown the three comparison stimuli labeled B, C, and D. If the infants had perceived the

triangular form in the Kanizsa stimulus, we might expect them to be less inclined to look at the real triangle (comparison object B) than at the other comparison figures. After all, they would have habituated to the Kanizsa triangle, so that another triangle would not be very interesting. This is precisely what Treiber and Wilcox found: infants who had habituated to the Kanizsa stimulus spent much less time gazing at the triangle than at either of the other comparison figures. Apparently babies as young as 1 month can perceive form—even when the boundary of that form is ambiguous, as is true of the Kanizsa triangle.

Yet a qualification is in order. Young infants will not perceive subjective contours such as the Kanizsa triangle unless they look at these stimuli for a long time. In contrast, 7-month-old infants perceive subjective contour after much shorter exposures (Bertenthal, Campos, & Haith, 1980). So it appears that form perception becomes much more sophisticated over the first six to seven months of life.

mothers rather than at strangers. In a second experiment, Barrera and Maurer (1981a) found that 3-month-old infants can discriminate the faces of two strangers, even when the strangers were thought to be quite similar in appearance by a panel of adult judges. So by the tender age of 12–13 weeks, infants have a schema for "faceness" and even prefer some facial patterns to others. What's more, strangers do not "all look alike" to them.

Let's note, however, that 3-month-old infants may rarely discriminate one face from another un-

less they examine these faces for a long time. By contrast, 5–6-month-old infants can quickly discriminate their regular companions from strangers, and they may even recognize that a line drawing of a woman and the woman's photograph represent the same person (Cohen, DeLoache, & Strauss, 1979). Finally, 5–7-month-old infants are unlikely to "forget a face," even if their exposure was brief (2–3 minutes) and they do not see the face again for two weeks (Fagan, 1979).

In sum, the ability to perceive faces seems to follow the same general course as the perception of other visual forms and patterns. During the neonatal period (the first month), babies scan the boundaries of faces as if they were trying to "construct" a form and/or determine its location in space. By age 3 months, infants are scanning the internal features of faces and responding to "faceness" as a distinctive pattern. With prolonged exposure to facial stimuli, 3-month-old infants can even discriminate different faces—a finding that indicates that they may be forming schemata for individual faces. By 5 to 7 months, not only are infants more proficient at discriminating facial configurations, but they remember them as well. In other words, the 5–7-month-old infant is forming *stable* recognition schemata for particular individuals, and as we will see in Chapter Eleven, this is precisely the time when infants begin to show strong emotional attachments to their parents and other close companions.

Spatial Perception

Once again try to imagine that you are a neonate. You are just about to take your first breast feeding. As you open your eyes, you see an object (the breast) before you. The question is this: Would you see a simple two-dimensional bull's-eye pattern formed by the nipple surrounded by breast tissue; or, rather, could you perceive that this object has some depth, or three-dimensionality?

Because we so easily perceive depth and the third dimension, it is tempting to conclude that neonates can too. However, empiricists have argued that poor visual acuity and an inability to bring objects into sharp focus (that is, to accommodate) prevent the neonate from making accurate spatial inferences. In addition, it appears that infants younger than 3½ months may not exhibit **stereopsis**—a convergence of the visual images of the two eyes to produce a singular, non-overlapping image that has depth (Fox, Aslin, Shea, & Dumais, 1980). All these biological limitations may make it difficult for infants to perceive depth and to locate objects in space.

However, nativists would argue that several cues to depth and distance are monocular—that is, detectable with only one eye. One important monocular depth cue is **perspective,** a principle that artists use to create the third dimension on a two-dimensional surface by drawing distant objects smaller than near objects and making linear

representations converge as they recede toward the horizon (see Figure 6-4). If neonates can detect these visual cues, then their world may be three-dimensional from the very beginning.

So when are infants capable of perceiving depth and making reasonably accurate inferences about size and spatial relations? Developmental psychologists have devised three kinds of experiments to answer these questions. Let's briefly consider the findings that have emerged from each of these research traditions and then see whether we can draw some general conclusions about the development of spatial abilities.

■ *Experiments on depth perception*

In the early 1960s, Eleanor Gibson and Richard Walk developed an apparatus they called the **visual cliff** to determine whether infants can perceive depth. The visual cliff (Photo 6-2) consists of an elevated glass platform divided into two sections by a center board. On the "shallow" side, a checkerboard pattern is placed directly under the glass. On the "deep" side, the pattern is placed several feet below the glass, creating the illusion of a sharp dropoff, or a "visual cliff." The investigator tests an infant for depth perception by placing him or her on the center board and then asking the child's mother to try to coax the infant to cross both the "shallow" and the "deep" sides. If the child crawls across the shallow side but refuses to cross the deep side, then he or she is said to perceive depth. Presumably the infant's hesitation to cross the deep side results from a fear of the perceived dropoff.[1]

In the original "visual cliff" studies, Gibson and Walk (1960) found that most babies aged 6-1/2 months and older would not crawl across the "deep" side to their mothers, although they showed no reluctance to cross the shallow side. Clearly, human infants are able to perceive depth by the middle of the first year.

The problem with the visual cliff is that infants must be able to crawl to show us they will avoid

---

[1]An alternative interpretation is that infants might avoid the "deep" side not because they *fear* the dropoff but simply because they see no "surface" over the cliff on which they can crawl (Rader, Bausano, & Richards, 1980). But even if this alternative interpretation is correct, the infant's refusal to cross the deep side would still imply that he or she perceives depth (that is, the "floor" is seen as too far away to permit any crawling).

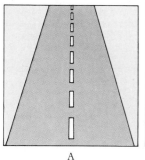
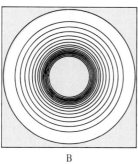

A   B   C   D

FIGURE 6-4. *Perspective or painter's cues. Artists use many monocular perspective cues to create the illusion of depth, or the third dimension, on a two-dimensional surface. One such cue is* linear perspective, *shown in panel A—linear features converge with increasing distance. The second painter's cue is* density gradient, *shown in panel B—the density of the lines increases over distance to produce the illusion of depth. Panel C shows the effect of* sizing *cues; one animal is drawn smaller to give the impression that it is farther away. Panel D illustrates* interposition, *in which a "near" figure is drawn to partly obscure a "far" figure to create the illusion of nearness and distance.*

the cliff, and unfortunately, babies younger than 6 months can't crawl. However, Joseph Campos and his associates (Campos, Langer, & Krowitz, 1970) devised a method of testing the depth perception of very young infants on the visual cliff. Campos et al. recorded changes in infants' heart rates when they were lowered face down over the "shallow" and the "deep" sides of the apparatus. Babies as young as 2 months showed a decrease in heart rate when they were over the cliff but no change in heart rate on the shallow side. A decrease in heart rate is a physiological indicator of attention that implies that the 2-month-old infants in this study considered the deep side of the apparatus more interesting than the shallow side (that is, they were probably perceiving depth although they had not yet learned to fear heights). In contrast, 1-month-old infants did not discriminate the deep and shallow sides, possibly because their visual abilities were too immature to allow them to detect the dropoff.

Although we cannot tell whether depth perception is innate from the visual-cliff research, we do know that babies are paying close attention to the deep side of the apparatus and detecting depth cues by the end of the second month.

■ *Experiments on size constancy*

If a friend who stands 5′8″ should leave your side and walk 20 feet away from you, the image of that person on your retina will become much smaller. Yet you realize that your friend is still 5′8″ and

simply *looks* smaller because he or she is now farther away. This realization is an example of **size constancy**—the ability to detect that the dimensions of an object will remain constant over a change in distance. Obviously, a person who displays size constancy has some understanding of depth and the third dimension. Specifically, he or she recognizes that increases in distance (or depth) can compensate for decreases in the size of a retinal image to preserve an object's absolute size. So if infants show some evidence of size constancy, we can conclude that they perceive depth, distance, and the third dimension.

Thomas Bower (1966) conducted an ingenious experiment to determine whether 6- to 12-week-old infants have size constancy. Bower first

---

stereopsis: *fusion of two flat images to produce a single image that has depth.*

perspective: *representation of depth on a two-dimensional surface by drawing distant objects smaller than near objects and making linear features converge as they recede toward the horizon.*

visual cliff: *an elevated platform that creates an illusion of depth, used to test the depth perception of infants.*

size constancy: *the tendency to perceive an object as the same size from different distances despite changes in the size of its retinal image.*

PHOTO 6-2. *An infant at the edge of the visual cliff.*

played peek-a-boo to train the infants to turn their heads to the left. The conditioned stimulus for this little game was a *12-inch cube* presented *at a distance of three feet.* If the infants turned their heads to the left in the presence of the conditioned stimulus, the experimenter would reinforce the response by popping up from below and saying "Peek-a-boo." Since young infants love peek-a-boo games, they soon learned to turn their heads to the left whenever they saw the 12-inch cube.

The next step was to see whether the infants would display size constancy by turning their heads to the cube when it was placed at a distance of nine feet. At nine feet, the 12-inch cube projects a retinal image only one-third the size of its image at three feet. Bower also included an equal number of test trials in which the infant was shown a 36-inch cube at nine feet. This second test stimulus produces a retinal image of exactly the same size as the original conditioned stimulus—the 12-inch cube at three feet (see Figure 6-5). An infant who does not have size constancy and is reacting on the basis of the size of the retinal image should respond more to the 36-inch cube than

to the 12-inch cube. But an infant who has size constancy and is *not* responding to the size of the retinal image should maintain a high rate of head-turning to the 12-inch cube and should show little or no response to the 36-inch cube.

The results of Bower's experiment were clear: when placed at nine feet, the 12-inch cube produced nearly three times the number of head-turning responses (average = 58) as the 36-inch cube (average = 22). In other words, these 6–12-week-old infants were displaying size constancy: they reacted to the *real* size of the 12-inch conditioned stimulus and did not rely on the size of the retinal image as a guide for responding.

Other investigators using other research techniques have found evidence for size constancy in infants as young as 4½ months (Day & McKenzie, 1981). So size constancy is present very early in life, although we don't know for sure whether this perceptual ability is innate.

■ *Experiments on visual looming*

As a moving object approaches the eye, its image will occupy a larger and larger portion of the

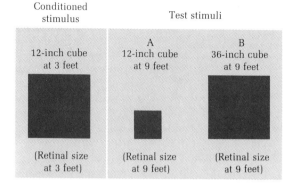

Conditioned stimulus

Test stimuli

12-inch cube at 3 feet	A 12-inch cube at 9 feet	B 36-inch cube at 9 feet
(Retinal size at 3 feet)	(Retinal size at 9 feet)	(Retinal size at 9 feet)

FIGURE 6-5. *The conditioned stimulus and test stimuli used in Bower's size-constancy experiment. Test stimulus B at 9 feet projects a retinal image of the same size as the original conditioned stimulus; test stimulus A at 9 feet projects a retinal image only one-third the size of the original conditioned stimulus.*

visual field. In fact, the approaching object may expand to occupy the entire field (that is, to **loom**) as it comes very close to the face. Do you think young infants would react to looming objects? If they do, we might infer that they can perceive movement across the third dimension (Bower, 1982).

Thomas Bower and his associates (Bower, Broughton, & Moore, 1970b) placed 6–20-day-old infants in infant seats and slowly moved a foam rubber cube toward the babies' faces. When the cube approached to within eight inches, the infants typically opened their eyes wide, threw their hands up in front of their faces, and retracted their heads. Bower (1982) interprets the babies' behavior as a defensive response indicating that the infants perceived distance and the approach of the cube. Although other investigators have not always observed the strong defensive reactions reported in Bower's research, it does appear that 3–4-week-old infants will reliably blink as moving stimuli approach their faces (Yonas, Petterson, & Lockman, 1979).

■ *Conclusions*

Taken together, the research we have reviewed suggests that both size constancy and the perception of a visual cliff may be present by 2 months of age and that the ability to detect the

approach of moving objects (visual looming) may be available during the first or second week of life. The visual-looming data provide the best evidence that depth or distance perception is innate—but even this research is not wholly conclusive. Thomas Bower (1982) tells us why:

> Since the ability is present at one week, it seems likely that it is an unlearned ability [and] that a learning theory explanation [is] implausible. How many times has a 1-week-old infant been struck in the face by an approaching object. [Yet I have been told that] during breast feeding, the infant of an inexperienced mother is quite likely to be struck in the face; indeed, overenthusiastic application of the breast can result in a response very much like that elicited by an approaching object. . . . [Although] it is possible that the response to an approaching object is learned on the basis of experience with the breast . . . I would prefer to conclude that these experiments do demonstrate a built-in capacity for perception of the third dimension [pp. 86–87].

But even if neonates have a "built in" capacity to perceive depth and the third dimension, these spatial abilities are not well developed at birth. Recent research indicates that all aspects of spatial perception improve rather dramatically over the first year (see Walk, 1981), and some of this improvement is attributable to the maturation of the infant's visual system. However, experience also comes into play: the first year is a time when children are learning more about distance, depth, and spatial relations by watching or reaching for moving objects and by exploring sloped surfaces, stairs, and other little "visual cliffs" in the natural environment (Bower, 1982; Walk, 1981).

Auditory cues may also help children to locate objects in space. For example, we know that neonates will turn their heads and look for objects that are making soft sounds (Bower, 1982). Children may also learn that noise-making stimuli sound louder as they approach and softer as they recede into the distance. So the sounds that an object emits may provide important clues about the object's distance and direction from the perceiver.

visual looming: *the tendency of an approaching object to take up the entire visual field as it draws very close to the face.*

AUDITORY PERCEPTION IN INFANCY

Although we often think of human beings as visual animals, babies are very responsive to many sounds that they hear. Not only do neonates pay attention to sounds, but it appears that they try to interpret them as well. In this section we will see that William James (1890) seems to have overstated the case when he inferred that the auditory world of the newborn is an unanalyzed buzz of confusion.

The fact that neonates will often turn their heads in the direction of a sound implies that sounds have meaning. Perhaps babies *interpret* a sound as an indication that there is something out there to see, and they turn their heads to catch a glimpse of the noise-making object (Bower, 1982). In other words, localization of sounds may be a primitive form of auditory *perception* (sounds imply sights) that is present at birth.

Although there is much we do not know about infants' auditory capabilities, researchers are beginning to ask some interesting questions. When, for example, will an infant first recognize his or her mother's voice or prefer it to the voice of a stranger? How soon are babies capable of discriminating the various vowel and consonant sounds that make up a language? Are infants inherently musical creatures who prefer marches and melodies to nonmusical forms of auditory stimulation? These are some of the issues we will explore in the pages that follow.

Voice Recognition

Many people would undoubtedly chuckle if a mother were to claim that her week-old infant already recognizes her voice. Yet the mother might have the last laugh, for a recent experiment by Anthony DeCasper and William Fifer (1980) suggests that babies can recognize their mothers' voices during the first three days of life. Infants were given a special pacifier that recorded their sucking rate. At first, the experimenters simply watched to see how often each baby sucked the pacifier. Once this "baseline" sucking rate had been established, the procedure began. For half the infants, sucking faster than the baseline rate activated a recording of the mother's voice, and sucking slower than baseline produced a record-

ing of a female stranger. Just the opposite was true for the remaining infants: fast sucking produced the stranger's voice, and slow sucking activated a recording of the mother. DeCasper and Fifer found that their 1–3-day-old infants did whatever it took (that is, sucked faster or slower) in order to hear their own mothers. In other words, not only did they recognize the sound of the mother's voice, but they clearly preferred it to the voice of a female stranger. Since very young infants cannot discriminate the mother's face from that of a stranger (Melhuish, 1982), they are apparently getting to know their companions through the auditory modality long before they recognize them by sight.

Reactions to Speech and Language

In Chapter Five we learned that neonates who listened to human speech (Chinese or English) synchronized their body movements with the rhythm of the language they were hearing (Condon & Sander, 1974). Such synchrony of movement was specific to language and did not occur while the infants were listening to recordings of disconnected vowel sounds and tapping noises. So babies may be biologically programmed to recognize and react to language from the moment of birth.

Very young infants are also capable of distinguishing the various vowel and consonant sounds that make up a language. For example, Marsha Clarkson and Keith Berg (1983) found that babies can tell the difference between the vowels *a* and *i* from the second day of life. And even consonant sounds that are very similar (for example, *b* and *p* or *d* and *t*) are easily discriminated by 2–3-month-old infants (Eimas, 1975b).

Are adults any better than infants at discriminating the auditory components of language? The answer is yes—and no. Adults can more readily discriminate some of the sounds of the language they have acquired, a finding that indicates that auditory discriminations become more refined as the individual listens to a language and begins to reproduce its sounds (see Walk, 1981). Yet each language uses only a subset of the sounds that human beings are capable of producing, and children will eventually lose the ability to differentiate certain sounds that are *not* components of their native tongue. For example, infants can easily discriminate the consonants /r/ and /l/ (Eimas, 1975a). So can you if your native language is English, French, Spanish, or German. However, Oriental languages such as Chinese and Japanese make no distinction between /r/ and /l/, and as a result, native speakers of these tongues lose the ability to make this auditory discrimination (Miyawaki, Strange, Verbrugge, Liberman, Jenkins, & Fujimura, 1975).

In sum, young infants place the auditory components of language into distinct vowel and consonant categories in much the same way that adults do. However, as children mature and begin to acquire the language of their culture, they will make finer distinctions among the components of that language and may actually lose the ability to discriminate certain sounds that are not used in their native tongue. The implication is that the language we acquire will influence our auditory perception. Richard Walk (1981, p. 61) concludes that "in some respects the Biblical story of the Tower of Babel is true—we have difficulty understanding each other's speech because to learn a new language is to change our auditory perception. We are always a foreigner in every language but our own."

The Sound of Music

Are neonates musical creatures? Do they prefer music to other auditory stimuli? And if they do, whom will they prefer: the Beatles or Beethoven?

Unfortunately, we know very little about how infants perceive music. We do know that babies only 1 day old will either increase or decrease their rate of sucking on a pacifier if this strategy permits them to hear a medley of classical, modern instrumental, and "pop" music (Butterfield, cited in Walk, 1981). However, this finding may simply indicate that infants prefer any kind of sound to silence. Do babies really like music?

Apparently so. In a second study (Butterfield & Siperstein, 1972), infants either sucked or refrained from sucking when that strategy produced folk music, but they did whatever it took to *avoid* listening to nonrhythmic noise (see Figure 6-6). The investigators concluded that babies do like music and that they find noise aversive.

By the age of 4–6 months, infants begin to "bounce" to music (Moog, 1976), and they can even discriminate musical features such as a

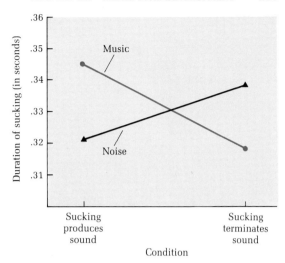

FIGURE 6-6. *Duration of sucking by infants as a function of whether sucking produces music or noise.*

change in melody or tempo (Chang & Trehub, 1977). Richard Walk (1981) has reviewed the infant literature and concluded that music appreciation "is a species-specific trait and a natural part of our auditory perceptual world" (p. 66). But if babies are inherently musical creatures, it is possible that they prefer some kinds of music to others. Perhaps future research will allow us to determine whether infants will choose marches over Muzak or the Beatles to Beethoven.

INTERSENSORY PERCEPTION

Suppose you are playing a game in which you are blindfolded and are trying to identify objects by touch. A friend then places a small, perfectly spherical object in your hand. As you finger it, you determine that it is 1.5 to 2 inches in diameter, that it weighs at most a couple of ounces, and that it is very hard and is covered with a large number of little indentations, or "dimples." You suddenly have an "aha" experience and conclude that the object is a _____.

A colleague who often conducts this exercise in class reports that most of his students easily identify the object as a golf ball—even if they have never touched or held a golf ball in their lives.

PHOTO 6-3. *Listening to music is a pleasurable activity for infants and toddlers.*

This is an example of **cross-modal perception**—the ability to recognize by one sensory modality (in this case, touch) an object that is familiar through another (vision). As adults, we can make many cross-modal inferences of this kind. But what about human infants? Are babies capable of cross-modal perception during the first year of life? Before we examine the evidence for ourselves, let's consider what some of the major theorists would have to say.

Theories of Intersensory Integration

Recall that William James (1890) believed that the senses are integrated at birth. Presumably, sensory inputs of any kind are global experiences that are not discriminated as "visual," "auditory," "tactile," or "olfactory" experiences; the child has to learn to differentiate the senses.

Thomas Bower (1982) and Eleanor Gibson (1969) can agree, in part, with James's viewpoint.

Both Bower and Gibson are **differentiation theorists:** they suggest that the senses are integrated at birth and are gradually differentiated through maturation and experience (perceptual learning). According to Bower (1982), the senses have to be integrated from the beginning—otherwise neonates would not look for sound-producing objects or reach for and try to touch objects they can see. Gibson (1969) adds that the "defining" features of various stimuli (features such as shapes, textures, forms, and patterns) are detectable by more than one modality. If she is correct, cross-modal perception may well be present at birth (or very soon thereafter).

Jean Piaget, in contrast, is an **enrichment theorist.** Piaget (1954, 1960) believes that the sensory modalities are separate at birth and will develop independently before they become more integrated at a later time (unfortunately, Piaget is not clear about when this sensory integration might occur). The enrichment perspective implies that cross-modal perception is not possible until the senses have become integrated. Presumably, a 6-week-old infant who "knows" an object by sight would be unable to recognize it by touch (as in the dark) or to discriminate it from other objects on the basis of tactile cues alone.

Which theory is correct? Let's see whether we can clarify the issue by examining the empirical record.

PHOTO 6-4. According to differentiation theory, the senses are integrated at birth, and babies expect to touch and feel objects that they can see and reach. However, vision and touch are soon differentiated, so that this year-old infant might even enjoy making an object disappear at her slightest touch.

Research on Intersensory Perception

Three kinds of research reflect on the intersensory capabilities of infants and older children: (1) studies of intersensory interaction, (2) studies of intersensory incongruity, and (3) studies of cross-modal perception.

■ *Intersensory interaction*

If the senses are integrated at birth, then babies should not distinguish visual stimulation from auditory or tactile stimulation. In other words, they should react to sensory inputs from different modalities as if these inputs were additive.

An example should clarify this point. Suppose you showed neonates three lights of different intensities and found that the infants preferred to look at the light of intermediate intensity (that is, the dim light was too dim to be interesting and the bright light was too bright). The next step in your procedure is to provide infants with short bursts of an auditory stimulus (**white noise**) just before showing them the three lights. If the senses are separate at birth (the enrichment position), the infants ought to differentiate the white noise from the lights and continue to look at the light of intermediate intensity. But if the senses are integrated (the differentiation position), the auditory and visual inputs should combine, producing one large, undifferentiated experience. Should that occur, one might hypothesize that the noise coupled with the light of intermediate intensity would be too arousing to be enjoyed. In other

cross-modal perception: *the ability to use one sensory modality to identify a stimulus or pattern of stimuli that is already familiar through another modality.*

differentiation theory: *a theory that the senses are integrated at birth and will gradually become more independent of one another as the child develops.*

enrichment theory: *a theory that the senses function independently at birth and will gradually become more integrated as the child develops.*

white noise: *a low-pitched hiss made up of all frequencies of sound presented simultaneously at an equal loudness so that no one frequency predominates.*

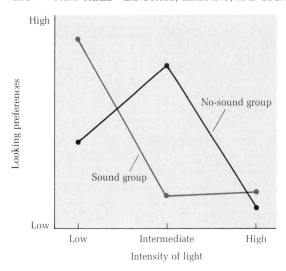

FIGURE 6-7. Visual preferences for lights of different intensities among children who either were or were not exposed to sounds (white noise).

words, the infant should now prefer the dim light, which, together with the noise, provides an optimal level of sensory arousal.

David Lewkowicz and Gerald Turkewitz (1981) have conducted this experiment with infants aged 11–48 hours. As we see in Figure 6–7, neonates who viewed the three lights without hearing white noise (the no-sound group) clearly preferred the light of *intermediate* intensity. In contrast, infants who first heard white noise clearly preferred to look at the light of *lowest* intensity. Apparently infants in the sound group did not treat auditory and visual stimulation as different experiences; instead, they seem to have reacted to these two inputs as if they were one large, undifferentiated sensory experience. Since these neonates were only 11–48 hours old, it appears that vision and audition are integrated at birth.

■ *Intersensory incongruity*

Suppose that you captured a baby's attention by floating a soap bubble in front of her face. Would she reach for it? If she did, how do you think she would react when the bubble disappeared at her slightest touch? Thomas Bower (1982), a differentiation theorist, would argue not only that the baby would reach for the bubble but that she

would be surprised and perhaps upset when it burst. According to Bower, the baby's surprise or discomfort over the disappearing object is an indication that her senses are integrated—that is, she expects to be able to touch or feel objects she can see and reach.

Bower, Broughton, and Moore (1970a) exposed neonates to a situation similar to the soap-bubble scenario. The subjects were 8–31-day-old infants who could see an object well within reaching distance while they were wearing special goggles. Actually, this **virtual object** was an illusion created by a shadow caster. If the infant reached for it, his or her hand would feel nothing at all. Bower et al. found that the infants did reach for the virtual object and that they became frustrated to tears when they failed to touch it. These results suggest that vision and touch are integrated: infants expect to "feel" objects they can see and reach, and an incongruity between vision and the tactile sense is discomforting.

Eric Aronson has studied the reactions of 1–2-month-old infants to incongruities between sights and sounds. In one experiment (Aronson & Rosenbloom, 1971), infants were placed in an infant seat where they were able to see their mothers through a soundproof screen. As the mother talked, the infant could see her mouth move and hear her voice through speakers located at each side of the infant seat (see Figure 6-8). When the speakers were equally loud, the mother's voice sounded as if it were coming from straight ahead (that is, from the mother's mouth). But if one speaker was turned up louder than the other, the voice sounded as if it were coming from the left or the right rather than from the mother's mouth. Such a visual/auditory discrepancy upset the infants in this study: they became agitated and stuck out their tongues (a sign of distress), and some even cried. In contrast, other infants who could not see their mothers were not at all upset by changes in the location of the mother's voice. Apparently vision and audition are integrated at birth—a baby who sees his or her mother speak expects to hear her voice coming from the general direction of her mouth.

Before we hastily chalk up a second point for the differentiation theorists (who claim that the senses are integrated at birth), it is important to note that there are studies in which young infants were *not* upset by auditory/visual or visual/tactile

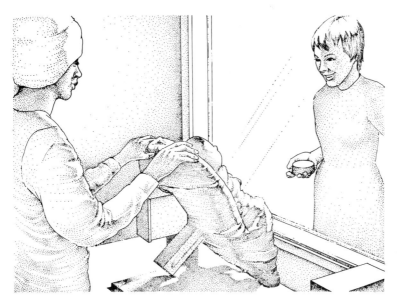

FIGURE 6-8. *The mother-voice apparatus used by Aronson and Rosenbloom.*

incongruities. In two recent reviews of this literature, Bower (1982) concludes that the bulk of the
data clearly supports differentiation theory, while
Walk (1981) gives the differentiation model a
more tentative endorsement.

■ *Cross-modal perception*
Can very young infants who have experienced an
object in one sensory modality "recognize" that
object through another modality? An experiment
by Meltzoff and Borton (1979) suggests that they
can. Meltzoff and Borton had 1-month-old infants
suck on an object that was placed directly into the
mouth so that it could not be seen. After sucking,
each infant was given an opportunity to look at
that object and a novel stimulus of a different
shape. Meltzoff and Borton's infants showed a
clear visual preference for the object they had
sucked, thereby indicating that they recognized by
sight a stimulus that was familiar only to the
"touch." Since these infants were only 26 to 33
days old, the results imply that certain kinds of
cross-modal perception may be innate.

Unfortunately, other investigators have been
unable to replicate Meltzoff and Borton's study.
Susan Rose, Allen Gottfried, and Wagner Bridger
(1978, 1981) have studied oral-to-visual and
tactile-to-visual perception in infants aged 6

months to 1 year. The infants either sucked or
touched an object and were then tested to see
whether they would recognize it by sight. The
6-month-old infants showed some limited evidence of cross-modal perception from touch to
vision but no evidence for oral-to-visual transfer.
In contrast, 12-month-old infants were generally
more proficient at both kinds of cross-modal tasks.

Research on cross-modal transfer between the
auditory and visual modalities paints a similar
picture. At 4 months of age, infants begin to recognize that a pattern (or rhythm) presented in the
auditory mode is either the same as or different
from another pattern of stimuli presented visually
(Mendelson & Ferland, 1982), and 6–8-month-old
infants are even better at this kind of auditory-to-
visual transfer (Allen, Walker, Symonds, &
Marcell, 1977).

Taken together, the bulk of the evidence suggests that cross-modal perception may not appear
until 4–6 months of age and then gradually improves. Here, then, is one set of findings that
seems consistent with Piaget's enrichment theory.

> **virtual object:** *an intangible object (optical illu-
> sion), produced by a shadow caster, that ap-
> pears to occupy a particular location in space.*

Another Look at the Enrichment/ Differentiation Controversy

From the data currently available, it appears that differentiation theory has received more support than enrichment theory. During the first two months of life, infants respond globally to sensory stimuli and do not clearly distinguish visual experiences from auditory or tactile input. Moreover, they may become upset by sensory incongruities such as not being able to touch objects they can see and reach. Both these findings suggest that the senses are integrated at birth and become differentiated later—precisely the position taken by differentiation theorists.

The one finding that seems consistent with enrichment theory is that cross-modal perception improves over time. In fact, studies of older children indicate that cross-modal judgments from vision to the **kinesthetic sense** (sensations produced by bodily movements) develop slowly and are not very accurate until 10–11 years of age (Birch & Lefford, 1963). How would differentiation theory explain gradual improvements in cross-modal abilities?

The differentiation theorist would first note that the senses begin to "differentiate" during the first year and will then continue to develop somewhat independently of one another from that point on. During the first six months of life, babies do begin to respond more selectively to sensory stimulation: At age 3 months, infants are less likely to turn in the direction of an auditory stimulus (Field, Muir, Pilon, Sinclair, & Dodwell, 1980), and they are no longer upset when they fail to touch a "virtual" object (Field, 1977). By 5 months of age, infants have stopped reaching for objects that make noise in the dark (Bower, 1982). All these findings suggest that the senses are gradually becoming more independent of one another.

As each sense continues to develop, it will become a more effective means of categorizing the properties or distinctive features of various objects and patterns. As a result, the child should become increasingly proficient at using any of his or her senses to recognize stimuli that are already familiar through another modality, and cross-modal perception will improve.

The reason some cross-modal judgments develop so very slowly is that the senses mature at different rates. For example, the kinesthetic sense is not fully developed until late in childhood, perhaps explaining why visual-to-kinesthetic perceptual comparisons are not very accurate until age 10 or 11. In sum, the accuracy of perception across any two senses is limited by the child's perceptual capabilities in the slower-developing modality (Walk, 1981).

Sensory Dominance

Psychologists have characterized human beings as visual creatures because it sometimes appears that vision dominates the other senses. In other words, we may eventually learn to rely on vision more than the other modalities when we interpret objects or events. One classic example of vision dominating audition is the case of the ventriloquist. A skillful ventriloquist can "throw" his or her voice because we judge the speech to be coming from the dummy's mouth, which we *see* moving, rather than from the ventriloquist's mouth, which moves very little (Walk, 1981).

Of course, you are not really "fooled" by a ventriloquist—but neither are young children. In fact, it is possible that children are less affected by the ventriloquist's illusion than adults are, for a study by Harry McGurk and J. MacDonald (1976) suggests that the tendency of vision to dominate hearing develops gradually over the course of childhood.

In McGurk and MacDonald's experiment, both adults and 3–5-year-old children listened to and tried to identify sounds such as "ba-ba" while watching a speaker on videotape. The rub was that the visual cues were inconsistent with the sounds. For example, if "ba-ba" played on the sound track, the speaker might be mouthing "ga-ga." Both the adults and the children could accurately report what they were hearing if they closed their eyes and did not attend to the conflicting visual cues. But with their eyes open, almost all the adults let their vision influence their hearing, and they misperceived the sound (reporting "ba-ba" as "da-da"). Although children also made errors of this kind, they were much more accurate than adults. Apparently visual cues are less likely to dominate the auditory perception of a young child because children are not yet as visually oriented as adults.

The ability of vision to dominate the tactile modality is illustrated in an experiment by Irvin Rock and Charles Harris (1967). Normally, adults who are allowed to feel an object without seeing it are able to use these tactile cues to estimate the object's size accurately. But if adults look through a reducing lens[2] at an object while they are feeling it, they will judge the object to be about the same size as the distorted visual image. In other words, the person's judgment is influenced more by visual cues than by tactile information. Recently, Harry McGurk and Roderick Power (1980) have shown that this particular form of visual dominance is already apparent by the time children enter school.

The findings reviewed to this point suggest that we human beings are *not* inherently visual creatures at birth, although we will eventually come to trust our eyes more than our ears (or touch) when these modalities give us conflicting information. Yet at least one sense seems to be *less* influenced by vision as we mature—the **proprioceptive** modality (that is, our sense of the orientation of the body in space). Herman Witkin (1959) has illustrated this point by seating subjects in a special chair within a small room and then independently tilting both the chair and the room. The subject's task is to align the chair to the true gravitational upright. Those who rely on visual cues to reposition themselves will err: they will end up aligning the chair to the tilted room. But subjects who rely on body position (proprioceptive cues) will align the chair to the gravitational upright, even though the visual environment still looks tilted. The results of Witkin's longitudinal study were clear: Between the ages of 8 and 17, children rely less and less on visual cues and more on proprioceptive information in the tilted-room task. Consequently, their performance improves.

Witkin also found that some children improved more than others. Those who became proficient at aligning themselves to the true vertical position were called **field independent** because their performance was hardly affected by the distracting visual field. Other children, called **field dependent**, were simply unable to ignore the tilted environment and align their chairs to the gravitational

upright. As it turns out, field dependence/independence is a most interesting perceptual attribute, which we will explore in greater detail later in the chapter.

PERCEPTUAL LEARNING AND DEVELOPMENT IN CHILDHOOD

Imagine that you are walking through a snow-covered forest when you notice what appears to be movement beside a bush on your left. You stop and stare, and lo and behold, you make out the shape of a white rabbit almost perfectly camouflaged against the sterile, white backdrop of a snowbank.

Now suppose that you had a 5-year-old child with you as you walked through the forest. Assuming that the child had also seen the movement beside the bush, do you think he could have unmasked the camouflaged form as well as you did? If the child sees the form, do you think he could easily identify it as a rabbit?

Rather than trying to answer these questions immediately, we will first consider several important perceptual changes that occur between infancy and adolescence—changes in visual search, selective attention, and the perception of visual forms. You should then not only have answers for our "camouflaged rabbit" questions but also be able to cite several lines of evidence to back your conclusions.

Development of Attention

In order to perceive a white rabbit against a snowy background, the child must first focus his attention on the area where movement was seen, tune

---

[2]A reducing lens produces an image of an object that is smaller than the object itself.

---

kinesthetic sense: *sensations of motion produced by movements of the muscles, joints, and tendons.*

proprioception: *the ability to locate the position of one's body (or body parts) in space.*

field dependence/independence: *a dimension of perceptual style—namely, the extent to which the surrounding context (the field) affects a person's perceptual judgments.*

out potentially distracting stimuli such as blowing snow or the rustling of trees, and then concentrate long enough to detect the white figure against a perceptually similar background. Can 5-year-old children do these things as well as older children, adolescents, or adults? Let's see for ourselves by "focusing our attention" on the pertinent research literature.

■ *Changes in visual search*

Earlier in the chapter, we learned that neonates will scan the exterior angles and edges of visual patterns, whereas 2–3-month-old infants have begun to examine a pattern's internal features. But as you might expect, the scanning patterns of a 3-month-old infant are rather unsystematic. Research with older children in the Soviet Union reveals that visual scanning becomes increasingly detailed, or "exhaustive," over the first six years of life (see Figure 6-9).

Older children are also more likely to follow a set strategy when scanning visual forms and patterns. Elaine Vurpillot (1968) recorded the eye movements of 4- to 10-year-olds who were trying to determine whether two objects were "the same" or "different." Children aged 4 and 5 displayed no systematic pattern of scanning, and as a result their judgments were often inaccurate. In contrast, children older than 6½ proceeded more slowly and systematically, looking back and forth at the corresponding features of each pair of stimuli. Not surprisingly, the older children were better able to detect the subtle (and not so subtle) differences

between stimuli—information that enabled them to make accurate judgments.

Since visual search becomes more organized, exhaustive, and efficient over the first six to seven years of life, our hypothetical 5-year-old may have problems identifying a small white figure that appears against a snowy backdrop. Of course, this conclusion assumes that the child would notice the white figure in the first place, and that is by no means assured, as we will see in the following section.

■ *Changes in selective attention*

At any given moment our attention is **selective**—we focus on only a small portion of the total stimulation impinging on our sensory receptors. If you are now studying this chapter in preparation for an upcoming quiz, you may scarcely be aware of the humming of a nearby appliance or the sounds of traffic outside. Whenever we concentrate on something, we are trying to focus our attention on that object or event while ignoring irrelevant or distracting sensations.

Even neonates are capable of selective attention. When babies scan the environment, they prefer the "contoured" and the "complex" to simpler, unpatterned stimulation. Moreover, they will focus intently on novel objects and events and will habituate (quit attending) to stimuli that have become overly familiar. Of course, it is not always easy to keep one's attention riveted to the situation or task at hand. For example, if eight hours has elapsed since you have eaten, the lus-

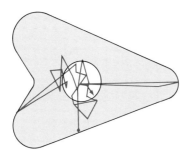

Trajectory of eye movements
of 3-year-old in familiarization
with figure (20 seconds)

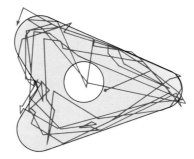

Trajectory of eye movements
of 6-year-old in familiarization
with figure (20 seconds)

FIGURE 6-9. *Typical visual search patterns of 3- and 6-year-old children who scan an unfamiliar figure for 20 seconds. Note that the visual search of the 6-year-old is much more detailed and exhaustive.*

cious aroma of spaghetti sauce from the crock pot in the kitchen may well be challenging your powers of concentration (on this passage, at least). Do you suppose that infants and young children are any more or less proficient than we adults at disregarding one source of stimulation in order to concentrate on another?

Eleanor Maccoby (1967) has tried to answer this question by placing children in a situation not unlike what we might experience at a cocktail party. At crowded social gatherings, it is often difficult to follow one conversation if other conversations nearby compete for our attention. Maccoby created this kind of scenario in the laboratory by asking kindergarten, second-grade, fourth-grade, and sixth-grade children to listen to simultaneous phrases spoken by a male and a female and then to identify what either the male or the female had said. The voices came from two loudspeakers placed 18 inches apart. On some occasions the children knew in advance which voice they would be asked to recall. These "preparatory" trials were similar to the situation in which we are trying to listen to one speaker while ignoring other conversations around us. On the remaining trials, the children did not know in advance which voice they would be asked to recall. These "nonpreparatory" trials were in some ways similar to a party situation in which we are trying to monitor two conversations at the same time.

The results of Maccoby's experiment appear in Figure 6-10. As you can see, older children clearly outperformed younger children on both the preparatory and the nonpreparatory trials—indicating that selective attention improves with age. In addition, performance in all age groups was much better on the preparatory than on the nonpreparatory trials. Clearly, it is easier to understand what someone has said if we listen to that person and do not try to monitor another voice (or conversation) at the same time.

Selective attention in the visual modality also improves with age. In one study, John Hagen (1967) had 7-, 9-, 11-, and 13-year-olds perform a visual learning task while listening to distracting sounds. Although the auditory distraction made visual learning more difficult for all, the performance of younger children (ages 7–9) was worse than that of their older counterparts (ages 11–13). Apparently the older children were better

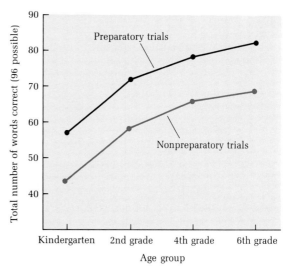

FIGURE 6-10. *Performance on a selective attention task as a function of age. Older children were more proficient than younger children at dividing their attention between two speakers (the nonpreparatory condition) and at concentrating on one speaker while ignoring the other (preparatory condition).*

able to concentrate on the pertinent visual information while "tuning out" the irrelevant sounds.

Taken together, these studies show that selective attention gradually improves over childhood and into early adolescence. Perhaps our hypothetical 5-year-old would have some difficulty visualizing a white rabbit on a snowy background, particularly if blowing snow, rustling limbs, or other irrelevant sensory inputs were present to divert his attention from the visual task at hand.

■ *Changes in attention span*

Research psychologists who work with young children are careful to limit their experimental sessions to no more than a few minutes. And nursery school teachers, who must often tend to young children for hours at a time, are likely to switch topics or change classroom activities every 15 to 20 minutes. The assumption that under-

---

selective attention: *the focusing of attention on certain aspects of experience while ignoring irrelevant or distracting sensations.*

lies these practices is that very young children have short **attention spans**—they cannot (or will not) concentrate on any single activity for long periods.

We now know that this assumption is quite correct. In one study of children's capacity for sustained attention (Yendovitskaya, 1971), subjects were asked to put strips of colored paper in appropriately colored boxes, and the time they devoted to this task was measured. Children aged 2½ to 3½ worked at the task for an average of 18 minutes and were easily distracted. In contrast, 5½–6-year-olds were much more persistent, often working at the task for an hour or more. Of course, capacity for sustained attention continues to improve throughout childhood and early adolescence, and these improvements may be due, in part, to important maturational changes occurring in the central nervous system. For example, the **reticular formation**, an area of the brain responsible for the regulation of attention, is not fully **myelinated** until puberty. Perhaps this neurological development helps to explain why adolescents and young adults are suddenly able to spend hours on end cramming for upcoming exams or typing furiously to make morning deadlines on term papers.

By now it should be apparent that our attentional capacities improve with age. Not only do we begin to extract more information from our sensory inputs, but we also become more selective in what we will attend to, and we develop an ability to concentrate on an object, a task, or a situation for extended periods of time. Do these developmental changes in attention affect our perception of the world around us? Perhaps the best way to answer this question is to consider some changes that occur in children's ability to perceive visual forms.

Development of Form Perception

We have seen that neonates are quite responsive to visual stimuli. They prefer to look at complex, contoured patterns. They are also able to perceive a variety of "forms," including highly ambiguous figures such as the Kanizsa triangle (see Box 6-2). These findings suggest that newborn infants will selectively attend to certain aspects of the environment and that they are capable of making the basic distinction between a visual form and its background.

As we noted earlier, an infant's visual preferences begin to change at about 2–4 months of age. Suddenly the child's attention to visual forms is no longer determined by their contour, complexity, or other physical attributes; infants are now captivated by stimuli that are moderately discrepant with their existing schemata. For example, a picture of an unfamiliar face is only moderately discrepant with the infant's schema for the faces of his or her caregivers. As a result, the 4-month-old infant will now prefer to look at an unfamiliar face rather than a highly discrepant "scrambled" face, even though the two stimuli have the same amount of complexity, contour, and curvature (Kagan, 1971).

Once children reach this second, or **"representational,"** stage, they will construct a variety of new schemata to represent the many new stimuli they encounter on a regular basis. But at some point near the end of the first year, form perception changes once again: infants suddenly become very interested in stimuli that are *highly discrepant* from existing schemata, and they begin to use their emerging cognitive abilities to "explain" these discrepancies (Kagan, 1971). For example, a 2-year-old is likely to find a "scrambled" face much more interesting than a normal face. In fact, the older child will typically stare at the unusual form as if trying to figure out why this face is different from other faces. And how do 2-year-olds interpret scrambled faces? They are likely to say things like "Who hit him in the nose?" or "Who that, mommy? A monster, mommy?" (Kagan, 1971).

We see, then, that 2-year-olds seem to enjoy the opportunity to interpret or explain new visual forms. But just how precise are the perceptual abilities of a young child? Could a 2-year-old or even a 5-year-old detect and correctly identify a white rabbit in the snow? If we analyze this perceptual task, we see that it presents the child with two basic challenges. First, the perceiver must unmask a camouflaged form from a perceptually similar background. Once the form has been detected, the perceiver must then recognize that it is indeed a rabbit rather than a dog, a cat, or a squirrel. Let's now turn to the research literature to see whether 2- to 5-year-old children are likely to accomplish either of these perceptual feats.

■ *Unmasking visual forms*

Apparently, young children are not very proficient at unmasking visual forms, even when they know a hidden figure is present and they devote their attention to finding it. If you have read the children's section of your newspaper, you have undoubtedly seen "embedded figures" puzzles in which the task is to find hidden objects (for example, a spoon, a dog) in a distracting visual context. L. Ghent (1956) administered an **"embedded figures" test** to children of different ages (see Figure 6-11) and found that the ability to unmask hidden objects develops very slowly. For example, only 25% of Ghent's 8-year-olds were able to ignore the distracting background and find all the embedded figures in his relatively simple test.

Another method of testing children's ability to unmask visual forms is to present them with an incomplete figure and then gradually add information until they recognize the stimulus. Eugene Gollin (1960, 1962) showed 3- to 5-year-olds sketchy outlines of common objects such as a pig, a shoe, and a fish (see Set I of Figure 6-12). If the child did not recognize the objects, progressively

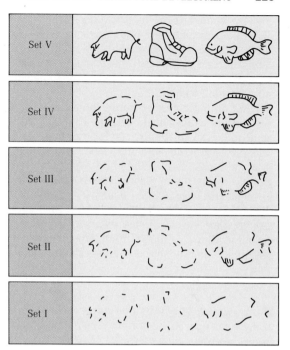

FIGURE 6-12. *Sample stimulus figures that vary in completeness. Children are first shown figures from Set I, then Set II, and so on until they can identify the object.*

more detail was added (Sets II-V) until he or she correctly identified them. Gollin found that many 3-year-olds went to Set IV before identifying the

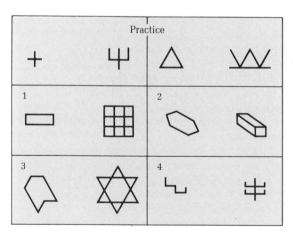

FIGURE 6-11. *The "embedded figures" test used by Ghent to measure children's ability to unmask visual forms. On this test, the child's task is to find the figure at the left of each card within the more complex figure to the immediate right.*

attention span: *a person's capacity for sustaining attention to a particular stimulus or activity.*

reticular formation: *an area of the brain that serves to activate the organism and is thought to be important in the regulation of attention.*

myelinization: *the process by which neurons are encased in waxy myelin sheaths that facilitate transmission of neural impulses.*

representational stage: *the period between 2 and 4 months of age when infants are beginning to construct perceptual schemata for familiar stimuli and to pay close attention to objects and events that are moderately discrepant from their existing schemata.*

embedded figures test: *a measure of the ability to locate hidden objects in a distracting visual context.*

objects, while 4-year-olds identified them at Set III, and 5-year-olds were often correct at Set II. A later study (Spitz & Borland, 1971) found that people become even more proficient at unmasking incomplete forms between kindergarten (age 5) and late adolescence.

What do these studies imply about the 5-year-old and the white rabbit? Perhaps we could conclude that even an attentive 5-year-old might have difficulty seeing an all-white object "embedded" in a snowbank. And if the child caught a quick glimpse of the "figure" before it ran behind a bush, he might still be unable to identify it as a rabbit on the basis of such sketchy information. Let's now see whether we can determine why preschool children require so much information in order to recognize common objects such as rabbits, fish, or shoes.

■ Perception of wholes and parts

Many years ago, Heinz Werner (1948) argued that form perception progresses from the "global," or "diffuse," to the "discrete," or "specific." In other words, Werner believed that younger children would react to a stimulus as a whole and pay little if any attention to its parts. In contrast, older children would eventually begin to attend to the "whole" figure *and* to its parts. Presumably, increased attention to the component parts of visual stimuli should help the older child to recognize or label objects that are initially unfamiliar or ambiguous.

For example, suppose we were to show children the object in Figure 6-13 and ask them "What do you think this is?" Apparently, younger children (aged 2–4) do react to the "whole," for they are likely to call the stimulus "some dirt," "a spot," or "a bird" without labeling its parts (Ames, Metraux, Roedell, & Walker, 1974). In contrast, 6- to 7-year-olds are more apt to describe the object as "a man wearing a hat" or "a bird with ears," suggesting that they are attending to both the whole stimulus and its component parts.

Why do children eventually stop responding only to the stimulus-as-a-whole and begin to pay more attention to its component parts? How do they come to appreciate those aspects of visual form that they may have previously ignored? And just what "parts" of a visual display are likely to capture their attention? Eleanor Gibson has pro-

FIGURE 6-13. *Children's classification of ambiguous figures. When asked to define a highly ambiguous figure, preschool children are apt to label the whole object without referring to its parts. For example, a 2–5-year-old might call this particular figure "a man," "a bird," or "some dirt." But a 6–7-year-old would respond to both the whole and its parts, perhaps by labeling this object "a bird with ears" or "a man wearing a hat."*

posed a theory of perceptual development that addresses these very issues.

■ Gibson's differentiation theory

According to Gibson (1969), **perceptual learning** occurs when we actively explore objects in our environment and discover their **distinctive features.** Simply defined, a distinctive feature is any cue that differentiates one form from another. A 3-year-old may initially confuse rabbits and cats, for both are furry animals of about the same size. However, the child will eventually discover that rabbits have big, floppy ears—a distinctive feature that differentiates them from cats, rats, squirrels, and all other small, furry animals.

Gibson believes that young children do not have to be taught to look for distinctive features; presumably perceptual learning is self-initiated and requires no external reinforcement. Thus, she views the young child as an active information seeker who is intrinsically motivated to look for

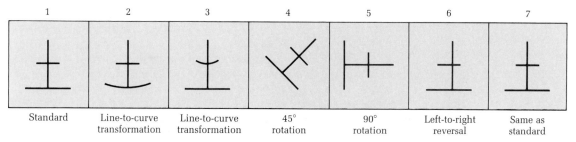

1	2	3	4	5	6	7
Standard	Line-to-curve transformation	Line-to-curve transformation	45° rotation	90° rotation	Left-to-right reversal	Same as standard

FIGURE 6-14. Examples of figures used to test children's ability to detect the distinctive features of letterlike forms. Stimulus 1 is the standard. The child's task is to examine each of the comparison stimuli (stimuli 2–7) and pick out those that are the same as the standard.

the properties that differentiate objects and events.

Of course, some distinctive features are easier to detect than others. Even a 4-year-old whose attentional strategies are relatively immature soon notices large distinctive features such as the trunk of an elephant or the long, floppy ears of a rabbit. However, 4-year-olds may not easily differentiate *b* from *d* because the distinctive feature that discriminates these letters (the direction of curvature) is subtle and not very meaningful to a child of this age.

Gibson and her colleagues have conducted an experiment to study the ability of young children to distinguish different letterlike forms (Gibson, Gibson, Pick, & Osser, 1962). Children aged 4 to 8 were shown a standard letterlike stimulus and several transformations of this "standard" form (examples appear in Figure 6-14). Their task was to pick out the stimuli that were identical to the standard. The 4- and 5-year-olds had difficulties with all the transformations in Figure 6-14: they often judged these stimuli to be identical to the standard. But 6- to 8-year-olds were generally able to detect the "distinctive features" that differentiated the transformations from the "standard" stimulus. Notice that these children are beginning to recognize subtle differences in letterlike forms at precisely the time (age 6) that they are learning to read in school. As it turns out, learning to read is a very complex task—one that deserves a closer look. Box 6-3 describes some of the perceptual hurdles that children must overcome in order to make sense of all those funny little squiggles on a printed page.

In sum, Eleanor Gibson is a *differentiation* theorist. She believes that young children are constantly extracting new information from the environment and thereby discovering the properties, patterns, and "distinctive features" that will enable them to differentiate objects and events. As this differentiation continues, a child will grow perceptually and become increasingly accurate at interpreting the broad array of stimuli that impinge on the sensory receptors.

We can now summarize the ground we have covered by returning to our 5-year-old who faces the task of detecting and identifying a stationary white object against a snowy background. A "best guess" is that the child would be much less proficient at this task than a typical adult. The reasoning is as follows:

1. Five-year-olds have much shorter attention spans than adults. Moreover, their visual search is not very exhaustive, and their focus of attention is less selective than an older person's. Taken together, these findings suggest that a 5-year-old might quickly scan the snowbank in an unsystematic fashion. And since a disorganized visual search is unlikely to detect a well-camouflaged visual form, the child may soon be attending to other distracting stimuli that are present (for example, rustling limbs or blowing snow) rather than continuing to search for the hidden object.

2. These attentional decrements may explain

---

perceptual learning: *changes in the ability to extract information from sensory stimulation that occur as a result of experience.*

distinctive feature: *a dimension on which two or more objects differ and can be discriminated.*

BOX 6-3
HOW DO WE LEARN TO READ?

By the time children receive their first formal instruction in reading, they are already quite familiar with the spoken language and rather adept at using it. Reading now presents a number of additional challenges. In order to read, a child must first realize that spoken words can be represented visually (in print). Once this milestone has been achieved, the child must then learn to recognize and to discriminate the letters of the alphabet and to associate these funny little figures with the sounds that make up the spoken word.

Eleanor Gibson and Harry Levin (1975) believe that children pass through three distinct phases while learning to read. During the first phase, children equate reading with storytelling: an adult who reads to them is simply telling a tale about the pictures in a book. In fact, a child at this phase of development may pick up an illustrated storybook and "read" very sensible sentences—most of which have no relation to the words on the page.

At the next phase, the child recognizes that the squiggles on the printed page represent words, which, in turn, will determine the content of the story to be told. Even before they have had any formal instruction in school, children whose parents read to them may learn a favorite story by heart and then try to match the spoken word to the symbols that appear in print (Smith, 1977). For example, a 3-year-old who knows that the title of her storybook is "Santa Is Coming to Town" might try to "read" the cover by touching each letter and verbalizing a word or syllable, as illustrated below. Eventually children learn that each letter is related to a particular sound and that combinations of letters (and sounds) make up printed words. However, the child who is just beginning to read is likely to skip over words that are unfamiliar.

Print on book cover:	S a n t a I s C o m...
Child's statements (as she touches each letter)	"San ta is com ing to town. What's this say?"

In the third and final phase of learning to read, children have become more proficient at recognizing the letters and sounds (the parts) that make up "whole" words. At this point the child may try to decipher unknown words by breaking them into their component parts and then attempting to reconstruct a meaningful whole. For example, if you learned to read by the "phonics" method, you were taught to deal with words you had not *seen* before by breaking them into familiar syllables and "sounding out" these auditory components. Presumably you would then be able to recognize the word because this combination of sounds would represent a familiar whole—a word that you had *heard* before.

For more than 30 years, experts in the field of reading education have argued about how reading should be taught. Proponents of the "whole word" method believe that children learn best if they are taught to recognize individual words by sight. Two arguments in favor of this method are (1) that young children perceive visual forms in a "holistic" manner and (2) that whole words have meaning, whereas letters and sounds do not. However, proponents of the "phonics" method believe that children will become much more skillful at reading if they first learn the relations between "whole words" and their component letters and sounds. One argument in favor of this technique is that it makes use of the child's developing ability to attend to the "parts" of visual stimuli. Moreover, the student of phonics who is taught to recognize words by their component parts is less likely to confuse stimuli such as *truck, trick, track,* and *trace,* which look alike but sound very different.

The "whole word" versus "phonics" controversy is difficult to resolve because both approaches are effective methods of teaching children to read. Whole-word training is particularly useful during the earlier phases, when the child must learn that abstract visual stimuli such as CAT or TREE represent spoken words and are therefore meaningful (Smith, 1977). However, many reading specialists believe that some phonics training is necessary if children are to become proficient at decoding words they have never seen before (Chall, 1967). Since each technique has something important to offer the child who is learning to read, many reading programs now make use of both kinds of instruction (Williams, 1979).

why young children are less proficient than adults at locating objects embedded in a distracting visual field. But even if the young child does momentarily detect a white object in the snow, he is likely to scan the form in a global, unsystematic fashion and thereby miss the "part" or "distinctive feature" (long, floppy ears) that will identify it as a rabbit (indeed, white ears may be very difficult to

PHOTO 6-5. *Perceiving the distinctive features of the letters of the alphabet is a tough task for preschool children.*

distinguish from a white background unless the perceiver has an opportunity to scan the figure extensively).

Of course, the research does not imply that all 5-year-olds will always fail to perceive stationary white rabbits in snowbanks. The point is simply that this perceptual task would be more difficult for a 5-year-old than for an older child or an adult.

ENVIRONMENTAL INFLUENCES ON PERCEPTION

We have seen that newborn infants are "perceiving" creatures who prefer to look at certain patterns and who will soon begin to avoid looming objects, to "construct" visual forms, and to respond in systematic ways to music, speech, and the sound of their mothers' voices. These findings are quite consistent with the nativist perspective, which implies that many basic perceptual tendencies are innate rather than learned.

But capable as neonates may be, their perceptual abilities are not very refined. Indeed, contemporary theorists generally acknowledge that the further development of *all* basic perceptual skills depends, in part, on the child's subsequent experiences.

Are there experiences that an individual *must* have in order to develop a normal repertoire of perceptual skills? Are the ways that we perceive the world at all influenced by the home and cultural settings in which we live? In this final section of the chapter, we will explore each of these issues and see that one's experiences are indeed important contributors to perceptual growth and development.

What Kinds of Experiences Are Important?

You have probably heard the expression "Use it or lose it," a cultural maxim implying that our basic abilities will deteriorate if we fail to exercise them. Students of perceptual development have tested this proposition by observing the perceptual growth of subjects (generally animals) that have been deprived of certain sensory or motor experiences. The logic underlying these "deprivation" experiments is straightforward. If subjects show a perceptual deficit of some kind after a period of sensory or motor deprivation, then the experiences that they did *not* have must be necessary for normal perceptual development.

■ *Physiological effects of visual deprivation*

A number of years ago, Austin Riesen and his associates found that chimpanzees raised in the dark will experience atrophy (degeneration) of the optic nerve, which seriously restricts their vision (Riesen, Chow, Semmes, & Nissen, 1951). This atrophy is reversible if the animal spends no more than seven months in the dark but is permanent if the deprivation lasts much longer. If dark-reared chimpanzees are exposed to diffuse, unpatterned light for brief periods every day, physical degeneration of the visual system will not occur. However, these visually deprived animals will later have difficulty in discriminating forms such

as circles and squares—a task that normal chimpanzees can easily master (Riesen, 1965).

Riesen's work is important because it indicates that the visual system requires a minimal amount of stimulation—presumably *patterned* stimulation—in order to develop normally. Although Riesen worked with chimpanzees, there is reason to believe that his findings would apply to human beings. Babies who are born with cataracts in both eyes (a cataract is an opacity of the lens of the eye that obstructs the passage of light) are often nearly blind at birth and will remain visually handicapped until the cataracts are removed. And once surgery restores their sight, these former cataract patients are like Riesen's dark-reared chimpanzees in that they have difficulty discriminating common forms such as spheres and cubes (Walk, 1981).

There is also evidence that our experiences may affect our ability to perceive objects in vertical, horizontal, or oblique (diagonal) orientations. Studies conducted with kittens reveal that individual cells in the **visual cortex** respond selectively to one of these three orientations. In other words, the visual area consists of "horizontal" cells, "vertical" cells, and "oblique" cells. Now suppose that we forced a young kitten to wear goggles all the time that allowed it to see lines in only one of the three visual orientations (for example, vertical stripes). The effect of this atypical visual environment is to change the orientation of cortical cells. Our goggle-wearing kitten would develop an abundance of "vertical" cells while losing some of those that would enable it to see lines in the horizontal and the oblique orientations (Stryker, Sherk, Leventhal, & Hirsch, 1978).

Although this research may seem rather artificial, the results probably do apply to human beings—at least to those human beings who have **visual astigmatisms** (Walk, 1981). The lenses of an astigmatic's eyes are optically distorted and will image more clearly in some visual orientations than in others. In this sense, the astigmatic's visual environment is restricted, though less severely than that of Stryker's goggle-wearing kittens. When tested, astigmatics often have trouble seeing some lines in the horizontal, the vertical, or the oblique orientation. Even when their optical errors have been corrected, astigmatics may still be unable to perceive lines equally well in all visual orientations (Mitchell,

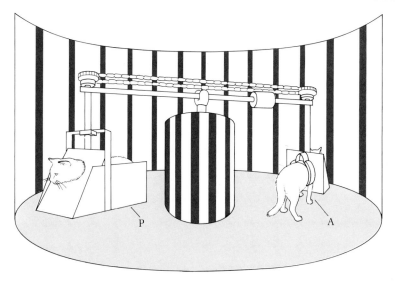

FIGURE 6-15. *The experimental apparatus used by Held and Hein to study the effects of locomotion on visual perception. An active kitten (A) pulls its passive litter mate (P). The two kittens have the same visual experiences, but only the active kitten is allowed to move about on its own.*

Freeman, Millodot, & Haegerstrom, 1973). This latter finding suggests that astigmatic distortions may alter the development of visual-cortical cells and produce some minor (but permanent) deficits in form perception.

■ *Are two eyes better than one?*

A childhood friend of mine who had been blind in one eye from birth eventually became a very skilled athlete. Indeed, his visual "handicap" seemed to bother him only when he boxed, for he had a hard time detecting punches directed to his "blind" side. However, many people who met this young man were quite unaware that he had but one working eye, for the one eye that he did have seemed to "work" as well as two.

Because the fusion of two flat images can create an impression of depth, people have often assumed that depth perception requires both eyes. Yet monocular (one-eyed) vision does not prevent depth perception, because some depth cues (for example, perspective) are detectable with only one eye. Richard Walk (1981) reports that a monocular infant in his sample clearly perceived depth, for she always avoided the deep side of a visual cliff. Moreover, binocular infants who have one eye covered with an eyepatch are just as likely to avoid the deep side of a visual cliff as infants who can see the dropoff with both eyes. Although

we have much to learn about monocular vision, the findings to date suggest that its effects on visual perception are probably rather subtle.

■ *Effects of movement on perception*

Suppose that an infant were tied to a cradleboard so that she could see the environment but could not move. Would this inability to reach for and to explore objects have an adverse effect on her visual perception later in life?

Richard Held and Alan Hein believe that it would. Held and Hein (1963) raised kittens in the dark for 8–12 weeks and then divided them into two experimental groups. Kittens assigned to an *active* condition were permitted to move about in a lighted environment while pulling the apparatus shown in Figure 6-15. Kittens assigned to the *passive* condition merely rode in the cartlike holder and were prevented from moving about on their own. Each pair of kittens spent three hours a day in this lighted environment and the rest of

---

visual cortex: *the area of the brain that receives and interprets visual impulses.*

visual astigmatism: *a refractive defect of the lens of the eye that prevents the formation of clear, distinct images.*

their time in the dark. After several days of experience in the light, the kittens were tested to see whether they would extend their paws when lowered to a visual surface. They were also tested on the visual cliff.

The results were clear. Active kittens soon began to pass the paw-placement tests, and they *always* avoided the deep side of the visual cliff. By contrast, passive kittens apparently did not perceive depth, for they showed absolutely no reluctance to venture out over the deep side of the apparatus. In fact, kittens in the passive group did not begin to extend their paws or to avoid the visual dropoff until they had had unrestrained access to a lighted environment for 48 hours. Held and Hein concluded that kittens (and possibly human infants) must be able to move around on their own in an environment that contains visual cues before they are likely to develop mature visual/spatial skills.

However, Held and Hein may have overstated the case. Note that their "active" kittens must necessarily attend to the visual environment as they walk, whereas the "passive" kittens are freer to doze off while riding in their holders. So increased attention to the visual environment (rather than self-produced motion) may be the factor that explains the superior visual/spatial performance of Held and Hein's active kittens.

There is some support for this alternative hypothesis in that children born without arms and legs can perceive depth and distance, even though their bodily movements are severely restricted (Gouin-DeCarie, 1969; James, 1890). Richard Walk (1981) suggests that "movement" may be essential for the development of visual perception, but he argues that this movement *need not be self-produced.* Presumably, even a paralyzed child might become proficient at estimating depth and distance relations if he or she is regularly exposed to moving stimuli that approach and recede from the child's location in space.

Walk tested his **"movement" hypothesis** by rearing kittens in the dark for seven weeks and then exposing them for three hours a day to different visual environments. Kittens that were passively exposed to an uninteresting environment tended to doze off in their holders. When tested, these subjects showed no more depth perception than "control" kittens that had remained in the dark. Another group of dark-reared kittens were

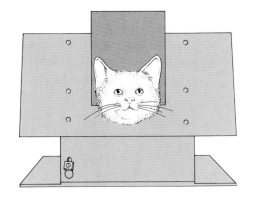

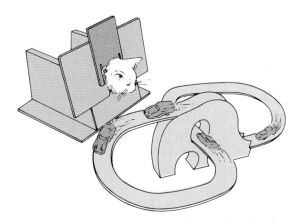

FIGURE 6-16. *Apparatus used in Richard Walk's passive attention experiment. Although the top kitten can see its environment, it has nothing interesting to look at. The bottom kitten is also confined and cannot move, but its visual environment contains interesting stimuli that move. Walk found that kittens that watched the moving objects were able to perceive depth but the passive kittens that stared at a static environment were not.*

exposed to an interesting visual environment: they sat passively in holders and watched as toy cars streaked around a racetrack (see Figure 6-16). When these "passive" animals were tested, they performed as well on the visual cliff as a group of "active" kittens that had been permitted to move about in a lighted environment.

If Walk's results hold for human beings, we could conclude that the child on the cradleboard will suffer no serious perceptual deficits as long as she is regularly exposed to moving objects that capture her attention. Of course, moving stimuli are very common in a typical home environment, a fact that might explain why children without arms and legs develop normal spatial abilities even though their motor activities are severely restricted.

Social and Cultural Influences

Do people who grow up in different societies and subcultures perceive the world in different ways? An initial reaction is to say "Of course they do" and to offer the following illustration. As Shakespeare notes in the lines that open this chapter, judgments of beauty are rather subjective. Moreover, they vary from culture to culture. In the United States, for example, people are led to believe that relatively trim women represent the ideal standard of feminine loveliness. Yet men in other societies would spurn the "Hollywood starlet" types in favor of heftier women with more rounded physiques. Clearly beauty is in the eye of the beholder—and the beholder is affected by the standards of his or her culture.

Although a culture may provide evaluative standards for judging other people and their behavior, it is by no means obvious that our sociocultural backgrounds affect our perceptions of inanimate objects. For example, would an igloo-dwelling Eskimo who lives on the flat, treeless tundra of northern Canada be any more or less proficient at perceiving lines in the oblique or vertical orientation than a resident of New York City who grew up in a visual environment dominated by skyscrapers? Would a poor child who hasn't much money be any more likely than a rich child to value a dime and thereby overestimate its size? Do the child-rearing techniques that parents use have any effect on the way children process information and make judgments about the physical environment? These are some of the issues that have been explored by researchers who have looked for "social" and "cultural" influences on perception.

■ Perception of the physical environment

Many people from modern, industrialized societies are subject to the **oblique effect**—that is, they are better able to detect objects oriented horizontally or vertically than those in the oblique orientation. One explanation for this insensitivity

to obliques is the **carpentered environment hypothesis:** People from "Westernized" societies are unlikely to see many obliques in a world full of rectangular buildings and furnishings (beds, bookcases, TV sets, and so forth) that are dominated by horizontals and verticals. However, people who live in a "noncarpentered" environment that contains many obliques should not show the "oblique effect." The implication, then, is that our architecture and the layout of objects in our everyday environment may have a dramatic effect on our visual perception.

Robert Annis and Barrie Frost (1973) tested the carpentered environment hypothesis by comparing the visual perception of Euro-Canadians with that of Cree Indians who lived in tepeelike structures in a "noncarpentered" forested setting. As expected, the Indians, who had grown up in an environment full of obliques, were better able to detect stimuli in an oblique orientation than the Euro-Canadians, who lived in a "carpentered" environment.

Although these findings appear to confirm the carpentered environment hypothesis, a genetic interpretation is also plausible. Cree Indians have an Oriental ancestry that is very different from that of Euro-Canadians. This is an important point, because Timney and Muir (1976) found that Chinese subjects (who share a genetic ancestry with the Crees) show little or no "oblique effect," even those raised in the carpentered environment of Hong Kong. Moreover, Richard Held and his associates report that infants of European ancestry display an "oblique effect " long before their visual perception could possibly have been modified by prolonged exposure to a carpentered

---

movement hypothesis: *the notion that individuals must attend to objects that move in order to develop a normal repertoire of visual/spatial skills.*

oblique effect: *the finding that people are better able to detect horizontal or vertical stimuli than those in the oblique (diagonal) orientation.*

carpentered environment hypothesis: *the notion that people living in human-made environments dominated by horizontal and vertical elements are more susceptible to the oblique effect.*

PHOTO 6-6. Some theorists believe that children who grow up in a carpentered environment are better able to detect stimuli oriented horizontally or vertically than those oriented obliquely.

environment (Leehy, Moskowitz-Cook, Brill, & Held, 1975). In sum, there are clear cross-cultural differences in the ability to perceive the oblique. However, it now appears that these perceptual variations may reflect cross-cultural differences in genotype and are probably not due to the visual characteristics of one's environment.

Of course, the cultural environment may well affect perceptual development in other ways. For example, we have already learned that the ability to discriminate certain sounds depends, in part, on one's linguistic environment. People from diverse cultural backgrounds may also differ in their ability to perceive the third dimension in pictures and drawings. In Box 6-4 we will take a closer look at "picture perception" and attempt to determine why a drawing may not always convey the same message to all perceivers.

■ *Social values and perception*

For years social psychologists have argued that important personal and social values may color our perceptions in any number of ways. Consider the following example. Leo Postman, Jerome Bruner, and Elliot McGinnies (1948) tested the religious, political, social, and economic values of 25 subjects. They then used a machine called a **tachistoscope** to flash words related to each of these values on a screen. Each word was presented for but a fraction of a second, and the exposure time was gradually lengthened across presentations until the subject could finally recognize it. The findings were clear: words related to values that the subject considered important were recognized much sooner (that is, after shorter exposures) than words related to "unimportant" values. So it appears that perception is selective and that we are most likely to notice stimuli that are in some way related to values we deem important.

The extent to which we value an object may also affect our perception of its physical attributes. Jerome Bruner and C. C. Goodman (1947) asked 10-year-olds to adjust a spot of light until it matched the size of a coin that had been presented in another part of the visual field. Children generally overestimated the sizes of all coins, and the overestimates were much greater for coins of high monetary value (dimes and quarters) than for coins of lesser value (pennies and nickels).

Bruner and Goodman also found that children from poorer homes overestimated the size of coins more than children from advantaged homes. Does this finding mean that the poorer children attached greater *value* to the coins or only that the poorer childeren were less *familiar* with the coins and their true sizes? Later research tends to support the value hypothesis: poorer children are

FIGURE 6-17. Find the termite. People who are field dependent find tasks of this sort much more difficult than people who are field independent.

more likely than advantaged children to overestimate the size of a valuable object such as a dime, but the two groups produce comparable size estimates judging an object without value, such as a metallic "slug" (Nelson & Lechelt, cited in Burtley, 1980).

■ *Effect of the home environment*

Does a child's home environment influence perceptual development? Psychologist Herman Witkin believes it does. Specifically, Witkin suggests that the techniques and strategies that parents use to raise their child will affect the child's standing on a perceptual dimension known as *field dependence/independence.*

Field dependence and field independence represent two different perceptual styles. The *field independent* person is able to process information and perceive objects and events without being distracted by background, or "contextual," factors. In contrast, the perceptions of a *field dependent* person are likely to be influenced by irrelevant or distracting information. One measure of field dependence/independence is the "tilted room" test, discussed earlier in the chapter. When placed on a tilted chair within a tilted room, the field-dependent person will align the chair to the tilted environment, whereas the field-independent person is better able to ignore the distracting visual "field" and align the chair to the true gravitational upright. Field independents are also better than field dependents at finding objects embedded in a distracting visual context. For example, a

field-independent person would soon find the hidden "termite" in Figure 6-17, whereas the field-dependent person would have to search much longer.

Witkin and his associates (Witkin, 1967; Witkin, Goodenough, & Oltman, 1979) believe that domineering parents who closely supervise their child's behavior and demand that the child conform to rigidly defined rules are likely to contribute to a field-dependent orientation. In contrast, parents who are less restrictive, less-rule oriented, and generally willing to allow their children some individual initiative are probably fostering the development of a field-independent orientation.

Sex differences. Although there are vast individual differences within each sex, females tend to be more field-dependent than males (Witkin & Goodenough, 1977). Witkin suggests that this sex difference may be attributable to the ways males and females are raised. Specifically, it appears that parents are more likely to stress obedience for daughters and to restrict girls' initiative (Barry, Bacon, & Child, 1957). And according to Witkin, this is precisely the pattern of child rearing that contributes to a field-dependent orientation.

---

tachistoscope: *an instrument for providing very brief exposures to visual stimuli such as pictures, letters, or words.*

BOX 6-4
SOCIOCULTURAL INFLUENCES ON PICTURE PERCEPTION

Pictures, paintings, and photographs are two-dimensional representations of a three-dimensional scene. Can children perceive depth and spatial relations as portrayed on a flat, two-dimensional surface? William Hudson (1960) tried to answer this question by showing a set of line drawings to groups of Black and White South Africans. Each subject scanned the drawings and then indicated his or her understanding of the depth and spatial cues by answering such questions as "Which animal is nearer the man?" and "What is the man doing (aiming at)?"

The answers to these questions may seem rather obvious to anyone who has grown up in a Western society, where two-dimensional representations of depth and space are common. However, many of Hudson's subjects failed to give three-dimensional responses to the drawings. Hudson did find that schoolchildren (both Black and White) were more likely to provide three-dimensional answers than pre-schoolers were; and the schoolchildren gave more accurate accounts of depth and spatial relations than groups of illiterate Black or White adult laborers did. Almost all subjects were better at describing depth and spatial relations as portrayed in a photograph, but at least one group of illiterate laborers were apparently unable to perceive depth and distance in a photo. Taken together, Hudson's findings suggest that both education and prior exposure to two-dimensional representations of space contribute to

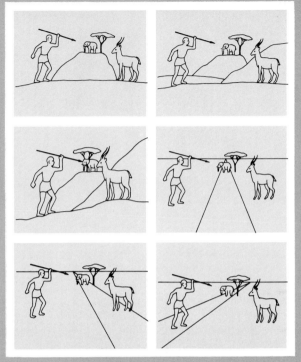

Drawings used by William Hudson to study depth perception in pictures.

the ability to perceive depth and spatial relations in pictures.

Later research indicated that education (or the lack thereof) cannot account for all group differences in picture perception. For example, Deregowski (1968) and Mundy-Castle (1966) have found that school-

Cross-cultural studies. Cross-cultural studies also tend to support Witkin's child-rearing hypothesis. Anthropologists sometimes classify non-industrialized societies into two basic categories: (1) *farming and pastoral* societies, in which a large number of relatively immobile families live and work together tending flocks and raising crops, and (2) *hunter-gatherer* societies, in which small groups earn their livelihood by moving about in search of food (edible plants, game, and fish). Parents in farming and pastoral societies stress the kinds of values that are necessary to maintain their way of life: children are expected to be obedient and cooperative and to place the needs of the group ahead of their own personal needs and goals. As expected, Witkin and Berry

(1975) found that people from this kind of society were quite field-*dependent*. Parents from hunter-gatherer societies also stress the values that would help to maintain their way of life. But for the hunter-gatherer, who most often works alone, these values include assertiveness, independence, and self-reliance rather than cooperation and obedience. Thus, Witkin and Berry (1975) were not surprised to find that children from hunter-gatherer societies were quite field-*independent*.

Perceptual style and personality. Recently, Herman Witkin and Donald Goodenough (1977) have proposed that field dependents are very different from field independents on dimensions other than perceptual style. After reviewing nearly 200 studies, Witkin and Goodenough con-

children from other African societies provided fewer three-dimensional responses to Hudson's pictures than Hudson's sample of South African school-children did. In fact, Hudson (1962) noted that Indian schoolchildren living in South Africa gave significantly fewer correct responses on pictorial tests of depth perception than either Black or White schoolchildren.

How can we account for these cross-cultural variations in picture perception? Perhaps they reflect societal or subcultural differences in genotype that affect visual perception (Pollack, 1976). It is also possible that children have very different *expectations* about what they are likely to see in a drawing—expectations that are based on the types or "styles" of artwork that are most common in their cultures. If the artwork of one's culture consists mostly of flat representations of isolated forms (people, game animals) with little or no spatial perspective, one may be unable to "see" anything other than a collection of objects in Hudson's pictures. Stated another way, a person from such a culture would not "expect" to see depth and spatial relations in a drawing.

Can our expectations, or "perceptual sets," really affect what we see in a picture or drawing? Yes, they can—and here is an example. Close your eyes and think for a second or two about a white rat. Now look at the drawing at the right, and lo and behold, you should see a white rat. However, if you had first been asked to think about an aging college professor with glasses, you would have approached the drawing with a different perceptual set and immediately perceived the "professor." Finally, note that the draw-

Ambiguous figure used to demonstrate the effects of perceptual sets on the interpretation of drawings.

ing of the "professor" is a relatively flat profile with few depth cues, whereas we (who are proficient with depth cues) tend to perceive more three-dimensionality in the "rat" figure—its tail looks closer to us than its body.

So our perception of pictures and drawings depends, in part, on our expectations or perceptual sets. If children from different cultures have very different expectations about what they are likely to see in a drawing, it is hardly surprising that their performance may differ from ours when they are asked to interpret what we "see" as indications of depth and spatial relations.

cluded that the field-dependent person is generally more interested in other people, better able to get along with others, more emotionally responsive, and somewhat less aggressive than the field-independent person. This is precisely the profile we might expect if field dependents have been encouraged by their parents to become cooperative individuals who are sensitive to the needs of others. In contrast, field independents tend to be more tolerant of ambiguous situations, better able to function without explicit guidance or supervision, and more interested in achievement than field dependents. Once again, these differences "make sense" if field independents are encouraged to be independent and assertive and to pursue individual goals.

WHAT IS PERCEPTUAL DEVELOPMENT?

Now that we have touched on the topic of perceptual development, here is a thought question that may seem rather strange: "What is perceptual development the development of?" Although there are many ways one might choose to answer this hopelessly ambiguous question, perhaps we can agree that perceptual development is the growth of interpretive skills—a complex process that depends, in part, on the expression of individual genotypes, the maturation of the sensory receptors, the kinds of sensory experiences that the child has available to analyze and interpret, the child's emerging cognitive abilities, and the social context in which all these other variables operate. Although this chapter has focused on perceptual growth, we should remember that development is a *holistic* process and that a child's maturing perceptual abilities are likely to have a meaningful effect on many other aspects of development. Indeed, as Herman Witkin points out (Witkin et al., 1979), the home environment in which a child is raised will contribute to the development of broad perceptual styles (such as field dependence/independence), which, in turn, may have far-reaching implications for intellectual growth and the child's developing personality.

SUMMARY

The term *perception* refers to the process by which we interpret sensory inputs. According to nativists, infants are born with many perceptual skills. Empiricists, however, believe that the neonate is merely a "sensory" creature and that all perceptual (interpretive) abilities must be learned. Although contemporary theorists continue to argue about what is innate and what is learned, they recognize that both innate abilities and learning are involved in perceptual growth and development.

During the first two months of life, infants prefer to look at complex, contoured stimuli. When scanning visual targets, very young infants focus on edges and boundaries as if they were concerned with "constructing" a form by differentiating it from its background. Over the next several months, infants begin to form mental representations, or schemata, for patterns and objects. They now scan forms as if they were trying to interpret them, and they soon become rather proficient at discriminating familiar and unfamiliar stimuli.

Babies are able to perceive depth and spatial relations very early in life: they respond to looming objects during the first month, and they may be able to perceive size constancy and the presence of a "visual cliff" by 2 months of age. Although the young infant's spatial abilities are quite primitive by adult standards, they will improve rather dramatically over the course of the first year.

The neonate's auditory capabilities are truly remarkable. In the first three days of life, an infant can already recognize its mother's voice. Neonates are quite responsive to human speech, and they place the auditory components of language into roughly the same vowel and consonant categories that adults do. Finally, babies prefer music to unpatterned auditory stimulation, and they begin to "bounce" to music and to recognize changes in melody and tempo by 4–6 months of age.

Apparently the senses are integrated at birth and differentiated later. For the neonate, sensations from all modalities may combine to produce a "global" experience. Moreover, young infants may look at and reach for noise-making objects, apparently recognizing that sounds imply there is something out there to be seen or touched. As the senses differentiate and continue to mature, the child becomes much more proficient at *cross-modal perception*—the ability to recognize by one modality an object that is already familiar through another modality. Eventually vision becomes the dominant sense because we learn to "trust our eyes" when other modalities provide us with conflicting information.

Several important perceptual changes take place between infancy and adolescence. Attentional abilities improve as children begin to examine sensory inputs more systematically. They also become more selective in what they will attend to and more proficient at concentrating on objects and tasks for long periods. As children become more attentive, they begin to identify the distinctive features that differentiate objects and events. This "perceptual learning" is a continuing process that enables the child to gradually become more proficient at interpreting the broad array of stimuli that impinge on the sensory receptors.

The environment influences perceptual development in many ways. Deprivation experiments suggest that young animals (and presumably children) must be exposed to patterned visual stimuli that capture their attention if their visual perception is to develop normally. Moreover, our social/cultural environments may influence our auditory perception, our interpretation of artwork, our ability to decode value-laden information, and our judgments about the physical characteristics of objects. Finally, it appears that the home environment contributes to the development of broad perceptual "styles" (field dependence or field independence) that may have important implications for many other aspects of development.

REFERENCES

Allen, T. W., Walker, K., Symonds, L., & Marcell, M. (1977). Intrasensory and intersensory perception of temporal sequences during infancy. *Developmental Psychology, 13,* 225–229.

Ames, L. B., Metraux, R. W., Roedell, J. L., & Walker, R. N. (1974). *Child Rorschach responses: Developmental trends from two to ten years.* New York: Brunner/Mazel.

Annis, R. C., & Frost, B. (1973). Human visual ecology and orientation anisotropies in acuity. *Science, 182,* 729–731.

Aronson, E., & Rosenbloom, S. (1971). Space perception within a common auditory-visual space. *Science, 172,* 1161–1163.

Banks, M. S. (1980). The development of visual accommodation during early infancy. *Child Development, 51,* 646–666.

Barrera, M. E., & Maurer, D. (1981a). Discrimination of strangers by the three-month-old. *Child Development, 52,* 558–563.

Barrera, M. E., & Maurer, D. (1981b). Recognition of mother's photographed face by the three-month-old infant. *Child Development, 52,* 714–716.

Barry, H., III, Bacon, M. K., & Child, I. L. (1957). A cross-cultural survey of some sex differences in socialization. *Journal of Abnormal and Social Psychology, 55,* 327–332.

Bertenthal, B. I., Campos, J. J., & Haith, M. M. (1980). Development of visual organization: The perception of subjective contours. *Child Development, 51,* 1077–1080.

Birch, H. G., & Lefford, A. (1963). Intersensory development in children. *Monographs of the Society for Research in Child Development, 25* (5, Serial No. 89).

Bower, T. G. R. (1966). The visual world of infants. *Scientific American, 215,* 80–92.

Bower, T. G. R. (1982). *Development in infancy.* San Francisco: W. H. Freeman.

Bower, T. G. R., Broughton, J. M., & Moore, M. K. (1970a). Infant responses to approaching objects: An indicator of response to distal variables. *Perception and Psychophysics, 9,* 193–196.

Bower, T. G. R., Broughton, J. M., & Moore, M. K. (1970b). The coordination of vision and tactile input in infancy. *Perception and Psychophysics, 8,* 51–53.

Bruner, J. S., & Goodman, C. C. (1947). Value and need as organizing factors in perception. *Journal of Abnormal and Social Psychology, 42,* 33–44.

Burtley, S. H. (1980). *Introduction to perception.* New York: Harper & Row.

Butterfield, E. C., & Siperstein, G. N. (1972). Influence of contingent auditory stimulation upon non-nutritional suckle. In J. F. Bosma (Ed.), *Third symposium on oral sensation and perception: The mouth of the infant.* Springfield, IL: Charles C Thomas.

Campos, J. J., Langer, A., & Krowitz, A. (1970). Cardiac responses on the visual cliff in prelocomotor human infants. *Science, 170,* 196–197.

Chall, J. S. (1967). *Learning to read: The great debate.* New York: McGraw-Hill.

Chang, H. W., & Trehub, S. E. (1977). Infants' perception of temporal grouping in auditory patterns. *Child Development, 48,* 1666–1670.

Clarkson, M. G., & Berg, W. K. (1983). Cardiac orienting and vowel discrimination in newborns: Crucial stimulus parameters. *Child Development, 54,* 162–171.

Cohen, L. B., DeLoache, J. S., & Strauss, M. S. (1979). Infant visual perception. In J. Osofsky (Ed.), *Handbook of infant development.* New York: Wiley.

Condon, W. S., & Sander, L. (1974). Neonate movement is synchronized with adult speech: Interactional participation and language acquisition. *Science, 183,* 99–101.

Day, R. H., & McKenzie, B. E. (1981). Infant perception of the invariant size of approaching and receding objects. *Developmental Psychology, 17,* 670–677.

DeCasper, A. J., & Fifer, W. P. (1980). Of human bonding: Newborns prefer their mother's voices. *Science, 208,* 1174–1176.

Deregowski, J. B. (1968). Difficulties in pictorial depth perception in Africa. *British Journal of Psychology, 59,* 195–204.

Descartes, R. (1965). La dioptrique. In R. J. Herrnstein & E. G. Boring (Eds.), *A sourcebook in the history of psychology.* Cambridge, MA: Harvard University Press. 1965. (Original work published 1638)

Eimas, P. D. (1975a). Auditory and phonetic cues for speech: Discrimination of the (r-l) distinction by young infants. *Perception and Psychophysics, 18,* 341–347.

Eimas, P. D. (1975b). Speech perception in early infancy. In L. B. Cohen & P. Salapatek (Eds.), *Infant perception: From sensation to cognition.* New York: Academic Press.

Fagan, J. F., III. (1979). The origins of facial pattern recognition. In M. H. Bornstein & W. Kessen (Eds.), *Psychological development from infancy: Image to intention.* Hillsdale, NJ: Erlbaum.

Fantz, R. L. (1961). The origin of form perception. *Scientific American, 204,* 66–72.

Fantz, R. L. (1963). Pattern vision in newborn infants. *Science, 140,* 296–297.

Fantz, R. L., & Fagan, J. F. (1975). Visual attention to size and number of pattern details by term and preterm infants during the first six months. *Child Development, 46,* 3–18.

Fantz, R. L., Fagan, J. F., & Miranda, S. B. (1975). Early visual selectivity. In L. B. Cohen & P. Salapatek (Eds.), *Infant perception: From sensation to cognition* (Vol. 1). New York: Academic Press.

Field, J. (1977). Coordination of vision and prehension in young infants. *Child Development, 48,* 97–103.

Field, J., Muir, D., Pilon, R., Sinclair, M., & Dodwell, P. (1980). Infants' orientation to lateral sounds from birth to three months. *Child Development, 51,* 295–298.

Fox, R., Aslin, R. N., Shea, S. L., & Dumais, S. T. (1980). Stereopsis in human infants. *Science, 207,* 323–324.

Ghent, L. (1956). Perception of overlapping and embedded figures by children of different ages. *American Journal of Psychology, 69,* 575–587.

Gibson, E. J. (1969). *Principles of perceptual learning and development.* New York: Appleton-Century-Crofts.

Gibson, E. J., Gibson, J. J., Pick, A. D., & Osser, H. A. (1962). A developmental study of the discrimination of letter-like forms. *Journal of Comparative and Physiological Psychology, 55,* 897–906.

Gibson, E. J., & Levin, H. (1975). *The psychology of reading.* Cambridge, MA: M.I.T. Press.

Gibson, E. J., & Walk, R. D. (1960). The "visual cliff." *Scientific American, 202,* 64–71.

Gollin, E. S. (1960). Developmental studies of visual recognition of incomplete objects. *Perceptual and Motor Skills, 11,* 289–298.

Gollin, E. S. (1962). Factors affecting the visual recognition of incomplete objects: A comparative investigation of children and adults. *Perceptual and Motor Skills, 15,* 583–590.

Gouin-DeCarie, T. (1969). A study of the mental and emotional development of the thalidomide child. In B. M. Foss (Ed.), *Determinants of infant behavior* (Vol. 4). London: Methuen.

Haaf, R. A., & Brown, C. J. (1976). Infants' response to face-like patterns: Developmental changes between 10 and 15 weeks of age. *Journal of Experimental Child Psychology, 22,* 155–160.

Haaf, R. A., Smith, P. H., & Smitley, S. (1983). Infant response to facelike patterns under fixed-trial and infant-control procedures. *Child Development, 54,* 172–177.

Hagen, J. W. (1967). The effect of distraction on selective attention. *Child Development, 38,* 685–694.

Haith, M. M. (1980). Visual competence in early infancy. In R. Held, H. Liebowitz, & H. R. Teuber (Eds.), *Handbook of sensory physiology* (Vol. 8). Berlin: Springer-Verlag.

Haith, M. M., Bergman, T., & Moore, M. J. (1977). Eye contact and face scanning in early infancy. *Science, 198,* 853–855.

Held, R., & Hein, A. (1963). Movement-produced stimulation in the development of visually guided behavior. *Journal of Comparative and Physiological Psychology, 56,* 872–876.

Hudson, W. (1960). Pictorial depth perception in subcultural groups in Africa. *Journal of Social Psychology, 52,* 183–208.

Hudson, W. (1962). Cultural problems in pictorial perception. *South African Journal of Science, 58,* 189–196.

James, W. (1890). *Principles of psychology* (2 vols.). New York: Holt.

Kagan, J. (1971). *Change and continuity in infancy.* New York: Wiley.

Kant, I. (1958). *Critique of pure reason.* New York: Modern Library. (Original work published 1781)

Leehy, S. C., Moskowitz-Cook, A., Brill, S., & Held, R. (1975). Orientational anisotropy in infant vision. *Science, 190,* 900–902.

Lewkowicz, D. L., & Turkewitz, G. (1981). Intersensory interaction in newborns: Modification of visual preferences following exposure to sound. *Child Development, 52,* 827–832.

Locke, J. (1939). An essay concerning human understanding. In E. A. Burtt (Ed.), *The English philosophers from Bacon to Mill.* New York: Modern Library. (Original work published 1690)

Maccoby, E. E. (1967). Selective auditory attention in children. In L. P. Lipsitt & C. C. Spiker (Eds.), *Advances in child development and behavior.* New York: Academic Press.

Maurer, D., & Salapatek, P. (1976). Developmental changes in the scanning of faces by young infants. *Child Development, 47,* 523–527.

McGurk, H., & MacDonald, J. (1976). Hearing lips and seeing voices. *Nature, 264,* 746–748.

McGurk, H., & Power, R. P. (1980). Intermodal coordination in young children: Vision and touch. *Developmental Psychology, 16,* 679–680.

Melhuish, E. C. (1982). Visual attention to mother's and stranger's faces and facial contrast in 1-month-old infants. *Developmental Psychology, 18,* 229–231.

Meltzoff, A. N., & Borton, R. W. (1979). Intermodal matching by human neonates. *Nature, 282,* 403–404.

Mendelson, M. J., & Ferland, M. B. (1982). Auditory-visual transfer in four-month-old infants. *Child Development, 53,* 1022–1027.

Mitchell, D. E., Freeman, R. D., Millodot, M., & Haegerstrom, G. (1973). Meridional amblyopia: Evidence for modification of the human visual system by early visual experience. *Vision Research, 13,* 535–558.

Miyawaki, K., Strange, W., Verbrugge, R., Liberman, A. M., Jenkins, J. J., & Fujimura, D. (1975). An effect of linguistic experience: The discrimination of [r] and [l] by native speakers of Japanese and English. *Perception and Psychophysics, 18,* 331–340.

Moog, H. (1976). *The musical experience of the pre-school child.* London: Schott.

Mundy-Castle, A. C. (1966). Pictorial depth perception in Ghanian children. *International Journal of Psychology, 1,* 289–300.

Piaget, J. (1954). *The construction of reality in the child.* New York: Basic Books.

Piaget, J. (1960). *Psychology of intelligence.* Paterson, NJ: Littlefield, Adams.

Pollack, R. H. (1976). Illusions and perceptual development: A tachistoscopic psychophysical approach. In K. F. Riegel & J. A. Meacham (Eds.), *The developing individual in a changing world* (Vol. 1). Chicago: Aldine.

Postman, L., Bruner, J. S., & McGinnies, E. (1948). Personal values as selective in perception. *Journal of Abnormal and Social Psychology, 42,* 142–154.

Rader, N., Bausano, M., & Richards, J. E. (1980). On the nature of the visual-cliff-avoidance response in human infants. *Child Development, 51,* 61–68.

Riesen, A. H. (1965). Effects of visual deprivation on perceptual function and the neural substrate. In J. de Ajuriaguerra (Ed.), *Dessaferentation experimental et clinique.* Geneva: Georg.

Riesen, A. H., Chow, K. L., Semmes, J., & Nissen, H. W. (1951). Chimpanzee vision after four conditions of light deprivation. *American Psychologist, 6,* 282.

Rock, I., & Harris, C. S. (1967). Vision and touch. *Scientific American, 216,* 96–104.

Rose, S. A., Gottfried, A. W., & Bridger, W. H. (1978). Cross-modal transfer in infants: Relationship to prematurity and socioeconomic background. *Developmental Psychology, 14,* 643–652.

Rose, S. A., Gottfried, A. W., & Bridger, W. H. (1981). Cross-modal transfer in 6-month-old infants. *Developmental Psychology, 17,* 661–669.

Salapatek, P. (1975). Pattern perception in early infancy. In L. B. Cohen & P. Salapatek (Eds.), *Infant perception: From sensation to cognition* (Vol. 1). New York: Academic Press.

Smith, F. (1977). Making sense of reading—and of reading instruction. *Harvard Educational Review, 47,* 386–395.

Spitz, H. H., & Borland, M. D. (1971). Redundancy in line drawings of familiar objects: Effects of age and intelligence. *Cognitive Psychology, 2,* 196–205.

Stryker, M. P., Sherk, H., Leventhal, A. G., & Hirsch, V. H. B. (1978). Physiological consequences for the cat's visual cortex of effectively restricting early visual experience with oriented contours. *Journal of Neurophysiology, 41,* 896–909.

Timney, H. H., & Muir, D. W. (1976). Orientation anisotropy: Incidence and magnitude in Caucasian and Chinese subjects. *Science, 193,* 699–701.

Treiber, F., & Wilcox, S. (1980). Perception of a "subjective contour" by infants. *Child Development, 51,* 915–917.

Vurpillot, E. (1968). The development of scanning strategies and their relation to visual differentiation. *Journal of Experimental Child Psychology, 6,* 632–650.

Walk, R. D. (1981). *Perceptual development.* Monterey, CA: Brooks/Cole.

Werner, H. (1948). *Comparative psychology of mental development.* New York: International Universities Press.

Williams, J. (1979). Reading instruction today. *American Psychologist, 34,* 917–922.

Witkin, H. A. (1959). The perception of the upright. *Scientific American, 200,* 50–56.

Witkin, H. A. (1967). A cognitive style approach to cross-cultural research. *International Journal of Psychology, 2,* 233–250.

Witkin, H. A., & Berry, J. W. (1975). Psychological differentiation in cross-cultural perspective. *Journal of Cross-Cultural Psychology, 6,* 4–87.

Witkin, H. A., & Goodenough, D. R. (1977). Field dependence and interpersonal behavior. *Psychological Bulletin, 84,* 661–689.

Witkin, H. A., Goodenough, D. R., & Oltman, P. K. (1979). Psychological differentiation: Current status. *Journal of Personality and Social Psychology, 37,* 1127–1145.

Yendovitskaya, T. V. (1971). Development of attention. In A. V. Zaporozhets & D. B. Elkonin (Eds.), *The psychology of preschool children.* Cambridge, MA: M.I.T. Press.

Yonas, A., Petterson, L., & Lockman, J. J. (1979). Young infants' sensitivity to optical information for collision. *Canadian Journal of Psychology, 33,* 268–276.

CHAPTER SEVEN

LEARNING AND DEVELOPMENT

■ *What is learning?*

■ *Habituation and mere exposure effects*
  Developmental trends
  Mere exposure and the development of positive
   attitudes

■ *Classical conditioning*
  Classical conditioning of emotions and attitudes
  Can neonates be classically conditioned?

■ *Operant (instrumental) conditioning*
  Reinforcement and punishment
  Operant conditioning in infancy
  Shaping of complex behaviors
  Factors that affect operant conditioning
  Why do reinforcers reinforce?
  Punishment: The aversive control of behavior

■ *Observational learning*
  How do we "learn" by observation?
  Developmental trends in imitation and
   observational learning
  Television as a modeling influence

■ *Complex processes in learning*
  Later developments in concept learning: The "5
   to 7 shift"

■ *Summary*

O ver the past four chapters, we have seen that human beings are biological creatures who inherit certain sensory and behavioral capacities and are "programmed" to change in a number of important ways as they mature. Yet it should be obvious that much of what we do or what we become is attributable to factors other than genetic or maturational programming. For example, there are no hereditary codes that instruct us to feel uncomfortable in public without clothing, to use toilets, to stop at traffic signals, to brush our teeth, to prefer weekends to weekdays, or to become slightly nauseated at the thought of eating fish-head soup. Clearly, these habits, feelings, and attitudes are *learned* as a result of the experiences we have had while growing up in a Western society.

In this chapter we will concentrate on the process of learning and see that it plays a very important role in many aspects of human development. Let's begin by trying to determine what learning is—and what it is not.

WHAT IS LEARNING?

Learning is one of those deceptively simple terms that are actually quite complex and difficult to define. Most psychologists think of learning as a change in behavior (or behavior potential) that meets the following three requirements (Domjan & Burkhard, 1982):

1. The individual now thinks, perceives, or reacts to the environment in a *new way.*
2. This change is clearly the result of one's *experiences*—that is, attributable to repetition, study, practice, or the observations one has made, rather than to hereditary or maturational processes or to physiological damage resulting from injury.
3. The change is *relatively permanent.* Facts, thoughts, and behaviors that are acquired and immediately forgotten have not really been

> learning: *a relatively permanent change in behavior (or behavioral potential) that results from one's experiences or practice.*

learned; and temporary changes attributable to fatigue, illness, or drugs do not qualify as learned responses.

There are at least three very general ways in which young children learn: (1) by *repetition,* (2) by *associating* a response with a particular stimulus or class of stimuli through some form of *conditioning,* and (3) by *observing* the behavior of social models. After examining each of these important and relatively simple kinds of learning, we will consider some complex learning processes that enable school-age children to become more proficient at forming concepts and solving problems.

HABITUATION AND MERE EXPOSURE EFFECTS

As we have seen on several occasions, newborn infants will eventually **habituate** (that is, stop attending or responding) to a strong auditory, visual, or olfactory stimulus that is presented over and over. This process of becoming familiar with a sight, sound, or odor is a very simple form of learning. As the infant stops responding to the stimulus, he is telling us that he recognizes it as something he has experienced before. In other words, he has already encoded that stimulus into memory, so that its further repetition is "old hat" and nothing to get excited about (Willemsen, 1979).

How do we know that an infant is not merely fatigued when he stops responding to a familiar stimulus? We know because when a child has habituated to one stimulus, he will often attend to or even react vigorously to the presentation of a slightly different stimulus. In so doing, he is telling us (1) that his sensory receptors are not simply fatigued and (2) that he can tell the difference between (that is, *discriminate*) the familiar and the unfamiliar.

Developmental Trends

Habituation clearly improves with age. Infants less than 4 months old may require many exposures to a stimulus before they habituate, and they soon **dishabituate**—that is, begin responding once again to something that they have previously

recognized as familiar. In contrast, 4–12-month-old infants show rapid habituation and are more likely than younger infants to prefer to gaze at novel rather than familiar stimuli (Lewis, 1971; Sigman, Kopp, Littman, & Parmelee, 1977).

This trend toward rapid habituation is probably due to the maturation of the cerebral cortex, which is beginning to assume control over subcortical reflexes during the first 4–6 months of life. As the cortex continues to develop, the child's memory improves: he or she is soon able to recognize something as familiar after only one or two brief exposures and will retain that "knowledge" for much longer periods (Fagan, 1979; Rose, 1981).

Mere Exposure and the Development of Positive Attitudes

Repeated exposure to a stimulus does not always lead to habituation in older children and adults. In fact, just the opposite may occur; most people can recall an occasion when they became more positive toward a song, a new food, an idea, or an acquaintance the more often they encountered that stimulus. Today we know that these **"mere exposure" effects** are real: over the past several years, social psychologists have discovered that we tend to develop favorable attitudes toward objects, activities, and individuals that we encounter regularly—even though we may never touch the objects, partake in the activities, or interact with the individuals (Worchel & Cooper, 1983). Although people say they know what they like, it seems that they often *learn* to like what they know (Domjan & Burkhard, 1982).

CLASSICAL CONDITIONING

A second way that young children learn is through **classical conditioning.** In classical conditioning, a neutral stimulus that initially has no effect on the child comes to elicit a response of some sort by virtue of its association with a second, nonneutral stimulus that always elicits the response. To illustrate the process, let's consider Ivan Pavlov's famous studies of classical conditioning in animals.

Pavlov was a Russian physiologist who discovered classical conditioning while studying the

PHOTO 7-1. *Ivan Pavlov (center) demonstrating an experiment in classical conditioning to students from the Russian Military Medical Academy.*

digestive processes of dogs. At one point in his research, Pavlov observed that his dogs would often salivate at the appearance of a caretaker who had come to feed them. Since it was unlikely that the dogs hoped to eat the caretaker, Pavlov wondered why they were salivating. He then speculated that the animals had probably associated the caretaker (an initially neutral stimulus) with food, a nonneutral stimulus that ordinarily makes dogs salivate (an unlearned, or "reflexive," response to food). In other words, salivation at the sight of the caretaker was said to be a learned response that the dogs acquired as they made a connection between the caretaker and the presentation of food.

Pavlov then designed a simple experiment to test his hypothesis. Dogs first listened to a bell, a neutral stimulus in that bells do not ordinarily make them salivate. Then this neutral stimulus was sounded just before the dogs were fed. Of course, food normally elicits salivation: in the language of classical conditioning, food is an **unconditioned stimulus (UCS),** and salivation is an unlearned or **unconditioned response (UCR)** to food. After the bell and the food had been paired several times, Pavlov then sounded the bell, withheld the food, and observed that the dogs now salivated to the sound of the bell alone. Clearly their behavior had changed as a result of their experiences. In the terminology of classical conditioning, the dogs were now emitting a **conditioned response (CR),** salivation, to an initially neutral or **conditioned stimulus (CS)**—the bell (see Figure 7-1).

As Pavlov continued to experiment with his dogs, he discovered a number of additional rules or characteristics of the conditioning process. One

such rule was the principle of **stimulus generalization:** stimuli that are very similar to a CS (for example, a bell with a slightly different ring) will also elicit the conditioned response. The opposite of generalizaton is the principle of **discrimination:** if a stimulus is very different from the original CS (for example, a bell with a much higher- or much lower-pitched ring), the subject apparently notices the difference and fails to emit a conditioned response. Finally, conditioned responses that occur repeatedly without occasionally being followed by the unconditioned stimulus will diminish in strength and eventually

habituation: *a simple form of learning in which an organism eventually stops responding to a stimulus that is repeated over and over.*

dishabituation: *recovery of a response to a previously habituated stimulus after the organism has been exposed to a novel stimulus.*

mere exposure effect: *the finding that repeated exposure to an object or activity produces more favorable attitudes toward that object or activity.*

classical conditioning: *a type of learning in which an initially neutral stimulus is repeatedly paired with a meaningful stimulus so that the neutral stimulus comes to elicit the response originally made only to the meaningful stimulus.*

unconditioned stimulus (UCS): *a stimulus that elicits a particular response without any prior learning.*

unconditioned response (UCR): *the unlearned response elicited by an unconditioned stimulus.*

conditioned response (CR): *a learned response to a stimulus that was not originally capable of producing the response.*

conditioned stimulus (CS): *an initially neutral stimulus that comes to elicit a particular response after being paired with a UCS that always elicits the response.*

stimulus generalization: *the process by which one stimulus can be substituted for another and produce the same response that the former stimulus did.*

discrimination: *the process of differentiating and responding differently to stimuli that vary on one or more dimensions.*

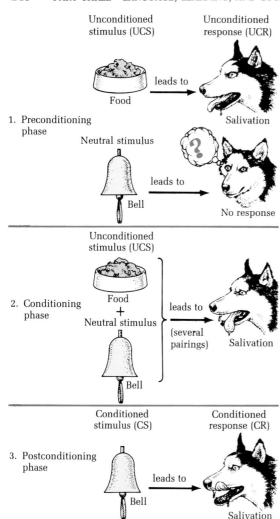

FIGURE 7-1. *The three phases of classical conditioning. In the preconditioning phase, the unconditioned stimulus (UCS) always elicits an unconditioned response (UCR), while the conditioned stimulus (CS) never does. During the conditioning phase, the CS and UCS are paired repeatedly and eventually associated. At this point, the learner passes into the postconditioning phase, in which the CS alone will elicit the original response (now called a conditioned response, or CR).*

disappear. This gradual weakening and elimination of a conditioned response is called **extinction.**

The Classical Conditioning of Emotions and Attitudes

Although the salivary responses that Pavlov conditioned may seem rather mundane, it is quite conceivable that every one of us has learned many things through classical conditioning—things that continue to affect us today. For example, some fears, phobias, and other emotional responses may be acquired in this way. In 1920 John Watson and Rosalie Raynor presented a gentle white rat to an 11-month-old infant named Albert. Albert's initial reactions were positive ones: he crawled toward the rat and played with it as he had previously with a dog and a rabbit. Then came the conditioning phase. Every time little Albert reached for the white rat, Watson would sneak up behind him and bang a steel rod loudly with a hammer. Little Albert would then cry and shy away from the rat. In this case, a loud noise is the unconditioned stimulus (UCS) because it elicits fearful behavior (the UCR) without any learning having taken place. Did little Albert eventually associate the white rat with the loud noise and come to fear his furry playmate? Indeed he did, and he also learned to shy away from other furry things, such as cats, balls of cotton, and a fur coat. This generalization of fear to objects other than the rat illustrates that the effects of classical conditioning can be powerful indeed.

Arthur Staats (1975) has argued that many of our attitudes and prejudices are acquired by classical conditioning. Imagine, if you can, that you are an 8-year-old who overhears your father say "Those redheads are really hot-tempered. Today Red Smith smashed the Coke machine just because it gypped him out of a quarter." Your mother then concurs, noting that a redheaded acquaintance of hers is often moody and temperamental. Two days later, you accuse a redheaded playmate of cheating at marbles, and he punches you. All these experiences may serve as conditioning "trials." Over the course of three days, you have associated redheadedness with destructive behavior, moodiness, cheating, and hostility—attitudes and activities that you are likely to view in a negative light. Suddenly an initially neutral stimulus, red hair, is apt to elicit negative feelings (a conditioned response). This conditioned "attitude" may then become a full-blown **prejudice** toward redheads if future contacts and experiences with redheaded people are not more positive.

Fortunately, prejudices, fears, and other undesirable responses can often be weakened or eliminated by a treatment known as *counterconditioning*. In Box 7-1 we will take a closer look at this interesting therapeutic technique.

Can Neonates Be Classically Conditioned?

Until very recently, many investigators believed that infants were not susceptible to classical conditioning for the first three or four weeks of life. But after carefully reviewing the literature, Hiram Fitzgerald and Yvonne Brackbill (1976) concluded that neonates can be classically conditioned. Consider the following example. Lewis Lipsitt and Herbert Kaye (1964) paired a neutral tone (the CS) with the presentation of a nipple (a UCS that normally elicits sucking) to infants 2–3 days old. After several of these conditioning trials, the infants began to make sucking motions at the sound of the tone—before the nipple was presented. Clearly, their sucking qualifies as a classically conditioned response because it is now elicited by a stimulus (the tone) that does not normally elicit sucking behavior.

Fitzgerald and Brackbill (1976) point out that only a small number of reflexes (such as sucking and blinking) can be classically conditioned during the first few weeks of life and that the infant must be alert and attentive for the conditioning to have any chance of success. Nevertheless, classical conditioning may be one mechanism through which very young infants learn important lessons such as that bottles or breasts give milk or that faces (caregivers) signify warmth and comfort.

OPERANT (INSTRUMENTAL) CONDITIONING

In classical conditioning, learned responses are *elicited* by a conditioned stimulus. **Operant** (or instrumental) **conditioning** is quite different: it requires the learner to first *emit* a response of some sort (that is, *operate* on the environment) and then associate this action with the positive or negative consequences it produces.

E. L. Thorndike (1898) was the first to demonstrate instrumental conditioning in the laboratory. In one series of experiments, Thorndike placed cats in cagelike "puzzle boxes" from which they could escape and obtain food by hitting a lever on the side of the apparatus. Typically these curious and active creatures would search for a means of escape, "accidentally" trip the lever, and run out of the box to their tasty treat. As they gained more experience with these puzzle boxes, the cats soon learned to hit the lever almost immediately in order to escape from confinement and obtain the food. Thorndike concluded that the "pleasure" (that is, escape and food) associated with lever pressing had the effect of "stamping in" this particular response and "stamping out" all other impulses that did not produce the desired outcomes. In other words, lever pressing was learned because it was *instrumental* for obtaining a reward.

Although Thorndike was the pioneer in this area of study, B. F. Skinner (1953) is the person who made operant conditioning famous. Skinner has argued that most human behaviors are responses that we emit freely and voluntarily. He calls them *operants*. According to Skinner, operant behaviors are modified by their consequences. If an operant is followed by a favorable (reinforcing) outcome, it is likely to be repeated in the future. Operants that generate less favorable outcomes are not as likely to be repeated and may be suppressed (see Figure 7-2). In sum, operant conditioning is a very common form of learning in which various acts become either more or less probable depending on the consequences they produce.

---

extinction: *gradual weakening and disappearance of a learned response that occurs because the CS is no longer paired with the UCS (in classical conditioning) or the response is no longer reinforced (in operant conditioning).*

prejudice: *an unjustified negative attitude toward an individual based solely on the person's membership in a particular group.*

operant conditioning: *a form of learning in which freely emitted acts (or operants) become either more or less probable depending on the consequences they produce.*

BOX 7-1
CLASSICAL CONDITIONING AS A
THERAPEUTIC TECHNIQUE

Many fears, phobias, and other undesirable reactions can be weakened or eliminated by *counterconditioning*—a treatment based on classical conditioning principles. The goal of counterconditioning is to extinguish an undesirable response to a person, object, or situation and to replace it with new and more adaptive behavior.

In *positive* counterconditioning, a stimulus or situation that initially elicits an undesirable reaction (for example, fear) is gradually associated with pleasant outcomes, thereby leading to the reduction or elimination of the maladaptive behavior. For example, Mary Cover Jones (1924) used positive counterconditioning to treat a 2-year-old named Peter who, like Watson's little Albert, had acquired a strong fear of furry objects. Peter was exposed to a rabbit (a CS for fearful behavior) while he ate some of his favorite foods (a UCS for pleasant feelings). While Peter ate, the rabbit was gradually moved closer and closer until Peter was finally able to hold the rabbit by himself. In this case, the rabbit came to be associated with a pleasant UCS (desirable foods), so that Peter's fearful reaction was eventually replaced by a more desirable response (playing with the rabbit).

Aversion therapy, a second form of counterconditioning, produces changes in behavior by pairing undesirable or maladaptive responses with *unpleasant* outcomes. One area to which mild aversion therapy has been applied with some success is enuresis (bedwetting). Most children eventually learn to wake up when they have to urinate because bladder tension (an initially neutral stimulus) has often been paired with a wet bed—an unpleasant UCS that wakes them up (the UCR). However, victims of enuresis do not learn this association between bladder tension and waking, probably because wetting the bed is not sufficiently unpleasant to rouse them from their sleep.

To treat enuresis by aversive counterconditioning, the therapist must devise a method that enables the child to associate bladder tension with an alternative UCS that will wake her up. One procedure that seems to work is to have the child sleep on a special sheet containing fine electrical wires. As soon as the child begins to wet, the urine (which conducts electricity) closes an electrical circuit and rings a loud buzzer or bell, a slightly unpleasant UCS that awakens the subject (Hansen, 1979). After several of these rude awak-

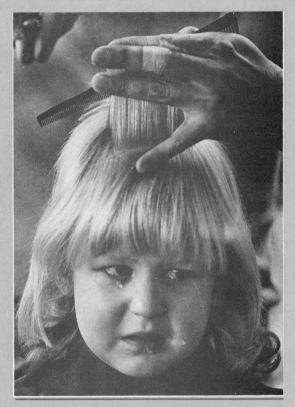

Those first haircuts are fearful events for many young children. With gentle treatment from the hairdresser—and perhaps a lollipop after the job is done—fear of the beauty parlor (or barbershop) will be weakened by counterconditioning.

enings, the child should associate bladder tension (the CS) with waking (the CR) and stop wetting the bed.

Here, then, are two of the many ways in which classical conditioning procedures have been used to modify the undesirable behavior of children and adults. Of course, counterconditioning is hardly a cure-all, for it is often necessary to supplement these techniques with other forms of therapy—particularly when treating very strong or long-term problems such as phobic reactions, test-taking fears, smoking, and drug or alcohol addiction. Nevertheless, the relatively simple principles of learning described by Pavlov have been applied in new and creative ways to provide solutions (or partial solutions) for a number of behavior disorders.

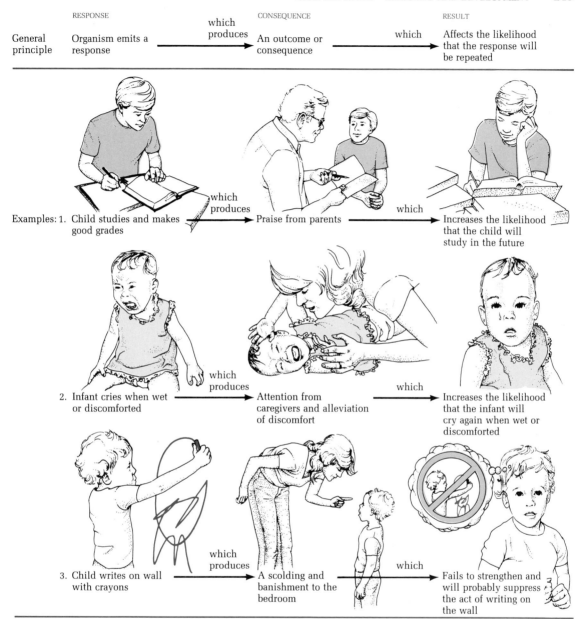

	RESPONSE		CONSEQUENCE		RESULT
General principle	Organism emits a response	which produces →	An outcome or consequence	which →	Affects the likelihood that the response will be repeated

Examples: 1. Child studies and makes good grades → which produces → Praise from parents → which → Increases the likelihood that the child will study in the future

2. Infant cries when wet or discomforted → which produces → Attention from caregivers and alleviation of discomfort → which → Increases the likelihood that the infant will cry again when wet or discomforted

3. Child writes on wall with crayons → which produces → A scolding and banishment to the bedroom → which → Fails to strengthen and will probably suppress the act of writing on the wall

FIGURE 7-2. *Basic principles of operant conditioning.*

Reinforcement and Punishment

In the language of operant conditioning, a **reinforcer** is any stimulus that *strengthens* a response by making it more likely to occur in the future. A reinforcer may be something pleasant

> **reinforcer:** *any consequence of an act that increases the probability that the act will recur.*

Conditions defining positive reinforcement, negative reinforcement, and punishment

| | Type of stimulus | |
Action	Positive (pleasant)	Negative (unpleasant)
Administered	Positive reinforcement (strengthens the response that produces it)	Punishment (suppresses the response that produces it)
Withdrawn	Punishment (suppresses the response that produces it)	Negative reinforcement (strengthens the response that produces it)

Have you ever missed an item on a test and felt that the item was unnecessarily confusing or picky? While taking a "pretest" on the first day of an upper-level psychology course, I and virtually everyone else in the class missed a true/false item that read "Negative reinforcement is a form of punishment." I now know that the answer to this question is "false," but oh, did the members of that class argue about that item! As the professor tried to explain, we students were confused by the fact that a negative stimulus could be involved in reinforcement. One disgruntled classmate thought that this particular issue (and the test question) was absurd. He expressed his frustration by saying "Where I come from, positive events are rewards and negative events are punishments. Isn't that really a whole lot simpler?"

The professor answered "No, that's an oversimplification." She then proceeded to explain that reinforcements and punishments are defined by their effects: reinforcers *strengthen* responses, while punishing stimuli *weaken* or *suppress* them. Finally, she drew a table on the board that helped the class to understand how, under certain circumstances, negative stimuli could help to strengthen (reinforce) a response, while positive stimuli could be implicated in suppressing a response (punishment). Perhaps this table will help you in the same way that it helped us.

such as a piece of candy or a pat on the head. These pleasant events are called *positive reinforcers.* A reinforcer may also be something *negative,* or unpleasant, that is *removed from the situation* once the subject has made a desired response. Suppose that every time a boy left his shoes in the kitchen, his mother were to scold him until he took them to his room. Since he would most likely find this experience unpleasant, the termination of the aversive scolding should reinforce his actions and help to ensure that he would take his shoes to his room in the future. In sum, both positive and negative reinforcers increase the probability that a particular response will be repeated.

Is *negative reinforcement* merely a fancy name for punishment? No, it is not! Recall that a negative reinforcer is an aversive stimulus that is *withdrawn* when the child performs a desirable act. In contrast, the most familiar form of punishment involves the *presentation* of an aversive stimulus when the child emits an undesirable response. In other words, the purpose of **punishment** is roughly opposite to that of reinforcement—to *suppress* unacceptable acts

rather than to strengthen acceptable ones. Another form of punishment that parents often use is to *withhold something desirable* when the child behaves inappropriately. For example, a mother may punish roughhousing behavior by refusing to allow her children to watch their favorite TV show. By withholding this desirable activity, she is trying to suppress their roughhousing behavior and *decrease* the probability that they will repeat these acts in the future.

One reason that people tend to confuse punishment and negative reinforcement is that these two processes often occur together. For example, the mother who scolds her son for leaving his shoes in the kitchen is punishing that oversight and then negatively reinforcing the *alternative* response of taking the shoes to his room. Moreover, people generally think of positive stimuli as reinforcers and negative ones as punishments. This source of confusion can be eliminated if we recall that reinforcements and punishments are defined not by their valences but by their effects: reinforcers strengthen responses, and punishing stimuli inhibit or suppress them. Perhaps the table in Box 7-2 will help you to remember the differences among positive and negative reinforcement and the two kinds of punishment.

Students of operant conditioning believe that punishment is generally less effective than reinforcement at producing desirable changes in behavior, because punishment merely suppresses ongoing or established responses without really teaching anything new. For example, a toddler who is punished for grabbing food with her hands is likely to stop eating altogether rather than to learn to use her spoon. A much simpler way to promote this desirable alternative response is to reinforce it (Skinnner, 1953).

■ *Primary and secondary reinforcers*

Learning theorists are careful to distinguish between two classes of reinforcers, each of which can be positive or negative. Some reinforcers can affect behavior in the absence of any learning. Activities such as sex and escape from electrical shock and substances such as food for the hungry and water for the thirsty are all examples of these natural, or unlearned, incentives. They are called **primary reinforcers** because they satisfy primary, or unlearned, needs.

A **secondary reinforcer** (or conditioned reinforcer) is something that *acquires* the capacity to reinforce by virtue of its repeated association with one or more primary reinforcers. A rat that accidentally presses a bar, hears a click, and receives a food pellet will eventually learn to press the bar (for food) and will continue to do so for a while even after food is withheld. The reason is that the clicking sound, which had always been associated with the delivery of food, has acquired the capacity to sustain bar pressing. Perhaps money is the clearest example of a secondary reinforcer for human beings. Toddlers will not alter their behavior for money; neither coin nor currency serves a useful purpose for them, except perhaps as something to play with. But children eventually learn that money can be used to purchase primary reinforcers (for example, candy), and suddenly it becomes a valuable commodity that will reinforce any number of responses.

■ *Generalized reinforcers*

Some secondary reinforcers have been paired so often with primary reinforcement that they remain powerful incentives that have the capacity to sustain almost *any* behavior—even though they may no longer be associated with the satisfaction of primary needs. For human beings, these **generalized reinforcers** include money, praise, attention, approval, respect, prestige, and power. Operant theorists such as Jacob Gewirtz (1969) have argued that much of human social behavior is established and maintained by these powerful sources of secondary reinforcement. For example, many adults will do almost anything to gain or to maintain the approval of their parents, even though their mothers and fathers have no money to lend or leave them and years have passed since they have satisfied any of their children's primary needs. Thus, parental approval can be a very powerful incentive for some people—one that may influence their behavior for several decades.

Operant Conditioning in Infancy

Will neonates alter their behavior in order to obtain positive outcomes? Indeed they will—as long as they are capable of emitting the response that you wish to reinforce. One interesting demonstration of operant conditioning in neonates is a study by Reuben Kron (1966), who found that 1-day-old infants will increase the rate at which they suck on a nipple when that sucking is reinforced by presentation of a sugary solution.

Although operant conditioning may begin at birth, we should remember that neonates are able (or biologically "prepared") to emit only a limited number of responses that are necessary for survival (for example, sucking, turning the head, and grasping). Nevertheless, these "prepared" re-

---

punishment: *any consequence of an act that suppresses the response and decreases the probability that it will recur.*

primary reinforcer: *a substance or activity that satisfies a primary (unlearned) drive.*

secondary reinforcer: *a stimulus or activity that becomes an effective reinforcer by virtue of its association with one or more primary reinforcers.*

generalized reinforcers: *powerful secondary incentives such as money or praise that acquire the capacity to reinforce many kinds of behavior.*

sponses can be organized into new and rather adaptive habits. Consider the work of Hanus Papousek (1961, 1967), who attempted to influence the behavior of neonates using a combination of classical and operant conditioning. In Papousek's studies, a bell (the CS) was sounded as the investigator touched the infant's cheek—a UCS that makes infants turn their heads in the direction of the touch (the rooting reflex). When the infants turned their heads, they found a nippleful of milk to suck on. Will neonates eventually learn to turn their heads at the sound of a bell in order to reward themselves with a drink of milk? Yes, they will, although they may require nearly 200 conditioning trials to acquire this simple operant response (Papousek, 1967).

Older infants learn much faster. By 3 months of age, they will require only about 40 trials to learn the head-turning response, and 5-month-old infants acquire this habit in fewer than 30 trials. Babies 3 to 4 months old have even learned to turn their heads to the left at the sound of a bell and to the right at the sound of a buzzer—and then to reverse these responses (turning right to the bell and left to the buzzer) when milk was withheld until they altered their previous habits and learned the reversal (Papousek, 1967). In sum, infants become much more susceptible to operant conditioning over the first few months of life.

What impact might early learning have on infants and their companions? Since even newborn infants are capable of associating their responses with various outcomes, they should soon learn that they can make some interesting things happen. For example, a baby may discover that crying brings forth her mother (or some other caregiver), who then unwittingly reinforces the baby's cries by giving food, attention, warmth, or comfort. Babbling and gazing are other responses that the infant may learn to use in order to attract the attention or nurturance of caregivers. As the child acquires these habits, her caregivers are also learning how to react to her, so that their social exchanges gradually become more satisfying for both the infant and her companions. It is fortunate, then, that neonates can learn, for in so doing, they are likely to become more responsive to benevolent caregivers, who, in turn, are becoming more responsive to them. As we will see in Chapter Eleven, these early reciprocal ex-

changes provide a foundation for the strong emotional attachments that often develop between young children and their closest companions.

Shaping of Complex Behaviors

Many of the responses that children are expected to learn are very unfamiliar to them and may seem rather complex. For example, preschool children often have a difficult time learning to dress themselves. It looks so easy when someone does it for them, but they invariably discover that looks can be deceiving when they become tangled in their shirts and put their shoes on the wrong feet. What is likely to happen then is that the child who can't get his shirt on or his shoe tied will seek the assistance of a parent or an older sibling.

How can we condition a complex response that the child has trouble performing? A student of operant conditioning would use a procedure called **shaping.** When shaping a complex pattern of behavior, the person doing the "teaching" reinforces the child for producing *successively closer approximations* of the behavior that he or she wishes the child to learn. For example, a boy who is learning to put on his shirt might be praised for getting his arms into the sleeves, even if he quits there and doesn't button up. Gradually, the "teacher" will require him to come closer to performing the desired response, perhaps by fastening a button or two, before giving any reinforcement. The next step might involve withholding praise until the boy properly aligns and fastens all the buttons on his shirt. And finally the boy might be required to align and fasten all buttons *and* to tuck his shirt into his trousers before praise or some other reinforcer is administered.

Shaping is a rather effective technique that works well even with very young children. In fact, B. F. Skinner has repeatedly shown that lower animals like pigeons can be taught to play an intricate game like table tennis if one simply takes the time to reinforce successive approximations and thereby "shape" the component responses of this complex behavioral sequence. Finally, the research described in Box 7-3 illustrates that shaping may be the most effective method of teaching language and social skills to some children who are severely disturbed.

Factors That Affect Operant Conditioning

A number of factors can affect the initial success of operant conditioning as well as the strength or durability of habits acquired in this way. Among the more important of these influences are the timing of reinforcement, the schedule on which it is administered, and the value of the reinforcer to the child.

■ *Timing of reinforcement*

Research with animals and young children shows that reinforcement is most effective when administered immediately after a response (Domjan & Burkhard, 1982). In fact, Stuart Millar and John Watson (1979) found that a delay of only three seconds in the presentation of a reinforcer is sufficient to prevent 6–8-month-old infants from learning to move their arms in order to see and hear an interesting audiovisual display (the reinforcer in this study). It is not that the infants are incapable of acquiring this habit, for a second group of 6–8-month-olds who were reinforced immediately after waving their arms soon learned to emit the arm-waving response.

Why do young infants fail to learn under conditions of delayed reinforcement? Probably because their memory is so poorly developed that they simply will not associate their actions with an outcome unless these events occur almost simultaneously. As children mature and their memories improve, they become better able to recall the acts that led to pleasant or unpleasant outcomes. If you receive an A in this course, for example, you will recognize that your hard work over a period of several months is the action that is most responsible for this favorable outcome. Of course, older children and adults often use verbal labels or other mediational strategies to help them to remember that certain actions are likely to pay off in the long run. This is precisely what students are doing when they say to themselves "I'll have to start studying this weekend if I hope to make an A or a B on the test next Tuesday."

■ *Frequency, or scheduling, of reinforcement*

To this point, we have been talking mainly about cases in which a response is reinforced every time it occurs—a schedule known as **continuous reinforcement**. But in a typical home, it is unlikely that a child's desirable behaviors will be reinforced every time they occur. Parents are often not around to observe them, or they may be too preoccupied with their own activities to carefully monitor and reinforce all the child's commendable actions. As a matter of fact, adults are often inconsistent—on some occasions when they are busy or moody, they may ignore or even punish a child who has done something praiseworthy. Why, then, do children continue to perform "desirable" responses if parents and other companions are less than consistent when it comes to reinforcing them?

The "partial reinforcement" effect. Extensive research with both animals and humans shows that habits may be acquired and then maintained for long periods with only occasional (that is, **partial** or *intermittent*) **reinforcement**. In fact, behaviors that have been partially reinforced will persist longer after reinforcement is totally withdrawn than behaviors that have been reinforced on a continuous schedule. In the language of operant conditioning, partial reinforcement makes a response *more resistant to extinction*. This seemingly paradoxical finding can be explained by analogy. If you've always found water when you go to the well, a nonproductive trip or two leads you to conclude that the well has gone dry. Consequently, you are not likely to return (rapid extinction following continuous reinforcement). However, if the well has produced water, say, 60% of the time, you will not be dismayed by a "dry" trip or two and are likely to return in the future (slow extinction following partial reinforcement).

---

shaping: *a method of teaching complex patterns of behavior by reinforcing successively closer approximations of these responses.*

continuous reinforcement: *a schedule of reinforcement in which every occurrence of an act is reinforced.*

partial reinforcement: *a schedule of reinforcement in which only some of the occurrences of an act are reinforced.*

The most severe emotional disturbance of early childhood is a condition called *autism*—a form of psychosis in which children are so self-involved that they barely recognize that other people exist. At home, autistic children pay little or no attention to parents and siblings, choosing instead to stimulate themselves for hours at a time with repetitive actions such as rocking, twirling, manipulating a toy, or perhaps even banging their heads against a wall. Not surprisingly, these profoundly disturbed youngsters acquire few if any basic social and behavioral skills, and their language is either absent or grossly retarded (Lovaas, 1976). Indeed, many therapists had found it difficult, if not impossible, to teach language and social skills to children who simply ignore the therapy and continue their ongoing activities as if no one else were present.

In the mid-1960s, Ivar Lovaas and his associates (1966; Lovaas, Freitas, Nelson, & Whalen, 1967) made some progress with autistic children using the "shaping" technique that Skinner and his associates had employed so successfully with animals. Since autistic youngsters do not respond to social overtures, the first step in the program was to pair verbal approval with a bit of food whenever the child made eye contact or merely attended to the therapist's speech or actions. This treatment has two effects: (1) to reinforce attention and (2) to associate a positive social gesture with food so that verbal approval eventually becomes a conditioned reinforcer. The next step is to reinforce the child with food and praise whenever he or she makes any kind of sound or even tries to imitate the therapist's actions. Once imitative attempts occur without prompting, the therapist gradually withholds reinforcement until the child successfully imitates entire acts or, in the case of language, utters particular vowel and consonant sounds, then syllables, then words, and finally word combinations.

Clearly, these advances do not come easy; often hundreds or even thousands of reinforcements are necessary before an autistic child will acquire a useful habit such as toothbrushing, begin to label objects with the appropriate words, or imitate simple phrases. Moreover, shaping is by no means a cure for autism. Children who receive this extensive training are likely to regress to their previous behavior if placed back in a nonsupportive institutional setting. And even under the best of circumstances, they never do achieve the creative use of language and the broad range of social skills that normal children develop without any special training. Nevertheless, Lovaas's shaping procedures have been extremely helpful at establishing a social dialogue with these disturbed

So this **"partial reinforcement" effect** helps to explain why children continue to perform commendable acts even when this praiseworthy conduct is not often reinforced by parents, teachers, and other social agents. But beware, for *undesirable* behaviors may persist for the same reason. For example, children may learn that they can nag their father until he "breaks down" and lets them do things that he was not inclined to allow. If they start several days ahead of time, persistently making their requests, occasionally a father may give in with a statement like "Oh, for Pete's sake, you can go." Although this hypothetical father may resist his children's nagging most of the time, those few occasions on which he wavers will have the effect of partially reinforcing and thus perpetuating their nagging behavior.

Schedules of partial reinforcement. B. F. Skinner and his associates have identified four major schedules of partial reinforcement and studied their effects on operant conditioning. The four schedules are:

1. *Fixed-ratio (FR) schedule.* The learner is reinforced after a set number of correct responses have been emitted. For example, one might say "That's good, Billy" every third time that the child shares a toy with his sister.

2. *Fixed-interval (FI) schedule.* The learner is reinforced for the first correct response emitted after a fixed amount of time has passed since the last reinforcement, but not for any response before then. Letting a child go to the movie on Saturdays provided that she keeps her room clean during the week is a "real world" approximation of a fixed-interval schedule.

3. *Variable-ratio (VR) schedule.* The learner is reinforced after a certain number of correct responses (say, four)—*on the average.* However, the ratio is not fixed—sometimes the learner might be reinforced after emitting two correct responses, sometimes after emitting six, after three, after five,

Autistic children prefer self-stimulation to stimulation from others.

young children, who do not respond to more traditional forms of therapy. In fact, the early indications are that autistic children will retain many of their therapeutic gains and even show some modest improvements at home if their parents have been trained to use the shaping techniques that were applied during therapy (Lovaas, Schreibman, & Koegel, 1976).

and so forth, on a random basis, the average being one reinforcement after every fourth response. Slot machines are generally programmed to pay off on a variable-ratio schedule that is just sufficient to entice the gambler to keep pulling the handle. Parents may also respond to their child's questions or requests on a VR schedule.

4. *Variable-interval (VI) schedule.* The learner is reinforced for the first correct response emitted after an *average time interval* of, say, five minutes. Sometimes only 30 seconds may elapse between reinforcements, sometimes 10 minutes, other times the interval may be two minutes, and so on, with an average interval of some specified value. Hitchhiking and door-to-door solicitation are examples of activities that are likely to be reinforced on a variable-interval schedule.

In general, both continuous reinforcement and the fixed-ratio (FR) schedule produce very rapid learning. However, responses that are reinforced on the FR schedule are the more resistant to ex-

tinction: because the child does not expect to be rewarded every time he or she performs the act, it will take longer to recognize that the act is no longer reinforcing once reinforcement is totally withdrawn (Bijou, 1957).

Variable-ratio (VR) schedules produce both high rates of responding and very strong resistance to extinction. Since the administration of reinforcement depends on the *number* of responses the child emits, he or she should perform these acts at a reasonably brisk rate. And because reinforcers have been administered *irregularly,* the child never knows exactly when a reinforcer will be forthcoming. Consequently, he or she

> **partial reinforcement effect:** *the finding that behaviors that have been partially reinforced are more resistant to extinction than those that have been reinforced on a continuous schedule.*

should continue to respond for long periods in the absence of any reinforcement (just as players of slot machines do when they have not received a payoff for a long while but keep playing in the hope of finally hitting the jackpot).

Many of the desirable habits that children acquire (for example, toothbrushing, toileting behavior, sharing) are probably reinforced on a variable schedule. Parents may begin by rewarding praiseworthy conduct almost every time they observe it and then gradually decrease the frequency of reinforcement until only an occasional acknowledgment or nod of approval is sufficient to sustain these behaviors. However, undesirable responses such as nagging or temper tantrums are also likely to be "reinforced" on a variable schedule, so that they may well persist long after an adult has begun to ignore (or punish) these habits.

■ *Value of the reinforcer*

The success of operant conditioning will also depend on the value of the stimulus that is offered as an incentive. For example, infants have little reason to value money and are less responsive to monetary incentives than older children or adults are. A girl who has just eaten all the sweets she wants is less likely to alter her behavior for another piece of candy than her brother who is hungry and hasn't had any sweets. So the learner's need for or evaluation of a reinforcer is an important determinant of its effectiveness at shaping operant responses.

Generalized reinforcers such as praise or approval may also assume different values. If a child has always received social approval from a particular companion, then further praise from that person is not valued as much as the same level of approval from a less familiar source (Aronson, 1976; Babad, 1972, 1973). This is one reason that a grandparent or a favorite aunt is often more effective than parents at persuading young children to play cooperatively, to brush their teeth, or to proceed quietly to bed. In addition, social reinforcers that provide the child with *information* about his or her performance (for example, "That's good! You can catch the ball when you hold your arms together") are much more likely to sustain an ongoing activity and promote new learning than uninformative praise or approval (for example,

"Good show!"), which will soon lose its effectiveness (Martin, 1977; Perry & Garrow, 1975).

Why Do Reinforcers Reinforce?

Earlier in the chapter, we defined a reinforcer as any stimulus that strengthens a response by making it more likely to occur in the future. If you are a bit of a logician, you have probably recognized that this definition is circular: it merely describes what happens when a response becomes more probable, rather than explaining how the response was strengthened. Suppose, for example, that a man wishes to know why his 10-month-old son repeatedly kicks at an overhead mobile while lying in his crib. To say that the kicking response leads to an event that is reinforcing, which, in turn, strengthens the kicking response, does not really tell the father much about his son's behavior. Indeed, many parents would want to know why the "reinforcing" events are reinforcing.

Literally hundreds of objects and events have been used as reinforcers in laboratory studies of operant conditioning. The list includes familiar incentives such as food, water, and sex (in animal studies), as well as less traditional activities such as playing pinball, having the brain stimulated with a mild electrical current, having the opportunity to explore visual scenes, and earning the privilege of yelling and screaming. Some of these objects and activities satisfy basic physiological needs, but others clearly do not. What do all these "incentives" have in common that makes them effective reinforcers? Why do reinforcers reinforce?

■ *The Premack principle*

Several years ago, David Premack (1965, 1971) proposed a theory of reinforcement that helps to explain why so many objects and events are capable of strengthening operant responses. The **"Premack principle"** of reinforcement says that *any event or activity can strengthen another event or activity as long as it is more probable than the response that one is trying to condition.* For example, food will reinforce maze running because eating is typically more probable than exploring a maze. Under ordinary circumstances maze running cannot reinforce eating. But suppose that we discovered a curious breed of malnourished animals that would rather explore new territories than eat. According to the Premack principle, we could reinforce these creatures for eating (the less probable activity) by then allowing them access to unfamiliar mazes (the more probable activity).

Teachers often use the Premack principle when they allow their students to play or to read a favorite story once they have completed their class work. Reading and playing are highly probable responses that are quite effective at reinforcing less probable activities such as schoolwork. Perhaps the most important implication of Premack's theory is that it is always the *learner,* rather than the teacher, who determines what is reinforcing. In Box 7-4 we will see how one team of investigators kept this point in mind as they designed a highly unusual and creative program aimed at teaching fidgety nursery school children to sit still and pay more attention to their teachers.

■ *Effect of unnecessary rewards on learning and performance*

A number of activities in which children take part are valued for their own sake and do not require external prompts or rewards in order to continue. These pastimes, which might include the kicking of an overhead mobile by a 10-month-old infant, watching television, reading storybooks, and solving puzzles, are said to be *intrinsically* satisfying.

As it turns out, many of the responses or habits that adults want children to acquire are not so intrinsically satisfying. In order to get a child to perform these responses or to develop an interest in initially unrewarding activities, parents and teachers typically offer inducements such as money, praise, or symbolic incentives (for example, gold stars for reading). These rewards, which are not inherent in the activities they are designed to encourage, are called *extrinsic* reinforcers.

There is a great deal of evidence that the offering and presentation of extrinsic reinforcement can promote new learning and motivate young children to undertake and complete activities that are not intrinsically satisfying to them (Danner & Lonky, 1981; Loveland & Olley, 1979; McLoyd, 1979). For example, a teacher who offers her "nonreaders" a gold star for every ten minutes that they spend reading may well increase the reading activities of these children, who would not ordinarily read on their own. But what effect would this incentive have on the class "bookworms," who read avidly because reading is intrinsically satisfying?

Mark Lepper (1980) suggests that children who perform intrinsically satisfying activities as a means of obtaining extrinsic reinforcement may come to like these activities less. In other words, intrinsic interest in an activity may be undermined if the child decides he or she is performing the activity to earn a tangible reward.

An experiment by Lepper, Greene, and Nisbett (1973) provides support for Lepper's hypothesis. Children aged 3 to 5 who showed considerable intrinsic interest in drawing with colored felt pens were promised a special certificate if they would draw a picture for a visiting adult (expected-reward condition). Other preschool children who were equally interested in drawing with felt pens engaged in the same drawing activities and either received an unexpected certificate for their work (unexpected-reward condition) or did not receive a certificate (no-reward condition). Then, 7 to 14 days later, the children were observed during free-play periods to determine whether they still wanted to draw with the felt pens. Lepper et al. found that children who had contracted to draw a picture for an extrinsic reinforcer now spent less of their free time drawing with the pens (8.6%) than children who had received no reward (16.7%) or those who had received the reward as a surprise (18.1%). Note that the reward itself did not undermine intrinsic motivation, for children in the unexpected-reward condition continued to show as much extrinsic interest in drawing as those who were not rewarded. It was only when children believed they were drawing *in order to obtain a reward* that extrinsic reinforcement undermined intrinsic interest.

Later research reveals that extrinsic reinforcement can sustain and even increase intrinsic interest in an activity if the reinforcer is given only for *successful* task performance rather than

> **Premack principle:** *the finding that less valued (or less probable) activities can be reinforced by providing the subject access to more valued (or more probable) activities.*

Nursery school children can be trying pupils because they often prefer to run around yelling, screaming, and visiting one another rather than sitting quietly in their seats listening to the teacher. Many teachers will try to suppress these aversive responses by punishing them, even though punishment rarely inhibits disruptive conduct for long. How, then, can a nursery school teacher establish control over restless young children so that they will pay more attention to the lessons of the day?

Disruptive behavior in the classroom is a problem that all teachers are faced with—and would like very much to eliminate.

One team of investigators (Homme, deBaca, Devine, Steinhorst, & Rickert, 1963) attempted to control the behavior of young preschool children by applying the Premack principle. They reasoned that disruptive behaviors that are so aversive to adults must be highly *reinforcing* for nursery school children, since they clearly prefer these activities to sitting still and listening to the teacher. If the Premack principle is correct, then highly probable behaviors such as running around, yelling, and screaming should be able to strengthen less probable responses such as sitting in one's seat and paying attention. But how? After all, these two classes of behavior seem quite incompatible.

Homme et al. solved the incompatibility problem in an ingenious way: they told the children that they could earn free time during which they could run around, yell, and scream if they sat in their seats and listened to the teacher. After three minutes of sitting quietly, a bell sounded, signaling the children to run, yell, jump, and scream. A short time later, another signal was given that informed the children that they must return to their seats and listen attentively for another three minutes. Gradually the sitting and listening requirements were increased, and the children began to earn tokens with which they could purchase yelling and screaming time at the end of the school day. Homme et al. (1963) found that their program was extremely effective at teaching children to sit still and attend to their schoolwork—even though these desirable habits were reinforced by the very activities that the teachers were trying to inhibit. These findings provide clear support for the Premack principle and remind us that it is the learner, not the teacher, who determines which activities are the most potent reinforcers for any particular behavior.

for merely working at the task (Pallak, Costomiris, Sroka, & Pittman, 1982). Why? Because rewards given for successes have *informational* value: they allow children to attribute their successful performance to their competence in that activity rather than to the need to obtain the extrinsic reward. Consequently, children are likely to perform the rewarded acts in the future because the external rewards have not undermined their intrinsic motivation.

The implications of this research are clear. Extrinsic reinforcers can be used both at home and in the classroom to strengthen or sustain those responses that children will not ordinarily perform. However, parents, teachers, and other social

agents must guard against creating unnecessary and uninformative reward systems that are likely to decrease children's interest in activities that they already like and will perform for the fun of it.

The fact that extrinsic rewards can undermine intrinsic interest once again implies that it is the learner, rather than the teacher, who determines what events are the most potent reinforcers for any given activity. At this point, it is tempting to conclude that reinforcers "reinforce" because they are somehow pleasant or pleasurable. However, we are about to see that either pleasurable or aversive events can actually *prevent* new learning if the subject has no control over their appearance or administration.

■ *Learned helplessness and*
the issue of control

Martin Seligman (1975, 1978) has found that a state of apathy, or **learned helplessness,** may develop if subjects perceive little or no connection between their actions and their outcomes. Consider the following example. Seligman and his associates administered severe electrical shocks to a group of dogs that were strapped into harnesses so that they could not escape. The next day, each dog was placed in one side of a two-compartment box and exposed to strong shocks that it could escape by merely jumping over the barrier into the other compartment. Naive dogs that have never experienced the inescapable shocks soon learn this jumping response because it is negatively reinforced (that is, jumping terminates the aversive shock). However, the dogs that had previously experienced uncontrollable shocks never did learn to escape. What these animals did learn from their prior experiences is that there was nothing they could do to control the shocks, so they did nothing. In other words, they had learned to be helpless.

Human infants can also develop these feelings of helplessness, even when the events that they cannot control are initially quite pleasant. In one study (Watson & Ramey, 1972), a group of 8-week-old infants learned to move their heads on a pressure-sensitive pillow, an act that closed an electrical switch in the pillow and caused a brightly colored mobile to rotate. The infants clearly seemed to enjoy this activity, for they smiled and cooed whenever they caused the mobiles to turn. A second group of infants were exposed to the same situation, with one important difference—they had *no* control over their mobiles, which rotated periodically on their own. Soon the infants in this second group seemed apathetic about the mobiles; they rarely smiled and were no longer interested in watching them turn. Later the investigators exposed all their young subjects to mobiles that they could control by moving their heads. Children who had previously learned to control the mobiles were soon turning their heads and exercising control once again. However, the infants who had not been able to control the mobiles in the earlier session made *no* further attempts to exercise control—even though they now had an opportunity to do so. Apparently

these children had learned that they were powerless to influence their environment, so they gave up and simply accepted their "learned helplessness."

Learning about the controllability of events is unquestionably an important aspect of human development. During the first year, most infants will discover that they can exercise some control over their caregivers by crying, cooing, or emitting other bids for attention that are likely to be reinforced with a smile, a hug, or other forms of social stimulation. Moreover, young infants tend to be wary of objects, people, or situations that they cannot control (Gunnar, 1980; Levitt, 1980), and they may stop trying to initiate social interactions with an aloof companion (Seligman, 1975). Indeed, we will see in Chapter Eleven that socially responsive children gradually become rather apathetic, depressed, and uninterested in human contact if they are raised in understaffed institutions where their social gestures rarely elicit reactions from anyone. It is almost as if they felt powerless to control the behavior of their caregivers, so that they simply stopped trying and became unresponsive to other people in much the same way that Watson and Ramey's "helpless" infants ceased responding to a rotating mobile that they had previously enjoyed.

In sum, the learned-helplessness research suggests that some reinforcers may "reinforce" not because they are inherently pleasant but, rather, because they provide *information* that allows the learner to associate actions with outcomes and thereby *control* his or her own fate. In fact, this sense of control over the environment (or at least the illusion of control) may ultimately prove to be the quality that makes many reinforcers "satisfying." Surely that was the case with the rotating mobile in Watson and Ramey's (1972) experiment: what the infants liked about the mobile was not that it moved but that *they could make it move.*

---

learned-helplessness effect: *the failure to learn how to respond appropriately in a situation because of previous exposures to uncontrollable events in the same or a similar situation.*

Punishment: The Aversive Control of Behavior

Earlier in the chapter, we defined *punishment* as an aversive event or experience that is administered in order to suppress an undesirable response. Although parents generally do not like to harm their children or see them unhappy, they will at least occasionally resort to punishment as a means of inhibiting a child's unacceptable behavior (Sears, Maccoby, & Levin, 1957; Shaffer, 1979). And there is a case to be made for its use, particularly if the prohibited act is something dangerous like playing with matches or probing electrical sockets with metallic objects. Yet many theorists believe that punishment is a two-edged sword that may prove counterproductive and even harmful in the long run.

Operant theorists are among the strongest critics of aversive control. They believe that punishment merely suppresses an undesirable response without teaching anything new. Moreover, advice columnists and authors of paperbacks on child rearing argue that punishment may engender anger, hostility, or resentment and, at best, a *temporary* suppression of the behavior it is designed to eliminate. Their point is that a fear of aversive consequences can never be a totally effective deterrent, because the potential transgressor will simply inhibit unacceptable conduct until it is unlikely to be detected and punished.

In spite of these criticisms, recent research indicates that punishment, properly applied, can be an effective method of controlling undesirable behavior. In this section we will first consider how and under what circumstances punishment is likely to work. Then we will look at some of the problems that may arise from an injudicious use of punitive tactics.

■ How does punishment suppress a response?

To understand the suppressive effects of punishment, we might consider the child's point of view. When an adult punishes a transgression, the aversive consequences that the child experiences will often produce some fear and anxiety. Now, since most transgressions are committed, detected, and punished on several occasions, it is likely that the fear or anxiety resulting from the punishment will become classically conditioned to

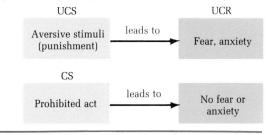
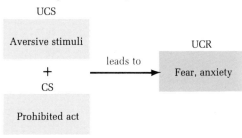
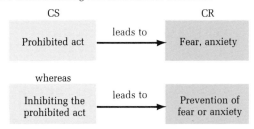

FIGURE 7-3. *A model of the suppressive effects of punishment.*

the punished act, as shown in Figure 7-3. Once this conditioning occurs, the child should then resist the temptation to commit the punished act in order to avoid the unpleasant consequences (conditioned fear or anxiety) now associated with its performance (Aronfreed, 1976; Parke, 1972).

■ When does punishment suppress a response?

Not all punishments are equally effective at suppressing or eliminating unacceptable behavior. Among the factors that influence the effectiveness of punishment are its timing, intensity, consistency, and underlying rationale, as well as the relationship between the child and the punitive agent.

Timing of punishment. Punishment is much more effective when it is administered "early," as the child prepares to commit the prohibited act, rather than "later," after the harm has been done (Aronfreed, 1968; Parke, 1977). In fact, the practice of delaying punishment for several hours until "Daddy comes home" is risky at best, for Justin Aronfreed (1968) found that the longer punishment is delayed, the less likely it is to prevent recurrences of the prohibited act.

There are probably several reasons that early or immediate punishments are more effective than those administered later. If children are punished as they initiate deviant acts, the anxiety associated with punishment is conditioned to their *preparatory* or *initiating* responses. As a result, they should experience anxiety when they prepare to commit the forbidden act and should inhibit the act in order to avoid this anxiety. In contrast, punishment that occurs after the transgression is completed has the effect of conditioning anxiety to the *end* of the deviant act. So children who are punished later may experience no ill feelings as they initiate future transgressions, although they may feel bad (or anxious about being caught) after the deed is done. In addition, transgressors who are punished later may have already experienced some pleasure from performing the prohibited act, and these pleasurable effects may partly offset the aversive aspects of punishment.

Recently, Gary Verna (1977) discovered that delayed punishments can be quite effective if the punitive agent explains to the child exactly what he or she has done to deserve these unpleasant consequences. So if punishment must be delayed until "Daddy comes home," the father will do well to remind his children why they are being punished just before the punishment is administered.

Intensity of punishment. Parents often assume that their child will "have something to think about" if they punish his or her transgressions forcefully. One implication of this point of view is that mild punishment will not generate enough anxiety to convince the child that forbidden acts should be inhibited.

Laboratory research with young children reveals that milder forms of punishment are generally less effective than stronger measures at inhibiting unacceptable behavior (see Parke,

1977). However, we must take care not to draw inappropriate conclusions from the results of these experiments. Although the "intense" punishments (loud buzzers or noises) used in this research were certainly discomforting, they are probably a whole lot less aversive than a spanking, a week's restriction to one's room, or the withdrawal of attention from a parent. There is evidence that young children tend to avoid punitive adults (Redd, Morris, & Martin, 1975), a finding that suggests that parents who punish their child too forcefully may produce an aloof son or daughter who is not often available to receive their instructions and guidance. And if the prohibition to be learned is difficult or subtle, the high levels of anxiety created by intense punishment may (1) prevent children from "learning their lesson" and (2) teach them to fear the punitive agent rather than the prohibited act.

In sum, it appears that the effectiveness of punishment increases as its intensity increases, as long as the punitive consequences are not so intense that they interfere with effective learning or are perceived by the child as "cruel and unusual."

Consistency of punishment. What will happen if an adult sometimes punishes and other times ignores unacceptable conduct or if two parents disagree about whether a particular type of behavior warrants a reprimand? Laboratory research designed to answer these questions paints a clear picture: acts that are punished in an erratic or irregular fashion tend to persist for long periods and are hard to eliminate, even after the disciplinary agent begins to punish them on a regular basis (Deur & Parke, 1970; Parke, 1977).

A student of operant learning can easily explain these findings. Since a prohibited act may be satisfying to the child, he or she should experience predominantly positive consequences on occasions when the act is *not* punished. In other words, inconsistent punishment may result in the "partial reinforcement" of unacceptable behavior, which will *strengthen* these habits and make them extremely resistant to the later use of punitive controls. If parents or teachers decide to use punishment as a means of suppressing an undesirable response, they would be well advised to punish the misbehavior on a regular basis from the day it first appears.

Warmth of the punitive agent. The effectiveness of punishment also depends on the relationship between the child and the punitive agent. Punishment delivered by a person who has previously established a warm and affectionate relationship with the child is much more likely to inhibit unacceptable behavior than the same punishment administered by a cold or impersonal agent (Parke, 1969; Sears et al., 1957). Children who are punished by a warm, caring person may perceive the reprimand as a loss of affection and will inhibit the punished act as a means of regaining approval. However, those who are punished by a cold or rejecting adult should not be highly motivated to inhibit forbidden acts, because they have no expectation of reestablishing a warm relationship with this cool or aloof disciplinarian.

Effects of verbal reprimands. It may have occurred to you that parents often give their children a rationale for the punishments they administer. Could it be that punishment becomes more effective when accompanied by an explanation that specifies why the punished act was wrong?

Both field and laboratory research suggests that this is indeed the case. Sears et al. (1957) found that mothers who combined physical punishment with the use of reasoning reported more success with punitive controls than did mothers who used punishment alone. Ross Parke (1969, 1977) reports similar findings from laboratory research and adds that factors such as the timing and intensity of punishment and the relationship between the child and the punitive agent are less important when a rationale accompanies punishment.

According to Justin Aronfreed (1976), rationales increase the effectiveness of punishment in two ways. First, they provide children with information about why they should inhibit an unacceptable response. Second, they allow the anxiety that stems from the aversive aspects of punishment to become conditioned to both the prohibited act and the verbal rationale. Once this conditioning occurs, the child should become rather anxious and may inhibit unacceptable responses whenever he or she even *thinks* about initiating a deviant act.

One final point: Many rationales may be ineffective with very young children, who have difficulty understanding why acts that they enjoy are wrong and should be inhibited. Ross Parke (1977), an authority on the use of punitive controls, finds that very brief rationales that are concrete ("Don't touch that toy, it's fragile and may break") and/or evoke anxiety ("You'll be sorry if you touch the toy") will work best with 3–4-year-olds. By contrast older children respond much more positively to longer rationales that justify response inhibition in terms of the negative impact a transgression would have on others (for example, "I will be sad if you touch the toy; you'll make me unhappy if you look at it now") (Kuczynski, 1983; Parke, 1977).

Combining punishment with positive reinforcement. Another way to enhance the suppressive effects of punishment is to reinforce alternative responses that are incompatible with the behavior you are trying to inhibit. David Perry and Ross Parke (1975) have demonstrated the usefulness of this approach in an experiment with 8-year-old boys who were told they were not to touch a group of attractive toys. The study revealed that punishment alone (a loud buzzer that sounded whenever a boy touched an attractive toy) was *less* effective at inhibiting this response than reward alone—that is, praise given whenever the boy decided to play with an *unattractive* toy (a desirable alternative response). However, a combination of punishment and praise proved more effective at instilling the prohibition than either of these treatments by itself. Apparently punishment will work better in the long run if the punitive agent takes the time to shape desirable alternative responses that can then substitute for the bad habits he or she is hoping to eliminate.

■ Some possible side effects of punishment

Those who have criticized the use of aversive controls are correct in arguing that punishment, when improperly applied, may produce undesirable side effects that limit its usefulness. For example, we have already seen that children may resent and will generally avoid punitive adults and that the anxiety generated by severe punishments may prevent the child from learning the lesson that the discipline was designed to teach. In addition, the children of highly punitive parents tend to be quite aggressive and difficult to control when away from the home setting in which punishment normally occurs (Eron, Walder, Huesmann, & Lef-kowitz, 1974; Sears et al., 1957). Albert Bandura (1977) explains this finding by noting that punitive adults, particularly those who rely on physical punishment, are serving as aggressive models for their children. A boy who learns that he will be hit when he displeases his parents will probably direct the same kind of response toward classmates who displease him.

Administration of aversive stimuli such as a slap or a spanking may also *reinforce the punitive agent* and become habitual if this form of discipline is particularly effective at inhibiting the child's undesirable behavior (Powers & Osborne, 1976). This is indeed unfortunate, for the regular use of physical punishment is often the first step along the road to child abuse (Parke & Collmer, 1975). In fact, child abuse may be a very real possibility if physical punishment is routinely administered to children who *misbehave as a means of attracting attention:* for a neglected or emotionally deprived youngster, the attention that accompanies punishment may be preferable to no attention at all.

■ *Removing positive stimuli: The "other side" of punishment*

Some of the potentially harmful effects of punishment are less likely to occur if adults choose to punish transgressions by withholding something desirable rather than administering aversive stimuli. One such punishment is the **response-cost technique**, in which the disciplinary agent removes a tangible reinforcer that the child already has (for example, candy) or would ordinarily receive in the future (a movie next Saturday). Another alternative is the **time-out technique** (that is, time out from the opportunity to receive positive reinforcement), in which the adult "punishes" by disrupting or preventing a prohibited activity that the child seems to enjoy (for example, sending a bossy, argumentative child to her room). Although both these techniques may generate some resentment or hostility, the punitive agent is not physically abusing the child, is not serving as an aggressive model, and is not likely to unwittingly reinforce the child who misbehaves as a means of attracting attention— particularly if the time-out procedure is used.

■ *The child's role in determining punitive outcomes*

We have talked as if parents alone determined how they would discipline their children. Yet recent laboratory and survey studies reveal that the discipline that parents use depends to a large extent on (1) what the child has done and (2) how he or she has reacted to previous disciplinary encounters (Grusec & Kuczynski, 1980; Holden, 1983; Mulhern & Passman, 1981). Joan Grusec and Leon Kuczynski (1980) found that transgressions producing psychological harm for others (stealing from a mother's purse; teasing a senile old man) are likely to elicit a "punishment" that is heavy on reasoning and designed to make children see why their behavior was wrong. In contrast, acts of disobedience such as fighting, refusing to share, and failing to comply with orders are more likely to result in physical punishment, a withdrawal of privileges, or a forced compliance with the original order. The child's reactions to discipline also affect the *severity* of the punishment he receives. For example, Ross Parke (1977) found that children who had ignored or defied the punitive agent or who had pleaded for mercy were punished much more forcefully during the next disciplinary encounter than children who had offered to undo the harm they had done. Thus, the flow of influence in punitive encounters is *reciprocal:* the nature of the child's transgression will influence the adult's choice of punishment, which will elicit a reaction from the child, which, in turn, will affect the adult's future use of punishment. Clearly, Parke (1977, p. 217) is correct in arguing that "children can play a role in sparing the rod!"

■ *Alternatives to punishment*

Punishment is only one of many techniques that adults can use to inhibit or eliminate undesirable

---

response-cost technique: *a form of punishment in which the punitive agent removes or withholds a valuable commodity from the transgressor.*

time-out technique: *a strategy in which the disciplinary agent "punishes" a child by disrupting or preventing the prohibited activity that the child seems to enjoy.*

behavior. One successful alternative to punishment is the **incompatible-response technique,** in which the adult in charge ignores undesirable behavior—for example, selfish acts—and provides lavish praise or other tangible reinforcers for responses such as sharing and cooperating that are incompatible with the conduct he or she is trying to eliminate. Another proven approach is the **self-instructional technique,** in which children are told why certain acts are wrong and then taught to verbalize these rationales when they feel the urge to deviate. Both these viable alternatives to punishment have an important advantage: they produce few if any of the undesirable side effects that often accompany the use of punitive tactics. Of course, there is a time and a place for punishment: Adults may occasionally have to resort to forceful or punitive strategies in order to command the attention of an unruly child. Yet parents and teachers who try these two alternative approaches may find that they rarely have to rely on punishment in order to control children's behavior.

OBSERVATIONAL LEARNING

In recent years a number of prominent developmentalists have argued that much of what we learn is acquired by observation. **Observational learning** is a relatively simple process in which the child acquires new responses by (1) observing the behavior of others (social models), (2) making mental notes of what he or she has witnessed, and (3) imitating these actions in situations where the new behaviors seem to be appropriate.

Albert Bandura is an important spokesman among observational-learning theorists—one who believes that the vast majority of the habits we acquire during our lifetimes are learned by observing and imitating other people. According to Bandura (1977), there are several reasons that observational learning plays such a prominent role in human development. First, learning by observation is much more efficient than the trial-and-error method. When observers can learn by watching a model perform flawlessly, they are spared the needless errors that might result from attempts to perfect the same skills and abilities on their own. Second, many complex behaviors could probably never be learned unless children were exposed to people who modeled them. Take

PHOTO 7-2. *Children acquire a variety of responses through observational learning.*

language, for example. It seems rather implausible that parents could ever shape their child's babbles into words, not to mention grammatical speech, merely by rewarding and punishing these random vocalizations.[1] Yet children who lack some bit of grammatical knowledge will soon alter their sentence constructions after hearing this rule of grammar reflected in the speech of a companion (Bandura & Harris, 1966; Zimmerman, 1977). Finally, observational learning permits the young child to acquire many new responses in a large number of settings where her "models" are simply

[1]Although Lovaas and his associates were able to shape the babbles of autistic children into words and word phrases (see Box 7-3), normal children do not acquire language in this way. Indeed, we will see in Chapter Eight that parents do not often reinforce a child's speech, and when they do, they are more likely to reward its truth value, or factual correctness, rather than its grammatical correctness.

pursuing their own interests and are not trying to teach her anything in particular. Of course, some of the behaviors that young children observe and may try to imitate are actions that adults display but would like to discourage—practices such as swearing, eating between meals, and smoking. Bandura's point is that children are continually learning both desirable and undesirable responses by "keeping their eyes (and ears) open," and he is not at all surprised that human development proceeds so very rapidly along so many different paths.

How Do We "Learn" by Observation?

In 1965 Bandura made what was then considered a radical statement: Children can learn by merely observing the behavior of a social model, *even though they have never attempted the responses that they have witnessed or received any reinforcement for performing them.* Note the implications here: Bandura is proposing a type of "no trial" learning in which the learned response is neither elicited by a conditioned stimulus nor strengthened by a reinforcer. Impossible, said many learning theorists, for Bandura's proposition seems to ignore important principles of both classical and instrumental conditioning.

■ An example of "no trial" learning without reinforcement

But Bandura was right, although he had to conduct what is now considered a classic experiment to prove his point (Bandura, 1965). At the beginning of this experiment, nursery school children were taken one at a time to a semidarkened room to watch a short film. As they watched, they saw an adult model direct an unusual sequence of aggressive responses toward an inflatable Bobo doll, hitting the doll with a mallet while shouting "Sockeroo," throwing rubber balls at the doll while shouting "Bang, bang, bang," and so on (see Photo 7-3). There were three experimental conditions. Children in the *model rewarded* condition saw the film end as a second adult appeared and gave the aggressive model some candy and a soft drink for a "championship performance." Children assigned to the *model punished* condition saw an ending in which a second adult scolded and spanked the model for beating up on Bobo.

Finally, children in the *no consequences* condition simply watched a model beat up on Bobo without receiving any reward or punishment.

When the film ended, each child was left alone in a playroom that contained a Bobo doll and many of the props that the model had used to work Bobo over. Hidden observers then watched the child, recording all instances in which he or she imitated one or more of the model's aggressive acts. These observations would reveal how willing the children were to *perform* the responses they had seen the model display. The results of this "performance" test appear on the left-hand (lighter) side of Figure 7-4. Here we see that children in the model-rewarded and the no-consequences conditions imitated more of the model's aggressive acts than children who had seen the model punished for aggressive behavior. At the very least, these results indicate that subjects in the first two conditions had learned some rather novel aggressive responses without being reinforced and without having had a previous opportunity to perform them. This looks very much like the kind of no-trial observational learning that Bandura had proposed.

■ The learning/performance distinction

But one question remained: Had the children in the model-rewarded and the no-consequences conditions actually *learned more* from observing the model than children who had seen the model punished? To find out, Bandura devised a second test in which he persuaded children to show just how much they had learned. Each child was offered some juice and trinkets for reproducing all of the model's behaviors that he or she could re-

---

incompatible-response technique: *a nonpunitive method of behavior modification in which adults ignore undesirable conduct while reinforcing acts that are incompatible with these responses.*

self-instructional technique: *a nonpunitive method of self-control in which children learn to verbalize the rationale for inhibiting an act whenever they feel the urge to perform it.*

observational learning: *learning that results from observing the behavior of others.*

PHOTO 7-3. *In Bandura's classic experiment, children who had watched an adult model show aggression toward a Bobo doll in several unusual ways (top row) performed similar acts themselves (middle and bottom rows), even though they hadn't been reinforced for committing such acts.*

call. The results of this "learning" test, which appear in the right-hand (darker) portion of Figure 7-4, clearly indicate that children in each of the three conditions learned about the same amount by observing the model. Apparently children in the model-punished condition had imitated fewer of the model's responses on the initial "performance" test because they felt that they too might be punished for striking Bobo. But offer them a reward, and they show that they have learned much more than their initial performances might have implied.

In sum, it is important to distinguish between what children *learn* by observation and their willingness to *perform* these responses. Bandura's (1965) experiment shows that reinforcement is not necessary for observational learning. What reinforcement does is to increase the likelihood

that the child will perform that which he or she has already learned by observing the model's behavior.

■ *What do children acquire in observational learning?*

In many cases, young children will not imitate a model's behavior for hours, days, or even weeks after observing it. For example, a boy who wants to "shave" himself after watching his father shave will have to wait until a time when he can be alone for a while, for few parents permit their youngsters to experiment with razors. What are children acquiring that enables them to reproduce the behavior of an absent model at some point in the future—often the distant future?

According to Bandura (1977), a child who carefully observes a model will acquire **symbolic rep-**

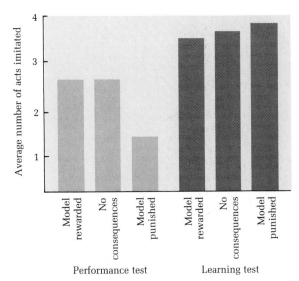

FIGURE 7-4. *Average number of aggressive responses imitated during the performance test and the learning test for children who had seen a model rewarded, punished, or receiving no consequences for his actions.*

resentations of the model's behavior, which are stored in memory and retrieved at a later date to guide his or her own attempts to imitate. These symbolic representations may be *images* of the model's actions or *verbal labels* that describe these responses in an economical way. Verbal representation is particularly important, for it enables the observer to retain information that would be difficult or impossible to remember by any other method. Imagine how hard it would be to open a combination safe if you simply formed images of the model turning the dials and had not translated these actions into a verbal label such as "L49, R37, L18."

Apparently, symbolic coding activities do facilitate observational learning. Bandura and his associates (Bandura, Grusec, & Menlove, 1966) found that 6–8-year-olds who were told to count out loud while watching a model later reproduced *fewer* of the model's actions than age mates whose symbolic activities were not "disrupted" by counting. In addition, Brian Coates and Willard Hartup (1969) found that 4–5-year-olds who had been explicitly instructed to describe what they were observing were able to reproduce about twice as many of the model's responses than age mates who had not been instructed to describe the model's behavior.

■ *Attentional processes: Choosing a model*

Virtually all children are exposed to a large number of social models, including parents, teachers, siblings, peers, Scout leaders, and media heroes. However, Bandura (1977) notes that (1) the child must attend carefully to any model to learn by observation and (2) that some models are more worthy of attention than others.

Whom are young children likely to select as social models? According to Bandura (1977), the most likely candidates are people who are warm and nurturant (socially responsive) and/or appear competent or powerful. Indeed, Joan Grusec and Rona Abramovitch (1982) found that nursery school children will often attend to and imitate their teachers (powerful, competent models) and those classmates who are typically warm, friendly, and responsive to them. Moreover, 5–8-year-olds prefer to imitate age mates or older children rather than a younger peer because they believe that younger children are less competent than they are (Brody & Stoneman, 1981; Graziano, Brody, & Bernstein, 1980).

The attainment of certain developmental milestones will also affect the child's choice of models. For example, once children are fully aware of their gender and know that it will never change (at about age 5–7), they will pay much more attention to models of their own sex (Grusec & Brinker, 1972). And as people mature, they develop certain interests, attitudes, and values and will normally prefer models who are in some way *similar* to themselves—friends or people in the same occupation, ethnic group, political party, and so on. But even though our choice of models may become somewhat more restricted over time, we will continue to learn by observing others for the rest of our lives.

---

symbolic representations: *the images and verbal labels that observers produce in order to retain the important aspects of a model's behavior.*

PHOTO 7-4. Older children tend to select models of their own sex.

Developmental Trends in Imitation and Observational Learning

Bandura's theory of observational learning assumes that an observer can form images and verbal labels to represent a model's behavior and then use these symbolic mediators to reproduce

what he or she has witnessed. Are all these abilities present at birth?

■ *Origins of imitation and imitative learning*

Although newborn infants may be biologically programmed to mimic certain facial expressions (Field, Woodson, Greenberg, & Cohen, 1982), it will be some time before they are capable of imitating other kinds of activities or constructing symbolic representations of a model's behavior. For example, Jean Piaget (1951) found that infants are not very proficient at reproducing an adult's simple motor responses until 9–12 months of age. And even then, the model must be present and must continue to perform the response before the child is able to imitate.

At about 20–24 months of age, infants are capable of **deferred imitation**—the ability to reproduce the actions of a model at some point in the future when the model is no longer present. Deferred imitation is an important developmental milestone that indicates that the child can now represent the model's behavior with mental images that will preserve the original scene and guide its later reproduction.

■ *Use of verbal mediators to represent experience*

Although preschool children are rapidly acquiring language and becoming accomplished conversationalists, they are less likely than older children to rely on verbal labels as a means of representing their experiences. In the study by Coates and Hartup (1969) mentioned earlier, 4–5-year-olds and 7–8-year-olds watched a short film in which an adult model displayed a number of unusual responses, such as shooting at a tower of blocks with a pop gun and throwing a bean bag between his legs. Some of the children from each age group were told to describe the model's actions as they observed them (induced-coding condition); others simply watched the model without having received any instructions (passive-observation condition). As we saw, the 4–5-year-olds who described what they were observing were later able to reproduce much more of the model's behavior than their counterparts in the passive-observation condition. In contrast, 7–8-year-olds reproduced the same number of the model's responses whether or not they had been told to describe what the model was doing. This latter finding suggests that 7–8-year-olds will use verbal labels to describe what they have seen, even if they are not explicitly instructed to do so. One important implication of this study is that preschool children may learn less from social models because they, unlike older children, do not spontaneously produce the verbal mediators that would help them retain what they have observed.

Television as a Modeling Influence

It has been estimated that the average American child between the ages of 2 and 11 watches almost four hours of television a day (Federal Trade Commission, 1978). Given this heavy exposure to television programming, it would be surprising if media models did not influence children's thinking and behavior.

■ *Age differences in children's reactions to television*

The extent to which children will process and retain televised information depends on a number of factors, including the child's age, the content and comprehensibility of the programming, and the presence of distractors such as toys, games, and other people. Robert McCall and his associates (McCall, Parke, & Kavanaugh, 1977) found that infants and toddlers become increasingly responsive to televised models between the ages of 18 months and 3 years. Eighteen-month-olds spend a far greater percentage of their time watching live models than TV models, and they are more likely to imitate the live model during a free-play session. In contrast, 3-year-olds attend equally to live and to televised models, and they are just as likely to imitate a TV model as a live one.

What do children attend to and remember from their exposure to television? According to recent research, preschool children pay more attention to the visual than to the auditory components of television programming (Hayes, Chemelski, & Birnbaum, 1981), particularly the perceptually salient features such as fast-paced action sequences, special effects, zooms, and segments in which there are rapid changes in the scenery or the number of characters (Anderson, Lorch, Field,

> **deferred imitation:** *the ability to reproduce a modeled sequence that has been witnessed at some point in the past.*

& Sanders, 1981). In contrast, aspects of programming that are subtle (information about a character's motives or intentions) or difficult to comprehend (adult narrations) are less likely to be noticed, understood, or retained (Calvert, Huston, Watkins, & Wright, 1982; Collins, Wellman, Keniston, & Westby, 1978).

During the elementary school years, children become less interested in the "captivating" visual effects of television programming and will attend more to features that provide information about the plot or the characters' motives and intentions. Compared with preschool children, who are apt to recall what actors have *done*, grade-school children are much more proficient at determining the *reasons* these actions were undertaken and the *consequences* they produce (Collins et al., 1978).

■ *What do children learn from television?*

Presumably children might learn any number of novel responses from TV if they pay close attention and construct symbolic representations of the behavior of the characters. In recent years, child developmentalists and the public at large have become concerned about two potentially important sources of media influence: televised violence and commercials aimed at children.

Does televised violence affect children's behavior? Children who grow up in the United States, Canada, and other Western nations can observe violent, aggressive episodes almost any time they care to by simply turning on their TV sets. In the United States, nearly 80% of prime-time programming contains at least one violent incident, with an average rate of about 7.5 incidents per hour. In fact, the most violent TV programs are those designed for children—especially Saturday morning cartoons, which contain nearly 25 violent incidents per hour (Gerbner, Gross, Morgan, & Signorelli, 1980).

Even though some people have argued that the comical violence portrayed in children's television programming is unlikely to affect the behavior of viewers, both anecdotal and research evidence suggests otherwise. Robert Liebert and his associates (Liebert, Sprafkin, & Davidson, 1982) provide several dramatic illustrations of how children have behaved in a violent or aggressive fashion after watching similar actions on television. Here is one example:

In Los Angeles, a housemaid caught a 7-year-old boy in the act of sprinkling ground glass into the family's lamb stew. There was no malice behind the act. It was purely experimental, having been inspired by curiosity to learn whether it would really work as well as it did on television [Liebert et al., 1982, p. 7].

A number of correlational surveys paint a similar picture: children and adolescents who watch a lot of televised violence at home tend to be more aggressive than their classmates who watch little violence (Belson, 1978; Eron & Huesmann, 1980; Huesmann, 1982; Liebert et al., 1982). And in one ten-year longitudinal study of children's aggression (Eron, Huesmann, Lefkowitz, & Walder, 1972), the investigators found that boys who preferred highly violent and aggressive programming at age 8 were much more aggressive at age 18 than their classmates who had not preferred to watch violent shows. So it appears that heavy exposure to televised violence during early and middle childhood may promote the development of aggressive habits that persist over time. Indeed, Eron et al. (1972) reported that children's television preferences at age 8 predicted aggression at age 18 better than any other factor they studied, including intelligence, social class, ethnicity, and parents' child-rearing practices.

We will return to the complex and controversial topic of televised violence when we take a closer look at media effects in Chapter Sixteen. At this point, let's simply note that the televised portrayal of aggression is one potentially important influence on children's interpersonal behavior.

Children's reactions to advertising. Children who watch commercial television are exposed to nearly 20,000 commercials a year, many of which are specifically targeted at them rather than their parents. Commercials typically contain production features such as brightly colored displays, action sequences, and exaggerated sound effects that are likely to command a young child's attention. In fact, many American children are already singing commercial jingles by age 3, and they can easily discriminate commercial messages from the programming that commercials sponsor (Levin, Petros, & Petrella, 1982; Lyle & Hoffman, 1972).

Parents are understandably concerned about the effects of television advertising on their children. A large percentage of the ads directed at children are for toys that adults are disinclined to purchase, for fast-food chains, and for sugary foods that pose a threat to the child's dental health (Barcus, 1978; Stoneman & Brody, 1981). And children are affected by these ads: They ask for the toys and products that they see advertised and will generally accept a commercial as an honest portrayal of a product that is designed to help people by showing them what they should be buying. Not until age 9–11 do children realize that ads are designed to persuade or sell, and by age 13–14 they will have acquired a healthy skepticism about product claims and advertising in general (Linn, de Benedictis, & Delucchi, 1982; Robertson & Rossiter, 1974). Nevertheless, older children and adolescents are often persuaded by the ads they see, particularly if the model who endorses the product is a celebrity (Campbell, Ross, Wright, Huston, Rice, & Turk, 1981).

So commercials are yet another modeling influence that may affect the behavior of young children. However, recent research indicates that a child's response to an advertised product will also depend on the reactions of adults and other children. For example, Joann Galst (1980) found that 3–6-year-olds who are allowed to choose between sugar-coated and nonsugary snacks are somewhat less likely to choose the sugary treats if they have heard an adult comment on an ad for sugary foods by stressing the product's poor nutritional value and its threat to dental health. In a similar vein, Zo Stoneman and Gene Brody (1981) have shown that the behavior of peers can dramatically alter the effects of advertising on school-age children. In this study, 9–10-year-olds saw four minutes of commercials for salty snacks and then either (1) watched a peer select salty snacks over other kinds of treats, (2) did not observe a peer model, or (3) watched a peer select other treats rather than salty snacks. All children then indicated their preferences for various kinds of snack foods. As we can see in Figure 7-5, children who had watched a peer choose salty snacks were more likely to prefer salty snacks themselves than children who had merely seen the ads for these products. By contrast, children who had seen peers shun the advertised products were *less* likely to prefer salty snacks than children who had only seen the salty-snack ads. In fact, they were no more likely to select these products than children

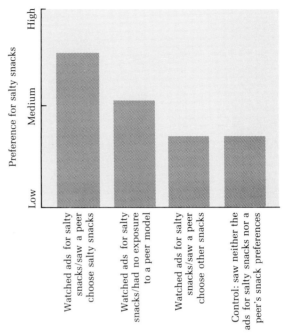

FIGURE 7-5. *Children's preference for salty snacks as a function of exposure to salty-snack ads and the choice of snacks made by peers.*

in a control group who had never seen the products advertised.

These findings clearly illustrate that television is not a unitary force that determines the child's thoughts, feelings, or behaviors. Children typically watch TV in a setting or context that includes family members, peers, and other important social agents who will react to the televised message in ways that may either enhance or reduce its impact.

Positive contributions of television. Although we have concentrated on the undesirable lessons that children may learn from watching television, it is important to note that this medium can have some very beneficial effects as well. For example, educational programming such as *Sesame Street* can transmit valuable information to preschool children and further their intellectual development (Ball & Bogatz, 1972). Children who often watch shows that stress positive values such as

BOX 7-5
MEDIA MODELS AS THERAPISTS

In Box 7-1 we saw how counterconditioning procedures were used to overcome a 2-year-old's fear of furry objects. As it happens, many preschool children develop a fear of a particular class of furry objects—those big old friendly *dogs* that may frighten them by barking a hello, licking their faces, knocking them over, and occasionally nipping playfully at their heels as the children flee in terror. Children who fear dogs also tend to have at least one parent who avoids dogs, so perhaps they acquire their dog-phobic reactions by observing the behavior of a fearful adult.

Albert Bandura and Frances Menlove (1968) have devised a treatment for dog phobia that they believe is both more efficient and more effective than counterconditioning. Their plan was to expose dog-phobic children to films in which one or more children react fearlessly to dogs. Presumably the observers would overcome their fears as they watched the films and learned that dogs can be pleasant companions for people like themselves.

Bandura and Menlove piloted their treatment in a nursery school. At the beginning of the project, all the children were asked to perform 14 acts to assess their fear of dogs. Each successive act required the child to initiate increasingly intimate contact with a live pooch. Forty-eight children who showed a strong fear of dogs were selected as participants for the treatment phase of the project.

The dog-phobics were then divided into three groups, each of which was exposed to a different set of films. Those assigned to a *single model* condition observed eight three-minute films (two a day for four days) that showed a 5-year-old boy engaging in progressively bolder interactions with a cocker spaniel. The final film showed the model fearlessly entering the dog's pen, where he petted the animal, fed it dog candies, and rested his head on the dog while taking a brief nap. Children assigned to the *multiple model* condition observed similar films, except that their materials showed several boys and girls interacting with a number of dogs ranging in size from very small

to quite large. Finally, children in the *control* group did not observe a fearless model; instead, they spent an equal amount of time watching films about Disneyland and Marineland of the Pacific.

On the day after the final film, the children were once again asked to perform the 14 acts that served as a test of their fear of dogs. Bandura and Menlove found that subjects who had been exposed to fearless peer models on film were now much more willing to approach and interact with a live dog than they had been during the original testing (the graph shows their results). In contrast, children in the control group showed absolutely no reduction in their fear of dogs. One month later, the children were tested a third time. This follow-up indicated that the reduced fear of dogs shown by children who had observed fearless peer models remained stable over time. The follow-up produced one other interesting outcome: children in the multiple-model condition were more willing than those who had observed a single model to initiate highly intimate contact with a dog, venturing alone into the dog's pen while feeding the dog from the hand, scratching the dog's stomach, and the like. Evidently several televised models are better than one as a means of eliminating a child's fear of a frightening object or situation.

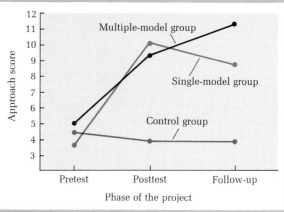

Willingness of dog-phobic children to approach a live dog at different phases of Bandura and Menlove's experiment.

sharing, cooperating, and helping others (for example, *Fat Albert and the Cosby Kids; Mister Rogers' Neighborhood*) are likely to become more considerate, cooperative, and helpful toward their siblings and peers, particularly when adults encourage them to think about and enact the prosocial lessons they have seen on TV (Friedrich & Stein, 1975; Friedrich-Cofer, Huston-Stein, Kipnis, Susman, & Clewett, 1979). Finally, the study described in Box 7-5 illustrates how televised information can be an invaluable aid in treating childhood fears and phobias.

Summing up. We have seen that children can learn many new responses from both live and televised models by merely attending to a model's behavior and retaining mental representations of what they have witnessed. Since observational learning requires neither formal instruction nor reinforcement, it probably occurs daily, even when models are simply pursuing their own interests and are not trying to teach the child anything in particular. Bandura (1977) reminds us that all developing children will learn from a variety of social models and that no two children are exposed to exactly the same pattern of modeling influences. Therefore, children should never be expected to emerge as carbon copies of their parents, siblings, or the child next door—individual differences are an inevitable consequence of observational learning.

COMPLEX PROCESSES IN LEARNING

Life would be rather chaotic if we had to learn how we should behave all over again every time we met a new person, took a seat in a strange classroom, or encountered a red light at an unfamiliar intersection. During the first few years of life, children are exposed to an enormous number of objects and situations that provide them with opportunities to acquire literally thousands of different responses. Yet even infants and toddlers do not have to learn how to respond to each novel stimulus or situation that they encounter. Like adults, they are able to recognize that new objects and situations are either similar or dissimilar to those they have experienced before and will call for a similar or a dissimilar response. In the pages that follow, we will consider how children form these simple **concepts**, and we will see that their concept-learning and problem-solving strategies become much more sophisticated over time.

One important aspect of all types of learning is the *stimulus generalization* principle, which states that *responses learned to one cue or situation are likely to recur whenever we encounter similar cues or situations.* A girl who has learned to fear a white rat may shy away from other white, furry objects; a boy who has learned to throw a tennis ball at home will probably throw baseballs, beach balls, beanbags, and other small, round objects at nursery school. This generalization of re-

sponses across cues and situations makes life much easier and somewhat less hazardous for all of us. For example, a child who burns herself on the stove in the kitchen quickly learns to avoid this appliance, and she will probably steer clear of the old stove in the basement, the one at Grandmother's house, and the home appliances display at the local department store. In sum, the stimulus generalization principle helps to explain how young children soon acquire very broad habits despite the great diversity of stimuli and experiences to which they are exposed.

Stimuli that are *physically* similar produce the greatest generalization among infants and toddlers. However, the ways objects are *labeled* or *classified* are probably a stronger determinant of generalization for older children and adults. Consider the following illustration. Leann Birch (1981) modified the food preferences of preschool children by reinforcing them whenever they selected a nonfavorite snack (for example, cashews) from an assortment of nuts, cheeses, fruits, and crackers. Once the children had learned to choose the reinforced snack, they were given a "generalization" test in which they could select either a similar snack (for example, peanuts) or a snack from one of the nonreinforced categories. Birch found that children who had earlier classified snack foods into distinct categories (that is, nuts, fruits, cheeses, and crackers) tended to generalize the response that they had learned by selecting another snack from the reinforced category—for example, peanuts. In contrast, children who had not classified snack foods into categories had less of a reason for judging cashews and peanuts as similar, and, as a result, they typically failed to select peanuts during the generalization test.

There are many occasions, however, when children are expected to respond quite differently to cues or situations that seem to be similar—a process known as *discrimination*. For example, toddlers must learn to discriminate the toilet from the bathtub when nature calls. They must recognize that certain objects (for example, toys) can be fondled while others (knives, vases) cannot. They

---

concept: *a classification of objects or events on the basis of one or more features they share.*

must learn to restrict their drawing activities to the pages of their coloring books and to refrain from marking up the encyclopedia or creating a mural on the living room wall. Indeed, many of the everyday lessons that parents try to teach are examples of discrimination training. And if they are successful, the child's behavior will soon begin to depend on the specific situation in which he finds himself.

Of course, there are some discriminations that children may learn the hard way. Consider the plight of a 2-year-old who assumes that all dogs are as docile as the family pooch, an even-tempered creature that tolerates acts such as tail pulling and an occasional slap in the face. Because many dogs will not react kindly to such abuse, it is in the child's best interest to discriminate the family dog from the hound next door—and to do so in a hurry. Fortunately, toddlers are not often left to make such monumental discoveries on their own; parents frequently accelerate the process by providing their children with distinctive verbal labels that mediate important discriminations. For example, a mother might tell her 2-year-old "You can play with *Shep* (the mild-mannered family dog), but don't you bother *Peppy*." By naming the two dogs, the mother has helped her child to discriminate them (Bandura & Walters, 1963).

Later Developments in Concept Learning: The "5 to 7 Shift"

Between the ages of 5 and 7, there are significant changes in both the character of children's learning and the strategies they use to form concepts and solve problems. Sheldon White (1965) cites 21 examples of this **"5 to 7 shift,"** and his list is not exhaustive by any means. In this final section of the chapter, we will consider a few of these changes and try to determine why they occur.

■ *Learning to learn*

Suppose that you devise a series of simple discrimination problems, each of which requires the learner to select one of two stimuli that differ on an attribute such as size, color, or shape. You then present your subject with the first problem and reward her with a peanut or a piece of candy whenever she selects the proper stimulus (say, a red rather than a green triangle). After six successive presentations of these stimuli (trials), you introduce a second discrimination problem, and then a third, a fourth, a fifth, and so on.

Harry Harlow (1949; Harlow & Harlow, 1949) conducted this kind of research with both monkeys and children and found that performance improved as subjects gained more experience solving simple discrimination problems. Note that each of these discriminations can be learned in a minimum of two trials if the subject selects a stimulus on Trial 1 and then, on Trial 2, either picks it again if it was reinforced or shifts to the other stimulus if the original choice did not pay off. Yet monkeys and young children did not operate this way for the first several problems. Instead, they made persistent errors such as choosing the bigger or brighter of the two stimuli, and their percentage of correct choices on second trials barely exceeded the chance level of 50%. But after working on a number of these simple discriminations, they eventually eliminated all their erroneous hypotheses and discovered the **"win–stay, lose–shift"** principle, which is appropriate for each successive problem. At this point their percentages of correct choices on second trials were far above the chance level (see Figure 7-6) because they had learned how to solve problems of this kind. In Harlow's words, they had **"learned how to learn."**

Although 3–5-year-olds are quite capable of "learning to learn," it will take them roughly twice as long as grade school children and three times as long as college students to eliminate their erroneous strategies and discover the win–stay, lose–shift principle, which permits them to solve successive discrimination problems in a trial or two (Levinson & Reese, 1967). Thus, "learning to learn" is a conceptual skill that improves dramatically between ages 5 and 7.

■ *The oddity concept*

Oddity problems are those in which the learner must select from three stimuli the one that is in some way different from the other two (for example, choose a red triangle rather than either of two red squares). The stimuli are frequently changed, but the child is always reinforced if he or she selects the odd stimulus.

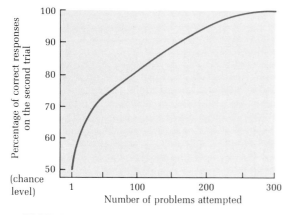

FIGURE 7-6. Learning to learn. Harlow gave 344 two-choice discrimination problems to monkeys. The curve shows the average percentage of correct responses on the second trial of each problem as a function of the number of problems they had previously worked on. After attempting some 30 problems, the monkeys were picking the correct object more than 70% of the time, and by the 300th problem, their performance was nearly errorless. What they had learned from their experiences was the "win–stay, lose–shift" principle, which enabled them to solve any problem of this type in only two trials. This is a simple form of concept learning.

In one study (Gollin & Shirk, 1966), 4-year-olds and 6-year-olds were asked to guess which light was correct on a series of oddity problems in which the stimuli consisted of all the possible binary combinations of red, green, and blue lights (that is, RRB, BBR, GBG, RGG, and so on). The position of the odd light in the three-light display was varied randomly across the 54 problems, and correct responses were always reinforced. Once children realize that the odd stimulus is always correct, they should solve each successive problem without making any errors. Although 88% of the 6-year-olds eventually discovered the oddity principle and responded accordingly, only 42% of the 4-year-olds ever picked the odd stimulus on as many as six successive problems. So oddity learning is another conceptual skill that improves between ages 5 and 7.

Note that oddity learning is not an example of simple operant conditioning. Suppose that the child has responded correctly to the following three problems: GGR, RBB, and GRG. That is, red was always reinforced. According to the operant analysis, the child should now pick one of the red lights on the problem BRR because the response "pick red" is the only one that has been strengthened. Although preschoolers may respond this way, older children are much more likely to select the "odd" (blue) light, which has *never* been reinforced! How do we account for this puzzling strategy that seems to defy the principles of operant conditioning? Before we try to answer this question, let's consider another line of evidence to suggest that older children learn in a different way than younger children do.

■ *Reversal and nonreversal learning*

Suppose that you present children with a discrimination problem in which the stimuli differ on the dimensions of size (large versus small) and color (black versus white), and you always reinforce them for choosing the *large* object, regardless of its color. Once they have learned to "pick large," you then divide the children into two groups. Those assigned to the **reversal** condition

---

"**5 to 7 shift**": *the dramatic changes in concept learning that are often observed between the ages of 5 and 7.*

"**win–stay, lose–shift**": *a strategy for solving two-choice discrimination problems in a minimum of two trials by staying with a response that is reinforced or switching to the alternative choice if the original response was not reinforced.*

learning to learn: *the improvement in one's ability to solve various problems as a result of previous experience with similar problems.*

oddity problem: *a discrimination task in which the subject is reinforced for responding to the stimulus that is different from all other comparison stimuli.*

reversal shift: *a type of discrimination learning in which subjects who have learned to respond to one aspect of a dimension (for example, large) must now learn to respond to the opposite aspect of the same dimension (small).*

are now reinforced only when they make the opposite response by picking the smaller of the two objects (color is still irrelevant). Children assigned to the **nonreversal** condition must now switch dimensions and learn to respond to color by picking the *black* object on each successive trial (see Figure 7-7). Which of these two new problems do you think would be easier to learn?

According to the operant analysis, nonreversals will be easier. Since the "large" stimuli rewarded during the training trials were "black" half the time, the response "pick black" has been partially reinforced. In contrast, the response necessary for reversal learning ("pick small") was *never* reinforced during the original training phase. Nonreversals should therefore be easier to learn, because it should be easier to strengthen a response ("pick black") that has already been reinforced.

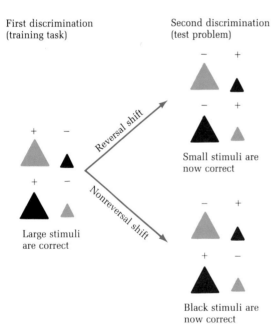

First discrimination
(training task)

Second discrimination
(test problem)

Reversal shift

Nonreversal shift

+   −

+   −

Large stimuli
are correct

−   +

−   +

Small stimuli are
now correct

−   +

+   −

Black stimuli are
now correct

FIGURE 7-7. Examples of a reversal and a nonreversal shift; + indicates the correct (rewarded) stimuli and − indicates the incorrect (nonrewarded) stimuli. All subjects are first trained to respond to large stimuli on the training task and then switched to a second problem set in which either small stimuli are reinforced (reversal learning) or black stimuli are reinforced (nonreversal learning).

Both animals and young (nursery school) children do find it easier to solve nonreversal problems (Kendler & Kendler, 1975; White, 1965). However, Howard Kendler and his associates (Kendler, Kendler, & Leonard, 1962) reported that about half of their 5–6-year-olds and a clear majority of their 8–10-year-olds learned reversal shifts more easily than nonreversal shifts. Once again, a simple operant analysis fails to explain the performance of older children.

■ *Explanations for the "5 to 7 shift"*

Why does the character of learning change so dramatically between the ages of 5 and 7? We will consider two possible answers.

The mediational model. Several years ago, Aleksandr Luria (1961) and Lev Vygotsky (1962) proposed that language and thinking become interrelated, so that the progress of one affects the progress of the other. Consider the following observations. When 2–3-year-olds play or work at a task, they say little if anything as they go about their business. But by age 4–5, children will typically describe what they are doing as they do it. Eventually, this "private speech" becomes more abbreviated, passing from complete sentences to incomplete phrases to whispers to lip movements, until it is not detectable at all. Luria and Vygotsky propose that young children are using private speech as a means of directing their ongoing activities and formulating new ideas or hypotheses. And once private speech is internalized (at ages 5–7), it becomes an effective "go-between," or **mediator,** that enables children to reflect on what they are doing *before* they do it—to think before they react (Luria, 1961).

Apparently, private speech can help young children to regulate ongoing activities and to find solutions for simple problems. Virginia Tinsley and Harriet Waters (1982) noted that 2-year-olds who were instructed to strike a peg only once with a hammer were generally unable to limit themselves to one blow until they had been trained to say "one" or "toy" as they hit the peg. Once trained, these toddlers were able to use overt speech to control their motor activities. In another recent experiment, Sherryl Goodman (1981) found that 3½–5-year-olds were most efficient at solving jigsaw puzzles during those work periods when they were frequently verbalizing their thoughts, plans, and intentions. Moreover, the rate of private speech increased whenever the children were having trouble with the puzzles—a finding that suggests they were talking to themselves in an attempt to generate solutions for their problems.

According to the **mediational** model, older children are better learners than younger children because they are more likely to rely on verbal mediators as a learning aid. Let's reconsider the hypothetical oddity experiment in which the child began by responding correctly to the problems GGR, RBB, and GRG (so that the red light was always reinforced). Presumably the older child who uses verbal mediators will label the features of the situation that seem to be important (that is, either "red" is correct or "odd" is correct). If the next problem is BRR, the child may again pick the red light and fail to receive a reward. At this point, he or she should immediately recognize that the mediator "red" is wrong and that picking the "odd" stimulus is the key to solving these problems. So children who use mediators are quick to acquire the oddity concept. In contrast, younger children who do not use these subvocal mediators are likely to keep selecting whatever stimulus has been reinforced most often in the recent past. After trying and eliminating many unsuccessful strategies (for example, different colors and positions), the child may eventually begin to pick the odd stimulus if he or she ever associates this strategy with the presentation of reinforcement.

The mediational model also explains why older children learn reversal shifts much more quickly than nonreversal shifts. If originally reinforced for picking the larger of two objects that also differ in color, the 7-year-old who uses mediators is likely to label size as the important dimension and color as irrelevant. When faced with a reversal shift in which the smaller stimulus is now rewarded, the child quickly learns this discrimination; after all, size is still the relevant mediator, and the learner merely has to change responses from "large" to "small." In contrast, nonreversal shifts are more difficult because the child has to switch mediators (from size to color) and then discover which of the two colors is correct.

It is interesting to note that younger children begin to perform like older children if they are told to use verbal mediators while working on reversal/nonreversal discrimination problems

(Kendler & Kendler, 1975). This finding is similar to the results of Coates and Hartup's (1969) experiment, in which 4-year-olds became much more proficient at reproducing the behavior of a model when they were instructed to describe the model's acts as they observed them. In sum, preschool children are quite capable of using verbal mediators to improve their performance on learning tasks, so there is no **mediation deficiency.** Their problem is best described as a **production deficiency**—that is, they do not ordinarily generate and use these verbal "learning aids" unless they are explicitly instructed to do so.

A cognitive explanation. The younger child's failure to produce verbal mediators suggests that language development may be in some way responsible for the "5 to 7 shift" and perhaps a number of other important cognitive advances as well. Several theorists have adopted this point of view, arguing that language, which is acquired very early, provides children with a remarkably effective method of representing and retaining any number of abstract experiences (Bruner, 1964; Vygotsky, 1962). Presumably, school-age children have become more proficient at reasoning and problem solving because they have acquired more language than their younger counterparts and have had more experience in using a wider variety of linguistic concepts to direct their thinking.

Jean Piaget (1970), however, argues that cognitive development comes first and provides the

---

nonreversal shift: *a type of discrimination learning in which subjects who have learned to respond to one aspect of a dimension (for example, large) must now learn to respond to some aspect of a different dimension (for example, black).*

mediator: *an event that intervenes between a stimulus and a response.*

mediational hypothesis: *the notion that older children are better learners than younger children because they are more likely to use verbal mediators as learning aids.*

mediation deficiency: *an inability to use verbal mediators to facilitate learning.*

production deficiency: *a failure to generate the verbal mediators that would facilitate learning.*

foundation for language development. Piaget's meticulous observations of intellectual growth during the first two years suggest that a number of cognitive advances are necessary before infants are even capable of using a word to label an object or represent an experience (these early intellectual developments are discussed at length in Chapter Nine). Moreover, Hans Furth (1971) reports that deaf children who have acquired little or no language perform at about the same level as speaking children on various reasoning and problem-solving tasks. These findings are quite consistent with Piaget's theory and imply that language is not absolutely necessary for children to acquire a normal range of intellectual abilities.

Piaget's **cognitive hypothesis** is that the "5 to 7 shift" is due to a number of impressive intellectual developments that occur at about this same time. For example, 5 to 7 is the period when children first begin to think about language and its properties and will recognize that speech can serve as something other than a means of communicating. Piaget believes that this emerging sense of **"metalinguistic awareness"** (a cognitive advance) is responsible for the spontaneous production and use of verbal mediators as learning aids. Moreover, Piaget has found that the thinking of preschool children tends to be focused, or **centered,** on only one aspect of a problem at a time. Not until age 5–7 will children *decenter* (a cognitive advance) and begin to evaluate several alternative hypotheses as they try to solve a problem.

Consider how Piaget might explain the preschool child's difficulties with oddity problems. We've seen that a younger child who is reinforced for picking the red light on the problems GGR, RBB, and GRG is likely to stay with red for the next several problems, even if this choice is no longer reinforced. Why? Piaget would argue that the child's thinking is centered on only one aspect of the problem—color—and hence he will fail to recognize that the colored light that has been reinforced was also the "odd" light. And since the younger child is merely responding to the perception of "redness" without labeling this feature, he may persist in picking the red light for several successive problems before switching to another strategy that may be equally inappropriate (for example, picking the green light or the one in the middle). In contrast, a 7-year-old who is exposed to the same problem set will consider (and probably label) all the features that may lead to reinforcement—the position of the light in the stimulus array, its color, and the fact that it is "different" from the two nonreinforced stimuli. As soon as he then sees that position and color are not the appropriate dimensions, he will quickly discard these alternative hypotheses and respond to the "odd" stimulus on all subsequent problems.

In sum, Piaget would agree that the production of verbal mediators will improve children's performance on a variety of learning tasks. However, he argues that several important cognitive advances that occur between the ages of 5 and 7 are responsible for both the spontaneous use of mediational strategies and the "5 to 7 shift."

SUMMARY

Learning is a relatively permanent change in behavior that occurs as a result of practice or experience. It is the process by which we acquire new information, attitudes, abilities, and behaviors.

Perhaps the simplest form of learning is habituation—a process in which infants come to recognize and cease responding to stimuli that are presented over and over. For older children and adults, repeated exposure to a stimulus may lead to the development of favorable attitudes toward that object, activity, or situation—a form of learning called the "mere exposure" effect.

In classical conditioning, an initially neutral, or conditioned, stimulus (for example, a bell) is repeatedly paired with a nonneutral, or unconditioned, stimulus (for example, food) that always elicits an unconditioned response (salivation). After several such pairings, the conditioned stimulus alone will acquire the capacity to evoke what is now called a "conditioned" response (in this case, salivation). Many of our attitudes and emotional responses (for example, fears) may be conditioned reactions that are acquired through classical conditioning.

In operant, or instrumental, conditioning, the subject first emits a response and then associates this action with a particular outcome. Reinforcers are outcomes that increase the probability that a response will be repeated; punishments are outcomes that suppress an act and decrease the likelihood that it will be repeated. Even very young infants can learn to alter their behavior to obtain reinforcement. Complex responses may be acquired through a process called "shaping" in which a subject is reinforced for emitting successively closer approximations of the desired behavior. Among the factors that determine the strength or effectiveness of operant conditioning are the timing of reinforcement, the scheduling of reinforcement, and the subject's need for (or valuation of) the stimulus offered as a reinforcer.

According to the "Premack principle" of reinforcement, any event or activity can reinforce a behavior as long as it is more probable than that behavior. However, stimuli offered as incentives may actually inhibit a response that a person would ordinarily perform for its intrinsic satisfaction. This finding indicates that it is the learner, rather than the teacher, who determines which events are the most potent reinforcers for any given activity.

Punishment is designed to inhibit undesirable responses. Factors that influence the effectiveness of punishment include its timing, intensity, consistency, and underlying rationale, as well as the relationship between the subject and the punitive agent. When applied improperly, punishment may produce a number of undesirable side effects that limit its usefulness. Reinforcement of incompatible behaviors and use of self-instructional techniques are viable alternatives to punishment that produce few if any side effects.

Much of what children learn is acquired by observing the behavior of social models. This "observational learning" occurs as the child attends to the model and constructs symbolic representations of the model's behavior. These symbolic codes are then stored in memory and may be retrieved at a later date to guide the child's attempts to imitate the behavior he or she has witnessed. Reinforcement is not necessary for observational *learning.* What reinforcement does is to increase the likelihood that children will *perform* that which they have already learned by observing a model.

Over the first two years, infants gradually become more proficient at imitating simple motor responses. At about age 2, children have progressed to the point that they can construct symbolic representations of a modeled sequence and imitate a model who is no longer present. Grade school children (aged 7–8) eventually begin to use verbal labels to represent and retain what they have observed, and as a result, they may learn more from social models than younger children do.

Between the ages of 18 months and 3 years, children become increasingly responsive to models on television. Advertising clearly affects the behavior of young children, and those who watch a lot of violence on TV are likely to acquire aggressive responses. However, media models can also promote new cognitive skills, help children to overcome their fears, and teach positive values such as cooperation and sharing.

Generalization is an important aspect of all types of learning. The generalization principle states that responses learned to one cue or situation are likely to recur whenever we encounter similar cues or situations. One reason that even very young children soon develop stable habits is that they recognize that many new objects or situations are similar to those they have experienced before and will call for a similar (generalized) response. But there are also many occasions when children are expected to respond quite differently to similar cues—a process called "discrimination." Parents often help their children to make important discriminations by applying different labels to the stimuli that the child is expected to distinguish.

Between the ages of 5 and 7, there are significant changes both in the character of children's learning and in the strategies they use to form concepts and solve problems. According to the mediational model, older children are better learners than younger ones because they are more likely to rely on verbal mediators as learning aids.

---

cognitive hypothesis: *the notion that older children are better learners than younger children because of a number of intellectual developments they have experienced.*

metalinguistic awareness: *a knowledge of language and its properties; an understanding that language can be used for purposes other than communicating.*

centration: *a tendency to focus on only one aspect of a problem when two or more aspects are relevant.*

Cognitive theorists concede that this may be true, although they add that important intellectual advances that occur between ages 5 and 7 are responsible for both the spontaneous use of verbal mediators and the "5 to 7 shift."

REFERENCES

Anderson, D. R., Lorch, E. P., Field, D. E., & Sanders, J. (1981). The effects of TV program comprehensibility on preschool children's visual attention to television. *Child Development, 52,* 151–157.

Aronfreed, J. (1968). Aversive control of internalization. In W. J. Arnold (Ed.), *Nebraska Symposium on Motivation* (Vol. 6). Lincoln: University of Nebraska Press.

Aronfreed, J. (1976). Moral development from the standpoint of a general psychological theory. In T. Lickona (Ed.), *Moral development and behavior.* New York: Holt, Rinehart and Winston.

Aronson, E. (1976). *The social animal.* San Francisco: W. H. Freeman.

Babad, E. Y. (1972). Person specificity of the "social deprivation-satiation effect." *Developmental Psychology, 6,* 210–213.

Babad, E. Y. (1973). Effects of informational input on the "social deprivation-satiation effect." *Journal of Personality and Social Psychology, 27,* 1–5.

Ball, S., & Bogatz, J. (1972). Summative research of Sesame Street: Implications for the study of preschool children. In A. D. Pick (Ed.), *Minnesota Symposia on Child Psychology* (Vol. 6). Minneapolis: University of Minnesota Press.

Bandura, A. (1965). Influence of models' reinforcement contingencies on the acquisition of imitative responses. *Journal of Personality and Social Psychology, 1,* 589–595.

Bandura, A. (1977). *Social learning theory.* Englewood Cliffs, NJ: Prentice-Hall.

Bandura, A., Grusec, J. E., & Menlove, F. L. (1966). Observational learning as a function of symbolization and incentive set. *Child Development, 37,* 499–506.

Bandura, A., & Harris, M. B. (1966). Modification of syntactic style. *Journal of Experimental Child Psychology, 4,* 341–352.

Bandura, A., & Menlove, F. L. (1968). Factors determining vicarious extinction of avoidance behavior through symbolic modeling. *Journal of Personality and Social Psychology, 8,* 99–108.

Bandura, A., & Walters, R. H. (1963). *Social learning and personality development.* New York: Holt, Rinehart and Winston.

Barcus, F. E. (1978). *Commercial children's television on weekends and weekday afternoons.* Newtonville, MA: Action for Children's Television.

Belson, W. A. (1978). *Television violence and the adolescent boy.* Westmead, England: Saxon House.

Bijou, S. W. (1957). Patterns of reinforcement and resistance to extinction in young children. *Child Development, 28,* 47–54.

Birch, L. L. (1981). Generalization of a modified food preference. *Child Development, 52,* 755–758.

Brody, G. H., & Stoneman, Z. (1981). Selective imitation of same-age, older, and younger peer models. *Child Development, 52,* 717–720.

Bruner, J. (1964). The course of cognitive growth. *American Psychologist, 19,* 1–15.

Calvert, S. L., Huston, A. C., Watkins, B. A., & Wright, J. C. (1982). The relation between selective attention to television forms and children's comprehension of content. *Child Development, 53,* 601–610.

Campbell, T., Ross, R. P., Wright, J. C., Huston, A. C., Rice, M., & Turk, P. (1981, May). *The effects of celebrity endorsement in television ads.* Paper presented at annual meeting of the International Communication Association, Minneapolis.

Coates, B., & Hartup, W. W. (1969). Age and verbalization in observational learning. *Developmental Psychology, 1,* 556–562.

Collins, W. A., Wellman, H., Keniston, A. H., & Westby, S. D. (1978). Age-related aspects of comprehension and inference from a televised dramatic narrative. *Child Development, 49,* 389–399.

Danner, F. W., & Lonky, E. (1981). A cognitive-developmental approach to the effects of rewards on intrinsic motivation. *Child Development, 52,* 1043–1052.

Deur, J. L., & Parke, R. D. (1970). The effects of inconsistent punishment on aggression in children. *Developmental Psychology, 2,* 403–411.

Domjan, M., & Burkhard, B. (1982). *The principles of learning and behavior.* Monterey, CA: Brooks/Cole.

Eron, L. D., & Huesmann, L. R. (1980). Adolescent aggression and television. *Annals of the New York Academy of Sciences, 347,* 314–331.

Eron, L. D., Huesmann, L. R., Lefkowitz, M. M., & Walder, L. O. (1972). Does television violence cause aggression? *American Psychologist, 27,* 253–263.

Eron, L. D., Walder, L. O., Huesmann, L. R., & Lefkowitz, M. M. (1974). The convergence of laboratory and field studies of the development of aggression. In J. deWit & W. W. Hartup (Eds.), *Determinants and origins of aggressive behavior.* The Hague: Mouton.

Fagan, J. F., III. (1979). The origins of facial pattern recognition. In M. H. Bornstein & W. Kessen (Eds.), *Psychological development from infancy: Image to intention.* Hillsdale, NJ: Erlbaum.

Federal Trade Commission. (1978). *FTC staff report on television advertising to children.* Washington, DC: U.S. Government Printing Office.

Field, T. M., Woodson, R., Greenberg, R., & Cohen, D. (1982). Discrimination and imitation of facial expressions by neonates. *Science, 218,* 179–181.

Fitzgerald, H. E., & Brackbill, Y. (1976). Classical conditioning in infancy: Development and constraints. *Psychological Bulletin, 83,* 353–376.

Friedrich, L. K., & Stein, A. H. (1975). Prosocial television and young children: The effects of verbal labeling and role-playing on learning and behavior. *Child Development, 46,* 27–38.

Friedrich-Cofer, L. K., Huston-Stein, A., Kipnis, D. M., Susman, E. J., & Clewett, A. S. (1979). Environmental enhancement of prosocial television content: Effects on interpersonal behavior, imaginative play, and self-regulation in a natural setting. *Developmental Psychology, 15,* 637–646.

Furth, H. G. (1971). Linguistic deficiency and thinking: Research with deaf subjects, 1964–69. *Psychological Bulletin, 75,* 58–72.

Galst, J. P. (1980). Television food commercials and pronutritional public service announcements as determinants of young children's snack choices. *Child Development, 51,* 935–938.

Gerbner, G., Gross, L., Morgan, M., & Signorelli, N. (1980). The "mainstreaming" of America: Violence profile no. 11. *Journal of Communication, 30,* 10–29.

Gewirtz, J. L. (1969). Mechanisms of social learning: Some roles of stimulation and behavior in early human development. In D. A. Goslin (Ed.), *Handbook of socialization theory and research.* Chicago: Rand McNally.

Gollin, E. S., & Shirk, E. J. (1966). A developmental study of oddity problem learning in young children. *Child Development, 37,* 213–217.

Goodman, S. H. (1981). The integration of verbal and motor behavior in preschool children. *Child Development, 52,* 280–289.

Graziano, W. G., Brody, G. H., & Bernstein, S. (1980). Effects of information about future allocation and peer's motivation on peer reward allocations. *Developmental Psychology, 16,* 475–482.

Grusec, J. E., & Abramovitch, R. (1982). Imitation of peers and adults in a natural setting: A functional analysis. *Child Development, 53,* 636–642.

Grusec, J. E., & Brinker, D. B. (1972). Reinforcement for imitation as a social learning determinant with implications for sex-role development. *Journal of Personality and Social Psychology, 21,* 149–158.

Grusec, J. E., & Kuczynski, L. (1980). Direction of effect in socialization: A comparison of the parent's versus the child's behavior as determinants of disciplinary techniques. *Developmental Psychology, 16,* 1–9.

Gunnar, M. R. (1980). Control, warning signals, and distress in infancy. *Developmental Psychology, 16,* 281–289.

Hansen, G. D. (1979). Enuresis control through fading, escape, and avoidance training. *Journal of Applied Behavior Analysis, 12,* 303–307.

Harlow, H. F. (1949). The formation of learning sets. *Psychological Review, 56,* 61–65.

Harlow, H. F., & Harlow, M. K. (1949). Learning to think. *Scientific American, 181,* 36–39.

Hayes, D. S., Chemelski, B. E., & Birnbaum, D. W. (1981). Young children's incidental and intentional retention of televised events. *Developmental Psychology, 17,* 230–232.

Holden, G. W. (1983). Avoiding conflict: Mothers as tacticians in the supermarket. *Child Development, 54,* 233–240.

Homme, L. E., deBaca, P. C., Devine, J. V., Steinhorst, R., & Rickert, E. J. (1963). Use of the Premack principle in controlling the behavior of nursery school children. *Journal of the Experimental Analysis of Behavior, 6,* 544.

Huesmann, L. R. (1982). Television violence and aggressive behavior. In D. Pearl, L. Bouthilet, & J. Lazer (Eds.), *Television and behavior: Ten years of scientific progress and implications for the eighties* (Vol. 2). Washington, DC: U.S. Government Printing Office.

Jones, M. C. (1924). A laboratory study of fear: The case of Peter. *Pedagogical Seminary, 31,* 308–315.

Kendler, H. H., & Kendler, T. S. (1975). From discrimination learning to cognitive development: A neobehavioristic odyssey. In W. K. Estes (Ed.), *Handbook of learning and cognitive processes* (Vol. 1). Hillsdale, NJ: Erlbaum.

Kendler, T. S., Kendler, H. H., & Leonard, B. (1962). Mediated responses to size and brightness as a function of age. *American Journal of Psychology, 75,* 571–586.

Kron, R. E. (1966). Instrumental conditioning of nutritive sucking behavior in the newborn. *Recent Advances in Biological Psychiatry, 9,* 295–300.

Kuczynski, L. (1983). Reasoning, prohibitions, and motivations for compliance. *Developmental Psychology, 19,* 126–134.

Lepper, M. R. (1980). Intrinsic and extrinsic motivation in children: Detrimental effects of superfluous social controls. In W. A. Collins (Ed.), *Minnesota Symposia on Child Psychology* (Vol. 14). Hillsdale, NJ: Erlbaum.

Lepper, M. R., Greene, D., & Nisbett, R. E. (1973). Undermining children's intrinsic interest with extrinsic reward: A test of the overjustification hypothesis. *Journal of Personality and Social Psychology, 28,* 129–137.

Levin, S. R., Petros, T. V., & Petrella, F. W. (1982). Preschoolers' awareness of television advertising. *Child Development, 53,* 933–937.

Levinson, B., & Reese, H. W. (1967). Patterns of discrimination learning set in preschool children, fifth graders, college freshmen, and the aged. *Monographs of the Society for Research in Child Development, 32* (Serial No. 115).

Levitt, M. J. (1980). Contingent feedback, familiarization, and infant affect: How a stranger becomes a friend. *Developmental Psychology, 16,* 425–432.

Lewis, M. (1971). Individual differences in the measurement of early cognitive growth. In J. Hellmuth (Ed.), *Exceptional infant: Studies in abnormality* (Vol. 2). New York: Brunner/Mazel.

Liebert, R. M., Sprafkin, J. N., & Davidson, E. S. (1982). *The early window: Effects of television on children and youth* (2nd ed.). New York: Pergamon Press.

Linn, M. C., de Benedictis, T., & Delucchi, K. (1982). Adolescent reasoning about advertisements: Preliminary investigations. *Child Development, 53,* 1599–1613.

Lipsitt, L. P., & Kaye, H. (1964). Conditioned sucking in the human newborn. *Psychonomic Science, 1,* 29–30.

Lovaas, O. I. (1966). A program for the establishment of speech in psychotic children. In J. Wing (Ed.), *Childhood autism.* London: Pergamon Press.

Lovaas, O. I. (1976). *Language acquisition programs for nonlinguistic children.* New York: Irvington.

Lovaas, O. I., Freitas, L., Nelson, K., & Whalen, C. (1967). The establishment of imitation and its use for the development of complex behavior in schizophrenic children. *Behavior Research and Therapy, 5,* 171–181.

Lovaas, O. I., Schreibman, L., & Koegel, R. L. (1976). A behavior modification approach to the treatment of autistic children. In E. Schopler & R. J. Reichler (Eds.), *Psychopathology and child development.* New York: Plenum Press.

Loveland, K. K., & Olley, J. G. (1979). The effect of external reward on interest and quality of task performance in children of high or low intrinsic motivation. *Child Development, 50,* 1207–1210.

Luria, A. R. (1961). *The role of speech in the regulation of normal and abnormal behavior.* New York: Liveright.

Lyle, J. L., & Hoffman, H. R. (1972). Explorations in patterns of television viewing by preschool-age children. In E. A. Rubinstein, G. A. Comstock, & J. P. Murray (Eds.), *Television and social behavior* (Vol. 4). Washington, DC: U.S. Government Printing Office.

Martin, J. A. (1977). Effects of positive and negative adult-child interactions on children's task performances. *Journal of Experimental Child Psychology, 23,* 493–502.

McCall, R. B., Parke, R., & Kavanaugh, R. (1977). Imitation of live and televised models in children 1–3 years of age. *Monographs of the Society for Research in Child Development, 42* (Serial No. 173).

McLoyd, V. C. (1979). The effects of extrinsic rewards of differential value on high and low intrinsic interest. *Child Development, 50,* 1010–1019.

Millar, W. S., & Watson, J. S. (1979). The effect of delayed feedback on infant learning reexamined. *Child Development, 50,* 747–751.

Mulhern, R. K., & Passman, R. H. (1981). Parental discipline as affected by sex of parent, the sex of the child, and the child's apparent responsiveness to discipline. *Developmental Psychology, 17,* 604–613.

Pallak, S. R., Costomiris, S., Sroka, S., & Pittman, T. S. (1982). School experience, reward characteristics, and intrinsic motivation. *Child Development, 53,* 1382–1391.

Papousek, H. (1961). Conditioned head rotation reflexes in infants in the first months of life. *Acta Pediatrica, 50,* 565–576.

Papousek, H. (1967). Experimental studies of appetitional behavior in human newborns and infants. In H. W. Stevenson, E. H. Hess, & H. L. Rheingold (Eds.), *Early behavior: Comparative and developmental approaches.* New York: Wiley.

Parke, R. D. (1969). Effectiveness of punishment as an interaction of intensity, timing, agent nurturance and cognitive structuring. *Child Development, 40,* 213–236.

Parke, R. D. (1972). Some effects of punishment on children's behavior. In W. W. Hartup (Ed.), *The young child* (Vol. 2). Washington, DC: National Association for the Education of Young Children.

Parke, R. D. (1977). Some effects of punishment on children's behavior—revisited. In E. M. Hetherington & R. D. Parke (Eds.), *Contemporary readings in child psychology.* New York: McGraw-Hill.

Parke, R. D., & Collmer, C. W. (1975). Child abuse: An interdisciplinary analysis. In E. M. Hetherington (Ed.), *Review of child development research* (Vol. 5). Chicago: University of Chicago Press.

Perry, D. G., & Garrow, H. (1975). The "social deprivation-satiation effect": An outcome of frequency or perceived contingency. *Developmental Psychology, 11,* 681–688.

Perry, D. G., & Parke, R. D. (1975). Punishment and alternative response training as determinants of response inhibition in children. *Genetic Psychology Monographs, 91,* 724–731.

Piaget, J. (1951). *Play, dreams, and imitation in childhood.* New York: Norton.

Piaget, J. (1970). Piaget's theory. In P. H. Mussen (Ed.), *Carmichael's manual of child psychology* (Vol. 1). New York: Wiley.

Powers, R. B., & Osborne, J. G. (1976). *Fundamentals of behavior.* St. Paul: West Publishing.

Premack, D. (1965). Reinforcement theory. In D. Levine (Ed.), *Nebraska Symposium on Motivation* (Vol. 13). Lincoln: University of Nebraska Press.

Premack, D. (1971). Catching up with common sense, or two sides of a generalization: Reinforcement and punishment. In R. Glaser (Ed.), *The nature of reinforcement.* New York: Academic Press.

Redd, W. H., Morris, E. K., & Martin, J. A. (1975). Effects of positive and negative adult-child interactions on children's social preferences. *Journal of Experimental Child Psychology, 19,* 153–164.

Robertson, T. S., & Rossiter, J. R. (1974). Children and commercial persuasion: An attribution theory analysis. *Journal of Consumer Research, 1,* 13–20.

Rose, S. A. (1981). Developmental changes in infants' retention of visual stimuli. *Child Development, 52,* 227–233.

Sears, R. R., Maccoby, E. E., & Levin, H. (1957). *Patterns of child rearing.* New York: Harper & Row.

Seligman, M. E. P. (1975). *Helplessness: On depression, development, and death.* San Francisco: W. H. Freeman.

Seligman, M. E. P. (1978). Comment and integration. *Journal of Abnormal Psychology, 87,* 165–179.

Shaffer, D. R. (1979). *Social and personality development.* Monterey, CA: Brooks/Cole.

Sigman, M., Kopp, C. B., Littman, B., & Parmelee, A. (1977). Infant visual attentiveness in relation to birth condition. *Developmental Psychology, 13,* 431–437.

Skinner, B. F. (1953). *Science and human behavior.* New York: Macmillan.

Staats, A. W. (1975). *Social behaviorism.* Homewood, IL: Dorsey Press.

Stoneman, Z., & Brody, G. H. (1981). Peers as mediators of television food advertisements aimed at children. *Developmental Psychology, 17,* 853–858.

Thorndike, E. L. (1898). Animal intelligence: An experimental study of the association processes in animals. *Psychological Review Monographs, 2* (Whole No. 8).

Tinsley, V. S., & Waters, H. S. (1982). The development of verbal control over motor behavior: A replication and extension of Luria's findings. *Child Development, 53,* 746–753.

Verna, G. B. (1977). The effects of a four-hour delay of punishment under two conditions of verbal instruction. *Child Development, 48,* 621–624.

Vygotsky, L. S. (1962). *Thought and language.* Cambridge, MA: M.I.T. Press.

Watson, J. B., & Raynor, R. (1920). Conditioned emotional reactions. *Journal of Experimental Psychology, 3,* 1–14.

Watson, J. S., & Ramey, C. T. (1972). Reactions to response-contingent stimulation in early infancy. *Merrill-Palmer Quarterly, 18,* 219–228.

White, S. H. (1965). Evidence for a hierarchical arrangement of learning processes. In L. P. Lipsitt & C. C. Spiker (Eds.), *Advances in child development and behavior* (Vol. 2). New York: Academic Press.

Willemsen, E. (1979). *Understanding infancy.* San Francisco: W. H. Freeman.

Worchel, S., & Cooper, J. (1983). *Understanding social psychology.* Homewood, IL: Dorsey Press.

Zimmerman, B. J. (1977). Modeling. In H. Hom & P. Robinson (Eds.), *Psychological processes in early education.* New York: Academic Press.

CHAPTER EIGHT ■

DEVELOPMENT OF LANGUAGE AND COMMUNICATION SKILLS

■ *Two basic questions about language development*
The "what" question
The "how" question

■ *Before language: The prelinguistic stage*
The infant's reactions to language
Producing sounds: The infant's prelinguistic vocalizations
Are prelinguistic vocalizations related to meaningful speech?
What do prelinguistic infants know about language?

■ *One word at a time: The holophrastic stage*
The infant's choice of words
Individual differences in language production
Early semantics: The development of word meanings

■ *From holophrases to simple sentences: The telegraphic stage*
Characteristics of telegraphic speech
Grammatical analyses of early speech
The pragmatics of early speech

■ *Language learning during the preschool period*
Acquiring grammatical morphemes
Mastering transformational rules
Semantic development
Pragmatics and communication skills

■ *Refinement of language skills*
Later syntactic development
Semantics and metalinguistic awareness
Growth of communication skills

■ *Theories of language development*
Learning theories
The nativist perspective
The interactionist perspective

■ *Summary*

*O*ne truly remarkable achievement that sets us humans apart from the rest of the animal kingdom is our creation and use of **language.** Although animals can **communicate** with one another, their limited number of calls and gestures are merely isolated signals that convey very specific messages (for example, a greeting, a threat, a summons to congregate) in much the same way that single words or stereotyped phrases do in a human language. By contrast, human languages are amazingly flexible and productive. From a small number of individually meaningless sounds, a person who is proficient in a language can generate thousands of meaningful auditory patterns (syllables, words) that can then be combined according to a set of grammatical rules to produce an infinite number of messages. Language is also an *inventive* tool. Most of what people say or hear in any given situation is not merely a repetition of what they have said or heard before; speakers create novel utterances on the spot, and the topics they talk about may not have anything to do with their current situation or the stream of ongoing events. Yet, creative as we may be in generating new messages, other people who know the language will be able to understand any and all of our ideas as long as each of our statements adheres to the rules and conventions of the language we are speaking.

Although language is one of the most abstract bodies of knowledge we will ever acquire, children in all cultures come to understand and use this intricate form of communication very early in life. Indeed, many infants are talking before they can walk. And by age 5, children not only understand most of the grammatical rules of their native tongue but are also constructing remarkably complex, adultlike sentences even though they have

---

language: *a small number of individually meaningless signals (sounds, letters, gestures) that can be combined according to agreed-on rules to produce an infinite number of messages.*
communication: *the process by which one organism transmits information to and influences another.*

285

PHOTO 8-1. *Animals communicate through a series of calls and gestures that convey a limited number of very specific messages.*

had no formal training in language. To a college student struggling with French, German, Spanish, or Russian, it may seem that children acquire language almost effortlessly.

The young child's remarkable capacity for language learning is a puzzling phenomenon that raises many questions. Are infants biologically programmed to acquire language? What kinds of linguistic input must they receive in order to become language users? Is there any relation between a child's cooing, gesturing, or babbling and the later production of meaningful words? How do infants and toddlers come to attach meaning to words? Do all children pass through the same steps or stages as they acquire their native language? And what must children learn to become truly effective communicators? These are but a few of the issues we will consider as we trace the development of children's linguistic skills and try to determine how youngsters become so proficient in using language at such an early age.

TWO BASIC QUESTIONS ABOUT LANGUAGE DEVELOPMENT

Those who study language development have tried to answer two very basic questions. The first is the "what" question—what is the normal course of language development, and just what are children acquiring that enables them to master the intricacies of their native tongue? The second is the "how" question—how is it that young children who have never had the benefit of formal schooling are nevertheless rather adept at using an abstract symbol system like language long before they ever set foot in a classroom? Before we start to grapple with these complex issues, it may be helpful to expand a bit on each of them so that we will see where we are headed and what we may be up against.

The "What" Question

What must children learn in order to become users of a language? Researchers have traditionally argued that three kinds of knowledge are essential: a knowledge of phonology, a knowledge of semantics, and a knowledge of syntax.

■ *Phonology*

Phonology refers to the basic units of sound, or **phonemes,** that are combined to produce words and sentences. Each language uses only a subset of the sounds that human beings are capable of generating. For example, English makes use of 45 phonemes, and no language uses more than 100. Each language has rules for combining phonemes and for pronouncing these phonemic combinations. For instance, speakers of English recognize that it is quite permissible to begin a word with *st-* (*stop, student*) or *sk-* (*skit, skull*) but not *sb-* or *sg-*. English-speaking people immediately discriminate the phonemic combinations "zip" and "sip," although Spanish speakers may not, because the Spanish language does not distinguish words on the basis of the difference between the phonemes *z* and *s*. The point for our purposes is that children must learn to hear and to pronounce a number of these speechlike sounds in order to make sense of the speech they hear and to be understood when they try to speak (de Villiers & de Villiers, 1979).

■ *Semantics*

Children must also learn how individually meaningless phonemes are combined to produce meaningful units of language called **morphemes.** Morphemes are words or grammatical markers (such as *-ed* for past tense) with "meanings" that are *arbitrarily* assigned. For example, the relation of the word *dog* to the furry, four-legged creature we know as a dog is completely arbitrary—a product of social convention. We could have just as easily labeled the animal in question a "chien," which is exactly what the French have done.

Semantics refers to the expressed meaning of words and sentences. Clearly, children must recognize that words convey meaning—that words refer to particular objects, actions, and relations—before they will comprehend the speech of others and be understood when they speak. How do children learn the meanings of individual words? How do they come to understand words that express relations, such as *in, on,* and *under; front* and *back;* or *large* and *small?* When do they first realize that the furry, four-legged family pet that they know as "doggie" is also an "animal" but at the same time is a fox terrier with a proper name such as "Fang" or "Pixie"? These are some of the questions that students of language development are now trying to answer.

■ *Syntax*

Syntax refers to the form, or structure, of a language—the rules that specify how words are combined to form meaningful sentences. Each language has its own set of syntactical rules that define the function of various words in a sentence and give the sentence a meaning. Consider the following examples:

1. John hit Jim.
2. Jim hit John.

These two statements contain precisely the same words but have very different meanings. In English there is a syntactical rule that in an active sentence the noun preceding the verb names the *agent* of action, and the noun following the verb names the *object* of that action. The sentence "Jim John hit" violates the rules of word order for English and is ungrammatical, although this order is perfectly acceptable in a language like French, where the noun naming the object of an action may immediately precede the verb.

The "Jim/John" example illustrates how the meanings of individual words in a sentence interact with sentence structure to give the entire sentence a meaning. This basic principle is true of all languages even though the rules of sentence construction (syntax) vary considerably from language to language. So it would seem that children must acquire a basic understanding of the syntactical features of their native tongue before they

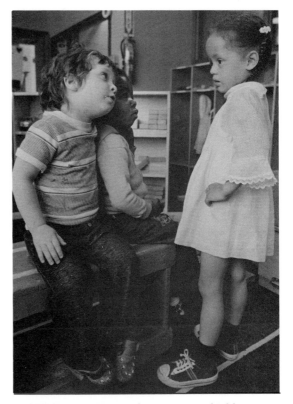

PHOTO 8-2. *Human languages are highly flexible and productive. By the age of 4 or 5, preschool children are able to combine a small number of individually meaningless sounds into thousands of words and phrases to produce an infinite number of messages.*

phonology: *the sound system of a language and the rules for combining these sounds to produce meaningful units of speech.*

phonemes: *the basic units of sound that are used in a spoken language.*

morphemes: *the smallest meaningful units of language; these include words and grammatical markers such as prefixes, suffixes, and verb-tense modifiers (for example, -ed, -ing).*

semantics: *the expressed meaning of words and sentences.*

syntax: *the structure of a language; the rules specifying how words and grammatical markers are to be combined to produce meaningful sentences.*

will become very proficient at speaking or understanding that language.

■ *Pragmatics—the fourth aspect of language learning*

A knowledge of phonology, semantics, and syntax will enable children to produce grammatical sentences, but there is no guarantee that the speech they generate will be appropriate for the setting in which they find themselves. Recently, psychologists such as Elizabeth Bates (1976b) have noted that young children must also acquire another important set of rules called the **pragmatics** of language—that is, the principles specifying how language is to be used in different contexts and situations. In other words, the child must learn "when" to say "what" to "whom" in order to communicate effectively and achieve his or her underlying objectives. Consider the case of a 6-year-old girl who is trying to explain a new game to her 2-year-old brother. Clearly, the older child cannot speak to this little toddler as if he were an adult or an age mate; she will have to adjust her speech to his linguistic capabilities if she hopes to be understood.

Children must learn not only *what* to say to other listeners but also *how* to say it appropriately. For example, a 3-year-old may not yet realize that the best way of obtaining a cookie from Grandma is to say "Grandma, may I please have a cookie?" rather than stating in a demanding tone "Gimme a cookie, Grandma!" In order to communicate most effectively, children must become "social editors" and take into account where they are, with whom they are speaking, what the listener already knows, and what the listener needs or wants to hear. These pragmatic abilities and social editing skills evolve rather gradually over the course of childhood and are now recognized as being important aspects of language development.

The "How" Question

As we noted, most 5-year-olds, who have had no formal linguistic training, have already mastered the basic syntax of their language and are quite capable of understanding all but the most complex sentences that they may hear. Perhaps even more remarkable, many severely retarded children who can neither count nor remember the rules of simple games are able to construct grammatical sentences and converse rather well (Lenneberg, 1967). How is this possible? How can we account for the young child's remarkable proficiency with this totally arbitrary and abstract symbol system that we know as language?

In reviewing the various theories of language development, we will once again run headlong into the *nativist/empiricist* (nature/nurture) controversy. *Learning theorists* represent the empiricist point of view. They contend that children will gradually learn a language as they imitate the speech they hear and are reinforced by adults for successive approximations of adult language. Presumably the process begins as parents and other close companions selectively reinforce those aspects of babbling (for example, "pa-pa"; "ma-ma") that sound most like words, thereby increasing the frequency of these vocalizations. Reinforcement is then gradually withheld until the child is imitating words, then word phrases, and finally grammatical utterances.

Clearly imitation must be involved in language learning, for children invariably acquire and use the same language that their caregivers do. However, *nativists* have argued that imitation cannot be the major mechanism by which children learn a language. If imitation were the central process in language learning, we wouldn't hear children producing utterances such as "poon" (for "spoon") or "I brushed my tooths" that do not appear in the speech of their older companions. Moreover, nativists contend that parents do not sit down with their children and attempt to shape their grammar; in fact, studies of vocal interactions between parents and young children suggest that parents pay little if any attention to the grammatical correctness or incorrectness of their children's statements (Slobin, 1979).

So how do nativists account for language acquisition? Theorists such as Noam Chomsky (1968, 1975) and David McNeill (1970) propose that human beings have inherited an inborn capacity for language learning called the **language acquisition device (LAD).** The LAD is not necessarily a particular structure or area of the brain but, rather, a set of perceptual and cognitive abilities that analyze linguistic input. Presumably these innate language-processing skills enable

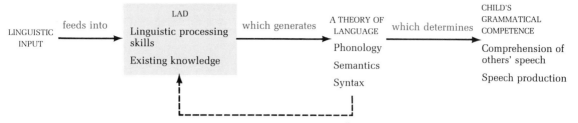

FIGURE 8-1. A model of language acquisition proposed by nativists.

young children to infer the phonological patterns, word meanings, and rules of syntax that characterize the speech they are listening to. These inferences about the meaning and structure of linguistic information represent a "theory" of language, which children will then use to guide their own attempts to communicate (see Figure 8-1). As a child matures and has the opportunity to process more and more linguistic input, his or her underlying theory of language will become increasingly sophisticated until it approximates that used by older children and adults. For the nativists, then, language acquisition is quite natural and almost automatic, as long as children have linguistic data to process and someone with whom to communicate.

Before we can decide anything about the relative merits of the nativist and the empiricist explanations of language acquisition, we must review the course of language development and see what it is that children are acquiring and when. Let's begin at birth and trace the steps that infants take on their way to uttering that memorable first word.

BEFORE LANGUAGE: THE PRELINGUISTIC STAGE

For the first 10 to 13 months of life, children are said to be in the **prelinguistic stage** of language development because they are not yet combining the sounds that they are capable of making into utterances that are easily interpretable as words. But even though young infants cannot produce any language, they are quite responsive to speech and other human vocalizations from the day they are born. Let's take a closer look.

The Infant's Reactions to Language

On several occasions, we have seen that young infants may be programmed to "tune in" to human speech. When spoken to, neonates will often open their eyes and look at their caregivers, begin to synchronize their bodily movements with the breaks and pauses in a companion's speech, and sometimes even vocalize themselves (Condon & Sander, 1974; Rosenthal, 1982). By 3 days of age, an infant already recognizes his or her mother's voice and clearly prefers it to the voice of a female stranger (DeCasper & Fifer, 1980). In the first few days of life, speech elicits greater electrical activity from the left half (cerebral hemisphere) of the infant's brain, while music produces greater activity from the right half (Molfese, 1977). This early pattern, which persists into adulthood, suggests that the two hemispheres of the brain are specialized for different acoustical functions from a very early age. Finally, young infants will suck faster to hear recorded speech than to hear instrumental music or other rhythmic sounds (Butterfield & Siperstein, 1972). So babies can discriminate speech from other sound patterns, and

pragmatics: *principles that underlie the effective and appropriate use of language in social contexts.*

language acquisition device (LAD): *a set of linguistic processing skills that nativists believe to be innate; presumably the LAD enables a child to infer the rules governing others' speech and then to use these rules to produce language.*

prelinguistic stage: *the period before children utter their first meaningful words.*

they pay particularly close attention to speech from the very beginning.

Do different samples of speech all sound alike to the very young infant? Apparently not. Peter Eimas (1975) has found that babies are as capable as adults of discriminating consonants such as *b* and *p* or *d* and *t*, even though infants have no idea that these phonetic contrasts are important aspects of language. In fact, 7-month-old infants from homes where English is spoken are better than English-speaking adults at differentiating certain phonemes that are *not* used in English (Werker, Gilbert, Humphrey, & Tees, 1981).

In sum, the abilities to discriminate speech from nonspeech and to differentiate a variety of speechlike sounds are either (1) innate or (2) learned in the first few days and weeks of life. In either case, it would seem that young infants are remarkably well prepared for language learning.

Producing Sounds: The Infant's Prelinguistic Vocalizations

All normal and healthy infants are capable of vocalizing at birth and will typically begin to produce a variety of speechlike sounds long before they utter their first recognizable word. In recent years, **psycholinguists** have found that the vocal abilities of prelinguistic children develop in a step- or stagelike fashion over the first 10–12 months of life. Although children may differ in the ages at which they move from one stage of vocalization to another, the overall sequence of vocal development is roughly the same for virtually all prelinguistic infants.

■ *Crying*
Neonates are capable of producing at least three kinds of cries—a "hunger" cry, a "mad" cry, and a "pain" cry. Although these vocalizations are probably reflexive responses to pain or discomfort rather than deliberate attempts to communicate, it is worth noting that cries—particularly pain cries—function as distress signals that serve to elicit the attention of caregivers (Wolff, 1969).

During the third week of life, many neonates begin to produce a "fake cry" that Peter Wolff (1969) describes as a "cry of low pitch and intensity; it consists of long drawn out moans which occasionally rise to more explicit cries, and then revert to poorly articulated moans" (p. 98). Wolff characterizes these vocalizations as "fake" cries because they are often emitted when the infant does not appear to be discomforted or distressed in any way. Although **fake cries** are often used to attract attention, that is probably not their only function. Wolff (1969) believes that calm, contented infants may sometimes "fake a cry" because they have discovered that they can make interesting noises and have decided to repeat the process for the sheer pleasure of experimenting with sounds.

■ *Cooing*
At about 3–5 weeks of age, infants begin to produce a variety of new sounds that appear to be associated with pleasant states of affairs rather than with discomfort or distress. These "noncrying" vocalizations are vowellike sounds such as "oooooh," "aaaaah," or "uuuuuh" that are likely to be heard after a feeding when the baby is awake, alert, dry, and seemingly contented. Such "sounds of contentment" are called **"coos"** (and the process known as "cooing") because infants tend to repeat the same vowel sound over and over, varying their tone ever so slightly, much as pigeons and doves do when they coo (Lenneberg, 1967; Menyuk, 1977).

■ *Babbling*
At 3 to 4 months of age children begin to add consonant sounds to their vocal repertoires, and by the middle of the first year, they are constructing some consonant/vowel combinations, such as *ka* and *ga*. Within weeks, infants begin to repeat these phonetic combinations and produce **babbles**—utterances such as "baba" or "papa" that sound very much like meaningful speech. But rarely are these early "words" intended as such by the 7–10-month-old infant, who is apt to follow an apparently meaningful utterance such as "papa" with a multisyllabic "papapapapapapa"— a process called **echolalia.** In the opinion of most psycholinguists, the vast majority of infants do not produce their first intelligible "word" until 10–13 months of age (de Villiers & de Villiers, 1979).

The patterns of sounds that infants make between 6 and 10 months of age are very similar across cultures, so that African, French, Japanese, and English babies sound pretty much alike at this stage (Dale, 1976). The babbling infant produces a wide variety of speechlike sounds, some of which do not occur in the language that he or she will acquire. For example, children who hear only English may make a clicking *tsk* sound that appears in South African languages or a blowing *pf* sound that is used in Japanese, even though they have never heard these sounds in anyone's speech (de Villiers & de Villiers, 1979). However, babbling infants do not produce all the sounds that appear in their native language; some of these phonemes will be added later—after children have begun to talk.

■ *Preparing for the transition to meaningful speech*

Babbling changes between 10 and 12 months of age. Infants are now producing a smaller number of phonetic elements than they did during the early babbling stage, and this smaller subset of speechlike sounds consists primarily of the phonemes that appear in the language the child has been listening to. In other words, the later babbling stage is a period when infants are preparing for meaningful speech by adding new sounds that they often hear and dropping others that they hear infrequently (de Villiers & de Villiers, 1979).

Before uttering their first "words," infants have already begun to use sounds to refer to actions, objects, or situations. Some of these early **vocables** may be approximations of adult words; others are the child's own creations (Ferguson, 1977). For example, children might utter the vocable "mmmmmm" when they see or hear a car coming or "aacccch" when they hope to engage a companion in a bout of rough-and-tumble play. According to Charles Ferguson (1977), infants who produce these vocables are about ready to talk. They are now aware that certain speech sounds have consistent meanings, and they have begun to construct their own unique "words" (vocables) from their babbles.

Are Prelinguistic Vocalizations Related to Meaningful Speech?

Does babbling contribute to the development of meaningful speech? Many linguists are skeptical, arguing that early vocal development follows a distinct maturational timetable and that the child's first vocalizations have little if anything to do with the later development of words and sentences (Jakobson, 1968). Surely maturation must play a prominent role in phonological development, for the early babbling of all infants sounds pretty much alike regardless of the language they have been listening to. In fact, deaf infants, who cannot hear the speech of their caregivers, will babble in much the same way that hearing infants do.

But even though the order in which infants produce speechlike sounds depends, in part, on the maturation of the brain and the vocal apparatus, there are reasons to believe that babbling is meaningfully related to later speech. For example, 6–10-month-old infants are already adjusting their babbling to the situation in which they find themselves. They will babble at a higher pitch to their mothers than to their fathers (Lieberman, 1967) and will match the intonation of their babbling to the tonal qualities of the language they are hearing (Weir, 1966). Let's also recall that 10–12-month-old infants have begun to restrict their babbling to the sounds that make up their native language, eliminating other patterns that they rarely hear. Finally, we've seen that the child's first "vocables" and meaningful words are composed of the very sounds that he or she has been producing in the later phases of the babbling stage (Ferguson, 1977). Taken together, these findings imply that the linguistic environment has a major influence on a child's babbling, which, in turn, is related to the language (that is, words and sentences) that the child will eventually produce.

---

psycholinguists: *those who study the structure and development of children's language.*

fake cries: *low-pitched moans that young infants make when seeking attention or experimenting with sounds.*

coos: *vowellike sounds that young infants repeat over and over during periods of contentment.*

babbles: *vowel/consonant combinations that infants begin to produce at about 4 to 6 months of age.*

echolalia: *the tendency of babbling infants to repeat the same sounds over and over.*

vocables: *unique patterns of sound that a prelinguistic infant uses to represent objects, actions, or events.*

BOX 8-1
*WHAT MOTHERS COMMUNICATE BY
THEIR TONE OF VOICE*

Before infants can hope to understand spoken language, they must first recognize that certain patterns of sound within the flow of speech represent meaningful units of information. How do babies begin to isolate and identify recurring speech patterns? How does a child recognize that his mother is trying to influence his behavior when she talks to him? Recently, Daniel Stern and his associates (Stern, Spieker, & MacKain, 1982) have proposed that very young infants might be able to infer an adult's communicative intent from a very subtle linguistic cue—the adult's tone of voice. Of course, this hypothesis implies that caregivers will reliably alter the pitch or intonation of their utterances when trying to communicate different messages to their young infants. But do they?

To find out, Stern et al. (1982) videotaped playful face-to-face interactions between 2- to 6-month-old infants and their mothers. Recordings of each mother's speech were then passed through an instrument called a "sound spectroscope" that provides a picture of the "pitch contour" (or intonational pattern) of an utterance. In addition, the investigators noted the *context* of each utterance—that is, what the infant had been doing just before the mother spoke.

Did mothers tailor their tones of voice to the particular situation or interactive context? Yes, indeed! When the infant looked away, the mother's speech assumed a rising intonation in an attempt to *recapture the baby's attention.* Sample utterances were

"Watcha looking at HUH?" or

"Look at mommy!"

When the infant gazed at the mother and smiled, mothers typically responded with a "bell" or a "sinusoidal" utterance—rhythmic patterns that are apparently intended to *maintain the baby's pleasant mood.* Sample utterances were

"comE On" (bell) or

"you're the cUTEst little thing in the wHOLe world" (sinusoidal)

Since smiles and bright-eyed expressions of glee appear and subside very quickly, the rising-falling intonation of the bell and sinusoidal patterns may be quite compatible with a baby's cycles of positive affect. Finally, if the infant gazed at the mother with a sober expression, mothers typically used the bell-right

(for example, "wHATCha doing")

or the fall

(for example, "HEY there")

—contours that exaggerate a drop in pitch. Stern et al. believe that these latter patterns have a coaxing quality that is designed to *elicit positive affect* (smiles, bright eyes) from a neutral infant.

In sum, mothers do vary their tones of voice when they try to communicate different "messages" to their infants. In fact, Stern and his colleagues report that mothers are likely to show greater exaggeration of intonation when speaking to 2- to 6-month-old infants than when talking to either neonates or 1- to 2-year-olds. It is tempting to conclude not only that these young infants can discriminate different intonational patterns but that they come to recognize that certain tones of voice have a particular meaning (for example, "Pay attention" or "Won't you smile for me?"). Indeed, Stern and his colleagues propose that the changing tone of the mother's voice is a signal that carries information about the mother's intentions and feelings. These signals may then be interpreted by the infant and serve as a stimulus for the development of responsive gesturing and early attempts at verbal communication.

What Do Prelinguistic Infants Know about Language?

Do young infants know more about language than they can possibly tell? It now appears that they do and that one of the first things they learn about speech is a practical lesson. During the first six months, babies are most likely to coo or babble *while* their caregivers are speaking (Freedle & Lewis, 1977; Rosenthal, 1982). It is almost as if young infants viewed "talking" as a game of noisemaking in which the object was to "harmonize" with their speaking companions. But by 7–8 months of age, infants are typically silent while a companion speaks and will then respond with a vocalization whenever their partner stops talking. In other words, they have apparently learned their first rule in the pragmatics of language: Don't talk while someone else is speaking, for you'll soon have an opportunity to have your say. Conversational turntaking may come about because parents who are talking to their 5–7-month-old infants will typically say something to the child, wait for the infant to cough, burp, coo, or babble, and then address the infant again, thereby inviting another response (Snow & Ferguson, 1977). So the ways in which parents structure their conversations with an infant may help the child to realize that "talking" is a form of communication that follows a definite set of rules. In Box 8-1 we consider yet other lessons that an infant may learn from the pitch or intonation of a caregiver's speech.

Although most children do not speak their first recognizable words until 10–13 months of age, parents are often convinced that their preverbal infants can understand at least some of what is said to them. For example, an 8-month-old boy may reliably reach for a ball when his father points to the object and says "Get the ball." Does this mean that the boy understands the meaning of the word *ball* even though he has never used a word to label the object? It's possible, for 9-month-old infants will often obey commands that are given in *familiar* contexts (Benedict, 1979). However, a skeptic might argue that 8–9-month-old infants can respond appropriately to a familiar command without really understanding the meaning of the words in that utterance. The boy who fetches the ball in response to his father's command may be treating his dad's gestures (pointing) and verbal prompts as simple "cues for action" in much the same way that a cocker spaniel does when told to fetch a ball. How can we tell whether preverbal infants really understand the meanings of various words?

One way is to see whether young infants will focus their attention on an object when told to look at the object by a parent who is out of sight and hence cannot point or use other gestures to direct the child's attention to the target. In one such study (Thomas, Campos, Shucard, Ramsay, & Shucard, 1981), 11- and 13-month-old infants sat in a highchair facing a square apparatus that contained an object (for example, a toy or a cookie) in each corner. One of these four stimuli had a name that the child's mother was sure her infant recognized and understood. As the experiment began, the mother sat behind her baby and faced away so that the infant could not see her *and* she could not tell what the infant was looking at. On some trials the mother told her infant to "look at the [known word]; see the [known word]" and

asked the child "Where is the [known word]?" On other trials she told the infant to look at an object designated by a "nonsense" word that the child would *not* understand (for example, "Look at the dosh"). If infants truly understand the meaning of the known word, then they should look longer at its referent on those trials when they are told to look at the known rather than the nonsense word.

Figure 8-2 shows the results. Apparently the 13-month-olds did understand the meaning of the known word, for they spent nearly twice as much time gazing at its referent on those trials when they had been told to look at the known rather than the nonsense word. But 11-month-olds did *not* understand the meaning of the "known" word, for they were just as likely to gaze at its referent when told to look at the nonsense word. In a similar study, Sharon Oviatt (1980) reported a similar outcome: few infants understood the meanings of individual words before their first birthday.

In sum, 9-month-old infants may respond appropriately when spoken to even though they do not yet understand the meanings of the words they are hearing. Although preverbal children are able to obey verbal commands only because they

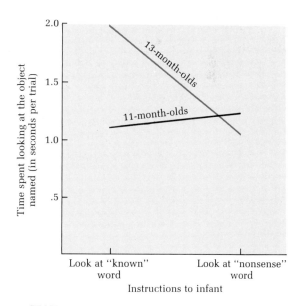

FIGURE 8-2. *Average amount of time that infants spent gazing at the referents of words that were presumably known or not known to them.*

correctly interpret nonlinguistic gestures and other contextual cues, they are quite aware that a vocal command is a communicative prompt for action. By 12 to 13 months of age, infants are beginning to realize that individual words have meaning. In fact, it is probably safe to assume that children know the meaning of that eagerly awaited "first word" before they use it in their own speech. Finally, Sharon Oviatt (1980) found that infants aged 12 to 17 months understood the meaning of many nouns (for example, *rabbit*) and verbs (for example, *press it*) long before these "object" and "action" words became part of their productive vocabularies. Taken together, these findings imply that infants know much more about language than they can possibly say. Apparently, **receptive language** (comprehension) is ahead of **productive language** (expression) from the 12th or 13th month of life and possibly even sooner.

ONE WORD AT A TIME: THE HOLOPHRASTIC STAGE

In the first stage of meaningful speech, the **holophrastic stage,** infants utter single words that may sometimes seem to represent an entire sentence's worth of meaning (that is, **holophrases**). At first the child's productive vocabulary is limited to one or two very simple words that may be intelligible only to close companions—for example, "ba" (for "ball") or "awa" (for "I want," as the child points to food or a glass of water). Initial language learning proceeds very slowly as infants simply expand their vocabularies "one word at a time" (Bloom, 1973). In fact, three to four months may pass before the "verbal" child develops a productive vocabulary of ten words (Nelson, 1973). But once they reach this ten-word milestone, infants begin to add new words at a faster pace. By 19 to 20 months of age, many children have working vocabularies of 50 words or more. And by age 24 months they are already producing an average of 186 words (Nelson, 1973).

The Infant's Choice of Words

What do young children talk about? Katherine Nelson (1973) studied 18 infants as they learned

their first 50 words and found that their one-word utterances fell into the six general categories that appear in Table 8-1. We can see that nearly two-thirds of these first 50 words are *nominals*—words that refer to unique objects (*Mama*) or to classes of objects (*ball, doggie*). And what kind of objects do children talk about? Nelson discovered that

> they do not learn the names of objects that are simply "there" such as tables, plates, towels, grass, or stoves. With few exceptions, all the words listed are terms applying to manipulable or movable objects. . . . [However, the objects that are named] are not only the ones the child acts upon in some way (shoes, bottle, ball), but also ones that do something themselves—trucks, clocks, buses, and animals [pp. 31–32].

In sum, children seem to talk about what interests them, and what interests them is something that moves, makes noise, or can be acted on.

PHOTO 8-3. *A large percentage of children's "first words" are the names of objects that move, make noise, or can be acted on.*

TABLE 8-1. Percentage of words in six categories used by children with productive vocabularies of 50 words

Word category	Description and examples	Percentage of utterances
1. General nominals	Words used to refer to classes of objects (*car, doggie, milk*)	51
2. Specific nominals	Words used to refer to unique objects (*Mommy, Rover*)	14
3. Action words	Words used to describe or accompany actions or to demand attention (*bye-bye, up, go*)	13
4. Modifiers	Words that refer to properties or quantities of things (*big, hot, mine, allgone*)	9
5. Personal/social words	Words used to express feelings or to comment about social relationships (*please, thank you, bye-bye, no, ouch*)	8
6. Function words	Words that have a grammatical function (*what, where, is, to, for*)	4

Individual Differences in Language Production

Even at the one-word stage, there are interesting individual differences in the kinds of words that children learn and use. Nelson found that most children can be classified as **referential**—that is, they tend to learn the names of things and to use general nominals far more than the other word categories (Nelson, 1973, 1981). However, a sizable minority of young children are **expressive** users of language. Their early vocabularies are much more diverse and include a large number of personal/social routines and action words such as *stop, no, don't, hi*, and *ouch*. Apparently language serves different functions for these two groups of children. Those at the referential end of the continuum seem most concerned with labeling and drawing attention to objects, while expressive children use language to call attention to their feelings and to regulate their social interactions (de Villiers & de Villiers, 1979). Nelson (1981) finds that "expressive" children tend to be later-borns from less highly educated families.

To some extent, a child's use of language reflects the mother's verbal style. Mothers who often use language to point out objects and their properties tend to have referential children; those who use language mainly to direct and respond to the child's actions are likely to have expressive children (de Villiers & de Villiers, 1979; Nelson, 1981). Perhaps the reason a large percentage of first-born children are referential users of language is that their mothers have the time to sit down and ask them questions about interesting objects and events. In contrast, mothers who have several small children to care for may end up spending less time talking to their later-borns about objects and events and more time uttering phrases designed to attract their attention or to control their behavior. Later-born children, then, may often conclude that the major function of language is to regulate social interactions and, as a result, be more likely than first-borns to adopt an expressive linguistic style (Nelson, 1973).

receptive language: *that which the individual comprehends when listening to others' speech.*

productive language: *that which the individual is capable of expressing (producing) in his or her own speech.*

holophrastic stage: *the period when the child's speech consists of one-word utterances, some of which are thought to be holophrases.*

holophrase: *a single-word utterance that represents an entire sentence's worth of meaning.*

referential communicators: *children whose first words are mostly nominals that name and call attention to people and objects.*

expressive communicators: *children whose early vocabularies include many action words and personal/social labels that are used to express emotions and regulate social interactions.*

Early Semantics: The Development of Word Meanings

Adults often chuckle at baby talk and consider it "cute" because young children use words differently than they do. For example, one 2-year-old boy called all furry, four-legged animals "doggie" and yet used the word cookie to refer only to chocolate chip cookies. If someone promised this child a cookie and gave him an Oreo, he would throw it down and look at the person as if to say "Come on, that's not a cookie!"

How do children come to infer the meaning of words? Why might they think that a cow or a horse is a "doggie" or that an Oreo is not a cookie? In recent years, psycholinguists have tried to answer these questions by looking carefully at the kinds of semantic errors (errors in word meaning) that children display in their speech.

■ Errors in word usage

When young children first attach a meaning to a word, it may or may not match the meaning that adults associate with the term. One kind of error that they often make is to use a word to refer to a wider variety of objects or events than an adult would. This phenomenon, called **overextension,** is illustrated by a child's use of the term *doggie* to refer to all furry, four-legged animals. **Underextension,** the opposite of overextension, is the tendency to use a general word to refer to a smaller range of objects than an adult would (for example, applying the term *cookie* only to chocolate chip cookies). Of course, children may match the adult meanings of some words from the very beginning. Indeed, many youngsters reserve the labels *daddy* and *mommy* to refer only to their parents (although others may overextend these terms to include several adult males and females). Jill and Peter de Villiers (1978) suggest that children are most likely to use a word as an adult would when that word is a proper noun (such as *Daddy*) that has a single referent.

Herbert and Eve Clark (1977) propose that children go through a series of stages in learning the meaning of a new word. These stages are (1) underextension, (2) appropriate use (without awareness of the word's true meaning), (3) overextension, and (4) correct use. For example, a child might start off using the word *kitty* to refer only to one cat—the family pet. She may later extend *kitty* to include other cats (a seemingly appropriate use), and then overextend the term to dogs and sheep, before finally understanding the meaning of *kitty* and using it only for domesticated felines.

■ How do children infer word meanings?

The tendency of young children to overextend or underextend the meaning of words suggests that they are forming hypotheses about what words signify and then gradually modifying these early guesses until their understanding matches an adult's. What do children attend to as they form their initial hypotheses about word meanings? According to Eve Clark's **semantic features hypothesis** (Clark, 1973), children infer the meaning of words from the *perceptual features* of their referents. For example, a verbal infant may hear her parents describe a number of small, round objects as "cookie" and conclude from these experiences that the term *cookie* describes any object that is small and round. The next step is to overextend the word to other small, round objects such as crackers, poker chips, and coins. In sum, the semantic features hypothesis contends that a child's initial ideas about word meanings are perceptually based. Presumably, young children will assume that words serve to classify or categorize objects on the basis of their size, shape, texture, or taste or the kinds of sounds they make (Clark & Clark, 1977).

Katherine Nelson (1978) has proposed a second theory of semantic development: that children infer the meanings of words from the *functions* of their referents. Nelson would argue that a child who overextends the word *cookie* to crackers, doughnuts, and other small, round, edible objects will do so on the basis of their **functional similarity** (the fact that these objects can be eaten) rather than their perceptual similarity (the fact that they look alike).

Recently, Richard Prawat and Susan Wildfong (1980) conducted an interesting experiment to test the merits of these two theories. Young children were asked to name items that were serving functions that did not jibe with the items' perceptual characteristics. For example, children saw cereal being poured into a cuplike container and were asked whether this container was a bowl or a cup (see Figure 8-3).

The results were generally consistent with the semantic features hypothesis; that is, the 3–4-year-olds in this study were more likely to call the

FIGURE 8-3. Is this item a cup or a bowl? If young children say it is a bowl, they apparently infer the meanings of words on the basis of the functions *served by their referents. But if they say the container is a cup, they must be inferring word meanings on the basis of the* perceptual characteristics *of their referents.*

container a cup (the perceptual choice) than a bowl (the functional choice). Even 2–3-year-olds tend to use perceptual rather than functional attributes as a basis for naming objects and inferring the meaning of words (Tomikawa & Dodd, 1980). In fact, overextensions based on shared perceptual features often cut across functional lines, so that a young child might well call a small, round poker chip a "cookie"—even though poker chips and cookies serve very different functions (Bowerman, 1977).

However, children know much more about the meaning of words than their semantic errors might indicate. Two-year-olds who call all four-legged animals "doggie" can often discriminate a dog from other animals if they are given a set of animal pictures and asked to "show the doggie" (Thompson & Chapman, 1977). Perhaps the reason young children overextend words like *doggie* in their speech is that they know so very few words. A young child who sees a horse may realize that this animal is not a doggie but will

nevertheless label it as such because she has no other words in her vocabulary to describe this large, four-legged creature (de Villiers & de Villiers, 1979). Children may also use this strategy to learn the names of new objects, for overextensions of a word such as *doggie* are likely to elicit reactions such as "No, Johnny, that's a *horsie*. Can you say 'horsie'? C'mon, say 'horsie'!"

Levels of semantic awareness. As adults, we can label objects in many ways. For example, we may call the family pet "Peppy" (a proper name), a collie, a dog, a mammal, or an animal. In contrast, 2–3-year-olds are likely to respond to a collie by calling it "doggie" rather than a collie (a more specific term) or an animal (a more general term).

Why are children's first words at an intermediate level of generality? Probably because adults often name objects at this level when talking with 2- to 3-year-olds, even though they may use other levels of generality when describing the same objects to an older child or an adult. For example, a mother might call a large, spotted feline a "leopard" (a specific term) when talking to her 5-year-old; however, the same animal becomes a "kitty cat" when she points it out to her infant or toddler (Mervis & Mervis, 1982). The 1- to 3-year-old has no need to distinguish leopards from house cats or golf balls from tennis balls; all "kitties" are animals that meow, and all "balls" are round objects that roll. So in naming objects at an intermediate level of generality, adults are providing verbal labels for those aspects of meaning

---

overextension: *the young child's tendency to use relatively specific words to refer to a wider set of objects, actions, or events than adults do (for example, using the word* car *to refer to all motor vehicles).*

underextension: *the young child's tendency to use general words to refer to a smaller set of objects, actions, or events than adults do (for example, using* candy *to refer only to mints).*

semantic features hypothesis: *the notion that children infer the meaning of new words from the perceptual characteristics of their referents.*

functional similarity hypothesis: *the notion that children infer the meaning of new words from the functions served by their referents.*

(or "semantic features") that their young children first notice and are able to understand (Blewitt, 1983).

First verbs and adjectives. Children first use verbs to describe actions that they undertake (for example, *jump, throw, hit, run*) or to call attention to changes in the objects they play with (*broke, fall, move*). Like nouns, verbs are often overextended. For example, a child may initially associate the word *kick* with any motion of the limbs and then say that she "kicks" when she swats at an object with her hand or that moths "kick" when they flutter their wings (Bowerman, 1977). Of course, children will eventually stop overextending the meaning of verbs as they learn the names for more and more activities and begin to limit the use of these words to their appropriate referents.

A child's first adjectives are terms such as *all-gone, broken,* or *open* that are used to describe the current status or condition of an object (Nelson, 1976). As children combine words, they begin to use adjectives such as *red, blue, pretty, big,* and *little* that not only describe objects but may also serve to differentiate them from other objects that are similar. However, 2–3-year-olds do not truly understand the meaning of relational adjectives such as *big* or *little*. If a toddler can easily handle an object, he is likely to describe it as "little"; but if the object is cumbersome or difficult to manipulate, it is "big" (de Villiers & de Villiers, 1979). Only later will children come to realize that *big* and *little* are relative terms, so that a motorbike might be described as "big" when compared with a tricycle but "little" when compared with a car.

■ When a word is more than a word

Many psycholinguists believe that children use single words as holophrases—that is, one-word "sentences" that derive their meaning from the word itself and the context in which it is spoken (Dale, 1976). It does often seem that a child's one-word utterances represent much more than an attempt to label objects. For example, one 17-month-old child named Shelley used the word *ghetti* (spaghetti) three times over a five-minute period. On the first occasion, she was simply pointing at a pan on the stove and seemed to be asking "Is that spaghetti?" When her older companion showed her the pan's contents, she grin-

ned and exclaimed "GHETTI!" as if to say "Heh, it *is* spaghetti!" Several minutes later, she once again approached her companion (who was now eating), tugged at his sleeve, and said "Ghetti" in a pleading way as if to request a bite of spaghetti.

Do we read too much into Shelley's speech when suggesting that she used a single word to express three different sentences' worth of meaning? Perhaps. But let's also note that on her third use of the term *ghetti*, Shelley added both a nonverbal gesture (tugging) and an intonational cue (a whine) that she had not previously used. These actions may well have been undertaken to differentiate her third utterance from the previous two, so that her companion would not misinterpret the message, "Give Shelley some spaghetti!"

In sum, children in the holophrastic stage of language learning may be expressing rather complex ideas in their one-word utterances—ideas that we would express in sentences. Toward the end of the holophrastic period, toddlers will often string holophrases together in ways that provide a more complete picture of their desires or their assessments of a situation. For example, the phrase "Daddy [long pause] car [long pause] ride" may represent the child's description of what she and dad are doing or perhaps an attempt to coax dad to take her for a ride in the country. At this point, children are on the verge of producing their first true sentences (Clark & Clark, 1977).

FROM HOLOPHRASES TO SIMPLE SENTENCES: THE TELEGRAPHIC STAGE

At about 18 to 24 months of age, children begin to combine words into simple "sentences" that are remarkably similar across languages (and cultures) as different as English, Finnish, German, Russian, and Samoan (see Table 8-2). These early combinations are sometimes called **telegraphic speech** because they resemble the abbreviated language of a telegram.

Although the two-word utterances in Table 8-2 are clearly ungrammatical by adult standards, they represent far more than strings of holophrases or random word combinations. Even the simplest of a child's early sentences show some systematic regularities in word order and word use. Moreover, early sentences are often quite cre-

TABLE 8-2. Similarities in children's spontaneous two-word sentences in several languages

Function of sentence	Language				
	English	Finnish	German	Russian	Samoan
To locate or name	There book	Tuossa Rina (there Rina)	Buch da (book there)	Tosya tam (Tosya there)	Keith lea (Keith there)
To demand	More milk Give candy	Annu Rina (give Rina)	Mehr milch (more milk)	Yeshche moloko (more milk)	Mai pepe (give doll)
To negate	No wet Not hungry	Ei susi (not wolf)	Nicht blasen (not blow)	Vody nyet (water no)	Le 'ai (not eat)
To indicate possession	My shoe Mama dress	Täti auto (aunt's car)	Mein ball (my ball) Mamas hut (Mama's hat)	Mami chashka (Mama's cup)	Lole a'u (candy my)
To modify or qualify	Pretty dress Big boat	Rikki auto (broken car)	Armer wauwau (poor dog)	Papa bol'shoy (Papa big)	Fa'ali'i pepe (headstrong baby)
To question	Where ball	Missa pallo (where ball)	Wo ball (where ball)	Gde papa (where Papa)	Fea Punafu (where Punafu)

ative. A 2-year-old who eats an Oreo and says "Allgone cookie" has created a novel statement—one that adults would not produce unless they were mimicking the child.

Why are children's earliest sentences incomplete? What kinds of messages and meanings are they trying to communicate in these telegraphic statements? And what have they learned about the pragmatics of language over the first two to two and a half years? Psycholinguists have tried to answer these questions by periodically recording and analyzing toddlers' speech. In conducting this research, investigators soon discovered that age is not a very good indicator of language development, because some children acquire language much faster than others. As a result, it is virtually impossible to specify the linguistic capabilities of the "average toddler" or the "typical 3-year-old."

According to Roger Brown (1973), the best estimate of a child's early language development is a measure called the **mean length of utterance (MLU)**—the average number of morphemes that the child uses in the sentences he or she produces. Earlier we defined a morpheme as the smallest unit of speech that conveys meaning. These meaningful elements of language may be whole words, such as *cat* or *jump*, or grammatical markers such as the *-s* at the end of a noun to signify plurality or the *-ed* at the end of a verb to indicate the past

tense. Thus, the phrase "See kitty" consists of only two morphemes, whereas the statements "Baby jumped" or "See doggies" each contain a total of three.

Characteristics of Telegraphic Speech

When adults send telegrams, they try to make them as short as possible because each word costs money. If you wanted to inform a friend that you were leaving Atlanta on Sunday and would be arriving home on Tuesday, you might write "Leaving Atlanta Sunday—home Tuesday." In the interest of economy, you would retain only the essential content words (typically nouns and verbs) and omit less important "function" words, such as articles, prepositions, pronouns, and auxiliary verbs. Young children follow roughly the same strategy when composing their earliest sentences.

---

telegraphic speech: *early sentences that consist solely of content words and omit the less meaningful parts of speech such as articles, prepositions, pronouns, and auxiliary verbs.*

mean length of utterance (MLU): *the average number of meaningful units (morphemes) in a child's utterances.*

The child's imitations of adult speech are also telegraphic. If you were to ask a 2-year-old to repeat the sentence "The doggie is chasing the kitty," she might say "Doggie chase kitty." That is, the child once again retains only the important nouns and verbs and deletes *the, is,* and the verb ending *-ing*—even though she has just heard these elements in the sentence she is trying to reproduce.

Why are children's first sentences telegraphic? One possibility is that toddlers don't know the meanings (or grammatical functions) of "function" words and therefore omit them from their speech (de Villiers & de Villiers, 1978). A second possibility is that children have some understanding of function words but simply lack the memory capacity that they would need to generate long sentences. If the child's memory will allow him to produce only two- or three-word sentences, then he is likely to choose the most meaningful words and omit all excess baggage (Glucksberg & Danks, 1975).

Grammatical Analyses of Early Speech

The structure of the sentences that children hear will vary considerably from culture to culture; each language has its own set of grammatical rules that permits certain word combinations and prohibits others. Yet we have seen in Table 8-2 that toddlers who have been exposed to very different languages will produce the same kinds of two-word utterances (Slobin, 1979). So children's earliest sentences are not merely shortened versions of adult language; they represent a universal "child language" that seems to have a structure of its own.

■ *Pivotal grammar*

Martin Braine (1963) was among the first to write a grammar for children's earliest sentences. Braine studied three toddlers and noticed that their two-word utterances seemed to consist of two kinds of words: *pivot class* words and *open class* words. A child's pivot class consisted of a small number of words (for example, *see, allgone, bye-bye*) that were used frequently in combination with other words. The larger number of words (mostly nouns and pronouns) that were combined with pivot words made up the child's open class.

After studying the speech of his three young subjects, Braine concluded that only open-class words are used in single-word utterances. In addition, the children seemed to be using a relatively simple principle to generate more than 80% of their two-word sentences: pick a pivot word and combine it with any open word (for example, "*See* sock," "*See* hot," "*See* boy"). Apparently this simple rule also signifies that some word combinations are not grammatical, for pivot words never occurred together in a two-word sentence, nor did they ever stand alone as a one-word utterance.

■ *A semantic analysis of early speech*

In recent years psycholinguists have discovered that children's earliest sentences are really much more complex than Braine had thought. Braine's **pivotal grammar** is a grammar based on the structure (or syntax) of children's utterances without any regard for their possible meanings. Accordingly, Braine treated sentences made up of two open-class words, such as "Mommy sleep" or "milk cup" as "unclassified" statements that are ungrammatical because they do not conform to the pivot + open combinational rule.

Perhaps you can see the problem. An open + open utterance such as "milk cup" is probably not a random combination of two words. Instead, it is a "nonpivotal" construction that the child may use to express a whole stentence's worth of meaning. Lois Bloom (1970) has noted that young children often produce these open + open sentences and that any one of these constructions may be used to express a number of semantic relations. For example, one of Bloom's young subjects said "mommy sock" on two occasions during the same day—once when she picked up her mother's sock and once while her mother was putting a sock on the child's foot. In the first instance, "Mommy sock" seems to imply a possessive relationship—"Mommy's sock." But in the second instance, the child is apparently expressing an agent/object relation such as "Mommy is putting on my sock." So here are two statements that fall outside the pivotal grammar described by Braine (1963) and yet clearly represent the child's attempts to express two very different ideas—ideas that adults would communicate with different kinds of sentences.

Actually, toddlers can and do express different semantic relations by simply varying the order of the words in their two-word utterances (Bloom,

1973). If they wish to talk about agent/action relations, they indicate who (or what) is undertaking the action by placing the subject noun *before* the verb. In contrast, they express action/object relations by locating the object of action *after* the verb. Applying this basic principle of syntax, the child might say something like "Billy hit" to indicate that Billy is hitting his sister—but "Hit Billy" to communicate that Billy is being (or has been) hit. So we see that children who produce alternative combinations of the same two words know much more than the meanings of the individual words: they also understand that the meaning of each word combination depends, in part, on the order of those words within the sentence (de Villiers & de Villiers, 1978).

Roger Brown (1970, 1973) has analyzed the "telegraphese" of several young children and written a **semantic grammar** to describe the basic categories of meaning that they often express in their two-word sentences. Several of these basic categories of meaning appear in Table 8-3.

The child's next accomplishment is to combine these semantic relations into longer telegraphic utterances. For example, an agent/action relation such as "Mommy drink" might be added to an action/object relation such as "drink milk" to yield an agent/action/object relation of the form "Mommy drink milk." Once children reach this milestone, they are about ready to acquire and use some of the rules of syntax that will make their sentences more "grammatical" within the framework of the language they are learning.

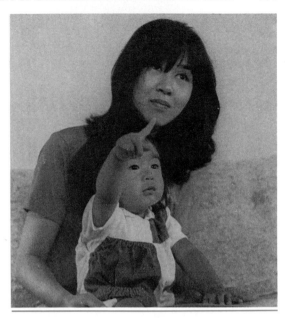

PHOTO 8-4. *Pointing is an early but very effective means of communication. By the end of the first year, children are calling attention to interesting objects and activities by pointing at them with the index finger.*

The Pragmatics of Early Speech

There are a number of very practical lessons that children must learn before they can become effective communicators. Obviously, they must learn how to attract the attention of their companions and how to use language as a means of sustaining social interactions. They must also learn how to supplement their limited vocabularies and productive skills to make their messages clear. And last but certainly not least, children must become good listeners, for the information they receive from their conversational partners may help them to restructure any of their messages that a partner has not understood.

The development of communication skills be-

TABLE 8-3. Common categories of meaning (semantic relations) expressed in children's earliest sentences

Semantic relation	Example
I. Reference operations	
To name	That book
To notice	Hi belt
To demand	More milk
To indicate nonexistence	Allgone cookie
II. Relational operations	
To indicate possession	Adam checker
To locate	Sweater chair
To modify	Big train
Agent/action	Eve read
Agent/object	Mommy sock
Action/object	Hit ball

pivotal grammar: *an analysis of the structure (syntax) of children's earliest sentences.*
semantic (or functional) grammar: *an analysis of the semantic relations (meanings) that children express in their earliest sentences.*

BOX 8-2
LEARNING A GESTURAL LANGUAGE

Children who are born deaf or who lose their hearing early in childhood will have a difficult time learning to use an oral language. Contrary to popular opinion, the deaf do not learn much from lip reading. In fact, many deaf children learn no language at all until they go to school and are exposed to a gestural system known as American Sign Language (ASL).

Even though ASL is produced by the hands rather than orally, it is a remarkably flexible medium that is similar to an oral language (Klima & Bellugi, 1975). For example, ASL has a distinct sign for each morpheme. Some signs represent entire words; others stand for grammatical morphemes (or inflections) such as the progressive ending -*ing,* the past tense -*ed,* and auxiliaries (Dale, 1976). Each sign is constructed from a limited set of gestural components in much the same way that the spoken word is constructed from a finite number of distinctive sounds (phonemes). In ASL the components that make up a sign are (1) the position of the signing hand(s), (2) the configuration of the hand(s) and fingers, and (3) the motions of the hand(s) and fingers. Syntactical rules specify how signs are to be combined to form declarative statements, to ask questions, and to negate a proposition. And like an oral language, ASL permits the user to sign plays on words (puns), metaphorical statements, and poetry. So people who are proficient in this gestural system can transmit and understand an infinite variety of highly creative messages—they are true language users.

Deaf children learn ASL in much the same way that hearing children acquire an oral language. If their parents are deaf and communicate in sign, deaf children will often produce their first signs during the first year (de Villiers & de Villiers, 1978). The deaf child usually begins by "babbling" in sign—that is, forming rough approximations of signs that parents use. The child then proceeds to one-word, or "holophrastic," phrases, in which a single sign is used to convey a number of different messages, and the kinds of signs that the child first uses (nominals, action words, modifiers) are virtually identical to the categories of words that speaking children first acquire (Bonvillian, Orlansky, & Novack, 1983). When deaf children begin to combine signs, their two-sign sentences are "telegraphic" statements that express the same set of semantic relations that appears in the early speech of hearing children. Finally, deaf children learning ASL and hearing children learning an oral tongue pass through roughly the same stages as they begin to acquire and use the grammatical rules of their respective languages. These striking parallels in the language learning of deaf and hearing children led Philip Dale (1976, p. 59) to conclude:

> The really important aspects of language and the really important abilities the child brings to the problem of language learning are independent of the modality in which the linguistic system operates. Language is a central process, not a peripheral one. The abilities that [deaf children share with hearing children] are so general, and so powerful, that [the deaf] proceed through the same milestones of development as do hearing children.

Today many educators believe that deaf children

gins long before children produce their first words. Three-month-old infants will learn to vocalize to their adult companions if this strategy is successful at attracting and maintaining an adult's attention (Weisberg, 1963). And by the middle of the first year, children are already using gestures to communicate with their parents. For example, a 6-month-old child might indicate her interest in a particular toy by picking it up and showing it to an adult. At 10–11 months, children will look in the direction in which adults are pointing, and by the end of the first year, the child begins to call the mother's attention to interesting objects and activities by pointing at them with the index finger.

How do mothers respond when their infants point? According to Eleanor Leung and Harriet Rheingold (1981), they will first determine what the child is pointing at and then name and describe whatever it is that the infant finds so fascinating. Thus, pointing is an important communicative gesture that the very young child may use to learn the *names* of interesting objects and activities—the very words that appear first in his or her vocabulary (Nelson, 1973).

When infants begin to speak, they will often combine a word and a gesture to make their "holophrases" less ambiguous for the listener. So if a 14-month-old child tugs at her father's shirt sleeve after pointing and saying "Cookie," her dad will undoubtedly realize that she is not simply naming the cookie for him. As children begin to combine words into telegraphic sentences, their use of gestures as aids to communication becomes more

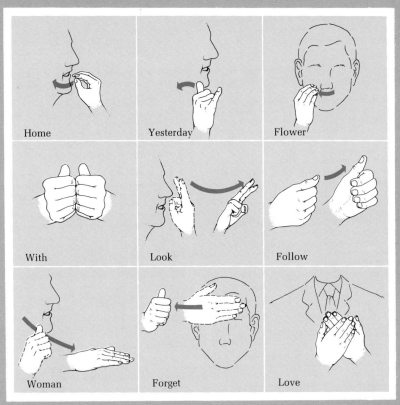

Some signs of American Sign Language.

should be exposed to both ASL and oral language as early as possible so that they can develop a broad range of general linguistic skills. Although this "total communication" training does not necessarily make it easier for deaf children to use the spoken language, it does make them more knowledgeable about communicating and may improve the quality of their social interactions with both their deaf and their hearing companions (de Villiers & de Villiers, 1978).

---

sophisticated. For example, 2-year-olds will often attempt to clarify the semantic relations they are trying to express by staring or pointing at the agent (or the object) of an action or by using hand and body movements to represent various actions and activities (Wilkinson & Rembold, 1981). Although we adults who are quite proficient with the spoken language may consider nonverbal gestures a rather primitive and inefficient form of communication, such an attitude is extremely short-sighted. Indeed, many deaf children come to know and use a rather sophisticated language that is based entirely on nonverbal signs and gestures (see Box 8-2).

Toddlers are also aware of many of the social and situational determinants of effective communication. For example, 2–3-year-olds know that they must either stand close to a listener or compensate for distance by raising their voices if they are to communicate with that person (Johnson, Pick, Siegel, Cicciarelli, & Garber, 1981; Wellman & Lempers, 1977). When talking to another toddler about some object or activity, the 2-year-old knows that he must stand close to the referent before his message is likely to be understood (Wellman & Lempers, 1977). And 2-year-olds listen carefully to the speech of their peers and will respond appropriately to many of the questions that other children ask (Garvey, 1975). In fact, Jeanne Wilcox and Elizabeth Webster (1980) found that children only 12–24 months of age are already monitoring the reactions of their conversational partners to determine whether their messages have been understood. When an adult responded to a holophrastic "request" such as "Cookie?" by saying "What?" or treating the utterance as a declarative ("There is a cookie"), these young toddlers immediately recognized their failure to communicate and proceeded to restate their message, to select another word to make their point (for example, "Give"), or to elaborate the utterance by adding one or more words (for example, "Give cookie").

In sum, most 2–2½-year-old children have learned many practical lessons about language and communication even before they begin to use the grammatical rules of their native tongue. But although toddlers can communicate with adults and other children, their conversational skills pale in comparison with those of a 5-year-old, a 4-year-old, or even many 3-year-olds. Our next task is to determine what it is that preschool children are learning that will enable them to become rather sophisticated users of language by the ripe old age of 5, when they are about ready to enter kindergarten.

LANGUAGE LEARNING DURING THE PRESCHOOL PERIOD

During the preschool period—ages 2½ to 5—children begin to produce some very lengthy sentences. Yet the most noteworthy aspect of preschool speech is not its length but its *complexity*. In Table 8-4 we see just how remarkably sophisticated a child's sentences can become over the brief span of seven to ten months.

What are children acquiring that enables them to produce complex sentences only a few short months after speaking in telegraphese? Surely they are mastering basic syntax. As we see in Table 8-4, a child of 35–38 months is now inserting articles, auxiliary verbs, and grammatical markers (for example, *-ed, - ing*) that were previously omitted, as well as negating propositions and occasionally asking a well-formed question. And although it is not as obvious from the table, we will see that preschool children are beginning to understand a number of complex semantic relations and are learning much more about the pragmatics of language and communication.

Acquiring Grammatical Morphemes

Grammatical morphemes are modifiers that give more precise meaning to the sentences we construct. These meaning modifiers usually begin to appear sometime during the third year as children begin to pluralize nouns by adding *-s*, to signify location with the prepositional morphemes *in* and *on*, to indicate verb tense with the present progressive *-ing* or the past tense *-ed*, and to describe possessive relations with the inflection *'s*.

Roger Brown (1973) kept records on three children as they acquired 14 grammatical morphemes that frequently appear in English sentences. He found that these three children varied considerably with respect to (1) the age at which they began to use grammatical markers and (2) the amount of time it took them to master all 14 rules. However, all three children in Brown's longitudinal study learned the 14 grammatical morphemes in precisely the order in which they

TABLE 8-4. Samples of one boy's speech at three ages

Age		
28 months *(telegraphic speech)*	*35 months*	*38 months*
Somebody pencil	No—I don't know	I like a racing car
Floor	What dat feeled like?	I broke my racing car
Where birdie go?	Lemme do again	It's broked
Read dat	Don't—don't hold with me	You got some beads
Hit hammer, Mommy	I'm going to drop it—inne dump truck	Who put dust on my hair?
Yep, it fit	Why—cracker can't talk?	Mommy don't let me buy some
Have screw	Those are mines	Why it's not working?

TABLE 8-5. Development of 14 grammatical markers in English: suffixes and function verbs

Morpheme	Meaning	Example
1. Present progressive: *-ing*	Ongoing process	He is sitt*ing* down
2. Preposition: *in*	Containment	The mouse is *in* the box
3. Preposition: *on*	Support	The book is *on* the table
4. Plural: *-s*	Number	The dog*s* ran away
5. Past irregular: for example, *went*	Earlier in time relative to time of speaking	The boy *went* home
6. Possessive: *-'s*	Possession	The girl*'s* dog is big
7. Uncontractible copula *be:* for example, *are, was*	Number; earlier in time	*Are* they boys or girls? *Was* that a dog?
8. Articles: *the, a*	Definite/indefinite	He has *a* book
9. Past regular: *-ed*	Earlier in time	He jump*ed* the stream
10. Third person regular: *-s*	Number; earlier in time	She run*s* fast
11. Third person irregular: for example, *has, does*	Number; earlier in time	*Does* the dog bark?
12. Uncontractible auxiliary *be:* for example, *is, were*	Number; earlier in time; ongoing process	*Is* he running? *Were* they at home?
13. Contractible copula *be:* for example, *-'s, -'re*	Number; earlier in time	That*'s* a spaniel
14. Contractible auxiliary *be:* for example, *-'s, -'re*	Number; earlier in time; ongoing process	They*'re* running very slowly

appear in Table 8-5—a finding confirmed in a cross-sectional study of 21 additional children (de Villiers & de Villiers, 1973).

Why do you suppose that children who have very different vocabularies would learn these 14 grammatical markers in one particular order? Brown (1973) first hypothesized that the order of acquisition might simply reflect the frequency of these 14 morphemes in parental speech. However, he soon rejected this "frequency" hypothesis when he found that the grammatical markers learned earliest appear no more often in parents' speech than the morphemes that are learned later.

Brown then considered the possibility that the morphemes acquired early may be less complex than those acquired late. A careful analysis of the semantic and syntactic complexity of each of the 14 morphemes revealed that simpler morphemes are indeed acquired earlier than the more complex forms. For example, the present progressive *-ing*, which describes an ongoing action, appears before the past regular *-ed*, which describes both action and a sense of "earlier in time." Moreover, *-ed*,

which conveys two semantic features, is acquired earlier than the uncontractible forms of the verb *to be* (*is, are, was, were*), which specify three semantic relations: number (singular or plural), tense (present or past), and action (ongoing process).

Young children also employ certain processing strategies that will make some morphemes easier to learn than others. For example, they seem to pay more attention to the ending of words and will find suffixes easier to learn than prefixes (Daneman & Case, 1981; Kuczaj, 1979). They also tend to look for regularities in the language they hear and to avoid (or discount) exceptions to the general rule (Slobin, 1979). Let's take a closer look at this latter strategy, for it is responsible for many of the interesting and rather creative sentences that preschool children come up with.

grammatical morphemes: *prefixes, suffixes, prepositions, and auxiliary verbs that modify the meaning of words and sentences.*

Once young children have acquired a new grammatical morpheme, they will apply this rule to novel as well as to familiar contexts. For example, if the child realizes that the way to pluralize a noun is to add the grammatical inflection -*s*, he or she will have no problem solving the puzzle in Figure 8-4—these two funny-looking creatures are obviously wug*s* (Berko, 1958).

Since children generally avoid or discount exceptions to a rule, they will often overextend new grammatical morphemes to cases in which the adult form is irregular—a phenomenon known as **overregularization.** For example, it is quite common to hear preschool children make statements such as "I brushed my *tooths*," "She *goed*," or "It *runned*." In so doing, the child is simply applying the regular morpheme for pluralization to the irregular noun *tooth* and the regular morpheme for past tense to the irregular verbs *go* and *run*.

Oddly enough, children often use the *correct* forms of many irregular nouns and verbs before they learn any grammatical morphemes. But once a new grammatical morpheme has been acquired, the child who has been correctly using irregulars such as *feet* and *went* will suddenly overregularize these words and say "foots" and "goed." Do these overgeneralizations represent giant leaps backward? Most psycholinguists say no. "Errors" of this kind merely indicate that children have discovered important new linguistic

principles and are now applying them in a "creative" way to their own speech. Although preschool children soon begin to refine their use of grammatical morphemes as they discover which words are regular and which are not, even a 5-year-old will occasionally overregularize unfamiliar words and say such things as "slided" rather than "slid," or "oxes" rather than "oxen" (Slobin, 1979).

Mastering Transformational Rules

In addition to grammatical morphemes, each language has rules for creating variations of the basic declarative sentence. For example, people who speak English learn to transform declaratives into *wh-* questions by placing an appropriate *wh-* word (*who, what, when, where, why*) at the beginning of the sentence and then inverting the order of the subject and auxiliary verb. Applying these rules, the declarative statement "I was eating pizza" can be modified to produce the question "What was I eating?" Other rules of **transformational grammar** that we have all mastered allow us to generate *negative* sentences ("I was *not* eating pizza"), *imperatives* ("Eat the pizza!"), *relative clauses* ("I, who hate cheese, was eating pizza"), and *compound sentences* ("I was eating pizza and John was eating spaghetti").

As the child's mean length of utterance (MLU) rises above 2.5, he or she will begin to produce some variations of declarative sentences (Dale, 1976). However, young children acquire the transformational rules of their language in a step-by-step fashion, and as a result, their earliest transformations are very different from those of an adult. Let's now consider the stages that children pass through as they begin to ask questions, to negate propositions, and to generate complex sentences.

■ *Learning to ask questions*

There are two kinds of questions that are common to virtually all languages. *Yes/no questions* ask whether particular declarative statements are true or false. In contrast, *wh- questions* ask the respondent to provide information other than a yes-or-no answer. These latter queries are called *wh-* questions because, in English, they almost always be-

This is a wug.

Now there is another one. There are two of them.

There are two _____

FIGURE 8-4. A linguistic puzzle used to determine young children's understanding of the rule for forming plurals in English.

TABLE 8-6. Transformational principles involved in generating yes/no and *wh-* questions

Declarative sentence	Transformation	Transformational rules
I. Yes/No questions		
I am swimming	Am I swimming?	1. Place the proper auxiliary verb (*am, is, are, do, does*) before the subject noun phrase
She is playing	Does she play often?	
II. Wh- questions		
They are going to church	Where are they going?	1. Insert *wh-* word at the beginning of the sentence
He sees the light	What does he see?	2. Invert the order of the subject noun and the auxiliary verb

gin with a *wh-* word such as *who, what, where, when, which,* or *why.* Table 8-6 illustrates some of the transformational rules we use when generating yes/no and *wh-* questions.

The child's earliest questions often consist of nothing more than two- or three-word phrases uttered with a rising intonation (for example, "See doggie?"). However, a few *wh-* words are occasionally placed at the beginning of telegraphic sentences to produce simple *wh-* questions such as "Where doggie?" or "What Daddy eat?"

During the second stage of question asking, grammatical morphemes begin to appear in the child's interrogative sentences. However, word order remains a problem because the child does not yet reverse the positions of the subject and the auxiliary verb. Here are some examples of Stage 2 questions:

What Daddy is eating?
Who doggie is barking at?
Where my ball goed?

Finally, children begin to place subjects and auxiliary verbs in the proper order, so that their questions sound pretty much like an adult's. However, they may occasionally produce utterances such as "Did I caught it?" or "What did you played?" because they do not yet realize that only the auxiliary verb is marked for tense in a simple interrogative sentence (Clark & Clark, 1977).

Several investigators have noted that children begin to ask "what," "where," and "who" questions long before they are requesting information about "why," "when," and "how" (Bloom, Merkin, & Wootten, 1982; Tyack & Ingram, 1977).

One possible explanation for this finding is that questions of the form "what ____," "where ____," or "who ____" have concrete referents (objects, locations, and persons) that a cognitively immature toddler can easily comprehend. The implication of this line of reasoning is that children will begin to ask more "when ____," "how ____," and "why ____" questions as they reach a point in their intellectual development at which they are better able to understand and appreciate abstract concepts such as time and causality.

■ *Learning to produce negative sentences*
The stages that children go through when learning to produce negative sentences are remarkably similar to the stages for asking questions. For example, the child's earliest negatives are formed by simply placing a negative marker at the beginning of an affirmative sentence to produce utterances such as—

No sit there
Not a teddy bear

The child's next step is to move the negative

---

overregularization: *the overgeneralization of grammatical rules to irregular cases where the rules do not apply (for example, saying "mouses" rather than "mice").*

transformational grammar: *rules of syntax that allow one to transform declarative statements into questions, negatives, imperatives, and other kinds of sentences.*

marker within the sentence, placing it next to the verb stem that is to be modified. At this second stage, children are producing negatives such as—

I no want milk
I not going there

Finally, children begin to combine their negative markers with auxiliary verbs such as *is, was, will, can,* and *do* to negate affirmative sentences in much the same way that adults do. Indeed, Peter and Jill de Villiers (1979) describe a delightful experiment in which young children were persuaded to argue with a talking puppet. Whenever the puppet made a declarative statement such as "He likes bananas," the child's task was to negate the proposition (argue) in any way he or she could. Most 3–4-year-olds thoroughly enjoyed this escalating verbal warfare between themselves and the puppet. But more important, these young children were quite capable of using a wide variety of negative auxiliaries—including *wouldn't, wasn't, hasn't,* and *mustn't*—to properly negate almost any sentence the puppet produced.

■ *Learning to produce complex sentences*
When MLU reaches 3.5–4.0 (a milestone that may occur as early as age 2 or as late as 3½), children begin to produce complex sentences. The first complex constructions are often embedded sentences in which a noun phrase or a *wh-* clause serves as the object of a verb (Dale, 1976). Here are two examples:

I mean *that's a D* (noun phrase as the object)
I remember *where it is* (*wh-* clause as the object)

Within weeks, children are producing *relative clauses* that modify noun phrases (for example, "That's a box *that they put it in*") and joining simple sentences with the conjunctions *and, because,* and *so*—for example, "He was stuck *and* I got him out"; "I want some milk *'cause* I have a cold" (Dale, 1976; Hood & Bloom, 1979). By the end of the preschool period (age 5–6), children's oral language is very much like that of an adult. They have now acquired a working knowledge of most of the grammatical principles of their native language and are able to produce a variety of complex sentences without ever having had a formal lesson in grammar.

Semantic Development

Another reason language becomes more complex during the preschool period is that children are beginning to understand and appreciate relational contrasts such as big/little, tall/short, in/on, before/after, here/there, and I/you (de Villiers & de Villiers, 1979). The I/you distinction in conversations provides an example of how a knowledge of semantic relations comes to affect the structure of child language. To use *I* and *you* properly, the child must first understand that speakers use the term *I* to refer to the self and *you* to refer to a listener. As it turns out, the I/you contrast (including my/your and mine/yours) is among the first semantic relations that preschool children master, even though they have always been called "you" by their companions and must learn never to use this label when referring to the self (de Villiers & de Villiers, 1979).

Words that specify relations between people, objects, and events occur quite early in child language, although young children do not fully appreciate the meaning of many of these terms. For example, the word *more* is often one of the child's first words—one that is used to request a repetition of some kind ("more milk"; "more tickle"). However, it will be some time before children use this relational term in its full comparative sense to specify relations such as "This glass contains *more* than that one" (de Villiers & de Villiers, 1978).

Big and *little* are usually the first spatial adjectives to appear, and even 4–5-year-olds may continue to use these general terms to refer to variations in height, length, and width. Several researchers have devised linguistic games such as the argumentative-puppet technique to test children's knowledge of relational opposites like big/little, tall/short, wide/narrow, and deep/shallow. They have found that children acquire spatial opposites in the following order:

	tall/short		wide/narrow	
big/little→		→high/low→		→deep/shallow
	long/short		thick/thin	

There appear to be two reasons that spatial adjectives are learned in this particular order. First, children hear some adjectives more than others:

big and *little* are by far the most *frequent* spatial terms in English, and even we adults seem to pay more attention to heights and lengths than to widths or thickness (for example, we are more apt to describe ourselves as tall or short than to mention whether we are thick or thin). Furthermore, the spatial adjectives that children acquire earliest are *less semantically complex* than those acquired later (Clark & Clark, 1977). For example, *big* and *little* refer to size along any and all spatial dimensions (physical extent) and are less precise than the adjectives *tall* and *short,* which convey two semantic relations (physical extent + verticality).

Although preschool children are becoming increasingly aware of a variety of meaningful relations and are learning how to express them orally, they continue to make some interesting semantic errors. Consider the following sentences:

1. *Before* you clean your teeth, brush your hair
2. Clean your teeth *after* you brush your hair
3. The girl hit the boy
4. The boy was hit by the girl

If a 4-year-old were to act out the instructions in either of the first two sentences, she would undoubtedly clean her teeth *before* she brushed her hair (Clark, 1971). Apparently the child pays little attention to the information specified by the word *before* or *after* because she mistakenly assumes that the two acts are to be performed *in the order that they are mentioned.* However, this semantic error does not imply that preschool children are totally ignorant of the meanings of *before* and *after.* In fact, Naomi Goodz (1982) has recently discovered that 3- to 4-year-olds who use an "order of mention" strategy and misinterpret the first two sentences are perfectly capable of answering *before/after* questions about events they have witnessed—for example, "When did the girl get out—before or after the boy?" So a preschool child may know the meaning of a word without understanding how that word is used in all grammatical constructions.

Children younger than 5 or 6 make similar errors when interpreting *passive* constructions, such as sentence number 4 above. Preschoolers can easily understand the *active* version of the same idea—that is, sentence 3. But if asked to point to a picture that shows "The boy was hit by the girl," they will select a drawing that shows a boy hitting a girl. What they have done is to assume that the first noun is the agent of the verb and that the second is the object; consequently, they interpret the passive construction as if it were an active sentence. The one exception to this rule is passives that make little sense when the child processes them as active sentences. For example, even a 3-year-old would correctly interpret "The candy was eaten by the girl" because it is nonsense to assume that the candy was the agent doing the eating (de Villiers & de Villiers, 1979).

Pragmatics and Communications Skills

During the preschool period, children are becoming increasingly aware of the pragmatics of language—that is, the rules specifying when to say what to whom in order to communicate effectively. For example, 3-year-olds already recognize that indirect commands such as "May I have some candy?" are more polite (and are probably more effective) than direct imperatives such as "Give me candy" (Bates, 1976a). Some 3-year-olds can even turn declarative statements into highly successful commands, as we see in an episode described by Kenneth Reeder (1981, p. 135):

> Shelia, who is almost 3 years old, was visiting me . . . while her parents were shopping. An ice cream van, loud speaker jangling its promise of syrupy confections, stopped nearby. "Every night I get an ice cream" declared Shelia. Nonplussed, I used my stock response: "That's very nice Shelia." "Yes, even when there's a babysitter, I get an ice cream" Shelia explained patiently. I had been backed into a corner by a 3-year-old's grasp of the language as a social tool.

Three- to five-year-olds are also learning that they must tailor their messages to their audience if they hope to communicate effectively. Marilyn Shatz and Rochel Gelman (1973) recorded the speech of several 4-year-olds as they introduced a new toy to either a 2-year-old or an adult. An analysis of the tapes revealed that 4-year-old children are already proficient at adjusting their speech to their listener's level of understanding. When talking to a 2-year-old, the children used short sentences and were careful to choose phrases such as "Watch," "Look, Perry," and

PHOTO 8-5. *Communication skills develop rapidly during the preschool period. Four-year-olds are already quite proficient at adjusting their messages to a listener's level of understanding.*

"Look here" that would attract and maintain the toddler's attention. In contrast, 4-year-olds explaining how the toy worked to an adult used complex sentences and were generally more polite.

REFINEMENT OF LANGUAGE SKILLS

Although 5-year-olds have learned a great deal about language in a remarkably brief period, many important strides in linguistic competence are made from ages 6 to 14—the grade school years. Not only do schoolchildren use bigger words and produce longer and more complex utterances, they also begin to think about and manipulate language in ways that were previously impossible.

Later Syntactic Development

During middle childhood, children are correcting many of their previous syntactical errors and beginning to use a number of complex grammatical forms that did not appear in their earlier speech.

For example, 5–8-year-olds are learning (or, in some cases, relearning) the correct past tenses for irregular verbs and the correct plurals for irregular nouns. They also begin to iron out the kinks in their use of personal pronouns, so that sentences such as "Him and her went" become much less frequent (Dale, 1976). Age 6–8 is the time that children begin to produce *tag questions* ("He will go, *won't he?*"; "You like candy, *don't you?*"), which are much more grammatically complex than yes/no or *wh-* questions (Dennis, Sugar, & Whitaker, 1982). And by age 7, children understand and may occasionally even produce simple passive sentences (de Villiers & de Villiers, 1979; Turner & Rommetveit, 1967).

When interpreting most English phrases, children can apply the **minimum distance principle (MDP)**—the rule of thumb that the subject of a verb in an active sentence is the noun (or pronoun) that immediately precedes it. Which of the following two sentences follows the minimum distance principle?

1. Bozo tells Donald to do a somersault
2. Bozo promises Donald to do a somersault

The answer, of course, is sentence 1, for the subject of the verb *tells* is the preceding noun, *Bozo*, and the subject of *to do* is the preceding noun, *Donald*. Sentence 2 is an exception to the MDP because *Bozo* is the subject of both the verb *promises* and the verb *to do*, even though *Donald* is the noun that immediately precedes *to do*. Carol Chomsky (1969) finds that children younger than 8 or 9 are likely to overextend the MDP to verbs (such as *promises*) that are exceptions to the rule. As a result, they will interpret sentence 2 to mean that Donald (not Bozo) will be doing the somersault.

Children younger than 9 or 10 also make errors in understanding sentences such as "Ask Ellen what to feed the doll." They often treat *ask* as if it meant *tell* and reply "hamburgers" or "eggs" rather than asking Ellen (Chomsky, 1969). The difficulty here is not the meaning of the word *ask*, for even a 6-year-old might correctly interpret "Ask John his last name." The problem with the first sentence seems to be that the child applies the MDP to the verb *to feed* and treats the preceding pronoun, *what*, as a request for information. Consequently, she *tells* Ellen what to feed the doll.

Clearly, middle childhood is a period of linguistic refinement: children are learning subtle exceptions to grammatical rules and coming to grips with the complex syntactical structures of their native tongue. However, this process of syntactic elaboration occurs very gradually, often continuing throughout junior high school and into the high school years (Clark & Clark, 1977).

Semantics and Metalinguistic Awareness

Children's knowledge of semantics and semantic relations continues to grow throughout the grade school years. Six-year-olds already understand some 8,000–14,000 words (Carey, 1977) and will continue to expand their productive vocabularies for many years to come. Grade school children are also becoming increasingly aware of the hierarchical relations among words and are able to label an object in many ways (for example, a big cat with spots is now recognized as a leopard, which, in turn, is a type of a cat, an animal, and a living creature). Finally, school-age children gradually become more proficient at making inferences about meaning, so that they can understand more than is actually said. For example, if a 6–8-year-old hears "John did not see the rock; the rock was in the path; John fell," he is now able to infer that John must have tripped over the rock. By age 10, children can make this kind of linguistic inference (semantic integration) even when the two or more pieces of information that are necessary to draw the "appropriate" conclusion are separated by a number of intervening sentences (Johnson & Smith, 1981). And once children begin to integrate different kinds of linguistic information, they are able to detect *hidden* meanings that are not immediately obvious from the content of an utterance. For example, if a noisy 8-year-old hears her teacher remark "My, but you're quiet today," the child will probably note the contradiction between the literal meaning of the sentence and its context and thereby detect the *sarcasm* in her teacher's remark (Ackerman, 1982).

One reason that school-age children are able to "go beyond the information given" when making linguistic inferences is that they are rapidly developing **metalinguistic awareness**—an ability to think about language and to comment on its properties. This reflective ability emerges rather late— usually after age 5. Before that time, children are not even consciously aware of the relation between words and their component sounds. Questions such as "If you take the *s* sound off *scream* (or the *a* off *address*), what's left?" will leave them scratching their heads (de Villiers & de Villiers, 1979). Moreover, preschool children find it difficult to see words as arbitrarily connected to meanings. They might think, for example, that a cow is called "cow" because it has horns—not because "cow" is what other people have arbitrarily decided to call members of this particular species.

As children reach school age, they begin to understand that language is a rule-bound system made up of sounds and words that can be fun to play with. This developing awareness of the structure and properties of language enables them to appreciate semantic ambiguities such as the "double meaning" of sentences like

The turkey is ready to eat
The shooting of the hunters was terrible

At about the time children begin to think about linguistic ambiguities, they come to appreciate various jokes, riddles, and puns that are "funny" because of their play on sounds or words or the double meanings of certain syntactic structures (see Box 8-3 for examples). Finally, language becomes increasingly "nonliteral" over the course of middle childhood. By age 10–11, children can appreciate and even generate some metaphors, and they are beginning to understand the proverbial meaning of figurative statements such as "When the cat's away, the mice will play" or "People who live in glass houses shouldn't throw stones" (Reynolds & Ortony, 1980; Saltz, 1979).

---

minimum distance principle (MDP): *the rule that in an active English sentence the subject of a verb is the immediately preceding noun.*
metalinguistic awareness: *a knowledge of language and its properties; an understanding that language can be used for purposes other than communicating.*

If you've ever tried to tell a 4-year-old a joke or a riddle, you may have been dismayed to find that your attempt at humor went over like a lead balloon. Preschool children rarely detect the plays on sounds or words that make jokes funny. And even if your young listener did laugh, it was probably for the wrong reasons, because young children who are asked to repeat jokes and riddles tend to paraphrase the meaning in ways that ignore the humor (de Villiers & de Villiers, 1979). For example, a 4-year-old who is told the following riddle:

Where does the fish keep its money?
Answer: In the riverbank.

is likely to retell it as:

Where does the fish keep its money?
Answer: In the bank.

In rephrasing the joke, the child has destroyed it. It's not that preschoolers have no sense of humor; indeed, they love the zany physical antics of clowns and cartoon characters. In fact, they may even laugh at the "fish" riddle, but their reason for doing so is likely to be that it's silly to imagine a fish having any money (admittedly true).

Between the ages of 5 and 7, children develop a metalinguistic awareness that enables them to appreciate linguistic humor. Typically, the first-grader's initial attempts at stand-up comedy are barbs that depend on *phonological ambiguities* such as the one in the following "knock knock" joke:

Knock knock. *Who's there?* Alan. *Alan who?* Al an' me, that's who!

The next type of joke to emerge is that based on lexical ambiguities—plays on words and word meanings. Paul McGhee (1974) tested children's understanding of this brand of humor by asking them to indicate which of two answers was funnier, a joking

answer or a plausible factual answer. Here is a sample item from that study:

Why did the old man tiptoe past the medicine cabinet?
Joking answer: Because he didn't want to wake up the *sleeping* pills.
Straight answer: Because he dropped a glass and didn't want to cut his foot.

McGhee found that 6-year-old first-graders chose serious answers as often as joking answers, thus indicating that they were merely guessing about what made these jokes funny. In contrast, second-graders (7–8-year-olds) clearly preferred the joking answers. Appreciation of lexical ambiguities continues to grow until the fourth or fifth grade (9–11 years of age), when the majority of jokes that children tell involve some kind of pun or play on words (McGhee & Chapman, 1980; Yalisove, 1978).

At about age 11 or 12, children begin to enjoy *absurdity riddles*—jokes that ask absurd questions (or make ridiculous assertions) and then provide an unexpected answer that is quite "logical" if the listener has accepted the absurd premise. Here are two examples:

1. I'll bet I can jump higher than that pine tree. *You're on!* (Jumps) Ha! I win because the tree can't jump.
2. Why did the elephant lie on his back with his feet in the air? *I don't know, why?* So he could trip birds!

The first joke plays on a *syntactical* ambiguity that is humorous once we become aware of it. However, the humor in the second absurdity riddle does not depend on a linguistic ambiguity. Children aged 11 to 12 find this joke funny because they are now able to *think* about absurd hypothetical situations and then appreciate an unexpected punch line that is "sensible" within the absurdity of the initial premise (Yalisove, 1978). Some theorists believe that important cognitive developments may underlie the child's increasing metalinguistic awareness and his or her growing appreciation of humor. We will explore this idea in greater detail in Chapter Nine.

Growth of Communication Skills

Earlier, we examined a study (Shatz & Gelman, 1973) in which preschool children adjusted the style and content of their speech to match a listener's level of understanding. Recall that the 4-year-olds in this study were face to face with

their 2-year-old or their adult companion and thus could see whether or not the listener was following their instructions. Could children this young have communicated effectively with their partners if they had been asked to deliver their messages over a telephone?

Probably not. Robert Krauss and Sam Glucksberg (1977) designed an interesting set of experiments to assess the communication skills of children from 4 to 10 years of age. Each child was asked to describe a set of unfamiliar graphic designs, printed on wooden blocks, to an age mate who had a duplicate set of designs. An opaque screen separated the speaker from the listener. The speaker's task was to stack his blocks and, at the same time, to tell the listener how to stack the duplicate blocks so that the two stacks would be identical. No restrictions were placed on communications between the speaker and listener, and their successes were rewarded with small plastic trinkets. To learn the game, the children were given practice trials with familiar, animal-shaped blocks under conditions where the speaker and listener could see each other. When they had learned the procedure, the speaker and listener were separated by the opaque screen and given eight opportunities to create identical stacks with the unfamiliar designs.

Preschool children failed miserably at this block-stacking task. As shown in Table 8-7, the younger speakers described each unfamiliar design in a highly idiosyncratic way, making it next to impossible for the listeners to know which of the six designs they were talking about. As a result, these younger participants were performing no better on the eighth block-stacking trial than they had on the first (see Figure 8-5). The third- and the fifth-graders, however, were soon communicating effectively, as indicated by their nearly errorless performances over the last three to four trials. Clearly, communication skills improve rather dramatically over the course of middle childhood. But why?

One possibility is that school-age children are gradually becoming more proficient at *thinking about* and *evaluating* the messages they send and receive (Flavell, 1981). At ages 4 to 6, children will occasionally recognize that a message is ambiguous or uninformative (see Patterson, Cos-

TABLE 8-7. Typical idiosyncratic descriptions offered by preschool children when talking about unfamiliar graphic designs in the Krauss and Glucksberg communication game

Form		*Child*				
		1	*2*	*3*	*4*	*5*
1		Man's legs	Airplane	Drapeholder	Zebra	Flying saucer
2		Mother's hat	Ring	Keyhold	Lion	Snake
3		Somebody running	Eagle	Throwing sticks	Strip-stripe	Wire
4		Daddy's shirt	Milk jug	Shoe hold	Coffeepot	Dog
5		Another Daddy's shirt	Bird	Dress hold	Dress	Knife
6		Mother's dress	Ideal	Digger hold	Caterpillar	Ghost

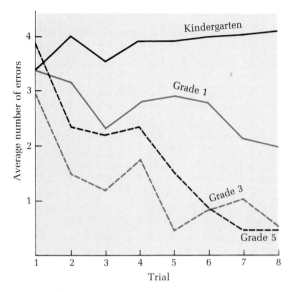

FIGURE 8-5. *Average numbers of errors in communication for kindergarten children and for first-, third-, and fifth-graders.*

grove, & O'Brien, 1980; Pratt & Bates, 1982). However, they are less likely than older (7–10-year-old) listeners to judge ambiguous messages "inadequate" or to request further information from the speaker (Beal & Flavell, 1983; Patterson, O'Brien, Kister, Carter, & Kotsonis, 1981). In addition, there seems to be a relationship between children's "listening" skills and their ability to generate effective communications: those who know (or who have been trained) how to recognize and to ask questions about the "uninformative" messages they receive are generally able to monitor their own speech and produce informative messages (Pratt & Bates, 1982). In sum, school-age children may become better communicators because they are acquiring the cognitive and metalinguistic abilities that enable them to *evaluate* the quality of their own and others' speech and to clarify these messages whenever the need arises.

THEORIES OF LANGUAGE DEVELOPMENT

As linguists began to chart the course of language development, they were amazed that children could learn this complex symbol system at such a breathtaking pace. After all, infants are using abstract signifiers (words) to refer to objects and activities before they can even walk. By age 2, toddlers are expressing hundreds of different messages in their telegraphic sentences. And by age 5, children already know and use most of the syntactical structures of their native tongue, even though they have yet to receive their first formal lesson in grammar. How do they do it? How can we possibly account for the fact that preschool children have such a rich understanding of this abstract symbol system that we call language?

At present, we have no truly definitive answers for these questions. What we do have available in the mid-1980s is a collection of theories, each of which has its strengths and weaknesses. In this final section of the chapter, we will review the three most influential of these approaches and see that each theory emphasizes certain mechanisms or processes that seem to play an important role in language development.

Learning Theories

Some disagreement exists among learning theorists about how children learn to talk. One group of researchers believe that language is learned through operant conditioning as adults *reinforce* children for their attempts to produce grammatical speech (Skinner, 1957; Staats & Staats, 1963). Others have argued that children acquire language by listening to and then *imitating* the speech of their older companions (Bandura, 1971).

■ *The reinforcement model*

In 1957 B. F. Skinner published a book entitled *Verbal Behavior* in which he argued that children learn to speak appropriately because they are reinforced for grammatical speech. Skinner believed that adults begin to shape a child's language by selectively reinforcing those aspects of babbling that are most like adult speech, thereby increasing the probability that these sounds will be repeated. Once they have "shaped" sounds into words, adults will presumably withhold further reinforcement (attention or approval) until the child begins combining words—first into primitive sentences and then into longer, grammatical utterances. So caregivers were said to teach language by reinforcing successive approximations of grammatical speech until the child is talking like an adult.

Another way that parents and other companions might reinforce language is to correctly interpret what the child is trying to say. According to the **communication pressure hypothesis,** children learn to speak more clearly and grammatically because they need to communicate their needs to others (Dale, 1976). The idea here is that adults are most likely to understand grammatical speech and then unwittingly reinforce these interpretable utterances by attending to the child's requests and satisfying his or her needs.

Do parents really "shape" their child's language? If reinforcement theory were a plausible explanation for language learning, we should find that parents often reinforce their children's grammatical speech (perhaps by saying "Very good" or nodding approval) while discouraging ungrammatical utterances. Roger Brown, Courtney Cazden, and Ursula Bellugi (1969) recorded conversations between mothers and their young children to determine whether a mother's reactions to her child's language depend on its syntactical correctness. They found that, in the majority of cases, a mother's approval or disapproval depended on the truth value of the child's statement rather than its grammatical properties. For example, when one child referred to her mother by saying "He a girl" (truthful but grammatically incorrect), her mother replied "That's right." When another child called attention to a lighthouse by stating "There's the animal farmhouse" (syntactically correct but untruthful), her mother corrected her. So it appears that parents pay very little attention to their child's early grammar and do not actively attempt to shape grammatical speech. What they are likely to reinforce when talking with their children is the *semantic* appropriateness, or "truth value," of the child's utterances.

According to the communication pressure hypothesis, children learn to speak appropriately because adults are more likely to (1) understand grammatical (rather than ungrammatical) speech and then (2) subtly reinforce these utterances by satisfying the child's needs. Roger Brown and Camille Hanlon (1970) evaluated this idea by recording and analyzing the conversations of three mothers and their young toddlers. They found that mothers were just as likely to answer a child's questions or to satisfy his needs when he generated a primitive (ungrammatical) utterance such as "Want milk" as when he produced a well-formed version of the same idea (for example, "I want some milk"). Thus, there was no support for the communication pressure hypothesis: mothers could easily understand their children's ungrammatical statements and would often reinforce this imperfect speech by attending to the child's needs. So why does the child's language eventually become more complex? Certainly not because of any need or "pressure" to communicate effectively.

■ *Imitation as a basis for language learning*

Imitation must play some part in language learning, for children end up speaking the same language as the other members of their families and usually will even acquire an accent that characterizes the subculture or the geographical region in which they are raised. Moreover, studies of language learning suggest that young children often learn to name things by listening to the words others use and then reproducing these labels (Ammon & Ammon, 1971; Leonard, Chapman, Rowan, & Weiss, 1983).

But what about syntax? Although children may learn new words by imitating the speech they hear, there are several reasons to believe they rely on other strategies to learn the rules of syntax. If 2–3-year-olds learned to construct sentences by imitating their parents' speech, then their utterances ought to reflect at least some principles of adult grammar from the very beginning. Yet what do children omit when they produce telegraphic statements? They drop the auxiliary verbs and other grammatical morphemes—precisely the information that they should be including if they

---

communication pressure hypothesis: *the idea that children learn to speak clearly and grammatically because clear, grammatical statements will effectively communicate their needs and desires.*

were acquiring grammatical knowledge by imitating the speech of their close companions. Moreover, we have seen that many of the child's earliest sentences are highly creative statements such as "Allgone cookie" or "It broked" that do not appear in adult speech and thus could not have been learned by imitation. Finally, when children do try to mimic an adult utterance, they usually condense or otherwise reformulate the statement so that it conforms to their own level of grammatical competence. Consider the following conversation in which a mother tried to teach a grammatical rule to her child by having him imitate her utterance (from McNeill, 1970, pp. 106–107):

Child: Nobody don't like me.
Mother: No, say "nobody like*s* me."
Child: Nobody don't like me.

[eight repetitions of this dialogue follow . . . then]

Mother: No, now listen carefully; say *"nobody likes me."*
Child: Oh! Nobody don't like*s* me.

This is hardly an atypical example. Lois Bloom and her colleagues (Bloom, Hood, & Lightbown, 1974) report that children do not readily imitate a grammatical rule until they have already used that principle at least once in their spontaneous speech. So imitation may help a child to properly apply rules that he understands and is beginning to use, but it is probably not the mechanism by which these rules are learned in the first place (Slobin, 1979).

■ *How do the child's companions promote language learning?*

Now we begin to see why language development is such a challenging topic. If a child does not directly imitate parental speech, and if parents do not "shape" the child's language, then just what role do others play in language learning? In recent years, psycholinguists have tried to answer this question by carefully analyzing the ways older people talk to young children. Let's see what they have learned.

Amount of conversation. Is a child's language development affected by the willingness of close

companions to initiate and maintain conversations? Apparently so. Alison Clarke-Stewart (1973) found that children whose mothers talked to them a lot had much larger productive vocabularies at age 17 months than children whose mothers were less talkative. Other investigators have found that parents who frequently encourage conversations by asking questions, making requests, and issuing commands that invite verbal responses have children who (1) produce longer utterances during the preschool period, (2) recognize more letters and numbers by age 5–6, and (3) score higher on tests of reading proficiency in the second grade, compared with children from similar backgrounds whose parents are less conversant (Norman-Jackson, 1982; Price, Hess, & Dickson, 1981).

But, interesting as these findings may be, several questions remain. How do children come to understand grammatical rules as they converse with others? Does it matter what close companions are saying; or, rather, could infants and toddlers learn to talk if they merely spent thousands of hours listening to people on television? Let's see whether we can shed some light on these issues by considering what parents seem to be doing when they talk to their children.

Talking the child's language. When adults converse with one another, their sentences tend to be long and grammatically complex. In contrast, parents and older siblings address infants and toddlers with very short, simple sentences that linguists call "baby talk" or **motherese** (see Gelman & Shatz, 1977). Typically these utterances are spoken slowly and in a high-pitched voice, with an emphasis on certain key words (usually words for objects and/or activities). Much of motherese consists of questions ("Where's the ball?") or simple imperatives ("Throw it") that may be paraphrased or repeated several times in order to attract the child's attention and help him to understand. As it turns out, parents and other adults are quite proficient at adjusting their speech to a child's level of understanding. In one study, the language used by 20 adult strangers was recorded as each of the adults conversed with a 2-year-old boy. The results were clear: whenever the 2-year-old gave some indication that he did not understand one of

PHOTO 8-6. *Older companions speak a simple, high-pitched, and repetitive language when talking to infants and toddlers—a language known as "motherese."*

the adult's statements, the adult's next sentence was shorter and less complex (Bohannon & Marquis, 1977).

Other investigators have found that mothers gradually increase both the length and complexity of their own sentences as their children's language becomes more elaborate (Newport, Gleitman, & Gleitman, 1977; Phillips, 1973). And at any given point in time, the adult's sentences are slightly longer and slightly more complex than the child's. Here, then, is a situation that would seem to be ideal for language learning. The child is constantly exposed to new semantic relations and grammatical rules that appear in simple utterances that he or she will probably understand— particularly if older companions frequently repeat or paraphrase the ideas they are trying to communicate. Clearly, this is a form of modeling by the parent. However, children do not acquire new grammatical principles by mimicking them directly, nor do adults make an active attempt to teach these principles by illustration. Parents

speak in "motherese" for one main reason—to communicate effectively with their children.

Expansions and recasts. Occasionally adults will react to a child's telegraphic utterances by re-forming or **expanding** them so that they include the missing grammatical morphemes. For example, if the child says "Doggie go," a parent might expand this sentence by saying "Yes, the doggie is going for a walk." What the adult has done is to draw a direct comparison between a child's primitive sentence and the grammatical forms that an

---

motherese: *the short, simple, high-pitched (and often repetitive) sentences that adults use when talking with young children.*

expansion: *responding to a child's ungrammatical utterance with a grammatically improved form of that statement.*

adult might use to express the same idea. Do children profit from these experiences?

The evidence on this issue is mixed. Courtney Cazden (1965) found that 3½-year-old children whose sentences had been expanded over a three-month period were no more linguistically advanced at the end of the study than a comparable group of 3½-year-olds who had received no special treatment. It may be that children in the "expansion" group did not profit from this experience because they were not very interested in listening to the speech of a companion who generally parroted back at them the very ideas that they had just expressed.

However, Keith Nelson (1977) reports that children may profit from a different kind of expansion in which the older companion **recasts** the child's sentences into new grammatical forms. In the recasting technique, a child who says "Doggie eat" might have her sentence restructured as "What is the doggie eating?" or "The doggie will eat more later." These recasts are moderately novel utterances that will probably command the child's attention and thereby ensure that she notices the new grammatical forms that appear in the adult's speech. Indeed, Nelson found that children whose sentences were often recast into complex questions subsequently began to produce these grammatical constructions, whereas other children whose sentences were recast into complex verb phrases later showed a significant improvement in their use of these verb forms.

Is conversation necessary for language learning? Adults who speak motherese and who recast their child's sentences may be providing an ideal environment for language learning—one that contains a rich variety of sentences that are moderately novel but, at the same time, are related to the ideas that the child is currently expressing. Yet we might wonder whether these modifications of adult speech are really necessary for normal language acquisition. Stated another way, could children learn to talk just as well by listening to adults converse with one another or by watching and listening to people on television?

Apparently not. Catherine Snow and her associates (Snow et al., 1976) studied a group of Dutch children who happened to watch a great deal of German television. Despite their prolonged ex-

posure to the German language, these Dutch-speaking subjects did not acquire any German words or grammar. The de Villierses (1979) also cite the case of a hearing child of deaf parents who saw his parents sign to each other (but not to him) and who had little opportunity to hear any oral speech other than that on television. This child learned no formal sign language from watching his parents, and his oral speech included only a few words like *Kool-aid* that had been taken from television jingles. By age 4, this boy was combining words into highly idiosyncratic strings (for example, "That enough two wing"; "Fall that back") that clearly reflected his ignorance of most grammatical principles. After reviewing this evidence, the de Villierses concluded that "at least some minimal exposure to [conversations] with speakers of the language and perhaps some degree of simplification of the speech that the child hears are necessary for normal language acquisition" (p. 105).

In sum, parents and other companions play a critical role in the child's language development by introducing new linguistic principles in simplified sentences that are carefully tailored to the child's level of understanding. But let's recall that children do not simply mimic these new linguistic forms and are not systematically reinforced for using them. How, then, do they ever acquire this information? Why do they continue to produce increasingly complex sentences? In recent years a number of linguists have proposed a biological theory of language development—*nativism*—in an attempt to answer these questions.

The Nativist Perspective

According to the nativists, human beings are biologically programmed to acquire language. Prominent linguists such as Noam Chomsky (1968, 1975) and David McNeill (1970) have proposed that only humans have a built-in *language acquisition device,* or *LAD*—a set of cognitive and perceptual abilities that are specialized for language learning. Presumably the LAD functions as a "language processor" that enables the child to infer the phonological, semantic, and syntactical regularities that appear in the speech of close companions. As children make inferences about semantic relations and sentence structures, they will then rely on these linguistic hypotheses to construct their own sentences.

Perhaps an example will help to illustrate how a LAD might operate. Let's suppose that a 2-year-old girl reliably produces the utterance "There doggie" every time she ventures into the back yard and sees the two family pets that live there. If her companions frequently recast these (or similar utterances) to illustrate the plural form of singular nouns (for example, "What are the doggie*s* doing?"), the LAD will eventually detect the rule for pluralization, and the child should begin to apply this principle in her own speech. In fact, nativists contend that overregularization errors such as "My *foots* are cold" or "I brushed my *tooths*" must surely mean that children have inferred the rule for pluralization on their own and are now merely demonstrating their newly acquired grammatical competence in these highly "creative" sentences. After all, these constructions would not have been taught by adults and do not appear in adult speech—unless, of course, an adult chooses to mimic a child.

If we assume that children have some unique, inborn capacity for language learning (such as a LAD), then it is easy to see how they might become rather proficient speakers without the benefit of any formal instruction. Recall that adults conversing with a child will carefully adjust their speech so that it is slightly more complex than that of their younger companion. Moreover, we have seen that parents will gradually increase the complexity of their own speech as their children's utterances become more elaborate. Nativists would argue that this changing pattern of parental speech is the ideal environment for language learning, for children are constantly being exposed to new linguistic principles that will be detected by the LAD and then applied to their own speech.

■ The evidence for nativism
The idea that children are biologically programmed to acquire language is very difficult to prove or disprove. It does seem as if human beings must have some unique, inborn capacity for language; after all, no subhuman species has devised anything that closely approximates a rule-bound linguistic system, whereas all normal, healthy children who are exposed to language will be-

come language users. Now suppose that we tried to teach a chimpanzee to use a form of language and found that our subject could produce two-, three-, and even four-word strings. Would this imply that chimps have an inborn linguistic capability that is simply not used in the natural environment? In recent years psycholinguists have had to grapple with this issue, for a small number of chimpanzees have now been trained to use "linguistic" signs and symbols as a means of communicating with human beings. A portion of this intriguing research is described in Box 8-4.

Even if we were to conclude that language is unique to human beings, it remains to be shown that children are biologically programmed for language learning. Over the years, nativists have made several observations that they believe to be consistent with their biological explanation of language development. Let's examine the record for ourselves.

Brain specialization and language. As we saw in Chapter Five, the brain is organized into hemispheres that are connected by a neurological bridge, the corpus callosum. Studies of people whose brains have been damaged by tumors, strokes, or bullet wounds clearly indicate that the major language centers are located in the left cerebral hemisphere. If one of these language areas is damaged, the individual will typically experience **aphasia**—a loss of one or more language functions (Lenneberg, 1967). Damage to the same areas of the right cerebral hemisphere is much less likely to affect the patient's language (Slobin, 1979). The symptoms that an aphasic displays will depend on the site and the extent of the injury. Injuries to Broca's area, near the frontal region of the left hemisphere, typically affect speech production rather than comprehension (Slobin, 1979). In contrast, patients who suffer an injury to Wernicke's area, at the back of the left hemisphere, may speak fairly well but will have difficulty understanding speech.

recasting: *responding to a child's ungrammatical utterance with a nonrepetitive statement that is grammatically correct.*
aphasia: *loss of one or more language functions due to an injury to the brain.*

BOX 8-4
LANGUAGE LEARNING IN CHIMPANZEES

Perhaps it's only natural for us humans to wonder whether chimpanzees and other primates that look so much like us could ever learn to express their ideas through some form of language. Earlier in this century, several attempts were made to raise chimpanzees like children and to teach them to speak English (Hayes, 1951; Kellogg & Kellogg, 1933). Unfortunately, these projects were destined to fail, for the vocal apparatus of a chimpanzee is structurally incapable of producing the many phonemes of human speech.

Washoe. Allen and Beatrice Gardner (1969, 1974) then tried a new approach that proved much more successful: they taught a young chimpanzee named Washoe to use the American Sign Language of the deaf (ASL).

At first Washoe learned the meanings of individual signs and increased her vocabulary one "word" at a time, just as young children do. Within a year, she was producing strings of two to three signs that expressed many of the semantic relations seen in children's telegraphic speech. Chimpanzees can also use signs in an inventive way to name new objects.

For example, on seeing a duck for the first time, Washoe signed "water bird," and another ASL-trained chimp, Lucy, invented the sign "drink fruit" (that is, drink + fruit) to describe a watermelon. By age 4, Washoe had a productive vocabulary of 160 signs and could understand many others that she did not produce. It is also apparent that she can carry on a simple dialogue with a human being, as we see in the following episode described by Dan Slobin (1979):

Human (pointing to Washoe's bed): What that?
Washoe: Bed.
Human: Whose?
Washoe: Mine.
Human: What color [is it]?
Washoe: Red.

Washoe also initiates conversations by describing objects and events, making requests, and asking simple questions (Gardner & Gardner, 1974; Slobin, 1979). She seems to have acquired the rudiments of a language, although she has not progressed beyond the capabilities of a 2–2½-year-old child.

Sarah. Anne and David Premack (1972; Premack, 1976) developed an artificial language in which magnetized plastic tokens that symbolize words can be arranged on a metal board to produce sentences. The

Until very recently, it was assumed that only humans had a capacity for language. This viewpoint is now being challenged by the progress of several chimpanzees (and at least one gorilla) who have learned to communicate simple and sometimes inventive messages using American Sign Language.

Premacks' star pupil, Sarah, first learned the meanings of individual tokens. Her productive vocabulary included names (symbols) for herself, each of her trainers, and a variety of other objects (apples, bananas, chocolate, and other foods; dishes, pails, and so on), as well as symbols for various actions (give, insert, take, and the like), adjectives (colors, this/that), and grammatical markers (plurals, negations, questions, and so on).

Over a 2½-year period, Sarah learned to construct hundreds of meaningful "sentences" in her plastic symbol-language. In the later phases of her training, she could quickly learn the names of new objects by "reading" sentences in which the symbol for *name of* was placed between the symbol for the new object and the object itself (for example, "Apple name of ◒ "). Sarah can also answer questions of the type "What name of ⍺ ?" by selecting the plastic symbol for *banana* from a number of alternatives. She seems to understand syntax as well. When presented with the symbol-sentence "Sarah banana pail cracker dish insert," Sarah dutifully inserts the banana in the pail and the cracker in the dish. If she had merely responded to each token in turn, she would not have realized that the verb *insert* refers to

two separate actions, both of which *she* is supposed to perform. Thus, failing to understand the syntax, Sarah would have tried to put everything in the dish (or perhaps would have carried out only the second insertion).

In sum, chimpanzees can learn that the structure (syntax) of a sentence conveys a message that goes beyond the meanings of its individual words. However, a chimp will require years of special training to achieve the basic level of "grammatical competence" that 2½- to 3-year-olds acquire without any formal instruction.

Lana. Lana is a chimpanzee who has learned to use hieroglyphics printed on a special keyboard to type messages to a computer (the locations of these hieroglyphic-words are changed frequently to ensure that Lana is responding to the symbolism rather than to the positions of particular keys). Apparently Lana's accomplishments are similar to Sarah's. She has learned to request a variety of foods, moving pictures, music, and even human contact by simply typing hieroglyphic sentences of the form "Please, machine, give _____." Lana asks the machine to

(*box continues*)

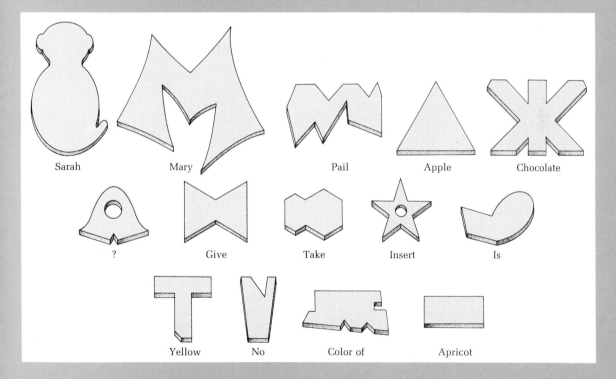

A sample of the plastic token-words learned by Sarah. The bottom row forms a symbol sentence that says "Yellow is not the color of an apricot"—a sentence Sarah is capable of producing.

BOX 8-4 (continued)
LANGUAGE LEARNING IN CHIMPANZEES

name new objects that she has never seen before. Moreover, she recognizes when she has made a productive error in a sentence by erasing her mistakes and starting the sequence over. However, her "language" is strictly pragmatic—once the machine gives her whatever she has requested, the "conversation" ends (Rumbaugh, 1977; Rumbaugh & Gill, 1976).

Criticisms of this monkey business. Remarkable as those accomplishments may seem, many psycholinguists are hesitant to conclude that Washoe, Sarah, or Lana has acquired a language. One of the more vocal critics, Herbert Terrace (1979; Terrace, cited in "Are Those Apes Really Talking?," 1980), actually began as an advocate of chimp language. He first taught sign language to a pupil named Nim Chimpsky (an obvious play on the name of nativist Noam Chomsky) and later discovered that Nim did not use the language to invent new sentences. In fact, Terrace reviewed reports and videotapes of other "linguistic" chimps and concluded that all of them were simply producing either routines that they had memorized or sentences that had been "cued" by the actions and gestures of a human trainer. Even Lana's interactions with a machine were viewed as nonlinguistic ploys

to gain a reward of some kind. The Gardners and the Premacks, however, insist that their pupils use language inventively and are capable of interpreting complex sentences that they have never seen before.

This debate will undoubtedly continue for some time unless chimps suddenly display much more of a linguistic capacity than they have shown to date. Clearly, the accomplishments of Washoe, Sarah, Lana, and Nim are similar in many respects to the language of young toddlers. However, let's keep in mind that even a severely retarded child will soon surpass the linguistic capabilities of the brightest of chimpanzees. Obviously, human beings have something chimps lack that enables them to acquire language as we know it. Is that something an inborn linguistic capacity (or LAD) that is unique to humans? Noam Chomsky says yes and adds: "It is about as likely that an ape will prove to have a language ability as that there is an island somewhere with a species of flightless birds waiting for human beings to teach them to fly" ("Are Those Apes Really Talking?," 1980, p. 57). However, David Premack (1976) suggests that the ape's relative incapacity for language may simply reflect the animal's limited intellectual capabilities rather than the absence of an innate language processor. It remains for future research to decide which of these two alternatives is correct.

Apparently the left hemisphere is sensitive to some aspects of language from birth. In the first day of life, speech sounds already elicit more electrical activity from the left side of an infant's brain, while music and other nonspeech sounds produce greater activity from the right cerebral hemisphere (Molfese, 1977). Moreover, we've seen that young infants are quite capable of discriminating important phonetic contrasts such as *b* and *p* or *d* and *t* during the first few weeks of life (Eimas, 1975). These findings would seem to imply that the neonate is "wired" for speech and is prepared to analyze speechlike sounds.

The critical-period hypothesis. It often seems as if preschool children acquired their first language a whole lot easier than college students learn a foreign tongue. Is this really the case? Nativists believe it is: they have argued that human beings are most proficient at language learning during the period between age 2 and puberty.

Eric Lenneberg (1967) is perhaps the strongest

proponent of a **critical period** for language learning. Lenneberg notes that prepubescent children can easily acquire two (or more) languages simultaneously and will speak each tongue without a trace of an accent from the other language(s). In contrast, those who acquire a second language after puberty must study intently to become fluent in that language, and they are likely to speak their new tongue with a "foreign" accent. In addition, the prognosis for recovering from traumatic aphasia depends on the age at which the injury was sustained. Children who suffer brain damage before puberty will recover most if not all of their lost language functions without special therapy, particularly if their injury occurred before age 5 (de Villiers & de Villiers, 1978). However, adolescent and adult aphasics often require extensive therapy to regain even a portion of their lost language skills. These observations suggest that the brain is particularly well suited for language acquisition before the onset of puberty. But why?

According to nativists, the critical period for

language learning is a product of biological maturation. Lenneberg (1967) proposes that the brain is not fully specialized for language functions until it is fully mature, at puberty. Presumably a young aphasic can recover lost language skills because the right hemisphere of his or her relatively unspecialized (immature) brain is able to assume the functions that would normally be served by the damaged areas of the left hemisphere. At puberty the prognosis changes. The brain is now completely specialized for language (and other neurological duties), so that the right hemisphere can no longer assume the linguistic functions lost when a person suffers an injury to the left side of the brain.

Linguistic universals. If language learning is unique to humans and heavily influenced by biological maturation, then all normal, healthy children should proceed through roughly the same stages when acquiring their first language. And apparently they do (this is what is meant by **linguistic universals**). Even though children are typically exposed to language from the first day or two of life, they do not begin to babble for several months or to produce meaningful words for about a year. All children in all cultures show a similar pattern of phonological development: consonants such as *g* and *k* from the back of the mouth always appear before frontal consonants such as *m* or *b*, while the sequencing of vowels is exactly reversed—frontal vowels such as *e* as in *beet* emerge before back vowels such as *a* as in *mama* (Glucksberg & Danks, 1975). It is only near the end of the babbling stage, after the vocal apparatus has become capable of producing a wide variety of speechlike sounds, that children will begin to restrict their babbling to the phonetic elements they hear in the speech of their companions.

As infants begin to "talk," they always start out with holophrastic utterances, progress to telegraphic sentences, and express precisely the same kinds of semantic and syntactic relations in their telegraphic speech (Slobin, 1979—review Table 8-2). All normal children will acquire and use the basic syntax of their native language by the time they enter school, and they almost invariably develop the ability to think about language and its properties (that is, metalinguistic awareness) between ages 6 and 10 (de Villiers & de Villiers,

1978). Children with Down's syndrome, who mature very slowly, will proceed through these same stages of language development—though at a much slower pace. Even severely retarded children who can neither count nor grasp the rules of kindergarten games will nevertheless acquire many abstract principles of syntax and become adequate conversationalists (Lenneberg, 1967).

Why is language easier to learn than counting or other sets of rules? A nativist would respond by arguing that *all* human beings (including retarded children) are born with certain cognitive and perceptual abilities (a LAD) that are specialized for language learning. As these abilities mature, all children should pass through the same sequence of linguistic "milestones," and they will require nothing other than regular interactions with speaking companions in order to learn any and all languages to which they are exposed.

■ *Problems with the nativist approach*

Today almost everyone agrees that language development is influenced by biological development. However, many contemporary researchers question the notion that human beings have an inborn language processor, or LAD, that functions most efficiently during a "critical period" between birth and puberty. Evidence against the critical-period hypothesis comes from many sources. Carroll (1969) reports that adults who receive intensive training in a foreign language will require only 250–500 hours of instruction to achieve a comfortable level of fluency. When acquiring a second language, adults and children learn grammar at about the same rate, and adults actually learn vocabulary items more rapidly than children do (Di Vesta, 1974). Although children are better than adults at the phonological aspects of language learning (pronouncing words), it is by no means impossible for an adult to learn to speak a foreign language without a detectable accent. Finally, if puberty were truly the end of a "critical

---

critical-period hypothesis: *the notion that human beings are most proficient at language learning between age 2 and puberty.*
linguistic universal: *an aspect of language development that all children share.*

BOX 8-5
*A CHILDHOOD WITHOUT LANGUAGE:
THE CURIOUS CASE OF GENIE*

In November of 1970, a neglected and abused child named Genie came to the attention of authorities in Los Angeles, California. Incredible as it may seem, Genie had been locked away in a back room as a toddler and had remained in solitary confinement until she was rescued at age 13 years, 7 months. During her long captivity, Genie had been tied down to a potty chair during the day and "caged" at night in a crib covered with wire. Her contacts with human beings were minimal. Genie's mother, who was nearly blind, would spend a few minutes with her every day as she fed the child soft baby food. However, Genie's abusive father (who believed that his daughter was hopelessly retarded) would not permit anyone to talk to her. Genie had never even heard a radio or a television, for her father would not tolerate these noisemaking appliances in his home. In fact, Genie was not permitted to make noise: whenever she made a sound, her father was likely to come into her room and beat her while barking and growling like a wild dog (Curtiss, 1977).

Although Genie was past puberty at the time of her liberation, she weighed less than 60 pounds and could not walk or even stand erect. Medical tests revealed that she had normal vision, hearing, and eye/hand coordination although, as you might expect, she was quite emotionally disturbed. When psycholinguists began to test Genie's language abilities, they found that she seemed to understand a word or two. However, Genie did not speak and gave absolutely no indication of understanding any grammar. So here is a child who had virtually no exposure to language from the middle of her second year until after puberty—precisely the time that nativists believe to be a "critical period" for language learning.

Genie soon surprised everyone with her progress. Within eight months of her rescue, she had learned most English phonemes, had acquired a working vocabulary of 200 words, and had already begun to produce two-word sentences. Genie's first sentences were telegraphic constructions that closely resembled the early speech of young toddlers, and her earliest negatives were produced by appending *no* to the beginning of a declarative sentence, just as normal children do (de Villiers & de Villiers, 1979).

Seven years after her rescue, Genie had come a long way. She could move around her neighborhood and use public transportation. She was functioning quite well in both her foster home and her special classes at school. She was also producing much longer sentences, although her speech was still far from normal. For example, she rarely used auxiliary verbs, personal pronouns, or the demonstrative adjectives *this* and *that*. Moreover, she often confused prepositional contrasts such as *over/under* and *front/back,* and she found it difficult to interpret many relative clauses and compound sentences. So even though Genie's early progress closely resembled the language learning of normal children, her language seven years later was much less sophisticated than that of a 5-year-old.

What can we say about the critical-period hypothesis in view of Genie's experiences? The de Villierses (1979) concluded that any strong version of the hypothesis that implies that first language learning is impossible after puberty must be incorrect. Genie had very little exposure to speech before puberty, and yet she has acquired a substantial amount of language. However, the de Villierses suggest that a weaker version of the hypothesis, which claims that language learning will be incomplete after puberty, may still be correct.

In sum, it appears that the time between 2 years of age and puberty is a *sensitive period* for first language learning, rather than an absolutely critical period.

---

period" for language learning, it would be difficult to explain the progress of Genie, a modern-day "wild child" who had already reached puberty before having an opportunity to converse with anyone (see Box 8-5).

Other investigators have argued that we don't really explain language development by attributing it to a built-in language acquisition device. Recall that the concept of a LAD arose as researchers began to discover that learning theories

could not explain language development. That being the case, the nativists concluded that the mechanism for language learning must be innate. Unfortunately, they have never specified *how* an inborn language processor might sift through linguistic input and infer the rules that govern language—they merely assume that these rules and relationships are eventually detected (in some unknown way) and applied to the child's own speech. The major shortcoming of this approach can be illustrated by analogy: attributing advances in linguistic competence to the mysterious workings of a LAD is like saying that physical growth is biologically programmed—*and then failing to identify the underlying variables (nutrition, hormones, and so forth) that explain why growth follows the course it takes.* Clearly, the nativist approach is woefully incomplete; it is really more a description of language learning than a true explanation.

The Interactionist Perspective

It should now be apparent that neither learning theory nor the nativist approach provides a complete explanation of language development, although each of these perspectives may be partly correct. We know that children must be exposed to speech, presumably simplified speech, before they will learn much of anything about language. Imitation obviously plays some part in the language-learning process, for children acquire the same language (and even the same accent) that their companions use. Reinforcement must also play some role, for we've seen that children talk more (and will become better readers) if their parents frequently encourage verbal interactions. Yet if language were learned through imitation and reinforcement, it would be difficult to explain why children who hear varying kinds and amounts of linguistic input will proceed through roughly the same steps when acquiring their first language. These "linguistic universals" suggest that language learning is related in some meaningful way to biological processes. But must we attribute language development to the mysterious workings of an inborn LAD in order to explain the similarities in children's early speech?

Apparently not. In recent years, cognitive theorists such as Jean Piaget (1970) have argued that both biological factors and the linguistic environment combine to influence language development. According to this **interactionist** viewpoint, young children talk alike because they are all members of the same species who *share many common experiences.* What may be innate is not any specialized linguistic capacity but, rather, a nervous system that predisposes children to develop similar ideas at about the same age.

Piaget suggests that infants are curious explorers who form intellectual schemata to explain interesting objects and events and then end up talking about that which they know and understand. In other words, he says that language development reflects the child's cognitive development. Since cognitive development is thought to be heavily influenced by the maturation of the brain and the nervous system, all children should proceed through the same stages of intellectual growth and show some very definite similarities in the patterning of their early speech.

What role does the environment play? Piaget suggests that as children develop intellectually, they will produce increasingly sophisticated utterances—statements that will prompt close companions to increase the complexity of their own speech as they address their children. This novel linguistic input will then provide children with information that they can use to form new linguistic schemata, produce even more complex utterances, and thereby influence the speech of their companions once again. Clearly the pattern of influence is reciprocal: the child's speech influences the speech of older companions, which, in turn, influences the child's speech, and so on. Stated another way, Piaget proposes that the language of young children is influenced by a linguistic environment that they have had a hand in creating.

Many observations are consistent with Piaget's theory. In our next chapter, we will see that the intellectual schemata of preverbal children are based largely on actions that these infants have witnessed or undertaken. Presumably an 8-month-old comes to know what a "ball" is by acting on it and discovering its properties. If one's cognitive competencies are reflected in language, then perhaps we should not be surprised to learn that children's first words usually focus on *objects they can manipulate* or *actions they have performed* (Nelson, 1973). Apparently these young infants are merely talking about aspects of their environment that they can understand.

---

interactionist theory: *the notion that biological factors and environmental influences combine to determine the course of language development.*

Consider another example. Children rarely produce hypothetical statements such as "If it is cold, we will shiver" or "If it had rained, we would have been soaked" until age 4 or 5 (de Villiers & de Villiers, 1979). Indeed, these are reasonably complex statements that require (1) the capacity to think about possibilities rather than actualities and (2) an ability to shift one's frame of reference to the future or the past. In English, the syntax required to express hypotheticals is reasonably complex, much more so than the grammatically simple forms used in Russian. Nevertheless, Russian children do not begin to produce hypothetical statements until about the same age as English-speaking children do (Slobin, 1966). So the appearance of hypotheticals in children's speech depends more on an understanding of the *concept* of the hypothetical than on the intricacies of the grammar necessary to produce these utterances.

In sum, the interactionist perspective is both a synthesis and an extension of the learning and the nativist theories and is probably more accurate than either of these approaches. Like the nativists, the interactionists believe that children are biologically prepared for language learning. However, they stress that the "universals" in children's language reflect a basic interplay among biological maturation, cognitive development, and the linguistic environment rather than the workings of an inborn language processor (or LAD).

What is new about the interactionist approach is its emphasis on cognitive development. This is not to say that cognitive development explains language development; it merely places some limits on what children will understand as they listen to others' speech. And even when children do grasp concepts such as time and causality, they must still discover how to express this knowledge in their own speech.

How do they make these discoveries? Here is where the interactionists propose that companions play an important role by continually introducing new linguistic concepts in simplified sentences tailored to the level of understanding of the child. And after several years of conversing with these responsive linguistic models, developing children will have acquired most of the important principles of their native language and will be speaking in much the same way that their older companions do.

SUMMARY

Students of language development have tried to answer two basic questions. The first is the "what" question: What is the normal course of language development, and just what are children acquiring that enables them to become language users? The four aspects of language that children acquire are phonology, a knowledge of the phonemes that are used in producing language; semantics, an understanding of the meaning of words and sentences; syntax, the rules that specify how words are combined to produce sentences; and pragmatics, the principles governing how language is to be used in different social situations. The second basic question is the "how" question: How do young children acquire a working knowledge of a highly abstract symbol system such as language? Empiricists have argued that children learn language as they imitate others' speech and are reinforced for grammatical statements. However, nativists contend that children are biologically programmed to acquire language and do not have to be reinforced for grammatical speech.

Although babies respond to speech at birth, they will not utter their first meaningful words for about a year. During this prelinguistic stage, infants vocalize by crying, cooing, and babbling. As children approach their first birthday, they begin to make the transition to meaningful speech by babbling those sounds that they often hear in their companions' speech and dropping other sounds that they hear infrequently.

At about 1 year of age, infants produce their first recognizable words and enter the holophrastic stage of language development. For the next several months, children talk in one-word utterances and will expand their vocabularies one word at a time. They talk most about those things that interest them—objects that move, make noise, and can be manipulated. Young children seem to infer the meanings of words from the perceptual characteristics of their referents (size, shape, and so on) and are likely to overextend the use of words—for example, applying *doggie* to all furry, four-legged animals. Some psycholinguists believe that a child's single words are often intended as holophrases—one-word messages that represent an entire sentence's worth of meaning.

At about 18–24 months of age, children enter the telegraphic stage of language development as they begin to combine words into simple sentences. These utterances are called "telegraphic" because they typically include only nouns, verbs, and occasionally adjectives, omitting prepositions, auxiliary verbs, articles, conjunctions, and other grammatical markers. Although telegraphic sentences are not grammatical by adult standards, they represent far more than random word combinations. Not only do all children follow the same rules of word order when combining words, but they also express the same categories of meaning (semantic relations) in their earliest sentences. So telegraphic speech is not merely a shortened version of adult speech; it is a universal "child language" that has a grammar of its own.

During the preschool period (ages 2½ to 5), the child's language becomes much more similar to an adult's. As children produce longer utterances, they begin to add grammatical morphemes such as the *-s* for plurality, the *-ed* for past tense, the *-ing* for present progressive, articles, prepositions, and auxiliary verbs. Although there are individual differences in the rate at which children will acquire grammatical markers, there is a striking uniformity in the order in which these morphemes appear. The preschool period is also the time when a child learns basic transformational rules that will enable him or her to change declarative statements into questions, negations, imperatives, relative clauses, and compound sentences. By the time they enter school, children have mastered most of the syntactical rules of their native language and can produce a variety of sophisticated, adultlike messages. Another reason language becomes increasingly complex during the preschool years is that youngsters are beginning to appreciate semantic and relational contrasts such as big/little, tall/short, wide/narrow, in/on, over/under, more/less, and before/after. Preschool children have also learned an important pragmatic lesson: If you hope to be understood, you must tailor your message to the listener's level of understanding.

Middle childhood (ages 6–14) is a period of linguistic refinement: children learn subtle exceptions to grammatical rules and begin to understand even the most complex syntactical structures of their native language. Vocabulary continues to grow, and children gradually develop metalinguistic awareness—an ability to think about language and to comment on its properties. School-age children are also becoming much better communicators as they acquire the cognitive skills and metalinguistic abilities that will enable them to detect and clarify the uninformative messages that they send and receive.

There are three major theories of language acquisition: learning theory, nativism, and the interactionist approach. Learning theorists believe that language is acquired as children imitate the speech of their companions and are reinforced for their grammatically correct imitations. However, careful analyses of conversations between parents and their young children reveal that children do not mimic the sentences they hear, nor do adults selectively reinforce their children's grammatical statements.

Nativists argue that human beings have an inborn linguistic processor, or language acquisition device, that is specialized for language learning. Presumably children require nothing other than speech to analyze and someone with whom to converse in order to learn any (and all) languages to which they are exposed. Two lines of evidence are consistent with the nativist approach. First, particular areas of the brain serve as centers of linguistic activity. Second, all children in all cultures go through the same stages of language acquisition, regardless of the structure of the language they are learning. However, nativists are not very clear about how children sift through verbal input and make the critical discoveries that will further their linguistic competencies.

Proponents of the interactionist position acknowledge that children are biologically prepared to acquire language. However, they suggest that what may be innate is not any specialized linguistic processor but, rather, a nervous system that gradually matures and predisposes children to develop similar ideas at about the same age. Thus, biological maturation is said to affect cognitive development, which, in turn, influences language development. However, interactionists recognize that the environment plays a crucial role in language learning, for children must hear simplified versions of adult speech in order to acquire the linguistic concepts that promote language development.

REFERENCES

Ackerman, B. P. (1982). Contextual integration and utterance interpretation: The ability of children and adults to interpret sarcastic utterances. *Child Development, 53,* 1075–1083.

Ammon, P. R., & Ammon, M. S. (1971). Effects of training black preschool children in vocabulary vs. sentence construction. *Journal of Educational Psychology, 62,* 421–426.

Are those apes really talking? (1980, March 10). *Time,* pp. 50–57.

Bandura, A. (1971). An analysis of modeling processes. In A. Bandura (Ed.), *Psychological modeling.* New York: Lieber-Atherton.

Bates, E. (1976a). *Language and context: The acquisition of pragmatics.* New York: Academic Press.

Bates, E. (1976b). Pragmatics and sociolinguistics in child language. In D. Morehead & A. Morehead (Eds.), *Normal and deficient child language.* Baltimore: University Park Press.

Beal, C. R., & Flavell, J. H. (1983). Young speakers' evaluations of their listener's comprehension in a referential communication task. *Child Development, 54,* 148–153.

Benedict, H. (1979). Early lexical development: Comprehension and production. *Journal of Child Language, 6,* 183–200.

Berko, J. (1958). The child's learning of English morphology. *Word, 14,* 150–177.

Blewitt, P. (1983). *Dog* versus *collie:* Vocabulary in speech to young children. *Developmental Psychology, 19,* 602–609.

Bloom, L. (1970). *Language development: Form and function in emerging grammars.* Cambridge, MA: M.I.T. Press.

Bloom, L. (1973). *One word at a time: The use of single word utterances before syntax.* The Hague: Mouton.

Bloom, L., Hood, L., & Lightbown, P. (1974). Imitation in language development: If, when and why. *Cognitive Psychology, 6,* 380–420.

Bloom, L., Merkin, S., & Wootten, J. (1982). Wh- questions: Linguistic factors that contribute to the sequence of acquisition. *Child Development, 53,* 1084–1092.

Bohannon, J. W., III, & Marquis, A. L. (1977). Children's control of adult speech. *Child Development, 48,* 1002–1008.

Bonvillian, J. D., Orlansky, M. D., & Novack, L. L. (1983). Developmental milestones: Sign language acquisition and motor development. *Child Development, 54,* 1435–1445.

Bowerman, M. (1977). Semantic factors in the acquisition of rules for word use and sentence construction. In D. Morehead & A. Morehead (Eds.), *Directions in normal and deficient child language.* Baltimore: University Park Press.

Braine, M. D. S. (1963). The ontogeny of English phrase structure: The first phrase. *Language, 39,* 1–13.

Brown, R. (1970). *Psycholinguistics.* New York: Free Press.

Brown, R. (1973). *A first language: The early stages.* Cambridge, MA: Harvard University Press.

Brown, R., Cazden, C., & Bellugi, U. (1969). The child's grammar from I–III. In J. P. Hill (Ed.), *Minnesota Symposia on Child Psychology* (Vol. 2). Minneapolis: University of Minnesota Press.

Brown, R., & Hanlon, C. (1970). Derivational complexity and order of acquisition. In J. R. Hayes (Ed.), *Cognition and the development of language.* New York: Wiley.

Butterfield, E. C., & Siperstein, G. N. (1972). Influence of contingent auditory stimulation on non-nutritional suckle. In J. F. Bosma (Ed.), *Third symposium on oral sensation and perception: The mouth of the infant.* Springfield, IL: Charles C Thomas.

Carey, S. (1977). The child as a word learner. In M. Halle, J. Bresnan, & G. A. Miller (Eds.), *Linguistic theory and psychological reality.* Cambridge, MA: M.I.T. Press.

Carroll, J. B. (1969). Psychological and educational research into second language teaching to young children. In H. H. Stern (Ed.), *Languages and the young school child.* London: Oxford University Press.

Cazden, C. (1965). *Environmental assistance to the child's acquisition of grammar.* Unpublished doctoral dissertation, Harvard University.

Chomsky, C. S. (1969). *The acquisition of syntax in children from 5 to 10.* Cambridge, MA: M.I.T. Press.

Chomsky, N. (1968). *Language and mind.* New York: Harcourt Brace Jovanovich.

Chomsky, N. (1975). *Reflections on language.* New York: Pantheon Books.

Clark, E. V. (1971). On the acquisition of the meaning of *before* and *after. Journal of Verbal Learning and Verbal Behavior, 10,* 266–275.

Clark, E. V. (1973). What's in a word? On the child's acquisition of semantics in his first language. In T. E. Moore (Ed.), *Cognitive development and the acquisition of language.* New York: Academic Press.

Clark, H. H., & Clark, E. V. (1977). *Psychology and language: An introduction to psycholinguistics.* New York: Harcourt Brace Jovanovich.

Clarke-Stewart, K. A. (1973). Interactions between mothers and their young children: Characteristics and consequences. *Monographs of the Society for Research in Child Development, 38* (Serial No. 153).

Condon, W. S., & Sander, L. W. (1974). Neonate movement is synchronized with adult speech: Interactional participation and language acquisition. *Science, 183,* 99–101.

Curtiss, S. (1977). *Genie: A psycholinguistic study of a modern-day "wild child."* New York: Academic Press.

Dale, P. S. (1976). *Language development: Structure and function.* New York: Holt, Rinehart and Winston.

Daneman, M., & Case, R. (1981). Syntactic form, semantic complexity, and short-term memory: Influences on children's acquisition of new linguistic structures. *Developmental Psychology, 17,* 367–378.

DeCasper, A. J., & Fifer, W. P. (1980). Of human bonding: Newborns prefer their mothers' voices. *Science, 208,* 1174–1176.

Dennis, M., Sugar, J., & Whitaker, H. A. (1982). The acquisition of tag questions. *Child Development, 53,* 1254–1257.

de Villiers, J. G., & de Villiers, P. A. (1973). A cross-sectional study of the acquisition of grammatical morphemes in child speech. *Journal of Psycholinguistic Research, 2,* 267–278.

de Villiers, J. G., & de Villiers, P. A. (1978). *Language acquisition.* Cambridge, MA: Harvard University Press.

de Villiers, P. A., & de Villiers, J. G. (1979). *Early language.* Cambridge, MA: Harvard University Press.

Di Vesta, F. J. (1974). *Language, learning, and cognitive processes.* Monterey, CA: Brooks/Cole.

Eimas, P. D. (1975). Speech perception in early infancy. In L. B. Cohen & P. Salapatek (Eds.), *Infant perception: From sensation to cognition* (Vol. 2). New York: Academic Press.

Ferguson, C. A. (1977). Learning to pronounce: The earliest stages of phonological development in the child. In F. D. Minifie & L. L. Lloyd (Eds.), *Communication and cognitive abilities: Early behavioral assessment.* Baltimore: University Park Press.

Flavell, J. H. (1981). Cognitive monitoring. In W. P. Dickson (Ed.), *Children's oral communication skills.* New York: Academic Press.

Flavell, J. H., Speer, J. R., Green, F. L., & August, D. L. (1981). The development of comprehension monitoring and knowledge about communication. *Monographs of the Society for Research in Child Development, 46* (Serial No. 192).

Freedle, R., & Lewis, M. (1977). Prelinguistic conversation. In M. Lewis & L. Rosenblum (Eds.), *Interaction, conversation, and the development of language.* New York: Wiley.

Gardner, B. T., & Gardner, R. A. (1974). Comparing the early utterances of child and chimpanzee. In A. Pick (Ed.), *Minnesota Symposia on Child Psychology* (Vol. 8). Minneapolis: University of Minnesota Press.

Gardner, R. A., & Gardner, B. T. (1969). Teaching sign language to a chimpanzee. *Science, 165,* 664–672.

Garvey, C. (1975). Requests and responses in children's speech. *Journal of Child Language, 2,* 41–63.

Gelman, R., & Shatz, M. (1977). Appropriate speech adjustments: The operation of conversational constraints on talk to two-year-olds. In M. Lewis & L. A. Rosenblum (Eds.), *Interaction, conversation, and the development of language.* New York: Wiley.

Glucksberg, S., & Danks, J. H. (1975). *Experimental psycholinguistics.* Hillsdale, NJ: Erlbaum.

Goodz, N. S. (1982). Is before really easier to understand than after? *Child Development, 53,* 822–825.

Hayes, C. (1951). *The ape in our house.* New York: Harper & Row.

Hood, L., & Bloom, L. (1979). What, when, and how about why: A longitudinal study of early expressions of causality. *Monographs of the Society for Research in Child Development, 44* (Serial No. 181).

Jakobson, R. (1968). *Child language, aphasia, and phonological universals.* The Hague: Mouton.

Johnson, C. J., Pick, H. L., Siegel, G. M., Cicciarelli, A. W., & Garber, S. R. (1981). Effects of interpersonal distance on children's vocal intensity. *Child Development, 52,* 721–723.

Johnson, H., & Smith, L. B. (1981). Children's inferential abilities in the context of reading to understand. *Child Development, 52,* 1216–1223.

Kellogg, W. N., & Kellogg, L. A. (1933). *The ape and the child.* New York: McGraw-Hill.

Klima, E. S., & Bellugi, I. (1975). Perception and production in a visually based language. In D. Aaronson & R. W. Rieber (Eds.), *Developmental psycholinguistics and communication disorders. Annals of the New York Academy of Science, 263,* 225–235.

Krauss, R. M., & Glucksberg, S. (1977). Social and nonsocial speech. *Scientific American, 236,* 100–105.

Kuczaj, S. A., II. (1979). Evidence for a language learning strategy: On the relative ease of acquisition of prefixes and suffixes. *Child Development, 50,* 1–13.

Lenneberg, E. H. (1967). *Biological foundations of language.* New York: Wiley.

Leonard, L. B., Chapman, K., Rowan, L. E., & Weiss, A. L. (1983). Three hypotheses concerning young children's imitations of lexical items. *Developmental Psychology, 19,* 591–601.

Leung, E. H. L., & Rheingold, H. L. (1981). Development of pointing as a social gesture. *Developmental Psychology, 17,* 215–220.

Lieberman, P. (1967). *Interaction, perception and language.* Cambridge, MA: M.I.T. Press.

McGhee, P. E. (1974). Cognitive mastery and children's humor. *Psychological Bulletin, 81,* 721–730.

McGhee, P. E., & Chapman, A. J. (1980). *Children's humour.* London: Wiley.

McNeill, D. (1970). *The acquisition of language.* New York: Harper & Row.

Menyuk, P. (1977). *Language and maturation.* Cambridge, MA: M.I.T. Press.

Mervis, C. B., & Mervis, C. A. (1982). Leopards are kitty-cats: Object labeling by mothers for their thirteen-month-olds. *Child Development, 53,* 267–273.

Molfese, D. L. (1977). Infant cerebral asymmetry. In S. J. Segalowitz & F. A. Gruber (Eds.), *Language development and neurological theory.* New York: Academic Press.

Nelson, K. (1973). Structure and strategy in learning to talk. *Monographs of the Society for Research in Child Development, 38* (Serial No. 149).

Nelson, K. (1976). Some attributes of adjectives used by young children. *Cognition, 4,* 13–30.

Nelson, K. (1978). Semantic development and the development of semantic memory. In K. E. Nelson (Ed.), *Children's language.* New York: Gardner Press.

Nelson, K. (1981). Individual differences in language development: Implications for development and language. *Developmental Psychology, 17,* 170–187.

Nelson, K. E. (1977). Facilitating children's syntax acquisition. *Developmental Psychology, 13,* 101–107.

Newport, E. L., Gleitman, H., & Gleitman, L. R. (1977). Mother, I'd rather do it myself: Some effects and non-effects of maternal speech style. In C. E. Snow & C. A. Ferguson (Eds.), *Talking to children: Language input and acquisition.* Cambridge: Cambridge University Press.

Norman-Jackson, J. (1982). Family interactions, language development, and primary reading achievement of Black children in families of low income. *Child Development, 53,* 349–358.

Oviatt, S. L. (1980). The emerging ability to comprehend language: An experimental approach. *Child Development, 51,* 97–106.

Patterson, C. J., Cosgrove, J. M., & O'Brien, R. G. (1980). Nonverbal indicants of comprehension and noncomprehension in children. *Developmental Psychology, 16,* 38–48.

Patterson, C. J., O'Brien, C. O., Kister, M. C., Carter, D. B., & Kotsonis, M. E. (1981). Development of comprehension monitoring as a function of context. *Developmental Psychology, 17,* 379–389.

Phillips, J. R. (1973). Syntax and vocabulary in mothers' speech to young children: Age and sex comparisons. *Child Development, 44,* 182–185.

Piaget, J. (1970). Piaget's theory. In P. H. Mussen (Ed.), *Carmichael's manual of child psychology* (Vol. 1). New York: Wiley.

Pratt, M. W., & Bates, K. R. (1982). Young editors: Preschoolers' evaluation and production of ambiguous messages. *Developmental Psychology, 18,* 30–42.

Prawat, R. S., & Wildfong, S. (1980). The influence of functional context on children's labeling responses. *Child Development, 51,* 1057–1060.

Premack, A. J., & Premack, D. (1972). Teaching language to an ape. *Scientific American, 227,* 92–99.

Premack, D. (1976). *Intelligence in ape and man.* Hillsdale, NJ: Erlbaum.

Price, G. C., Hess, R. D., & Dickson, W. P. (1981). Processes by which verbal-educational abilities are affected when mothers encourage preschool children to verbalize. *Developmental Psychology, 17,* 554–564.

Reeder, K. (1981). How young children learn to do things with words. In P. S. Dale & D. Ingram (Eds.), *Child language—an international perspective.* Baltimore: University Park Press.

Reynolds, R. E., & Ortony, A. (1980). Some issues in the measurement of children's comprehension of metaphorical language. *Child Development, 51,* 1110–1119.

Rosenthal, M. K. (1982). Vocal dialogues in the neonatal period. *Developmental Psychology, 18,* 17–21.

Rumbaugh, D. M. (1977). *Language learning by a chimpanzee: The Lana project.* New York: Academic Press.

Rumbaugh, D. M., & Gill, T. V. (1976). Language and the acquisition of language-type skills by a chimpanzee. *Annals of the New York Academy of Science, 270,* 90–135.

Saltz, R. (1979). Children's interpretation of proverbs. *Language Arts, 56,* 508–514.

Shatz, M., & Gelman, R. (1973). The development of communication skills: Modifications in the speech of young children as a function of listener. *Monographs of the Society for Research in Child Development, 38* (Serial No. 152).

Skinner, B. F. (1957). *Verbal behavior.* New York: Appleton-Century-Crofts.

Slobin, D. I. (1966). The acquisition of Russian as a native language. In F. Smith & G. A. Miller (Eds.), *The genesis of language: A psycholinguistic approach.* Cambridge, MA: M.I.T. Press.

Slobin, D. I. (1979). *Psycholinguistics.* Glenview, IL: Scott, Foresman.

Snow, C. E., Arlman-Rupp, A., Hassing, Y., Jobse, J., Joosken, J., & Vorster, J. (1976). Mother's speech in three social classes. *Journal of Psycholinguistic Research, 5,* 1–20.

Snow, C. E., & Ferguson, C. A. (Eds.). (1977). *Talking to children.* Cambridge: Cambridge University Press.

Staats, A. W., & Staats, C. K. (1963). *Complex human behavior.* New York: Holt, Rinehart and Winston.

Stern, D., Spieker, S., & MacKain, K. (1982). Intonational contours as signals in maternal speech to prelinguistic infants. *Developmental Psychology, 18,* 727–735.

Terrace, H. S. (1979, November). How Nim Chimpsky changed my mind. *Psychology Today,* pp. 65–76.

Thomas, D., Campos, J. J., Shucard, D. W., Ramsay, D. S., & Shucard, J. (1981). Semantic comprehension in infancy: A signal detection approach. *Child Development, 52,* 798–803.

Thompson, J. R., & Chapman, R. S. (1977). Who is "Daddy" revisited? The status of two-year-olds' overextended words in use and comprehension. *Journal of Child Language, 4,* 359–375.

Tomikawa, S. A., & Dodd, D. H. (1980). Early word meanings: Perceptually or functionally based. *Child Development, 51,* 1103–1109.

Turner, E. W., & Rommetveit, R. (1967). Experimental manipulation of the production of active and passive voice in children. *Language and Speech, 10,* 169–180.

Tyack, D., & Ingram, D. (1977). Children's production and comprehension of questions. *Journal of Child Language, 4,* 211–224.

Weir, R. H. (1966). Some questions on the child's learning of phonology. In F. Smith & G. Miller (Eds.), *The genesis of language.* Cambridge, MA: M.I.T. Press.

Weisberg, P. (1963). Social and nonsocial conditioning of infant vocalizations. *Child Development, 34,* 377–388.

Wellman, H. M., & Lempers, J. D. (1977). The naturalistic communicative abilities of two-year-olds. *Child Development, 48,* 1052–1057.

Werker, J. F., Gilbert, J. H. V., Humphrey, K., & Tees, R. C. (1981). Developmental aspects of cross-language speech perception. *Child Development, 52,* 349–355.

Wilcox, M. J., & Webster, E. J. (1980). Early discourse behavior: An analysis of children's responses to listener feedback. *Child Development, 51,* 1120–1125.

Wilkinson, L. C., & Rembold, K. L. (1981). The form and function of children's gestures accompanying verbal directives. In P. S. Dale & D. Ingram (Eds.), *Child language: An international perspective.* Baltimore: University Park Press.

Wolff, P. H. (1969). The natural history of crying and other vocalizations in early infancy. In B. M. Foss (Ed.), *Determinants of infant behavior* (Vol. 4). London: Methuen.

Yalisove, D. (1978). The effect of riddle structure on children's appreciation of humor. *Developmental Psychology, 14,* 173–180.

CHAPTER NINE ◼

COGNITIVE DEVELOPMENT

■ *What are cognition and cognitive development?*

■ *Piaget's basic ideas about cognition*
What is intelligence?
Cognitive schemata: The structural aspects of intelligence
How is knowledge gained? The functional basis of intelligence

■ *Piaget's stages of cognitive development*
The sensorimotor stage (birth to 2 years)
The preoperational stage (2 to 7 years)
The concrete-operational stage (7 to 11 years)
The formal-operational stage (age 11–12 and beyond)

■ *An evaluation of Piaget's theory*
The issue of timing
Does cognitive development occur in stages?
Does Piaget's theory "explain" cognitive development?
Present and future directions

■ *The information-processing approach*
Attentional processes: Getting information into the system
Memory processes: Retaining what one has experienced
Hypothesis testing and problem solving: Using information one has retained
The current status of information-processing theory

■ *Individual differences in cognitive style*
Implications of reflective and impulsive styles
Can conceptual tempo be modified?

■ *Summary*

*T**eacher*** (to a class of 9-year-olds): For artwork today, I'd like each of you to draw me a picture of a person who has three eyes.
Billy: I can't do it. Nobody has three eyes!

If you were asked to account for the reaction of this 9-year-old, you might be tempted to conclude that the boy either lacks imagination or is being sarcastic. Actually, the child's feelings about the art assignment may be rather typical, for many 9-year-olds find it extremely difficult to think about hypothetical propositions that have no basis in reality.

Our next two chapters will focus on the development of children's mental abilities. In this chapter we will chart the course of cognitive (intellectual) development from birth through adolescence and see how the changing character of children's thinking affects their relationships with other people as well as their understanding of the world around them. In Chapter Ten we will take up the topic of intelligence testing and discuss the many factors that contribute to individual differences in children's intellectual performance.

WHAT ARE COGNITION AND COGNITIVE DEVELOPMENT?

The *American Heritage Dictionary* (1982) defines **cognition** as "the mental process or faculty by which knowledge is acquired." The cognitive processes that help us to "know" and "understand" include a wide variety of activities, such as attending, perceiving, learning, thinking, and remembering—in short, the unobservable events and undertakings that characterize the human mind (Ault, 1977; Flavell, 1982). Almost everything we do while awake involves some kind of mental activity. We are constantly attending to objects and events, interpreting them, comparing them with past experiences, placing them into categories, and encoding them into memory. Human beings are truly cognitive beings.

> cognition: *the activity of knowing and the processes through which knowledge is acquired.*

The term **cognitive development** refers to the changes that occur in children's mental skills and abilities between birth and early adulthood, when cognitive growth is essentially complete. In this chapter we will consider two very different perspectives on intelligence and intellectual development. One of these theories arises from the work of information theorists who have likened the human intellectual apparatus to a sophisticated computer system that processes, categorizes, stores, and retrieves information according to a set of programmed strategies. The primary goals of this *information-processing* theory are (1) to describe how children process information to make sense of their surroundings and (2) to specify how these basic informational strategies change over time.

However, the major theory of cognitive development is Jean Piaget's *structural-functional* approach—a model that emphasizes the biological functions and environmental influences that promote intellectual growth. Although certain aspects of Piaget's theory have become rather controversial in recent years, the Piagetian approach remains the most detailed and systematic statement on human intellectual development presently available. Consequently, much of this chapter will be devoted to Piaget's insightful and provocative theoretical formulations.

PIAGET'S BASIC IDEAS ABOUT COGNITION

In Chapter Two we learned that Piaget was a trained zoologist who developed a strong interest in cognitive development while standardizing intelligence tests. This particular job required him to administer a large number of precisely worded questions to his young test takers in order to determine the age at which the majority of them could *correctly* answer each item. However, Piaget soon became interested in the children's *wrong* answers when he discovered that children of roughly the same age were making similar kinds of mistakes—errors that were typically quite different from the incorrect responses of younger or older children. Could these age-related differences in children's error patterns reflect developmental steps, or stages, in the process of intellectual growth? Piaget thought so, and he began

to suspect that *how* children think is probably a much better indicator of their cognitive abilities than *what* they may know (Flavell, 1963).

When his own three children were born, Piaget made detailed notes on their intellectual abilities, carefully observing how they reacted to various objects, events, and problems that he presented to them. Many of Piaget's ideas about intelligence and about intellectual development during infancy are based on these naturalistic observations of his own children.

Piaget's theory gradually took shape over a number of years as he broadened his horizons and began to study a larger sample of developing children. Many of Piaget's theoretical insights came from his use of the *clinical method* (see Box 9-1), a question-and-answer technique that he devised to measure the ways children attacked various problems and thought about everyday issues. By carefully questioning a large number of children in several age groups, Piaget was able to identify four methods (or patterns) of reasoning that are age-related and, in his opinion, represent different "stages" of intellectual growth.

In order to appreciate Piaget's structural-functional theory of cognitive development, it is necessary to understand what he means by *intelligence, cognitive structures* (or *schemata*), and *intellectual functions*.

What Is Intelligence?

Piaget's background in the life sciences is apparent when he defines **intelligence** as a *basic life function* that helps the organism *to adapt to its environment* (Piaget, 1952). Children are viewed as active explorers who, from the moment of birth, are constantly observing, investigating, and experimenting in an attempt to understand what people do and how things work (Cowan, 1978).

According to Piaget, the child is a **constructivist**—an organism that acts on novel objects and events and thereby gains some understanding of their essential features. Piaget stresses that the child's constructions of reality (that is, interpretations of objects and events) will depend on the knowledge base available to him at that point in time: the more immature the child's cognitive system, the more limited his interpretation of an environmental event. Consider the following example:

A four-year-old child and his father are watching the setting sun. "Look Daddy. It's hiding behind the mountain. Why is it going away? Is it angry?" The father grasps the opportunity to explain to his son how the world works. "Well, Mark, the sun doesn't really feel things. And it doesn't really move. It's the earth that's moving. It turns on its axis so that the mountain moves in front of the sun . . ." The father goes on to other explanations of relative motion, interplanetary bodies and such. The boy . . . firmly and definitely responds, "But *we're* not moving. *It* is. Look, it's going down" [Cowan, 1978, p. 11].

This child is making an important assumption here that dominates his attempt at understanding—namely, that the way he sees things must correspond to the way they are. Obviously, it is the sun that is moving, ducking behind the mountain as if it were a live being who was expressing some feeling or serving a definite purpose by hiding. However, the father knows the characteristics that distinguish animate from inanimate objects (and a little about astronomy as well), so that he is able to construct a very different interpretation of the "reality" that he and his son have witnessed.

Cognitive Schemata: The Structural Aspects of Intelligence

Piaget uses the term *schemata* to describe the models, or mental structures, that we create to represent, organize, and interpret our experiences. A **schema** is a pattern of thought or action that is similar in certain respects to what the layperson calls a strategy or a concept. Piaget (1952, 1977) has described three kinds of intellectual structures: behavioral (or sensorimotor) schemata, symbolic schemata, and operational schemata.

■ *Behavioral (or sensorimotor) schemata*

A **behavioral schema** is an organized pattern of behavior that a child uses to represent and respond to an object or an experience. Piaget believes that children are born with a number of reflexive schemata that are programmed to respond to certain eliciting stimuli and thereby further the infant's adaptation to the environment. For example, a sucking reflex is activated whenever an object touches the infant's lips; cries are elicited by biological needs such as hunger; a grasping reflex is activated if a small object

touches the infant's palm. These early schemata are soon modified and combined into new and more complex behavioral sequences as the child seeks out, manipulates, and thereby comes to know more and more about the objects and events in his or her everyday world.

■ *Symbolic schemata*

During the second year, children reach a point at which they can solve problems and think about objects and events without having acted on them. In other words, they are now capable of representing actions mentally and using these mental symbols, or **symbolic schemata,** to satisfy their objectives. Consider the following observation of the antics of Jacqueline, Piaget's 16-month-old daughter:

> Jacqueline had a visit from a little boy [18 months of age] . . . who, in the course of the afternoon got into a terrible temper. He screamed as he tried to get out of a playpen and pushed it backward, stamping his feet. Jacqueline stood watching him in amazement, never having witnessed such a scene before. The next day, she herself screamed in her playpen and tried to move, stamping her foot . . . several times in succession [Piaget, 1951, p. 63].

Clearly, Jacqueline was imitating the responses of her absent playmate, even though she had not

---

cognitive development: *changes that occur in mental activities such as attending, perceiving, learning, thinking, and remembering.*

intelligence: *in Piaget's theory, a basic life function that enables an organism to adapt to its environment.*

constructivist: *one who gains knowledge by acting or otherwise operating on objects and events to discover their properties.*

schema: *an organized pattern of thought or action that one constructs to interpret some aspect of one's experience (also called cognitive structure).*

behavioral schemata: *organized patterns of behavior that are used to represent and respond to objects and experiences.*

symbolic schemata: *internal mental symbols (such as images or verbal codes) that one uses to represent aspects of experience.*

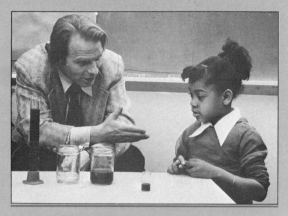

Investigator using the clinical method. All children are asked the same questions at first, but the way each child answers those initial questions determines what the researcher will ask next.

Piaget relied on a question-and-answer technique known as the *clinical method* to assess the cognitive capabilities of children who could converse well enough to answer questions. In the clinical procedure, the child is asked a question or presented with a problem of some sort and then invited to respond. Once the child answers, the investigator will ask a second question or introduce a variation of the original problem in order to clarify the child's reasoning. All children are asked the same questions at first, but the way each child responds to these initial probes will determine what the investigator will do next. The following exchange illustrates the clinical procedure in a setting where an adult is trying to determine whether a 7-year-old named Pie understands the concept of mass:

E: You see these two little balls here. Is there as much dough in this one as in this one?
Pie: Yes.
E: Now watch. (*The experimenter changes one of them into the shape of a sausage.*)
Pie: The sausage has more dough.
E: And if I roll it up again?
Pie: Then I think there will be the same amount. (*The clay is rolled into a ball once more and the other ball is molded into the shape of a disc.*)
E: There's still as much dough (*in the disc*)?
Pie: There is more dough in the ball [Piaget & Inhelder, 1941, as cited by Flavell, 1963, p. 26].

This series of questions and answers suggested to Piaget that young Pie has only a primitive concept of mass, for the child apparently fails to recognize that a quantity of dough remains constant when its appearance is altered.

Methodological purists cringe at this approach. If the research procedure is tailored to the individual child, how does one ever compare the answers of different children to identify general trends? Can we

be certain that the data are reliable? After all, observations collected through unstandardized procedures are difficult if not impossible to replicate. This is particularly true of Piaget's work, for he did not normally report the number of children he had tested, their exact ages, or an overall summary of their behavior.

Piaget (1929) was aware of the shortcomings of his clinical method. However, he made a very important point in its defense. He noted that discovering the many cognitive concepts and stages that characterize children's intellectual development requires a *flexible* methodology—that is, an approach that enables the investigator to probe the child's line of reasoning without deforming it by suggestion or imposing his or her own views on the child. The clinical method is very flexible. The experimenter is free to phrase questions in a language that the child understands and then respond in a manner dictated by the child's answer. In sum, Piaget considered his clinical methodology to be quite appropriate for the scientific task that he had set out to accomplish.

performed those actions at the time they were modeled. It appears that she must have represented the model's behavior in some internal, symbolic form that preserved the original scene and guided her later imitation.

■ *Operational schemata*

The thinking of children aged 7 and older is characterized by a third type of schema, the oper-

ational structure. A **cognitive operation** is an internal mental activity that a person performs on his or her objects of thought. Common cognitive operations include mental activities such as **reversibility** (reversing an action in one's head) and all the actions implied in mathematical symbols such as $+$, $-$, $\times$, $\div$, $=$, $<$, and $>$. As we will see later in the chapter, these cognitive operations permit children to construct rather complex in-

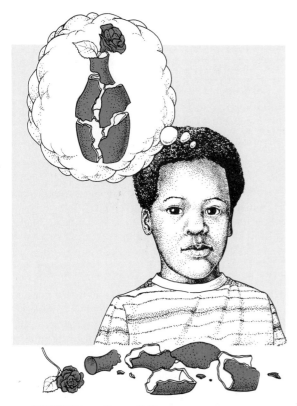

FIGURE 9-1. *Reversibility is a cognitive operation that develops during middle childhood.*

tellectual schemata that will enable them to think logically and systematically—first about their actual experiences and eventually about abstract or hypothetical events.

How Is Knowledge Gained? The Functional Basis of Intelligence

How do children construct and modify their intellectual schemata? Piaget believes that all cognitive structures are created through the operation of two inborn intellectual functions that he calls *organization* and *adaptation*. **Organization** is the process by which children combine existing schemata into new and more complex intellectual structures. For example, a young infant who has "gazing," "reaching," and "grasping" reflexes will soon organize these initially unrelated schemata into a complex structure—*visually directed reaching*—that enables her to reach out and dis-

cover the characteristics of many interesting objects in the environment. Although intellectual schemata may assume radically different forms at different phases of development, the process of organization is unchanging. Piaget believes that children are constantly organizing their available schemata into higher-order systems or structures.

The goal of organization is to further the adaptive function. As its name implies, **adaptation** is the process of adjusting to the demands of the environment. According to Piaget, adaptation occurs through two complementary activities, *assimilation* and *accommodation*.

Assimilation is the process by which the child tries to interpret new experiences in terms of her existing models of the world—the schemata that she already possesses. The young child who sees a horse for the first time will try to assimilate it into one of her existing schemata for four-legged animals and thus may think of this creature as a "doggie." In other words, she is trying to adapt to this novel stimulus by construing it as something familiar.

However, truly novel objects, events, and experiences may be difficult or impossible to interpret in terms of one's existing schemata. Horses differ in important ways from dogs, and the young child may begin to recognize these differences even as she is attempting to assimilate the horse into her "doggie" schema. Piaget believes that as we assimilate new experiences, we will also accommodate to these experiences. **Accommodation,** the com-

---

cognitive operation: *an internal mental activity that one performs on objects of thought.*

reversibility: *the ability to reverse or negate an action by mentally performing the opposite action.*

organization: *one's inborn tendency to combine and integrate available schemata into coherent systems or bodies of knowledge.*

adaptation: *one's inborn tendency to adjust to the demands of the environment.*

assimilation: *the process of interpreting new experiences by incorporating them into existing schemata.*

accommodation: *the process of modifying existing schemata in order to incorporate or adapt to new experiences.*

plement of assimilation, is the process of modifying existing structures in order to account for new experiences. So the child who recognizes that a horse is not a dog may invent a name for this strange new creature or perhaps say "What dat?" and adopt the label that her companions use. In other words, she has modified (accommodated) her schema for four-legged animals to include a new category of experience—horses.

Although Piaget distinguishes assimilation from accommodation, he believes that they occur together as complementary aspects of all adaptive acts. Every assimilation of an experience involves an accommodation to that experience. And what motivates the child to assimilate environmental stimuli and to accommodate to these objects and events? Piaget is clear on this point: "His position is simply that there is an intrinsic need for *cognitive . . . structures, once generated by functioning, to perpetuate themselves by more functioning.* Schemas are [active], and one of their important, built-in properties is that of repeated assimilation of anything assimilable in the environment" (Flavell, 1963, p. 78; italics added).

In sum, Piaget describes intellectual growth as an active process in which children are repeatedly assimilating new experiences and accommodating their cognitive structures to those experiences. And even during the times when they are not experiencing anything new, children are apt to be growing intellectually as they organize their existing schemata into new and more complex structures. Thus, two innate activities—adaptation and organization—make it possible for children to construct a progressively greater understanding of the world in which they live.

PIAGET'S STAGES OF COGNITIVE DEVELOPMENT

Piaget has identified four major periods of cognitive development: the *sensorimotor* stage (birth to 2 years), the *preoperational* stage (2 to 7 years), the stage of *concrete operations* (7 to 11 years), and the stage of *formal operations* (11 years and beyond). These stages of intellectual growth represent completely different levels of cognitive functioning and form what Piaget calls an **invariant developmental sequence.** The invariant

sequence notion implies that all children progress through the stages in precisely the same order. According to Piaget, there can be no skipping of stages, because each successive stage builds on the accomplishments of previous stages.

Nevertheless, there are tremendous individual differences in the ages at which children enter or emerge from any particular stage. Piaget has argued that cultural practices and other environmental factors may accelerate or retard a child's intellectual growth. So it is important to remember that the age norms that accompany each of Piaget's stages (or substages) are only rough approximations and that any given child may spend either more or less time in a particular stage than is indicated by the "norm."

The Sensorimotor Stage (Birth to 2 Years)

The **sensorimotor stage** spans the first two years, or the period that psychologists refer to as infancy. The dominant cognitive structures are behavioral schemata, which evolve as infants begin to coordinate their *sensory* input and *motor* responses in order to "act on" and get to "know" the environment.

During the first two years of life, infants evolve from reflexive creatures with very limited knowledge into planful problem solvers who have already learned a great deal about themselves, their close companions, and the objects and events in their everyday world. Piaget divides this sensorimotor period into six substages that describe the child's gradual transition from a reflexive to a *reflective* organism. Let's keep in mind that the age norms that accompany each substage are only *rough approximations,* even though all children pass through the stages in the order in which we will discuss them.

■ Substage 1: Reflexive activity (birth to 1 month)

During the first month of life, infants are exercising and refining their innate reflexes. New objects are assimilated into reflexive schemata, so that the child who initially sucked only on nipples may begin to suck on blankets, fingers, and toys and will gradually accommodate his reflexes to the objects that are assimilated. According to Piaget, these first primitive adaptations represent the beginning of cognitive growth.

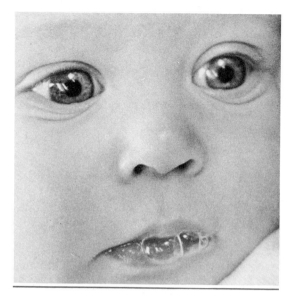

PHOTO 9-1. Blowing bubbles is an accommodation of the sucking reflex and one of the infant's earliest primary circular reactions.

■ Substage 2: Primary circular reactions (1 to 4 months)

In the second substage, the infant begins to organize sensory experiences and motor responses into behavioral structures known as **primary circular reactions.** Responses that occur by chance and prove satisfying are now performed over and over for the pleasure they bring. One example of a primary circular reaction is Laurent's thumb-sucking schema, which was described in detail in Chapter Two. Clearly, this act was *not* a reflex. Laurent had previously displayed a sucking reflex, but the act of raising his thumb to his mouth and then sucking was a new behavior. Primary circular reactions are always centered on the child's own body. They are called "primary" because they are the first coordinated "habits" to appear. They are called "circular" reactions because the pleasure they bring stimulates their repetition.

■ Substage 3: Secondary circular reactions (4 to 8 months)

At about 4 months of age, infants begin to display a new kind of activity: **secondary circular reactions.** These responses are circular in that they are pleasurable events that stimulate their own repetition. But they differ from primary circular re-

actions because they are centered on objects and events in the *external* environment.

The following observation provides an example of a secondary circular reaction. Piaget had just attached a string to Laurent's left arm so that the infant's arm movements would shake a rattle tied to the other end of the string:

> I attached the string to the left arm. . . . The first shake is given by chance: [Laurent shows] fright, curiosity, etc. Then, at once, there is a coordinated circular reaction: . . . the right arm is outstretched and barely mobile while the left one swings. . . . It is therefore possible to speak definitely of a secondary circular reaction [1951, pp. 161–162].

In this instance, Laurent discovers that he can produce an interesting effect (shaking the rattle) by simply swinging his left arm. Is this planful (*intentional*) thinking? Piaget says no: the secondary circular reaction is not a fully intentional response, because the result it produces was discovered by chance and was not an intended goal at the time the action was first performed.

■ Substage 4: Coordination of secondary schemata (8 to 12 months)

Truly planful responding first appears during Piaget's fourth substage of sensorimotor intelligence. For the first time, the infant is able to coordinate previously unrelated acts to produce interesting outcomes or solve simple problems. Consider the following account of Laurent's be-

---

invariant developmental sequence: *a series of developments that occur in one particular order because each development in the sequence is a prerequisite for those appearing later.*

sensorimotor stage: *Piaget's first intellectual stage (from birth to 2 years), when infants are relying on behavioral schemata as a means of exploring and understanding the environment.*

primary circular reaction: *a pleasurable response, centered on the infant's own body, that is discovered by chance and performed over and over.*

secondary circular reaction: *a pleasurable response, centered on an external object, that is discovered by chance and performed over and over.*

havior at 9 months of age when Piaget showed him an attractive object and then placed it under a cushion:

> Laurent lifts the cushion . . . to look for a cigar case. . . . When one end of the case appears, Laurent removes the cushion with one hand and with the other tries to extricate the objective. The act of lifting the [cushion] is therefore entirely separate from that of grasping the desired object and constitutes an autonomous "means" [to an end] [1952, p. 222].

On this occasion, Laurent's lifting of the cushion is not accidental but *intentional:* he had hoped to obtain the cigar case. Thus, a lifting schema and a grasping schema are coordinated to achieve the goal.

Voluntary imitation of novel responses.   Although Stage 3 infants may occasionally imitate (repeat) their *own* actions when these responses are mimicked by a companion, the infant at Stage 4 can imitate *new* responses by emitting behaviors that were not previously in his or her repertoire. See how 9-month-old Jacqueline struggles and eventually succeeds at imitating a novel behavior displayed by her father:

> I alternatively bent and straightened my finger, and she opened and closed her hand. . . . [One week later] I tried the same experiment. She imitated me but used her whole hand which she straightened and bent without taking her eyes off my finger. . . . Finally [three days later] she succeeded in isolating and imitating correctly the movement of the forefinger [Piaget, 1951, pp. 46–47].

Note that it took Jacqueline nearly two weeks to correctly imitate this very simple yet novel activity. Kenneth Kaye and Janet Marcus (1981) have recently found that Stage 4 infants will typically "imitate" a novel response by first assimilating it to existing schemata (as Jacqueline did by opening and closing her entire hand) and then gradually working up to a precise imitation by accommodating their imitative schemata over a period of weeks and months. So it is unreasonable for parents to expect an 8- to 12-month-old infant to imitate their playtime activities after seeing these responses displayed once or twice. Dozens of demonstrations may be required before the child will catch on and

will come to enjoy sensorimotor games such as pat-a-cake.

■ *Substage 5: Tertiary circular reactions (12 to 18 months)*

In Substage 4, infants are combining actions to solve simple problems. During the fifth substage, they begin to experiment with objects and will try to invent totally new methods of solving problems or reproducing interesting outcomes. Suppose, for example, that an infant squeezes a rubber duck, causing it to "quack." At Substages 3 and 4, the child may continue to squeeze the duck in order to reproduce the quacking sound; that is, she will repeat this basic secondary circular reaction. However, the infant at Substage 5 will probably convert the original squeezing response into a **tertiary circular reaction** by exploring new means to the same end. The older child may now step on the duck, drop it, or crush it with another object to see whether these new activities will have the same or different effects on the toy. The infant's behavior is still "circular" because the effect of her response (the quack) stimulates its repetition. But tertiary circular reactions are not fixed patterns of action; they are trial-and-error exploratory schemata that signal the emergence of true curiosity.

Voluntary imitation of novel responses.   Although infants at Substage 4 can imitate novel responses, we've seen that it often takes them days, weeks, or even months to faithfully reproduce the relatively simple actions of a close companion. Imitation is much more precise and systematic in the fifth substage, as we see in the following example:

> At [1 year and 16 days of age, Jacqueline] discovered her forehead. When I touched the middle of mine, she first rubbed her eye, then felt above it and touched her hair, after which she brought her hand down a little and finally put her finger on her forehead [Piaget, 1951, p. 56].

■ *Substage 6: Invention of new means through mental combinations (18 months to 2 years)*

A dramatic development takes place during the sixth and final sensorimotor substage: infants are internalizing their behavioral schemata to construct mental symbols, or images. Once children begin to create mental representations of objects, actions, and events, they can reproduce (imitate) the behavior of models who are no longer present. In addition to deferred imitation, Stage 6 infants are also capable of generating solutions to simple problems on a mental (symbolic) level, without resorting to trial-and-error experimentation. Piaget calls this ability **inner experimentation** or the "invention of new means through internal mental combinations." Consider the following example:

> Laurent is seated before a table and I place a bread crust in front of him, out of reach. Also, to the right of the child I place a stick, about 25 cm. long. At first, Laurent tries to grasp the bread . . . and then he gives up . . . Laurent again looks at the bread, and without moving, looks very briefly at the stick, then suddenly grasps it and directs it toward the bread. . . . [He then] draws the bread to him [Piaget, 1952, p. 335].

Clearly, Laurent has an important insight: the stick can be used as an extension of his arm to obtain a distant object. Trial-and-error experimentation is not apparent in this case, for Laurent's "problem solving" occurred at an internal, symbolic level.

■ *Object permanence: Out of sight is no longer out of mind*

To this point we have talked about the development of two basic intellectual activities: (1) imitation and (2) the evolution of problem-solving schemata that permit the child to produce or reproduce interesting outcomes. However, infants are also forming some simple *concepts* as they begin to recognize similarities and differences among objects and events and to treat perceptually similar phenomena as if they were alike (Sugarman, 1981). One of the more notable achievements of the sensorimotor period is the development of the **object concept**—the idea that people, places, and things continue to exist when they are no longer visible or detectable through the other senses.

According to Piaget, an "object" is something that the child conceives of as having an identity of its own, something that exists independent of his immediate perceptions. We adults have well-developed object concepts. If you were to take off your watch and cover it with a coffee mug, you would be well aware that the watch continued to exist even though you could no longer see it. Objects have a permanence for us; out of sight is not necessarily out of mind.

This is not so for very young infants. Throughout the first two stages of the sensorimotor period, children will not search for an object that vanishes. Even at Substage 3, the infant has a poor understanding of the permanence of objects. Although a 4–8-month-old will retrieve a partly concealed object or one that is covered by a transparent cloth, he will not search for an attractive object that is completely concealed. In other words, the Stage 3 infant acts as if the disappearing object no longer existed.

In the fourth sensorimotor substage (coordination of secondary schemata), infants show some evidence of an object concept by searching for items that disappear from view. However, object permanence is far from complete, as we see in Piaget's observation of Jacqueline at 10 months of age:

> Jacqueline is seated on a mattress without anything to disturb or distract her. . . . I take her [toy] parrot from her hands and hide it twice in succession under the mattress, on her left [point A]. Both times Jacqueline looks for the object immediately and grabs it. Then I take it from her hands and move it very slowly *before her eyes* to the corresponding place on her right, under the mattress [point B]. Jacqueline watches this movement . . . but at the moment when the parrot disappears [at point B] she turns to her left and looks where it was before [at point A] [1954, p. 51; italics added].

---

tertiary circular reaction: *an exploratory schema in which the infant devises a new method of acting on objects to reproduce interesting results.*

inner experimentation: *the ability to solve simple problems on a mental, or symbolic, level without having to rely on trial-and-error experimentation.*

object concept: *the realization that objects continue to exist when they are no longer visible or detectable through the other senses.*

Jacqueline's response is typical of children at this stage. When searching for a disappearing object, the Stage 4 infant will look in the place where it was previously found rather than the place where it was last seen. In other words, the child assumes that her behavior determines where the object is to appear, and consequently she does not treat the object as if it existed independent of her own activity.

At Substage 5 (tertiary circular reactions), object permanence improves. The 12–18-month-old will track the visible movements of objects and search for them where they were last seen. However, the object concept is not yet complete, for Stage 5 infants cannot make the mental inferences necessary to represent and understand *invisible* displacements. Suppose, for example, that you conceal an attractive toy in your hand, place your hand behind a barrier and deposit the object there, remove your hand, and then ask the child to find the toy. At Substage 5 the child will search for the object *where it was last seen*—in your hand— rather than looking for it behind the barrier.

At Substage 6 (invention of new means through

PHOTO 9-2. *Playing peek-a-boo is an exciting activity for infants who are acquiring object permanence.*

mental combinations), the object concept is complete. Children are now capable of mentally representing sequences of invisible displacements, and they will use these mental inferences to guide their search for an object that has disappeared. For example, at 18 months of age,

> Jacqueline throws a ball under a sofa. But instead of . . . searching for it on the floor [where it was last seen] she looks at the place, realizes that the ball must have crossed under the sofa, and sets out to go behind it. . . . she begins by turning her back on the place where the ball disappeared, goes around the table, and finally arrives behind the sofa at the right place [Piaget, 1954, p. 205].

In Chapter Eleven we will see that the object concept may play an important role in the development of the child's first true emotional attachments. Many cognitive theorists have proposed that infants cannot form close emotional ties to regular companions unless these individuals have a "permanence" about them. After all, it would seem rather difficult to establish a meaningful and lasting relationship with a person who "ceases to exist" whenever he or she passes from view.

Before we summarize the developments of the sensorimotor period, a caution is in order. In recent years, investigators have questioned several of Piaget's ideas about the object concept when they began to discover that very young infants seem to understand much more about objects than Piaget gives them credit for. Box 9-2 discusses some of these intriguing discoveries and their implications for Piaget's theory.

■ *An overview of sensorimotor development*

The child's intellectual achievements during the sensorimotor period are truly remarkable. In two short years, infants have evolved from reflexive and largely immobile creatures into planful thinkers who can move about on their own, solve some problems in their heads, form simple concepts, and even communicate many of their thoughts to their companions. Table 9-1 presents a brief summary of the major intellectual accomplishments of the first two years.

Although the sensorimotor period is divided into a series of substages, Piaget emphasizes that the *process* of intellectual growth is gradual and continuous. Infants are not at Substage 3 on one

BOX 9-2
DO INFANTS KNOW MORE ABOUT
OBJECTS THAN PIAGET ASSUMES?

Are babies aware that disappearing objects continue to exist before the age when they will begin to search for them? Thomas Bower (1982) thinks so, and to prove his point, he has conducted experiments in which infants at Piaget's Substage 2 (1–4 months) watched as a screen blocked an attractive toy from view. A few seconds later, the screen was removed, revealing either the toy or an empty space where the toy had been. If the child thinks the toy no longer exists when it is out of sight, he should be surprised to see it when the screen is taken away. But if he believes the object is there, hidden behind the screen, then he should be more perplexed when it does *not* reappear. Bower found that his young subjects were quite surprised on those occasions when the screen was removed and the toy was not there. In other words, they showed some evidence of an object concept several months before they were capable of searching for and finding a hidden object.

Bower also describes a study (Mundy-Castle & Anglin, 1974) that demonstrates that 4-month-old infants (at the beginning of Substage 3) can follow and anticipate the path of a moving object that is hidden from view. The illustration shows the apparatus used in this experiment. The infant sees the object only when it passes by the portholes at points A and B. Of course, the object continues to move in an elliptical orbit as it passes behind the screen, so that it periodically travels from the bottom to the top of porthole A and from the top to the bottom of porthole B. Infants who watched this display were observed to move their eyes in an elliptical pattern and to anticipate the reappearance of the object at the proper location for each porthole. Apparently these 4-month-old children recognized that the object was still present and moving when it was hidden behind the screen.

If young infants understand that objects have a "permanence," then why don't they search for and locate items that disappear? Clearly, 4–8-month-olds have the motor capabilities to uncover hidden objects, for they show little hesitancy to retrieve a toy that they can see beneath a transparent cloth. Bower (1982) believes that a deficit in *spatial reasoning* accounts for the failure of Stage 3 infants to search for hidden objects. Presumably the infant will not look for an object that disappears into a box (or under a cup) because she suspects that two entities cannot occupy the same space and will think the box (or cup) has simply replaced the disappearing object. If Bower's hypothesis is correct, infants should successfully retrieve objects from behind two-

dimensional barriers such as a screen before they retrieve them from three-dimensional hiding places such as a cup or the inside of a box. The rationale for this prediction is that it is much harder to perceive a flat two-dimensional screen (or cover) as occupying the same space and thereby replacing the object that has disappeared.

Recently, Carl Dunst, Penelope Brooks, and Pamela Doxsey (1982) observed the search patterns of 6–10-month-old infants who had seen objects disappear behind a screen, under a cloth or a cup, or into a box. The findings were generally consistent with Bower's hypothesis: 7-month-olds were better able to locate objects hidden by two-dimensional barriers such as the cloth or the screen than those hidden by three-dimensional obstructions such as the cup or the box. But by 10 months of age, the children had apparently learned that two items can occupy the same space, for they were now quite capable of finding objects that had disappeared under (or into) a three-dimensional barrier.

In sum, the inability of young infants to locate hidden objects may reflect their lack of knowledge about spatial relations rather than ignorance of the object concept. By relying solely on studies involving search procedures, Piaget seems to have underestimated what infants may know about objects and their properties during the first three sensorimotor stages.

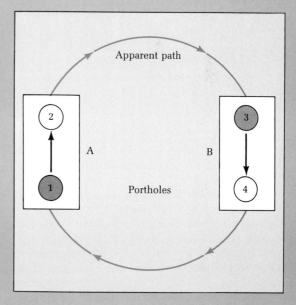

Apparatus used in Mundy-Castle and Anglin's experiment. The object appears at point 1, progresses to point 2, and is later seen moving between points 3 and 4 before disappearing behind the screen and reappearing at point 1.

TABLE 9-1. Summary of the substages and intellectual accomplishments of the sensorimotor period

Substage	Methods of solving problems or producing interesting outcomes	Imitation	Object concept
1. Reflex activity (0–1 month)	Exercise and accommodation of inborn reflexes	Some imitation of facial expressions[a]	Tracks moving object but ignores its disappearance[b]
2. Primary circular reactions (1–4 months)	Repeating interesting acts that are centered on one's own body	Repetition of own behavior that is mimicked by a companion	Looks intently at the spot where an object disappeared
3. Secondary circular reactions (4–8 months)	Repeating interesting acts that are directed toward external objects	Same as in Substage 2	Searches for partly concealed object
4. Coordination of secondary schemata (8–12 months)	Combining actions to solve simple problems (first evidence of intentionality)	Ability to eventually imitate novel responses after gradually accommodating a crude initial attempt at imitation	First glimmering of object permanence; searches for and finds concealed object that has *not* been visibly displaced
5. Tertiary circular reactions (12–18 months)	Experimenting to find new ways to solve problems or reproduce interesting outcomes	Systematic imitation of novel responses	Searches for and finds object that has been *visibly* displaced
6. Invention of new means through mental combinations (18–24 months)	First evidence of insight as the child solves problems at an internal, symbolic level	Deferred imitation of the actions of absent models	Object concept is complete; searches for and finds objects that have been hidden through *invisible* displacements

[a]Imitation of facial expressions such as surprise or sadness is apparently an inborn ability that may bear little relation to the voluntary imitation that appears later in the first year (Field, Woodson, Greenberg, & Cohen, 1982; Meltzoff & Moore, 1983).
[b]Some researchers believe that object permanence may be present very early and that young infants simply lack the eye/hand coordination and/or the spatial reasoning abilities that would permit them to search for and find hidden objects (see Box 9-2).

day and at Substage 4 on the next. In fact, the child's behavior is not always consistent across all aspects of functioning, for it is possible for the object concept to be at one stage of development (say, Substage 4) while imitation and problem-solving schemata are at the preceding or the following stage. But even though intellectual growth occurs continuously and is somewhat uneven, the important advances in each aspect of cognitive functioning do emerge in a particular sequence. This is the reason Piaget talks about substages of sensorimotor development.

Keep in mind that 2-year-olds are relatively unpracticed and inefficient in the use of symbolic schemata at the end of the sensorimotor period. But they will soon improve. In fact, mental symbols quickly become the most important instruments of thought as the child enters the second, or preoperational, stage of intellectual development.

The Preoperational Stage (2 to 7 Years)

During the **preoperational stage,** children are becoming increasingly proficient at constructing and using mental symbols to think about the objects, situations, and events they encounter. But despite these advances in symbolic reasoning, Piaget's descriptions of preoperational intelligence focus mainly on the limitations or deficiencies in children's thinking. Indeed, he calls this period "preoperational" because he believes that preschool children have not yet acquired the cognitive operations (and operational schemata) that would enable them to think logically. Let's consider what Piaget has to say about the intellectual capabilities of preschool children and then contrast his somewhat negative viewpoint with a more positive outlook that is beginning to emerge from recent research.

Piaget divides the preoperational period into two substages: the *preconceptual* period (2–4 years of age) and the *intuitive* period (4–7 years).

■ *The preconceptual period*

Emergence of symbolic thought. The **preconceptual period** is marked by the sudden appearance of the **symbolic function:** the ability to make one thing—a word or an object—stand for, or represent, something else. For example, words soon come to represent objects, persons, and events, so that the child can now easily reconstruct and make reference to the past and talk about items that are no longer present. Pretend play also emerges at this time. Toddlers often pretend to be people they are not (mommies, superheroes), and they may play these roles with props such as a shoebox or a stick that symbolize other objects such as a baby's crib or a ray gun. These kinds of symbolic play activities enable the 2–4-year-old to construct what adults often call a make-believe or a fantasy world. Although some parents are concerned when their preschool children immerse themselves in a world of make-believe and begin to invent imaginary playmates, Piaget feels that these are basically healthy activities. In Box 9-3 we will take a closer look at children's play and see how these "pretend" activities may contribute in a positive way to the child's social, emotional, and intellectual development.

Deficits in preconceptual reasoning. Piaget calls this period "preconceptual" because he believes that the ideas, concepts, and cognitive processes of 2–4-year-olds are rather primitive by adult standards. One of the flaws that characterize the child's thinking is **animism**—a willingness to attribute life and lifelike qualities (for example, motives and intentions) to inanimate objects. The 4-year-old who believed that the setting sun was alive, angry, and hiding behind the mountain provides a clear example of the animistic logic that children often use during the preconceptual period.

Several other illogical schemata, or "preconcepts," stem from the child's **transductive reasoning.** The transductive thinker reasons from the particular to the particular: when any two events occur together (covary), the child is likely to assume that one has caused the other. One day when Piaget's daughter had missed her usual afternoon nap, she remarked "I haven't had a nap, so it isn't afternoon." In this case, Lucienne reasoned from one particular (the nap) to another (the afternoon) and erroneously concluded that her nap determined when it was afternoon.

According to Piaget, the most striking deficiency in children's preoperational reasoning is a characteristic that he calls **egocentrism**—a tendency to view the world from one's own per-

---

preoperational stage: *Piaget's second stage of cognitive development, lasting from about age 2 to age 7, when children are thinking at a symbolic level but are not yet using cognitive operations (hence the name "preoperational").*

preconceptual period: *the early substage of preoperations (from age 2 to age 4), characterized by the appearance of primitive ideas, concepts, and methods of reasoning.*

symbolic function: *the ability to use symbols (for example, images and words) to represent objects and experiences.*

animism: *attributing life and lifelike qualities to inanimate objects.*

transductive reasoning: *reasoning from the particular to the particular, so that events that occur together are assumed to be causally related.*

egocentrism: *the tendency to view the world from one's own perspective while failing to recognize that others may have different points of view.*

BOX 9-3
PLAY IS SERIOUS BUSINESS

Play is an intrinsically satisfying activity—something that young children do for the fun of it (Rubin, Fein, & Vandenberg, 1983). Since toddlers and preschool children spend a large percentage of their waking hours at one form of play or another, we might wonder what effects these pleasurable activities will have on their social, emotional, and intellectual development.

Piaget (1951) is one theorist who views play as an adaptive activity. Play begins early in the sensorimotor period as infants begin to repeat acts that they find satisfying or pleasurable. Piaget suggests that play activities permit children to practice their competencies in a relaxed and carefree way. Presumably the opportunity to manipulate novel objects and to play social games such as peek-a-boo will help to nurture curiosity, object permanence, inner experimentation, and other cognitive advances.

At 11–13 months of age, *pretend play* begins (Rubin et al., 1983). The earliest forms of pretend play are simple acts in which infants pretend to engage in familiar activities such as eating, sleeping, or drinking from a cup. As children enter the preoperational stage, their play becomes further removed from everyday activities and much more complex. They can now substitute one object (for example, a block) for another (a car) and use language

in inventive ways to construct rich fantasy worlds for themselves. One notable example is that many preoperational children create "imaginary playmates" who are given names and personality traits and who will remain near and dear to their creators during this period (Singer, 1973). Once again, Piaget views these symbolic play activities as a means for energetic young children to practice and perfect their emerging conceptual skills, thereby setting the stage for further social and intellectual growth.

Recently investigators have begun to confirm some of Piaget's ideas about play. Jeffrey Dansky (1980) observed a group of preschool children and divided them into *players* (those who often engage in pretend play) and *nonplayers* (those who rarely do). One week later, these children were observed after they had been given a number of unusual play objects such as clothespins, matchboxes, and paper clips. Dansky found that his "players" were more likely than "nonplayers" to use these objects in a novel, creative way. In a similar vein, Hutt and Bhavnani (1976) found that children who were judged low in exploratory play as toddlers tended five years later to be low in curiosity and to experience problems in their personal and social adjustment. In contrast, those who had been active explorers as toddlers were more likely to score high on tests of creativity and to be judged curious and independent during the grade school years. Finally, Jennifer Connolly (1982) reports that preschool children who "pretend" a lot are

spective and to have difficulty recognizing another person's point of view. Examples of this self-centeredness can be found in children's speech as well as their thinking. Here is a sample conversation in which the egocentrism of a 4-year-old named Sandy comes through as she describes an event she has witnessed:

Sandy: Uncle David, it got on your car and scratched it.
Adult: What did?
Sandy: Come, I'll show you. (*She takes her uncle outside and shows him a scratch on the top of his new car.*)
Adult: Sandy, what made the scratch?
Sandy: Not me!
Adult (laughing): I know, Sandy, but how did the scratch get there?
Sandy: It got on the car and scratched it with its claws.

Adult: What did?
Sandy (looking around): There! (*She points to a cat that is walking across the street.*)
Adult: Oh, a cat! Why didn't you tell me that in the first place?
Sandy: I did [Shaffer, 1979, p. 111].

Note that Sandy has made little or no attempt to adapt her speech to the needs of her listener, because she assumes that her uncle shares her perspective and must already know what has caused the scratch on his car. On another occasion, Sandy was asked how many sisters she had, and she said "Two." Next she was asked whether Shelley (her older sister) had two sisters, and she replied "No, Shelley has one sister—Shannon!" Can you see the egocentrism in Sandy's reasoning? Her problem is that she does not assume Shelley's perspective and realize that she too is Shelley's sister.

more advanced on Piagetian tests of cognitive development and more popular with their peers than children of the same age who "pretend" less often. After reviewing these and other studies of children's play, Rubin et al. (1983) concluded that play is clearly an adaptive activity that (1) reflects current conceptual abilities and (2) helps children to develop additional cognitive and social skills.

Play may also serve as a means of coping with emotional crises and reducing interpersonal conflicts. Piaget points out that young children are often obliged to follow rules and adapt to a social world that they do not fully understand. When children are upset by the imposition of a rule, they can cope with these conflicts and crises by retreating into a fantasy world that permits them to reflect on the incidents that have been so discomforting. Piaget argues that

> it is primarily [emotional] conflicts that reappear in symbolic play. . . . If there is a [disciplinary] scene at lunch . . . one can be sure that an hour or two afterward it will be re-created with dolls and brought to a happier solution. Either the child disciplines her doll . . . or in play she accepts what had not been accepted at lunch (such as finishing a bowl of soup she does not like, especially if it is the doll who finishes it symbolically). . . . Generally speaking, symbolic play helps in the resolution of conflicts and also in the compensation of unsatisfied needs, [and] *the inversion of roles* such as obedience and authority [Piaget & Inhelder, 1969, p. 60; italics added].

The italicized portion of Piaget and Inhelder's statement hints at another major function of symbolic play—*role taking*. During the preschool period, children become cowboys, firefighters, doctors, lawyers, nurses, or space travelers by simply donning the appropriate attire and pretending to be these things. They can become powerful authority figures (such as parents) by enacting that role with dolls or with younger brothers and sisters. In other words, pretend play enables preschool children to try out roles that other people play while encouraging them to think about the feelings of the individuals who actually live these roles. In the process, they will learn from their enactments and further their understanding of the social world in which they live (Rubin et al., 1983).

Instead, she operates strictly from her own point of view.

■ *The Intuitive Period*

Piaget calls the phase between age 4 and age 7 the **intuitive period.** Intuitive thought is little more than an extension of preconceptual thought, although children are now slightly less egocentric and somewhat more proficient at using images and symbols in their reasoning. The child's thinking is called "intuitive" because his or her understanding of objects and events is centered on their single most salient perceptual feature—the way things appear to be.

Classification and whole/part relations. The limitations of a perceptually based, intuitive logic

are apparent when 4–7-year-olds work on **class-inclusion** problems that require them to think about whole/part relations. One such problem presents children with a set of wooden beads, most of which are brown, with a few white ones thrown in. If the preoperational child is asked whether these are all wooden beads, he answers yes. If asked whether there are more brown beads than white beads, he will once again answer cor-

> intuitive period: *the later substage of preoperations (from age 4 to age 7), when the child's thinking about objects and events is dominated by salient perceptual features.*
>
> class inclusion: *the ability to compare a class of objects with its subclasses without confusing the two.*

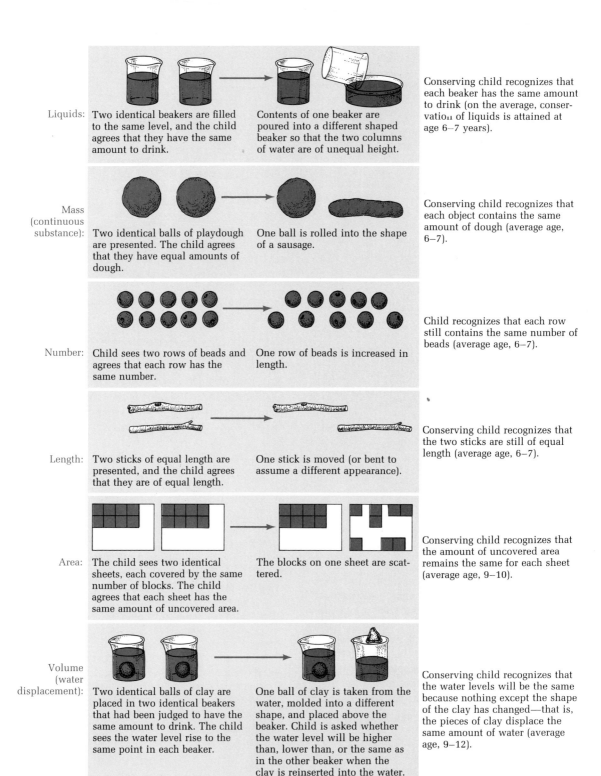

FIGURE 9-2. *Some common tests of the child's ability to conserve.*

rectly. However, if he is then asked "Are there more brown beads or more wooden beads?," he will usually say "More brown beads." Notice that the child can conceive of a whole class (wooden beads) when responding to the first question and of two distinct classes (brown and white beads) when responding to the second. Yet the third question, which requires him to *simultaneously* relate a whole class to its component parts, is too difficult. The child's thinking about class inclusion is now centered on the one most salient perceptual feature—the color of the beads—so that he fails to consider that brown beads and white beads can be combined to form a larger class of wooden beads.

The conservation problem. Other examples of children's intuitive reasoning come from Piaget's famous conservation studies (Flavell, 1963). One of these experiments begins with the child adjusting the volumes of liquid in two identical containers until each is said to have "the same amount to drink." Next the child sees the experimenter pour the liquid from one of these tall, thin containers into a short, broad container. He is then asked whether the remaining tall, thin container and the shorter, broader container have the same amount of liquid (see Figure 9-2 on p. 348 for an illustration of the procedure). Children younger than 6 or 7 will usually say that the tall, thin receptacle contains *more* liquid than the short, broad one. The child's thinking about liquids is apparently centered on one perceptual feature: the relative heights of the columns (tall column = more liquid). In Piaget's terminology, preoperational children are incapable of **conservation:** they do not yet realize that certain properties of a substance (such as its volume or mass) remain unchanged when its appearance is altered in some superficial way.

Why do preoperational children fail to conserve? Simply because their thinking is not yet *operational.* According to Piaget, two cognitive operations appear to be necessary for conservation. The first is *reversibility*—the ability to mentally undo, or reverse, an action. At the intuitive level, the child is incapable of mentally reversing the flow of action and therefore does not realize that the liquid in the short, broad container would attain its former height if it were poured back into a tall, thin container.

A second problem that prevents preoperational children from conserving is their **centration**—the tendency to center, or focus, on a single aspect of a problem while ignoring other information that would help them to answer correctly. Piaget suggests that children begin to overcome their "centered" thinking as they acquire a cognitive operation called **compensation**—the ability to focus on several aspects of a problem at the same time. Children at the intuitive stage are unable to attend simultaneously to both height and width when trying to solve the liquid conservation problem. Consequently, they fail to recognize that increases in the width of a column of liquid compensate for decreases in its height to preserve its absolute amount.

■ *Does Piaget underestimate the preoperational child?*

Are preschool children really as intuitive, illogical, and egocentric as Piaget assumes? Can a child who has no understanding of cognitive operations be taught to conserve? We will now consider some of the recent research designed to answer these questions.

New evidence on egocentrism. Several experiments indicate that Piaget has badly underestimated the ability of preschool children to recognize and appreciate another person's point of view. In one study, John Flavell (Flavell, Everett, Croft, & Flavell, 1981) showed 3-year-olds a card with a dog on one side and a cat on the other. The card was then held vertically between the child (who could see the dog) and the experimenter (who could see the cat), and the child was

---

> conservation: *the recognition that the properties of an object or substance do not change when its appearance is altered in some superficial way.*
> centration: *the tendency to focus on only one aspect of a problem when two or more aspects are relevant.*
> compensation: *the ability to consider more than one aspect of a problem at a time (also called decentration).*

asked which animal the experimenter could see. The 3-year-olds performed flawlessly, indicating that they could assume the experimenter's perspective and infer that he must be seeing the cat rather than the animal they could see.

In another study (Mossler, Marvin, & Greenberg, 1976), 2- to 6-year-olds watched a movie in which a boy expressed a strong desire for cookies as he sat at a table. Next, the mother of the child who had seen the movie entered the room and watched the same movie, except that this time the sound track was turned off. Finally, the experimenter asked each child whether his or her mother knew that the boy in the movie was sitting at the table and that he wanted cookies. Since the mother had not heard the sound track, the nonegocentric child should say that his or her mother could see the boy at the table but would *not* know that he wanted any cookies. The results were clear. Although 2- and 3-year-olds gave egocentric answers, the majority of the 4- to 6-year-olds easily recognized that their mothers had no way of knowing of the boy's desire for cookies. Clearly, these older, preoperational children were correctly inferring what their mothers knew and then determining that their mothers' information did not match their own.

It appears, then, that preoperational children are not nearly so egocentric as Piaget had thought. However, we shouldn't assume that 4–5-year-olds are capable of seeing and appreciating another person's point of view in all circumstances and situations, particularly those in which they must infer abstract, nonobservable information such as a person's motives or intentions. Rochel Gelman (1978) nicely summarizes the current viewpoint on egocentrism by noting that children become less egocentric and better able to appreciate others' points of view as they learn more and more—particularly about other people and their behavior. Perspective-taking abilities are not totally absent at one stage and suddenly present at another; they are gradually developing and becoming more refined from early in life into adulthood (Gelman, 1978).

Another look at children's causal reasoning.
Piaget is quite correct in stating that pre-operational children make many logical errors when thinking about cause-and-effect relationships. However, a review of more than 100 recent studies on children's causal reasoning suggests that even 3-year-olds recognize that (1) causes precede rather than follow effects and (2) an event that always precedes an effect (100% covariation) is more likely to be its cause than are other events that occasionally precede the effect (Sedlak & Kurtz, 1981). These are very simple kinds of causal inferences, but they nevertheless indicate that 3–4-year-olds have some understanding of causality and will not always resort to transductive reasoning.

If we look carefully at Piaget's research, it becomes clearer why he believed that preschool children did not understand cause and effect. Piaget's tests of causal reasoning presented the child with questions such as "What causes the wind?," "Why do rivers flow?," and "How do bicycles work?" Gelman (1978) points out that few if any preschoolers would have had an opportunity to learn about these natural events or about the workings of a bicycle. And in the absence of any information, preschool children have little choice but to formulate some kind of "transductive" or "animistic" answer (for example, pedals make a bicycle work) based on what they have seen or what little they do know.

Can preoperational children conserve?
According to Piaget (1970b), children younger than 6 or 7 cannot solve conservation problems, because they have not yet acquired reversibility and compensation—the two cognitive operations that would enable them to discover the constancy of attributes such as mass and volume. Piaget has also argued that one cannot teach conservation to subjects younger than 6 or 7 years of age, for these *pre*operational children are much too intellectually immature to understand and use logical operations such as reversibility and compensation.

Are preschool children really incapable of learning to conserve? Irving Sigel and his associates (Sigel, Roeper, & Hooper, 1968) tested this hypothesis by coaxing 4–5-year-olds who had failed various conservation tests to focus on several dimensions at once (compensation training) and to think about what might happen if an action were reversed or undone (reversibility training). The majority of children who were trained in these logical operations showed at least some modest improvement in their performance on conservation tests.

Other investigators (see Beilin, 1980; Field, 1977) have had much greater success with **identity training**—teaching children to recognize that the object or substance transformed in a conservation task is still the *same* object or substance, regardless of its new appearance. For example, a child being trained to recognize identities on a "conservation of liquids" task might be told "It may look like less water when we pour it from a tall, thin glass into this shorter one, but it is the *same* water, and there has to be the same amount to drink." Recently, Dorothy Field (1981) has shown that 4-year-olds who received this training not only conserved on the training task but could also use their new knowledge about identities to solve a number of conservation problems on which they had not been trained. Field also reports that nearly 75% of the 4-year-olds who had received some kind of identity training were able to solve at least three (out of five) conservation problems that were presented to them two and one-half to five months *after* their training had ended. In contrast, only 35% of the 4-year-olds who had been trained in the logical operations of reversibility and compensation were able to conserve on this delayed posttest. We see, then, that 4-year-olds can learn to conserve and that their understanding of this "law of nature" seems to depend more on their ability to recognize identities than on their use of logical operations. In fact, 5–6-year-olds who have never been trained will often conserve by identity long before they acquire the logical operations of reversibility and compensation (Acredolo & Acredolo, 1979, 1980).

Summing up. Taken together, the evidence we have reviewed suggests that preschool children are not as illogical and egocentric as Piaget assumes. Nevertheless, Piaget is undoubtedly correct in arguing that their thinking will become much more orderly and rational once they begin to understand and use cog-

nitive operations such as reversibility and compensation.

The Concrete-Operational Stage (7 to 11 Years)

During the **concrete-operational** period, children are rapidly acquiring cognitive operations and applying these important new skills when thinking about objects, situations, and events that they have seen, heard, or otherwise experienced. Recall from our earlier discussion that a cognitive operation is an internal mental schema that enables the child to modify and reorganize her images and symbols and to reverse these transformations in her head (Flavell, 1977). For example, the operation of reversibility allows the child to mentally reverse the flow of action and thereby recognize that a column of water would once again look the same if she were to pour it back into its original container. The operations of cognitive *addition* and *subtraction* permit the child to discover the logical relation between whole classes and subclasses by mentally adding the parts to form a superordinate whole and then reversing this action (subtracting) to once again think of the whole class as a collection of subclasses. In sum, the ability to operate on one's objects of thought takes the 7- to 11-year-old far beyond the static and centered thinking of the preoperational stage.

Why does Piaget call this period *concrete* operations? Because he believes that children at this stage of development can apply their operational schemata only to objects, situations, and events that are *real* or *imaginable*. Indeed, we will see that 7- to 11-year-olds find it very diffi-

---

identity training: *an attempt to promote conservation by teaching nonconservers to recognize that a transformed object or substance is the same object or substance, regardless of its new appearance.*

concrete operations: *Piaget's third stage of cognitive development, lasting from about age 7 to age 11, when children are acquiring cognitive operations and thinking more logically about real objects and experiences.*

cult to think about any abstract idea or hypothetical proposition that has no basis in reality.

■ Some characteristics of concrete- operational thinking

To this point, we have talked about two operational structures: class inclusion and conservation. Let's briefly consider three more.

Mental representation of actions.   According to Piaget, the concrete operator is finally able to construct accurate mental representations of a complex series of actions. Suppose, for example, that we were to ask a 5-year-old preoperational child and his 10-year-old sister to sketch a map of the route to their grandmother's house across town. Even if the younger child walks there every day, he will probably fail to produce an accurate map. His problem, according to Piaget, is that he cannot conjure up a mental representation of the entire route. By contrast, the older, operational child will find this mapmaking task rather easy, for it simply requires her to transcribe the "cognitive map" in her head (Piaget & Inhelder, 1956).

But caution is required in interpreting Piaget's mapmaking studies. In a recent experiment, Linda Anooshian and her colleagues (Anooshian, Hartman, & Scharf, 1982) found that many 3- to 6-year-olds are able to describe the steps they have taken through a familiar environment by placing photographs of the various landmarks into their proper sequence. In other words, these preoperational children must be able to represent their past actions in some internal, symbolic fashion that enables them to recall the route they traveled. Perhaps cognitive operations do help older children to think about distances, directions, and action sequences; but it appears that they are not absolutely necessary for either the mental representation of actions or the development of cognitive maps.

Relational logic.   A better understanding of relations and relational logic is one of the hallmarks of concrete-operational thinking. For example, concrete operators are capable of **seriation,** an operation that enables them to arrange a set of stimuli along a quantifiable dimension, such as length. A related ability is the concept of **transitivity,** which describes the relations among the elements in a serial order. If, for example, John is taller than Mark, who is taller than Sam, then John has to be taller than Sam. Although this inference seems elementary to us, children show little awareness of the transitivity principle before the stage of concrete operations.

Two additional observations are worthy of note. First, preoperational children can be trained to seriate and to make simple transitive inferences, so that the basic ability to understand the relations "less than" and "greater than" must precede the development of cognitive operations (Gelman, 1978). Second, the transitive inferences of concrete operators are generally limited to real objects that are physically present. Indeed, 7- to 11-year-olds do not yet apply this relational logic to abstract signifiers such as the xs, ys, and zs that we use in algebra.

Linguistic humor.   In Chapter Eight we learned that children begin to appreciate linguistic humor at about the time that they develop metalinguistic awareness—the ability to think about language and its properties. Suddenly, puns and jokes that depend on the double meaning of words and sounds become hilarious to the 6- to 8-year-old. For example, the humor in the riddle "What has an eye but can't see? *Answer:* A needle" stems from the double meaning of the word *eye.* The child who is metalinguistically aware can quickly compare these two meanings and see the humorous incongruity between the typical use of the term *eye* and its unusual or unexpected use in the punchline.

Cognitive theorists such as Paul McGhee (1979) have argued that the development of concrete-operational abilities may be responsible for both the emergence of metalinguistic awareness and

the child's growing appreciation of humor. In cognitive terms, an understanding of jokes such as the "eye" riddle depends on the child's ability to *classify* the double meaning of words and then to quickly *reverse* his perspective to think about the two meanings at the same time. Although a pre-operational child may know the two meanings for a word such as *eye*, he will center on the more common usage (an organ of sight) and will not reclassify the punchline or reverse perspectives quickly enough to find the eye riddle humorous. Consequently, he either "doesn't get it" or may consider the riddle stupid when and if he finally sees the play on words.

■ *The sequencing of concrete operations*
While examining Figure 9-2, you may have noticed that some forms of conservation (for example, mass) are understood much sooner than others (area or volume). Piaget was aware of this and other developmental inconsistencies, and he coined the term **horizontal decalage** to describe them.

Why does the child display different levels of awareness or understanding on a series of conservation tasks that seem to require the same mental operations? According to Piaget, horizontal decalage occurs because problems that appear quite similar may actually differ in complexity. For example, conservation of volume (see Figure 9-2) is not attained until age 9 to 12 because it is a complex task that requires the child to simultaneously consider the operations involved in the conservation of both liquids and mass *and* then to determine whether there are any meaningful interactions between these two phenomena. Although we have talked as if concrete operations were a set of skills that appeared rather abruptly over a brief period, this is not Piaget's point of view. Piaget has always maintained that operational abilities evolve gradually and sequentially as the simpler skills that appear first are consolidated, combined, and reorganized into increasingly complex mental structures.

Recently, Carol Tomlinson-Keasey and her associates (Tomlinson-Keasey, Eisert, Kahle, Hardy-Brown, & Keasey, 1979) studied the growth of logical reasoning between ages 6 and 9. In this longitudinal study they found that the various concrete-operational abilities did develop very gradually and in approximately the same se-

quence for all the children they tested. By age 6, most of the children could seriate and understood the concept of number. The next abilities to emerge were conservation of mass and weight, which, in turn, appeared to be necessary for the development of class-inclusion skills. Finally, children were able to conserve volume only after they had a firm understanding of mass and could classify objects in a variety of ways. In sum, there is a coherence, or consistency, to development during the concrete-operational period. Concrete operations emerge gradually and in a particular sequence because the skills that develop earliest are simpler schemata that serve as prerequisites for those developing later (Tomlinson-Keasey et al., 1979).

■ *Piaget on education*
After reviewing the accomplishments of the concrete-operational period, we can see why many societies begin to formally educate their young at 6 to 7 years of age. This is precisely the time when children are decentering from perceptual illusions and acquiring the cognitive operations that will enable them to comprehend arithmetic, to think about language and its properties, to classify animals, people, objects, and events, and to understand the relations between upper- and lower-case letters, letters and the printed word, words and sentences, and so on.

Although Piaget's theory is not a theory of education, it offers some helpful hints to the elementary school teacher. Perhaps the most important single proposition that educators can derive from Piaget's work is that children are naturally inquisitive souls who learn best by exploring their environments. In addition, it helps to recall that 7–11-year-olds think most logically and systematically about *real* objects

---

seriation: *a cognitive operation that allows one to order a set of stimuli along a quantifiable dimension such as height or weight.*

transitivity: *the ability to recognize relations among elements in a serial order (for example, if A > B and B > C, then A > C).*

horizontal decalage: *an inability to solve certain problems even though one can solve similar problems requiring the same mental operations.*

and events and about activities that can be concretized in some way. For these reasons, Piaget advises teachers to spend less time lecturing and allow children to learn by doing. He believes that arithmetic operations may be best illustrated by having children add and subtract buttons rather than showing them how to solve problems on a blackboard. He advocates "teaching" the concepts of space and distance by allowing children to measure their heights or the widths of their desks, as opposed to lecturing them on the relations between inches, feet, and yards. In other words, Piaget contends that the teacher's job is not so much to transmit facts and concepts as to provide the setting and materials that will enable curious children to *discover* this knowledge for themselves. He sees a discovery-based education as critical because he believes that "the principal goal of education is to create [adults] who are capable of doing new things, not simply of repeating what other generations have done—[people] who are creative, inventive, discoverers" (Piaget, as cited in Elkind, 1977, p. 171).

The Formal-Operational Stage (Age 11–12 and Beyond)

By age 11 or 12, many children are entering the last of Piaget's intellectual stages—**formal operations.** Perhaps the most important characteristic of formal-operational thinking is its flexibility. No longer is thinking tied to the observable or imaginable, for formal operators can now reason quite logically about abstract ideas that may have no basis in reality.

■ *Reactions to hypothetical propositions*
One way to determine whether a preadolescent has crossed over into the stage of formal operations is to present a thought problem that violates her views about the real world. The concrete operator, whose thinking is tied to objective reality, will often balk at hypothetical propositions. In fact, she may even reply that it is impossible to think about objects that don't exist or events that could never happen. In contrast, formal operators enjoy thinking about hypotheticals and are likely to generate some very unusual and creative responses. In Box 9-4 we can see the differences

between concrete-operational and formal-operational thinking as children consider a hypothetical proposition that was presented in the form of an art assignment.

■ *Hypothetical-deductive reasoning: The systematic search for answers and solutions*
The formal operator's approach to problem solving becomes increasingly systematic and abstract —not at all unlike the **hypothetical-deductive reasoning** of a scientist. We can easily compare the reasoning of formal operators with that of their younger counterparts by examining their responses to Piaget's famous "four beaker" problem:

> The child is given four similar flasks containing colorless, odorless liquids which are perceptually identical [but contain different chemicals]. We number them (1) . . . (2) . . . (3) . . . and (4). We add a bottle (with an eyedropper) which we call *g*. Mixing chemicals 1 + 3 + *g* will yield a yellow color. The experimenter presents to the subject two glasses, one containing chemicals 1 + 3, the other containing chemical 2. In front of the subject, he pours several drops of *g* into each of the two glasses and notes the different reactions. Then the subject is asked to simply reproduce the yellow color in a test tube, using flasks 1, 2, 3, 4, and *g* as he wishes [Inhelder & Piaget, 1958, pp. 108–109].

Children at the concrete-operational stage attack this problem by *doing what they saw the experimenter do:* they mix a few drops of *g* with chemicals from each of the four flasks and thus fail to produce the yellow color. At this point, concrete operators may say something like "I tried them all and nothing works." Usually they have to be coaxed to go beyond their visual experiences to mix three chemicals, and their higher-order combinations tend to be unsystematic. In fact, concrete operators who stumble on the correct solution by this trial-and-error approach are often unable to reproduce the yellow color when asked to repeat the process.

The formal operator begins in the same way as the concrete operator, but he subsequently proceeds to test every possible combination of three chemicals when the binary combinations (that is, 1 + *g*, 2 + *g*, 3 + *g*, 4 + *g*) fail to solve the problem. Furthermore, the formal operator generates the higher-order combinations according to a rational, systematic plan, often begin-

PHOTO 9-3. *A systematic approach to problem solving is one of the characteristics of formal-operational thinking.*

ning with 1 + 2 + *g* and proceeding through 1 + 3 + *g*, 1 + 4 + *g*, 2 + 3 + *g*, and so on until all possible combinations have been tested and the one correct solution identified. The verbalizations that accompany the formal operator's problem-solving behavior are likely to include many "if/then" propositional statements that characterize the logic used in hypothetical-deductive reasoning. These statements rarely appear in the protocols on concrete-operational children.

In sum, formal-operational thinking is rational, systematic, and abstract. The formal operator can now "think about thinking" and operate on *ideas* as well as tangible objects and events. Piaget believes that these new cognitive abilities are almost certain to have a dramatic impact on the adolescent's feelings, goals, and behaviors, for teenagers are suddenly able to reflect on weighty abstractions such as morality and justice, as well as more personal concerns such as their present and future roles in life, their beliefs and values, and the way things "are" as opposed to the way things

"ought to be." Consequently, the adolescent approaching intellectual maturity is apt to become a bit of a philosopher, and his or her preoccupation with thinking and its products is the hallmark of the formal-operational period.

■ *Some questions about formal operations*

Piaget (1970b) has argued that the transition from concrete-operational to formal-operational reasoning takes place very gradually over a period of several years. For example, 11–13-year-olds who are entering formal operations are able to consider simple hypothetical propositions such as the three-eye problem (see Box 9-4). However, they are not yet proficient at generating and testing hypotheses, and it may be another three to four years before they are capable of the planful, systematic reasoning that is necessary to solve the "four beaker" problem or to determine the factor that explains how fast a pendulum will swing.[1] Piaget has never identified a stage of reasoning beyond formal operations, and he believes that most people will reach this highest level of intellect by age 15–18.

---

[1]The pendulum problem is another of Piaget's famous tests for formal-operational thinking. The subject is given a number of weights that can be tied to a long string to make a pendulum. He or she is allowed to vary the length of the string, the amount of weight attached to it, and the height from which the weight is released in order to determine which of these factors alone or in combination will determine how quickly the pendulum swings. The trick is to test each variable singly while holding the others constant. Formal operators, who are capable of this planful and systematic reasoning, soon discover that the critical variable is the *length* of the string: the shorter it is, the faster the pendulum swings.

---

formal operations: *Piaget's fourth and final stage of cognitive development (from age 11 or 12 and beyond), when the individual begins to think more rationally and systematically about abstract concepts and hypothetical events.*

hypothetical-deductive reasoning: *a style of problem solving in which the possible solutions to a problem are generated and then systematically evaluated to determine the correct answer.*

BOX 9-4
CHILDREN'S RESPONSES TO A
HYPOTHETICAL PROPOSITION

Piaget (1970a) has argued that the thinking of concrete operators is reality-bound. Presumably most 9-year-olds would have a difficult time thinking about objects that don't exist or events that could never happen. By contrast, children entering the stage of formal operations were said to be quite capable of considering hypothetical propositions and carrying them to a logical conclusion. Indeed, Piaget suspected that many formal operators would even enjoy this type of cognitive challenge.

Several years ago, a group of concrete operators (9-year-old fourth-graders) and a group of children who were at or rapidly approaching formal operations (11- to 12-year-old sixth-graders) completed the following assignment:

> Suppose that you were given a third eye and that you could choose to place this eye anywhere on your body. Draw me a picture to show where you would place your "extra" eye, and then tell me why you would put it there.

All the 9-year-olds placed the third eye *on the forehead between their two natural eyes.* It seems as if these children called on their concrete experiences to complete their assignment: eyes are found some-where around the middle of the face in all people. One 9-year-old boy remarked that the third eye should go between the other two because "that's where a cyclops has his eye." The rationales for this eye placement were rather unimaginative. Consider the following examples:

Jim (age 9½): I would like an eye beside my two other eyes so that if one eye went out, I could still see with two.

Vickie (age 9): I want an extra eye so I can see you three times.

Tanya (age 9½): I want a third eye so I could see better.

In contrast, the older, formal-operational children gave a wide variety of responses that were not at all dependent on what they had seen previously. Furthermore, these children thought out the advantages of this hypothetical situation and provided rather imaginative rationales for placing the "extra" eye in unique locations. Here are some sample responses:

Ken (age 11½): (*Draws the extra eye on top of a tuft of hair.*) I could revolve the eye to look in all directions.

John (age 11½): (*Draws his extra eye in the palm of his left hand.*) I could see around corners and see what kind of cookie I'll get out of the cookie jar.

Tony (age 11): (*Draws a close-up of a third eye in his mouth.*) I want a third eye in my mouth because I want to see what I am eating.

When asked their opinions of the "three eye" assignment, many of the younger children considered it

---

Does everyone reach formal operations? Recently investigators have been finding that adolescents are much slower to acquire formal operations than Piaget had thought. In fact, Edith Neimark's (1979) review of the literature suggests that a sizable percentage of American adults do not reason at the formal level and that there are some societies where no one solves Piaget's formal-operational problems.

Why is it that some people fail to attain formal operations? One possibility is that they may not have had the kinds of schooling that stress logic, mathematics, and science—experiences that Piaget believes will help the child to reason at the formal level. Another possibility is that some individuals may not have the intellectual capacity to move from concrete to formal operations. Indeed, adolescents and adults who score below average on standardized intelligence tests rarely if ever reason at the formal level (Inhelder, 1966; Jackson, 1965).

Of course, it may be that nearly all adults are *capable* of reasoning at the formal level but will do so only on problems that hold their interest or are of vital importance to them. For example, a competent auto mechanic may engage in hypothetical-deductive reasoning when troubleshooting an engine problem but then revert to a more concrete level of functioning when thinking about most other issues (Flavell, 1977). Hunters from preliterate societies will often reason at the formal level when tracking prey—a vitally important activity that requires the systematic testing of inferences and hypotheses (Tulkin & Konner, 1973). Finally, Robert Siegler and his associates (Siegler & Liebert, 1975; Siegler, Liebert, & Liebert, 1973) found that 10–11-year-old concrete operators can learn to solve Piaget's formal-operational

Tanya's, Ken's, and John's responses to the "third eye" assignment.

rather silly and uninteresting. One 9-year-old remarked "This is stupid. Nobody has three eyes." However, the 11–12-year-olds enjoyed the task and continued to pester their teacher for "fun" art assignments "like the eye problem" for the remainder of the school year.

So the results of this demonstration are generally consistent with Piaget's theory. Older children who are at or rapidly approaching formal operations are more likely than younger concrete operators to generate logical and creative responses to a hypothetical proposition and to enjoy this type of reasoning.

problems if certain scientific concepts are defined for them and if they are encouraged to think logically and systematically about the problems. In sum, we must be careful not to underestimate the cognitive capabilities of adolescents and adults who do not seem to reason at the formal level. Since the majority of issues that people consider on a daily basis do not require formal reasoning, it is quite conceivable that the failure of many to think logically and systematically about Piaget's test problems reflects their lack of experience with formal operations rather than their inability to reason at that level.

Are there higher stages of intellectual development? According to Piaget, formal-operational thinking is the structural equivalent of adult intelligence—the most mature form of reasoning of which human beings are capable. Not everyone

agrees. Patricia Arlin (1975, 1977) has called formal operations a *problem-solving* stage that describes how bright adolescents and adults think about problems that someone else presents to them. However, she believes that truly creative and insightful thinkers—people like Aristotle, Einstein, and Piaget himself—operate on a higher plane that enables them to rethink or reorganize existing knowledge and then to *ask* important questions or define totally new problems. Arlin refers to this higher intellectual ability as a **problem-finding stage.**

> **problem-finding stage:** *according to Arlin, a stage beyond formal operations in which the individual is now capable of using knowledge to ask questions and define new problems.*

Michael Commons and his associates (Commons, Richards, & Kuhn, 1982) suggest that there may be two levels of intellectual functioning beyond Piaget's formal operations. The first is what they call **systematic reasoning**—the ability to combine sets of formal operations into higher-order structures, or "systems." The next level of intellect, called **metasystematic reasoning**, is the ability to operate on and organize general systems into supersystems. As a first step in evaluating these hypotheses, Commons et al. (1982) asked college undergraduates and graduate students to read four story-problems and to indicate how the stories were similar or dissimilar to one another. This story-comparison test required the reader to think about abstract similarities and dissimilarities among the pieces of information within the stories and to organize these properties into *systems* (axioms that describe all the relations within a story) and *supersystems* (an overall classification of all the stories based on *systematic* principles that make certain stories similar and others dissimilar). Although the vast majority of the research participants could solve Piaget's tests of formal operations, fewer than 20% of the undergraduate students organized the information within the stories into abstract systems or supersystems. In contrast, nearly 70% of the graduate students showed at least some evidence of systematic or metasystematic reasoning. Thus, the majority of the graduate students recognized abstract similarities and dissimilarities that most undergraduates did not detect.

Do these findings indicate that there are levels of intellectual development beyond formal operations? Commons et al. (1982) believe they do, although other interpretations are possible. For example, a Piagetian could argue that the inability of a formal operator to construct abstract "systems" and "supersystems" simply represents a form of horizontal decalage that is comparable to that of a concrete operator who conserves liquids and mass but not volume. In other words, the cognitive abilities that Arlin and Commons have described may represent very complex formal-operational schemata rather than higher stages of intellect that are qualitatively different from formal reasoning. At this point, it is not clear whether the Piagetian perspective or the Arlin/Commons (higher-stage) perspective is correct. But regardless of how this debate is eventually

resolved, a task for future research will be to determine why some people are able to pose new questions or think at the "systematic" or "metasystematic" levels while the vast majority of adults may never reach these intellectual plateaus.

AN EVALUATION OF PIAGET'S THEORY

Jean Piaget had a profound impact on the study of cognitive development in particular and child development in general. Perhaps the most important and far-reaching of his many insights was the realization that developing children are naturally curious beings who will *actively* explore the environment and seek to explain phenomena that they don't understand. This perspective on human nature was a dramatic departure from the then-traditional view of children as passive recipients of environmental influence who must be taught the ways of the world and trained to think for themselves.

After nearly 60 years of collaborating with his young informants, Piaget died in 1980 and left us with the most detailed and integrated theory of cognitive development that currently exists. Like all good theories, this one has generated an enormous amount of research. And as often happens when theories are scrutinized, some of this research points to possible problems and shortcomings in Piaget's approach. Among the more common criticisms of Piaget's theory are the issue of timing, the issue of stages, and the question of whether Piaget really "explains" cognitive development.

The Issue of Timing

The most frequent complaint about Piaget's theory is that children do not always display various intellectual skills or enter a particular stage of development when Piaget says they should. Recall that Piaget was overly pessimistic about the cognitive abilities of preschool children and much too optimistic about the rate at which adolescents acquire formal operations. Part of the problem stems from Piaget's methods. He often asked younger children to think about objects or concepts that were very unfamiliar to them—a practice that is almost certain to underestimate what the children may know and understand. Moreover, he frequently phrased his questions in ways that might confuse the child or somehow obscure the concept being tested. For example, Barbara Hodkin (1981) finds that 3–5-year-olds perform much better on class-inclusion problems that call attention to hierarchical classes ("Are there more smarties *or* more of *all* the candies?") than they do when asked the standard Piagetian questions, which may cloud the relation between a whole class and its subclasses ("Are there more smarties *or* more candies?")

Piagetians often dismiss the timing issue. They note that Piaget was interested mainly in identifying the *sequencing* of intellectual stages and that his age norms are rough approximations at best. As it turns out, later research has generally confirmed Piaget's sequential hypotheses: the sequencing of intellectual abilities that Piaget observed in his Swiss samples also describes the course and content of intellectual growth for children from the hundreds of countries, cultures, and subcultures that have now been studied (Cowan, 1978; Flavell, 1977). Although cultural factors do influence the *rate* of cognitive growth, the direction of development is always from sensorimotor intellect to preoperational thinking to concrete operations to (in many cases) formal operations.

Does Cognitive Development Occur in Stages?

Other researchers have begun to question Piaget's idea that the child's thinking develops in stages (Brainerd, 1978; Flavell, 1982). From their perspective, a "stage" of intellect implies that abrupt changes in intellectual functioning occur as the child acquires several new skills and abilities over a very brief period. Yet our review of the literature suggests that cognitive growth doesn't happen that way: major changes or transitions in intellect occur quite gradually, and there is often very little consistency in the child's performance on tasks that presumably measure the abilities that define a "stage." For example, we've seen that it may be months or even years before a 6-year-old who can seriate and conserve number will pass other concrete-operational tests such as class inclusion or conservation of volume (Tomlinson-Keasey et al., 1979).

Piaget's reply is to attribute inconsistencies in intellectual performance to horizontal decalage. Presumably children who can conserve liquid and mass but not volume are at a *stage* (concrete operations) where operational schemata are the dominant mental structures. Their problem is that they have not yet organized their operational structures in a way that would enable them to solve the very difficult "conservation of volume" problem.

Perhaps you can anticipate the critics' response. They argue that if cognitive growth is gradual and continuous, without sudden transformations to higher levels of functioning, then it is misleading to talk about distinct *stages* of intellectual growth. Although cognitive abilities do seem to emerge in a particular sequence, this intellectual progression is probably not as "stage-like" as Piaget assumed (Brainerd, 1978; Flavell, 1982).

Does Piaget's Theory "Explain" Cognitive Development?

The major shortcoming of Piaget's theory is that it does not *clearly* indicate how children move from one stage of intellect to the next. After considering the issue, Piaget (1970a) concluded that the maturation of the brain and the nervous system interacts with the child's experiences to promote cognitive growth. Presumably children are always assimilating new experiences, accommodating to those experiences, and reorganizing their schemata into increasingly complex mental structures. Maturation was thought to influence intellectual development by affecting the ways children can act on objects and events, which, in turn, will determine what they can learn from their experiences. As children continue to construct and reorganize their cognitive schemata, they will eventually come to think about old information in new ways and begin the gradual transition from one stage of intellect to the next.

---

systematic reasoning: *the ability to combine formal-operational schemata into higher-order structures called systems.*

metasystematic reasoning: *the ability to operate on systems to construct higher-order structures (or supersystems).*

Clearly, this rather vague explanation of cognitive growth raises more questions than it answers. For example, we might wonder what maturational changes are necessary before children can progress from sensorimotor to preoperational functioning or from concrete operations to formal operations. What kinds of experiences must a child have before he will construct mental symbols, understand cognitive operations, or begin to operate on ideas and think about hypotheticals? Piaget is simply not very explicit about these or any other mechanisms that might enable a child to move to a higher stage of intellect. As a result, a growing number of researchers now look on his theory as an elaborate *description* of cognitive development that has little if any explanatory value (Brainerd, 1978).

When we critique a theory as broad as Piaget's, it is easy to lose sight of the fact that researchers have been testing and confirming many of Piaget's hypotheses for more than 60 years. Although we now recognize that this theory has some very real shortcomings and may eventually be discarded in favor of a better alternative, Piaget surely qualifies as the father of cognitive psychology and as a leading figure in the history of the behavioral sciences. Indeed, it is almost inconceivable that our knowledge of intellectual development could have progressed to its present level had Piaget pursued his early interests in zoology and never worked with developing children.

Present and Future Directions

Today researchers are branching out in several directions as they try to gain a better understanding of cognitive growth and its relation to other aspects of development. Many investigators continue to study Piagetian phenomena as they try to fill in the gaps in this influential theory. Others have looked for maturational correlates of intellectual growth and are beginning to ask some interesting questions. For example, is there any connection between the end of the brain growth spurt at age 2 and the appearance of symbolic schemata? Is it merely a coincidence that children begin to acquire and use cognitive operations at age 6 or 7—about the time that higher brain centers are rapidly myelinating and neural impulses are traveling much faster than they were during the preschool period? Do the changes in

hormonal balance that occur as the body prepares for puberty have anything to do with the onset of formal-operational abilities at about the same age? Although no one can yet answer these important questions, investigators are now pursuing these early leads and continuing to search for other meaningful links between neurological maturation and intellectual growth (Kohen-Raz, 1977).

Perhaps the best-known alternative to Piaget's theory is the *information-processing* approach, a "new look" at cognitive development that arose from the work of information theorists and experimental psychologists in Canada and in the United States. Proponents of information-processing theory view cognition as an extremely complex activity involving a number of related processes. As a result, they approach the topic of intellectual development by studying the growth of specific cognitive-processing skills such as attending, perceiving, thinking, learning, and remembering.

Before we take a closer look at the information-processing approach, a caution is in order. Since much of what we know about children's ability to process and use information is itself recent information, the cognitive-processing approach lacks the elegant coherence that we saw in Piaget's work. In the following section, we will try to tie up a few of the loose ends as we discuss some of the interesting findings that are beginning to emerge from this new look at children's intellectual growth.

THE INFORMATION-PROCESSING APPROACH

In the mid-1950s, information theorists such as Allen Newell and Herbert Simon began to compare the human mind with that wondrous new invention called the "electric brain" (Carey, Foltz, & Allan, 1983). Simon and his colleagues noted that both the mind and the electronic computer are devices that have a finite capacity for storing, retrieving, and analyzing information. Moreover, each of these information-processing systems consists of *hardware* and *software*. Computer hardware is the physical parameters of the machine—its keyboard (or input) system, memory, and logic units. The software consists of the plans, or programmed instructions, that tell the machine how to organize, retrieve, and operate on the information it receives. The mind's physical machinery, or "hardware," consists of the brain, nervous system, and sensory receptors. For "software" the mind relies on rules, plans, motives, and intentions—mental "programs" that affect the ways information is registered, interpreted, stored, retrieved, and analyzed.

Over the years, electronic computers have become increasingly sophisticated: each new generation of these remarkable machines is more capable than its predecessors because of improvements in its hardware and software. Information-processing theorists suggest that the same may be true of the developing mind: as the brain and nervous system mature (hardware improvements) and children adopt new strategies for attending to stimuli, interpreting them, and remembering what they have experienced (software improvements), they should become much more proficient at acting on information to solve important problems (Klahr & Wallace, 1976).

Of course, we can take this mind/computer analogy only so far, because these two systems differ in important respects. A computer processes information rapidly and *sequentially* (one unit at a time) as it executes a preprogrammed series of logical operations to arrive at a solution to the problem it has been given. A computer does not define problems, and its processing strategies remain unchanged unless the machine is reprogrammed to execute a different set of logical operations. By contrast, human beings process information much more slowly than a computer does. However, humans are able to consider several units of information *simultaneously* and perhaps even create *new* information by altering their processing strategies and redefining the nature of the problems they face (Carey et al., 1983; Reynolds & Flagg, 1983).

The primary goal of information-processing theory is to explain how children of different ages process information about objects and events to "construct" knowledge and solve various problems. In the pages that follow, we will trace the development of three important cognitive processing skills that are thought to influence the character of children's thinking: (1) the ability to gather task-relevant information (attention), (2) the ability to retain this input (memory), and (3) the strategies or rules that children use when evaluating what they have noticed and retained (hypothesis testing).

Attentional Processes: Getting Information into the System

On several occasions we have noted that toddlers and preschool children have short attention spans. When asked to work on a repetitive task, 2- to 4-year-olds will often persist for no more than a few minutes, and they are easily distracted (Wellman, Ritter, & Flavell, 1975). Even when doing things that they like, such as watching television, 2- and 3-year-olds will frequently get up and wander around the room to talk to people or play with toys (Anderson, Alwitt, Lorch, & Levin, 1979). So very young children may fail to solve many problems because they are unable (or unwilling) to sustain their attention long enough to gather the necessary information.

By about age 5, children are becoming much more persistent in their attempts to solve problems. However, their strategies for gathering information are typically unsystematic and reveal a lack of planfulness. In a recent study, Alice Vlietstra (1982) had 5-, 8-, and 11-year-olds examine a mock-up of a house. She then asked the children to search six similar houses until they (1) found *one* difference between the sample house and the comparison houses or (2) found *all* differences between the sample and the comparison houses. The 5-year-olds in this experiment clearly failed to follow the instructions, choosing instead to explore the stimuli in a haphazard way. The 8-year-olds searched the stimulus displays much more systematically than the 5-year-olds did, but they failed to limit their attention to "one difference" when asked to find a single difference between the sample and the comparison houses. Only the 11-year-olds were very planful; they followed the two sets of instructions equally well by confining their visual search to the information that was necessary to perform each task. In sum, the tendency of younger children to seek out and *explore* interesting new stimuli may interfere with the planful gathering of information that would help them to solve problems or perform well on tasks they are asked to undertake.

Would young children perform as well as older children if they knew in advance which infor-

PHOTO 9-4. *Although the ability to concentrate improves dramatically during middle childhood, grade school students are not always successful at overcoming distractions.*

mation was relevant to the task at hand? Apparently not. In one study, Patricia Miller and Michael Weiss (1981) told 7-, 10-, and 13-year-olds to remember the locations of a number of animals, each of which was hidden behind a different cloth flap. When each flap was lifted to reveal an animal, the children could also see a household object positioned either above or below the animal. Here, then, is a learning task that requires the child to attend selectively to certain information (the animals) while ignoring other potentially distracting input (the household objects). When the children were tested to see whether they had learned where each animal was located, the 13-year-olds outperformed the 10-year-olds, who, in turn, performed slightly better than the 7-year-olds. Miller and Weiss then tested to see whether children had attended to the incidental (irrelevant) information by asking them to recall which household object had been paired with

each animal. They found exactly the opposite pattern on this incidental learning test: 13-year-olds recalled *less* about the household objects than either 7- or 10-year-olds. In fact, both of the younger groups actually recalled as much about the irrelevant objects as about the locations of the animals. Taken together, these findings indicate that older children are much better than younger ones at concentrating on relevant information and filtering out extraneous input that may interfere with task performance.

■ *What do children know about attention?*

Young children may know much more about selective attention than their behavior would indicate. Patricia Miller and Michael Weiss (1982) asked 5-, 7-, and 10-year-olds to answer a series of questions about factors known to affect performance on an incidental learning task (that is, a task like the "animals and objects" test in which children are told to remember only one category of objects when other distracting stimuli are present). Although knowledge about attentional processes generally increased with age, even the 5-year-olds realized that one should at least *look first* at task-relevant stimuli and then *label* these objects as an aid to remembering them. The 7- and 10-year-olds further understood that one must *attend selectively* to task-relevant stimuli and *ignore* irrelevant or incidental information in order to do well on the problem that one was asked to undertake.

Why, then, do younger children fail to use these attentional strategies when they actually work on an incidental learning task? It may be that any strategy the younger child knows about and hopes to apply is soon overwhelmed by a desire to *explore* those fascinating incidental stimuli that compete for his attention. However, Miller and Weiss believe that children will gradually learn to translate their knowledge into appropriate attentional strategies as they encounter more and more situations that require them to shut out irrelevant distractions in order to accomplish important objectives.

■ *Training children to attend*

Can younger children be trained to attend more selectively to the relevant features of their environment? Apparently so. Alice Vlietstra (1982) reports that 7-year-olds become much more plan-

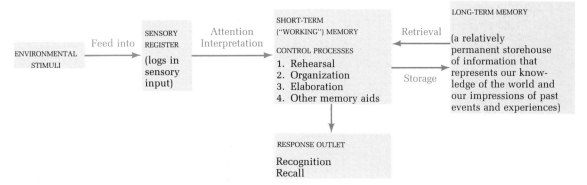

FIGURE 9-3. *A cognitive-processing model of the flow of information within the memory system.*

ful when searching for task-relevant information if they are shown how to search and then reinforced (with a marble) for following this strategy. In another recent experiment, Pamela Cole and Nora Newcomb (1983) have shown that 7-year-olds can learn to focus their attention on a central task and to shut out distracting verbal stimuli by either instructing themselves not to listen or imagining that they have shut a door between themselves and the verbal distractor.

The successful attempts to teach preschool children to conserve can also be viewed as methods of fostering selective attention. Recall that children who undergo identity training are taught to recognize that the object or substance that is transformed in a conservation task remains the same object or substance, regardless of its new appearance. In other words, they are encouraged to attend to certain task-relevant information (identities) and to ignore all potentially distracting input (altered shapes, heights, widths, and so forth) that could prevent them from conserving (Field, 1981). Since even 4-year-olds have learned to conserve simple quantities after being trained in this way, it is clear that attentional processes play a major role in determining what young children may know and understand.

Memory Processes: Retaining What One Has Experienced

Once children have attended to information of some kind, they must find a way to remember it if they are to learn from their experiences or use this input to solve a problem. **Memory** is a term that cognitive psychologists use to describe the ways in which people retain information and then re-

trieve it for use at a later time. In years past, researchers thought of the mind as a receptacle for ideas and facts. Presumably, young children remembered less than older children and adults because they had smaller minds with less capacity for storing information (Brown & DeLoache, 1978). Today we know that this "container model" of memory is inappropriate: Mental images of our experiences do not simply trickle into a warehouse in our heads. Instead, memory is both an *active* and a *selective* process in which we devise strategies for reconstructing, storing, and retrieving a portion of the many experiences we have had.

■ *A model of memory*

As we see in Figure 9-3, information-processing theorists have described memory as a flow of information through a number of separate but interrelated processing units. The first component of memory is the **sensory register**—a mechanism for logging in environmental input (sensory images) and holding this information for a second or so. If we then interpret or categorize incoming information, it passes into **short-term memory (STM),**

> **memory:** *the process by which people retain information and retrieve it for use at a later time.*
> **sensory register:** *the first step in information processing, in which stimuli are noticed and are briefly available for further processing.*
> **short-term memory (STM):** *the second step in information processing, in which stimuli are examined and retained for a minute or so (also called working memory).*

or "working memory," where it is retained in consciousness for perhaps as long as a minute. Finally, input that is operated on while in short-term memory may pass into **long-term memory (LTM)**—a vast and relatively permanent storehouse of information that represents our knowledge of the world and our impressions of past events and experiences.

An example will illustrate how the system is thought to work. Suppose that you are taking notes in a history class and you hear your instructor mention that the U.S. Constitution was ratified in 1789. If you think that this date is one you will need to remember, it should pass from your sensory register into short-term memory, where it remains until you can record it in your notebook. As you later study your notes in preparation for an upcoming exam, you will probably review this information several times and eventually register it in long-term memory, where it may remain for days, months, or even years.

According to the memory model presented in Figure 9-3, all conscious intellectual activity is thought to take place in short-term, or working, memory. So if your teacher asks you how many years passed between the signing of the Declaration of Independence (in 1776) and the ratification of the U.S. Constitution, you must transfer two dates from long-term to short-term memory and then compare them in order to arrive at the correct answer.

Short-term memory is usually studied by allowing subjects a minute or so to look at a list of items and then noting their recall of the last few items on the list. Presumably these items will be easier to recall than the earlier ones (a recency effect) because they are still in short-term memory. A number of studies indicate that people can hold very little information (perhaps fewer than ten discrete facts) in short-term memory at any one time. Although the capacity of STM does increase over the course of childhood (Dempster & Rohwer, 1983; Myers & Perlmutter, 1978), these changes are relatively modest compared with the developments occurring in long-term memory.

In contrast to STM, the capacity of LTM is very large, and once information is stored there, it is relatively permanent (or at least difficult to lose). Yet the most important developments that occur

in long-term memory center not on its capacity or its contents but, rather, on the strategies, or control processes, that children devise to transfer information into and out of this huge repository of knowledge.

Up to now we have been talking about the "hardware" of memory—that is, the structural components of the system where information is registered, interpreted, classified, and eventually deposited. But memory also has a "software"—a set of mental programs, or "control processes," that we use to shift information from short-term to long-term storage and to retrieve this input whenever we may need it to answer a question or solve a problem. Among the strategies that we use to facilitate or improve memory are *rehearsal, organization,* and *elaboration.*

Suppose that you had two minutes to learn the 12 objects in Figure 9-4. One strategy that you might use to remember these items is to repeat them to yourself by saying "Apple, truck, grapes, . . ." or perhaps "Apple goes with horse, truck goes with baseball, . . ." This process of repetition, or **rehearsal,** is perhaps the simplest way of transferring information from short-term to long-term memory. Of course, naming the objects is only one type of rehearsal that you might attempt. You could also construct a mental image for each item or perhaps devise a symbolic code for the item (for example, apple = a, truck = t, grapes = g, horse = h) and rehearse the code. Although some strategies may be more effective than others, stimuli that are rehearsed are less likely to be forgotten than those that are not rehearsed (Flavell, 1977).

A second strategy for retaining information is a process called **organization**. Since the working capacity of short-term memory is so very limited, it may be necessary to group, or organize, large numbers of stimuli into categories or clusters and then rehearse one category or cluster at a time. For the items in Figure 9-4, you might first lump the apple, grapes, and hamburger into a category, "foods," and rehearse its components before performing the same operations on the "animals," the "motor vehicles," and the "baseball equipment." When the material to be recalled is not easily categorized, one might adopt a second organizational strategy, "chunking"—that is, grouping large amounts of information into smaller, more man-

FIGURE 9-4. *Imagine that you have 120 seconds to learn the 12 objects pictured here. What tricks or strategies might you devise to make your task easier?*

ageable units. For example, the number 565622720 is difficult to remember in its nine-digit format, but it becomes much easier to recall if we store it in chunks (565-62-2720), as Americans do with their Social Security numbers.

Finally, we are more likely to remember if we add to, or **elaborate** on, the items we are trying to retain. One way we might use elaboration to retain the information in Figure 9-4 is to construct sentences or images that in some way associate the stimuli we are trying to remember. Thus, the sentence "The horse eats the apple" or an image of this action should help the learner to retain these items. Elaboration is a particularly effective way of recalling any two or more stimuli that are to be linked in some way or remembered as a unit (Pressley, 1982).

Now that we have discussed the basic "memory model" outlined in Figure 9-3, let's consider how children learn to remember.

■ *The development of memory*
Investigators who study memory are careful to distinguish between recognition and recall. **Recognition memory** occurs when we encounter some information and realize that we have seen or experienced it before. **Recall memory** requires us to *retrieve* for comparative purposes a piece of information that is not currently being presented. As it turns out, recognition tasks are much easier than recall tasks. More people could correctly an-

swer the question "Is Mick Jagger the lead singer for the Rolling Stones?" (recognition test) than the related item "Who is the lead singer for the Rolling Stones?" (recall test).

The ability to recognize the familiar is apparently inborn, for neonates who habituate to the repeated administration of a stimulus are indi-

> **long-term memory (LTM):** *the third step in information processing, in which information that has been examined and interpreted is stored for future use.*
>
> **rehearsal:** *a strategy for remembering that involves repeating the items one is trying to retain.*
>
> **organization:** *in information-processing theory, a strategy for remembering that involves grouping or classifying stimuli into meaningful (or manageable) clusters that are easier to retain.*
>
> **elaboration:** *a strategy for remembering that involves adding something to (or creating meaningful links between) the bits of information one is trying to retain.*
>
> **recognition memory:** *realizing that an object or event that one experiences has been experienced before.*
>
> **recall memory:** *recollecting objects, events, and experiences when examples of these bits of information are not available for comparative purposes.*

cating that they recognize this object or event as something they have experienced before. As a matter of fact, very young infants are also storing information in long-term memory: by 2 to 3 months of age, babies who have been taught to kick an overhead mobile will remember this act and perform it two or three weeks later if they are "reminded" of the response by simply seeing the mobile move as it had earlier when they had learned to kick it (Davis & Rovee-Collier, 1983; Sullivan, 1982). Moreover, 5- to 7-month-old infants are unlikely to forget a face, even if their initial exposure was brief (two to three minutes) and they do not see the face again for two weeks (Fagan, 1979). So infants are capable of remembering, and their ability to recognize familiar stimuli and to recall their previous experiences will gradually improve over the first two years of life (Brody, 1981; Rose, 1981).

During the preschool period, recognition memory develops much faster than recall memory. If a 4-year-old were shown the 12 items in Figure 9-4, she would *recognize* nearly all of them if asked to select these objects from a larger set of pictures (Brown, 1975). But if asked to *recall* the objects, she might remember only 2–4 of them, a far cry from the 7–9 items that an 8-year-old would recall.

Why do young children fail to recall so many of their experiences? Could it be that their memory deficits stem from a failure to use planful strategies such as rehearsal, organization, and elaboration—activities that could help them to store information and to retrieve this input later? Let's explore this idea by looking at the ways children of different ages approach the task of remembering.

Rehearsal.   John Flavell and his associates (see Flavell, 1977) have conducted a series of experiments in which 5- to 10-year-olds were told to remember the order in which an experimenter pointed to a series of pictures. The results were clear: children who rehearsed (as indicated by their lip movements) performed much better than nonrehearsers on this recall task. In addition, spontaneous use of verbal rehearsal increased with age. Whereas only 10% of the 5-year-olds named the objects that they were to recall, more than half of the 7-year-olds and 85% of the

10-year-olds adopted this rehearsal strategy. In a second study, Flavell and his colleagues trained "nonrehearsers" to rehearse and found that their performance on recall tasks soon matched that of children who spontaneously rehearsed. So younger children are unlikely to produce the verbal mediators that will improve memory—that is, they show a **production deficiency** (Flavell, 1977). However, they can certainly use these mediators to their advantage if they are taught how to produce them, so there is no **mediation deficiency.**

The child's earliest attempts at spontaneous rehearsal are rather clumsy and inefficient compared with the strategies of older children. If asked to recall a list of words, 8-year-olds will rehearse them one word at a time. In contrast, 12-year-olds are more likely to bunch the words in groups of three or four and then rehearse these clusters (Ornstein, Naus, & Liberty, 1975). This second form of rehearsal is apparently a more effective strategy, because the older children who use it perform better on recall tests than younger children who rehearse an item at a time. However, younger children can be taught to rehearse more effectively, and they will continue to use these strategies once they realize that they work, (Gelabert, Torgesen, Dice, & Murphy, 1980; Ornstein, Naus, & Stone, 1977).

Organization.   In one sense, rehearsal is a rather unimaginative memory device because it is simply a form of mimicry or imitation. If a rehearser merely labels the items to be remembered, he or she may fail to notice certain meaningful relations among the stimuli that should make them easier to recall (Flavell, 1977). Consider the following example:

List 1: boat, match, hammer, coat, grass, sentence, pencil, dog, cup, picture

List 2: knife, shirt, car, fork, boat, pants, sock, truck, spoon, plate

Although these ten-item lists should be equally difficult to recall if one simply rehearses them, the second list is actually much easier for many people. The reason is that its items can by grouped into three semantically distinct categories (eating utensils, clothes, and vehicles) that can serve as cues for storage and retrieval. In contrast, items in the first list are harder to organize (and thus harder to remember) because they represent ten different categories (Flavell & Wellman, 1977).

Until about age 9 to 10, children are not much better at recalling items that can be categorized (such as list 2) than those that are difficult to categorize (such as list 1). This finding suggests that young children make few attempts to organize information that they are trying to remember. And even when they begin to categorize as an aid to recall, the organizational schemes of grade school children are generally less useful than those of adults. For example, Liberty and Ornstein (1973) report that fewer than 60% of their fourth-grade sample placed words such as *flower, seed, tree* into a single category when asked to organize 28 words that they were supposed to remember. As a result, these children recalled fewer items than young adults who had grouped the 28 words into four distinct clusters.

The failure of younger children to spontaneously organize the materials they are trying to remember is apparently a production deficiency rather than a mediation deficiency. This conclusion is based on studies showing that 6- to 8-year-olds will use organizational cues to improve their recall if they have been told how to group items into meaningful clusters (Kee & Bell, 1981; Lange, 1978). However, this same type of organizational prompting is unlikely to affect the recall of 4- to 5-year-olds, who appear not to notice or use the organizational "hints" they are given.

In sum, the tendency to organize information is another "control process" that gradually evolves over the grade school years and helps to explain why older children outperform younger ones on tests of recall memory.

Elaboration.   Another effective strategy for improving recall is to add to, or elaborate on, the information that we hope to remember. Elaboration is particularly useful whenever our task is to associate two or more stimuli, such as a foreign word and its English equivalent. For example, one way to remember the Spanish word for "duck," *pato* (pronounced "pot-o"), is to elaborate on the word *pato* by creating an image of a pot that is in some way linked to a duck (see Figure 9-5 for an example). Foreign-language students who receive

FIGURE 9-5. *An example of an elaborative image that one might create to associate* pato *(pronounced "pot-o"), the Spanish word for "duck," with its English translation.*

this kind of "elaborative" training learn and retain much more new vocabulary than those who simply rehearse the meanings of foreign words (Atkinson, 1975). A *verbal* elaboration such as "The duck goes into the pot-o" may also help the student to remember the Spanish word for "duck" (Pressley, 1982).

In a review of literature, Michael Pressley (1982) found that the spontaneous use of elaborative techniques is a "latecomer to the memorizer's bag of tricks" that is rarely seen before adolescence. Moreover, a sizable percentage of adolescents do not elaborate as a strategy for improving their recall, and these "nonelaborators" typically perform at lower levels on tests of associative learning than their counterparts who use elaborative techniques.

---

production deficiency: *a failure to generate the mediators that would improve learning and memory.*

mediation deficiency: *an inability to use the mediators that would improve learning and memory.*

There may be several reasons that elaboration is so late in developing. Some investigators suspect that the very limited capacity of a younger child's short-term "working" memory may prevent him or her from generating complex elaborative mediators (Pressley, 1982). And since one must "go beyond the information given" to create an elaborative sentence or image, it is possible that spontaneous elaboration will not occur until the child reaches formal operations (Greer, 1979). Finally, there is a third possibility that is certainly not inconsistent with the other two: adolescents may be more proficient at elaboration because they know more about the world than younger children do and are better able to imagine how any two (or more) stimuli might be linked (Rohwer, 1980).

Retrieval processes. We have talked about rehearsal, organization, and elaboration as if they were only methods of storing information in long-term memory. However, there are now indications that these control processes may also help us to search for and *retrieve* information from long-term storage. An interesting study by Daniel Kee and Terace Bell (1981) nicely illustrates how organization may serve as a "retrieval" cue.

Kee and Bell (1981) showed subjects from three age groups (7-year-olds, 11-year-olds, and college students) 36 pictures that they would later be asked to recall. The pictures fell into six categories (for example, zoo animals, bathroom accessories), with six items per category (a tiger, a zebra, a towel, a brush, and so on). Also available for some participants were "categorical pictures" (for example, a picture of a zoo, a picture of a bathroom) that might serve as cues for grouping and later retrieving items in each category. Subjects were allowed 2½ minutes to study the pictures and then were given a recall test. The most important experimental conditions were the following:

1. *No cues available.* These subjects had no categorical cues available during the time they were studying the pictures (storage) or at the time of the recall test (retrieval).

2. *Cues available at storage.* While these subjects studied, they were shown the categorical pictures and told that these pictures would help them to remember the items. However, the categorical cues were not available during the recall test.

3. *Cues available at retrieval.* These subjects had no categorical cues available while they studied; however, they were shown the categorical pictures and asked to recall the 36 items by categories during the recall test.

4. *Cues available at storage and retrieval.* Categorical pictures were present throughout. Subjects were instructed to use the categorical cues to help them study. They were also asked to recall the items by categories during the recall test.

The results of this rather elaborate experiment appear in Figure 9-6. To interpret the findings, let's first consider conditions 1–3. Note that, for each age group, the presence of categorical cues at either storage (condition 2) or retrieval (condition 3) led to greater recall than when no cues were present (condition 1). Now compare condition 4 with the first three conditions. Here we see that subjects who had categorical cues available during *both* storage and retrieval recalled more items than their age mates in any of the other three conditions. The implications of these findings are clear: organizational activities not only help us to store information but may also serve as a strategy or code for *retrieving* the data we have placed in long-term storage.

In a similar study, Michael Pressley and Joel Levin (1980) prompted 6- and 11-year-olds to *elaborate* on 18 pairs of stimuli that they were trying to learn. When later taking a recall test, half the children from each age group were told to use their elaborative images to help them remember the items; the remaining children were not given any retrieval instructions. Pressley and Levin found that 11-year-olds remembered nearly 65% of the items, regardless of whether they had been told to use their elaborative images to help them recall. In contrast, the 6-year-olds recalled nearly twice as many items when given retrieval instructions (42.5%) as when left to their own devices (23%). This latter result is important, for it suggests that the poor performance of younger children on tests of recall memory may stem, in part, from their *retrieval deficiencies.* In other words, even when 6–10-year-olds do "organize" and

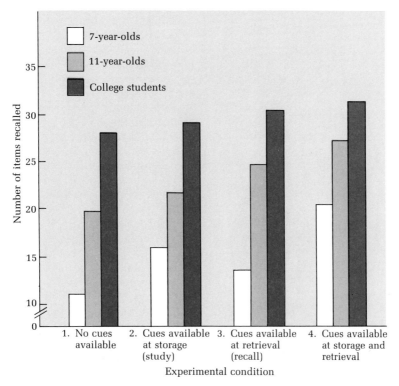

FIGURE 9-6. *Mean number of items correctly recalled as a function of age and the presence of categorical cues at storage and retrieval.*

"elaborate" in order to register information in long-term memory, they are less likely than older children to use these same strategies to retrieve that which they have worked so intently to store. But why?

One possible explanation is that younger children simply know less about memory aids and the circumstances when it is appropriate to use them. In recent years, investigators have begun to study what children know about memory and how this knowledge may influence their performance on memory tests. Let's consider what they have learned.

■ *Metamemory*

The term **metamemory** refers to our knowledge about memory and memory processes. To measure this knowledge, investigators often describe one or more memory problems and ask subjects how much information they think they will remember

(anticipated performance) or which of two memory tasks will be the more difficult (knowledge of memory processes and variables that affect memory). Suppose, for example, that we showed children the two sets of pictures in Figure 9-7 and asked them which girl in each set will have an easier time remembering her material. The answers should help us to determine whether children know that memory depends on the number of items to be recalled (set 1) and the ease with which these materials can be categorized (set 2).

Knowledge about memory increases rather dramatically between the ages of 5 and 10. Compared with older children, 5- to 7-year-olds consistently overestimate the number of items they

metamemory: *one's knowledge about memory and memory processes.*

FIGURE 9-7. Two simple metamemory questions. The child is shown the pictures in each set and asked which girl will have an easier time remembering her items. These two questions are designed to measure the child's knowledge that memory depends on the amount of information one is trying to recall (set 1) and how easily the information can be categorized (set 2).

will remember on a recall test while underestimating the amount of study that is necessary to learn the materials (Kreutzer, Leonard, & Flavell, 1975; Yussen & Levy, 1975). Most 5- to 7-year-olds will also fail to recognize that *related* items or those that can be *organized* are easier to recall than unrelated items or those that are difficult to organize (Kreutzer et al., 1975; Moynahan, 1973). Indeed, this deficit in metamemory is yet another reason that younger children may not spontaneously organize or elaborate on the materials they are trying to remember.

Finally, it appears that younger children know very little about how they retrieve information from long-term memory. David Bjorklund and Barbara Zeman (1982) found that 7- and 9-year-olds had no preexisting strategies for recalling the names of children in their classroom, although they performed reasonably well at this task (approximately 75% recall). But nearly 60% of a sample of 11-year-olds professed to have a retrieval strategy, and they clearly outperformed the younger children on this exercise (approximately 88% recall). One reason that younger children may know little about retrieval is that they tend to rely on external prompts such as written notes to help them remember (Flavell, 1977). But even though 7-year-olds may recognize that a written note can help them to remember something, they are less likely than 9- or 11-year-olds to know where to place such "reminders" to ensure that they will have the intended effect (Fabricius & Wellman, 1983).

What is the relation between memory and metamemory: does a person's knowledge of the memory process determine how well he or she will perform on various memory tests? The answer to this question is not as straightforward as we might hope. In their review of the literature, John Cavanaugh and Marion Perlmutter (1982) found several studies reporting low to moderate positive correlations between memory and metamemory. However, there are several reasons for believing that one's level of metamemory may *not* determine performance on memory tests. For example, Bjorklund and Zeman's 7- to 9-year-olds were able to recall the names of more than 75% of their classmates, even though they knew very little about the strategies that might help them to retrieve this information. Apparently *good meta-*

memory is not required for good recall. In addition, children who know that categorized lists are easier to remember may themselves fail to categorize items when studying for a recall test (Salatas & Flavell, 1976). So *good metamemory does not guarantee good recall.*

One reason that good metamemory may not always predict good recall is that children who know the most about memory processes could be confused about which of these strategies works best. For example, youngsters who recognize the merits of organization may fail to organize the material they are trying to remember if they think rehearsal is a more effective strategy. Consequently, these "knowledgeable" children may perform no better on a recall test than less knowledgeable youngsters who know all about rehearsal and nothing about organization. To understand how metamemory influences memory, we must begin to pay more attention to what children know about *combinations* of memory variables (Wellman, Collins, & Glieberman, 1981).

Hypothesis Testing and Problem Solving: Using Information One Has Retained

In recent years, cognitive-processing theorists have tried to explain how developing children use information to generate hypotheses and solve problems. Although this "problem solving" research is itself at a very early stage of development, we will see that the types of inferences children make when attempting to solve a problem clearly depend on the information they have processed.

Robert Siegler (1978, 1981) believes that children who are faced with a problem of some kind will first gather information and then formulate a *rule*, or strategy, to account for what they have witnessed. Presumably the kind of rule that the child generates and applies to the task at hand will depend on the type of information that he or she has encoded (that is, noticed and interpreted). According to Siegler, an investigator who hopes to understand the development of problem-solving skills must first identify the rules that children use to solve problems and then determine how and why these rules may change over time.

Among the many tasks that Siegler uses to study children's problem-solving behavior is a set

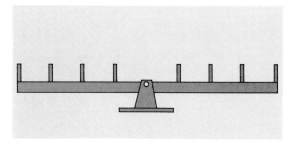

FIGURE 9-8. *The balance-scale apparatus used by Siegler to study children's problem-solving abilities.*

of balance-scale problems. The balance-scale apparatus (Figure 9-8) has four equally spaced pegs on each of its arms. Once weights are placed on various pegs, the child is asked to predict what will happen (for example, will the arms remain balanced? will the left arm go up? down?) when a brake that holds the arms motionless is released. Clearly, two aspects of this problem are important: the number of weights on each arm and the distance of those weights from the fulcrum. Siegler proposes that children might adopt any of four rules for solving balance problems and that the rule they use will depend on the type of information that they encode. The four rules are as follows:

Rule 1: The child considers only the *number of weights* and concludes that the arm with more weight will drop. If the number of weights on each arm is the same, the child concludes that the scale will remain balanced.

Rule 2: The child pays more attention to weight and consistently predicts that the arm with more weight will drop. Only when the weight on each arm is equal will the child consider the distance of the weights from the fulcrum.

Rule 3: The child always considers both weight and distance when making a prediction. But if one side has more weight while the other has its weights farther from the fulcrum, the child is conflicted and simply guesses at what will happen.

Rule 4: The child always considers both weight and distance and knows that the torque on each arm is a function of weight × distance. For example, if there are three weights on the second peg to the left and two weights on the fourth peg to the right, then left torque = 3 × 2 = 6; right torque = 2 × 4 = 8; therefore the right arm will go down.

To measure a child's strategy for solving balance problems, Siegler presents the child with the six problems in Table 9-2 and notes the patterning of responses across all six tasks. If a child consistently uses one of Siegler's four rules, then his or her answers should conform to one of the four patterns shown in the columns of the table. For example, children who make use of the "rule 1" strategy (encode only weight) will solve problems 1, 2, and 4 but will erroneously conclude that the scale will balance in problem 3 and that the right arm will drop on problems 5 and 6. In contrast, a user of rule 3 will correctly solve problems 1, 2, and 3 and respond at chance levels (guess) on problems 4, 5, and 6.

When Siegler (1981) administered his six balance-scale problems to subjects between ages 3 and 20, he found that 91% of the 4- to 20-year-olds responded as if they were using one of his four rules. Moreover, there were age differences in the use of various rules. Whereas almost no 3-year-olds used a rule, more than 80% of the 4- to 5-year-olds were encoding weight and relying on rule 1 to solve balance problems. By age 8, children were generally using rule 2 or 3, and the vast majority of 12-year-olds had settled on rule 3 as a problem-solving strategy. And although most 20-year-olds continued to use rule 3 to solve balance-scale problems, 30% of these adults had discovered the weight × distance principle and were relying on rule 4.

At first glance, this study seems remarkably similar to Piaget's work on age differences in problem solving. However, the critical difference is that Siegler's rule-assessment approach allows the investigator to specify exactly how children are processing (or failing to process) relevant information and thus to indicate why they will fail to solve a particular problem or set of related problems. The advantage of this approach is that if we know exactly what the child fails to encode when trying to solve a problem, it may be possible to design a training technique or a learning experience to overcome this processing deficit. For example, Dean Richards and Robert Siegler (1981) have shown that 3-year-olds, who normally fail to

TABLE 9-2. Six balance-scale problems and the patterning of answers that follows from using a systematic rule for solving problems

	Problem	Correct answer	Siegler's rule			
			1	2	3	4
1.		Balance	100% correct	100% correct	100% correct	100% correct
2.		Left down	100% correct	100% correct	100% correct	100% correct
3.		Left down	0% correct (will say balance)	100% correct	100% correct	100% correct
4.		Left down	100% correct	100% correct	33% correct (chance responding)	100% correct
5.		Left down	0% correct (will say right down)	0% correct (will say right down)	33% correct (chance responding)	100% correct
6.		Balance	0% correct (will say right down)	0% correct (will say right down)	33% correct (chance responding)	100% correct

process any task-relevant information on balance-scale problems, can be trained to encode weight (and use rule 1) if they are encouraged to think about and explain what they have witnessed (for example, "Why did that side go down?"; "Try to figure out what made this side drop").

In sum, information-processing theorists can agree with Piaget that children progress through a series of "alternative understandings" before mastering certain concepts (Siegler, 1981). However, they believe that their rule-assessment approach is more precise than Piaget's theory at indicating why a child's thinking takes the form it does and at specifying the information that the child must now consider in order to move from one level of understanding to the next.

The Current Status of Information-Processing Theory

If a history of psychology were written today, Piaget's theory would surely dominate the chapter on cognitive development. At this point, the Piagetian approach is a much more orderly and elaborate account of children's intellectual growth than that presently available from the information processors. Moreover, information-processing theorists have focused on cognitive changes that occur between the ages of 5 and 12, so that the scope of their theory is much narrower than that of Piaget's.

Clearly, there is some order to the data we have considered, for attention, memory, and hypothesis testing are all becoming more systematic and planful between ages 5 and 12. And although much of the relevant research remains to be conducted, these important developments in information processing may help to explain the "5 to 7 shift" in children's concept learning (discussed in Chapter Seven), as well as the appearance and refinement of abilities such as seriation, classification, perspective taking, conservation, and hypothetical-deductive reasoning (Flavell, 1977; Rosser, 1983).

In sum, the information-processing approach is itself a developing theory—one that is probably best described as a complement to, rather than a replacement for, Piaget's earlier framework. Surely this "new look" at cognitive growth will continue to evolve and perhaps even fill in some of the gaps in Piaget's model, thereby contributing to a comprehensive theory of intellectual development that retains the best features of both approaches.

INDIVIDUAL DIFFERENCES IN COGNITIVE STYLE

Several years ago, Jerome Kagan and his associates (Kagan, Rosman, Day, Albert, & Phillips, 1964) found that children clearly differ on an aspect of cognitive style that they called *reflectivity/impulsivity*. Children described as **impulsive** seem to have a quick conceptual tempo. When faced with a problem, these youngsters tend to favor the first hypothesis they think of, without carefully considering the merits of alternative solutions. In contrast, **reflective** children seem to have a slower conceptual tempo; they take the time to evaluate many possible hypotheses before answering questions or proposing solutions for a problem.

The most common instrument for measuring a child's tendency to be reflective or impulsive is the *Matching Familiar Figures test*. This test consists of several problems, each of which requires the child to select from six similar alternatives the one stimulus that exactly matches a standard (see Figure 9-9). Two pieces of information are used to classify the child: the *time* that the child takes to select his or her answers and the *number of errors* made. Children who answer quickly and make many errors are labeled impulsive, while those who answer slowly and make few errors are said to be reflective. Although virtually all children become more reflective as they mature (Salkind & Nelson, 1980), individual differences in conceptual tempo are reasonably stable over time: a child who is very impulsive (or very reflective) at one age is likely to remain more impulsive (or

---

impulsivity: *a problem-solving style characterized by impatience and unsystematic evaluation of alternative solutions.*

reflectivity: *a problem-solving style characterized by patience and careful evaluation of alternative solutions.*

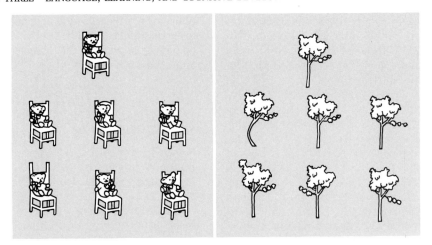

FIGURE 9-9. *Sample items from the Matching Familiar Figures test for reflectivity/impulsivity.*

more reflective) than his or her classmates over the next several years (Kagan, Lapidus, & Moore, 1978; Messer & Brodzinsky, 1981).

Implications of Reflective and Impulsive Styles

Conceptual tempo is an attribute that seems to affect children's intellectual performance and their interpersonal behaviors. In the classroom, reflective children are more attentive and less distractible than impulsives and may have an easier time learning to read (Kagan et al., 1978; Messer, 1976). This latter finding makes sense when we recall that the initial phases of reading instruction require children to inspect and discriminate various letters and letter combinations, a task that would seem to favor the careful, reflective thinker. Moreover, reflective children and adolescents usually outperform impulsives on tests of recall memory as well as a number of Piagetian tasks, such as taking others' perspectives, conserving simple quantities, and solving formal-operational problems (Brodzinsky, 1982; Neimark, 1975; Pascual-Leone, 1980). Stanley Messer (1976) has also reported that impulsive boys are more likely than their reflective classmates to fail a grade at school.

Although it is tempting to conclude that impulsive children are simply less intelligent than reflectives, this is not always true. For example, Messer's impulsive "retainees" scored no lower on standardized intelligence tests than their classmates who were promoted to the next grade. And in his review of more than 20 studies, Messer (1976) found that the typical correlation between IQ and conceptual tempo is low to moderate at best. So it appears that the performance deficits that impulsives often exhibit on various cognitive tests are attributable to their careless methods of problem solving rather than to a lack of intellectual ability.

The personalities of reflectives and impulsives may also differ in important ways. In the school setting, impulsives are more likely than reflectives to run around the room or the playground and to initiate social interactions with their classmates. Unfortunately, these social gestures are not always positive, for Stanley Messer and David Brodzinsky (1979) found that impulsive fifth-graders (10- to 11-year-olds) were rated more physically aggressive by teachers and peers than their less impulsive classmates were. There is also a link between conceptual tempo and various personality disorders. Disturbed children who internalize their conflicts and feel anxious, guilty, or self-critical tend to be reflectives. Children who "act out," or externalize, their conflicts by lying, stealing, or being rebellious are typically impulsives (Messer, 1976).

Can Conceptual Tempo Be Modified?

Many attempts have been made to alter the conceptual tempo of impulsive children in order to improve their performance on cognitive tasks.

Changes in cognitive style have been induced by reinforcing impulsive children for slowing down and spending more time on their work (see Messer, 1976). In addition, impulsive children may become more reflective after watching a teacher or a peer use a reflective approach to solve problems (Cohen & Przybycien, 1974; Yando & Kagan, 1968). However, these techniques are of limited usefulness, for they often persuade impulsive children to work more deliberately without appreciably reducing the number of errors they make (Messer, 1976).

Other investigators have tried to modify conceptual tempo by teaching impulsive children how to consider alternative hypotheses and then requiring them to verbalize these strategies as they use them. For example, an impulsive child might be trained to scan all the figures and to compare each with the standard before offering solutions to problems from the Matching Familiar Figures test. As he scans, the child would be told to describe what he is doing: "I have to look carefully at this one, then this one. . . ." Stanley Messer (1976) reports that this "direct training—self-instructional" approach is quite effective at altering the conceptual tempo of impulsive children and reducing the number of errors they make. Moreover, children who receive this training may apply their new strategies to other cognitive tasks, and often they are continuing to use them and making fewer errors when tested again several months after the original training.

Since most classroom learning requires a child to attend carefully to important details and places a premium on accuracy, perhaps we are on the right track by coaxing impulsive children to function more like reflectives. However, a little impulsiveness training just might be a positive experience for those extremely reflective children who are anxious, self-critical, and unresponsive to their peers.

SUMMARY

In this chapter we considered two theories of intellectual development: Jean Piaget's "structural-functional" viewpoint and the more recent "information-processing" approach. Piaget's model is a comprehensive theory of intellectual growth that evolved from his naturalistic observations of developing children. According to Piaget, intellectual activity is a basic life function that helps the child to adapt to the environment. He describes children as active, inventive explorers who construct knowledge (schemata) and modify these cognitive structures through the processes of organization and adaptation. Organization is the process by which children rearrange their existing knowledge into higher-order structures, or schemata. Adaptation consists of two complementary activities: assimilation and accommodation. Assimilation is the process by which the child attempts to fit new experiences to existing schemata. Accommodation is the process of modifying existing schemata in response to new experiences. Presumably, cognitive growth results from the interplay of these intellectual functions: assimilations stimulate accommodations, which induce the reorganization of schemata, which allow further assimilations, and so on.

Piaget believes that intellectual growth proceeds through an invariant sequence of stages that can be summarized as follows:

Sensorimotor period (0–2 years). Over the first two years, infants come to know and understand objects and events by acting on them. The sensorimotor schemata that a child creates to adapt to his or her surroundings are eventually internalized to form mental symbols that enable the child to understand the permanence of objects, to imitate the actions of absent models, and to solve simple problems at a mental level without resorting to trial and error.

Preoperational period (roughly 2 to 7 years). Symbolic reasoning becomes increasingly apparent during the preoperational period as children begin to use words and images in inventive ways in their play activities. Although 2- to 7-year-olds are becoming more and more knowledgeable about the world around them, their thinking tends to be animistic, egocentric, and unidimensional. Consequently, they may fail to solve problems that require them to consider several pieces of information simultaneously or to assume another person's point of view.

Concrete operations (roughly 7 to 11 years). During the period of concrete operations, children can think logically and systematically about concrete objects, events, and experiences. They can now add and subtract in their heads, and they recognize that the effects of many physical actions are reversible. The acquisition of these and other cognitive operations permits the child to conserve, seriate, make transitive inferences, think in numerical terms, and construct mental representations of a complex series of actions.

Formal operations (age 11 to 12 and beyond). Formal-operational reasoning is rational, abstract, and much like the hypothetical-deductive reasoning of a scientist. However, not all adolescents and adults reason at this level. Formal-operational thinking may elude those who score below average on intelligence tests or who have not been exposed to the kind of educational experiences that promote the development of this highest form of intellect.

Although Piaget has accurately described the sequence of intellectual development, he often underestimates and occasionally overestimates the child's cognitive capabilities. Some investigators have challenged Piaget's assumption that development occurs in stages, and others have criticized his theory for failing to specify how children progress from one "stage" of intellect to the next. Although the Piagetian approach remains the most comprehensive statement on intellectual growth that currently exists, contemporary researchers recognize its shortcomings and are trying to improve on this influential theory.

Information-processing theorists approach the topic of intellectual growth by charting the development of cognitive processing skills such as attention, memory, and problem solving. In order to understand something or to solve a problem, one must first pay attention to the right kinds of information. Between the preschool period and adolescence, children become better able to sustain attention for longer periods, more planful and systematic in their search for information, and more knowledgeable about the strategies that they can use to attend selectively to task-relevant information and ignore sources of distraction.

Memory also improves over the course of childhood. During the grade school years, children become better at using strategies such as rehearsal, organization, and elaboration to register information in long-term storage and to retrieve this input whenever it is needed to answer a question or to solve a problem. Metamemory, one's knowledge about memory, also improves dramatically with age. Children become more aware of the limitations of their own memory and more knowledgeable about the variables and cognitive strategies that will influence their ability to recall what they have experienced.

Like Piaget, information-processing theorists have sought to explain how developing children generate hypotheses and solve problems. As children mature, they use increasingly complex problem-solving strategies, or rules, that are based on the information they have encoded. Cognitive-processing theorists can agree with Piaget that children progress through a series of "alternative understandings" before mastering certain concepts, but they argue that their rule-assessment approach is better able than Piaget's theory to specify why children of different ages approach problems in different ways.

Children differ in an aspect of cognitive style known as reflectivity/impulsivity. Reflective children work slowly and methodically on cognitive tasks and tend to outperform fast-paced, impulsive children on problems that require attention to detail. Because most classroom learning requires attention to detail and places a premium on accuracy, researchers have developed successful strategies for coaxing impulsive children to become more reflective in their approach to problem solving.

REFERENCES

Acredolo, C., & Acredolo, L. P. (1979). Identity, compensation, and conservation. *Child Development, 50,* 524–535.

Acredolo, C., & Acredolo, L. P. (1980). The anticipation of conservation phenomenon: Conservation or pseudo-conservation? *Child Development, 51,* 667–675.

American Heritage dictionary of the English language (2nd ed.). (1982). Boston: Houghton Mifflin.

Anderson, D. R., Alwitt, L. F., Lorch, E. P., & Levin, S. R. (1979). Watching children watch television. In G. Hale & M. Lewis (Eds.), *Attention and the development of cognitive skills.* New York: Plenum Press.

Anooshian, L. J., Hartman, S. R., & Scharf, J. S. (1982). Determinants of young children's search strategies in a large-scale environment. *Developmental Psychology, 18,* 608–616.

Arlin, P. K. (1975). Cognitive development in adulthood: A fifth stage? *Developmental Psychology, 11,* 602–606.

Arlin, P. K. (1977). Piagetian operations in problem finding. *Developmental Psychology, 13,* 297–298.

Atkinson, R. C. (1975). Mnemotechnics in second-language learning. *American Psychologist, 30,* 821–828.

Ault, R. L. (1977). *Children's cognitive development.* New York: Oxford University Press.

Beilin, H. (1980). Piaget's theory: Refinement, revision, or rejection? In R. Kluwe & H. Spada (Eds.), *Developmental models of thinking.* New York: Academic Press.

Bjorklund, D. F., & Zeman, B. R. (1982). Children's organization and metamemory awareness in their recall of familiar information. *Child Development, 53,* 799–810.

Bower, T. G. R. (1982). *Development in infancy.* San Francisco: W. H. Freeman.

Brainerd, C. J. (1978). The stage question in cognitive-developmental theory. *Behavioral and Brain Sciences, 2,* 173–213.

Brody, L. R. (1981). Visual short-term cued recall memory in infancy. *Child Development, 52,* 242–250.

Brodzinsky, D. M. (1982). Relationship between cognitive style and cognitive development: A 2-year longitudinal study. *Developmental Psychology, 18,* 617–626.

Brown, A. L. (1975). The development of memory: Knowing, knowing about knowing, and knowing how to know. In H. W. Reese (Ed.), *Advances in child development and behavior* (Vol. 10). New York: Academic Press.

Brown, A. L., & DeLoache, J. S. (1978). Skills, plans, and self-regulation. In R. S. Siegler (Ed.), *Children's thinking: What develops?* Hillsdale, NJ: Erlbaum.

Carey, J., Foltz, K., & Allan, R. A. (1983, February 7). The mind of the machine. *Newsweek,* pp. 44–45.

Cavanaugh, J. C., & Perlmutter, M. (1982). Metamemory: A critical examination. *Child Development, 53,* 11–28.

Cohen, S., & Pryzbycien, C. A. (1974). Some effects of sociometrically selected peer models on the cognitive styles of impulsive children. *Journal of Genetic Psychology, 124,* 213–220.

Cole, P. M., & Newcomb, N. (1983). Interference effects of verbal and imaginal strategies for resisting distraction on children's verbal and visual recognition memory. *Child Development, 54,* 42–50.

Commons, M. L., Richards, F. A., & Kuhn, D. (1982). Systematic and metasystematic reasoning: A case for levels of reasoning beyond Piaget's stage of formal operations. *Child Development, 53,* 1058–1069.

Connolly, J. (1982). Social pretend play and social competence in preschoolers. In D. J. Pepler & K. Rubin (Eds.), *The play of children: Current theory and research.* Basel: Karger.

Cowan, P. A. (1978). *Piaget: With feeling.* New York: Holt, Rinehart and Winston.

Dansky, J. (1980). Make-believe: A mediator of the relationship between play and associative fluency. *Child Development, 51,* 576–579.

Davis, J. M., & Rovee-Collier, C. K. (1983). Alleviated forgetting of a learned contingency in 8-week-old infants. *Developmental Psychology, 19,* 353–365.

Dempster, F. N., & Rohwer, W. D., Jr. (1983). Age differences and modality effects in immediate and final free recall. *Child Development, 54,* 30–41.

Dunst, C. J., Brooks, P. H., & Doxsey, P. A. (1982). Characteristics of hiding places and the transition to stage IV performance in object permanence tasks. *Developmental Psychology, 18,* 671–681.

Elkind, D. (1977). Giant in the nursery—Jean Piaget. In E. M. Hetherington & R. D. Parke (Eds.), *Contemporary readings in child psychology.* New York: McGraw-Hill.

Fabricius, W. V., & Wellman, H. M. (1983). Children's understanding of retrieval cue utilization. *Developmental Psychology, 19,* 15–21.

Fagan, J. F., III. (1979). The origins of facial pattern recognition. In M. H. Bornstein & W. Kessen (Eds.), *Psychological development from infancy: Image to intention.* Hillsdale, NJ: Erlbaum.

Field, D. (1977). The importance of verbal content in the training of Piagetian conservation skills. *Child Development, 48,* 1583–1592.

Field, D. (1981). Can preschool children really learn to conserve? *Child Development, 52,* 326–334.

Field, T. M., Woodson, R., Greenberg, R., & Cohen, D. (1982). Discrimination and imitation of facial expressions by neonates. *Science, 218,* 179–181.

Flavell, J. H. (1963). *The developmental psychology of Jean Piaget.* New York: Van Nostrand Reinhold.

Flavell, J. H. (1977). *Cognitive development.* Englewood Cliffs, NJ: Prentice-Hall.

Flavell, J. H. (1982). On cognitive development. *Child Development, 53,* 1–10.

Flavell, J. H., Everett, B. H., Croft, K., & Flavell, E. R. (1981). Young children's knowledge about visual perception: Further evidence for the level 1–level 2 distinction. *Developmental Psychology, 17,* 99–103

Flavell, J. H., & Wellman, H. M. (1977). Metamemory. In R. V. Kail & J. W. Hagen (Eds.), *Memory in cognitive development.* Hillsdale, NJ: Erlbaum.

Gelabert, T., Torgesen, J., Dice, C., & Murphy, H. (1980). The effects of situational variables on the use of rehearsal by first-grade children. *Child Development, 51,* 902–905.

Gelman, R. (1978). Cognitive development. *Annual review of psychology, 29,* 297–332.

Greer, R. N. E. (1979). Spontaneous elaboration of paired associates and formal operational thinking: A developmental analysis. *Dissertation Abstracts International, 39,* 5410A–5411A.

Hodkin, B. (1981). Language effects in the assessment of class-inclusion ability. *Child Development, 52,* 470–478.

Hutt, C., & Bhavnani, R. (1976). Predictions from play. In J. S. Bruner, A. Jolly, & K. Sylva (Eds.), *Play.* New York: Penguin Books.

Inhelder, B. (1966). Cognitive development and its contribution to the diagnosis of some phenomena of mental deficiency. *Merrill-Palmer Quarterly, 12,* 299–319.

Inhelder, B., & Piaget, J. (1958). *The growth of logical thinking from childhood to adolescence.* New York: Basic Books.

Jackson, S. (1965). The growth of logical thinking in normal and subnormal children. *British Journal of Educational Psychology, 35,* 255–258.

Kagan, J., Lapidus, D. R., & Moore, M. (1978). Infant antecedents of cognitive functioning: A longitudinal study. *Child Development, 49,* 1005–1023.

Kagan, J., Rosman, B. L., Day, D., Albert, J., & Phillips, W. (1964). Information processing in the child: Significance of analytic and reflective attitudes. *Psychological Monographs, 78* (Whole No. 578).

Kaye, K., & Marcus, J. (1981). Infant imitation: The sensorimotor agenda. *Developmental Psychology, 17,* 258–265.

Kee, D. W., & Bell, T. S. (1981). The development of organizational strategies in the storage and retrieval of categorical items in free-recall learning. *Child Development, 52,* 1163–1171.

Klahr, D., & Wallace, J. C. (1976). *Cognitive development: An information-processing view.* Hillsdale, NJ: Erlbaum.

Kohen-Raz, R. (1977). *Psychobiological aspects of cognitive growth.* New York: Academic Press.

Kreutzer, M. A., Leonard, C., & Flavell, J. H. (1975). An interview study of children's knowledge about memory. *Monographs of the Society for Research in Child Development, 40* (1, Serial No. 159).

Lange, G. (1978). Organization-related processes in children's recall. In P. A. Ornstein (Ed.), *Memory development in children.* Hillsdale, NJ: Erlbaum.

Liberty, C., & Ornstein, P. A. (1973). Age differences in organization and recall: The effects of training in categorization. *Journal of Experimental Child Psychology, 15,* 169–186.

McGhee, P. E. (1979). *Humor: Its origin and development.* San Francisco: W. H. Freeman.

Meltzoff, A. N., & Moore, M. K. (1983). Newborn infants imitate adult facial gestures. *Child Development, 54,* 702–709.

Messer, S. B. (1976). Reflection-impulsivity: A review. *Psychological Bulletin, 83,* 1026–1052.

Messer, S. B., & Brodzinsky, D. M. (1979). The relation of conceptual tempo to aggression and its control. *Child Development, 50,* 758–766.

Messer, S. B., & Brodzinsky, D. M. (1981). Three year stability of reflection-impulsivity in young adolescents. *Developmental Psychology, 17,* 848–850.

Miller, P. H., & Weiss, M. G. (1981). Children's attention allocation, understanding of attention, and performance on the incidental learning task. *Child Development, 52,* 1183–1190.

Miller, P. H., & Weiss, M. G. (1982). Children's and adults' knowledge about what variables affect selective attention. *Child Development, 53,* 543–549.

Mossler, D. G., Marvin, R. S., & Greenberg, M. T. (1976). Conceptual perspective taking in two- to six-year-old children. *Developmental Psychology, 12,* 85–86.

Moynahan, E. D. (1973). The development of knowledge concerning the effect of categorization upon free recall. *Child Development, 44,* 238–246.

Mundy-Castle, A. C., & Anglin, J. (1974). Looking strategies in infancy. In L. J. Stone, H. T. Smith, & L. B. Murphy (Eds.), *The competent infant.* London: Tavistock.

Myers, N. A., & Perlmutter, M. (1978). Memory in the years from two to five. In P. A. Ornstein (Ed.), *Memory development in children.* Hillsdale, NJ: Erlbaum.

Neimark, E. D. (1975). Longitudinal development of formal operations thought. *Genetic Psychology Monographs, 91,* 171–225.

Neimark, E. D. (1979). Current status of formal operations research. *Human Development, 22,* 60–67.

Ornstein, P. A., Naus, M. J., & Liberty, C. (1975). Rehearsal and organizational processes in children's memory. *Child Development, 46,* 818–830.

Ornstein, P. A., Naus, M. J., & Stone, B. P. (1977). Rehearsal training and development of differences in memory. *Developmental Psychology, 13,* 15–24.

Pascual-Leone, J. (1980). Constructive problems for constructive theories: The current relevance of Piaget's work and a critique of information processing simulation psychology. In H. Speda & P. Kluwe (Eds.), *Psychological models of thinking.* New York: Academic Press.

Piaget, J. (1929). *The child's conception of the world.* New York: Harcourt Brace Jovanovich.

Piaget, J. (1951). *Play, dreams, and imitation in childhood.* New York: Norton.

Piaget, J. (1954). *The construction of reality in the child.* New York: Basic Books.

Piaget, J. (1954). *The construction of reality in the child.* New York: Basic Books.

Piaget, J. (1970a; May). A conversation with Jean Piaget. *Psychology Today, 3,* pp. 25–32.

Piaget, J. (1970b). Piaget's theory. In P. H. Mussen (Ed.), *Carmichael's manual of child psychology* (Vol. 1). New York: Wiley.

Piaget, J. (1977). The role of action in the development of thinking. In W. F. Overton & J. M. Gallagher (Eds.), *Knowledge and development* (Vol. 1). New York: Plenum Press.

Piaget, J., & Inhelder, B. (1941). *Le développement des quantités chez l'enfant.* Neuchâtel: Delachaux et Niestlé.

Piaget, J., & Inhelder, B. (1956). *The child's conception of space.* New York: Norton.

Piaget, J., & Inhelder, B. (1969). *The psychology of the child.* New York: Basic Books.

Pressley, M. (1982). Elaboration and memory development. *Child Development, 53,* 296–309.

Pressley, M., & Levin, J. R. (1980). The development of mental imagery retrieval. *Child Development, 51,* 558–560.

Reynolds, A. G., & Flagg, P. W. (1983). *Cognitive psychology.* Boston: Little, Brown.

Richards, D. D., & Siegler, R. S. (1981). Very young children's acquisition of systematic problem-solving strategies. *Child Development, 52,* 1318–1321.

Rohwer, W. D., Jr. (1980). An elaborative conception of learner differences. In R. E. Snow, P. A. Frederico, & W. E. Montague (Eds.), *Aptitude, learning, and instruction.* Hillsdale, NJ: Erlbaum.

Rose, S. A. (1981). Developmental changes in infants' recognition of visual stimuli. *Child Development, 52,* 227–233.

Rosser, R. A. (1983). The emergence of spatial perspective taking: An information-processing alternative to egocentrism. *Child Development, 54,* 660–668.

Rubin, K. H., Fein, G., & Vandenberg, B. (1983). *Play.* In E. M. Hetherington (Ed.), *Carmichael's manual of child psychology: Social development.* New York: Wiley.

Salatas, H., & Flavell, J. H. (1976). Behavioral and meta-mnemonic indicators of strategic behaviors under remember instructions in first grade. *Child Development, 47,* 81–89.

Salkind, N. J., & Nelson, C. F. (1980). A note on the developmental nature of reflection-impulsivity. *Developmental Psychology, 16,* 237–238.

Sedlak, A. J., & Kurtz, S. T. (1981). A review of children's use of causal inference principles. *Child Development, 52,* 759–784.

Shaffer, D. R. (1979). *Social and personality development.* Monterey, CA: Brooks/Cole.

Siegler, R. S. (1978). The origin of scientific reasoning. In R. S. Siegler (Ed.), *Children's thinking: What develops.* Hillsdale, NJ: Erlbaum.

Siegler, R. S. (1981). Developmental sequences within and between concepts. *Monographs of the Society for Research in Child Development, 46* (Serial No. 189).

Siegler, R. S., Liebert, D. E., & Liebert, R. M. (1973). Inhelder and Piaget's pendulum problem: Teaching preadolescents to act as scientists. *Developmental Psychology, 9,* 97–101.

Siegler, R. S., & Liebert, R. M. (1975). Acquisition of formal scientific reasoning by 10- and 13-year-olds: Designing a factorial experiment. *Developmental Psychology, 11,* 401–402.

Sigel, I. E., Roeper, A., & Hooper, F. H. (1968). A training procedure for the acquisition of Piaget's conservation of quantity: A pilot study and its replication. In I. E. Sigel & F. H. Hooper (Eds.), *Logical thinking in children: Research based on Piaget's theory.* New York: Holt, Rinehart and Winston.

Singer, J. (1973). *The child's world of make believe.* New York: Academic Press.

Sugarman, S. (1981). The cognitive basis of classification in very young children: An analysis of object-ordering trends. *Child Development, 52,* 1172–1178.

Sullivan, M. W. (1982). Reactivation: Priming forgotten memories in human infants. *Child Development, 53,* 516–523.

Tomlinson-Keasey, C., Eisert, D. C., Kahle, L. R., Hardy-Brown, K., & Keasey, B. (1979). The structure of concrete-operational thought. *Child Development, 50,* 1153–1163.

Tulkin, S. R., & Konner, M. J. (1973). Alternative conceptions of intellectual functioning. *Human Development, 16,* 33–52.

Vlietstra, A. G. (1982). Children's responses to task instructions: Age changes and training effects. *Child Development, 53,* 534–542.

Wellman, H. M., Collins, J., & Glieberman, J. (1981). Understanding the combination of memory variables: Developing conceptions of memory limitations. *Child Development, 52,* 1313–1317.

Wellman, H. M., Ritter, K., & Flavell, J. H. (1975). Deliberate memory behavior in the delayed reactions of very young children. *Developmental Psychology, 11,* 780–787.

Yando, R., & Kagan, J. (1968). The effect of teacher tempo on the child. *Child Development, 39,* 27–34.

Yussen, S. R., & Levy, V. M. (1975). Developmental changes in predicting one's own memory span of short-term memory. *Journal of Experimental Child Psychology, 19,* 502–508.

CHAPTER TEN

INTELLIGENCE: MEASURING MENTAL PERFORMANCE

■ *What is intelligence?*
The nature/nurture controversy
Is intelligence a single attribute or many
   attributes?

■ *How is intelligence measured?*
The first intelligence tests
Modern IQ tests

■ *What do intelligence tests predict?*
IQ as a predictor of scholastic achievement
IQ as a predictor of occupational status
IQ as a predictor of health, adjustment, and life
   satisfaction

■ *Factors that influence IQ scores*
The evidence for heredity
Environmental influences

■ *Sociocultural correlates of intellectual
   performance*
The home environment as a determinant of
   intellectual growth
Effects of birth order and the family
   configuration
Social-class, racial, and ethnic differences in IQ
Why do groups differ in intellectual
   performance?

■ *Improving intellectual performance through
   compensatory education*
Long-term follow-ups
Home-based interventions
Limitations of compensatory education

■ *Some common uses (and abuses) of IQ tests*

■ *Summary*

W hat does it mean to say that someone is bright or intelligent? To Piaget, it suggests that the individual has acquired a number of cognitive structures that enable him or her to solve problems and adapt successfully to the demands of the environment. Piaget thought of intelligence as a particular type of logic that children use when answering questions and thinking about everyday issues. He believed that these logical structures change with age and that all children will go through exactly the same steps, or "stages," of reasoning as they progress toward intellectual maturity.

In contrast, the person on the street often thinks of intelligence as an indication of how smart someone is compared with other people. The implication is that intelligence is a "quantity" that reflects a person's ability to learn new material or to solve various problems. Recently a group of Cornell undergraduates were asked to list the characteristics of "intelligent people." They attributed a wide range of qualities to the intellectually exceptional person, including a broad general knowledge, an ability to think logically, common sense, wit, creativity, openness to new experience, and a sensitivity to one's own limitations (Neisser, 1980). Presumably these students would have mentioned roughly the opposite attributes had they been asked to list the characteristics of "dull," or unintelligent, persons.

Our focus in this chapter is on individual differences in intelligence. We will begin by looking at how intelligence is defined and measured by scientists who have constructed intelligence tests. We will then consider what a person's score on an intelligence test implies about his or her ability to learn, to perform in academic settings, and to succeed at a job. Finally, we will discuss several important sociocultural factors that are known to affect intellectual performance and conclude by evaluating the merits of preschool educational programs, such as Project Head Start, designed to enhance the intellectual development of children who perform poorly on intelligence tests.

WHAT IS INTELLIGENCE?

In 1921 the *Journal of Educational Psychology* asked 17 leading investigators to define intelligence in their own words. Fourteen of these scientists were bold enough to reply, but unfortunately their answers were contradictory and provided little insight into what it was that they were measuring with their "intelligence" tests. Although few topics in psychology have generated as much research as intelligence and intelligence testing, even today there is little consensus about what intelligence is.

The Nature/Nurture Controversy

One reason investigators have not agreed on a definition of intelligence is that they disagree about the origins of intellectual abilities. Many of the early theorists believed that intelligence was a capacity for thinking and problem solving that was genetically determined and thus fixed at conception. This nativist viewpoint can be traced to Charles Darwin, whose theory of evolution implied that most individual differences among the members of a species stemmed from their different genotypes. Darwin believed that some members of a species were simply "better off" (or more *fit*) than others because they had inherited certain physical and behavioral characteristics that would enable them to survive and propagate in a rapidly changing environment.

Darwin's cousin Sir Francis Galton was the first to apply evolutionary theory to the study of human intelligence. Galton believed that the ability to think clearly and accurately was essential for success (if not survival) in the rapidly changing world of the 19th century. Moreover, he concluded that these intellectual abilities must be inherited after observing that (1) successful people tend to come from successful families and (2) family members are more similar than unrelated persons in their mental abilities and accomplishments. What Galton overlooked was the possibility that children of successful parents may accomplish a great deal themselves because of the environments in which they were raised. Surely the offspring of illustrious families of 19th-century England were afforded numerous opportunities, privileges, and social connections that

PHOTO 10-1. *Sir Francis Galton (1822–1911) was among the first to study individual differences in intellectual performance.*

helped them to succeed in life—advantages rarely available to the children of commoners. But despite this important oversight, Galton's views on the origins of intelligence have remained influential. Even today there are theorists who believe that 70–80% of the intellectual variation among the members of a population is attributable to the genes that people have inherited at conception (Eysenck, 1981a; Jensen, 1969).

Most contemporary psychologists acknowledge that genetic factors contribute to intellectual performance, but they feel that a heritability estimate of 70–80% is simply too high.[1] As we will see later in the chapter, the scores that a person makes on

---

[1]The term *heritability* refers to the amount of variation in a trait that is attributable to genetic factors (see Chapter Three). When we talk about the heritability of an attribute, it is extremely important to remember that heritability ratios apply only to populations, *never to individuals*. If a researcher were to estimate that the heritability of IQ is .80, this simply means that, within the population he has studied, 80% of the *differences* among examinees in their intelligence-test scores can be explained by hereditary influences. But since a heritability ratio does not apply to individuals, it is clearly inappropriate to conclude that 80% of John Smith's IQ is inherited and 20% is due to the environment.

intelligence tests may vary considerably over time, suggesting that intelligence is not a fixed capacity that is determined at conception. Even more intriguing is the finding that a person's intelligence quotient, or IQ, can be modified either upward or downward depending on the kinds of experiences to which he or she is exposed. In other words, it now appears that both hereditary and environmental factors play crucial roles in determining how well people perform on intelligence tests.

Is Intelligence a Single Attribute or Many Attributes?

Consider the following definitions of intelligence that appeared before 1960:

1. "The ability to carry on abstract thinking" (Terman, 1921).
2. "The . . . capacity of an individual to act purposefully and think rationally and to deal effectively with the environment" (Wechsler, 1944).
3. "Adaptive thinking or action" (Piaget, 1950).
4. "Innate, general cognitive ability" (Burt, 1955).

At first glance, all these definitions seem to imply that intelligence is a *singular* ability that resides within the individual and determines his or her performance on various kinds of cognitive tasks. When the first intelligence tests began to appear, early in this century, investigators typically found that children's scores on different intelligence tests were positively correlated with one another. This is precisely the pattern that we might expect if intelligence is a general ability to think, learn, and solve problems.

However, people who take an intelligence test are usually asked to perform a *variety* of tasks, such as defining concepts, recalling lists of words or numbers, reproducing geometric designs with blocks, and solving arithmetic puzzles. Many investigators believe that these "subtests" measure a number of distinct mental abilities rather than a singular cognitive capacity. According to this multifactorial viewpoint, an individual may score high on tests of some cognitive abilities (for example, verbal comprehension) and actually test below average on other, presumably independent mental skills (such as memory or arithmetic reasoning).

■ *The factor-analytic approach*

One way of determining whether intelligence is a single ability or many different abilities is to ask a group of subjects to work at a number of mental tasks and then analyze their performances using a statistical procedure called **factor analysis**. Simply stated, factor analysis is a correlational technique that groups test items or problems that are highly correlated with one another and yet unrelated to all the remaining items or problems on the test. Clusters of related items are called *factors*, and each factor (if any are found) will presumably represent a unique mental ability. Suppose, for example, we found that examinees performed very similarly on two tests of verbal comprehension and on three tests of arithmetic reasoning but that their "comprehension" scores were only marginally related to their "arithmetic reasoning" scores. Under these circumstances, we might conclude that verbal comprehension and arithmetic reasoning represent distinct intellectual factors. But if subjects' verbal comprehension scores were highly correlated with their arithmetic reasoning scores (and with their scores on all other kinds of mental problems), we might conclude that intelligence is a singular attribute rather than a number of distinct mental abilities.

■ *Factor-analytic studies of intelligence*

Spearman's "general mental ability." Charles Spearman (1927) was among the first to apply the logic of factor analysis to the study of intelligence. Spearman looked at the correlations between children's scores on a variety of cognitive tests and their grades in different subjects at school. He found that many of these measures were moderately correlated, thereby reflecting the contribution of a primary intellectual ability that he called **g** (for general mental ability). However,

> **factor analysis:** *a statistical procedure for identifying clusters of tests or test items that are highly correlated with one another and unrelated to other tests or test items.*
>
> *g: Spearman's abbreviation for neogenesis, which, roughly translated, means one's ability to understand relations (or general mental ability).*

Spearman was intrigued by the finding that people were often inconsistent in their intellectual performance. For example, a student who excelled at most cognitive tasks might score very low on a particular measure (for example, musical aptitude or verbal memory). He then proposed that intelligence consists of two factors: *g*, or general ability, and **s**, or special abilities, each of which is specific to a particular test. Thus, one's score on a test of arithmetic reasoning would depend not only on *g* but also on the specific numerical skills (*s*) that are involved in this kind of problem solving.

Thurstone's "primary mental abilities." The two-factor theory of intelligence proposed by Spearman was only the beginning. Several years later, Louis Thurstone (1938; Thurstone & Thurstone, 1941) administered a large number of cognitive tasks to groups of eighth-grade children and college students. When he factor-analyzed his results, Thurstone came up with seven distinct intellectual factors that he called *primary mental abilities:*

S. *Spatial*: Ability to recognize spatial relationships

P. *Perceptual speed*: Quick and accurate noting of visual detail

N. *Numerical reasoning*: Ability to perform arithmetic operations quickly and accurately

V. *Verbal meaning*: Understanding of the meaning of words and verbal concepts

W. *Word fluency*: Speed in recognizing single and isolated words

M. *Memory*: Ability to recall lists of words, numbers, and other materials

I. *Inductive reasoning*: Ability to generate a rule or relationship that describes a set of observations

When Thurstone constructed tests to measure each of his primary mental abilities, he found that subjects' scores on the seven scales were moderately correlated. For example, a person who scored high on spatial ability might also tend to do well on tests of perceptual speed, memory, and inductive reasoning. So even though the seven primary mental abilities that Thurstone identified do seem to require different cognitive operations, the fact that they are not totally independent suggests that they may tap a common intellectual

dimension of some sort—something similar to what Spearman had called *g*, or general mental ability.

The Cattell/Horn theory of fluid and crystallized intelligence. Raymond Cattell and John Horn have formulated a theory of intelligence that attempts to explain the findings of Spearman and Thurstone. Cattell and Horn argue that Spearman's *g* and Thurstone's primary mental abilities are divisible into two major dimensions of intellect: **fluid intelligence** and **crystallized intelligence** (Cattell, 1963; Horn & Cattell, 1967, 1982). Fluid intelligence (g_f) is described as an ability to solve abstract relational problems of the sort that are *not* taught and are relatively free of cultural influences. The kinds of problems that are used to measure g_f include verbal analogies, memory for lists of unrelated items (for example, paired associates such as *dog–hoe*), and tests of one's ability to recognize relationships among abstract figures. In contrast, crystallized intelligence (g_c) is an ability to understand relationships or solve problems that depend on knowledge acquired as a result of schooling and other life experiences. Presumably, tests of general information (for example, "At what temperature does water boil?"), word comprehension ("What is the meaning of *duplicate*?"), and numerical abilities are all measures of g_c, or crystallized intelligence.

The Cattell/Horn theory has a distinct developmental flavor. Crystallized intelligence is said to increase throughout the life span, since it is primarily a reflection of one's cumulative learning experiences. Fluid intelligence, in contrast, is said to increase gradually throughout childhood and adolescence as the nervous system matures. It should then level off during young adulthood and begin a steady decline with age. Many investigators have found that individuals do seem to improve with age on measures of crystallized intelligence. However, longitudinal studies of adults often fail to find the steady age-related declines in fluid intelligence that the Cattell/Horn theory predicts (Labouvie-Vief, 1977; Schaie & Hertzog, 1983; Schaie & Labouvie-Vief, 1974).[2]

[2]Indeed, evidence from a recent longitudinal study (Schaie & Hertzog, 1983) indicates that neither fluid nor crystallized intelligence shows an appreciable decline until after age 60.

TABLE 10-1. Guilford's components of mental structure: Contents, operations, and products of intellect

Contents: What the person is thinking about
1. *Figural*—properties of stimuli that we can experience through the basic senses, such as color, loudness, shape, texture
2. *Symbolic*—numbers, letters, symbols, and designs
3. *Semantic*—ideas
4. *Behavioral*—actions and expressions of other people

Operations: Mental actions or processes the person performs
1. *Cognition*—recognizing or discovering
2. *Memory*—retaining or recalling the contents of thought
3. *Divergent production*—producing a variety of ideas or solutions to a problem
4. *Convergent production*—producing a single, best solution to a problem
5. *Evaluation*—deciding whether intellectual contents are positive or negative, good or bad, and so on

Products: The outcomes of thinking (or results) of thinking
1. *Units*—a single number, letter, or word
2. *Classes*—a higher-order concept (for example, rats and gerbils are rodents)
3. *Relations*—a connection between concepts
4. *Systems*—an ordering or classification of relations
5. *Transformation*—altering or restructuring intellectual contents
6. *Implication*—making inferences from separate pieces of information

Guilford's "structure of intellect" model. The factor-analytic approaches that we have reviewed suggest that there are anywhere from two to seven primary mental abilities that make up the concept we call "intelligence." A very different point of view has been voiced by J. P. Guilford, who proposes that there may be more than 100 distinct mental abilities. He arrived at this figure by first classifying cognitive tasks along three major dimensions: (1) *content* (what must the person think about), (2) *operations* (what kind of thinking is the person asked to perform), and (3) *products* (what kind of answer is required). Guilford (1967) argued that there are four kinds of intellectual contents, five classes of mental operations, and six kinds of intellectual products (see Table 10-1). Thus, his **"structure of intellect" model** allows for as many as 120 primary mental abilities, based on all the possible combinations of the various intellectual contents, operations, and products (that is, 4 × 5 × 6 = 120).

Guilford then set out to construct tests to measure each of his 120 mental abilities. For example, the test of "social intelligence" illustrated in Figure 10-1 measures the mental ability that requires the test taker to act on a *behavioral* content (the figure's facial expression), using a particular operation, *cognition*, to produce a particular product,

the probable *implication* of that expression. To date, tests have been constructed to assess more than 70 of the 120 mental abilities in Guilford's model of intellect. However, the scores that people make on those presumably independent intellectual factors are often correlated—a finding that implies that the number of basic mental abilities is much smaller than Guilford had assumed (Brody & Brody, 1976).

Summary and critique of the factor-analytic approach. During the 1940s and 1950s, researchers were quite enthusiastic about the factor-

> *s:* Spearman's term for mental abilities that are specific to particular tests.
>
> **fluid intelligence** (g_f): *the ability to perceive relations and solve relational problems of the type that are not taught and are relatively free of cultural influences.*
>
> **crystallized intelligence** (g_c): *ability to understand relations or solve problems that depend on knowledge acquired from schooling and other cultural influences.*
>
> **"structure of intellect" model:** *Guilford's factor-analytic model of intelligence, which proposes that there are 120 distinct mental abilities.*

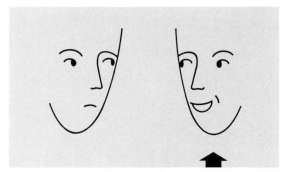

1. I'm glad you're feeling a little better.
2. You make the funniest faces!
3. Didn't I tell you she'd say "No"?

FIGURE 10-1. An item from one of Guilford's tests of social intelligence. The task is to read the characters' expressions and to decide what the person marked by the arrow is most probably saying to the other person. You may wish to try this item yourself (the correct answer appears below).

analytic study of intelligence. Some of that initial optimism has waned, and for very good reasons.

Consider, for example, that independent investigators typically disagree about the number and type of basic mental abilities that compose human intelligence. Part of the problem stems from the fact that different researchers have administered different batteries of tests to their research participants. Since the number and type of factors that emerge from a factor analysis depend largely on the tests administered and the range of problems that these tests pose to subjects, it is hardly surprising that these researchers might draw different conclusions about the structure of intellect.

Let's also note that the "products" of a factor analysis are merely clusters of interrelated items and problems. Once these clusters emerge, it is the theorist who must then scan these patterns of correlations in order to interpret and label them. Clearly, a technique that allows this much subjectivity is bound to produce some interpretive inconsistencies. Moreover, the labels that investigators give to their factors are only "best guesses" about the meanings of these clusters, and these guesses may or may not be accurate.

Answer to task in Figure 10-1: 3.

What we have learned from the factor-analytic method is that intelligence is not merely a singular attribute that determines how well people perform on *all* cognitive tasks. The model of intelligence that best fits the data is one that includes a general intellectual factor and a small number of "specialized" abilities that have not yet been clearly identified. One particularly intriguing notion is Cattell's (1971) idea that some components of intelligence may be genetically determined whereas others depend primarily on experiences and learning. Later in the chapter, we will see that both hereditary and environmental influences do affect the scores that people make on *global* assessments of their intelligence. However, it remains for future research to firmly establish that specific mental abilities such as verbal comprehension, memory, and arithmetic reasoning are influenced to different degrees by the forces of nature and nurture.

HOW IS INTELLIGENCE MEASURED?

When psychologists first began to construct intelligence tests, at the beginning of this century, their concern was not with defining the nature of intelligence but, rather, with devising a method to determine who among groups of schoolchildren were likely to be slow learners. In this section of the chapter we will trace the development of this mental-testing movement and briefly consider the characteristics of some of the most respected and widely used intelligence tests.

The First Intelligence Tests

Although Sir Francis Galton was the first to attempt to measure mental ability, it was a French psychologist named Alfred Binet who produced the forerunner of our modern intelligence tests. In 1904 Binet and a colleague, Theophile Simon, were commissioned by the French government to devise a test that would identify "dull" children—slow learners who might profit from remedial instruction. Since their task was a practical one—to predict success at school—Binet and Simon began by constructing a large battery of cognitive tasks that measured skills presumed necessary for classroom learning: processes such as attention, perception, memory, reasoning, and verbal com-

PHOTO 10-2. *Alfred Binet (1857–1911), the father of modern intelligence testing.*

prehension. These problems were then administered to normal schoolchildren and to those described by their instructors as dull or retarded. Items that did not discriminate between dull and normal children (for example, measures of motor skills) were systematically eliminated from the battery. After several such refinements, Binet and Simon had produced a test that sampled several cognitive abilities, could be administered in a little more than an hour, and reliably discriminated children described as dull, average, and bright by their teachers.

■ *The concept of mental age*
Binet assumed that intelligence develops with age and that older children and adolescents should be able to perform a wider variety of intellectual tasks than their younger counterparts. In 1908 the Binet-Simon test was revised and all test items were age-graded. For example, problems that were passed by most 6-year-olds but few 5-year-olds were assumed to reflect the mental performance of a typical 6-year-old; those passed by most 12-year-olds but few 11-year-olds were said to measure the intellectual skills of an average 12-year-old; and so on. This age-grading of test items for ages 3–13 allowed for a more precise assessment of a child's

level of intellectual functioning. A child who passed all items at the 5-year-old level but none at the 6-year-old level was said to have a **mental age (MA)** of 5 years. A child who passed all items at the 10-year-old level and half of those at the 11-year old level would have an MA of 10½ years, and so on.

■ *The intelligence quotient (IQ)*
Mental age is a useful concept that gives an absolute assessment of the child's level of intellectual development. However, a mental age, by itself, does not tell us how smart someone is. To determine whether a child is bright, average, or dull, it is necessary to compare the child's mental age with his or her chronological age. Suppose that a 7-year-old girl has a mental age of 8 years. We would consider this child reasonably bright because she can perform intellectual tasks that most 7-year-olds will fail. But the same mental age of 8 would be taken as an indication of retarded intellectual development if our test taker had a chronological age of 13.

William Stern, a German psychologist, later proposed a ratio measure of intelligence that came to be known as the **intelligence quotient,** or **IQ.** A person's IQ was calculated by simply dividing her mental age by her chronological age and then multiplying by 100:

$$IQ = MA/CA \times 100$$

Notice that an IQ of 100 indicates average intelligence; it means that the child has passed all the items that age mates typically pass and none of the items at the next level higher, so that *her mental age is exactly equal to her chronological age.* An IQ greater than 100 indicates that the child's performance is superior to that of other children her age; an IQ less than 100 means that her intellectual performance is below average.

One advantage of the IQ measure is that it al-

---

mental age (MA): *a measure of intellectual development that reflects the level of age-graded problems a child is able to solve.*

intelligence quotient (IQ): *a numerical measure of a person's performance on an intelligence test relative to the performance of other examinees of the same age.*

lows us to compare the intellectual development of children of different ages. For example, a 6-year-old with a mental age of 3 has an IQ of 50—the same IQ as a 10-year-old with a mental age of 5. These two children are considered equally retarded even though the mental age of the second child is two years greater.

In sum, Binet had created a test that enabled him to identify slow learners and to estimate their levels of intellectual development. This information proved particularly useful to school administrators, who began to use children's mental ages as a guideline for planning curricula for both normal and retarded students.

Modern IQ Tests

Binet's work soon attracted the attention of psychologists in other countries. In 1916 Louis Terman of Stanford University translated and published a revised version of the Binet scale for use with American children. This test came to be known as the Stanford-Binet.

■ The Stanford-Binet

Like the Binet scale, the original version of the Stanford-Binet consisted of a series of age-graded tasks designed to measure the average intellectual performance of subjects aged 3 through 13 (see Table 10-2 for some sample problems). Terman first gave his test to a sample of about 1000 American schoolchildren in order to establish performance norms against which the individual child could be compared. But unlike Binet, who classified children according to mental age, Terman favored the use of Stern's intelligence quotient, or IQ. Thus, the 1916 version of the Stanford-Binet became the first true "IQ test."

The norms for this 1916 test were based on the intellectual performance of White children from middle-class backgrounds. Furthermore, the earliest version of the Stanford-Binet did not adequately measure the intellectual skills of either very young children or adults. To correct these problems, investigators have revised the Stanford-Binet on several occasions. Norms for the most recent version of the test are based on a representative sample of people (2-year-olds through young adults) from many racial and socioeconomic backgrounds. The concept of mental age is no longer used to determine a child's IQ. Today IQs from all intelligence tests are calculated by comparing the number of items a child passes against the average number of items passed by other children of the same age. The child who hits this "average" is assigned an IQ of 100. Any child

---

TABLE 10-2. Sample problems from the Stanford-Binet

Age 3—Child should be able to:	Point to objects that serve various functions such as "goes on your feet" Name pictures of objects such as *chair, flag* Repeat a list of 2 words or digits—for example, *car, dog*
Age 4—Child should be able to:	Discriminate visual forms such as squares, circles, and triangles Define words such as *ball* and *bat* Repeat 10-word sentences Count up to 4 objects Solve problems such as "In daytime it is light; at night it is . . ."
Age 6—Child should be able to:	State the difference between similar items such as a *bird* and a *dog* Count up to 9 objects Solve analogies such as "An inch is short; a mile is . . ."
Age 9—Child should be able to:	Solve verbal problems such as "Tell me a number that rhymes with *tree*" Solve simple arithmetic problems such as "If I buy 4 cents worth of candy and give the storekeeper 10 cents, how much money will I get back?" Repeat 4 digits in reverse order
Age 12—Child should be able to:	Define words such as *skill* and *muzzle* Repeat 5 digits in reverse order Solve verbal absurdities such as "One day we saw several icebergs that had been entirely melted by the warmth of the Gulf Stream. What is foolish about that?"

TABLE 10-3. The meaning of various IQs obtained from the Stanford-Binet

An IQ of	Equals or exceeds __ % of the population	An IQ of	Equals or exceeds __ % of the population
160	99.99	100	50
140	99.3	95	38
135	98	90	27
130	97	85	18
125	94	80	11
120	89	75	6
115	82	70	3
110	73	65	2
105	62	62	1

who does better than that average has an IQ above 100, and those who pass fewer problems than average obtain IQs lower than 100.

The distribution of IQ scores. If a young girl scores 130 on the Stanford-Binet, we know that her IQ is above average. But how bright is she? In order to tell, we would have to know something about the way IQs are distributed within the population at large.

One interesting feature of all modern IQ tests is that people's scores are **normally distributed** around an IQ of 100 (see Figure 10-2). This pat-

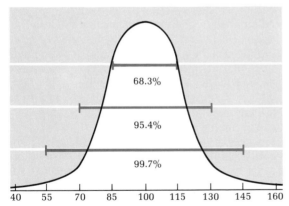

FIGURE 10-2. *The approximate distribution of IQ scores people make on contemporary intelligence tests. These tests are constructed so that the average score made by examinees in each age group is equivalent to an IQ of 100. Note that more than two-thirds of all examinees score within 15 points of this average (that is, IQs of 85–115) and that 95% of the population score within 30 points of average (IQs of 70–130).*

terning of scores is hardly an accident. By definition, the average score made by examinees from each age group is set at 100, and this is the most common score that people make. Note that approximately half the population scores below 100 and half above. Moreover, roughly equal numbers of examinees will obtain IQs of 85 and 115 (15 points from the average) or 70 and 130 (30 points from average). To determine the meaning of an IQ of 130, we can look at Table 10-3, which shows what percentage of the population the person outperforms by scoring at that level. Here we see that an IQ of 130 equals or exceeds the IQs of 97% of the population; it is a very high IQ indeed.

■ *The Wechsler scales*

Professor David Wechsler of the New York University–Bellevue Medical School has constructed two intelligence tests for children, both of which are now widely used. The Wechsler Intelligence Test for Children–Revised (WISC-R) is appropriate for schoolchildren aged 6 to 16 (Wechsler, 1974). A second test, the Wechsler Preschool and Primary Scale of Intelligence (WPPSI), is designed for preschoolers between the ages of 4 and 6½ (Wechsler, 1967).

One reason that Wechsler constructed his own intelligence scales is that he believed tests such as

---

normal distribution: *a symmetrical (bell-shaped) curve that describes the variability of certain characteristics within a population; most people fall at or near the average score, with relatively few high or low scores.*

the Stanford-Binet are too heavily loaded with items that require verbal skills. Wechsler suggested that there are many intellectual skills that are predominantly *nonverbal*—abilities that are not adequately represented on Binet-type scales. He also argued that the heavily verbal bias of the Binet test discriminates against children who have certain language handicaps—for example, those for whom English is a second language or those who have reading difficulties or are hard of hearing.

Wechsler tried to overcome these problems by constructing intelligence scales that contain both a verbal subtest and a nonverbal, or "performance," subtest. Items on the verbal subtest are very similar to those on the Stanford-Binet. They are designed to measure the child's vocabulary, general knowledge, understanding of ideas and concepts, arithmetic reasoning, and the like. In contrast, items on the performance subtest are designed to assess predominantly nonverbal skills, such as the ability to assemble puzzles, to solve mazes, to reproduce geometric designs with colored blocks, and to rearrange sets of pictures so that they tell a meaningful story. When the examinee's performance is evaluated, he or she is assigned three scores: a verbal IQ, a performance IQ, and a full-scale IQ based on a combination of the first two measures.

Although the Wechsler scales differ in format from the Stanford-Binet, IQs derived from these instruments tend to be highly correlated. Those who work with preschoolers typically favor the Stanford-Binet because this scale has items designed for children as young as 2. However, many educators and school psychologists prefer to use the WISC when working with school-age children. Not only does the WISC tap a wider variety of intellectual abilities than the Stanford-Binet, but it is also sensitive to inconsistencies in intellectual performance that may be early indications of brain damage or learning disorders (for example, children who have had difficulty learning to read often do much worse on the verbal component of the WISC). Of course, the WISC cannot specify the reasons for a child's uneven performance. It merely alerts the examiner to the possibility that a problem exists—one that may call for diagnostic testing and treatment.

■ *Group tests of mental ability*

Both the Stanford-Binet and the Wechsler scales are expensive and time-consuming. These tests must be administered individually by a professional examiner, and it can take more than an hour to assess the IQ of a single examinee. If one's task is to measure the intellectual performance of a large number of people—army recruits, job applicants, or thousands of students in a city's public schools—the costs of administering individual intelligence tests can become prohibitive.

The first group intelligence test was developed for the U.S. Army. During World War I, a team of psychologists was commissioned to devise an instrument that could be administered to hundreds of thousands of inductees in order to weed out the very dull and to place the others into military occupations in accordance with their intellectual capabilities. The psychologists came up with a paper-and-pencil measure that included many of the same kinds of items that appeared on individual intelligence tests and yet was suitable for assessing the IQs of large numbers of men in a group setting (Yerkes, 1921). Once developed, this *Army Alpha Intelligence Test* was routinely used to classify and assign military personnel. As Wrightsman and Sanford (1975, p. 124) noted, "Many of our fathers and grandfathers had their military careers—and perhaps their lives—determined by their performance on this test."

It is likely that you have taken a group test of intelligence (or scholastic aptitude) at some point in your academic career. Among the more widely used of these tests are the Lorge-Thorndike Test, which is designed for grade school and high school students, the Scholastic Aptitude Test (SAT) and the American College Test (ACT), taken by many college applicants, and the Graduate Record Examination (GRE), often required of applicants to graduate school. These instruments are sometimes called "achievement" tests because they call for specific information that the examinee has learned at school (that is, what Cattell and Horn call crystallized intelligence) and are designed to predict future academic achievement.

One clear disadvantage of group testing is that the examiner has less direct contact with each examinee and may fail to notice a child who is anxious, inattentive, or simply not trying very hard. Thus, a group test may underestimate the intellectual abilities of examinees who, for one reason or another, are not very enthusiastic about the task at hand. This problem occurs less frequently with individual intelligence tests because the examiner can temporarily halt the proceedings in order to reassure an anxious child or perhaps inspire one who becomes tired, bored, or discouraged.

■ *Assessing infant intelligence*

None of the tests that we have reviewed can be used with children much younger than 3. Infants and toddlers have very short attention spans, and they do not talk very well. Consequently, long exams that depend heavily on the use of language are not well suited for assessing their intellectual skills.

One of the first infant "intelligence" tests was developed by Arnold Gesell, a Yale University pediatrician. During the 1920s and 1930s, Gesell and his colleagues studied hundreds of middle-class infants and toddlers to chart the sequence and timing of various developmental milestones. The resulting developmental norms were then used as a basis for constructing the *Gesell Developmental Schedules* (Gesell & Amatruda, 1947), a series of tests designed to evaluate the child's progress in four areas: *motor development* (for example, posture, balance, and locomotion), *adaptive behavior* (that is, alertness, eye/hand coordination, exploration, and problem solving), *language development* (including facial expressions, gestures, and verbal comprehension), and *personal-social behavior* (responsiveness to people, ability to feed and dress oneself, maturity of one's play activities, and the like). Since a **developmental schedule** assesses so many aspects of development, the child's performance yields a score called a **DQ, or developmental quotient,** rather than an IQ. A DQ of 100 means that the child has passed all problems listed as appropriate for his or her age group and none for the next age group higher. A DQ greater than 100 is a sign of accelerated development, whereas a DQ less than 100 means that the child's developmental progress is slower than that of a typical age mate.

Perhaps the best known and most widely used of today's infant (or DQ) tests is the *Bayley Scales of Infant Development* (Bayley, 1969). This instrument, designed for infants aged 2 to 30 months, consists of three subtests: (1) the *Motor* scale (including problems such as grasping a cube and throwing a ball), (2) the *Mental* scale (adaptive behaviors such as reaching for a desirable object, searching for a hidden toy, and following directions), and (3) the *Infant Behavioral Record* (a rating of the child's behavior on dimensions such as goal-directedness, fearfulness, and social responsivity). The child's rate of development, or DQ, is determined by comparing the number of items passed with the number passed by the "average" child of the same age.

Today it is fashionable to criticize infant tests because these instruments often fail to predict a child's later IQ score or scholastic achievements (Honzik, 1976; Rubin & Balow, 1979). Moreover, the younger children are when an infant test is administered, the lower the correlation between their DQ scores and their later performance on standardized IQ tests (Anderson, 1939; Honzik, 1976).

Why do infant scales not do a better job of predicting children's later IQs? Perhaps the main reason is that infant tests and IQ tests tap very different kinds of abilities. The infant scales are designed to measure sensory, motor, language, and social skills, whereas standardized IQ tests such as the WISC and the Stanford-Binet emphasize more abstract abilities such as verbal reasoning, concept formation, and problem solving. So to expect an infant test to predict the later results of an IQ test is like expecting a yardstick to tell us how much someone weighs. There may be some correspondence between the two measures (a yardstick indicates height, which is correlated with weight; DQ indicates developmental prog-

---

developmental schedules: *standardized tests designed to measure an infant's progress in the areas of motor, mental, social, and emotional development (also called infant tests).*

developmental quotient (DQ): *a numerical measure of an infant's performance on a developmental schedule relative to the performance of other infants the same age.*

ress, which is related to IQ), but the relationship is not very great.

However, infant tests are useful for diagnosing neurological deficits and mental retardation—even when these conditions are reasonably mild and difficult to detect through standard pediatric or neurological examinations (Escalona, 1968; Honzik, 1976). Moreover, Linda Siegal (1981) reports that it is possible to predict which children are likely to be developmentally delayed at age 2 (as indicated by a DQ of less than 85) from their score on the Bayley Mental Development subtest at age 4, 8, 12, or 18 months. Siegal also found that children's earlier performances on the Bayley scale (which includes language items) were positively correlated with their scores on a standardized test of language development at 2 years of age. So infant scales may well predict the child's future performance on assessments of those particular skills and abilities that the infant tests are designed to evaluate.

■ Is IQ a stable attribute?

When intelligence testing became widespread, during the first half of this century, it was generally assumed that a person's IQ was a reflection of his or her mental *capacity*—an attribute that was genetically determined and therefore would remain reasonably stable over time. In other words, a child with an IQ of 120 at age 5 was expected to obtain a similar IQ when retested at age 10, 15, or 20.

Although infant tests do not predict later intelligence-test scores, the IQs that children obtain in middle childhood are related to their performances on IQ tests later in life. Table 10-4 summarizes the results of a longitudinal study of more than 250 children conducted at the University of California (Honzik, Macfarlane, & Allen, 1948). In examining these correlations, we see that the shorter the interval between testings, the higher the correlation betweeen children's IQ scores. Thus, the correlation between IQs measured at ages 8 and 10 (+.88) is greater than the correlation between IQs measured at ages 6 and 10 (+.76) or at ages 8 and 18 (+.70).

At first glance, these data seem to imply that one's IQ is a very stable attribute. After all, the scores that children obtain at age 6 are clearly related to those that they obtain *12 years later at age 18!* However, it is important to note that these correlations, or "stability coefficients," are based

TABLE 10-4. Correlations of IQs measured during the preschool years and middle childhood with IQs measured at ages 10 and 18

Age of child	Correlation with IQ at age 10	Correlation with IQ at age 18
4	.66	.42
6	.76	.61
8	.88	.70
10	—	.76
12	.87	.76

on a large *group* of subjects, and they do not necessarily imply that the IQs of *individual children* will remain stable over time.

When individual profiles are examined, we find that many children show wide variations in their IQ scores over the course of childhood (see Figure 10-3 for some sample profiles). Robert McCall and his associates (McCall, Applebaum, & Hogarty, 1973) looked at the IQ scores of 140 children who had taken intelligence tests at regular intervals from age 2½ to age 17. Their findings were remarkable. More than half of these individuals displayed wide fluctuations in IQ over time, and the average range of variation in their IQ scores was a whopping 28.5 points. One child in seven showed changes of at least 40 points, and changes of more than 70 points are not unknown (Hindley & Owen, 1978). More boys than girls posted long-term gains in IQ. However, girls who had developed interests in masculine activities were more likely to show increases in IQ than girls who were more traditionally sex-typed (McCall et al., 1973).

So we see that IQ is reasonably stable for some children but extremely variable for many others. These findings suggest that an IQ score is not an indication of one's absolute potential for learning or intellectual capacity; if it were, the intellectual profiles of virtually all children would be highly stable, showing only minor variations due to errors of measurement.

What, then, does an IQ represent, if not one's intellectual competence or ability? Today, many experts believe that an IQ score is merely an estimate of the examinee's intellectual *performance* at one particular point in time—an estimate that may or may not be a good indication of the examinee's intellectual capabilities. The fact that IQs can wander upward or downward suggests that the environment may play a crucial role in deter-

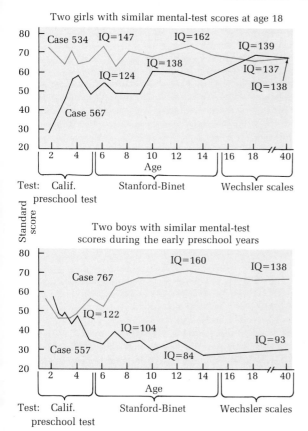

FIGURE 10-3. *The intellectual profiles of four individuals tested on several occasions between the ages of 21 months and 40 years. The IQ scores of the two girls in this example were quite different during the preschool period and then converged with age. Just the opposite was true of the two boys, whose scores diverged more and more over the course of childhood. Note that all four of these individuals showed considerable variability in their IQ scores over the years.*

mining intellectual performance. Indeed, the authors of the California longitudinal study were intrigued to find that the children whose IQ scores fluctuated the most were those from unstable home environments—that is, youngsters whose life experiences had also fluctuated between periods of happiness and turmoil (Honzik et al., 1948).

In reviewing several of the more widely respected intelligence tests, we have seen that these instruments vary considerably in structure and

format. Some must be administered to individuals; others are appropriate for testing large groups. Many tests are heavily loaded with items requiring verbal skills; others give equal weight to nonverbal abilities. Tests are designed to serve many purposes, ranging from assessing the developmental progress of infants to predicting the ability of adults to profit from higher education or to succeed at various occupations. Although there is no simple answer to the question "How is intelligence measured?" psychologists do follow a common set of procedures when constructing and evaluating intelligence tests. In Box 10-1 we will take a closer look at these important principles of test construction and see why they must be followed if a test is to be at all useful.

WHAT DO INTELLIGENCE TESTS PREDICT?

We have seen that IQ tests measure intellectual performance rather than competence and that a person's IQ may vary considerably over time. At this point, it seems reasonable to ask whether IQ scores can tell anything very meaningful about the people who were tested. For example, does IQ predict future academic accomplishments? Is it in any way related to a person's health, occupational status, or general life satisfaction? Research designed to answer these questions suggests some tentative answers. Let's first consider the relationship between IQ and academic achievement.

IQ as a Predictor of Scholastic Achievement

Since the original purpose of IQ testing was to estimate how well children would perform at school, it should come as no surprise that modern intelligence tests do predict academic achievement. The average correlation between children's IQ scores and their *current* grades at school is about .50 (Minton & Schneider, 1980). Moreover, assessments of IQ (or scholastic aptitude) can predict *future* academic performance. In one short-term longitudinal study, children's IQs measured in the fourth grade were highly correlated (+.73) with their scores on standardized achievement tests in the sixth grade (Crano, Kenny, & Campbell, 1972). Scholastic aptitude tests such as the ACT or SAT are also reliable predictors of the

BOX 10-1
PRINCIPLES OF TEST CONSTRUCTION

Tests designed to measure various psychological attributes vary considerably in quality. Some are virtually worthless; others are reasonably proficient at estimating how people differ along important dimensions such as anxiety, creativity, and intelligence. What makes for a good or useful test? At least four qualities: a *careful selection of items, reliability, validity,* and the establishment of *normative standards* against which to interpret an examinee's score.

Item selection. The first task when constructing any kind of psychological test is to carefully select items that reflect or represent the attribute that you hope to measure. When Binet set out to construct the first intelligence test, his purpose was to identify mentally retarded children who would not profit from traditional classroom instruction. He then selected items that seemed to tap the skills children use in completing school assignments, under the assumption that examinees who perform poorly on these tasks would also founder in the classroom. Of course, Binet would almost certainly have made different assumptions and chosen different items had his task been to assess the mechanical aptitude of students in a high school shop class. Clearly, the items that one selects for a test will depend on the purpose of that test and the assumptions that are made about the attribute(s) being measured.

Reliability. One characteristic of all useful tests is that they are highly reliable. Reliability means that *the test measures consistently,* even though different persons may administer and/or score it. If an IQ test is reliable, a person who takes it several times over a short period should obtain similar IQs on all testings. We could hardly consider a particular IQ test to be a very useful measure of intellectual functioning if a child who took it three times in a week scored 130 on Saturday, 85 on Monday, and 105 on the following Thursday.

The most common method of assessing the reliability of a test is to administer it twice to the same individuals and see how closely the two sets of scores are correlated. Fortunately, the IQ tests that we have reviewed are all fairly reliable, giving "test-retest" correlations of approximately .90. Whatever it is that these tests are measuring, they are measuring it consistently.

Validity. Good tests are not only reliable but *valid* as well. Simply stated, a test is valid if *it is measuring whatever it claims to measure.*

The validity of a test is usually estimated by comparing the scores that people make on this instrument with one or more criterion measures that are known to reflect the attribute in question. But how do we validate an IQ test when there are no absolute criteria for intellectual performance and theorists cannot even agree on what intelligence is? Admittedly, the problem is formidable—but hardly insur-

---

grades that high school students will make in college.

Not only do children with high IQs tend to do better in school, but they stay there longer (Brody & Brody, 1976): students who perform well on IQ tests are less likely to drop out of high school and more likely than other high school graduates to attempt and to complete college.

So intelligence-test scores do predict academic achievements. Yet it is important to note that the correlational findings we have reviewed are based on large numbers of students and that the IQ score of any particular student may not be a very good indicator of her current or future academic accomplishments. When trying to predict how well a particular student will perform in the future, a well-trained guidance counselor would undoubtedly consider the student's IQ score. However, he or she would also want to know about other variables that are related to academic success—factors such as the student's work

habits, interests, and motivation to succeed. Although IQ (and aptitude) tests predict academic achievement better than *any other type of test*, judgments about an individual's future accomplishments *should never be based on a test score alone*. Indeed, studies have shown that the best single predictor of a student's future grades is not an IQ (or aptitude) score but, rather, the grades that the student has previously earned (Minton & Schneider, 1980).

IQ as a Predictor of Occupational Status

Do people with higher IQs land the better jobs? Are they more successful in their chosen occupations than coworkers who test lower in intelligence?

The answer to the first question seems to be yes. In one study of military personnel during World War II, recruits' IQ scores on the Army General Classification Test were clearly related to the

mountable. What is typically done is to determine whether the scores that people make on an IQ test are correlated with one or more criterion measures that are *presumed* to reflect individual differences in intelligence—measures such as grades in school, teachers' ratings of intellectual ability, and the examinees' performance on other IQ tests (or tests of academic achievement). Thus, Binet's first intelligence test was considered valid because it accomplished precisely what it was designed to do—it discriminated those students who had been labeled as dull, average, and bright by their teachers.

Normative standards. A child's performance on an IQ test has little if any meaning unless we have norms against which to compare and evaluate the child's score. These normative standards are obtained by administering the IQ test to a *standardization group*—that is, a large sample of the population for which the test was designed. Data from the standardization sample would then tell us what score represents "average" performance as well as how scores are distributed in the population as a whole.

For norms to be useful, the standardization sample must truly represent the population for which the test is intended. For example, an IQ test designed for 6–10-year-old schoolchildren in the United States should be standardized on a 6–10-year-old sample that includes the appropriate proportions of youngsters from all the racial, ethnic, socioeconomic, and geographical backgrounds that make up the population of U.S. schoolchildren. If a test is improperly standardized on a nonrepresentative segment of the population—say, schoolchildren from urban settings—the norms that result may be inappropriate for children from other groups and settings. Suppose, for example, that the item "What is an escalator?" was passed by 50% of the 7-year-olds in the urban standardization sample but by only 10% of the 7-year-olds from a rural school in Arizona. In this case, the urban norms would almost certainly underestimate the intellectual functioning of rural schoolchildren; their poor performance on the "escalator" item (and other items tapping predominantly "urban" experiences) is probably due to cultural differences between themselves and the standardization group rather than to any true differences in their intellectual abilities. So it is not enough to merely standardize a test—the test must be standardized on a representative sample of the population to which it will be administered.

An important aspect of the standardization process is the *standardization of test procedures*. This simply means that a single testing procedure has been established and that the test apparatus, instructions, and scoring are identical for all children, regardless of who is administering the test. The purpose of this standardization is to ensure that children from all backgrounds and settings have taken the same test under exactly the same set of circumstances so that their scores may be compared.

prestige of their civilian occupations (Harrell & Harrell, 1945). Table 10-5 (p. 396) shows the rank order (from most to least prestigious) of some of the civilian occupations, as well as the average IQs and the range of IQs that characterized the men who worked at those jobs. Notice that the average IQ score increases as the prestige of the occupation increases—that is, the more prestigious jobs were generally held by the more intelligent men. However, a high IQ was certainly no guarantee that one would be working at a prestigious job. As we see in the "range of IQs" column, there were some very bright men working at low-status occupations such as farmhand or miner.

Do brighter people just naturally select the more prestigious occupations; or, rather, do prestigious occupations demand higher intellectual performances? Although there may be some truth to both these assertions, the second is probably closer to the mark. High-status occupations such as law, engineering, and chemistry are simply not open to all who might choose them; one must first earn a college degree and then make a reasonably high score on an IQ or aptitude test before it is even possible to obtain the training to pursue these careers. So it is hardly surprising that the average "professional" has a high IQ and that we rarely, if ever, find accountants, lawyers, doctors, or scientists who score much below average on IQ tests.

We can also ask whether IQ scores predict job *performance*. Are bright lawyers, electricians, or farmhands more successful or productive than their less intelligent colleagues? Erness and Nathan Brody (1976) have reviewed the literature and concluded that the relationship between IQ and occupational success depends on the nature of the work and the range of IQs that are found in the work force. Specifically, they noted that—

1. In high-status occupations where high intelligence scores are required as a condition for train-

TABLE 10-5. Average IQs and range of IQs for enlisted military personnel who had worked at various civilian occupations

Occupation	Average IQ	Range of IQs
Accountant	128.1	94–157
Lawyer	127.6	96–157
Engineer	126.6	100–151
Chemist	124.8	102–153
Reporter	124.5	100–157
Teacher	122.8	76–155
Pharmacist	120.5	76–149
Bookkeeper	120.0	70–157
Sales manager	119.0	90–137
Purchasing agent	118.7	82–153
Radio repairman	115.3	56–151
Salesman	115.1	60–153
Artist	114.9	82–139
Stock clerk	111.8	54–151
Machinist	110.1	38–153
Electrician	109.0	64–149
Riveter	104.1	50–141
Butcher	102.9	42–147
Bartender	102.2	56–137
Carpenter	102.1	42–147
Chauffeur	100.8	46–143
Cook and baker	97.2	20–147
Truck driver	96.2	16–149
Barber	95.3	42–141
Farmhand	91.4	24–141
Miner	90.6	42–139

ing and employment, there is *no* relationship between IQ and job performance. Scientists with IQs of 150 publish no more experiments than their colleagues with IQs of 115; extremely bright lawyers win no higher percentage of their cases than lawyers whose IQs are merely "above average." However, the range of IQs among workers in high-status professions is severely restricted (everybody is reasonably bright), and it is likely that intelligence would predict job performance if individuals with low IQs were allowed to enter these professions.

2. IQ scores do seem to predict job performance in professions of intermediate status where (a) cognitive skills are helpful and (b) the range of IQs among workers is quite large. For example, bright bookkeepers outperform their relatively dull co-workers; bright life insurance agents sell more insurance than their less intelligent colleagues.

3. IQ scores are not systematically related to job performance in relatively low-status occupations that make few intellectual demands of the workers (for example, routine clerical work, factory work, and waitressing). However, the more intelligent workers tend to be more dissatisfied with these jobs and less likely to remain in them very long.

In sum, it appears that the relationship between IQ and the status of one's occupation is much simpler and more clear-cut than the relationship between IQ and job performance (Brody & Brody, 1976).

IQ as a Predictor of Health, Adjustment, and Life Satisfaction

Are bright people any healthier, happier, or better adjusted than those of average or below-average intelligence? A longitudinal project begun by Louis Terman in 1922 provides some relevant information (Fincher, 1973; Terman, 1954; Terman & Oden, 1959). The subjects for Terman's study were more than 1500 California schoolchildren who had IQs of 140 or higher. The purpose of the project was to collect as much information as possible about the abilities and personal characteristics of these "gifted" children and to follow up on them every few years to see what they were accomplishing.

It soon became apparent that these children were exceptional in many respects other than intelligence. For example, they had weighed more at birth and had learned to walk and talk much sooner than most toddlers. They reached puberty somewhat earlier than normal, and their general health, as determined from physicians' reports, was much better than average. The gifted children were rated by teachers as better adjusted emotionally and more morally mature than their less intelligent peers. And although they were no more popular, on the average, than their classmates, the gifted children were quicker to take charge and assume positions of leadership. Taken together, these findings demolish the stereotype of child prodigies as frail, sickly youngsters who are socially inadequate and emotionally immature.

As adults, the individuals in Terman's gifted sample were still remarkable in many respects. Fewer than 5% were rated seriously maladjusted, and the incidence of problems such as ill health, insanity, alcoholism, and delinquent behavior was but a fraction of that normally observed in the general population (Terman, 1954). The marriage rate for these individuals was as high as it is for the population as a whole, and members of the gifted sample were more satisfied with their marriages and better adjusted sexually than were husbands and wives in general. Finally, a large percentage of these gifted individuals were high achievers, both in school and later in life. About 90% of the group had entered college, and 70% had graduated. Although many of the gifted women did not pursue a career outside the home, the occupational attainments of the gifted men were quite impressive. By age 40, 86% were working at professional or semiprofessional positions, compared with only 15–20% of California males as a whole. Many of these men were listed in *Who's Who* and *American Men of Science*, and as a group, they had taken out more than 200 patents and written some 2000 scientific reports, 100 books, 375 plays or short stories, and more than 300 essays, sketches, magazine articles, and critiques. All things considered, it would appear that the majority of Terman's gifted sample were very well-adjusted people who were living healthy, happy, and (in many cases) highly productive lives.

Interesting as Terman's results may be, they do not clearly establish that a high IQ guarantees good health, happiness, or occupational success. Psychologist David McClelland points out that

> neither Professor Terman nor anyone else has yet brought forward conclusive evidence that it is giftedness *per se* . . . that is responsible for these happy life outcomes. [Terman's] gifted children were drawn very disproportionately from the ranks of the educated, the wealthy, and the powerful. This means that they not only had a better chance to acquire the characteristics measured in the test, but also to be happier (since they had more money), and also to have access to higher occupations and better social standing [as cited in Fincher, 1973, p. 14].

In other words, McClelland suggests that many of the positive outcomes that characterized Terman's gifted subjects may have stemmed not from their high IQs but, rather, from their superior family environments.

As it turns out, there are data to support Mc-

Clelland's "family environment" hypothesis. When Terman (1954) contrasted the 150 gifted individuals who were most successful in a career (the As) with the 150 who were least successful (the Cs), he found that the childhood IQs of the members of these groups were comparable, averaging about 150. However, the academic achievements and intellectual profiles of those in the successful (A) group had remained fairly stable over time, whereas the scholastic performance and average IQ of those in the unsuccessful (C) group had declined since childhood. But why?

When Terman compared the family backgrounds of the As and Cs, he found some interesting differences. For example, the fathers of the As had more education and held better jobs than the fathers of the Cs, and twice as many of the As had siblings who had graduated from college. Moreover, the intellectual climate of the home (as indexed by number of books present and the parents' involvement in the child's learning activities) was generally richer or more stimulating for As than for Cs. Finally, twice as many Cs had experienced a disruption of family ties due to their parents' divorce, and the later divorce rate of the C subjects themselves was twice that observed among members of the A group.

So we see that a high IQ, by itself, does not guarantee good health, happiness, or success. Even among a select sample of children with superior IQs, the quality of the home environment contributes in important ways to future outcomes and accomplishments.

FACTORS THAT INFLUENCE IQ SCORES

To this point, we have seen that both heredity and environment seem to influence the scores that people make on IQ tests. Recall that Galton believed that intelligence must be inherited, since family members are so similar in their intellectual abilities and accomplishments. However, it is clear that a person's IQ score may fluctuate considerably over time and that the children whose IQs fluctuate the most are often the ones who have experienced many changes in their home and family environments.

Few if any issues in the history of psychology

have sparked more debate than the question "Is intelligence due mainly to heredity or mainly to the environment?" In the pages that follow, we will review some of the classic evidence for the hereditary and the environmental sides of this nature/nurture controversy and then see that the forces of nature and nurture combine, or *interact*, to determine intellectual performance.

The Evidence for Heredity

In Chapter Three we reviewed three lines of evidence to suggest that intelligence is a heritable attribute:

1. *Animal (selective breeding) studies*. Many characteristics (including something that resembles intelligence) can be influenced by selective breeding. For example, Tryon (1940) produced two strains of rats that differed in maze-learning ability by systematically breeding the best maze runners from each generation together while also inbreeding the "dullest" members of each cohort. After 18 generations, the worst performer among the "maze-bright" group was better at running mazes than the very best performer from the "maze-dull" group.

2. *Family studies*. The intellectual resemblance between pairs of individuals living in the same household increases as a function of the individuals' degree of kinship (that is, genetic similarity). For example, the IQ correlation for monozygotic twins (who inherit identical genes) approaches .90, whereas the IQ correlations for dizygotic twins and for normal siblings (who have half their genes in common) is closer to .50. Indeed, monozygotic twins raised in *different* households are more similar in IQ than dizygotic twins raised together in the *same* household.

3. *Adoption studies*. Adopted children are more similar intellectually to their biological parents than to their adoptive parents. This finding can be interpreted as evidence for a genetic influence on IQ, for adoptees share genes with their biological parents but not with their adoptive caregivers.

Just how heritable is IQ? The estimates vary considerably depending on the data that theorists choose to emphasize and the ways they interpret these findings. For example, Arthur Jensen (1969) and H. J. Eysenck (1981b) have focused on the family studies and inferred that 80% of the variation among IQ scores within a particular population is attributable to the genes that people inherit. Other influential behavior geneticists such as Robert Plomin (Plomin & DeFries, 1980, 1983) and Sandra Scarr (Scarr & Weinberg, 1977, 1983) have conducted adoption studies and concluded that both heredity and environment play prominent (and perhaps equal) roles in the determination of intellectual performance. Finally, Leon Kamin (1974, 1981) has taken an extreme environmentalist position, arguing that there is really no clear evidence that IQ is a heritable attribute. A brief summary and evaluation of Kamin's rather provocative viewpoint appears in Box 10-2.

Although few developmentalists would endorse Kamin's radical position, most are of the opinion that the environment is an important contributor to one's intellectual development. Let's now review some of the evidence to support this claim.

Environmental Influences

The evidence for environmental effects on intelligence comes from a variety of sources. For example, we have noted that (1) unstable home environments are associated with fluctuations in children's IQ scores and (2) there is a moderate intellectual resemblance between pairs of genetically unrelated children who live together in the same household (see Box 10-2). There are also data to indicate that living in a barren intellectual environment may inhibit cognitive growth while exposure to a more stimulating environment can have the opposite effect.

■ *The effects of an impoverished environment* Several investigators have studied the intellectual development of children who live in isolated, poverty-stricken communities where the literacy rate among adults is low and the educational facilities are substandard. Youngsters living in these impoverished settings scored far below average on standardized intelligence tests, and their IQs actually decreased with age (Ascher, 1935; Gordon, 1923; Sherman & Key, 1932; Wheeler, 1932). Otto Klineberg (1963) has proposed a **"cumulative deficit" hypothesis** to explain these findings. According to Klineberg's cumulative-deficit theory, impoverished environments inhibit intellectual growth, and these inhibiting effects will accumulate over time. Consequently, the longer children remain in a barren intellectual environment, the more poorly they will perform on standardized IQ tests.

Arthur Jensen (1977) tested the cumulative-deficit hypothesis by comparing the intellectual performance of economically disadvantaged Black siblings living in California and Georgia. Jensen proposed that if a "cumulative deficit" mechanism is operating, older siblings should obtain lower IQs than their younger brothers and sisters. This is precisely what he found for children in the Georgia sample, whose environmental disadvantages were markedly greater than those of the California group.[3]

■ *Effects of environmental enrichment*

Can we promote intellectual development by enriching the environment in which children live? Apparently so, if the results of two studies of isolated mountain children are any guide (Wheeler, 1932, 1942). When children from a mountain community in Eastern Tennessee were first tested, in the early 1930s, they obtained an average IQ of 82. Ten years later, the children in this same community were retested. During the interval between testings, this community had changed in many ways: roads had been built, the school system had been drastically overhauled, and economic conditions had improved to the point that most people could now afford radios. In other words, this formerly isolated and impoverished community was coming into the social and economic mainstream of American life. As a result, the average IQ of children there rose by 11 points (from 82 to 93) in the ten years between testings. Other studies conducted in Hawaii and the American Midwest found similar increases in children's intellectual performance in communities

where dramatic social and educational improvements had taken place (Finch, 1946; Smith, 1942).

Other investigators have charted the intellectual growth of adopted children who had been placed in their new homes before their first birthday (Scarr & Weinberg, 1977, 1983; Skodak & Skeels, 1947, 1949). Many of these adoptees came from disadvantaged family backgrounds where their biological parents were poorly educated and somewhat below average in IQ. They were placed in middle-class homes with adoptive parents who were highly educated and above average in intelligence. By the time these adoptees were 4–7 years old, they were scoring well above average on standardized IQ tests (about 110 in Scarr and Weinberg's study and 112 in Skodak and Skeels's). In fact, their intellectual performance was considerably higher than what one would expect on the basis of the IQs and educational levels of their biological parents or the IQs of other children from disadvantaged backgrounds. Since the adopting parents were known to be highly educated and above average in intelligence, it seems reasonable to assume that they were providing enriched, intellectually stimulating home environments that fostered the cognitive development of their adoptive children.

As these studies clearly indicate, the environment is a powerful force that may either promote or inhibit intellectual growth. Yet the term *environment* is a very global concept, and the evidence that we have reviewed does not really tell us which of the many life experiences that children have are most likely to affect their intellectual development. In the next section of the chapter, we will take a closer look at environmental influences and see that a child's performance on IQ tests depends to some extent on the child-rearing practices used by parents, the structure and socioeconomic status of the family, and perhaps even the racial or ethnic group to which the family belongs.

---

[3]The California children showed a small cumulative deficit on tests of verbal IQ but no age-related performance deficits on tests of nonverbal IQ.

---

cumulative-deficit hypothesis: *the notion that impoverished environments inhibit intellectual growth and that these inhibiting effects accumulate over time.*

Princeton psychologist Leon Kamin (1974, 1981) has examined the "evidence" for the heritability of intelligence and concluded that these data are flawed and inconclusive. His argument centers on the following observations:

The problem with twin studies. Perhaps the strongest evidence for a genetic contribution to intelligence comes from twin studies. Monozygotic (MZ) twins, who have identical genotypes, are much more similar intellectually than dizygotic (DZ) twins, who have only half their genes in common. In fact, the IQ scores for pairs of MZ twins reared *apart* are more highly correlated than those of DZ twins reared *together*. As Eysenck has noted, *"IQs of identical twins reared apart . . . are perhaps the most cogent evidence in favor of the genetic determination of intelligence. . . . If the genetic case rested on just one kind of support, this would be the one chosen by most experts"* (cited in Kamin, 1981, p.106).

Kamin (1981) offers several criticisms of the twin studies. He begins by noting that the most widely cited of these projects appears to have been a fraud. He then reviews the remaining "separated twin" studies and finds each to have important shortcomings. The most serious of these problems was that separated MZ twins were typically placed in very similar home environments; and this practice,

> no less than identical genes, might easily be responsible for the [separated twins'] resemblance in IQ. We cannot guess what the IQ correlation might be if . . . we separated pairs of identical twins at birth and scattered them at random across the full range of available environments. It could conceivably be zero—which would force us to conclude that the heritability of IQ is zero [Kamin, 1981, p. 113].

To carry the argument one step further, Kamin suggests that MZ twins raised together are treated alike and share a nearly identical home environment,

whereas DZ twins (who may be of different sexes) are often treated very differently by their families. The implication of this line of reasoning is that twin studies overestimate the heritability of IQ. If MZ twins experience more similar environments than DZ twins do, then perhaps it is their "identical environments," rather than their identical genes, that explain why they are so similar in intelligence.

Reinterpreting the adoption studies. We've noted that adopted children bear a closer intellectual resemblance to their biological parents than to their adoptive parents. Since adoptees share genes with their biological parents, this finding seems to indicate that intelligence is a heritable attribute.

Kamin challenges this interpretation by suggesting that the IQ correlation between adoptees and their biological parents is the result of *selective placement.* The idea here is that adoption agencies will try to place infants in homes that are quite similar to the home environments of their biological parents. So if a child's IQ is determined largely by the home environment, and the adoption agency is successful in matching the home environments of biological and adoptive parents, then there will be an inevitable and highly spurious correlation between the IQs of adoptees and those of their biological parents (Kamin, 1974).

According to Kamin (1981), the most conclusive adoption studies are those of adoptive families who have also had a biological child of their own. These studies are interesting because they allow one to determine the correlations between parents' IQs and those of both their adopted and their biological children. Now, adoptees and natural children have been raised in the same household by the same parents. So if IQ is a highly heritable attribute, the IQ correlations between parents and their biological children should be much greater than those between parents and their adopted children.

The table shows the results of the two studies that have used this improved design. Note that, in both

SOCIOCULTURAL CORRELATES OF INTELLECTUAL PERFORMANCE

When searching for social/cultural variables that may affect intellectual performance, it makes some sense to start with the first social system to which children are exposed—the family.

The Home Environment as a Determinant of Intellectual Growth

We have suggested that the quality of the home environment plays an important role in determining how well children perform on IQ tests. Recently, Bettye Caldwell and Robert Bradley have developed an instrument called the **HOME**

Mother/child and sibling/sibling IQ correlations in adoptive families with one or more biological children

	Texas study	Minnesota study
Mother/child comparisons		
Mother/biological child	.20 ($N = 162$)	.34 ($N = 100$)
Mother/adopted child	.22 ($N = 151$)	.29 ($N = 66$)
Sibling/sibling comparisons		
Biological/biological pairs	.35 ($N = 46$)	.37 ($N = 75$)
Biological/adopted pairs	.29 ($N = 167$)	.30 ($N = 134$)
Adopted/adopted pairs	—	.49 ($N = 21$)

Note: N = the number of pairs on which each correlation is based.

the Texas and the Minnesota studies, the intellectual resemblance between mothers and their biological children is not appreciably greater than that between mothers and their adoptive children. Thus, "children who are reared by the same mother resemble her in IQ to the same degree, whether or not they share her genes" (Kamin, 1981, p. 119). This finding suggested to Kamin that the heritability of IQ is very low.

Kamin then reinforces his conclusion by comparing the IQs of adopted and biological children raised in the same homes. As the table shows, the IQ correlations between pairs of biological siblings are not appreciably higher than those between pairs of biological and adopted siblings. So *whether or not they share common genes, two children who are raised in the same environment resemble each other in IQ to about the same degree.* Kamin (1981) concludes that

> this review of adoption studies . . . has failed to yield convincing evidence for the heritability of IQ. Though early studies appeared to suggest a high heritability, . . . they also ignored the profound [and confounding] effects of selective placement. With improved designs and increased sophistication of analysis, the more recent studies of adoption produce a radically lower estimate of heritability. In fact, the possibility cannot be excluded that IQ heritability is actually zero [p. 125].

An evaluation of Kamin's perspective. Although Kamin's critiques have convinced many developmentalists that the environment plays a prominent role in determining IQ, most are unwilling to accept his premise that the heritability of intelligence is close to zero. Consider Kamin's argument that separated twins are placed in similar home environments. Although this may well be true, it seems somewhat implausible to argue that the home environments of *MZ* twins *raised apart* are more similar than those of *DZ* twins *who live together*. Yet the IQ correlations for pairs of separated MZ twins (about .75) are substantially higher than those for DZ twins who live in the same home (about .50)—a finding that indicates IQ is a heritable attribute. Kamin also makes little of the fact that the father/child IQ correlations in recent adoption studies are much higher for father/biological-child pairings (about .31) than for father/adopted-child pairings (about .10)—a finding that again suggests IQ is a heritable attribute.

In sum, Kamin is undoubtedly correct in arguing that much of the early research overestimated the heritability of IQ. However, a careful examination of all the literature suggests that (1) there are clear genetic influences on intellectual performance and (2) Kamin badly overstates the case when arguing that compelling evidence for these influences does not exist.

inventory (Home Observation for Measurement of the Environment) that allows an interviewer/observer to visit an infant or a preschool child at home and to gain a good idea of just how intellectually stimulating (or impoverished) that home environment is (Caldwell & Bradley, 1978). The HOME inventory consists of 45 statements, each of which is scored *yes* (the statement is true

of this family) or *no* (the statement is not true of this family). In order to gather the information to complete the inventory, the researcher will (1) ask

> **HOME inventory:** *a measure of the amount and type of intellectual stimulation provided by a child's home environment.*

the child's parent (usually the mother) to describe her daily routine and child-rearing practices, (2) carefully observe the parent as she interacts with her child, and (3) note the kinds of play materials that the parent makes available to the child. The 45 bits of information collected are then grouped into the six categories, or subscales, that appear in Table 10-6. The home then receives a score on each subscale. The higher the scores across all six subscales, the more intellectually stimulating the home environment.

■ *Does the HOME predict IQ?*

As it turns out, there is a clear relationship between the quality of the home environment, as measured by the HOME, and children's performance on IQ tests. In fact, both Bradley and Caldwell (1976) and Helen Bee and her associates (1982) found that the quality of the home environment measured when children were either 6 or 12 months of age is a better predictor of their IQs at ages 3 and 4 than is their own first-year performance on infant intelligence tests.

Which aspects of the home environment are most important for furthering the child's intellectual development? As we see in Table 10-7, all the HOME subscales seem to be important, although the pattern differs somewhat for boys and girls. Boys who obtain high IQs have mothers who are highly involved with them and who provide an orderly environment with lots of age-appropriate toys. And although these same factors are equally important for the intellectual development of girls, the girls who score highest on IQ tests are also likely to have responsive and nonpunitive caregivers who provide them with a variety of new experiences on a regular basis (Bradley & Caldwell, 1980).

The quality of a mother's language may also make a difference. Patrick Dickson and his associates (Dickson, Hess, Miyake, & Azuma, 1979) asked American and Japanese mothers to describe a series of abstract pictures to their 4-year-olds. After hearing each description, the child was to select the picture the mother had described from a set of four similar pictures. Of course, a child's

---

TABLE 10-6. Subscales and sample items from the HOME inventory

Subscale 1: Emotional and Verbal Responsivity of the Mother (11 items)
  Sample items: Mother responds to child's vocalizations with a verbal response
            Mother's speech is clear, distinct, and audible
            Mother caresses or kisses child at least once during visit

Subscale 2: Avoidance of Restriction and Punishment (8 items)
  Sample items: Mother neither slaps nor spanks child during visit
            Mother does not scold or derogate child during visit
            Mother does not interfere with the child's actions or restrict child's movements more than three times during visit

Subscale 3: Organization of Physical and Temporal Environment (6 items)
  Sample items: Child gets out of house at least four times a week
            Child's play environment appears safe and free of hazards

Subscale 4: Provision of Appropriate Play Materials (9 items)
  Sample items: Child has push or pull toy
            Parents provide learning equipment appropriate to age—mobile, table and chairs, highchair, playpen, and so on
            Mother provides toys or interesting activities for child during interview

Subscale 5: Maternal Involvement with Child (6 items)
  Sample items: Mother "talks" to child while doing her work
            Mother structures the child's play periods

Subscale 6: Opportunities for Variety in Daily Stimulation (5 items)
  Sample items: Father provides some caretaking every day
            Mother reads stories at least three times weekly
            Child has three or more books of his own

PHOTO 10-3. *Contrasting home environments. The photograph at the left shows an orderly home environment, and one in which family members are warm, responsive, and eager to be involved with one another. This is precisely the kind of setting that seems to promote children's intellectual development. In the photograph at the right we see an example of a barren, disorderly, and unattractive home environment—one that is likely to inhibit intellectual development.*

ability to identify the correct picture will depend on how well the mother describes its distinguishing features—that is, her **referential communication accuracy**. Dickson and his colleagues found that a mother's communication accuracy as assessed when her child was 4 years old predicted the child's IQ at age 6. Moreover, the size of the correlation between the mothers' communication skills and their children's later IQ scores was the same (about .60) in both the American and the Japanese samples. So it appears that a mother who communicates information clearly

and accurately is making an important contribution to her child's intellectual development.

Other investigators have found that students who make good grades and who score high on IQ tests have parents who emphasize achievement and are actively involved in their children's learning activities (Crandall & Battle, 1970; Hanson, 1975; Sontag, Baker, & Nelson, 1958).

In sum, an intellectually stimulating home environment is one in which parents are warm, responsive, and eager to be involved with their child. They describe new objects, concepts, and experiences clearly and accurately, and they provide the child with a variety of play materials that are appropriate for her age or developmental level. They encourage the child to ask questions, to solve problems, and to think about what she is learning. As the child matures and enters school, they stress the importance of academic achievement and expect her to get good grades. When you stop and think about it, it is not at all surprising that children from these "enriched" home settings

TABLE 10-7. Correlations between HOME scores at 12 months of age and children's IQs at age 3

HOME subscale	Boys	Girls
Responsivity of Mother	.27[a]	.49[a]
Avoidance of Restriction and Punishment	.03	.37[a]
Organization of Environment	.40[a]	.46[a]
Play Materials	.61[a]	.55[a]
Maternal Involvement	.41[a]	.53[a]
Variety in Stimulation	.19	.42[a]
Total HOME score	.36[a]	.53[a]

[a]This aspect of the home environment was a significant predictor of IQ scores at 3 years of age.

referential communication accuracy: *a measure of a person's tendency to communicate clearly and accurately with another person.*

often have very high IQs; after all, their parents are obviously concerned about their cognitive development and have spent several years encouraging them to acquire new information and to practice many of the cognitive skills that are measured on intelligence tests.

■ *Is the home environment really all that important?*

Langdon Longstreth and his associates (1981) have argued that *bright* mothers are likely to provide the most intellectually stimulating home environments. One implication of this point of view is that any correlation between the quality of the home environment and children's intellectual performance may simply reflect a hidden *genetic* effect on intelligence—that is, intelligent mothers

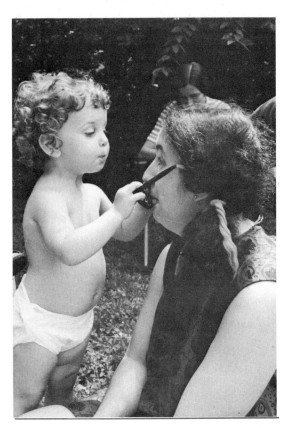

PHOTO 10-4. *Some studies have shown that there is a correlation between a mother's communication skills and her children's later IQ scores.*

(who just happen to provide stimulating home environments) have intelligent offspring. If this view is correct, it is possible that the quality of the home environment has few if any direct effects on children's intellectual development.

Recently, Keith Yeates and his colleagues (Yeates, MacPhee, Campbell, & Ramey, 1983) evaluated this hypothesis in a longitudinal study of 112 mothers and their 2–4-year-old children. The mothers' IQs were measured just before the birth of their children, and the children's IQs were measured at 24, 36, and 48 months of age. The HOME inventory was used to assess the quality of the families' home environments when the children were 6, 18, 30, and 42 months of age. By using a statistical procedure called multiple regression, Yeates and his associates were able to determine whether the home environment had any effect on children's IQ scores beyond that predicted on the basis of their mothers' IQs.

The results of this study were interesting and rather complex. The best predictor of a child's IQ at age 24 months was the mother's IQ, and the quality of the home environment had little if any direct effect on the intellectual performance of these toddlers. This finding is quite consistent with Longstreth's genetic reinterpretation of "home environment" effects. However, the picture had changed by the time the children were 4 years old. Now the quality of the home environment not only predicted their IQ scores but was actually a better predictor than maternal IQ. So we see that the home environment is truly an important factor in a child's intellectual development. It also seems that these environmental effects may accumulate over time, so that the full impact of the parent's behavior on the child's IQ may not be apparent until the child is 4 or older.

Effects of Birth Order and the Family Configuration

Two other "family" characteristics that seem to affect children's performance on IQ tests are *family size* and the child's position within the family, or *birth order*. These effects are clearly illustrated in a large-scale study conducted in Holland (Belmont & Marolla, 1973). The investigators had a very large data base indeed—the military records of 386,114 males who represented nearly the entire population of young men born in Holland

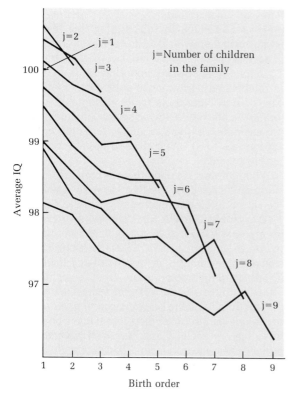

FIGURE 10-4. *Average scores on a nonverbal measure of intelligence as a function of the examinee's birth order and the size of his family. Note that subjects from smaller families score higher on this test than subjects from large families. We also see that, within a given family size, children born early tend to obtain higher IQs than those born late.*

between 1944 and 1947. Data available for each man included an IQ score and other biographical information that was used to determine his social class, birth order, and family size. Controlling for both social class and birth order, Belmont and Marolla found that family size had a significant effect on IQ. As we see in Figure 10-4, *the brightest children tended to come from the smaller families*. When Belmont and Marolla then looked at the effects of birth order within any given family size, they found a clear birth-order effect: on the average, *first-borns outperformed second-borns, who outperformed third-borns*, and so on down the line. These findings are not unique to Dutch males—they have now been replicated in samples of males and females from several countries

(Berbaum & Moreland, 1980; Markus & Zajonc, 1977).

One possible explanation for these birth-order and family-size effects is that first-borns and children from small families may receive more intellectual stimulation from their parents than do later-borns and children from large families. A study by Mary Rothbart (1971) is certainly relevant. Rothbart asked 56 mothers to supervise the performance of their 5-year-olds on a series of achievement tasks. Half the children were first-borns and half later-borns. To control for family size, Rothbart selected her participants from two-child families in which both children were the same sex. Experimental sessions were tape-recorded to determine whether mothers were behaving differently toward first-borns and later-borns while supervising their performance.

Rothbart discovered that mothers spent an equal amount of time interacting with first-born and later-born children. However, the quality of the interaction differed: Mothers gave more complex technical explanations to the first-borns. In addition, mothers put more pressure on first-borns to achieve and were more anxious about their performance. When Rothbart then looked at the children's performance, she found that first-borns attained higher scores than later-borns on all but one of the experimental tasks. These findings are clearly consistent with the notion that first-borns receive more direct achievement training from their parents than later-borns.

■ *Zajonc's hypothesis on family-size and birth-order effects*

Robert Zajonc (1975; Zajonc & Markus, 1975; Zajonc, Markus, & Markus, 1979) has proposed a slightly different explanation for these birth-order and family-size effects. According to Zajonc's theory, a child's intellectual development depends on the *average intellectual level of all family members*, including the child himself. Clearly, first-borns should have an advantage because they are initially exposed *only* to adults, whose intellectual levels are very high. In contrast, a second child experiences a less stimulating intellectual environment because she must deal with a cognitively immature older sibling as well as with her parents. The third child is further disadvantaged by the presence of *two* relatively immature older siblings. Zajonc (1975) suggests that

> with each additional child, the family's intellectual environment depreciates. . . . Children who grow up surrounded by people with higher intellectual levels [that is, first-borns and children from small families] have a better chance to achieve their maximum intellectual powers than . . . children from large families who spend more time in a world of child-sized minds . . . , develop more slowly, and therefore attain lower IQs [p. 39].

Although Zajonc's theory is appealing for its simplicity, its predictions do not always ring true. For example, children who grow up in homes with *three* mature adults (say, two parents and a grandparent) should score higher on IQ tests than those who are exposed only to their parents; yet they don't (Brackbill & Nichols, 1982). Moreover, longer intervals between births should be to the advantage of both older and younger siblings. When children are widely spaced, the older sib has more time alone with parents, and the younger child is exposed to a much older child companion who is now reasonably mature. However, at least two recent studies have failed to confirm Zajonc's "sibling spacing" hypothesis (Brackbill & Nichols, 1982; Galbraith, 1982). So even though Zajonc's theory is an interesting explanation for birth-order and family-size effects on intelligence, it remains for future research to firmly establish its usefulness.

Finally, a caution is in order. These birth-order and family-size effects tend to be quite small and are observed only when large numbers of families are compared. Hence, the trends that emerge for the population as a whole may not apply to the members of any *particular* family. Clearly not all first-borns are brighter than average; nor do all later-borns score lower in IQ than their older brothers and sisters.

■ Intellectual development in a single-parent household

Are children raised in a single-parent home at an intellectual disadvantage? Zajonc's theory suggests that they are, for they have only one parent to provide intellectual stimulation.

Most of the early research (reviewed in Shinn, 1978) found that children from single-parent homes did indeed score lower on IQ tests than their age mates from two-parent families. But there is a problem in interpreting this research because single-parent families are generally lower in socioeconomic status than two-parent families. Therefore, it is quite possible that the decrements in intellectual performance among children from single-parent homes are really attributable to factors associated with lower socioeconomic status (for example, having less money for books or age-appropriate toys) rather than to the absence of a second parent.

Which of these explanations is correct? The results of two recent studies seem to favor the "social status" interpretation (Brackbill & Nichols, 1982; Svanum, Bringle, & McGlaughlin, 1982). For example, when we consider only those children *within a particular social class*, then those from single-parent families do *not* score any lower on IQ tests than their counterparts from intact homes. These findings suggest (1) that there may be no distinct intellectual disadvantages to growing up in a single-parent home but (2) that one's position in society, or social class, may well have an important effect on intellectual development.

Social-Class, Racial, and Ethnic Differences in IQ

One of the most reliable findings in the intelligence literature is that children from lower- and working-class homes average some 10–20 points below their middle-class age mates on standardized intelligence tests. Infants are apparently the only exception to this rule, as Mark Golden and his associates find no social-class differences in intellectual performance for children less than 2 years old (Golden & Birns, 1976; Golden, Birns, Bridger, & Moss, 1971).

Which abilities are most affected by one's class standing? It appears that those associated with academic performance (for example, verbal, numerical, and spatial abilities) are more closely related to social status. By contrast, social-class differences in mental abilities such as memory and reasoning are negligible or nonexistent (Globerson, 1983; Minton & Schneider, 1980).

There are also racial and ethnic differences in intellectual performance. In the United States, for example, children of Black, Native American, or Hispanic ancestry tend to score well below the White norms on standardized intelligence tests

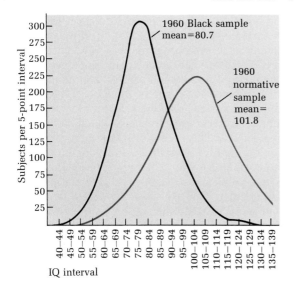

FIGURE 10-5. *IQ distributions on the Stanford-Binet for the 1960 normative sample of White schoolchildren and for 1800 Black schoolchildren living in the Southeast.*

(Minton & Schneider, 1980; Tyler, 1965). One team of investigators (Kennedy, van de Reit, & White, 1963) administered the Stanford-Binet to 1800 Black elementary school children living in the Southeastern United States. As we see in Figure 10-5, these youngsters obtained an average IQ of 80.7, compared with the White average of 101.8. Black children living in the North or in metropolitan areas of the South do perform better on intelligence tests, obtaining an average IQ of about 85–88. Nevertheless, they continue to score some 12–15 IQ points lower than their White age mates (Loehlin, Lindzey, & Spuhler, 1975).

Before we try to interpret these social-class, racial, and ethnic differences, an important truth is worth stating here—one that is often overlooked when people discover that White children outperform their Black or Hispanic classmates on IQ tests. This "important truth" is that we cannot predict anything about the IQ or the future accomplishments of an *individual* on the basis of his ethnicity or color. As we see in Figure 10-5, the IQ distributions show considerable overlap between the Black and the White samples. So even though the average IQ of Blacks is somewhat lower than that of Whites, the overlapping distributions mean that many Black children obtain higher IQ scores than many White children. In

fact, approximately 15–25% of the Black population scores higher—in many cases, substantially higher—than *half* of the White population (Shuey, 1966).

Why Do Groups Differ in Intellectual Performance?

Over the years, psychologists have proposed three hypotheses to account for racial, ethnic, and social-class differences in IQ: (1) a *test bias* hypothesis, which argues that standardized IQ tests do not adequately measure the intellectual capabilities of lower-class children or those from minority subcultures, (2) a *genetic* hypothesis, which implies that group differences in IQ are hereditary, and (3) an *environmental* hypothesis, which states that the groups scoring lower in IQ come from culturally deprived backgrounds—that is, neighborhoods and home environments that are far less conducive to intellectual growth than those typically experienced by members of the middle class.

■ The test-bias hypothesis

Those who favor the **"test bias" hypothesis** believe that group differences in IQ are an artifact of our testing procedures. They point out that the IQ tests now in use were designed to measure the cognitive skills of the White middle class and were never formally standardized on people from minority subcultures. When such a test is then given to youngsters with different values, interests, and customs, there is almost certain to be a built-in "cultural bias" that makes the instrument a less than adequate measure of their intellectual capabilities (Minton & Schneider, 1980; Sarason, 1973).

IQ tests probably are culturally biased to some extent. For example, it has been argued that subtests measuring vocabulary and word usage may be harder for Blacks and Hispanics, who often speak a different English dialect from that of the White middle class. Not only might these children

---

"test bias" hypothesis: *the notion that IQ tests have a built-in, middle-class bias that explains the substandard performance of children from lower-class and minority subcultures.*

be working under a linguistic handicap while trying to understand the test instructions, but many common words do not even have the same meanings for Blacks and Hispanics as for Whites. Moreover, the content of general-information subtests is based largely on concepts and experiences that may be more familiar to White, middle-class examinees than to their disadvantaged age mates (for example, "What is a 747?"). Adrian Dove, a Black sociologist, has attempted to illustrate the kinds of biases that minority children encounter on IQ tests by constructing his own "culturally biased" test—one that relies very heavily on the language and experiences of American Blacks (see Table 10-8). If this test were to be interpreted as a valid measure of intellectual performance, the average Black would undoubtedly obtain a higher IQ score than most Whites.

Does "test bias" explain group differences in IQ? Even though standardized intelligence tests have a distinct middle-class flavor, there are

---

TABLE 10-8. Sample items from Dove's Counterbalance General "Intelligence" Test (the "Chitling Test")

1. Cheap chitlings (not the kind you purchase at a frozen food counter) will taste rubbery unless they are cooked long enough. How soon can you quit cooking them to eat and enjoy them? (A) 45 minutes, (B) 2 hours, (C) 24 hours, (D) one week (on a low flame), (E) 1 hour

2. A "handkerchief head" is: (A) a cool cat, (B) a porter, (C) an Uncle Tom, (D) a preacher

3. A "gas head" is a person who has a: (A) fast-moving car, (B) stable of "lace," (C) "process," (D) habit of stealing cars, (E) long jail record for arson

4. "Hully Gully" came from: (A) East Oakland, (B) Filmore, (C) Watts, (D) Harlem, (E) Motor City

5. If you throw the dice and a seven is showing on the top, what is facing down? (A) seven, (B) snake eyes, (C) boxcars, (D) little Joes, (E) eleven

6. T-Bone Walker got famous for playing what? (A) trombone, (B) piano, (C) "T-flute," (D) guitar, (E) "Hambone"

Correct answers: 1, C; 2, C; 3, C; 4, C; 5, A; 6, D. How did you do on this test?

---

reasons to believe that group differences in IQ are not solely attributable to test bias. Several attempts have now been made to construct **"culture-fair" IQ tests** that do not place poor people or those from minority subcultures at an immediate disadvantage. For example, the *Raven Progressive Matrices Test* requires the examinee to scan a series of abstract designs, each of which has a missing section. The examinee's task is to complete each design by selecting the appropriate section from a number of alternatives (see Figure 10-6). These problems are assumed to be equally familiar (or unfamiliar) to people from all ethnic groups and social classes. There is no time limit on the test, and the instructions are very simple. But despite such attempts to eliminate cultural bias from the test content, middle-class Whites continue to outperform their lower-class and/or Black age mates on these "culture-fair" measures of intelligence (Anastasi, 1976; Jensen, 1980).

Other investigators have tried to reduce test bias by administering IQ tests in the dialects that children speak and understand. In one study (Quay, 1971), two versions of the Stanford-Binet were given to groups of urban Black preschool children. One version was administered in standard English; the second was translated into the Black English dialect that these children spoke at home. The two groups' performances were virtually identical. Evidently the middle-class dialect used to administer intelligence tests is not the critical factor that explains Black/White differences in IQ.

Finally, IQ tests and various tests of intellectual aptitude (such as the Scholastic Aptitude Test) predict future academic successes just as well for Blacks and other minorities as they do for Whites (Cleary, Humphries, Kendrick, & Wesman, 1975; Cole, 1981). Here, then, is another line of evidence that group differences in IQ are not entirely the result of biases in our tests or testing procedures.

Zigler's motivational hypothesis. Edward Zigler and his associates (Zigler, Abelson, Trickett, & Seitz, 1982) believe that social-class and ethnic differences in IQ are largely attributable to motivational factors. Presumably, lower-class and minority children score lower than they should on IQ tests because they tend to be wary of strange examiners and see little point in trying to do well on abstract and seemingly irrelevant test items—

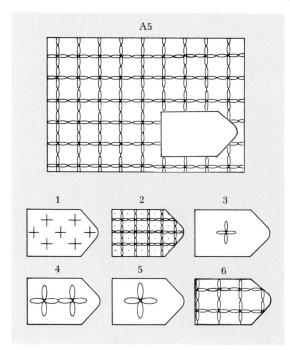

FIGURE 10-6. An item similar to those appearing in the Raven Progressive Matrices Test.

particularly if they have a history of academic failure and are anxious in testing situations.

Attempts to increase the motivation of these children by first allowing them time to play with a friendly examiner (or by mixing easy items with the harder ones to prevent examinees from becoming discouraged by a long string of errors) have a clear effect on test performance: disadvantaged children score some 7–10 points higher than they normally would when tested in the traditional way by a strange examiner (Zigler et al., 1982; Zigler & Butterfield, 1968). But as it turns out, middle-class youngsters also score higher on IQ tests when tested by a friendly examiner (Sacks, 1952). The implications of this latter finding are that (1) *all* children perform better when taking intelligence tests under optimal conditions, so that (2) Zigler's motivational hypothesis is not a totally adequate explanation for group *differences* in IQ.

■ *The genetic hypothesis*

The most controversial explanation for group differences in intelligence is that they are hereditary.

Those who favor the **genetic hypothesis** note that members of various social-class, ethnic, and racial groups tend to marry within their own populations rather than mating with outsiders. Although this selective mating is obviously not universal, it will nevertheless result in a restriction in the gene flow between subgroups if it continues over many generations. In other words, the argument is that people in various racial, ethnic, and social-class groupings have genotypes drawn from different gene pools. Presumably these gene pools differ in the frequency and distribution of the genes that determine IQ.

Perhaps the strongest proponent of this genetic interpretation is Arthur Jensen of the University of California (Jensen, 1969, 1980). Jensen believes that there are two kinds of intellectual abilities, which are equally heritable within different subgroups of the population. **Level I abilities** include attentional processes, short-term memory, and associative skills—abilities that are important for simple kinds of rote learning. **Level II abilities** are those that allow one to reason abstractly and to manipulate words and symbols to form concepts and solve problems. According to Jensen, Level II abilities are highly correlated with school achievement, while Level I abilities are not. Of course, it is predominantly Level II abilities that are measured on IQ tests.

Jensen finds that Level I tasks are performed equally well by children from all races, ethnic groups, and social classes. However, middle-class and White children outperform lower-class and Black children on the more advanced Level II tasks. Since Level I and Level II tasks are equally heritable *within* each social class and ethnic

"culture-fair" tests: *intelligence tests constructed to minimize any irrelevant cultural biases that could influence test performance.*

genetic hypothesis: *the notion that group differences in IQ are hereditary.*

level I abilities: *Jensen's term for lower-level intellectual abilities (such as attention and short-term memory) that are important for simple association learning.*

level II abilities: *Jensen's term for higher-level cognitive skills that are involved in abstract reasoning and problem solving.*

Let's suppose that a group of White children obtain an average IQ of 101 and their Black classmates average 87 on the same test. Further, we will assume that the heritability estimates for the Black and the White populations are comparable. Jensen might use these data to argue that the 14-point difference in IQ between the White and the Black children is attributable to the genetic differences between Blacks and Whites. On the surface, this reasoning seems to make sense because IQ is equally heritable within each group.

However, the argument is flawed. Let's recall that heritability is the amount of variation in a trait that is attributable to genetic factors. If two groups have comparable heritability estimates for a trait, this simply means that, *within* each group, the amount of variability on that trait that is attributable to genetic factors is approximately the same. It says nothing about any differences *between* the groups on that trait.

An example should clarify the point. Suppose a farmer randomly draws corn seed from a bag containing several genetic varieties. He then plants half the seed in a barren field and half in soil that is quite fertile. When the plants are fully grown, the farmer discovers that those *within* each field have grown to different heights. Since all plants within each field were grown in the same soil, their different heights reflect the genetic variability among the seeds that were planted. Therefore, the heritability estimates for plants within each plot should be very high. But notice that the plants grown in the fertile soil are taller, on the average, than those grown in the barren soil. The most logical explanation for this *between-field variation* is an environmental one: plants grown in fertile soil simply grew taller than those grown in barren soil, and this is true even though the heritability estimates for the heights of the plants *within* each field are comparable (Lewontin, 1976).

Why within-group differences do not necessarily imply anything about between-group differences. Here we see that the difference in the heights of the plants within each field reflects the genetic variation in the seeds that were planted there, whereas the difference in the average *heights of the plants across the fields is attributable to an environmental factor—the soils in which they were grown.*

The same argument can be applied in explaining group differences in intellectual performance. Even though the heritability estimates for IQ are comparable *within* our samples of Black and White schoolchildren, the 14-point difference in average IQ *between* the groups may reflect differences in the home environments of Blacks and Whites rather than a genetic difference between the races.

group, Jensen proposes that the IQ differences *between* groups must be hereditary.

Criticisms of the genetic hypothesis.
Although Jensen's arguments may sound convincing, there are reasons to believe that genetic influences do not explain group differences in IQ. For example, Jensen's critics have noted that within-group heritability estimates imply absolutely nothing about between-group variability in an attribute (Layzer, 1972; Lewontin, 1976). As we see in the examples in Box 10-3, it is possible for individual differences *within* a group to be entirely genetic in character while differences *between* two groups are largely the result of the environments in which they are raised.

Now let's consider the idea that, owing to selective mating, members of different groups come from populations that differ in the frequency and distribution of IQ-determining genes. If this were true, we would have to assume that groups scoring low on IQ tests have fewer of these "smart genes" in their gene pool than groups that score high. Therefore, if members of a low-scoring group, such as Blacks, were to mate with members of a high-scoring group, such as Whites, the children they produce should inherit an intermediate number of IQ-determining genes and score somewhere between the Black and the White norms on IQ tests.

Data available on mixed-race children provide little support for the genetic hypothesis. Eyferth (as cited in Loehlin et al., 1975) obtained the IQ scores of illegitimate German children fathered by Black American servicemen. These mixed-race children were then compared with a group of illegitimate White children of the same age and social background. Clearly, the mixed-race group should have scored lower than their White age mates if their Black fathers had had fewer IQ-determining genes to pass along to them. However, Eyferth found that these two groups of illegitimate children did not differ in IQ.

If the genetic hypothesis were correct, we might also predict that Blacks who score extremely high on IQ tests would have a higher percentage of White ancestors than would Blacks who obtain lower IQs. Yet at least one study of extremely bright Black children found that these youngsters had no more White ancestors than is typical for the Black population as a whole (Witty & Jenkins, 1936).

Although studies of mixed-race children do not support the genetic hypothesis, neither do they disprove it. Consider, for example, that Eyferth had no data on the IQs of the Black servicemen who had fathered mixed-race children. So if these men were brighter than the average Black American, the genetic hypothesis predicts that their children would score much higher on IQ tests than mixed-race children normally do—perhaps even high enough to match the IQs of the illegitimate White children. But regardless of how we choose to interpret the results of Eyferth's study, it is worth noting that there is simply no evidence that conclusively demonstrates that group differences in IQ are genetically determined.

■ *The environmental hypothesis*

A third explanation for group differences in IQ is the **environmental hypothesis**—that poor people and members of various minority groups tend to grow up in environments that are much less conducive to intellectual development than those experienced by most Whites and other members of the middle class. As we saw in Chapter Five, many children from low-income families are undernourished—a circumstance that may inhibit brain growth and make them somewhat listless and inattentive. Moreover, low-income parents are often poorly educated and may have neither the time nor the money to provide an intellectually stimulating home environment for their children, particularly if they have several youngsters to feed, clothe, and care for. Poor people and ethnic minorities are often the targets of prejudicial and discriminatory acts that may contribute to a negative self-image and undermine their motivation to do well on tests, including IQ tests. In fact, many teachers (and some parents) expect their lower-class and minority children to perform poorly at school, and as we will see in Chapter Sixteen, these negative expectations do seem to inhibit the intellectual performances of students from disadvantaged backgrounds.

One implication of the environmental hypothesis is that disadvantaged children who score low on IQ tests should begin to show some improvement if their environments change for the better. A study by E. S. Lee (1951) is certainly relevant. Lee compared the intellectual performance of Black children who were born and raised in the Northern part of the United States (Philadelphia) with that of Blacks who had migrated from the rural South and its substandard, segregated school systems. The children who had migrated north were tested several times during the grade school years in order to assess the long-term effects of this change in their environment. As we see in Table 10-9, the IQs of Philadelphia-born Blacks remained fairly stable, whereas the IQs of Black children who had migrated from the South clearly

---

environmental hypothesis: *the notion that groups differ in IQ because the environments in which they are raised are not equally conducive to intellectual growth.*

TABLE 10-9. Average IQ of Black children as a function of length of time living in the North and attending Northern schools

Group	IQ in grade					Number of children
	1	2	4	6	9	
Philadelphia-born; attended kindergarten	97	96	97	98	97	212
Philadelphia-born; no kindergarten	92	93	95	94	94	424
Southern-born; entered Northern schools at beginning of first grade	87	89	92	93	93	182
Southern-born; entered Northern schools during first or second grade		87	88	91	91	109
Southern-born; entered Northern schools during third or fourth grade			86	87	89	199
Southern-born; entered Northern schools in fifth or sixth grade				88	90	221
Southern-born; entered Northern schools in seventh, eighth, or ninth grade					87	219

improved over time. In fact, the longer the Southern Blacks had spent in the North (and in Northern schools), the more their IQs increased.

And what happens to children from disadvantaged backgrounds who grow up in middle-class homes? Sandra Scarr and Richard Weinberg (1976, 1977, 1983) have studied 99 Black (or interracial) children who were adopted during the first year of life by White, middle-class families. The adoptive parents in these families were above average in IQ and highly educated, and many had biological children of their own. Although Scarr and Weinberg found that the Black children averaged about 6 points lower on IQ tests than the White offspring of these same families, this small racial difference seems rather insignificant when we look at the absolute performance of the transracial adoptees. As a group, the Black adoptees obtained an average IQ of 110—10 points above the average for the population as a whole and 20 points above comparable children who are raised in the Black community. Moreover, the Black adoptees from these middle-class families were also scoring well above the national average on standardized achievement tests at school. So the major findings of this study suggest that the social environment plays a dominant role in determining the average IQ of Black children. Scarr and Weinberg (1983) believe that

the high IQ scores for the black and interracial children . . . mean that (a) genetic differences do not account for a major portion of the IQ performance difference between racial groups, and (b) black and interracial children reared in the [middle-class] culture of the tests and the schools perform as well as other adopted children in similar families [p. 261].

Would disadvantaged children be "better off" if they were routinely placed in White, middle-class homes? This question is impossible to answer, for as Scarr and Weinberg (1976) note,

Our emphasis on IQ scores . . . is not an endorsement of IQ as the ultimate human value. Although important for functioning in middle-class educational environments, IQ tests do not sample a huge spectrum of human characteristics that are requisite for social adjustment. Empathy, sociability, and altruism, to name a few, are important human attributes that are not guaranteed by a high IQ. Furthermore, successful adaptation within ethnic subgroups may be less dependent on the intellectual skills tapped by IQ measures than is adaptation in middle-class white settings [p. 739].

And even if we psychologists and educators were to assume that intelligence is the ultimate human attribute, it would obviously be impractical (not to mention morally objectionable) to recommend that disadvantaged youths be taken from their parents and placed in more stimulating adoptive homes. However, there are other, less objectionable strategies that researchers have used to supplement the life experiences of disadvantaged children in the hope of furthering their intellectual and academic accomplishments. In our next section, we will take a closer look at these cognitive interventions and attempts at compensatory education.

IMPROVING INTELLECTUAL PERFORMANCE THROUGH COMPENSATORY EDUCATION

During the 1960s a number of preschool educational programs were implemented in an attempt to enrich the learning experiences of disadvantaged children. Project Head Start is perhaps the best known of these **compensatory** interventions. Simply stated, the goal of **Head Start** (and similar programs) was to provide disadvantaged children with the kinds of educational experiences that middle-class youngsters were presumably getting in their homes and nursery school classrooms. It was hoped that these early interventions would compensate for the disadvantages that these children may have already experienced and place them on a roughly equal footing with their middle-class age mates by the time they entered the first grade.

The earliest reports suggested that Head Start and comparable programs were a smashing success. Children participating in compensatory education were posting an average gain of about 10 points on IQ tests, whereas the IQs of nonparticipants from similar social backgrounds remained unchanged. However, this initial optimism soon began to wane. When program participants were reexamined after completing a year or two of grade school, the gains they had made on IQ tests had largely disappeared (Bronfenbrenner, 1975; Gray & Klaus, 1970; Klaus & Gray, 1968). In other words, few if any lasting intellectual benefits seemed to be associated with these interventions—a finding that led Arthur Jensen (1969, p. 2) to conclude that "compensatory education has been tried and it apparently has failed."

However, many investigators were reluctant to accept Jensen's conclusion. They felt that it was shortsighted to place so much emphasis on IQ scores as an index of program effectiveness. After all, the ultimate goal of compensatory education is not so much to boost IQ as to improve children's academic performance. Others have argued that the impact of these early interventions could be cumulative, so that it may be several years before children who have participated in compensatory education begin to outperform their disadvantaged classmates who did not participate.

Long-Term Follow-Ups

As it turns out, Jensen's critics may have been right on both counts. In 1982 Irving Lazar and Richard Darlington reported on the long-term effects of 11 early intervention programs implemented during the 1960s. The program participants were disadvantaged preschool children from several areas of the United States. At regular intervals throughout the grade school years, the investigators examined the participants' scholastic records and administered IQ and achievement tests. The participants and their mothers were also interviewed to determine the children's feelings of self-worth, attitudes about school and scholastic achievement, and vocational aspirations, as well as the mothers' aspirations for their children and their feelings about the children's progress at school. A very similar follow-up of Head Start participants is currently underway, and some preliminary results are now available (Collins, 1983). Briefly, these long-term follow-ups indicate the following:

1. Children who participate in early intervention programs show immediate gains on IQ tests

---

compensatory education: *special educational programs designed to further the cognitive growth and scholastic achievements of disadvantaged children.*

Head Start: *a large-scale preschool educational program designed to provide children from low-income families with a variety of social and intellectual experiences that might better prepare them for school.*

and other indicators of cognitive development, whereas nonparticipants from similar social backgrounds do not. Although the cognitive gains may persist for three to four years after the program has ended, participants and nonparticipants do not differ in IQ by the time they reach junior high school.

2. Program participants tend to score somewhat higher than nonparticipants on tests of reading, language, and mathematics achievement. In addition, there is some evidence that the "achievement gap" between participants and nonparticipants widens between the first and the eighth grades.

3. Program participants are more likely to meet their school's basic requirements. In other words, they are less likely to be assigned to special education classes or to be retained in grade than their low-income classmates who did not participate in compensatory education. Program participants are also less likely than nonparticipants to drop out of high school.

4. Compensatory education seems to have long-term effects on children's attitudes about achievement. When asked to indicate something they have done that has made them feel proud of themselves, program participants are more likely than nonparticipants to mention their scholastic or (in the case of 15–18-year-olds) job-related successes.

5. Finally, compensatory education seems to affect maternal attitudes. Mothers of program participants are more satisfied with their children's school performance and hold higher occupational aspirations for their children than mothers of nonparticipants.

In sum, the longitudinal evaluations suggest that compensatory education has been tried and *apparently it works!* Although these programs rarely produce long-term gains in IQ, they clearly foster positive attitudes about achievement and improve children's chances of succeeding in the classroom. In fact, the lasting educational benefits of these early interventions have been sufficiently impressive to persuade the Reagan administration to stand behind and continue to fund compensatory education during an era of severe cutbacks in other social programs (Collins, 1983).

Home-Based Interventions

Some of the most successful of all the interventions are those that begin rather early and take place in the home so that parents are involved in the child's learning experiences. One notable example of a **home-based intervention** is Phyllis Levenstein's (1970) "toy demonstration" program. Levenstein worked with disadvantaged 2-year-olds and their mothers. About twice a week, members of Levenstein's research team visited participants' homes to deliver various educational toys and books. During these half-hour visits, the researcher showed the mother how to use these materials to stimulate her child. Children who took part gained an average of 17 IQ points during the seven months that the program was in effect, whereas disadvantaged "nonparticipants" showed no changes in IQ over the same period. And was this merely a temporary gain? Apparently not, for follow-up evaluations conducted during the fourth, fifth, and sixth grades revealed that Levenstein's program participants were still outperforming the disadvantaged nonparticipants on measures of IQ and academic achievement (see Lazar & Darlington, 1982).

An important advantage of a home-based intervention is that parents who become more competent at stimulating their children may then continue to provide intellectually stimulating experiences long after the program formally ends. Indeed, this may be the reason that participants in Levenstein's project showed *long-term* gains in IQ. It may also explain why the younger brothers and sisters of program participants often benefit from home-based enrichment programs (Bronfenbrenner, 1975; Madden, Levenstein, & Levenstein, 1976).

Another type of home intervention is the "discussion group" technique, in which small groups of low-income mothers meet regularly with a trained group leader to present their parenting problems and learn about various methods of stimulating their children. Diana Slaughter (1983) finds that the discussion-group approach is just as effective as a toy-demonstration program at fostering the intellectual development of preschool children. Yet the outcomes *for mothers* seemed to be better in the discussion-group approach. At the end of her two-year study, Slaughter found that mothers who had experienced social support from other mothers in the context of group discussions were (1) expressing more mature social attitudes and (2) spending more time interacting with their children and structuring their play than mothers who had participated in a toy-demonstration program. Unfortunately, the children in Slaughter's study were only about 4 years old at the end of her project. If we presume that home interventions work because of their positive effects on parents and parenting styles, then it would certainly be interesting to follow Slaughter's subjects through grade school to see whether the beneficial impact of the group discussions on mothers would have any measurable effects on the later scholastic performance of their children.

Limitations of Compensatory Education

Now let's note what compensatory education has failed to accomplish. To date, none of these interventions has succeeded in transforming a disadvantaged population into a group of "high achievers" who score significantly above average in IQ or scholastic aptitude (Ramey, 1982). The more typical finding is that children who take part in an enrichment program will continue to score 5–15 points below the national average on IQ tests and somewhat below their grade level on measures of academic achievement. But even though these interventions do not place program participants at the same intellectual level as their middle-class age mates, they do serve a critically important function in helping to prevent the progressive decline in IQ and academic achievement so often observed among children from disadvantaged backgrounds.

Can we ever expect to do better than this in the future? The results of Scarr and Weinberg's transracial adoption study certainly provide some hope. Yet it is important to note that Scarr and Weinberg's adoptees may have fared so well because their enriching experiences *began very early and continued on a daily basis over a period of several years*. By contrast, a formal intervention that lasts but a few hours a week for a year or two at most is probably far too limited in scope to achieve such favorable outcomes.

Perhaps the most valuable lesson that we have learned from the early-intervention research is that it is important to get the parents involved in the child's education at an early age. Urie Bronfenbrenner (1975) has presented a set of guidelines for the successful enrichment program—one that he believes would help disadvantaged youths to realize their full intellectual and academic potentials. He suggests that the optimal long-range intervention might consist of five uninterrupted phases:

1. *Preparation for parenthood*. This includes child care, nutrition, and medical training.
2. *Setting the stage*. Before children come, parents should procure adequate housing and economic security (that is, a steady source of income).
3. *The first three years of life*. Establish a warm and responsive relationship with the child, one that is based on reciprocal interactions centered on activities that are challenging for the child. Home visits or group meetings should be used to establish the parent as the primary agent of intervention.
4. *Ages 4 through 6*. Expose the child to a cognitively oriented preschool program that is reinforced at home by parents who have learned about (or even participated in) the preschool curriculum and who continue to provide intellectual stimulation.
5. *Ages 6 through 12*. Parents should continue to support the child's educational activities at home and at school. Ideally, they would remain the primary figures responsible for the child's social, emotional, and intellectual development.

Note that Bronfenbrenner would have parents involved in the program long before their child is born and would keep them involved long after a traditional intervention has ended. Obviously his proposals (particularly Phase 2) will be diffi-

---

home-based interventions: *compensatory interventions that take place in the home and involve one or more family members in the child's learning experiences.*

cult to implement, even among the wealthiest nations of the world. Nevertheless, our experiences with compensatory education suggest that *long-term* interventions, emphasizing both active, continuous *parental* support and quality preschool education, would undoubtedly produce more favorable outcomes than the piecemeal interventions of the past.

SOME COMMON USES (AND ABUSES) OF IQ TESTS

Schools are by far the biggest users of intelligence tests. Virtually all American children take one or more IQ tests during the grade school years, and their scores are generally kept on file and made readily available to teachers and counselors (Brody & Brody, 1976). Traditionally, this information has been used to identify youngsters who may have difficulties in the classroom and to sort and classify students according to their presumed intellectual abilities. As we will see, both these uses of IQ tests have the potential for serious abuse.

The diagnostic function. IQ tests are often used as a diagnostic tool to identify children who may have problems at school or to explain why slow learners are performing so poorly in the classroom. For example, a lackadaisical first-grader who obtains an IQ of 70 might be considered mildly retarded and a candidate for special education. However, a marginal student who obtains an IQ of 125 would seem to have some sort of motivational or emotional problem that is undermining her academic performance, and no one would recommend placing her in classes for the mentally retarded.

The sorting function. A related use of IQ tests is to sort children into relatively homogeneous groups on the basis of their presumed mental abilities. It is often assumed that students will learn best when surrounded by classmates of comparable intellect. And since IQ scores seem to predict later academic and vocational accomplishments, it is not at all unusual for school systems to use IQ tests to channel students into the curricula for which they are presumably "best

suited"—college preparatory courses for the bright children and vocational training for those who are not so bright.

Problems and pitfalls. Perhaps you can see some of the problems involved in relying on IQ tests to diagnose, sort, and classify children. Many educators (and some school psychologists) have erroneously assumed that an IQ score reflects a relatively permanent intellectual "capacity" rather than an index of mental *performance* that may fluctuate widely over the course of childhood (Brody & Brody, 1976). If a 7-year-old boy were to obtain an IQ of 70, people would be apt to conclude that the child had a definite *lack* of ability. They might then characterize him as mildly "retarded"—a label that could follow the child throughout life and effectively bar the doors to any number of academic or vocational opportunities.

Surely many youngsters who score 70 on an IQ test are mildly retarded. But as it turns out, a low IQ merely reflects a *performance* deficit that may be caused by motivational and emotional problems or other physically based but treatable learning disabilities—factors that IQ tests are hardly designed to detect (Brody & Brody, 1976; Scarr, 1981). The implications for educational policy are clear: in the absence of other diagnostic information that points in the same direction, a low IQ score is not sufficient justification for labeling a child "retarded" or placing her in special classes.

Many of the same arguments can be made against the practice of using IQ tests to sort children into "ability groups." As we will see in Chapter Sixteen, grade school students do not seem to learn any better or faster when surrounded by classmates who obtain similar IQs. And even if they did, many of those children whose IQs fluctuate by 20–40 points over the grade school years would undoubtedly end up in the wrong "ability" groups. Ability grouping by IQ may also have some unintended but harmful effects on children who are "correctly" classified. For example, students of average intelligence may be discouraged by their classification (or their counselors) from attempting college preparatory curricula that they are perfectly capable of mastering—particularly if they are highly motivated to do so. Moreover, children who are placed in the lower ability groups often develop negative attitudes toward themselves and school (Rutter, 1983). And when we recall that IQ scores often fail to predict the future accomplishments of *any particular individual*, we have to wonder whether intelligence tests are at all useful for sorting students into groups or channeling them into various educational curricula (Brody & Brody, 1976).

In sum, an IQ score is a potentially useful piece of information that, *when considered along with many other pieces of information*, can help to specify the causes of certain learning difficulties. But it is important to recognize that an intelligence quotient is merely an estimate of the child's intellectual performance at *one point in time*—an index that, *by itself*, tells us very little about what that child is capable of accomplishing in the years ahead. Indeed, even the educable mentally retarded usually blend into the general population after leaving school, and their later successes in life depend more on their social adjustment and motivation to succeed than on their tested mental abilities (Scarr, 1981).

SUMMARY

Intelligence is extremely difficult to define. Some theorists argue that it is a singular "capacity" for thinking and problem solving that is genetically determined; others believe that intelligence consists of several distinct mental abilities that are influenced by both heredity and environment. Most of the available evidence seems to support the latter point of view.

The first intelligence tests were designed to predict children's academic performance and to identify slow learners who might profit from special education. Today there are literally hundreds of intelligence tests. These instruments differ considerably in format and content, but most of them present the examinee with a variety of cognitive tasks and then evaluate his or her performance by comparing it with the average performance of age mates. An examinee whose performance equals that of the average age mate is assigned an intelligence quotient (IQ) of 100. An IQ greater than 100 indicates that the child's performance is superior to that of other children her age; an IQ less than 100 means that the child's intellectual performance is below that of a typical age mate.

IQ is a relatively stable attribute for some individuals. However, many others will show wide variations in their IQ scores over the course of childhood. The fact that IQ can wander upward or downward over time suggests that IQ tests are measuring intellectual *performance* rather than ability.

When we consider trends for the population as a whole, IQ scores seem to predict important outcomes such as future academic accomplishments, occupational status, and even health and happiness. However, a closer examination of individual profiles suggests that an IQ score is not always a reliable indicator of one's future health, happiness, or success. Many people with very high IQs are not very prosperous or well adjusted, while other people of average intelligence are happy, healthy, and highly successful. So a high IQ, by itself, does not guarantee success. Other factors such as one's work habits and motivation to succeed are also important contributors to future outcomes and accomplishments.

Psychologists are still debating whether IQ scores are due mainly to heredity or mainly to environmental forces. The evidence from family studies and studies of adopted children indicates that much of the variation among individuals in IQ is attributable to hereditary factors. Yet the environment interacts with the forces of heredity to determine intellectual performance. Indeed, barren intellectual environments clearly inhibit cognitive growth, while an enriched, intellectually stimulating environment can have the opposite effect.

Parents who provide a stimulating home environment by becoming involved in their child's learning activities, carefully explaining new concepts, furnishing age-appropriate toys, and consistently encouraging the child to achieve are likely to have children who score high on IQ tests. Two other family characteristics that affect intellectual performance are family size and birth order: first-borns and children from smaller families tend to obtain higher IQs than later-borns and children from large families.

On the average, children from lower-class and minority backgrounds score lower on IQ tests than White children and other members of the middle class. Apparently these group differences in IQ are not simply an artifact of our tests and testing procedures. Nor is there any evidence that they are attributable to genetic differences among the various social-class, racial, and ethnic groups. Perhaps the best explanation for group differences in IQ is the environmental hypothesis: poor people and minority-group members score lower on IQ tests because they often grow up in impoverished environments that are much less conducive to intellectual development than those of their middle-class age mates.

Several enrichment programs for disadvantaged preschoolers have now been evaluated. Although these early interventions do not produce dramatic long-term gains in IQ, they do improve children's chances of succeeding in the classroom, and they help to prevent the progressive decline in intellectual performance so often observed among students from disadvantaged backgrounds.

REFERENCES

Anastasi, A. (1976). *Psychological testing*. New York: Macmillan.

Anderson, L. D. (1939). The predictive value of infant tests in relation to intelligence at 5 years. *Child Development, 10,* 202–212.

Ascher, E. J. (1935). The inadequacy of current intelligence tests for testing Kentucky mountain children. *Journal of Genetic Psychology, 46,* 480–486.

Bayley, N. (1969). *Bayley Scales of Infant Development*. New York: Psychological Corporation.

Bee, H. L., Barnard, K. E., Eyres, S. J., Gray, C. A., Hammond, M. A., Spietz, A. L., Snyder, C., & Clark, B. (1982). Prediction of IQ and language skill from perinatal status, child performance, family characteristics, and mother-infant interaction. *Child Development, 53,* 1134–1156.

Belmont, L., & Marolla, F. A. (1973). Birth order, family size, and intelligence. *Science, 182,* 1096–1101.

Berbaum, M. L., & Moreland, R. L. (1980). Intellectual development within the family: A new application of the confluence model. *Developmental Psychology, 16,* 506–518.

Brackbill, Y., & Nichols, P. L. (1982). A test of the confluence model of intellectual development. *Developmental Psychology, 18,* 192–198.

Bradley, R. H., & Caldwell, B. M. (1976). Early home environment and changes in mental test performance in children from 6 to 36 months. *Developmental Psychology, 12,* 93–97.

Bradley, R. H., & Caldwell, B. M. (1980). The relation of home environment, cognitive competence, and IQ among males and females. *Child Development, 51,* 1140–1148.

Brody, E. B., & Brody, N. (1976). *Intelligence: Nature, determinants, and consequences*. New York: Academic Press.

Bronfenbrenner, U. (1975). Is early intervention effective? Some studies of early education in familial and extrafamilial settings. In A. Montagu (Ed.), *Race and IQ*. New York: Oxford University Press.

Burt, C. (1955). The evidence for the concept of intelligence. *British Journal of Educational Psychology, 25,* 158–177.

Caldwell, B. M., & Bradley, R. H. (1978). *Manual for the Home Observation for Measurement of the Environment*. Little Rock: University of Arkansas at Little Rock.

Cattell, R. B. (1963). Theory of fluid and crystallized intelligence: A critical experiment. *Journal of Educational Psychology, 54,* 1–22.

Cattell, R. B. (1971). The structure of intelligence in relation to the nature-nurture controversy. In R. Cancro (Ed.), *Intelligence: Genetic and environmental influences*. New York: Grune & Stratton.

Cleary, T. A., Humphries, L. G., Kendrick, S. A., & Wesman, A. (1975). Educational uses of tests with disadvantaged students. *American Psychologist, 30,* 15–41.

Cole, N. (1981). Bias in testing. *American Psychologist, 36,* 1067–1077.

Collins, R. C. (1983, Summer). Head Start: An update on program effects. *Newsletter of the Society for Research in Child Development*, pp. 1–2.

Crandall, V. C., & Battle, E. S. (1970). The antecedents and adult correlates of academic and intellectual achievement effort. In J. Hill (Ed.), *Minnesota Symposia on Child Development* (Vol. 4). Minneapolis: University of Minnesota Press.

Crano, W. D., Kenny, J., & Campbell, D. T. (1972). Does intelligence cause achievement: A cross-lagged panel analysis. *Journal of Educational Psychology, 63,* 258–275.

Dickson, W. P., Hess, R. D., Miyake, N., & Azuma, H. (1979). Referential communication accuracy between mother and child as a predictor of cognitive development in the United States and Japan. *Child Development, 50,* 53–59.

Escalona, S. (1968). *The roots of individuality: Normal patterns of individuality*. Chicago: Aldine.

Eysenck, H. J. (1981a). The nature of intelligence. In M. P. Freidman, J. P. Das, & N. O'Connor (Eds.), *Intelligence and learning*. New York: Plenum Press.

Eysenck, H. J. (1981b). Rejoinder to Kamin. In H. J. Eysenck versus L. Kamin, *The intelligence controversy*. New York: Wiley.

Finch, F. H. (1946). Enrollment increases and changes in the mental level of the high school population. *Applied Psychology Monographs*, No. 10.

Fincher, J. (1973). The Terman study is 50 years old: Happy anniversary and pass the ammunition. *Human Behavior, 2,* 8–15.

Galbraith, R. C. (1982). Sibling spacing and intellectual development: A closer look at the confluence models. *Developmental Psychology, 18,* 151–173.

Gesell, A., & Amatruda, C. S. (1947). *Developmental diagnosis* (2nd ed.). New York: Hoeber-Harper.

Globerson, T. (1983). Mental capacity and cognitive functioning: Developmental and social class differences. *Developmental Psychology, 19,* 225–230.

Golden, M., & Birns, B. (1976). Social class and infant intelligence. In M. Lewis (Ed.), *Origins of intelligence: Infancy and early childhood.* New York: Plenum Press.

Golden, M., Birns, B., Bridger, W., & Moss, A. (1971). Social class differentiation in cognitive development among black preschool children. *Child Development, 42,* 37–46.

Gordon, H. (1923). *Mental and scholastic tests among retarded children.* Pamphlet No. 44. London: Board of Education.

Gray, S. W., & Klaus, R. A. (1970). The early training project: A seventh-year report. *Child Development, 41,* 909–924.

Guilford, J. P. (1967). *The nature of human intelligence.* New York: McGraw-Hill.

Hanson, R. A. (1975). Consistency and stability of home environmental measures related to IQ. *Child Development, 46,* 470–480.

Harrell, T. W., & Harrell, M. S. (1945). Army General Classification Test scores for civilian occupations. *Educational and Psychological Measurement, 5,* 229–239.

Hindley, C. B., & Owen, C. F. (1978). The extent of individual changes in IQ for ages between 6 months and 17 years in a British longitudinal sample. *Journal of Child Psychology and Psychiatry, 19,* 329–350.

Honzik, M. P. (1976). Value and limitations of infant tests: An overview. In M. Lewis (Ed.), *Origins of intelligence: Infancy and early childhood.* New York: Plenum Press.

Honzik, M. P., Macfarlane, J. W., & Allen, L. (1948). The stability of mental test performance between two and eighteen years. *Journal of Experimental Education, 17,* 309–324.

Horn, J. L., & Cattell, R. B. (1967). Age differences in fluid and crystallized intelligence. *Acta Psychologica, 26,* 107–129.

Horn, J. L., & Cattell, R. B. (1982). Whimsy and misunderstandings of G_f–G_c theory: A comment on Guilford. *Psychological Bulletin, 91,* 623–633.

Jensen, A. R. (1969). How much can we boost IQ and scholastic achievement? *Harvard Educational Review, 39,* 1–123.

Jensen, A. R. (1977). Cumulative deficit in the IQ of blacks in the rural South. *Developmental Psychology, 13,* 184–191.

Jensen, A. R. (1980). *Bias in mental testing.* New York: Free Press.

Kamin, L. (1974). *The science and politics of IQ.* Hillsdale, NJ: Erlbaum.

Kamin, L. (1981). Separated identical twins [chap. 14]; Studies of adopted children [chap. 15]. In H. J. Eysenck versus L. Kamin, *The intelligence controversy.* New York: Wiley.

Kennedy, W. Z., van de Reit, V., & White, J. C. (1963). A normative sample of intelligence and achievement of Negro elementary school children in the Southeastern United States. *Monographs of the Society for Research in Child Development, 28* (6, Serial No. 90).

Klaus, R. A., & Gray, S. W. (1968). The early training project for disadvantaged children: A report after five years. *Monographs of the Society for Research in Child Development, 33* (4, Serial No. 120).

Klineberg, O. (1963). Negro-white differences in intelligence test performance: A new look at an old problem. *American Psychologist, 18,* 198–203.

Labouvie-Vief, G. (1977). Adult cognitive development: In search of alternative interpretations. *Merrill-Palmer Quarterly, 23,* 227–263.

Layzer, D. (1972). Science or superstition: A physical scientist looks at the IQ controversy. *Cognition, 1,* 265–300.

Lazar, I., & Darlington, R. (1982). Lasting effects of early education: A report from the Consortium for Longitudinal Studies. *Monographs of the Society for Research in Child Development, 47* (2–3, Serial No. 195).

Lee, E. S. (1951). Negro intelligence and selective migration: A Philadelphia test of the Klineberg hypothesis. *American Sociological Review, 16,* 227–233.

Levenstein, P. (1970). Cognitive growth in preschoolers through verbal interaction with mothers. *American Journal of Orthopsychiatry, 40,* 426–432.

Lewontin, R. C. (1976). Race and intelligence. In N. J. Block & G. Dworkin (Eds.), *The IQ Controversy.* New York: Pantheon.

Loehlin, J. C., Lindzey, G., & Spuhler, J. N. (1975). *Race differences in intelligence.* San Francisco: W. H. Freeman.

Longstreth, L., Davis, B., Carter, L., Flint, D., Owen, J., Rickert, M., & Taylor, E. (1981). Separation of home intellectual environment and maternal IQ as determinants of child IQ. *Developmental Psychology, 17,* 532–541.

Madden, J., Levenstein, P., & Levenstein, S. (1976). Longitudinal IQ outcomes of the mother-child home program. *Child Development, 47,* 1015–1025.

Markus, G. B., & Zajonc, R. B. (1977). Family configuration and intellectual development: A simulation. *Behavioral Science, 22,* 137–142.

McCall, R. B., Applebaum, M. I., & Hogarty, P. S. (1973). Developmental changes in mental test performance. *Monographs of the Society for Research in Child Development, 38* (3, Serial No. 150).

Minton, H. L., & Schneider, F. W. (1980). *Differential psychology.* Monterey, CA: Brooks/Cole.

Neisser, U. (1980). The concept of intelligence. In R. J. Sternberg & D. K. Detterman (Eds.), *Human intelligence: Perspectives on its theory and measurement.* Norwood, NJ: Ablex.

Piaget, J. (1950). *The psychology of intelligence.* New York: Harcourt Brace Jovanovich.

Plomin, R., & DeFries, J. C. (1980). Genetics and intelligence: Recent data. *Intelligence, 4,* 15–24.

Plomin, R., & DeFries, J. C. (1983). The Colorado adoption project. *Child Development, 54,* 276–289.

Quay, L. C. (1971). Language dialect, reinforcement, and the intelligence-test performance of Negro children. *Child Development, 42,* 5–15.

Ramey, C. T. (1982). In I. Lazar & R. Darlington, Lasting effects of early education: A report from the Consortium for Longitudinal Studies. *Monographs of the Society for Research in Child Development, 47* (2–3, Serial No. 195).

Rothbart, M. K. (1971). Birth order and mother-child interaction in an achievement situation. *Journal of Personality and Social Psychology, 17,* 113–120.

Rubin, R., & Balow, B. (1979). Measures of infant development and socioeconomic status as predictors of later intelligence and school achievement. *Developmental Psychology, 15,* 225–227.

Rutter, M. (1983). School effects on pupil progress: Research findings and policy implications. *Child Development, 54,* 1–29.

Sacks, E. L. (1952). Intelligence scores as a function of experimentally established social relationships between child and examiner. *Journal of Abnormal and Social Psychology, 47,* 354–358.

Sarason, S. B. (1973). Jewishness, blackness, and the nature-nurture controversy. *American Psychologist, 28,* 962–971.

Scarr, S. (1981). Testing for children: Assessment and the many determinants of intellectual competence. *American Psychologist, 36,* 1159–1166.

Scarr, S., & Weinberg, R. A. (1976). IQ test performance of black children adopted by white families. *American Psychologist, 31,* 726–739.

Scarr, S., & Weinberg, R. A. (1977). Intellectual similarities within families of both adopted and biological children. *Intelligence, 32,* 170–191.

Scarr, S., & Weinberg, R. A. (1983). The Minnesota adoption studies: Genetic differences and malleability. *Child Development, 54,* 260–267.

Schaie, K. W., & Hertzog, C. (1983). Fourteen-year cohort-sequential analyses of adult intellectual development. *Developmental Psychology, 19,* 531–543.

Schaie, K. W., & Labouvie-Vief, G. (1974). Generational versus ontogenetic components of change in adult cognitive behavior: A fourteen-year cross-sequential study. *Developmental Psychology, 10,* 305–320.

Sherman, M., & Key, C. B. (1932). The intelligence of isolated mountain children. *Child Development, 3,* 279–290.

Shinn, M. (1978). Father absence and children's cognitive development. *Psychological Bulletin, 85,* 295–324.

Shuey, A. (1966). *The testing of Negro intelligence.* New York: Social Science Press.

Siegal, L. S. (1981). Infant tests as predictors of cognitive and language development at two years. *Child Development, 52,* 545–557.

Skodak, M., & Skeels, H. M. (1947). A follow-up study of the development of one-hundred adopted children in Iowa. *American Psychologist, 2,* 278.

Skodak, M., & Skeels, H. M. (1949). A final follow-up study of children in adoptive homes. *Journal of Genetic Psychology, 75,* 85–125.

Slaughter, D. T. (1983). Early intervention and its effects on maternal and child development. *Monographs of the Society for Research in Child Development, 48* (4, Serial No. 202).

Smith, S. (1942). Language and nonverbal test performance of racial groups in Honolulu before and after a 14-year interval. *Journal of General Psychology, 26,* 51–93.

Sontag, L. W., Baker, C. T., & Nelson, V. L. (1958). Mental growth and personality development: A longitudinal study. *Monographs of the Society for Research in Child Development, 23* (Serial No. 68).

Spearman, C. (1927). *The abilities of man.* New York: Macmillan.

Svanum, S., Bringle, R. G., & McGlaughlin, J. E. (1982). Father absence and cognitive performance in a large sample of six- to eleven-year-old children. *Child Development, 53,* 136–143.

Terman, L. M. (1921). In symposium: Intelligence and its measurement. *Journal of Educational Psychology, 12,* 127–133.

Terman, L. M. (1954). The discovery and encouragement of exceptional talent. *American Psychologist, 9,* 221–238.

Terman, L. M., & Oden, M. H. (1959). *The gifted group at mid-life.* Stanford, CA: Stanford University Press.

Thurstone, L. L. (1938). *Primary mental abilities.* Chicago: University of Chicago Press.

Thurstone, L. L., & Thurstone, T. G. (1941). Factorial studies of intelligence. *Psychometric Monographs,* No. 2.

Tryon, R. C. (1940). Genetic differences in maze learning in rats. *Yearbook of the National Society for Studies in Education, 39,* 111–119.

Tyler, L. E. (1965). *The psychology of human differences.* New York: Appleton-Century-Crofts.

Wechsler, D. (1944). *The measurement of adult intelligence* (3rd ed.). Baltimore: Williams and Wilkins.

Wechsler, D. (1967). *Wechsler Preschool and Primary Scale of Intelligence.* New York: Psychological Corporation.

Wechsler, D. (1974). *Wechsler Intelligence Scale for Children.* New York: Psychological Corporation.

Wheeler, L. R. (1932). The intelligence of East Tennessee children. *Journal of Educational Psychology, 23,* 351–370.

Wheeler, L. R. (1942). A comparative study of the intelligence of East Tennessee mountain children. *Journal of Educational Psychology, 33,* 321–334.

Witty, P. A., & Jenkins, M. D. (1936). Intrarace testing and Negro intelligence. *Journal of Psychology, 1,* 179–192.

Wrightsman, L. S., & Sanford, F. H. (1975). *Psychology: A scientific study of human behavior.* Monterey, CA: Brooks/Cole.

Yeates, K. O., MacPhee, D., Campbell, F. A., & Ramey, C. T. (1983). Maternal IQ and home environment as determinants of early childhood intellectual competence: A developmental analysis. *Developmental Psychology, 19,* 731–739.

Yerkes, R. M. (1921). Psychological examining in the U. S. Army. *Memoirs: National Academy of Science, 15,* 1–890.

Zajonc, R. B. (1975, August). Birth order and intelligence: Dumber by the dozen. *Psychology Today*, pp. 39–43.

Zajonc, R. B., & Markus, G. B. (1975). Birth order and intellectual development. *Psychological Review, 82,* 74–88.

Zajonc, R. B., Markus, H., & Markus, G. B. (1979). The birth order puzzle. *Journal of Personality and Social Psychology, 37,* 1325–1341.

Zigler, E., Abelson, W. D., Trickett, P. K., & Seitz, V. (1982). Is an intervention program necessary to improve economically disadvantaged children's IQ scores? *Child Development, 53,* 340–348.

Zigler, E., & Butterfield, E. C. (1968). Motivational aspects of changes in IQ test performance of culturally deprived nursery school children. *Child Development, 39,* 1–14.

PART FOUR

H uman beings are social animals, and our focus in Part Four shifts to social and personality development. We begin in Chapter Eleven by examining the social and emotional developments of infancy and by discussing the consequences that children may face if they fail to establish affectional ties to other people during the first two or three years of life.

SOCIAL AND PERSONALITY DEVELOPMENT

In Chapter Twelve we will trace the development of children's knowledge about themselves and others and see that a person's understanding of the "self" and of the social environment contributes in important ways to his or her personality and social behavior.

Our attention in Chapter Thirteen turns to the interesting and often controversial subject of sex differences and sex-role development. We will first look beyond the myths and attempt to establish how males and females differ psychologically. Then we will consider several theories of sex-role development and try to

determine whether the psychological differences between the sexes are culturally or biologically determined.

Many theorists have argued that establishing a sense of morality is the toughest task that parents face when raising a child. In Chapter Fourteen we will consider the topic of moral development and learn how children and adolescents come to distinguish right from wrong and to act on this distinction.

CHAPTER ELEVEN ■

ATTACHMENT: THE DEVELOPMENT OF INTIMATE RELATIONSHIPS

■ *A definition of attachment*

■ *The caregiver's attachment to the infant*
Early emotional bonding
Infant characteristics that promote caregiver-to-infant attachments
Problems in establishing caregiver-to-infant attachments

■ *The infant's attachment to caregivers*
Development of primary social attachments
Theories of attachment

■ *Development of fearful reactions*
Stranger anxiety
Separation anxiety

■ *Long-term effects of early social and emotional development*
Individual differences in the quality of attachments
The unattached infant: Effects of restricted social contacts during infancy

■ *Summary*

I n 1891 G. Stanley Hall stated that adolescence is the most crucial stage of the life cycle for the development of personality. Hall characterized the teenage years as a time when interests are solidified, long-lasting friendships emerge, and important decisions are made about one's education, career, and (in those days) choice of a mate. In other words, he viewed adolescence as the period when individuals assume personal and interpersonal identities that will carry them through their adult lives.

This viewpoint was soon challenged by Sigmund Freud (1905/1930), who believed that many of the decisions that an adolescent makes about the future are predetermined by his or her reactions to earlier life experiences. In fact, Freud proclaimed that the foundations of the adult personality are laid during the first five to six years of life and that the process of personality development begins the moment that a baby is first handed to his or her parents.

Today we know that Freud was right in at least one respect: Social and emotional development does begin very early in life. Although few contemporary theorists believe that our personalities are "set in stone" during the first five or six years, it is now apparent that the kinds of emotional relationships that infants develop with their close companions may well affect the ways they relate to other people later in life. Early social experiences are important experiences—and infancy is truly a sensitive period for personality development.

Our focus in this chapter is on a major social and emotional milestone of infancy—the development of affectional ties between children and their closest associates. We will begin by considering how developmentalists define a true emotional attachment. We will then concentrate on the *process* of becoming attached and will try to determine how infants and their companions establish these close emotional ties. Next, we will consider two common fears that attached infants often display and see why these fearful reactions often emerge during the latter part of the first year. Finally, we will review a rapidly expanding base of evidence that suggests that the kind of emotional attachments that infants are able to establish (or the lack thereof) may have important implications for their later social, emotional, and intellectual development.

A DEFINITION OF ATTACHMENT

Researchers have found that the young of many species soon form close emotional ties to their mother or a "mother figure." To the layperson, this "attachment" appears to be a bond of love that is often attributed to maternal tendencies such as "mother instinct" or "mother love." Developmentalists are willing to concede that mothers and other close companions are likely to become attached to an infant long before the infant is attached to them. However, it now appears that mother love must be nurtured and that most infants are capable of promoting such a caregiver-to-infant bond from the moment of birth.

Just what is a social **attachment**? John Bowlby (1958, 1973) uses the term to describe the strong affectional ties that bind a person to his or her most intimate companions. According to Bowlby, people who are attached will interact often and will try to *maintain proximity* to each other. Accordingly, an 8-month-old boy who is attached to his mother may show his attachment by doing whatever it takes—crying, clinging, approaching, or following—in order to establish or to maintain contact with her. Leslie Cohen (1974) adds that attachments are *selective* in character and imply that the company of some people (**attachment objects**) is more pleasant or reassuring than that of others. For example, a 2-year-old girl who is attached to her mother should prefer the mother's company to that of a stranger whenever she is upset, discomforted, or afraid.

Although our focus in this chapter is on the attachments that develop between infants and their close companions, there are many other kinds of attachments that individuals may form. For example, children may become attached to playmates and form solid friendships. Adults are

PHOTO 11-1. *Infants and caregivers who are attached interact often and try to maintain proximity.*

typically attached to their mates. In fact, people often develop intense attachments to those cuddly kittens, puppies, or other house pets that respond to them and seem to enjoy their company. All these relationships are similar in that the attachment object is someone (or something) special with whom we are motivated to maintain contact.

How do infants and caregivers become attached to each other? Let's address this important issue by looking first at caregivers' reactions to infants.

THE CAREGIVER'S ATTACHMENT TO THE INFANT

People sometimes find it hard to understand how a parent might become attached to a neonate. After all, newborn infants can be demanding little creatures who drool, spit up, fuss, cry, dirty their diapers on a regular basis, and often require a lot of attention at all hours of the day and night. Since babies are associated with so many unpleasant consequences, why don't their parents learn to dislike them?

One reason that parents may overlook or discount the negative aspects of child care is that they have often begun to form emotional attachments to their infant *before* they experience many of the unpleasantries of parenthood. Marshall Klaus and John Kennell (1976) believe that caregivers can become emotionally bonded to an infant during the first few hours after birth —provided that they are given an opportunity to get to know their baby. And just what kinds of contact are necessary to promote this early emotional bonding? Let's see what Klaus and Kennell have to say.

Early Emotional Bonding

Several years ago, Klaus and Kennell (1976) proposed that a mother's attitude toward her infant may depend, in part, on her experiences with that child during the first few days after giving birth. Specifically, they hypothesized that extended skin-to-skin contact between mothers and their babies would make mothers more responsive to their infants and thereby promote the development of strong mother-to-infant emotional bonds.

To test this hypothesis, Klaus and Kennell studied 28 young mothers who had just delivered full-term, healthy infants. During their three-day stay in the hospital, half the mothers followed the traditional routine: they saw their babies briefly after delivering, visited with them 6–12 hours later, and then had half-hour feeding sessions with their infants every four hours. The mothers in the second, or "extended contact," group were permitted five "extra" hours a day to cuddle their babies, including an hour of skin-to-skin contact that took place within three hours of birth. At the end of these three-day routines, the two groups of mothers went home and began to care for their infants on a full-time basis.

One month later, Klaus and Kennell interviewed the 28 mothers, examined their babies, and filmed each mother feeding her infant. The results of this follow-up were striking: mothers who had had extended early contact with their infants seemed much more involved with them and held them much closer during their feeding sessions than mothers who had experienced the normal hospital routine. Perhaps even more remarkable were the results of a second follow-up conducted when the babies were a year old: mothers from the extended-contact group were still more soothing, cuddling, and nurturing, and they were also more likely than mothers from the "normal routine" group to report that they missed their babies while away from home at work. As for the infants, those who had had extended early contacts with their mothers outperformed those who had not on tests of physical and mental development.

Klaus and Kennell believe that the amount of early contact a mother has with her infant is less important than the *timing* of that contact. In the hospital setting, mothers who have had some close contact with their babies in the first 10–12 hours of life tend to caress their infants more and hold them closer while feeding than do mothers whose initial contacts with their infants were delayed or abbreviated (Gaulin-Kremer, Shaw, & Thoman, 1977; Grossmann, Thane, & Grossmann,

---

attachment: *a close emotional relationship between two persons, characterized by mutual affection and a desire to maintain proximity.*
attachment object: *a close companion to whom one is attached.*

1981). Kennell, Voos, and Klaus (1979) suggest that the first 6–12 hours is a **sensitive period** for the emotional bonding of a mother to her infant: presumably mothers are most likely to develop the strongest possible affection for their babies if they have had skin-to-skin contact with them during this particular time.

■ *Why might early contact be important?*

Why do mothers build these emotional bridges to their infants just after giving birth? Kennell, Voos, and Klaus (1979) have suggested that hormones present at the time of delivery may help to focus the mother's attention on her baby and make her more susceptible to forming an early attachment. If these hormones should dissipate before a mother has any extended contact with her infant, she will presumably become less responsive to her baby, much as animals do if separated from their offspring in the first few hours after giving birth.

Although the "hormonal mediation" hypothesis may seem to account for the findings we have reviewed, there are reasons to question this interpretation of early emotional bonding. For one thing, mothers who have had close contact with their infants soon after giving birth are not always more nurturant or more involved with their babies (Svejda, Campos, & Emde, 1980), particularly if their pregnancies were unplanned (Grossmann et al., 1981). Moreover, the hormonal hypothesis cannot explain why fathers who are present at the birth often become so fascinated with their neonate, wishing to touch, hold, or caress the baby. As we saw in Chapter Four, this initial "engrossment" seems to be a form of early emotional bonding that increases a father's sense of involvement with his child.

There may be a simple explanation for the early affection that parents display toward their newborn infants. Perhaps the intense emotional arousal (fear or apprehension) that parents experience during childbirth is reinterpreted in a positive light when they are handed an infant who gazes attentively at them, grasps their fingers, and seems to snuggle in response to their caresses. If parents should then attribute these positive feelings *to the baby and its behavior,* it is easy to see how they might feel rather affectionate toward their neonate and become emotionally involved with him or her. However, parents who have little or no early contact with their neonates are unable to attribute their existing emotional arousal to a beautiful, responsive baby. In fact, they often end up labeling their emotions as exhaustion or a sense of relief that the ordeal of pregnancy and childbirth is finally over (Grossman, Eichler, Winickoff, & Associates, 1980). Perhaps you can see that these latter attributions are unlikely to make parents feel especially affectionate toward the child they have just borne.

■ *Is early contact necessary for optimal development?*

Klaus and Kennell's sensitive-period hypothesis implies that new parents show a basic "readiness" to become attached to their infant during the first few hours after the baby is born. As we have seen, there is some evidence to support this proposition. However, Klaus and Kennell also claim that parents who have had little or no contact with their neonates during the sensitive period may never become as attached to these infants as they might had they had skin-to-skin contact with them during the first few hours. This second theoretical proposition is much more controversial.

In her recent review of the emotional-bonding literature, Susan Goldberg (1983) reports that mothers who have had early contact with their infants do seem to be somewhat more responsive and affectionate toward their babies for the first three days of life. But in contrast to Klaus and Kennell's research, Goldberg finds that these "early contact" effects are not large and may not last very long. In the one study in which mothers and infants were carefully observed over a nine-day period, the advantages of early contact steadily declined over time. By the ninth day after birth, early-contact mothers were no more affectionate or responsive toward their infants than mothers who had had no skin-to-skin contact with their babies for several hours after delivery. Indeed, the delayed-contact mothers showed a dramatic increase in responsiveness over the nine-day observation period—suggesting that the hours immediately after birth are not nearly as critical as Klaus and Kennell assumed (Goldberg, 1983).

Michael Rutter (1979) is another theorist who believes that the events of the first few hours are unlikely to have a permanent effect on mother/infant relationships. To support his claim, Rutter notes that adoptive parents develop close emotional ties to their children even though they have rarely had *any* contact with their adoptees during the neonatal period. Moreover, Sara Rode and her associates (Rode, Chang, Fisch, & Sroufe, 1981) recently followed up on a number of 12–19-month-old infants who had been born prematurely (or seriously ill) and had spent the first several weeks of their lives in intensive care. Although many of the parents occasionally visited their children in the hospital, they did not have the close early contact with their babies that Klaus and Kennell believe to be necessary for optimal parent-to-infant emotional bonding. Nevertheless, Rode et al. found that the vast majority of these infants were closely attached to their parents during the second year of life. In fact, the percentage of securely attached infants in Rode's sample (71%) compares favorably with the 66–70% typically observed among 12-month-old, full-term infants who have had a fair amount of early contact with their caregivers (Ainsworth, Blehar, Waters, & Wall, 1978). Rode and her associates concluded that

> although prematurity and physical separation place stress on the family system, of greater importance to the infant-caregiver attachment relationship may be the length of time that the infant has been at home with the caregiver and the quality of care experienced. The quality of the infant-caregiver attachment relationship is a product of the entire history of infant-caregiver interaction. While the earliest days and hours are important . . . attachment is a process that evolves during the first year of life [p. 190].

In sum, research on early emotional bonding suggests that parents can become highly involved with their infants during the first few hours if they are permitted to touch, hold, cuddle, and play with their babies. As a result, many hospitals have altered their routines to allow and encourage these kinds of experiences. However, it appears that this early contact is neither crucial nor sufficient for the development of strong parent-to-infant or infant-to-parent attachments. Stable attachments between infants and caregivers are not formed in a matter of minutes, hours, or days: they build rather slowly from social interactions that take place over many weeks and months. In other words, there is no reason for parents who do not have early skin-to-skin contact with their infant to assume that they will have problems establishing a warm and loving relationship with the child.

Infant Characteristics That Promote Caregiver-to-Infant Attachments

John Bowlby (1958, 1969) believes that human infants are born with a repertoire of reflexes and other physical characteristics that are likely to elicit highly favorable reactions from their caregivers. For example, the rooting, sucking, and grasping reflexes may lead parents to believe that their infant enjoys being close to them. Other reactions such as the reflexive smile (see Box 11-1), laughter, or spontaneous babbling are also likely to have a positive effect on close companions. In fact, parents may interpret their infant's smiles, laughs, and babbles as indications that the child is contented and that they are effective caregivers. Thus, a smiling or babbling infant can reinforce caregiving activities and thereby increase the likelihood that parents or other nearby companions will want to attend to this happy little person in the future.

Even the reflexive cry, which is sometimes described as aversive, can promote caregiver-to-infant attachments. Bowlby views the cry as a "distress signal" that elicits the approach of those who are responsible for the infant's care and safety. Presumably, responsive caregivers who are successful at quieting their babies will then become the beneficiaries of positive responses, such as smiling and babbling, that should reinforce their caregiving behavior and make them feel even closer to their contented infants.

■ Physical characteristics

Konrad Lorenz (1943) has argued that a baby's **"kewpie doll"** appearance (large forehead;

---

sensitive-period hypothesis: *Klaus and Kennell's notion that mothers will develop the strongest possible affection for their babies if they have close contact with them during the first 6–12 hours after giving birth.*

kewpie-doll effect: *the notion that infantlike facial features are perceived as cute and lovable and will elicit favorable responses from others.*

BOX 11-1
THE ASOCIAL SMILE BECOMES
A SOCIAL SMILE

John Bowlby (1958, 1969) believes that smiling is a biologically programmed response that will play an important role in the development of affectional ties between caretakers and their infants. Smiling does begin very early, although the neonate's first smiles are not necessarily "social": soft sounds, changes in brightness, and the appearance of a new visual pattern are examples of nonsocial stimuli that may elicit smiles from very young infants (Ambrose, 1963; Bower, 1982). Some neonates will even smile while in a drowsy state or during periods of REM (rapid eye movement) sleep (Emde, Gaensbauer, & Harmon, 1976). So these early smiles appear to be *reflexive* responses to a variety of internal or external events. In fact, this smile often strikes observers as more of a grimace than a true smile.

True *social smiling* begins as early as 3 weeks of age, when the sound of a female voice may produce a grin. In the fifth or sixth week of life, the human face (particularly the eyes) replaces the female voice as the most potent elicitor of smiling (Wolff, 1963). By 3–4 months of age, infants are apt to crack broad smiles in response to either a familiar or a strange face, although they may be quicker to smile at familiar company (Bowlby, 1969; Dunkeld, 1978). Apparently the onset of social smiling is influenced by both genetic and maturational factors. For example, identical twins are more similar than fraternal twins in

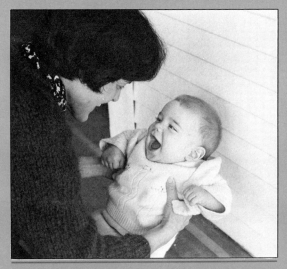

Few signals will attract as much attention as a baby's social smile.

the age at which they begin to smile at faces (Freedman, 1965). Moreover, infants who are born six weeks premature do not begin to smile at social stimuli until 12 weeks of age—about six weeks behind full-term infants (Dittrichova, 1969). However, premature and full-term infants start to smile at approximately the same *conceptional* age—46 weeks—indicating that maturation plays an important role in the emergence of social smiling.

Once infants begin to smile at caregivers, their tendency to keep smiling at them may depend, in

chubby, protruding cheeks; soft, rounded features) makes the infant appear cute or lovable to caregivers. Recently, Thomas Alley (1981) found that adults aged 18–47 judged line drawings of "babyish" faces (and profiles) to be much "cuter" than those of 4-year-old children. When commenting on the babyish figures, Alley's subjects often described them as "adorable" or "pleasant to look at" or noted that "you receive pleasure from a cute person" (p. 653). Younger boys and girls also react positively to babyish facial features, although girls begin to show an even stronger interest in infants after reaching menarche (Goldberg, Blumberg, & Kriger, 1982). Finally, infants clearly differ in physical attractiveness (Hildebrandt, 1983), and adults often respond more favorably to attractive babies than to unattractive ones (Hildebrandt & Fitzgerald, 1981; Stephan & Langlois,

1984). So it seems that infantlike facial features (or the "kewpie doll" look) may help to elicit the kinds of attention from caregivers that will promote social attachments. However, research is needed to tell us whether adults actually find it easier to become attached to highly attractive infants than to babies whose facial features are somewhat less than attractive.

■ Interactional synchrony

One thing that many parents find so fascinating about infants is that their babies often seem so responsive to them. In Chapter Six we learned that full-term, healthy neonates are particularly responsive to the sound of the human voice (particularly high-pitched "feminine" voices) and will synchronize their movements with the starts, stops, and pauses in the speech they hear.

part, on caregivers' reactions to these signals. Parents often interpret the infant's smile as a wonderful thing; in fact, one study found that an adult's most typical response to a baby's smile was to smile back at the baby (Gewirtz & Gewirtz, 1968). And how do infants react to smiles and other social gestures? They smile all the more at their playful companions (Brackbill, 1958; Wahler, 1967). At about 6 months of age, most infants who have been raised in a home setting with their parents become quite selective, generally saving their smiles for familiar company. This *discriminated smiling response* is one sign that an infant is becoming attached to his close companions.

Learning theorists explain the increasingly social character of an infant's smile by analyzing the interactions that occur between infants and caregivers. Presumably an infant will smile more and more at faces because her parents, siblings, and other caregivers will reinforce these greetings by smiling at, speaking to, or otherwise entertaining her. Moreover, a baby's smile can reinforce caregiving activities and increase the amount of time that parents and other caregivers will *want* to spend with their happy, responsive infant. So continued interactions between a smiling infant and a responsive caregiver should lead to an increase in reciprocal smiling and to the development of a "special" relationship that both parties enjoy. Here, then, is what seems a very plausible explanation for the origin of a discriminated smiling response in young infants.

Cognitive theorists stress that the development of the social smile may also depend on the child's cognitive and perceptual growth. According to Jerome Kagan (1971), infants are active information processors who try to understand what they are experiencing by matching these events to their existing schemata. Presumably, when infants can assimilate events into their cognitive schemata, they will indicate their pleasure at this accomplishment by cracking a broad smile.

Cognitive-perceptual theorists would point out that infants are developing schemata for familiar patterns during the second month of life—precisely the time that they begin to smile regularly at faces. Perhaps the first social smiles simply indicate that the infant recognizes the human face as a familiar pattern. At 3 to 4 months of age, when infants are first capable of discriminating faces, they suddenly become quicker to smile at a familiar face. However, the fact that the infant still smiles at unfamiliar faces suggests that his schema for faces is very general. As the child's facial schema becomes more differentiated, only familiar faces will be recognized and will elicit smiles. Thus, the discriminated smiling response may arise because strange faces are now simply too discrepant with the child's existing schemata to be assimilated and "understood."

In sum, the smile is initially an asocial, reflexive response that becomes increasingly "social" in character over the first six months of life. Although biological factors may determine the onset of social smiling, the further development of the smile from an indiscriminate social signal to a greeting reserved for close companions depends on the child's cognitive development and experiences with caregivers.

Moreover, Craig Peery (1980) reports that 1-day-old infants are already synchronizing their head movements with those of adults: frame-by-frame photographic analyses of the interactions between infants and an admiring female adult revealed that each infant reliably (1) withdrew his or her head at the approach of the adult and (2) approached the adult as she withdrew her head. Clearly, infants are capable of engaging in synchronized interactions with caregivers from the first day of life.

Over the next several weeks and months, caregivers and infants will ordinarily have many opportunities to interact and to develop and perfect **synchronized routines** that both parties will probably enjoy. Psychologists who have observed these exquisite interactions have likened them to "dances" in which the partners take turns responding to each other's lead. Daniel Stern (1977) has provided a written account of one such "dance" that occurred as a mother was feeding her 3-month-old infant:

> A normal feeding, not a social interaction, was underway. Then a change began. While talking and looking at me, the mother turned her head and gazed at the infant's face. He was gazing at the ceiling, but out of the corner of his eye he saw her head turn toward him and he turned to gaze back at her . . . now he broke

---

synchronized routines: *generally harmonious interactions between two persons in which each participant adjusts his or her behavior in response to the partner's actions.*

rhythm and stopped sucking. He let go of the nipple . . . as he eased into the faintest suggestion of a smile. The mother abruptly stopped talking and, as she watched his face begin to transform, her eyes opened a little wider and her eyebrows raised a bit. His eyes locked on to hers, and together they held motionless for an instant. . . . This silent and almost motionless instant continued to hang until the mother suddenly shattered it by saying "Hey!" and simultaneously opened her eyes wider, raising her eyebrows further, and throwing her head up toward the infant. Almost simultaneously, the baby's eyes widened. His head tilted up and, as his smile broadened, the nipple fell out of his mouth. Now she said, "Well, hello! . . . Heello . . . Heeelloo," so that her pitch rose and the "hellos" became longer and more emphatic on each successive repetition. With each phrase, the baby expressed more pleasure, and his body resonated almost like a balloon . . . filling a little more with each breath. The mother then paused and her face relaxed. They watched each other expectantly for a moment . . . then the baby suddenly took an initiative. . . . His head lurched forward, his hands jerked up, and a fuller smile blossomed. His mother was jolted into motion. She moved forward, mouth open and eyes alight, and said "Oooooh . . . ya wanna play do ya . . . yeah? . . ." And off they went [p. 3].

In this example, it was the mother who started the episode by gazing at the baby's face and capturing his attention. However, young infants are quite capable of initiating, maintaining, and even terminating these synchronized exchanges if they become overly excited or discomforted in some way. In the interaction that Stern describes, the mother soon became much more boisterous in her play and raised her voice to a level where her baby appeared apprehensive. At this point, the baby attempted to withdraw from the game by looking away. Once he had composed himself, he gazed again at his mother and "exploded into a big grin." The mother then became even more playful than before, and the baby immediately frowned and looked away. Clearly, he had had enough excitement for the moment. The mother picked up on this signal and gave the baby his nipple, and he began to feed once again. Their synchronized social exchange was suddenly over.

In sum, infants seem naturally responsive to other people—almost as if they had an innate capacity for engaging in sychronized interaction. Stern (1977) has suggested that these synchronized routines may occur several times a day and are important contributors to social attachments. As an infant continues to interact with a particular caregiver, he will learn what this person is like and how he can regulate her attention. Of course, the caregiver should become more proficient at interpreting the baby's signals and will learn how to adjust her behavior to successfully capture and maintain his attention. As the caregiver and the infant practice their routines and become better "dance partners," their relationship should become more satisfying for both parties and may eventually blossom into a strong reciprocal attachment.

Problems in Establishing Caregiver-to-Infant Attachments

Although we have talked as if caregivers invariably became attached to their infants, this does not always happen. As we will see, some babies are hard to love, some caregivers are hard to reach, and some environments are not very conducive to the establishment of secure emotional relationships.

■ Some babies may be hard to love

Caregivers may find it rather difficult to become emotionally attached to an infant who is extremely active, irritable, or unresponsive to their bids for attention. Babies who are "at risk" of alienating their close companions can often be identified in the first week of life: their performances on the Brazelton Neonatal Behavioral Assessment Scale are characterized by mild irritability, inalertness, lack of attention to social stimuli, and poor motor control (Brazelton, 1979; Waters, Vaughn, & Egeland, 1980). Recent research indicates that adults have a difficult time establishing stable and synchronized routines with these irritable and unresponsive infants (Greene, Fox, & Lewis, 1983; Thoman, Acebo, & Becker, 1983). Indeed, Jamie Greene, Nathan Fox, and Michael Lewis (1983) report that infants who often cry during social interactions seem to disrupt the development of a positive reciprocal relationship with their caregivers. Although the mothers of these fretful infants are quite willing to provide comfort and attend to basic needs, they spend less time in playful and affectionate social exchanges than mothers whose babies are less fretful and more responsive to social play.

Fortunately, many parents will eventually establish satisfying routines and become quite attached to their difficult or unresponsive infants. One way to help the process along is to identify neonates who may be difficult to love and then to teach their caregivers how to elicit favorable reactions from these sluggish or irritable companions. The Brazelton testing and training programs reviewed in Chapter Five (see Box 5-2) were designed with these objectives in mind.

■ *Some caregivers are hard to reach*

Caregivers sometimes have personal quirks or characteristics that seriously hinder or prevent them from establishing close emotional ties to their infants. For example, parents who were themselves unloved, neglected, or abused as children may expect their babies to be "perfect" and to love them right away. When the infant is irritable, fussy, and inattentive (as all infants will be at times), these emotionally insecure adults are apt to feel as if the baby had rejected them. They may then withdraw their affection—sometimes to the point of neglecting the child—or become physically abusive (Rutter, 1979; Steele & Pollack, 1974).

Problems may also arise if caregivers try to follow preconceived notions about how infants should be raised rather than adjusting their parenting to the infant's state or temperamental characteristics. For example, a father who believes that his baby requires a large amount of stimulation may end up overexciting an "excitable" infant; a mother who is afraid of spoiling her baby may be reluctant to soothe a child who has become overly excited (Korner, 1974). Unfortunately, caregivers who often misread their baby's signals and end up trying to fit a square peg into a round hole may be less likely to establish the kind of interactional synchrony with their infant that would help them to become attached to him or her.

Finally, some caregivers may be disinclined to love their babies because their pregnancies were unplanned and their infants are unwanted. In one study conducted in Czechoslovakia (Matějček, Dytrych, & Schüller, 1979), mothers who had been denied permission to abort an unwanted pregnancy were judged to be less closely attached to their children than a group of same-aged mothers of similar marital and socioeconomic status who had not requested an abortion. Although both the "wanted" and the "unwanted" children were physically healthy at birth, over the next nine years the unwanted children were more frequently hospitalized, made lower grades in school, had less stable family lives and poorer relations with peers, and were generally more irritable than the children whose parents had wanted them. Here, then, are data suggesting that failure of a caregiver to become emotionally attached to an infant could have long-term effects on the child's physical, social, emotional, and intellectual well-being.

Of course, these findings do not imply that all wanted children will be loved or that all unwanted children will remain unloved. Nevertheless, it would appear that mothers who give birth to an unplanned and unwanted child are less likely than mothers who plan their pregnancies to become closely attached to their infants.

■ *Some environments are hazardous to the formation of healthy attachments*

To this point, we have noted that the character of an adult's attachment to his or her infant is influenced by the adult's characteristics as well as those of the infant. However, we should also recognize that interactions between infants and caregivers take place within a broader social and emotional context that may affect how a particular caregiver and infant will react to each other. For example, mothers who must care for several small children with little or no assistance may find themselves unwilling or unable to devote much attention to their newest baby, particularly if the infant is at all irritable or unresponsive (Belsky, 1980; Crockenberg, 1981). Indeed, researchers have consistently reported that the more children a woman has had, the more negative her attitudes toward children become, and the more difficult she thinks her children are to raise (Garbarino & Sherman, 1980; Hurley & Hohn, 1971).

In recent years, family sociologists have argued that the quality of a caregiver's relationship with his or her spouse can have a dramatic effect on parent/infant interactions. For example, parents who are depressed about an unhappy marriage sometimes look to their babies for love and attention

PHOTO 11-2. *Mothers who have several young children to care for may feel harassed and react negatively to their "newest" baby, particularly if the infant is irritable or unresponsive.*

when their spouses fail to satisfy these emotional needs (Steele & Pollack, 1974). However, they will probably fail to find the support they are seeking, for Jeffrey Cohn and Edward Tronick (1982) report that 3-month-old infants soon become wary and begin to protest should their mothers behave as if they were depressed. Cohn and Tronick suggest that the infant's negative reaction to depression may further depress the adult and make it difficult for him or her to establish a satisfying routine with the child. This problem may be particularly apparent if the baby has already shown a tendency to be irritable and unresponsive. Indeed, Jay Belsky (1981) finds that neonates who are "at risk" for later emotional difficulties (as indicated by their poor performance on the Brazelton scale) are likely to have nonsynchronous interactions with their parents only when the parents are unhappily married. Taken together, these findings indicate that a stormy marriage is a major environmental hazard that can hinder or even prevent the establishment of close emotional ties between parents and their infants.

THE INFANT'S ATTACHMENT TO CAREGIVERS

Although adults may become emotionally attached to an infant very soon after the baby is born, the infant will require a little more time in order to form a genuine attachment to his or her caregivers. Many theories have been proposed to explain how and why infants become emotionally involved with the people around them. But before we consider these theories, we should briefly discuss the stages that babies go through in becoming attached to a close companion.

Development of Primary Social Attachments

Several years ago, Rudolph Schaffer and Peggy Emerson (1964) studied the development of social attachments by following a group of Scottish infants from early infancy to 18 months of age. Once a month, mothers were interviewed to determine (1) how the infant responded when separated from close companions in seven situations (for example, being left in a crib; being left in the presence of strangers) and (2) the persons to whom the infant's separation responses were directed. A child was judged to be attached to someone if separation from that person reliably elicited a protest.

Schaffer and Emerson found that infants pass through the following steps, or stages, as they develop close ties with their caregivers:

1. *The asocial stage (0–6 weeks).* The very young infant is largely an asocial creature: many kinds of social and nonsocial stimuli will elicit favorable reactions, and few produce any kind of protest. By the end of this period, infants are beginning to show a distinct preference for social stimuli, such as a smiling face.

2. *The stage of indiscriminate attachment (6 weeks to 6–7 months).* During this period, infants prefer human company, and they are apt to protest when an adult puts them down or leaves them alone. However, the children's protests are truly indiscriminate: they dislike being separated from anyone, whether strangers or regular companions.

3. *The stage of specific attachments (about age 7 months).* At about 7 months of age, infants begin to protest only when separated from one particular individual, usually the mother (see Figure 11-1). In addition, many infants begin to fear strangers at about this time. Schaffer and Emerson interpret these data as an indication that the infants have formed their first genuine attachments.

4. *The stage of multiple attachments.* Within weeks after forming their initial attachments,

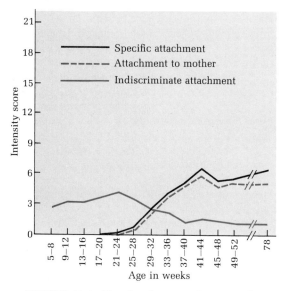

FIGURE 11-1. *The developmental course of attachment during infancy.*

about half the infants in Schaffer and Emerson's study were becoming attached to other people (fathers, siblings, grandparents, or perhaps even a regular babysitter). By 18 months of age, very few infants were attached to only one person, and some were attached to five or more.

Schaffer and Emerson originally believed that infants who are multiply attached have a "hierarchy" of attachment objects and that the individual at the top of the list is their most preferred companion. However, later research indicates that each of the infant's attachment objects may serve slightly different functions, so that the person whom an infant prefers most may depend on the situation. For example, most infants prefer the mother's company if they are upset or frightened (Lamb & Stevenson, 1978). However, fathers seem to be preferred as playmates, possibly because much of the time they spend with their infants is "play time," and fathers are more likely than mothers to play unusual, rough-and-tumble games that infants seem to enjoy (Clarke-Stewart, 1978; Lamb, 1981). Schaffer (1977) is now convinced that "being attached to several people does not necessarily imply a shallower feeling toward each one, for an infant's capacity for attachment is not like a cake that has to be [divided]. Love, even in babies, has no limits" (p. 100).

Theories of Attachment

If you have ever cared for a kitten or a puppy, you may have noticed that pets seem most responsive to the person who feeds them. Is this true of human infants? Some theorists think so, but many others disagree. We will now look at several theories that attempt to explain how (or why) infants might become attached to their regular companions.

For years, theorists have argued about the reasons that babies come to "love" their caregivers. The history of this theoretical controversy is interesting because each theory makes different assumptions about the part that infants play in their social relationships and the roles that caregivers must enact in order to win the baby's affection. The four theories that have been most influential are those reviewed in Chapter Two—psychoanalytic theory, learning theory, cognitive-developmental theory, and ethological theory.

■ *Psychoanalytic theory: Attachments develop from oral activities*

According to Freud, infants are "oral" creatures who derive pleasure from activities such as sucking, biting, and mouthing objects. Presumably the infant will invest psychic energy in and become attached to any person or object that provides oral pleasure. Thus, infants were thought to become emotionally involved with their mothers because it is usually the mother who gives pleasure to the oral child by feeding her. Freud believed that infants will become securely attached to their mothers if the mother is relaxed and generous in her feeding practices, thereby allowing the child a lot of oral pleasure.

Erik Erikson also believes that the feeding situation is a major contributor to social attachments. According to Erikson, a mother who allows her infant to go hungry at times or who weans her baby too early is likely to have an anxious child who fails to develop a sense of trust in other people. Erikson contends that an untrusting child may become overdependent—one who will "lean on" others, not necessarily out of love or a desire to be near but solely to ensure that his or her needs are met. Presumably children who have not learned to trust others during infancy are likely to avoid close mutual-trust relationships throughout their lives.

Before we examine the research on feeding practices and their contribution to social attachments, we need to consider another viewpoint that assumes that feeding is important—learning theory.

■ Learning theory: Rewardingness leads to love

Learning theorists consider the mother a logical attachment object for her baby. Not only do mothers feed their infants, they also change them when they are wet or soiled, provide warmth, tender touches, and soft, reassuring vocalizations when they are upset or afraid, and promote changes in the "scenery" in what otherwise could be a rather monotonous environment for babies who cannot get up and move about on their own. What will a baby make of all this? According to learning theorists, an infant will eventually associate the mother with pleasant feelings and pleasurable sensations, so that she becomes a conditioned stimulus for positive outcomes (in the language of learning theory, a *secondary reinforcer*). Once the mother (or any other caregiver) has attained the status of a conditioned, or secondary, reinforcer, the infant is attached—he or she will now do whatever is necessary (smile, coo, babble, or follow) in order to attract the caregiver's attention or to remain near this valuable and rewarding individual.

Like psychoanalysts, many learning theorists believe that feeding plays an important role in determining the quality of an infant's attachment to the primary caregiver. Robert Sears (1963) suggests two reasons that feeding may be a special kind of caregiving activity. First, the mother is often able to sit down with her infant and provide *many comforts*—including warmth and tactile, visual, and vocal stimulation, as well as satisfying the baby's hunger and thirst—*all at once*. Second, feeding is an activity that should elicit positive responses from the infant (smiling, cooing) that are likely to increase a caregiver's affection for the child. In sum, feeding is thought to be important because it provides positive reinforcers to both the caregiver and her infant—reinforcers that will strengthen their feelings of affection for each other.

Just how important is feeding? In 1959 Harry Harlow and Robert Zimmerman reported the results of a study designed to compare the importance of feeding and tactile stimulation for the development of social attachments in infant monkeys. The monkeys were separated from their mothers in the first day of life and reared for the next 165 days by two surrogate mothers. As you can see in Photo 11-3, each surrogate mother had a face and well-proportioned body constructed of wire. However, the body of one surrogate (the "cloth mother") was wrapped in foam rubber and covered with terrycloth. Half the infants were always fed by this warm, comfortable cloth mother, the remaining half by the rather uncomfortable "wire mother." At several points during the experiment, the attachment of each infant to its surrogate mothers was measured by noting the amount of time that the infant spent in close contact with each mother as well as the mother to whom the infant would run when frightened.

If feeding is especially important to the development of primary social attachments, we would expect the monkeys to spend more time in contact with the mother who had fed them, regardless of the amount of contact comfort she provided. We would also expect the monkeys to run

PHOTO 11-3. *The "wire" and "cloth" surrogate mothers used in Harlow's research. This infant remains with the cloth mother even though it must stretch to the wire mother in order to feed.*

to the feeding mother whenever they were upset or afraid. However, Harlow and Zimmerman found that all the infants spent more time on the cloth mother, *regardless of which mother had fed them* (see Figure 11-2). In addition, all infants showed a clear preference for the cloth mother when they were frightened by novel stimuli (marching toy bears, wooden spiders) that were placed in their cages. Apparently the cloth mothers provided the reassurance the infants were seeking, for Harlow and Zimmerman (1959) noted that

> in spite of their abject terror, the infant monkeys, after reaching the cloth mother and rubbing their bodies about hers, rapidly come to lose their fear of the frightening stimuli. Indeed, within a minute or two most of the babies were visually exploring the thing which so shortly before had seemed an object of evil. The bravest of the babies would actually leave the mother and approach the fearful monsters, under, of course, the protective gaze of their mothers (p. 423).

Clearly, the implication of Harlow and Zimmerman's classic study is that feeding is *not* the most

important determinant of an infant's attachment to caregivers.

Although Harlow's subjects were monkeys, research with human infants paints a similar picture. In their study of Scottish infants, Schaffer and Emerson (1964) asked each mother the age at which her child had been weaned, the amount of time it had taken to wean the child, and the feeding schedule (regular interval or demand feeding) that she had used with her baby. None of these feeding practices predicted the character of an infant's attachment to his or her mother. In fact, Schaffer and Emerson found that, in 39% of cases, the person who usually fed, bathed, and changed the child (typically the mother) was not even the child's primary attachment object! These findings are clearly damaging to any theory that states that feeding and feeding practices are the primary determinants of the child's first social attachment.

How, then, do attachments develop? Contemporary learning theorists would argue that feeding plays a role in the process but that satisfying the child's hunger is only one of the many nice things that caregivers do for their infants. Presumably the visual, tactile, and vocal stimulation that adults provide when they interact with their infants will also make these regular companions seem rather attractive or rewarding (Gewirtz, 1969). In fact, Harlow's research with infant monkeys suggests that warmth and **"contact comfort"** may be a more powerful contributor to attachments than feeding and the reduction of hunger.

In sum, learning theorists believe that infants are attracted to those individuals who are quick to respond to their signals and who provide them with a variety of pleasant or rewarding experiences. Indeed, Schaffer and Emerson (1964) found that the two aspects of a mother's behavior that predicted the character of her infant's attachment to her were (1) her responsiveness to the infant's behavior and (2) the total amount of stimulation that she provided. Mothers who responded quickly to their infants' social signals and who

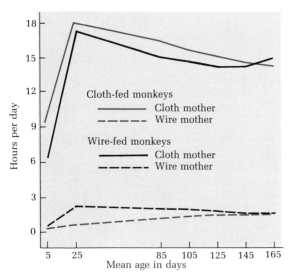

FIGURE 11-2. Average amount of time infant monkeys spent in contact with their cloth and wire mother surrogates. The monkeys spent the majority of their time clinging to the cloth mother, regardless of which mother had fed them.

contact comfort: *the term used by Harlow to describe the pleasure infant monkeys derive from clinging to their mothers' bodies or to a soft, warm terrycloth mother surrogate.*

often played with their babies had infants who were closely attached to them.

■ *Cognitive-developmental theory: Attachments depend on cognitive development*

Proponents of Jean Piaget's cognitive-developmental theory believe that an infant's ability to form social attachments depends, in part, on his or her level of intellectual development. Before an attachment can occur, the infant must be able to discriminate familiar persons (that is, potential attachment objects) from strangers. He or she must also recognize that close companions continue to exist even when they are absent (Kohlberg, 1969; Schaffer, 1971). This latter ability is an example of the object concept (or *object permanence*) discussed in Chapter Nine. Presumably infants who recognize that objects (or persons) have a permanent existence will develop stable schemata for people with whom they regularly interact. They should then prefer these people to all others and may even protest when they cannot locate their close companion(s).

Is the timing of social attachments related to cognitive development? Apparently so. In their classic study of Scottish infants, Schaffer and Emerson (1964) noted that attachments normally appear during the third quarter of the first year (age 7–9 months)—precisely the time that infants begin to show some evidence of acquiring the object concept. Drawing from these observations and the work of Piaget, Schaffer (1971) then proposed that attachments will not occur until the fourth sensorimotor substage, when infants first begin to search for and find objects hidden behind a screen.

An experiment by Barry Lester and his associates (Lester, Kotelchuck, Spelke, Sellers, & Klein, 1974) was designed to evaluate Schaffer's hypothesis. In this study, 9-month-old and 12-month-old infants were given a test that measured their level of object permanence. Then each infant was exposed to a number of brief separations from the mother, the father, and a stranger. The results lend some support to the cognitive-developmental viewpoint. The 9-month-old infants who scored high (Stage 4 or above) in object permanence showed stronger protests when separated from their mothers than infants who scored lower (Stage 3 or below). Among the 12-month-old infants, those who scored high in object permanence

showed more separation protest at the departure of *either the mother or the father* than infants whose object permanence was less well developed. Neither age group protested separations from a stranger. Using separation protest as evidence of attachments, it would appear that the cognitively advanced 9-month-olds were attached to their mothers, while the cognitively advanced yearlings were attached to both parents. Thus, Lester's findings not only are consistent with the developmental stages of attachment reported by Schaffer and Emerson (1964) but also indicate that the timing of the primary attachment is related to the child's level of object permanence.

■ *Ethological theory: Attachments may be biologically programmed*

Ethologists have proposed an interesting explanation for social attachments that is sometimes called "evolutionary" theory because of its distinct evolutionary overtones. The major assumption of the ethological approach is that all animals, including human beings, are born with a number of species-specific "signals," or behavioral tendencies, that promote certain social behaviors (Ainsworth, Bell, & Stayton, 1974; Bowlby, 1969, 1973). Presumably these innate signals are products of a species' evolutionary history, and each of these attributes is designed to serve some purpose that increases the chances of survival for the individual and the species.

What is the purpose of a social attachment? According to John Bowlby (1969, 1973), infant/caregiver attachments serve the same function for all species—namely, to protect the young from prolonged discomfort, from predators, and perhaps from fear itself. Of course, ethologists would argue that the long-range purpose of the primary social attachment is to ensure that the young of each successive generation live long enough to reproduce, thereby enabling the species to survive.

Let's briefly consider some of the evidence that led Bowlby to propose his evolutionary theory of attachment.

Attachment in precocial birds. More than 100 years ago, investigators first noted that chicks would follow almost any moving object—another chicken, a duck, or a human being—as soon as they were able to walk (Spaulding, 1873). Konrad Lorenz (1937) observed the same "following response" in young goslings, a behavior he labeled **imprinting** (or stamping in). Lorenz also noted that (1) imprinting is automatic—the young fowl does not have to be taught to follow, (2) imprinting occurs only within a narrowly delimited **critical period** after the bird has hatched, and (3) imprinting is irreversible—once the bird begins to follow a particular object, it will remain attached to it. Although later research has challenged some of Lorenz's original conclusions (see Rajecki, 1977), contemporary ethologists remain firm in their belief that imprinting is an innate response that attaches an infant to its mother, thereby increasing the infant's chances of survival.

Attachment in mammals. The tendency to cling to or to maintain physical contact with the mother is commonly observed among infants of many mammalian species. We have previously touched on Harry Harlow's work showing the importance of tactile stimulation and contact comfort for the development of primary attachments in infant monkeys. Although the attachment of a young monkey to its primary caregiver is certainly not an example of imprinting, Harlow's research convinced John Bowlby that the tendency of young animals to cling to their mothers is an inborn, **preadapted** response that promotes the development of social attachments.

Attachment in human infants. According to Bowlby (1969, 1973), human infants have inherited a number of responses that help them to maintain contact with a caregiver. Three of these response systems—sucking, grasping, and following (first by keeping the caregiver in sight and later by crawling or walking)—are said to serve an **executive function:** they are initiated by the infant and require only a minimal response from the caregiver. Two other responses, smiling and vocalizing (crying or babbling), serve a **signaling function** by encouraging caregivers to approach the infant and to provide some kind of attention or comfort. A baby's "kewpie doll" appearance is yet another inborn characteristic that may make an infant seem desirable to others (Alley, 1981). Thus, infants are said to be *active* participants in the attachment process: their role (initially, at least) is to emit a number of preprogrammed signals that are likely to attract attention or influence the behavior of caregivers.

According to Bowlby, adults are biologically programmed to respond to an infant's signals in much the same way that infants are programmed to react to the sight, sound, warmth, and touch of their caregivers. As a mother (or other primary caregiver) becomes more proficient at reading and reacting to her baby's signals, the infant should become ever more responsive to her. The end result of these increasingly personal interactions is the development of a *mutual* bond or attachment between the infant and his or her most intimate companion(s).

A common misunderstanding. A hasty reading of ethological theory might lead one to conclude that attachments are "automatic"—that all the child requires to form one is a caregiver with whom to interact. This view is incorrect. Although infants may be preprogrammed to beam various signals to other people, these innate responses may eventually wane if they fail to produce favorable reactions from an unresponsive caregiver (Ainsworth et al., 1978). So infants are not biologically programmed to attach themselves to the closest available human; attachments are a product of a history of interaction in which each participant has learned to respond in a mean-

---

imprinting: *an innate or instinctual form of learning in which the young of certain species will follow and become attached to moving objects (usually their mothers).*

critical period: *a brief period in the development of an organism when it is particularly sensitive to certain environmental influences; outside this period, the same influences will have little if any effect.*

preadapted characteristic: *an innate attribute that is a product of evolution and serves some function that increases the chances of survival for the individual and the species.*

executive responses: *behaviors such as sucking, grasping, and following that an infant initiates in order to establish or maintain contact with a close companion.*

signaling responses: *behaviors such as smiling and vocalizing that an infant emits in order to attract the attention or influence the behavior of a close companion.*

ingful way to the social signals of his or her partner. A little later in the chapter, we will see that infants may fail to establish warm, affectionate relationships with primary caregivers who are slow to react to their bids for attention.

■ *Comparing the four theoretical approaches*
Although the four theories we have reviewed are different in many respects, each theory has had something to offer. Even though feeding practices are not as important as psychoanalysts had originally thought, it was Sigmund Freud who stressed that we will need to know more about mother/infant interactions if we are to understand how babies form emotional attachments. Learning theorists followed up on Freud's ideas and concluded that caregivers play an important role in the infant's emotional development. Presumably the infant is likely to view a responsive companion who provides many comforts as a rewarding individual who is worthy of affection. Ethologists can agree with this point of view, but they would add that the infant is an active participant in the attachment process. That is, infants are born with a number of preprogrammed responses that enable them to promote the very interactions from which attachments are likely to develop. Finally, cognitive theorists have contributed to our understanding of early emotional development by showing that the timing of social attachments is related to the child's level of intellectual development. In sum, it makes no sense to tag one of these theories as "correct" and to ignore the other three, for each theory has helped us to understand how and why infants become attached to their most intimate companions.

DEVELOPMENT OF FEARFUL REACTIONS

At about the same time that infants are establishing close affectional ties to a caregiver, they often begin to display negative emotional outbursts that may puzzle or perhaps even annoy their close companions. In this section we will look at two of the common fears of infancy—stranger anxiety and separation anxiety—and try to determine why these negative reactions are likely to emerge during the second half of the first year.

Stranger Anxiety

Nine-month-old Billy is sitting on the floor in the den when his mother leads a strange person into the room. The stranger suddenly walks toward the child, bends over, and says "Hi, Billy! How are you?" If Billy is like many 9-month-olds, he may stare at the stranger for a moment and then turn away, whimper, and crawl toward his mother.

This wary reaction to a stranger, or **stranger anxiety,** stands in marked contrast to the smiling, babbling, and other positive greetings that infants often emit when approached by a familiar companion. Schaffer and Emerson (1964) noted that most of the infants in their sample reacted positively to strangers up until the time they had formed an attachment (usually at about 7 months of age) but then became fearful of strangers shortly thereafter. Studies of North American children tend to confirm this finding: wary reactions to strangers often emerge at 6–7 months of age, peak at 8–10 months, and gradually decline in intensity over the second year (Sroufe, 1977). However, stranger anxiety may never completely subside, for 2-, 3-, and even 4-year-olds are apt to show at least some signs of wariness when approached by a stranger in an unfamiliar setting (Greenberg & Marvin, 1982).

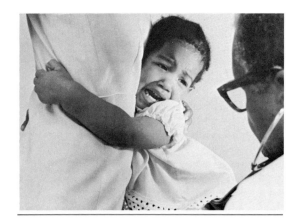

PHOTO 11-4. *Although infants become more tolerant of strangers during the second year, stranger anxiety is a reaction that may never completely subside. Unavoidable contact with an intrusive stranger is likely to upset many 2-, 3-, and even 4-year-olds.*

At one time, stranger anxiety was thought to be a true developmental milestone—that is, an inevitable response to unfamiliar company that supposedly characterized all infants who had become attached to a caregiver. However, recent research indicates that infants are not always afraid of strangers and, in fact, may sometimes react rather positively to an unfamiliar companion (Bretherton, Stolberg, & Kreye, 1981; Rheingold & Eckerman, 1973). Before we try to understand why 6–12-month-old infants are sometimes wary of strangers, it may be helpful to note the circumstances under which stranger anxiety is most likely to occur.

■ *When will infants fear a stranger?*

Among the many factors that affect an infant's reactions to a stranger are the availability of a familiar companion, the setting in which the stranger appears, the ways the stranger responds to the infant, and the stranger's physical characteristics.

Availability of familiar companions. Infants react much more negatively to the approach of a stranger when they are separated from their mothers or other close companions. In one study, strangers approached 6–12-month-old infants who were sitting either on their mothers' laps or in infant seats a few feet away. Although fewer than one-third of the infants showed a wary reaction when seated with their mothers, about two-thirds of them frowned, turned away, whimpered, or cried if they were seated only four feet from their mothers (Morgan & Ricciuti, 1969). Apparently contact with a loved one provides a sense of security that enables infants to respond more constructively to the approach of a stranger. This is particularly true if caregivers use a positive tone of voice when talking to their infants about the stranger (Feinman & Lewis, 1983).

The setting. A number of years ago, a student noted that her baby reacted much more negatively to strangers while visiting the supermarket than at home. Her hypothesis was that babies are apprehensive in unfamiliar settings and that this wariness is then magnified by the approach of an unfamiliar person.

Later research suggests that this young woman was a rather astute observer. Alan Sroufe and his associates (Sroufe, Waters, & Matas, 1974) found that few 10-month-old infants were wary of strangers when tested within the familiar confines of the home but that most of them reacted negatively to strange companions when tested in an unfamiliar laboratory. Sroufe et al. also found that an infant's familiarity with a strange setting made a difference: whereas only 50% of the infants were apprehensive when they had had ten minutes to get used to a strange room, over 90% became upset if a stranger approached within a minute after they had been placed there. Clearly, the setting in which a stranger appears is an important determinant of an infant's reactions to him or her.

The stranger's behavior. After reviewing the literature, Alan Sroufe (1977) concluded that an infant's response to a stranger often depends on the stranger's behavior. Strangers who initially keep their distance and then approach slowly while smiling, talking, or offering a familiar toy are likely to elicit a positive reaction from a 10–12-month-old. Presumably some of the apprehension surrounding the approach of an unfamiliar person can be offset if the stranger behaves in a friendly manner (like a caregiver) and offers a familiar object (such as a toy) with which the child will feel comfortable. In contrast, intrusive strangers who approach rapidly and force themselves on the child (for example, by trying to pick her up) are likely to elicit a fearful reaction.

Some investigators have argued that an infant will react quite favorably to any stranger who allows the child to regulate their initial interactions. Mary Levitt (1980) tested this hypothesis by exposing 10-month-old infants to a stranger who wanted to play peek-a-boo. In the contingent-response condition, the infant could control the stranger's peek-a-boo behavior: every time the child touched a cylinder in front of him or her, the stranger opened a curtain and said "Hi, [baby's name]." In the noncontingent-response condition,

---

stranger anxiety: *a wary or fretful reaction that infants often display when approached by an unfamiliar person.*

the stranger simply opened the curtain and vocalized a total of 14 times according to a schedule that the infant could not control. After playing peek-a-boo for seven minutes, the stranger reappeared, approached the child, and lifted him or her. Figure 11-3 shows the results. Note that infants who had been able to control the stranger's peek-a-boo behavior reacted much more positively to the stranger's later intrusions than infants who had had no prior control over the stranger. Apparently, strange adults can become "friends" if they allow the infant to regulate their earliest interactions.

Do Levitt's findings imply that strangers should never initiate games or activities with a potentially wary infant? *No, they do not.* Recently, Inge Bretherton and her associates (Bretherton et al., 1981) have found that 12–24-month-old children are quite willing to play with a friendly stranger who actively bids for their attention as long as the

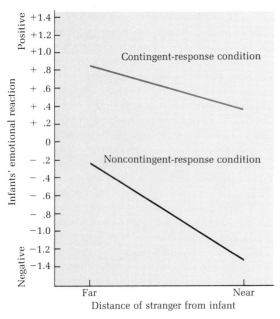

FIGURE 11-3. *Emotional reactions of 10-month-old infants to the approach of a stranger. Infants in the contingent condition, who had had some control over the stranger's peek-a-boo behavior, reacted favorably to the stranger's approach. In contrast, infants in the noncontingent condition were quite wary of a stranger they could not control, and their wariness increased as the stranger became more intrusive.*

stranger (1) is not overly intrusive and (2) offers a toy (or suggests an activity) with which the infant is familiar. In fact, friendly strangers are apt to be more successful at establishing rapport with an infant if they cautiously take the initiative and allow the infant to control the pace of their activities rather than sitting back and waiting for the child to initiate an interaction with them (Bretherton et al., 1981).

The strange child: Friend or fiend.   A number of years ago, Michael Lewis and Jeanne Brooks (1974) exposed 7–19-month-old infants to strange adults and a strange child (a 4-year-old girl). As the adults approached, the infants became quite wary. However, the approach of the strange child typically elicited a mildly *positive* reaction. Could the infants have been responding favorably to the child because she was relatively small, as they were? To find out, Brooks and Lewis (1976) exposed 7–24-month-old infants to a strange adult, a strange child, and an adult midget who was the same size as the strange child. The infants reacted much more negatively to both the normal-sized adult and the midget than to the child. Surely these subjects did not prefer the strange child solely on the basis of size; otherwise they would have reacted positively to the "child-sized" midget. Apparently, adultlike facial features were the cues that elicited a wary response.

Although infants may initially react to other children as if they were friends rather than fiends, it is not at all unusual for a youngster to become wary of peers at some point during the second year (Jacobson, 1980; Kagan, Kearsley, & Zelazo, 1975). In the following section, we will take a closer look at this "delayed reaction" to unfamiliar peers as we consider how various developmental theorists would explain stranger anxiety.

■ Why are infants wary of strangers?

We have seen that stranger anxiety follows a regular developmental course, normally emerging at about the same time as the primary social attachment. But why do children who are attached to someone suddenly become wary of strangers? Let's consider three points of view.

The "fear of separation" hypothesis.   Psychoanalytic and social-learning theorists (Sears, 1963;

Spitz, 1950) have proposed that a child's stranger anxiety actually represents a fear of becoming separated from or losing the person(s) to whom he or she is attached. Consistent with this point of view are the observations that wary reactions first appear after the infant has become attached to someone and that attached infants will often cling to their mothers or other close companions when a stranger approaches (Morgan & Ricciuti, 1969; Schaffer & Emerson, 1964). However, the "fear of separation" hypothesis does not explain why infants sometimes react very positively to strangers and may continue to do so even after they have seen their mothers leave the room (Ainsworth et al., 1978). How can we explain these findings?

The ethological perspective. John Bowlby (1973) suggests that there are a number of events that qualify as natural clues to danger. In other words, some situations have been so frequently associated with danger throughout a species' evolutionary history that a fear or avoidance response has become innate, or "biologically programmed." Avoidance or wariness of strangers is presumably one example of a class of preprogrammed fears that are elicited by stimuli that are unfamiliar to the child.

Why does stranger anxiety become less intense during the second year? Mary Ainsworth (Ainsworth et al., 1974) believes that infants become less wary of strangers as they begin to use their attachment objects as **secure bases** who encourage a second preprogrammed behavior—exploring the environment. According to Ainsworth and her associates (1974),

> The dynamic balance between exploratory and attachment behavior has significance from an evolutionary point of view. Whereas attachment behaviors . . . serve a protective function during the long, helpless infancy of a species such as the human . . . exploratory behaviors reflect a genetic basis for an infant to be interested in novel features of the environment, to approach them, manipulate them, . . . to play, and to learn more about the nature of his environment and the properties of the objects in it. It is an advantageous arrangement for an infant . . . to explore without straying too far from an adult who can protect him [p. 104].

In sum, stranger anxiety is thought to wane as the child explores the environment and finds that many novel stimuli (including friendly strangers) can be interesting and enjoyable in their own right.

Two questions remain. If 7–10-month-old infants are programmed to fear unfamiliar people, then (1) why don't they fear strange children, and (2) why do they then become wary of peers in the second year of life? Cognitive theorists have proposed an explanation for stranger anxiety that addresses both these issues.

The cognitive-developmental viewpoint.
Jerome Kagan (1972) believes that stranger anxiety is a natural outgrowth of the infant's perceptual and cognitive development. Kagan suggests that 6–8-month-olds have developed stable schemata for the faces of familiar companions and that a strange face now represents a discrepant and potentially fear-producing stimulus. He notes that children of this age will typically stare at a stranger before they begin to protest. Presumably this short visual fixation is not a fear-induced "freezing" but, rather, a period of *hypothesizing:* the infant is examining the discrepant stimulus and trying to explain what it is or what has become of the familiar faces that match his or her schema for human beings. Failing to answer these questions, the child becomes wary of the stranger and may cry in an attempt to summon familiar company. As infants mature, they are gradually exposed to many strangers, and their schema for faces will become more generalized. Therefore, a 2-year-old is unlikely to be upset at the sight of a strange face, because strangers are now easily assimilated into the infant's very broad facial schema.

According to the cognitive viewpoint, infants who see only a small number of people should soon develop stable schemata for these regular companions and perhaps come to fear strangers at an early age. In contrast, infants who are often exposed to strangers (for example, relatives, babysitters, and family friends) should be slow to develop a stable schema for "caregivers" and therefore may be relatively unperturbed by a stranger. Support for this proposition comes from

---

secure-base phenomenon: *the tendency of infants to venture away from a close companion to explore the environment.*

a study by Rudolph Schaffer (1966), who found that infants who are wary of strangers at an early age are likely to come from small families and to have had very little contact with people from outside the immediate household.

Why are 7–10-month-old infants *not* afraid of strange children? Perhaps because babies of this age are cared for mainly by adults and do not have well-developed schemata for children. As a result, an unfamiliar child may simply represent an interesting stimulus that is far too discrepant from the infant's schema for "caregivers" to generate much anxiety. However, Jerome Kagan and his associates (Kagan et al., 1975) believe that an unfamiliar child will become an object of apprehension once the infant has developed a schema for children (based on siblings or playmates) and then discovers that the small stranger does not match this "child schema."

In a longitudinal study, Joseph Jacobson (1980) found that infants do become wary of unfamiliar peers at some point between the ages of 10 and 14½ months. Moreover, all Jacobson's infants had been given a test of cognitive development at 10 months of age. Jacobson discovered that the infants who had scored highest on this cognitive test were most wary of strange peers at 12 months of age, while those who had scored lower showed their greatest anxiety at age 14½ months. So the time at which infants are most apprehensive around other children will depend, in part, on their rate of cognitive development.

Summing up.   We have seen that stranger anxiety is a rather complex emotional response that depends, in part, on the availability of familiar companions, the setting, the identity and behavior of the stranger, and the infant's developmental level. Clearly, there is no one correct explanation for this interesting phenomenon: each of the above explanations has received some support and has helped us to understand why infants are sometimes wary when they come face to face with a stranger.

Separation Anxiety

At 7–12 months of age, many infants begin to show signs of discomfort when separated from their mothers or other familiar companions. For example, 10-month-old Tony, restrained in his playpen,

is likely to cry if he sees his mother put on a coat and pick up a purse as she prepares to go shopping. If unrestrained and exposed to the same scene, 15-month-old Ben might run and cling to his mother or at least follow her to the door. As she leaves and closes the door behind her, Ben will probably cry. These reactions reflect the infants' **separation anxiety.** Separation anxiety normally appears during the latter half of the first year (at about the time infants are forming primary social attachments), peaks at 14–18 months, and gradually becomes less frequent and less intense throughout infancy and the preschool period (Kagan, 1976; Weinraub & Lewis, 1977).

Children raised in some cultural settings protest separations from their mothers at an earlier age than North American or European infants. For example, Mary Ainsworth (1967) found that Ugandan infants begin to fear separations from their mothers as early as 5–6 months of age. Why? One reason may be that Ugandan babies have much more close contact with their mothers than is typical in Western cultures—these infants sleep with their mothers, nurse for at least two years, and go wherever their mothers go, riding on the mother's hips or across her back in a cotton sling. So Ugandan infants may be quick to protest separations from their mothers because these separations are very unusual events.

■ *Explanations for separation anxiety*

There are several reasons that an infant might protest a separation from loved ones. Let's consider three very different points of view.

The "conditioned anxiety" hypothesis.   Psychoanalysts and some learning theorists have proposed that infants may learn to fear separations from their caregivers if prior discomforts (for example, hunger, wet diapers, and pain) have been especially frequent or intense during periods when caregivers were not present to relieve them. In other words, infants may associate prolonged or intense discomfort with the caregiver's absence and then express their "conditioned anxiety" by protesting whenever the caregiver is about to depart.

One problem with the "conditioned anxiety" hypothesis is that it cannot explain why infants are *less* likely to protest separations from their mothers at home (where they have previously suf-

PHOTO 11-5. Separation anxiety appears very early in infants who spend most of their time close to their caregivers.

fered many discomforts) than in a laboratory environment where they have never been before (Rinkoff & Corter, 1980). In addition, "conditioned anxiety" cannot explain the *early* separation protests seen among Ugandan infants, who have rarely been separated from their mothers and therefore have had little or no opportunity to associate pain and discomfort with the mother's absence. Let's now consider a second point of view that offers an explanation for both these findings.

The ethological viewpoint. Ethologists have argued that children are biologically programmed to fear many strange or uncertain situations, including strange people, strange settings, and the "strange circumstance" in which they are separated from their familiar companions (Bowlby, 1973; Stayton, Ainsworth, & Main, 1973). According to the ethological viewpoint, infants should show stronger separation protests in a strange laboratory environment because this unfamiliar setting magnifies the apprehension they will

ordinarily experience when separated from a caregiver. Moreover, ethologists would argue that Ugandan infants are quick to protest separations from their mothers because these separations occur so very infrequently that they qualify as highly unusual (that is, fear-provoking) events (Ainsworth, 1967).

Why does separation anxiety become less intense toward the end of the second year? According to ethologists, a fear of separation will gradually wane as the child's innate exploratory activities become increasingly apparent and he or she begins to initiate brief separations by using the mother (or another close companion) as a secure base from which to explore.

Apparently infants are much less likely to fear separations *that they initiate themselves.* Harriet Rheingold and Carol Eckerman (1970) found that 10-month-olds were perfectly willing to leave their mothers and venture alone into a strange room in order to play there. However, a second group of 10-month-olds typically cried when they were placed in this strange room and then were left alone as their mothers departed. It appears that the first group of infants were not discomforted in the strange setting because they knew where their mothers were and were using them as a secure base from which to explore the environment.

Of course, the infant's willingness to explore will depend on the setting, the accessibility of caregivers, and the presence of other people. Alan Sroufe (1977) reports that infants are much more likely to explore an unfamiliar setting if a caregiver is physically present. Moreover, Helen Samuels (1980) found that infants will venture much farther from their mothers and stay away longer when a brother or sister is present to pull them away from their "secure bases." However, an exploring infant will typically retreat in the direction of a caregiver if confronted by a stranger (Bretherton & Ainsworth, 1974) or if the caregiver should become less accessible by moving away from the child or pursuing an interest of her own,

> **separation anxiety:** *a wary or fretful reaction that infants often display when separated from the person(s) to whom they are attached.*

such as reading or sewing (Rinkoff & Corter, 1980; Sorce & Emde, 1981).

In sum, ethologists view separation anxiety as an innate reaction that helps to protect the young of a species from harm or discomfort by ensuring that they will remain near their caregivers. Yet the caregivers who serve this protective function are also instrumental in alleviating separation anxiety. By serving as a secure base for exploratory activities, the caregiver encourages the infant to venture into the unknown and to become increasingly familiar with the environment. As a result, the child should eventually become more tolerant of separations and much less wary of stimuli (strangers and unfamiliar settings) that have previously been a source of concern.

The cognitive viewpoint. Cognitive-developmental theorists propose another explanation of separation anxiety that complements the ethological viewpoint. Jerome Kagan (1972, 1976) believes that infants develop not only schemata for familiar faces (caregivers) but also schemata for a familiar person's probable whereabouts. In other words, the infant may schematize "familiar faces in familiar places." Kagan notes that infants are often separated from their mothers in the course of day-to-day living and generally do not protest these brief separations. For example, if a mother proceeds into the kitchen, leaving her 10-month-old son on the living-room floor, the infant is likely to stop playing and watch her depart and then resume his previous activity without protesting her absence. This separation is not protested, because the child is able to explain where his mother has gone; that is, he has previously developed a schema for mother-in-the-kitchen. But should the mother pick up her coat and purse and walk out the front door, the child will find it difficult to account for her whereabouts and will probably cry. In sum, cognitive theorists believe that infants are most likely to protest separations when they cannot understand where their absent companions may have gone or when they are likely to return.

The results of a home-based observational study (Littenberg, Tulkin, & Kagan, 1971) are quite consistent with Kagan's cognitive hypothesis. In this study, 15-month-old infants showed little separation protest when mother departed through a doorway she used often but considerable protest when she left through a door that she used infrequently, such as the entry to a closet or the cellar. The children were separated from their mothers in both cases, but they protested only when they could not account for the mother's whereabouts.

Kagan's theory also explains the results of an interesting study by Carl Corter and his associates (Corter, Zucker, & Galligan, 1980). Nine-month-old infants first accompanied their mothers to a strange room (room A) and shortly thereafter watched the mothers exit into a second room (room B). Few of the infants protested this separation; most of them continued to play for a while with the toys that were present before crawling into the adjoining room and finding their mothers. In cognitive terms, it is reasonable to assume that the infants had formed a schema for the mother's whereabouts once they had found her in room B. At this point, the infants and their mothers reentered room A and spent a short time together before the mother departed once again. But on this second trial, she proceeded into another room (room C) and thus violated the infant's schema for her probable whereabouts. This time the majority of the infants fussed or cried! And where did these distressed youngsters go to search for their mothers? Generally, they crawled to the doorway that matched their schemata (room B) rather than to the location where they had most recently seen the mother depart (room C). Here, then, is another demonstration that infants are most likely to protest separations from a caregiver when they are uncertain of her whereabouts.

Apparently the development of object permanence is necessary before a child can schematize the probable location of an absent caregiver. If an infant did not recognize that a caregiver continued to exist, he or she would not try to determine her location and might not even protest her absence. As it turns out, we have already discussed a study that supports this line of reasoning. Recall that Barry Lester and his associates (Lester et al., 1974) found that infants who had not yet developed the concept of object permanence generally failed to protest when separated from their mothers and fathers.

■ *On easing the pain of separations*
At some point, virtually all parents will find it necessary to leave their infants and toddlers in an

unfamiliar setting (such as a nursery or a day-care center) or in the company of a stranger (for example, a babysitter) for hours at a time. Are there ways to make these separations easier or more tolerable for a young child?

Indeed there are. Marsha Weinraub and Michael Lewis (1977) found that toddlers who were separated from their mothers in an unfamiliar setting cried less and played more constructively if the mother took the time to explain that she was leaving and would soon return. Apparently, brief explanations that inform the child that he or she should "play until Mommy returns" are more effective at reducing separation distress than lengthy explanations (Adams & Passman, 1981). The problem with a lengthy discourse is that it is probably quite discrepant with the caregiver's usual practices. In other words, if the child has no schema for lengthy explanations, he or she may perceive the upcoming separation as something "out of the ordinary" and become very concerned.

PHOTO 11-6. *A brief explanation can help ease the pain of separation from a loved one.*

Some parents try to prepare their toddlers for an upcoming separation by explaining the situation to the child anywhere from a few hours to a few days in advance. This approach may work with preschool children who have the language skills and cognitive abilities to ask pertinent questions and to rehearse the situation in their own minds, but it may backfire with younger children who lack these problem-solving capabilities. Indeed, Roderick Adams and Richard Passman (1980) found that 2-year-olds who had been prepared at home for an upcoming separation later played less constructively and were more likely to follow their departing mothers than were toddlers who had not been told of the separation in advance.

Recently, Richard Passman and Kathleen Longeway (1982) found that toddlers who were given sharply focused photographs of their mothers were reasonably tolerant of separations: they played more and stayed longer in an unfamiliar playroom than toddlers who were given unrecognizable (blurred) photographs of their mothers. Apparently a clear physical representation of the mother reduces the separation distress, and it may help a child to remember whatever explanation a mother has given for her departure (although this latter assumption remains to be tested). Although all the children in Passman and Longeway's study were at least 20 months of age, we know that infants are capable of recognizing photographs of their mothers early in the first year (Barrera & Maurer, 1981) and that they have already begun to carefully examine and to smile at photographs of their parents by age 9–12 months (Brooks Gunn & Lewis, 1981). So it is possible that even a 9–12-month-old infant, who is unlikely to understand a verbal explanation, can be made less discomforted during necessary separations if a substitute caregiver is able to produce a photograph of the infant's absent companion(s).

LONG-TERM EFFECTS OF EARLY SOCIAL AND EMOTIONAL DEVELOPMENT

Do the emotional events and experiences of infancy have any long-term effects on developing children? Most developmental theorists believe that they do. Sigmund Freud (1905/1930) argued that the formation of a stable mother/infant bond

TABLE 11-1. The eight episodes that make up the strange-situations test

Number of episode	Persons present	Duration	Brief description of action
1	Mother, baby, and observer	30 seconds	Observer introduces mother and baby to experimental room, then leaves. (Room contains many appealing toys scattered about.)
2	Mother and baby	3 minutes	Mother is nonparticipant while baby explores; if necessary, play is stimulated after 2 minutes.
3	Stranger, mother, and baby	3 minutes	Stranger enters. First minute: stranger silent. Second minute: stranger converses with mother. Third minute: stranger approaches baby. After 3 minutes mother leaves unobtrusively.
4	Stranger and baby	3 minutes or less	First separation episode. Stranger's behavior is geared to that of baby.
5	Mother and baby	3 minutes or more	First reunion episode. Mother greets and/or comforts baby, then tries to settle him again in play. Mother then leaves, saying "bye-bye."
6	Baby alone	3 minutes or less	Second separation episode.
7	Stranger and baby	3 minutes or less	Continuation of second separation. Stranger enters and gears her behavior to that of baby.
8	Mother and baby	3 minutes	Second reunion episode. Mother enters, greets baby, then picks him up. Meanwhile stranger leaves unobtrusively.

is necessary for normal social and personality development. Erik Erikson agrees. His point of view is that emotional attachments provide the child with a basic sense of trust that will permit him or her to form close affectional ties to other people later in life. Learning theorists such as Harry Harlow (who studied monkeys) and Robert Sears (who studied humans) believe that close contact with a mother figure allows the infant to acquire a repertoire of social skills that will enable him or her to interact efficiently and appropriately with other members of the species. In sum, almost everyone agrees that the emotional events of infancy are very influential in shaping one's future development.

There are at least two ways to evaluate this **"early experience" hypothesis.** First, one could try to determine whether infants who do not become securely attached to their parents turn out any different from those who do. Second, one could look at what happens to infants who have had little or no contact with a mother figure during the first two years and do not become attached to anyone. In the pages that follow, we will consider the findings and implications of both these lines of inquiry.

Individual Differences in the Quality of Attachments

Mary Ainsworth and her associates (Ainsworth et al., 1978) have found that infants differ in the type (or quality) of attachments that they have with their caregivers. Ainsworth measures the quality of an infant's attachment by exposing the child to a **"strange situations" test** consisting of a series of eight episodes designed to gradually escalate the amount of stress that the baby will experience (see Table 11-1). By recording and analyzing the total pattern of crying, exploratory activities, and reunion behaviors that a child displays across all eight of the strange situations, we can usually place the infant's attachment into one of the following categories:

1. *Secure attachment.* About 70% of 1-year-old infants fall into this category. The **securely attached** infant actively explores while alone with the mother and is visibly upset by separation. The infant greets the mother when she returns and will welcome physical contact with her. The child is outgoing with strangers while the mother is present.

2. *Insecure attachment (anxious and resistant).* About 10% of 1-year-olds fall into this category. Although they appear quite anxious and are unlikely to explore while the mother is present, they become very distressed when the mother departs. When the mother returns, these infants are ambivalent: they will try to remain near her, although they resent her for having left them, and they are likely to resist contact initiated by the mother. **Anxious/resistant** infants are quite wary of strangers, even when their mothers are present.

3. *Insecure attachment (anxious and avoidant).* These infants (approximately 20% of 1-year-olds) seem uninterested in exploring when alone with their mothers. Moreover, they show little distress when separated from the mother and will generally avoid contact with her when she returns. **Anxious/avoidant** infants are not particularly wary of strangers but may sometimes avoid or ignore them in much the same way that they avoid or ignore their mothers.

From these descriptions, it would appear that securely attached infants are reasonably happy individuals who have established an affectionate relationship with their primary caregivers. In contrast, infants in the anxious/resistant category are drawn to their mothers but seem not to trust them, while infants who are anxious and avoidant appear to derive little if any comfort from their mothers, almost as if they were somewhat "detached" from them.

■ *How do infants become securely or insecurely attached?*

Ainsworth (1979) has suggested that the quality of an infant's attachment to his or her mother depends largely on the kinds of interactions that the mother and the infant have had. For example, it appears that mothers of *securely attached* infants are responsive caregivers from the very beginning: they are highly sensitive to their infants' signals, emotionally expressive, and likely to encourage their infants to explore; moreover, they seem to enjoy close contact with their babies (Ainsworth, 1979; Ainsworth et al., 1978). Ainsworth believes that infants learn what to expect from other people from their early experiences with primary caregivers. When a caregiver is sensitive to the infant's needs and easily accessible, the infant should derive comfort and pleasure from their interactions and become securely attached.

Mothers of *anxious and resistant* infants seem interested in their babies and willing to provide close physical contact. However, they frequently misinterpret their infants' signals and have generally failed to establish synchronized routines with them. In some cases, part of the problem may be attributable to a "difficult" infant, for Everett Waters and his associates found that infants

---

early-experience hypothesis: *the notion that the social and emotional events of infancy are very influential in determining the course of one's future development.*

strange-situations test: *a series of eight mildly stressful situations to which infants are exposed in order to determine the quality of their attachments to one or more close companions.*

secure attachment: *an infant/caregiver bond in which the child welcomes contact with a close companion and uses this person as a secure base from which to explore the environment.*

anxious and resistant attachment: *an insecure infant/caregiver bond, characterized by strong separation protest and a tendency of the child to resist contact initiated by the caregiver, particularly after a separation.*

anxious and avoidant attachment: *an insecure infant/caregiver bond, characterized by little separation protest and a tendency of the child to avoid or ignore the caregiver.*

BOX 11-2
FATHERS AS ATTACHMENT OBJECTS

We have seen that infants usually become attached to their primary caregivers (typically their mothers) before forming attachments to other close companions. What do we know about infants' attachments to their fathers? Are these relationships different from those that infants establish with their mothers? And just how important is the father to a child's emotional development?

Michael Lamb (1981) reports that many infants form attachments to their fathers during the third quarter of the first year, particularly if the fathers spend a lot of time with them. Lamb also notes that fathers and mothers respond in different ways to their babies. Mothers are more likely than fathers to hold their infants, to soothe them, to play traditional games, and to care for their needs; fathers are more likely than mothers to provide playful physical stimulation and to initiate unusual or unpredictable games that infants often enjoy (Lamb, 1981). Although many infants prefer their mothers' company when upset or afraid, fathers are generally preferred as playmates. However, the playmate role is only one of many that fathers assume. Most fathers are quite skillful at soothing and comforting their distressed infants, and they may also serve as a "secure base" from which their babies will venture to explore the environment (Lamb, 1981). In other words, fathers are rather versatile companions who can assume any and all of the functions normally served by the other parent (of course, the same is true of mothers).

Now, if parents are so versatile, why do you suppose fathers and mothers often behave so very differently toward their infants? Many investigators be-

The "playmate" role is only one of many that fathers assume.

lieve that the answer is simple—the mother quickly assumes the role of primary caregiver, thereby pushing the father in another direction if he hopes to play a special role in the infant's life. Although this "social roles" hypothesis seems reasonable, it cannot easily account for the results of a recent study by Michael Lamb and his associates (Lamb, Frodi, Hwang, Frodi, & Steinberg, 1982). Lamb et al. found that, even in nontraditional families where the father has served as the child's primary caregiver, mothers continue to be the more nurturant or comforting parent. The implication of these findings is that a parent's biological gender or early sex typing may have a greater influence on his or her reactions to an infant

classified as anxious/resistant at 1 year of age had often been rather irritable and unresponsive as neonates (Waters et al., 1980). Yet the infant's behavior cannot be the only contributor to an anxious/resistant attachment, since many difficult babies will eventually become securely attached to their caregivers. Ainsworth (1979) has noted that mothers of anxious/resistant infants tend to be inconsistent in their caregiving—at times they react very enthusiastically to their babies, although their responses to the infant may depend more on their own moods than on the infant's behavior. As a result, the infant becomes both anxious and resentful when he learns that he cannot necessarily count on the mother for the emotional

support and comfort that he needs (see also Belsky, Rovine, & Taylor, 1984).

The mothers of *anxious and avoidant* infants are different from other mothers in several respects. For example, they are very impatient with their babies, angry or resentful when the infant interferes with their own plans and activities, and quite unresponsive to the infant's signals (Ainsworth, 1979; Egeland & Farber, 1984). Moreover, they often express negative feelings about their infants, and on those occasions when they do respond positively to their children, they tend to limit their expressions of affection to brief kisses rather than hugging or cuddling (Tracy & Ainsworth, 1981). Ainsworth (1979) believes that these

Average levels of social responsiveness and emotional conflict shown by infants who were either securely or insecurely attached to their mothers and fathers

	Patterns of attachment			
Measure	Securely attached to both parents	Secure with mother, nonsecure with father	Nonsecure with mother, secure with father	Nonsecurely attached to both parents
Social responsiveness	6.04	4.87	3.30	2.45
Emotional conflict	1.17	1.00	1.80	2.50

Note: Social responsiveness ratings could vary from 1 (wary, distressed) to 9 (happy, responsive). Conflict ratings could vary from 1 (no conflict) to 5 (very conflicted).

than the parent's actual involvement in caregiving activities.

Does the kind of attachment that an infant establishes with his or her mother affect the infant's relationship with the father? Not necessarily. Mary Main and Donna Weston (1981) used the strange-situations test to measure the quality of infants' attachments to both their mothers and their fathers. They found that the quality of the child's attachment to one parent did not predict the type of attachment relationship that the infant had with the second parent. Of the 43 infants tested, 12 were securely attached to both parents, 11 were secure with the mother but insecure with the father, 10 were insecure with the mother but secure with the father, and 11 were insecurely attached to both parents.

Main and Weston then exposed these infants to a friendly stranger in a clown outfit who first spent several minutes trying to play with the child and then turned around and cried when a person at the door told the clown he would have to leave. As the clown went through his routine, the infants were each observed and rated for (1) the extent to which

they were willing to establish a positive relationship with the clown (low ratings indicated that the infant was wary or distressed) and (2) signs of emotional conflict (that is, indications of psychological disturbance such as curling up in the fetal position on the floor or vocalizing in a "social" manner to a wall). The table shows the results of this stranger test. Note that infants who were securely attached to both parents were the most socially responsive group. Equally important is the finding that infants who were securely attached to *at least one parent* were more friendly toward the clown and less emotionally conflicted than infants who had insecure relationships with both parents. In sum, this study illustrates the important role that fathers play in their infants' social and emotional development. Not only are infants more socially responsive when they are securely attached to *both* the mother and the father, but it also appears that a secure attachment to the father can help to prevent harmful consequences (emotional disturbances, an exaggerated fear of other people) that could otherwise result when infants are insecurely attached to their mothers.

mothers are rigid, self-centered people who are likely to reject their babies. Indeed, Byron Egeland and Alan Sroufe (1981) found that rejecting mothers (particularly those who express their rejection by abusing their infants) are the ones who are likely to have infants classified as anxious and avoidant.

To this point we have focused only on the quality of the infant's attachment to his or her mother. Do you think the kind of attachment an infant has with the mother will have any effect on the infant's relationship with the father? In Box 11-2 we will explore this issue as we take a closer look at the ways fathers contribute to their infants' social and emotional development.

■ *Long-term correlates of secure and insecure attachments*

Does the type of attachment that an infant has with the mother predict his or her later behavior? Apparently so, and the long-term correlates of secure and insecure attachments are very interesting. For example, Susan Londerville and Mary Main (1981) found that infants who were securely attached at 12 months of age are more likely than those who were insecurely attached to obey their mothers and to cooperate with female strangers at 21 months of age. Moreover, infants who were securely attached at 18 months are more curious at age 2, more likely to enjoy solving problems, and more sociable with peers than infants who were insecurely attached (Matas, Arend, & Sroufe, 1978; Pastor, 1981).

The relationship of early attachments to social and intellectual behavior during the *preschool* period is nicely illustrated in a study by Everett Waters and his associates. Waters, Wippman, and Sroufe (1979) first measured the quality of children's attachments at 15 months of age and then observed these children in a nursery school setting at age 3½. Children who had been securely attached to their mothers at age 15 months were now social leaders in the nursery school setting: they often initiated play activities, were generally sensitive to the needs and feelings of other children, and were very popular with their peers. Observers described these children as curious, self-directed, and eager to learn. In contrast, children who had been insecurely attached at age 15 months were socially and emotionally withdrawn, were hesitant to engage other children in play activities, and were described by observers as less curious, less interested in learning, and much less forceful in pursuing their goals. By age 4 to 5, children who had been securely attached as infants were still more curious, more responsive to peers, and much less dependent on adults, in comparison with classmates who had been insecurely attached (Arend, Gove, & Sroufe, 1979; Sroufe, Fox, & Pancake, 1983).

These findings are consistent with Erik Erikson's ideas about the importance of developing an early sense of "trust" in other people. Perhaps securely attached infants who have learned to trust an easily accessible and responsive caregiver become curious problem solvers later in life because they feel comfortable at venturing away from an attentive parent to explore and, as a result, they learn how to answer questions and to solve problems on their own. Moreover, securely attached infants may be quite sociable and rather popular with their peers because they have already established pleasant relationships with responsive caregivers and have learned from these experiences that human beings are likely to react positively to their social gestures. In contrast, an anxious, insecure infant who has not learned to trust her caregivers may find it exceedingly difficult to trust other people. In fact, the insecurities surrounding her interpersonal relationships may make the child less interested in the novel aspects

of her environment, thereby hindering her exploratory activities and preventing her from developing the individual initiative that would help her to answer questions and to solve problems.

Fortunately, the future is not always so bleak for infants who are insecurely attached. As we saw in Box 11-2, a secure relationship with another person such as the father (or perhaps a grandparent or an older sibling) may help to prevent the harmful consequences of an insecure attachment to the mother. In addition, it is quite possible for an initially insecure attachment to become more secure over time. One reason infants become insecurely attached in the first place is that their mothers have often withdrawn from caregiving activities because of life stresses of their own, such as health and marital problems, financial woes, and a lack of emotional support from friends and family members. Recently, researchers have been finding that initially insecure infants are likely to become securely attached if the lives of their close companions become less stressful (Vaughn, Egeland, Sroufe, & Waters, 1979). Often these positive developments take place as highly stressed and emotionally unresponsive mothers begin to receive emotional support and assistance from a close friend, a spouse, or a grandparent (Crockenberg, 1981; Egeland & Sroufe, 1981).

However, it is also possible for securely attached infants to become insecurely attached if their caregivers experience life changes that make them less accessible and less responsive to their children. Ross Thompson and his colleagues (Thompson, Lamb, & Estes, 1982) have found that secure attachments sometimes change for the worse if the mother returns to work or if the child begins to receive regular caregiving from someone else (for example, a babysitter or a day-care agency). Unlike diamonds, attachments are not forever: any event that drastically alters the ways an infant and caregiver respond to each other is likely to have a significant effect on the quality of their emotional relationship.

But it would be wrong to create the impression that all mothers will undermine the security of their infants' attachments by returning to work or enrolling their children in a day-care center. As it turns out, the effects of maternal employment and alternative caregiving are bidirectional: although some securely attached infants become insecure, at least as many insecure infants will develop secure attachments to their mothers after the mother has returned to work or enrolled them in a day-care facility (Thompson et al., 1982). In Box 11-3 we will take a closer look at the effects of maternal employment and alternative caregiving and try to determine why these events and experiences do not affect all children in the same way.

The Unattached Infant: Effects of Restricted Social Contacts during Infancy

Some infants have very limited contacts with adults during the first year or two of life and do not appear to become attached to anyone. Occasionally these socially deprived youngsters are reared at home by very abusive or neglectful caregivers, but most of them are found in understaffed institutions where they may see a caregiver only when it is time to be fed, changed, or bathed. Will these unattached infants suffer as a result of their early experiences? If so, how are they likely to differ from children raised at home with a responsive caregiver, and what, if anything, can be done to "normalize" their developmental progress? These are the issues we will consider in the pages that follow .

We will begin by looking at the immediate and long-range effects of social deprivation on infant monkeys. Although this may seem a strange way to approach questions about socially deprived humans, there are several good reasons for reviewing the animal literature. For one thing, socially deprived humans are rather hard to come by; very few babies are raised without a primary caregiver, and it is clearly unethical to subject human infants to conditions of prolonged social deprivation when we have reason to suspect that these experiences will prove harmful to their development. But monkeys can be subjected to varying degrees of deprivation in controlled experiments that permit the investigator to infer cause-and-effect relationships. This is hardly the ideal solution, for one can never be absolutely certain that findings obtained for monkeys will hold for humans. However, monkeys do develop, and their development, like that of human infants, takes place over a period of years. Infant monkeys also form emotional attachments to their mothers—attachments that closely resemble the human infant's emotional ties to close companions. So it would seem that tightly controlled experimental studies of socially deprived monkeys may help us to understand the behavior of those human beings who have not had an opportunity to become attached to a primary caregiver.

■ Harlow's studies of socially deprived monkeys

Many investigators have studied the effects of early social deprivation on rhesus monkeys, and their findings are remarkably consistent: monkeys isolated for the first six months of life or longer show extremely abnormal patterns of behavior that persist into adulthood. One of the best known of these research programs is that of Harry and Margaret Harlow (1977). The Harlows isolated rhesus monkeys at birth by placing them in individual wire cages where they could see and hear but could not touch other monkeys (partial social deprivation) or in stainless-steel cubicles in which all light was diffused, sounds were filtered, temperature and air flow were controlled, and even feeding and cleaning of the chambers were automated (total social deprivation). These two kinds of isolation produced similar effects.

Three months of social deprivation left infants in a state of emotional shock. When removed from isolation, the infant avoided other monkeys and generally gave the appearance of being terrified by clutching at itself, crouching, or burying its head in its arms as if trying to shut out this strange new world (see Photo 11-7). The isolates also showed

PHOTO 11-7. *Isolate monkeys often display unusual postures.*

Working mothers are no longer exceptions to the rule. In the United States, over half of all mothers who live with their husbands are now employed outside the home, and the percentage of working mothers in single-parent households is even higher (Hoffman, 1979). Not only does work take a mother away from her child for several hours a day, but her infants or preschool children will also have to adjust to some kind of alternative caregiving—either in-home or out-of-the-home care by a babysitter or relative, or care provided by a group day-care center (Etaugh, 1980). Are these daily separations and contacts with alternative caregivers likely to undermine an infant's attachment to the mother? Will they have a harmful effect on a child's social and emotional development?

Two recent reviews of the literature suggest that neither maternal employment nor alternative caregiving is likely to have adverse effects on the vast majority of young children (Etaugh, 1980; Hoffman, 1979). According to Lois Hoffman (1979), maternal employment is unlikely to disrupt a child's emotional development because a working mother will often compensate for her absences by spending more time with the child when she is home. Indeed, most children who receive group day care continue to prefer their mothers to their substitute caregivers if given a choice (Cummings, 1980; Ragozin, 1980). And there is even some evidence that *excellent* day care improves the social skills and furthers the in-

tellectual development of children from economically disadvantaged homes (O'Connell & Farran, 1982; Zeskind & Ramey, 1981). In sum, these findings paint a very rosy picture, suggesting that mothers need not worry about harming their youngsters or undermining their own emotional relationships with them when they return to work or leave their children with a substitute caregiver.

Yet there is another side to this story—one that we must consider before drawing any firm conclusions of our own. Most of the studies that show no differences between day-care children (or children of working mothers) and children raised at home have looked at *middle-class samples* in which the alternative caregiving was of *unusually high quality* (Anderson, Nagle, Roberts, & Smith, 1981). Unfortunately, we cannot be sure that the results of these studies would apply to economically disadvantaged children, who may often receive much less stimulating kinds of day care. In addition, we have already seen that some securely attached infants from middle-class homes become insecurely attached when their mothers return to work and/or arrange for them to receive alternative care on a part-time basis (Thompson et al., 1982). So although many youngsters are not adversely affected by their mothers' employment or by alternative caregiving, the fact remains that these events and arrangements can disrupt the emotional development of some children.

Why do children differ in their reactions to job-related separations and substitute caregiving? Let's consider two possibilities.

Age at separation. One factor that may affect a child's adjustment to the mother's return to work or

abnormal behaviors such as self-biting, rocking, and pulling out tufts of their hair. However, these three-month isolates eventually recovered. Daily 30-minute play periods with a normal age mate soon led to the development of effective social relationships that persisted into adolescence and adulthood.

The prognosis was not nearly as optimistic for infants isolated six months or longer. The six-month isolates clearly avoided normal age mates during free-play sessions, preferring instead to play by themselves with toys. What little social responsiveness they did show was directed toward other isolates, leading the Harlows to conclude that *misery prefers miserable company.*

Normally reared infant monkeys usually go through a phase of aggressive play as they near their first birthday. Yet when the isolates were attacked by other infants, they accepted the abuse without offering much defense. Bad as this behavioral pattern may sound, the effects of 12 months of social isolation were even worse. The 12-month isolates were extremely withdrawn and apathetic, and they often had to be separated from their normal age mates, who were likely to injure or even kill these passive creatures during periods of aggressive play (Harlow & Harlow, 1977).

Follow-up studies of monkeys isolated six months or longer have found that the isolates develop bizarre patterns of social and sexual be-

to alternative caregiving is the child's age at the time these events first occur. Recently, researchers have been finding that infants from both lower-class and middle-class backgrounds are much more likely to develop insecure (anxious-avoidant) attachments to their mothers if the mother returns to work before the child's first birthday and the child receives full-time (all-day) alternative care (Schwartz, 1983; Vaughn, Gove, & Egeland, 1980). Moreover, 3- and 4-year-olds who began day care early in infancy are sometimes found to be more aggressive toward their peers and less cooperative with adults than are children who began day care as toddlers (Belsky & Steinberg, 1978; Etaugh, 1980). By contrast, Jerome Kagan found that one group of infants who began to participate in a very high-quality day-care program at age 3½ to 5½ months were not adversely affected: they developed secure attachments to their mothers (Kagan, Kearsley, & Zelazo, 1978). Unfortunately, this kind of high-quality day care is not always available, particularly to mothers from economically disadvantaged backgrounds who often have very limited resources and must soon return to work in order to get by. Perhaps you can see the irony here: the families that may have the greatest need for excellent day care are those that are least able to afford it.

Quality of alternative care. According to experts on alternative care, an excellent day-care facility is one that has (1) a reasonable child-to-caregiver ratio (4–12 children per adult), (2) caregivers who are warm, emotionally expressive, and responsive to children's bids for attention, (3) little staff turnover so that children can become familiar and feel comfortable with their new adult companions, (4) a curriculum made up of games and activities that are age-appropriate, and (5) an administration that is willing (or, better yet, eager) to confer with parents about the child's progress (Anderson et al., 1981; Kagan et al., 1978).

It is now apparent that the quality of alternative care that children receive does make a difference, whether that care is provided by a babysitter at home, a relative, or a group day-care center. For example, we have seen that even very young infants who experience alternative caregiving are likely to become securely attached to their parents if the care they receive is outstanding (Kagan et al., 1978). In addition, children are more likely to become attached to their substitute caregivers and to profit from the day-care curriculum when they interact with the same caregiver over a long period and when the caregiver is knowledgeable about children and responsive to their needs (Anderson et al., 1981; Cummings, 1980; Ruopp, Travers, Glantz, & Coelen, 1979). The size of the day-care group is also important: children who are cared for in smaller groups (15 or fewer) are more outgoing with their peers and score higher on standardized tests than children who are part of larger aggregations (Ruopp et al., 1979).

Perhaps we can summarize by concluding that most children who receive excellent alternative care are unlikely to suffer any adverse effects as a result of their day-to-day separations from working parents. However, the outcome may not be so favorable for a very young infant who receives substandard day care from an unresponsive caregiver (or series of caregivers), particularly if the working mother lacks the time, patience, or energy to respond to her baby's signals when she does come home (Vaughn et al., 1980).

havior during adolescence and adulthood. Harlow describes the adult sexual behavior of these monkeys as follows:

When the females were smaller than the [normally reared] males, the girls would back away and sit down facing the males [an inadequate attempt at sexual posturing], looking appealingly at their would-be consorts. Their hearts were in the right place but nothing else was. . . . [Isolate] males were equally unsatisfactory. They approached the females with a blind . . . misdirected enthusiasm. Frequently, they would grasp the females by the side of the body and thrust laterally, leaving them working at cross purposes with reality [1962, p. 5].

Harlow and his associates initially believed that the first six months of life was a critical period for the social development of rhesus monkeys. Presumably rhesus infants who were denied social stimulation and who remained unattached to another monkey for six months or longer would become forever incapable of establishing normal social and emotional relationships. However, a later experiment by Steven Suomi and Harry Harlow (1972) challenged this point of view by showing that the isolation syndrome can be reversed.

Suomi and Harlow isolated four male rhesus infants for a six-month period and then exposed the isolates to 26 weeks of "therapy." The therapists in this case were younger rhesus females who were 3 months of age at the beginning of the therapy sessions. Why younger therapists? For two reasons. First, normally reared age mates are likely to attack the passive isolates and will accept these strangers only if they defend themselves. Unfortunately, the isolates do not defend themselves; instead, they withdraw and their condition worsens. By contrast, a 3-month-old infant has not yet become active and aggressive in its play; the initial response of the younger infant is to approach and cling tenaciously to the passive isolate rather than working him over. Suomi and Harlow reasoned that an emotionally disturbed isolate might be able to tolerate the presence of a relatively passive, nonaggressive infant and perhaps would even learn to respond to the younger therapist's playful antics. Once the isolate had been "drawn out of his shell," both he and his younger companion might then progress together toward the development of normal social behaviors.

For the first four weeks of the project, each isolate saw his therapist for two-hour periods, three days a week. Contact time was gradually increased so that, by the 12th week of therapy, each isolate and his younger therapist had contact with each other and with a second isolate/therapist pair several times a week. All the isolates were severely disturbed when they emerged from isolation, and their abnormal behaviors persisted for the first 60 days of the program. But by the end of the 26 weeks of therapy, the isolates had recovered. Their behavioral abnormalities had largely disappeared, and their play antics were virtually indistinguishable from those of their socially competent therapists. In no way did these isolates resemble the rather pitiful, socially inept creatures described in earlier reports. Follow-up studies of these "rehabilitated" monkeys found their behavior to be perfectly normal and age-appropriate two years later (Cummins & Suomi, 1976).

Melinda Novak (1979) has now used this **younger-peer therapy** to treat rhesus monkeys that were isolated for their entire first year. Novak reports that even these profoundly disturbed 12-month isolates will eventually become socially and sexually competent as adults if they are eased into a rehabilitative program with a younger therapist.

Clearly, these dramatic reversals contradict the critical-period hypothesis—a viewpoint that implied that the devastating social and emotional consequences of prolonged isolation were permanent and irreversible. Perhaps it is more accurate to say that the first six months of life is a "sensitive" period when normally reared monkeys are rapidly developing important social skills and becoming attached to their mothers. Although social deprivation interferes with these activities and produces a rather disturbed young monkey, recovery is possible if the patient is given the proper therapy.

■ *Social deprivation in humans: The institutionalized child*

Fortunately, there are both legal and ethical constraints to prevent researchers from isolating human infants for scientific purposes. Yet in the recent past, physicians and psychologists began to discover that infants in some orphanages and foundling homes were being raised under conditions that resembled those experienced by Harlow's socially deprived monkeys. For example, it was not uncommon for an impoverished institution to have but one caregiver for every 8–12 infants. Moreover, the adults in these understaffed institutions rarely saw the infants except to bathe and change them or to prop a bottle against the infant's pillow at feeding times. Infants were often housed in separate cribs with sheets hung over the railings so that, in effect, they were isolated from the world around them. To make matters worse, babies in the more impoverished of these institutions had no crib toys to manipulate and few if any opportunities to get out of their cribs and practice motor skills. Compared with infants raised in a typical home setting, these institutionalized children received very little in the way of social or sensory stimulation.

Since the early 1940s, several investigators have reported the same reliable and quite alarming outcome: children raised for the first year of life in impoverished and understaffed institutions are likely to show signs of severe developmental retardation (Goldfarb, 1943, 1945, 1947; Provence & Lipton, 1962; Ribble, 1943; Spitz, 1945). Typically these infants appear quite normal for the first three to six months of life: they cry for attention, smile and babble at caregivers, and make all the proper postural adjustments when they are about to be picked up. But in the second half of the first year their behavior begins to change. Compared

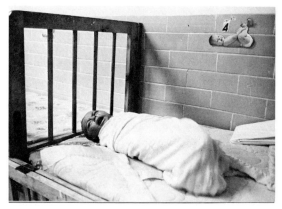

PHOTO 11-8. Children raised in barren, understaffed institutions show many signs of developmental retardation.

with home-reared infants, institution children seldom cry, coo, or babble; they adopt rigid body postures and often fail to accommodate to the handling of caregivers when such contact is forthcoming; their language is grossly retarded; and they often appear either forlorn and uninterested in their caretakers or emotionally starved with an insatiable need for affection. Here are two descriptions of these children:

> While the children in 'nursery' [who were cared for by their mothers] developed into normal, healthy toddlers, a two-year observation of 'Foundling-home' showed that these emotionally starved children never learned to speak, to walk, to feed themselves. With one or two exceptions . . . those who survived were human wrecks who behaved in a manner of agitated or apathetic idiots [Spitz, 1949, p. 149].

> Outstanding were his soberness, his forlorn appearance, and lack of animation. . . . He did not turn to adults to relieve his distress. . . . He made no demands. . . . As one made active and persistent efforts at a social exchange he became somewhat more responsive, animated and . . . active, but lapsed into his depressed . . . appearance when the adult became less active . . . if you crank his motor you can get him to go a little; but he can't start on his own [Provence & Lipton, 1962, pp. 134–135].

What are these institutionalized infants like as schoolchildren, adolescents, and adults? The answer depends, in part, on how long they stay in the bleak, barren institutional setting. William Goldfarb (1943, 1947) compared the developmen-

tal progress of two groups of children: a group who left an understaffed orphanage for foster homes during the first year of life (foster children) and a second group who had spent their first three years at the orphanage before departing for foster homes (institution children). The children in these two groups were comparable in age, sex, and the socioeconomic backgrounds of their biological parents. The developmental progress of each group was periodically assessed by interviewing and observing the children and by giving them a battery of tests. The children were studied at four ages: 3½, 6½, 8½, and 12.

Goldfarb found that the institution children performed less well than the foster children on almost all the tests he administered. The institution children scored lower on all tests of intelligence, particularly those emphasizing conceptual skills and abstract reasoning. Compared with foster children, the institution children were socially immature and remarkably dependent on adults, even when adult assistance appeared unnecessary. Language and speech problems often plagued these children, and they were much more prone than the foster children to displays of temper, hyperactivity, aggression, deception, and acts of destruction. Goldfarb reported that the institution children seemed almost incapable of forming close interpersonal attachments. By adolescence, they were often loners who had a difficult time relating to peers or family members. Barbara Tizard (Tizard, 1977; Tizard & Hodges, 1978) compared similar groups of institutionalized and early-adopted children and found that many of the developmental impairments described by Goldfarb also characterized her sample of late adoptees. Clearly, prolonged social and sensory deprivation can have any number of adverse effects on the developing child.

■ Why is social and sensory deprivation harmful?

Studies of institutionalized children are "experiments of nature" that were not designed in a lab-

---

younger-peer therapy: *a method of rehabilitating emotionally withdrawn individuals by regularly exposing them to younger but socially responsive companions.*

oratory and are subject to a variety of methodological criticisms (Longstreth, 1981; Pinneau, 1955). However, the results we have reviewed are so consistent across studies that researchers have stopped arguing about whether deprivation effects are real; today the issue is "Why do they occur?"

The maternal deprivation hypothesis. Psychologists such as John Bowlby (1973) and Rene Spitz (1965) believe that infants will not develop normally unless they receive the warm, loving attention of a mother figure to whom they can become attached. Presumably children raised in understaffed institutions and monkeys reared in isolation will show developmental impairments because they have not had an opportunity to become emotionally involved with a primary caregiver.

Popular as this explanation was when it first appeared, there is no evidence to suggest that infants need to be "mothered" by a single caregiver in order to develop normally. Studies of adequately staffed institutions in the Soviet Union, the People's Republic of China, and Israel reveal that infants who are cared for by many responsive caregivers appear quite normal and are as well adjusted at 2–3 years of age as noninstitutionalized infants who are reared at home (Bronfenbrenner, 1970; Kessen, 1975; Levy-Shiff, 1983). Moreover, we have seen that Harlow's infant monkeys who were isolated for three months eventually recovered from their early developmental abnormalities without ever being exposed to a mother figure. All they needed was stimulation provided through daily contacts with other monkeys of the same age. So infants need not become attached to a single mother figure in order to develop normally.

The stimulus deprivation hypothesis. Other psychologists have proposed a stimulus deprivation hypothesis to explain the behavioral abnormalities of children raised in understaffed institutions. The central theme of this explanation is that infants require a variety of sensory inputs, or "stimulus feedings," in order to become responsive to the environment and to show a normal pattern of development. Proponents of the stimulus deprivation hypothesis argue that impoverished, understaffed institutional settings are breeding grounds for developmental abnormalities because they provide the infant with a monotonous sensory environment where *there is*

little if any stimulation to encourage any sort of responsiveness, be it social responsiveness, exploratory behavior, cognitive functioning, or emotional expression. And what kind of stimulation is most important? Lawrence Casler (1965) suggests that "perhaps any source—an impersonal caretaker, or even a machine—would be satisfactory, so long as the dosage of stimulation were approximately correct" (p. 141).

Would infants in understaffed institutions develop normally if they received periodic doses of sensory stimulation? Probably not. C. L. Pratt (1967, 1969) attempted to reverse the effects of social isolation on infant monkeys by providing enriched visual stimulation in the form of "slide shows" (pictures of inanimate objects and other monkeys). This treatment had no real therapeutic effect—the infants remained socially inept. In contrast, isolates who received *social* stimulation through contacts with age mates did eventually overcome their deficiencies and develop age-appropriate patterns of social behavior.

The social stimulation hypothesis. Many investigators now believe that infants in poorly run institutions develop abnormally because they have very little exposure to anyone who reacts to their social signals. Sally Provence and Rose Lipton (1962) studied a sample of institutionalized infants who had toys to play with, some visual and auditory exposure to other infants, but limited contact with adult caregivers. In other words, these infants were "socially deprived" although they were certainly not "stimulus deprived." In spite of the variety of stimulation that the infants received, they showed roughly the same patterns of social, emotional, and intellectual impairment that characterized the institutionalized children from earlier studies. If we contrast this finding with the normal development of Chinese, Russian, and Israeli infants who are raised by a multitude of caregivers in communal settings, we can draw an interesting conclusion: *infants apparently need sustained interactions with responsive companions in order to develop normally.* Recall that we came to the same conclusion when we looked at the origins of the primary social attachment: infants who have regular interactions with *responsive* caregivers are the ones who are likely to become securely attached to their close companions.

Why are interactions with responsive people so important? Probably because the social stimulation an infant receives is likely to depend on the infant's own behavior: people often attend to the infant *when* he or she cries, smiles, babbles, or gazes at them. This kind of association between one's own behavior and the behavior of caregivers may lead infants to believe that they have some *control* over their social environment. Thus, the infant may become more sociable as she learns that she can use her social signals to attract the attention and affection of her responsive companions.

Now consider the plight of institutionalized infants who may emit many signals and rarely receive a response from their overburdened or inattentive caregivers. What are these children likely to learn from their early experiences? Probably that attempts to attract the attention of others are useless, for nothing they do seems to matter to anyone. Consequently, they may develop a sense of **"learned helplessness"** and simply stop trying to exercise any control over the environment (Finkelstein & Ramey, 1977). Here, then, is a very plausible explanation for the finding that socially deprived infants are often rather passive, withdrawn, and apathetic.

■ Can children recover from early developmental impairments?

Earlier we noted that severely disturbed young monkeys can overcome the effects of prolonged social isolation if they receive the proper kinds of therapy. Is the same true of human beings? Can children who start out in an understaffed institutional setting recover from their initial handicaps, and if so, what will they require in the way of corrective therapy?

There is now a wealth of evidence that socially deprived infants can recover from their handicaps if they are placed in homes where they receive ample doses of individualized attention from affectionate and responsive caregivers (Clarke & Clarke, 1976; Rutter, 1979). One notable example is a study by Wayne Dennis (1973), who compared the development of two groups of children who had lived in an understaffed Lebanese institution. Children in one group were adopted into good homes before their second birthday. Although they had developmental quotients in the mentally retarded range at the time of their adoptions, these

children eventually attained average IQ scores after spending several years in a stimulating home environment. By contrast, children who remained in the institution continued to score in the mentally retarded range on all intelligence tests.

The *quality* of the home environment in which children live affects their chances of recovering from early developmental impairments. Lee Willerman and his associates found that 1-year-olds with social, motor, and mental handicaps are unlikely to recover if they live in economically disadvantaged homes where they receive little social or intellectual stimulation from their caregivers (Willerman, Broman, & Fiedler, 1970). However, children who are placed in "enriched" home environments may show dramatic recoveries. Audrey Clark and Jeanette Hanisee (1982) studied a group of Asian children who were adopted by highly educated and relatively affluent American parents, many of whom were teachers, ministers, or social workers. The adoptees had all been separated from their biological parents and had lived in institutions, foster homes, or hospitals before coming to the United States. Many were war orphans who had early histories of malnutrition or serious illness. But in spite of the severe environmental insults they had endured, these children made remarkable progress. After only two to three years in their highly stimulating adoptive homes, the Asian adoptees scored significantly *above* average on both a standardized intelligence test and an assessment of social maturity.

The prognosis for recovery may also depend on the amount of time the child has spent in a depriving early environment. It appears that prolonged social and sensory deprivation that begins early in the first year and lasts as long as three years is likely to produce serious social, emotional, and intellectual handicaps that are difficult to overcome (Dennis, 1973; Goldfarb, 1943, 1947; Rutter, 1979). For example, we have noted that Goldfarb's institution children, who had spent their first three years in an understaffed orphan-

---

learned-helplessness effect: *the failure to learn how to respond appropriately to a situation because of previous exposures to uncontrollable events in the same or similar situations.*

age, remained somewhat socially, emotionally, and intellectually deficient as adolescents despite having lived in foster homes during the preceding eight to nine years. Do such findings imply that the first three years is a critical period for the social, emotional, and intellectual development of human beings?

At this point, no one can say for sure that the effects of prolonged social and sensory deprivation are completely reversible. However, many theorists believe that those who favor a critical-period hypothesis are being overly pessimistic. It stands to reason that children who develop severe problems when deprived for long periods might take longer to overcome their handicaps than children whose early deprivation was relatively brief. Moreover, we have to wonder how Goldfarb's institution children would have fared had they been adopted into enriched home environments such as those experienced by the Asian adoptees in Clark and Hanisee's (1982) study. Clearly, the fact that Goldfarb's institution children showed some deficiencies as adolescents in no way implies that they were *incapable* of recovery, as proponents of the critical-period hypothesis might have us believe.

It was only a short time ago that six months of isolation was thought to have irreversible effects on the social and emotional development of rhesus monkeys. Yet Harry Harlow and his associates were able to perfect a therapy to treat the harmful consequences of early social deprivation and bring even their most profoundly disturbed 12-month isolates back to a state of normalcy. This younger-peer therapy has now been used by Wyndol Furman, Don Rahe, and Willard Hartup (1979) to modify the behavior of socially withdrawn preschool children. Children who had been identified as social isolates in a day-care setting were exposed to a series of play sessions with a partner who was either their age or 18 months younger. The results were clear: withdrawn children who had played with a partner became much more socially outgoing in their day-care classrooms than social isolates who had not taken part in any play sessions. In addition, the improvements in sociability were greatest for those withdrawn children who had played with a *younger* partner (see Figure 11-4). So Furman et al. (1979)

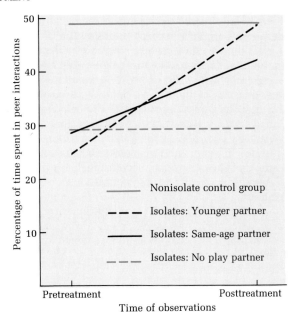

FIGURE 11-4. *Percentages of time that children spent interacting with peers before and after engaging in play sessions with a younger or a same-age partner.*

obtained results with humans that are similar to those reported earlier for emotionally disturbed monkeys. Although Furman's withdrawn children could hardly be classified as emotionally ill, the results of this study are sufficiently encouraging to suggest the younger-peer treatment as one possible therapy for children who are more severely disturbed.

In sum, infants who have experienced social and sensory deprivation over the first two years show a strong capacity for recovery when they are placed in a stimulating home environment and receive individualized attention from responsive caregivers. Even severely disturbed children who are adopted after spending several years in understaffed institutions will show dramatic improvements, compared with their counterparts who have remained in a barren institutional setting (Dennis, 1973; Rutter, 1979). And rather than being discouraged by handicaps that continue to plague many late adoptees, we could just as easily treat their partial recoveries as an encouraging sign—one that may lead to the discovery of environmental interventions and therapeutic techniques that will enable these victims of prolonged social and sensory deprivation to put their lingering deficiencies behind them.

SUMMARY

Infants begin to form affectional ties to their close companions during the first year of life. These "bonds of love," or attachments, serve many purposes and are important contributors to social and emotional development. Attachments are usually reciprocal relationships, for parents and other intimate companions will often become attached to the infant.

Parents may become emotionally involved with an infant during the first few hours if they have close contact with their baby during this period. An initial bond may then be strengthened as the infant begins to emit social signals (smiles, vocalizations) that attract the attention of caregivers and make them feel that the baby enjoys their company. Eventually the infant and a close companion will establish highly synchronized interactive routines that are satisfying to both parties and are likely to blossom into a reciprocal attachment. However, some parents may have a difficult time becoming attached to their infant if the child is irritable, unresponsive, or unwanted, if they are unhappily married or have other problems that prevent them from devoting much attention to the baby, or if they follow preconceived notions about child rearing rather than adjusting their parenting to the infant's state and temperament.

The infant's primary social attachment occurs at about 6–8 months of age and is normally limited to one person. But within weeks most infants are forming attachments to other regular companions. Many theories have been proposed to explain how and why infants form attachments. Among the most influential theories of attachment are the psychoanalytic, the learning, the cognitive-developmental, and the ethological viewpoints. Although these theories make different assumptions about the roles played by infants and caregivers in the formation of attachments, each viewpoint has contributed to our understanding of early social and emotional development.

At about the time infants are becoming attached to a close companion, they often begin to display two negative emotions, or "fears." Stranger anxiety is the child's wariness of unfamiliar people. It is by no means a universal reaction and is most likely to occur in response to an intrusive stranger who appears in an unfamiliar setting where loved ones are unavailable. Separation anxiety is the discomfort infants may feel when separated from the person or persons to whom they are attached. As infants develop intellectually and begin to move away from attachment objects to explore the environment, they will become increasingly familiar with strangers and better able to account for the absences of familiar companions. As a result, both stranger anxiety and separation anxiety will decline in intensity toward the end of the second year.

Children differ in the security of their attachments to caregivers. A securely attached infant is one who derives comfort from close companions and can use them as safe bases for exploration. Insecurely attached infants do not venture far from their attachment objects even though they derive very little comfort or security from their contacts with them. A secure attachment is fostered by caregivers who are very responsive and affectionate toward their babies. The quality of the infant's attachments may affect his or her later behavior: Those who are securely attached are generally more curious than insecurely attached infants and more interested in learning, more cooperative, and friendlier toward adults and peers. Moreover, these differences persist throughout the preschool period and possibly much longer.

Some infants have had very limited contacts with caregivers during the first year or two of life, and as a result they do not become attached to anyone. Both monkeys and children who experience little social contact during infancy are likely to be withdrawn, apathetic, and (in humans) intellectually deficient. The longer infants suffer from social and sensory deprivation, the more disturbed they become. However, both monkeys and humans have a strong capacity for recovery and may overcome many of their initial handicaps if placed in settings where they will receive ample amounts of individualized attention from responsive companions.

REFERENCES

Adams, R. E., & Passman, R. H. (1980, March). *The effects of advance preparation upon children's behavior during brief separation from their mother.* Paper presented at annual meeting of the Southeastern Psychological Association, Washington, DC.

Adams, R. E., & Passman, R. H. (1981). The effects of preparing two-year-olds for brief separations from their mothers. *Child Development, 52,* 1068–1070.

Ainsworth, M. D. S. (1967). *Infancy in Uganda: Infant care and the growth of love.* Baltimore: Johns Hopkins University Press.

Ainsworth, M. D. S. (1979). Attachment as related to mother-infant interaction. In J. S. Rosenblatt, R. A. Hinde, C. Beer, & M. Busnel (Eds.), *Advances in the study of behavior* (Vol. 9). New York: Academic Press.

Ainsworth, M. D. S., Bell, S. M., & Stayton, D. J. (1974). Infant-mother attachment and social development: Socialization as a product of reciprocal responsiveness to signals. In M. P. M. Richards (Ed.), *The integration of the child into a social world.* London: Cambridge University Press.

Ainsworth, M. D. S., Blehar, M., Waters, E., & Wall, S. (1978). *Patterns of attachment.* Hillsdale, NJ: Erlbaum.

Alley, T. R. (1981). Head shape and the perception of cuteness. *Developmental Psychology, 17,* 650–654.

Ambrose, J. A. (1963). The concept of a critical period in the development of social responsiveness in early infancy. In B. M. Foss (Ed.), *Determinants of infant behavior* (Vol. 2). London: Methuen.

Anderson, C. W., Nagle, R. J., Roberts, W. A., & Smith, J. W. (1981). Attachment to substitute caregivers as a function of center quality and caregiver involvement. *Child Development, 52,* 53–61.

Arend, R., Gove, F. L., & Sroufe, L. A. (1979). Continuity of individual adaptation from infancy to kindergarten: A predictive study of ego-resiliency and curiosity in preschoolers. *Child Development, 50,* 950–959.

Barrera, M. E., & Maurer, D. (1981). Recognition of mother's photographed face by the three-month-old infant. *Child Development, 52,* 714–716.

Belsky, J. (1980). Child maltreatment: An ecological integration. *American Psychologist, 35,* 320–335.

Belsky, J. (1981). Early human experience: A family perspective. *Developmental Psychology, 17,* 3–23.

Belsky, J., Rovine, M., & Taylor, D. G. (1984). The Pennsylvania infant and family development project, III: The origins of individual differences in infant-mother attachment: Maternal and infant contributions. *Child Development, 55,* 718-728.

Belsky, J., & Steinberg, L. D. (1978). The effects of day care: A critical review. *Child Development, 49,* 929–949.

Bower, T. G. R. (1982). *Development in infancy.* San Francisco: W. H. Freeman.

Bowlby, J. (1958). The nature of the child's tie to his mother. *International Journal of Psychoanalysis, 39,* 350–373.

Bowlby, J. (1969). *Attachment and loss.* Vol. 1: *Attachment.* London: Hogarth Press.

Bowlby, J. (1973). *Attachment and loss.* Vol. 2: *Separation.* London: Hogarth Press.

Brackbill, Y. (1958). Extinction of the smiling response in infants as a function of reinforcement schedule. *Child Development, 29,* 114–124.

Brazelton, T. B. (1979). Behavioral competence of the newborn infant. *Seminars in Perinatology, 3,* 35–44.

Bretherton, I., & Ainsworth, M. D. S. (1974). Responses of one-year-olds to a stranger in a strange situation. In M. Lewis & L. Rosenblum (Eds.), *The origins of fear.* New York: Wiley.

Bretherton, I., Stolberg, U., & Kreye, M. (1981). Engaging strangers in proximal interaction: Infants' social initiative. *Developmental Psychology, 17,* 746–755.

Bronfenbrenner, U. (1970). *Two worlds of childhood: U.S. and U.S.S.R.* New York: Russell Sage Foundation.

Brooks, J., & Lewis, M. (1976). Infants' responses to strangers: Midget, adult, and child. *Child Development, 47,* 323–332.

Brooks-Gunn, J., & Lewis, M. (1981). Infant social perception: Responses to pictures of parents and strangers. *Developmental Psychology, 17,* 647–649.

Casler, L. (1965). The effects of extra tactile stimulation on a group of institutionalized infants. *Genetic Psychology Monographs, 71,* 137–175.

Clark, E. A., & Hanisee, J. (1982). Intellectual and adaptive performance of Asian children in adoptive American settings. *Developmental Psychology, 18,* 595–599.

Clarke, A. M., & Clarke, A. D. B. (1976). *Early experience: Myth and evidence.* New York: Free Press.

Clarke-Stewart, K. (1978). And daddy makes three: The father's impact on the mother and the young child. *Child Development, 49,* 466–478.

Cohen, L. J. (1974). The operational definition of human attachment. *Psychological Bulletin, 4,* 207–217.

Cohn, J. F., & Tronick, E. Z. (1982). Three-month-old infants' reactions to simulated maternal depression. *Child Development, 53,* 185–193.

Corter, C. M., Zucker, K. J., & Galligan, R. F. (1980). Patterns in the infant's search for mother during brief separation. *Developmental Psychology, 16,* 62–69.

Crockenberg, S. B. (1981). Infant irritability, mother responsiveness, and social support influences on the security of infant-mother attachment. *Child Development, 52,* 857–865.

Cummings, E. M. (1980). Caregiver stability and day care. *Developmental Psychology, 16,* 31–37.

Cummins, M. S., & Suomi, S. J. (1976). Long-term effects of social rehabilitation in rhesus monkeys. *Primates, 17,* 43–51.

Dennis, W. (1973). *Children of the crèche.* New York: Appleton-Century-Crofts.

Dittrichova, J. (1969). The development of premature infants. In R. J. Robinson (Ed.), *Brain and early development.* London: Academic Press.

Dunkeld, J. (1978). *The function of imitation in infancy.* Unpublished doctoral dissertation, University of Edinburgh.

Egeland, B., & Farber, E. A. (1984). Mother-infant attachment: Factors related to its development and changes over time. *Child Development, 55,* 753-771.

Egeland, B., & Sroufe, L. A. (1981). Attachment and early maltreatment. *Child Development, 52,* 44–52.

Emde, R. N., Gaensbauer, T. J., & Harmon, R. J. (1976). *Emotional expression in infancy: A biobehavioral study.* New York: International Universities Press.

Etaugh, C. (1980). Effects of nonmaternal care on children: Research evidence and popular views. *American Psychologist, 35,* 309–319.

Feinman, S., & Lewis, M. (1983). Social referencing at 10 months: A second-order effect on infants' responses to strangers. *Child Development, 54,* 878–887.

Finkelstein, N. W., & Ramey, C. T. (1977). Learning to control the environment in infancy. *Child Development, 48,* 806–819.

Freedman, D. G. (1965). Hereditary control of early social behavior. In B. M. Foss (Ed.), *Determinants of infant behavior* (Vol. 3). London: Methuen.

Freud, S. (1930). *Three contributions to the theory of sex.* New York: Nervous and Mental Disease Publishing Co. (Original work published 1905)

Furman, W., Rahe, D. F., & Hartup, W. W. (1979). Rehabilitation of socially withdrawn preschool children through mixed-age and same-age socialization. *Child Development, 50,* 915–922.

Garbarino, J., & Sherman, D. (1980). High-risk neighborhoods and high-risk families: The human ecology of child maltreatment. *Child Development, 51,* 188–198.

Gaulin-Kremer, E., Shaw, J. L., & Thoman, E. B. (1977, March). *Mother-infant interaction at first encounter: Effects of variation in delay after delivery.* Paper presented at biennial meeting of the Society for Research in Child Development, New Orleans.

Gewirtz, H. B., & Gewirtz, J. L. (1968). Caretaking settings, background events, and behavior differences in four Israeli child-rearing environments: Some preliminary trends. In B. M. Foss (Ed.), *Determinants of infant behavior* (Vol. 4). London: Methuen.

Gewirtz, J. L. (1969). Mechanisms of social learning: Some roles of stimulation and behavior in early human development. In D. A. Goslin (Ed.), *Handbook of socialization theory and research.* Chicago: Rand McNally.

Goldberg, S. (1983). Parent-infant bonding: Another look. *Child Development, 54,* 1355–1382.

Goldberg, S., Blumberg, S. L., & Kriger, A. (1982). Menarche and interest in infants: Biological and social influences. *Child Development, 53,* 1544–1550.

Goldfarb, W. (1943). The effects of early institutional care on adolescent personality. *Journal of Experimental Education, 12,* 107–129.

Goldfarb, W. (1945). Effects of psychological deprivation in infancy and subsequent stimulation. *American Journal of Psychiatry, 102,* 18–33.

Goldfarb, W. (1947). Variations in adolescent adjustment in institutionally reared children. *Journal of Orthopsychiatry, 17,* 449–457.

Greenberg, M. T., & Marvin, R. S. (1982). Reactions of preschool children to an adult stranger: A behavioral systems approach. *Child Development, 53,* 481–490.

Greene, J. G., Fox, N. A., & Lewis, M. (1983). The relationship between neonatal characteristics and three-month mother-infant interaction in high-risk infants. *Child Development, 54,* 1286–1296.

Grossman, F. K., Eichler, L. S., Winickoff, S. A., & Associates. (1980). *Pregnancy, birth, and parenthood: Adaptations of mothers, fathers, and infants.* San Francisco: Jossey-Bass.

Grossmann, K., Thane, K., & Grossmann, K. E. (1981). Maternal tactile contact of the newborn after various postpartum conditions of mother-infant contact. *Developmental Psychology, 17,* 158–169.

Hall, G. S. (1891). The contents of children's minds on entering school. *Pedagogical Seminary, 1,* 139–173.

Harlow, H. F. (1962). The heterosexual affectional system in monkeys. *American Psychologist, 17,* 1–9.

Harlow, H. F., & Harlow, M. K. (1977). The young monkeys. In *Readings in developmental psychology today* (2nd ed.). Del Mar, CA: CRM Books.

Harlow, H. F., & Zimmerman, R. R. (1959). Affectional responses in the infant monkey. *Science, 130,* 421–432.

Hildebrandt, K. A. (1983). Effect of facial expression variations on ratings of infants' physical attractiveness. *Developmental Psychology, 19,* 414–417.

Hildebrandt, K. A., & Fitzgerald, H. E. (1981). Mothers' responses to infant physical appearance. *Infant Mental Health Journal, 2,* 56–61.

Hoffman, L. W. (1979). Maternal employment: 1979. *American Psychologist, 34,* 859–865.

Hurley, J. R., & Hohn, R. L. (1971). Shifts in child-rearing attitudes linked with parenthood and occupation. *Developmental Psychology, 4,* 324–328.

Jacobson, J. L. (1980). Cognitive determinants of wariness toward unfamiliar peers. *Developmental Psychology, 16,* 347–354.

Kagan, J. (1971). *Change and continuity in infancy.* New York: Wiley.

Kagan, J. (1972). Do infants think? *Scientific American, 226,* 74–82.

Kagan, J. (1976). Emergent themes in human development. *American Scientist, 64,* 186–196.

Kagan, J., Kearsley, R. B., & Zelazo, P. R. (1975). The emergence of initial apprehension to unfamiliar peers. In M. Lewis & L. Rosenblum (Eds.), *Friendship and peer relations.* New York: Wiley.

Kagan, J., Kearsley, R. B., & Zelazo, P. R. (1978). *Infancy: Its place in human development.* Cambridge, MA: Harvard University Press.

Kennell, J. H., Voos, D. K., & Klaus, M. H. (1979). Parent-infant bonding. In J. D. Osofsky (Ed.), *Handbook of infant development.* New York: Wiley.

Kessen, W. (1975). *Childhood in China.* New Haven, CT: Yale University Press.

Klaus, H. M., & Kennell, J. H. (1976). *Maternal-infant bonding*. St. Louis: Mosby.

Kohlberg, L. (1969). Stage and sequence: The cognitive-developmental approach to socialization. In D. A. Goslin (Ed.), *Handbook of socialization theory and research*. Chicago: Rand McNally.

Korner, A. F. (1974). The effect of the infant's state, level of arousal, sex, and ontogenetic stage on the caregiver. In M. Lewis & L. A. Rosenblum (Eds.), *The effect of the infant on its caregiver*. New York: Wiley.

Lamb, M. E. (1981). The development of father-infant relationships. In M. E. Lamb (Ed.), *The role of the father in child development*. New York: Wiley.

Lamb, M. E., Frodi, A. M., Hwang, C., Frodi, M., & Steinberg, J. (1982). Mother- and father-infant interaction involving play and holding in traditional and nontraditional Swedish families. *Developmental Psychology, 18*, 215–221.

Lamb, M. E., & Stevenson, M. (1978). Father-infant relationships: Their nature and importance. *Youth and Society, 9*, 277–298.

Lester, B. M., Kotelchuck, M., Spelke, E., Sellers, M. J., & Klein, R. E. (1974). Separation protest in Guatemalan infants: Cross-cultural and cognitive findings. *Developmental Psychology, 10*, 79–85.

Levitt, M. J. (1980). Contingent feedback, familiarization, and infant affect: How a stranger becomes a friend. *Developmental Psychology, 16*, 425–432.

Levy-Shiff, R. (1983). Adaptation and competence in early childhood: Communally-raised kibbutz children versus family raised children in the city. *Child Development, 54*, 1606–1614.

Lewis, M., & Brooks, J. (1974). Self, others, and fear: Infant's reactions to people. In M. Lewis & L. A. Rosenblum (Eds.), *The origins of fear*. New York: Wiley.

Littenberg, R., Tulkin, S., & Kagan, J. (1971). Cognitive components of separation anxiety. *Developmental Psychology, 4*, 387–388.

Londerville, S., & Main, M. (1981). Security of attachment, compliance, and maternal training methods in the second year of life. *Developmental Psychology, 17*, 289–299.

Longstreth, L. E. (1981). Revisiting Skeels' final study: A critique. *Developmental Psychology, 17*, 620–625.

Lorenz, K. Z. (1937). The companion in the bird's world. *Auk, 54*, 245–273.

Lorenz, K. Z. (1943). Die angebornen Formen möglicher Erfahrung. *Zeitschrift für Tierpsychologie, 5*, 233–409.

Main, M., & Weston, D. R. (1981). The quality of the toddler's relationship to mother and to father: Related to conflict and the readiness to establish new relationships. *Child Development, 52*, 932–940.

Matas, L., Arend, R. A., & Sroufe, L. A. (1978). Continuity of adaptation in the second year: The relationship between quality of attachment and later competence. *Child Development, 49*, 547–556.

Matějček, Z., Dytrych, Z., & Schüller, V. (1979). The Prague study of children born from unwanted pregnancies. *International Journal of Mental Health, 7*, 63–74.

Morgan, G. A., & Ricciuti, H. N. (1969). Infants' responses to strangers during the first year. In B. M. Foss (Ed.), *Determinants of infant behavior* (Vol. 4). London: Methuen.

Novak, M. A. (1979). Social recovery of monkeys isolated for the first year of life: II. Long-term assessment. *Developmental Psychology, 15*, 50–61.

O'Connell, J. C., & Farran, D. C. (1982). Effects of day-care experience on the use of intentional communicative behaviors in a sample of socioeconomically depressed infants. *Developmental Psychology, 18*, 22–29.

Passman, R. H., & Longeway, K. P. (1982). The role of vision in maternal attachment: Giving 2-year-olds a photograph of their mother during separation. *Developmental Psychology, 18*, 530–533.

Pastor, D. L. (1981). The quality of mother-infant attachment and its relationship to toddlers' initial sociability with peers. *Developmental Psychology, 17*, 326–335.

Peery, J. C. (1980). Neonate and adult head movement: No and yes revisited. *Developmental Psychology, 16*, 245–250.

Pinneau, S. R. (1955). The infantile disorders of hospitalism and anaclitic depression. *Psychological Bulletin, 52*, 429–452.

Pratt, C. L. (1967). *Social behavior of rhesus monkeys reared with varying degrees of peer experience*. Unpublished master's thesis, University of Wisconsin.

Pratt, C. L. (1969). *Effect of different degrees of early stimulation on social development*. Unpublished doctoral dissertation, University of Wisconsin.

Provence, S., & Lipton, R. C. (1962). *Infants in institutions*. New York: International Universities Press.

Ragozin, A. S. (1980). Attachment behavior of day-care children: Naturalistic and laboratory observations. *Child Development, 51*, 409–415.

Rajecki, D. W. (1977). Social psychology from an ethological perspective. In C. Hendrick (Ed.), *Perspectives on social psychology*. Hillsdale, NJ: Erlbaum.

Rheingold, H. L., & Eckerman, C. D. (1970). The infant separates himself from his mother. *Science, 168*, 78–83.

Rheingold, H. L., & Eckerman, C. D. (1973). Fear of the stranger: A critical examination. In H. W. Reese (Ed.), *Advances in child development and behavior* (Vol. 8). New York: Academic Press.

Ribble, M. (1943). *The rights of infants*. New York: Columbia University Press.

Rinkoff, R. F., & Corter, C. M. (1980). Effects of setting and maternal accessibility on the infant's response to brief separation. *Child Development, 51*, 603–606.

Rode, S. S., Chang, P., Fisch, R. O., & Sroufe, L. A. (1981). Attachment patterns of infants separated at birth. *Developmental Psychology, 17*, 188–191.

Ruopp, R., Travers, J., Glantz, F., & Coelen, C. (1979). *Children at the center: Final report of the National Day Care Study*. Cambridge, MA: Abt Associates.

Rutter, M. (1979). Maternal deprivation, 1972–1978: New findings, new concepts, new approaches. *Child Development, 50*, 283–305.

Samuels, H. R. (1980). The effect of an older sibling on infant locomotor exploration of a new environment. *Child Development, 51,* 607–609.

Schaffer, H. R. (1966). The onset of fear of strangers and the incongruity hypothesis. *Journal of Child Psychology and Psychiatry, 7,* 95–106.

Schaffer, H. R. (1971). *The growth of sociability.* Baltimore: Penguin Books.

Schaffer, H. R. (1977). *Mothering.* Cambridge, MA: Harvard University Press.

Schaffer, H. R., & Emerson, P. E. (1964). The development of social attachments in infancy. *Monographs of the Society for Research in Child Development. 29* (3, Serial No. 94).

Schwartz, P. (1983). Length of day-care attendance and attachment behavior in eighteen-month-old infants. *Child Development, 54,* 1073–1078.

Sears, R. R. (1963). Dependency motivation. In M. Jones (Ed.), *Nebraska Symposium on Motivation* (Vol. 11). Lincoln: University of Nebraska Press.

Sorce, J. F., & Emde, R. N. (1981). Mother's presence is not enough: Effect of emotional availability on infant exploration. *Developmental Psychology, 17,* 737–745.

Spaulding, D. A. (1873). Instinct with original observation in young animals. *MacMillans Magazine, 27,* 282–283.

Spitz, R. A. (1945). Hospitalism: An inquiry into the genesis of psychiatric conditions in early childhood. In A. Freud (Ed.), *The psychoanalytic study of the child* (Vol. 1). New York: International Universities Press.

Spitz, R. A. (1949). The role of ecological factors in emotional development in infancy. *Child Development, 20,* 145–155.

Spitz, R. A. (1950). Anxiety in infancy. *International Journal of Psychoanalysis, 31,* 139–143.

Spitz, R. A. (1965). *The first year of life: A psychoanalytic study of normal and deviant object relations.* New York: International Universities Press.

Sroufe, L. A. (1977). Wariness of strangers and the study of infant development. *Child Development, 48,* 1184–1199.

Sroufe, L. A., Fox, N. E., & Pancake, V. R. (1983). Attachment and dependency in developmental perspective. *Child Development, 54,* 1615–1627.

Sroufe, L. A., Waters, E., & Matas, L. (1974). Contextual determinants of infant affectional response. In M. Lewis & L, A. Rosenblum (Eds.), *The origins of fear.* New York: Wiley.

Stayton, D. J., Ainsworth, M. D. S., & Main, M. B. (1973). Development of separation behavior in the first year of life: Protest, following, and greeting. *Developmental Psychology, 9,* 213–225.

Steele, B. F., & Pollack, C. B. (1974). A psychiatric study of parents who abuse infants and small children. In R. E. Helfer & C. H. Kempe (Eds.), *The battered child.* Chicago: University of Chicago Press.

Stephan, C. W., & Langlois, J. H. (1984). Baby beautiful: Adult attributions of infant competence as a function of infant attractiveness. *Child Development, 55,* 576–585.

Stern, D. (1977). *The first relationship: Infant and mother.* Cambridge, MA: Harvard University Press.

Suomi, S. J., & Harlow, H. F. (1972). Social rehabilitation of isolate reared monkeys. *Developmental Psychology, 6,* 487–496.

Svejda, M. J., Campos, J. J., & Emde, R. N. (1980). Mother-infant "bonding": Failure to generalize. *Child Development, 51,* 775–779.

Thoman, E. B., Acebo, C., & Becker, P. T. (1983). Infant crying and stability in the mother-infant relationship: A systems analysis. *Child Development, 54,* 653–659.

Thompson, R. A., Lamb, M. E., & Estes, D. (1982). Stability of infant-mother attachment and its relationship to changing life circumstances in an unselected middle-class sample. *Child Development, 53,* 144–148.

Tizard, B. (1977). *Adoption: A second chance.* London: Open Books.

Tizard, B., & Hodges, J. (1978). The effect of early institutional rearing on the development of eight-year-old children. *Journal of Child Psychology and Psychiatry, 19,* 99–118.

Tracy, R. L., & Ainsworth, M. D. S. (1981). Maternal affectionate behavior and infant-mother attachment patterns. *Child Development, 52,* 1341–1343.

Vaughn, B. E., Egeland, B. R., Sroufe, L. A., & Waters, E. (1979). Individual differences in infant-mother attachment at twelve and eighteen months: Stability and change in families under stress. *Child Development, 50,* 971–975.

Vaughn, B. E., Gove, F. L., & Egeland, B. R. (1980). The relationship between out-of-home care and the quality of infant-mother attachment in an economically disadvantaged population. *Child Development, 51,* 1203–1214.

Wahler, R. G. (1967). Infant social attachments: A reinforcement theory interpretation and investigation. *Child Development, 38,* 1079–1088.

Waters, E., Vaughn, B. E., & Egeland, B. R. (1980). Individual differences in mother-infant attachment relationships at age one: Antecedents in neonatal behavior in an urban, economically disadvantaged sample. *Child Development, 51,* 208–216.

Waters, E., Wippman, J., & Sroufe, L. A. (1979). Attachment, positive affect, and competence in the peer group: Two studies in construct validation. *Child Development, 50,* 821–829.

Weinraub, M., & Lewis, M. (1977). The determinants of children's responses to separation. *Monographs of the Society for Research in Child Development, 42* (4, Serial No. 172).

Willerman, L., Broman, S. H., & Fiedler, M. (1970). Infant development, pre-school IQ, and social class. *Child Development, 41,* 69–77.

Wolff, P. H. (1963). Observations on the early development of smiling. In B. M. Foss (Ed.), *Determinants of infant behavior* (Vol. 2). London: Methuen.

Zeskind, P. S., & Ramey, C. T. (1981). Preventing intellectual and interactional sequelae of fetal malnutrition: A longitudinal, transactional, and synergistic approach to development. *Child Development, 52,* 213–218.

CHAPTER TWELVE ■

THE SELF AND
SOCIAL DEVELOPMENT

■ *Development of the self-concept*
The self as separate from others
When do children recognize themselves?
The preschooler's conceptions of self
Conceptions of self in middle childhood and
  adolescence
Self-esteem: The affective component of self

■ *Knowing about others*
Age trends in impression formation
Role taking as a determinant of social cognition

■ *Sociability: Development of the social self*
Sociability during the first three years
Individual differences in sociability
Sociability during the preschool period
Is sociability a stable attribute?

■ *Altruism: Development of the prosocial self*
Developmental trends in altruism
Training altruism: Cultural and social influences
Cognitive and affective contributors to altruism
Who raises altruistic children?

■ *The development of aggression*
What is aggression?
Origins of aggression
Age-related changes in the nature of aggression
Is aggression a stable attribute?
Sex differences
Cultural influences
Familial influences
Methods of controlling aggression

■ *Achievement: Development of the
  competent self*
What is achievement motivation?
Home and family influences on achievement
Can I achieve? The role of expectancies in
  children's achievement behavior
Why do I succeed (or fail)? Locus of control and
  children's achievement behavior

■ *Summary*

W ho am I?

I am a free man, an American, a liberal, a conservative, a taxpayer, a rancher, a businessman, a consumer, a parent, a voter, and not as young as I used to be nor as old as I expect to be and I am all these things in no fixed order.

PRESIDENT LYNDON B. JOHNSON
(as quoted by Gordon, 1968, p. 123)

How would you answer the "Who am I" question? If you are like most adults, you would probably respond by mentioning attributes such as your gender, those of your interpersonal characteristics that you consider particularly noteworthy (for example, honesty, sincerity, friendliness, or kindness), your political leanings, religious preferences (if any), and occupational aspirations, and your strongest interests and values. In so doing, you would be describing that elusive concept that psychologists call the **self.**

Although no one else knows you the way you do, it is a safe bet that much of what you know about yourself stems from your contacts and experiences with other people. When a college sophomore tells us that she is a friendly, outgoing person who is active in the Phi Mu sorority, the Young Republicans, and the Campus Crusade for Christ, she is saying that her past experiences with others and the groups to which she belongs are important determinants of her personal identity. Several decades ago, sociologists Charles Cooley (1902) and George Herbert Mead (1934) proposed that the self-concept evolves from social interactions and will undergo many changes over the course of a lifetime. They used the term **looking-glass self** to emphasize that a person's understanding of his or her identity is a reflection of how other people react to him or her: one's self-concept is the image cast by a social mirror.

> **self:** *the combination of attributes, motives, values, and behaviors that is unique to each individual.*
> **looking-glass self:** *the idea that a child's self-concept is largely determined by the ways other people respond to him or her.*

Cooley and Mead believed that the self and social development are completely intertwined—that they emerge together and that neither can progress far without the other. Presumably, neonates experience people and events as simple "streams of impressions" and will have absolutely no concept of "self" until they realize that they exist independent of the objects and individuals that they encounter on a regular basis. Once infants make this important distinction between self and nonself, they will establish interactive routines with their close companions (that is, develop socially) and will learn that their behavior elicits predictable reactions from others. In other words, they are acquiring information about the "social self" based on the ways people respond to their overtures. As they acquire some language and begin to interact with a larger number of other people, children's self-concepts will change. Soon toddlers are describing themselves in categorical terms such as age ("I this many"), size and gender ("I big boy, not a baby"), and activities ("I'm a runner—zoom") that are reflections of how others respond to or label them. Mead (1934) concluded that

> the self has a character that is different from that of the physiological organism proper. The self is something which . . . is not initially there at birth but arises in the process of social development. That is, it develops in a given individual as a result of his relations to that process as a whole and to other individuals within the process.

Do babies really have no sense of self at birth? This issue is explored in the first section of the chapter, where we will trace the growth of the self-concept from infancy through adolescence. We will then consider what developing children know about other people and see that this aspect of social cognition parallels the development of the self-concept. Finally, we will look at some of the important "outcomes" of social development that help children to define a sense of self. In this chapter we will focus on sociability (social responsiveness), altruism (cooperation, sharing, and helping), aggression, and achievement (instrumental competence). In Chapter Thirteen we will examine the sex-typing process and note that the child's emerging conception of self as a male or a female may exert a powerful influence on his or her thoughts, feelings, and patterns of conduct.

Our focus in Chapter Fourteen shifts to moral and ethical issues as we follow the child's transformation from an egocentric and self-indulgent organism to a moral philosopher of sorts who has internalized certain ethical principles to evaluate his or her own conduct and the behavior of others.

Let's now return to the starting point and see how children come to know and understand this entity that we call the "self."

DEVELOPMENT OF THE SELF-CONCEPT

When do infants first distinguish themselves from other people, objects, and environmental events? At what point do they sense their uniqueness and form self-images? What kinds of information do young children use to define the self? And how do their self-images and feelings of self-worth change over time? These are some of the issues we will explore as we trace the development of the **self-concept** from infancy through adolescence.

The Self as Separate from Others

Like Mead, many developmentalists believe that infants are born without a sense of self. Psychoanalyst Margaret Mahler (Mahler, Pine, & Bergman, 1975) likens the newborn to a "chick in an egg" who has no reason to differentiate the self from the surrounding environment. After all, every need that the child has is soon satisfied by his or her ever-present companions, who are simply "there" and have no identities of their own. Only as the ego begins to form, at 3–6 months of age, will infants recognize that they are separate from their caregivers. In Mahler's words, the child is now in the process of "hatching" from the mother's protective shell and spreading his wings to establish an identity of his own.

Piaget agrees that neonates are born without any knowledge of self. But as they apply their reflexive schemata to the world around them, things begin to change. During the stage of primary circular reactions (1–4 months), infants are repeating pleasurable acts that are centered on their own bodies (for example, sucking their thumbs and waving their arms). At 4–8 months (the stage of secondary circular reactions), they have begun to repeat actions centered on some aspect of the *external* environment (for example, shaking a rattle or squeezing a noise-making toy). Thus, children may learn the limits of their bodies during the first four months and recognize that they can operate on objects external to this "physical self" by the middle of the first year. If 8-month-old infants could talk, they might answer the "Who am I" question by saying "I am a looker, a chewer, a reacher, and a grabber who acts on objects and makes things happen."

When Do Children Recognize Themselves?

Recognizing that one is separate from objects and close companions is only the first step in the development of a personal identity. Although a 5–6-month-old infant may have a subjective sense of physical self (me) and nonself (they, it), we might wonder whether she perceives herself as an object that continues to exist in space and over time. In other words, does the child have a firm self-image? Can she recognize herself?

Michael Lewis and Jeanne Brooks-Gunn (1979) have studied the development of self-recognition by applying a spot of rouge to infants' noses and then placing them before a mirror. If infants have schemata for their own faces and recognize their mirror images as themselves, they should soon notice the discrepant red dot and reach for or wipe their *own* noses. When Lewis and Brooks-Gunn subjected 9–24-month-olds to this rouge test, they found that a few of the 15–17-month-olds and the vast majority of the 18–24-month-olds touched their own noses rather than those of their mirror images. In other words, they recognized the images as reflections of themselves and inferred that they must have a strange dot on their faces—something that warranted further investigation.

By 18 months of age, many infants recognize static representations of themselves, such as a photograph taken earlier (Lewis & Brooks-Gunn, 1979). Recall that this is precisely the age when the object concept is maturing and infants are internalizing their sensorimotor schemata to form mental images. So it seems that the ability to recognize the self is closely related to the child's level of cognitive development. Even children with Down's syndrome and a variety of other mental deficiencies can recognize themselves in a mirror if they have attained a mental age of at least 18–20 months (Hill & Tomlin, 1981).

PHOTO 12-1. Recognizing one's mirror image is a milestone in the development of "self."

Although a certain level of cognitive development seems necessary for self-recognition, social experiences are probably of equal importance. Gordon Gallup (1979) finds that adolescent chimpanzees can easily recognize themselves in a mirror (as shown by the rouge test) unless they have been reared in complete social isolation. In contrast to normal chimps, social isolates react to their mirror images as if they were looking at another animal! So the term *looking-glass self* applies to chimpanzees as well as to humans: reflections cast by a "social mirror" enable normal chimps to develop a knowledge of self, whereas a chimpanzee that is denied these experiences will fail to acquire a personal identity.

The Preschooler's Conceptions of Self

Once children acquire language, they begin to tell us what they know about their emerging self-concepts. By the end of the second year, some toddlers are already using the personal pronouns *I, me, my,* and *mine* when referring to the self and *you* when addressing a companion (Lewis & Brooks-Gunn, 1979). This linguistic distinction between *I* and *you* suggests that 2-year-olds now

self-concept: *one's sense of oneself as a separate individual who possesses a unique set of characteristics.*

have a firm concept of "self" and "others" (who are also recognized as selves) and have inferred from their conversations that *I* means the person (or self) who is speaking whereas *you* refers to whomever is spoken to.

■ *Emergence of the categorical self*

Once children realize that they are separate and distinct from their companions, they begin to notice some of the ways that people differ and to categorize themselves on these dimensions, a classification called the **categorical self.** Age is one of the first social categories that children recognize and incorporate into their self-concepts. By the end of the first year, children can easily discriminate a strange baby from a strange adult, and given a choice, they much prefer to play with the infant (Lewis & Brooks-Gunn, 1979). Apparently infants classify others as "children" or "adults" on the basis of perceptual cues such as size, tone of voice, and facial configuration. The importance of facial features was illustrated by Brooks and Lewis (1976), who found that infants react much more enthusiastically when approached by a 4-year-old (with childlike features) than by an adult midget of the same height.

The child's use of age as a social category becomes much more refined during the preschool period (Edwards, 1984). Children aged 3 to 5 who examine photographs of people aged 1 to 70 can easily classify them as "little boys and girls" (photographs of 2- to 6-year-olds), "big boys and girls" (7- to 13-year-olds), "mothers and fathers" (14- to 49-year-olds), and "grandmothers and grandfathers" (age 50 and older).

Gender is another social category that children recognize and react to very early in life. Brooks-Gunn and Lewis (1981) found that 9- to 12-month-old infants can easily discriminate photographs of strange women from those of strange men, and they are more likely to smile at the women. Those 2- to 3-year-olds who have acquired gender labels such as *mommy* and *daddy* or *boy* and *girl* can correctly identify photographs as males and females, even though they are not always certain about their own gender identities (Brooks-Gunn & Lewis, 1982; Thompson, 1975). Further, 3- to 4-year-olds are quite aware that they are "boys" or "girls," although they often feel that they could change sex if they really wanted to (Kohlberg, 1969). And by the time they enter school, children know that they will always be males or females and have already learned many cultural stereotypes about men and women (Williams, Bennett, & Best, 1975). Clearly, one's gender identity is an extremely important aspect of "categorical self"—one that we will discuss at length in Chapter Thirteen.

■ *Who am I? Responses of preschool children*

When asked to describe themselves, preschoolers dwell on their physical characteristics, their possessions and interpersonal relationships, and the actions they can perform (Damon & Hart, 1982). In one study (Keller, Ford, & Meachum, 1978), 3- to 5-year-olds were asked to say ten things about themselves and to complete the sentences "I am a ———" and "I am a boy/girl who ———." Approximately 50% of the children's responses to these probes and questions were *action* statements such as "I play baseball" or "I walk to school." By contrast, psychological descriptions such as "I'm happy" or "I like people" were rare among these 3- to 5-year-olds. So it seems that preschool children have a somewhat "physicalistic" conception of self that is based mainly on their ability to perform various acts and make things happen.

These findings would hardly surprise Erik Erikson. In his theory of psychosocial development, Erikson (1963) proposes that 2- to 3-year-olds are struggling to become independent or autonomous, while 4- to 5-year-olds who have achieved a sense of **autonomy** are now acquiring new skills, achieving important objectives, and taking great pride in their accomplishments. According to Erikson, it is a healthy sign when preschool children define themselves in terms of their activities, for an activity-based self-concept reflects the sense of **initiative** they will need in order to cope with the difficult lessons they must learn at school.

■ *Origins of the "private" self*

When adults think about the self, they know that they have a **"public" self** (or selves) that others see and a **"private," thinking self** that is not available for public scrutiny. Do young children make this distinction between public self (or "self as known") and private self ("self as knower")?

One way to find out is to ask young children "how" or "where" they think and whether other people can observe them thinking. John Flavell (as

PHOTO 12-2. Young children's sense of self is based on the activities they can perform.

cited in Maccoby, 1980) tried this approach and found that children older than 3½ generally know (1) that dolls can't think, even though they have heads, (2) that their own thinking goes on inside their heads, and (3) that another person cannot observe their thought processes. In addition, most 4- to 5-year-olds know that private mental activities are controlled by their brains (or their minds), whereas they mistakenly assume that this unseen organ is not responsible for the overt acts that others can see, such as making a face or telling a story (Johnson & Wellman, 1982). Finally, Lev Vygotsky (1934) noted that 4- to 5-year-olds are beginning to make a clear distinction between "speech for self" and "speech for others." Speech for self, which often accompanies problem-solving activities, is now abbreviated, may be nearly inaudible, and contains many indefinite referents such as "this" or "get it" that are not likely to be understood by anyone other than the child. In contrast, communicative speech that is intended for others is boldly articulated and usually consists of complete sentences.

In sum, it appears that children begin to acquire the concept of a private, thinking self that others can't see between the ages of 3½ and 5. However, we still don't know the point at which a child will first recognize that the *products* of thinking are private, so that other people are often unable to determine exactly what he or she is thinking about.

---

categorical self: *a person's classification and definition of self along such dimensions as age, size, gender, activity preferences, beliefs, and values.*

autonomy vs. shame and doubt: *the second of Erikson's eight psychosocial stages, in which toddlers must establish a sense of independence and self-control or else experience feelings of shame and self-doubt.*

initiative vs. guilt: *the third of Erikson's eight psychosocial stages, in which preschool children must learn to initiate new activities and achieve important objectives or else become self-critical and experience guilt.*

public self: *those aspects of the self that others can see or infer.*

private self: *those aspects of the self that are known only to the individual and are not available for public scrutiny.*

Conceptions of Self in Middle Childhood and Adolescence

In Chapter Nine we learned that children's thinking gradually becomes less concrete and much more abstract as they progress from middle childhood through adolescence. Is the same true of one's personal identity, or self-concept? To find out, Raymond Montemayor and Marvin Eisen (1977) asked 4th-, 6th-, 8th-, 10th-, and 12th-graders to write 20 different answers to the question "Who am I?" They found that younger children (9- to 10-year-olds) do describe themselves in much more concrete terms than preadolescents (11- to 12-year-olds), who, in turn, are more concrete and less abstract than adolescents. Generally speaking, the younger children mentioned categorical information such as name, age, gender, and address, as well as their physical attributes and favorite activities. However, adolescents defined themselves in terms of their traits, beliefs, motivations, and interpersonal affiliations. This developmental shift toward a more abstract or "psychological" view of self can be seen in the responses of three participants:

> *9-year-old:* My name is Bruce C. I have brown eyes. I have brown hair. I love! sports. I have seven people in my family. I have great! eye site. I have lots! of friends. I live at . . . . I have an uncle who is almost 7 feet tall. My teacher is Mrs. V. I play hockey! I'm almost the smartest boy in the class. I love! food . . . I love! school.

> *11½-year-old:* My name is A. I'm a human being . . . a girl . . . a truthful person. I'm not pretty. I do so-so in my studies. I'm a very good cellist. I'm a little tall for my age. I like several boys . . . I'm old fashioned. I am a very good swimmer . . . I try to be helpful . . . Mostly I'm good, but I lose my temper. I'm not well liked by some girls and boys. I don't know if boys like me . . .

> *17-year-old:* I am a human being . . . a girl . . . an individual . . . I am a Pisces. I am a moody person . . . an indecisive person . . . an ambitious person. I am a big curious person . . . I am lonely. I am an American (God help me). I am a Democrat. I am a liberal person. I am a radical. I am conservative. I am a pseudoliberal. I am an Athiest. I am not a classifiable person (i.e., I don't want to be) [pp. 317–318].

On those occasions when grade school children use psychological labels to describe the self, they apply them in a concrete fashion, viewing these attributes as absolute and unchanging. For example, an 8- to 11-year-old who says that she is "kind" is likely to believe that kindness is a stable and enduring aspect of her personality that will always characterize her interactions with others (Mohr, 1978; Rotenberg, 1982). But adolescents who describe themselves with a trait such as "kindness" may recognize that any number of extenuating circumstances can cause them to act in a way that is inconsistent with their self-descriptions. For example, a "kindly" 20-year-old might say "I help my brother with his homework, but I don't help my sister with hers because my brother really needs help, while my sister is lazy. I mean it's fair to help him and not her" (Damon & Hart, 1982, p. 858). What the adolescent has done is to integrate a stable attribute (kindness) with a belief (help only those who need help) to produce an abstract conception of self that provides a logical explanation for two actions that appear inconsistent (Bernstein, 1980).

Robert Selman (1980) has studied children's awareness of their *private* selves by asking them to consider the following dilemma:

> Eight-year-old Tom is trying to decide what to buy his friend Mike for a birthday present. By chance, he meets Mike on the street and learns that Mike is extremely upset because his dog Pepper has been lost for two weeks. In fact, Mike is so upset that he tells Tom "I miss Pepper so much that I never want to look at another dog . . ." Tom goes off only to pass by a store with a sale on puppies. Only two are left and these will soon be gone.

Children were first asked whether Tom should buy Mike one of the puppies. To probe their understanding of the distinction between the private self and one's public image, they were then asked questions such as "Can you ever fool yourself into thinking that you feel one way when you really feel another?" and "Is there an inside and an outside to a person?"

Selman found that children younger than 6 did not distinguish between private feelings and public behavior, responding to the questions with statements such as "If I say that I don't want to see a puppy again, then I really won't ever want to."

FIGURE 12.1

Really true for me	Sort of true for me			Sort of true for me	Really true for me
☐	☐	Some kids often but forget what they learn	Other kids can remember things easily	☐	☐

In contrast, most 8-year-olds recognize the difference between inner states and outward appearances, and they are likely to say that Mike would really be happy to have another puppy. So somewhere between the ages of 6 and 8, children become much more aware of their subjective, "inner" selves and will think of this private self as the true self.

In early adolescence, thinking about the private self becomes much more complex. Selman (1980) proposes that young adolescents are "aware of their own self-awareness" and believe that they can *control* their inner feelings. For example, a 14-year-old might react to the loss of a pet by noting "I can fool myself into not wanting another puppy if I keep saying to myself, I don't want a puppy; I don't ever want to see another puppy." However, older adolescents eventually realize that they cannot control all their subjective experiences because their feelings and behaviors may be influenced by factors of which they are not consciously aware. Consider the response of one older adolescent when asked "Why did Mike say he didn't want to ever see another puppy?"

> [Mike] might not want to admit that another dog could take Pepper's place. He might feel at one level that it would be unloyal to Pepper to just go out and replace the dog. He may feel guilty about it. He doesn't want to face these feelings, so he says no dog. (Experimenter: Is he aware of this?) Probably not [Selman, 1980, p. 106].

In sum, children's understanding of their public and private selves becomes increasingly abstract from middle childhood through adolescence. The concrete 6-year-old who feels that her public image is an accurate portrayal of self will gradually become a reflective adolescent who not only distinguishes between the public and private selves but also recognizes that the private "self as knower" may not always understand why the public self behaves as it does.

Self-Esteem: The Affective Component of Self

There is another side to the self-concept that we have not considered: children's feelings about (or evaluations of) the qualities that they perceive themselves as having. This aspect of self is called **self-esteem.** Children with high self-esteem generally feel quite positive about their perceived characteristics, whereas those with low self-esteem view the self in a less favorable light.

Susan Harter (1982) has developed a 28-item self-concept scale that asks children to evaluate their competencies in four areas:

1. *Cognitive competence.* Doing well in school, feeling smart, remembering things easily, understanding what they read.
2. *Social competence.* Having a lot of friends, being popular, being important to one's classmates, feeling liked.
3. *Physical competence.* Doing well at sports, being chosen early for games, being good at new games, would rather play than watch.
4. *General self-worth.* Sure of myself, am a good person, happy the way I am, want to stay the same.

Each of the 28 items requires the child to select one of two statements that is "most like me" and then to indicate whether that statement is "sort of true for me" or "really true for me." Figure 12-1 shows a sample item from the cognitive competencies subscale. Each item is scored from 1 to 4—a score of 1 (far left-hand box) indicates low perceived competence on that item and a score of 4 (far right-hand box) indicates high perceived competence. Responses to items on each of the

---

self-esteem: *a person's feelings about the qualities and characteristics that make up his or her self-concept.*

four subscales are then summed and averaged to determine how positively the child evaluates his or her cognitive competencies, social competencies, physical competencies, and general self-worth.

Harter (1982) administered her self-concept scale to 2097 third- through ninth-graders and also asked teachers to rate each child on a similar 28-item scale. Several interesting findings emerged from this study. First, even third-graders (8-year-olds) perceive themselves in either favorable or unfavorable terms on each of the four subscales—indicating that children's feelings about the self (or self-esteem) are well established by middle childhood. Second, children make important distinctions about their competencies in different areas, so that their "self-esteem" depends on the situation in which they find themselves. For example, a star student who considers himself bad at sports and other physical activities may enjoy high self-esteem in the classroom while feeling inadequate on the playground. Finally, Harter found that children's evaluations of self seem to be accurate reflections of how others perceive them. For example, subjects' ratings of their cognitive competencies were positively correlated with their own achievement scores and their teachers' ratings of their cognitive competencies. Their ratings of interpersonal skills and competencies in the social area were confirmed by peers who had been asked to rate each classmate in terms of how good a friend that person was. Moreover, children who had rated themselves high in physical competencies were more frequently chosen for sporting activities and were rated higher on physical competence by gym teachers than were classmates who had rated themselves low in physical competencies. Taken together, these results suggest that both self-knowledge and self-esteem may depend to a large extent on the way others perceive and react to our behavior. This is precisely the point that Charles Cooley (1902) was making when he coined the term *looking-glass self* to explain how we construct a self-image.

■ *Which competencies are most important?*

Although children evaluate their competencies in many areas, it appears that some attributes are more important than others. For example, fourth-, fifth-, and sixth-graders typically define their self-

PHOTO 12-3. *Children who do well in school and who have lots of friends are likely to enjoy high self-esteem.*

worth in terms of their cognitive and social competencies, so that children who enjoy the highest self-esteem are those who do well in school and have lots of friends (Coopersmith, 1967; Kokenes, 1974). Once again, these findings would not surprise Erik Erikson, who believed that the major psychosocial crisis that grade school children face is **industry versus inferiority.** According to Erikson, 6- to 12-year-olds are beginning to "measure" themselves against their peers to determine who they are and what they are capable of. The major goal of the grade school child is to achieve a sense of personal and interpersonal competence by acquiring important technological and social skills—reading, writing, an ability to cooperate, and a sense of fair play—that are necessary to win the approval of both adults and peers. Children who acquire these skills should feel good about themselves because they are developing the sense of "industriousness" that will prepare them for their next developmental hurdle—the identity crisis of adolescence. Those who fail to acquire important academic and social skills will feel inferior (that is, have low self-esteem) and may have a difficult time establishing a stable identity later in life (Erikson, 1963).

Erikson believed that the determinants of self-esteem will change as children enter adolescence and begin the long process of establishing stable social, sexual, and occupational identities. Recent research suggests that he may have been right: eighth- to tenth-graders who feel good about themselves and who have made a preliminary commitment to a social or occupational identity are those who have warm and supportive relationships with their parents, a teacher who cares about them, and/or a close circle of friends (Berndt, 1982; Kokenes, 1974; Waterman, 1982). In other words, the social looking glass by which young adolescents define and evaluate the self now consists of a smaller group of "significant others" rather than most or all others.

■ *Changes in self-esteem from middle childhood through adolescence*

Recently a number of investigators have found that self-esteem often declines at age 12 to 13 (Simmons, Blyth, Van Cleave, & Bush, 1979; Simmons, Rosenberg, & Rosenberg, 1973) and then gradually increases over the next several years (McCarthy & Hoge, 1982; O'Malley & Bachman, 1983). One explanation for the 12- to 13-year-old's declining self-esteem is that many children of this age are experiencing puberty and becoming overly critical and self-conscious about their changing body images. Indeed, those 12–16-year-olds who are least satisfied about their physical appearance tend to have negative self-images (Lerner, Iwawaki, Chihara, & Sorell, 1980; Simmons et al., 1979). Other possible explanations for a decline in perceived self-worth are (1) that young adolescents are moving from elementary school, where they are the oldest and most revered pupils, to junior high, where they are the youngest and least competent, and (2) that these young "formal operators" are beginning to think about the concept of an "ideal self" (the person they ought to be), so that any major discrepancies between who they are and "what they should be" will lower their self-esteem.

According to Erikson (1963), adolescents experience a decline in self-worth because they are now reevaluating themselves and their goals as they search for a stable identity. Erikson proposed that the many physical, cognitive, and social changes that occur at puberty force the young adolescent to conclude "I ain't what I ought to be, I ain't what I'm gonna be, but I ain't what I was" (1950, p. 139). In other words, 12- to 15-year-olds face an **"identity crisis"** in that they are no longer sure who they are and yet must also grapple with the question "Who will I become?" A failure to answer these questions leaves them confused and uncertain about their self-worth. However, Erikson proposed that adolescents would eventually view themselves in more positive terms if they achieved a stable identity with which to approach the tasks of young adulthood.

In recent years, investigators have taken a closer look at the adolescent identity crisis and found that many people go through several phases, or "identity statuses," before establishing a stable self-concept. In Box 12-1 we will consider some of these findings and see that the development of a firm, future-oriented self-image is a gradual and somewhat uneven process that may take longer than Erikson assumed.

■ KNOWING ABOUT OTHERS

There are some interesting parallels between the child's knowledge of self and knowledge of others. For example, infants begin to form attachments to their caregivers and to become wary of strangers shortly *after* they discover that other people are separate entities and not merely extensions of the self (Mahler et al., 1975). They recognize their regular companions and know that these people continue to exist long *before* they recognize themselves in a mirror or a photograph. As we learned earlier, many 2–3-year-olds can

---

industry vs. inferiority: *the psychosocial crisis of the grade school years, in which children must acquire important social and intellectual skills, or they may view themselves as incompetent.*
identity crisis: *Erikson's term for the uncertainty and discomfort that adolescents experience when they become confused about their present and future roles in life.*

Perhaps you can recall a time during the teenage years when you were confused about who you were, what you should be, and what you were likely to become. Do you remember how you resolved your adolescent identity crisis? Is it possible that you have not resolved it yet? And what role do you think an experience like college might play in the process of identity formation?

James Marcia (1966) has carefully analyzed what Erik Erikson had to say about the adolescent identity crisis and has concluded that, at any given point in time, adolescents and young adults can be classified into one of four "identity statuses":

1. *Identity diffusion.* The least mature of the identity statuses. Adolescents classified as diffuse either have not yet experienced an identity crisis or have failed to resolve it. No commitments have been made to important attitudes, values, or plans for the future.

2. *Identity foreclosure.* A person is classified as a foreclosure if he or she has never experienced an identity crisis but has made preliminary commitments to particular goals, values, and beliefs. This may occur when parents or other authority figures suggest an identity to the adolescent (for example, "You'll go to med school, Johnny") and he or she accepts their wishes without really evaluating them.

3. *Moratorium.* This status describes the person who is currently experiencing a strong identity crisis and is actively exploring a number of values, interests, ideologies, and prospective careers in an attempt to find a stable identity in which to grow and embrace the challenges of young adulthood.

4. *Identity achievement.* The identity achiever has resolved his or her crisis by making relatively strong commitments to an occupation, a sexual orientation, and/or a political or religious ideology. Both Marcia and Erikson believe that adolescents must experience an identity crisis and the moratorium status before achieving a stable identity. However, it is possible to progress from identity diffusion to the moratorium phase, skipping the foreclosure status.

Although Erikson assumed that the identity crisis occurred in early adolescence and was typically resolved by age 15–18, it appears that his age norms were overly optimistic. Philip Meilman (1979) used a structured interview to access the identity statuses of college-bound boys between 12 and 18, 21-year-old college males, and 24-year-old adult males. As shown in the graph, only 20% of the 18-year-olds, 40% of the college students, and slightly over half of the 24-year-olds had established a mature identity status. Note, however, that there was evidence of a clear developmental progression: identity diffusion and the foreclosure status became less common among older subjects, whereas nearly 25% of the 18-year-olds, 52% of the 21-year-olds, and 68% of the 24-year-olds had either reached the moratorium status or achieved stable identities.

One problem with Meilman's study is that subjects came from a very restricted sample; all were college-bound or college-educated males. Sally Archer (1982) has recently studied a broader cross-section of male and female 6th-, 8th-, 10th-, and 12th-graders and reported a similar set of findings. The vast majority of Archer's subjects were classified as identity diffuse or foreclosures, the largest increase in identity achievement coming between the 10th and 12th grades. However, Archer reports that only 19% of the

---

correctly label pictures of males and females, even though they are not always certain of their own gender identities. And although 3-year-olds can easily place photographs into age categories such as "little children" and "big children," they are not always sure about the category to which they belong (Edwards & Lewis, 1979). In sum, it appears that infants and toddlers are first noticing how other people differ and then using the information to formulate a self-concept. Perhaps Gordon Gallup (1979) was right in arguing that a person must have some knowledge of others before he or she can understand the self.

What kinds of information do children use when forming impressions of other people? How do their impressions of others change over time? And what skills might children be acquiring that would explain these changes in **social cognition**? These are the issues we will consider in the pages that follow.

Age Trends in Impression Formation

Children younger than 6 or 7 are likely to characterize their friends and acquaintances in the same concrete, observable terms that they use to describe themselves. For example, preschool children often say that they like their "best friend" because (1) the friend lives nearby, so that they can play together (availability and shared ac-

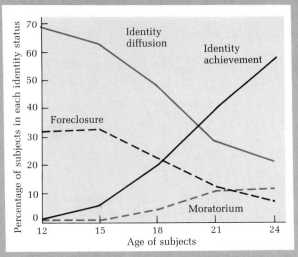

Percentages of subjects in each of Marcia's four identity statuses as a function of age. Note that resolution of the identity crisis occurs much later than Erikson assumed: only 4% of the 15-year-olds and 20% of the 18-year-olds had achieved a stable identity.

12th-graders' responses could be classified as moratoriums or identity achievement—a figure that is remarkably similar to the 24% of all 18-year-olds who had achieved these statuses in Meilman's study. Taken together, the results of these studies indicate that American youth do not experience a strong identity crisis until late adolescence. It also appears that a substantial percentage of young adults are still searching for and trying to establish a personal identity.

Not only does the formation of a stable identity take longer than Erikson assumed, it is apparently an uneven process. Archer's structured interview assessed subjects' identity statuses in four areas: occupational choice, sex-role attitudes, religious beliefs, and political ideologies. Only 5% of her adolescents were found to have the same identity status in each area, and more than 90% had two or three identity statuses across the four areas. Vocational choice was the area in which subjects were most likely to have achieved a stable identity; the largest number of identity diffusions came in the area of political ideology.

Gordon Munro and Gerald Adams (1977) compared college students with their working peers in order to assess the effects of college attendance on the process of identity formation. Although the two groups were comparable in the area of occupational identity, the working youth were further along in terms of establishing stable religious and political identities. Munro and Adams concluded that full-time employment "might stimulate rapid movement toward identity formation, while college attendance might be seen as an extended moratorium period" (p. 523). Indeed, one recent longitudinal study found that college students often regress from identity achievement to the moratorium status at some point in their academic careers (Adams and Fitch, 1982).

In sum, the establishment of a stable adult identity (or identities) is a very gradual process that often extends into young adulthood, particularly if the individual is exposed to a college community in which old viewpoints are likely to be challenged and new alternatives presented. However, let's not be too critical of the college environment, for the vast majority of college students emerge from their four years of higher education with "identity statuses" that are much more mature than those they had as entering freshmen (Waterman, 1982).

tivities), (2) the friend is good-looking (physical appearance), and/or (3) the friend has interesting toys (possessions). When these youngsters do use a psychological term to describe a liked or disliked other, it is typically a very general attribute such as "He is *nice*" or "She is *naughty*"—the same kind of diffuse psychological labels that they occasionally use to describe the self (Hayes, Gershman, & Bolin, 1980; Livesley & Bromley, 1973).

Between the ages of 7 and 10, children begin to rely less on concrete attributes (for example, possessions and physical characteristics) and more on psychological terms when describing the self and others (Livesley & Bromley, 1973; Peevers & Secord, 1973). Carl Barenboim (1981) has recently proposed a three-step developmental sequence to describe the changes in children's impressions during the grade school years. The three steps are as follows:

1. *Behavioral comparisons phase.* If asked to talk about people they know, 6- to 8-year-olds will compare and contrast their acquaintances in concrete *behavioral* terms such as "Billy *runs* faster

> social cognition: *the ability to understand the thoughts, feelings, motives, and intentions of oneself and other people.*

than Jason," or "She *draws* best in our whole class." Before this phase, children usually describe the behavior of their companions in absolute terms (for example, "Billy's fast") without making explicit comparisons.

2. *Psychological constructs phase.* As they continue to observe definite regularities in a companion's behavior, 8- to 10-year-olds should begin to base their impressions on the stable *psychological* attributes, or traits, that the person is now presumed to have. For example, an 8- to 10-year-old might describe well-known classmates with statements such as "He's a stubborn idiot" or "She's generous." However, children at this phase are not yet comparing their acquaintances on these psychological dimensions.

3. *Psychological comparisons phase.* By preadolescence (age 11 or 12), children should begin to *compare and contrast* others on important psychological dimensions. The statement "Bill is much more shy than Ted" is an example of a psychological comparison.

Barenboim evaluated his proposed developmental sequence by asking 6-, 8-, and 10-year-olds to describe three persons whom they knew well. Each of the child's descriptive statements was classified as a behavioral comparison, a psychological construct (or traitlike statement), or a psychological comparison. The children were then retested one year later, so that data were available for subjects at all ages between 6 and 11.

Several interesting findings emerged. As we see in Figure 12-2, the impressions of younger children were usually stated in behavioral terms. Use of behavioral comparisons increased between the ages of 6 and 8 and began to decline at age 9. However, 9- to 11-year-olds were relying much more heavily on psychological constructs during the same period that the use of behavioral comparisons was becoming less common. The longitudinal data were also consistent with Barenboim's proposed developmental sequence: over the year between the original test and the retest, virtually all the subjects had either stayed at the same phase of impression formation or moved forward (for example, from behavioral comparisons to the psychological constructs phase). Note, however, that even the 11-year-olds rarely used psychological comparisons when stating their impressions of other people.

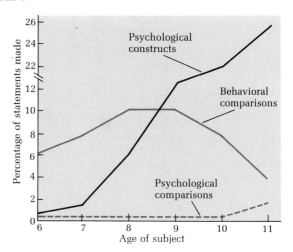

FIGURE 12-2. *Percentages of descriptive statements classified as behavioral comparisons, psychological (traitlike) constructs, and psychological comparisons for children between the ages of 6 and 11.*

When do children begin to compare others on important psychological dimensions? To find out, Barenboim repeated his study with 10-, 12-, 14-, and 16-year-olds and found that the vast majority of 12–16-year-olds had progressed to this third level of impression formation. In contrast, fewer than 15% of the 10-year-olds *ever* used a psychological comparison when talking about their companions.

Why do children progress from behavioral comparisons to psychological constructs to psychological comparisons? Barenboim suggests that this three-step sequence probably reflects changes that are occurring in children's intellectual abilities. His conclusion seems quite reasonable when we recall that the use of concrete behavioral comparisons begins at about the same time that children are entering Piaget's concrete-operational stage and that the more abstract psychological comparisons appear at about age 12—precisely the time when many children are approaching formal operations. Robert Selman (1976, 1980) goes one step further in arguing that a child's impressions of other people (that is, interpersonal understanding) depend to a large extent on one particular aspect of cognitive growth—the development of **role-taking skills**. Let's take a closer look.

Role Taking as a Determinant of Social Cognition

According to Selman (1980), children will become much more proficient at understanding other people as they acquire the ability to discriminate their own perspectives from those of their companions and to see the relationships between these potentially discrepant points of view. The underlying assumption of Selman's theory is straightforward: in order to "know" a person, one must be able to assume his perspective and understand his thoughts, feelings, motives, and intentions—in short, the *internal* factors that account for his behavior. If a child has not yet acquired these important role-taking skills, she may have little choice but to describe her acquaintances in terms of their external attributes—that is, their appearance, their activities, and the things they possess.

Selman has studied the development of role-taking skills by asking children to comment on a number of interpersonal dilemmas. Here is one example (from Selman, 1976, p. 302):

Holly is an 8-year-old girl who likes to climb trees. She is the best tree climber in the neighborhood. One day while climbing down from a tall tree, she falls . . . but does not hurt herself. Her father sees her fall. He is upset and asks her to promise not to climb trees any more. Holly promises.

Later that day, Holly and her friends meet Shawn. Shawn's kitten is caught in a tree and can't get down. Something has to be done right away or the kitten may fall. Holly is the only one who climbs trees well enough to reach the kitten and get it down but she remembers her promise to her father.

After listening to the dilemma, the children were asked:

1. Does Holly know how Shawn feels about the kitten?
2. How will Holly's father feel if he finds out she climbed the tree?
3. What does Holly think her father will do if he finds out she climbed the tree?
4. What would you do in this situation?

After analyzing children's responses to these questions, Selman concluded that role-taking abil-

ities progress through a series of stages, which appear in Table 12-1.

Apparently these role-taking stages represent a true developmental sequence, for 40 of 41 boys who were repeatedly tested over a five-year period showed a steady forward progression from stage to stage with no skipping of stages (Gurucharri & Selman, 1982). Perhaps the reason these role-taking skills develop in one particular order is that they are closely related to Piaget's invariant sequence of cognitive stages (Keating & Clark, 1980). As we see in Table 12-2 on p. 481, most concrete operators are at Selman's second or third level of role taking, whereas many formal operators have reached the fourth and final role-taking stage.

■ *Role taking and social behavior*

As children acquire important role-taking skills, their relationships with other people will begin to change. For example, we've seen that preschool children (at Selman's egocentric stage) think of "friends" as people who live nearby and play together. But once they recognize that playmates may have different motives and intentions (Selman's Stage 1), children begin to think of a friend as anyone who tries to do nice things for another person. Later, at Stage 2, children understand that the term *friend* implies a *reciprocal* relationship in which the parties involved act with mutual respect, kindness, and affection (Furman & Bierman, 1983; Selman, 1980). Finally, young adolescents who are becoming more knowledgeable about the preferences and personalities of their acquaintances begin to view a "friend" as a person with similar interests and values who is willing to share intimate information with them (Berndt, 1982). In sum, children become much more selective about whom they call a friend as they begin to understand the viewpoints of their peers and are better able to determine who among these companions has an outlook on life that is reasonably well coordinated with their own.

A child's role-taking skills may also affect his or her status in the peer group. Lawrence Kurdek

> **role taking:** *the ability to assume another person's perspective and understand his or her thoughts and feelings.*

TABLE 12-1. Selman's stages of social perspective taking

Stage	*Typical responses to the "Holly" dilemma*
0. Egocentric or undifferentiated perspective (roughly 3 to 6 years) Children are unaware of any perspective other than their own. They assume that whatever they feel is right for Holly to do will be agreed on by others.	Children often assume that Holly will save the kitten. When asked how Holly's father will react to her transgression, these children think he will be "happy because he likes kittens." In other words, these children like kittens themselves, and they assume that Holly and her father also like kittens. They do not recognize that another person's viewpoint may differ from their own.
1. Social-informational role taking (roughly 6 to 8 years) Children now recognize that people can have perspectives that differ from their own but believe that this happens *only* because these individuals have received different information. The child is still unable to think about the thinking of others and know in advance how others will react to an event.	When asked whether Holly's father will be angry because she climbed the tree, the child may say "If he didn't know why she climbed the tree, he would be angry. But if he knew why she did it, he would realize that she had a good reason." Thus, the child is saying that if both parties have exactly the same information, they will reach the same conclusion.
2. Self-reflective role taking (roughly 8 to 10 years) Children now know that their own and others' points of view may conflict even if they have received the same information. They are now able to consider the other person's viewpoint. They also recognize that the other person can put himself in their shoes, so that they are now able to anticipate the person's reactions to their behavior. However, the child cannot consider his own perspective and that of another person at the same time.	If asked whether Holly will climb the tree, the child might say "Yes. She knows that her father will understand why she did it." In so doing, the child is focusing on the father's consideration of Holly's perspective. But if asked whether the father would want Holly to climb the tree, the child usually says no, thereby indicating that he is now assuming the father's perspective and considering the father's concern for Holly's safety.
3. Mutual role taking (roughly 10–12 years) The child can now simultaneously consider her own and another person's points of view and recognize that the other person can do the same. At this point, each party can put the self in the other's place and view the self from that vantage point before deciding how to react. The child can also assume the perspective of a disinterested third party and anticipate how each participant (self and other) will react to the viewpoint of his or her partner.	At this stage, a child might describe the outcome of the "Holly" dilemma by taking the perspective of a disinterested third party and indicating that she knows that both Holly and her father are thinking about what each other is thinking. For example, one child remarked: "Holly wanted to get the kitten because she likes kittens, but she knew that she wasn't supposed to climb trees. Holly's father knew that Holly had been told not to climb trees, but he couldn't have known about [the kitten]. He'd probably punish her anyway just to enforce his rule."
4. Social and conventional system role taking (roughly 12 to 15 and older) The young adolescent now attempts to understand another person's perspective by comparing it with that of the social system in which he operates (that is, the view of the "generalized other"). In other words, the adolescent expects others to consider and typically assume perspectives on events that most people in their social group would take.	A Stage 4 adolescent might think that Holly's father would become angry and punish her for climbing the tree because fathers generally punish children who disobey. However, adolescents sometimes recognize that other people are nontraditional or may have a personal viewpoint quite discrepant from that of the "generalized other." If so, the subject might say the reaction of Holly's father will depend on the extent to which he is unlike other fathers and does not value absolute obedience.

TABLE 12-2. Percentages of children and adolescents at each of Selman's role-taking stages as a function of their level of cognitive development

| | Role-taking stage | | | | |
| | 0 | 1 | 2 | 3 | 4 |
Piaget's stage	Egocentric	Social-informational	Self-reflective	Mutual	Social systems
Concrete operations	0	14	32	50	4
Transitional (late concrete)	1	3	42	43	10
Early formal operations	0	6	6	65	24
Consolidated formal operations	0	12[a]	0	38	50

[a]Since only 8 consolidated formal operators were found in the sample, this figure of 12% represents only one subject.

and Donna Krile (1982) recently found that the most popular children among groups of third- to eighth-graders are those who have well-developed role-taking skills. Moreover, children who have established intimate friendships score higher on tests of role-taking abilities than do classmates without close friends (McGuire & Weisz, 1982).

Why are mature role takers likely to enjoy such a favorable status in the peer group? A recent study by Lynne Hudson and her associates (Hudson, Forman, & Brion-Meisels, 1982) provides one clue. Second-graders who had tested either high or low in role-taking ability were asked to teach two kindergarten children how to make caterpillars out of construction paper. As each tutor worked with the kindergartners, his or her behavior was videotaped for later analysis. Hudson et al. found that all the older tutors were willing to assist their younger pupils if the kindergartners *explicitly asked for help.* However, good role takers were much more likely than poor role takers to respond to a kindergartner's subtle or *indirect* requests for help. For example, exaggerated straining with scissors and frequent glances at the tutor usually elicited a helpful response from a good role taker but nothing more than a smile from a poor role taker. Apparently, good role takers are better able to infer the needs of their companions so that they can respond accordingly—an ability that may help to explain why they are so popular with their peers and quite successful at establishing close friendships.

■ *Effects of social interactions on role taking*
Although our understanding of self and others will influence our social behavior, it appears that the reverse is also true: our social experiences can affect the ways we think about the self and other people. For example, Jean Piaget (1965) has argued that playful interactions among grade school children promote the development of important role-taking skills. By assuming different roles while playing together, young children should become more aware of discrepancies between their own perspectives and those of their playmates. And when conflicts arise in play, children must learn to integrate their points of view with those of their companions (that is, compromise) in order for play to continue. So Piaget assumes that equal-status contacts among peers are an important contributor to social perspective taking and the growth of interpersonal understanding.

Diane Bridgeman (1981) has recently tested this hypothesis in an interesting study with fifth-graders. Students in a *cooperative interdependence* condition were divided into six-person study groups. Each person in each group was assigned various lessons that he or she was required to learn and then teach to the other group members. Since each student had access only to his or her own materials, the members of each group were clearly dependent on one another. Indeed, the tutors had to be good listeners and recognize what their pupils didn't understand and would need to know (a form of perspective taking)

PHOTO 12-4. *Equal-status contacts with peers are an important contributor to role-taking skills and the growth of interpersonal understanding.*

in order for the group members to learn all the material for which they were ultimately responsible. Students assigned to the *control condition* were required to learn exactly the same material, which was taught in the classroom by their teachers.

When tested before the experiment, students in the control condition were found to be comparable in role-taking abilities to their counterparts in cooperative interdependence groups. But by the end of the eight-week experiment, children in the cooperative learning groups had typically become better role takers, while those in the control condition had not. Apparently Piaget was right in arguing that a person's role-taking skills will depend, in part, on the kinds of social experiences that he or she has had.

Although many questions remain to be answered about the development of self and interpersonal understanding, this much is certain: Cooley and Mead were quite correct in suggesting that social cognition and social development are completely intertwined—that they occur together and that neither can progress very far without the other. Lawrence Kohlberg (1969) reached the same conclusion, arguing that social development

produces changes in both the child's self-concept and his or her impressions of other people. These latter developments then influence the child's future social interactions, which, in turn, will affect his or her impressions of the self and the social environment. Let's now consider some of the important social events, experiences, and outcomes that seem to influence the self-concepts of developing children.

SOCIABILITY: DEVELOPMENT OF THE SOCIAL SELF

Sociability is a term that researchers use to describe the child's willingness to engage others in social interaction and to seek their attention or approval. Although sociable interactions and emotional attachments are sometimes confused, they are easily distinguished. Recall that an attachment is a relatively *strong* and *enduring* affectional tie between the child and a particular person (for example, the mother or father). In contrast, *sociability* refers to the friendly gestures that the child makes to a much wider variety of targets (peers, strange adults, teachers), and the resulting social relationships are often temporary and emotionally uninvolving (Ainsworth, 1972; Clarke-Stewart, Umeh, Snow, & Pederson, 1980). Some of the confusion surrounding these two constructs stems from the fact that both originate from the child's earliest interactions with caregivers, who usually become both attachment objects and targets for sociable gestures. But even though children may eventually become sociable with any number of other people, they will form attachments to very few.

Sociability during the First Three Years

Months before infants form their first attachments, they are already smiling, cooing, and trying to attract the attention of their companions. By 6 weeks of age, many infants prefer human company to nonsocial forms of stimulation, and they are apt to protest whenever *any* adult puts them down or walks off and leaves them alone (Schaffer & Emerson, 1964). Even another baby may elicit a sociable response from an infant. Touching first occurs at 3 to 4 months of age (Vincze, 1971), and by the middle of the first year, infants will often smile at their tiny companions, vocalize, offer toys, and take turns gesturing to one another (Hay, Nash, & Pedersen, 1983; Vandell, Wilson, & Buchanan, 1980). Perhaps children become sociable at such an early age because other people—even little people—are likely to notice and respond to their bids for attention.

Do infants become more sociable over time? Alison Clarke-Stewart attempted to answer this question by observing 60 infants as they interacted with their mothers and an adult stranger at 12, 18, 24, and 30 months of age (Clarke-Stewart et al., 1980). The results of this longitudinal study were clear: children became much more friendly and outgoing toward both their mothers and the adult stranger over the period between 12 and 30 months of age. These findings parallel the results of an earlier study (Maccoby & Feldman, 1972) in which children became much less anxious around strangers between the ages of 2 and 3. In fact, Maccoby and Feldman (1972) reported that many distressed 3-year-olds could be comforted by a strange adult and did not require that their mothers be present in order to sustain a friendly interaction with a stranger.

Individual Differences in Sociability

Researchers who study infants and toddlers have found that some youngsters are simply more sociable than others. At least three hypotheses have been proposed to account for these individual differences in sociability: the genetic hypothesis, the "security of attachment" hypothesis, and the "ordinal position" hypothesis.

■ *The genetic hypothesis: Sociability as a heritable attribute*

There is now evidence to suggest that one's genotype influences responsiveness to other people (Goldsmith, 1983). Over the first year, identical twins are much more similar than fraternal twins in their frequency of social smiling and their fear of strangers (Freedman, 1974), and these differences in sociability are still apparent when pairs of identical and fraternal twins are retested at 18 and 24 months of age (Matheny, 1983). In fact, Sandra Scarr's (1966, 1968) studies of 6–10-year-old twin pairs suggests that genetic influences on sociability are often detectable well into middle childhood. Scarr found that identical

twins were more similar than fraternal twins on measures of their desire to affiliate with others (as rated by their mothers) as well as their "friendliness" and "shyness" (as rated by an adult observer). Moreover, some of the mothers in Scarr's study were mistaken about whether their twins were monozygotic (identical) or dizygotic (fraternal). Yet in each case of mistaken identity, the degree of similarity between members of a twin pair was more in line with their actual zygosity than with their mother's belief about their zygosity. That is, identical twins raised mistakenly as fraternals were as much alike as identical twins raised as identicals. Fraternal twins raised mistakenly as identicals were as dissimilar as fraternals raised as fraternals. The results for these older, misclassified twin pairs are very important, for they indicate that genetic influences on sociability are long-lasting and may never be completely overridden by social influences.

Although sociability appears to be a heritable attribute, environmental influences can play a major role in its expression. One environmental factor that seems to have such an effect is the quality of a child's emotional attachments.

■ *The "security of attachment" hypothesis*

Although attachment and sociability represent different social systems, Mary Ainsworth (1979) believes that the quality of a child's attachments will affect his or her reactions to other people. Ainsworth's position is that children who are insecurely attached to one or more unresponsive companions will be rather anxious and inhibited in the presence of others and much less sociable than children who are securely attached.

Most of the available evidence is consistent with Ainsworth's hypothesis. Infants who are securely attached to their mothers at 12 to 19 months of age are more likely than those who are insecurely attached to (1) obey their mothers, (2) cooperate and make positive social gestures toward a strange adult, (3) act sociably around other infants, and (4) be friendly, outgoing, and popular with their peers some three years later in

---

> **sociability:** *a person's tendency to interact with others and to seek their attention or approval.*

nursery school (Londerville & Main, 1981; Pastor, 1981; Thompson & Lamb, 1983; Waters, Wippman, & Sroufe, 1979). Moreover, two secure attachments are apparently better than one: toddlers who are secure with their mothers and their fathers are more socially responsive and less conflicted about interacting with a strange adult than are children who are insecure with one or both parents (Main & Weston, 1981). Perhaps Ainsworth is right in arguing that securely attached children are sociable children because they have learned to trust their responsive caregivers and assume that other people will also welcome their bids for attention.

■ The "ordinal position" hypothesis

Several years ago, Stanley Schachter (1959) reported an interesting finding: in times of stress or uncertainty, first-borns prefer to affiliate with other people, while later-borns would rather face their problems alone. Although his subjects were adults, Schachter suspected that first-born children, who have enjoyed an exclusive relationship with their parents, are generally more sociable than later-borns.

Deborah Vandell (Vandell, Wilson, & Whalen, 1981) evaluated this **"ordinal position" hypothesis** by placing pairs of 6-month-old infants together and watching them play. Vandell found that first-borns were more likely than later-borns to approach and take turns gesturing to each other. In a similar study of 3-year-olds, Margaret Snow, Carol Jacklin, and Eleanor Maccoby (1981) found that first-borns (particularly "only" children) were both more socially outgoing and more aggressive than later-borns. The later-borns in this study often stood around watching others play, and they were somewhat more likely than first-borns to withdraw from social contacts.

There are at least two reasons that a child's ordinal position in the family may influence responsiveness to peers. For one, only children and other first-borns tend to receive more attention from parents than later-borns do (Lewis & Kreitzberg, 1979). Thus, first-borns may be particularly sociable because they have had many positive social experiences at home—experiences that encourage them to be more outgoing with their peers. In addition, it is possible that later-borns have learned to be wary and somewhat inhibited

around other people—particularly little people—because they are often dominated, bullied, or ridiculed by their older and more powerful siblings (Abramovitch, Corter, & Lando, 1979). Vandell et al. (1981) reported a finding that is consistent with this "social power" hypothesis: first-borns who had often interacted with an older child from outside the family were less sociable than first-borns who had had little contact with an older child. Apparently, frequent exposure to older, more powerful companions (siblings or little friends of the family) can make a child a bit hesitant to approach and interact with a new playmate.

Perhaps parents could help their later-borns to become more friendly and outgoing by reserving special play periods for these youngsters—times when the younger child can be at the center of their attention. In this way, they may help these newer members of the family to feel important and loved and to learn that other people can be pleasant, responsive companions. Another strategy that parents might follow is to find other children about the same age for their later-borns to play with. This suggestion is based on the finding that infants and toddlers who often play with children their own age are friendlier and more outgoing than those who are rarely exposed to age mates (Mueller & Brenner, 1977; Vandell et al., 1981).

Sociability during the Preschool Period

Between the ages of 2 and 5, children not only become more outgoing but also direct their social gestures to a wider audience. Observational studies suggest that 2- to 3-year-olds are more likely than older children to remain near an adult and to seek physical affection, while the sociable behaviors of 4- to 5-year-olds normally consist of playful bids for attention or approval that are directed at peers rather than adults (Hartup, 1970; Sullivan, 1953).

■ Effects of nursery school on children's sociability

Does the nursery school experience have any noticeable effect on children's sociability? John Shea (1981) addressed this issue by observing 3- and 4-year-olds as they entered nursery school and began to attend classes two, three, or five days a week. As children mingled on the playground, their behavior was videotaped, and individual acts were classified on five dimensions: aggression, rough-and-tumble play, distance from the nearest child, distance from the teacher, and frequency of peer interaction. Over a ten-week observation period, children gradually ventured farther from the teacher as they became much more playful and outgoing with one another and much less forceful and aggressive. Moreover, these changes in sociability were most noticeable for the children who attended school five days a week and least apparent (but detectable nevertheless) for those who attended twice a week. Shea concluded that nursery school attendance has a very positive effect on children's reactions to other children.

However, there are exceptions to the rule. James Pennebaker and his associates (Pennebaker, Hendler, Durrett, & Richards, 1981) found that children rated *low* in sociability by their parents and teachers miss more days of nursery school because of illness than children who are rated highly sociable. This was a particularly interesting finding, for the health records of the less sociable (and presumably sickly) children indicated that they had been no less healthy than their more sociable classmates before entering nursery school. Pennebaker et al. suggest that shy and otherwise unsociable children often find the nursery school setting threatening and aversive. As a result, they may feign illnesses in order to stay home, or they may actually suffer from stress-induced disorders such as gastric problems and tension headaches. Unfortunately, these socially distressed "absentees" may be the ones who would profit most from the social curriculum of nursery school—if only they could acquire a few basic skills that would enable them to interact more effectively with their classmates. In Box 12-2 we will consider some of the strategies that researchers have used to improve the social skills of extremely unsociable children.

■ *Who raises sociable children?*

Although the data are somewhat limited, it appears that parents who are warm and supportive and who *require* their children to follow certain rules of social etiquette (for example, "Be nice"; "Play quietly"; "Don't hit") are likely to raise well-adjusted sons and daughters who relate well to both adults and peers (Baumrind, 1971). In contrast, permissive parents who set few standards and exert little control over their children often raise youngsters who are aggressive and unpopular with their peers and who may resist or rebel against rules set by other adults (for example, teachers). There is also evidence that children of overprotective mothers (particularly boys) are quite sociable when interacting with adults but are often anxious and inhibited around their peers (Kagan & Moss, 1962; Shaffer, 1979). This finding might be explained by the fact that a highly protective mother frequently encourages her children to remain near her side. As a result, an overprotected son may be rejected as a sissy by other children, an experience that may prompt him to seek the company of friendly adults and to avoid peers.

Is Sociability a Stable Attribute?

Several longitudinal studies suggest that sociability is a reasonably stable attribute (Kagan & Moss, 1962; Schaefer & Bayley, 1963). In other words, if a child is quite friendly and outgoing during nursery school or the early grade school years, chances are that he or she will become a highly sociable adolescent or young adult.

Merrill Roff and his associates (Roff, 1974; Roff, Sells, & Golden, 1972) have collected longitudinal data on the interpersonal behavior of thousands of developing children. One of the most reliable findings in this research is that unsociable children who are *rejected by their peers* run the risk of experiencing serious emotional disturbances later in life—problems such as neuroses, psychoses, and sexual deviations. Clearly, the task of becoming appropriately sociable is an important developmental hurdle—one that may call for therapeutic intervention if children are extremely shy, uncomfortable, or aggressive around their peers.

> ordinal-position effect: *the finding that first-borns tend to be more socially responsive to their peers than later-borns do.*

BOX 12-2
IMPROVING THE SOCIAL SKILLS OF
UNSOCIABLE CHILDREN

Unsociable children are usually deficient at a number of very basic social skills, such as successfully initiating play activities, cooperating, communicating their needs, giving help, affection, and approval to their peers, and resolving interpersonal conflicts (Asher, 1983). During the past few years, investigators have devised a number of "therapies" aimed at improving the social skills of withdrawn or otherwise unpopular children who can't seem to get along with others. Among the more common of these approaches are the following:

Reinforcing socially appropriate behaviors. In their excellent review of the literature on social-skills training, Melinda Combs and Diana Slaby (1978) point out that adults can shape socially appropriate responses such as cooperation and sharing by reinforcing these actions and ignoring examples of "inappropriate" behavior, such as aggression and solitary play. Another method of encouraging children to make social contacts is to place them in charge of valuable resources that they must dispense to the peer group. Frank Kerby and Curt Tolar (1970) tried this approach with a withdrawn 5-year-old. Each day for several days, the boy was given a large bag of candies. He was then told to ask his classmates what kind of candy they wanted and to give them the candy of their choice. After distributing all the candies, the boy was praised by his teacher and given some candy (and a nickel) for his efforts. Observations during later free-play periods revealed that this child became much more outgoing and cooperative with his peers. It seems that the candy gave him a reason to initiate social interactions. And in the process he acquired some basic social skills and enhanced his status as he dispensed valuable commodities to his classmates.

Modeling social skills. In Chapter Seven we learned that modeling techniques are an effective method of teaching children to approach objects (dogs) that they have previously avoided. Would a similar form of therapy help shy or solitary children overcome any fears they might have about approaching and interacting with peers?

Apparently so. In one study (Cooke & Apolloni, 1976), live models demonstrated certain social skills—for example, smiling at others, sharing, initiating positive physical contacts, and giving verbal compliments—to withdrawn grade school children. This procedure proved effective at increasing each type of behavior that the model had enacted. The training also had two desirable side effects. First, the withdrawn children began to show increases in other positive social behaviors that had not been modeled. Second, the frequency of positive social responses among *untrained* children also increased, apparently in direct response to the friendly gestures made by their classmates who had received the social-skills training. Thus, modeling strategies can produce marked changes in a child's social skills—changes that benefit both the child and the peers with whom he or she interacts.

ALTRUISM: DEVELOPMENT OF THE PROSOCIAL SELF

One value that many adults hope their children will acquire is a sense of **altruism**—that is, a concern for the welfare of other people. In fact, parents often begin to encourage altruistic acts such as sharing, cooperating, or helping while their children are still in diapers. Until very recently, experts in child development would have claimed that these well-intentioned adults were wasting their time, for young egocentric infants were thought to be incapable of considering the needs of anyone other than themselves. But in this case the experts were wrong!

Developmental Trends in Altruism

Long before children receive any deliberate moral or religious training, they may act in ways that resemble the prosocial behavior of older people. At 12 months of age, infants are often "sharing" interesting experiences by pointing, and they will occasionally offer toys to their companions (Hay, 1979; Leung & Rheingold, 1981). And by age 18 months, some children are already jumping in and trying to help with household chores such as sweeping, dusting, or setting the table (Rheingold, 1982). Demonstrations of sympathy or compassion are not at all uncommon among young children . Consider the reaction of 21-month-old John to his distressed playmate, Jerry:

"Coaching" can be effective at improving the social skills of withdrawn children.

Cognitive approaches to social-skills training. There are now a number of therapies that teach social skills by persuading children to *think about* how they might deal with everyday social situations (Urbain & Kendall, 1980). *Coaching* is a technique in which the therapist discusses the "how to's" of and rationales for various social skills. Sherrie Oden and Steve Asher (1977) coached third- and fourth-grade social isolates on four important social skills—how to participate in play activities, how to take turns and share, how to communicate effectively, and how to give attention and help to peers. Not only did the children who were coached become more outgoing and positive, but follow-up measures a year later revealed that these former isolates had achieved even

further gains in social status (see also Bierman & Furman, 1984; Ladd, 1981).

Role-playing techniques are another type of cognitive therapy that seems to improve children's social skills. Myrna Shure and George Spivack (1978) devised a ten-week program to help preschool children generate and then evaluate solutions to a number of interpersonal problems. Children role-played these situations with puppets and were encouraged to discuss the impact of their solutions on the feelings of all parties involved in a conflict. Shure and Spivack found that fewer aggressive solutions were offered the longer the children had participated in the program. Moreover, the children's classroom adjustment (as rated by teachers) improved as they became better able to think through the social consequences of their own actions.

Summing up. Clearly, there are several methods that might be used to improve the social skills of unsociable children and head off the potentially harmful effects of poor peer relations. Perhaps the way to treat extremely shy and withdrawn children is to begin with a technique that produces fairly immediate results—for example, contingent reinforcement or modeling. Once these isolates have been drawn out of their shells and have seen that peer contacts can be rewarding, they may then be ready for coaching or the kinds of role-playing and problem-solving experiences that are apparently quite effective at producing long-term gains in sociability and peer acceptance.

Today Jerry was kind of cranky; he just started . . . bawling and he wouldn't stop. John kept coming over and handing Jerry toys, trying to cheer him up.... He'd say things like "Here Jerry," and I said to John "Jerry's sad; he doesn't feel good; he had a shot today." John would look at me with his eyebrows wrinkled together like he really understood that Jerry was crying because he was unhappy.... He went over and rubbed Jerry's arm and said "Nice Jerry," and continued to give him toys [Zahn-Waxler, Radke-Yarrow, & King, 1979, pp. 321–322].

Clearly, John was concerned about his little playmate and did what he could to make him feel better.

Although some toddlers will often try to comfort distressed companions, others rarely do. In an attempt to explain these individual differences in compassionate behavior, Carolyn Zahn-Waxler and her associates (1979) asked mothers to keep records of (1) the reactions of their 1½- to 2½-year-olds to the distress of other children and (2) their own reactions when their child had been the cause of that distress. The results of this study

> **altruism:** *a concern for the welfare of others that is expressed through prosocial acts such as sharing, cooperating, and helping.*

were indeed interesting. Mothers of less compassionate toddlers tended to discipline acts of harm-doing with physical restraint ("I just moved him away from the baby"), physical punishment ("I swatted her a good one"), or unexplained prohibitions ("I said 'Stop that'"). In contrast, mothers of highly compassionate toddlers frequently disciplined harm-doing with *affective explanations* that helped the child to see the relation between his or her own acts and the distress they had caused (for example, "You made Doug cry; it's not nice to bite"; "You must never poke anyone's eyes!"). According to Eleanor Maccoby (1980), these affective explanations may be a form of **empathy** training—that is, the mother's scolding will distress the child and simultaneously draw attention to the discomfort of another person. Once children begin to associate their own distress with that of their victims, the foundation for compassionate behavior has been laid. All that the child now needs to learn is that he can eliminate his own conditioned discomfort by relieving the distress of others.

Sharing, helping, and other forms of altruism become much more common as children mature (Underwood & Moore, 1982). Observational studies in nursery schools indicate that 2½- to 3½-year-olds are more likely than their older classmates to perform acts of kindness during pretend play. However, 4–6-year-olds perform more *real* helping acts and will rarely "play-act" the role of an altruist (Bar-Tal, Raviv, & Goldberg, 1982). At age 7 to 12, children are even more altruistic and will show a greater variety of other-oriented behavior. In one study (Green & Schneider, 1974),

boys from four age groups—5–6, 7–8, 9–10, and 13–14—had opportunities to (1) share candy with classmates who wouldn't otherwise receive any, (2) help an experimenter who had accidentally dropped a number of pencils, and (3) volunteer to work on a project that would benefit poor children. As we see in Table 12-3, both sharing and helping increased with age. The one exception was the "volunteering to work" index: virtually all the boys were willing to sacrifice some of their play time in order to help needy children.

People often assume that girls are generous, friendly, and helpful while boys are selfish, unsympathetic, and aggressive (see Hartshorne, May, & Maller, 1929; Shigetomi, Hartmann, & Gelfand, 1981). Yet recent reviews of the literature dispute the notion that girls are more altruistic than boys (Rushton, 1980). When differences are found, females are likely to be the more helpful sex. However, many studies find no sex differences in altruism, and boys are often more helpful than girls on some measures, such as active rescue behavior.

Does the sex of the person who needs help or comforting affect children's altruism? Apparently so, at least for young children. Roslind Charlesworth and Willard Hartup (1967) observed the interactions of nursery school children over a five-week period and found that these youngsters generally directed their acts of kindness to playmates of the same sex. In a recent laboratory study (Ladd, Lange, & Stremmel, 1983), kindergartners and first-, third-, and fourth-graders were given an opportunity to help other children complete some schoolwork. Some of these potential recipients

TABLE 12-3. Altruistic behavior of boys from four age groups

	Age group			
Altruistic response	*5–6*	*7–8*	*9–10*	*13–14*
Average number of candy bars shared	1.36 (60%)	1.84 (92%)	2.88 (100%)	4.24 (100%)
Percentage of children who picked up pencils	48	76	100	96
Percentage of children who volunteered to work for needy children	96	92	100	96

Note: Figures in parentheses indicate percentage of children sharing at least one candy bar.

clearly needed more help than others. Ladd et al. found that kindergartners and first-graders generally chose to help children of their own sex. However, this same-sex bias was much less apparent among third- and fourth-graders, who typically based their helping decisions on a recipient's need for help rather than his or her gender.

Training Altruism: Cultural and Social Influences

How do children become concerned (or unconcerned) about the welfare of other people? Perhaps it can be argued that altruism begins at home, for as we've noted, a mother's reactions to harmdoing can influence the amount of compassion that her toddler displays toward distressed companions. Yet the lessons that a mother is teaching at home may or may not be reinforced by other members of the family, the peer group, or the society in which the child is raised. All these factors must be considered when attempting to specify the reasons that some children are more altruistic than others.

■ Cultural Influences

Cultures clearly differ in their endorsement of altruistic values. Many Western societies place a tremendous emphasis on *competition* and stress individual rather than group goals. In contrast, Native American and Mexican children are taught to cooperate with others and to avoid interpersonal conflicts. The impact of these cultural teachings can be seen when children are asked to play games that require partners to cooperate in order to win prizes: Mexican children, who are taught to cooperate, clearly outperform their more competitive Mexican-American and Anglo-American age mates (Kagan & Masden, 1971, 1972). In fact, many 7- to 9-year-old American children are so competitive at these games that they will attempt to lower their partner's outcomes even though they receive no direct benefits for doing so (Kagan & Masden, 1972). Apparently this competitive orientation can be acquired very early and may interfere with prosocial activities such as sharing. In a study of nursery school children, Eldred Rutherford and Paul Mussen (1968) found that boys who were judged highly competitive by their teachers were less likely than

other preschoolers to share candy with their two best friends.

In an interesting cross-cultural study, Beatrice and John Whiting (1975) observed the altruistic behavior of 134 children aged 3 to 10 in six cultures—Kenya, Okinawa, Mexico, the Philippines, India, and the United States. The cultures in which children were most altruistic were the less industrialized societies (Kenya, Mexico, and the Philippines) where people live together in large families and everyone contributes to the family welfare. The Whitings concluded that children who are assigned important responsibilities, such as producing and processing food or caring for infant brothers and sisters, are likely to develop an altruistic orientation at an early age.

Although cultures may differ in the emphasis they place on altruism, most people in most societies endorse the **norm of social responsibility**—a rule of thumb prescribing that one should help others who need help (Krebs, 1970). Let's now consider some of the ways that parents, teachers, and other social agents might persuade young children to adopt this important value and to become more concerned about the welfare of other people.

■ Reinforcing altruism

Perhaps the most obvious method of promoting altruism among young children is to reward them for their generous or helpful acts. In one study (Fischer, 1963), 4-year-olds were given material reinforcement (bubble gum) or social reinforcement (verbal approval) for sharing marbles with a child they did not know. Material reinforcement produced much more sharing than social reinforcement. Apparently a small amount of praise from an unfamiliar experimenter is simply not enough of a reinforcer to elicit self-sacrificing responses from preschool children.

Verbal reinforcement can promote altruistic behavior if it is administered by a warm and chari-

---

empathy: *the ability to experience the same emotions that someone else is experiencing.*

norm of social responsibility: *the principle that we should help others who are in some way dependent on us for assistance.*

BOX 12-3
*PROMOTING ALTRUISM THROUGH
COOPERATIVE GAMES*

Teaching children to get along well, to share, and to cooperate are important goals of preschool educational programs. How might we accomplish these objectives? Terry Orlick (1981) has been experimenting with a "cooperative activities" program in which children must join forces in order to meet a challenge or achieve the goals of various games. In a game called "bridges," for example, children are instructed to band together in groups of two or three to make bridges with their bodies. They then connect their bridges until the whole group forms one long bridge. Orlick compares the behavior of these youngsters with that of children in a "traditional activities" group who are encouraged to undertake individual pursuits. When children in the traditional program play "bridges," the objective is for each child to make his or her own unique bridge.

Preschool children who participate in a "cooperative activities" program do become more cooperative with their peers, both in the training environment and during unstructured free-play sessions in the gym and the classroom (Orlick & Foley, 1979; Orlick, McNally, & O'Hara, 1978). But does this cooperative training stimulate other altruistic acts such as sharing?

To find out, Orlick (1981) had one group of kindergarten children play cooperative games four times a week for 18 weeks. Children in a traditional games group spent the same amount of time playing very similar but individualized games that did not require a partner. At both the beginning and the end of the 18-week training period, each child received a bag containing five candies to keep or to share with other kindergartners (the afternoon class) who would otherwise not receive any candy. All children were then given an opportunity to donate some of their

Number of children showing change in willingness to share after participating in a "cooperative activities" or a "traditional activities" program

| Training condition | Change in generosity | |
	Increase	Decrease
Cooperative games	11	5
Traditional games	5	17

candies anonymously to their less fortunate peers in the other class. The table summarizes the results. Note that 11 of the children from the "cooperative games" program became more generous as a result of their training, while only 5 children became less willing to share. The pattern was reversed in the "traditional games" program, where 17 children became less willing to donate candy to others and only 5 showed an increase in sharing.

In sum, a program designed to teach young children to cooperate not only accomplishes that objective but may also promote completely different forms of altruism such as sharing. This finding is even more impressive when we recall that the recipients of the children's generosity were not familiar playmates but, rather, peers from another kindergarten class.

Gerald Sagotsky and his colleagues report that normally competitive American schoolchildren can be taught to cooperate at games that require cooperation in order for participants to win prizes (Sagotsky, Wood-Schneider, & Konop, 1981). In fact, Sagotsky et al. report that 7–8-year-olds who learn to work together while playing one set of games will usually adopt cooperative strategies for new games introduced *seven weeks later*. If our goal is to increase our children's prosocial behavior, we should probably be spending much more time teaching youngsters to play cooperative games and persuading them to pull together to achieve important objectives.

table individual whom children respect or admire (Midlarsky, Bryan, & Brickman, 1973; Yarrow, Scott, & Waxler, 1973). However, Elizabeth Midlarsky and her associates (Midlarsky et al., 1973) found that children often become reluctant to share if their charitable acts are praised by a *selfish* model. Perhaps the approving responses of a selfish model made the inconsistency between the model's self-serving actions and her verbal behavior obvious to the child. This inconsistency

may then have prompted the child to think about the inequity of the situation and wonder "Why should I share when this person has not?"

One way that adults might subtly reinforce altruism is to structure play activities so that children are likely to discover the benefits of cooperating and helping one another. In Box 12-3 we will see how one investigator has used this strategy to increase both the cooperative behavior and the generosity of preschool children.

■ *Practicing and preaching altruism*

Social-learning theorists have assumed that adults who encourage altruism and who practice what they preach will affect children in two ways. By practicing altruism, the adult model may induce the child to perform similar acts of kindness. In addition, regular exposure to the model's **altruistic exhortations** provides the child with opportunities to internalize principles such as the norm of social responsibility that should contribute to the development of an altruistic orientation.

When young children observe charitable or helpful models, they generally become more altruistic themselves—particularly if they have established a warm and friendly relationship with these benevolent companions (Rushton, 1980; Yarrow et al., 1973). Moreover, it appears that exposure to an altruistic model can have long-term effects on children's behavior. Elizabeth Midlarsky and James Bryan (1972) found that a model who donated valuable tokens to a charity increased children's willingness to donate candy to the same charity, even though the candy donations were solicited ten days later in a different setting by a person the children had never seen. Other investigators have noted that children who observe charitable models are more generous than those who observe selfish models, even when they are tested *two to four months later* (Rice & Grusec, 1975; Rushton, 1975). Taken together, these findings suggest that encounters with altruistic models promote the development of prosocial habits and altruistic values.

Although most parents encourage their children to be kind, generous, or helpful to others, they don't always practice what they preach. How do children respond to these inconsistencies? James Bryan and his associates (Bryan & Schwartz, 1971; Bryan & Walbek, 1970) addressed this issue by exposing grade school children to models who behaved either charitably or selfishly and who preached either charity ("It's good to donate to poor children") or greed ("Why should I give my money to other people?"). When the children were given an opportunity to donate their own valuable resources to charity, the size of their donations was determined by the model's behavior rather than his exhortations. In other words, children who saw a model refuse to donate while preaching charity (or greed) showed a low level of altruism themselves, while those who ob-

PHOTO 12-5. *Children learn many prosocial responses by observing the behavior of altruistic models. In the photo at the top, a number of children look on as an adult helps a child by tying her shoe. When the photographer returned to the same nursery school the very next day, he saw one of the onlookers performing a similar act of kindness for a classmate.*

served a charitable model who exhorted greed (or charity) gave sizable amounts to charity. These findings have important implications for child rearing: parents would be well advised to back up their verbal exhortations with altruistic deeds if they hope to instill a strong sense of altruistic concern in their children.

---

altruistic exhortations: *verbal encouragements to help, comfort, share, or cooperate with others.*

■ *Creating an altruistic self-concept*

Can we promote altruism by persuading children to think of themselves as generous or helpful individuals? Joan Grusec and Erica Redler (1980) tried to answer this question by urging 5- and 8-year-olds to (1) donate marbles to poor children, (2) share colored pencils with classmates who hadn't any, and (3) help an experimenter with a dull and repetitive task. Once children had made an initial donation or begun to work on the repetitive task, either they were told that they were "nice" or "helpful" persons (self-concept training condition) or nothing was said (control condition). One to two weeks later, the children were asked by another adult to donate drawings and craft materials to help cheer up sick children at a local hospital.

Grusec and Redler found that self-concept training had a much greater effect on the 8-year-olds than the 5-year-olds. The 8-year-olds who were told that they must be "nice" or "helpful" individuals were more likely than those in the control condition to share their possessions and to make drawings for sick children. Perhaps the reason self-concept training was so effective with the older children is that 8-year-olds are just beginning to describe the self in psychological terms and to see these "traits" as relatively stable aspects of their character. Thus, when told that they are "nice" or "helpful," older children will incorporate these attributions into their self-concepts and try to live up to this new self-image by sharing with or helping others.

Cognitive and Affective Contributors to Altruism

Earlier in the chapter, we saw that children with well-developed role-taking abilities may appear to be more charitable than poor role takers because they are better able to infer a companion's needs for assistance—a skill that enables them to perform the appropriate act of kindness. However, role taking is only one of several abilities that seem to play a part in the development of altruistic behavior. Two other contributors are children's level of moral reasoning and their empathic reactions to the distress of other people.

■ *Moral reasoning*

In their recent review of the literature, Bert Underwood and Bill Moore (1982) concluded that the maturity of a child's moral reasoning (as defined by responses to moral-conflict stories) predicts his or her altruistic behavior.[1] Not only are mature moral reasoners quite willing to help others who need help, they are also more likely than immature moral reasoners to comfort distressed companions, to share, and to criticize selfishness after observing the miserly behavior of an uncharitable model. In fact, mature moral reasoners may even help someone they *dislike* if that person really needs their assistance, whereas immature moral reasoners are apt to ignore the needs of an individual they do not like (Eisenberg, 1983).

Why are mature moral reasoners so sensitive to the needs of others—even disliked others? Although we don't yet know the answer to this question, it's possible that morally mature individuals experience strong empathic responses to the distress of other people and that these emotional reactions trigger some form of altruistic behavior. In the following section, we will take a closer look at the relationship between empathy and altruism.

■ *Empathy*

Empathy refers to a person's ability to experience the emotions of other people. According to Martin Hoffman (1981), empathy is a universal human response that has a neurological basis and is subject to environmental influences. Hoffman believes that empathic arousal will eventually become an important mediator of altruism, a viewpoint shared by Eleanor Maccoby (1980):

> With empathic distress the process would work in the following way: A twelve-month-old has cried on hundreds of different occasions and the sound of crying has repeatedly been associated with the child's own distress. And so by a process of [classical conditioning], the sound of crying—anyone's crying—can now evoke feelings of distress . . . and even tears. If the young listener thinks of a way to make the other person stop crying, he

---

[1]The development of moral reasoning is described in detail in Chapter Fourteen.

or she will feel better. From the standpoint of simple self-interest, then, we should expect children to learn to perform such "altruistic" actions [Maccoby, 1980, p. 347].

Although infants and toddlers do seem to recognize and will often react to the distress of their companions (Zahn-Waxler et al., 1979; see also Box 2-4), their responses are not always helpful ones. In fact, the evidence for a link between empathy and altruism is weak at best for young children, though much stronger for preadolescents, adolescents, and adults (Underwood & Moore, 1982).

One possible explanation for these age trends is that younger children often make situational inferences about another person's emotions, so that they may not even understand why they are experiencing the same feelings as that person. For example, when kindergartners see slides of a boy who becomes dejected after his dog runs away, they attribute his sadness to a situational cause (the dog's disappearance) rather than to a more personal cause such as the boy's love for his pet (Hughes, Tingle, & Sawin, 1981). And although kindergartners report that they feel sad after seeing the slides, they provide egocentric explanations for their empathic arousal (for example, "I might lose my dog"). However, 7–9-year-olds are beginning to associate their own empathic emotions with those of the story character as they put themselves in his place and infer the psychological basis for his sadness (for example, "I'm sad because he's sad . . . because if he really liked the dog, then . . ."). So empathy may become an important mediator of altruism once children become more proficient at inferring others' points of view (role taking) and understanding the causes of their own empathic emotions.

The relationship among role taking, empathy, and altruism is illustrated in a recent experiment by Mark Barnett and his associates (Barnett, Howard, Melton, & Dino, 1982). Sixth-graders rated high or low in empathy by their teachers were first asked to reminisce about a sad event that had happened to themselves or to another person. A few minutes later, they had an opportunity to construct "color and activity" booklets to cheer up some hospitalized children. As we see in

the left-hand portion of Figure 12-3, a child's capacity for empathy, by itself, does not predict his or her willingness to help sick children when the child has been thinking about his or her own misfortunes. The only time that the highly empathic 12-year-olds were more helpful than their less empathic classmates was when they had been thinking about another person's misfortune—a form of *role taking* that triggers a strong empathic response from high empathizers, which then increases their motivation to aid and comfort a group of unfortunate children.

Who Raises Altruistic Children?

Studies of unusually charitable adults indicate that these "altruists" have enjoyed a warm and affectionate relationship with parents who themselves were highly concerned about the welfare of others. For example, Christians who risked their lives to save Jews from the Nazis during World War II reported that they had had close ties to moralistic parents who always acted in accordance with their ethical principles (London, 1970). And in Box 1-2 we learned that fully committed civil rights workers in the 1960s differed

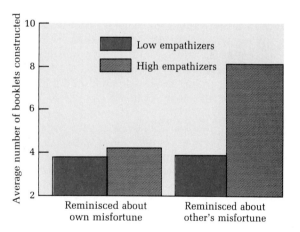

FIGURE 12-3. *Average number of "color and activity" booklets constructed by high- and low-empathic 12-year-olds who had reminisced about a sad event that had happened to themselves or to another person.*

from those who were only partially committed in two important ways: they had enjoyed warmer relations with their parents, and they had had parents who advocated altruism and backed up these exhortations by performing many kind and compassionate acts. By contrast, parents of partially committed civil rights workers had often preached but rarely practiced altruism (Rosenhan, 1972). Clearly, these findings are reminiscent of the laboratory evidence we have reviewed, which indicates that warm and compassionate models who practice what they preach are especially effective at eliciting prosocial responses from young children.

Parental reactions to a child's harm-doing also play a significant role in the development of altruism. Martin Hoffman (1975) has argued that the use of **power-assertive** discipline, such as spankings, or **love-oriented** techniques, such as the withdrawal of affection, are likely to (1) arouse resentment or anxiety and focus the child's attention on his own negative consequences, (2) contribute nothing to the child's appreciation of the other person's distress, and (3) expose the child to a punitive rather than an altruistic model. By comparison, **inductive** (or **victim-centered**) discipline is a nonpunitive technique that informs the child of the harm that he has caused, encourages the child to imagine himself in the victim's place, and urges the child to direct some sort of comforting or helpful response toward the victim. Hoffman believes that children are likely to develop a strong altruistic orientation if their parents often use victim-centered disciplinary techniques.

Most of the available evidence supports Hoffman's contention. Parents who rely mainly on inductive discipline do tend to raise children who are sympathetic, self-sacrificing, and concerned about the welfare of other people, whereas the frequent use of power assertion or love withdrawal appears to inhibit altruism and lead to the development of self-centered values (Brody & Shaffer, 1982; Dlugokinski & Firestone, 1974).

If we think about it, there are several reasons that inductive discipline might inspire children to become more altruistic. First, it encourages the child to assume another person's perspective (role taking) and to experience his or her distress (empathy training). It also teaches the child to perform helpful or comforting acts that make both the self and the other person feel better. And last but not least, these reparative responses might convince older (grade school) children that they are "nice" or "helpful" people, a positive self-image that they may try to perpetuate by performing other acts of kindness in the future (Grusec & Redler, 1980).

THE DEVELOPMENT OF AGGRESSION

Although toddlers and preschool children will often respond to one another with kindness and affection, they may also fight over toys, punch, kick, or tease their companions, or call them names. Why do children behave aggressively? How does aggression change over time? And what can adults do to control these hostile outbursts? These are some of the issues we will consider in the pages that follow.

What Is Aggression?

Before reading further, you may wish to jot down your own definition of *aggression* so you can compare it with the following points of view.

Could aggression be an instinct—a basic component of human nature? Freud thought so (remember the Thanatos), as did ethologist Konrad Lorenz (1966), who argued that human beings (particularly males) are biologically programmed to fight over sources of food, territories, and members of the other sex. Other theorists think of aggression as a particular class of social behavior. For example, Arnold Buss (1961) defines aggression as any response that delivers noxious stimuli to another organism. Note that this *behavioral* definition emphasizes the *consequences* of the action and ignores the intentions of the actor. A strict interpretation of this viewpoint suggests that klutzy dance partners who inflict pain by stepping on our toes would have to be considered aggressive. Does this seem like an aggressive act to you?

Many people would say no, because dancers usually intend no harm when they step on a partner's toes. Today, researchers generally favor an *intentional* definition of **aggression,** which states that an aggressive act is any form of behavior designed to harm or injure another living being who is motivated to avoid such treatment (Baron & Byrne, 1981). This intentional definition would classify as aggressive all acts in which harm was intended but not done (for example, a violent kick that misses its target) while excluding accidental injuries or activities such as rough-and-tumble play in which participants are enjoying themselves with no harmful intent.

Aggressive acts are often divided into two categories: **hostile aggression** and **instrumental aggression**. If an actor's major goal is to injure a victim, his or her behavior qualifies as hostile aggression. By contrast, instrumental aggression describes those situations in which one person harms another as a means to a nonaggressive end. Clearly, the same overt act could be classified as either hostile or instrumental aggression depending on the circumstances. If a young boy clobbered his sister and then teased her for crying, we would consider this hostile aggression. But these same actions could be labeled instrumentally aggressive (or a mixture of hostile and instrumental aggression) had the boy also grabbed a toy that his sister was using.

Origins of Aggression

Although infants do get angry and may occasionally strike people, it is difficult to think of these actions as having an aggressive intent. Piaget (1952) describes an incident in which he frustrated 7-month-old Laurent by placing his hand in front of an interesting object that Laurent was trying to reach. The boy then smacked Piaget's hand as if to knock it out of the way. Although this looks very much like an example of instrumental aggression, it is unlikely that Laurent intended to frighten or harm his father. Instead, he seems to have been treating his father's hand as a simple obstruction that had to be removed. Even 12- to 15-month-olds will rarely look at each other as they struggle over a toy; their attention is usually riveted on the toy itself, and their goal seems to be to gain possession of the object rather than to intimidate or harm their adversary (Bronson, 1975).

Near the end of the second year, things begin to change. Dale Hay and Hildy Ross (1982) observed pairs of 20–23-month-olds at play, noting all instances of conflict. Unlike their younger counterparts, these toddlers began most of their tussles by communicating with an opponent (for example, "Mine," "No! Kenny have phone") rather than treating him or her as an inanimate obstacle. As these disputes wore on, they occasionally escalated into incidents of forcible contact—actions that might be interpreted as attempts to intimidate or to force an adversary to withdraw. Although sociable reactions such as sharing were actually more common than these "shows of force," it appears as if the seeds of instrumental aggression may have already been sown by the age of 20–23 months.

Age-Related Changes in the Nature of Aggression

Much of what we know about the aggressive behavior of preschool children comes from two studies. The first is a project conducted by Florence Goodenough (1931), who asked mothers of 2- to 5-year-olds to keep diaries recording each angry outburst displayed by their children, its apparent cause, and its consequences. The second is an observational study by Willard Hartup (1974), who analyzed the causes and consequences of aggressive acts that occurred over a five-week period in groups of children aged 4 to 6 and 6 to 7. These studies indicate the following:

1. Unfocused temper tantrums diminish during the preschool period and are uncommon after

---

power-assertive discipline: *a form of discipline in which an adult relies on his or her superior power (for example, by administering spankings or withholding privileges) to modify or control a child's behavior.*

love-oriented discipline: *a form of discipline in which an adult withholds attention, affection, or approval in order to modify or control a child's behavior.*

inductive (victim-centered) discipline: *a nonpunitive form of discipline in which reasoning is used to inform the child of the harm that he or she has caused a victim and to encourage the child to make the victim feel better.*

aggression: *behavior performed with the intention of harming another living being who is motivated to avoid this treatment.*

hostile aggression: *aggressive acts for which the actor's major goal is to harm or injure a victim.*

instrumental aggression: *aggressive acts that are undertaken as a means to a nonaggressive end.*

age 4. However, the total amount of aggression that children display increases over the preschool period, *peaking at about age 4.*

2. The tendency to retaliate in response to attack or frustration increases dramatically for children over age 3.

3. *The primary instigators of aggression vary with the age of the child.* At age 2–3, children are most often aggressive after parents have thwarted or angered them by exerting authority; older children are much more likely to aggress after conflicts with siblings or peers.

4. The *form* of aggression also changes over time. Children aged 2 or 3 are likely to hit or kick an adversary. Most of the squabbles among youngsters of this age concern toys and other possessions, so that their aggression is usually *instrumental* in character. Older nursery-schoolers (and young grade school children) show less and less physical aggression as they choose instead to tease, taunt, tattle, and call their victims uncomplimentary names. Although older children continue to fight over objects, an increasing percentage of their aggressive outbursts are *hostile* in character—designed primarily to harm another person.

Why are aggressive exchanges less common among 5-year-olds than 3- and 4-year-olds? One reason may be that parents and teachers are actively preparing older nursery-schoolers for kindergarten by refusing to tolerate aggressive acts and encouraging alternative responses such as cooperation and sharing (Emmerich, 1966). Of course, older children may have also learned from their own experiences that negotiation can be a relatively painless and efficient method of achieving the same objectives that they used to attempt through a show of force.

Although the overall incidence of aggression declines with age, hostile aggression shows a slight increase. Hartup (1974) attributes this finding to the fact that older children (particularly grade school children) are acquiring the role-taking skills that enable them to infer the intentions of other people and to retaliate when they believe that someone means to hurt them. "To the extent that hostile aggression is dependent upon attributions about [the aggressive *intent* of another person], this type of aggression should be less evident in younger than older children" (p. 338).

Apparently, younger children are less likely to consider an actor's intent when evaluating the naughtiness of an aggressive act or responding to a person who has harmed them (Ferguson & Rule, 1980; Shantz & Voydanoff, 1973). In one study (Shantz & Voydanoff, 1973), 7-, 9-, and 12-year-old boys were asked how they would react to a number of situations in which they had been hurt (either physically or verbally) by another child. Some of these incidents were described so as to suggest that they might be accidental, whereas others appeared to be intentional. Shantz and Voydanoff found that 7-year-olds favored a highly aggressive form of retaliation whether the harm done to them was accidental or intentional, but 9- and 12-year-olds responded much more aggressively to intentional attacks than to accidents.

Although even highly aggressive grade school children will overlook harm-doing that is obviously accidental, they are more likely than nonaggressive classmates to retaliate against someone who has harmed them under *ambiguous* circumstances—for example, after being hit hard

PHOTO 12-6. As children mature, an increasing percentage of their aggressive acts qualify as examples of hostile aggression.

from behind by a ball (Dodge, 1980). As it turns out, these aggressive youngsters may have an excellent reason for attributing hostile intentions to their peers: not only do aggressive children provoke a large number of fights, but they are also more likely than nonaggressive children to become the targets of aggression. In fact, nonaggressive children who are harmed under ambiguous circumstances are much more likely to retaliate *if the harm-doer has a reputation as an aggressive child* (Dodge & Frame, 1982). So by virtue of their own hostile inclinations, highly aggressive children ensure that they will often be attacked by their peers.

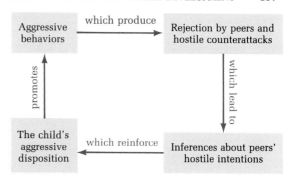

FIGURE 12-4. *A cyclical model to explain the stability of aggression over time.*

Is Aggression a Stable Attribute?

We've seen that the kinds of aggression that children display will change over time. But what about aggressive dispositions? Do aggressive preschoolers remain highly aggressive throughout the grade school years, during adolescence, and as young adults?

Apparently aggression is a reasonably stable attribute from the preschool period through early adolescence. Not only are highly aggressive 3-year-olds likely to become aggressive 5-year-olds (Emmerich, 1966), but the amount of physical and verbal aggression that a child displays at ages 6 to 10 is a fairly good predictor of his or her tendency to threaten, insult, tease, and compete with peers at ages 10 to 14 (Kagan & Moss, 1962; Olweus, 1979). The model presented in Figure 12-4 may help to explain why aggression is reasonably stable over time. Highly aggressive children who fight a lot will probably have few friends and will often be attacked by their peers. These negative social encounters should then lead aggressive youngsters to attribute hostile motives to their classmates, which triggers further aggression and starts the vicious cycle all over again.

Will aggressive adolescents become aggressive adults? Data collected in the Fels longitudinal study suggest that between early adolescence and young adulthood *aggression is stable for males but not for females.* Jerome Kagan and Howard Moss (1962) propose a simple "sex typing" explanation for these results. They contend that aggressive activities among young adolescents are more likely to be tolerated if displayed by a male. Although many girls are allowed to roughhouse dur-

ing the grade school years, they will face strong pressures to suppress these tendencies and to assume nurturant, cooperative attitudes during the adolescent period. In other words, postpubescent females are expected to become "appropriately feminine," and aggression is incompatible with the feminine role.

Sex Differences in Aggression

Not only are girls less likely than boys to remain aggressive, *they are less aggressive in the first place.* More than 100 studies conducted in several cultures indicate that (1) males are more aggressive than females and (2) these sex differences in aggressive behavior are already detectable among groups of 2- to 3-year-olds (Hyde, 1984; Maccoby & Jacklin, 1974, 1980). The probability of becoming a *target* of aggression also depends on one's sex: even young children will reduce the intensity of their attacks on an adversary if that person is a female (Hoving, Wallace, & LaForme, 1976).

In Chapter Thirteen we will see that there may be a biological basis for sex differences in aggression. However, biology is hardly destiny, for social influences combine with biological predispositions to shape the aggressive behavior of both boys and girls. Let's now consider two important "social" influences on aggression: (1) the norms and values endorsed by one's society and (2) the family settings in which children are raised.

Cultural Influences

The notion that aggression is instinctual, or biologically programmed, does not explain why some societies are more aggressive than others. In the United States and Canada, religious sects such as the Amish, the Mennonites, and the Hutterites advocate cooperation and sharing while strongly discouraging aggressive behavior. Peoples such as the Arapesh of New Guinea, the Lepchas of Sikkim, and the Pygmies of the central Congo all use weapons to procure food but rarely show any kind of interpersonal aggression. When these peace-loving societies are invaded by outsiders, their members will retreat to inaccessible regions rather than stand and fight (Gorer, 1968).

In marked contrast to these groups is the Ik tribe of Uganda, whose members live in small bands and will steal from, deceive, or even kill one another in order to ensure their own survival (Turnbull, 1972). Another aggressive society is the Mundugumor of eastern New Guinea, who teach their children to be independent, combative, and emotionally unresponsive to the needs of others (Mead, 1935). These are values that serve the Mundugumor well, for during some periods of their history, the Mundugumor were cannibals who routinely killed human beings as prey and considered almost anyone other than close kinfolk to be fair game. The United States is also an aggressive society. On a percentage basis, the incidence of rape, assault, robbery, and homicide is higher in the United States than in any other stable democracy (National Commission on the Causes and Prevention of Violence, 1969).

In sum, a person's tendency toward violence and aggression will depend, in part, on the extent to which his or her society condones such behavior. Yet not all people in pacifistic societies are kind, cooperative, and helpful, nor are all members of aggressive societies prone to violence. One reason that there are dramatic individual differences in aggression within any society is that individual children are raised in very different families. In our next section, we will see how the home setting can sometimes serve as a breeding ground for violent, aggressive behavior.

Familial Influences

When investigators began to study the development of aggression, they operated under the assumption that parents' attitudes and child-rearing strategies play a major role in shaping children's aggressive behavior. Clearly, there is some truth to

this assumption. One of the most reliable findings in the child-rearing literature is that *cold and rejecting* parents who *apply physical punishment in an erratic fashion* and often *permit their child to express aggressive impulses* are likely to raise hostile, aggressive children (Eron, 1982; Olweus, 1980; Sears, Maccoby, & Levin, 1957). Surely these findings make good sense. Cold and rejecting parents are frustrating their children's emotional needs and modeling a lack of concern for others by virtue of their aloofness. By ignoring many of the child's aggressive outbursts, a permissive parent is legitimizing combative activities and failing to provide many opportunities for the child to control his or her aggressive urges. And when aggression escalates to the point that a permissive parent steps in and spanks the child, the adult is serving as a model for the very behavior (aggression) that he or she is trying to suppress. So it is hardly surprising to find that parents who rely on physical punishment to discipline aggression have children who are highly aggressive outside the home setting in which the punishment normally occurs (Eron, 1982; Sears et al., 1957). A child who learns that she will be hit when she displeases her parents will probably direct the same kind of response toward playmates who displease her.

Although parental attitudes and child-rearing techniques may contribute to children's aggression, the chain of influence may also flow in the opposite direction, from child to parent. For example, Dan Olweus (1980) reports that a child's temperament during the early years influences his mother's reactions to aggression. According to Olweus, "A boy with an impetuous and active temperament may . . . exhaust his mother, resulting in her becoming more permissive of the boy's aggression, which in turn may be conducive to a higher level of aggression in the boy" (p. 658).

Gerald Patterson (1976, 1980) has observed patterns of interaction among children and their parents in families that have at least one highly aggressive child. The aggressive children in Patterson's sample fought a lot at home and at school and were generally unruly and defiant. These families were then compared with other families of the same size and socioeconomic status that had no problem children.

Patterson found that his problem children were growing up in highly **coercive home environ-**

ments where family members were constantly struggling with one another. He also noted that *negative reinforcement* was important in maintaining these coercive interactions: when one family member is making life unpleasant for another, the second will learn to whine, yell, scream, tease, or hit because these actions often force the antagonist to stop. Consider the following sequence of events, which may be fairly typical in families with problem children:

1. A girl teases her older brother, who makes her stop teasing by yelling at her (yelling is negatively reinforced).

2. A few minutes later, the girl calls her brother a nasty name. The boy then chases and hits her.

3. The girl stops calling him names (which negatively reinforces hitting). She then whimpers and hits him back, and he withdraws (negatively reinforcing her hits). The boy then approaches and hits his sister again, and the conflict escalates.

4. At this point the mother intervenes. However, her children are too emotionally disrupted to listen to reason, so she finds herself applying punitive and coercive tactics to make them stop fighting.

5. The fighting stops (thus reinforcing the mother for using punitive methods). However, the children now begin to whine, cry, or yell at the mother. These countercoercive techniques are then reinforced if the mother backs off and accepts peace at any price. Unfortunately, backing off is only a temporary solution. The next time the children antagonize each other and become involved in an unbearable conflict, the mother is likely to use even more coercion to get them to stop. The children once again apply their own methods of countercoercion to induce her to "lay off," and the family atmosphere becomes increasingly unpleasant for everyone.

Children who live in such highly coercive family settings eventually become resistant to punishment. They have learned to fight coercion with countercoercion and will often do so by defying the parent and repeating the very act that she is trying to suppress. No wonder Patterson calls these children "out of control." By contrast, parents from noncoercive families are more successful when they punish a child's undesirable behavior because they stand firm and will not "cave in" to countercoercion (Patterson, 1976).

So we see that the flow of influence in the family setting is bidirectional; coercive *interactions* between parents and children affect the behavior of all parties and may contribute to the development of a hostile family environment—a true breeding ground for aggression. Unfortunately, these problem families may never break out of this destructive pattern of attacking and counterattacking one another unless they receive help. In Box 12-4 we will look at one particularly effective approach to this problem—a method that necessarily focuses on the family as a system rather than simply concentrating on the aggressive child who has been referred for treatment.

Another possible contributor to children's aggression is the violence and destruction that they see at home while watching television. We will return to this point and take an in-depth look at the effects of TV violence when we consider children's reactions to the mass media in Chapter Sixteen.

Methods of Controlling Aggression

How might parents and teachers control children's aggression? Over the years, a variety of solutions have been offered, including the catharsis technique, the incompatible response technique, the creation of nonaggressive environments, and the suggestion that children be trained to empathize with the victims of aggression.

■ *Catharsis: A dubious strategy*

The **catharsis hypothesis** states that angry people who commit aggressive acts will "drain away" their hostile, aggressive impulses (that is, experience catharsis) and become less likely to commit another act of aggression in the near future. Freud, a proponent of this idea (which he credited to Aristotle), believed that people should be encouraged to express their aggressive urges every

---

coercive home environment: *a home in which family members often annoy one another and use aggressive tactics as a method of coping with these aversive experiences.*
catharsis hypothesis: *the notion that aggressive urges are reduced when people commit aggressive acts.*

BOX 12-4
HELPING CHILDREN (AND PARENTS) WHO ARE "OUT OF CONTROL"

How does one treat a problem child who is hostile, defiant, and "out of control"? Rather than focusing on the problem child, Gerald Patterson's (1976, 1980) approach is to work with the entire family. Patterson begins by carefully observing the family's interactions and determining just how family members are reinforcing one another's coercive activities. The next step is to describe the nature of the problem to parents and to teach them a new approach to managing their children's behavior. Some of the principles, skills, and procedures that Patterson stresses are the following:

1. Don't give in to the child's coercive behavior.
2. Don't escalate your own coercion when the child becomes coercive.
3. Control the child's coercion with the *time out* procedure—a method of punishment (described in Chapter Seven) in which the child is sent to her room (or some other location) until she calms down and stops using coercive tactics.
4. Identify those of the child's behaviors that are most irritating and then establish a point system in which the child can earn credits (rewards, privileges) for acceptable conduct or lose them for unacceptable behavior. Parents with older problem children are taught how to formulate "behavioral contracts" that specify how the child is expected to behave at home and at school, as well as how deviations from this behavioral code will be punished. Whenever possible, children should have a say in negotiating these contracts.
5. Be on the lookout for occasions when one can respond to the child's prosocial conduct with warmth and affection. Although this is often difficult for parents who are accustomed to snapping at their children and accentuating the negative, Patterson believes that parental affection and approval will reinforce good conduct and eventually elicit displays of affection from the child—a clear sign that the family is on the road to recovery.

A clear majority of problem families respond quite favorably to these methods. Not only do problem children become less coercive, defiant, and aggressive, but the mother's depression fades as she gradually begins to feel better about herself, her child, and her ability to resolve family crises (Patterson, 1980). Some problem families show an immediate improvement. Others respond more gradually to the treatment and may require periodic "booster shots"—that is, follow-up treatments in which the clinician visits the family, determines why progress has slowed (or broken down), and then retrains the parents or suggests new procedures to correct the problems that are not being resolved. Clearly, this therapy works because it recognizes that "out of control" behavior stems from a *family system* in which both parents and children are influencing each other and contributing to the development of a hostile family environment. Therapies that focus exclusively on the problem child are not enough!

now and then before they build to dangerous levels and trigger a truly violent or destructive outburst. The implications of this viewpoint are clear: Presumably we could teach children to vent their anger or frustrations on inanimate objects such as Bobo dolls. In so doing, an angry child should experience catharsis and become less likely to commit aggressive acts against other people.

Popular as this **cathartic technique** has been, it does *not* work and *may even backfire*. In one study (Walters & Brown, 1963), children who had been encouraged to slap, punch, and kick an inflatable Bobo doll were found to be much more aggressive in their later interactions with peers than were classmates who had not had an opportunity to beat on the doll. Other investigators have noted that children who are first angered by a peer and then given an opportunity to aggress against an inanimate object become no less aggressive toward the peer who had angered them in the first place (Mallick & McCandless, 1966). So cathartic techniques do not reduce children's aggressive urges. In fact, they may teach youngsters that hitting and kicking are acceptable methods of expressing their anger or frustrations.

■ *The incompatible response technique*

One proven method of reducing children's aggression is to ignore their hostile outbursts *while reinforcing acts that are incompatible with aggression*. In a classic study of this **incompatible response technique**, Paul Brown and Rogers Elliot (1965) instructed nursery school teachers to turn their backs on all but the most severely aggressive exchanges among their pupils. At the same time, they were asked to reward all instances of prosocial behavior, such as sharing toys or playing together cooperatively. Within two weeks this treatment had significantly reduced the incidence of both physical and verbal aggression among the children, and the program was ended. A follow-up treatment given several weeks later brought about further reductions in aggressive behavior. In a second study, Ron Slaby (Slaby & Crowley, 1977) found that merely encouraging children to say nice things about one another produced an increase in prosocial behavior and a corresponding decrease in aggression. Clearly the reinforcement of responses that are incompatible with aggression can inhibit hostile behavior. The beauty of this nonpunitive approach is that it does not reinforce children who seek attention through their hostile acts, it does not make children angry or resentful, and it does not expose them to a punitive or aggressive model. Thus, many of the negative side effects associated with punishment can be avoided.

■ Creating nonaggressive environments

Another method that adults may use to reduce children's aggression is to create play areas that minimize the likelihood of interpersonal conflict. For example, providing ample space for vigorous play helps to eliminate the kinds of accidental body contacts such as tripping and shoving that often provoke aggressive incidents (Hartup, 1974). Paul Gump (1975) points out that shortages in play materials also contribute to conflicts and aggression. Perhaps parents and teachers could create nonaggressive environments by making available a variety of interesting playthings so that children can keep themselves occupied without having to compete for scarce resources.

Finally, toys that suggest aggressive themes (guns, knives, and so on) are likely to provoke aggressive incidents. In one study, 5- to 8-year-olds who had been encouraged to use aggressive toys in a classroom play session were more likely than those who had played with neutral toys to get into fights in other settings, such as the playground (Feshbach, 1956). If our goal is to reduce the incidence of aggression, we may be better off in the long run to advise parents and teachers against making aggressive toys available to young children.

■ Empathy as a deterrent to aggression

Grade school children, adolescents, and adults will normally back off and stop attacking a victim who shows signs of pain or suffering (Baron, 1971; Perry & Bussey, 1977). However, many preschool children and *highly aggressive* grade school boys will continue to attack a suffering victim or one who denies that he has been hurt (Patterson, Littman, & Bricker, 1967; Perry & Perry, 1974). One possible explanation for this seemingly sadistic behavior is that preschoolers and other highly aggressive individuals do not empathize with their victims. In other words, they may not feel bad or suffer themselves when they have harmed another person.

Does empathy inhibit aggression? Apparently so. Grade school children who score high in empathy are rated low in aggression by their teachers, whereas classmates who test very low in empathy tend to be more aggressive (Bryant, 1982; Feshbach, 1978). Moreover, Michael Chandler (1973) found that highly aggressive 11–13-year-old delinquents who participated in a ten-week program designed to make them more aware of other people's feelings subsequently became less hostile and aggressive, compared with a second group of delinquents who had not participated in the program.

In the home setting, parents can foster the development of empathy by modeling empathic concern (Zahn-Waxler et al., 1979) and by using inductive techniques that (1) point out the harmful consequences of the child's aggressive actions while (2) encouraging the child to put himself in the victim's place and imagine how the victim feels. As we have seen, parents who rely mainly on inductive discipline tend to raise sympathetic children who are concerned about the welfare of other people.

---

cathartic technique: *a strategy for reducing aggression by encouraging children to vent their anger or frustrations on inanimate objects.*
incompatible response technique: *a nonpunitive method of behavior modification in which adults ignore undesirable conduct while reinforcing acts that are incompatible with these responses.*

ACHIEVEMENT: DEVELOPMENT OF THE COMPETENT SELF

Two basic aims of socialization are to urge children to pursue important goals and to take pride in their accomplishments. In many Western societies, including our own, children are encouraged to be independent and competitive and to do well at whatever they may attempt—in short, to become "achievers." Although the meaning of achievement varies somewhat from society to society, a recent survey of 30 cultures reveals that people from all over the world value personal attributes such as self-reliance, responsibility, and a willingness to work hard to attain important objectives (Fyans, Salili, Maehr, & Desai, 1983).

Must these valued attributes be taught? Social-learning theorists think so, but others disagree. Psychoanalyst Robert White (1959) proposes that children are intrinsically motivated to "master" the environment. He calls this **effectance motivation,** after the young child's tendency to "effect" various acts, with little or no parental prompting, that will enable her to cope with the demands of the environment and the people within it. Note the similarity of White's position to that of Piaget, who believes that children are intrinsically motivated to adapt to the environment by assimilating new experiences and then accommodating to these experiences.

Throughout this text, we have stressed that human infants are curious, active explorers who are constantly striving to understand and to exert some control over the world around them. But even though the basic propensity for competence and achievement may be innate, it is obvious that some children try harder than others to master their school assignments, their music lessons, or the positions they play on the neighborhood softball team.

How can we explain these individual differences? Is there a "motive to achieve" that children must acquire? What kinds of home and family experiences are likely to promote achievement behavior? And how do children's self-images and their expectations about succeeding or failing affect their aspirations and accomplishments? These are the issues we will consider in this final section of the chapter.

What Is Achievement Motivation?

When developmentalists talk about an "independent" person, they mean an individual who is able to accomplish many goals without assistance. The concept of achievement motivation is more complex. David McClelland and his associates (McClelland, Atkinson, Clark, & Lowell, 1953) define the **need for achievement (*n* Ach)** as a learned motive to compete and to strive for success whenever one's behavior can be evaluated against a standard of excellence. In other words, high "need-achievers" have learned to take pride in their ability to meet or exceed high standards, and it is this sense of self-fulfillment that motivates them to work hard, to be successful, and to outperform others when faced with new challenges.

Achievement motivation is usually measured by asking subjects to examine a set of four pictures and then write a story about each as part of a test of "creative imagination." These four pictures show people working or studying, although each is sufficiently ambiguous to suggest any number of themes (see Photo 12-7). The subject's need for achievement (*n* Ach) is then determined by counting the number of achievement-related statements that he or she includes in the four stories (the assumption being that subjects are projecting themselves and their motives into their themes). For example, a high need-achiever might respond to Photo 12-7 by saying that these men have been working for months on a new scientific breakthrough that will revolutionize the field of med-

PHOTO 12-7. *Scenes like this one were used by David McClelland and his associates to measure achievement motivation.*

icine, whereas a low need-achiever might say that the workers are glad the day is over so that they can go home and relax.

Recently, Susan Harter (1981) has argued that children may attempt to achieve for either of two reasons: (1) to satisfy their own needs for competence or mastery (an **intrinsic orientation** very similar to McClelland's *n* Ach) or (2) to earn *external* incentives such as grades, prizes, or approval (an **extrinsic orientation** that other theorists have called social achievement). Harter measures achievement orientation with a 30-item questionnaire that asks children to indicate whether the reasons they perform various activities are intrinsic (I like challenging tasks; I like to solve problems myself) or extrinsic (I do things to get good grades; to win the teacher's approval). Preliminary research with this new measure indicates that children who are intrinsically oriented to achieve are more likely than those who are extrinsically oriented (1) to prefer challenging problems over simpler ones and (2) to view themselves as highly competent at schoolwork and other cognitive activities.

Home and Family Influences on Achievement

As early as 6 months of age, infants already differ in their willingness to explore the environment and their attempts to control objects, situations, and the actions of other people (Yarrow et al., 1983). Although the amount of mastery motivation that these infants show is related to their level of maturity (as measured by the Bayley Scales of Infant Development), social experiences will soon begin to affect the child's curiosity and problem-solving behavior. For example, we have seen that infants who are securely attached to their mothers at 12–15 months of age are more likely than those who are insecurely attached (1) to venture away from the mother to explore a strange environment and (2) to display a strong sense of curiosity, self-reliance, and eagerness to solve problems some four years later in kindergarten (Matas, Arend, & Sroufe, 1978; Arend, Gove, & Sroufe, 1979). So it appears that a secure emotional bond to a primary caregiver may be an important contributor to achievement motivation.

TABLE 12-4. Relation between quality of home environment at 12 months of age and children's grade school academic achievement five to nine years later

Quality of home environment at age 12 months	Academic achievement	
	Average or high (top 70%)	Low (bottom 30%)
Stimulating	20 children	10 children
Unstimulating	6 children	14 children

The young child's tendency to explore, to acquire new skills, and to solve problems will also depend on the character of the home environment and the challenges it provides. In one recent study (van Doorninck, Caldwell, Wright, & Frankenberg, 1981), investigators visited the homes of 50 12-month-old infants from lower-class families and used the HOME inventory (described in Chapter Ten) to classify the child's early environment as intellectually stimulating or unstimulating (stimulating homes were those with emotionally responsive caregivers who structured the child's play periods and provided a variety of age-appropriate toys that he or she could manipulate and control). Five to nine years later, the research team followed up on these children by looking at their standardized achievement test scores and the grades they had earned at school. As we see in Table 12-4, the quality of the home environment at 12 months of age predicted children's academic achievement several years later. Two out of three

effectance motivation: *an inborn motive to explore, understand, and control one's environment.*

need for achievement (*n* Ach): *a learned motive to compete and to strive for success in situations where one's performance can be evaluated against some standard of excellence.*

intrinsic orientation: *a desire to achieve in order to satisfy one's personal needs for competence or mastery.*

extrinsic orientation: *a desire to achieve in order to earn external incentives such as grades, prizes, or the approval of others.*

children from stimulating homes were now performing quite well at school, whereas 70% of those from unstimulating homes were doing very poorly. Although the seeds of mastery motivation may well be innate, it seems that the joy of discovery and problem solving is unlikely to blossom in a barren home environment where the child has few problems to solve and limited opportunities for learning.

The demands that parents make of their child and the ways they respond to his or her accomplishments can also influence the child's will to achieve. In Box 12-5 we will take a closer look at some of the child-rearing practices that seem to encourage (or discourage) the development of achievement motivation.

Can I Achieve? The Role of Expectancies in Children's Achievement Behavior

Children differ not only in their motivation to achieve but in their *expectations* of achieving as well. Do these expectations of doing well (or poorly) have any effect on children's achievement behavior? Apparently so! In Chapter Ten we learned that IQ is an important determinant of academic achievement. Yet it is not uncommon for children with high IQs and low academic expectancies to earn *poorer* grades than their classmates who have low IQs and high expectancies (Battle, 1966; Crandall, 1967). In other words, expectations of success or failure are a powerful determinant of achievement behavior: children who expect to achieve usually do, whereas those who expect to fail may spend little time and effort pursuing goals that they believe to be "out of reach."

Although there are tremendous individual differences among members of each sex, girls generally outperform boys during elementary school, and boys eventually close the gap and may even outperform girls in certain subjects (for example, mathematics) during high school and college. But despite their early accomplishments, grade school girls often *underestimate* their capacity for academic achievement, while boys consistently *overestimate* their academic capabilities (Crandall, 1969). In fact, kindergarten and first-grade girls already think they are not as good as boys at concept-formation tasks and arithmetic, even though they are earning higher grades in arith-

metic and have outperformed their male classmates on tests of concept learning (Entwisle & Baker, 1983; Ruble, Parsons, & Ross, 1976).

Where do these sex differences in achievement expectancies come from? Many theorists believe that they begin at home. For example, parents "model" different roles for their children in families where the father pursues a career while the mother stays home to manage the household. Even if both parents work, children can form different impressions of the academic competencies of males and females if it is the father who usually helps them with their "tough" math and science homework. Finally, it seems that parents often expect more in the way of academic achievement from adolescent sons than from adolescent daughters (Parsons, Ruble, Hodges, & Small, 1976). In one recent study, Jacquelynne Parsons and her associates (Parsons, Adler, & Kaczala, 1982) found that parents of 5th- through 11th-graders believe that mathematics courses are easier, more important, and somewhat more enjoyable for their boys than for their girls. Do these parental attitudes affect children's own impressions of their mathematical aptitude and their prospects for future success in math? Yes, indeed! Even though the males and females in Parsons's sample *did not differ* in their previous performance in math, the children's beliefs about their own mathematical *abilities* were more in line with their parents' beliefs about their math aptitude and potential than with their own past experiences in math! So it appears that parents' sex-stereotyped beliefs about their children's academic potential may be an important determinant of the sex differences we find in children's academic self-concepts. "By attributing their daughters' performances to hard work and their sons' to high ability, parents may be teaching their sons and daughters to draw different inferences regarding their . . . abilities from equivalent achievement experiences" (Parsons et al., 1982, p. 320).

Why Do I Succeed (or Fail)? Locus of Control and Children's Achievement Behavior

Children's expectations of achieving success will also depend on the extent to which they believe that their behavior determines their outcomes.

What kinds of child-rearing practices encourage achievement motivation? In their book *The Achievement Motive,* McClelland et al. (1953) propose that parents of high need-achievers (1) stress independence training and (2) expect their children to be self-reliant at an earlier age than parents of low need-achievers.

Marian Winterbottom (1958) tested these hypotheses by measuring the achievement motivation of 29 boys aged 8 to 10 and then comparing their scores against the child-rearing strategies their mothers had used. The results supported McClelland's hypotheses: mothers of high need-achievers expected their sons to be independent at an earlier age than mothers of low need-achievers. In addition, mothers of high need-achievers were more likely than mothers of low need-achievers to reinforce self-reliance with a hug and a kiss. Winterbottom concluded that *early* independence training given with lots of warmth and affection is an important contributor to children's achievement motivation.

Bernard Rosen and Roy D'Andrade (1959) suggest that direct *achievement training* (encouraging children to do things well) is at least as important to the development of achievement motivation as independence training (encouraging children to do things on their own). To evaluate their hypothesis, Rosen and D'Andrade visited the homes of boys who had tested either high or low in achievement motivation and asked these 9- to 11-year-olds to work at difficult and potentially frustrating tasks—for example, building a tower of irregularly shaped blocks while blindfolded and using only one hand. To assess the kind of independence and achievement training the boys received at home, the investigators asked parents to watch their son work and to give any encouragement or suggestions that they cared to. The results were clear. Both the mothers and fathers of high need-

Parents who encourage independence and achievement are likely to raise children who are motivated to achieve.

achievers set lofty standards for their boys to accomplish while working on the experimental tasks, and they were noticeably concerned about the quality of their sons' performance. They gave many helpful hints and were quick to praise their sons for meeting one of their performance standards. In contrast, parents of low need-achievers (particularly fathers) stressed neither independence nor achievement training. They often told their sons how to perform the tasks and became rather irritated whenever the boys experienced any difficulty. Finally, the high need-achievers tended to outperform the low need-achievers, and they seemed to enjoy the tasks more as well. So it appears that independence, achievement motivation, and achievement behavior are more likely to develop when parents encourage children to do things on their own *and to do them well.*

However, a caution is in order. Early independence and achievement training can backfire and cause a child to shy away from challenging tasks if parents accentuate the negative by *punishing failures and responding neutrally to successes* (Teeven & McGhee, 1972). Children who show the highest levels of achievement motivation are those who are encouraged to "do their best" by parents who *reward successes and respond neutrally to failures.*

Some children, called **internalizers,** assume that they are personally responsible for their successes and failures. If an internalizer were to receive an A on an essay, she would probably attribute the high mark to her ability to write or to the hard work that she had expended in preparing the paper (internal causes). Other children, known as **externalizers,** believe that their successes and failures depend more on luck, fate, or the actions of others

internalizers: *people who believe that they are personally responsible for their successes and failures.*

externalizers: *people who believe that their successes and failures depend more on external factors such as luck or fate than on their own efforts and abilities.*

than on their own abilities or efforts. Thus, an externalizer is likely to attribute an A grade on an essay to luck (the teacher just happened to like this one), indiscriminate grading, or some other external cause.

Virginia Crandall and her associates believe that an internal locus of control (internality) is conducive to achievement: children must necessarily assume that their efforts will lead to positive outcomes if they are to strive for success and become high achievers. Externalizers are not expected to strive for success or to become high achievers, because they assume that their efforts are generally irrelevant to their outcomes.

Crandall measures children's locus of control by administering the Intellectual Achievement Responsibility Questionnaire, a 34-item scale that taps one's perceptions of responsibility for pleasant and unpleasant outcomes. Each item describes an achievement-related experience and asks the child to select an internal or an external cause for that experience (see Figure 12-5 for sample items). The more "internal" responses the child selects, the higher his internality score; children who choose few internal responses are classified as externalizers.

In their recent review of more than 100 studies, Maureen Findley and Harris Cooper (1983) found that internalizers do earn higher grades and will typically outperform externalizers on standardized tests of academic achievement. In fact, one rather extensive study of minority students in the

PHOTO 12-8. *If youngsters believe that they are personally responsible for their successes, they are more likely to become high achievers.*

United States found that children's beliefs in internal control were a better predictor of academic achievements than were *n* Ach scores, the child-rearing practices of parents, or the type of classroom and the teaching styles to which the students had been exposed (Coleman et al., 1966). So striking were these results that researchers set out to determine how a sense of internality develops.

It appears that parents who encourage self-reliance while setting clear performance standards for their children to live up to are likely to raise internalizers (Buriel, 1981; MacDonald, 1971). In contrast, protective parents who set few performance standards and allow little autonomy or freedom of expression are likely to raise youngsters who score higher in externality (Davis & Phares, 1969; Wichern & Nowicki, 1976). Perhaps there is a simple explanation for these findings. If children are often protected by parents who solve their problems for them and set few standards for them to live up to, it is easy to see how they might be confused about what constitutes acceptable performance and assume that parents or other adults will make those judgments for them. By contrast, parents who stress self-reliance and set clear performance standards are creating a "predictable" world for their children—one that will enable them to determine whether their own efforts to achieve important goals have been successful or unsuccessful.

Parental reactions to a child's successes and failures may also influence the child's locus of

---

FIGURE 12-5 *Sample items from the Intellectual Achievement Responsibility Questionnaire.*

1. *If a teacher passes you to the next grade, it would probably be*
   _____ a. because she liked you
   * _____ b. because of the work that you did

2. *When you do well on a test at school, it is more likely to be*
   * _____ a. because you studied for it
   _____ b. because the test was especially easy

3. *When you read a story and can't remember much of it, it is usually*
   _____ a. because the story wasn't well written
   * _____ b. because you weren't interested in the story

*Denotes the "internal" response for each sample item.

control. Children who take credit for their accomplishments and score high in internality tend to have parents who frequently reward successes and do not criticize an occasional failure (Katkovsky, Crandall, & Good, 1967). By contrast, youngsters who deny personal responsibility for their outcomes and score high in externality often have parents who are neutral toward successes and who punish failures. So it seems that adults who react in a generally positive manner to a child's accomplishments are probably fostering the development of an internal orientation, while those who accentuate the negative by punishing failures may be encouraging their children to defend themselves against the threat of punishment by adopting an external locus of control (Katkovsky et al., 1967).

SUMMARY

This chapter has traced the development of children's knowledge about the self and others and then considered how these aspects of social cognition are related to the process of social development.

Infants do not distinguish between the self and nonself (objects, other people) until 4–6 months of age. By age 15–24 months, they will recognize their images in a mirror, and they soon begin to categorize themselves along socially significant dimensions such as age and sex. The self-concepts of preschoolers and young grade school children are very concrete, focusing on physical features, possessions, and the activities they can perform. Older grade school children typically describe the self in terms of psychological attributes, whereas adolescents have a more abstract conception of self that includes not only their stable attributes but also their beliefs, attitudes, and values.

Grade school children differ in their perceived self-worth, or self-esteem. Children who feel good about their cognitive and social competencies tend to do better at school and have more friends than their classmates who feel that they are socially and intellectually inadequate.

There are some interesting parallels between children's knowledge of self and their knowledge of others. Children younger than 6 or 7 are likely to describe friends and acquaintances in the same concrete, observable terms (physical attributes

and activities) that they use to describe the self. By age 8 to 10, children begin to see regularities in the behavior of both themselves and others and will often base their impressions of an acquaintance on the stable psychological constructs, or "traits," that this individual is presumed to have. When they approach adolescence, their impressions become much more abstract as they begin to compare and contrast their friends and acquaintances on a number of psychological attributes. The growth of self-knowledge and interpersonal understanding is related to changes occurring in children's intellectual abilities and role-taking skills. To truly "know" a person, one must be able to assume his perspective and understand his thoughts, feelings, motives, and intentions—in short, the internal factors that account for his behavior.

Sociability is the child's tendency to approach and interact with other people and to seek their attention or approval. Although children become much more sociable over the first three years, some infants are more outgoing than others. Three factors that may contribute to these individual differences in sociability are the child's genotype, the security of his or her interpersonal attachments, and the child's ordinal position in the family. During the preschool period, children become more playful and outgoing with one another and much less likely to fight. Parents who are warm and supportive and who require their children to follow certain rules of social etiquette are likely to raise sons and daughters who establish good relations with both adults and peers. In contrast, permissive parents who exert little control are likely to have children who resist adult authority and are aggressive and unpopular with their classmates.

Although infants and toddlers will occasionally offer toys to playmates, help their parents with household chores, and try to soothe distressed companions, examples of altruism become increasingly common over the first 10–12 years of life. Parents can promote altruistic behavior by encouraging their child to perform acts of kindness, by reinforcing the child's prosocial deeds, and by practicing what they preach. Older children may incorporate altruism into their self-concepts if adults tell them that they are "kind" or "helpful" people whenever they behave charitably. Empathy and role-taking skills both contribute to the development of altruistic behavior, and parents who discipline harm-doing with inductive, or victim-centered, techniques are likely to raise children who are sympathetic, self-sacrificing, and concerned about the welfare of others.

Aggression emerges in the second year as infants begin to quarrel with siblings and peers over toys and other possessions. During the preschool period, children become less likely to throw temper tantrums or to hit others and more likely to resort to verbally aggressive tactics such as name calling or ridiculing. Although 6–7-year-olds continue to fight over objects, an increasing percentage of their aggressive exchanges are person-directed hostile outbursts. Boys are more aggressive than girls, and aggression is a much more stable attribute for males than for females. A person's tendency toward violence and aggression depends, in part, on cultural influences and the family setting. Cold and rejecting parents who rely on physical punishment and often permit aggression are likely to raise aggressive children. Highly aggressive youngsters who are "out of control" often live in coercive home environments where family members are constantly struggling with one another. In order to help these highly combative children, it is often necessary to treat the entire family.

Proceeding in accordance with the catharsis hypothesis, the belief that children become less aggressive after behaving aggressively toward an inanimate object, is an ineffective control tactic that may instigate aggressive behavior. Some proven methods of controlling children's aggression are (1) rewarding incompatible responses such as cooperation and sharing, (2) creating play environments that minimize the likelihood of conflict, and (3) encouraging children to recognize the harmful effects of their aggressive acts and to empathize with the victims of aggression.

Children differ in their willingness to strive for success and to master new challenges. Infants who are securely attached to responsive caregivers who provide them with age-appropriate toys and problems are likely to become curious nursery school children who will later do well at school. Parents can contribute to their child's achievement motivation by reinforcing self-reliant behavior and encouraging the child to do things well. Children who expect to succeed are likely to work longer at new problems and to outperform those who expect to fail. A child's achievement expectancies are related to parental expectations, and some parents may expect more of their sons than of their daughters. The belief that a person is responsible for his or her outcomes—that is, an internal locus of control—is an important contributor to academic achievement. Parents who hope to foster a sense of internal control are well advised to stress self-reliance, to set clear standards for their child to live up to, and to encourage achievement behavior by rewarding successes without becoming overly concerned about an occasional failure.

REFERENCES

Abramovitch, R., Corter, C., & Lando, B. (1979). Sibling interaction in the home. *Child Development, 50,* 997–1003.

Adams, G. R., & Fitch, S. A. (1982). Ego stage and identity status development: A cross-sequential analysis. *Journal of Personality and Social Psychology, 43,* 574–583.

Ainsworth, M. D. S. (1972). Attachment and dependency: A comparison. In J. L. Gewirtz (Ed.), *Attachment and dependency.* Washington, DC: Winston.

Ainsworth, M. D. S. (1979). Attachment as related to mother-infant interaction. In J. G. Rosenblatt, R. A. Hinde, C. Beer, & M. Busnel (Eds.), *Advances in the study of behavior* (Vol. 9). New York: Academic Press.

Archer, S. L. (1982). The lower age boundaries of identity development. *Child Development, 53,* 1551–1556.

Arend, A., Gove, F. L., & Sroufe, L. A. (1979). Continuity of individual adaptation from infancy to kindergarten: A predictive study of ego-resiliency and curiosity in preschoolers. *Child Development, 50,* 950–959.

Asher, S. R. (1983). Social competence and peer status: Recent advances and future directions. *Child Development, 54,* 1427–1434.

Barenboim, C. (1981). The development of person perception in childhood and adolescence: From behavioral comparisons to psychological constructs to psychological comparisons. *Child Development, 52,* 129–144.

Barnett, M. A., Howard, J. A., Melton, E. M., & Dino, G. A. (1982). Effect of inducing sadness about self or other on helping behavior in high- and low-empathic children. *Child Development, 53,* 920–923.

Baron, R. A. (1971). Magnitude of victim's pain cues and level of prior anger arousal as determinants of adult aggressive behavior. *Journal of Personality and Social Psychology, 17,* 236–243.

Baron, R. A., & Byrne, D. (1981). *Social psychology: Understanding human interaction.* Boston: Allyn & Bacon.

Bar-Tal, D., Raviv, A., & Goldberg, M. (1982). Helping behavior among preschool children: An observational study. *Child Development, 53,* 396–402.

Battle, E. S. (1966). Motivational determinants of academic competence. *Journal of Personality and Social Psychology, 4*, 634–642.

Baumrind, D. (1971). Current patterns of parental authority. *Developmental Psychology Monographs, 4* (No. 1, Part 2).

Berndt, T. J. (1982). The features and effects of friendship in early adolescence. *Child Development, 53*, 1447–1460.

Bernstein, R. M. (1980). The development of the self-system during adolescence. *Journal of Genetic Psychology, 136*, 231–245.

Bierman, K. L., & Furman, W. (1984). The effects of social skills training and peer involvement on the social adjustment of preadolescents. *Child Development, 55*, 151-162.

Bridgeman, D. L. (1981). Enhanced role-taking through cooperative interdependence: A field study. *Child Development, 51*, 1231–1238.

Brody, G. H., & Shaffer, D. R. (1982). Contributions of parents and peers to children's moral socialization. *Developmental Review, 2*, 31–75.

Bronson, W. C. (1975). Developments in behavior with age mates during the second year of life. In M. Lewis & L. A. Rosenblum (Eds.), *The origins of behavior: Friendship and peer relations*. New York: Wiley.

Brooks, J., & Lewis, M. (1976). Infants' response to strangers: Midget, adult, and child. *Child Development, 47*, 323–332.

Brooks-Gunn, J., & Lewis, M. (1981). Infant social perception: Responses to pictures of parents and strangers. *Developmental Psychology, 17*, 647–649.

Brooks-Gunn, J., & Lewis, M. (1982). The development of self-knowledge. In C. B. Kopp & J. B. Krakow (Eds.), *The child: Development in a social context*. Reading, MA: Addison-Wesley.

Broughton, J. (1978). Development of concepts of self, mind, reality, and knowledge. *New Directions for Child Development, 1*, 75–100.

Brown, P., & Elliot, R. (1965). Control of aggression in a nursery school class. *Journal of Experimental Child Psychology, 2*, 103–107.

Bryan, J. H., & Schwartz, T. H. (1971). The effects of filmed material upon children's behavior. *Psychological Bulletin, 75*, 50–59.

Bryan, J. H., & Walbek, N. (1970). Preaching and practicing self-sacrifice: Children's actions and reactions. *Child Development, 41*, 329–353.

Bryant, B. K. (1982). An index of empathy for children and adolescents. *Child Development, 53*, 413–425.

Buriel, R. (1981). The relation of Anglo- and Mexican-American children's locus of control beliefs to parents' and teachers' socialization practices. *Child Development, 52*, 104–113.

Buss, A. H. (1961). *The psychology of aggression*. New York: Wiley.

Chandler, M. J. (1973). Egocentrism and antisocial behavior: The assessment and training of social perspective taking skills. *Developmental Psychology, 9*, 326–332.

Charlesworth, R., & Hartup, W. W. (1967). Positive social reinforcement in the nursery school peer group. *Child Development, 38*, 993–1002.

Clarke-Stewart, K. A., Umeh, B. J., Snow, M. E., & Pederson, J. A. (1980). Development and prediction of children's sociability from 1 to 2½ years. *Developmental Psychology, 16*, 290–302.

Coleman, J. S., Campbell, E. Q., Hobson, C. J., McPartland, J., Mood, A. M., Weinfeld, F. D., & York, R. L. (1966). *Equality of educational opportunity*. Report from U.S. Office of Education. Washington, DC: U.S. Government Printing Office.

Combs, M. L., & Slaby, D. A. (1978). Social skills training with children. In B. B. Lahey & A. E. Kazdin (Eds.), *Advances in clinical child psychology*. New York: Plenum Press.

Cooke, T., & Apolloni, T. (1976). Developing positive social-emotional behaviors: A study of training and generalization effects. *Journal of Applied Behavior Analysis, 9*, 65–78.

Cooley, C. H. (1902). *Human nature and the social order*. New York: Scribner's.

Coopersmith, S. (1967). *The antecedents of self-esteem*. San Francisco: W. H. Freeman.

Crandall, V. C. (1967). Achievement behavior in young children. In *The young child: Reviews of research*. Washington, DC: National Association for the Education of Young Children.

Crandall, V. C. (1969). Sex differences in expectancy of intellectual and academic reinforcement. In C. P. Smith (Ed.), *Achievement-related motives in children*. New York: Russell Sage Foundation.

Damon, W., & Hart, D. (1982). The development of self-understanding from infancy through adolescence. *Child Development, 53*, 841–864.

Davis, W. L., & Phares, E. J. (1969). Parental antecedents of internal-external control of reinforcement. *Psychological Reports, 24*, 427-436.

Dlugokinski, E. L., & Firestone, I. J. (1974). Other centeredness and susceptibility to charitable appeals: Effects of perceived discipline. *Developmental Psychology, 10*, 21–28.

Dodge, K. A. (1980). Social cognition and children's aggressive behavior. *Child Development, 51*, 162–170.

Dodge, K. A., & Frame, C. L. (1982). Social cognitive biases and deficits in aggressive boys. *Child Development, 53*, 620–635.

Edwards, C. P. (1984). The age group labels and categories of preschool children. *Child Development, 55*, 440-452.

Edwards, C. P., & Lewis, M. (1979). Young children's concepts of social relations: Social functions and social objects. In M. Lewis & L. Rosenblum (Eds.), *The child and its family: The genesis of behavior* (Vol. 2). New York: Plenum Press.

Eisenberg, N. (1983). Children's differentiations among potential recipients of aid. *Child Development, 54*, 594–602.

Emmerich, W. (1966). Continuity and stability in early social development: II. Teacher's ratings. *Child Development, 37*, 17–27.

Entwisle, D. R., & Baker, D. P. (1983). Gender and young children's expectations for performance in arithmetic. *Developmental Psychology, 19*, 200–209.

Erikson, E. H. (1950). In M. J. E. Senn (Ed.), *Symposium on the healthy personality.* New York: Josiah Macy, Jr., Foundation.

Erikson, E. H. (1963). *Childhood and society* (2nd ed.). New York: Norton.

Eron, L. D. (1982). Parent-child interaction, television violence, and aggression of children. *American Psychologist, 37,* 197–211.

Ferguson, T. J., & Rule, B. G. (1980). Effects of inferential set, outcome severity, and basis for responsibility on children's evaluations of aggressive acts. *Developmental Psychology, 16,* 141–146.

Feshbach, N. (1978). Studies of the development of children's empathy. In B. Maher (Ed.), *Progress in experimental personality research.* New York: Academic Press.

Feshbach, S. (1956). The catharsis hypothesis and some consequences of interaction with aggressive and neutral play objects. *Journal of Personality, 24,* 449–461.

Findley, M. J., & Cooper, H. M. (1983). Locus of control and academic achievement: A literature review. *Journal of Personality and Social Psychology, 44,* 419–427.

Fischer, W. F. (1963). Sharing in pre-school children as a function of the amount and type of reinforcement. *Genetic Psychology Monographs, 68,* 215–245.

Freedman, D. G. (1974). *Human infancy: An evolutionary perspective.* Hillsdale, NJ: Erlbaum.

Furman, W., & Bierman, K. L. (1983). Developmental changes in young children's conceptions of friendship. *Child Development, 54,* 549–556.

Fyans, L. J., Jr., Salili, F., Maehr, M. L., & Desai, K. A. (1983). A cross-cultural exploration into the meaning of achievement. *Journal of Personality and Social Psychology, 44,* 1000–1013.

Gallup, G. G., Jr. (1979). Self-recognition in chimpanzees and man: A developmental and comparative perspective. In M. Lewis & L. A. Rosenblum (Eds.), *Genesis of behavior.* Vol. 2: *The child and its family.* New York: Plenum Press.

Goldsmith, H. H. (1983). Genetic influences on personality from infancy to adulthood. *Child Development, 54,* 331–355.

Goodenough, F. L. (1931). *Anger in young children.* Minneapolis: University of Minnesota Press.

Gordon, C. (1968). Self-conceptions: Configurations of content. In C. Gordon & K. J. Gergen (Eds.), *The self in social interaction.* New York: Wiley.

Gorer, G. (1968). Man has no "killer" instinct. In M. F. A. Montague (Ed.), *Man and aggression.* New York: Oxford University Press.

Green, F. P., & Schneider, F. W. (1974). Age differences in the behavior of boys on three measures of altruism. *Child Development, 45,* 248–251.

Grusec, J. E., & Redler, E. (1980). Attribution, reinforcement, and altruism: A developmental analysis. *Developmental Psychology, 16,* 525–534.

Gump, P. V. (1975). Ecological psychology and children. In M. Hetherington (Ed.), *Review of child development research* (Vol. 5). Chicago: University of Chicago Press.

Gurucharri, C., & Selman, R. L. (1982). The development of interpersonal understanding during childhood, preadolescence, and adolescence: A longitudinal follow-up study. *Child Development, 53,* 924–927.

Harter, S. (1981). A new self-report scale of intrinsic versus extrinsic orientation in the classroom: Motivational and informational components. *Developmental Psychology, 17,* 300–312.

Harter, S. (1982). The perceived competence scale for children. *Child Development, 53,* 87–97.

Hartshorne, H., May, M. A., & Maller, J. B. (1929). *Studies in the nature of character: II. Studies in service and self-control.* New York: Macmillan.

Hartup, W. W. (1970). Peer interaction and social organization. In P. H. Mussen (Ed.), *Carmichael's manual of child psychology* (Vol. 2). New York: Wiley.

Hartup, W. W. (1974). Aggression in childhood: Developmental perspectives. *American Psychologist, 29,* 336–341.

Hay, D. F. (1979). Cooperative interactions and sharing among very young children and their parents. *Developmental Psychology, 15,* 647–653.

Hay, D. F., Nash, A., & Pedersen, J. (1983). Interaction between six-month-old peers. *Child Development, 54,* 557–562.

Hay, D. F., & Ross, H. S. (1982). The social nature of early conflict. *Child Development, 53,* 105–113.

Hayes, D. S., Gershman, E., & Bolin, L. J. (1980). Friends and enemies: Cognitive bases for preschool children's unilateral and reciprocal relationships. *Child Development, 51,* 1276–1279.

Hill, S. D., & Tomlin, C. (1981). Self-recognition in retarded children. *Child Development, 52,* 145–150.

Hoffman, M. L. (1975). Altruistic behavior and the parent-child relationship. *Journal of Personality and Social Psychology, 31,* 937–943.

Hoffman, M. L. (1981). Is altruism part of human nature? *Journal of Personality and Social Psychology, 40,* 121–137.

Hoving, K. L., Wallace, J. R., & LaForme, G. L. (1976). *The expression of interpersonal aggression in a competitive situation as a function of age, sex, amount and type of provocation.* Unpublished manuscript, Kent State University.

Hudson, L. M., Forman, E. R., & Brion-Meisels, S. (1982). Role-taking as a predictor of prosocial behavior in cross-age tutors. *Child Development, 53,* 1320–1329.

Hughes, R., Jr., Tingle, B. A., & Sawin, D. B. (1981). Development of empathic understanding in children. *Child Development, 52,* 122–128.

Hyde, J. S. (1984). How large are gender differences in aggression? A developmental meta-analysis. *Developmental Psychology, 20,* 722-736.

Johnson, C. N., & Wellman, H. M. (1982). Children's developing conceptions of the mind and brain. *Child Development, 53,* 222–234.

Kagan, J., & Moss, H. A. (1962). *Birth to maturity.* New York: Wiley.

Kagan, S., & Masden, M. C. (1971). Cooperation and competition of Mexican, Mexican-American, and Anglo-American children of two ages and four instructional sets. *Developmental Psychology, 5,* 32–39.

Kagan, S., & Masden, M. C. (1972). Rivalry in Anglo-American and Mexican children of two ages. *Journal of Personality and Social Psychology, 24,* 214–220.

Katkovsky, W., Crandall, V. C., & Good, S. (1967). Parental antecedents of children's beliefs in internal-external control of reinforcements in intellectual achievement situations. *Child Development, 38,* 765–776.

Keating, D., & Clark, L. V. (1980). Development of physical and social reasoning in adolescence. *Developmental Psychology, 16,* 23–30.

Keller, A., Ford, L. H., Jr., & Meachum, J. A. (1978). Dimensions of self-concept in preschool children. *Developmental Psychology, 14,* 483–489.

Kerby, F. D., & Tolar, H. C. (1970). Modification of preschool isolate behavior: A case study. *Journal of Applied Behavior Analysis, 3,* 309–314.

Kohlberg, L. (1969). Stage and sequence: The cognitive-developmental approach to socialization. In D. A. Goslin (Ed.), *Handbook of socialization theory and research.* Chicago: Rand McNally.

Kokenes, B. (1974). Grade level differences in factors of self-esteem. *Developmental Psychology, 10,* 954–958.

Krebs, D. L. (1970). Altruism—an examination of the concept and a review of the literature. *Psychological Bulletin, 73,* 258–302.

Kurdek, L. A., & Krile, D. (1982). A developmental analysis of the relation between peer acceptance and both interpersonal understanding and perceived social self-competence. *Child Development, 53,* 1485–1491.

Ladd, G. W. (1981). Effectiveness of a social learning method for enhancing children's social interaction and peer acceptance. *Child Development, 52,* 171–178.

Ladd, G. W., Lange, G., & Stremmel, A. (1983). Personal and situational influences on children's helping behavior: Factors that mediate compliant helping. *Child Development, 54,* 488–501.

Lerner, R. M., Iwawaki, S., Chihara, T., & Sorell, G. T. (1980). Self-concept, self-esteem, and body attitudes among Japanese male and female adolescents. *Child Development, 51,* 847–855.

Leung, E. H. L., & Rheingold, H. L. (1981). Development of pointing as a social gesture. *Developmental Psychology, 17,* 215–220.

Lewis, M., & Brooks-Gunn, J. (1979). *Social cognition and the acquisition of self.* New York: Plenum Press.

Lewis, M., & Kreitzberg, V. S. (1979). Effects of birth-order and spacing on mother-infant interactions. *Developmental Psychology, 15,* 617–625.

Livesley, W. J., & Bromley, D. B. (1973). *Person perception in childhood and adolescence.* London: Wiley.

Londerville, S., & Main, M. (1981). Security of attachment, compliance, and maternal training methods in the second year of life. *Developmental Psychology, 17,* 289–299.

London, P. (1970). The rescuers: Motivational hypotheses about Christians who saved Jews from the Nazis. In J. Macaulay & L. Berkowitz (Eds.), *Altruism and helping behavior.* New York: Academic Press.

Lorenz, K. (1966). *On aggression.* New York: Harcourt Brace Jovanovich.

Maccoby, E. E. (1980). *Social development: Psychological growth and the parent-child relationship.* New York: Harcourt Brace Jovanovich.

Maccoby, E. E., & Feldman, S. (1972). Mother-attachment and stranger-reactions in the third year of life. *Monographs of the Society for Research in Child Development, 37* (1, Serial No. 146).

Maccoby, E. E., & Jacklin, C. N. (1974). *The psychology of sex differences.* Stanford, CA: Stanford University Press.

Maccoby, E. E., & Jacklin, C. N. (1980). Sex differences in aggression: A rejoinder and reprise. *Child Development, 51,* 964–980.

MacDonald, A. P. (1971). Internal-external locus of control: Parental antecedents. *Journal of Clinical and Consulting Psychology, 37,* 141–147.

Mahler, M. S., Pine, F., & Bergman, A. (1975). *The psychological birth of the infant.* New York: Basic Books.

Main, M., & Weston, D. R. (1981). The quality of the toddler's relationship to mother and father: Related to conflict and the readiness to establish new relationships. *Child Development, 52,* 932–940.

Mallick, S. K., & McCandless, B. R. (1966). A study of the catharsis of aggression. *Journal of Personality and Social Psychology, 4,* 591–596.

Marcia, J. E. (1966). Development and validation of ego identity status. *Journal of Personality and Social Psychology, 3,* 551–558.

Matas, L., Arend, R. A., & Sroufe, L. A. (1978). Continuity of adaptation in the second year: The relationship between quality of attachment and later competence. *Child Development, 49,* 547–556.

Matheny, A. P. (1983). A longitudinal twin study of the stability of components from Bayley's Infant Behavior Record. *Child Development, 54,* 356–360.

McCarthy, J. D., & Hoge, D. R. (1982). Analysis of age effects in longitudinal studies of adolescent self-esteem. *Developmental Psychology, 18,* 372–379.

McClelland, D. C., Atkinson, J. W., Clark, R. A., & Lowell, E. L. (1953). *The achievement motive.* New York: Appleton-Century-Crofts.

McGuire, K. D., & Weisz, J. R. (1982). Social cognition and behavioral correlates of preadolescent chumship. *Child Development, 53,* 1478–1484.

Mead, G. H. (1934). *Mind, self, and society.* Chicago: University of Chicago Press.

Mead, M. (1935). *Sex and temperament in three primitive societies.* New York: Morrow.

Meilman, P. W. (1979). Cross-sectional age changes in ego identity status during adolescence. *Developmental Psychology, 15,* 230–231.

Midlarsky, E., & Bryan, J. H. (1972). Affect expressions and children's imitative altruism. *Journal of Experimental Research in Personality, 6,* 195–203.

Midlarsky, E., Bryan, J. H., & Brickman, P. (1973). Aversive approval: Interactive effects of modeling and reinforcement on altruistic behavior. *Child Development, 8,* 99–104.

Mohr, D. M. (1978). Development of attributes of personal identity. *Developmental Psychology, 14,* 427–428.

Montemayor, R., & Eisen, M. (1977). The development of self-conceptions from childhood to adolescence. *Developmental Psychology, 13,* 314–319.

Mueller, E., & Brenner, J. (1977). The origins of social skill and interaction among playgroup toddlers. *Child Development, 48,* 854–861.

Munro, G., & Adams, G. R. (1977). Ego-identity formation in college students and working youth. *Developmental Psychology, 13,* 523–524.

National Commission on the Causes and Prevention of Violence. (1969). *To establish justice, to insure domestic tranquility.* New York: Award Books.

Oden, S., & Asher, S. R. (1977). Coaching children in social skills for friendship making. *Child Development, 48,* 495–506.

Olweus, D. (1979). Stability of aggressive reaction patterns in males: A review. *Psychological Bulletin, 86,* 852–875.

Olweus, D. (1980). Familial and temperamental determinants of aggressive behavior in adolescent boys: A causal analysis. *Developmental Psychology, 16,* 644–660.

O'Malley, P. M., & Bachman, J. G. (1983). Self-esteem: Change and stability between ages 13 and 23. *Developmental Psychology, 19,* 257–268.

Orlick, T. D. (1981). Positive socialization via cooperative games. *Developmental Psychology, 17,* 426–429.

Orlick, T. D., & Foley, C. (1979). Pre-school cooperative games: A preliminary perspective. In M. J. Melnick (Ed.), *Sport sociology: Contemporary themes* (2nd ed.). Dubuque, IA: Kendall/Hunt.

Orlick, T. D., McNally, J., & O'Hara, T. (1978). Cooperative games: Systematic analysis and cooperative impact. In F. Smoll & R. Smith (Eds.), *Psychological perspectives in youth sports.* Washington, DC: Hemisphere.

Parsons, J. E., Adler, T. F., & Kaczala, C. M. (1982). Socialization of achievement attitudes and beliefs: Parental influences. *Child Development, 53,* 310–321.

Parsons, J. E., Ruble, D. N., Hodges, K. L., & Small, A. W. (1976). Cognitive-developmental factors in emerging sex differences in achievement-related expectancies. *Journal of Social Issues, 32,* 47–61.

Pastor, D. L. (1981). The quality of mother-infant attachment and its relationship to toddlers' initial sociability with peers. *Developmental Psychology, 17,* 326–335.

Patterson, G. R. (1976). The aggressive child: Victim and architect of a coercive system. In E. J. Mash, L. A. Hamerlynck, & L. C. Handy (Eds.), *Behavior modification and families.* Vol. 1: *Theory and research.* New York: Brunner/Mazel.

Patterson, G. R. (1980). Mothers: The unacknowledged victims. *Monographs of the Society for Research in Child Development, 45* (5, Serial No. 18b).

Patterson, G. R., Littman, R. A., & Bricker, W. (1967). Assertive behavior in children: A step toward a theory of aggression. *Monographs of the Society for Research in Child Development, 32,* (5, Serial No. 113).

Peevers, B. H., & Secord, P. F. (1973). Developmental changes in attribution of descriptive concepts to persons. *Journal of Personality and Social Psychology, 27,* 120–128.

Pennebaker, J. W., Hendler, C. S., Durrett, M. E., & Richards, P. (1981). Social factors influencing absenteeism due to illness in nursery school children. *Child Development, 52,* 692–700.

Perry, D. G., & Bussey, K. (1977). Self-reinforcement in high- and low-aggressive boys following acts of aggression. *Child Development, 48,* 653–657.

Perry, D. G., & Perry, L. C. (1974). Denial of suffering in the victim as a stimulus to violence in aggressive boys. *Child Development, 45,* 55–62.

Piaget, J. (1952). *The origins of intelligence in children.* New York: International Universities Press.

Piaget, J. (1965). *The moral judgment of the child.* New York: Free Press.

Rheingold, H. L. (1982). Little children's participation in the work of adults, a nascent prosocial behavior. *Child Development, 53,* 114–125.

Rice, M. E., & Grusec, J. E. (1975). Saying and doing: Effects on observer performance. *Journal of Personality and Social Psychology, 32,* 584–593.

Roff, M. F. (1974). Childhood antecedents of adult neurosis, severe bad conduct, and psychological health. In D. F. Ricks, A. Thomas, & M. Roff (Eds.), *Life history research in psychopathology* (Vol. 3). Minneapolis: University of Minnesota Press.

Roff, M. F., Sells, S. B., & Golden, M. M. (1972). *Social adjustment and personality development in children.* Minneapolis: University of Minnesota Press.

Rosen, B. C., & D'Andrade, R. (1959). The psychosocial origins of achievement motivation. *Sociometry, 22,* 185–218.

Rosenhan, D. L. (1972). Prosocial behavior of children. In W. W. Hartup (Ed.), *The young child* (Vol. 2). Washington, DC: National Association for the Education of Young Children.

Rotenberg, K. J. (1982). Development of character constancy of self and other. *Child Development, 53,* 505–515.

Ruble, D. N., Parsons, J. E., & Ross, J. (1976). *Self-evaluative responses in an achievement setting.* Unpublished manuscript, Princeton University.

Rushton, J. P. (1975). Generosity in children: Immediate and long term effects of modeling, preaching, and moral judgment. *Journal of Personality and Social Psychology, 31,* 459–466.

Rushton, J. P. (1980). *Altruism, socialization, and society.* Englewood Cliffs, NJ: Prentice-Hall.

Rutherford, E., & Mussen, P. H. (1968). Generosity in nursery school boys. *Child Development, 39,* 755–765.

Sagotsky, G., Wood-Schneider, M., & Konop, M. (1981). Learning to cooperate: Effects of modeling and direct instruction. *Child Development, 52,* 1037–1042.

Scarr, S. (1966). The origins of individual differences in adjective check list scores. *Journal of Consulting Psychology, 30,* 354–357.

Scarr, S. (1968). Environmental bias in twin studies. *Eugenics Quarterly, 15,* 34–40.

Schachter, S. (1959). *The psychology of affiliation.* Stanford, CA: Stanford University Press.

Schaefer, E. S., & Bayley, N. (1963). Maternal behavior, child behavior, and their intercorrelations from infancy through adolescence. *Monographs of the Society for Research in Child Development, 28* (Serial No. 87).

Schaffer, H. R., & Emerson, P. E. (1964). The development of social attachments in infancy. *Monographs of the Society for Research in Child Development, 29* (3, Serial No. 94).

Sears, R. R., Maccoby, E. E., & Levin, H. (1957). *Patterns of child rearing.* New York: Harper & Row.

Selman, R. L. (1976). Social-cognitive understanding: A guide to educational and clinical practice. In T. Lickona (Ed.), *Moral development and behavior: Theory, research and social issues.* New York: Holt, Rinehart & Winston.

Selman, R. L. (1980). *The growth of interpersonal understanding.* New York: Academic Press.

Shaffer, D. R. (1979). *Social and personality development.* Monterey, CA: Brooks/Cole.

Shantz, D. W., & Voydanoff, D. R. (1973). Situational effects on retaliatory aggression at three age levels. *Child Development, 44,* 149–153.

Shea, J. D. C. (1981). Changes in interpersonal distances and categories of play behavior in the early weeks of preschool. *Developmental Psychology, 17,* 417–425.

Shigetomi, C. C., Hartmann, D. P., & Gelfand, D. M. (1981). Sex differences in children's altruistic behavior and reputations for helpfulness. *Developmental Psychology, 17,* 434–437.

Shure, M. B., & Spivack, G. (1978). *Problem-solving techniques in childrearing.* San Francisco: Jossey-Bass.

Simmons, R. G., Blyth, D. A., Van Cleave, E. F., & Bush, D. M. (1979). Entry into early adolescence: The impact of school structure, puberty, and early dating on self-esteem. *American Sociological Review, 44,* 948–967.

Simmons, R. G., Rosenberg, F., & Rosenberg, M. (1973). Disturbance in self-image at adolescence. *American Sociological Review, 38,* 553–568.

Slaby, R. G., & Crowley, C. G. (1977). Modification of cooperation and aggression through teacher attention to children's speech. *Journal of Experimental Child Psychology, 23,* 442–458.

Snow, M. E., Jacklin, C. N., & Maccoby, E. E. (1981). Birth-order differences in peer sociability at thirty-three months. *Child Development, 52,* 589–595.

Sullivan, H. S. (1953). *The interpersonal theory of psychiatry.* New York: Norton.

Teeven, R. C., & McGhee, P. E. (1972). Childhood development of fear of failure motivation. *Journal of Personality and Social Psychology, 21,* 345–348.

Thompson, R. A., & Lamb, M. E. (1983). Security of attachment and stranger sociability in infancy. *Developmental Psychology, 19,* 184–191.

Thompson, S. K. (1975). Gender labels and early sex-role development. *Child Development, 46,* 339–347.

Turnbull, C. M. (1972). *The mountain people.* New York: Simon & Schuster.

Underwood, B., & Moore, B. (1982). Perspective-taking and altruism. *Psychological Bulletin, 91,* 143–173.

Urbain, E. S., & Kendall, P. C. (1980). Review of social-cognitive problem-solving interventions with children. *Psychological Bulletin, 88,* 109–143.

Vandell, D. L., Wilson, K. S., & Buchanan, N. R. (1980). Peer interaction in the first year of life: An examination of its structure, content, and sensitivity to toys. *Child Development, 51,* 481–488.

Vandell, D. L., Wilson, K. S., & Whalen, W. T. (1981). Birth-order and social experiences differences in infant-peer interaction. *Developmental Psychology, 17,* 438–445.

van Doorninck, W. J., Caldwell, B. M., Wright, C., & Frankenberg, W. K. (1981). The relationship between twelve-month home stimulation and school achievement. *Child Development, 52,* 1080–1083.

Vincze, M. (1971). The social contacts of infants and young children reared together. *Early Child Development and Care, 1,* 99–109.

Vygotsky, L. S. (1934). *Thought and language.* Cambridge, MA: M.I.T. Press.

Walters, R. H., & Brown, M. (1963). Studies of reinforcement of aggression: Transfer of responses to an interpersonal situation. *Child Development, 34,* 562–571.

Waterman, A. S. (1982). Identity development from adolescence to adulthood: An extension of theory and a review of research. *Developmental Psychology, 18,* 341–358.

Waters, E., Wippman, J., & Sroufe, L. A. (1979). Attachment, positive affect, and competence in the peer group: Two studies in construct validation. *Child Development, 50,* 821–829.

White, R. W. (1959). Motivation reconsidered: The concept of competence. *Psychological Review, 66,* 297–333.

Whiting, B. B., & Whiting, J. W. M. (1975). *Children of six cultures.* Cambridge, MA: Harvard University Press.

Wichern, F., & Nowicki, S. (1976). Independence training practices and locus of control orientation in children and adolescents. *Developmental Psychology, 12,* 77.

Williams, J. E., Bennett, S. M., & Best, D. L. (1975). Awareness and expression of sex stereotypes in young children. *Developmental Psychology, 11,* 635–642.

Winterbottom, M. (1958). The relation of need for achievement to learning experiences in independence and mastery. In J. Atkinson (Ed.), *Motives in fantasy, action, and society.* Princeton, NJ: Van Nostrand.

Yarrow, L. J., McQuiston, S., MacTurk, R. H., McCarthy, M. E., Klein, R. P., & Vietze, P. M. (1983). Assessment of mastery motivation during the first year of life: Contemporaneous and cross-age relationships. *Developmental Psychology, 19,* 159–171.

Yarrow, M. R., Scott, P. M., & Waxler, C. Z. (1973). Learning concern for others. *Developmental Psychology, 8,* 240–260.

Zahn-Waxler, C., Radke-Yarrow, M., & King, R. A. (1979). Child rearing and children's prosocial initiations toward victims of distress. *Child Development, 50,* 319–330.

CHAPTER THIRTEEN ■

SEX DIFFERENCES AND SEX-ROLE DEVELOPMENT

■ *Categorizing males and females: Sex-role standards*

■ *Some facts and fictions about sex differences*
Sex differences that appear to be real
Attributes that may differentiate the sexes
Cultural myths
Evaluating the accomplishments of males and females

■ *Developmental trends in sex typing*
Development of the gender concept
Acquiring sex-role stereotypes
Development of sex-typed behavior

■ *Theories of sex typing and sex-role development*
The biological approach
Freud's psychoanalytic theory
Social-learning theory
Kohlberg's cognitive-developmental theory
An attempt at integration

■ *Sex typing in the nontraditional family*
Effects of maternal dominance
Effects of father absence
Effects of maternal employment

■ *Psychological androgyny: A new look at sex roles*
Is androgyny a desirable attribute?
Who raises androgynous offspring?
Implications and prescriptions for the future

■ *Summary*

How important is a child's gender to his or her eventual development? The answer seems to be "Very important!" Often the first bit of information that parents receive about their child is his or her sex, and the ramifications of this sex labeling are normally swift in coming and rather direct. In the hospital nursery or delivery room, parents often call an infant son things like "big guy" or "tiger," and they are apt to comment on the vigor of his cries, kicks, or grasps. In contrast, female infants are more likely to be labeled "sugar" or "sweetie" and described as soft, cuddly, and adorable (Maccoby, 1980; MacFarlane, 1977). A newborn infant is usually blessed with a name that reflects his or her sex, and in many Western societies children are immediately adorned in either blue or pink. Mavis Hetherington and Ross Parke (1975, pp. 354–355) describe the predicament of a developmental psychologist who "did not want her observers to know whether they were watching boys or girls":

> Even in the first few days of life some infant girls were brought to the laboratory with pink bows tied to wisps of their hair or taped to their little bald heads. . . . When another attempt at concealment of sex was made by asking mothers to dress their infants in overalls, girls appeared in pink and boys in blue overalls, and "Would you believe overalls with ruffles?"

This gender indoctrination continues during the first year as parents provide their children with "sex-appropriate" clothing, toys, and hairstyles. Moreover, they often play differently with and expect different reactions from their young sons and daughters. Clearly, gender is an important attribute that frequently determines how other people will respond to an infant.

Why do people react differently to males and females—especially *infant* males and females? One explanation centers on the biological differences between the sexes. Recall that fathers determine the gender of their offspring. A zygote that receives an X chromosome from each parent is a genetic (XX) female that will develop into a baby girl, whereas a zygote that receives a Y chromosome from the father is a genetic (XY) male that will normally assume the appearance of a baby boy. Could it be that this basic genetic difference

515

PHOTO 13-1. Sex-role socialization begins very early as parents provide their infants with "gender-appropriate" clothing, toys, and hairstyles.

between the sexes is ultimately responsible for *sex differences in behavior*—differences that might explain why parents often fail to treat their sons and daughters alike? We will explore this interesting idea in some detail in a later section of the chapter.

However, there is more to sex differences than biological heritage. Virtually all societies expect males and females to behave differently and to assume different roles. In order to conform to these expectations, the child must understand that he is a boy or that she is a girl and must incorporate this information into his or her self-concept. In this chapter we will concentrate on the interesting and controversial topic of **sex typing**—the process by which children acquire not only a gender identity but also the motives, values, and behaviors considered appropriate in their culture for members of their biological sex.

We begin the chapter by summarizing what people generally believe to be true about sex differences in personality and social behavior. As it turns out, some of these stereotypes appear to be reasonably accurate, although many others are best described as fictions or fables that have no basis in fact. We will then look at developmental trends in sex typing and see that youngsters are

often well aware of sex-role stereotypes and are displaying sex-typed patterns of behavior long before they are old enough to go to kindergarten. And how do children learn so much about the sexes and sex roles at such an early age? We will address this issue by reviewing several influential theories of sex typing—theories that indicate how biological forces, social experiences, and cognitive development might combine or interact to influence the sex-typing process. Next we will look at sex typing in the nontraditional family and see that factors such as a mother's employment or the absence of a father figure can influence a child's sex-role development. Finally, we will consider a new perspective on sex typing and learn why many theorists now believe that traditional sex roles have outlived their usefulness in the more egalitarian social climate of the 1980s.

CATEGORIZING MALES AND FEMALES: SEX-ROLE STANDARDS

Most of us have learned a great deal about males and females by the time we enter college. In fact, if you and your classmates were asked to jot down ten psychological dimensions on which men and women are thought to differ, it is likely that every member of the class could easily generate such a list. Here's a head start: Which gender is most likely to display emotions? to be tidy? to be competitive? to use harsh language?

A **sex-role standard** is a value, a motive, or a class of behavior that is considered more appropriate for members of one sex than the other. Taken together, a society's sex-role standards describe how males and females are expected to behave and, thus, reflect the stereotypes by which we categorize and respond to members of each sex.

The female's role as childbearer is largely responsible for the sex-role standards that characterize many societies, including our own. Girls are typically encouraged to assume a nurturant, **expressive role,** for as a wife and mother, the female is often assigned the tasks of raising the children she has borne and keeping the family functioning on an even keel. To serve this end, girls are expected to become warm, friendly, cooperative, and sensitive to the needs of others (Parsons, 1955). In contrast, boys are encouraged to adopt an **instrumental** orientation, for as a husband and father, the male faces the tasks of providing for the family and protecting it from harm. Thus, young boys are expected to become dominant, independent, assertive, and competitive—in short, to acquire those attributes that will prepare them to make a living and to serve as intermediaries between the family and society. Roger Brown (1965) describes how this sexual "division of labor" has affected the sex-role stereotypes of American society:

> In the United States, a *real* boy climbs trees, disdains girls, dirties his knees, plays with soldiers, and takes blue for his favorite color. A real girl dresses dolls, jumps rope, plays hopscotch, and takes pink as her favorite color. When they go to school, real girls like English, music, and "auditorium"; real boys prefer manual training, gym, and arithmetic. In college, the boys smoke pipes, drink beer, and major in engineering or physics; the girls chew gum, drink cokes, and major in fine arts. The real boy matures into a "man's man" who plays poker, goes hunting, drinks brandy, and dies in the war; the real girl becomes a "feminine" woman who loves children, embroiders handkerchiefs, drinks weak tea, and "succumbs" to consumption [p. 161].

Needless to say, these traditional standards of masculinity and femininity have become rather controversial in recent years. At this writing, the Equal Rights Amendment to the United States Constitution is being reintroduced in the U.S. Congress, and advocates of women's rights have fought for and won major legal concessions (such as the Equal Opportunity Employment Act) that allow women more freedom to assume the instrumental role so long enjoyed by American males. But in spite of these important (and long overdue) advances, a homogenization of the sex roles is not likely in the foreseeable future. Several recent studies (see Broverman, Vogel, Broverman, Clarkson, & Rosenkrantz, 1972; Shaffer & Johnson, 1980; Werner & LaRussa, 1983) indicate that young adults of both sexes still endorse many traditional standards of masculinity and femininity and prefer other members of their own and the other sex who conform to these stereotypes. Table 13-1 illustrates the traits and characteristics that U.S. college students and mental health professionals assign to "typical" men and women.

Note that most desirable feminine characteristics reflect warmth and emotional expressiveness, whereas the desirable masculine attributes seem to signify a competent or instrumental orientation.

Cross-cultural studies (Best et al., 1977; D'Andrade, 1966) reveal that a large number of societies endorse the sex-role standards and stereotypes shown in Table 13-1. In one rather ambitious project, Herbert Barry, Margaret Bacon, and Irvin Child (1957) analyzed the sex-typing practices of 110 nonindustrialized societies. Two judges rated each society for sex differences in the socialization of five basic attributes: nurturance, obedience, responsibility, achievement, and self-reliance. The results are summarized in Table 13-2. Note that achievement and self-reliance were more often expected of young boys, while young girls were encouraged to become nurturant, responsible, and obedient. The societies that placed the greatest emphasis on this pattern of sex typing were (1) those in which people live in large, cooperative family units where a division of labor is absolutely necessary and (2) those that depend on strength or physical prowess (for example, hunting skills or herding large animals) as a means of obtaining food and earning a living.

Children in modern industrialized societies also face strong sex-typing pressures, even though most people in these countries neither live in extended families nor depend on hunting and herding skills for their livelihood. Although parents may play a major role in this sex-typing process, they hardly stand alone. As we will see, other significant adults (for example, teachers), peers,

---

sex typing: *the process by which a child becomes aware of his or her gender and acquires certain motives, values, and behaviors considered appropriate for members of that sex.*

sex-role standard: *a behavior, value, or motive that members of a society consider more typical or appropriate for members of one sex.*

expressive role: *a social prescription, usually directed toward females, that stresses that one should be cooperative, kind, nurturant, and sensitive to the needs of others.*

instrumental role: *a social prescription, usually directed toward males, that stresses that one should be dominant, independent, assertive, competitive, and goal-oriented.*

TABLE 13-1. Common stereotypes of men and women

Competency cluster (masculine descriptions are considered more desirable)	
Feminine descriptions	*Masculine descriptions*
Not at all aggressive	Very aggressive
Not at all independent	Very independent
Does not hide emotions at all	Almost always hides emotions
Very subjective	Very objective
Very submissive	Very dominant
Very passive	Very active
Not competitive	Very competitive
Very home-oriented	Very worldly
Very sneaky	Very direct
Not adventurous	Very adventurous
Has difficulty making decisions	Can make decisions easily
Not at all self-confident	Very self-confident

Warmth-expressive cluster (feminine descriptions are considered more desirable)	
Feminine descriptions	*Masculine descriptions*
Doesn't use harsh language	Uses very harsh language
Very tactful	Very blunt
Very gentle	Very rough
Very aware of others' feelings	Not at all aware of others' feelings
Very quiet	Very loud
Very neat	Very sloppy
Very strong need for security	Very little need for security
Enjoys art and literature	Does not enjoy art and literature
Easily expresses tender feelings	Does not easily express tender feelings

and even the television set are important in shaping children's attitudes about the sexes and encouraging them to adopt culturally prescribed sex roles.

SOME FACTS AND FICTIONS ABOUT SEX DIFFERENCES

The old French maxim "Vive la difference" reflects a fact that we all know to be true: males and females are anatomically different. Adult males are typically taller, heavier, and more muscular than adult females, while females may be hardier in the sense that they live longer and are less susceptible to many diseases. But although these physical variations are fairly obvious, the evidence for sex differences in psychological functioning is not as clear as most of us might think.

Eleanor Maccoby and Carol Jacklin (1974) have conducted a major review of the literature and concluded that very few of the stereotyped views of men and women are accurate. Maccoby and Jacklin place traditional sex-role standards into the following three basic categories: (1) those that are probably correct, (2) open questions (stereotypes that may be overstated), and (3) those that qualify as "cultural myths" having no basis in fact. Let's begin with the stereotypes that seem to be correct.

TABLE 13-2. Sex differences in the socialization of five attributes

Attribute	Percentage of societies in which socialization pressures were greater for:	
	Boys	Girls
Nurturance	0	82
Obedience	3	35
Responsibility	11	61
Achievement	87	3
Self-reliance	85	0

Note: The percentages for each attribute do not add to 100, because some of the societies did not place differential pressures on boys and girls with respect to that particular attribute. For example, 18% of the societies for which pertinent data were available did not differentiate between the sexes in the socialization of nurturance.

Sex Differences That Appear to Be Real

After reviewing more than 1500 studies, Maccoby and Jacklin state that only four common sex-role stereotypes are reasonably accurate. First, females seem to have greater *verbal abilities* than males. Girls develop verbal skills at an earlier age than boys, although differences between the sexes are very small until adolescence, when female superiority in verbal ability becomes increasingly apparent. However, males outperform females on tests of *visual/spatial ability* (block designs, identifying the same figure from different angles) and *arithmetic reasoning*. Again, sex differences on these measures are not extensive until puberty (ages 12 to 13). Finally, Maccoby and Jacklin came to the conclusion that males are more physically and verbally *aggressive* than females.

Since the publication of Maccoby and Jacklin's influential work, researchers have identified a few additional sex-role stereotypes that seem to be accurate. For example, males are usually found to be more active than females (Eaton & Keats, 1982; Phillips, King, & Dubois, 1978), more willing to take risks (Ginsburg & Miller, 1982), and more receptive to bouts of nonaggressive rough-and-tumble play (DiPietro, 1981). Girls and women appear to be more interested in and more responsive to infants than boys and men are (Blakemore,

1981; Maccoby, 1980). Girls are also less demanding than boys (Martin, 1980) and are more likely to respond playfully to parents' social overtures and to comply with their requests (Gunnar & Donahue, 1980; Hetherington, Cox, & Cox, 1976). After reviewing many of these recent studies, Maccoby (1980) suggests that perhaps there is some truth to the old wives' tale that boys are harder to raise than girls.

However, let's keep in mind that these sex differences reflect *group averages* that may or may not characterize the behavior of any particular individual. For example, some males are as interested in infants as the most nurturant of females, and many girls and women are just as mathematically inclined as the best-performing boys and men. So even though one *group* may differ from another on certain attributes, there are many people within a group who do not fit the pattern. Stated another way, it is impossible to predict the aggressiveness, the mathematical skills, or the verbal abilities of any individual simply by knowing his or her gender. Only when group averages are computed do the sex differences emerge.

PHOTO 13-2. *Rough-and-tumble play is more common among boys than among girls.*

Attributes That May Differentiate the Sexes

The evidence for sex differences on several other social attributes is suggestive at best. As we review these findings, keep in mind that more research will be necessary before we will be able to draw any firm conclusions.

People commonly assume that females are more timid, fearful, and anxious than males, although the data on this issue are mixed. Observational studies of children who are exposed to a variety of situations usually find no sex differences in fearful behavior. However, females are more likely than males to *report* feeling timid, anxious, or fearful. Studies of dominance and competitive behavior often find no sex differences, although males tend to be the more dominant or competitive gender when differences are found. In childhood, girls appear to be more compliant with the demands of parents, teachers, and other authority figures. But girls are no more compliant than boys with the demands and directives of age mates. And although there are data to indicate that 6- to 10-year-old girls are more nurturant than their male counterparts (and perhaps more empathic as well), the findings reviewed in Chapter Twelve indicate that girls are no more altruistic than boys.

Cultural Myths

Several popular sex-role stereotypes are best described as unfounded opinions or "cultural myths" that have no basis in fact. Among the most widely accepted of these "myths" are those in Table 13-3.

Why do these inaccuracies persist? Maccoby and Jacklin (1974) propose that

> a . . . likely explanation for the perpetuation of "myths" is the fact that stereotypes are such powerful things. An ancient truth is worth restating here: if a generalization about a group of people is believed, whenever a member of the group behaves in the expected way the observer notes it and his belief is confirmed and strengthened; when a member of the group behaves in a way that is not consistent with the observer's expectations, the instance is likely to pass unnoticed, and the observer's generalized belief is protected from disconfirmation. We believe that

this well-documented [selective attention] process occurs continually in relation to the expected and perceived behavior of males and females, and results in the perpetuation of myths that would otherwise die out under the impact of negative evidence [p. 355].

In other words, sex-role stereotypes are well-ingrained cognitive schemata that we use to interpret (or misinterpret) the behavior of males and females (Martin & Halverson, 1981). People even use these schemata to classify the behavior of infants. In one study (Condry & Condry, 1976), college students watched a videotape of a 9-month-old child who was introduced as either a girl ("Dana") or a boy ("David"). As the students observed the child at play, they were asked to interpret his/her reactions to toys such as a teddy bear or a jack-in-the-box. The resulting impressions of the child's behavior clearly depended on his or her presumed sex. For example, a strong reaction to the jack-in-the-box was labeled "anger" when the child was presumed to be a male and "fear" when the child had been introduced as a female. Later research indicates that even 3- to 5-year-olds are using sex-role stereotypes to interpret the play activities of infants described as boys or girls (Haugh, Hoffman, & Cowan, 1980).

As it turns out, the persistence of unfounded or inaccurate sex-role stereotypes has important consequences for both males and females. Some of the more negative implications of these cultural myths are discussed in the following section.

Evaluating the Accomplishments of Males and Females

In 1968 Phillip Goldberg asked female college students to judge the merits of several professional articles that were attributed to a male author ("John McKay") or to a female author ("Joan McKay"). Although these manuscripts were identical in every other respect, subjects perceived the articles written by a male to be of higher quality than those by a female.

This tendency to undervalue the accomplishments of females is apparent even when males and females are asked to explain their *own* successes. Kay Deaux (1977) has reviewed several studies in which males and females have succeeded at unfamiliar tasks and finds that "it is far

TABLE 13-3. Some unfounded beliefs about sex differences

Belief	Facts
1. Girls are more "social" than boys.	Research indicates that the two sexes are equally interested in social stimuli, equally responsive to social reinforcement, and equally proficient at learning through the imitation of social models. At certain ages, boys actually spend more time than girls with playmates.
2. Girls are more "suggestible" than boys.	Most studies of children's conformity find no sex differences. However, some researchers have found that boys are more likely than girls to accept peer-group values that conflict with their own.
3. Girls have lower self-esteem than boys.	The sexes are highly similar in their overall self-satisfaction and self-confidence throughout childhood and adolescence. However, men and women differ in the areas in which they have their greatest self-confidence: girls rate themselves higher in social competence, while boys see themselves as dominant or potent. Thus, males and females apply questionable sex-role stereotypes to themselves.
4. Girls are better at simple repetitive tasks, whereas boys excel at tasks that require higher-level cognitive processing.	The evidence does not support these assertions. Neither sex is superior at rote learning, probability learning, or concept formation.
5. Boys are more "analytic" than girls.	Overall, boys and girls do not differ on tests of analytic cognitive style or logical reasoning, although boys do excel if the task requires visual/spatial abilities. .
6. Girls lack achievement motivation.	Under "neutral" conditions girls actually score higher than boys on tests of achievement motivation. Under competitive conditions, the achievement motivation of boys increases to about the level that girls have already attained. Perhaps the myth of lesser achievement motivation for females has persisted because males and females have generally directed their achievement strivings toward different goals.

more common for the female to explain her performance on the basis of luck, whether the outcome is a good or a bad one. Males, on the other hand, are much more likely to claim that ability was responsible for their successes" (p. 467).

Even when luck is not a plausible explanation, people are reluctant to attribute a female's accomplishments to her abilities. Consider the following example. Shirley Feldman-Summers and Sara Kiesler (1974) asked subjects to explain the achievements of either a male or a female physician who had established a highly successful practice after years of work. Luck was seldom used to explain the success of either the male or the female physician. But subjects did tend to attribute the male's success to ability and the female's success to effort. In other words, people believe that women must try harder in order to accomplish the same feats as men. This attitude may explain the finding that employers who must choose between equally qualified male and female applicants will frequently offer a more advanced position or a higher starting salary to the male (Forisha & Goldman, 1981; Terborg & Ilgen, 1975).

Parents may contribute to these sexist attitudes by virtue of the expectancies they have for their children. Recall from Chapter Twelve that mothers and fathers believe that math and science courses are harder and less enjoyable for daughters than for sons. By attributing their daughters' academic accomplishments to "hard work" and their sons' to "high ability," parents seem to be conveying an impression that girls are less competent than boys (Parsons, Adler, & Kaczala, 1982).

Teachers may also reinforce these sex-typed attitudes if they react differently to the accomplishments of their male and female students. Jacquelynne Parsons and her associates (Parsons, Kaczala, & Meese, 1982) report that some elementary school teachers are more likely to praise girls whom they expect to do poorly than girls whom they expect to do well. But just the opposite is true for boys, who are likely to receive more praise when the teacher expects them to achieve. So the praise received by female students may not reflect the teacher's true expectations about their future academic accomplishments. Perhaps you can see how a star female student who is rarely praised for her achievements might eventually conclude that she must lack ability or that academic success is not very important for girls, particularly when both the star male students and her less competent female classmates receive far more praise from the teacher than she does.

Will the picture become brighter for females as they become increasingly prominent in business and the professions? Almost certainly, although the prospects of immediate change are not terribly encouraging. In one interesting experiment, John Touhey (1974) asked males and females to rate the prestige and desirability of five high-status occupations—architect, professor, lawyer, physician, and scientist—after receiving information that the proportion of women entering these fields was either increasing or unchanged. Both male and female subjects rated these professions lower in prestige when they were led to believe that the proportion of women practitioners was increasing. The implication is clear: when women are likely to make significant contributions to a high-status profession, people tend to reassess the value of these contributions (or the value of the profession) rather than the competencies of women. Sex-role stereotypes are very powerful indeed.

When do children first begin to think that males are more competent than females? Very early, or so it seems. Susan Haugh and her colleagues (Haugh et al., 1980) asked 3- and 5-year-olds to watch two infants on film, one of whom was presumed to be a male. When told to point to the baby who was "smart," these preschool children typically chose whichever infant had been labeled the boy. Nick Pollis and Donald Doyle (1972) found that first-grade boys were judged by their male and female classmates to be more competent at a number of unfamiliar tasks and more worthy of leadership roles than first-grade girls. Finally, Claire Etaugh and Barry Brown (1975) asked 10-, 13-, 16-, and 18-year-olds to explain the performance of a male or a female who had either succeeded or failed at some mechanical tasks. The female's success at mechanics was attributed to her untiring efforts to succeed, while the male's success was attributed to his mechanical abilities. However, failure at mechanics was more likely to be attributed to a definite *lack of ability* when the person who had failed was a female. There were no age or "sex of subjects" effects in these studies. So it appears that the tendency to underestimate the abilities and accomplishments of females is well established in both boys and girls by the age of 6 to 10 and possibly much sooner.

DEVELOPMENTAL TRENDS IN SEX TYPING

Sex-typing research has traditionally focused on three separate but interrelated topics: (1) the development of **gender identity**, or the knowledge that one is either a boy or a girl and that gender is an unchanging attribute, (2) the development of sex-role stereotypes, or ideas about what males and females are supposed to be like, and (3) the development of sex-typed patterns of behavior—that is, the child's tendency to favor same-sex activities over those normally associated with the other sex. Let's look first at the child's understanding of gender and its implications.

Development of the Gender Concept

Children initially discriminate "maleness" from "femaleness" on the basis of clothing and hairstyles rather than body types and other morphological characteristics (Katcher, 1955; Thompson & Bentler, 1971). Spencer Thompson (1975) found that some 2-year-olds can readily identify the sex of people shown in pictures, even if the females are wearing short hair or pants. However, these toddlers are often uncertain about their own gender identities. By age 2½ to 3, almost all children can accurately label themselves as either boys or girls, although they have not yet developed a sense of **gender constancy**—a form of conservation in which they recognize that biological sex is unchanging. Indeed, it is not at all uncommon for 3- to 5-year-olds to think that boys can become mommies and girls daddies or that a person who alters his or her appearance (by changing hairstyle and clothing) has become a member of the other sex (Marcus & Overton, 1978; Slaby & Frey, 1975). Children normally begin to conserve gender between the ages of 5 and 7, precisely the time that they are beginning to conserve physical quantities such as liquids and mass (Marcus & Overton, 1978). Apparently 5- to 7-year-olds will apply gender constancy to themselves before they recognize that the gender of other people is invariant (Gouze & Nadelman, 1980). The sequence that youngsters seem to follow is (1) gender constancy for self, (2) gender constancy for same-sex others, (3) gender constancy for members of the other sex (Eaton & Von Bargen, 1981).

Acquiring Sex-Role Stereotypes

Remarkable as it may seem, toddlers begin to acquire sex-role stereotypes at roughly the same time that they first become aware of their gender identities. Deanna Kuhn and her associates (Kuhn, Nash, & Brucken, 1978) showed a male doll ("Michael") and a female doll ("Lisa") to 2½–3½-year-olds and then asked each child which of the two dolls would engage in sex-stereotyped activities such as cooking, sewing, playing with dolls, trucks, or trains, talking a lot, giving kisses, fighting, or climbing trees. Almost all the 2½-year-olds had some knowledge of sex-role stereotypes. For example, boys and girls agreed that girls talk a lot, never hit, often need help, like to play with dolls, and like to help their mothers with chores such as cooking and cleaning. In contrast, these young children felt that boys like to play with cars, like to help their fathers, like to build things, and are apt to make statements such as "I can hit you." The children who knew the most about sex-role stereotypes were those who had some idea that gender is a stable attribute.

Over the next several years, children learn much more about the behavior of males and females and eventually begin to differentiate the sexes on *psychological* dimensions. In a well-known cross-cultural study, Deborah Best and her colleagues (Best et al., 1977) found that fourth- and fifth-graders in England, Ireland, and the United States generally agree that women are weak, emotional, soft-hearted, sophisticated, and affectionate, while men are ambitious, assertive, aggressive, dominating, and cruel. However, the stereotypes held by older grade school children are far more flexible than those of their younger counterparts. For example, a 7-year-old might say that carpentry is a masculine occupation that is not appropriate for a woman, while an 11- to 13-year-old is more likely to argue that females can and perhaps should pursue a "masculine" occupation such as carpentry if they really want to (Carter & Patterson, 1982; Meyer, 1980).

Development of Sex-Typed Behavior

The most common method of assessing the "sex-appropriateness" of children's behavior is to observe whom and what they like to play with. Sex differences in toy preferences develop very early—even before the child has established a clear gender identity or can correctly label various toys as "boy things" or "girl things" (Blakemore, LaRue, & Olejnik, 1979). Boys aged 14 to 22 months usually prefer trucks and cars to other objects, while girls of this age would rather play with dolls and soft toys (Smith & Daglish, 1977). By the time they enter nursery school, children generally play at sex-typed or gender-neutral activities, and they have often segregated into male and female play groups (Strayer, 1977).

Apparently this preference for same-sex playmates also develops very early. In one study (Jacklin & Maccoby, 1978), pairs of 33-month-old

gender identity: *one's awareness of one's gender and its implications.*
gender constancy: *the realization that biological sex is invariant despite superficial changes in a person's appearance, attire, or activities.*

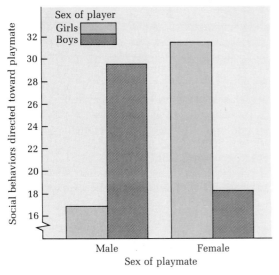

FIGURE 13-1. *Do toddlers prefer playmates of their own sex? Apparently so, for boys are much more sociable with boys than with girls, whereas girls are more outgoing with girls than with boys.*

toddlers were dressed in gender-neutral clothing (T-shirts and pants) and taken to a laboratory playroom that contained several interesting toys. Some of these dyads were same-sex pairs (two boys or two girls), and others were mixed-sex pairs (a boy and a girl). As the children played, an adult observer recorded the frequency with which they engaged in solitary activities and in socially directed play. As we see in Figure 13-2, social play varied as a function of the sex of one's playmate: boys directed more social responses to boys than to girls, while girls were more sociable with girls than with boys.

Many cultures, including our own, assign greater status to the male role (D'Andrade, 1966; Rosenblatt & Cunningham, 1976), and boys face stronger pressures than girls to adhere to sex-appropriate codes of conduct. Consider that fathers of baby girls are generally willing to offer a truck to their 12-month-old daughters, while fathers of baby boys are likely to withhold dolls from their sons (Snow, Jacklin, & Maccoby, 1983). Moreover, parents of 2- to 9-year-olds (particularly fathers) express more concern about their

child's cross-sex play activities if the child is a male (Fagot, 1978; Langlois & Downs, 1980; Tauber, 1979b), and they perceive a wider range of behaviors as appropriate for girls than for boys (Fagot, 1978). Perhaps it can be argued that we live in a male-oriented society where "tomboys" are at least tolerated while "sissies" are ridiculed and rejected. In other words, the male role is more clearly defined than the female role, and boys, who face stronger sex-typing pressures than girls, will soon learn what is or is not expected of them as they are criticized for deviating from approved sex-role standards. Walter Emmerich (1959) has suggested that the major accomplishment for young girls is to learn how not to be babies, while young boys must learn how not to be girls.

Indeed, males are quicker than females to adopt sex-typed preferences and patterns of behavior. Judith Blakemore and her associates (Blakemore et al., 1979) found that 2-year-old boys already favor sex-appropriate toys while 2-year-old girls do not. Even at age 3, many girls will not prefer feminine to masculine toys unless they are first reminded that the feminine toys are more "appropriate" for them (Blakemore et al., 1979). Finally, 3- to 4-year-old boys are more likely than 3- to 4-year-old girls to say that they dislike opposite-sex toys (Eisenberg, Murray, & Hite, 1982).

Between the ages of 4 and 10, both males and females are becoming more aware of what is expected of them and conforming to these cultural prescriptions. However, girls are more likely than boys to retain an interest in cross-sex toys, games, and activities (Brown, 1957; Ward, 1973). For example, John Richardson and Carl Simpson (1982) recorded the toy preferences of 750 children aged 5 to 9 years as expressed in their letters to Santa Claus. Although their requests were clearly sex-typed, we see in Table 13-4 that more girls than boys were asking for "opposite sex" items. With respect to their actual sex-role preferences, young girls often wish they were boys, but it is unusual for a boy to wish he were a girl (Brown, 1957; Nash, 1975).

There are probably several reasons that girls are drawn to male activities and the masculine role during middle childhood. For one thing, they are becoming increasingly aware that masculine behavior is more highly valued, and perhaps it is only natural that girls would want to be what is "best" (or at least something other than a second-class citizen). And as we have noted, girls are much freer than boys to engage in cross-sex pursuits. Finally, it is conceivable that fast-moving masculine games and "action" toys are simply more interesting than the playthings and pastimes (dolls, dollhouses, dish sets, cleaning and caretaking activities) often imposed on girls to encourage their adoption of a nurturant, expressive orientation. Consider the reaction of Gina, a 5-year-old who literally squealed with delight when she received an "action garage" (complete with lube racks, gas pumps, cars, tools, and spare parts) from Santa one Christmas. At the unveiling of this treasure, Gina and her three female cousins (aged 3, 5, and 7) immediately ignored their dolls, dollhouses, and other unopened gifts to cluster around and play with this unusual and intriguing toy.

In spite of their earlier interest in masculine activities, most girls come to prefer the feminine role as they reach puberty, become preoccupied with their changing body images, and face strong

"Please don't bring me anything that requires my acting out traditional female roles."

social pressures to be "little ladies" (Brown, 1957; Kagan & Moss, 1962).

■ *Social-class differences in sex typing*

Patterns of sex typing differ somewhat for children from the lower and the middle classes. In 1950 Meyer Rabban found that youngsters from lower-class backgrounds were more likely than middle-class age mates to prefer sex-appropriate toys and activities. Lower-class boys indicated a strong preference for masculine activities by age 4 or 5. Lower-class girls and middle-class boys were firmly sex-typed by age 7. However, middle-class girls did not clearly prefer feminine pastimes until the age of 9. These class differences in sex typing are still apparent today. In both England and the United States, children from the lower socioeconomic strata usually show stronger preferences for sex-typed behaviors and hold a more stereotyped view of males and females than middle-class children (Angrist, Mickelson, & Penna, 1977; Morgan, 1982; Nadelman, 1970, 1974).

Several factors contribute to social-class differences in sex typing. For example, we know that parents from the lower socioeconomic strata are more likely than middle-class parents to accept traditional, nonegalitarian sex-role standards (Meyer, 1980; Thompson, 1975). Furthermore, lower-class mothers emphasize and encourage sex typing to a greater degree than middle-class

TABLE 13-4. Percentages of boys and girls who requested popular "masculine" and "feminine" items from Santa Claus

	Percentage of boys requesting	Percentage of girls requesting
Masculine items		
Vehicles	43.5	8.2
Sports equipment	25.1	15.1
Spatial-temporal toys (construction sets, clocks, and so on)	24.5	15.6
Race cars	23.4	5.1
Real vehicles (tricycles, bikes, motorbikes)	15.3	9.7
Feminine items		
Dolls (adult female)	.6	27.4
Dolls (babies)	.6	23.4
Domestic accessories	1.7	21.7
Dollhouses	1.9	16.1
Stuffed animals	5.0	5.4

mothers (Kohn, 1959). Finally, lower-class and middle-class parents may act as very different kinds of models for their children. Many lower-class fathers are employed as heavy laborers, mechanics, or construction workers—occupations that are generally regarded as highly masculine. In contrast, middle-class fathers are often employed at white-collar jobs that may not be perceived as exclusively masculine, and they are more likely than lower-class fathers to take part in "feminine" activities such as housekeeping and child care. Although a large percentage of women from each social class have entered the labor force, mothers from the lower socioeconomic strata tend to work at traditionally feminine jobs such as waitressing or clerking, while middle-class mothers may work at occupations such as business, law, and medicine that are not exclusively feminine. In sum, it appears that many children from lower-class backgrounds are more firmly sex-typed than those from the middle class because their parents are more likely than middle-class parents to *encourage* and to *display* sex-typed patterns of behavior.

■ *Stability of sex-typed behaviors*

Are highly sex-typed children likely to become highly sex-typed adults? The Fels longitudinal project attempted to answer this question by measuring the stability of several types of behavior in a group of middle-class children who were studied from birth to early adulthood (Kagan & Moss, 1962). Seven classes of behavior were examined: passivity, dependence, behavior disorganization (for example, angry outbursts, aggression), heterosexual activity, spontaneity, achievement, and sex-typed activities (for example, interest in mechanics for boys and cooking for girls). Figure 13-2 summarizes the relationships between childhood and adult measures for each of these attributes. In examining the figure, we see that certain behaviors—namely, achievement, sex-typed activity, and spontaneity—were found to be reasonably stable over time for members of each sex. By contrast, aggression and heterosexual activities were stable for males but not for females, whereas passivity and dependence were much more stable for females than males.

How can we account for this pattern of results? Kagan and Moss (1962) suggest that a particular class of behavior will remain stable over time if

these actions are consistent with culturally prescribed sex roles. In the United States, achievement and sex-typed activities are encouraged in *both* boys and girls, so that these attributes should remain stable over time for members of each sex. However, aggression and the initiation of heterosexual activities are generally considered more appropriate for (or characteristic of) males, and these attributes were stable only for males. Finally, passivity and dependence, which many people think of as "feminine" attributes, were stable for females but not for males. So it appears that childhood behaviors that match traditional sex-role standards are encouraged and will remain stable over time, while behaviors that conflict with these cultural prescriptions are apt to be discouraged and will not predict similar behaviors in adulthood. Although there are undoubtedly many exceptions to the rule, the Fels longitudinal data suggest that highly sex-typed 6- to 10-year-olds will often become highly sex-typed adults.

THEORIES OF SEX TYPING AND SEX-ROLE DEVELOPMENT

Several theories have been proposed to account for sex differences and the development of sex roles. On the one hand, theorists who stress biological processes suggest that genetic, anatomical, and hormonal variations between the sexes are largely responsible for sex-linked behavioral differences, which, in turn, will predispose males and females to adopt gender-consistent sex roles. On the other hand, many developmentalists believe that *social* factors are crucial in determining both sex differences in behavior and the outcomes of the sex-typing process. Historically, the most influential of these "social" theories have been Freud's psychoanalytic model, social-learning theory, and Lawrence Kohlberg's cognitive-developmental approach. In this section of the chapter, we will briefly review these theories and discuss the strengths and weaknesses of each.

The Biological Approach

From a biological perspective, males differ from females in five important respects:

1. *Sex chromosomes*—XY for males, XX for females.
2. *Hormonal balance*—for example, males higher in androgen; females higher in estrogen.
3. *Composition of gonads*—testicular tissue for males; ovarian tissue for females.
4. *Internal reproductive system*—testes, seminal vesicles, and prostate for males; vagina, uterus, ovaries, and fallopian tubes for females.
5. *External genitalia*—penis and scrotum for males; labia and clitoris for females.

How do these physical variations affect sex typing? Some theorists have argued that genetic and hormonal differences between the sexes are responsible for several sex-linked characteristics that are apparent at birth or shortly thereafter. For example, female infants are said to be hardier, to mature faster, to talk sooner, and to be more sensitive to pain than male infants, while larger, more muscular males tend to sleep less, to cry more, and to be somewhat more active, more irritable, and harder to comfort than female infants (see Bell, Weller, & Waldrip, 1971; Hutt, 1972; Maccoby, 1980; Moss, 1967). If these sex differences are constitutionally based, it might seem that males and females are biologically programmed for certain activities that are congruent with the masculine or the feminine role. Could boys, for example, be predisposed toward activities such as aggression, assertiveness, and rough-and-tumble play by virtue of their higher pain thresholds, heightened activity, irritable or demanding dispositions, and muscular physiques? Could docile, undemanding, and highly verbal females be ideally suited for adoption of a nurturant, cooperative, expressive orientation?

People often assume that most sex differences are biologically determined, since biology is responsible for some (namely, the five physical

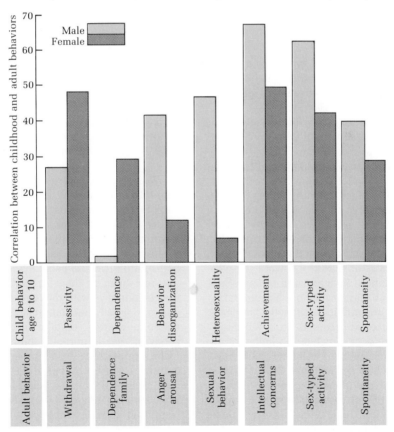

FIGURE 13-2. *Stability of seven classes of behavior between childhood and early adulthood.*

PHOTO 13-3. Are young girls genetically predisposed toward cooperative forms of play? Biological theories of sex typing suggest that this may be the case.

characteristics listed above). A more likely possibility is that sex-linked constitutional factors *interact* with environmental events to produce sex-typed patterns of behavior (Maccoby, 1980). For example, parents may play more vigorously with active, muscular sons than with docile, less muscular daughters. Or perhaps they become more impatient with irritable and demanding sons who are difficult to quiet or comfort. In the first case, adults would be encouraging young boys to partake in the kinds of fast-paced, vigorous activities from which aggressive outbursts may emerge. In the second case, a parent's irritability with an agitated son could have the effect of making the child hostile or resentful toward the parent. So sex differences in aggression or any other form of sex-typed behavior may not be automatic, or "biologically programmed." Indeed, it appears that a child's biological predispositions are likely to affect the *behavior* of caregivers and other close companions, which, in turn, will elicit certain reactions from the child and influence the activities and interests that the child is likely to display. The implication of this interactive model is that biological factors and social influences are completely intertwined and that both nature and nur-

ture are important contributors to a child's sex-role development.

In the pages that follow, we will first consider some of the biological factors that contribute to sex differences and sex-typed patterns of behavior. Then we will take a look at the research suggesting that biology is not destiny.

■ *Chromosomal differences between the sexes*

Corinne Hutt (1972) believes that genetic differences between the sexes may account for the finding that boys are more vulnerable to problems such as reading disabilities, speech defects, various emotional disorders, and certain forms of mental retardation. Since genetic (XY) males have but one X chromosome, they are necessarily more susceptible to any X-linked recessive disorder for which their mother is a carrier (genetic [XX] females would have to inherit a recessive gene from each parent to have the same disorder). And since males have more genetic information (by virtue of having some genes that appear only on a Y chromosome), they show a wider variety of attributes, including some negative ones.

Psychological theories of sex typing cannot easily explain why males face greater risks of developmental disorders than females do. Hutt's chromosomal hypothesis is an interesting explanation for this puzzling difference between the sexes—one that should be investigated further.

■ *Hormonal influences*

Some sex differences are at least partly attributable to the uneven distribution of sex hormones between males and females. Studies of lower animals reveal that changes in a developing organism's hormonal balance are likely to have both anatomical and behavioral effects. For example, one team of investigators injected pregnant rhesus monkeys with the male hormone testosterone and noted that the female offspring showed malelike external genitalia and a pattern of social behavior that is normally more characteristic of males (Young, Goy, & Phoenix, 1964). These masculinized females often threatened other monkeys, engaged in rough-and-tumble play, and would try to "mount" a partner as males do at the beginning of a sexual encounter. Frank Beach (1965) reports that female rat pups that received testosterone injections in the first three days of life frequently displayed masculine sexual responses such as "mounting" as adults. The reverse was true for males. That is, castrated pups, which could not produce testosterone, exhibited feminine sexual characteristics such as receptive posturing as adults. Similar cross-sex mating behaviors occur among female hamsters that receive injections of the male hormone androgen as infants (Doty, Carter, & Clemens, 1971).

Although the evidence is limited, it appears that human beings may be subject to the same kinds of hormonal influences. For example, a small percentage of males are affected by a genetic anomaly known as **testicular feminization syndrome.** A male fetus who inherits this trait is insensitive to the male hormone androgen and will develop external genitalia that resemble those of a female.

John Money and his associates (Ehrhardt & Baker, 1974; Money, 1965; Money & Ehrhardt, 1972) call our attention to the reverse effect in females. Before the consequences were known, some mothers who had had problems carrying pregnancies to term were given an androgenlike drug to prevent miscarriage. This treatment had the effect of masculinizing female fetuses: if their mothers were taking the drug during the period when the genitals were developing, these genetic (XX) females were born with a female internal reproductive system and external organs that resembled those of a male (for example, a large clitoris that looked like a penis and fused labial folds that resembled a scrotum).

Money and Ehrhardt (1972; Ehrhardt & Baker, 1974) have followed several of these **androgenized females** whose external organs were surgically altered and who were then raised as girls. Compared with their sisters and other female age mates, many of the androgenized girls were little tomboys who preferred to dress in slacks and shorts, showed almost no interest in jewelry and cosmetics, and clearly favored vigorous athletic activities (and male playmates) over traditionally feminine pastimes. Moreover, their attitudes toward sexuality and achievement were similar to those of males. They expressed some interest in marriage and motherhood but thought in terms of a late marriage with few children—events that should be delayed until they had es-

tablished themselves in a career.[1] Although it could be argued that other family members had reacted to the girls' abnormal genitalia and treated them more like boys, interviews with the girls' parents suggested that they had not (Ehrhardt & Baker, 1974). So we must seriously consider the possibility that prenatal exposure to male hormones affects the attitudes, interests, and activities of human females.

Sex differences in aggression appear so early (about age 2) in so many cultures that it is difficult to attribute them solely to parental child-rearing practices (Maccoby & Jacklin, 1980). It has been suggested that males are more aggressive than females because of their higher levels of androgen and testosterone—male sex hormones that are thought to promote aggressive responses. Indeed, Dan Olweus and his associates (Olweus, Mattsson, Schalling, & Low, 1980) found that 16-year-old boys who label themselves physically and verbally aggressive do have higher testosterone levels than boys who view themselves as non-aggressive. And in their study of androgenized females, Ehrhardt and Baker (1974) report that, in the majority of families, it was the androgenized sibling who started fights with her nonandrogenized sister, rather than the other way around. However, we must be cautious in interpreting these findings, for a person's hormone level may depend on his or her experiences. For example, Irwin Bernstein and his associates (Rose, Bernstein, & Gordon, 1975) found that the testosterone levels of male rhesus monkeys rose after they had won a fight and fell after they had been defeated.

---

[1]Although these androgenized females began dating somewhat later than other girls, they were heterosexually inclined, choosing males as sex partners in real life and in their fantasies.

> **testicular feminization syndrome:** *a genetic anomaly in which a male fetus is insensitive to the effects of male sex hormones and will develop femalelike external genitalia.*
>
> **androgenized females:** *females who develop malelike external genitalia because of an exposure to male sex hormones during the prenatal period.*

So it appears that higher concentrations of the male sex hormones may be either a cause or an effect of aggressive behavior (Maccoby & Jacklin, 1980).

■ The "timing of puberty" effect

In recent years, investigators have found a relationship between the timing of puberty and children's performance on tests of visual/spatial abilities: both males and females who mature late perform better on spatial tests than those who mature early (Newcombe & Bandura, 1983; Waber, 1977). Since boys reach puberty some two years later than girls, this **"timing of puberty" effect** may help to explain why males outperform females on tests of spatial reasoning.

Why should the timing of puberty affect spatial abilities? One hypothesis is that the lateralization of spatial functions in the right cerebral hemisphere continues until puberty, so that those who mature early will be less specialized for spatial abilities than those who mature late (Waber, 1977). Although this is an interesting and highly controversial idea, the available evidence is far too limited to allow any firm conclusions.

■ Why biology is not destiny

Even though biological factors may predispose males and females toward different patterns of behavior, many developmentalists believe that these "forces of nature" can be modified by social experience. There are at least three lines of evidence to support this contention: John Money's work with androgenized females, Margaret Mead's cross-cultural studies of sex typing, and Nora Newcombe's recent research on the "timing of puberty" effect.

Recall that Money's androgenized females were born with the internal reproductive organs of a normal female even though their external genitalia resembled a penis and scrotum. These children are sometimes labeled boys at birth and raised as such until their abnormalities are detected. Money (1965; Money & Ehrhardt, 1972) reports that the discovery and correction of this condition (by surgery and gender reassignment) presented few if any adjustment problems for the child, provided that the sex change took place *before the age of 18 months*. But after age 3, sexual reassignment was exceedingly difficult because these genetic females had experienced prolonged

masculine sex typing and had already labeled themselves as boys. These data led Money to conclude that there is a "critical period" between 18 months and 3 years of age for the establishment of gender identity.[2] At the very least, Money's findings (see also Box 13-1) indicate that social labels and sex-role socialization play a prominent and perhaps crucial role in determining a child's sex-role preferences and behaviors.

Margaret Mead's (1935) observations of three primitive tribes lead to the same conclusion. Mead noted that both males and females of the Arapesh tribe were taught to be cooperative, non-aggressive, and sensitive to the needs of others. This behavioral profile would be considered "expressive" or "feminine" in most Western cultures. In contrast, both men and women of the Mundugumor tribe were expected to be hostile, aggressive, and emotionally unresponsive in their interpersonal relationships—a masculine pattern of behavior by Western standards. Finally, the Tchambuli displayed a pattern of sex-role development opposite to that of Western societies: males were passive, emotionally dependent, and socially sensitive, whereas females were dominant, independent, and aggressive. In sum, members of these three tribes developed in accordance with the sex roles prescribed by their culture—even when these roles were quite inconsistent with sex-linked biological predispositions.

Nora Newcombe and Mary Bandura (1983) have recently found a "timing of puberty" effect for 11- to 12-year-old girls: those who mature late perform better on tests of spatial abilities than those who mature early. But in this study, measures of hemispheric lateralization of the brain were *unrelated* to either the timing of puberty or spatial performance. The factors that did predict the spatial abilities of these normal, nonandrogenized females were (1) timing of puberty, of course (a biological variable), and (2) measures of the girls' desire to be boys and their interest in masculine activities—interests that appear to be *socially*

---

[2]It is probably more accurate to call the first three years a *sensitive* period, for recent research indicates that one group of genetic males who had been raised as females were able to accept a masculine identity at *puberty* once their bodies assumed a more malelike appearance (Imperato-McKinley, Peterson, Gautier, & Sturla, 1979).

BOX 13-1
A CASE STUDY IN SEXUAL
REASSIGNMENT

The impact of socialization on sex-role development is readily apparent in a case study reported by Money and Tucker (1975). The patient was a male identical twin whose penis was damaged beyond repair during circumcision. After seeking medical advice and considering the alternatives, the parents subjected their 21-month-old child to a surgical procedure designed to make him a female.

After the operation, the child's mother began to actively sex-type her new daughter by changing the child's hairstyle and dressing her in pink slacks, frilly blouses, dresses, and the like. The child soon learned many sex-appropriate attitudes and behaviors such as aspiring to motherhood and sitting to urinate, and within a year or two people could easily determine which of the identical twins was the female. By the age of 5, the girl had developed strong preferences for feminine toys, activities, and apparel. Unlike her brother, she was neat and dainty. If similar cases of early gender reassignment provide any guidelines, this young girl will retain her preference for feminine interests and activities and will lead a reasonably satisfying life as a female.

The implications are obvious. Here is a circumstance in which a *normal* genetic male was sexually reassigned and socialized into the feminine role. The male twin was very dissimilar in his sex-role orientation, preference, and pattern of sex-typed behaviors, even though his genetic constitution was identical to that of his sister. Thus, biology alone does not determine the course of sex typing. Assigned sex and sex-role socialization are important factors that in this case overcame biological predispositions.

transmitted. Finally, timing of puberty itself was not related to the girls' preferences for the male role or masculine activities. The investigators concluded that

> the sexes differ not only in timing of puberty but also in possession of masculine personality traits and interests. . . . Since timing of puberty and [measures of masculine interests] were found to be independently related to spatial ability, either factor could potentially explain sex-differences in spatial ability. . . . Both possibilities need investigation [p. 222].

In sum, the evidence we have reviewed indicates that biology is not destiny; sex-linked biological predispositions can be modified and possibly even reversed by social and cultural influences. John Money and Anke Ehrhardt (1972) take note of this fact in their recent biosocial theory of sex typing. This theory is appropriately labeled *bio*social because it emphasizes the biological factors that determine how other people will respond to the child.

■ *Money and Ehrhardt's biosocial theory*

Money and Ehrhardt (1972) propose that there are a number of critical episodes or events that will affect a person's eventual preference for the masculine or the feminine sex role. The first critical event occurs at conception as the child inherits either an X or a Y chromosome from the father. Over the next six weeks, the developing embryo has only an undifferentiated gonad, and the sex chromosomes determine whether this structure becomes the male testes or the female ovaries. If a Y chromosome is present, the embryo develops testes; otherwise ovaries will form.

These newly formed gonads then determine the outcome of episode 2. The testes of a male embryo secrete two hormones—*testosterone,* which stimulates the development of a male internal reproductive system, and *mullerian inhibiting substance* (MIS), which inhibits the development of female organs. In the absence of these hormones, the embryo develops the internal reproductive system of a female.

At choice point 3 (three to four months after conception), testosterone secreted by the testes leads to the development of a penis and scrotum. If testosterone is absent (as in normal females) or if the male fetus is insensitive to the male sex hormones, the female external genitalia will form. This is the point at which a female fetus may develop the external genitalia of a male if exposed to a heavy dose of male sex hormones through drugs that the mother is taking or because of a genetic dysfunction of its own adrenal glands (of

"timing of puberty" effect: *the finding that people who reach puberty late perform better on visual/spatial tasks than those who mature early.*

course, these androgenized females have no testes; their saclike "scrotums" are empty). Money and Ehrhardt also believe that testosterone alters the development of the brain and the nervous system, thereby suppressing the production of female sex hormones in males, which will ultimately prevent males from experiencing menstrual cycles at puberty.

The next major development occurs during the first three years after birth. Parents and other social agents label and begin to sex-type the child on the basis of the appearance of his or her genitals. In addition, the child will become more aware of his or her body type and learn how males and females are supposed to look. By age 3, most children have established a basic gender identity and are now well aware that they are boys or girls. Money considers this a critical development because he has found that children who undergo gender reassignment after age 3 usually experience serious adjustment problems and may never feel comfortable with their newly assigned sex.

Later, at puberty, changes in hormonal functioning are responsible for the growth of the reproductive system, the appearance of secondary sex characteristics, and the development of sexual

urges. These events, in combination with one's earlier self-concept, provide the basis for adult gender identity and sex-role preferences (see Figure 13-3).

Although Money and Ehrhardt believe that social forces play an important role in the sex-typing process, their theory emphasizes the early biological developments that people are responding to when deciding how to raise a child. Other theorists have focused more intently on the socialization process itself, trying to identify the kinds of experiences that will convince children that they are boys who should adopt a masculine orientation or girls who should favor feminine pursuits. The first of these "social" theories was Sigmund Freud's psychoanalytic approach—a highly controversial perspective on sex typing to which we will now turn.

Freud's Psychoanalytic Theory

Freud's explanation of psychosexual development acknowledges the contributions of both social and biological factors. Recall from our discussion of psychoanalytic theory in Chapter Two

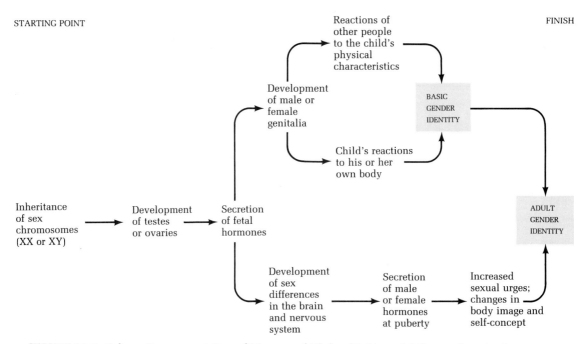

FIGURE 13-3. *Schematic representation of Money and Ehrhardt's biosocial theory of sex typing.*

that sexuality (the sex instinct) was said to be innate. Freud also believed that everyone is constitutionally bisexual, having inherited, in varying proportions, the biological attributes of both sexes. What, then, is responsible for the child's adoption of a sexual identity consistent with his or her (predominant) biological sex?

Freud's answer was that sex typing occurs through the process of **identification.** Recall that identification is the child's tendency to emulate another person, usually the parent of the same sex. Freud argued that a 3- to 6-year-old boy will internalize masculine attitudes and behaviors when he is forced to identify with his father (the aggressor) as a means of renouncing his incestuous desires for his mother, reducing his **castration anxiety,** and thus resolving the **Oedipus complex.** According to Freud, a boy may show inadequate sex typing or homosexual tendencies later in life if his father is inadequate as a masculine model, often absent from the home, or not sufficiently threatening to foster a strong identification; if the boy inherited a relatively strong feminine constitution; or if some combination of these factors is operating.

Freud argued that sex typing is somewhat more difficult for girls. During the oedipal period, a young girl's affectional ties to her mother are normally weakened because the mother is now perceived as a competitor for the father's love. But unlike her brother, the girl does not fear castration for her rivaling conduct; indeed, there is no analogue of castration anxiety that would compel a daughter to identify with her mother and resolve her **Electra complex.**

Why, then, would a girl ever develop a preference for the feminine role? For two reasons: (1) the mother retains some of her attractiveness from the pre-oedipal period, when she had served as the girl's benevolent caretaker, and (2) the father is likely to reinforce his daughter for "feminine" behavior—an act that increases the attractiveness of the mother, who serves as the girl's model of femininity. Freud believed that a girl could become a tomboy or perhaps even a lesbian later in life if she failed to identify with her mother (or overidentified with her father), if she had inherited a relatively strong masculine constitution, or if her mother proved inadequate as a feminine model.

Some of the evidence we have reviewed is gen-

PHOTO 13-4. *According to psychoanalytic theory, children become appropriately "masculine" or "feminine" by identifying with the same-sex parent.*

erally consistent with Freudian theory. Recall that young children are rapidly acquiring sex-role stereotypes and developing sex-typed behaviors at roughly the same age that Freud says they will (3 to 6). And the finding that sex typing takes a little longer for girls than for boys is also in line with Freudian theory. Finally, the notion that fathers play an important role in the sex typing of their daughters has now been confirmed (Hetherington,

---

identification: *Freud's term for the child's tendency to emulate another person, usually the same-sex parent.*

castration anxiety: *in Freud's theory, a young boy's fear that his father will castrate him as punishment for his rivalrous conduct.*

Oedipus complex: *Freud's term for the conflict that 4- to 6-year-old boys were said to experience when they develop an incestuous desire for their mothers and a jealous and hostile rivalry with their fathers.*

Electra complex: *female version of the Oedipus complex, in which a 4- to 6-year-old girl was thought to envy her father for possessing a penis and would choose him as a sex object in the hope that he would share with her this valuable organ that she lacked.*

1967; Lamb, 1981; Langlois & Downs, 1980; Snow et al., 1983).

However, the results of several other studies are very damaging to psychoanalytic theory. The idea that young children experience an Oedipus complex including castration anxiety for boys and penis envy for girls assumes that 3- to 6-year-olds are well aware of the differences between the male and female genitalia. Yet, as we saw in Chapter Two, 4- to 5-year-olds are inept at assembling dolls so that the genitals match other parts of the dolls' bodies (Katcher, 1955). These oedipal-aged children, who knew that they were boys or girls, made mistakes that showed they were ignorant about sex differences in genital anatomy (see also McConaghy, 1979). So it is hardly plausible that 3- to 6-year-olds would experience an Oedipus (or Electra) complex with castration anxiety or penis envy.

Other investigators have found that boys show a stronger identification with their fathers and heightened masculinity when fathers are warm and nurturant rather than overly punitive or threatening (Hetherington & Frankie, 1967; Mussen & Rutherford, 1963). These data are clearly inconsistent with the Freudian notion that a boy's sex-role development is furthered by experiencing a hostile relationship with a threatening father.

In sum, Freud's explanation of sex typing has not received much empirical support even though children begin to develop sex-role preferences at about the time that he specified. Let's now consider the social-learning interpretation of sex typing to see whether this approach looks any more promising.

Social-Learning Theory

Prominent social-learning theorists (Bandura, 1977; Mischel, 1970) have argued that children acquire their gender identities, sex-role preferences, and sex-typed behaviors in two ways: through direct tuition and observational learning. *Direct tuition* refers to the tendency of parents, teachers, and other social agents to reinforce the child's sex-appropriate responses and to punish those behaviors that they consider more appropriate for members of the other sex. Thus, boys are encouraged to be tough, assertive, and competitive and to play with action toys such as

trucks or guns; girls are encouraged to be gentle and cooperative and to play with toys such as dolls or dish sets that require them to assume a nurturant, caretaking role. In addition, every child learns a variety of sex-typed attitudes and behaviors by observing the activities of same-sex models, including peers, teachers, older siblings, and media personalities, as well as the mother or the father. Walter Mischel (1970) has noted that children do not necessarily identify with (that is, hope to emulate) all the models who contribute to their sex-role development. Indeed, imitative responses that psychoanalysts call "identification" are just as easily described as examples of observational learning.

■ *Direct tuition of sex roles*

Are parents actively involved in the sex typing of their children? Yes, indeed, and the shaping of sex-typed behaviors begins rather early. Beverly Fagot (1978) studied 24 families, each of which included a mother, a father, and a single child between the ages of 20 and 24 months. Each family was observed in the home for five one-hour periods, during which the child's behaviors and the reactions of the parents were carefully recorded. Fagot noted that parental responses to certain classes of behavior *clearly depended on the sex of the toddler*. On the one hand, parents reinforced their daughters for dancing, dressing up (as women), following them around, asking for assistance, and playing with dolls. Daughters were discouraged from manipulating objects, running, jumping, and climbing. On the other hand, boys were punished for "feminine" activities (playing with dolls, seeking help) and encouraged to play with "masculine" items such as blocks, trucks, and push-and-pull toys that require large-muscle activity. Parents perceived aggression and rough-and-tumble play as more appropriate for boys than for girls, although they did not encourage their sons to display these behaviors. Fagot also noted that boys were more likely to be punished for feminine behaviors than were girls for masculine behaviors.

Encouragement of sex-appropriate behavior is even more apparent during the preschool years. A glance at the bedrooms of boys and girls is revealing in itself: boys' rooms are likely to contain outer-space toys, sporting equipment, construction sets, and vehicles, while girls' rooms will typically include dolls, domestic toys, floral furnishings, and ruffles (MacKinnon, Brody, & Stoneman, 1982).

Judith Langlois and Chris Downs (1980) recently compared the reactions of mothers, fathers, and peers to 3–5-year-old children who were asked (by the experimenter) to play with either same-sex or cross-sex toys. Fathers showed the clearest pattern by rewarding their children for playing with same-sex items and punishing cross-sex play. Mothers showed this same pattern with their daughters but tended to reward their sons for playing with either masculine or feminine toys. Finally, peers were especially critical of children who played with cross-sex toys, often ridiculing the offender or disrupting this "inappropriate" play.

In sum, it appears that the child's earliest preferences for sex-typed toys and activities may result from the tendency of parents (particularly fathers) to actively encourage sex-appropriate behavior and to punish acts that they consider sex-inappropriate. As the child grows older, other people, such as teachers, Scout leaders, and especially peers, will become increasingly important as sources of reinforcement for sex-typed attitudes and behaviors (Roopnarine, 1984).

■ *Observational learning*

According to Albert Bandura (1977), children acquire a large percentage of their sex-typed attributes by observing and imitating the actions of same-sex models. Bandura believes that there are two reasons a child might pay particular attention to models of his or her own sex. First, young children may often be reinforced for imitating same-sex siblings or parents. Indeed, you have probably heard a proud parent make statements such as "That's my little man; you're just like daddy!" or "You're as pretty as your mommy when you dress up like that!" As the child acquires a firm gender identity, a second factor comes into play. Same-sex models are now more worthy of attention because children perceive them as *similar* to themselves.

One problem with Bandura's hypothesis is that children do *not* pay more attention to same-sex models until relatively late—about 6 to 7 years of age (Ruble, Balaban, & Cooper, 1981; Slaby & Frey, 1975). In fact, John Masters and his associates (Masters, Ford, Arend, Grotevant, & Clark, 1979)

found that preschool children are much more concerned about the sex-appropriateness of the *behavior* they are observing than the sex of the model who displays it. For example, 4- to 5-year-old boys will play with objects labeled "boys' toys" even after they have seen a girl playing with them. However, these youngsters are reluctant to play with "girls' toys" that boy models have played with earlier. In other words, children's toy choices are affected more by the labels attached to the toys than by the sex of the child who served as a model. But once children recognize that gender is an unchanging aspect of their personalities (at age 6 to 7), they do begin to attend selectively to same-sex models and are now likely to avoid toys and activities that members of the other sex seem to enjoy (Ruble et al., 1981).

A central tenet of social-learning theory is that a large number of same-sex models will contribute to the child's sex-role development. If this is so, we might expect that the child will become less like the father or the mother as he or she matures and is frequently exposed to same-sex teachers, peers, media personalities, and the like. Indeed, studies of parent/child similarities reveal that school-age children and adolescents are not notably similar to either parent (Maccoby & Jacklin, 1974). One investigator (Tolar, 1968) found that college males actually resembled their mothers more than their fathers! Surely these findings are

PHOTO 13-5. *According to social-learning theory, many same-sex models will contribute to a child's sex-role development.*

damaging to any theory (particularly the psycho-analytic approach) that claims that children acquire important personality traits by identifying with the same-sex parent.

The family as a social system.   The number of children in a family and their distribution by age and sex affect the sex-role behaviors of *all* family members (Rosenberg & Sutton-Smith, 1964; Sutton-Smith & Rosenberg, 1970; Tauber, 1979a). For example, fathers who have two daughters tend to portray a more "masculine" image than fathers who have a son and a daughter. At first, this finding seems puzzling. But it is conceivable that fathers in girl/girl families must spend a large amount of time playing the complementary (masculine) role in order to successfully encourage the femininity of *two* girls.

The impact of siblings on sex typing is not well understood. It might seem as if both boys and girls would be more traditionally sex-typed if they had a large number of same-sex sibs to encourage and model sex-appropriate behavior. Yet Margaret Tauber (1979a) reports that school-age girls who have older sisters and boys from all-boy families are the children who are most likely to enjoy *cross-sex* games and activities. Moreover, Harold Grotevant (1978) found that adolescent girls who have sisters develop a less "feminine" pattern of interests than girls who have brothers. These findings make some sense if children are concerned about establishing a personal niche within the family. A child with other-sex sibs could easily achieve such an individual identity by behaving in an appropriately "masculine" or "feminine" manner. However, a child who is surrounded by same-sex sibs may have to engage in cross-sex activities in order to distinguish the self from brothers (or sisters) and avoid being categorized as one of the "boys" (or "girls").

Although we are only beginning to understand how the structure of the family affects children's sex typing, this much is clear: the child's sex-role socialization within the home depends more on the total family environment than on the influence of the same-sex parent.

Media influences.   For the most part, males and females are portrayed in a highly stereotyped fashion in children's storybooks and on television.

The majority of children's readers feature males as the central characters, and it is almost invariably a male who responds to emergencies, makes important decisions, and assumes a position of leadership. In contrast, females are usually depicted as passive, dependent, excitable, and lacking in ability (Brooks-Gunn & Matthews, 1979; Kolbe & LaVoie, 1981). Sex roles on television are similar to those found in children's books: males are dominant characters who work at a profession, whereas females are passive, emotional creatures who usually manage a home or work at "feminine" occupations such as nursing (Liebert, Sprafkin, & Davidson, 1982). Even TV commercials are sex-stereotyped; males are more often portrayed as experts on the advertised product, while females are typically the ones who are "convinced" by demonstrations of the product's superiority (McArthur & Resko, 1975).

Do these media models affect the sex-role development of young children? Indeed they do if the child is frequently exposed to these stereotyped portrayals of men and women. For example, 5- to 11-year-olds who watch more than 25 hours of television a week are more likely to choose sex-appropriate toys and to hold stereotyped views of males and females than their classmates who watch little television (Frueh & McGhee, 1975; Rothschild, 1979). Even adolescents are quite susceptible to the media typing of sex roles, particularly those aspects of masculinity and femininity portrayed in advertising (Tan, 1979). In recent years, steps have been taken to design television programming aimed at reducing the sex-role stereotypes of grade school children. We will evaluate the merits of these programs when we return to the topic of media influences in Chapter Sixteen.

Kohlberg's Cognitive-Developmental Theory

Lawrence Kohlberg (1966, 1969) has proposed a cognitive theory of sex typing that is strikingly different from the other theories we have considered. Recall that both psychoanalytic theory and social-learning theory specify that boys learn to do "boy things" and girls learn to do "girl things" because their companions encourage these activities and discourage cross-sex behavior. Presumably children will eventually begin to identify with (or habitually imitate) same-sex models, thereby acquiring a stable gender identity and sex-appropriate attitudes and behaviors.

The cognitive theory of sex typing turns this sequence upside down. Kohlberg suggests that a child's gender identity is a cognitive judgment about the self that *precedes* his or her selective attention to (or identification with) same-sex models. Furthermore, the child's conception of gender, which is of central importance to the sex-typing process, will depend on his or her level of cognitive development. Kohlberg believes that children progress through the following three stages as they acquire an understanding of gender and its implications:

1. **Basic gender identity.** The child recognizes that he or she is a male or a female. Three-year-olds have usually reached this stage, although they fail to realize that gender is an unchanging attribute.
2. **Gender stability.** Gender is now perceived as stable over time. The child at this stage knows that boys invariably become men and that girls grow up to be women.
3. **Gender consistency.** The gender concept is now complete, for the child realizes that gender is stable over time *and* across situations. Children of 6 to 7 who have reached this stage are no longer fooled by appearances. They know, for example, that one's gender cannot be altered by superficial changes such as dressing up as a member of the other sex or partaking in cross-sex activities.

According to Kohlberg, a child's basic interests and values will begin to change once he or she acquires a mature gender identity. For example, a boy who realizes that he will always be a male should come to value male attributes and the masculine role. At this point, he will begin to seek out male models and imitate their mannerisms in order to learn sex-appropriate patterns of behavior. The encouragement that he receives for successfully imitating males informs him that he is behaving the way boys should behave and thereby strengthens his masculine self-concept. Thus, Kohlberg's model is a cognitive-consistency theory: children are motivated to acquire values, interests, and behaviors that are consistent with their cognitive judgments about the self. It is

worth repeating that, for Kohlberg, a child's conservation of gender (gender consistency) is the *cause*, rather than the consequence, of attending to same-sex models.

■ *Support for Kohlberg's viewpoint*
The results of several experiments are consistent with various aspects of Kohlberg's theory. For example, studies of 3- to 7-year-olds indicate that children's understanding of gender develops gradually and is clearly related to other aspects of their cognitive development such as the conservation of mass and liquids (DeVries, 1974; Marcus & Overton, 1978). Ron Slaby and Karin Frey (1975) have also noted that the gender concept develops *sequentially,* progressing through the three stages Kohlberg describes (see also Munroe, Shimmin, & Munroe, 1984; Wehren & De Lisi, 1983). There was a second interesting finding in Slaby and Frey's experiment: children who were at the higher stages of gender constancy were more likely to attend to same-sex models in a movie than were children whose gender concepts were less well developed (see also Ruble et al., 1981). Finally, the research presented in Box 13-2 suggests that a child's understanding of gender may affect his or her interpretation of sex-role stereotypes and expectations.

■ *Limitations of Kohlberg's theory*
The one major problem with Kohlberg's cognitive approach is that sex typing is already well underway before the child acquires a mature gender identity. As we have noted, 2-year-old boys prefer masculine toys before they are even aware that these playthings are more appropriate for boys than for girls (Blakemore et al., 1979). Moreover,

---

basic gender identity: *the stage of gender identity in which the child first labels the self as a boy or a girl.*

gender stability: *the stage of gender identity in which the child recognizes that gender is stable over time.*

gender consistency: *the stage of gender identity in which the child recognizes that a person's gender is invariant despite changes in the person's activities or appearance (also known as gender constancy).*

BOX 13-2
CHILDREN'S CONCEPTIONS OF
SEX-ROLE STEREOTYPES

What do young children think about the sex-role standards and stereotypes that they have learned? Must they conform to these expectations; or, rather, do they feel free to do their own thing?

According to Lawrence Kohlberg, the answers to these questions will depend on the child's understanding of gender. Until they realize that gender is unchanging, young, egocentric children may feel that cross-sex behavior is acceptable as long as a child really wants to partake in these activities. But once the child achieves gender constancy at age 6 to 7, he or she should become something of a chauvinist and interpret sex-role standards as absolute laws or moral imperatives that everyone should follow. Finally, Kohlberg proposes that older children who are approaching formal operations will be capable of thinking more abstractly and thus seeing the arbitrary nature of many sex-role stereotypes. In other words, preadolescents should become more flexible about sex-role standards, viewing them more as social conventions rather than moral absolutes that everyone must obey.

William Damon (1977) has tested Kohlberg's hypotheses in an interesting study of 4- to 9-year-olds. Each child was told a story about a little boy named George who insists on playing with dolls, even though his parents have told him that dolls are for girls and that boys should play with other toys. The children were then asked a series of questions about this story—questions designed to assess their own impressions of sex-role stereotypes. For example:

1. Why do people tell George not to play with dolls? Are they right?
2. Is there a rule that boys shouldn't play with dolls? Where does it come from?
3. What should George do?
4. What if George wanted to wear a dress to school? Can he do that?

Damon's findings were generally consistent with Kohlberg's cognitive explanation of stereotyping. Four-year-olds (who do not conserve gender) believe that doll play and other cross-sex behaviors are OK if that is what George really wants to do. Here are some of the answers provided by a 4-year-old named Jack:

(*Is it ok for boys to play with dolls?*) Yes. (*Why?*) Because they wanted to. . . . (*So what should George do?*) Play with dolls. (*Why?*) Because it's up to him. . . . (*Can boys have dresses?*) No. (*Why not?*) Because boys don't wear them. (*Does George have the right to wear a dress to school if he wants to?*) Yes, but he didn't want to. (*Is it ok if he wanted to?*) It's up to him [Damon, 1977, p. 249; italics added].

By age 6, about the time that they acquire gender

3-year-olds of each sex have learned many sex-role stereotypes and already prefer same-sex activities and playmates long before they begin to attend more selectively to same-sex models (Kuhn et al., 1978; Maccoby, 1980). And let's not forget the work of John Money (Money & Ehrhardt, 1972), who found that gender reassignment is exceedingly difficult once children have reached the age of 3 (or Kohlberg's basic identity stage) and have *tentatively* categorized themselves as boys or girls. In sum, it appears that Kohlberg overstates the case in arguing that a mature understanding of gender is necessary for sex typing and sex-role development.

An Attempt at Integration

Perhaps some combination of the biosocial, social-learning, and cognitive-developmental approaches provides the most accurate explanation of sex differences and the sex-typing process. Money and Ehrhardt (1972) have contributed to our understanding of sex typing by describing the important biological developments that people use to label the child as a boy or a girl and treat him or her accordingly. Yet their biosocial model is not very explicit about the psychological determinants of sex differences and sex-role development.

Kohlberg's cognitive-developmental theory emphasizes the period between age 3, when the child acquires a basic gender identity, and age 7, when most children recognize that gender is truly an unchanging attribute. However, an integrative theorist would surely point out that the cognitive approach ignores the important events of the first three years, when a boy, for example, develops a preference for masculine toys and activities be-

constancy, children become extremely intolerant of a person who violates traditional standards of masculinity or femininity. Consider the reaction of 6-year-old Michael to George's doll play:

(*Why do you think people tell George not to play with dolls?*) Well, he should only play with things that boys play with. The things that he is playing with now is girls' stuff.... (*Can George play with Barbie dolls if he wants to?*) No sir! ... (*What should George do?*) He should stop playing with girls' dolls and start playing with G.I. Joe. (*Why can a boy play with G.I. Joe and not a Barbie doll?*) Because if a boy is playing with a Barbie doll, then he's just going to get people teasing him ... and if he tries to play more, to get girls to like him, then the girls won't like him either [Damon, 1977, p. 255; italics added].

The oldest children in Damon's sample were only 9, but these youngsters were already less chauvinistic about sex-role standards and sex-typed activities. Note how 9-year-old James makes a distinction between moral rules that imply a sense of obligation and sex-role standards that are customary but nonobligatory:

(*What do you think his parents should do?*) They should ... get him trucks and stuff, and see if he will play with those. (*What if ... he kept on playing with dolls? Do you think they would punish him?*) No.

(*How come?*) It's not really doing anything bad. (*Why isn't it bad?*) Because ... if he was breaking a window, and he kept on doing that, they could punish him, because you're not supposed to break windows. But if you want to you can play with dolls. (*What's the difference ... ?*) Well, breaking windows you're not supposed to do. And if you play with dolls, you can, but boys usually don't [Damon, 1977, p.263; italics added].

Why do 6–7-year-olds interpret sex-role stereotypes so literally, as if these social conventions must be obeyed? One possibility is that these young concrete operators simply view any rule or custom as a natural law like the law of gravity—a principle that describes the natural order of things and must always be correct (Carter & Patterson, 1982). Eleanor Maccoby (1980) suggests another possibility: children may be exaggerating sex-role stereotypes in order to "get them cognitively clear." A clear understanding of sex-role standards might help "children establish their own sex identity firmly, and only after this identity is established can they become more flexible and less sex-bound." So Maccoby is proposing that the sexist attitudes of the early school years may represent "a developmentally useful phase that children pass through" (p. 237)—and something that they should eventually outgrow *if* they are exposed to a less stereotyped and more egalitarian environment.

cause parents, siblings, and other social agents frequently tell him that he is a boy, reinforce him for doing "boy things," and discourage those of his behaviors that they consider feminine. In other words, it appears that very young children display sex-appropriate behaviors *because other people encourage these activities*.

As a result of this early socialization, children acquire a basic gender identity. This is an important development, for Money's research suggests that as soon as a child first labels himself or herself as a boy or a girl, this self-concept is difficult to change. One reason that 3- to 5-year-olds prefer same-sex activities prior to achieving gender consistency may be that they are satisfied with their "current" sexual identity and mistakenly assume that they must either continue to display gender-appropriate behavior or else become a member of

the other sex (Ullian, 1976). However, these preschool children do not selectively attend to same-sex models, perhaps because they do not yet realize that the model's gender is invariant. Indeed, this may explain why many 4- to 5-year-olds (who typically prefer sex-stereotyped activities) are much less concerned about the model's gender than about the sex-appropriateness of the model's behavior whenever they must decide whether to imitate these activities (Masters et al., 1979).

Once children achieve a mature understanding of gender, at age 6 to 7, their reasons and strategies for incorporating sex-typed characteristics will begin to change. For example, a 7-year-old girl will typically select females as her models, not because she hopes to remain a girl or expects rewards for imitating females, but because she now realizes that *she will always be a female* and is highly motivated to make her behavior consistent with her feminine self-concept.

In sum, biological characteristics and social-learning mechanisms such as direct tuition and observational learning play a central role in the sex-typing process. However, these factors clearly interact with the child's cognitive structuring abilities to determine the course and the outcome of sex-role development (see Table 13-5 for an overview of the integrative viewpoint).

SEX TYPING IN THE NONTRADITIONAL FAMILY

Much of the work we have reviewed is based on studies of children growing up in a standard family setting—that is, an intact home where the father is the primary breadwinner. But in today's rapidly changing society, the so-called standard family is becoming less and less common. Economic realities have forced many mothers to work

full time, and in some families where the mother's earning capacity is substantial, it is the father who remains at home and assumes the role of house-husband. One issue that has intrigued developmental psychologists is the impact of changing parental roles on sex-role development of young children. In this section of the chapter, we will consider the effects of one type of role reversal: the case in which the mother could be described as the dominant parent.

Fatherless homes are now rather common. Recent statistics reveal that nearly 50% of U.S. marriages end in divorce, and about 40% of all children born in the United States during the 1970s will spend an average of six years living in a single-parent home (Hetherington, 1979; MacKinnon et al., 1982). In 1979, 19% of American families were headed by a single parent, nearly always the mother ("One-Parent Families," 1980). In view of the important role that fathers play in the sex-typing process, it seems legitimate to wonder whether children from fatherless

TABLE 13-5. An overview of the sex-typing process from the perspective of an integrative theorist

Developmental period	Events and outcomes
Prenatal period	The fetus develops the morphological characteristics of a male or a female, which others will react to once the child is born.
Birth to 3 years	Parents and other companions label the child as a boy or a girl, frequently remind the child of his or her gender, and begin to encourage gender-consistent behavior while discouraging cross-sex activities. As a result of these social experiences and the development of very basic classification skills, the young child acquires some sex-typed behavioral preferences and the knowledge that he or she is a boy or a girl (basic gender identity).
3 to 6 years	Although children in this age range are aware of their genders and generally prefer gender-consistent activities, they are not certain that gender is unchanging. Consequently, they attend to models of both sexes and will learn many of the cultural stereotypes about both males and females. Toward the end of this phase, children acquire a sense of gender stability and are likely to imitate behaviors considered appropriate for their sex, regardless of the sex of the model who displays them.
Age 6 to 7 and beyond	Children finally acquire a sense of gender consistency—a firm, future-oriented image of themselves as boys who must necessarily become men or girls who will obviously become women. At this point they begin to attend selectively to same-sex models in order to acquire mannerisms and attributes that are consistent with their firm categorization of self as a male or a female. Direct tuition of sex-roles may then no longer be necessary, for the cognitively sophisticated child who recognizes that gender is invariant is now intrinsically motivated to incorporate sex-appropriate characteristics into his or her personality.

homes will show an atypical pattern of sex-role development.

We know much less about the effects of mother absence because motherless homes are still relatively uncommon. Mothers are usually awarded custody of their children in divorce proceedings, and should a mother die or lose a custody hearing, the father often remarries or hires a female caretaker, thereby providing his children with a mother surrogate (Santrock & Warshak, 1979). However, an increasing number of young mothers are taking jobs that render them unavailable to their children for several hours of a typical workday. In 1979 almost 42% of mothers with preschool children and more than 50% of mothers with school-age children were employed outside the home (Hoffman, 1979; U.S. Department of Commerce, 1979). In the pages that follow, we will look at some of the research that seeks to determine whether a mother's work activities and her temporary absences from the home have any systematic effects on the sex-role development of her children.

Effects of Maternal Dominance

The balance of power between mothers and fathers varies considerably from family to family. In the United States, the father tends to be the dominant parent (Lavine, 1982), although mother-dominant households are not particularly uncommon. The obvious question is "What happens if the mother is clearly the dominant parent?" Will her daughters be less feminine and her sons less masculine than girls and boys from father-dominant homes?

Mavis Hetherington (1965) attempted to answer these questions in a study of 4- to 11-year-old children and their parents. The sex-role preferences of each child were measured by the **It scale**, a test in which the child projects his or her own toy and activity preferences by guessing the choices that a sexually ambiguous stick figure, "It," would make when presented with pairs of masculine and feminine items (for example, a dress versus a pair of trousers, cosmetics versus shaving implements, a doll versus a ball). In addition, children took an "identification" test that measured their willingness to imitate each parent. Finally, the child's parents were asked to work out

mutually agreeable solutions to 12 hypothetical child-rearing problems, such as "Your son/daughter loses his/her temper while playing with a toy and intentionally breaks it." The dominant parent was determined by noting which spouse spoke first, which spoke the most, and which tended to accept the other's influence as they worked out their cooperative solutions.

Hetherington found that boys from mother-dominant households made significantly fewer masculine choices on the It test than boys from father-dominant homes. Furthermore, the identification test revealed that boys from father-dominant homes imitated their fathers more than their mothers, while boys from mother-dominant homes *imitated their mothers more than their fathers*. It appears that a dominant mother clearly affects the sex typing of her son, for boys from mother-dominant homes were apparently reluctant to identify with their passive fathers (for additional evidence see Biller & Borstelmann, 1967; Lynn, 1974).

Mother dominance did not seem to affect the sex typing of daughters; that is, girls from mother-dominant homes were no less feminine on the It test than girls from father-dominant households. This result may come as a surprise, since a dominant mother would seem to offer her daughter a rather "unfeminine" role model. But Hetherington (1965) notes that "the measure of maternal dominance in this study was one of dominance relative to the spouse and not to other members of her own sex. Thus a mother could be more dominant than a passive husband and still not be dominant or unfeminine relative to other women" (p. 90).

A recent article by Linda Lavine (1982) suggests that dominant mothers may have at least one effect on the sex typing of their daughters. In her study of 7- to 11-year-olds, Lavine found that girls from mother-dominant or egalitarian families were more likely than those from father-dominant homes to aspire to traditionally masculine occupations such as law or medicine. Apparently a girl feels more comfortable about accepting the chal-

> **It scale:** *a test for measuring children's sex-typed toy and activity preferences.*

lenges of a "male-dominated" occupation if she has seen her mother make important decisions or demonstrate an ability to influence an adult male (namely, her father).

Effects of Father Absence

Fatherless homes resemble mother-dominant households in that the mother is, by necessity, the parent who exerts more influence over her children. Therefore, we might expect that the absence of a father (or father figure) would hinder the sex-role development of sons who haven't an adequate masculine role model in the home. However, fatherless daughters should show fewer disruptions in sex typing, for their mothers are present to serve as models of femininity. The data are generally consistent with these hypotheses.

■ Effects on sons

Boys who are separated from their fathers early in life tend to be more emotionally dependent, less aggressive, less achievement-oriented, and less masculine in their sex-role preferences than boys from homes where the father is present (Biller, 1974; Drake & McDougall, 1977; Hetherington, 1966; Levy-Shiff, 1982). Sons of military personnel who are separated from their fathers for extended periods during the first five years may find it particularly difficult to incorporate various aspects of the masculine role. Many of these boys are considered "sissies" by their fathers, and they often remain somewhat effeminate in their overt behavior (for example, submissive and unassertive) even after their fathers have returned to the home (Leichty, 1960; Stolz, 1954).

An interesting study by Mavis Hetherington (1966) indicates that the age at which father separation occurs is an important consideration. Hetherington's subjects were 9- to 12-year-old boys who were rated on a number of sex-typed dimensions by recreation directors who knew the boys well. In addition, the sex-role preferences of each boy were assessed by means of the It test. Hetherington found few differences between boys from intact homes and boys who had been separated from their fathers *after age 6*. But boys who had been separated from their fathers *before age 4* were less masculine on the It test, more dependent, less aggressive, and less willing to engage in rough-and-tumble play than boys from intact homes.

PHOTO 13-6. Early contacts with a father or father figure promote the development of masculine interests and attitudes. Boys who are separated from their fathers early in life may find it difficult to incorporate certain aspects of the male sex role.

gage in rough-and-tumble play than boys from intact homes.

Why is early separation from the father more likely to influence a boy's sex typing? Hetherington proposes that "adequate masculine identification has occured by age 6 . . . and this identification can be maintained in the absence of the father. If the father leaves in the first four years before [a masculine identity] has been established, long-lasting disruption of sex-typed behaviors may result" (p. 193).

The persistence of sex-role disruptions among father-absent boys depends on many factors, including the boy's social class, the availability of substitute masculine models such as uncles, older brothers, and male teachers, and the extent to which the mother encourages the development of masculine interests and attitudes. Several investigators (Douvan & Adelson, 1966; Lynn & Sawrey, 1959) have found that older boys from father-absent homes often display a pattern of exaggerated masculine behaviors such as toughness, proclaimed self-confidence, rebelliousness, and sexual boldness that is curiously intertwined with "feminine" attributes such as dependency. This **compensatory masculinity** is particularly common among father-absent boys from the lower class, who often appear no less masculine in their overt behavior than lower-class adolescents from intact homes (Barclay & Cusumano, 1967). By contrast, fatherless boys from the middle and upper classes are more likely to retain some interests and attitudes that are characteristic of females (see Shaffer, 1979).

Why are boys from fatherless homes often less sex-typed than those from intact families? Certainly the boys' lack of a masculine role model during the early years is one contributing factor. However, we should also note that father absence has *indirect* effects that may influence a son's sex-role development. For example, mothers in fatherless homes are often found to be more irritable and overprotective, more likely to use power-assertive discipline, and less likely to encourage sons to be active and outgoing than mothers from intact families (Hetherington, Cox, & Cox, 1978; Levy-Shiff, 1982; Santrock, 1975). So part of the impact of "father absence" on young boys may be attributable to the attitudes and child-rearing practices of their mothers.

And perhaps we should not be surprised to find that fatherless boys from the middle and upper classes are more likely to retain feminine interests than their lower-class age mates. We have already seen that lower-class mothers are more likely to encourage their children to display sex-appropriate behavior (Kohn, 1959). Moreover, studies of American teenagers reveal that the lower-class peer group endorses (and encourages) traditional sex-role standards with a fervor not observed among adolescents from the middle class (Kagan, 1964; Pope, 1953).

■ *Effects on daughters*

It appears that the absence of the father from the home has little if any effect on the sex-role development of preadolescent daughters (Hether-

ington, 1972; Santrock, 1970). In fact, some researchers have reported that father-absent girls are actually more feminine in certain respects (for example, more dependent on the mother) than girls from intact homes (Baggett, 1967; Lynn & Sawrey, 1959).

Although father absence does not disrupt a girl's sex typing, it may affect the way she relates to males in later life. Mavis Hetherington (1972) has studied a group of lower- to lower-middle-class adolescent females who fell into three categories: (1) girls from intact homes, (2) girls from homes where the father was absent because of divorce, and (3) girls whose fathers had died. None of the father-absent families had had any males living in the home since the father's departure. Hetherington collected several pieces of information about each girl, including her performance on tests of sex typing, observations of her behavior at a community recreation center, and data from interviews with the girl and her mother.

The results were interesting. As noted earlier, the father-absent girls did not differ from the father-present group on traditional measures of sex typing: girls in all three groups clearly preferred female activities and the feminine role. However, many of the father-absent girls reacted to males in one of two ways that distinguished them from the father-present group.

The *daughters of widows* tended to be shy and noticeably discomforted in the presence of males. At recreation center dances, these girls assumed the role of "wallflowers," clustering at one end of the room away from the boys and remaining there unless asked to dance. When interviewed by a male experimenter, the daughters of widows often sat in an upright (uptight?) posture with their legs together and their arms crossed. They frequently chose to sit in the chair farthest from the interviewer, and they maintained little eye contact with him. These girls were generally described by

---

compensatory masculinity: *a pattern of exaggerated masculine behavior said to characterize father-absent boys from the lower socioeconomic strata.*

their mothers as very outgoing with the girls but shy and retiring around boys and men.

In contrast, *daughters of divorcees* tended to be rather assertive and uninhibited in their interactions with males. They initiated contacts with boys on a regular basis and often asked them to dance at recreation center socials. When interviewed by a male, the daughters of divorcees frequently sat near the interviewer and assumed a sprawling posture, leaning forward with their legs apart and their arms hooked around the back of the chair. They seemed quite receptive to the male interviewer, smiling and maintaining more eye contact with him than girls from intact homes or daughters of widows. One divorcee described her daughter as follows:

> That kid is going to drive me over the hill. . . . She was so good . . . then Pow! At eleven she really turned on. She went boy crazy. When she was only twelve, I . . . found her in bed with a young hood and she's been bouncing from bed to bed ever since. She doesn't seem to care who it is, she can't keep her hands off men. . . . Her uncle is a 60-year-old priest and she even made a "ha-ha" type pass at him. It almost scared him to death. . . . We still have a good time together when we are alone. . . . We both like to cook and get a lot of good laughs when we're puttering around in the kitchen [Hetherington, 1972, p. 322].

Apparently the differences between daughters of widows and daughters of divorcees were not attributable to variations in their mothers' child-rearing practices or affection for their daughters. Both groups of mothers loved their daughters and held positive attitudes toward men in general. But the divorcees were often anxious and unhappy. Their attitudes toward their former husbands and their memories of marriage were negative, and they usually felt that they had received little support from other people during the crisis of divorce and the times of stress they experienced while trying to raise a child by themselves. By contrast, widows expressed favorable attitudes toward marriage and their departed husbands, and they frequently reported that they had received the emotional support of friends and relatives during the period since the death of their spouses. Hetherington suggests that the daughters of divorcees are well aware of their mothers' unhappiness and are likely to conclude that men are

essential for a happy life. As a result, these girls may feel that they must do whatever it takes to secure a man. However, daughters of widows may have an aggrandized image of their fathers that prompts them to avoid males for either of two reasons: (1) they believe that few men can compare favorably with their fathers, or (2) they have come to regard all males as superior and as objects of deference and apprehension.

Hetherington (1977) has followed up on these girls, noting that the daughters of divorcees married younger than daughters of widows (several of whom were not yet married) and were more often pregnant at the time of their marriages. The daughters of divorcees tended to marry immature and inconsiderate husbands who were poorly educated and had unstable work histories, whereas the daughters of widows were more likely to marry nurturant, ambitious, and somewhat inhibited men who were characterized by one interviewer as "repulsively straight." When asked to select adjectives from an adjective checklist that best described the men in their lives, daughters from father-absent homes tended to report more similarities between their husbands and fathers than daughters from intact homes. According to Hetherington, father-absent girls seemed to be selecting mates who matched their images of their fathers, whereas girls from intact homes were much less constrained by father-fantasies when choosing (and later evaluating) their husbands.

Surely not all girls from father-absent homes will show the extreme reactions to males that characterized the father-absent females in Hetherington's sample. We must remember that Hetherington's father-absent subjects were atypical in that they had had *no* males living in the home from the day that father separation occurred. In other words, they were not only father-deprived but male-deprived. In a more recent study, Louise Hainline and Ellen Feig (1978) report that, among a sample of *middle-class* college students, neither daughters of widows nor daughters of divorcees were radically different in their reactions to males from female students who came from intact homes. What these data may indicate is that father-absent girls (at least older girls from middle-class backgrounds) are likely to overcome whatever social deficiencies they have had once they "have the opportunity to engage in social interactions of varying intensities with males" (Hainline & Feig, 1978, p. 42). Nevertheless, Hetherington's research does point to some problems that *young* adolescent girls may face if they are denied an opportunity to establish a stable relationship with a father or father figure.

Effects of Maternal Employment

There are several reasons that we might expect maternal employment to influence the sex-role development of young children. First, working mothers expend a sizable amount of time and effort at job-related activities outside of the home. As a result, they are less available to serve as models of femininity for their daughters or have less energy to do so when they are at home. And if both parents are employed, the child may find it more difficult to discriminate the mother's role from the father's; both parents share the instrumental function traditionally assigned to males, and fathers may often assist working mothers with household chores and child-rearing responsibilities that are usually associated with the feminine role. So it seems reasonable to assume that children of working mothers (especially daughters) will be less traditional in their sex-role attitudes and behaviors than children of nonworking mothers.

Most of the available evidence is consistent with this hypothesis. Sonia Marantz and Annick Mansfield (1977) report that 7- to 11-year-old daughters of working mothers already perceive men and women in less stereotyped ways than daughters of homemakers do. Apparently traits such as competence, independence, and competitiveness that are normally associated with working fathers are likely to be attributed to working mothers as well. In a study of 10-year-olds, Delores Gold and David Andres (1978) found that both sons and daughters of working mothers (particularly mothers who were satisfied with their work roles) have more egalitarian sex-role concepts than children of homemakers. Moreover, daughters' perceptions of sex-role standards were influenced more by maternal employment than sons' were (see Vogel, Broverman, Broverman, Clarkson, & Rosenkrantz, 1970, for a similar set of findings with American college students).

Other investigators have found that daughters of working mothers are more independent, have fewer feminine interests, and are less likely than daughters of homemakers to devalue the competence or achievements of women (Baruch, 1972; Hoffman, 1979; Stein, 1973). Adolescent daughters of working mothers view work as something they will want to do when they are mothers; in fact, they are more likely to have jobs already than adolescent daughters of nonworking mothers (Etaugh, 1974). There is even some evidence that maternal employment contributes positively to a girl's personal adjustment and self-esteem, particularly if her mother enjoys her work or is a professional (Hoffman, 1979; Kappel & Lambert, 1972).

In sum, children of working mothers do grow up with a less stereotyped view of men and women than their counterparts whose mothers remain at home and provide a "sex-typed" contrast to the role played by working fathers. Is this a positive sign? Lois Hoffman (1979) thinks so. She notes that maternal employment is a part of modern family life—a pattern that may be

> better suited to socializing the child for the adult roles that he or she will occupy. This is particularly true for the daughter, but for the son too, the broader range of emotions and skills that each parent [displays] are more consistent with his adult role. Just as his father shares his breadwinning role and the child-rearing role with his mother, so the son too, will be likely to share these roles. The rigid sex-role stereotyping perpetuated by the division of labor in the traditional family is not appropriate for the demands children of either sex will have made on them as adults [p. 864].

PSYCHOLOGICAL ANDROGYNY: A NEW LOOK AT SEX ROLES

Throughout this chapter, we have used the term *sex-appropriate* to describe the mannerisms and behaviors that societies consider more suitable for members of one sex than the other. Today many psychologists believe that these rigidly defined sex-role standards are actually harmful or maladaptive because they constrain the behavior of both males and females. Indeed, Sandra Bem (1978) has stated that her major purpose in studying sex roles is "to help free the human personality from the restrictive prison of sex-role stereotyping and to develop a conception of mental health that is free from culturally imposed definitions of masculinity and femininity."

Psychologists have traditionally assumed that masculinity and femininity are at opposite ends of a single dimension: masculinity supposedly implies the absence of femininity, and vice versa. Bem challenges this assumption by arguing that a person can be androgynous—that is, both masculine and feminine, instrumental and expressive, assertive and nonassertive, competitive or noncompetitive, depending on the utility or situational appropriateness of these attributes. The underlying assumption of Bem's model is that masculinity and femininity are *two separate dimensions*. A person who has many masculine and few feminine characteristics is defined as a *masculine sex-typed individual*. One who has many feminine and few masculine characteristics is said to be *feminine sex-typed*. Finally, the **androgynous** individual is a person who has a large number of both masculine and feminine characteristics (see Figure 13-4).

Do androgynous people really exist? To find out, Bem (1974, 1979) and other investigators (Spence & Helmreich, 1978) have developed sex-role inventories that contain both a masculinity and a femininity scale. One testing of a large sample of college students (Spence & Helmreich, 1978) revealed that roughly 33% of the test takers were sex-typed, 27–32% were androgynous, and

the remaining subjects were either "undifferentiated" (low in both masculinity and femininity) or "sex-reversed" (masculine sex-typed females or feminine sex-typed males). Judith Hall and Amy Halberstadt (1980) have constructed a similar sex-role inventory for grade school children and found that 27–32% of their 8- to 11-year-olds could be classified as androgynous. So androgynous individuals do indeed exist, and in sizable numbers.

Is Androgyny a Desirable Attribute?

Bem (1975, 1978) has argued that androgynous people are "better off" than their sex-typed counterparts because they are not constrained by rigid sex-role concepts and are freer to respond effectively to a wider variety of situations. Seeking to test this hypothesis, Bem exposed masculine, feminine, and androgynous men and women to situations that called for independence (a masculine attribute) or nurturance (a feminine attribute). The test for masculine independence assessed the subject's willingness to resist social pressure by refusing to agree with peers who gave bogus judgments when rating cartoons for funniness (for example, several peers might say that a very funny cartoon was unfunny or that unfunny cartoons were hilarious). Nurturance, or feminine expressiveness, was measured by observing the behavior of the subject when left alone for ten minutes with a 5-month-old baby. The results confirmed Bem's hypotheses. Both the masculine sex-typed and the androgynous subjects were more independent (less conforming) on the "independence" test than feminine sex-typed individuals. Furthermore, both the feminine sex-typed and the androgynous subjects were more "nurturant" than the masculine sex-typed individuals when interacting with the baby. Thus, the androgynous subjects were quite flexible; they performed as masculine subjects did on the "masculine" task and as feminine subjects did on the "feminine" task.

If androgynous people are truly "better off," as Bem has argued, then we might expect them to be popular and to score higher on measures of self-esteem than traditional males and females do. As a matter of fact, recent research indicates that androgynous adolescents and college students do enjoy higher self-esteem and are perceived by

Femininity

		High	Low
Masculinity	High	Androgynous	Masculine sex-typed
	Low	Feminine sex-typed	Undifferentiated

FIGURE 13-4. Categories of sex-role orientation (masculinity and femininity are conceptualized as separate and independent dimensions).

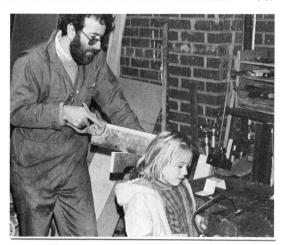

PHOTO 13-7. *Parents who are themselves androgynous are likely to raise androgynous children.*

peers to be more likable and better adjusted than classmates who are traditionally sex-typed (Major, Carnevale, & Deaux, 1981; Massad, 1981; Spence, 1982). Clearly, these data seem to imply that androgyny is a desirable attribute.

However, a caution is in order as we try to interpret these results. Since the androgynous person has a large number of masculine and feminine traits, we might wonder whether it is the masculine or the feminine component of androgyny that is primarily responsible for the higher levels of self-esteem and personal adjustment that seem to characterize androgynous individuals. Those who have researched the question find that it is the masculine component of androgyny that contributes most heavily to self-esteem while the feminine component has a much smaller effect (Lamke, 1982; Whitley, 1983). Perhaps this finding makes good sense when we recall that both males and females perceive masculine attributes and activities as more desirable and socially prestigeful than feminine qualities and pastimes.

Who Raises Androgynous Offspring?

Although the data are sketchy at this point, we are beginning to get some idea about how androgyny originates. There is some evidence that androgynous adolescents and college students come from homes in which the parents are androgynous themselves (Orlofsky, 1979; Spence & Helmreich, 1978). Moreover, parents who are *nurturant* and

highly involved with their children tend to foster the development of both masculine and feminine attributes (Orlofsky, 1979). Finally, daughters of working mothers are more likely to be androgynous than daughters of nonworking mothers (Hansson, Chernovetz, & Jones, 1977). So it appears that adults who model both "masculine" instrumentality and "feminine" expressiveness are the ones who are most likely to raise androgynous offspring.

Do androgynous adults make better parents than those who are traditionally sex-typed? At first glance it may seem so if androgynous parents raise androgynous children, who, in turn, enjoy high self-esteem and are perceived as likable and well-adjusted by their peers. Yet in one recent study (Baumrind, 1982), 9-year-old daughters of androgynous parents were actually found to be somewhat *less* competent than their female classmates whose parents were traditionally sex-typed.

Do these findings imply that traditional adults make better parents than those who are androgynous? Diana Baumrind (1982) thinks so, although other interpretations are possible. For ex-

---

androgyny: *a sex-role orientation in which the individual has incorporated a large number of both masculine and feminine attributes into his or her personality.*

ample, it may be that the benefits of having androgynous parents are minimal until adolescence, when teenagers (1) become more interested in close interpersonal relationships (in which nurturance and a concern for others are adaptive attributes) and (2) are planning and preparing for a career (so that independence, assertiveness, and other "masculine" attributes might be advantageous). In fact, there is some evidence that the benefits of being androgynous oneself are much more apparent for adolescents and young adults than for grade school children (see Perry & Bussey, 1984). So at this point, whether androgynous parents are any more or less effective than traditional parents is an open question—one that developmentalists will be trying to answer in the years ahead.

Implications and Prescriptions for the Future

The androgyny concept has generated an enormous amount of research within a brief time, and these early returns are fascinating. Perhaps the major implication of this work is that the notion of masculine superiority is a myth; androgynous individuals of each sex seem to be adaptable to a wide variety of situations, and they need not fear rejection from either same-sex or other-sex peers for having incorporated both masculine and feminine attributes into their personalities. Advocates of the women's movement have long argued that women should be freer to become more like men, and many of us may have barely noticed their support for the opposite premise—namely, that men might be "better off" if they became a little more like women. Although some people react quite negatively to the androgyny concept, thinking that it implies a drab, unisex society is "best," it is worth repeating that androgynous females are perceived as no less feminine, nor are androgynous males perceived as any less masculine, simply because they have characteristics normally associated with the other sex (Major et al., 1981). In other words, the research to date provides little or no evidence of any disadvantage associated with being androgynous, and it illustrates that androgynous people are adaptive, well-adjusted individuals who are liked and respected by their peers. Although the androgyny concept is in its

infancy and we are a long way from becoming an androgynous society, Sandra Bem (1975) may ultimately be correct in speculating that "the androgynous individual will someday come to define a new and more human standard of psychological health" (p. 643).

SUMMARY

Males and females differ in many respects. Some sex differences are biological in origin, whereas others stem from socialization pressures. Interests, activities, and attributes that are considered more appropriate for members of one sex than the other are called sex-role standards (or sex-role stereotypes). Sex typing is the process by which children acquire a gender identity and assimilate the motives, values, and behaviors considered appropriate in their culture for members of their biological sex.

Some sex-role stereotypes are more accurate than others. Males tend to be more active and aggressive than females and to outperform them on tests of spatial abilities and arithmetic reasoning; females are less irritable and demanding than males, more compliant with parents' requests, and somewhat more responsive to infants, and they tend to outperform males on tests of verbal abilities. But on the whole, males and females are more similar than they are different. Among the stereotypes that have *no* basis in fact are the notions that females are more sociable, suggestible, and illogical and less analytical and achievement-oriented than males. The persistence of these "cultural myths" is particularly damaging to women. For example, members of both sexes tend to devalue women's accomplishments by attributing them to luck or hard work rather than competence. This tendency to degrade the achievements of females is well established among boys and girls by middle childhood.

Sex typing begins very early. By age 2½, most children know whether they are boys or girls, they tend to favor sex-typed toys and activities, and they are already aware of several sex-role stereotypes. By the time they enter school (or shortly thereafter), they know that gender is an unchanging aspect of their personalities, and they have learned most of the sex-role standards of their society. Boys face stronger sex-typing pressures than girls do, and consequently males are quicker to develop a preference for sex-appropriate patterns of behavior. In Western societies such as the United States and Canada, children from the lower socioeconomic strata are more firmly sex-typed than children from the middle class.

Several theories have been proposed to account for sex differences and the sex-typing process. Money and Ehrhardt's biosocial theory emphasizes the biological developments that occur before a child is born—developments that parents and other social agents will react to when deciding how to socialize the child. Other theorists have focused more intently on the socialization process itself. Psychoanalytic theorists suggest that sex typing is one result of the child's identification with the same-sex parent. Social-learning theorists offer two mechanisms to explain how children acquire sex-typed attitudes and behaviors: (1) direct tuition (reinforcement for sex-appropriate behaviors and punishment for sex-inappropriate activities) and (2) observational learning. Finally, cognitive-developmental theorists point out that the course of sex-role development will depend, in part, on the child's cognitive development.

Family structure affects the sex typing of both boys and girls. A boy may have difficulties incorporating certain aspects of the masculine role if his mother is the dominant parent. Boys whose fathers are absent from the home during the first five years are often less aggressive, more dependent, and less masculine in their sex-role preferences than boys from intact families. Father absence has a lesser effect on daughters, although girls from fatherless homes may experience some difficulties in their relationships with males during adolescence and young adulthood. Maternal employment has no disruptive effects on sex typing. However, children of working mothers, particularly daughters, develop less traditional views of men and women and more favorable impressions of the feminine role.

The psychological attributes "masculinity" and "femininity" are generally considered to be at opposite ends of a single dimension. However, one "new look" at sex roles proposes that masculinity and femininity are two separate dimensions and that the androgynous individual is someone who possesses both masculine and feminine characteristics. Recent research indicates that such individuals do exist and that they may be better adjusted and more adaptable to the environment than people who are traditionally sex-typed.

REFERENCES

Angrist, S. S., Mickelson, R., & Penna, A. N. (1977). Sex differences in sex-role conceptions and family orientation of high school students. *Journal of Youth and Adolescence, 6,* 179–186.

Baggett, A. T. (1967). The effect of early loss of father upon the personality of boys and girls in late adolescence. *Dissertation Abstracts, 28*(1-B), 356–357.

Bandura, A. (1977). *Social learning theory.* Englewood Cliffs, NJ: Prentice-Hall.

Baruch, G. K. (1972). Maternal influences upon college women's attitudes toward women and work. *Developmental Psychology, 6,* 32–37.

Barclay, A., & Cusumano, D. R. (1967). Father absence, cross-sex identity, and field dependent behavior in male adolescents. *Child Development, 38,* 243–250.

Barry, H., III, Bacon, M. K., & Child, I. L. (1957). A cross-cultural survey of some sex differences in socialization. *Journal of Abnormal and Social Psychology, 55,* 327–332.

Baumrind, D. (1982). Are androgynous individuals more effective persons and parents? *Child Development, 53,* 44–75.

Beach, F. A. (1965). *Sex and behavior.* New York: Wiley.

Bell, R. Q., Weller, G. M., & Waldrip, M. F. (1971). Newborn and preschooler: Organization of behavior and relations between periods. *Monographs of the Society for Research in Child Development, 36* (1–2, Serial No. 142).

Bem, S. L. (1974). The measurement of psychological androgyny. *Journal of Consulting and Clinical Psychology, 42,* 155–162.

Bem, S. L. (1975). Sex-role adaptability: One consequence of psychological androgyny. *Journal of Personality and Social Psychology, 31,* 634–643.

Bem, S. L. (1978). Beyond androgyny: Some presumptuous prescriptions for a liberated sexual identity. In J. A. Sherman & F. L. Denmark (Eds.), *The psychology of women: Future directions in research.* New York: Psychological Dimensions.

Bem, S. L. (1979). Theory and measurement of androgyny: A reply to the Podhazer-Tetenbaum and Locksley-Colten critiques. *Journal of Personality and Social Psychology, 37,* 1047–1054.

Best, D. L., Williams, J. E., Cloud, J. M., Davis, S. W., Robertson, L. S., Edwards, J. R., Giles, H., & Fowles, J. (1977). Development of sex-trait stereotypes among young children in the United States, England, and Ireland. *Child Development, 48,* 1375–1384.

Biller, H. B. (1974). *Paternal deprivation.* Lexington, MA: Heath.

Biller, H. B., & Borstelmann, L. J. (1967). Masculine development: An integrative review. *Merrill-Palmer Quarterly, 13,* 253–294.

Blakemore, J. E. O. (1981). Age and sex differences in interaction with a human infant. *Child Development, 52,* 386–388.

Blakemore, J. E. O., LaRue, A. A., & Olejnik, A. B. (1979). Sex-appropriate toy preference and the ability to conceptualize toys as sex-role related. *Developmental Psychology, 15,* 339–340.

Brooks-Gunn, J., & Matthews, W. S. (1979). *He and she.* Englewood Cliffs, NJ: Prentice-Hall.

Broverman, I. K., Vogel, S. R., Broverman, D. M., Clarkson, F. E., & Rosenkrantz, P. S. (1972). Sex-role stereotypes: A current appraisal. *Journal of Social Issues, 28,* 59–78.

Brown, D. G. (1957). Masculinity-femininity development in children. *Journal of Consulting Psychology, 21,* 197–202.

Brown, R. (1965). *Social psychology.* New York: Free Press.

Carter, D. B., & Patterson, C. J. (1982). Sex roles as social conventions: The development of children's conceptions of sex-role stereotypes. *Developmental Psychology, 18,* 812–824.

Condry, J., & Condry, S. (1976). Sex differences: A study in the eye of the beholder. *Child Development, 47,* 812–819.

Damon, W. (1977). *The social world of the child.* San Francisco: Jossey-Bass.

D'Andrade, R. G. (1966). Sex differences and cultural institutions. In E. E. Maccoby (Ed.), *The development of sex differences.* Stanford, CA: Stanford University Press.

Deaux, K. (1977). The social psychology of sex roles. In L. Wrightsman, *Social psychology.* Monterey, CA: Brooks/Cole.

DeVries, R. (1974). Relationship among Piagetian, IQ, and achievement assessments. *Child Development, 45,* 746-756.

DiPietro, J. A. (1981). Rough and tumble play: A function of gender. *Developmental Psychology, 17,* 50–58.

Doty, R. L., Carter, C. S., & Clemens, L. G. (1971). Olfactory control of sexual behavior in male and early-androgenized female hamsters. *Hormones and Behavior, 2,* 325–335.

Douvan, E., & Adelson, J. (1966). *The adolescent experience.* New York: Wiley.

Drake, C. T., & McDougall, D. (1977). Effects of the absence of the father and other male models on the development of boys' sex-roles. *Developmental Psychology, 13,* 537–538.

Eaton, W. O., & Keats, J. G. (1982). Peer presence, stress, and sex differences in the motor activity levels of preschoolers. *Developmental Psychology, 18,* 534–540.

Eaton, W. O., & Von Bargen, D. (1981). Asynchronous development of gender understanding in preschool children. *Child Development, 52,* 1020–1027.

Ehrhardt, A. A., & Baker, S. W. (1974). Fetal androgens, human central nervous system differentiation, and behavioral sex differences. In R. C. Friedman, R. M. Rickard, & R. L. Van de Wiele (Eds.), *Sex differences in behavior.* New York: Wiley.

Eisenberg, N., Murray, E., & Hite, T. (1982). Children's reasoning regarding sex-typed toy choices. *Child Development, 53,* 81–86.

Emmerich, W. (1959). Parental identification in young children. *Genetic Psychology Monographs, 60,* 257–308.

Etaugh, C. (1974). Effects of maternal employment on children: A review of recent research. *Merrill-Palmer Quarterly, 20,* 71–98.

Etaugh, C., & Brown, B. (1975). Perceiving the causes of success and failure of male and female performers. *Developmental Psychology, 11,* 103.

Fagot, B. I. (1978). The influence of sex of child on parental reactions to toddler children. *Child Development, 49,* 459–465.

Feldman-Summers, S., & Kiesler, S. B. (1974). Those who are number two try harder: The effect of sex on attribution of causality. *Journal of Personality and Social Psychology, 30,* 846–855.

Forisha, B. L., & Goldman, B. H. (1981). *Outsiders on the inside: Women & organizations.* Englewood Cliffs, NJ: Prentice-Hall.

Frueh, T., & McGhee, P. H. (1975). Traditional sex-role development and the amount of time spent watching television. *Developmental Psychology, 11,* 109.

Ginsburg, H. J., & Miller, S. M. (1982). Sex differences in children's risk-taking behavior. *Child Development, 53,* 426–428.

Gold, D., & Andres, D. (1978). Developmental comparisons between ten-year-old children with employed and nonemployed mothers. *Child Development, 49,* 75–84.

Goldberg, P. (1968). Are women prejudiced against women? *Trans/Action, 5,* 28–30.

Gouze, K. R., & Nadelman, L. (1980). Constancy of gender identity for self and others in children between the ages of three and seven. *Child Development, 51,* 275–278.

Grotevant, H. D. (1978). Sibling constellations and sex-typing of interests in adolescence. *Child Development, 49,* 540–542.

Gunnar, M. R., & Donahue, M. (1980). Sex differences in social responsiveness between six months and twelve months. *Child Development, 51,* 262–265.

Hainline, L., & Feig, E. (1978). The correlates of childhood father absence in college-aged women. *Child Development, 49,* 37–42.

Hall, J. A., & Halberstadt, A. G. (1980). Masculinity and femininity in children: Development of the Children's Personal Attributes Questionnaire. *Developmental Psychology, 16,* 270–280.

Hansson, R. O., Chernovetz, M. E., & Jones, W. H. (1977). Maternal employment and androgyny. *Psychology of Women Quarterly, 2,* 76–78.

Haugh, S. S., Hoffman, C. D., & Cowan, G. (1980). The eye of the very young beholder: Sex-typing of infants by young children. *Child Development, 51,* 598–600.

Hetherington, E. M. (1965). A developmental study of the effects of sex of the dominant parent on sex-role preference, identification, and imitation in children. *Journal of Personality and Social Psychology, 2,* 188–194.

Hetherington, E. M. (1966). Effects of paternal absence on sex-typed behaviors in Negro and white preadolescent males. *Journal of Personality and Social Psychology, 4,* 87–91.

Hetherington, E. M. (1967). The effects of familiar variables on sex-typing, on parent-child similarity, and on imitation in children. In J. P. Hill (Ed.), *Minnesota Symposia on Child Psychology* (Vol. 1). Minneapolis: University of Minnesota Press.

Hetherington, E. M. (1972). Effects of father absence on personality development in adolescent daughters. *Developmental Psychology, 7,* 313–326.

Hetherington, E. M. (1977). *My heart belongs to daddy: A study of the marriages of daughters of divorcees and widows.* Unpublished manuscript, University of Virginia.

Hetherington, E. M. (1979). Divorce: A child's perspective. *American Psychologist, 34,* 851–858.

Hetherington, E. M., Cox, M., & Cox, R. (1976). Divorced fathers. *Family Coordinator, 25,* 417–428.

Hetherington, E. M., Cox, M., & Cox, R. (1978). The aftermath of divorce. In J. H. Stevens and M. Matthews (Eds.), *Mother-child, father-child relations.* Washington, DC: National Association for the Education of Young Children.

Hetherington, E. M., & Frankie, G. (1967). Effect of parental dominance, warmth, and conflict on imitation in children. *Journal of Personality and Social Psychology, 6,* 119–125.

Hetherington, E. M., & Parke, R. D. (1975). *Child psychology: A contemporary viewpoint.* New York: McGraw-Hill.

Hoffman, L. W. (1979). Maternal employment: 1979. *American Psychologist, 34,* 859–865.

Hutt, C. (1972). *Males and females.* Baltimore: Penguin Books.

Imperato-McKinley, J., Peterson, R. E., Gautier, T., & Sturla, E. (1979). Androgyns and the evolution of male gender identity among male pseudohermaphrodites with 5a-reducase deficiency. *New England Journal of Medicine, 300,* 1233–1237.

Jacklin, C. N., & Maccoby, E. E. (1978). Social behavior at 33 months in same-sex and mixed-sex dyads. *Child Development, 49,* 557–569.

Kagan, J. (1964). Acquisition and significance of sex-typing and sex-role identity. In M. Hoffman & L. Hoffman (Eds.), *Review of child development research* (Vol. 1). New York: Russell Sage Foundation.

Kagan, J., & Moss, H. A. (1962). *Birth to maturity.* New York: Wiley.

Kappel, B. E., & Lambert, R. D. (1972). *Self worth among children of working mothers.* Unpublished manuscript, University of Waterloo.

Katcher, A. (1955). The discrimination of sex differences by young children. *Journal of Genetic Psychology, 87,* 131–143.

Kohlberg, L. (1966). A cognitive-developmental analysis of children's sex-role concepts and attitudes. In E. E. Maccoby (Ed.), *The development of sex differences.* Stanford, CA: Stanford University Press.

Kohlberg, L. (1969). Stage and sequence: The cognitive-developmental approach to socialization. In D. A. Goslin (Ed.), *Handbook of socialization theory and research.* Chicago: Rand McNally.

Kohn, M. L. (1959). Social class and parental values. *American Journal of Sociology, 64,* 337–351.

Kolbe, R., & LaVoie, J. C. (1981). Sex-role stereotyping in preschool children's picture books. *Social Psychology Quarterly, 44,* 369–374.

Kuhn, D., Nash, S. C., & Brucken, L. (1978). Sex-role concepts of two- and three-year-olds. *Child Development, 49,* 445–451.

Lamb, M. E. (1981). *The role of the father in child development.* New York: Wiley.

Lamke, L. K. (1982). The impact of sex-role orientation on self-esteem in early adolescence. *Child Development, 53,* 1530–1535.

Langlois, J. H., & Downs, A. C. (1980). Mothers, fathers, and peers as socialization agents of sex-typed play behaviors in young children. *Child Development, 51,* 1237–1247.

Lavine, L. O. (1982). Parental power as a potential influence on girls' career choice. *Child Development, 53,* 658–663.

Leichty, M. M. (1960). The effect of father absence during early childhood upon the oedipal situation as reflected in young adults. *Merrill-Palmer Quarterly, 6,* 212–217.

Levy-Shiff, R. (1982). Effects of father absence on young children in mother-headed families. *Child Development, 53,* 1400–1405.

Liebert, R. M., Sprafkin, J. N., & Davidson, E. S. (1982). *The early window: Effects of television on children and youth.* New York: Pergamon Press.

Lynn, D. B. (1974). *The father: His role in child development.* Monterey, CA: Brooks/Cole.

Lynn, D. B., & Sawrey, W. L. (1959). The effects of father absence on Norwegian boys and girls. *Journal of Abnormal and Social Psychology, 59,* 258–262.

Maccoby, E. E. (1980). *Social development.* New York: Harcourt Brace Jovanovich.

Maccoby, E. E., & Jacklin, C. N. (1974). *The psychology of sex differences.* Stanford, CA: Stanford University Press.

Maccoby, E. E., & Jacklin, C. N. (1980). Sex differences in aggression: A rejoinder and reprise. *Child Development, 51,* 964–980.

MacFarlane, A. (1977). *The psychology of childbirth.* Cambridge, MA: Harvard University Press.

MacKinnon, C. E., Brody, G. H., & Stoneman, Z. (1982). The effects of divorce and maternal employment on the home environments of preschool children. *Child Development, 53,* 1392–1399.

Major, B., Carnevale, P. J. D., & Deaux, K. (1981). A different perspective on androgyny: Evaluations of masculine and feminine personality characteristics. *Journal of Personality and Social Psychology, 41,* 988–1001.

Marantz, S. A., & Mansfield, A. F. (1977). Maternal employment and the development of sex-role stereotyping in five- to eleven-year-old girls. *Child Development, 48,* 668–673.

Marcus, D. E., & Overton, W. F. (1978). The development of cognitive gender constancy and sex-role preferences. *Child Development, 49,* 434–444.

Martin, C. L., & Halverson, C. F., Jr. (1981). A schematic processing model of sex typing and stereotyping in children. *Child Development, 52,* 1119–1134.

Martin, J. A. (1980). A longitudinal study of the consequences of early mother-infant interaction: A microanalytic approach. *Monographs of the Society for Research in Child Development, 46* (3, Serial No. 190).

Massad, C. M. (1981). Sex-role identity and adjustment during adolescence. *Child Development, 52,* 1290–1298.

Masters, J. C., Ford, M. E., Arend, R., Grotevant, H. D., & Clark, L. V. (1979). Modeling and labeling as integrated determinants of children's sex-typed imitative behavior. *Child Development, 50,* 364–371.

McArthur, L. Z., & Resko, B. G. (1975). The portrayal of men and women in American television commercials. *Journal of Social Psychology, 97,* 209–229.

McConaghy, M. J. (1979). Gender permanence and the genital basis of gender: Stages in the development of constancy of gender identity. *Child Development, 50,* 1223–1226.

Mead, M. (1935). *Sex and temperament in three primitive societies.* New York: William Morrow.

Meyer, B. (1980). The development of girls' sex-role attitudes. *Child Development, 51,* 508–514.

Mischel, W. (1970). Sex-typing and socialization. In P. H. Mussen (Ed.), *Carmichael's manual of child psychology* (Vol. 2). New York: Wiley.

Money, J. (1965). Psychosexual differentiation. In J. Money (Ed.), *Sex research: New developments.* New York: Holt, Rinehart & Winston.

Money, J., & Ehrhardt, A. (1972). *Man and woman, boy and girl.* Baltimore: Johns Hopkins University Press.

Money, J., & Tucker, P. (1975). *Sexual signatures: On being a man or a woman.* Boston: Little, Brown.

Morgan, M. (1982). Television and adolescents' sex-role stereotypes: A longitudinal study. *Journal of Personality and Social Psychology, 43,* 947–955.

Moss, H. A. (1967). Sex, age, and state as determinants of mother-infant interaction. *Merrill-Palmer Quarterly, 13,* 19–36.

Munroe, R. H., Shimmin, H. S., & Munroe, R. L. (1984). Gender understanding and sex-role preferences in four cultures. *Developmental Psychology, 20,* 673–682.

Mussen, P. H., & Rutherford, E. (1963). Parent-child relations and parental personality in relation to young children's sex-role preferences. *Child Development, 34,* 589–607.

Nadelman, L. (1970). Sex identity in London children: Memory, knowledge, and preference tests. *Human Development, 13,* 28–42.

Nadelman, L. (1974). Sex identity in American children: Memory, knowledge, and preference tests. *Developmental Psychology, 10,* 413–417.

Nash, S. C. (1975). The relationship among sex-role stereotyping, sex-role preference, and the sex difference in spatial visualization. *Sex Roles, 1,* 15–32.

Newcombe, N., & Bandura, M. M. (1983). Effect of age at puberty on spatial ability in girls: A question of mechanism. *Developmental Psychology, 19,* 215–224.

Olweus, D., Mattsson, A., Schalling, D., & Low, H. (1980). Testosterone, aggression, physical and personality dimensions in normal adolescent males. *Psychosomatic Medicine, 42,* 253–269.

One-parent families and their children: The school's most significant minority. (1980). *Principal, 60,* 31–37.

Orlofsky, J. L. (1979). Parental antecedents of sex-role orientation in college men and women. *Sex Roles, 5,* 495–512.

Parsons, J. E., Adler, T. F., & Kaczala, C. M. (1982). Socialization of achievement attitudes and beliefs: Parental influences. *Child Development, 53,* 310–321.

Parsons, J. E., Kaczala, C. M., & Meese, J. L. (1982). Socialization of achievement attitudes and beliefs: Classroom influences. *Child Development, 53,* 322–339.

Parsons, T. (1955). Family structure and the socialization of the child. In T. Parsons & R. F. Bales (Eds.), *Family socialization and interaction processes.* Glencoe, IL: Free Press.

Perry, D. G., & Bussey, K. (1984). *Social development.* Englewood Cliffs, NJ: Prentice-Hall.

Phillips, S., King, S., & Dubois, L. (1978). Spontaneous activities of female versus male newborns. *Child Development, 49,* 590–597.

Pollis, N. P., & Doyle, D. C. (1972). Sex role, status, and perceived competence among first-graders. *Perceptual and Motor Skills, 34,* 235–238.

Pope, B. (1953). Socioeconomic contrasts in children's peer culture prestige values. *Genetic Psychology Monographs, 48,* 157–220.

Rabban, M. (1950). Sex-role identification in young children in two diverse social groups. *Genetic Psychology Monographs, 42,* 81–158.

Richardson, J. G., & Simpson, C. H. (1982). Children, gender, and social structure: An analysis of the contents of letters to Santa Claus. *Child Development, 53,* 429–436.

Roopnarine, J. L. (1984). Sex-typed socialization in mixed-aged preschool classrooms. *Child Development, 55,* 1078–1084.

Rose, R. M., Bernstein, I. S., & Gordon, T. P. (1975). Consequences of social conflict on plasma testosterone levels in rhesus monkeys. *Psychosomatic Medicine, 37,* 50–61.

Rosenberg, B. G., & Sutton-Smith, B. (1964). Ordinal position and sex-role identification. *Genetic Psychology Monographs, 70,* 297–328.

Rosenblatt, P. C., & Cunningham, M. R. (1976). Sex differences in cross-cultural perspective. In B. Lloyd & J. Archer (Eds.), *Exploring sex differences.* London: Academic Press.

Rothschild, N. (1979). *Group as a mediating factor in the cultivation process among young children.* Unpublished master's thesis, Annenberg School of Communications, University of Pennsylvania.

Ruble, D. N., Balaban, T., & Cooper, J. (1981). Gender constancy and the effects of sex-typed televised toy commercials. *Child Development, 52,* 667–673.

Santrock, J. W. (1970). Paternal absence, sex-typing, and identification. *Developmental Psychology, 2,* 264–272.

Santrock, J. W. (1975). Father absence, perceived maternal behavior, and moral development in boys. *Child Development, 46,* 753–757.

Santrock, J. W., & Warshak, R. A. (1979). Father custody and social development in boys and girls. *Journal of Social Issues, 35,* 112–125.

Shaffer, D. R. (1979). *Social and personality development.* Monterey, CA: Brooks/Cole.

Shaffer, D. R., & Johnson, R. D. (1980). Effects of occupational choice and sex-role preferences on the attractiveness of competent men and women. *Journal of Personality, 48,* 505–519.

Slaby, R. G., & Frey, K. S. (1975). Development of gender constancy and selective attention to same-sex models. *Child Development, 46,* 849–856.

Smith, P. K., & Daglish, L. (1977). Sex differences in parent and infant behavior in the home. *Child Development, 48,* 1250–1254.

Snow, M. E., Jacklin, C. N., & Maccoby, E. E. (1983). Sex-of-child differences in father-child interaction at one year of age. *Child Development, 54,* 227–232.

Spence, J. T., (1982). Comment on Baumrind's "Are androgynous individuals more effective persons and parents?" *Child Development, 53,* 76–80.

Spence, J. T., & Helmreich, R. L. (1978). *Masculinity and femininity: Their psychological dimensions, correlates, and antecedents.* Austin, TX: University of Texas Press.

Stein, A. H. (1973). The effects of maternal employment and educational attainment on the sex-typed attributes of college females. *Social Behavior and Personality, 1,* 111–114.

Stolz, L. M. (1954). *Father relations of war-born children.* Stanford, CA: Stanford University Press.

Strayer, F. F. (1977). Peer attachment and affiliative subgroups. In F. F. Strayer (Ed.), *Ethological perspectives on preschool social organization.* Memo de Recherche #5, University of Quebec.

Sutton-Smith, B., & Rosenberg, B. G. (1970). *The sibling.* New York: Holt, Rinehart & Winston.

Tan, R. S. (1979). TV beauty ads and role expectations of adolescent female viewers. *Journalism Quarterly, 56,* 283–288.

Tauber, M. A. (1979a). Parental socialization techniques and sex differences in children's play. *Child Development, 50,* 225–234.

Tauber, M. A. (1979b). Sex differences in parent-child interaction styles during a free-play session. *Child Development, 50,* 981–988.

Terborg, J. R., & Ilgen, D. R. (1975). A theoretical approach to sex discrimination in traditionally masculine occupations. *Organizational Behavior and Human Performance, 13,* 352–376.

Thompson, S. K. (1975). Gender labels and early sex-role development. *Child Development, 46,* 339–347.

Thompson, S. K., & Bentler, P. M. (1971). The priority of cues in sex discrimination by children and adults. *Developmental Psychology, 5,* 181–185.

Tolar, C. J. (1968). An investigation of parent-offspring relationships. *Dissertation Abstracts, 28*(8-B), 3465.

Touhey, J. C. (1974). Effects of additional women professionals on ratings of occupational prestige and desirability. *Journal of Personality and Social Psychology, 29,* 86–89.

Ullian, D. Z. (1976). The development of conceptions of masculinity and femininity. In B. Lloyd & J. Ascher (Eds.), *Exploring sex differences.* London: Academic Press.

U.S. Department of Commerce, Bureau of the Census. (1979). *Population profile of the United States: 1978, population characteristics.* Washington, DC: U.S. Government Printing Office.

Vogel, S. R., Broverman, I. K., Broverman, D. M., Clarkson, F. E., & Rosenkrantz, P. S. (1970). Maternal employment and perception of sex roles among college students. *Developmental Psychology, 3,* 384–391.

Waber, D. P. (1977). Sex differences in mental abilities, hemispheric lateralization, and rate of physical growth at adolescence. *Developmental Psychology, 13,* 29–38.

Ward, W. D. (1973). Patterns of culturally defined sex-role preference and parental imitation. *Journal of Genetic Psychology, 122,* 337–343.

Wehren, A., & De Lisi, R. (1983). The development of gender understanding: Judgments and explanations. *Child Development, 54,* 1568–1578.

Werner, P. D., & LaRussa, G. W. (1983). *Persistence and change in sex-role stereotypes.* Unpublished manuscript, California School of Professional Psychology.

Whitley, B. E., Jr. (1983). Sex-role orientation and self-esteem: A critical meta-analytic review. *Journal of Personality and Social Psychology, 44,* 765–778.

Young, W. C., Goy, R. W., & Phoenix, C. H. (1964). Hormones and sexual behavior. *Science, 143,* 212–218.

CHAPTER FOURTEEN ■

MORAL DEVELOPMENT AND SELF-CONTROL

■ *A definition of morality*

■ *Psychoanalytic explanations of moral development*
Freud's theory of oedipal morality
Erikson's views on moral development

■ *Cognitive-developmental theory: The child as a moral philosopher*
Piaget's theory of moral development
Tests of Piaget's theory
Kohlberg's theory of moral development
Tests of Kohlberg's theory

■ *Morality as a product of social learning*
How consistent is moral behavior?
Determinants of children's resistance to temptation
Is morality a stable and unitary attribute?

■ *Who raises children who are morally mature?*

■ *The development of self-control*
Motor inhibition
Delay of gratification
A final note on self-control

■ *Summary*

S uppose that a large sample of parents were asked "What is the most important aspect of a child's social development?" Surely this is a question that could elicit any number of responses. However, it's a good bet that many parents would hope above all that their children would acquire a strong sense of morality—right and wrong—to guide their everyday exchanges with other people.

The **moral development** of each successive generation is of obvious significance to society. One of the reasons that people can live together in peace is that they have evolved codes of ethics that sanction certain practices and prohibit others. Although moral standards may vary from culture to culture (Garbarino & Bronfenbrenner, 1976), every society has devised rules that its constituents must obey in order to remain members in good standing. Thus, the moral education of each succeeding generation serves two important functions: (1) to maintain the social order while (2) making it possible for the individual to function appropriately within his or her culture (or subculture).

Sigmund Freud once argued that moral education is the largest hurdle that parents face when raising a child, and many of his contemporaries agreed. In one of the first social psychology texts, William McDougall (1908) suggested:

> The fundamental problem of social psychology is the moralization of the individual into the society into which he was born as an amoral and egoistic infant. There are successive stages, each of which must be traversed by every individual before he can attain the next higher: (1) the stage in which . . . [innate] impulses are modified by the influence of rewards and punishments, (2) the stage in which conduct is controlled . . . by social praise or blame, and (3) the highest stage in which conduct is regulated by an ideal that enables a man to act in

---

moral development: *the process by which children acquire society's standards of right and wrong.*

a way that seems to him right regardless of the praise or blame of his immediate social environment [p.6].

The third stage in McDougall's theory suggests that children do not go through life submitting to society's moral dictates because they expect rewards for complying or fear punishments for transgressing. Rather, they eventually *internalize* the moral principles that they have learned and will behave in accordance with these ideals even when authority figures are not present to enforce them. As we will see, many contemporary theorists consider **internalization** to be a very important part of the development of moral controls.

Society also makes many other demands that do not take the form of right versus wrong. Consider a dilemma that you could be facing right now: You have an important midterm tomorrow morning but would really like to see the movie that is playing downtown. Should you fall prey to your wishes and see the flick or, rather, ignore this impulse and study for the exam? In an achievement-oriented society such as ours, many people would advise you to control your impulses and study for the exam because, after all, "doing well in school is your ticket to future success." Clearly it is not immoral to go to a movie rather than studying for a test. However, an individual who often gives in to temptations of this sort may risk others' disapproval and find it very difficult to accomplish long-range goals.

Of course, this hypothetical dilemma may pose few if any problems for the majority of college students, who have become reasonably proficient at resisting those momentary pleasures that interfere with important long-range objectives. But how might a young child accomplish this difficult feat, particularly when there is no one around to remind him to exercise "will power"? In a later section of the chapter, we will return to this important issue and see what experimental psychologists have learned about the development of patience and **self-control.**

A DEFINITION OF MORALITY

Virtually all adults have some idea of what morality is, although the ways they define the term will depend, in part, on their general outlooks on life. A theologian, for example, might mention the relationship between human beings and their creator. A philosopher's definition of morality may depend on the assumptions that he or she makes about human nature. Psychologists are generally concerned with the feelings, thoughts, and actions of people who are facing moral dilemmas. But most adults would probably agree that **morality** implies *an ability to distinguish right from wrong and to act on this distinction.*

Psychological research has focused on three basic components of morality: the *affective,* or emotional, component, the *cognitive* component, and the *behavioral* component. Psychoanalytic theorists emphasize the emotional aspects of moral development. According to Freud, the kind of emotional relationship a child has with his or her parents will determine the child's willingness

PHOTO 14-1. *Learning to resist temptation is an important aspect of moral development.*

to internalize parental standards of right and wrong. Freud also believed that a child who successfully internalizes the morality of his parents will experience negative emotions such as shame or guilt—that is, **moral affect**—if he then violates these ethical guidelines. Cognitive-developmental theorists have concentrated on the cognitive aspects of morality, or **moral reasoning**, and have found that the ways children think about right and wrong may change rather dramatically as they mature. Finally, the research of social-learning theorists has helped us to understand how children learn to resist temptation and to practice **moral behavior**, inhibiting actions such as lying, stealing, and cheating that violate moral norms.

We will begin by examining each of these theories and the research it has generated. After we have seen how each theory approaches the topic of moral development, we will look at the relationships among moral affect (that is, guilt, shame), moral reasoning, and moral behavior. This research should help us to decide whether a person really has a "moral character" that is stable over time and across situations. Finally, we will consider how various child-rearing practices may affect a child's moral development before turning to the related topic of children's self-control.

PSYCHOANALYTIC EXPLANATIONS OF MORAL DEVELOPMENT

According to Freud (1935/1960), the personality consists of three basic components—the id, the ego, and the superego. Recall from Chapter Two that the id is impulsive and hedonistic. Its purpose is to gratify the instincts. The function of the ego is to restrain the id until "realistic" means for satisfying needs can be worked out. The superego is the final component of the personality to develop. Its role is to determine whether id impulses and the means of impulse satisfaction produced by the ego are acceptable or unacceptable (moral or immoral).

Freud believed that infants and toddlers are basically amoral and hedonistic because they are dominated by their ids. Before the formation of the superego, parents must reward behaviors that they consider acceptable and punish those that they consider unacceptable if they hope to restrain the child's hedonistic impulses. Once the

superego develops, it will monitor the child's thoughts and actions and become an internal censor. Indeed, Freud argued that a well-developed superego is a harsh master that will punish the ego for moral transgressions by producing feelings of guilt, shame, or a loss of self-esteem.

Freud's Theory of Oedipal Morality

According to Freud, the superego develops during the phallic stage (age 3–6), when children were said to experience a hostile rivalry with the same-sex parent that stemmed from their incestuous desire for the other-sex parent (that is, an Oedipus complex for males and an Electra complex for females). Freud proposed that hostilities arising from the Oedipus complex would build until a boy came to fear his father and would be forced to identify with him in order to reduce this fear. By identifying with the father, the boy should internalize many of his father's attributes, including the father's moral standards. In other words, Freud assumed that the male superego will emerge during the preschool period and mature by the age of 6 to 7, when most boys will have resolved their oedipal conflicts.

Girls were assumed to experience similar conflicts during the phallic stage as they begin to compete with their mothers for the affection of their fathers. But Freud argued that girls are never

---

internalization: *the process of adopting the attributes or standards of other people—taking these standards as one's own.*

self-control: *the ability to control one's immediate impulses in the service of more important, valuable, or acceptable long-range objectives.*

morality: *one's ability to distinguish right from wrong and to act on this distinction.*

moral affect: *the emotional component of morality, including feelings such as guilt, shame, and pride in ethical conduct.*

moral reasoning: *the cognitive component of morality; the thinking that people display when resolving moral dilemmas and deciding whether various acts are right or wrong.*

moral behavior: *the behavioral component of morality; actions that are consistent with one's moral standards in situations in which one is tempted to violate a prohibition.*

quite as afraid of their mothers as boys are of their fathers, because in the worst of all imaginable circumstances, their mothers could never castrate them. The implication is that a young girl might find it difficult to resolve her Electra complex because she experiences no overriding fear that would absolutely force her to identify with her mother. For this reason, Freud believed that females develop weaker superegos than males do!

Studies of moral development provide very little support for any of Freud's hypotheses. Cold, threatening parents do not raise children who are morally mature. Quite the contrary; parents who rely on punitive forms of discipline, such as spankings, tend to have youngsters who often misbehave and who rarely express feelings of guilt, remorse, shame, or self-criticism (Brody & Shaffer, 1982; Hoffman, 1970). Furthermore, there is simply no evidence that males develop stronger superegos than females. In fact, investigators who have left children alone so that they are tempted to violate a prohibition usually find no sex differences in moral behavior, or they find differences favoring females (Hoffman, 1975b). Finally, there is little evidence that children are morally mature at age 6 or 7, when they have supposedly resolved their oedipal conflicts. As we will see later in the chapter, at least one aspect of morality—moral reasoning—continues to develop well into young adulthood. In view of the repeated failures to confirm these and other Freudian hypotheses, many developmentalists now believe that it is time to lay Freud's theory of **oedipal morality** to rest.

Erikson's Views on Moral Development

Other psychoanalysts such as Erik Erikson (1963) have rejected Freud's theory of oedipal morality and argued that children internalize the moral principles of *both* parents in order to win their approval and to avoid losing their love. According to Erikson, both the ego and the superego play important roles in moral development. The superego dictates to the ego the kinds of behavior that are morally acceptable and unacceptable. But unless the ego is strong so that it has the capacity to inhibit the id's undesirable impulses, the child will be unable to resist the id, regardless of the strength of the superego. In other words, Erikson assumes that moral behavior is a product of both the internalized rules of the superego and the re-

straining forces of the ego that permit the child to obey these rules.

Since the ego is the rational component of the personality—the seat of all higher intellectual functions—Erikson is arguing that moral development depends, in part, on intellectual development. The cognitive-developmentalists definitely agree.

COGNITIVE-DEVELOPMENTAL THEORY: THE CHILD AS A MORAL PHILOSOPHER

Cognitive-developmentalists study morality by looking at the development of *moral reasoning*—that is, the thinking that children display when deciding whether various acts are right or wrong. The most basic assumption of the cognitive approach is that moral development depends on cognitive development. Moral reasoning is said to progress through an **invariant sequence** of "stages," each of which is a consistent way of thinking about moral issues that is different from the stages preceding or following it. Presumably each moral stage evolves from and replaces its immediate predecessor, so that there can be no "skipping" of stages. If these assumptions sound familiar, they should, for they are the same ones that Piaget made about his stages of intellectual development.

In this section of the chapter we will consider two cognitive-developmental theories of moral reasoning—Jean Piaget's (1932/1965) model and Lawrence Kohlberg's (1969, 1981) revision and extension of Piaget's approach.

Piaget's Theory of Moral Development

According to Piaget (1932/1965), moral maturity implies both a respect for rules and a sense of social justice—that is, a concern that all people be treated fairly and equitably under the socially defined rules of order. Piaget studied the development of a respect for rules by rolling up his sleeves and playing marbles with a large number of Swiss children. As he played with children of different ages, Piaget would ask them questions about the rules of the game—questions such as "Where do these rules come from? Must everyone obey a rule? Can these rules be changed?" Once he had identified developmental stages in the understanding and use of rules, he proceeded to study children's conceptions of social justice by presenting them with moral dilemmas in the form of stories. Here is one example:

Story A. A little boy who is called John is in his room. He is called to dinner. He goes into the dining room. But behind the door there was a chair, and on the chair there was a tray with 15 cups on it. John couldn't have known that there was all this behind the door. He goes in, the door knocks against the tray, bang go the 15 cups, and they all get broken.

Story B. Once there was a little boy whose name was Henry. One day when his mother was out he tried to reach some jam out of the cupboard. He climbed onto a chair and stretched out his arm. But the jam was too high up, and he couldn't reach it. . . . While he was trying to get it, he knocked over a cup. The cup fell down and broke [Piaget, 1932/1965, p. 122].

Having heard the stories, subjects were asked "Are these children equally guilty?" and "If not, which child is naughtier? Why?" Subjects were also asked how the naughtier child should be punished. Through the use of these research techniques, Piaget formulated a theory of moral development that includes a premoral period and two moral stages.

■ The premoral period

According to Piaget, preschool children show little concern for or awareness of rules. In a game of marbles, these **premoral** children do not play systematically with the intent of winning. Instead, they seem to make up their own rules, and they think the point of the game is to take turns and have fun. Toward the end of the premoral period (ages 4 to 5), the child becomes more aware of rules by watching older children and imitating their rule-bound behavior. But the premoral child does not yet understand that rules represent a cooperative agreement about how a game should be played.

■ The stage of moral realism, or heteronomous morality

Between the ages of 6 and 10, the child develops a strong respect for rules and a belief that they must be obeyed at all times. Children at this **heter-** **onomous** stage assume that rules are laid down by authority figures such as God, the police, or their parents, and they think these regulations are sacred and unalterable. Try breaking the speed limit with a 6-year-old at your side and you may see what Piaget was talking about. Even if you are rushing to the hospital in a medical emergency, the young child may note that you are breaking a "rule of the road" and consider your behavior unacceptable conduct that deserves to be punished. In sum, heteronomous children think of rules as *moral absolutes.* They believe that there are a "right" side and a "wrong" side to any moral issue, and right always means following the rules.

Children at this first moral stage are apt to judge the naughtiness of an act by its objective consequences rather than the actor's intent. For example, Piaget found that many 6–10-year-olds judged John, who accidentally broke 15 cups while performing a well-intentioned act, to be naughtier than Henry, who broke one cup while stealing jam. Perhaps this focus on objective harm done, or **moral realism,** stems from the fact that young children may be punished if and when their behavior produces harmful consequences. For example, a girl who bumps into a table without doing any harm is less likely to be rep-

---

oedipal morality: *Freud's theory that moral development occurs during the phallic period (ages 3 to 6) when children internalize the moral standards of the same-sex parent as they resolve their Oedipus or Electra conflicts.*

invariant sequence: *a series of developments that occur in one particular order because each development in the sequence is a prerequisite for those appearing later.*

premoral period: *in Piaget's theory, the first 4 to 6 years of life, when children have little respect for or awareness of socially defined rules.*

heteronomous morality: *Piaget's first stage of moral development; when children think of rules as moral absolutes that are not to be challenged (also known as the stage of moral realism).*

moral realism: *a characteristic of Piaget's heteronomous stage; when judging whether acts are right or wrong, children focus on the objective harm done rather than on the actor's intentions.*

PHOTO 14-2. According to Piaget, young children display a form of "moral realism" by judging the naughtiness of an act by its objective consequences rather than the actor's intent.

rimanded for her clumsiness than a second youngster who nudges the table and knocks over a number of her mother's plants in the process.

Heteronomous children favor **expiatory punishment**—punishment for its own sake with no concern for its relation to the nature of the forbidden act. For example, a 6-year-old might favor spanking a boy who had misbehaved and broken a window rather than making the boy pay for the window from his allowance. Moreover, the heteronomous child believes in **immanent justice**—the idea that violations of social rules will invariably be punished in one way or another. So if a 6-year-old boy were to fall and skin his knee while stealing cookies, he might conclude that this injury was the punishment he deserved for his transgression. Life for the morally realistic person is fair and just.

■ The stage of moral relativism, or autonomous morality

By age 10 or 11 most children are entering Piaget's second moral stage—the stage of moral relativism, or **autonomous morality**. Older, autonomous children now realize that social rules are arbitrary agreements that can be challenged and even changed with the consent of the people they govern. They also feel that rules can be violated in the service of human needs. Thus, a driver who speeds during a medical emergency will no longer be considered a wrongdoer, even though she is

breaking the law. Judgments of right and wrong now depend more on the actor's intent to deceive or to violate social rules rather than the objective consequences of the act itself. For example, 10-year-olds reliably say that Henry, who broke one cup while stealing some jam (bad intent), is naughtier than John, who broke 15 cups while coming to dinner (good or neutral intent).

When deciding how to punish a transgression, the morally autonomous individual usually favors **reciprocal punishments**—that is, treatments that shape the punitive consequences to the "crime" so that the rule breaker will understand the implications of a transgression and perhaps be less likely to repeat it. For example, an autonomous child may decide that the boy who deliberately breaks a window should pay for it out of his allowance (and learn that windows cost money) rather than simply submitting to a spanking. Children at this higher stage of moral reasoning no longer believe in immanent justice, because they have learned from experience that violations of social rules often go undetected and unpunished.

■ Moving from heteronomous to autonomous morality

Piaget believes that two cognitive deficits contribute to the young child's rigid and absolutistic moral reasoning. The first is **egocentrism**—an inability to recognize perspectives other than one's own. The second is **realism**—the tendency to confuse subjective experience (one's own thoughts) with external reality. Perhaps you can see how these cognitive shortcomings might lead to a sense of moral realism. When parents or other authority figures enforce a rule, the young child assumes that this dictate must be sacred and unalterable, particularly since it comes from a powerful individual who can make the rule stick (realism). And since the child at this age assumes that other people see things as she does (egocentrism), she will conclude that various rules must be "absolutes" that apply to everyone.

According to Piaget, both cognitive maturation and social experience play a role in the transition from heteronomous to autonomous morality. The cognitive advances that are necessary for this shift are a general decline in egocentrism and the development of role-taking skills that will enable the child to view moral issues from several perspectives. The kind of social experience that

Piaget considers important is *equal-status* contact with peers. Beginning at about age 6, the child spends 4–6 hours a day at school surrounded by other children of approximately the same age. When with peers, conflicts will often arise because the members of the peer group will not always agree on how they should play games or solve various problems. Since everyone has roughly equal status, children will soon learn that they must compromise on a course of action, often without any assistance from adults, if they are to play together cooperatively or accomplish other group goals. While settling disputes, each child will assume the roles of "governor" and "governed" and see that rules are merely social contracts that derive their power from the mutal consent of the group members rather than from an external authority figure. In sum, Piaget believes that equal-status contacts with peers lead to a more flexible morality because they (1) lessen the child's unilateral respect for adult authority, (2) increase his or her self-respect and respect for peers, and (3) illustrate that rules are arbitrary agreements that can be changed with the consent of the people they govern.

And what role do parents play? According to Piaget, parents may actually slow the progress of moral development by reinforcing the child's unilateral respect for authority figures. If, for example, a parent enforces a demand with a threat or a statement such as "Do it because *I* told you to," it is easy to see how the young moral realist might conclude that rules are "absolutes" that derive their "teeth" from the parent's power to enforce them. Although Piaget believes that the peer group plays the greater role in the development of autonomous morality, he suggests that parents could help by relinquishing some of their power to establish a more egalitarian relationship with their children.

Tests of Piaget's Theory

Many researchers have used Piaget's methods in an attempt to replicate his findings, and much of the data that they have collected are consistent with his theory. In Western cultures, there is a clear relationship between children's ages and stages of moral reasoning: younger children are more likely than older children to think about rules as moral absolutes, to believe in immanent justice, and to consider the objective consequences of an act rather than the actor's intent when making moral judgments (Hoffman, 1970; Lickona, 1976). Apparently the child's level of moral reasoning does depend, in part, on his or her level of cognitive development. For example, IQ and moral maturity are positively correlated (Lickona, 1976), and children who score high on tests of role taking tend to make more advanced moral judgments than age mates whose role-taking skills are less well developed (Ambron & Irwin, 1975; Selman, 1971). Finally, there is even some support for Piaget's "peer participation" hypothesis: popular children who often take part in social activities and who assume positions of leadership in the peer group tend to make mature moral judgments (Keasey, 1971).

Yet in spite of this supportive evidence, there is reason to believe that Piaget's theory has some very real shortcomings. Let's take a closer look.

■ *Did Piaget underestimate the heteronomous child?*

Recent research indicates that younger children can and often do consider an actor's intentions when evaluating his behavior. One problem with Piaget's moral-decision stories is that they confounded intentions and consequences by asking

---

expiatory punishment: *punitive consequences that bear no relation to the nature of the forbidden act.*

immanent justice: *the notion that unacceptable conduct will invariably be punished.*

autonomous morality: *Piaget's second stage of moral development, in which children realize that rules are arbitrary agreements that can be challenged and even changed with the consent of the people they govern (also called the stage of moral relativism).*

reciprocal punishment: *punitive consequences that are tailored to the forbidden act so that a rule breaker will understand the implications of a transgression.*

egocentrism: *a tendency to view the world from one's own perspective while failing to recognize that others may have different points of view.*

realism: *the tendency of younger children to confuse their own thinking with external reality.*

the child whether a person who caused a small amount of harm in the service of bad intentions was naughtier than one who caused a larger amount of damage while serving good intentions. Since younger children give more weight to concrete evidence that they can see than to abstract information that they must infer (Surber, 1982), it is hardly surprising that they would consider the person who did more damage to be the naughtier of the two.

Sharon Nelson (1980) unconfounded information about an actor's motives and intentions in an interesting experiment with 3-year-olds. Each child listened to stories in which a character threw a ball to a playmate. The actor's motive was described as *good* (his friend had nothing to play with) or *bad* (the actor was mad at his friend), and the consequences of his act were described as *positive* (the friend caught the ball and was happy to play with it) or *negative* (the ball hit the friend in the head and made him cry). To ensure that these young subjects would understand the actor's motives, some of them were shown drawings such as Figure 14-1, which happens to depict a negative intent. The remaining subjects simply had the actor's motives described to them in words by the experimenter. The children were then asked to evaluate the "goodness" or "badness" of the actor's behavior.

The results were rather interesting. As we see in Figure 14-2, Nelson's 3-year-olds did consider acts that produced positive consequences to be more favorable than those producing negative outcomes. Yet the more interesting finding was that the good-intentioned actor who had wanted to play was evaluated much more favorably than the actor who intended to hurt his friend, *regard-*

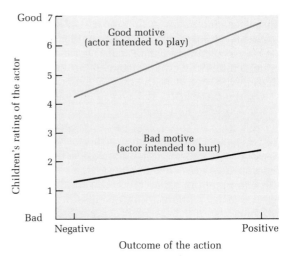

FIGURE 14-2. *Average ratings of an actor's behavior for actors who produced positive or negative outcomes while serving either good or bad intentions.*

less of the consequences of his actions. So 3-year-olds can use intentions when making moral judgments if this information is made clear to them.

Why do younger children not appear more "intentional" on Piaget's moral-decision stories? Probably because (1) intentional information was not made explicit by Piaget (while consequences were), and (2) young children may generally assume that motives and outcomes are logically related. Indeed, Nelson (1980) found that if intentions are not made clear, 3-year-olds assume that actors who produce negative consequences must have had a negative intent. Their problem is not that they fail to consider an actor's intentions but, rather, that they are less proficient than older children at discriminating intentions from consequences and using these separate pieces of information to make moral judgments. When do children first recognize that intentions and consequences are distinctly different kinds of information? Colleen Surber (1982) finds that many youngsters reach this milestone by age 5—some two to four years earlier than Piaget had assumed.

■ *Do heteronomous children respect all rules?* According to Piaget, young children think of rules as sacred and obligatory prescriptions that are laid down by respected authority figures and are not to

FIGURE 14-1. *Example of drawings used by Nelson to convey an actor's intentions to preschool children.*

be questioned or changed. However, Elliot Turiel (1978) notes that children actually encounter two kinds of rules: (1) **moral rules,** which focus on the rights and privileges of individuals, and (2) **social-conventional rules,** which are determined by consensus and serve to govern interpersonal behavior within a particular social setting. The procedures followed while playing marbles are examples of social-conventional rules, whereas prescriptions such as "Thou shalt not steal [shove, hit, lie]" are examples of moral rules. Do children treat these two kinds of rules as equivalent?

Apparently not. In a recent observational study conducted on ten playgrounds, Larry and Maria Nucci (1982) noted the reactions of younger (7–10-year-old) and older (11–14-year-old) children to violations of moral and social-conventional rules. Social-conventional transgressions included acts such as spitting or eating grass—deviations from social norms. Moral transgressions consisted in acts such as throwing sand at smaller children or snatching away a child's playthings—violations of individual rights. Nucci and Nucci found that children from both age groups were much more likely to react to moral than to social-conventional violations. Moreover, children's responses clearly depended on the nature of the transgression. Moral breaches elicited comments about the injury or loss that the victim had suffered, comments about the unfairness of the transgressor's behavior, and retaliatory acts. In contrast, social-conventional violations were greeted with statements that admonished the actors for deviating ("You're not supposed to spit") or ridiculed them in some way ("Bobby and Allison sitting in a tree, K-I-S-S-I-N-G"). Clearly, these 7–14-year-olds showed some respect for both moral and social-conventional rules, although they did not treat them as one and the same.

Judith Smetana (1981) found that even 2½–5-year-olds make important distinctions between moral and social-conventional rules. Moral transgressions such as hitting, stealing, or refusing to share are considered much more serious and deserving of punishment than social-conventional violations such as not staying in one's seat at nursery school or not saying grace before eating. When asked whether a violation would be OK if there were no rule against it, children said that

moral transgressions are always wrong but that social-conventional violations are OK in the absence of any explicit prohibitions. So not only did these preschoolers fail to see social-conventional rules as sacred and unalterable, they actually showed a strong respect for the moral prescriptions at 2½ to 3—much sooner than Piaget had assumed they would.

Piaget was among the first to suggest that children's moral reasoning may develop in stages. His early work stimulated an enormous amount of research and several new insights, some of which were inconsistent with his original theory. One theorist who was profoundly influenced by Piaget and who has contributed many of these new insights is Lawrence Kohlberg of Harvard University.

Kohlberg's Theory of Moral Development

Kohlberg (1963, 1969, 1981) has refined and extended Piaget's theory of moral development by asking 10-, 13-, and 16-year-old boys to resolve a series of "moral dilemmas." Each dilemma challenged the respondent by requiring him to choose between (1) obeying a rule, law, or authority figure and (2) taking some action that conflicts with these rules and commands while serving a human need. The following story is the best known of Kohlberg's moral dilemmas:

> In Europe, a woman was near death from a special kind of cancer. There was one drug that doctors thought might save her. It was a form of radium that a druggist in the same town had recently discovered. The drug was expensive to make, but the druggist was charging $2000, or 10 times the cost of the drug, for a small (possibly life-saving) dose. Heinz, the sick woman's husband, borrowed all the money he could, about $1000, or half of what he needed. He told the druggist that his wife was dying and asked him to

---

moral rules: *standards of acceptable and unacceptable conduct that focus on the rights and privileges of individuals.*

social-conventional rules: *standards of conduct determined by social consensus that serve to regulate behavior within a particular social context.*

sell the drug cheaper or to let him pay later. The druggist replied "No, I discovered the drug, and I'm going to make money from it." Heinz then became desperate and broke into the store to steal the drug for his wife.

Should Heinz have done that?

Kohlberg was actually less interested in the subject's decision (that is, what Heinz should have done) than in the underlying rationale, or "thought structures," that the subject used to justify his decision. To determine the "structure" of a subject's moral reasoning, Kohlberg asked probing questions. Should Heinz be punished for stealing the drug? Did the druggist have a right to charge so much? Would it be proper to charge the druggist with murder? If so, should his punishment be greater if the woman who died was an important person? And so on.

Kohlberg soon discovered some interesting discrepancies between his data and the findings reported earlier by Piaget. First, he noted that the adherence to rules shown by his younger subjects stemmed from a *fear of punishment* rather than a "unilateral respect" for rules or the authority figures who proposed them. Second, Kohlberg found that moral development was far from complete when the child reached age 10 to 12, or Piaget's autonomous stage. Indeed, moral reasoning seemed to evolve and become progressively more complex throughout adolescence and into young adulthood. Careful analyses of his subjects' responses to several dilemmas led Kohlberg to conclude that moral growth progresses through an *invariant sequence* of three moral levels, each of which is composed of two distinct moral stages. According to Kohlberg, the order of these moral levels and stages is invariant because each depends on the development of certain cognitive abilities that evolve in an invariant sequence. Like Piaget, Kohlberg assumes that each succeeding stage evolves from and replaces its predecessor; once the individual has attained a higher stage of moral reasoning, he or she should never regress to earlier stages.

Before looking at Kohlberg's sequence of stages, it is important to emphasize that each stage represents a particular perspective, or *method of thinking* about moral dilemmas, rather than a particular type of moral decision. Decisions are not very informative in themselves, because subjects

at each moral stage might well endorse either of the alternative courses of action when resolving one of these ethical dilemmas.

The basic themes and defining characteristics of Kohlberg's three moral levels and six stages are as follows:

*Level 1: **Preconventional morality.*** At this level, morality is truly external. The child conforms to rules imposed by authority figures in order to avoid punishment or to obtain personal rewards. The preconventional level consists of two stages:

Stage 1: Punishment-and-obedience orientation. At this stage, the child determines the goodness or badness of an act on the basis of its consequences. The child will defer to authority figures and obey their commands in order to avoid punishment. There is no true conception of rules, however; if the child can "get away with" an act, it is not considered bad. The seriousness of a violation depends on the magnitude of its consequences (that is, the amount of punishment received or the amount of objective harm done).

Stage 2: Naive hedonism, or instrumental orientation. A person at the second stage of moral development conforms to rules in order to gain rewards or to satisfy personal needs. Doing things for others is "right" if the actor will benefit in the long run. This low-level reciprocity is quite pragmatic; "You scratch my back and I'll scratch yours" is the guiding philosophy of the individual at Stage 2. The seriousness of a violation now depends, in part, on the actor's intent.

*Level 2: **Conventional morality.*** At this level, the individual strives to obey the rules set forth by others (such as parents, peers, social groups) in order to win praise and recognition for virtuous conduct or to maintain social order.

Stage 3: "Good boy" or "good girl" orientation. Moral behavior is that which pleases, helps, or is approved of by others. Actions are evaluated on the basis of the actor's intent. "He means well" is a common expression of moral approval at this stage. A primary objective of a Stage 3 respondent is to be thought of as a "nice" person.

Stage 4: Authority and social-order-maintaining morality. At this stage, one accepts and conforms to social rules and conventions in order to avoid censure by legitimate authorities. The reason for conformity is not so much a fear of punishment as a belief that rules and laws maintain a social order that is worth preserving. Thus, behavior is judged as "good," or moral, to the extent that it conforms to rules that maintain social order.

Level 3: ***Postconventional morality,*** *or the morality of self-accepted moral principles.* The individual who has attained this third level of moral reasoning is personally committed to a set of principles that are often shared with others and yet transcend particular authority figures. In other words, moral standards are internalized and become the person's own.

Stage 5: Morality of contract, individual rights, and democratically accepted law. There is a flexibility in moral judgments at this stage. Moral actions are those that express the will of the majority or maximize social welfare. To be acceptable, rules must be arrived at by democratic procedures and must be impartial. Laws that are imposed or that compromise the rights of the majority are considered unjust and worthy of challenge. By contrast, the person at Stage 4 will not ordinarily challenge an established law and may be suspicious of those who do. This fifth stage of moral reasoning represents the official morality of the United States Constitution.

Stage 6: Morality of individual principles of conscience. At this "highest" stage of moral reasoning, the individual defines right and wrong on the basis of the self-chosen ethical principles of his or her own conscience. These principles are not concrete rules such as the Ten Commandments. They are abstract moral guidelines or principles of universal justice (and respect for individual rights) that are to be applied in all situations. Deviations from one's self-chosen moral standards produce feelings of guilt or self-condemnation; for example, the Stage 6 conscientious objector may refuse to conform to a draft law that violates his pacifist beliefs. To comply would bring self-degradation, a punishment that may be much more aversive to the conscientious objector than a short prison sentence.

Examples of how subjects at each stage might respond to the Heinz dilemma appear in Box 14-1. Although these particular responses were constructed for illustrative purposes, they represent precisely the kinds of logic that Kohlberg's sub-

jects often use to justify stealing or not stealing the drug.

Tests of Kohlberg's Theory

The data from which Kohlberg fashioned his theory of moral development came from his doctoral research, in which boys aged 10, 13, and 16 each spent up to two hours resolving nine moral dilemmas. In analyzing the data, Kohlberg found that each child showed a fairly consistent pattern of reasoning when justifying his answers to different dilemmas. The kinds of judgments that these boys made seemed to fall into six general categories, which became Kohlberg's six moral stages.

■ *Age trends in the use of Kohlberg's moral stages*

If Kohlberg's stages represent a true developmental sequence, then we might expect that the use of Stage 1 and Stage 2 reasoning will decline with age, while judgments at stages 3 through 6 will become more frequent. Figure 14-3 presents age trends in the use of Kohlberg's moral stages for a sample of American males. Note that preconventional reasoning (stages 1 and 2) declines sharply with age: 80% of the moral judgments of 10-year-olds were preconventional (stages 1 and 2), as opposed to about 18% at age 16–18 and only 3% at age 24. The use of conventional reasoning

> **preconventional morality:** *Kohlberg's term for the first two stages of moral reasoning, in which moral judgments are based on the consequences of an act rather than the relationship of that act to society's rules and customs.*
> **conventional morality:** *Kohlberg's term for the third and fourth stages of moral reasoning, in which moral judgments are based on a desire to maintain good interpersonal relations (Stage 3) or to comply with formal laws and customs (Stage 4).*
> **postconventional morality:** *Kohlberg's term for the fifth and sixth stages of moral reasoning, in which moral judgments are based on social contracts and democratic law (Stage 5) or on universal principles of ethics and justice (Stage 6).*

BOX 14-1
EXAMPLES OF HOW SUBJECTS AT EACH OF KOHLBERG'S SIX MORAL STAGES MIGHT RESPOND TO THE HEINZ DILEMMA

Stage 1: Punishment-and-obedience orientation

Protheft: It isn't really bad to take it—he did ask to pay for it first. He wouldn't do any other damage or take anything else and the drug he'd take is only worth $200, not $2000.

Antitheft: Heinz doesn't have permission to take the drug. He can't just go and break through a window. He'd be a bad criminal doing all that damage. That drug is worth a lot of money and stealing anything so expensive would be a big crime.

Note: Both these answers disregard Heinz's intentions and judge the act in terms of its consequences. The "pro" answer minimizes the consequences while the "con" answer maximizes them. The implication is that big crimes warrant severe punishment.

Stage 2: Instrumental hedonism

Protheft: Heinz isn't really doing any harm to the druggist, and he can always pay him back. If he doesn't want to lose his wife, he should take the drug.

Antitheft: The druggist isn't wrong, he just wants to make a profit like everybody else. That's what you're in business for, to make money.

Note: Heinz's intentions are apparent in the pro answer, while the intentions of the druggist come out in the con answer. Both Heinz and the druggist are "right" for satisfying their own needs or goals.

Stage 3: "Good boy" or "Good girl" morality

Protheft: Stealing is bad, but this is a bad situation. Heinz is only doing something that it is natural for a good husband to do. You can't blame him for doing something out of love for his wife. You'd blame him if he didn't save her.

Antitheft: If Heinz's wife dies, he can't be blamed. You can't say he is heartless for failing to commit a crime. The druggist is the selfish and heartless one. Heinz tried to do everything he really could.

Note: Both the pro and con answers seek to resolve the dilemma by doing what others would approve of under the circumstances. In either case, Heinz is described as a well-intentioned person who is doing what is right.

Stage 4: Authority and social-order-maintaining morality

Protheft: The druggist is leading the wrong kind of life if he just lets somebody die; so it's Heinz's duty

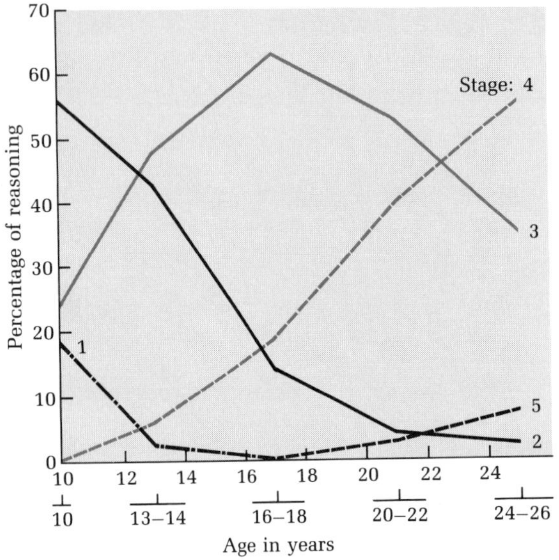

FIGURE 14-3. Use of Kohlberg's moral stages by male subjects aged 10 through 26 years.

(stages 3 and 4) increased until about age 22 and then stabilized at roughly 90% of all moral statements. Postconventional reasoning also increased with age. Whereas the 10- to 16-year-olds in this sample never used Stage 5 or Stage 6 reasoning, approximately 10% of the moral judgments of the 24-year-olds were at the postconventional level (Stage 5). Finally, a few of the 16–24-year-old subjects made statements that Kohlberg had originally interpreted as examples of Stage 6. However, a careful analysis of the rationales underlying these judgments suggested that they were more appropriately classified at stages 3, 4, or 5 (Colby, Kohlberg, Gibbs, & Lieberman, 1983).

Similar age trends have been reported in Mexico, the Bahamas, Taiwan, Turkey, Central America, India, Kenya, and Nigeria (Edwards, 1981; Kohlberg, 1969; Magsud, 1979; Parikh, 1980; Turiel, Edwards, & Kohlberg, 1978). In all these cultures, adolescents and young adults typically reason about moral issues at a higher level

to save her. But Heinz can't just go around breaking laws—he must pay the druggist back and take his punishment for stealing.

Antitheft: It's natural for Heinz to want to save his wife, but it's still always wrong to steal. You have to follow the rules regardless of your feelings or the special circumstances.

Note: The obligation to the law transcends special interests. Even the pro answer recognizes that Heinz is morally wrong and must pay for his transgression.

Stage 5: Morality of contract, individual rights, and democratically accepted law

Protheft: Before you say stealing is wrong, you've got to consider this whole situation. Of course the laws are quite clear about breaking into a store. And even worse, Heinz would know that there were no legal grounds for his actions. Yet it would be reasonable for anybody in this kind of situation to steal the drug.

Antitheft: I can see the good that would come from illegally taking the drug, but the ends don't justify the means. You can't say that Heinz would be completely wrong to steal the drug, but even these circumstances don't make it right.

Note: The judgments are no longer black and white. The pro answer recognizes that theft is legally wrong but that an emotional husband may be driven to steal the drug—and that is understandable (although not completely moral). The con answer recognizes exactly the same points. Heinz would be committing an immoral act in stealing the drug, but he would do so with good intentions.

Stage 6: Morality of individual principles of conscience

Protheft: When one must choose between disobeying a law and saving a human life, the higher principle of preserving life makes it morally right to steal the drug.

Antitheft: With many cases of cancer and the scarcity of the drug, there might not be enough to go around to everybody who needs it. The correct course of action can only be the one that is "right" by all people concerned. Heinz ought to act, not on emotion or the law, but according to what he thinks an ideally just person would do in this case.

Note: Both the pro and con answers transcend the law and self-interest and appeal to higher principles (individual rights, the sanctity of life) that all "reasonable" persons should consider in this situation. The pro answer is relatively straightforward. However, it is difficult to conceive of a "con" Stage 6 response unless the drug was scarce and Heinz would be depriving other equally deserving people of life by stealing the drug to save his wife.

than children do. So it seems that Kohlberg's levels and stages of moral reasoning are "universal"—as we would expect if they represent a true developmental sequence based, in part, on one's intellectual development.

Although Kohlberg has argued that his stages represent an invariant developmental sequence, he believes that only a small minority of any group will actually reach Stage 5 or 6—the postconventional level. In fact, the dominant level of moral reasoning among adults from virtually all societies is conventional morality (stages 3 and 4), and it is not at all unusual to find that people from rural villages in underdeveloped countries show absolutely no evidence of postconventional reasoning (Harkness, Edwards, & Super, 1981; Kohlberg, 1969). Kohlberg suggests that fixation (or arrested development) may occur at any stage if the individual is not exposed to persons or situations that force a reevaluation of current moral concepts. The implication is that people in many societies will not reason at the postconventional level because they are never exposed to the kinds of judgments and experiences that might enable them to progress beyond a sense of conventional morality.

Perhaps we can illustrate this point by briefly contrasting life in an urban, industrialized society with that in a small village in a nonindustrialized country. In industrialized societies consisting of many political, religious, racial, and ethnic groups, people are often governed by a system of justice that transcends these subgroups and is designed (in theory, at least) to maximize the welfare of all social factions. This is precisely the type of sociopolitical climate in which Stage 5 reasoning (the social-contract orientation) could evolve (Harkness et al., 1981). In contrast, people in many rural, nonindustrialized societies are governed at the village or the tribal level, and they need to be concerned only with the laws and customs of their immediate social group. These individuals have little if any experience with the kinds of political compromise and governmental control on which Stage 5 reasoning seems to depend, so that they may never reason about moral issues at the postconventional level. Nevertheless, their conventional reasoning (stages 3 and 4) is perfectly adaptive and hence "mature" within their own social systems (Harkness et al., 1981).

■ Are Kohlberg's stages an invariant sequence?

Although Kohlberg's early research and the cross-cultural studies are generally consistent with his developmental scheme, they do not establish that his moral stages develop in a fixed or invariant sequence. The major problem with the cross-sectional studies is that subjects at each age level were *different* children, and we cannot be certain that a 24-year-old at Stage 5 has progressed through the various moral levels and stages in the order specified by Kohlberg's theory. How can we evaluate the invariant-sequence hypothesis? By examining two important sources of evidence: (1) experimental attempts to modify children's moral judgments and (2) longitudinal studies of the moral development of individual children.

The experimental evidence. If Kohlberg's stages represent an invariant sequence, as he has proposed, then children should be influenced by models who reason about moral issues at one stage higher than their own. However, reasoning that is less advanced should be rejected as too simplistic, and moral judgments that are two stages higher should be too difficult for subjects to comprehend.

Most of the available evidence is consistent with these hypotheses. When exposed to moral reasoning that is one stage above (+1) or one stage below (−1) their own, children generally favor and are more influenced by the more sophisticated set of arguments (Arbuthnot, 1975; Rest, 1983; Turiel, 1966). And yet Lawrence Walker (1982) found that the moral judgments of 10- to 13-year-olds can be influenced by arguments that are *two stages higher* than their own—a level that Kohlberg assumes to be too difficult for them to understand. Does this finding invalidate Kohlberg's invariant-sequence hypothesis? Not necessarily. Walker's subjects were a very select sample of children who had already achieved all

the cognitive prerequisites for the next higher (+1) stage of moral development, even though they were not yet reasoning at that level. By contrast, children who are not ready to move to the next moral stage are generally not influenced by moral arguments that are two stages higher than their own (Turiel, 1966).

The longitudinal evidence. Clearly the most compelling evidence for Kohlberg's invariant-sequence hypothesis would be a demonstration that individual children progress through the moral stages in precisely the order that Kohlberg says that they should. Ann Colby and her associates (Colby et al., 1983) have recently reported the results of a 20-year longitudinal study of 58 American males who were 10, 13, or 16 years old at the beginning of the project. These boys responded to nine of Kohlberg's moral dilemmas when the study began and again in five follow-up sessions administered at three- to four-year intervals. Colby et al. found that subjects proceeded through the stages in the order Kohlberg predicted and that no subject ever skipped a stage between testings. Furthermore, the answers a subject gave during any single testing were remarkably consistent in that about 70% fell within the subjects' dominant moral stage, the remainder falling at an immediately adjacent level (that is, either one stage higher or one stage lower than the person's dominant stage). Similar results have been reported in a three-year longitudinal study of children in the Bahamas (White, Bushnell, & Regnemer, 1978) and a twelve-year longitudinal project conducted in Turkey (Nisan & Kohlberg, 1982). So it would appear that Kohlberg's moral stages do represent a true developmental sequence.

However, regression from higher to lower stages is not unknown, particularly when subjects are retested over very short intervals. The most common reversal is for people who have attained Stage 5 to regress to Stage 4 (or to a point intermediate between stages 4 and 5) at a later testing (Gilligan & Murphy, 1979; Holstein, 1976). Although these reversals may be true developmental regressions (which would disconfirm Kohlberg's invariant-sequence hypothesis), they could also represent the minor fluctuations in performance that people often show when taking the same test twice over a brief interval. Indeed, the "test-retest" explanation is supported by a short-term longitudinal study (Kohlberg & Kramer, 1969) in which the few subjects who had seemed to regress from Stage 4 in high school to a lower stage of moral reasoning in college were later reasoning at either Stage 4 or Stage 5 when retested during their midtwenties.

Finally, the only way that we can consider movement from Stage 5 to Stage 4 to be a true developmental regression is if we also assume that stages 5 and 6 are somehow better or more "mature" than Stage 4 reasoning. It may be that Kohlberg is only partly correct—that stages 1–4 represent an invariant developmental sequence and that stages 5 and 6 will require a very special kind of environment to ever emerge (Gibbs, 1979; Harkness et al., 1981; Saltzstein, 1983). At one point, Kohlberg himself suggested that stages 4, 5, and 6 may be "alternative types of mature [reasoning] rather than an invariant sequence" (1969, p. 385). Additional research is needed to clarify this point. Yet it is worth noting that whenever Stage 5 reasoning first appears, it has always evolved from the subject's Stage 4 reasoning—a finding that supports Kohlberg's invariant-sequence hypothesis (Colby et al., 1983).

■ *The relationship of Kohlberg's stages to cognitive development*

According to Kohlberg (1963), the young, preconventional child reasons about moral issues from an egocentric point of view. At Stage 1 the child thinks that certain acts are bad because they are punished. At Stage 2 the child shows a limited awareness of the needs, thoughts, and intentions of others but still judges self-serving acts as "right," or appropriate. However, conventional reasoning clearly requires an ability to role-take, or assume the perspective of others. For example, a person at Stage 3 must necessarily recognize others' points of view before she will evaluate intentions that would win their approval as "good" or morally acceptable. Furthermore, postconventional, or "principled," morality would seem to require much more than a loss of egocentrism and a capacity for reciprocal-role taking: the person who bases moral judgments on abstract principles must be able to reason abstractly rather than simply adhering to concrete moral norms. In other words, Kohlberg believes that the highest level of cognitive development, *formal oper-*

ations, is necessary for principled moral reasoning (stages 5 and 6).

Much of the available research is consistent with Kohlberg's hypotheses. For example, John Moir (1974) administered Kohlberg's "dilemmas test" and several measures of role taking to a group of 11-year-old girls, many of whom showed a mixture of Stage 2 (preconventional) and Stage 3 (conventional) reasoning on the moral dilemmas. Moir found a very substantial positive correlation between role-taking abilities and moral maturity; girls who were more proficient at role taking were more likely to reason at Kohlberg's conventional level (Stage 3). In another study of 10–13-year-olds, Lawrence Walker (1980) found that the only subjects who had reached Kohlberg's third stage of moral reasoning ("good boy/good girl" morality) were those who were quite proficient at reciprocal-role taking. However, not all the proficient role takers had reached Stage 3 in their moral reasoning. So Walker's results imply that reciprocal-role-taking skills are *necessary but not sufficient* for the development of conventional morality.

Carol Tomlinson-Keasey and Charles Keasey (1974) administered Kohlberg's moral dilemmas and three tests of cognitive development to sixth-grade girls (age 11–12) and to college women. An interesting pattern emerged. All the subjects who reasoned at the postconventional level (Stage 5) on the dilemmas showed at least some formal-operational thinking on the cognitive tests. But not all the formal operators reasoned at the postconventional level on the dilemmas test. This same pattern also emerged in a later study by Deanna Kuhn and her associates (Kuhn, Kohlberg, Langer, & Haan, 1977). So it seems that formal operations are *necessary but not sufficient* for the development of postconventional morality.

In sum, Kohlberg's moral stages are clearly related to one's level of cognitive development. Proficiency at role taking may be necessary for the onset of conventional morality, and formal operations appear to be necessary for postconventional, or "principled," morality. Yet it is important to emphasize that intellectual growth does not guarantee moral development, for a person who has reached Piaget's highest stages of intellect may continue to reason at the preconventional level about moral issues. The implication, then, is that both *intellectual growth* and *relevant social experiences* (exposure to persons or situations that force a reevaluation of one's current moral concepts) are necessary before children can progress from preconventional morality to Kohlberg's higher stages.

■ Some lingering questions about Kohlberg's approach

The relationship between moral reasoning and moral behavior. One common criticism of Kohlberg's theory is that it is based on subjects' responses to hypothetical and somewhat artificial dilemmas that they do not have to face themselves (Baumrind, 1978). Would children reason in the same way about the moral dilemmas they actually encounter? Would an individual who said that Heinz should steal the drug actually do so if he were in Heinz's shoes? Can we ever predict a person's moral behavior from a knowledge of his or her stage of moral reasoning?

Many researchers have found that the moral judgments of young children do *not* predict their actual behavior in situations where they are induced to cheat or violate other moral norms (Nelson, Grinder, & Biaggio, 1969; Santrock, 1975; Toner & Potts, 1981). However, studies of older grade school children, adolescents, and young adults often find at least some consistency between moral reasoning and moral conduct (see Blasi, 1980, for a review of the evidence). Kohlberg (1975), for example, found that only 15% of those students who reasoned at the postconventional level actually cheated when given an opportunity, compared with 55% of the "conventional" students and 70% of those at the preconventional level. Yet Kohlberg is hardly surprised that moral reasoning often fails to predict moral behavior; after all, he has argued that subjects at any of his moral stages may favor either course of action when resolving an ethical dilemma. It is the *structure* of their reasoning that sets them apart into different "stages" of moral development, not the decisions they reach.

In sum, Kohlberg expects a significant but imperfect relationship between moral reasoning and moral behavior, and this is precisely what the data seem to show (Blasi, 1980). A person who reasons at Stage 5 will often act differently in moral situations than one who reasons at Stage 4 or at Stage 2. However, the correlations between moral reasoning and moral conduct that are reported in this research are based on *group* trends, and it is not always possible to specify how an *individual* will behave from a knowledge of his or her stage of moral reasoning.

Situational influences on moral reasoning. One interesting aspect of Kohlberg's research is that subjects are fairly consistent in the type (or stage) of reasoning that they use to resolve different moral issues. Does this coherence simply reflect the fact that all Kohlberg's dilemmas are abstract and hypothetical? Would subjects be so consistent when reacting to more common moral issues—ones that they may often face? Apparently not, for Leming (1978) found that adolescents use lower levels of moral reasoning when asked to resolve practical dilemmas that could have negative consequences *for them.*

The impact of negative consequences on moral reasoning is nicely illustrated in a recent study by William Sobesky (1983). High school and college students read and resolved a version of the Heinz dilemma in which the consequences of stealing the drug were described as rather severe (Heinz would definitely be caught and sent to prison) or quite mild (Heinz could take such a small amount of the drug that it would not be missed). Subjects were asked to imagine themselves in Heinz's position and to describe what they would do and why. Sobesky found that when the consequences were severe, people were less likely to advocate stealing the drug, and the levels of moral reasoning used to justify their decisions were lower. We see, then, that both the content and the structure of moral reasoning depend to some extent on the situation. Subjects reason at a higher level when resolving hypothetical dilemmas (or those without serious personal consequences) than when thinking about practical moral issues that could have negative implications for themselves.

The question of sex differences. Some investigators have reported an interesting sex difference in moral reasoning: adult females are typically at Stage 3 of Kohlberg's stage sequence, while adult males are usually at Stage 4 (Holstein, 1976; Kohlberg, 1969; Parikh, 1980). Does this mean that females are less morally mature than males (as Freud had assumed)? Carol Gilligan (1977, 1982) says no, arguing that Kohlberg's moral stages were derived from interviews with males and that they may not capture the essence of feminine moral reasoning. In Box 14-2, we will consider the basis for Gilligan's provocative claim as we examine the kinds of moral judgments that her female subjects displayed when deciding whether to have abortions.

■ Summing up

Kohlberg's theory is an important statement about children's moral growth. He has identified a sequence of moral stages that does seem to be related to cognitive development. Yet the theory applies most directly to the cognitive aspects of morality—specifically, to the reasoning that people use to justify moral decisions that they make when resolving hypothetical dilemmas. There is some question whether the theory applies equally well to males and females. We've also seen that moral reasoning does not always predict moral behavior and that both these components of morality depend to some extent on the situation that one faces. In the next section, we will examine a third theory—the social-learning approach—that attempts to specify some of the important social and situational influences on a child's moral development.

MORALITY AS A PRODUCT OF SOCIAL LEARNING

Unlike psychoanalytic theorists, who assume that the development of the superego implies a consistent moral orientation, social-learning theorists propose a *"theory of specificity."* The implications of these opposing viewpoints can be seen in the following example. Suppose we expose a young girl to two tests of moral conduct. In the first test, the child is told not to play with some attractive toys and is then left alone with the toys. The second test is one in which the child is left to play a game that is "rigged" in such a way that she must cheat in order to win a valuable prize. Each situation requires the child to resist the temptation to do something she is not supposed to do before we would label her behavior morally responsible. If morality is a general attribute, as the psychoanalysts contend, our subject should either resist temptation on both of the tests or transgress on both. However, if morality is specific to the situation, the child might resist temp-

tation on both tests, transgress on both, or resist on one and transgress on the other.

Prominent social-learning theorists such as Justin Aronfreed (1976) and Albert Bandura (1977) think of moral behavior as a class of "socially acceptable" responses that are self-reinforcing (for example, it feels good to help) or instrumental for avoiding guilt, anxiety, or punishment. Bandura argues that specific moral responses or habits are acquired in much the same way as any other type of social behavior—through direct tuition and observational learning. Thus, if the girl in our example had often been punished for violating verbal prohibitions (or rewarded for following instructions) and had been reinforced in the past for her honesty (or exposed to honest models), she might well resist temptation on both of the "moral conduct" tests. But inconsistent behavior could occur if one of these moral habits (for example, complying with verbal instructions) had been established while the other (honesty) had not.

How Consistent Is Moral Behavior?

Perhaps the most extensive study of children's moral conduct is one of the oldest—the Character Education Inquiry reported by Hugh Hartshorne and Mark May (1928–1930). The purpose of this five-year project was to investigate the moral "character" of 10,000 children (aged 8–16) by tempting them to lie, cheat, or steal in a variety of situations. The most noteworthy finding of this massive investigation was that children tended *not* to be consistent in their moral behavior; a child's willingness to cheat in one situation did not predict his or her willingness to lie, cheat, or steal in other situations. Of particular interest was the finding that children who cheated in a particular setting were just as likely as those who did not to state that cheating is wrong! Hartshorne and May concluded that "honesty" is largely specific to the situation rather than a stable character trait.

> doctrine of specificity: *a viewpoint shared by many social-learning theorists which holds that moral reasoning and moral behavior depend more on the situation one faces than on an internalized set of moral principles.*

BOX 14-2
GILLIGAN'S THEORY OF FEMALE
MORAL DEVELOPMENT

Do females have a different orientation to moral issues than males do? Are there fundamental differences between the sexes in the character of moral reasoning? Carol Gilligan (1977, 1982) believes that males and females do adopt different perspectives on moral issues and that these sex differences in moral reasoning stem from the ways in which boys and girls are raised. Gilligan suggests that boys learn to be independent, assertive, and achievement-oriented—experiences that encourage them to consider moral dilemmas as inevitable conflicts of interest between two or more parties that laws and other social conventions are designed to resolve (a perspective that represents Stage 4 reasoning in Kohlberg's scheme). By contrast, girls are taught to be nurturant, empathic, and concerned about the needs of others—in short, to define their sense of "goodness" in terms of their relationships with other people. These experiences should encourage females to think of moral dilemmas as conflicts between one's own selfishness and the needs or desires of others (a perspective that approximates Stage 3 in Kohlberg's scheme). According to Gilligan, the interpersonal orientation that women adopt when thinking about moral issues is neither more nor less mature than the rule-bound morality of men. Instead, she views these two moralities as "separate but equal" and suggests that females go through a different series of moral stages than males do.

Gilligan's next step was to study the moral development of females by asking pregnant women to discuss an important dilemma that they were currently facing—should they continue their pregnancies or have abortions? After analyzing the responses of her 29 subjects, Gilligan proposed that women's moral judgments progress through a sequence of three levels (and two transitions between levels), where each level represents a more complex understanding of the relationship between one's own perspective and the rights and concerns of others.

These moral levels (and transitions) are described as follows.

Level I: Orientation to individual survival

At this first level, a woman's thinking about abortion centers on her own needs and desires. The issue is individual survival, and the needs of others are largely ignored. For example, one 18-year-old, when asked what she thought when she found herself pregnant, replied: "I really didn't think anything except that I didn't want it . . . I wasn't ready for it, and next year will be my last year and I want to go to school" (Gilligan, 1977, p. 492).

The first transition: From selfishness to responsibility. According to Gilligan, there is a transitional period between Level I and Level II reasoning when women first recognize that there may be a clash between their own desires and the responsible course of action—a conflict between "doing something for oneself" and "doing the right thing." For example, one young woman stated: "What I want to do is to have the baby, . . . but what I feel I should do is to have an abortion right now. . . . Sometimes what is necessary comes before what you want, because [what you want] might not always lead to the right thing" (Gilligan, 1977, p. 494). Gilligan believes that females must experience this transitional conflict between selfishness and responsibility before they can move to the second level of moral reasoning.

Level II: Goodness as self-sacrifice

At this level, women have adopted many traditional feminine values and have come to evaluate themselves in terms of their interpersonal relationships. Now the orientation is to do right by others and to avoid hurting them if at all possible—even if one's decision represents a personal sacrifice. Clearly, the issue of hurting others is of primary concern when women reason about an abortion. When there is no decision that she can make that seems in the best interests of everyone, a female finds it exceedingly difficult to choose the "right" course of action. For example, a woman who feels protective toward her unborn fetus, and yet knows that her mate wishes her

---

This "doctrine of specificity" has been questioned by other researchers. Roger Burton (1963) reanalyzed Hartshorne and May's data using newer and more sophisticated statistical techniques. His analyses provide some evidence for a character trait of honesty. A similar outcome was reported by Nelson, Grinder, and Mutterer (1969), who administered six resistance-to-temptation tests to sixth-grade children and found that "temptation behavior is at least moderately consistent across a variety of tasks" (p. 265). Finally, Philippe Rushton (1980) reports some consistency in children's altruistic behavior: those who are most helpful in one particular context are likely to provide assistance in related contexts. So we see that moral behavior is not nearly so "situationally

to abort it, is clearly in a no-win situation. If she aborts, she does the "right" thing in terms of the father's wishes but ignores her own feelings and the rights of the child. However, a decision not to abort might be construed as doing right by the fetus while ignoring the father's wishes. When forced to choose between two things she loves, the woman feels that she must make a large personal sacrifice, regardless of whether she serves the needs of her mate by aborting or those of her fetus by continuing the pregnancy.

The second transition: From goodness to truth.
Between Level II and Level III comes a transitional period in which women begin to question the logic of moral self-sacrifice. Once again, the issue of selfishness versus responsibility comes to the forefront, but this time the woman also considers the "rightness" of hurting oneself as well as the issue of hurting others. She strives to be responsible to others and thus "good" but also to be responsible to herself and, thus, truthful or "honest." One Catholic woman illustrated this transitional logic by stating "I am doing it [abortion] because I have to do it. I'm not doing it the least bit because I want to. . . . Keeping the child . . . was impractical" (Gilligan, 1977, p. 500). This woman went on to state that, in the beginning, she had decided to have an abortion not so much for herself as for her parents (that is, to be good to others). But in the final analysis, she admitted to herself that she honestly didn't want to be a mother and that it is not always right to hurt oneself in the name of morality.

Level III: The morality of nonviolence
At this third level, women have largely rejected the notion of moral self-sacrifice as immoral in its power to hurt the self. The principle of nonviolence—an injunction against hurting—becomes the basic premise underlying all moral judgments. Looking after the welfare of people is now a self-chosen and *universal* obligation that permits the woman to recognize a moral equality between herself and others that must be considered when making moral judgments. This morality of nonviolence is apparent in the justifi-cation that one 25-year-old gave for having an abortion: "I would not be doing myself or the child a favor by having this child . . . I don't need to pay off my imaginary debts to the world through this child, and I don't think that it is right to bring a child into the world and use it for that purpose" (Gilligan, 1977, p. 505). Note that the concern here is to hurt neither oneself nor the baby. Although the decision to terminate the pregnancy was described as a "very heavy thing" that obviously compromised the woman's principles of nonviolence, she felt that the ultimate harm to herself and to an unwanted child could be greater had she decided to continue her pregnancy. Gilligan concludes that this Level III moral reasoning is every bit as abstract and "postconventional" as Kohlberg's highest stages, even though Kohlberg's scheme places it at Stage 3 (and hence less mature) because of its focus on personal and interpersonal obligations.

Evaluating Gilligan's approach
Although Gilligan's theory represents an exciting new perspective on female moral development, many questions remain to be answered. For example, will men who are affected by an abortion decision show similar patterns of moral reasoning when thinking about this issue? Gilligan's theory seems to suggest that they will not. Will females reason in the same ways about practical dilemmas other than abortion (for example, mercy killing or capital punishment)? Do Gilligan's moral levels and transitions represent an invariant developmental sequence that is related to cognitive development in the same way that Kohlberg's stages seem to be? And how might Gilligan explain the fact that the vast majority of studies using the Kohlberg scheme find no sex differences in moral reasoning? (See Walker, 1984, for a review.) These are some of the issues that must now be resolved before we will know whether Gilligan's model is a more accurate account of female moral development than the sequence of moral levels and stages described earlier by Lawrence Kohlberg.

specific" as Hartshorne and May had thought. However, these results do not minimize the importance of the setting, for a child's willingness to lie, cheat, or violate other moral prohibitions is definitely influenced by a variety of situational factors such as the importance of the goal that can be achieved by transgressing, the probability of being detected, and the amount of encouragement provided by peers for deviant behavior (Burton, 1976).

Determinants of Children's Resistance to Temptation

From society's standpoint the most important index of morality is the extent to which an individual is able to resist pressures to violate moral norms *even when the possibility of detection and punishment is remote* (Hoffman, 1970). A person who resists temptation in the absence of external surveillance not only has learned a moral rule but also is internally motivated to abide by that rule. How do children acquire moral standards, and what motivates them to obey these learned codes of conduct? Social-learning theorists have attempted to answer these questions by studying the effects of reinforcement, punishment, and social modeling on children's moral behavior.

■ *The resistance-to-temptation paradigm*

When studying children's resistance to temptation, an experimenter will first establish a prohibition of some sort and then leave the child alone so that he or she is tempted to violate that edict. A common procedure is to inform children that they are not to touch certain attractive toys but that they are free to play with any number of other unattractive objects. Once a child has learned the prohibition and refrains from playing with the attractive items, the experimenter leaves the room and thereby tempts the child to violate the rule. As we will see, this **"forbidden toy" paradigm** has proved quite useful at determining whether various forms of praise, punishment, and other disciplinary techniques affect the child's willingness to comply with rules and regulations.

■ *Reinforcement as a determinant of moral conduct*

We have seen on several occasions that the frequency of many behaviors can be increased if these acts are reinforced. Moral behaviors are certainly no exception. For example, sharing among

PHOTO 14-3. *Sometimes it is difficult to tell whether children are working together, helping each other, or using each other's work. Although there is some consistency to moral behavior, a child's conduct in any particular situation is likely to be influenced by factors such as the importance of the goal that might be achieved by breaking a moral rule and the probability of being caught should he or she commit a transgression.*

preschool children becomes more common when adults reinforce these acts of kindness with bubble gum (Fischer, 1963). But the role played by external reward in the establishment and maintenance of **inhibitory controls** is difficult to determine, because parents, teachers, and peers will often fail to recognize that the child has *resisted* a temptation and is deserving of praise. By contrast, other people are quick to inform the child of his or her misdeeds by *punishing* moral transgressions!

Does punishment play a larger role than reinforcement in the establishment of moral controls? Although many children would probably say yes, it appears that reinforcement may be a very important part of a child's moral education. David Perry and Ross Parke (1975) found that children were less likely to violate a prohibition against touching attractive toys if they had been reinforced for playing with other unattractive items. Thus, rewarding alternative behaviors that are incompatible with prohibited acts can be an effective method of instilling moral controls. In addition, physical punishment administered by a warm, loving (socially reinforcing) parent is more effective at producing resistance to temptation than the same punishment given by a cold, rejecting parent (Sears, Maccoby, & Levin, 1957). Although adults may often use punishment as a means of establishing moral prohibitions, the effectiveness of this strategy will depend, in part, on their past history as *reinforcing* agents.

■ *The role of punishment in establishing moral controls*

Parents often assume that the best way to restrain a child's undesirable antics is to punish them. Yet many psychologists believe that punishment produces anger, resentment, and at best a temporary suppression of the behavior that it is designed to eliminate. Their point is that a fear of aversive consequences can never be a totally effective deterrent, because the child will simply inhibit unacceptable conduct until it is unlikely to be detected and punished.

Both arguments have some merit. Parents who are severely punitive do tend to raise hostile, antisocial children (Bandura & Walters, 1959), and few contemporary theorists believe that a person's internal morality, or capacity for *self*-control, is based on a fear that unacceptable behavior will

be detected and punished. Nevertheless, punishment can have a beneficial effect on children's moral development if it is not overly harsh and if it attaches negative affect to the acts that are punished. In other words, fear of detection and punishment is not enough; children must wish to avoid the prohibited act itself before they will inhibit that response when there is no one around to oversee their activities.

Early research on the effects of punishment. Ross Parke and his associates have used the "forbidden toy" paradigm to study the effects of punishment on children's resistance to temptation. During the first phase of a typical experiment, subjects are punished (usually by hearing a loud and noxious buzzer) whenever they touch an attractive toy; however, nothing happens when they play with unattractive toys. Once the child has learned the prohibition, the experimenter leaves the room. The child is then surreptitiously observed to determine whether he or she plays with the forbidden objects.

Parke found that not all punishments are equally effective at promoting the development of moral controls. You may recall that we discussed much of this research when we looked at the effects of punishment in Chapter Seven. By way of review, Table 14-1 briefly summarizes the conditions under which punishment was most effective at inhibiting the child's undesirable conduct after the disciplinarian had left the room.

Effects of cognitive rationales. When parents punish a child, they often will indicate why he or she is being punished and will explain why the prohibited act was wrong. Ross Parke (1977) believes that virtually any form of punishment be-

---

"forbidden toy" paradigm: *a method of studying children's resistance to temptation by noting whether youngsters will play with forbidden toys when they believe that this transgression is unlikely to be detected.*

inhibitory control: *an ability to display acceptable conduct by resisting the temptation to commit a forbidden act.*

TABLE 14-1. Characteristics of punishment and the punitive context that influence a child's resistance to temptation

Timing of punishment	Punishment administered as children initiate deviant acts is more effective than punishment given after the acts have been performed. Early punishment makes children apprehensive as they prepare to commit a transgression, so that they are less likely to follow through. By contrast, late punishment makes children apprehensive *after* the act is completed, so that they may perform the act again and only then feel anxious.
Intensity of punishment	High-intensity punishment (a loud buzzer or forceful *NO!*) is more effective at inhibiting undesirable conduct than mild punishments are. However, a caution is in order, for very intense punishments such as a forceful spanking can backfire by making children hostile toward the punitive agent and willing to deviate "out of spite" when the disciplinarian is not around to oversee their activities.
Consistency of punishment	To be effective, punishment must be administered consistently. Satisfying acts that are punished erratically or inconsistently persist for long periods and are difficult to eliminate even after the punitive agent begins to punish them on a regular basis.
Relationship to the punitive agent	Punishment is more effective at establishing moral prohibitions when administered by someone who has previously established a warm and friendly (rewarding) relationship with the child.

comes more effective if it is accompanied by a **cognitive rationale** that provides the child with reasons for inhibiting a forbidden act. Even a simple statement such as "Don't touch these toys because I don't have any others like them" may be effective with young children. In fact, Parke (1972, 1977) found that when rationales accompany punishment, (1) mild forms of punishment become just as effective at producing resistance to temptation as strong punishment, (2) delayed punishment becomes as effective as early punishment, and (3) punishment from an aloof, impersonal adult becomes as effective as that administered by a warm and rewarding disciplinarian. Parke also noted that resistance to temptation is much more stable over time if children are told why their deviant acts are inappropriate when they receive their punishment. This finding is extremely important, for it suggests that the establishment of long-term (internalized) moral controls "may *require* the use of cognitively oriented training procedures. Punishment techniques that rely solely on anxiety induction, such as the noxious noises employed . . . in many experiments . . . or the more extreme forms of physical punishment sometimes used by parents may be effective mainly in securing only short-term inhibition" (Parke, 1972, p. 274).

Do rationales alone produce any resistance to temptation? Indeed they do. In fact, Parke reports that rationales are more effective than mild punishment at persuading children not to touch attractive toys. However, let's not conclude that parents should abandon punishment in favor of rationales, for a combination of a punishment and a rationale is much more effective than either of these treatments by itself (Parke, 1972).

Why are rationales important for the establishment of moral controls? Justin Aronfreed (1976) suggests two reasons. First, the anxiety stemming from the aversive aspects of a disciplinary encounter may become conditioned to both the deviant act *and the cognitive rationale*, particularly if the disciplinary agent has stressed the child's intentions when punishing a transgression (for example, "You shouldn't have wanted to touch that toy because it might break"). Once this conditioning occurs, the child should become rather anxious or apprehensive at the mere thought of committing the deviant act. Second, the rationale provides the child with a *good reason* for inhibiting undesirable behavior, so that he or she can reduce anxiety by refusing to deviate and, at the same time, feel good about this "mature and responsible" conduct.

Parke (1974, 1977) finds that not all rationales

are equally effective at producing resistance to temptation. Preschool children are much more responsive to concrete, *object-oriented* rationales such as "Don't touch the toy; it's fragile and may break" than to abstract rationales based on ownership (for example, "Don't touch the toy; it belongs to someone else"). By contrast, older children tend to be more responsive to abstract, *person-oriented* rationales that indicate ownership or justify response inhibition in terms of the negative effects that a transgression would have on others (for example, "I'll be sad if you touch the toy"). So it appears that rationales are most effective when they are consistent with the ways in which children normally think about moral rules and issues: young, morally realistic children seem to require concrete rationales, whereas older, morally autonomous children are affected more by reasoning that focuses on the rights, privileges, and feelings of other people.

■ *Effects of social models on children's moral behavior*

Social-learning theorists have generally assumed that modeling influences play an important role in the child's moral development. And they are undoubtedly correct, for as we have seen, young children often imitate the compassionate and helpful acts of altruistic models. But helpful acts are *active* responses that will capture a child's attention. Will children learn *inhibitory controls* from models who exhibit socially desirable behavior in a "passive" way by failing to commit forbidden acts?

Apparently they will, as long as they recognize that the "passive" model is actually resisting the temptation to violate a moral norm. Nace Toner and his associates (Toner, Parke, & Yussen, 1978) exposed preschool and second-grade boys to rule-following models and found that this experience did indeed promote resistance to temptation. In fact, some of the children who had been exposed to the rule-following models were still following the rule when retested a week later. In a similar study, Joan Grusec and her associates (Grusec, Kuczynski, Rushton, & Simutis, 1979) found that a model who resists temptation can be particularly effective at inspiring children to behave in kind if he clearly verbalizes that he is following a rule and states a rationale for not committing the devi-

ant act. Finally, the type of rationale that the model provides to justify his resistance to temptation is important. Rule-following models whose rationales match the child's customary level of moral reasoning are more influential than models whose rationales are beyond that level (Toner & Potts, 1981).

Of course, a model who violates a moral norm may *disinhibit* observers by giving them reason to think that they too can break the rule, particularly if the model is not punished for his deviant acts (Rosenkoetter, 1973; Walters & Parke, 1964). Thus, social models play two roles in a child's moral development, sometimes leading him or her to resist temptation and at other times serving as "bad influences" who encourage inappropriate conduct.

On serving as a model of moral restraint. An experiment by Nace Toner and his associates produced a very interesting outcome: 6- to 8-year-olds who were persuaded to serve as models of moral restraint for other children became more likely than age mates who had not served as exemplary models to obey rules during later tests of resistance to temptation (Toner, Moore, & Ashley, 1978). It was almost as if serving as a model had produced a change in the children's self-concepts, so that they now defined themselves as "people who follow rules." The implications for child rearing are obvious: perhaps parents could succeed in establishing inhibitory controls in their older children by appealing to their maturity and persuading them to serve as models of self-restraint for their younger brothers and sisters.

Promoting honesty through self-instruction. Recently, William Casey and Roger Burton (1982) found that 7- to 10-year-olds became much more honest while playing games if "honesty" was stressed and the players had learned to remind themselves to follow the rules. Yet when honesty was *not* stressed, the players were likely to cheat—

---

cognitive rationale: *reasoning that describes why a forbidden act is wrong and should not be performed.*

PHOTO 14-4. A child who has served as a rule-following model is likely to obey that rule in the future.

even when they had been taught to periodically tell themselves how they were supposed to be playing. So it appears that children can become effective allies in their own moral socialization if they are often encouraged to be good or "honest" persons and have learned to remind themselves of the rules they must follow in order to establish a good or an "honest" self-image.

Is Morality a Stable and Unitary Attribute?

Earlier in the chapter, we saw that psychoanalytic theorists think of morality as a reasonably stable attribute that is controlled by the superego, whereas social-learning theorists argue that morality is unstable, or situation-specific. Can you guess where the cognitive-developmentalists stand on this issue? As it turns out, they side with the psychoanalysts; moral reasoning is said to be reasonably consistent across situations and a strong determinant of both moral affect and moral behavior.

If morality is a stable and **unitary** attribute, we should find that the three basic components of moral character—affect, reasoning, and behavior—bear some meaningful relationship to one another. Yet we've already learned that the moral reasoning of young children does not predict their moral conduct and that a child's willingness to lie, cheat, or steal in one particular situation is not a very good indicator of how he or she will behave in other situations.

However, studies of adolescents and young adults often find that (1) the moral behavior of these older subjects is more consistent across situations than that of younger children and (2) there is some consistency between their moral reasoning and moral behavior. And at least one study of young adults (MacKinnon, 1938) found a link between moral affect (guilt) and moral behavior: subjects who did not cheat on a problem-solving task reported that they would have felt guilty if they had, whereas those who cheated and denied their transgression said that they would not have felt guilty about cheating.

So we see that morality is neither a unified whole, as envisioned by the psychoanalytic and the cognitive-developmental theorists, nor totally specific to the situation, as the social-learning theorists argue. It is possible that moral affect, moral reasoning, and moral behavior emerge as three separate "moralities" that older children eventually integrate *to some extent* as they reach that point in their intellectual development when they are able to recognize the basic commonalities among these three moral components. However, it is unlikely that the "moral character" of even the most mature of adults is perfectly consistent across all settings and situations.

WHO RAISES CHILDREN WHO ARE MORALLY MATURE?

Several years ago, Martin Hoffman (1970) carefully reviewed the child-rearing literature to determine whether the techniques that parents use to discipline transgressions have any effect on the moral development of their children. Much of the research that he reviewed was designed to test the hypothesis that **love-oriented discipline** (withdrawing affection or approval), which generates

TABLE 14-2. Relationships between parents' use of three disciplinary strategies and children's moral development

Direction of relationship (between parent's use of a disciplinary strategy and children's moral maturity)	Type of discipline		
	Power assertion	Love withdrawal	Induction
+ (positive correlation)	7	8	38
− (negative correlation)	32	11	6

Note: Table entries represent the number of occasions on which a particular disciplinary technique was found to be associated (either positively or negatively) with a measure of children's moral affect, reasoning, or behavior.

anxiety over a loss of love, would prove more effective at furthering the child's moral development than **power-assertive discipline** (physical punishment or withholding privileges), which generates anger or resentment.

Hoffman discovered that neither love withdrawal nor power assertion is particularly effective at promoting moral development. In fact, parents who often rely on power-assertive techniques have children who can be described as morally immature. The one disciplinary strategy that seems to foster the development of moral affect (guilt, shame), moral reasoning, and moral behavior is an approach called **induction**. Induction

> includes techniques in which the parent gives explanations or reasons for requiring the child to change his behavior. Examples are pointing out physical requirements of the situation or the harmful consequences of the child's behavior for himself or others. These techniques are . . . an attempt to . . . convince the child that he should change his behavior in the prescribed manner. Also included are techniques that appeal to conformity-inducing agents that already exist with the child. Examples are appeals to the child's pride, strivings for mastery and to be "grown up," and concern for others [Hoffman, 1970, p. 286].

Hoffman noted that inductive parents who regularly stress the needs and emotions of others as part of their discipline have children who show the highest levels of moral maturity. This "other-oriented" induction is accomplished by

> directly pointing out the nature of the consequence (e. g., If you throw snow on their wall, they will have to clean it up all over again; Pulling the

leash like that can hurt the dog's neck; That hurts my feelings); pointing out the relevant needs or desires of others (e. g., he is afraid . . . , so please turn the lights back on); or explaining the motives underlying the other person's behavior toward the child (e. g., Don't yell at him. He was only trying to help) [Hoffman, 1970, p. 286].

Table 14-2 summarizes the relationships among the three patterns of parental discipline (power assertion, love withdrawal, and induction) and various measures of children's moral development. Clearly these data confirm Hoffman's conclusion: parents who rely on inductive discipline tend to have children who are morally mature, whereas frequent use of power assertion may actually inhibit the child's moral development.

Why is induction such an effective disciplinary

---

unitary morality: *the notion that moral affect, moral reasoning, and moral behavior are interrelated components of a "moral character" that is consistent across situations.*

love-oriented discipline: *a form of discipline in which an adult withholds attention, affection, or approval in order to modify or control a child's behavior.*

power-assertive discipline: *a form of discipline in which an adult relies on his or her superior power (for example, by administering spankings or withholding privileges) to modify or control a child's behavior.*

inductive discipline: *a nonpunitive form of discipline in which an adult relies on cognitive rationales to modify or control a child's behavior.*

technique? Hoffman suggests several reasons. First, the inductive disciplinarian provides *cognitive standards* (or rationales) that children can use to evaluate their actions. And when inductive discipline is other-oriented, parents are furnishing their child with the kinds of experiences that should foster the development of empathy and reciprocal-role taking—two cognitive abilities that contribute to the growth of mature moral reasoning. Second, use of inductive discipline allows parents to talk about the affective components of morality, such as guilt and shame, that are not easily discussed with a child who is made emotionally insecure by love-oriented discipline or angry by power-assertive techniques. Finally, parents who use inductive discipline are likely to explain to the child (1) what he or she *should have done* when tempted to violate a prohibition and (2) what he or she *can now do* to make up for a transgression. So it appears that induction is an effective method of moral socialization because it clearly illustrates the affective, cognitive, and behavioral aspects of morality and may help the child to integrate them.

Does induction promote moral maturity; or, rather, do morally mature children elicit more inductive forms of discipline from their parents? Since the child-rearing studies are correlational in nature, either of these possibilities could explain Hoffman's findings. Yet Hoffman (1975a) believes that the direction of influence is primarily from parent to child, so that parental use of inductive discipline promotes moral maturity rather than the other way around. As we see in Box 14-3, there is some experimental support for Hoffman's argument. Nevertheless, it is likely that moral socialization is a two-way street and that children who respond more favorably to discipline are the ones who are apt to be treated in a rational and nonpunitive manner by their parents.

Finally, it is important to note that few if any parents are totally inductive, love-oriented, or power-assertive in their approach to discipline; most make at least some use of all three disciplinary techniques. Although parents classified as "inductive" frequently use inductive methods, they occasionally take punitive measures whenever punishment is necessary to command the child's attention or to discipline repeated transgressions. So the style of parenting that Hoffman calls induction may be very similar to the "rationale + mild punishment" treatment that is so effective at producing resistance to temptation in the laboratory.

THE DEVELOPMENT OF SELF-CONTROL

One of the more important lessons that children must learn is that it is often necessary to control immediate impulses and to regulate their behavior in order to have any chance of attaining desirable long-range objectives. In achievement-oriented societies where individual accomplishments are stressed, children must exercise self-restraint daily if they are to behave appropriately and satisfy the expectations of parents, teachers, and the society at large. Consider the plight of high school students who, for years, have been encouraged to set momentary pleasures aside in order to acquire important academic skills that will serve them well later in life. On graduating from high school, many students face an important decision: should they take a job and finally begin to accomplish some of the things that may seem desirable to them now (for example, economic security, independence, or purchasing a new car) or, rather, put off these pleasures and embark on a four-year college education in the hope that their eventual career opportunities (and financial rewards) will be much better? The college graduate,

"If you're tryin' to get something into my head, you're workin' on the wrong end!"

Dennis the Menace ® and © by Field Enterprises, Inc.

of course, will face similar decisions: Should I now go to graduate school or take one of the two jobs I was offered? OK, I'll take a job—but which one? The job with the best salary, or the lower-paying job where the prospects for advancement are greater? Since people will face these kinds of decisions throughout their lives, it is hardly surprising that students of human behavior are interested in the topic of *self-control*—the ability to defer immediate gratification and to successfully regulate one's behavior in order to achieve more valuable, interesting, or socially desirable outcomes in the future.

If you have worked with toddlers and preschool children, you are probably aware that these youngsters are often impulsive, impatient, and notoriously uninhibited. Parents who give birthday parties for children of this age often find that their young guests feast ravenously on small pieces of candy, only to discover that they are unable to manage a slice of the more desirable birthday cake a few minutes later. When confronted with a choice between an immediately available but less valued outcome and a delayed outcome of greater value, the young child may seem unable or unwilling to postpone immediate gratification and wait patiently for the delayed incentive. In contrast, adults are much more proficient at controlling their immediate impulses because they have learned that delayed incentives are often worth waiting for and have acquired some useful strategies that enable them to work (or wait) patiently until they receive these valuable outcomes.

How do children learn to delay immediate gratification? What strategies do they use to exercise self-restraint during the interval when they must wait patiently for a delayed incentive? These are two of the important issues we will discuss in the pages that follow. Let's begin by considering the most rudimentary form of self-control—the child's ability to inhibit an overt motor act when instructed to do so (**motor inhibition**).

Motor Inhibition

At one time or another, all parents become perturbed when their young children continue an activity after being told to stop. In fact, it is not at all unusual for a toddler or a preschool child to respond to a demand such as "Don't pull the cat's

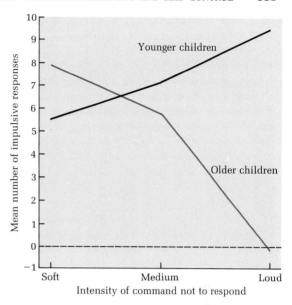

FIGURE 14-4. *Average number of impulsive responses by younger (3–4-year-old) and older (5–6-year-old) children as a function of the intensity of the verbal command not to respond.*

tail!" by pulling all the harder. It is not that the young child intends to be disobedient but, rather, that the command "Don't pull . . ." has a positive instructional component, the verb *pull*, that seems to stimulate the ongoing response (Luria, 1961). Indeed, Eli Saltz and his associates (Saltz, Campbell, & Skotko, 1983) found that the louder an adult's instruction to inhibit a response, the greater the likelihood that 3- to 4-year-olds will continue to perform that behavior, at least for short periods (see Figure 14-4). But while preschool children have difficulty inhibiting an ongoing response, 5–6-year-olds are more likely to respond appropriately to verbal commands—particularly if the command is loud or forceful (Saltz et al., 1983).

Other researchers have measured children's motor inhibition with the "Draw-a-line" (DAL) and the "Walk-a-line" (WAL) tests. Briefly, these tests require the child either to draw a line or to walk between two points *as slowly as possible*

---

motor inhibition: *the ability to regulate or inhibit a motor act when instructed to do so.*

Do inductive procedures make children more willing to obey rules or to comply with the requests of an authority figure? Leon Kuczynski (1983) attempted to answer this question in a recent experiment with 9–10-year-olds. Each child took part in a project in which he or she was asked to evaluate the merits of a highly attractive group of toys. After ten minutes of play, the child was informed that it was now time to put these toys aside and test the desirability of a simple crank-turning device. Each subject was then seated at a table with his or her back to the attractive items and was told to keep turning the toy crank. The experimenter gave one of three sets of instructions to keep the child working and to prohibit him or her from even looking at the attractive toys:

1. *Unelaborated prohibition* (a form of power assertion): "Listen, don't look at those toys again until I let you!"
2. *Self-oriented induction:* Don't look at those other toys. "You'll be unhappy if you look at them. . . . If you don't work hard enough you'll have to do some of this work later and you'll have little time to play with those toys."
3. *Other-oriented induction:* Don't look at those other toys. "You'll make me unhappy if you look at them now. If you don't work hard enough, I'll have to do some of this work later and I'll have little time to do what I want to do."

The child's willingness to comply with the experimenter's request was then observed in three contexts: (1) a two-minute period while the experimenter remained in the room, (2) a seven-minute period while the experimenter was out of the room making a phone call, and (3) a second seven-minute period after the experimenter had returned, said that he would be away for a while longer and that he would not be angry if the child looked at the toys (disinhibition instructions), and then departed once again. The measures of compliance were (1) the rate at which the child worked at the dull crank-turning chore and (2) the amount of time that the child spent looking at (or playing with) the attractive toys.

The results were clear. As we see in the first graph, other-oriented induction was more effective than either self-oriented induction or the unelaborated prohibition at persuading children to keep working at the crank-turning task. Note that children in the other-oriented condition, who believed that they would be hurting the experimenter by not working, were willing to keep working hard, even after the experimenter had implied that it was OK to look at the toys.

How long did the children spend looking at the attractive toys? As we see in the second graph, subjects who had received an other-oriented rationale spent much less time gazing at the prohibited items

when told to do so. The most common finding is that children's ability to inhibit these motor acts (by performing them very slowly) increases with age, the most dramatic improvements occurring toward the end of the preschool period (Toner, Holstein, & Hetherington, 1977).

According to Aleksandr Luria (1961), young children are slow to respond to inhibitory commands because they pay less attention to the *semantic* content of the message (the *don't* or *stop* that would suppress the response) than to the tone, or *physical energy*, of a forceful command (which tends to energize the response). Are children who are brighter than average any more capable of separating these two message components and reacting appropriately to an inhibitory command? Apparently so, for 3–5-year-olds who perform well on IQ tests are better able to slow down their movements on the "Draw-a-line" and the "Walk-a-line" tests (Maccoby, Dowley, Hagen, & Degerman, 1965; Toner et al., 1977). There is also a relationship between motor inhibition and cognitive style: *reflective* children (that is, those who work slowly and accurately on Kagan's Matching Familiar Figures test) are much better at inhibiting motor activities than their more *impulsive* age mates (Harrison & Nadelman, 1972; Toner et al., 1977).

If preschool children often have difficulty controlling their own motor activities, can we expect them to forgo immediate pleasures and wait patiently for delayed incentives? Let's see what researchers have found in trying to answer this question.

Delay of Gratification

Excited at the prospect of buying a new toy, two

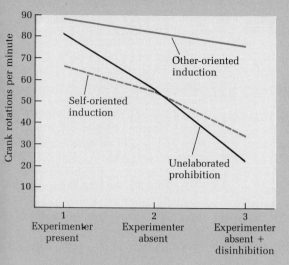

Average rate of work as a function of the type of rationale children received and the context in which they were observed.

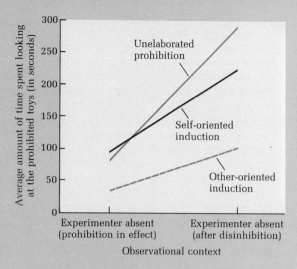

Average amount of time spent looking at prohibited toys as a function of the type of rationale given for not looking and the context in which the observations occurred.

than did those who had received a self-oriented rationale or unelaborated prohibition. In fact, the experimenter's statement that he would not be angry if they looked only increased the looking time of the "other-oriented" subjects to the level that the other children had already shown before receiving these disinhibiting instructions.

So inductive reasoning can increase children's

motivation to comply with the wishes or demands of an authority figure. And as Hoffman had found in his review of the child-rearing literature, the type of reasoning that was most effective at gaining compliance was an *other-oriented* induction in which children were informed of the negative consequences that their noncompliant acts would have on someone other than themselves.

young boys approach their fathers, who give them roughly the same choice: each may either buy the toy now with money borrowed against next week's allowance or wait until next week to buy the toy without having to forgo the triple-decker ice-cream cone that he normally purchases at the end of each week's shopping trip. One boy decides to buy the toy now, giving little thought to the fact that he will miss out on this week's ice-cream cone by refusing to delay his purchase for a week. The second child recognizes that patience is a virtue, for if he delays his purchase, he will have ice cream today and the toy (and another ice-cream cone) on his next shopping trip. Although these two children were given the same choice under similar circumstances, they made very different decisions. But why? What determines the child's ability or willingness to postpone immediate gratification in favor of more

desirable outcomes at some point in the future?

Research on children's delay of gratification suggests that this important aspect of self-control consists of two distinct phases. To illustrate the process, let's suppose that a young girl has been offered a choice between receiving only one piece of candy immediately (so as not to ruin her dinner) and receiving three pieces of candy if she is willing to wait and enjoy these treats later as her dessert. In the first phase of the delay process, the child must make a **delay choice**—that is, choose between the immediate and the deferred incen-

delay choice: *the decision one makes when faced with a choice between a lesser incentive available immediately or a greater incentive available at some point in the future.*

tive. If she opts for the delayed incentive, she then enters the second phase, in which **patience** is required to stick by her decision and actually receive her "just desserts." But all too often, this waiting is difficult and frustrating—particularly if the child has the option of terminating her self-imposed delay of gratification and settling for the lesser incentive. As we will see, a young child's decision to defer immediate gratification does not necessarily imply that she will maintain her resolve and end up with the delayed incentive. Patience is a virtue that may take some time to develop.

■ *The decision phase: To wait or not to wait?*
Two sets of factors seem to affect a person's preference for immediate or delayed incentives: (1) the characteristics of the individual who must make these decisions and (2) situational influences such as the context in which the decision is made and the specific options available to the chooser.

Who chooses to delay gratification? One of the most reliable findings in the delay-of-gratification literature is a positive correlation between age and delay choice: older children are more likely than younger ones to choose a valuable, delayed incentive over a less valuable incentive given immediately. Children begin to show a clear preference for delayed incentives at about age 10, although younger subjects may also be willing to defer immediate gratification if the advantages of this course of action are obvious to them (Mischel & Metzner, 1962). Of course, delaying gratification can sometimes be difficult for people of any age, particularly if the immediate incentive is enticing and the wait for the more valuable outcome is likely to be a long one.

In one of the first studies of children's delay of gratification, John Washburne (1929) hypothesized that "all children are irresponsible but that bad children are even more so" (p. 1). To test this notion, Washburne presented delinquent and nondelinquent children with three hypothetical and two actual choices between immediate incentives and more valuable, delayed outcomes. He found that delinquent children, particularly those older than 12, were more likely than their nondelinquent age mates to choose the incentives immediately available to them. Washburne con-

cluded that an inability to defer immediate gratification is a clear indicator of moral immaturity.

Although Washburne has overstated the implications of his correlational result, it does appear that children who consistently choose to delay gratification have other qualities that society views as valuable. Compared with youngsters who favor immediate rewards, those who choose delayed outcomes (1) score higher on IQ tests, (2) perform better at school, (3) display stronger achievement motivation, (4) are rated as more responsible and socially mature, and (5) are more likely to resist the temptation to violate rules when working alone without supervision (Mischel, 1966).

When will children delay gratification? Walter Mischel has identified three variables that affect children's willingness to delay immediate gratification. The first is their *confidence* that they will receive the delayed incentive should they decide to wait for it. Two factors that influence children's confidence are (1) the trustworthiness of the people who must deliver on their promises and (2) their own assessments of whether they can be patient and/or accomplish whatever it is they must do in order to earn the delayed incentive. A second factor that influences children's delay choices is the *relative value* that they attach to the immediate and the delayed incentives. Children are more likely to defer immediate gratification and to wait for the delayed outcome if its subjective value is much greater than that of the immediately available incentive (Mischel, 1966). Finally, the *length of the delay* that children must endure is an important consideration: longer delays make immediate choices more likely (Mischel, 1974; Schwarz, Schrager, & Lyons, 1983).

A study by Bandura and Mischel (1965) suggests that children's preferences for immediate or delayed incentives depend, in part, on the amount of self-restraint shown by their companions. The 9–10-year-olds who participated in this experiment first took a "delay of gratification" test in which they made 14 choices between small, immediate incentives and larger, delayed incentives (for example, $.15 now or $.30 a week later). On the basis of these decisions, each child was classified as one who consistently preferred immediate incentives (that is, an **impulsive**) or one who typically chose delayed incentives (a **nonimpulsive**). Then some of the children in each group watched an adult model make a number of choices between immediately available incentives of lesser value or delayed incentives of greater value. Those children who preferred immediate gratification always observed a model who picked delayed incentives, whereas those who preferred to delay watched the model select immediate incentives. Children assigned to a control group did not observe a model. Finally, all children retook the delay-of-gratification test at the end of the experimental session and again one month later.

Bandura and Mischel found that children were definitely influenced by the model's choices. Impulsive children who watched the model select delayed incentives subsequently chose delayed incentives on about half the items on the immediate posttest. Even after a month, these children were still showing more willingness to delay immediate gratification than they had shown before observing the model. By contrast, nonimpulsive children who had initially favored delayed incentives were now much less willing to choose the more valuable, delayed outcomes after watching an impulsive model who displayed little self-control. The implications for child rearing are clear: parents who hope to teach their children to delay immediate gratification in the interest of achieving desirable, long-range objectives are likely to be much more successful if they control their own immediate impulses and take care to explain the advantages of their self-restraint.

The effects of verbal persuasion on children's delay of gratification are illustrated in an experiment by Ervin Staub (1972). Staub gave seventh-graders a number of rationales for choosing a valuable delayed incentive over a less valuable incentive offered immediately. He found that children were more likely to choose the delayed incentive when they were told that (1) the waiting time would seem short, (2) they could trust the researchers to deliver the delayed incentives, and (3) individuals who choose delayed outcomes are likely to be considered more mature and intelligent by parents and teachers. Yet when Staub explicitly recommended that children choose the delayed incentives without justifying his recommendation, the children were not influenced. Apparently, power-assertive suggestions or commands are no more effective at promoting delay of

gratification than at persuading children to exercise moral restraint.

Will children choose to defer immediate gratification in order to produce larger delayed incentives for someone other than themselves? Indeed they will, although the research presented in Box 14-4 suggests that their willingness to make this kind of sacrifice depends to a large extent on who will become the beneficiary of their self-restraint.

Cultural influences.   We have been talking as if one's willingness to defer immediate gratification while working toward "bigger and better" things in the future were unquestionably a desirable attribute. However, a preference for delayed outcomes seems to be more adaptive in some societies than in others.

One culture that evaluates delay of gratification very differently than we do is the Aboriginal society of northern Australia. Unlike youngsters in Western societies, Aboriginal children do not show a greater preference for delayed incentives as they grow older. On the contrary, the older and the more intelligent the Aboriginal child, the greater the likelihood that he or she will choose incentives that are immediately available (Bochner & David, 1968). This interesting developmental trend makes perfectly good sense given the lifestyle of the Aborigines. Since these people are nomadic hunters who must often move in search of food and water, the conservation of resources for later use might create a burden. As a result, aboriginal youth are taught to consume their resources immediately—a practice that seems well suited to their nomadic way of life.

Mischel (1958, 1961) found that lower-class subjects from the island of Trinidad were another group who seemed to live for the present and rarely chose to wait for delayed incentives. How-

---

patience: *the ability to overcome the frustrations of a delay while waiting (or working) for a deferred incentive.*

impulsives: *those who favor smaller incentives available immediately rather than larger incentives available later.*

nonimpulsives: *those who favor larger incentives available later rather than smaller incentives available immediately.*

BOX 14-4
ME SACRIFICE FOR SOMEONE ELSE!
WELL . . . THAT DEPENDS

Recently, Frederick Kanfer and his associates (Kanfer, Stifter, & Morris, 1981) designed an interesting experiment to see whether 3½–6-year-olds would delay immediate gratification in order to produce a desirable outcome for somebody else. Each of Kanfer's young subjects first learned how to perform a dull chip-sorting task and earned five prize tokens that could be used later to purchase a toy. The child was then given a choice between playing with an array of attractive toys (small immediate incentive) and continuing to sort chips in order to earn more prize tokens with which to buy additional toys (larger delayed incentive). Some of the children were led to believe that they would be using their later "earnings" to buy *themselves* attractive toys. Others were told that their future earnings would be used to buy toys for (1) *another little boy or girl* (anonymous-other condition), (2) a *"classmate"* whom the experimenter would select as the recipient, or (3) a *"friend"* whom the child liked very much. Finally, children in the *control* condition were simply told that they could either play with the toys or sort chips if they wanted to but that no more prize tokens would be given for chip sorting. If the child began to sort chips (the delay choice), the experimenter left the room and observed the child's activities from an adjacent area for a maximum of 15 minutes. After 15 minutes had elapsed (or the child had quit working and started to play with the toys), the experimenter returned and praised the child for his or her work. The subject was then allowed to exchange the tokens earned at the beginning of the session for a toy.

The results of the experiment appear in the table. In evaluating these data, let's first note that not one child in the control condition chose to continue the chip-sorting task when his efforts would earn him no more tokens. Even preschool children won't work for nothing. And will they work for themselves? Yes, indeed, for 75% of those who could earn tokens to buy themselves additional toys chose to work rather than play, and most of these youngsters worked for the entire 15 minutes. Now for the question that stimulated this research: Will preschool children set aside personal pleasures in order to do something nice for somebody else? As we see in the table, the answer depends on who it is that they would be working for. The majority of these 3½–6-year-olds refused to do anything to benefit an anonymous child or a "classmate" whose identity was left unspecified. However, 55% of the children were willing to defer immediate gratification and perform the dull chip-sorting task when the person who would benefit from their sacrifice was a friend.

Number of children who worked at the dull chip-sorting task for all, part, or none of the 15-minute delay interval

	Condition				
	Control (no tokens earned)	Self as recipient	Anonymous other as recipient	Classmate as recipient	Friend as recipient
No work	20 (100%)	5 (25%)	19 (95%)	15 (75%)	9 (45%)
Part-time work	0 (0%)	2 (10%)	1 (5%)	2 (10%)	1 (5%)
Maximum work	0 (0%)	13 (65%)	0 (0%)	3 (15%)	10 (50%)

ever, their impulsive behavior is actually quite adaptive, for they live in a culture where immediate gratification is modeled and encouraged and where promises of future rewards are often broken.

In sum, the ability to defer gratification is a desirable attribute only to the extent that other people value and reinforce this kind of self-restraint. In many impoverished cultures, particularly those in which people survive by gathering food, an individual who is always delaying immediate gratification to plan for the future may be considered selfish, foolhardy, or otherwise maladjusted.

On making the "wise" choice.   What do young children think about choosing a delayed incentive? Do they feel that this is the wiser choice? Mordecai Nisan and Asher Koriat (1977) tried to answer these questions by first asking 5- to 6-year-olds to make a series of choices between small immediate and larger delayed incentives. The children were also asked to guess the choices that a "smart" child and a "stupid" child would make when faced with these same decisions. Apparently these youngsters believed that the larger delayed incentives are the wiser choices, for they said that the "smart" child would choose to delay while the "stupid" one would prefer immediate gratification. Yet the children themselves chose fewer of the delayed outcomes than they expected of the "smart" child. Perhaps they had already adopted a philosophy that many of us adults seem to follow: "It's OK to indulge ourselves now and then, even if it isn't always the *smart* thing to do."

■ *On maintaining one's resolve: The development of patience*

Once children have made the decision to wait for delayed incentives, they must now find a way of passing the time until these incentives become available. All too often, young children who have decided to wait for something will become frustrated during the delay and end up settling for a lesser incentive that is immediately available. Indeed, saving one's allowance to buy an expensive toy might be a trying experience for a 6-year-old girl who is sorely tempted to tap into her funds whenever she passes a candy counter. If she often yields to these immediate temptations, she may never reach her long-range objective and could end up concluding that waiting or working for delayed incentives is too difficult. What this girl needs is a strategy that enables her to be patient and to resist momentary pleasures until she accumulates enough money to buy the coveted toy. But what can she do to maintain her resolve?

Early research on patience.   Sigmund Freud (1911/1959) argued that a child can reduce the frustration of waiting by creating mental images of the delayed incentive—images that allow him or her to fantasize about the goal object and the pleasures it will bring. Walter Mischel and Ebbe Ebbesen (1970) went one step further, arguing that

waiting for a delayed incentive will be easiest whenever the goal object is physically present and serves as a vivid reminder that it is something worth waiting for. Of course, the assumption underlying these predictions is that anything that focuses the child's attention on the desirable qualities of a delayed incentive will make the waiting easier.

Mischel and Ebbesen (1970) tested this **attentional hypothesis** in the following way. First, 3- to 5-year-olds were asked whether they preferred cookies or pretzels. Each child was then told that, by waiting alone in a room until the experimenter returned, he or she would receive the preferred treat. However, if the children decided they couldn't wait that long for their snack, they could signal the experimenter to return and would receive the nonpreferred treat. The experimenter then left the room, leaving behind both foods, the preferred snack only, the nonpreferred snack only, or neither snack. He returned after 15 minutes had elapsed, or earlier if the impatient child had signaled to him by ringing a bell.

According to the attentional hypothesis, children should have found it easier to wait whenever the preferred snack was present to remind them that it was worth waiting for. But as we see in Figure 14-5, the presence of the preferred snack produced very little waiting. It seemed that when children could see what they were waiting for, they became even more frustrated by the delay and were motivated to end this aversive waiting. The subjects who showed the *most* patience were those who had *neither* incentive present as they waited.

A few of the children who waited with the preferred snack in front of them were able to bridge the entire 15-minute delay period and receive their tasty treat. How did they maintain their resolve? Mischel and Ebbesen noted:

> Instead of focusing prolonged attention on the objects for which they were waiting, they avoided looking at them. Some children covered their eyes

---

attentional hypothesis: *the notion that it is easier to wait patiently for a delayed incentive if one's attention is focused on the desirable qualities of that incentive.*

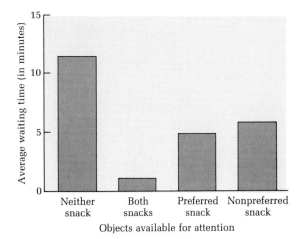

FIGURE 14-5. *Average amount of time that children waited for their preferred snack. The presence of either or both of the snack foods undermined children's resolve and often persuaded them to signal the experimenter before the 15 minutes was up, thus forfeiting the preferred snack. When neither incentive was present, children were much more patient: 75% of them waited the entire 15 minutes and received their preferred snack.*

with their hands, rested their heads on their arms, and found other similar techniques for averting their eyes from the reward objects. Many seemed to try to reduce the frustration of delay . . . by generating their own diversions: they talked to themselves, sang, invented games with their hands and feet, and even tried to fall asleep while waiting—as one child successfully did [1970, p. 335].

So it appears that learning *not* to think about a delayed incentive is an important lesson for children who are struggling to be patient.

After rejecting the attentional hypothesis, Mischel and his associates predicted that children would become more patient whenever they distracted themselves from the aversive aspects of waiting by transforming the delay into a more pleasant experience. In one experiment to test this **distraction hypothesis**, children who were instructed to think about "fun things" waited much more patiently for a delayed incentive than those who either thought "sad thoughts" or were not

encouraged to distract themselves (Mischel, Ebbesen, & Zeiss, 1972).

Of course, it is difficult not to focus on a deferred incentive that is physically present. Yet the ways in which children think about these objects can influence their willingness to wait for them. When subjects are encouraged to think about a desirable commodity in an imaginative way (for example, picturing marshmallows as round, white clouds), they often wait long and patiently for their delayed rewards. However, children who are told to think about the actual characteristics of the delayed incentive (such as the marshmallow's sweet, soft taste) are able to wait only briefly before settling for a lesser incentive (Mischel & Baker, 1975; Moore, Mischel, & Zeiss, 1976). After reviewing several of his own studies, Mischel (1976) concluded that it's "what is in the children's heads—not what is physically in front of them—that determines their ability to delay" (p. 447).

Maintaining one's resolve through self-instructions. If a child's willingness to defer immediate gratification is under cognitive control, as Mischel has suggested, then it should be possible to teach young children how to instruct themselves to be more patient. To test this hypothesis, Walter Mischel and Charlotte Patterson (1976) asked preschool children to work on a dull task in the presence of a talking "clown box" that tried to persuade these youngsters to stop working and come play with him. Children who had been taught to say to themselves "I'm not going to look at Mr. Clown box . . . when Mr. Clown box says to look at him" were better able than those who had received no **self-instructional** strategy to resist this tempting distraction and keep on working.

In another study (Toner & Smith, 1977), preschool girls played a "waiting" game in which they received one piece of candy for every 30 seconds that they continued to wait. The rules were simple. As long as the child continued to wait, candies would accumulate in front of her. But if she told the experimenter to stop so that she could enjoy her treats, the game was over and could not be restarted. As the game began, the young subjects were either (1) given no further instructions, (2) told to talk about how good the candy would

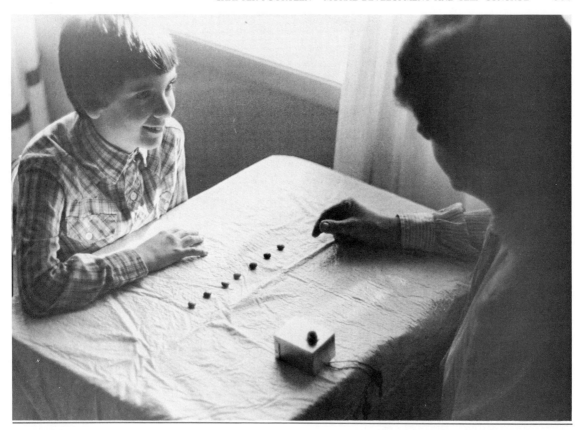

PHOTO 14-5. *Toner's waiting game. Candies accumulate at the rate of one every 30 seconds as long as the subject waits patiently for them. However, waiting can be a trying experience for preschool children, who do not yet realize that, in order to maintain their resolve, they must* avoid *thinking about the candy's positive qualities.*

taste, or (3) told to instruct themselves "It is good if I wait." The results were clear. Children who instructed themselves that it was a good idea to wait did in fact wait much longer before ending the game than their peers who either received no further instructions or talked about how good the candy would be.

When first- and second-grade girls were tested, the results were similar—with one notable exception. If these older girls had not been instructed to say anything to themselves while waiting, they waited quite a while before ending the game. It appeared as if the older subjects were more patient because they knew that they must distract themselves from the candy's positive qualities in

order to maintain their resolve. By contrast, the preschool children apparently preferred to focus on the candy itself and were not very patient unless they were specifically instructed to think dis-

> **distraction hypothesis:** *the notion that it is easier to wait patiently for a delayed incentive if one thinks distracting thoughts and does not focus on the desirable qualities of that incentive.*
> **self-instructional technique:** *a strategy for becoming more patient by instructing oneself to be more patient and/or to ignore immediate temptations.*

tracting thoughts (for example, "It's good to wait").

In a follow-up study, Toner (1981) asked preschool children to play the waiting game and gave them a choice between saying "The candy is good" or "It is good to wait" while they played. Nearly 70% of these preschoolers chose to talk about how good the candy was, thereby selecting a very ineffective strategy for coping with the frustrations of a delay.

In sum, we see that what children say to themselves while waiting for a delayed incentive clearly affects their ability to postpone immediate gratification. And one reason preschool children may appear so impatient is that they do not spontaneously produce the kinds of self-instructions that would enable them to overcome the unpleasant aspects of a long wait.

Instilling a "patient" self-concept. Will children wait more patiently for a delayed incentive if they are **labeled** as "patient" by an adult? Nace Toner and his associates (Toner, Moore, & Emmons, 1980) tested this hypothesis with 5½–9-year-old girls. Before playing the "waiting" game in which she could accumulate candies, each subject chatted briefly with the experimenter. During this conversation, half the subjects heard the experimenter say "I hear that you are very patient because you can wait for nice things when you can't get them right away" (relevant-label group). The remaining children heard the experimenter remark "I hear that you have some very nice friends here at school" (irrelevant-label group). A few minutes later, the girls began the waiting game and played under one of three conditions: (1) with the experimenter present, (2) with another adult present who knew nothing of the label the child had been given, or (3) alone with no adult surveillance. The measure of patience was the amount of time that elapsed between the release of the first candy by the candy dispenser and the point at which the child ended the game by eating one or more of her treats.

Toner et al. found that their elder (7½–9-year-old) subjects waited more patiently for candies to accumulate than the 5½– 7-year-olds. But the more interesting result appears in Figure 14-6. Note that, in all three playing conditions, children who had been labeled as "patient" by the experi-

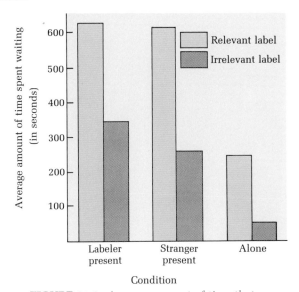

FIGURE 14-6. *Average amount of time that children waited patiently for candies to accumulate before ending the game and eating their treats. In each of the three conditions under which they played, children labeled as "patient" waited longer than those who were labeled in an irrelevant way as "having nice friends."*

menter waited about twice as long before ending the game as their age mates who had been labeled as "having nice friends." In a follow-up study, Ritchie and Toner (in press) found that even 3-year-olds became more patient after being labeled as such by an adult. Recall that these labels were given only once as part of a much longer conversation, and yet they affected the behavior of even those children who waited *alone*. Imagine, then, what parents might accomplish by appealing to their child's maturity and stressing what the child *can* do (be patient) as well as what he or she should do. If Toner's results are any guide, children who are often labeled as patient by their parents should incorporate this information into their self-concepts and try to live up to their new self-image by waiting more patiently for the delayed incentives that they have chosen to pursue.

■ *A "child's eye" view of patience*

The research we have reviewed suggests that strategies such as distraction or self-instruction

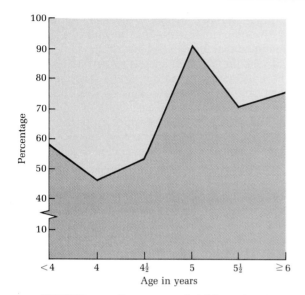

FIGURE 14-7. *Percentage of children choosing to instruct themselves to wait, by age.*

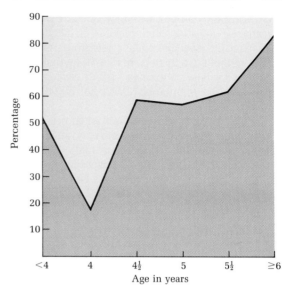

FIGURE 14-8. *Percentage of children choosing to cover the incentives, by age.*

that are *suggested by adults* can help children to be more patient while waiting for delayed incentives. Yet until very recently, no one had tried to determine when children begin to recognize and use these strategies on their own. Harriet and Walter Mischel (1983) have now traced the development of children's understanding of patience in two interesting studies of 3- to 11-year-olds. Let's see what they learned.

In one study, 3–8-year-olds were asked to imagine that they could have either two marshmallows if they waited until the experimenter returned to the room or one marshmallow if they couldn't wait that long and signaled the experimenter to return by ringing a bell. To measure their understanding of the processes that would assist them in maintaining their resolve, the experimenter began by saying "Suppose you really want to get the two marshmallows" and then asked the children the following two questions:

1. Would you cover the rewards or leave them exposed? Why? [Note: Covering the rewards is the more effective strategy.]
2. Would you say "I'm waiting for the two marshmallows" [self-instructions to wait] or "The marshmallows are yummy and chewy" [consummatory ideation]? Why? [Note: We've

seen that self-instruction to wait is the more effective strategy.]

The results were indeed interesting. As we see in Figure 14-7, children know that self-instruction is more effective than consummatory ideation by age 5. Yet it is not until age 6 that they seem to understand that covering the rewards is a better procedure than leaving them exposed. In fact, 4- to 4½-year-olds actually believe that leaving the rewards exposed so that they can think about them will prove more effective at delaying immediate gratification than covering them up (see Figure 14-8). Clearly, these children were making the same *incorrect* prediction that Freud and Mischel had made from their "attentional" hypothesis. They do not yet realize that they will think about the *positive qualities* of an exposed incentive and become so aroused that it is difficult to delay—even if they tell themselves they must wait. The Mischels concluded that "in the delay of

---

labeling technique: *a strategy for increasing a child's patience by labeling the child as a "patient" person who is able to wait for nice things.*

gratification paradigm, young 4-year-olds seem to create self-defeating dilemmas for themselves by choosing (or even creating) a tempting environment without adequately anticipating that they will not be able to execute [other] strategies to overcome the temptation" (Mischel & Mischel, 1983, p. 617).

In another study, the Mischels asked preschool, third-grade, and sixth-grade subjects to imagine they wanted to wait for two marshmallows and to indicate which of two strategies would better help them to achieve this objective. The strategies were:

1. Think "The marshmallows are puffy like clouds" [abstract ideation]

or

2. Think "The marshmallows taste yummy and chewy" [consummatory ideation]

Earlier we saw that young children who are *instructed* to use abstract ideation will often wait for long periods for a delayed incentive. Yet the Mischels found that their subjects were not *aware* of the effectiveness of this strategy until the sixth grade (age 11–12). One reason an awareness of abstract ideation may develop so late is that it requires a metaphorical transformation of the incentive (for example, marshmallows are like clouds; pretzels are like logs), which, in turn, may require a capacity for abstract thought. Indeed, the sixth-graders who knew that abstract ideation would help them to wait were 11–12 years old, precisely the age at which children are approaching Piaget's stage of formal operations and are now more capable of thinking more abstractly.

A Final Note on Self-Control

We have seen that delay of gratification is a two-step process in which the child must first *decide* to pursue a delayed incentive and then *wait patiently* until this valuable outcome becomes available. At both steps, younger children are less willing than their older counterparts to inhibit immediate impulses and pursue the more valuable options that will require them to wait. Do these findings mean that younger children are less capable of self-control?

The answer seems to be yes—and no. Young children are less capable of deferring immediate gratification in the sense that they may be (1) less confident that the delayed incentive will be available should they wait and (2) less aware of either the advantages of waiting or the strategies that they can use to maintain their resolve. However, we have seen that younger children will often choose to defer immediate gratification if the advantages of that course of action are obvious to them. Moreover, they seem to be as patient as older children when they are told to use effective delay strategies that they may not know about. So it appears that the impulsive behavior that preschoolers often display does not necessarily reflect an *inability* to demonstrate self-control. Instead, they may simply be reluctant to wait for delayed incentives because they either don't recognize the benefits of waiting or don't know how to ward off their frustrations and successfully bridge the delay interval.

On a practical note, parents who hope to instill self-control in their preschool children might begin by (1) pointing out the advantages of waiting for delayed incentives and (2) enlisting the child as an ally by convincing him or her that "you can be patient." At the very least, these techniques should make waiting seem more reasonable to the child—something that he or she wants to do. Of course, it is of no advantage to wait if one chooses to do so, becomes frustrated during the delay, and ends up settling for a lesser incentive. In fact, such experiences may undermine self-control and lead to impulsive behavior in the future. To be effective, the parents' training program should provide the child with a plan or a "blueprint for action" that he or she can use to overcome frustration and wait patiently for delayed incentives. To wait or not to wait may be "the question"; but when it comes to making *reasonable* decisions, a knowledge of when, why, and how to wait is surely "the answer."

SUMMARY

The present chapter focuses on two important aspects of social and personality development: morality (or moral development) and the development of self-control.

Morality has been defined in many ways, although almost everyone agrees that it implies an ability to distinguish right from wrong and to act on this distinction. Morality has three basic components: moral affect, moral reasoning, and moral behavior.

Psychoanalytic theorists emphasize the affective, or "emotional," aspects of morality. According to Freud, the character of the parent/child relationship largely determines the child's willingness to internalize the moral standards of his or her parents. This internalization is said to occur during the phallic stage and results in the development of the superego. Once formed, the superego functions as an internal censor that will reward the child for virtuous conduct and punish moral transgressions by making the child feel anxious, guilty, or shameful. Many tests of Freudian theory have now been conducted, and most of the evidence does *not* support Freud's explanation of moral development.

Cognitive-developmental theorists have emphasized the cognitive component of morality by studying the development of moral reasoning. Jean Piaget was the pioneer. He formulated a two-stage model of moral development based on changes that occur in children's conceptions of rules and their sense of social justice. Although Piaget did identify some important processes and basic trends in the development of moral reasoning, recent research suggests that his two-stage theory is too simplistic. Lawrence Kohlberg believes that moral development progresses through an invariant sequence of three moral levels, each composed of two distinct stages. According to Kohlberg, the order of progression through the levels and stages is invariant because each of these modes of thinking depends, in part, on the development of certain cognitive abilities that evolve in a fixed sequence. Each successive stage represents a reorganization of previous stages; and once the individual has attained a higher stage of moral reasoning, he or she will not regress to earlier stages.

Attempts to verify the cognitive theories reveal that moral reasoning is related to cognitive development. Moreover, children progress through the first four of Kohlberg's six stages in the order that Kohlberg specifies. Yet most people never reach Kohlberg's highest moral stages, which

seem to require a special kind of environmental support in order to develop.

Social-learning theorists emphasize the behavioral component of morality, and their research has helped us to understand how children are able to resist temptation and to inhibit acts that violate moral norms. Among the processes that are important in establishing inhibitory controls are reinforcing the child for acceptable behavior and punishing unacceptable conduct. However, some punishments are more effective than others. Among the factors that determine the effectiveness of punishment are its timing, intensity, consistency, and accompanying rationale, as well as the emotional warmth of the punitive agent. Children may also acquire inhibitory controls by observing models who show moral restraint or by themselves serving as rule-following models for other children.

Measures of moral affect, moral reasoning, and moral behavior are not highly interrelated, even among adults. Moreover, people are sometimes inconsistent in their moral behavior from situation to situation. So morality is neither a "unified whole," as envisioned by psychoanalytic and cognitive theorists, nor totally specific to the situation, as argued by social-learning theorists.

Martin Hoffman has looked at the relationship between parental disciplinary practices and children's moral development. His findings indicate that warm and loving parents who rely mainly on inductive discipline tend to raise children who are morally mature. Induction is an effective method of moral socialization because it often illustrates and may help the child to integrate the affective, cognitive, and behavioral aspects of morality.

The development of self-control has also been the focus of a great deal of speculation and research. One important lesson that children must learn is that it is often necessary to delay gratification—that is, to control their immediate impulses and to regulate their behavior in order to achieve desirable long-range objectives. Research on children's delay of gratification suggests that this important aspect of self-control consists of two phases: (1) the decision to defer gratification in order to seek a delayed incentive and (2) the ability to be patient and maintain one's resolve until the delayed incentive becomes available.

Among children in Western societies, willingness to delay immediate gratification increases with age and is related to factors such as the child's confidence that the delayed incentive will be available later, the relative value of the immediate and the deferred incentives, and the length of delay that children must endure to obtain a delayed incentive.

Once young children have decided to forgo immediate gratification in favor of a larger, delayed incentive, they often become frustrated with their decision and impatient and will end up settling for a lesser incentive that is immediately available. Their problem is not that they are incapable of self-control but, rather, that they know little about the strategies that they could use to reduce the frustrations of waiting. Indeed, preschool children can be as patient as older children if they are taught to substitute effective delay strategies for their own ineffective procedures that make waiting difficult.

REFERENCES

Ambron, S. R., & Irwin, D. M. (1975). Role-taking and moral judgment in five- and seven-year-olds. *Developmental Psychology, 11,* 102.

Arbuthnot, J. (1975). Modification of moral judgment through role-playing. *Developmental Psychology, 11,* 319–324.

Aronfreed, J. (1976). Moral development from the standpoint of a general psychological theory. In T. Lickona (Ed.), *Moral development and behavior.* New York: Holt, Rinehart & Winston.

Bandura, A. (1977). *Social learning theory.* Englewood Cliffs, NJ: Prentice-Hall.

Bandura, A., & Mischel, W. (1965). Modification of self-imposed delay of reward through exposure to live and symbolic models. *Journal of Personality and Social Psychology, 2,* 698–705.

Bandura, A., & Walters, R. H. (1959). *Adolescent aggression.* New York: Ronald Press.

Baumrind, D. (1978). A dialectical materialist's perspective on knowing social reality. In W. Damon (Ed.), *New directions for child development* (No. 2): *Moral development.* San Francisco: Jossey-Bass.

Blasi, A. (1980). Bridging moral cognition and moral action: A critical review of the literature. *Psychological Bulletin, 88,* 1–45.

Bochner, S., & David, K. H. (1968). Delay of gratification, age, and intelligence in Aboriginal culture. *International Journal of Psychology, 3,* 167–174.

Brody, G. H., & Shaffer, D. R. (1982). Contributions of parents and peers to children's moral socialization. *Developmental Review, 2,* 31–75.

Burton, R. V. (1963). The generality of honesty reconsidered. *Psychological Review, 70,* 481–499.

Burton, R. V. (1976). Honesty and dishonesty. In T. Lickona (Ed.), *Moral development and behavior.* New York: Holt, Rinehart & Winston.

Casey, W. M., & Burton, R. V. (1982). Training children to be consistently honest through verbal self-instructions. *Child Development, 53,* 911–919.

Colby, A., Kohlberg, L., Gibbs, J., & Lieberman, M. (1983). A longitudinal study of moral judgment. *Monographs of the Society for Research in Child Development, 48* (Nos. 1–2, Serial No. 200).

Edwards, C. P. (1981). The development of moral reasoning in cross-cultural perspective. In R. H. Munroe, R. L. Munroe, & B. B. Whiting (Eds.), *Handbook of cross-cultural human development.* New York: Garland Press.

Erikson, E. H. (1963). *Childhood and society* (2nd ed.). New York: Norton.

Fischer, W. F. (1963). Sharing in pre-school children as a function of the amount and type of reinforcement. *Genetic Psychology Monographs, 68,* 215–245.

Freud, S. (1959). Formulations regarding the two principles of mental functioning. *Collected papers* (Vol. 4). New York: Basic Books. (Original work published 1911)

Freud, S. (1960). *A general introduction to psychoanalysis.* New York: Washington Square Press. (Original work published 1935)

Garbarino, J., & Bronfenbrenner, U. (1976). The socialization of moral judgment and behavior in cross-cultural perspective. In T. Lickona (Ed.), *Moral development and behavior.* New York: Holt, Rinehart & Winston.

Gibbs, J. (1979). Kohlberg's moral stage theory: A Piagetian revision. *Human Development, 22,* 89–112.

Gilligan, C. (1977). In a different voice: Women's conceptions of self and morality. *Harvard Educational Review, 47,* 481–517.

Gilligan, C. (1982). *In a different voice: Psychological theory and women's development.* Cambridge, MA: Harvard University Press.

Gilligan, C., & Murphy, J. M. (1979). Development from adolescence to adulthood: The philosopher and the dilemma of the fact. In D. Kuhn (Ed.), *New directions for child development* (No. 5): *Intellectual development beyond childhood.* San Francisco: Jossey-Bass.

Grusec, J. E., Kuczynski, L., Rushton, J. P., & Simutis, Z. (1979). Learning resistance to temptation through observation. *Developmental Psychology, 15,* 233–240.

Harkness, S., Edwards, C. P., & Super, C. M. (1981). Social roles and moral reasoning: A case study in a rural African community. *Developmental Psychology, 17,* 595–603.

Harrison, A., & Nadelman, L. (1972). Conceptual tempo and inhibition of movement in black preschool children. *Child Development, 43,* 657–668.

Hartshorne, H., & May, M. S. (1928–1930). *Studies in the nature of character.* Vol. 1: *Studies in deceit.* Vol. 2: *Stud-*

ies in self-control. Vol. 3: *Studies in the organization of character.* New York: Macmillan.

Hoffman, M. L. (1970). Moral development. In P. H. Mussen (Ed.), *Carmichael's manual of child psychology* (Vol. 2). New York: Wiley.

Hoffman, M. L. (1975a). Moral internalization, parental power, and the nature of parent-child interaction. *Developmental Psychology, 11,* 228–239.

Hoffman, M. L. (1975b). Sex differences in moral internalization and values. *Journal of Personality and Social Psychology, 32,* 720–729.

Holstein, C. (1976) Irreversible, stepwise sequence in the development of moral judgment: A longitudinal study of males and females. *Child Development, 47,* 51–61.

Kanfer, F. H., Stifter, E., & Morris, S. J. (1981). Self-control and altruism: Delay of gratification for another. *Child Development, 52,* 674–682.

Keasey, C. B. (1971). Social participation as a factor in the moral development of preadolescents. *Developmental Psychology, 5,* 216–220.

Kohlberg, L. (1963). The development of children's orientations toward a moral order: I. Sequence in the development of moral thought. *Vita Humana, 6,* 11–33.

Kohlberg, L. (1969). Stage and sequence: The cognitive-developmental approach to socialization. In D. A. Goslin (Ed.), *Handbook of socialization theory and research.* Chicago: Rand McNally.

Kohlberg, L. (1975, June). The cognitive-developmental approach to moral education. *Phi Delta Kappan,* pp. 670–677.

Kohlberg, L. (1981). *Essays on moral development* (Vol. 1). New York: Harper & Row.

Kohlberg, L., & Kramer, R. (1969). Continuities and discontinuities in childhood and adult moral development. *Human Development, 12,* 93–120.

Kuczynski, L. (1983). Reasoning, prohibitions, and motivations for compliance. *Developmental Psychology, 19,* 126–134.

Kuhn, D., Kohlberg, L., Langer, J., & Haan, N. (1977). The development of formal operations in logical and moral judgment. *Genetic Psychology Monographs, 95,* 97–188.

Leming, J. (1978). Intrapersonal variation in stage of moral reasoning among adolescents as a function of situational context. *Journal of Youth and Adolescence, 7,* 405–416.

Lickona, T. (1976). Research on Piaget's theory of moral development. In T. Lickona (Ed.), *Moral development and behavior.* New York: Holt, Rinehart & Winston.

Luria, A. R. (1961). *The role of speech in the regulation of normal and abnormal behavior.* London: Pergamon Press.

Maccoby, E. E., Dowley, E. M., Hagen, J., & Degerman, R. (1965). Activity level and intellectual functioning in normal preschool children. *Child Development, 36,* 761–770.

MacKinnon, D. W. (1938). Violation of prohibitions. In H. W. Murray (Ed.), *Explorations in personality.* New York: Oxford University Press.

Magsud, M. (1979). Resolution of moral dilemmas by Nigerian secondary school pupils. *Journal of Moral Education, 7,* 40–49.

McDougall, W. (1908). *An introduction to social psychology.* London: Methuen.

Mischel, H. N., & Mischel, W. (1983). The development of children's knowledge of self-control strategies. *Child Development, 54,* 603–619.

Mischel, W. (1958). Preference for delayed reinforcement: An experimental study of a cultural observation. *Journal of Abnormal and Social Psychology, 56,* 57–61.

Mischel, W. (1961). Preference for delayed reinforcement and social responsibility. *Journal of Abnormal and Social Psychology, 62,* 1–7.

Mischel, W. (1966). Theory and research on the antecedents of self-imposed delay of reward. In B. A. Maher (Ed.), *Progress in experimental personality research* (Vol. 3). New York: Academic Press.

Mischel, W. (1974). Processes in the delay of gratification. In L. Berkowitz (Ed.), *Advances in experimental social psychology* (Vol. 7). New York: Academic Press.

Mischel, W. (1976). *Introduction to personality.* New York: Holt, Rinehart & Winston.

Mischel, W., & Baker, N. (1975). Cognitive transformations of reward objects through instructions. *Journal of Personality and Social Psychology, 31,* 254–261.

Mischel, W., & Ebbesen, E. B. (1970). Attention in delay of gratification. *Journal of Personality and Social Psychology, 16,* 329–337.

Mischel, W., Ebbesen, E. B., & Zeiss, A. R. (1972). Cognitive and attentional mechanisms in delay of gratification. *Journal of Personality and Social Psychology, 21,* 204–218.

Mischel, W., & Metzner, R. (1962). Effects of attention to symbolically presented rewards upon self-control. *Journal of Abnormal and Social Psychology, 64,* 425–431.

Mischel, W., & Patterson, C. J. (1976). Substantive and structural elements of effective plans for self-control. *Journal of Personality and Social Psychology, 34,* 942–950.

Moir, J. (1974). Egocentrism and the emergence of conventional morality in preadolescent girls. *Child Development, 45,* 299–304.

Moore, B., Mischel, W., & Zeiss, A. R. (1976). Comparative effects of the reward stimulus and its cognitive representation on voluntary delay. *Journal of Personality and Social Psychology, 34,* 419–424.

Nelson, E. A., Grinder, R. E., & Biaggio, A. M. B. (1969). Relationships between behavioral, cognitive-developmental, and self-report measures of morality and personality. *Multivariate Behavioral Research, 4,* 483–500.

Nelson, E. A., Grinder, R. E., & Mutterer, M. L. (1969). Sources of variance in behavioral measures of honesty in temptation situations: Methodological analyses. *Developmental Psychology, 1,* 265–279.

Nelson, S. A. (1980). Factors influencing young children's use of motives and outcomes as moral criteria. *Child Development, 51,* 823–829.

Nisan, M., & Kohlberg, L. (1982). Universality and variation in moral judgment: A longitudinal and cross-sectional study in Turkey. *Child Development, 53,* 865–876.

Nisan, M., & Koriat, A. (1977). Children's actual choices and their conception of the wise choice in a delay-of-gratification situation. *Child Development, 48,* 488–494.

Nucci, L. P., & Nucci, M. S. (1982). Children's responses to moral and social conventional transgressions in free-play settings. *Child Development, 53,* 1337–1342.

Parikh, B. (1980). Moral judgment development and its relation to family factors in Indian and American families. *Child Development, 51,* 1030–1039.

Parke, R. D. (1972). Some effects of punishment on children's behavior. In W. W. Hartup (Ed.), *The young child* (Vol. 2). Washington, DC: National Association for the Education of Young Children.

Parke, R. D. (1974). Rules, roles, and resistance to deviation: Explorations in punishment, discipline, and self-control. In A. Pick (Ed.), *Minnesota Symposia on Child Psychology* (Vol. 8). Minneapolis: University of Minnesota Press.

Parke, R. D. (1977). Some effects of punishment on children's behavior—revisited. In E. M. Hetherington & R. D. Parke (Eds.), *Contemporary readings in child psychology.* New York: McGraw-Hill.

Perry, D. G., & Parke, R. D. (1975). Punishment and alternative response training as determinants of response inhibition in children. *Genetic Psychology Monographs, 91,* 257–279.

Piaget, J. (1965). *The moral judgment of the child.* New York: Free Press. (Original work published 1932)

Rest, J. (1983). Morality. In J. H. Flavell & C. Markman (Eds.), *Carmichael's manual of child psychology* (Vol. 4). New York: Wiley.

Ritchie, F. K., & Toner, I. J. (in press). Direct labeling, tester expectancy, and delay maintenance behavior in Scottish preschool children. *International Journal of Behavioral Development.*

Rosenkoetter, L. I. (1973). Resistance to temptation: Inhibitory and disinhibitory effects of models. *Developmental Psychology, 8,* 80–84.

Rushton, J. P. (1980). *Altruism, socialization, and society.* Englewood Cliffs, NJ: Prentice-Hall.

Saltz, E., Campbell, S., & Skotko, D. (1983). Verbal control of behavior: The effects of shouting. *Developmental Psychology, 19,* 461–464.

Saltzstein, H. D. (1983). Commentary: Critical issues in Kohlberg's theory of moral reasoning. In A. Colby, L. Kohlberg, J. Gibbs, & M. Lieberman, A longitudinal study of moral development. *Monographs of the Society for Research in Child Development, 48,* Nos. 1–2 (Serial No. 200).

Santrock, J. W. (1975). Moral structure: The interrelations of moral behavior, moral judgment, and moral affect. *Journal of Genetic Psychology, 127,* 201–213.

Schwarz, J. C., Schrager, J. B., & Lyons, A. E. (1983). Delay of gratification by preschoolers: Evidence for the validity of the choice paradigm. *Child Development, 54,* 620–625.

Sears, R. R., Maccoby, E. E., & Levin, H. (1957). *Patterns of child rearing.* New York: Harper & Row.

Selman, R. L. (1971). The relation of role-taking to the development of moral judgment in children. *Child Development, 42,* 79–91.

Smetana, J. G. (1981). Preschool children's conceptions of moral and social rules. *Child Development, 52,* 1333–1336.

Sobesky, W. (1983). The effects of situational factors on moral judgments. *Child Development, 54,* 575–584.

Staub, E. (1972). Effects of persuasion and modeling on delay of gratification. *Developmental Psychology, 6,* 166–177.

Surber, C. F. (1982). Separable effects of motives, consequences, and presentation order on children's moral judgments. *Developmental Psychology, 18,* 257–266.

Tomlinson-Keasey, C., & Keasey, C. B. (1974). The mediating role of cognitive development in moral judgment. *Child Development, 45,* 291–298.

Toner, I. J. (1981). Role involvement and delay maintenance behavior in preschool children. *Journal of Genetic Psychology, 138,* 245–251.

Toner, I. J., Holstein, R. B., & Hetherington, E. M. (1977). Reflection-impulsivity and self-control in preschool children. *Child Development, 48,* 239–245.

Toner, I. J., Moore, L. P., & Ashley, P. K. (1978). The effect of serving as a model of self-control on subsequent resistance to deviation in children. *Journal of Experimental Child Psychology, 26,* 85–91.

Toner, I. J., Moore, L. P., & Emmons, B. A. (1980). The effect of being labeled on subsequent self-control in children. *Child Development, 51,* 618–621.

Toner, I. J., Parke, R. D., & Yussen, S. R. (1978). The effect of observation of model behavior on the establishment and stability of resistance to deviation in children. *Journal of Genetic Psychology, 132,* 283–290.

Toner, I. J., & Potts, R. (1981). Effect of modeled rationales on moral behavior, moral choice, and level of moral judgment in children. *Journal of Psychology, 107,* 153–162.

Toner, I. J., & Smith, R. A. (1977). Age and overt verbalization in delay maintenance behavior in children. *Journal of Experimental Child Psychology, 24,* 123–128.

Turiel, E. (1966). An experimental test of the sequentiality of developmental stages in the child's moral judgments. *Journal of Personality and Social Psychology, 3,* 611–618.

Turiel, E. (1978). The development of concepts of social structure: Social convention. In J. Glick & A. Clarke-Stewart (Eds.), *The development of social understanding.* New York: Gardner Press.

Turiel, E., Edwards, C. P., & Kohlberg, L. (1978). Moral development in Turkish children, adolescents, and young adults. *Journal of Cross-Cultural Psychology, 9,* 75–86.

Walker, L. J. (1980). Cognitive and perspective-taking prerequisites for moral development. *Child Development, 51,* 131–139.

Walker, L. J. (1982). The sequentiality of Kohlberg's stages of moral development. *Child Development, 53,* 1330–1336.

Walker, L. J. (1984). Sex differences in the development of moral reasoning: A critical review. *Child Development, 55,* 677–691.

Walters, R. H., & Parke, R. D. (1964). Influences of response consequences to a social model on resistance to deviation. *Journal of Experimental Child Psychology, 1,* 269–280.

Washburne, J. N. (1929). An experiment in character measurement. *Journal of Juvenile Research, 13,* 1–18.

White, C. B., Bushnell, W., & Regnemer, J. L. (1978). Moral development in Bahamian school children: A three-year examination of Kohlberg's stages of cognitive development. *Developmental Psychology, 14,* 58–65.

PART FIVE

Y ou may have heard the saying that we are products of our environments and are influenced by the company we keep. The truth in this assertion will become quite apparent as we explore in this final section of the book the contexts or settings in which people develop.

THE ECOLOGY OF DEVELOPMENT

Virtually all children are raised in a family setting, although families differ considerably and no two individuals ever experience exactly the same family environment. Chapter Fifteen concentrates on the family as an agent of socialization and outlines the many ways in which families (and the cultural contexts in which families live) influence the social, emotional, and intellectual development of their young.

Of course, the family is only one source of influence for developing children, who soon reach a point in their lives when they spend many of their waking hours away from the watchful eyes of parents and other family members. In our sixteenth and final chapter we will look beyond the family to see how children and adolescents react to the messages they receive from television, their schooling, and the society of their peers.

CHAPTER FIFTEEN ■

THE FAMILY

■ *Basic features and functions of the family*
The functions of a family
The goals of parenting

■ *Some cautionary comments about the study of families*
The middle-class bias
The directionality issue
Reconceptualizing family effects: The family as a social system
The changing American family

■ *Interactions between parents and their infants*
The transition to parenthood
The effects of parents on their infants

■ *Parental effects on preschool and school-age children*
Two major dimensions of child rearing
Patterns of parental control
Parental warmth/hostility
Patterns of parental discipline
Social-class differences in parenting

■ *Effects of siblings and the family configuration*
The nature of sibling interactions
Origins and determinants of sibling rivalry
Positive effects of sibling interaction
Characteristics of first-born and later-born children

■ *The impact of divorce*
The immediate effects
The crisis phase
Long-term reactions to divorce
Children in reconstituted families

■ *Effects of maternal employment*

■ *When parenting breaks down: The problem of child abuse*
Who is abused?
Who are the abusers?
Social-situational triggers: The ecology of child abuse

■ *Summary*

A t some point during the prehistoric era, human beings became social animals. Groups of men, women, and children began to form collectives, or tribal units, that provided increased protection against common enemies and allowed individuals to share the many labors necessary for their survival (Hoffman, 1978; LeVine, 1979). These early societies evolved codes of conduct that defined the roles of various members and sanctioned certain motives and practices while prohibiting others. Once a workable social order was established, it then became necessary to socialize each succeeding generation.

Socialization is the process by which children acquire the beliefs, values, and behaviors deemed significant and appropriate by the older members of their society. The socialization of each generation serves society in at least three ways. First, it is a means of regulating children's behavior and controlling their undesirable or antisocial impulses. Second, the socialization process helps to promote the personal growth of the individual. As children interact with and become like other members of their culture, they acquire the knowledge, skills, motives, and aspirations that should enable them to adapt to their environment and function effectively within their communities. Finally, socialization perpetuates the social order. Socialized children become socialized adults who will impart what they have learned to their own children.

All societies have developed various mechanisms, or institutions, for socializing their young. Examples of these socializing institutions are the family, the church, the educational system, children's groups (for example, Boy and Girl Scouts), and the mass media.

Central among the many social agencies that impinge on the child is that institution we call the family. More than 99% of children in the United States are raised in a family of one kind or another (U.S. Department of Commerce, 1979), and most

---

socialization: *the process by which children acquire the beliefs, values, and behaviors considered desirable or appropriate by the society to which they belong.*

children in most societies grow up in a home setting with at least one biological parent or other relative. Often children have little exposure to people outside the family for several years until they are placed in day care or nursery school or until they reach the age at which they will begin formal schooling. So it is fair to say that the family has a clear head start on other institutions when it comes to socializing a child. And since the events of the early years are very important to the child's social, emotional, and intellectual development, it is perhaps appropriate to think of the family as society's most important instrument of socialization.

Our focus in this chapter is on the family as a social system—an institution that both influences and is influenced by its young. What is a family and what functions do families serve? How does the birth of a child affect other family members? Do the existing (or changing) relationships among other members of the family have any effect on the care and training that a young child receives? Are some patterns of child rearing better than others? Do parents decide how they will raise their children—or might children be influencing their parents? Does the family's socioeconomic status affect parenting and parent/child interactions? Do siblings play an important part in the socialization process? How do children react to divorce, maternal employment, or a return to the two-parent family when a single parent remarries? And why do some parents mistreat their children? These are the issues we will consider as we look at the important roles that families play in the cognitive, social, and emotional development of their children.

BASIC FEATURES AND FUNCTIONS OF THE FAMILY

The characteristics of a family are difficult to summarize in a sentence or two. Many family sociologists prefer to think of the family unit as a social system consisting of three basic roles: wife/mother, husband/father, and child/sibling. Of course, there are many variations on this traditional **nuclear family.** In the United States, for example, there are nearly as many childless married couples as there are families with children, and about 40–50% of American children will spend some time in a **single-parent home** (Clarke-Stewart, 1982; Hetherington, 1981; U.S. Department of Commerce, 1979). Although the nuclear family is the norm in contemporary Western society, people in many cultures live in **extended families**—an arrangement in which grandparents, parents and their children, aunts, uncles, nieces, and nephews may live under the same roof and share the responsibility for maintaining the household.

The Functions of a Family

Families serve society in many ways. They produce and consume goods and services, thereby playing a role in the economy. Traditionally, the family has served as an outlet for the sexual urges of its adult members and as the means of replacing the elements of society who succumb to illness, accidents, or old age. Indeed, few societies sanction the birth of "illegitimate" children (that is, those born out of wedlock), who are often treated as second-class citizens and called uncomplimentary names such as "bastard." Historically, families have cared for their elderly, although this function is now less common in Western societies with the advent of institutions such as Social Security, socialized medical care, and nursing homes. But perhaps the most widely recognized functions of the family—those that are served in all societies—are the caregiving, nurturing, and training that parents and other family members provide for young children.

The Goals of Parenting

After studying the child-rearing practices of several cultures, Robert LeVine (1974, p. 230) concluded that all families have three basic goals for their children:

1. The **survival goal**—to promote the physical survival and health of the child, ensuring that the child lives long enough to have children of his or her own.
2. The **economic goal**—to foster the skills and behavioral capacities that the child will need for economic self-maintenance as an adult.

3. The **self-actualization goal**—to foster behavioral capabilities for maximizing other cultural values (for example, morality, religion, achievement, wealth, prestige, and a sense of personal satisfaction).

According to LeVine, these universal goals of parenting form a hierarchy. Parents and other caregivers are initially concerned about maximizing the child's chances of survival, and higher-order goals such as teaching the child to talk, count, or abide by moral rules are placed on the back burner until it is clear that the youngster is healthy and is likely to survive. When physical health and security can be taken for granted, then parents begin to encourage those characteristics that are necessary for economic self-sufficiency. Only after survival and the attributes necessary for economic productivity have been established do parents begin to encourage the child to seek status, prestige, and self-fulfillment.

LeVine's ideas stem from his observations of child-rearing practices in societies where infants often die before their second birthday. Regardless of whether one is observing African Bushmen, South American Indians, or Indonesian tribes, parents in societies where infant mortality is high tend to maintain close contact with their infants 24 hours a day, often carrying them on their hips or their backs in some sort of sling or cradleboard. LeVine suggests that these practices increase the infants' chances of survival by reducing the likelihood of their becoming ill or dehydrated, crawling into the river or the campfire, or ambling off to be captured by a predator. Although infants are kept close at all times, their parents rarely chat with or smile at them and may seem almost uninterested in their future psychological development. This pattern of psychologically aloof yet competent physical caregiving may be a defensive maneuver that prevents parents from becoming overly attached to an infant who could well die. As we saw in Chapter Five, many cultures in which infant mortality is high still institutionalize practices such as not speaking to neonates as if they were human beings or not naming them until late in the first year, when it is more probable that they will survive (Brazelton, 1979).

The next task that parents face is to promote those characteristics and competencies that will enable children to care for themselves and their own future families. Anthropologist John Ogbu (1981) points out that the economy of a culture (that is, the way in which people support themselves, or subsist) will determine how families socialize their young. To illustrate his point, he cites a well-known cross-cultural study by Herbert Barry and his associates (Barry, Child, & Bacon, 1959), who hypothesized that societies that depend on an agricultural or pastoral economy (those that accumulate food) would stress obedience, cooperation, and responsibility when raising their children. By contrast, groups that do not accumulate food (hunting, trapping, and fishing societies) were expected to train their children to be independent, assertive, and venturesome. In other words, both types of society were expected to emphasize the values, competencies, and attributes that are necessary to maintain their way of life. Barry et al. used existing anthropological records to review the economic characteristics and child-rearing techniques of 104 **preliterate societies** all over the world. As predicted, they found

---

nuclear family: *a family unit consisting of a wife/ mother, a husband/father, and their dependent child(ren).*

single-parent family: *a family unit consisting of one parent (either the mother or the father) and the parent's dependent child(ren).*

extended family: *a group of blood relatives from more than one nuclear family (for example, grandparents, aunts, uncles, nieces, and nephews) who live together, forming a household.*

survival goal: *LeVine's first priority of parenting—to promote the physical health and safety (survival) of young children.*

economic goal: *LeVine's second priority of parenting—to promote skills that children will need for economic self-sufficiency.*

self-actualization goal: *LeVine's third priority of parenting—to promote the child's cognitive and behavioral capacity for maximizing such cultural values as morality, achievement, prestige, and personal satisfaction.*

preliterate society: *a society in which there is little or no formal schooling, so that many children never learn to read and write.*

BOX 15-1
METHODS OF STUDYING THE FAMILY

Investigators who study family relationships have traditionally used one of three research strategies: the *interview* or *questionnaire* technique, *direct observation* of family interactions, or *laboratory analogue studies* (that is, experimental simulations of parent/child interactions). Although these approaches have generated a lot of very useful information about families, it is important to understand the strengths and weaknesses of each.

Interview and questionnaire studies

In an interview or questionnaire study, parents are asked to recall and describe the child-rearing practices they have used and to indicate the ways their children have acted at different times and in a variety of situations. The major advantage of this approach is that one can collect an enormous amount of information about a parent and his or her children in a short time.

Unfortunately, the interview/questionnaire method can generate inaccurate and misleading data if parents cannot recall how they or their child behaved earlier or if they confuse the child-rearing practices they used while raising different children. When asked to describe the previous behavior of any one of their children, parents are likely to become confused about which child did what and when, and thus they may end up providing a composite description of all their children. Finally, most parents have heard noted authorities express opinions about "proper" child-rearing practices, and often the practices advocated by experts differ from those that the parent has used. If even a small percentage of parents say that they relied on these "socially desirable" practices rather than the ones that they actually used, this

response bias could obscure any real relationships that may exist between parenting styles and behavior of young children.

Today few investigators rely exclusively on the interview and questionnaire technique when studying family relations. Perhaps the most common research strategy is to observe family members interacting with one another at home or in the laboratory and to supplement these observations with questionnaire data or interviews.

Observational methodologies

One excellent method of studying family relations and learning how family members influence one another is to observe them interacting at home or in the laboratory. Researchers who conduct observational studies are able to look at *behavioral sequences* among various family members and determine who did what to whom with what effect. By focusing on behavioral sequences, the investigator can answer questions such as: What does the mother typically do when her son ignores her? Does she raise her voice to ensure that he listens; threaten to take away a cherished privilege; spank him? How does the child respond to his mother's influence attempts? Does he comply; argue with her; cry? Does the father become involved in these exchanges; how; when? Of course, use of an observational methodology requires the researcher to assess the *reliability* of his or her observations. Reliability is most often measured by asking a second person to observe at least some of the interactions that the first observer witnesses and then comparing the observational records of the two observers. If independent observers have recorded similar information and can agree on what has occurred, their observational records are considered reliable.

One problem with the observational approach is that the mere presence of an observer making notes

that agricultural and pastoral societies did place strong pressures on their children to be cooperative and obedient, whereas hunting and fishing societies stressed assertiveness, self-reliance, and individual achievement.

Even in industrialized societies such as the United States, a family's social position or socioeconomic status affects the child-rearing practices that parents will use. For example, parents from the lower socioeconomic strata who typically work for a boss and must defer to his or her authority tend to stress obedience, neatness, cleanli-

ness, and respect for power—attributes that should enable their children to function effectively within a blue-collar economy. In contrast, middle-class parents, particularly those who work for themselves or who are professionals, are more likely to stress ambition, curiosity, creativity, and independence when raising their children (Hess, 1970; Kohn, 1969). The latter finding would hardly surprise LeVine, who would argue that middle-class parents who have the resources to promote their child's eventual economic security are freer to encourage his or her initiative,

and recording data can affect the ways family members relate to one another. For example, Leslie Zegoib and her associates (Zegoib, Arnold, & Forehand, 1975) report that mothers are warmer, more patient, and more involved with their children when they know they are being observed. Some investigators have tried to minimize these "observer effects" by capturing family interactions on videotape recorders placed in unobtrusive locations in the lab or the home. Another strategy is to mingle with the family for a few days before any data are collected so the family members will gradually become accustomed to the observer's presence and behave more naturally.

Naturalistic observation is not a very efficient method of studying socially undesirable interactions or those that occur infrequently. Indeed, a young researcher might turn gray before witnessing an instance of child abuse or coming across a youngster who is bold enough to play with matches, steal cookies, or masturbate in his or her presence. Another way of determining how various child-rearing techniques may affect children's behavior—particularly those undesirable behaviors that may occur infrequently—is to conduct an analogue experiment.

The analogue experiment

In a laboratory analogue, an adult experimenter behaves in a way that simulates a particular pattern of child rearing and then observes the effect of this experimental manipulation on the child's behavior. For example, we've seen in Chapter Fourteen how Ross Parke and his associates used the analogue technique to study the impact of various forms of punishment on children's resistance to temptation.

One problem with this approach is that the sequential complexities of parent/child interactions are difficult if not impossible to simulate in a situation where the child interacts on a *single occasion* with a *strange* adult. Moreover, the experimental tasks that children face in an analogue and the rules they must follow are often very dissimilar to those that they encounter at home, at school, or on the playground. Consider that children are often required to play with unattractive objects and to refrain from touching attractive toys in laboratory tests of resistance to temptation. Such a "prohibition" may seem rather arbitrary or irrational to youngsters whose experience in the home and at school suggests that it is acceptable to play with whatever toys are present in their play areas. Finally, prevailing ethical standards prevent experimenters from exposing children to the kinds of *intense* child-rearing practices (for example, spanking, ridicule, name calling, and rejection) that may occur in the home setting. So laboratory simulations of a particular child-rearing strategy are often rather weak approximations of their naturalistic referents, and they may have very different effects on the behavior of young children (Brody & Shaffer, 1982).

In spite of these limitations, the laboratory analogue serves an important "sufficiency" function by demonstrating that various child-rearing practices can (and often do) have immediate effects on children's behavior. Clearly, the observational and interview methodologies are invaluable because they provide data on the relationships between the patterns of child rearing that *parents* use and the behavior of *their* children. Once those relationships are known, the experimental analogue can then be used to tease apart the effects of the many child-rearing practices that make up a general style or pattern of parenting and thus allow us to draw meaningful conclusions about the ways parents and children are likely to influence one another.

achievement, and personal self-fulfillment (the third set of parenting goals) at a very early age.

SOME CAUTIONARY COMMENTS ABOUT THE STUDY OF FAMILIES

As we progress through the chapter looking at the ways families influence the development of their young, there are several important points to keep in mind. First, there is no "best way" to study families; each of the methods that investigators have used has very definite strengths and weaknesses (see Box 15-1), and the most convincing information that we have about family effects consists of findings that have been replicated using several methods.

In addition, much of the research that we will review assumes that the child-rearing practices that parents use largely determine how their children will behave. But as we will see, this unidirectional model of family effects is much too simplistic. Not only do children seem to influence the behavior and the child-rearing strategies of

PHOTO 15-1. In many cultures, parents increase their babies' chances of survival by keeping them close at all times.

their parents, but there is also reason to believe that a family is a complex social system in which each family member influences the thinking and behavior of every other family member.

Finally, some of the research that we will examine might seem to suggest that certain patterns of parenting are better or "more competent" than others. Now let's see why many family researchers are reluctant to endorse this conclusion.

The Middle-Class Bias

Much of the data that we will review were collected from White, middle-class samples in Western cultures and apply most directly to the development of White, middle-class children.

Should we assume that the patterns of child rearing that are most effective for these youngsters are "better" or more appropriate than other parenting techniques? If we do, we may be making a serious mistake, for as John Ogbu (1981) aptly notes, what passes as "competent parenting" for middle-class youngsters may fall far short of the mark if applied to children in other sociocultural groups.

Consider the case of disadvantaged children who grow up in urban ghettos in the United States. According to Ogbu (1981), these youngsters must acquire a very different set of competencies from those learned by middle-class age mates if they are to function effectively in the "street economy" of their subculture. While Johnny from the suburbs may strive to perfect skills such as reading and math that will prepare him for a traditional job, Johnny from the ghetto may come to view academics as a waste of time and choose instead to pursue other "survival-strategies" such as fighting, hustling, or working on his jump shot. Ogbu notes that ghetto parents are warm enough toward their infants but tend to use harsh and inconsistent discipline with their preschool and school-age children. When applied on a regular basis, these child-rearing techniques foster the development of assertiveness, self-reliance, and a mistrust of authority figures—precisely the attributes that ghetto youngsters may need in order to make it within their street culture. Of course, Ogbu is not implying that ghetto children will grow up to be deviant or abnormal by anyone's standards. His point is simply that the practices that qualify as "competent parenting" will depend on the particular skills and abilities that children will need for success within any given culture or subculture. So let's keep this point in mind and not automatically assume that deviations from middle-class patterns of child rearing are somehow "deficient" or "pathological."

The Directionality Issue

Until very recently, social scientists have assumed that influence within families was a one-way street—from parents, who did the shaping, to their children, whose personalities were molded by the caregiving practices and disciplinary techniques used by their elders. Indeed, much of the work that we will discuss has attempted to deter-

PHOTO 15-2. *A child's behavior is an important contributor to the treatment that he or she receives from parents.*

mine the correspondence between various patterns of parenting and the development of young children. When relationships were found, it was generally assumed that the behavior of parents determined the behavior of their children.

Today we have reason to believe that the pattern of influence in most, if not all, social relationships is **reciprocal** in character. Parents do indeed influence the behavior of their children. But at the same time, children play an important role in shaping the child-rearing practices used by their parents.

An excellent example of how children influence their parents comes from a study by David Buss (1981). Buss measured the activity level of 117 children at age 3 and again at age 4. When these children were 5 years old, they were placed in an experimental setting in which either their mothers or their fathers watched as they performed a battery of four cognitive tasks. The parent was encouraged to provide whatever assistance might be necessary to enable the child to complete the problems. Buss found that parents of active children often got into power struggles with their youngsters, tended to intrude physically and to become somewhat hostile, and had a difficult time establishing good working relationships with the

children. In contrast, interactions between parents and less active children were much more peaceful and harmonious. Since activity level is a moderately heritable component of temperament, one could argue that active children have active parents and that interactions between two reasonably active individuals are bound to lead to power struggles. But even if this is so, the data clearly indicate that the child's activity level is contributing in an important way to the treatment that he or she receives from parents. And as we have seen on several occasions, the techniques that parents use to discipline transgressions depend to a large extent on (1) the particular act the *child* committed and (2) the *child's reactions* to previous disciplinary encounters (Grusec & Kuczynski, 1980; Holden, 1983; Mulhern & Passman, 1981). So influence in parent/child interactions is a two-way street: children may have nearly as much effect on the behavior of their parents as parents have on the behavior of their children.

> **reciprocal influence:** *the notion that each person in a social relationship influences and is influenced by the other person(s).*

Reconceptualizing Family Effects: The Family as a Social System

Another limitation of the early research on families is that investigators concentrated on mother/child and father/child interactions and failed to treat the family as a true **social system.** Jay Belsky (1981) notes that the family consisting of a mother, a father, and a first-born child is a complex entity. Not only does the infant enter into a reciprocal relationship when alone with each parent, but the presence of *both* parents "transforms the mother-infant dyad into a *family system* [comprising] a husband-wife as well as mother-infant and father-infant relationships" (Belsky, 1981, p. 17). As it turns out, the mere presence of the second parent does affect the way the first parent interacts with his or her child. For example, fathers talk less to their toddlers when the mother is present (Stoneman & Brody, 1981), and mothers are less likely to play with or hold their youngsters when the father is around (Belsky, 1981). Moreover, the quality of the marriage (that is, the husband/wife relationship) can affect parent/child interactions, which, in turn, can have an effect on the quality of the marriage. So the patterns of influence in even the simplest of nuclear families are a whole lot more complex than researchers have generally assumed (see Figure 15-1). Of course, the social system becomes much more intricate with the birth of the second child and the addition of sibling/sibling and sibling/parent relationships.

We should also recognize that families exist within a larger cultural or subcultural setting and that the ecological niche that a family occupies (for example, the family's religion, its social class, and the values that prevail within a subculture or even a neighborhood) can affect family interactions and the development of a family's children (Bronfenbrenner, 1979). According to Belsky (1981), future advances in the study of family relations will stem from interdisciplinary efforts in which developmentalists, family sociologists, and community psychologists pool their expertise to gain a better understanding of the ways in which families (within particular social contexts) influence and are influenced by their young. Belsky argues:

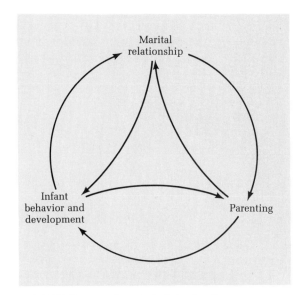

FIGURE 15-1. *A model of the family as a social system. As implied in the diagram, a family is bigger than the sum of its parts. Parents affect infants, who affect each parent and the marital relationship. Of course, the marital relationship may affect the parenting the infant receives, the infant's behavior, and so on. Clearly, families are complex social systems. As an exercise, you may wish to rediagram the patterns of influence within a family after adding a sibling or two.*

It is no longer acceptable to focus narrowly on parent-infant interaction. Such experience must be examined from the perspective of the family system, and thus, the marital relationship (as well as sibling relations) must be considered. The family too . . . needs to be examined within the wider ecology in which it is embedded. . . . Such [interdisciplinary research] should . . . thoroughly revitalize the study, and enhance our understanding of [the family and its impact on developing children] [1981, p. 19].

The Changing American Family

To date, most family research is based on traditional nuclear families consisting of a mother, a father, and one or more children. Although the times are definitely changing, the nuclear family remains the dominant living arrangement in modern industrialized societies. In the United States, for example, more than 80% of children live in an intact family setting with their parents, stepparents, or legal guardians such as foster parents or grandparents (U.S. Bureau of the Census, 1982). The major changes in the American nuclear family are that (1) more mothers are working outside the home and (2) people are having fewer children.

Even though most children live in nuclear families, the number of single-parent households is steadily increasing. Mavis Hetherington (1981) reports that the number of children living in single-parent homes doubled between 1960 and 1978 (rising from 5.8 million to 11.7 million), and it is worth repeating that 40–50% of all children born in the 1970s will spend some time living in a single-parent family. Two trends are responsible for this dramatic increase in the number of single-parent households: (1) the increasing number of children born out of wedlock and (2) the large number of divorces. Of these two factors, divorce is by far the major contributor. Only 16% of single-parent homes are the result of an illegitimate birth. However, the divorce rate in the United States has doubled between 1965 and 1978 (Hetherington, 1981). It is now estimated that nearly 50% of marriages between young adults will end in divorce (MacKinnon, Brody, & Stoneman, 1982).

As these statistics clearly indicate, marital disruptions and a restructuring of family ties are experiences that many children are now facing or will face in the years ahead. How do they cope? Does a divorce leave permanent emotional scars on the developing child? Is it possible that children may be better off in a single-parent home than in a strife-ridden nuclear family where the parents are constantly bickering? These are issues that family researchers are currently exploring as they study the impact of divorce on both parents and their children.

Although recent research has increased our knowledge about the effects of divorce and family dissolution, much less is known about how children are affected by a common by-product of divorce: the remarriage of the custodial parent. Over 6 million children now live in stepparent homes, and these **reconstituted families** represent about 11% of all American households (Santrock, Warshak, Lindbergh, & Meadows, 1982). Later in the chapter, we will take a closer look at the reconstituted family and see whether there is any evidence for the Cinderella syndrome—the notion that many stepparents are cool, aloof caregivers who tend to favor their own biological offspring and may even abuse a stepchild.

The ways in which researchers think about and study family relations are changing almost as fast as the families themselves. Our upcoming review of the literature represents a blend of (1) the old unidirectional research in which parents were assumed to mold the character of their children and (2) the "new look" at the family as a complex social system in which each family member interacts with and thereby influences every other family member. The older research is definitely worth reviewing, for it gives us some idea of how various patterns of child rearing contribute to positive or negative developmental outcomes. But as we discuss this work, let's keep in mind that children are active participants in the socialization process who play a major role in determining the character of the home environment to which they are exposed.

INTERACTIONS BETWEEN PARENTS AND THEIR INFANTS

A child begins to influence the behavior of other family members long before he or she is born. Adults who have hoped to conceive and who eagerly anticipate their baby's arrival will often plan for the blessed event by selecting names for the infant, buying or making baby clothes, decorating a nursery, moving to larger quarters, changing or leaving jobs, and preparing older children in the

---

family social system: *the complex network of relationships, interactions, and patterns of influence that characterizes a family with three or more members.*

reconstituted families: *new families that form after the remarriage of a single parent.*

family for the changes that are soon to come (Grossman, Eichler, Winickoff, & Associates, 1980). Of course, the impact of an unborn child may be far less pleasant for an unwed mother or a couple who do not want their baby, who cannot afford a child, or who receive very little encouragement and support from friends, relatives, and other members of the community (David & Baldwin, 1979).

How is the birth of a child likely to influence the mother, the father, and the marital relationship? Do the changes that parents experience affect their reactions to the baby? Are some parents more capable than others of coping with a difficult infant? Is there any truth to the claim that shaky marriages can be strengthened by having a child? In attempting to answer these questions, we will see why researchers like to think of families as complex entities that they are only now beginning to understand. However, this much is certain: the arrival of an infant transforms the marital dyad into a rather intricate social system that can influence the behavior and emotional well-being of all family members.

The Transition to Parenthood

The birth of a baby is a highly significant event that alters the behavior of both mothers and fathers and may affect the quality of their marital relationship. Shirley Feldman and Barbara Aschenbrenner (1983) find that the transition to parenthood affects the sex typing of new parents. New mothers not only feel more "feminine," they also begin to display more feminine behaviors and to perform fewer masculine activities. In other words, women behave in more traditionally sex-typed ways after the birth of a first child. By contrast, new fathers become less traditionally sex-typed. Although the frequency of their masculine role behaviors does not change, fathers show an increase in feminine activities, and their self-concepts become somewhat less "masculine" after the birth of a first child. Clearly, these findings are at odds with the stereotype that men are not affected by a transition to parenthood.

Does the birth of a child affect the marital relationship? Many family sociologists believe that the advent of parenthood is a "crisis" of sorts for a marriage. Couples must now cope with greater

financial responsibilities, a possible loss of income, changes in sleeping habits, and less time to themselves—events that may be perceived as aversive and could well disrupt the bond between husbands and wives (Miller & Sollie, 1980). Yet the research on this issue is mixed: some investigators find that the birth of a first child leads to a reduction in spousal intimacy and affection, while others report that the adjustment to parenthood is only mildly stressful (Belsky, 1981).

How do we explain these inconsistencies? After reviewing the available literature, Belsky (1981) concluded that the impact of a new baby on the marital relationship tends to be less severe or disruptive when parents are older, conceive after the marriage ceremony, and have been married longer before conceiving. Taken together, these findings suggest that mature, well-adjusted couples who have chosen to have a child are likely to experience few if any major problems as they make the transition to parenthood.

Of course, the behavior of the infant can also influence the couple's adjustment to parenthood. Parents of temperamentally difficult infants who cry a lot, have feeding problems, and are often "on the move" report experiencing more disruption of normal activities than parents of "quiet" babies (Russell, 1974). Moreover, many parents of infants who require special care (for example, babies with Down's syndrome or those who are at risk for sudden infant death) have problems with their spouses and believe that rearing a "special" child has made their marriages worse (Cain, Kelly, & Shannon, 1980; Gath, 1978). But for every set of parents who experience marital disharmony as a result of caring for a special child, there is at least one other couple who say that their abnormal infant has brought them closer together! So it appears that the arrival of a baby who requires special attention may disrupt the balance of a vulnerable marriage without shaking the foundation of one that is already on firm ground (Gath, 1978).

The Effects of Parents on Their Infants

In recent years, a number of investigators have begun to collect longitudinal data on parent/child interactions in an attempt to determine how parents affect the social, emotional, and intellectual development of their infants and toddlers. The results of these studies are remarkably consistent: warm and sensitive mothers who often talk to their infants and try to stimulate their curiosity are contributing in a positive way to the establishment of secure emotional attachments (Ainsworth, 1979) as well as to the child's exploratory competence (Belsky, Goode, & Most, 1980) and intellectual growth (Bradley, Caldwell, & Elardo, 1979; Cohen & Beckwith, 1979). Jay Belsky (1981) notes that the importance of warm and responsive mothering is

> underscored by several studies indicating that one of the products of maternal sensitivity, a secure attachment to the caregiver, forecasts skill in problem-solving and peer competence when the child is 2 and 5 years of age. . . . Block and Block . . . have also shown that the kinds of skills assessed by Sroufe and his students during the preschool years are . . . related to [the competencies children display] during the elementary school years. These findings strengthen the argument that sensitivity is *the* influential dimension of mothering in infancy: It not only fosters healthy psychological functioning during this developmental epoch, but it also lays the foundation on which future experience will build [pp. 7–8].

Recently, Christoph Heinicke and his associates (Heinicke, Diskin, Ramsey-Klee, & Given, 1983) have found that it is possible to predict who is likely to become a sensitive, responsive mother even before the child is born. A testing of 46 mothers at midpregnancy revealed that those who were warm and outgoing, high in ego strength (a measure of adaptive functioning and self-esteem), and confident in visualizing themselves as mothers were later found to be highly sensitive and responsive to their infants' needs throughout the first year.

■ Effects of the mother's age on mother/infant interactions

Popular wisdom suggests that women should have their children between the ages of 18 and 35. In Chapter Four we reviewed the medical evidence for this claim: teenage mothers and those over 35 are much more likely than those in their twenties to experience severe obstetrical complications and to deliver infants who are premature, are stillborn, or have some kind of birth defect. But are younger and older mothers any less

responsive to their infants than those who give birth during the "optimal" childbearing years?

Most of the research on this issue has focused on the child-rearing practices of young adolescent mothers. Teenage mothers express less favorable attitudes about child rearing and are apt to be less responsive to their infants than mothers in their twenties (Field, Widmayer, Stringer, & Ignatoff, 1980; Jones, Green, & Krauss, 1980). This finding may simply reflect the fact that many adolescent mothers are unmarried and hence receive little in the way of intimate support and encouragement from the baby's father, their own relatives, or other members of the community.

Recently, Arlene Ragozin and her associates (Ragozin, Basham, Crnic, Greenberg, & Robinson, 1982) observed the behavior of mothers aged 16 to 38 as they interacted with their 4-month-old infants. As shown in Figure 15-2, older mothers were quite responsive to their children (particularly first-borns), and they seemed to derive more satisfaction from interacting with their first-born or second-born infants than younger mothers did. Clearly these data argue against the popular belief that women in their twenties are the ones who are best suited psychologically for the responsibilities of motherhood.

■ Father/infant interactions

Until very recently, investigators have concentrated on mother/infant interactions and all but ignored the influence of fathers. One reason for this emphasis is that mothers attend more to their infants than fathers do, even when the fathers are home from work (Clarke-Stewart, 1978). Several years ago, Freda Rebelsky and Cheryl Hanks (1971) attached microphones to ten infants and recorded how often their fathers spoke to them between the ages of 2 weeks and 3 months. On an average day, the fathers in this study addressed their infants only 2.7 times for a total of approximately 40 seconds. However, these results are somewhat deceiving. One reason that American fathers in earlier reports may have seemed so detached from or unresponsive to their infants is that very few fathers were allowed in delivery rooms to greet their neonates and become involved with them. Today, birthing practices have changed so that fathers are often encouraged to be present for the baby's arrival. These changes

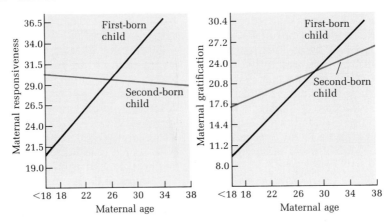

FIGURE 15-2. *Effects of maternal age on mothers' responsiveness to their infants and amount of gratification received from mother/infant interactions.*

are largely due to the finding that fathers who are present in the nursery or delivery room often appear to be just as intrigued, or engrossed, by their neonates as mothers are (Greenberg & Morris, 1974; Peterson, Mehl, & Liederman, 1979).

And even when fathers have had very little contact with their neonates, they will typically become much more involved with them over the next several months (Easterbrooks & Goldberg, 1984). Unlike mothers, who are likely to hold, soothe, care for, or play quietly with their infants, fathers are much more boisterous, choosing to initiate physically stimulating, rough-and-tumble activities that infants seem to enjoy (Lamb, 1981). In assuming the role of "special playmate," the father is in a unique position to influence the activities and preferences of his children. Indeed, fathers of 12-month-old infants are already beginning to encourage their children (particularly their sons) to play with sex-typed toys and to avoid playful activities that are considered more appropriate for children of the other sex (Snow, Jacklin, & Maccoby, 1983). However, let's note that fathers are more than mere playmates; they are often successful at soothing or comforting a distressed infant, and they may also serve as a "secure base" from which their infant will venture to explore the environment. Finally, a secure attachment to the father can help to offset the social deficiencies and emotional disturbances that could otherwise result when an infant is insecurely attached to the mother (Main & Weston, 1981).

■ *Indirect effects*

Parents may also have **"indirect" effects** on their infants by virtue of their ability to influence the behavior of their spouses. For example, marital tension following the birth of a baby can disrupt a mother's caretaking routines and interfere with her ability to enjoy her infant (Belsky, 1981). Moreover, Frank Pedersen and his associates (Pedersen, Anderson, & Cain, 1977) found that both mothers and fathers were likely to be unresponsive or negative toward their 5-month-old infants in families characterized by marital strife. So it would seem that unhappily married couples are ill advised to have children as a means of solidifying a shaky marriage. Not only is this practice unlikely to strengthen the marital bond, but it is almost guaranteed to lead to poor parent/child relations.

Of course, the indirect effects of either parent may often be positive ones. Belsky (1979; Belsky, Gilstrap, & Rovine, 1984) found that fathers were much more involved with their infants in families where the parents frequently talked about the baby. In this case, it appeared that mothers were exerting an indirect influence on father/infant interactions by helping the fathers to become more knowledgeable about and interested in the development of their children. Happily married couples seem to function as sources of mutual support and encouragement, so that many child-rearing problems are easier to overcome (Crnic, Greenberg, Ragozin, Robinson, & Basham, 1983; Goldberg &

PHOTO 15-3. Fathers play a central role in a child's life, serving as playmates, caregivers, and confidants, as well as an important source of emotional security.

Easterbrooks, 1984). For example, parents of babies who are at risk for later emotional problems (as noted by the child's disorganized performance on the Brazelton Neonatal Assessment Scale) will typically establish "synchronous" and satisfying relationships with their infants *unless they are unhappily married* (Belsky, 1981).

After examining the data on parent/infant interactions, we see that even the simplest of families is a true social system that is bigger than the sum of its parts. Not only does each family member influence the behavior of every other family member, but the relationship that any two family members have can indirectly affect the interactions and relationships among all other members of the family. Clearly, socialization within the family setting is not merely a two-way street— it is more accurately characterized as the busy intersection of many avenues of influence.

PARENTAL EFFECTS ON PRESCHOOL AND SCHOOL-AGE CHILDREN

During the second and the third years, parents spend less time caring for and playing with their child as they begin to impose restrictions on the child's activities and try to teach him or her how to behave (or how not to behave) in a variety of situations. According to Erik Erikson (1963), this is the period when socialization begins in earnest. Parents must now limit the child's autonomy in the hope of instilling a sense of social propriety and self-control, while taking care not to undermine the child's curiosity, initiative, and feelings of personal competence. Erikson believed that two aspects of parenting are especially important during the preschool and school-age years: parental warmth and parental control (that is, permissiveness/restrictiveness).

Two Major Dimensions of Child Rearing

A number of studies suggest that parents do differ on the two attributes that Erikson thought to be so important. Let's first consider the dimension of parental control.

Permissiveness/restrictiveness refers to the amount of autonomy that parents allow their children. Restrictive parents limit their children's freedom of expression by imposing many demands and actively surveying their children's behavior to ensure that these rules and regulations are followed. Permissive parents are much less controlling. They make relatively few demands of their children and allow them considerable freedom in exploring the environment, expressing their opinions and emotions, and making decisions about their own activities. A common finding is that parents become less restrictive as

---

indirect parental effect: *an occasion when one parent influences the behavior of his or her spouse, which, in turn, influences the behavior of their children.*

permissiveness/restrictiveness: *a dimension of parenting that describes the amount of autonomy (or freedom of expression) that a parent allows his or her children.*

their children mature, although some parents are more likely to loosen the reins than others (Schaefer & Bayley, 1963).

Parental warmth (or **warmth/hostility**) refers to the amount of affection and approval that an adult displays toward his or her children. Parents described as warm and nurturant are those who often smile at, praise, and encourage their child while limiting their criticisms, punishments, and signs of disapproval. In contrast, the hostile or rejecting parent is one who is quick to criticize, belittle, punish, or ignore a child while limiting his or her expressions of affection and approval. It is important to note that measures of parental warmth reflect the character of an adult's reactions to the child *across a large number of situations.* For example, a parent who is cool and critical when a child misbehaves but warm and accepting in most other contexts would be classified as high in parental warmth. One who is warm and nurturant whenever her child praises her but critical, punitive, or indifferent in many other situations would be considered a more aloof or rejecting parent.

These two dimensions of child rearing are reasonably independent, so that we find parents who are warm and restrictive, warm and permissive, cool (rejecting) and restrictive, and cool and permissive. Are these aspects of parenting related in any meaningful way to the child's social, emotional, and intellectual development?

Patterns of Parental Control

Perhaps the best-known research on the effects of parental control is that of Diana Baumrind (1971, 1977). Baumrind's sample consisted of 134 preschool children and their parents. Each child was observed on several occasions in a nursery school setting and at home. These data were used to rate the child on several dimensions of *instrumental competence* (for example, sociability, self-reliance, self-control, and achievement). Parents were also interviewed and observed while interacting with their children at home. When Baumrind analyzed the parental data, she found that individual parents generally used one of three patterns of parental control, which she describes as follows:

The **authoritarian** parent attempts: to shape, control, and evaluate the behavior of the child in accordance with a set standard of conduct, usually an absolute standard, theologically motivated and formulated by a higher authority. She values obedience as a virtue and favors punitive, forceful measures to curb self-will at points where the child's actions or beliefs conflict with what she thinks is right conduct. . . . She does not encourage verbal give and take, believing that the child should accept her word for what is right. . . .

The **authoritative** parent, by contrast with the authoritarian parent, attempts: to direct the child's activities but in a rational . . . manner. She encourages verbal give and take, and shares with the child the reasoning behind her policy. She values . . . both *autonomous self-will and disciplined conformity*. Therefore, she exerts firm control at points of parent-child divergence, but does not hem the child in with restrictions. She [balances] her own special rights as an adult [against] the child's individual interests. . . . The authoritative parent sets standards for future conduct and uses reason as well as power to achieve her objectives. She . . . does not regard herself as infallible or divinely inspired. . . .

The **permissive** parent attempts: to behave in a nonpunitive, acceptant, and affirmative manner toward the child's impulses, desires, and actions. She consults with him about policy decisions and gives explanations for family rules. She makes few demands . . . [and] presents herself as a resource for him to use as he wishes, not as an active agent responsible for altering . . . his behavior. She allows the child to regulate his own activities, . . . avoids the exercise of control, and does not encourage him to obey externally defined standards. She uses reason but not overt power to accomplish her ends [1971, pp. 22–23].

Baumrind found that authoritative parents are more likely than either authoritarian or permissive parents to have preschool children who are friendly and cooperative with adults and peers, socially responsible, self-reliant, and interested in achievement. Note that both authoritative and authoritarian parents set many standards for their children and are quite controlling. But there is a clear difference in the way control is exercised. The authoritarian parent dominates the child, allowing little if any freedom of expression, whereas the authoritative parent is careful to per-

TABLE 15-1. Relationship between patterns of parental control during the preschool period and children's cognitive and social competencies during the grade school years

Pattern of parenting during preschool period	Children's competencies at age 8–9	
	Girls	Boys
Authoritative	Very high cognitive and social competencies	High cognitive and social competencies
Authoritarian	Average cognitive and social competencies	Average social competencies; low cognitive competencies
Permissive	Low cognitive and social competencies	Low social competencies; very low cognitive competencies

mit the child enough autonomy so that he or she can develop a sense of initiative, self-reliance, and a feeling of pride in personal accomplishments. Baumrind's results indicate that maintaining a firm sense of control over a child can be a very beneficial child-rearing practice. It is only when the controlling parent severely restricts the child's autonomy and uses arbitrary or irrational methods of control that the child is likely to be surly, defiant, uncomfortable in social situations, and lacking in independence.

Permissive parents do not demand much of their children, do not discourage immature responses, and do not actively encourage self-reliant behavior. Children of permissive parents (particularly boys) tend to be selfish, rebellious, aggressive, rather aimless, and quite low in independence and achievement. Perhaps we are not too far off if we describe their behavioral profile as the "spoiled brat" syndrome.

Ninety-eight of Baumrind's subjects (and their parents) were observed once again when the children were 8 to 9 years old (Baumrind, 1977). As we see in Table 15-1, children of authoritative parents were still relatively high in both *cognitive competencies* (that is, shows originality in thinking, has high achievement motivation, likes intellectual challenges) and *social skills* (for example, is sociable and outgoing, participates actively and shows leadership in group activities), whereas children of permissive parents were relatively unskilled in both areas. Baumrind also reported an interesting sex difference in the effects of authoritarian parenting: among children whose parents had remained highly authoritarian during the school-age years, boys were more likely than

girls to lose interest in achievement and to withdraw from social contacts.

One limitation of Baumrind's research is that almost all the parents in her sample were rather warm and accepting. As it turns out, the effects of either restrictive or permissive parenting will depend, in part, on the extent to which the parent displays warmth and affection toward the child (Becker, 1964). Children of *restrictive and rejecting* parents are often found to be extremely withdrawn and inhibited, and they may even show **masochistic** or suicidal tendencies. By contrast, children of *permissive and rejecting* parents tend

---

warmth/hostility: *a dimension of parenting that describes the amount of affection and approval that a parent displays toward his or her children.*

authoritarian parenting: *a restrictive pattern of parenting in which adults set many rules for their children, expect strict obedience, and do not explain why it is necessary to comply with these regulations.*

authoritative parenting: *a flexible style of parenting in which adults allow their children autonomy but are careful to explain the restrictions they impose and will ensure that their children follow these guidelines.*

permissive parenting: *a pattern of parenting in which adults make few demands of their children and rarely attempt to control their behavior.*

masochist: *a person who derives pleasure from beatings or other forms of abuse administered by the self or others.*

PHOTO 15-4. *Warmth and affection are crucial components of effective parenting.*

to be very hostile, rebellious, and prone to delinquency. What these findings seem to suggest is that the undesirable effects of either extremely restrictive (authoritarian) or extremely permissive parenting are exaggerated when parents are also hostile toward their children or unconcerned about their welfare.

Parental Warmth/Hostility

Although most parents are typically warm and loving, a small minority in any sample are clearly rejecting—expressing a lack of concern or feelings of dislike for their youngsters, who are often perceived as burdensome (Maccoby, 1980). Throughout this text, we have taken care to note the relationships between parental warmth and various aspects of children's social, emotional, and intellectual development. Here are but a few of the attributes that characterize the children of warm and accepting parents:

1. They are securely attached at an early age. Of course, secure attachments are an important contributor to the growth of curiosity, exploratory competence, problem-solving skills, and positive social relations with both adults and peers (see Chapter Eleven).

2. They are relatively altruistic, especially when their parents preach altruistic values and practice what they preach (see Chapter Twelve).

3. They are generally obedient, noncoercive youngsters who get along reasonably well with parents and peers (see Chapter Twelve).

4. They tend to be high in self-esteem and role-taking skills, and when they are disciplined, they usually feel that their parents' actions are justified (Brody & Shaffer, 1982; Coopersmith, 1967).

5. They are satisfied with their gender identities and are likely to be firmly sex-typed or androgynous (Mussen & Rutherford, 1963; see Chapter Thirteen).

6. They will often refer to internalized norms rather than fear of punishment as a reason for complying with moral rules (Brody & Shaffer, 1982).

Recently, Thomas Crook, Allen Raskin, and John Eliot (1981) proposed that adults who are clinically depressed and view themselves as inferior or worthless are often the product of a home environment in which they were clearly rejected by one or both parents. To evaluate their hypothesis, Crook et al. asked 714 adults who were hospitalized for depression to describe their childhood relationships with their mothers and fathers by indicating whether each of 192 statements characterized the behavior of either or both parents (for example, Did your mother [father] worry about you when you were away? Threaten not to love you if you misbehaved? Often make you feel guilty? Set firm standards? Consistently enforce her [his] rules? Often ridicule you?). As a comparison group, 387 nondepressed adults answered the same questions. Since an adult's self-reports of childhood experiences may be distorted and unreliable, the investigators also interviewed siblings, relatives, and long-time friends of the subjects as a check on the accuracy of their reflections. Data collected from these "independent sources" were then used to rate each subject's mother and father on the warmth/hostility and the autonomy/control (permissiveness/restrictiveness) dimensions.

The results of this study were straightforward. Subjects hospitalized for depression rated *both their mothers and their fathers* as less "accepting" and more "hostile," "detached," and "rejecting" than nondepressed adults in the comparison sample. Although the parents of depressed patients were not rated as any more "restrictive" or "controlling" than parents of nondepressed adults, they were perceived as exercising control in a more derisive way, often choosing to ridicule, belittle, or withdraw affection from their children. So even the guidance and discipline that depressed adults received during childhood were administered in a hostile, rejecting manner.

Data collected from the "independent sources" were quite consistent with the subjects' own reports. Both the mothers and fathers of the depressed patients were described as less affectionate and less involved with their children than the parents of nondepressed adults.

In sum, it appears that a primary contributor to adult depression is a family setting in which one or both parents have treated the individual as if he or she were unworthy of their love and affection. Perhaps it is fair to say that parents who blatantly reject their children are committing an extremely powerful form of child abuse—one that could leave emotional scars that will last a lifetime.

Now compare this behavioral profile with that of a group of "unwanted" Czechoslovakian children whose mothers had tried repeatedly to gain permission to abort them during the prenatal period. Compared with a group of "wanted" Czech children from similar family backgrounds, the unwanted children had less stable ties to their mothers and fathers and were described by the researchers as anxious, emotionally frustrated, and irritable (Matějček, Dytrych, & Schüller, 1979). Although they were all physically healthy at birth, the unwanted children were more likely than those in the "wanted" group to have spotty medical histories that had required them to be hospitalized. Children in the unwanted group made significantly poorer grades at school even though they were comparable in intelligence to their "wanted" classmates. Finally, the unwanted children were less well integrated into the peer group and more likely to require psychiatric attention for serious behavior disorders. (For another look at the long-term consequences of cool, aloof parenting, see Box 15-2.)

Is parental warmth alone likely to lead to positive developmental outcomes? Probably not, for we've seen that children of warm but permissive parents tend to be low in both cognitive and social competencies (Baumrind, 1971, 1977). Nevertheless, warmth and affection are clearly important components of effective parenting. As Eleanor Maccoby (1980) has noted,

Parental warmth binds children to their parents in a positive way—it makes children responsive and more willing to accept guidance. If the parent-child relationship is close and affectionate, parents can exercise what control is needed without having to apply heavy disciplinary pressure. It is as if parents' responsiveness, affection, and obvious commitment to their children's welfare have earned them the right to make decisions and exercise control [p. 394].

Patterns of Parental Discipline

In earlier chapters we saw that parents differ in the strategies they use to enforce their demands and to discipline transgressions. Both *power-assertive* discipline (use of forceful commands, physical punishment, and control over valuable resources) and *love withdrawal* (expressions of ridicule, disliking, or withdrawing affection) may threaten the child. Children whose parents rely heavily on these disciplinary practices are motivated to comply with parental demands in order *to avoid negative consequences.* By contrast, *induction* is a relatively nonpunitive form of discipline in which parents attempt to reason with their children. The goal of the inductive disciplinarian is to make children understand (1) why they need to follow various rules and regulations, (2) why their transgressions are wrong, and (3) how they might alter their behavior to prevent future transgressions or undo whatever harm they may have done.

In one recent review of the literature, Gene Brody and David Shaffer (1982) found that parents who rely on power assertion to enforce their demands are likely to have extremely self-centered children who score low on tests of moral development. By contrast, parents who use inductive discipline, particularly those who also have a warm, affectionate relationship with their children, have youngsters who are highly altruistic and who score above average on tests of moral development. Note that the inductive disciplinarian who is warm and accepting and who appeals to reason in order to enforce his or her demands sounds very much like Baumrind's authoritative parent. In contrast, adults who use arbitrary forms of punishment such as spankings or a withdrawal of affection are in some ways similar to Baumrind's authoritarian parent. So the research on parental discipline dovetails nicely with the earlier work on other aspects of child rearing. The implication is that parents who are warm, controlling, and inductive in their role as disciplinarians are likely to raise children who are quite friendly, outgoing, intellectually competent, and morally mature.

Of course, the extent to which parents are able to function as warm, controlling, and inductive caregivers will depend, in part, on the behavior of their children. In Chapter Seven we reviewed a study by Joan Grusec and Leon Kuczynski (1980) in which mothers were asked how they would respond if their 4–8-year-olds had committed each of 12 transgressions. The mothers' responses clearly depended on what their children had done. Each of the 12 transgressions elicited *similar* forms of discipline from virtually all the mothers, and individual mothers were generally not very consistent in their disciplinary practices from one situation to the next. Moreover, Douglas Sawin and Ross Parke (as cited in Parke, 1977) found that defiant children are disciplined more severely than those who generally accept their punishment without complaining. Even temperamental characteristics such as the child's activity level are important, for we've seen that parent/child interactions are much more stressful and coercive when the parent must deal with a highly active child (Buss, 1981).

The way parents react to their children will also depend on the child's age or developmental level. During the first year of an infant's life, parent/child interactions gradually become less centered on routine caregiving activities and increasingly playful, with the infant doing more of the initiating (Green, Gustafson, & West, 1980). At this age, mothers are usually successful at terminating undesirable behavior by simply repositioning their infants or directing their attention elsewhere (Holden, 1983). During the second and third years, when curious, active children are now turning knobs, fondling breakables, and harassing the family pet, parents will often handle disciplinary issues by physical manipulations such as swatting the child's hands, placing fragile or dangerous items out of reach, or carrying the child away from the scene of mischievous behavior (Maccoby, 1980). One reason that adults use these power-assertive techniques is that toddlers and preschool children may have a difficult time understanding cognitive appeals and are simply more responsive to power assertion. Indeed, young, egocentric preschoolers believe that most acts of disobedience are all right if they are not detected, and they equate parental authority with the parent's power to punish (Damon, 1977; Kohlberg, 1969). But over the next several years, the child develops the role-taking skills to recognize and appreciate the perspectives of other people—

BOX 15-3
WHY "MOM IS THE GREATEST"

After reviewing the literature, many people would undoubtedly conclude that "great parents" are those who are generally warm, accepting, and authoritative in their approach to child rearing. Do children agree with this point of view? To find out, John Weisz (1980) analyzed the contents of letters submitted by 7–17-year-olds to a newspaper contest entitled "Why Mom Is the Greatest." If children and developmental researchers see eye to eye on the determinants of effective parenting, then youngsters should stress maternal attributes such as nurturance and a willingness to give praise, to be supportive, and to grant some autonomy as their reasons for thinking that "mom is the greatest."

Weisz found that young grade school children clearly value the *physical nurturance* that their mothers provide (that is, the mother's willingness to attend to the child's physical needs—to provide toys, clothes, meals, and transportation). One 7-year-old named April wrote that her mom was the greatest because "she cooks the best chili and she kisses me every day on the nose." Older children and adolescents also valued their mothers' physical nurturance, but they were more likely than their younger counterparts to stress their mothers' *psychological nurturance* (for example, willingness to listen to problems, counsel, and give emotional support) and to think highly of her for *"just being there"* (a form of security in knowing that mom is always there when she is needed). For example, a 15-year-old named Bill wrote "She teaches me right from wrong even though it may hurt. She's very heart warming when your down in the blues [*sic*]." The older child's emphasis on psychological nurturance seems to reflect the development of important role-taking skills— namely, the ability to recognize that mom makes an active attempt to understand his or her point of view. Indeed, many adolescents said mom is the greatest because "she always seems to know how I feel" or "when I'm sad, she knows what's on my mind."

How did children feel about parental control over their activities? Younger children generally valued mothers who gave them lots of autonomy. Ten-year-old Melissa wrote "My mother is the greatest because she lets us do almost anything." However, older children and adolescents seemed to favor a little more control. They apparently recognized that maternal restraints reflect love and concern about their welfare, whereas extreme permissiveness may indicate laxity or disinterest.

Although Weisz's findings are based on only 244 letters that were written by children who had obviously established good relationships with their mothers, it is interesting to note that these youngsters stressed the very attributes that child developmentalists consider important dimensions of effective parenting. In fact, statements indicative of aloof, authoritarian parenting almost never appeared in the letters of these young respondents. Since the data apply only to mothers, it would be interesting to see whether children mention the same attributes and child-rearing practices when they tell us "why dad is the greatest."

a cognitive advance that helps to explain why many parents become much more inductive with their grade school children.

What do children think of the parenting they receive? What do they view as competent or effective parenting? As we see in Box 15-3, the answers to these questions depend, in part, on the child's developmental level.

Social-Class Differences in Parenting

Social class (or *socioeconomic status*) refers to one's position within a society that is stratified according to status or power (Maehr, 1974). In many countries (such as India) a person's social standing is determined at birth by the status of his or her parents. If you were to grow up in this kind of society, you would be compelled by virtue of your origins to pursue one of a limited number of occupations, to live in a designated neighborhood, and to marry someone who occupies a similar position in the social hierarchy.

This scenario sounds rather dismal to those of us who live in Western industrialized societies, where the most common measures of social class—family income, prestige of father's occupation, and parents' educational level—are indications of the family's achievements. In the United States, we are fond of saying that virtually anyone can rise above his or her origins if that person is willing to work extremely hard toward the pursuit of success. Indeed, this proverb is the cornerstone of the American dream.

However, sociologists tell us that the "American dream" is a belief that is more likely to be endorsed by members of the middle and upper classes—those elements of society that have the economic resources to maintain or improve on their lofty economic status (Hess, 1970). As we will see, many people from the lower and working classes face very different kinds of problems, pursue different goals, and often adopt different values. In short, they live in a different world than middle-class people do, and these ecological considerations may well affect the methods and strategies that they use to raise their children.

■ Social-class differences in attitudes, values, and lifestyles

Perhaps the most obvious differences between middle- and lower-class families are economic: middle-class families usually have more money and material possessions. A more subtle difference between **high-SES** (middle- and upper-class) and **low-SES** (lower- and working-class) families centers on their feelings of power and influence. People from the lower socioeconomic strata often believe that, without material resources, they have few opportunities to get ahead and no direct access to those in power, and consequently they feel that their lives are largely controlled by the "advantaged" members of society. In order to qualify for housing, financial, or medical assistance, they must often live where the bureaucrats tell them to live or otherwise do as the bureaucrats say. Many low-SES parents cannot afford the luxury of health or disability insurance, and their resources are likely to be insufficient to cope with problems such as an accident, an extended illness, or the loss of a job. Is it any wonder, then, that many lower- and working-class adults feel insecure or helpless and are apt to develop an external locus of control (Hess, 1970; Phares, 1976)?

The powerlessness and sense of insecurity so often seen in low-SES families clearly affect the expectations that parents have for their children. Middle- and upper-class children are expected to get good grades in elementary school, to attend college, and to become professionals or enter other high-status vocations. In contrast, lower- and working-class parents are less likely to emphasize the importance of attending college or striving toward a high-status career; instead, they are apt to encourage their children to prepare for a steady line of work, regardless of its prestige value

(Hess, 1970). So we see that middle- and upper-class children are expected to "get ahead," while lower- and working-class children are encouraged to "get by." By midadolescence these class-linked expectations are apparently having an effect, for middle- and upper-class high school students expect to enter higher-status occupations than students of comparable intelligence from lower-class families (Sewell, Haller, & Strauss, 1957).

A low income may also mean that living quarters are crowded, that family members must occasionally make do without adequate food or medical care, and that parents are constantly tense or anxious about living under these marginal conditions. Eleanor Maccoby (1980) suggests that low-income living is probably more stressful for parents and that stress affects the ways in which parental functions are carried out. Recently, John Zussman (1980) has studied the impact of stress on parent/child interactions in an interesting analogue experiment. Either mothers or fathers were asked to perform a distracting cognitive activity (a mental anagram task) in the presence of their two young children (in this study, families with one nursery school child and one toddler were recruited). The room in which the experiment took place included toys that were difficult to operate without the parent's assistance as well as attractive nuisances such as a filled ashtray and stacks of papers and index cards. Parent/child interactions were observed during two ten-minute periods: one in which the parent was instructed simply to observe the play of his or her children (low-stress condition) and one in which the parent was preoccupied with the distracting cognitive activity (high-stress condition). Zussman found that the stress created by trying to concentrate on the cognitive task while keeping one's children out of mischief had a dramatic effect on the quantity and quality of parent/child interactions. Under the stressful conditions, parents became much less responsive and helpful toward their nursery school children. And although they continued to show as much attention to their toddlers under the stressful circumstances, the character of their interactions changed as the parents became more critical, restrictive, and punitive toward the younger child.

In sum, Zussman's study indicates that even very mild and temporary forms of stress can affect the ways adults react to their children. When we consider that low-SES families are more likely to experience major and prolonged life stresses such as inadequate housing, losses of employment due to economic uncertainties, anxieties about being able to pay bills or put food on the table, and family disruptions because of divorce or desertion, we have good reason to believe that low-SES parents may end up raising their children differently than middle- and upper-class parents do.

■ *Social-class differences in parent/infant and parent/toddler interactions*

Class-linked differences in mother/infant interactions are already apparent in the first year. Tiffany Field and Susan Pawlby (1980) found that middle-class mothers in both England and the United States did not differ from working-class mothers in the amount of *close contact* (touching, caregiving) they had with their 4-month-old infants. However, the middle-class mothers in both societies were more likely to provide **distal stimulation** by gazing or smiling at their infants, vocalizing or singing to them, or engaging them in some form of play. Dale Farran and Craig Ramey (1980) observed the interactions between 60 lower- and middle-class mother/infant pairs on two occasions, once when the children were 6 months of age and again when they were 20 months old. By noting the frequency of both close contact and distal interaction, Farran and Ramey assigned each mother/infant dyad a score that represented how "involved" they were with each other. The results of this study appear in Figure 15-3. Note that social-class differences in "dyadic involvement" were quite small when children were 6 months of age but that a much higher percentage of middle-class dyads were rated as positively involved at age 20 months. When Farran and Ramey then looked at the absolute *amount* of involvement that characterized each mother/infant dyad, they found that middle-class mothers generally interacted more with their youngsters as the children grew older, whereas lower-class mothers typically were no more involved with their older infants or interacted with them even less than they had at age 6 months.

Mothers often function as "teachers" in their everyday interactions with toddlers and preschool children, and there is now a good deal of evidence that the character of this "informal curriculum" depends, in part, on the mother's sociocultural

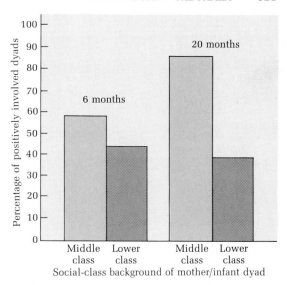

FIGURE 15-3. *Percentages of mother/infant dyads rated as positively involved at ages 6 months and 20 months. Note that middle-class mothers seem to become more involved with their infants as they mature, whereas lower-class mothers show exactly the opposite pattern.*

background (Laosa, 1981). When encouraging the child to complete a puzzle or a cognitive task, middle-class mothers tend to focus on the child's attention by using very precise verbal labels in their instructions, making suggestions in the form of questions, and including praise or approval in their communications. In contrast, lower-class mothers are more likely to issue "unfriendly orders" (or commands), to employ nonverbal gestures as a means of focusing attention, and to use criticism and punishment (see Laosa, 1981, for a review of the literature). Of course, these differences represent *group averages* rather than abso-

---

high-SES: *a term that refers to the middle and upper classes—that is, the economically advantaged members of society.*

low-SES: *a term that refers to the lower and working classes—that is, the economically disadvantaged members of society.*

distal stimulation: *stimulation provided from a distance; smiling, vocalizing, and gesturing are examples.*

lute contrasts: some middle-class mothers use teaching strategies more commonly observed among the lower-class dyads, and many lower-class mothers function more like their counterparts from the middle class. But on the average, it appears that lower-class mothers are somewhat less precise in their verbal instructions and somewhat more critical, punitive, and controlling when cast into the role of a teacher.

■ Patterns of child rearing in high-SES and low-SES families

Eleanor Maccoby (1980) has reviewed the child-rearing literature and concluded that high-SES parents differ from low-SES parents in at least four respects:

1. Low-SES parents tend to stress obedience and respect for authority, neatness, cleanliness, and staying out of trouble. Higher-SES parents are more likely to stress happiness, curiosity, independence, creativity, ambition, and self-control.
2. Lower-SES parents are more restrictive and authoritarian, often setting arbitrary standards and enforcing them with power-assertive forms of discipline. Higher-SES parents tend to be either permissive or authoritative, and they are more likely to use inductive forms of discipline.
3. Higher-SES parents talk more with their children, reason with them more, and may use somewhat more complex language than lower-SES parents.
4. Higher-SES parents tend to show more warmth and affection toward their children.

According to Maccoby, these relationships seem to be true in many cultures and across racial and ethnic groups within the United States. However, there is some evidence that differences between high-SES and low-SES parenting are much more pronounced for boys than for girls. For example, John Zussman (1978) found that lower-class parents were more likely than middle-class parents to use power assertion with their sons, although parents from both social classes used very low levels of power assertion with their daughters.

There are undoubtedly many factors that contribute to social-class differences in child rearing. Earlier we saw that the stresses associated with low-income living may cause parents to become more critical, controlling, and punitive and less responsive to a child's needs—in short, to seem somewhat aloof or uninvolved with their children. And as John Ogbu (1981) and others have noted, the way a family earns its livelihood may affect the strategies that parents use to raise their children. Low-SES parents may emphasize respect, obedience, neatness, and staying out of trouble because these are precisely the attributes that they view as critical for success in the blue-collar economy. In contrast, high-SES parents may reason or negotiate more with their children while emphasizing individual initiative and achievement because these are the skills, attributes, and abilities that high-SES parents find necessary in their own roles as businesspersons, white-collar workers, or high-salaried professionals. Finally, let's note that the children themselves may contribute to social-class differences in child rearing. Low-SES mothers, who are often younger and may receive less adequate prenatal care, are more likely than middle-class mothers to deliver prematurely or to experience other complications of childbirth (Kessner, 1973). In other words, low-SES families are more likely to have irritable, unresponsive, or otherwise difficult babies who may be harder to care for and love.

When we look at the data, it may seem that high-SES parenting is somehow "better" or more competent. After all, the responsive, authoritative parenting often observed in middle-class families produces highly sociable children who are curious, outgoing, intellectually capable, and morally mature. Yet there is another side to this issue—one that researchers in Western societies sometimes fail to consider. Perhaps middle-class parenting is "better" for children who are expected to grow up and become productive members of a middle-class subculture. However, a middle-class pattern of parenting that stresses individual initiative, intellectual curiosity, and competitiveness may actually represent "incompetent" parenting among the Temne of Sierra Leone, a society in which everyone must pull together and suppress individualism if the community is to successfully plant, harvest, and ration the meager crops on which its livelihood absolutely depends (Berry, 1967). And since many children from Western, industrialized societies will choose a career within the so-called blue-collar economy, it hardly seems reasonable to conclude that a pattern of child rearing that prepares them for this undertaking is in some way deficient or "incompetent."

The closest thing to a general law of parenting is that warm, sensitive, and responsive caregiving seems to be associated with positive developmental outcomes in virtually all the cultures and subcultures that social scientists have studied. But people are being somewhat **ethnocentric** when they suggest that a particular pattern or style of child rearing (for example, authoritative parenting) that produces favorable outcomes in one culture (middle-class Western societies) is the optimal pattern for children in all other cultures and subcultures. Louis Laosa (1981, p. 159) makes this same point, noting that "indigenous patterns of child care throughout the world represent largely successful adaptations to conditions of life that have long differed from one people to another. Women are 'good mothers' by the only relevant standards, those of their own culture."

EFFECTS OF SIBLINGS AND THE FAMILY CONFIGURATION

Perhaps the one aspect of family socialization that we know least about is the effects that siblings have on one another. The vast majority of American children grow up with siblings, and there is certainly no shortage of speculation about the roles that brothers and sisters play in a child's life. For example, parents are often concerned about the fighting and bickering that their youngsters display, and they may wonder whether this rivalrous conduct is good for their children. At the same time, the popular wisdom is that "only" children are likely to be lonely, overindulged "brats" who would profit both socially and emotionally from having siblings to teach them that they are not nearly as "special" or important as they think they are.

Although our knowledge about sibling influences is not extensive, we will see that brothers and sisters may often play an important role in a child's life. Moreover, it appears that the influence that siblings are likely to have will depend, in part, on whether they are older or younger than the child.

The Nature of Sibling Interactions

Do children respond differently to siblings than to parents? Linda Baskett and Stephan Johnson (1982) tried to answer this question by visiting with 47 families in their homes. Each family was observed for 45 minutes on five occasions. The children in these two- or three-child families ranged from 4 to 10 years of age.

Baskett and Johnson found that interactions between children and their parents were much more positive in character than those that occurred between siblings. Children often laughed with, talked to, and showed affection toward their parents, and they were more likely to comply with parental commands. In contrast, hitting, yelling, and other annoying physical antics were more often directed toward siblings. Although positive social responses outnumbered negative ones in both parent/child and sibling/sibling interactions, brothers and sisters were more coercive than parents and tended to respond less positively to a child's social overtures.

Origins and Determinants of Sibling Rivalry

Sibling rivalry often begins rather early, while the younger child is still in diapers. Carol Kendrick and Judy Dunn (1980) found that older toddlers and preschool children receive less attention from their mothers after the birth of a baby, and they are likely to respond to this "neglect" by demanding attention or doing something naughty while the mother cares for the infant. By the time the younger child is 8 months of age, older siblings will occasionally harass him or her by hitting, poking, pinching, or taking away objects that the infant is playing with (Dunn & Kendrick, 1981b). Quarrels are usually initiated by the older sibling, and they are likely to become more frequent and intense as the younger child matures and is better

---

ethnocentrism: *the tendency to view one's own culture as "best" and to use one's own cultural standards as a basis for evaluating other cultures.*

sibling rivalry: *the spirit of competition, jealousy, and resentment that may arise between two or more siblings.*

PHOTO 15-5. *Coercive and rivalrous conduct between siblings is a normal aspect of family life.*

able to retaliate (Dunn & Kendrick, 1981b; Pepler, Abramovitch, & Corter, 1981). In their study of 14-month-old infants and their older siblings, Dunn and Kendrick (1981b) found that same-sex sibs display more positive social behaviors (for example, smiling, laughing, sharing, and showing affection) and are less frequently negative toward one another than cross-sex sibs. The reason for this "sex of sibling" effect may be indirectly attributable to the behavior of mothers. Dunn and Kendrick reported that mothers spent much more time playing with the younger child when he or she differed in gender from the older sibling. Thus, an infant sibling of the other sex may represent a greater threat to the older child's security,

which, in turn, leads him or her to resent the other-sex sib and to respond less positively to this little intruder.

Additional evidence that mothers influence sibling interactions comes from a second study by Dunn & Kendrick (1981a). In this project, the investigators found that older girls who had received lots of attention during the weeks after a baby was born were the ones who played *least* with and were *most negative* toward their baby brother or sister 14 months later. The older children who were most positive toward their infant brothers or sisters were those whose mothers had not permitted them to brood or respond negatively toward the baby. Although parents should set some time aside for their older children to let them know that they are still loved and considered important, it appears that this practice can promote rivalrous conduct if a mother becomes *overly* attentive or solicitous toward her older children.

Competition among siblings is commonplace, particularly among those who are nearly the same age (Minnett, Vandell, & Santrock, 1983). And there is some evidence that sibling rivalries may increase over time, for John Santrock and Ann Minnett (1981) found that interactions between older female sibs (for example, an 8-year-old and a 12-year-old) were more negative and included fewer positive acts than interactions between pairs of younger sisters (for example, a 4-year-old and an 8-year-old). But even though sibling rivalries are a normal aspect of family life, we should keep in mind that brothers and sisters do nice things for one another and that these acts of kindness are typically more common than hateful or rivalrous conduct (Baskett & Johnson, 1982; Pepler et al., 1981).

Positive Effects of Sibling Interaction

One recent survey of child-rearing practices in 186 societies found that older children were the principal caregivers for infants and toddlers in 57% of the groups studied (Weisner & Gallimore, 1977). Even in industrialized societies such as the United States, older siblings (particularly females) are often asked to look after and care for their younger brothers and sisters (Cicirelli, 1977). So there is reason to believe that older children may play a major role in the lives of younger siblings, often serving as their teachers, playmates, and advocates and occasionally as their disciplinarians.

■ Siblings as attachment objects

Do infants become attached to their older brothers and sisters? To find out, Robert Stewart (1983) exposed 10–20-month-old infants to a variation of Ainsworth's "strange situations" test. Each infant was left with a 4-year-old sibling in a strange room that a strange adult soon entered. The infants typically showed signs of distress as their mothers departed, and they were wary in the company of the stranger. Stewart noted that these distressed infants would often approach their older brother or sister, particularly when the stranger appeared. Moreover, a majority of the 4-year-olds offered some sort of comforting or caregiving to their baby brothers and sisters. So it appears that older preschool children can become sources of emotional support who help younger siblings to cope with uncertain situations when their parents are not around. In addition, Helen Samuels (1980) found that infants are likely to venture much farther away from their mothers if an older sibling is nearby to serve as a "secure base" for exploration.

■ Siblings as social models

In addition to providing a sense of security and facilitating the child's exploratory competencies, older siblings serve as models for their younger brothers and sisters. Between 12 and 20 months of age, infants become very attentive to their older sibs, often choosing to imitate their actions or to take over toys that the older children have abandoned (Abramovitch, Corter, & Pepler, 1980; Samuels, 1977). By contrast, an older child will pay much less attention to the behavior of a younger sib unless they happen to be playing together or the younger sibling is interfering with the older child's activities.

■ Siblings as teachers

Recently, Gene Brody and his associates (Brody, Stoneman, & MacKinnon, 1982) asked 8- to 10-year-olds to play a popular board game with (1) a younger (4½- to 7-year-old) sibling, (2) an 8- to 10-year-old peer, and (3) a younger sib and a peer. As the children played, observers noted how often each child assumed the following roles:

teacher, learner, manager (child requests or commands an action), *managee* (child is the target of management), and *equal-status playmate*. Brody et al. found that older children dominated the sibling/sibling interactions by assuming the teacher and manager roles much more often than younger sibs did. Yet when playing with a peer, these 8- to 10-year-olds took the role of equal-status playmate and rarely tried to dominate their friends. When all three children played together, it was the older sibling rather than the peer who assumed responsibility for "managing" the younger child, although neither the older sib nor the peer did much teaching in this situation. So older siblings are likely to make an active attempt to instruct their younger brothers and sisters, particularly when they are playing alone with them. Although the teaching that older sibs performed in this study may seem rather trivial, other research indicates that younger siblings who expe-

PHOTO 15-6. *Older siblings often serve as teachers for their younger brothers and sisters.*

rience little difficulty in learning to read are likely to have older brothers and sisters who played "school" with them and who taught them important lessons such as the ABCs (Norman-Jackson, 1982).

Do older children benefit from teaching their younger siblings? Indeed they may. Studies of peer tutoring, in which older children teach academic lessons to younger pupils, consistently find that the tutors show significant gains in academic achievement—bigger gains than those posted by age mates who have not had an opportunity to tutor a younger child (Feldman, Devin-Sheehan, & Allen, 1976). Moreover, Robert Zajonc and his associates (Zajonc, Markus, & Markus, 1979) report that first-born children with younger sibs tend to score higher on tests of IQ and academic achievement than "only" children who have no younger siblings to tutor. Finally, Delroy Paulhus and David Shaffer (1981) found that the greater the number of younger siblings (up to three) that college women have, the higher these women score on the Scholastic Aptitude Test (SAT).

So it appears that the teacher/learner roles that siblings often assume at play are beneficial to all parties involved: older siblings learn by tutoring their younger brother and sisters, while the young tutees seem to profit from the instruction they receive.

Characteristics of First-Born and Later-Born Children

For more than 100 years social scientists have speculated that a child's **ordinal position** within the family will affect his or her personality (Henderson, 1981). One popular notion was that first-born children, who initially enjoy an exclusive relationship with their parents, will remain forever closer to their mothers and fathers than later-borns. Another was that later-borns will eventually become more likable and popular than first-borns because they have had to acquire important social skills in order to negotiate with their older and more powerful siblings. Do these claims have any merit? Do first-borns reliably differ from later-borns, and if so, why?

■ Characteristics of first-borns

There is now a great deal of evidence that first-borns are more achievement-oriented than later-borns. First-borns are overrepresented among populations of eminent people and college students (Schachter, 1963; Warren, 1966), and they tend to score higher than later-borns on tests of English and mathematics achievement (Eysenck & Cookson, 1969), verbal achievement (Breland, 1974), and verbal reasoning (Kellaghan & Mac-Namara, 1972). In addition, first-borns score somewhat higher on tests of achievement motivation and hold higher educational aspirations than later-borns (Glass, Neulinger, & Brim, 1974; Sampson & Hancock, 1967).

In Chapter Twelve we learned that first-born toddlers, nursery school children, and college students are more sociable than their later-born age mates. However, they also tend to be less confident in social situations, and first-born males are more likely than later-borns to exhibit behavior disorders and to be rated by teachers as anxious and aggressive toward their peers (Lahey, Hammer, Crumrine, & Forehand, 1980; Schachter, 1959). As a result, many first-borns are not terribly popular, even though they may be outgoing and seem to enjoy being around other people.

First-born children (particularly females) tend to be more obedient and somewhat more socially responsible than later-borns. Brian Sutton-Smith and B. G. Rosenberg (1970) propose that this obedience may stem from the special and exclusive early relationship that first-borns have had with their parents. Parents seem to expect more of their first-borns and are often critical of their behavior (Hilton, 1967; Rothbart, 1971). However, they also appear to be more attentive and affectionate toward their first-born children (Jacobs & Moss, 1976), a finding that may help to explain why first-borns often feel closer to their parents than later-borns do (Sutton-Smith & Rosenberg, 1970).

■ Characteristics of later-borns

It is difficult to characterize later-borns because they occupy many different sibling statuses (for example, second-born female in a family of two; fourth-born and male in a family with three elder sisters) and are not really a homogeneous group. In two-child families, the behavior of the later-born child is clearly influenced by the sex of his or her sibling. For example, a boy who has an older sister is likely to develop more "feminine" interests than a boy with an older brother (Sutton-Smith & Rosenberg, 1970).

As a group, later-borns seem to establish better relations with peers than first-borns do. In one study of 1750 first-born, middle-born, and last-born schoolchildren (Miller & Maruyama, 1976), the investigators found that the "babies of the family" (that is, last-borns) were most popular with their classmates, while middle-borns enjoyed intermediate popularity, and first-borns were least popular. Only children were similar in popularity to the first-borns.

Let's keep in mind that these "ordinal position" effects represent group averages. Many first-borns are extremely popular with their peers, just as many later-borns are highly obedient, socially responsible, and motivated to achieve. Only when group averages are compared do the differences between first-borns and later-borns emerge.

■ *Explaining birth-order effects*

It appears that parents contribute to ordinal-position effects by treating first-borns differently from later-borns. For example, first-borns receive more direct achievement training than their younger siblings. In one study of two-child families, Mary Rothbart (1971) asked mothers to supervise their first-born or second-born 5-year-olds as they worked on a series of achievement tasks. Although mothers spent equal amounts of time interacting with first-born and later-born children, they gave more complex technical explanations to first-borns. In addition, mothers put more pressure on their first-borns to achieve, and they were more anxious about the quality of their performances (which were better than those of the later-borns). In a similar study, Hilton (1967) found that mothers of first-borns were more likely than mothers of later-borns to be extremely warm and affectionate when their 4-year-olds succeeded at a cognitive task. However, mothers of first-borns were also more likely to *withhold affection* if their children scored below average on the tasks. Taken together, these findings help to explain why first-borns are so obedient and interested in pleasing their parents and are also higher in achievement motivation than later-borns.

Why are first-borns *more sociable* and yet *less popular* than later-borns? Many researchers believe that these findings are attributable to the character of sibling interactions. If you grew up with brothers and sisters, you know very well that power is unequally distributed among siblings.

We have already seen that older sibs will try to dominate younger brothers and sisters in order to achieve their objectives—a tendency that may suppress the affiliative tendencies of later-borns and make them somewhat cautious and concerned about interacting with others (Brody et al., 1982; Schachter, 1959). However, later-borns may eventually become more popular than first-borns because

> if later-born children are to obtain . . . a fair share of positive outcomes, they must develop their interpersonal skills—powers of negotiation, accommodation, tolerance, and a capacity to accept less favorable outcomes—to a degree not found in first-born children . . . who may simply take or achieve what they want quite arbitrarily. . . . The acquisition of [these] interpersonal skills should facilitate social interactions with peers and thereby increase a [later-born] child's popularity [Miller & Maruyama, 1976, pp. 123–124].

THE IMPACT OF DIVORCE

Earlier in the chapter, we saw that nearly 50% of contemporary American marriages will end in divorce and that about 40–50% of American children born in the 1970s will spend some time in a single-parent household—usually one headed by the mother. Only recently have investigators begun to conduct longitudinal studies to determine how children cope with a divorce and whether this disruption of the nuclear family is likely to have any long-term effects on their social, emotional, and intellectual development. Let's see what they have learned.

The Immediate Effects

In her review of the literature, Mavis Hetherington (1981) notes that divorce is a stressful and painful event for many children. At first, these youngsters are likely to feel angry, fearful, depressed, or guilty about a divorce, and these initial reactions often strike hardest at young, egocentric preschoolers, who are likely to perceive themselves

---

ordinal position: *the child's order of birth among siblings (also called birth order).*

as somehow responsible for the dissolution of their parents' marriages. Although adolescents may experience considerable pain and anger when their parents divorce, they are better able to infer why the divorce has occurred, to resolve any loyalty conflicts that may arise, and to understand and cope with the financial and other practical problems that the family now faces. Yet it may be as long as a year after the divorce before children of any age recover from the initial shock and begin to feel more positively about themselves and their new living arrangements (Hetherington, 1981).

The Crisis Phase

Hetherington (1981) proposes that most children go through two phases when adjusting to a divorce: the **crisis phase,** which often lasts a year or more, and the **adjustment phase,** in which they settle down and begin to adapt to life in a single-parent home.

The emotional upheaval that often accompanies the crisis phase is likely to affect the relationship that children have with their custodial parent. Children may become quite cranky, disobedient, or otherwise "difficult," while the parent who has custody (usually the mother) may suddenly become more punitive and controlling. To use Patterson's terminology, mother/child relationships may tend to be more **coercive** in the year following a divorce. In addition, the stresses resulting from the divorce and this new coercive lifestyle may disrupt the child's peer relations and undermine the quality of his or her work at school (Hetherington, Cox, & Cox, 1978).

■ The question of sex differences
According to Hetherington (1981), the effects of marital disharmony and divorce are much more powerful and enduring for boys than for girls. At least two longitudinal studies found that girls had largely recovered from their social and emotional disturbances by the end of the second year after a divorce (Hetherington et al., 1978; Wallerstein & Kelly, 1980). Although boys improved dramatically over this same period, many of them continued to show signs of emotional distress and problems in their relationships with parents, siblings, teachers, and peers.

However, other investigators have found no sex differences in children's short-term or long-term reactions to divorce (Kurdek, Blisk, & Siesky, 1981; J. A. Powell, personal communication, November 1983). One factor that does seem to predict children's postdivorce relations with their parents is the quality of their relations with each parent during the year *preceding* the divorce (Fine, Moreland, & Schwebel, 1983). Perhaps boys who show a very poor adjustment to divorce are those who were very close to their fathers. Separation from the father is undoubtedly quite stressful and frustrating for these youngsters, who may then express their anger and resentment toward the closest available targets—namely, their mothers, siblings, and peers. However, this hypothesis has not been tested, and it remains for future research to specify the conditions under which boys and girls are likely to differ in their reactions to divorce.

■ On staying together for the good of the children
The conventional wisdom used to be that unhappily married couples should remain together for the good of the children. Yet recent research suggests that, after the first year, children in single-parent homes are usually better adjusted than those who remain in conflict-ridden nuclear families (Hetherington, Cox, & Cox, 1979; Wallerstein & Kelly, 1980). Hetherington (1981) believes that an eventual escape from conflict may be the most positive outcome of divorce for many children. Judith Wallerstein and Joan Kelly (1980) definitely agree, adding that "today's conventional wisdom holds . . . that an unhappy couple might well *divorce* for the good of the children; that an unhappy marriage for the adults is also unhappy for the children; and that a divorce that promotes the happiness of the adults will benefit the children as well" (p. 67).

■ The role of the noncustodial parent
The fact that children of divorce are often better off than those in strife-ridden homes suggests that marital separation doesn't always disrupt the child's social, emotional, and intellectual development. However, Mavis Hetherington (1981) points out that the quality of the child's eventual adjustment to a divorce depends to a large extent

PHOTO 15-7. Youngsters who live in conflict-ridden nuclear families often suffer physically as well as emotionally. In the long run, children of divorce are usually better adjusted than those whose unhappily married parents stay together "for the sake of the children."

on the amount of support that the family receives from the noncustodial parent.

Let's first consider the *financial* support. Following a divorce, mother-headed families must often get by on a fraction of the income that they had when the father was present. This often necessitates a move to more modest housing in a poorer neighborhood and thus may take the family away from important sources of emotional support such as friends and neighbors. And if the mother begins to work at the time of the divorce or soon thereafter, she may have less time for her children and could become more erratic and inconsistent in the parenting that she is able to provide (Hetherington, 1981). So it should hardly come as a surprise that children who adjust well to a divorce often live in homes where the family finances and level of economic support are not seriously undermined by marital separation (Desimone-Luis, O'Mahoney, & Hunt, 1979; Hodges, Wechsler, & Ballantine, 1979).

The amount of *emotional* support that the noncustodial parent provides is perhaps the most important contributor to the child's eventual ad-justment. If parents continue to squabble after a divorce and are generally hostile toward each other, the quality of the mother's parenting is apt to suffer. This is the circumstance under which children of divorce are most likely to show serious disruptions in their academic performance and interpersonal relationships. By contrast, children from divorced families may experience few if any long-term problems in adjusting when their parents maintain reasonably warm and friendly relations. Mothers who have cordial ex-husbands tend to be more involved with their children and sensitive to their needs, particularly when the parents agree on child-rearing strategies and disciplinary issues (Berg & Kelly, 1979; Hetherington et al., 1978). Regular visitation by fathers also helps children (particularly sons) to make a positive adjustment to their new life in a single-parent home (Hess & Camara, 1979; Rosen, 1979). In summarizing this research, Hetherington (1981, p. 50) suggests that "a continued, mutually supportive relationship including involvement of the father with the child is the most effective support system for divorced mothers in their parenting role."

How do children react to a divorce when the father is the custodial parent? In recent years, investigators have tried to answer this question by comparing the behavior of children growing up in father-headed and mother-headed single-parent homes. In Box 15-4, we will look at this research and see that fathers may be more competent as single parents than many people (and the legal system) have generally assumed.

---

crisis phase: *the period during and immediately after a divorce (often lasting a year or more), when many children suffer emotional distress and disruptions in their schoolwork and interpersonal relations.*

adjustment phase: *the period following the crisis phase, when the emotional conflicts surrounding a divorce begin to subside and children are adapting to life in a single-parent home.*

coercive relationship: *a pattern of interaction in which the two parties often annoy each other and use assertive or aggressive tactics as a method of coping with these unpleasant experiences.*

BOX 15-4
THE FATHER AS A CUSTODIAL PARENT

Although the overwhelming majority of children from broken homes live with their mothers, about 10% of custody hearings now award children to the father, and joint custody is becoming more and more common (National Center for Health Statistics, 1980). How do fathers fare as custodial parents? Are they able to cope with the emotional distress that their children may be experiencing? Do they establish good relations with their children? Are children in father-custody homes any different from those living in mother-headed families?

Fathers who have custody of their children report many of the same problems as divorced mothers do: they feel overburdened with responsibilities, are somewhat depressed, and are concerned about their competence as parents and their ability to cope with their children's emotional needs (Hetherington, 1981). As a group, custodial fathers are more likely than custodial mothers to make use of alternative caregiving and support systems such as babysitters, relatives, day-care facilities, or even the noncustodial parent (Santrock & Warshak, 1979). Single-parent fathers typically demand more assistance with household tasks and more independence from their children than custodial mothers do. But most fathers in single-parent households perceive their relationships with their children to be reasonably sound (Hetherington, 1981), and they are more likely than custodial mothers to report that their children are well behaved (Ambert, 1982).

As for the children, it appears that both boys and girls react differently to the parenting they receive when the father is the custodial parent. For boys, the differences are positive ones. John Santrock and Richard Warshak (1979) report that boys are much less coercive and demanding with custodial fathers than in mother-headed families. Moreover, boys in father-custody homes are more independent than girls, while just the reverse is true when the mother is the custodial parent. If there is a weakness in the father-custody arrangement, it is centered on the father/daughter relationship. Custodial fathers are often quite concerned about their ability to cope with the problems and emotional needs of their daughters and the fact that their daughters have no feminine role model in the home (Mendes, 1976; Santrock & Warshak, 1979). And they have reason to be concerned, for at least one study has found that girls in families where the father has custody are less well adjusted than girls who live with their divorced mothers (Santrock & Warshak, 1979). However, boys in homes where the father has custody were found to be better adjusted than boys who were living with their mothers. As Hetherington (1981, p. 50) points out, "These findings need to be replicated and will have important implications for custody assignments if they are confirmed."

Long-Term Reactions to Divorce

Recently, Lawrence Kurdek and his associates (Kurdek et al., 1981) asked 8- to 17-year-olds how they felt about their parents' divorce at four years and again at six years after the marriage was dissolved. They found that many children still had negative feelings about the divorce, even though the youngsters now understood that they had not been personally responsible for the break-up. Children generally described their parents in positive or neutral terms (thus harboring few grudges), and most of them felt that the divorce had not adversely affected their peer relationships. In fact, those who had showed positive changes in their feelings about the divorce during the interval between the fourth and sixth years often reported that having friends whose parents were also divorced had helped them to cope with their earlier feelings of bitterness and resentment. Finally, Kurdek et al. found that the older children in their sample had made the most positive adjustments to divorce, particularly those youngsters who tested high in interpersonal understanding (that is, role-taking skills) and who had an internal locus of control.

In sum, a divorce is an unsettling experience—one that few children feel very positive about some four to six years after the fact. But despite their sentiments, it seems that a conflict-ridden nuclear family is much more detrimental to the child's development than the absence of a divorced parent. Indeed, the children of divorce may actually benefit in the long run if the dissolution of the marriage leads to an overall reduction in stress that enables either or both parents to be more sensitive and responsive to their needs (Hetherington, 1981; Wallerstein & Kelly, 1980).

Children in Reconstituted Families

Within three years of a divorce, about half of all children from broken homes will experience yet another major change in their lives: a return to the nuclear family when the custodial parent remarries and they suddenly acquire a stepparent. Apparently children from divorced families want to live in two-parent homes, even if it means having their mothers marry someone other than their fathers (Santrock et al., 1982). But are children happy with their new living arrangements once the mother remarries? Do they prosper in these reconstituted families; or, rather, are they more likely to experience problems with their stepparent that could affect their cognitive, social, and emotional development?

John Santrock and his associates (Santrock et al., 1982) have studied the effects of remarriage on children's social behavior by comparing 6- to 11-year-olds from stepparent families with age mates from two other groups: divorced families in which the mother had not remarried and intact families in which the biological father was present. The families were matched on important variables such as age and sex of the children, family size, and socioeconomic status. All the children in the reconstituted families had been living with their stepfathers for at least 18 months. The data consisted of videotaped records of the children interacting with their parents (or stepparents). The children's behaviors and those of their parents were coded separately.

When the data were analyzed, some interesting sex differences emerged. Boys in stepfather families showed more warmth, higher levels of self-esteem, less anxiety, and less anger than boys in intact families. But girls in stepfather families were much more anxious than girls from intact homes. Moreover, girls in stepfather families showed more anger toward their mothers than boys did, and boys were warmer than girls toward their stepfathers.

Apparently these sex differences in children's responses to remarriage are not attributable to the behavior of stepfathers, for these substitute parents were at least as attentive and authoritative with their stepdaughters as with their stepsons. Part of the stepdaughters' anxiety may have resulted from the behavior of their mothers, who were somewhat less attentive and authoritative than mothers in intact homes. Finally, it is interesting to note that the parenting provided by *stepfathers* was at least as "competent" (by middle-class standards) as that given by biological fathers to their daughters and somewhat more competent than that given by biological fathers to their sons.

Earlier research (Chapman, 1977; Santrock, 1972) had suggested that children from stepfather families (particularly boys) are less likely than those from single-parent homes to show personality disorders or deficiencies in cognitive development. So on the basis of very limited evidence, it appears that boys in stepfather families may actually fare rather well, whereas girls are probably no worse and possibly better off than they would be in a single-parent home. Finally, there is little or no evidence for the notion that stepparents are cool, aloof disciplinarians who are unconcerned about their stepchildren. On the contrary, the stepfathers whom Santrock studied seemed to be competent parents who were involved with their stepchildren and sensitive to their needs.

EFFECTS OF MATERNAL EMPLOYMENT

We have previously seen that a majority of young mothers now work outside the home and that this arrangement need not disrupt the emotional development or the sex typing of their children. Infants and toddlers are likely to become securely attached to their working mothers if they receive quality day care and responsive caregiving when their mothers return home from work (Belsky, Steinberg, & Walker, 1982; Hoffman, 1979; see also Box 11-3). Moreover, children of working mothers hold higher educational and occupational aspirations and less stereotyped views of men and women than children whose mothers are not employed (Hoffman, 1979).

Recent research suggests that children of working mothers are at least as outgoing and adaptable to social situations as children of homemakers. Frances Schachter (1981) studied a group of 20- to 36-month-old toddlers, about half of whom had mothers who were employed outside the home.

She found no differences between the two groups in maturity of emotional development. However, children with employed mothers were more self-sufficient, less dependent on adults, and more sociable with peers. In a similar vein, studies of nursery school children, grade school children, and adolescents consistently indicate that both sons and daughters of working mothers show more independence and tend to score higher on tests of social and personal adjustment than children whose mothers remain at home (Gold & Andres, 1978a, 1978b; Gold, Andres, & Glorieux, 1979).

Does maternal employment have any effect on a child's cognitive development? The answer to this question is by no means clear at present. In her review of the literature, Lois Hoffman (1979) noted that most studies find no differences in either cognitive or scholastic performance between children of homemakers and those whose mothers work. However, at least two recent studies of infants and toddlers suggest that the *very young* children of working mothers perform at lower levels on developmental tests and score lower on standardized measures of intelligence than children of homemakers (Cohen, 1978; Schachter, 1981). Even more sobering is a recent report published by the U.S. Department of Education (Ginsburg, cited in "Study: Children with Working Mothers," 1983) indicating that high school students from two-parent families in which the mother works score significantly lower on tests of academic achievement than their classmates whose mothers have never worked. This latter study is particularly important because it is based on a large national sample, and the findings seem to hold in every region of the country for families from all racial and socioeconomic backgrounds.

Clearly, these are provocative results that we should interpret cautiously until they are replicated in other large, national samples. But even if these findings are confirmed in future research, it may make little sense to advise working mothers that they should abandon their careers in order to stay home with their children. Economic realities have forced many mothers to work, and in one survey the vast majority of working women (76%) stated that they would continue to work even if they did not have to (Dubnoff, Veroff, & Kulka,

1978). One implication of the latter finding is that many women might resent a life of full-time mothering if they were pressured to assume that role, and it is possible that they would vent their frustrations on their children. Indeed, Francine Stuckey and her associates (Stuckey, McGhee, & Bell, 1982) found that the amount of complaining and criticism expressed among mothers, fathers, and their preschool children was significantly greater in families with *unemployed mothers who wanted to work* than in families where the mothers either were unemployed and preferred it that way or were employed and happy about it. So it appears that family interactions are most likely to be amiable and conducive to the child's development when the mother's employment status matches her attitudes about working.

In sum, maternal employment is an integral part of modern family life—a role that often satisfies a mother's personal needs as well as providing for the economic welfare of the family. An important task for future research is to discover exactly how, why, and under what circumstances a mother's working is likely to have a negative effect on her child's intellectual and academic development. Once these parameters are known, it should then be possible to help working mothers adjust their caretaking routines or obtain outside support (day care, tutoring, and the like) so that they can promote their children's cognitive and academic competencies while continuing in the careers that they must or desperately hope to pursue.

WHEN PARENTING BREAKS DOWN: THE PROBLEM OF CHILD ABUSE

In recent years, researchers and child-care professionals have coined terms such as *the mistreated child* or **the battered-child syndrome** to describe those youngsters who are burned, bruised, beaten, starved, suffocated, neglected, sexually abused, or otherwise mistreated by their caregivers. Child abuse is a very serious problem in the United States—one that seems to be increasing at an alarming rate. Between 1968 and 1972, the number of *reported* cases of seriously battered children rose from 721 to 30,000 in the state of Michigan and from 4000 to nearly 40,000

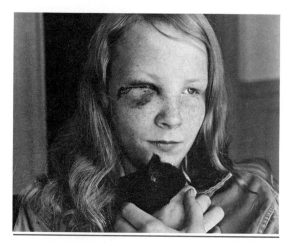

PHOTO 15-8. Although children receive scrapes, cuts, and bruises from playtime activities, sometimes, because of lack of communication, it is difficult to detect cases of possible child abuse.

in California (Kempe & Kempe, 1978). Since many cases of child abuse are neither detected nor reported, these statistics may represent the tip of the iceberg. Raymond Starr (1979) estimates that every year, in the United States, as many as 1.4–1.9 *million* children are subjected to forms of violence or neglect that could cause them serious physical or emotional harm.

Clearly, there are many factors that contribute to a problem as widespread as child abuse. To date, researchers have attempted to understand the battered-child syndrome by seeking answers for three basic questions: (1) who gets abused? (2) who are the abusers? and (3) under what circumstances is abuse most likely to occur?

Who Is Abused?

Although just about any child could become a target of neglect or abuse, some youngsters are more vulnerable than others. For example, children who react to discipline by defying or ignoring an adult are likely to elicit even stronger forms of punishment from the disciplinarian. And if these high-intensity tactics are reinforced by inhibiting the undesirable antics of a defiant child, they are likely to become the disciplinarian's preferred method of behavior control. This is indeed unfortunate, for reliance on physically coercive forms of discipline is often the first step along the road to child abuse (Parke & Lewis, 1981).

Children of all ages can contribute to their own abuse—even tiny infants! Babies who are emotionally unresponsive, hyperactive, irritable, or ill face far greater risks of being abused than quiet, responsive infants who are easy to care for. Indeed, premature babies, who are often active, irritable, and unresponsive, represent nearly 25% of the population of battered children—even though only 8% of the total infant population is born prematurely (Klein & Stern, 1971). Of course, this does not mean that 25% of all premature infants are abused but, rather, that the premature baby is more likely than a full-term infant to display certain characteristics that may trigger abusive responses from *some* caregivers. The emphasis on "some" caregivers is important, for the vast majority of difficult children are not mistreated by their parents or guardians, while other seemingly normal and happy children do become targets of abuse. Thus, the implication is that certain people may be "primed" to become abusive when their children irritate or anger them.

Who Are the Abusers?

Strange as it may seem, only about 1 child abuser in 10 has a serious mental illness that is difficult to treat (Kempe & Kempe, 1978). The fact is that people who abuse their children come from all races, ethnic groups, and social classes, and many of them appear to be rather typical, loving parents—except for their tendency to become extremely irritated with their children and to do things they will later regret.

However, overt appearances can be very deceiving. Recently, Ann Frodi and Michael Lamb (1980) presented videotapes of smiling and crying

> **battered children:** *the victims of child abuse— that is, children who are beaten, bruised, neglected, or otherwise mistreated by their caregivers.*

infants to groups of abusive and nonabusive mothers who were matched for age, marital status, and the number of children they had had. While the subjects watched the tapes, their physiological responses were monitored. Moreover, each subject described the emotional reactions that she had experienced while observing the infants. Frodi and Lamb reported that the *nonabusive* parents showed increases in physiological arousal to the infant's cries but not to his or her smiles; cries were described as unpleasant, while smiles generally made the nonabusers feel happy. In contrast, the *abusive* parents had much stronger physiological reactions to both cries and smiles, and they felt less happy and less willing to interact with a smiling infant than nonabusers. Frodi and Lamb suggest that child abusers may find all of an infant's social signals aversive. Thus, even a smile might trigger a hostile response from an abusive caregiver.

Some child abusers may react very negatively to their infants because they themselves were abused or unloved as children (Belsky, 1980; Steele & Pollack, 1974). Harry Harlow and his associates have observed a similar phenomenon among rhesus monkeys: Female monkeys who were either abused as infants or raised without caregivers later became indifferent or abusive toward their own offspring (Harlow, Harlow, Dodsworth, & Arling, 1966; Suomi, 1978). Not only did they push their babies away, refusing to let them nurse, but some of the reluctant caregivers even killed their infants by biting off their fingers and toes. Apparently these abusive mother monkeys who had never received love from a caregiver simply did not know how to attend to an infant or how to respond to its signals. They treated infants as if they were irritants.

Fortunately, many human beings who were abused or neglected during childhood learn how to respond appropriately to other people long before they have children of their own. In fact, recent research indicates that individuals who were mistreated or emotionally deprived as children are likely to become abusive parents *only* if they are currently experiencing other kinds of social or environmental stresses (Conger, Burgess, & Barrett, 1979). Let's now consider some of the social and situational factors that can contribute to child abuse.

Social-Situational Triggers: The Ecology of Child Abuse

Child abuse is most likely to occur in families under stress. Consider, for example, that the battered child often comes from a large family in which overburdened caregivers have many small children to attend to (Light, 1973). Other significant life changes such as the death of a family member, the loss of a job, or moving to a new home can disrupt the social and emotional relationships within a family and thereby contribute to abusive and neglectful parenting (Conger et al., 1979; Steinberg, Catalano, & Dooley, 1981). Finally, children are much more likely to be abused or neglected if their parents are unhappily married (Belsky, 1980; Kempe & Kempe, 1978).

Of course, families are embedded in a broader social context (for example, a neighborhood, a community, and a culture) that may well affect a child's chances of being abused. Some neighborhoods can be labeled **"high risk"** areas because they have much higher rates of child abuse than other neighborhoods of the same demographic and socioeconomic backgrounds. What are these high-risk areas like? According to James Garbarino and Deborah Sherman (1980), they tend to be deteriorating neighborhoods in which families "go it alone" without interacting much with their neighbors or making use of community services such as Scouting or recreation centers. Unlike mothers in low-risk areas, those in high-risk areas take very little pride in their neighborhoods and see them as poor places to raise children. Gabarino and Sherman (1980) describe the high-risk neighborhood as a physically unattractive and socially impoverished setting in which parents not only are struggling financially but also are isolated from formal and informal support systems (for example, friends, relatives, the church, and a sense of "community"). Although the quality of a neighborhood will depend, in part, on the people who live there, let's also note that the actions of government and industry can have an effect. For example, a decision to rezone a low-risk area or to locate a highway there can lead to a destruction of play areas, declining property values, a loss of pride in the neighborhood, and the eventual isolation of families from friends, community services (which may no longer exist),

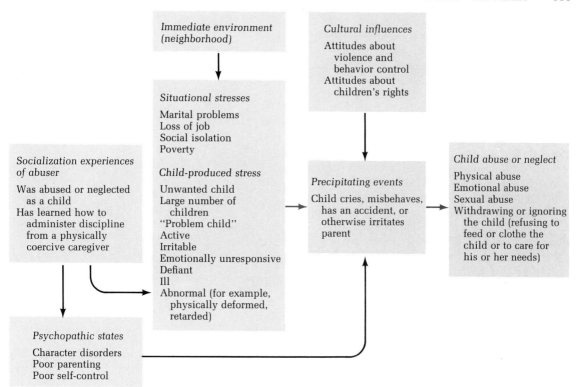

FIGURE 15-4. *A social-ecological model of child abuse.*

and other bases of social support. James Garbarino (1982) is one of many theorists who believe that large numbers of American children are likely to be mistreated because of political or economic decisions that have undermined the health and stability of low-risk, family-oriented neighborhoods.

Some researchers have argued that child abuse is rampant in the United States because people in this society (1) have a permissive attitude about violence and (2) generally sanction the use of physical punishment as a means of controlling children's behavior. Indeed, there may be some truth to these assertions, for cross-cultural studies reveal that children are rarely abused in societies that discourage the use of physical punishment (see Belsky, 1980).

In sum, child abuse is a very complex phenomenon that has many causes and contributing factors. An examination of Figure 15-4 indicates that we have come a long way from those early theories that focused almost exclusively on the abu-

sive parent (and his or her personality) as the primary contributor to the battered-child syndrome. But despite our better understanding of the causes of child abuse, we are still a long way from solving the problem. Rather than conclude on that depressing note, let's look at some of the methods that have been used to assist the abused child and his or her abusers.

■ *How can we help abusive parents and their children?*

A number of strategies have been devised in an attempt to prevent or control the problem of child

---

"high risk" neighborhood: *a residential area in which the incidence of child abuse is much higher than in other neighborhoods with the same demographic and socioeconomic characteristics.*

abuse. For example, Kempe and Kempe (1978) report that a large percentage of abusive parents will stop physically mistreating their children if they can be persuaded to use certain services, such as 24-hour "hotlines" or crisis nurseries, that will enable them to discuss their hostile feelings with a volunteer or to get away from their children for a few hours when they are about to lose control. However, these are only stopgap measures that will probably not work for long unless the abuser also takes advantage of other services— such as **Parents Anonymous** or family therapy— that are designed to help the caregiver to understand his or her problem while providing the friendship and emotional support that an abusive parent so often lacks.[1]

Babies who are at risk for later emotional difficulties can be identified through neonatal assessment programs, and their parents can be taught how to make these infants respond more favorably to their caregiving. Indeed, we have already seen that Brazelton testing and training programs (see Box 5-2) are effective methods of preventing the "miscommunications" between infants and caregivers that could lead to child abuse. The Kempes (1978) also note that potential child abusers can often be identified in the delivery room by their reluctance to look at, touch, hold, or cuddle their infants. However, many of these reluctant caregivers will never abuse their child if they are visited regularly by a child-care professional who provides them with emotional support and encouragement, as well as the information and guidance they will need to establish a sound relationship with their baby (Kempe & Kempe, 1978).

Although its potential is largely untapped, television could become an effective ally in our efforts to prevent child abuse (Parke & Lewis, 1981).

---

[1]Fortunately these services are often free. Chapters of Parents Anonymous are now located in many cities and towns in the United States (for the location of a nearby chapter, one can consult a telephone directory or write to Parents Anonymous, 2230 Hawthorne Blvd., Suite 93102, Torrance, Calif. 90505). In addition, many cities and counties provide free family therapy to abusive parents. Often the therapists are lay volunteers who have been trained to serve in this capacity and who do so quite effectively.

4 out of 5 convicts were abused children.

In the United States, an average of 80% of our prisoners were abused children. That is why we are working so hard to help these children today, before they develop into a threat to others tomorrow. With your support, we can have a full staff of trained people available 24 hours a day. Abused children desperately need us. Please let us be there to help. Write for our free brochure, or send in your tax-deductible donation today.

San Francisco Child Abuse Council, Inc.
4093 24th Street, San Francisco, CA 94114

PHOTO 15-9. A number of programs and services have been created in an attempt to prevent or control the problem of child abuse.

Thirty-second public service announcements might be an excellent method of publicizing formal support systems (for example, Parents Anonymous or crisis nurseries) that are locally available to abusive parents. Programming could be developed to teach parents effective, nonpunitive child-care techniques that would minimize social conflicts within the family and decrease the probability of child abuse (see McCall, Gregory, & Murray, 1984). Finally, television could be used to modify our attitudes about the rights of parents and their children. In the United States, the courts and welfare agencies are often hesitant to take children from their abusive parents, even when there is a history of repeated physical abuse (Rosenheim, 1973). One reason for their reluctant attitude is that, historically, children have been treated as their parents' possessions. Another is that abused children and their parents are often firmly attached to each other, so that neither the abusive adult nor the battered child wishes to be separated. However, it is essential that we carefully weigh the child's rights against the rights and wishes of the parents in cases of child abuse, for some abusive adults will continue to seriously harm and occasionally even kill their battered children, regardless of the counseling they receive (Fontana, 1973; Kempe & Kempe, 1978).

Clearly, no caregiver has the right to abuse a child. In cases of severe abuse or neglect, our first priority must be to provide for the health and safety of mistreated children, even if that means terminating the abusers' legal rights of parenthood and placing their children in foster care or adoptive homes.

![black rectangular marker]

SUMMARY

The family is the primary agent of socialization—the setting in which children begin to acquire the beliefs, attitudes, and values of their society. The most common arrangement in Western societies is the nuclear family—a social system that consists of three basic roles: wife/mother, husband/father, and child/sibling. Parents in all societies pursue three goals in raising their children: (1) ensuring the child's survival, (2) preparing the child for economic self-sufficiency, and (3) training the child to maximize other cultural values such as morality, religion, intellectual achievement, and personal satisfaction.

Traditionally, researchers have assumed that the flow of influence within a family was from parents, who did the shaping, to children, whose characters were molded by the child-rearing strategies of their elders. Today we recognize that families are complex social systems: parents influence each of their children, who, in turn, may influence one another, each parent, and the parents' marital relationship. Families also live within a broader social context (for example, in a particular neighborhood, community, and society) that may affect family interactions and ultimately the development of the children within a family. To understand the influence of the family on developing children, one must treat the family as a social system rather than focusing exclusively on the ways in which parents may influence the child.

The birth of a child is a highly significant event that alters the behavior of both parents and may change the character of their marital relationship. The transition to parenthood tends to be less severe or disruptive when parents are older and have been married for some time before the child is conceived. Warm, responsive parenting during infancy contributes to the establishment of secure parent/child attachments and promotes the child's exploratory competence and intellectual growth. Although fathers interact less with their very young infants than mothers do, they soon become more involved with their children and begin to play a very special role in the child's life.

Two important aspects of parenting are warmth/hostility and permissiveness/restrictiveness (parental control). These two parental dimensions are independent, so that we find parents who are warm and restrictive, warm and permissive, cool (rejecting) and restrictive, and cool and permissive. Generally speaking, warm and restrictive parents who appeal to reason in order to enforce their demands are likely to raise cheerful, friendly children who are intellectually curious, self-confident, and morally mature.

Parents from different social classes have different values, concerns, and outlooks on life that influence their child-rearing strategies. Lower- and working-class parents stress obedience, respect, neatness, cleanliness, and staying out of trouble—precisely the characteristics that their children will need to adapt to a position within a blue-collar economy. In contrast, middle-class parents are less restrictive and authoritarian and more likely than low-SES parents to stress independence, creativity, ambition, and self-control—the attributes that their children will need for success in business or the professions. Thus, parents from all socioeconomic strata tend to emphasize the characteristics that contribute to

---

Parents Anonymous: *an organization of reformed child abusers (modeled after Alcoholics Anonymous) that functions as a support group and helps parents to understand and overcome their abusive tendencies.*

success *as they know it,* and it is inappropriate to conclude that one particular style of parenting is somehow "better" or more competent than all others.

Interactions between siblings are generally more negative than those between children and their parents. But even though sibling rivalries are a normal aspect of family life, there is a positive side to having a sibling. Older sibs serve as attachment objects who may comfort their distressed brothers and sisters and provide a "secure base" for exploration. Moreover, the teacher/learner roles that siblings often assume at play are beneficial to all parties: older siblings learn by tutoring their younger brothers and sisters, while the younger tutees appear to profit from the instruction they receive. First-born children, who receive more attention and achievement training from their parents, tend to be more obedient, anxious, and achievement-oriented than later-borns. However, later-borns, who must acquire important social skills in order to negotiate with older, more powerful sibs, tend to establish better relations with peers than first-borns do.

Divorce represents a drastic change in family life that is stressful and unsettling for many children. Their initial reactions often include feelings of anger, fear, depression, and guilt—feelings that may last more than a year. The emotional upheaval that follows a divorce may influence the parent/child relationship. Children often become cranky, disobedient, or otherwise difficult, while the custodial parent may suddenly become more punitive and controlling. The stresses resulting from a divorce and this new coercive lifestyle often affect the child's peer relations and the quality of his or her schoolwork. But after the first year, the children of divorce are usually better adjusted than those who remain in conflict-ridden nuclear homes. Moreover, children from divorced homes may experience few if any long-term problems in adjustment when their parents are cordial and can agree on child-rearing strategies and when the noncustodial parent continues to provide financial assistance.

Maternal employment does not seem to disrupt children's social and emotional development; in fact, children of working mothers are often found to be more independent and more sociable and to have less stereotyped views of men and women than children whose mothers are not employed. Although the data are scanty at this point, there is some evidence that children of working mothers score lower on tests of academic achievement than their classmates whose mothers have never worked. If this finding proves to be reliable, we will need to learn why maternal employment affects academic achievement so that working mothers can take the steps necessary to prevent these problems while continuing in the careers that they must or very much hope to pursue.

Child abuse is a serious problem that is becoming more common. Just about any child could become the target of abuse, although defiant children and those who are active, irritable, emotionally unresponsive, or ill are more vulnerable than happy, healthy children who are easy to care for. Child abusers come from all social strata, but many of them were themselves victims of abuse as children. Child abuse is more likely to occur in families under social, financial, or environmental stress. Programs designed to assist abused children and their abusive parents have achieved some success. However, we are still a long way from solving the problem.

REFERENCES

Abramovitch, R., Corter, C., & Pepler, D. J. (1980). Observations of mixed-sex sibling dyads. *Child Development, 51,* 1268–1271.

Ainsworth, M. D. S. (1979). Attachment as related to mother-infant interaction. In J. S. Rosenblatt, R. A. Hinde, C. Beer, & M. Busnel (Eds.), *Advances in the study of behavior* (Vol. 9). New York: Academic Press.

Ambert, A. (1982). Differences in children's behavior toward custodial mothers and custodial fathers. *Journal of Marriage and the Family, 44,* 73–86.

Barry, H., Child, I. L., & Bacon, M. K. (1959). The relation of child training to subsistence economy. *American Anthropologist, 61,* 51–63.

Baskett, L. M., & Johnson, S. M. (1982). The young child's interaction with parents versus siblings: A behavioral analysis. *Child Development, 53,* 643–650.

Baumrind, D. (1971). Current patterns of parental authority. *Developmental Psychology Monographs, 4,* (1, Part 2).

Baumrind, D. (1977, March). *Socialization determinants of personal agency.* Paper presented at the biennial meeting of the Society for Research in Child Development, New Orleans.

Becker, W. C. (1964). Consequences of different kinds of parental discipline. In M. L. Hoffman & L. W. Hoffman (Eds.), *Review of child development research* (Vol. 1). New York: Russell Sage Foundation.

Belsky, J. (1979). The interrelation of parent and spousal behavior during infancy in traditional nuclear families: An exploratory analysis. *Journal of Marriage and the Family, 41,* 62–68.

Belsky, J. (1980). Child maltreatment: An ecological integration. *American Psychologist, 35,* 320–335.

Belsky, J. (1981). Early human experience: A family perspective. *Developmental Psychology, 17,* 3–23.

Belsky, J., Gilstrap, B., & Rovine, M. (1984). The Pennsylvania infant and family development project, I: Stability and change in mother-infant and father-infant interaction in a family setting at one, three, and nine months. *Child Development, 55,* 692–705.

Belsky, J., Goode, M. K., & Most, R. K. (1980). Maternal stimulation and infant exploratory competence: Cross-sectional, correlational, and experimental analyses. *Child Development, 51,* 1168–1178.

Belsky, J., Steinberg, L., & Walker, A. (1982). The ecology of day care. In M. Lamb (Ed.), *Childrearing in nontraditional families.* Hillsdale, NJ: Erlbaum.

Berg, B., & Kelly, R. (1979). The measured self-esteem of children from broken, rejected, and accepted families. *Journal of Divorce, 2,* 363–370.

Berry, J. W. (1967). Independence and conformity in subsistence-level societies. *Journal of Personality and Social Psychology, 7,* 415–418.

Bradley, R. H., Caldwell, B. M., & Elardo, R. (1979). Home environment and cognitive development in the first 2 years: A cross-lagged panel analysis. *Developmental Psychology, 15,* 246–250.

Brazelton, T. B. (1979). Behavioral competence of the newborn infant. *Seminars in Perinatology, 3,* 35–44.

Breland, H. M. (1974). Birth order, family configuration, and intelligence. *Science, 45,* 1011–1019.

Brody, G. H., & Shaffer, D. R. (1982). Contributions of parents and peers to children's moral socialization. *Developmental Review, 2,* 31–75.

Brody, G. H., Stoneman, Z., & MacKinnon, C. E. (1982). Role asymmetries in interactions among school-aged children, their younger siblings, and their friends. *Child Development, 53,* 1364–1370.

Bronfenbrenner, U. (1979). Contexts of child rearing: Problems and prospects. *American Psychologist, 34,* 844–850.

Buss, D. M. (1981). Predicting parent-child interactions from children's activity level. *Developmental Psychology, 17,* 59–65.

Cain, L., Kelly, D., & Shannon, D. (1980). Parents' perceptions of the psychological and social impact of home monitoring. *Pediatrics, 66,* 37–40.

Chapman, M. (1977). Father absence, stepfathers, and the cognitive performance of college students. *Child Development, 48,* 1155–1158.

Cicirelli, V. (1977). Family structure and interaction: Sibling effects on socialization. In M. McMillan & M. Sergio

(Eds.), *Child psychiatry: Treatment and research.* New York: Brunner/Mazel.

Clarke-Stewart, K. A. (1978). And daddy makes three: The father's impact on the mother and young child. *Child Development, 49,* 466–478.

Clarke-Stewart, K. A. (1982). *Daycare.* Cambridge, MA: Harvard University Press.

Cohen, S. E. (1978). Maternal employment and mother-child interaction. *Merrill-Palmer Quarterly, 24,* 189–197.

Cohen, S. E., & Beckwith, L. (1979). Preterm infant interaction with the caregiver in the first year of life and competence at age two. *Child Development, 50,* 767–776.

Conger, R., Burgess, R., & Barrett, C. (1979). Child abuse related to life change and perceptions of illness: Some preliminary findings. *Family Coordinator, 28,* 73–78.

Coopersmith, S. (1967). *The antecedents of self-esteem.* San Francisco: W. H. Freeman.

Crnic, K. A., Greenberg, M. T., Ragozin, A. S., Robinson, N. M., & Basham, R. B. (1983). Effects of stress and social support on mothers and premature and full-term infants. *Child Development, 54,* 209–217.

Crook, T., Raskin, A., & Eliot, J. (1981). Parent-child relationships and adult depression. *Child Development, 52,* 950–957.

Damon, W. (1977). *The social world of the child.* San Francisco: Jossey-Bass.

David, H. P., & Baldwin, W. P. (1979). Childbearing and child development: Demographic and psychosocial trends. *American Psychologist, 34,* 866–871.

Desimone-Luis, J., O'Mahoney, K., & Hunt, D. (1979). Children of separation and divorce: Factors influencing adjustment. *Journal of Divorce, 3,* 37–42.

Dubnoff, S. J., Veroff, J., & Kulka, R. A. (1978, August). *Adjustment to work: 1957–1976.* Paper presented at the meeting of the American Psychological Association, Toronto.

Dunn, J., & Kendrick, C. (1981a). Interaction between young siblings: Association with the interaction between mother and firstborn child. *Developmental Psychology, 17,* 336–343.

Dunn, J., & Kendrick, C. (1981b). Social behavior of young siblings in the family context: Differences between same-sex and different-sex dyads. *Child Development, 52,* 1265–1273.

Easterbrooks, M. A., & Goldberg, W. A. (1984). Toddler development in the family: Impact of father involvement and parenting characteristics. *Child Development, 55,* 740–752.

Erikson, E. H. (1963). *Childhood and society* (2nd ed.). New York: Norton.

Eysenck, H. J., & Cookson, D. (1969). Personality in primary school children: 3. Family background. *British Journal of Educational Psychology, 40,* 117–131.

Farran, D. C., & Ramey, C. T. (1980). Social class differences in dyadic involvement during infancy. *Child Development, 51,* 254–257.

Feldman, R. S., Devin-Sheehan, L., & Allen, V. L. (1976). Children tutoring children: A critical review of research.

In V. L. Allen (Ed.), *Children as teachers: Theory and research on tutoring*. New York: Academic Press.

Feldman, S. S., & Aschenbrenner, B. (1983). Impact of parenthood on various aspects of masculinity and femininity: A short-term longitudinal study. *Developmental Psychology, 19*, 278–289.

Field, T. M., & Pawlby, S. (1980). Early face-to-face interactions among British and American working- and middle-class mother-infant dyads. *Child Development, 51*, 250–253.

Field, T. M., Widmayer, S. M., Stringer, S., & Ignatoff, E. (1980). Teenage, lower-class, black mothers and their preterm infants: An intervention and developmental follow-up. *Child Development, 51*, 426–436.

Fine, M. A., Moreland, J. R., & Schwebel, A. I. (1983). Long-term effects of divorce on parent-child relationships. *Developmental Psychology, 19*, 703–713.

Fontana, V. J. (1973). *Somewhere a child is crying: Maltreatment—causes and prevention*. New York: Macmillan.

Frodi, A. M., & Lamb, M. E. (1980). Child abusers' responses to infant smiles and cries. *Child Development, 51*, 238–241.

Garbarino, J. (1982). The human ecology of school crime. In B. Emrich (Ed.), *Theoretical perspectives on school crime*. Davis, CA: National Council on Crime and Delinquency.

Garbarino, J., & Sherman, D. (1980). High-risk neighborhoods and high-risk families: The human ecology of child maltreatment. *Child Development, 51*, 188–198.

Gath, A. (1978). *Down's syndrome and the family: The early years*. New York: Academic Press.

Glass, D. C., Neulinger, J., & Brim, O. G. (1974). Birth order, verbal intelligence, and educational aspiration. *Child Development, 45*, 807–811.

Gold, D., & Andres, D. (1978a). Developmental comparisons between adolescent children with employed and nonemployed mothers. *Merrill-Palmer Quarterly, 24*, 243–254.

Gold, D., & Andres, D. (1978b). Developmental comparisons between 10-year-old children with employed and nonemployed mothers. *Child Development, 49*, 75–84.

Gold, D., Andres, D., & Glorieux, J. (1979). The development of Francophone nursery-school children with employed and nonemployed mothers. *Canadian Journal of Behavioral Science, 11*, 169–173.

Goldberg, W. A., & Easterbrooks, M. A. (1984). Role of marital quality in toddler development. *Developmental Psychology, 20*, 504–514.

Green, J. A., Gustafson, G. E., & West, M. J. (1980). Effects of infant development on mother-infant interactions. *Child Development, 51*, 199–207.

Greenberg, M., & Morris, N. (1974). Engrossment: The newborn's impact upon the father. *American Journal of Orthopsychiatry, 44*, 520–531.

Grossman, F. K., Eichler, L. S., Winickoff, S. A., & Associates. (1980). *Pregnancy, birth, and parenthood: Adap-*

tations of mothers, fathers, and infants. San Francisco: Jossey-Bass.

Grusec, J. E., & Kuczynski, L. (1980). Direction of effect in socialization: A comparison of the parent's versus the child's behavior as determinants of disciplinary techniques. *Developmental Psychology, 16*, 1–9.

Harlow, H. F., Harlow, M. K., Dodsworth, R. O., & Arling, G. L. (1966). Maternal behavior of rhesus monkeys deprived of mothering and peer associations as infants. *Proceedings of the American Philosophical Society, 110*, 88–98.

Heinicke, C. M., Diskin, S. D., Ramsey-Klee, D. M., & Given, K. (1983). Pre-birth parent characteristics and family development in the first year of life. *Child Development, 54*, 194–208.

Henderson, R. W. (1981). Home environment and intellectual performance. In R. W. Henderson (Ed.), *Parent-child interaction: Theory, research, and prospects*. New York: Academic Press.

Hess, R. D. (1970). Social class and ethnic influences upon socialization. In P. H. Mussen (Ed.), *Carmichael's manual of child psychology* (Vol. 2). New York: Wiley.

Hess, R. D., & Camara, K. A. (1979). Post divorce family relationships as mediating factors in the consequences of divorce for children. *Journal of Social Issues, 35*, 79–96.

Hetherington, E. M. (1981). Children and divorce. In R. W. Henderson (Ed.), *Parent-child interaction: Theory, research, and prospects*. New York: Academic Press.

Hetherington, E. M., Cox, M., & Cox, R. (1978). The aftermath of divorce. In J. H. Stevens, Jr., & M. Matthews (Eds.), *Mother-child, father-child relations*. Washington, DC: National Association for the Education of Young Children.

Hetherington, E. M., Cox, M., & Cox, R. (1979). Family interaction and the social, emotional, and cognitive development of children following divorce. In V. Vaughn & T. B. Brazelton (Eds.), *The family: Setting priorities*. New York: Science and Medicine Publishing Co.

Hilton, I. (1967). Differences in the behavior of mothers toward first and later born children. *Journal of Personality and Social Psychology, 7*, 282–290.

Hodges, W. F., Wechsler, R. C., & Ballantine, C. (1979). Divorce and the preschool child: Cumulative stress. *Journal of Divorce, 3*, 55–68.

Hoffman, L. W. (1979). Maternal employment: 1979. *American Psychologist, 34*, 859–865.

Hoffman, M. L. (1978). Empathy, its development and pro-social implications. In H. E. Howe (Ed.), *Nebraska Symposium on Motivation* (Vol. 25). Lincoln: University of Nebraska Press.

Holden, G. W. (1983). Avoiding conflict: Mothers as tacticians in the supermarket. *Child Development, 54*, 233–240.

Jacobs, B. S., & Moss, H. A. (1976). Birth order and sex of sibling as determinants of mother-infant interaction. *Child Development, 47*, 315–322.

Jones, F. A., Green, V., & Krauss, D. R. (1980). Maternal responsiveness of primiparous mothers during the post-partum period: Age differences. *Pediatrics, 65*, 579–583.

Kellaghan, T., & MacNamara, J. (1972). Family correlates of verbal reasoning ability. *Developmental Psychology, 7*, 49–53.

Kempe, R. S., & Kempe, C. H. (1978). *Child abuse.* Cambridge, MA: Harvard University Press.

Kendrick, C., & Dunn, J. (1980). Caring for the second baby: Effects on interaction between mother and firstborn. *Developmental Psychology, 16*, 303–311.

Kessner, D. M. (1973). *Infant death: An analysis by maternal risk and health care.* Washington, DC: National Academy of Sciences.

Klein, M., & Stern, L. (1971). Low birth weight and the battered child syndrome. *American Journal of Diseases of Childhood, 122*, 15–18.

Kohlberg, L. (1969). Stage and sequence: The cognitive-developmental approach to socialization. In D. A. Goslin (Ed.), *Handbook of socialization theory and research.* Chicago: Rand McNally.

Kohn, M. L. (1969). *Class and conformity: A study of values.* Homewood, IL: Dorsey Press.

Kurdek, L. A., Blisk, D., & Siesky, A. E., Jr. (1981). Correlates of children's long-term adjustment to their parents' divorce. *Developmental Psychology, 17*, 565–579.

Lahey, B. B., Hammer, D., Crumrine, P. L., & Forehand, R. L. (1980). Birth order × sex interactions in child behavior problems. *Developmental Psychology, 16*, 608–615.

Lamb, M. E. (1981). *The role of the father in child development.* New York: Wiley.

Laosa, L. M. (1981). Maternal behavior: Sociocultural diversity in modes of family interaction. In R. W. Henderson (Ed.), *Parent-child interaction: Theory, research, and prospects.* New York: Academic Press.

LeVine, R. A. (1974). Parental goals: A cross-cultural view. *Teachers College Record, 76*, 226–239.

LeVine, R. A. (1979, March). *Cross-cultural research on child development.* Invited address presented at the biennial meeting of the Society for Research in Child Development, San Francisco.

Light, R. J. (1973). Abused and neglected children in America: A study of alternative policies. *Harvard Educational Review, 43*, 556–598.

Maccoby, E. E. (1980). *Social development.* New York: Harcourt Brace Jovanovich.

MacKinnon, C. E., Brody, G. H., & Stoneman, Z. (1982). The effects of divorce and maternal employment on the home environments of preschool children. *Child Development, 53*, 1392–1399.

Maehr, M. L. (1974). *Sociocultural origins of achievement.* Monterey, CA: Brooks/Cole.

Main, M., & Weston, D. R. (1981). The quality of the toddler's relationship to mother and to father: Related to conflict and the readiness to establish new relationships. *Child Development, 52*, 932–940.

Matějček, Z., Dytrych, Z., & Schüller, V. (1979). The Prague study of children born from unwanted pregnancies. *International Journal of Mental Health, 7*, 63–74.

McCall, R. B., Gregory, T. G., & Murray, J. P. (1984). Communicating developmental research results to the general public through television. *Developmental Psychology, 20*, 45–54.

Mendes, H. A. (1976). Single fathers. *Family Coordinator, 25*, 439–440.

Miller, B. C., & Sollie, D. L. (1980). Normal stresses during the transition to parenthood. *Family Relations, 29*, 459–465.

Miller, N., & Maruyama, G. (1976). Ordinal position and peer popularity. *Journal of Personality and Social Psychology, 33*, 123–131.

Minnett, A. M., Vandell, D. L., & Santrock, J. W. (1983). The effects of sibling status on sibling interaction: The influence of birth order, age spacing, sex of child and sex of sibling. *Child Development, 54*, 1064–1072.

Mulhern, R. K., & Passman, R. H. (1981). Parental discipline as affected by sex of parent, sex of child, and the child's apparent responsiveness to discipline. *Developmental Psychology, 17*, 604–613.

Mussen, P. H., & Rutherford, E. (1963). Parent-child relations and parental personality in relation to young children's sex-role preferences. *Child Development, 34*, 589–607.

National Center for Health Statistics. (1980). *Provisional statistics.* Monthly Vital Statistics Report. Washington, DC: U.S. Department of Health, Education and Welfare.

Norman-Jackson, J. (1982). Family interactions, language development, and primary reading achievement of Black children in families of low income. *Child Development, 53*, 349–358.

Ogbu, J. U. (1981). Origins of human competence: A cultural-ethological perspective. *Child Development, 52*, 413–429.

Parke, R. D. (1977). Some effects of punishment on children's behavior—revisited. In E. M. Hetherington & R. D. Parke (Eds.), *Contemporary readings in child psychology.* New York: McGraw-Hill.

Parke, R. D., & Lewis, N. G. (1981). The family in context: A multilevel interactional analysis of child abuse. In R. W. Henderson (Ed.), *Parent-child interaction: Theory, research, and prospects.* New York: Academic Press.

Paulhus, D., & Shaffer, D. R. (1981). Sex differences in the impact of number of older and number of younger siblings on scholastic aptitude. *Social Psychology Quarterly, 44*, 363–368.

Pedersen, F., Anderson, B., & Cain, R. (1977, March). *An approach to understanding linkages between parent-infant and spouse relationships.* Paper presented at the biennial meeting of the Society for Research in Child Development, New Orleans.

Pepler, D. J., Abramovitch, R., & Corter, C. (1981). Sibling interaction in the home: A longitudinal study. *Child Development, 52*, 1344–1347.

Peterson, G. H., Mehl, L. E., & Liederman, P. H. (1979). The role of some birth-related variables in father attachments. *American Journal of Orthopsychiatry, 49,* 330–338.

Phares, E. J. (1976). *Locus of control in personality.* Morristown, NJ: General Learning Press.

Ragozin, A. S., Basham, R. B., Crnic, K. A., Greenberg, M. T., & Robinson, N. M. (1982). Effects of maternal age on parenting role. *Developmental Psychology, 18,* 627–634.

Rebelsky, F., & Hanks, C. (1971). Father verbal interaction with infants in the first three months of life. *Child Development, 42,* 63–68.

Rosen, R. (1979). Some crucial issues concerning children of divorce. *Journal of Divorce, 3,* 19–26.

Rosenheim, M. K. (1973). The child and the law. In B. M. Caldwell & H. N. Ricciuti (Eds.), *Review of child development research* (Vol. 3). Chicago: University of Chicago Press.

Rothbart, M. K. (1971). Birth order and mother-child interaction in an achievement situation. *Journal of Personality and Social Psychology, 17,* 113–120.

Russell, C. (1974). Transitions to parenthood: Problems and gratifications. *Journal of Marriage and the Family, 36,* 294–301.

Sampson, E. E., & Hancock, F. T. (1967). An examination of the relationship between ordinal position, personality, and conformity: An extension, replication, and partial verification. *Journal of Personality and Social Psychology, 5,* 398–407.

Samuels, H. R. (1977, March). *The sibling in the infant's social environment.* Paper presented at the biennial meeting of the Society for Research in Child Development, New Orleans.

Samuels, H. R. (1980). The effect of older sibling on infant locomotor exploration of a new environment. *Child Development, 51,* 607–609.

Santrock, J. W. (1972). The relations of type and onset of father absence to cognitive development. *Child Development, 43,* 455–469.

Santrock, J. W., & Minnett, A. (1981, April). *Sibling interaction: An observational study of sex of sibling, age spacing, and ordinal position.* Paper presented at the biennial meeting of the Society for Research in Child Development, Boston.

Santrock, J. W., & Warshak, R. A. (1979). Father custody and social development in boys and girls. *Journal of Social Issues, 35,* 112–125.

Santrock, J. W., Warshak, R. A., Lindbergh, C., & Meadows, L. (1982). Children's and parents' observed social behavior in stepfather families. *Child Development, 53,* 472–480.

Schachter, F. F. (1981). Toddlers with employed mothers. *Child Development, 52,* 958–964.

Schachter, S. (1959). *The psychology of affiliation.* Stanford, CA: Stanford University Press.

Schachter, S. (1963). Birth order, eminence, and higher education. *American Sociological Review, 28,* 757–767.

Schaefer, E. S., & Bayley, N. (1963). Maternal behavior, child behavior, and their intercorrelations from infancy through adolescence. *Monographs of the Society for Research in Child Development, 28* (3, Serial No. 87).

Sewell, W. H., Haller, A. O., & Strauss, M. A. (1957). Social status and educational and occupational aspiration. *American Sociological Review, 22,* 67–73.

Snow, M. E., Jacklin, C. N., & Maccoby, E. E. (1983). Sex-of-child differences in father-child interaction at one year of age. *Child Development, 54,* 227–232.

Starr, R. H., Jr. (1979). Child abuse. *American Psychologist, 34,* 872–878.

Steele, B. F., & Pollack, C. B. (1974). A psychiatric study of parents who abuse infants and small children. In R. E. Hefler & C. H. Kempe (Eds.), *The battered child.* Chicago: University of Chicago Press.

Steinberg, L. D., Catalano, R., & Dooley, D. (1981). Economic antecedents of child abuse and neglect. *Child Development, 52,* 975–985.

Stewart, R. B. (1983). Sibling attachment relationships: Child-infant interactions in the strange situation. *Developmental Psychology, 19,* 192–199.

Stoneman, Z., & Brody, G. H. (1981). Two's company, three makes a difference: An examination of mothers' and fathers' speech to their young children. *Child Development, 52,* 705–707.

Stuckey, M. F., McGhee, P. E., & Bell, N. J. (1982). Parent-child interaction: The influence of maternal employment. *Developmental Psychology, 18,* 635–644.

Study: Children with working mothers score lower on tests. (1983, June 26). *Atlanta Journal,* p. 4-A.

Suomi, S. J. (1978). Maternal behavior by socially incompetent monkeys: Neglect and abuse of offspring. *Journal of Pediatric Psychology, 3,* 28–34.

Sutton-Smith, B., & Rosenberg, B. G. (1970). *The sibling.* New York: Holt, Rinehart & Winston.

U. S. Bureau of the Census. (1982). *Characteristics of American children and youth: 1980.* Current Population Reports, Series P-23, No. 114. Washington, DC: U.S. Government Printing Office.

U.S. Department of Commerce. (1979). *Marital status and living arrangements: March 1978.* Current Population Reports, Series P-20, No. 338. Washington, DC: U.S. Government Printing Office.

Wallerstein, J. S., & Kelly, J. B. (1980, January). California's children of divorce. *Psychology Today,* pp. 67–76.

Warren, J. R. (1966). Birth order and social behavior. *Psychological Bulletin, 65,* 38–49.

Weisner, T. S., & Gallimore, R. (1977). My brother's keeper: Child and sibling caretaking. *Current Anthropology, 18,* 169–190.

Weisz, J. R. (1980). Autonomy, control, and other reasons why "Mom is the greatest": A content analysis of children's Mother's Day letters. *Child Development, 51,* 801–807.

Zajonc, R. B., Markus, H., & Markus, G. B. (1979). The birth order puzzle. *Journal of Personality and Social Psychology, 37,* 1325–1341.

Zegoib, L. E., Arnold, S., & Forehand, R. (1975). An examination of observer effects in parent-child interactions. *Child Development, 46,* 509–512.

Zussmán, J. U. (1978). Relationship of demographic factors to parental disciplinary techniques. *Developmental Psychology, 14,* 685–686.

Zussman, J. U. (1980). Situational determinants of parental behavior: Effects of competing cognitive activity. *Child Development, 51,* 792–800.

CHAPTER SIXTEEN ■

BEYOND THE HOME SETTING: EXTRAFAMILIAL INFLUENCES

■ *The early window: Effects of television on children and youth*
Children's use of television
Effects of televised violence
Television as a source of social stereotypes
Children's reactions to commercial messages
Television as a prosocial instrument
Television as a contributor to cognitive development
Should television be used to socialize children?

■ *The school as a socialization agent*
Does schooling promote cognitive development?
Determinants of effective and ineffective schooling
The teacher's influence
The school as a middle-class institution: Effects on disadvantaged youth

■ *The second world of childhood: Peers as socialization agents*
Who or what is a peer?
The role of peers in the socialization process
Peer versus adult influence: The question of cross-pressures
The role of the peer group in other societies

■ *Summary*

I n Chapter Fifteen we focused on the family as an instrument of socialization, looking at the ways parents and siblings affect developing children. Although families have an enormous impact on their young throughout childhood and adolescence, it is only a matter of time before other societal institutions begin to exert their influence. For example, infants and toddlers are often exposed to alternative caregivers and a host of new playmates when their working parents place them in some kind of day care. Even those toddlers who remain at home will soon begin to learn about the outside world once they develop an interest in television. Between the ages of 2 and 5, many American children spend several hours of every weekday away from home as they attend nursery school. And by the age of 6 to 7, virtually all children in Western societies are going to elementary school, a setting that requires them to interact with other little people who are similar to themselves and to adjust to the rules and regulations of a brave new world—one that may be very dissimilar to the home environment from which they came.

So as they mature, children are becoming increasingly familiar with the outside world and will spend much less time under the watchful eyes of their parents. How do these experiences affect their lives? This is the issue to which we will now turn as we consider the impact of three "**extrafamilial**" agents of socialization: television, schools, and children's peer groups.

THE EARLY WINDOW: EFFECTS OF TELEVISION ON CHILDREN AND YOUTH[1]

It seems almost incomprehensible that only 40 years ago the average person in the United States could not have answered the question "What is a

---

extrafamilial influences: *social agencies other than the family that influence a child's cognitive, social, and emotional development.*

television?" When first introduced in the late 1940s, television was an expensive luxury for the wealthy—one that made the children of well-to-do parents immensely popular with their peers. Today a television occupies a prominent location in virtually all American homes, and 70% of American families have more than one set. Robert Liebert and his associates (Liebert, Sprafkin, & Davidson, 1982) believe that television has changed our daily lives more than any other technological innovation of the 20th century. And they may be correct, for the average TV set in the United States runs for more than six hours a day, and it is not at all uncommon for people to alter their sleeping habits or plan their meals and leisure activities to accommodate television (Steinberg, 1980).

Does television undermine the quality of family life, as some critics have maintained? Are children who watch a lot of television likely to be socially withdrawn and less interested in schoolwork? How do children react to televised violence and to the social stereotyping of women and minorities that often appears in commercial programming? Can television be used to reduce social prejudices and to teach prosocial lessons such as cooperation and sharing? Does educational programming promote cognitive growth? In the pages that follow, we will discuss each of these issues as we consider what is known about the effects of television on children's social and intellectual development.

Children's Use of Television

In the United States, children between the ages of 3 and 11 watch an average of three to four hours of television a day. As we see in Figure 16-1, time spent in front of the television gradually increases until about age 12 and then declines somewhat during adolescence. A recent survey of television usage in Australia, Canada, and several European countries reported virtually the same develop-

mental trends in children's viewing habits (Murray, 1980). To place these findings in perspective, we need only note that by age 18 a child born today will have spent more time watching television than in any other single activity except sleeping (Liebert et al., 1982). Is it any wonder, then, that parents, educators, and those who study children are curious and often concerned about the possible effects of this incredible exposure to the electronic media?

■ *What do children watch?*

It is often assumed that children spend most of their TV time watching programs designed for children. In fact, many 7–8-year-olds are already watching programs intended for adults at least half the time (Brown, 1976). The production features that are most likely to capture a young child's attention are fast-paced action sequences, special effects, zooms, and segments in which there are rapid changes in the scenery or the number of characters (Anderson, Lorch, Field, & Sanders, 1981). Shows containing a lot of violence typically incorporate all these attention-grabbing features. However, it appears that 2–11-year-olds actually prefer situation comedies to violent programming, even though they end up watching a

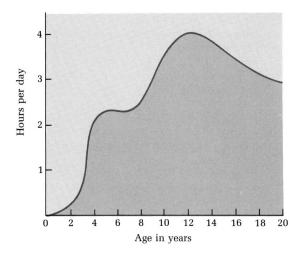

FIGURE 16-1. *Average number of hours per day that American children and adolescents spend watching television.*

---

[1]The title of this section is taken from a book of the same name (Liebert, Sprafkin, & Davidson, 1982). I highly recommend this volume to those who are seeking a reasonably comprehensive and readable overview of the effects of television on developing children.

lot of violence on television (Huston & Wright, 1982).

■ *Has television changed family life?*

The presence of a television in the home has a significant impact on parents, children, and the structuring of family life. One survey found that a majority of families altered their sleeping patterns and mealtimes once they had purchased a television (Johnson, 1967). The introduction of television also had the effect of decreasing the amount of time parents spent with their youngsters in non-TV-related leisure activities (that is, games and family outings), and most parents at least occasionally used television as an "electronic baby-sitter." Although parents and children may spend many hours in close proximity as they watch television together, many critics believe that this form of family interaction is not very meaningful for the younger set—particularly if they are often told to sit still or keep their mouths shut until the commercials come on. Urie Bronfenbrenner (1970b) has argued:

> The primary danger of . . . television . . . lies not so much in the behavior it produces—although there is danger there—as in the behavior that it prevents: the talks, games, the family festivities and arguments through which much of the child's learning takes place and through which his character is formed. Turning on the television set can turn off the process that transforms children into people.

Does television really transform children into social isolates who are so captivated by their visual experiences that they become less interested in playing games, making friends, or doing their homework? The answer to this question is a qualified no. Children who live in remote areas without television do spend significantly more time reading comics, going to movies, or listening to the radio than age mates who live in similar communities served by television (Huston & Wright, 1982; Schramm, Lyle, & Parker, 1961). But when television comes to an isolated area, children simply substitute TV viewing for these other roughly equivalent forms of entertainment. Apparently the availability of television does not affect the amount of time children spend on

homework—or leisure reading, for that matter, if we exclude comic books. Moreover, popular children who partake in many sports and extracurricular activities tend to read a lot and to watch a lot of TV (Lyle & Hoffman, 1972). So it is clearly inappropriate to argue that television viewing has replaced valuable pastimes and activities such as reading or playing with one's peers.

The impact of television on academic achievement is not well understood. At least one researcher found that the reading comprehension of elementary school students declined once television was introduced to an isolated community (Williams, 1977, cited in Huston & Wright, 1982). However, a recent study published by the U. S. Department of Education suggests that students in the lower grades may actually learn a great deal of useful information from watching television—particularly educational programming ("Study: Children with Working Mothers," 1983). It may be that the effects of television on academic performance depend largely on what the children are watching. An educational program such as *The Electric Company,* which is designed to teach reading concepts, may well reinforce the elementary school curriculum and have a positive effect on academic achievement, whereas popular programs such as *The Three Stooges* or *Starsky and Hutch* have little educational value and could undermine academic achievement if they keep children from their lessons. Indeed, the authors of the Department of Education study reported that high school students perform better on standardized achievement tests when they spend more time on homework and watch less commercial television.

Effects of Televised Violence

As early as 1954, complaints raised by parents, teachers, and students of human development prompted Senator Estes Kefauver, then chairman of the Senate Subcommittee on Juvenile Delinquency, to question the need for violence in television programming. As it turns out, American television is incredibly violent. Eighty percent of all prime-time television programs contain at least one incident of physical violence, with an average

PHOTO 16-1. *Although families spend much of their leisure time watching television, there is little evidence that TV viewing has undermined the quality of family life or replaced other valuable activities and pastimes such as reading and being with friends.*

rate of 7.5 violent acts per hour (Gerbner, Gross, Morgan, & Signorelli, 1980). It is estimated that the average child of 16, who has already spent more time watching TV than in school, will have witnessed more than 13,000 killings on television (Waters & Malamud, 1975). This remarkable statistic often shocks college students, particularly those who have young children of their own. Yet they would probably not be surprised by these figures were they to sit down and watch Saturday morning television. George Gerbner and his associates (Gerbner et al., 1980) report that the most violent programs on commercial television are those designed for children—especially Saturday morning cartoon shows, which contain nearly 25 violent incidents per hour.

Does a heavy exposure to televised violence encourage spectators to behave aggressively? Do children who watch a lot of violent programming become more tolerant of the aggressive acts that they may witness at home, at school, or on the playground? Let's see what researchers have learned in trying to answer these questions.

■ *Experimental data*

One method of determining whether violent films instigate aggression is to expose children to these materials and then provide them with an opportunity to make aggressive responses. As early as 1972, 18 such experiments had been conducted, and 16 of them (89%) found that children become more aggressive after watching violent sequences on television (Liebert & Baron, 1972).

Would children behave aggressively after watching violent programming if they were given an opportunity to *help* another child? Apparently so. In one study (Collins & Getz, 1976), fourth-, seventh-, and tenth-graders watched an episode of *Mod Squad* that had been edited so that the protagonist responded either aggressively or constructively to an interpersonal conflict. After viewing one of the episodes, each child was given an opportunity to assist or to hinder a peer by pressing either a "help" button that would make the peer's task very easy or a "hurt" button that would make it very difficult. The results were clear: despite the availability of an alternative helping response, children were much more likely to hinder the efforts of a peer if they had watched the violent program.

Several field experiments paint a similar picture. For example, Aletha Stein and Lynette Friedrich (1972) observed 97 preschool children over a three-week period to establish a "baseline" level of aggression for each child. The children were then randomly assigned to three experimental conditions. For a month, those who watched *violent programming* saw one *Batman* or one *Superman* cartoon a day in their nursery school classrooms. Children exposed to **prosocial television** watched daily episodes of *Mister Rogers' Neighborhood*, while those in the third group saw *neutral* (neither aggressive nor prosocial) films of circuses and farm scenes. After the month had passed, the children were observed at play for two additional weeks in order to measure the effects of the programming. Stein and Friedrich found that the children who had watched violent programming were subsequently more aggressive in nursery school than their classmates who had watched either prosocial or neutral programming. Although the impact of the violent programming was greatest for children who had been above average in aggressiveness during the initial baseline period, these "initially aggressive" children were by no means extreme or deviant. They simply represented the more aggressive members of a typical nursery school peer group. So watching violent programming does indeed instigate aggression in many young children. Stein and Friedrich remind us that "these effects occurred in [a naturalistic setting] that was removed both in time and place from the viewing experience. They occurred with a small amount of exposure . . . and they endured during the postviewing period" (1972, p. 247).

Correlational research

In Chapter Seven we saw that children and adolescents who watch a lot of televised violence at home tend to be more aggressive than their classmates who watch little violence. Indeed, Leonard Eron and his associates (Eron, Huesmann, Lefkowitz, & Walder, 1972) found that one of the best predictors of aggression among adolescent males was the boys' preference for violent television programming as expressed ten years earlier, when they were in the third grade. In other words, boys

who favored violent programming at age 8 to 9 tended to be highly aggressive at age 19. Although this is correlational research and does not demonstrate causality, the findings are at least consistent with the argument that early exposure to a heavy diet of televised violence may lead to the development of aggressive habits that persist over time.

One reason that violence may instigate aggression is that children younger than 8 or 9 cannot easily distinguish fantasy from reality and are likely to believe that much of what they see on television is quite realistic. A steady diet of violent programming may convince the child that the outside world is a violent place inhabited by people who typically rely on aggressive strategies when faced with interpersonal conflicts. Indeed, Leonard Eron and his associates (Eron, Huesmann, Brice, Fischer, & Mermelstein, 1983) found that 7- to 9-year-old boys *and girls* who were judged highly aggressive by their peers not only preferred violent television programs—they also believed that violent shows were an accurate portrayal of everyday life.

Desensitization effects

In addition to instigating aggressive behavior, a steady diet of televised violence may increase children's *tolerance* for aggression, even aggression that takes place around them in the real world. Ronald Drabman and Margaret Thomas (1974) tested this **desensitization hypothesis** with 8- to 10-year-olds. Half the children watched a violent Hopalong Cassidy film that contained several gun battles and fist fights. The remaining subjects were assigned to a control condition and did not see a film. Each child was then asked to watch a television monitor to ensure that two kindergarten children who were playing in another room didn't get into any trouble while the ex-

---

prosocial television: *television programming that emphasizes socially desirable themes such as cooperation, helping, sharing, or comfort giving that benefit other people.*

desensitization hypothesis: *the notion that people who watch a lot of media violence will become less aroused by aggression and more tolerant of violent and aggressive acts.*

perimenter was away at the principal's office. The experimenter took great care to explain to the child that he or she was to come to the principal's office for help should *anything* go wrong. Each child then observed the same videotaped sequence, in which the two kindergartners got into an intense battle. The tape ended with a loud crash that occurred shortly after the camera had been knocked over and the video had gone dead.

The results of this study were straightforward: children who had watched the violent film reacted much more slowly to what they believed to be a real-life altercation than their classmates who had not seen a film. Drabman and Thomas suggested that exposure to media violence may blunt viewers' emotional reactions to later aggressive episodes and perhaps even make them feel that aggressive acts are a part of everyday life that do not necessarily warrant a response.

In a second experiment, Margaret Thomas and her colleagues (Thomas, Horton, Lippincott, & Drabman, 1977) exposed 8- to 10-year-olds to either a *violent* film from the popular police series *S.W.A.T.* or a *nonviolent* but exciting film of a championship volleyball match. The viewers were hooked up to a physiograph that recorded their emotional reactions to the films (which were equally arousing). After the film, the experimenter switched channels and asked the child to monitor the activities of two younger children who were playing in an adjacent room. At this point the experimenter departed, leaving the subject hooked up to the physiograph. The child then observed the

PHOTO 16-2. Heavy exposure to media violence may blunt children's emotional reactions to real-life aggression and lead them to believe that the world is a violent place populated mainly by hostile and aggressive people.

same videotaped altercation that Drabman and Thomas had used, and his or her emotional reactions to these events were recorded.

Once again, the results were clear: children who had watched the violent programming were subsequently less aroused by the real-life altercation than classmates who had seen the nonviolent film. Apparently an exposure to media violence does lessen a viewer's emotional sensitivity to later acts of aggression—a finding that may help to explain why children are more likely to *tolerate* aggression after witnessing violent acts on television.

■ *Reducing the harmful effects of televised violence*

Perhaps the most obvious method of reducing the impact of violent programming is to carefully monitor what children are watching and to try to interest them in programs that contain little or no violence. Anyone who would like a list of programs that the experts consider too violent for young children can obtain one by writing to Action for Children's Television, 46 Austin Street, Boston, Mass. 02160.

Of course, it would be next to impossible for parents to shield their children from televised violence, because violence is widespread in the media, and curious youngsters who are not allowed to watch it at home may be eager to see what they are missing while watching TV at a community recreation center or in the homes of their friends. In recent years, organizations such as Action for Children's Television, the American Medical Association, and the National Association for Better Broadcasting have campaigned against TV violence and recommended that concerned parents write to both the commercial networks and their local network affiliates to complain about the highly violent and aggressive programming directed at their children. These protests have not always fallen on deaf ears, for several advertisers (for example, Best Foods, Miracle White, and Samsonite) have pledged to avoid sponsoring extremely violent television shows ("Cooling Off the Tube," 1976). So there is some evidence that organized protests and write-in campaigns can be effective at reducing the level of violence on TV—but only if a sufficient number of concerned citizens become involved.

In the meantime, parents can help their children to critically evaluate media violence by pointing out subtleties that young viewers often miss—content such as the aggressor's motives, his or her intentions, and the unpleasant consequences that perpetrators suffer as a result of their aggressive acts (Collins, Sobol, & Westby, 1981). When adults highlight this information while strongly disapproving of a perpetrator's conduct, young children gain a much better understanding of media violence and are less affected by what they have seen—particularly if the adult commentator also suggests how these perpetrators might have approached their problems in a more constructive way (Corder-Bolz & O'Bryant, 1977; Horton & Santogrossi, 1978).

Television as a Source of Social Stereotypes

Television is often the young child's first exposure to the outside world and the people who live there. Indeed, many children have had little or no contact with police officers, lawyers, teachers, people from different racial and ethnic groups, or the elderly, and their "knowledge" of these individuals is likely to consist of what they have seen on television.

Sex-role stereotyping is common on television, both in programs and in commercial messages. Males on TV outnumber females nearly 2 to 1, and men are typically portrayed as high-status individuals who are more powerful, dominant, rational, and intelligent than women (Gerbner et al., 1980; Liebert et al., 1982). Although children may encounter an occasional female lawyer or doctor, most women on TV are assigned marital, romantic, or family roles, and those who work are rarely holding prestigious positions (Liebert et al., 1982). Perhaps we should not be surprised to learn that children who watch a lot of commercial TV and are often exposed to these sex-role stereotypes are more traditionally sex-typed themselves and are more likely to hold stereotyped views of males and females than their classmates who watch little television (Frueh & McGhee, 1975; Rothschild, 1979). In one recent longitudinal study of young adolescents, Michael Morgan (1982) found that the youngsters who are affected most by watching sex-role stereotypes on television are girls of above-average intelligence from middle-class homes—precisely the group that is otherwise least likely to hold traditionally sexist attitudes.

■ *Stereotyping of minorities*
Until the middle to late 1970s, ethnic minorities other than Blacks were practically ignored on television. When foreigners or non-Black minorities did appear, they were presented in an unfavorable light, often cast in the roles of swindlers or villains (Liebert et al., 1982). Blacks were almost always placed in minor roles, and the one Black show that appeared in the early days of television—*Amos and Andy*—presented such an unfavorable image of Black Americans that the National Association for the Advancement of Colored People (NAACP) demanded that CBS take it off the air. Today the representation of minorities on television has increased to approximate their proportions in the population. Yet compared with Whites, a greater percentage of non-White characters are depicted as very poor people who work at service occupations, are prone to violence, or are involved in illegal activities (Liebert et al., 1982).

A study by Sheryl Graves (1975) suggests that these media stereotypes may affect children's racial attitudes. In Graves's experiment, both Black and White children watched a series of cartoons in which Black people were portrayed either positively (as competent, trustworthy, and hardworking) or negatively (as inept, lazy, and powerless). On a later test of racial attitudes, both Black and White children became more favorable toward Blacks if they had seen the positive portrayals. But when the depictions of Blacks were negative, an interesting racial difference emerged: Black children once again became more favorable in their racial attitudes, while Whites became much *less* favorable. So the way Blacks are portrayed on television may have a striking effect on the racial attitudes of White viewers, whereas the mere presence of Black TV characters may be sufficient to produce more favorable attitudes toward Blacks among a young Black audience.

■ *Countering stereotypes on television*
In recent years, attempts have been made to design programs for the younger set that counter inaccurate racial, sexual, and ethnic stereotypes

while fostering goodwill among children from different backgrounds. In 1969 *Sesame Street* led the way with positive portrayals of Blacks and Hispanics. Indeed, one study (Gorn, Goldberg, & Kanungo, 1976) found that White preschool children became more willing to include non-Whites in their play activities after watching episodes of *Sesame Street* that depicted minority youngsters as cheerful companions. Among the other shows that have been effective at fostering international awareness and reducing children's ethnic stereotypes are *Big Blue Marble,* a program designed to teach children about people in other countries, and *Vegetable Soup,* a show that portrays many ethnic groups in a favorable light (Liebert et al., 1982).

In 1975 the National Institute of Education funded a program named *Freestyle,* designed to counter sex-role stereotypes and to make grade school children more aware of various career options that may be available to them. *Freestyle* is

> a television intervention aimed at 9 to 12-year-olds . . . a carefully articulated package designed to influence the attitudes and behaviors of this age group in a way that would reduce sex-role stereotypes and expand the "career awareness" of children, especially girls, in non-traditional ways. The task was to be accomplished by focusing on non-traditional possibilities in the 9 to 12-year-old's own world. . . . Its purpose would be to have children relate non-traditional childhood interests to educational and ultimately to occupational choices [Johnston, Ettema, & Davidson, 1980].

Although it is too early to tell whether *Freestyle* will accomplish its long-term objectives, the early returns are encouraging. For example, one group of grade school children showed the following changes after viewing 13 episodes of the program (Johnston et al., 1980):

1. Boys became more tolerant of girls who attempted sporting or mechanical activities, and girls became much more interested in these endeavors.
2. Both boys and girls became more accepting of boys who engage in "feminine" activities such as housework or caring for younger children.
3. Both boys and girls became more accepting of men and women who have nontraditional jobs.
4. Both boys and girls became less traditional and more egalitarian in their views about family

roles such as who should cook, clean, or repair the house.

So we see that television can either reinforce or reduce inaccurate and potentially harmful social stereotypes, depending, of course, on the type of programming to which people are exposed. Unfortunately, the stereotyped depictions of gender, race, and ethnicity that often appear on commercial TV are presently far more numerous than the nonstereotyped portrayals, which are largely limited to selected programs that appear on public (educational) television.

Children's Reactions to Commercial Messages

In the United States, the average child is exposed to nearly 20,000 television commercials each year—many of which extol the virtues of various toys, fast-food products, and sugary treats that adults may not wish to purchase. Nevertheless, young children continue to ask for products that they have seen advertised on television, and conflicts often ensue when parents refuse to honor their requests (Atkin, 1978). In one study, 4- and 5-year-olds saw a program that had either no commercials or two commercials for a particular toy. The children were later shown photographs of a father and son and were told that the father had refused to buy the advertised toy after his son had requested it. More than 60% of the youngsters who had seen the commercials felt that the boy would be resentful and would not want to play with his father, while the comparable figure among the no-commercial group was less than 40% (Goldberg & Gorn, 1977, as cited in Liebert et al., 1982).

In addition to making children angry or resentful toward adults who refuse to buy advertised products, commercials may have an indirect effect on a child's peer relations. In the experiment by Goldberg and Gorn described above, children were asked whether they would rather play with the advertised toy or with friends in a sandbox. Those who had seen the commercials for the toy were much more likely to choose the toy over their friends than children who had not seen the commercials. When asked whether they would rather play with a "nice boy" without the toy or a "not-so-nice boy" with the toy, 65% of the commercial viewers chose the "not-so-nice boy" who possessed the advertised item, compared with only 30% of those in the no-commercial group. Is it any wonder, then, that parents are often concerned about the impact of commercials on their children? Not only do children's ads often push products that are unsafe or of poor nutritional value, they may also contribute to coercive family interactions and poor peer relations.

Television as a Prosocial Instrument

Thus far, we've cast a wary eye at television, talking mostly about its capacity to do harm. Yet the medium itself is not to blame; it is the programming that comes over the airwaves that is primarily responsible for these harmful effects.[2] There is now reason to believe that television could become a most effective means of teaching prosocial lessons if only its content were altered to reflect these principles. In the pages that follow, we will examine some of the evidence to support this claim.

■ *Prosocial effects of commercially broadcast programs*

Although network programming designed for children is often violent, each of the commercial networks has made an attempt to broadcast some programs with prosocial themes (Liebert et al., 1982). For example, CBS consulted with educators and child psychologists to develop *Fat Albert and the Cosby Kids,* a program designed to teach elementary school children how to deal with a host of social issues, such as divorce, the arrival of a new baby, discrimination, being honest, and being helpful. Moreover, several commercial series such as *Lassie* or *The Waltons* occasionally present episodes that revolve around one character's predicaments and the helpful acts of a protagonist. Do young children learn these

[2]John Wright and Aletha Huston (1983) believe that the medium *is* partly to blame. To back their argument, they cite some of their own research in which children who watched programs containing fast-paced motion and other attention-grabbing production features often became more aggressive in their play—even when these programs contained no violence. So it is possible that the medium may have some undesirable effects, regardless of its message.

prosocial lessons? If so, are they likely to put them into practice?

The answer to both questions is a qualified yes. In the formative stages of *Fat Albert and the Cosby Kids,* the Columbia Broadcasting System (1974) reported that about 90% of the children who watched the program were able to verbalize the prosocial themes conveyed in these episodes. Joyce Sprafkin and her associates (Sprafkin, Liebert, & Poulos, 1975) then examined the effects of prosocial programming on children's behavior. In their experiment, 6-year-olds watched one of three programs: an episode from the popular *Lassie* series in which a boy risked his life to save a puppy (prosocial programming), a *Lassie* episode that contained no outstanding prosocial acts (neutral programming), or a light-hearted but nonaltruistic episode from *The Brady Bunch* (neutral programming). After viewing the program, children began to play a game in an attempt to win prizes. While they played, they could hear some puppies that apparently needed help. As we see in Figure 16-2, children who had watched the prosocial episode persisted longer in their attempts to relieve the puppies' distress (and thereby stood

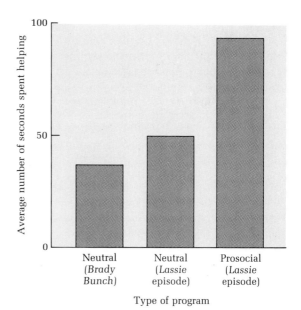

FIGURE 16-2. *Average amount of time that children spent helping distressed puppies after watching prosocial or neutral programming on commercial TV.*

less chance of winning a nice prize) than children who had watched the neutral programs. In a similar study (Baran, Chase, & Courtright, 1979), 8- to 10-year-olds who had watched a *Waltons* episode that portrayed a cooperative solution to a conflict later behaved more cooperatively while playing a game than age mates who had seen a non-cooperative film or no film. Finally, Sprafkin discovered that children who prefer and often watch prosocial programming tend to behave more prosocially at school than their classmates who rarely watch such shows (Sprafkin & Rubinstein, 1979). Taken together, these findings suggest that "it is possible to produce [commercial] programming that features action and adventure, appeals to child and family audiences, and still has a salutary rather than a negative social influence on viewers" (Sprafkin et al., 1975, p. 125).

■ *Educational television and children's prosocial behavior*

A number of programs broadcast on the Public Broadcasting System are designed to supplement the everyday learning experiences of preschool children. For example, *Sesame Street* was created to entertain preschoolers while fostering their intellectual and social development. A typical episode combines fast action and humorous incidents with a carefully designed educational curriculum designed to teach (among other things) letters of the alphabet, numbers, counting, vocabulary and many affective lessons. Another program, *Mister Rogers' Neighborhood*, is designed to facilitate the child's social and emotional development. To accomplish these objectives, Mister Rogers talks directly to his audience about things that may interest or puzzle children (for example, crises such as the death of a pet); he reassures them about common fears such as riding in airplanes; he encourages viewers to learn from and to cooperate with children of different races and social backgrounds; and he helps children to see themselves in a favorable light by repeatedly emphasizing that "there is only one person in the whole wide world like you, and I like you just the way you are."

Both these programs have a positive influence on the social behavior of young viewers. When preschool children watch either program over a long period, they often become more affectionate, considerate, cooperative, and helpful toward their nursery school classmates, particularly if adults watch these shows with them and encourage them to verbalize or role-play the prosocial lessons they have observed (Coates, Pusser, & Goodman, 1976; Friedrich & Stein, 1973, 1975; Paulson, 1974). Yet it is interesting to note that children who are exposed to prosocial programming may become more helpful or cooperative without becoming any less aggressive (Friedrich-Cofer, Huston-Stein, Kipnis, Susman, & Clewett, 1979). This puzzling finding may simply reflect the fact that children who watch prosocial programming typically become more outgoing and thus will have more opportunities to argue with their peers. Nevertheless, it seems that the positive effects of prosocial programming greatly outweigh the negatives, particularly if adults encourage children to pay close attention to episodes that emphasize constructive methods of resolving interpersonal conflicts.

Television as a Contributor to Cognitive Development

In 1968 the U.S. government and a number of private foundations contributed the funding to create the **Children's Television Workshop (CTW)**, an organization committed to producing TV programs that would hold children's interest and hopefully facilitate their intellectual development. CTW's first production, *Sesame Street*, became the world's most popular chil-

PHOTO 16-3. *Children learn many valuable lessons from educational TV programs such as* Sesame Street.

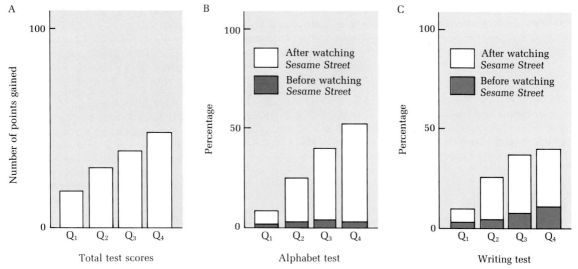

FIGURE 16-3. *Relationship between amount of viewing of* Sesame Street *and children's abilities: A, improvement in total test scores for children grouped into different quartiles according to amount of viewing; B, percentage of children who recited the alphabet correctly, grouped according to quartiles of amount of viewing; C, percentage of children who wrote their first names correctly, grouped according to quartiles of amount of viewing.*

dren's TV series—one that now reaches approximately 85% of the 3–5-year-olds in the United States and is broadcast to nearly 70 other countries around the world (Liebert et al., 1982; Wright & Huston, 1983).

■ *The objectives of Sesame Street*
As noted earlier, production artists, educators, and experts in child development worked together to design a program for preschool children that would foster important cognitive skills such as recognizing and discriminating numbers and letters, counting, ordering and classifying objects, and solving simple problems. It was hoped that children from disadvantaged backgrounds would be much better prepared for school after viewing this programming on a regular basis. In 1969 *Sesame Street* was unveiled and became an immediate hit. But was it accomplishing its objectives?

■ *The evaluations*
During the first season that *Sesame Street* was broadcast, its impact was assessed by the Educational Testing Service. About 950 children from five areas of the United States participated in the study. At the beginning of the project, children took a pretest that measured their cognitive skills

and determined what they knew about letters, numbers, and geometric forms. At the end of the season, they took this test again to see what they had learned. Originally the sample had been divided into an experimental group that was encouraged to watch *Sesame Street* and a control group that received no such encouragement. However, the program proved so popular that the control children ended up watching nearly as often as the experimental group. As a result, the sample was divided into quartiles (a quartile equals 25% of the viewers) on the basis of the frequency of viewing. Children in Q_1 rarely watched *Sesame Street;* those in Q_2 watched two or three times a week; Q_3 watched about four or five times a week; and Q_4 watched more than five times a week.

When the data were analyzed, it was clear that *Sesame Street* was achieving its objectives. In Figure 16-3, we see that the children who watched

> **Children's Television Workshop (CTW):** *an organization committed to producing TV programs that hold children's interest and facilitate their social and intellectual development.*

Sesame Street the most (Q_3 and Q_4) were the ones who showed the biggest improvements in their total test scores (panel A), their scores on the alphabet test (panel B), and their ability to write their names (panel C). The 3-year-olds posted bigger gains than the 5-year-olds, probably because the younger children knew less to begin with.

During the second year a new sample of urban disadvantaged youngsters was selected from cities where *Sesame Street* had not been available during the first year. The investigators also followed up on 283 of the disadvantaged children from the original sample, many of whom were now in kindergarten or the first grade. The results of the second-year evaluation paralleled those of the original study—children who often watched *Sesame Street* posted larger cognitive gains than those who watched infrequently (Bogatz & Ball, 1972). In addition, the heavy viewers from the original sample were rated by their teachers as better prepared for school and more interested in school activities than their classmates who rarely watched the program.

■ *The Electric Company*

In 1970 CTW consulted with reading specialists to create *The Electric Company,* a TV series designed to teach reading skills to young elementary school children. The programming was heavily animated, and well-known personalities such as Bill Cosby often appeared to interest children in the content. The curriculum attempted to teach children the correspondence between letters (or letter combinations) and sounds—knowledge that should help them to decode words. Reading for meaning and syntax were also taught (Liebert et al., 1982).

The success of *Electric Company* was evaluated by administering a battery of reading tests to first-through fourth-grade children. Although home viewing had little or no effect on children's reading skills, those who watched *Electric Company* at school attained significantly higher scores on the reading battery than nonviewers (Ball & Bogatz, 1973). In other words, *Electric Company* was achieving many of its objectives when children watched the program with an adult, in this case the teacher, who could help them to apply what they had learned. *The Electric Company* is now used in many elementary schools in the United

States, and in some ways the program is quite a bargain: while a typical Saturday morning children's show costs about $70,000 to produce, an average episode of *Electric Company* costs only about $32,000 (Liebert et al., 1982).

■ *Other educational programs*

In recent years, CTW and other noncommercial producers have created children's programs designed to teach subjects such as math (*Infinity Factory*), logical reasoning (*Think About*), science (*3-2-1 Contact*), and social studies (*Big Blue Marble*), to name a few. Most of these offerings have been quite popular in the areas where they are broadcast, although it remains to be seen whether they are achieving their stated objectives.

■ *Limitations of educational programming*

One criticism of educational television is that it is essentially a one-way medium in which the pupil is a passive recipient rather than an active processor of information. Indeed, we've seen that programs such as *The Electric Company* are unlikely to achieve their stated objectives unless children watch with an adult who then encourages them to apply what they have learned. Perhaps John Wright and Aletha Huston (1983) are correct in arguing that television will soon be a much more powerful teaching device as it becomes computer-integrated and interactive, thereby allowing the viewer to be more actively involved in the learning process.

Even the highly successful educational programs are not without their critics. Some have argued that the fast-paced *Sesame Street* will shorten the attention spans of frequent viewers and make the classroom seem a boring place. Yet the evidence available to date suggests that habitual consumers of *Sesame Street* are actually rated by their teachers as better adjusted to the school environment than their classmates who rarely watch the show (Bogatz & Ball, 1972).

Although *Sesame Street* was primarily targeted at disadvantaged preschoolers in an attempt to narrow the intellectual gap between these youngsters and their advantaged peers, it seems that children from advantaged backgrounds are the ones who are more likely to watch the program. As a result, *Sesame Street* may actually end up *widening* the intellectual and academic gaps between advantaged and disadvantaged youth (Cook et al., 1975). Yet it seems fruitless to blame the program itself, for disadvantaged youngsters who watch it regularly learn just as much as their more advantaged classmates (Bogatz & Ball, 1972). In other words, *Sesame Street* is *potentially* a valuable resource for all preschool children. The formidable task lies ahead—that being to convince parents that episodes of *Sesame Street* (and other educational programs) are indeed rewarding and valuable experiences, ones that their children should not be missing.

Should Television Be Used to Socialize Children?

Although television is often criticized as a harbinger of violence or an "idiot box" that undermines the intellectual curiosity of our young, we have seen that the medium can have many positive effects on children's social, emotional, and intellectual development. Should we now work at harnessing television's potential—at using this "early window" as a means of socializing our children? Many developmentalists think so, although not everyone agrees, as we see in the following newspaper account of a conference on behavioral control through the media. To set the stage, the conference participants were reacting to the work of Dr. Robert M. Liebert, a psychologist who had produced some 30-second TV spots to teach children cooperative solutions to conflicts. Here is part of the account that appeared in the *New York Times*:

> The outburst that followed Liebert's presentation flashed around the conference table. Did he believe that he had a right to . . . deliberately impose values on children? Should children . . . be taught cooperation? Did ghetto kids perhaps need to be taught to slug it out in order to survive in this society? Was it not . . . immoral to create a TV advertisement . . . to influence kids' behavior? Liebert was accused of . . . manipulation and even brainwashing. One would have thought he had proposed setting up Hitler Youth Camps on Sesame Street. . . .
>
> However, I understand why the hackles had gone up around the . . . table. I am one of those

people who is terrified of manipulation. A Skinnerian world filled with conditioned people scares the daylights out of me—even if those people do hate war and . . . love their fellow man. [Behavior control through technology may come] . . . at the cost of our freedom [Rivers, 1974, as cited in Liebert et al., 1982, pp. 210–211].

The concern of those conference participants is perhaps understandable, for television is often used as a means of political indoctrination in many countries. And is the use of television for socialization not a subtle form of brainwashing? Perhaps it is. However, one could argue that television in this country is already serving as a potent agent of socialization and that much of what children see in the media helps to create attitudes and to instigate actions that the majority of us may not condone. Perhaps the question we should be asking is "Can we somehow alter television to make it a more effective agent of socialization—one that teaches attitudes, values, and behaviors that more accurately reflect the mores of a free society?" Surely we can, although it remains to be seen whether we will.

THE SCHOOL AS A SOCIALIZATION AGENT

Of all the formal institutions that children encounter in their lives away from home, few have as much of an opportunity to influence their behavior as the schools they attend. Starting at age 6, the typical child in the United States spends about five hours of each weekday at school. And children are staying there longer than ever before. In 1870 there were only 200 public high schools in the United States, and only half of all American children were attending during the three to five months that school was in session. Today the school term is about nine months long (180 school days); more than 75% of American youth are still attending high school at age 17; and nearly 50% of U.S. high school graduates enroll in some form of higher education. Yet these figures are somewhat unusual, even in the Western world. Only 29% of all Australians, 47% of Belgians, and 9% of West Germans complete their final year of high school (Copperman, 1978).

If asked to characterize the mission of the schools, we are likely to think of them as the place where children acquire basic knowledge and academic skills: reading, writing, arithmetic, and, later, computer skills, foreign languages, social studies, higher math, and science. But schools seem to have an **informal curriculum** as well. Children are expected to obey rules, to cooperate with their classmates, to respect authority, to learn about the American way of life, and to become upstanding citizens. Today we see the schools providing information and moral guidance in an attempt to combat social problems such as racism, teenage sex, and drug abuse. Although many social critics believe that educators should stick to academics and leave other forms of socialization to the church and family, it is interesting to note that the push for compulsory education in the United States arose from the need to "Americanize" an immigrant population—to teach them the values and principles on which this country was founded so that they could be assimilated into the mainstream of American society and become productive citizens. Ironically, the need to train a highly uneducated work force was of only secondary importance, for most people earned a living from unskilled labor or farming—occupations that required little or no formal schooling (Boocock, 1976; Rudolph, 1965).

So it is proper to think of the school as a socializing agent—one that is likely to affect children's social and emotional development as well as imparting knowledge and helping to prepare them for a job and economic self-sufficiency.

In this section of the chapter, we will take a closer look at the ways in which schools influence children. First, we will consider whether formal classroom experiences are likely to promote children's intellectual development. Then we will see that schools clearly differ in "effectiveness"—that is, the ability to accomplish both curricular goals and noncurricular objectives that contribute to what educators often call "good citizenship." After reviewing the characteristics of effective and less effective schools, we will examine some of the ways in which teachers influence the social behavior and academic progress of their pupils. Finally, we will discuss a few of the problems that disadvantaged youth may encounter as they enter the middle-class environment of the schools.

Does Schooling Promote Cognitive Development?

Perhaps the most basic question we might ask is "Does school have any measurable effects on a child's cognitive development?" In one sense, the answer has to be yes, for students will acquire a vast amount of knowledge about their world from the classes they attend. Indeed, it is very likely that if you have completed the first two years of college, you already know far more biology, chemistry, or physics than many of the brightest college professors of only 100 years ago.

But when developmentalists ask "Do schools make a difference?," they want to know whether formal instruction hastens intellectual development or encourages modes of thinking and methods of problem solving that are less likely to develop in the absence of schooling. This question is difficult to answer in modern industrialized societies where schooling is widely available and all children are required by law to receive some kind of formal instruction. Accordingly, the strategy that researchers have followed is to study the intellectual growth of children from developing countries where schooling is not yet available throughout the society. If children who attend school demonstrate higher-order cognitive skills than their age mates from similar backgrounds who receive no formal instruction, then the investigator can conclude that schooling facilitates intellectual development.

Studies of this type generally find that children who attend school are quicker to reach a number of Piagetian milestones (for example, conservation) and will perform better on tests of memory and categorization skills than those from similar backgrounds who do not go to school (Bruner, Olver, & Greenfield, 1966; Rogoff, 1981; Sharp, Cole, & Lave, 1979; Stevenson, Parker, Wilkinson, Bonnevaux, & Gonzalez, 1978). Yet it is important to note that the differences between educated and uneducated subjects are likely to be small on tasks that do not depend on the use of cognitive processes that are acquired in school. In Figure 16-4, for example, we see that people with lower levels of education make fewer errors and perform more like educated subjects when trying to learn "related" paired associates (for example, *hoe–machete; bull–sheep*) that require little if any cognitive strategizing. But when trying to learn "unrelated" paired associates (for example, *hoe–sheep; bull–machete*) that may require the use of a strategy such as **elaboration** in order to do well, educated subjects clearly outperform those with less education.

So we see that schooling does seem to promote cognitive development, although no one can say for sure exactly why this is so. Michael Cole (1978) has argued that schooling teaches children general rules or strategies that they can apply to many kinds of information. In so doing, they will make important discoveries and "learn how to learn." Donald Sharp and his associates (Sharp et al., 1979) add that "it's what you do with what you have that counts" after noting that their highly educated subjects were more likely to use intellectual strategies such as rehearsal or elaboration "which are not rigidly predetermined by the structure of the task and which promote efficient performance" (p. 77). However, it's possible that some of the differences between educated and uneducated subjects may stem from the fact that people who have been to school are more experienced at taking tests and perhaps more comfortable (less anxious) about being evaluated (Rogoff,

1981). Clearly, there is a need for additional research to determine exactly how, why, and under what circumstances formal education is likely to promote children's intellectual growth and development.

Determinants of Effective and Ineffective Schooling

One of the first questions that parents often ask when searching for a residence in a new town is "What are the schools like here?" or "Where should we live so that our children will get the best education?" These concerns reflect the common belief that some schools are "better" or "more effective" than others. But are they?

Michael Rutter (1983) is one theorist who thinks so. According to Rutter, **effective schools** are those that promote academic achievement, social skills, polite and attentive behavior, positive attitudes toward learning, low absenteeism, continuation of education beyond the age at which attendance is mandatory, and acquisition of skills that will enable students to find and hold a job. Rutter argues that some schools are more successful than others at accomplishing these objectives, regardless of the students' racial, ethnic, or socioeconomic backgrounds. Let's examine some of the evidence for this claim.

In one study, Rutter and his associates (Rutter, Maughan, Mortimore, Ouston, & Smith, 1979) conducted extensive interviews and observations in 12 secondary schools serving lower- to lower-middle-class populations in London, England. As

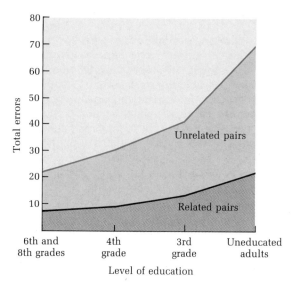

FIGURE 16-4. Average number of errors made by subjects of four educational levels as they attempted to learn lists of related or unrelated paired associates.

---

informal curriculum: *noncurricular objectives of schooling such as teaching children to cooperate, to respect authority, to obey rules, and to become good citizens.*

elaboration: *a strategy for remembering that involves adding something to (or creating meaningful links between) the bits of information that one is trying to remember.*

effective schools: *schools that are generally successful at achieving curricular and noncurricular objectives, regardless of the racial, ethnic, or socioeconomic backgrounds of the student population.*

the children entered these schools, they were given a battery of achievement tests to measure their prior academic accomplishments. At the end of the secondary school experience, the pupils took another major exam to assess their academic progress. Other information such as attendance records and teacher ratings of classroom behavior was also available. When the data were analyzed, Rutter et al. found that the 12 schools clearly differed in "effectiveness": students from the "better" schools exhibited fewer problem behaviors, attended school more regularly, and made more academic progress than students from the less effective schools. We get some idea of the importance of these "schooling effects" from Figure 16-5. The "bands" on the graph refer to the pupils' academic accomplishments *at the time they entered* the secondary schools (band 3, low achievers; band 1, high achievers). In all three bands,

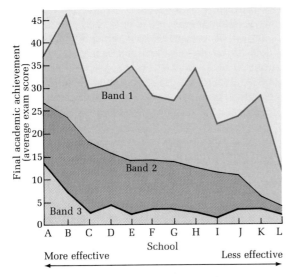

FIGURE 16-5. *Average level of academic achievement in secondary school as a function of initial achievement at the time of entry (bands 1–3) and the school that pupils were attending (schools A–L). Note that pupils in all three bands performed at higher levels on this final academic assessment if they attended the more effective schools. Moreover, students in band 2 performed like band 1 students in the more effective schools but like band 3 students in the least effective schools.*

students attending the "more effective" schools outperformed those in the "less effective" schools on the final assessment of academic achievement. Even more revealing is the finding that the initially poor students (band 3) who attended the "better" schools ended up scoring just as high on this final index of academic progress as the initially good (band 1) students who attended the least effective schools. Similar findings were also obtained in a large study of elementary schools in the United States. Even after controlling for potentially important variables such as the racial composition and socioeconomic backgrounds of the student bodies and the type of communities served, some elementary schools were found to be much more "effective" than others (Brookover, Beady, Flood, Schweitzer, & Wisenbaker, 1979; see also Rutter, 1983).

So the school that children attend can make a difference. And although the evidence is sketchy at this point, we are beginning to understand why some schools are able to accomplish many of their objectives while others are not. In the pages that follow, we will first consider some of the variables that are thought to contribute to an effective school environment and then try to determine how individual teachers might influence their students.

■ *Monetary resources and the physical plant*

Surprising as it may seem, factors such as the amount of money spent per pupil, the number of books in the school library, teachers' salaries, and teachers' academic credentials play only a minor role in determining student outcomes (Rutter, 1983). In two studies of secondary schools in England, the investigators found that neither the age nor the physical appearance of the school buildings predicted children's conduct or their academic accomplishments (Reynolds, Jones, St. Leger, & Murgatroyd, 1980; Rutter et al., 1979). Similar studies in the United States indicate that the level of "personnel support" (that is, teacher credentials and salaries) is positively related to student achievement only in the predominantly Black, inner-city schools where resources in some school districts are marginal at best (Brookover et al., 1979). The latter finding implies that there is some basic minimum level of support that is required for effective schooling. However, Rutter (1983) concludes:

Within the general range of resources usually available to schools, the precise level [of support] seems to be of limited importance with respect to pupil outcomes. We may conclude that an increase in resources is not likely to be an effective means of improving standards. Of course, the way resources are employed may well be important [p. 15].

■ *School and class size*

Is the size of the school that children attend in any way important? It may well be. Roger Barker and Paul Gump (1964) tried to determine whether students from small high schools are more likely than those in larger schools to participate in extracurricular activities. Schools ranging from fewer than 100 to more than 2000 students participated in the study. Although the larger schools offered more extracurricular activities to their students, it was the pupils in the smaller schools who were more heavily involved in these activities. Moreover, students in the smaller schools were more likely than those in larger schools to say that they enjoyed the challenge of working in and actually contributing to their extracurricular groups. Finally, there were few "isolates" in the small schools, where almost everyone was encouraged to join in one or more activities. In contrast, the marginal student in larger schools felt few pressures to participate and could easily get lost in the crowd. To the extent that a sense of belonging is an important aspect of schooling, these findings suggest that there may be some advantages to attending smaller schools.

Does the size of one's school have any effects on academic achievement? Those who have studied this issue focus on *average class size* rather than the size of the institution, and the results of their research are not always consistent. One recent review of the literature concluded that, in classes ranging from 20 to 40 students, class size has little if any effect on academic achievement (Rutter, 1983). However, there are some exceptions to this very general rule. It appears that smaller classes are advantageous to students in the primary grades who are just learning to read and to perform arithmetic operations (Educational Research Service, 1978). Smaller classes also seem to aid the academic progress of economically disadvantaged students and those who are handicapped.

These findings may have important policy implications. Clearly, an across-the-board decrease in class size—say, from 35 to 24 students—is unlikely to have any major effects on academic standards. So if a school district were to have the money to hire additional instructors, the wisest course might be to devote these "personnel resources" to the primary grades, to remedial instruction, or to classes for the handicapped—precisely the settings in which smaller classes will have a beneficial effect on children's academic achievement (Rutter, 1983).

■ *Organizational structure of the school and the classroom*

Ability tracking.   If you attended high school within the past 20 years, you may well have experienced **ability tracking**—a procedure in which students are placed in categories based on IQ scores or academic achievement and then taught in classes with pupils of comparable academic or intellectual standing. The pros and cons of this practice have been debated for years. Some theorists argue that students learn best when surrounded by peers of comparable ability. Others believe that ability tracking undermines the self-esteem of low-ability students and actually contributes to their poor academic achievement and high dropout rate.

In his recent review of the literature, Rutter (1983) found that neither ability tracking nor mixed-ability teaching has decisive advantages: both procedures are common in highly effective and less effective schools. A closer inspection of the data suggested that mixed-ability instruction may be advantageous with younger children and that ability tracking makes more sense in secondary schools, where it is difficult to teach advanced subjects to students who vary considerably in their background knowledge. However, ability tracking is occasionally found to have negative effects on the self-esteem and academic

---

ability tracking: *the practice of placing students in categories on the basis of IQ or academic achievement and then educating them in classes with pupils of comparable academic or intellectual ability.*

BOX 16-1
EDUCATING THE HANDICAPPED—IS
"MAINSTREAMING" THE ANSWER?

Public Law 94-142 is a significant piece of legislation. It requires public schools in the United States to provide an education roughly equivalent to that received by normal children to all handicapped youth—regardless of whether they are blind, deaf, mentally retarded, or experiencing neurological and motor impairments. The law also specifies that, wherever possible, the educational setting for handicapped children should be the same as that provided for the nonhandicapped. Not surprisingly, many school districts caught in the squeeze between the federal mandate and local budget cutbacks interpreted the provision for equal education to mean that handicapped children should be integrated into the regular classroom—a practice known as *mainstreaming* (Zigler & Muenchow, 1979).

Mainstreaming has its advocates. One argument often cited in its defense is that handicapped youngsters (particularly the mentally retarded) are likely to learn from the interactions with classmates who are brighter than they are. Supporters of mainstreaming also believe that placement in special classes could prevent handicapped children from developing social skills and cause them to be stigmatized as those "weirdniks" or "retardos" down the hall. However, the skeptics argue that handicapped youngsters who are "mainstreamed" will suffer a serious loss of self-esteem (not to mention an undermining of their achievement motivation) should they fail to keep pace with their nonhandicapped classmates and make poor grades. Indeed, these failure experiences may lead to even more stigmatizing of the handicapped than occurs when handicapped children are educated away from the mainstream in special classes.

How do handicapped children fare when placed in regular classrooms? The data on academic progress are inconclusive; some investigators find that mainstreamed children perform no better or worse than handicapped youngsters in special classes, while others report that mainstreaming leads to somewhat higher levels of academic achievement (Zigler & Muenchow, 1979). In contrast, the social adjustment of handicapped children may be better when they are educated in special classrooms away from their nonhandicapped peers. Few nonhandicapped children choose the handicapped as friends or playmates, and it seems that normal children are more likely to reject or ridicule the handicapped when they have had extensive contact with these youngsters in a regular classroom (Gottlieb, 1978; Karnes & Lee, 1979; Zigler & Muenchow, 1979). Yet there is some evidence that the social consequences of mainstreaming may be more positive at the high school level, for at least one investigator found that secondary students who were exposed to the educable mentally retarded in their classes viewed these handicapped classmates more favorably than did nonhandicapped students who had not been exposed (Shere, as cited in Zigler & Muenchow, 1979).

Perhaps the major limitation of mainstreaming programs is that most classroom instructors are not adequately prepared to meet the needs of special students who may by placed in their care. Zigler and Muenchow (1979) are undoubtedly correct in arguing that "without adequate support personnel to assist regular-class teachers with the education of handicapped students, mainstreaming is doomed to fail" (p. 994). Since these conditions are rarely met, it is really too early to know whether mainstreaming can be a more effective educational policy than the practice of teaching the handicapped in special classes. Zigler and Muenchow (1979) suggest that

> mainstreaming can have ... positive effects on handicapped children, but this policy will be an empty slogan ... if not accompanied by adequate teacher training and support services. ... Moreover much more work is needed to determine not only which children, with which handicaps, can benefit from mainstreaming, but also what the environmental nutrients are that promote [their] development [p. 995].

achievement of low-ability students. After reviewing the tracking systems of effective and ineffective schools, Rutter (1983) concluded that effective ability tracking—

1. Categorizes students on the basis of their *tested abilities* in *particular subjects* rather than using an across-the-board assignment based on teachers' ratings or IQ scores.

2. Ensures that students in *all* ability groups have some exposure to the more experienced, popular, or "effective" teachers rather than simply assigning the best teachers to the high-ability groups.

3. Takes steps to integrate the bottom-track students into the nonacademic aspects of schooling such as music, sports, and extracurricular activities. By taking part in these activities and

occasionally being picked for positions of responsibility, bottom-track students are less likely to be stigmatized in a negative way or to suffer a loss of self-esteem.

In 1975 the United States Congress passed the Education for All Handicapped Children Act (P. L. 94-142), a law that guarantees a "free public education" in the "least restrictive environment" to all *handicapped* children between the ages of 3 and 18. Here was one act of Congress that proved to be a bombshell to many school administrators. How were they to cope with the need to educate handicapped children, many of whom had never attended public schools? The costs alone seemed insurmountable, particularly in the 1970s, when budget cutbacks were the rule of the day. In Box 16-1 we take a closer look at the implications of Public Law 94-142 for both the schools and the handicapped children whom it was designed to serve.

Open versus traditional classrooms.   Although it may be difficult to remember your elementary school days, chances are you were educated in **traditional classrooms** where the seats were arranged in neat rows facing the teacher, who lectured and gave demonstrations at a desk or a blackboard. In a traditional classroom, the curriculum is highly structured. Normally, everybody will be studying the same subject at a given moment, and students are expected to interact with the teacher rather than with one another. One interesting aspect of this classroom arrangement is that teachers end up interacting with some students more than others. As we see in Figure 16-6, children who sit in the front and/or the center of the class are more likely to catch the teacher's eye and participate in classroom discussions than their classmates who sit outside this **"zone of activity"** (Adams & Biddle, 1970).

In recent years, many American classrooms have become much less formal or structured. "Open" education is a philosophy based on the premise that children are curious explorers who will achieve more by becoming actively involved in the learning process rather than simply listening to a teacher recite facts, figures, and principles. In an **open classroom**, all the children are rarely doing the same thing at once. A more typical scenario is for students to distribute them-

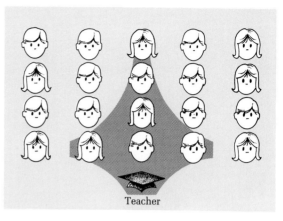

Teacher

FIGURE 16-6. *In a traditional classroom, the students in the shaded area are more likely to capture the teacher's attention and to participate in classroom activities than their classmates who sit outside this "zone of activity."*

selves around the room working individually or in small groups. For example,

> Two youngsters may be stretched out on a rug reading library books. The teacher is at the math table, showing four children how to use scales to learn about weights. Two children in the writing corner play a word game. Another takes notes about the nursing behavior of the class guinea pig. A sense of purpose pervades the room [Papalia & Olds, 1979, p. 401].

Is the open classroom more effective than the highly structured setting? This question is difficult to answer because students who attend open nursery and elementary schools often come from

---

traditional classroom: *a classroom arrangement in which all pupils sit facing an instructor, who normally teaches one subject at a time by lecturing or giving demonstrations.*

classroom "zone of activity": *areas in the front and center of a traditional classroom where students are more likely to attract the teacher's attention and participate in class discussions.*

open classroom: *a less structured classroom arrangement in which there are separate areas for each educational activity and children distribute themselves around the room, working individually or in small groups.*

PHOTO 16-4. Students at work in an open classroom.

different (usually more affluent) backgrounds than those who receive traditional instruction. It does appear that many students prefer the open classroom and that this arrangement may be more effective in helping young elementary school children to develop novel ideas and concepts (Rutter, 1983; Thomas & Berk, 1981). Moreover, one recent study found that boys who had attended relatively unstructured nursery schools at age 4 were later performing at higher levels in reading and math during the sixth, seventh, and eighth grades than their classmates who had attended structured preschool programs (Miller & Bizzell, 1983). This finding is particularly intriguing, for the children who participated in the research had been randomly assigned to the structured or the unstructured nursery schools, and the two groups did not initially differ in either intelligence or socioeconomic background.

However, open education is hardly the answer for all instructional problems. Many investigators find no differences in the performance (or the conduct) of students in open and traditional classrooms; others have concluded that students will actually learn more in a structured classroom whenever the subject matter requires teachers to illustrate very difficult concepts or transmit a lot of factual information (Good, 1979; Good, Biddle, & Brophy, 1975; Rutter, 1983). Finally, a particular instructional format will not affect all children in the same way. Students who are restless, distractible, and low in achievement motivation seem to do better in a highly structured setting, while those who are less fidgety and more achievement-oriented may do rather well in an open classroom (Grimes & Allinsmith, 1961; Peterson, 1977). Michael Rutter (1983) is probably correct in arguing that "the debates on whether 'open classrooms' are better than traditional approaches . . . or whether 'formal' methods are preferable to 'informal' methods . . . are probably misplaced. Neither system has an overall superiority, but both include elements of good practice" (p. 21).

In sum, the findings suggest that some schools might be more successful at motivating students and accomplishing instructional goals by (1) providing more unstructured learning experiences to stimulate curiosity and active involvement while (2) retaining an element of formal structure and guidance that many students (and some academic subjects) seem to require.

■ *Composition of the student body*

To some extent, the "effectiveness" of a school reflects the composition of the student body. On the average, academic achievement is lowest in schools with a preponderance of economically disadvantaged students (Brookover et al., 1979; Rutter et al., 1979), and it appears that *any* child is likely to make more academic progress if taught in a school with a relatively high concentration of intellectually capable peers (Rutter, 1983).

Do these findings imply that the quality of schooling that children receive makes little if any difference and that the "effectiveness" of a school depends mainly on the clientele that it is educating? *No, they do not!* As it turns out, many schools that draw heavily from disadvantaged minority populations are highly effective at motivating students and preparing them for jobs or higher education (Rutter, 1983). Moreover, school desegregation in the United States has often led to increases in academic achievement for minority students without undermining the progress of the "advantaged" pupils in these integrated settings (Stephan, 1978; St. John, 1975). So the quality of schooling and the composition of the student body do make a difference—particularly to students from a socially disadvantaged background. We will have more to say about this issue later when we discuss the impact of school desegregation on minority students in the United States.

■ *Other contributors to an "effective" school environment*

In his review of the literature, Rutter (1983) lists several additional values and practices that seem to characterize "effective" schools. For example:

1. *Academic emphasis.* Effective schools have a clear focus on academic goals. Children are regularly assigned homework, which is checked, corrected, and discussed with them. Teachers expect a lot of their students and devote a high proportion of their time to active teaching and planning lessons so that their expectations can be met. Instructors often plan their curriculum in groups and then monitor one another to ensure that they are doing what they can to achieve their objectives.

2. *Classroom management.* In effective schools, teachers spend little time setting up equipment, handing out papers, and dealing with disciplinary problems. Lessons begin and end on time. Pupils are told exactly what is expected of them and receive clear and unambiguous feedback about their academic performance. The classroom atmosphere is comfortable; all students are actively encouraged to work to the best of their abilities, and ample praise is given to acknowledge good work.

3. *Discipline.* In effective schools, the staff is firm in enforcing rules and does so on the spot rather than sending offenders off to the principal's office. Rarely do instructors resort to physical punishment. In fact, several studies suggest that corporal punishment and unofficial physical sanctions (slapping, cuffing) contribute to truancy, disobedient behavior, delinquency, and the establishment of a tense, negative atmosphere that is hardly conducive to effective learning.

4. *Staff organization and teacher morale.* Student conduct and academic achievement are better in schools where both the curriculum and approaches to discipline are agreed on by the staff working together as a team. Although it may be necessary for administrators to make decisions that individual instructors don't like, pupil outcomes are best in schools where all teachers feel that their points of view are taken seriously, even if they are not adopted.

In sum, we see that effective schools are those in which staff members work together to achieve well-defined educational objectives based on what children want and need to know. Teachers are encouraged to offer helpful guidance and to refrain from commanding, ridiculing, or punishing their pupils. The emphasis in effective schools is on successes rather than failures, and ample praise and recognition are given to students for a job well done. In other words, the effective school environment is a comfortable but business-like setting in which students are *motivated* to learn. After reviewing the literature, Michael Rutter (1983) concluded that the task of motivating students was of critical importance, for "in the long run, good pupil outcomes were [nearly always] dependent on pupils *wanting* to participate in the educational process" (p. 23).

And whose job is it to motivate students? Traditionally we have assigned this responsibility to the classroom instructor.

The Teacher's Influence

Once they reach school age, many children spend nearly as much time around their teachers as they do around their parents or guardians. Indeed, teachers are often the first adults outside the immediate family to play a major role in a child's life, and children's reactions to school usually depend on how well they like their teachers. Generally speaking, children like instructors who are kind, patient, fair, and interested in them as persons; they dislike teachers who ridicule, scold, or punish them, as well as those who are rigid or ill-tempered or who assign too much homework (Jersild, 1968).

Of course, teachers are only human, and they too will form definite impressions of their pupils. One impression that can make a difference is the teacher's evaluation of a student's academic capabilities.

■ Teacher expectancies and children's achievements: The Pygmalion effect

Several years ago, Robert Rosenthal and Lenore Jacobson (1968) conducted an interesting experiment to measure the effects of teacher expectancies on children's intellectual and academic progress. Students in grades 1 through 6 took a nonverbal IQ test. Teachers were led to believe that this test predicted which students would show sudden bursts of intellectual growth during the academic year. Each teacher was given the names of five students who might very well prove to be "rapid bloomers." In fact, the so-called rapid bloomers had been randomly selected from the class rosters. The only way that they differed from the other children was that their teachers expected more of them. Yet, when the students were retested eight months later, Rosenthal and Jacobson found that, among the first- and second-graders, *the so-called rapid bloomers showed significantly greater gains in IQ and reading achievement than other students in the class*. In other words, the children who were expected to do well did, in fact, do better than other students of comparable ability.

Since the publication of this study, several other investigators have reported similar findings (Beez, 1968; Seaver, 1973), so that the "teacher expectancy" effect appears to be real. Somehow teachers must be communicating their expec-

tancies to students, thereby improving the self-concepts (and the will to achieve) of the "rapid bloomers" while making other students feel that they are not especially bright or expected to do well. The implication is that students are becoming the objects of their teachers' self-fulfilling prophecies in what Rosenthal and Jacobson call the **Pygmalion effect**.

Jere Brophy and Thomas Good (1970) observed student/teacher interactions in four first-grade classrooms in an attempt to identify the processes that underlie the Pygmalion effect. They found that students who were expected to do well were treated very differently from those who were expected to do poorly. For example, teachers demanded better performance from the "high expectancy" students and were more likely to praise these children for answering questions correctly. In contrast, "low expectancy" students were more likely to receive criticism from the teacher when they answered questions incorrectly (for example, "That's a stupid answer"). On those occasions when high-expectancy students did answer incorrectly, the teacher often responded by rephrasing the question, thus giving these children another opportunity to succeed. Clearly, there is nothing magical about the Pygmalion effect. Brophy and Good argue that "teachers do, in fact, communicate different performance expectations to different children through their classroom behavior, and the nature of this differential treatment is such as to encourage the children to begin to respond in ways which would confirm teacher expectancies" (p. 373).

How do teachers derive these impressions of their students? Probably from the students' prior academic backgrounds, achievement test scores, and performance during the first few weeks of a school year. In addition, many teachers get some idea of what they can expect from a student from their experiences with the student's older brothers and sisters. When a teacher has taught a child's older siblings, the child's performance in the classroom depends, in part, on how the older siblings performed (Seaver, 1973). If the older sibs were good students, the younger sib ends up achieving more than students of comparable ability whose older siblings were taught by a different instructor. However, if the older sibs were poor students, then the younger sib achieves less than students of comparable ability whose older sibs were taught by a different instructor. So the Pygmalion effect works both ways: teacher expectancies may either facilitate or inhibit a child's academic growth, depending on the direction of these expectancies.

But let's not be too critical of teachers for forming opinions of their students. All of us form impressions of the people in our lives, and these impressions often affect their behavior for better or worse. However, teachers probably should be made aware of the impact that their expectancies may have on their students. Perhaps the clever instructor can use this knowledge to "get the most out of" nearly every child in the class by setting educational objectives that the child can realistically achieve, communicating these *positive* expectancies to the child, and then praising the child whenever he or she reaches one or more of these academic milestones.

■ Teaching styles and instructional techniques

Earlier we saw that teachers in "effective" schools will typically set clear-cut standards for their students to achieve, emphasize successes more than failures, firmly enforce rules without derogating an offender or becoming overly punitive, and use praise rather than threats to encourage each child to work to the best of his or her ability. Perhaps you have noticed that these managerial characteristics are in some ways similar to the pattern of control that Diana Baumrind calls authoritative parenting. Indeed, Baumrind (1972) believes that the three major patterns of control that characterize parent/child interactions are also found in the classroom. Teachers who use an **authoritarian** style tend to dominate their pupils, relying on power-assertive methods to enforce their demands. The **authoritative** teacher is also controlling but will rely on reason to explain his or her demands, encourage verbal give and take, and value autonomy and creative expression so long as the child is willing to live within the rules that the teacher has established. Finally, the **laissez-faire** (or permissive) instructor makes few demands of students and provides little or no active guidance. Baumrind believes that teachers who use an authoritative style will contribute in a positive way to children's intellectual curiosity, their academic achievement, and their social and emotional development.

A classic study by Kurt Lewin and his associates (Lewin, Lippitt, & White, 1939) is certainly relevant. The subjects were 11-year-old boys who met in groups after school to partake in hobby activities (such as making papier-mâché theater masks). Each group was led by an adult who behaved in one of three ways. The *authoritarian* leaders assigned jobs and work partners to each boy, dictated policy, frequently criticized the boys' work, remained somewhat aloof, and gave little or no explanation of the reasons for their policies. In contrast, *democratic* leaders talked about long-range goals, allowed the boys to participate in policy making, permitted them to select their own work partners, evaluated them honestly, and remained open and receptive to all questions. (The "democratic" leadership in this study represents a pattern of control roughly equivalent to what Baumrind calls the authoritative style.) Finally, *laissez-faire* leaders gave their groups free rein—they provided the necessary equipment and would answer questions if any were asked, but they remained noncommittal for the most part.

Lewin et al. found that boys responded very differently to these three supervisory styles. Authoritarian leadership produced tension, restlessness, aggressive outbursts, damage to play mate-

---

Pygmalion effect: *the tendency of students to perform better in the classroom when their teachers expect them to do well and to perform worse than they ordinarily would when the teacher expects them to do poorly (also called the teacher-expectancy effect).*

authoritarian instruction: *a restrictive style of instruction in which the teacher makes absolute demands and uses threats or force (if necessary) to ensure that students comply.*

authoritative instruction: *a controlling style of instruction in which the teacher makes many demands but also allows some autonomy and individual expression as long as students are staying within the guidelines that the teacher has set.*

laissez-faire instruction: *a permissive style of instruction in which the teacher makes few demands of students and provides little or no active guidance.*

rials, and a general dissatisfaction with the group experience. Productivity (as indexed by the number of theater masks the groups constructed) was high under authoritarian leadership while the leader was present. But when the leader left the room, work patterns disintegrated. Democratic leadership was more effective; the boys were much less hostile and generally happier with the leader and their group. Although the boys did not produce as many masks under democratic leadership, they continued to work when the leader left the room. Moreover, the work they did complete was of higher quality than that produced under authoritarian or laissez-faire leaders. Finally, the laissez-faire approach generally resulted in an apathetic group atmosphere and very low productivity. All but 1 of the 20 boys in this experiment clearly favored democratic supervision.

These findings also seem to hold in the school setting. Students prefer a democratic atmosphere in the classroom (Rosenthal, Underwood, & Martin, 1969), and it appears that a flexible, non-dictatorial instructional style is conducive to academic achievement (Brookover et al., 1979; Prather, 1969). But a word of caution is in order, for the instructional techniques that a teacher uses will not affect all children in the same way. For example, Brophy (1979) notes that teachers get the most out of high-ability students by moving at a quick pace and requiring high standards of performance. In other words, brighter students perform best when they are challenged. In contrast, low-ability and disadvantaged children respond much more favorably to slow-paced instruction from a teacher who is warm and encouraging rather than intrusive and demanding.

In sum, authoritative instruction does seem to contribute in a positive way to academic achievement. Yet there are many ways that authoritative instructors might attempt to motivate their pupils, and the techniques that work best will depend, in part, on the type of student they are trying to reach.

The School as a Middle-Class Institution: Effects on Disadvantaged Youth

Public schools in the United States are middle-class institutions largely staffed by middle-class instructors who preach middle-class values. Some theorists have argued that this particular emphasis places children from lower-class or minority subcultures at an immediate disadvantage. After all, these youngsters must adjust to an environment that may seem altogether foreign and somewhat foreboding to them—a problem with which middle-class students do not have to contend.

Many lower-class and minority students do have problems at school. They are more likely than middle-class youngsters to make poor marks, to be disciplined by the staff, to be "held back" in one or more grades, and to drop out before completing their high school education. Among the factors that are thought to contribute to these sociocultural differences in scholastic achievement are (1) the nature of the educational materials that schools provide their students, (2) the attitudes of parents about the importance of schooling, and (3) the tendency of teachers to respond differently to students from different social backgrounds.

■ Educational materials and academic achievement

The textbooks that children read are clearly centered on the lives and experiences of middle-class people. These characters live in suburban homes, work at white-collar jobs, ride in fancy cars, take airplane trips, go on picnics, give parties, and are never unhappy—experiences that may seem unimportant or irrelevant to many disadvantaged children. But does the use of "irrelevant" instructional materials have any effect on their will to achieve?

Maybe so. Spencer Kagan and Lawrence Zahn (1975) compared groups of Anglo-American and Mexican-American children on two measures of academic achievement: math and reading proficiency. Although Anglo students performed better than Mexican-Americans on both achievement tests, the cultural gap was much wider on the reading measure. Furthermore, the reading deficit of Mexican-American children was not attributable to differences between the groups in IQ or cognitive style, to teacher prejudices, or to the use of English in the classroom (almost all these children were third-generation Mexican-Americans who spoke only English). Kagan and Zahn believe that Mexican-American students may simply lack the motivation to master traditional reading materials that adequately represent the White culture but are largely irrelevant to their own experiences and values. According to this line of reasoning, the Mexican-American students showed much less deficiency in mathematics because math texts contain less culturally irrelevant information. If Kagan and Zahn are correct in their interpretation, then perhaps we should be using more "culturally relevant" educational materials in school systems heavily populated by underachieving ethnic minorities.

■ *Parents' attitudes and values*

In Chapter Fifteen we saw that many lower- and working-class parents encourage their children to "get by" in school, while middle- and upper-class parents are more likely to stress "doing well" and "getting ahead." Parents from the lower socioeconomic strata are generally less knowledgeable about the school system and less involved in school activities, and this lack of participation may convince their children that school is really not all that important. Yet when lower-class parents are interested and involved in school activities, their children do well in school (Brookover et al., 1979). So it appears that parental encouragement and involvement can make a big difference.

■ *Teachers' reactions to disadvantaged students*

In a book entitled *Dark Ghetto*, Kenneth Clark (1965) argues that the classroom represents a "clash of cultures" in which adults who have

PHOTO 16-5. Children are more likely to do well in school if their parents value education and are interested and involved in school activities.

adopted middle-class values fail to appreciate the difficulties faced by students from different subcultural and socioeconomic backgrounds. According to Clark, teachers in schools serving lower-income minority populations make nearly three times as many negative comments to their students than their colleagues in middle-income schools. Teachers often have lower expectancies for children from low-income families (Minuchin & Shapiro, 1983). Even before they have any academic information about their students, many instructors are already placing them into "ability groups" on the basis of their grooming, the quality of their clothing, and their use or misuse of standard English (Rist, 1970). In one study (Gottlieb, 1966), teachers were asked to select from a checklist those attributes that best described their lower-class pupils. Middle-class respondents consistently checked adjectives such as *lazy, fun-loving,* and *rebellious.* Clearly, these instructors did not expect much of their disadvantaged students—an attitude that undoubtedly contributes to social-class differences in achievement.

Ironically, disadvantaged children may be convinced that they are doing well if their teachers assign them passing marks and routinely promote them from grade to grade, regardless of their actual accomplishments (Plummer, 1982). Indeed, Katherine Fulkerson and her associates (Fulkerson, Furr, & Brown, 1983) report that the academic expectancies of minority students increase and become more unrealistic from the third to the ninth grade. Is it a wise practice to give **"social promotions"** to children whose accomplishments are clearly substandard? Probably not. In fact, it could be argued that this practice actually perpetuates social inequalities by denying these underachievers the opportunity to repeat a grade and thereby acquire critical academic skills that they will need to do well in the future. But how do children feel about repeating a grade? Does it really help? As we see in Box 16-2, grade retention is a controversial practice that could have either positive or negative effects on re-

social promotion: *the practice of promoting students to the next grade when their scholastic performance indicates that they should repeat their present grade.*

If children do not attain the "minimal competencies" necessary for success in the next grade, they are often required to repeat the work that they have failed to master. Advocates of grade retention argue that repeating a grade is a beneficial experience—one that provides the underachieving child an opportunity to mature both socially and intellectually and to acquire academic skills that are absolutely essential to perform well in the higher grades (Kerzner, 1982). Yet the critics have argued that retained children may often be stigmatized as "different" or even "stupid," an experience that could undermine their self-concepts, their academic expectancies, and their relations with teachers and peers.

For the most part, parents and teachers support grade retention because they believe that the positive aspects of this policy outweigh the negatives (Chase, 1968). Let's now consider the evidence to see whether there is any basis for this claim.

Grade retention and academic achievement. The primary purpose of retaining a child is to allow him or her to acquire important academic skills and thereby do better in school. Yet an examination of the evidence available before 1970 suggests that the policy of holding children back in school was not meeting these objectives. The majority of nonpromoted children performed no better while repeating a grade than they had the first time around. Moreover, children of comparable ability who had been promoted generally outscored retainees on standardized achievement tests (see Plummer, Hazzard-Lineberger, & Graziano, 1984, for review of these data). Yet even the most critical of these early reports acknowledged that about 20% of the retainees were doing better academically after repeating a grade.

The recent literature on grade retention is more encouraging. Nonpromoted children are generally found to make better grades the second time around and to show definite improvements on standardized tests of academic achievement, particularly when they are retained in the lower grades (Ames, 1981; Kerzner, 1982). Retainees are more likely to make good academic progress if (1) their parents support the decision to retain them, (2) they have a positive self-concept before being retained, (3) they have good social skills, and (4) *their academic deficiencies are not too extensive* (Plummer et al., 1984; Sandoval & Hughes, 1981). The last point is important, for it suggests that children who have received several "social promotions" and were not ready for the grade they failed may not profit by repeating it.

Grade retention and peer relations. Do peers stigmatize an older retainee as dumb, incompetent, or otherwise undesirable? Diane Plummer (1982) attempted to answer this question by showing second- and fifth-graders photographs of retained and nonretained peers (whom they did not know) and then asking them who would be liked better, who could give more help on schoolwork, and who would be a better playmate. The results were indeed interesting. On the liking item, 55% of the respondents felt that the older, retained child would be liked better than a younger, nonretained classmate. On the academic item, 86% of the second-graders and 66% of the fifth-

tainees, depending on their age, the extent of their deficiencies, their self-esteem, and the amount of support they receive from parents, teachers, and peers.

■ *Effects of school desegregation on minority youth*

In 1954 the U.S. Supreme Court issued a landmark decision in *Brown* v. *Board of Education* —one that mandated an end to segregated schooling in the United States. After listening to the testimony of many social scientists, the high court concluded:

> To separate [minority students] from others of similar age and qualifications solely because of race generates a feeling of inferiority as to their status in the community that may affect their hearts and minds in a way unlikely ever to be undone. . . . We conclude that in the field of public education, the doctrine "separate but equal" has no place. Separate educational facilities are inherently unequal.

The *Brown* decision was expected to have at least three positive effects on minority students (in this case, Blacks) and one favorable effect on Whites (Stephan, 1978):

1. For Whites, school desegregation was to lead to more positive attitudes toward Blacks.
2. For Blacks, desegregation was to lead to (a) more positive attitudes toward Whites,

graders felt that the older, retained child would be of more assistance with schoolwork. When asked why, they usually stated that the retainee had more experience with such assignments and would know more about them. Finally, more than half (52%) of the second-graders preferred the older, retained child as a playmate, and even 40% of the fifth-graders chose the retainee as a preferred companion. As a cautionary note, it is important to recall that the respondents were evaluating children whom they did not know. Nevertheless, their responses clearly question the notion that a child who has "failed" a grade will automatically be stigmatized as dull, incompetent, or otherwise undesirable.

Grade retention and self-esteem. How do children feel when they fail a grade? It is often assumed that they will be upset and depressed and may begin to lower their academic expectations or to question their self-worth. In fact, some theorists have argued that grade retention can produce a serious loss of self-esteem, which leads to further failure and eventually to feelings of learned helplessness (Johnson, 1981). Do these reactions often occur when a child must repeat a grade?

Apparently not. In one study (Chase, 1968), only 10 of 65 children (15%) showed any emotional discomfort when held back in the first, second, or third grade, and their reactions to being retained were only temporary. However, it could be argued that these retainees were somewhat atypical in that their parents strongly supported the decision to retain them and stated that their children were benefiting from repeating a year at school.

Diane Plummer (1982) looked at the effects of grade retention in a rural school district in Georgia where a substantial percentage of Black and White students were retained at least once while in elementary school. Second- and fifth-grade retainees and nonretainees were asked to estimate the grades they would receive on their next report card (academic expectancy measure) and to indicate verbally how they viewed themselves on 20 personal and social dimensions such as "lazy," "smart," "popular," "successful," and "honest" (self-esteem measure). The results were clear: Retained students did not differ from their nonretained classmates on the measure of academic expectancies. Moreover, retainees in both the second and fifth grades actually had more favorable self-concepts than students who had not been retained. We must be cautious in interpreting these results because nearly 40% of the children in this school had been held back at one time or another, so that being a "retainee" was in no way unusual. Nevertheless, there was little support for the idea that retainees view themselves as less capable of achieving or less "worthy" than nonretainees.

The policy of holding children back to facilitate their eventual academic progress remains highly controversial, and it is possible that alternative strategies such as promoting a child and providing special instruction in areas of deficiency will prove more effective than grade retention—if and when these techniques are tried on a large scale. Nevertheless, it appears that many children can benefit academically from repeating a grade without experiencing poor peer relations or a serious loss of self-esteem.

(b) increases in self-esteem, and (c) increases in academic achievement.

Since the *Brown* decision, several investigators have studied the impact of school desegregation on both Black and White students. Were the early predictions borne out? Let's take a look at the findings.

Has desegregation reduced racial prejudice? As we see in Table 16-1, the data on this issue are mixed. Black prejudice toward Whites was observed to decrease in 50% of the schools studied, whereas integration led to reduction of White prejudice toward Blacks in only 13% of the studies (Stephan, 1978). However, it is not at all un-

common for both Blacks and Whites in integrated schools to have more negative attitudes toward the other group than their counterparts in *segregated* schools. And this is often true even where integration was achieved voluntarily and without serious incidents (Green & Gerard, 1974; Stephan, 1977).

One reason that school desegregation has not been more successful at reducing racial prejudice is that members of various racial and ethnic groups tend to stick together without interacting much with their classmates from other groups. In fact, Neal Finkelstein and Ron Haskins (1983) found that kindergartners who were just entering an integrated school already preferred same-race peers. Moreover, these racial cleavages became even stronger over the course of the school year. After reviewing their findings, Finkelstein and Haskins concluded that "school desegregation will not, by itself, inevitably lead to a destruction of the color barriers that have plagued our society . . . if such barriers are to be reduced, schools will need to design, implement, and monitor programs aimed at facilitating social contacts between blacks and whites" (p. 508).

Has desegregation increased Black children's self-esteem?
In his review of the literature, Walter Stephan (1978) found few differences in self-esteem between Black children in segregated and in integrated schools. In fact, none of the 20 studies found that desegregation had had a positive effect on Black self-esteem, while 5 studies (25%) reported that desegregation had had a negative effect. Unfortunately, this research has considered only the short-term effects of desegregation, and it remains to be seen whether the self-concepts of minority children will improve after spending several years in integrated schools.

Has desegregation increased academic achievement?
Do minority students achieve more in desegregated classrooms? In many cases they do, particularly if they begin to attend an integrated school early in their academic careers (Mahan & Mahan, 1970; Stephan, 1978; St. John, 1975). Although the academic gains that result from desegregation are often rather modest, it is worth noting that in only 1 of 34 studies have minority students in integrated classrooms performed at lower levels than their counterparts in segregated schools (Stephan, 1978).

Of course, the effects of desegregation may vary considerably, depending on the ability and the personality of the child. Are sociable children who make friends easily any more likely to develop favorable attitudes toward students of other races? Will minority students who are high in achievement motivation benefit more from desegregation than their counterparts who are apprehensive about competing with Whites? Walter Stephan (1978) suggests that we should now be trying to answer these kinds of questions by studying the effects of desegregation on *individuals* rather than groups. After studying groups, we have some idea what the effects of desegregation are—*but not why they occur.* By looking at how desegregation affects individuals, we may be able to determine the conditions under which different children will react most favorably to desegregation and then to use this information to produce more favorable social and academic consequences in our integrated schools.

THE SECOND WORLD OF CHILDHOOD: PEERS AS SOCIALIZATION AGENTS

Although youngsters spend an enormous amount of time and energy playing with one another, only within the past 20 years have child developmentalists given much thought to how peer contacts affect developing children. Willard Hartup (1979) notes that peers have often been characterized as potentially subversive agents who may erode the influence of adults and lead the child into a life of delinquency and antisocial conduct. Popular novels and films such as *Lord of the Flies* and *A Clockwork Orange* reinforce this point of view.

However, this perspective on peer relations is distorted and unnecessarily negative. Although peers are occasionally "bad influences," they clearly have the potential to affect their playmates

TABLE 16-1. Effects of desegregation on prejudice toward Blacks and Whites

Subjects	Number of studies finding increased prejudice	Number of studies finding no change	Number of studies finding decreased prejudice
Blacks (Black prejudice toward Whites)	5	1	6
Whites (White prejudice toward Blacks)	8	5	2

in positive ways. Try to imagine what your life would be like if other children had not been available as you were growing up. Would you have acquired the social skills to mix comfortably with others, to cooperate and to engage in socially acceptable forms of competition, or to make appropriate social (or sexual) responses to love objects other than your parents? No one can say for sure, but the following letter written by a farmer from the Midwestern United States provides a strong clue that interactions with other children may be an important aspect of the socialization process.[3]

Dear Dr. Moore:

I read the report in the Oct. 30 issue of _____ about your study of only children. I am an only child, now 57 years old, and I want to tell you some things about my life. Not only was I an only child, but I grew up in the country where there were no nearby children to play with. My mother didn't want children around. She used to say "I don't want my kid to bother anybody and I don't want nobody's kids bothering me." . . .

From the first year of school, I was teased and made fun of. For example, in about third or fourth grade, I dreaded to get on the school bus and go to school because the other children on the bus called me "Mommy's baby." In about the second grade I heard the boys use a vulgar word. I asked what it meant and they made fun of me. So I learned a lesson—don't ask questions. This can lead to a lot of confusion to hear talk one doesn't understand and not be able to learn what it means. . . .

I never went out with a girl while I was in school—in fact I hardly talked to them. In our school the boys and girls did not play together. Boys were sent to one part of the playground and girls to another. So I didn't learn anything about girls. When we got into high school and boys and girls started dating, I could only listen to their stories about their experiences.

I could tell you a lot more, but the important thing is I have never married or had any children. I have not been very successful in an occupation or vocation. I believe my troubles are not all due to being an only child . . . but I do believe you are right in recommending playmates for preschool children, and I will add playmates for . . . school agers and not have them strictly supervised by adults. I believe I confirm the experiments with monkeys in being overly timid sometimes and overly aggressive sometimes. Parents of only children should make special efforts to provide playmates for them.

Sincerely yours,

_____

If we assume that peers are important agents of socialization, there are a number of questions that remain to be answered. For example, who qualifies as a peer? How do peers influence one another? What is it about peer influence that is unique? What are the consequences (if any) of poor peer relations? Do peers eventually become a more potent source of influence than parents or other adults? Are there cultural differences in the roles that peers play in a child's socialization? These are some of the issues that researchers are currently exploring as they turn in ever-increasing numbers to the study of children's peer groups.

Who or What Is a Peer?

Webster's New Collegiate Dictionary defines a **peer** as "one that is of equal standing with another." Developmentalists also think of peers as "social equals" or as individuals who, for the moment at least, are operating at similar levels of behavioral complexity (Lewis & Rosenblum, 1975).

We get some idea of why peer contacts are important by contrasting them to exchanges that occur within the family setting. A child's interactions with parents and older siblings are rarely equal-status contacts; typically children are placed in a subordinate position by an older member of the family who is trying to teach them something, issuing an order, or otherwise overseeing their activities. In contrast, peers are much less critical and directive, and children are freer to try out new roles, ideas, and behaviors when interacting with someone of similar status. And in

[3]This letter appears by permission of its author and its recipient, Dr. Shirley G. Moore.

> **peers:** *two or more persons who are operating at similar levels of behavioral complexity.*

so doing, they are likely to learn important lessons about themselves and others—lessons such as "She quits when I don't take turns," "He hits me when I push him," or "Nobody likes a cheater." Many theorists believe that peer contacts are important precisely because they are *equal-status* contacts—that is, they teach children to understand and appreciate the perspectives of people *just like themselves* and will thereby contribute to the development of social competencies that are difficult to acquire in the nonegalitarian atmosphere of the home.

■ *Frequency of peer contacts*

As you might expect, the amount of contact that children have with their peers increases with age. Recently, Sharri Ellis and her colleagues (Ellis, Rogoff, & Cromer, 1981) observed the activities of 436 children between the ages of 2 and 12 as they played in their homes and other locales around the neighborhood. The purpose of this research was to determine how often children interacted with adults, age mates, and other children who differed in age by more than a year. As we see in Figure 16-7, children's exposure to other children increases steadily from infancy through preadolescence, while their contacts with adult companions show a corresponding decrease.

■ *Same-age versus mixed-age interactions*

Since children attend age-graded schools, it seems reasonable to conclude that they would play most often with age mates. However, Ellis et al. (1981) found that they do not! As we see in Figure 16-8, youngsters of all ages spend much less time with age mates than with children who differ in age by more than a year. In another study of children's interactions in a neighborhood setting, Roger Barker and H. F. Wright (1955) found that 65% of peer contacts involved individuals who differed in age by more than 12 months.

■ *Same-sex versus mixed-sex interactions*

In Chapter Thirteen we found that preschool children already prefer playmates of their own sex. In their observational study, Ellis et al. found that even 1- to 2-year-olds were playing more often with same-sex companions and that this like-sex bias became increasingly apparent with age. The fact that infants and toddlers play more often with children of their own sex probably reflects their parents' idea that boys should be playing with boys and girls with girls. And as children acquire

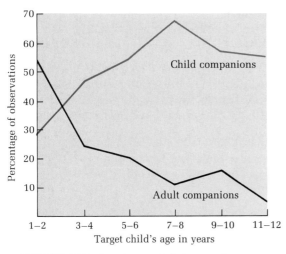

FIGURE 16-7. *Developmental changes in children's companionship with adults and other children.*

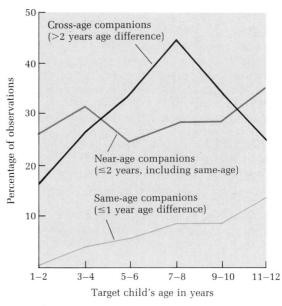

FIGURE 16-8. *Developmental changes in children's companionship with children of different ages.*

gender stereotypes and sex-typed interests, it is hardly surprising that they would begin to choose same-sex playmates who enjoy the same kind of activities that they do.

What may be most surprising about the naturalistic studies of peer interaction is the sheer amount of contact that children have with one another before they go to school. Even 5–6-year-olds are spending as much leisure time (or more) in the company of children as around adults (Barker & Wright, 1955; Ellis et al., 1981). And what is the "peer group" like? It consists primarily of same-sex children of *different* ages. Now we see why developmentalists define peers as "people who interact at similar levels of behavioral complexity," for only a small percentage of a child's associates are actually age mates.

The Role of Peers in the Socialization Process

What roles do peers play in the developmental process? Are they as important as parents or siblings? Developmentalists became very interested in these questions after Harry Harlow showed that rhesus monkeys require peer contacts in order to get along with other monkeys. Let's take a closer look.

■ Peer contacts and social competence

Will youngsters who have little or no contact with their peers turn out to be abnormal or maladjusted? To find out, Harry Harlow and his associates (Alexander & Harlow, 1965; Suomi & Harlow, 1975) raised a group of rhesus monkeys with their mothers and denied them the opportunity to play with their peers. The results revealed that these **"mother only" monkeys** failed to develop normal patterns of social behavior. When finally exposed to age mates, the peer-deprived youngsters preferred to avoid them. On those occasions when they did approach a peer, these social misfits tended to be highly (and inappropriately) aggressive. Moreover, their antisocial tendencies often persisted into adulthood, particularly if they had been denied peer contacts for long periods.

Is peer contact the key to normal social development? Not entirely. In later experiments,

PHOTO 16-6. *Monkeys raised only with peers form strong mutual attachments and will often attack other monkeys from outside their peer group.*

Harlow and his colleagues separated rhesus monkeys from their mothers and raised them so that they had continuous exposure to their peers. These **"peer only" monkeys** were observed to cling tenaciously to one another and to form strong mutual attachments. Yet their social development was somewhat atypical. Suomi and Harlow (1975) noted: "It is somewhat difficult for a baby monkey to explore its environment with another monkey hanging on for dear life and [when] even the most enthusiastic attempts at play are terminated by a big bearhug" (p. 167). The peer-only monkeys were often disturbed by minor stresses or frustrations, and as adults they became unusually aggressive toward monkeys from outside their peer groups.

In 1951 Anna Freud and Sophie Dann reported a startling human parallel to Harlow's peer-only monkeys. During the summer of 1945, six 3-year-olds were found living by themselves in a German concentration camp. By the time these children were 12 months old, their parents had been put to death. Although they had received minimal care-

"mother only" monkeys: *monkeys who are raised with their mothers and denied any contacts with peers.*

"peer only" monkeys: *monkeys who are separated from their mothers (and other adults) soon after birth and raised with peers.*

giving from a series of inmates who were period-ically executed, these children had, in effect, reared themselves.

When rescued at the war's end, the six orphans were flown to a special treatment center in Eng-land, where attempts were made to "rehabilitate" them. How did these "peer only" children re-spond to this treatment? They began by breaking nearly all their toys and damaging their furniture. Moreover, they often reacted with cold indiffer-ence or open hostility toward the staff at the center. And like Harlow's monkeys, these children

> had no other wish than to be together and became upset when they were separated . . . , even for short moments. No child would remain upstairs while the others were downstairs. . . . If anything of the kind happened, the single child would constantly ask for the other children, while the group would fret for the missing child. . . .
>
> There was no occasion to urge the children to "take turns"; they did it spontaneously. They were extremely considerate of each other's feelings. . . . At mealtimes handing food to the neighbor was of greater importance than eating oneself [Freud & Dann, 1951, pp. 131–133].

Although these orphans were closely attached to one another and very suspicious of outsiders, they were certainly not psychotic. In fact, they eventu-ally established positive relationships with their adult caregivers and even acquired a new lan-guage during the first year at the center.

These studies suggest that parents and peers each contribute something different and perhaps unique to a monkey's (or a child's) social de-velopment. Under normal circumstances, parents may provide a sense of *security* that enables their young to explore the environment and discover that other people can be interesting companions. By contrast, contacts with peers seem to promote the development of competent and adaptive pat-terns of social behavior. Indeed, Harlow's "peer only" monkeys behaved in strange ways as adults only when exposed to strange companions; within their own peer groups, they generally displayed normal patterns of social and sexual behavior (Suomi & Harlow, 1978).

Just how important is it that children establish and maintain adequate relations with their peers? Apparently it is very important. Merrill Roff and his associates (Roff, 1961, 1974; Roff, Sells, &

Golden, 1972) have collected longitudinal data on a large number of children who were clients at a child guidance center. After tracking these indi-viduals for many years, Roff and his associates found that poor peer relations during childhood (being rejected by many and accepted by few) were a reliable predictor of severe emotional dis-turbances later in life. Children who had been rejected or largely ignored by their classmates were more likely to be delinquent as adolescents, to receive bad-conduct discharges from the mili-tary service, and to display a large number of seri-ous adjustment problems, including neuroses, psychoses, and sexual deviations. A second longi-tudinal study painted a similar picture: children who had been rejected by their peers in the third grade were more likely than those with good peer relations to be seeking treatment for emotional disturbances 11 years later as young adults (Cowen, Pederson, Babigan, Izzo, & Trost, 1973).

Why are poor peer relations such good prognos-tic indicators of later adjustment problems? It may be that children who are rejected or ignored by their peers have difficulties later in life because they have paid little attention to the values and teachings of the peer group and failed to learn socially appropriate patterns of behavior. Indeed, Wyndol Furman and John Masters (1980) found that unpopular 5-year-olds were less likely than their popular classmates to follow rules endorsed by either peers or adults.

Of course, it is likely that poor peer relations are not entirely responsible for the adjustment prob-lems of unpopular children. Often an unpopular child may be insecurely attached to parents or live in a conflict-ridden home, experiences that may create their own emotional difficulties and pre-vent the child from developing adequate peer relations (Hetherington, 1981; Lewis, Feirig, Mc-Guffog, & Jaskir, 1984). But since regular contacts with peers do seem to promote the development of adaptive social responses, children who fail to establish positive links to the peer group will run a far greater risk of displaying inappropriate and perhaps even pathological patterns of behavior as adolescents and young adults.

How do children establish and maintain good relations with their peers? In Box 16-3 we will try to answer this question as we take a closer look at the determinants of one's social standing in the peer group.

To this point, we have seen that it is important for children to establish and maintain good peer relations because they will acquire many competent and adaptive patterns of social behavior through their interactions with peers. And exactly how do peers influence one another? In many of the same ways that parents do—by reinforcing, modeling, and discussing the behaviors and values that they condone.

■ Peers as reinforcing agents

It is easy to see how parents, teachers, and other powerful authority figures are in a position to reward or punish the behavior of children. Yet we might legitimately wonder whether a peer, who shares a similar status with the child, can become an effective agent of reinforcement. Wonder no longer—the evidence is clear: peers are rather potent sources of reinforcement and punishment.

In one study (Wahler, 1967), groups of nursery school children were trained to ignore several of a classmate's social responses and to reinforce others by attending to them. To illustrate the procedure, we will consider the case of Dick, a 5-year-old who frequently threw toys and shouted at his classmates. Two other members of the class were trained to "shape" Dick's behavior by refusing to play with him whenever he made an aggressive response. This particular form of "punishment" brought about a drastic reduction in the frequency of Dick's aggressive behavior and a corresponding increase in the number of socially appropriate acts, such as playing carefully with the toys. Wahler next instructed the two classmates to reinforce (that is, attend to) Dick's acts of aggression, and the result was a sharp increase in Dick's aggressive activity. Clearly, Dick was modifying his behavior in response to the reinforcements and punishments offered by peers.

Although Wahler's study demonstrates that peers *can* become effective agents of reinforcement, we might wonder whether children *do* reinforce one another to any great extent in their "unprogrammed" day-to-day exchanges on the playground or in the classroom. Michael Lamb and his associates (Lamb, Easterbrooks, & Holden, 1980) hoped to find out by carefully observing how 3- to 5-year-olds reacted when playmates engaged in sex-appropriate or sex-inappropriate (cross-sex) activities. They found that children generally reinforced their companions for sex-

appropriate play and were quick to criticize or disrupt a playmate's cross-sex activities. But were these playmates influenced by the treatment they received? Indeed they were. Children who were reinforced for sex-appropriate play tended to keep playing, while those who were punished for sex-inappropriate play usually terminated these activities in less than a minute.

The reinforcers that children provide one another are often subtle or unintentional. For example, if Joey cries or withdraws when Rocky snatches a toy away from him, Joey may be unintentionally *reinforcing* his tormentor's aggressive behavior by allowing Rocky to obtain the toy at little or no cost. If so, Rocky should become more likely to attack Joey in the future. In an observational study of 3–5-year-olds, Gerald Patterson and his associates (Patterson, Littman, & Bricker,

PHOTO 16-7. Sometimes nothing is as reassuring as the affection and encouragement of a friend.

At many points throughout the text, we have discussed factors that contribute in a positive way to children's popularity or social status. By way of review:

1. *Parenting styles.* Warm, sensitive, and authoritative caregivers tend to raise children who are securely attached and who establish good relations with both adults and peers. Unresponsive caregivers, particularly those who are also permissive, tend to raise children who are hostile and aggressive, while the children of authoritarian parents are often shy and anxious around their peers.
2. *Physical correlates.* Children with an athletic, or "mesomorphic," body build tend to be more popular than those with linear (ectomorphic) or rounded (endomorphic) physiques. Rate of maturation may also affect one's social status. Boys who reach puberty early tend to be more popular than boys who mature late.
3. *Ordinal-position effects.* Later-born children who must learn to negotiate with older and more powerful siblings tend to be more popular than first-borns.
4. *Role-taking skills.* Among groups of third- through ninth-graders, the most popular children are those who have well-developed role-taking skills. Children who have established intimate friendships score higher on tests of role taking than do classmates without close friends.

At least three additional characteristics may affect children's standing in the peer group: their names, their facial features, and their typical patterns of behavior.

Names. What's in a name? Apparently quite a lot, in the eyes (or ears) of young children. John McDavid and Herbert Harari (1966) asked four groups of 10- to 12-year-olds to rate the attractiveness of a large number of first names. At a later date, the subjects were asked to indicate the three most popular and three least popular children in their classes. McDavid and Harari found that children with attractive names (for example, Steven, John, Susan, or Kim) were rated more popular by their peers than were children with unusual and less attractive names (for example, Herman or Chastity).

This outcome, like all correlational findings, must be interpreted with caution. Perhaps having a strange name does handicap children by making them the object of scorn or ridicule. However, we must consider the possibility that parents who give their children unusual names may also encourage unusual behaviors that contribute to the problems that the Dorises and the Mortimers may have with their peers.

Facial attractiveness. Despite the maxim that "beauty is only skin deep," many of us (children included) seem to think otherwise. Although it is difficult to specify exactly what combinations of features contribute to facial attractiveness, even 3–5-year-olds can discriminate attractive from unattractive children, and they apparently use the same criteria as adults when making their judgments (Styczynski & Langlois, 1977). Attractive youngsters are often described in more favorable terms (for example, friendlier, more intelligent) than their less attractive playmates by both adults and other children—even preschool children (Adams & Crane, 1980; Styczynski & Langlois, 1977). And when unattractive children do something wrong, they are judged to be "meaner" or more "chronically antisocial" than an attractive child who commits the same act (Dion, 1972; Lerner & Lerner, 1977). So it seems that we are often swayed by a pretty face and will act as if whatever is beautiful must be good—or at least not too bad.

Attractive children are generally more popular than their less attractive companions, although a pretty face seems to be more of an asset for girls than for

1967) found that the most frequent victims of aggression were those children who often reinforced their attackers by crying, withdrawing, or giving in. And what happens if a victim suddenly begins to "punish" his tormenters by fighting back? Patterson et al. found that this strategy often persuaded the attackers to back off and seek new victims. Of course, victims who learn to repel their tormentors by counterattacking may conclude that aggression is a very rewarding activity and become more aggressive themselves. Indeed, few children remained chronic victims from session to session, and it was not at all unusual for one week's victim to become a later week's victimizer (Patterson et al., 1967).

So peers *are* important sources of social reinforcement. Although we have sampled but three studies from a voluminous literature, the evidence clearly indicates that children's social behaviors are often strengthened, maintained, or virtually

boys (Vaughn & Langlois, 1983). The fact that even 3- to 5-year-olds prefer attractive playmates suggests that they have already learned the "beautiful is good" stereotype and are using this "knowledge" to evaluate their peers. Some theorists have argued that parents, teachers, and other children may be contributing to a self-fulfilling prophecy by subtly (or not so subtly) communicating to attractive youngsters that they are expected to do well in school, behave in a pleasant manner, and achieve good relations with their peers. Information of this sort undoubtedly has an effect on children's behavior. Attractive youngsters may become more confident, friendly, and outgoing, whereas unattractive children who receive less favorable feedback may suffer a loss of self-esteem and become more resentful, defiant, and aggressive. This is precisely the way in which stereotypes about physically attractive and unattractive children could become a "reality" (Langlois & Downs, 1979).

Behavioral characteristics. Although attractiveness is an important contributor to peer acceptance, even a highly attractive child may be very unpopular if playmates consider his conduct inappropriate or antisocial (Langlois & Styczynski, 1979). What behaviors seem to be important in determining a child's status in the peer group? In her study of preschoolers, Shirley Moore (1967) found that popular children were perceived by their classmates as friendlier, more compliant, and less aggressive than unpopular children. Studies of third- through eighth-graders find pretty much the same things: popular children are described as calm, outgoing, cooperative, and supportive, while unpopular youngsters are often viewed as disruptive braggarts who are snobbish, short-tempered, and aggressive (Coie, Dodge, & Coppotelli, 1982).

Do popular children become popular because they are friendly, cooperative, and nonaggressive? Or is it that children become friendlier, more cooperative, and less aggressive after achieving their popularity?

One way to distinguish these two hypotheses is to place children in play groups with *unfamiliar* peers and then see whether the patterns of behavior they display will predict their eventual status in the peer group. Several studies of this type have been conducted (Coie & Kupersmidt, 1983; Dodge, 1983; Putallaz, 1983), and the results are reasonably consistent: The patterns of behavior that children display do predict the statuses they will achieve with their peers. Children who attain high status in the peer group are quite effective at initiating social interactions and at responding positively to others' bids for attention. Moreover, they first attempt to understand the group's activities and then slowly work their way into the group, so as not to be perceived as pushy, disruptive, and self-serving. By contrast, children who are eventually rejected by their peers are more likely to force themselves on the group and to insult, threaten, hit, or otherwise mistreat their new playmates—particularly when their intrusive social overtures are not well received. Finally, children who initiate few interactions with their new playmates and who shy away from others' bids for attention are likely to be ignored and neglected.

In sum, children who are accepted by their peers tend to be warm, outgoing, and above all, reinforcing in their interactions with other children. Several kinds of behavior such as giving attention or approval, cooperating, and sharing will contribute to a child's "rewardingness" and promote his or her acceptance in the peer group. By contrast, selfish, demanding, and aggressive children who are frequently at odds with their playmates are apt to be disliked and rejected, whereas passive youngsters who shy away from social contacts run the risk of becoming neglected. Fortunately, both these groups of unpopular children can often be helped to achieve better peer relations through the kinds of social-skills training described in Box 12-2.

eliminated by the favorable or unfavorable reactions that they elicit from peers.

■ *Peers as social models*

Peers influence one another by serving not only as reinforcing and punishing agents but also as social models. For example, we have seen that children who are afraid of dogs will often overcome their phobic reactions after witnessing another child

playing with these once-terrifying creatures (see Box 7-5). Among the other attributes and activities that are easily acquired by observing peer models are socially responsive behaviors (Cooke & Apolloni, 1976), achievement behaviors (see Sagotsky & Lepper, 1982), moral judgments (Dorr & Fey, 1974), an ability to delay gratification (Stumphauzer, 1972), and sex-typed attitudes and behaviors (Ruble, Balaban, & Cooper, 1981), to name a few. You may recall that several of these findings were discussed at length in earlier chapters.

Another function that peer models serve is to inform the child how he or she is supposed to behave in different contexts and situations. For example, a new child at school may not know whether it is acceptable to visit the water fountain during a study period without first asking the teacher. Yet she will quickly conclude that this behavior is allowed if she sees her classmates doing it.

Whom do children prefer to imitate? In 1965 David Hicks designed an interesting experiment to compare the effectiveness of peers and adults as models for aggressive behavior. Children aged 3 to 6 watched an eight-minute film in which either an adult or a peer made several unusual aggressive responses toward an inflatable plastic doll. Children assigned to a control group did not observe an aggressive model. In the second phase of the experiment, each child was mildly frustrated and then was led to a playroom that contained an inflatable doll and many of the same implements that the model had used to strike the doll. For the next 20 minutes an observer watched the child's play and recorded the number of aggressive responses similar to those displayed earlier by the model. Figure 16-9 shows the results. Notice that children who had observed either the adult or the peer model displayed more imitative aggression than those in the control group. However, the most interesting finding was that peer models were every bit as effective as adults at eliciting imitative responses. In fact, it was a male peer model who produced the highest levels of imitative aggression.

Yet not all peer models are equally influential. At age 5 to 9, children are less likely to imitate the behavior of a younger child than that of an age mate or an older peer (Brody & Stoneman, 1981). And once children acquire gender constancy, they begin to attend more selectively to and would rather imitate models of their own sex (Ruble et al., 1981).

The imitator's effect on the imitated. Do children like to be imitated by their peers? Apparently so. In a recent observational study, Joan Grusec and Rona Abramovitch (1982) found that when

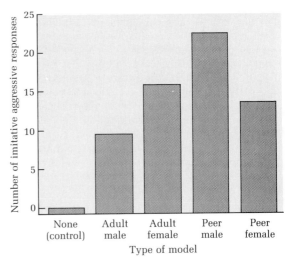

FIGURE 16-9. *Average number of imitative aggressive responses displayed by children who had observed the aggressive behavior of an adult model, a peer model, or no model.*

one preschool child imitated another, the model usually reacted very positively to his or her mimic by smiling, laughing, and even imitating the imitator, thereby prolonging a pleasant social interaction. This finding raises an interesting question: Do children learn to imitate their peers as a means of establishing friendly relations or influencing their companions? To find out, Mark Thelen and his associates (Thelen, Miller, Fehrenbach, Frautschi, & Fishbein, 1980) asked some fourth-, fifth-, and sixth-graders to do whatever they could to influence a younger peer to eat some horrible-tasting crackers (social-influence condition). Other children were not asked to influence the behavior of the peer (control condition). Before the crackers were to be eaten, each subject and his or her companion played a game, and the investigators noted the frequency with which subjects chose to imitate the strategies of their younger playmates. The results were clear: children who had been told to influence a younger child chose to imitate that child's behavior to a much greater extent than those in the control group did. So it seems that children do like to be imitated and that their imitators know it. And when do children learn to imitate as a means of establishing friendly relations or influencing their playmates? Perhaps as early as age 3, for Steve Dollinger and Melissa Gasser (1981) report that 3–5-year-olds who were instructed to influence a companion reliably chose to imitate the companion's behavior.

Can you imagine a circumstance in which children prefer not to be imitated? Although imitation is generally perceived as a form of flattery, a child who has had a creative idea copied by classmates may be anything but flattered. There is also evidence that children do not like to be imitated by a companion whose status is lower than their own. In one experiment (Thelen & Kirkland, 1976), 8–9-year-olds had solved two problems when they discovered that either an older (high-status) or a younger (low-status) child was imitating their work. The subjects seemed to enjoy being imitated by the high-status peer, and they were likely to imitate their imitator on later problems. In contrast, children whose efforts had been imitated by the low-status child reported that being imitated was unpleasant, and they often voiced the opinion that their younger imitator had copied their solutions because "he couldn't decide for himself." One implication of these findings is that younger (or other low-status) children may not be very successful at influencing older (or higher-status) associates by imitating their behavior. Indeed, children of higher status may simply consider these imitative responses as additional evidence that their low-status companions are incompetent and perhaps even undesirable as prospective playmates.

Do older children enjoy being imitated by younger companions if the older child is explicitly trying to teach something to a young understudy? Apparently they do, and as we see in Box 16-4, older children themselves may benefit when they tutor a younger child.

■ *The normative function of peer groups*

It is difficult to specify the exact age at which group membership becomes important to a child. When social psychologists talk about true "**peer groups**," they are referring not merely to a collection of playmates but, rather, to a confederation that (1) interacts on a regular basis, (2) defines a sense of belonging, (3) shares implicit or explicit norms that specify how members are supposed to behave, and (4) develops a structure or hierarchal organization that enables the membership to work together toward the accomplishment of mutual goals. Older nursery school children do share common interests, assume different roles while playing together, and conform to loosely defined norms or rules of conduct. But the membership of these preschool "play groups" may fluctuate from day to day, and the guidelines to which the children conform are often laid down by adults. By contrast, the group activities of elementary school children are very different. Members now share norms that they have had a hand in creating, and they begin to assume stable roles or "statuses" within the peer society. Moreover, elementary school children clearly identify with their groups; to be a "Brownie," a "Blue Knight," or "one of Smitty's gang" is often a source of great personal pride. So it seems that middle childhood (ages 6–10) is the period when children are assuming membership in what we can call true peer groups.

One of the most important ways that peers influence one another is by forming groups and setting norms that define how group members are supposed to look, think, and act. You may recall from your own childhood that pressures to conform to group norms are often intense and that those who ignore the dictates of their peers risk all sorts of penalties, ranging from simply being labeled a "nerd" to outright rejection. For many youngsters, it is quite an accomplishment to be accepted as "one of the gang" while somehow maintaining respectability in the eyes of parents, teachers, and other important adults.

People often assume that children become more conforming with age and that adolescence is the period when the peer group has its greatest influence. This assumption is only partly correct. Suppose, for example, that a group of peers tries to influence a child to partake in socially unacceptable conduct or to conform to a judgment that he suspects is definitely *wrong*. Under these circumstances, there is a curvilinear relationship between age and conformity: children become more conforming between the ages of 6 and 13 and then

> **peer group:** *a confederation of peers who interact regularly, share norms, and work together toward the accomplishment of mutual goals.*

BOX 16-4
CHILDREN AS TEACHERS—A SPECIAL
KIND OF PEER INFLUENCE

Several investigators have proposed that children can have a positive influence on their peers by serving as tutors in the classroom. Although most American schools are age-graded, an increasing number are experimenting with cross-age peer-tutoring programs. It is too early to tell whether these tutorials will become standard procedure in our schools, but the research to date suggests that peer tutoring may have several beneficial effects (see Feldman, Devin-Sheehan, & Allen, 1976). Let's look at some of the findings.

If you have ever had a teaching position or made an oral presentation in the classroom, you may have experienced a feeling that is common among classroom instructors—one invariably learns by teaching others. The same is apparently true of children who teach their peers, for several studies (reviewed in Feldman et al., 1976) indicate that low achievers who serve as tutors for younger students show an improvement in their own academic achievement. For example, Allen and Feldman (1974) designed a project in which fifth-graders who were low achievers in reading either tutored third-graders or spent the same amount of time studying by themselves. At the end of a two-week period the performance of tutors on the subject matter was better than that of their low-achieving classmates who had merely studied on their own. Clearly, there is *something* about playing the role of a tutor (other than additional time spent studying) that results in improved academic performance. How are we to explain this finding?

Perhaps older tutors (especially the low achievers) acquire a new perspective on school as they begin to derive many benefits—prestige, rewards from adults, respect from their tutees, and so on—from their tutoring experiences. Indeed, children who serve as tutors often show an improvement in their *self-concepts* and their *attitudes toward school* (Mohan, 1972; Yamamoto & Klentschy, 1972). In fact, one investigator (Elder, 1967) reported that children from the lower socioeconomic strata frequently *raised their levels of aspiration* after a year's experience as a tutor and began to aspire to occupations associated with a higher social class. Any or all of these factors may underlie the gains made by tutors in peer-tutoring studies.

Do peer-tutoring programs benefit the children who are tutored? Unfortunately, the results on this issue are mixed. Children apparently like to be tutored by students who are two to three years older than they (Allen & Feldman, 1976), and several investigators have reported increases in the academic performance of children instructed by their peers. But other researchers have found that peer tutees fared no better than classmates who simply studied on their own (see Feldman et al., 1976). Feldman et al. suggest that the benefits accruing to tutees may well depend on the difference in competence between the tutor and the tutee. If the tutor's academic competence is clearly superior to that of the child who is being tutored, the tutee should profit from the experience.

show less and less conformity from early adolescence into young adulthood (Berndt, 1979; Costanzo & Shaw, 1966). But in unfamiliar or ambiguous situations where the appropriate response is not immediately obvious, adolescents are more likely than younger children to conform to the actions or judgments of the peer group (Hoving, Hamm, & Galvin, 1969).

Age is only one of the many variables that affect a child's willingness to accept influence from peers. For example, children of all ages may find it harder to resist peer pressure in groups where virtually everyone endorses the group norms and a potential deviate has little or no prospect of gaining any social support for a nonconforming response (Berenda, 1950). Children are also likely to yield to their peers if the sources of this influence are older or more competent than they are (Cohen, Bornstein, & Sherman, 1973; Gelfand, 1962). In contrast, peer pressure from the younger or less competent members of the group is likely to fall on deaf ears. Finally, children of intermediate status conform the most, probably because they hope to become more popular and are trying to improve their status by publicly endorsing the actions and opinions of the peer group (Harvey & Consalvi, 1960).

In sum, we cannot draw any simple conclusions about age trends in conformity, for the patterns that emerge will depend on the type of judgments that children are asked to make, as well as the prestige or competence of the source of influence, the homogeneity of group opinion, and the child's own status within the peer group. But we can say that the stereotype of adolescents as "blind conformists" is a myth, for the evidence we have reviewed indicates that adolescents can easily tolerate differences in opinion when they believe that their own views are correct, and they are more likely than preadolescent children to resist peer pressures in all but the most uncertain situations.

Peer versus Adult Influence: The Question of Cross-Pressures

Adolescence is often characterized as a stormy period when all children experience **cross-pressures**—severe conflicts between the practices advocated by parents and those favored by peers. How do they react to these conflicting demands? It is commonly assumed that parents and other adults make a stronger impression on the young child but that peers gradually become more influential than parents as children approach adolescence.

Ken Hoving and his associates tested this hypothesis by asking 8-, 10-, 12-, 14-, and 16-year-olds what a child should do in each of ten situations in which parents and peers gave conflicting advice. For example:

Susan likes music and is trying to decide whether to join the band or the choir. Her *mother and father think* that being in the band would be more fun because the band plays at all the basketball and football games. Susan's *friends think* that she would have more fun in the choir because the choir goes to many different towns to sing. What do you think Susan will decide to do?

1. Do as her parents say and join the *band*.
2. Do as her friends say and join the *choir*.

Conformity to peers increased with age. In other words, the older the subjects, the more likely they were to ignore the advice of parents and endorse the opinions of the peer group (Hamm & Hoving, 1971; Utech & Hoving, 1969). In another study, Ed Bixenstine and his colleagues (Bixenstine, DeCorte, & Bixenstine, 1976) found an increase between the ages of 9 and 16 in children's readiness to participate in antisocial acts designed to annoy adults (for example, soaping windows on Halloween).

■ *Situational determinants of children's reactions to cross-pressures*

Although children become increasingly responsive to peer influence as they mature, there are some situations in which they typically react to cross-pressures by siding with parents rather than peers. *Peers* are likely to be more influential than parents in conflicts involving status norms, friendship choices, or questions of personal and group identity (Brittain, 1963; Sebald & White, 1980). However, adolescents generally prefer the advice of *parents* to that of peers whenever the situation involves scholastic achievement, academic choices, or future aspirations. Perhaps it is fair to say that peers are the primary reference group for questions of the form "Who am I?," whereas the advice of parents, teachers, and other significant adults will carry more weight whenever a teenager grapples with the question "Who am I to be?"

■ *Just how important are these cross-pressures?*

After reviewing much of the available literature, Willard Hartup (1970) concluded that cross-pressures are not nearly as disruptive as they were once thought to be. Adolescents who have established warm relationships with conventional and controlling (that is, nonpermissive) parents seem to experience fewer conflicts of this type (Bixenstine et al., 1976; Brook, Whiteman, & Gordon, 1983). And even when teenagers are at odds with a parent over status issues, privileges, or academic matters, these disagreements do not necessarily make them any more susceptible to peer influence. In fact, Raymond Montemayor (1982) finds that adolescents who argue a lot with their mothers will often react to these conflicts by spending more time alone or with their fathers rather than becoming more involved with peers.

But perhaps the major reason that the cross-pressures "problem" is not a problem for most adolescents is that the values of the peer group are rarely as deviant as people have commonly as-

---

cross-pressures: *conflicts between the practices advocated by parents and those favored by peers.*

PHOTO 16-8. *Although teenagers are often characterized as wild or rebellious, typically their norms and values are a reflection of adult society.*

sumed. And often when parental and peer norms do conflict, the child's behavior is the product of *both* parental and peer influences. Consider the following example. Denise Kandel (1973) studied a group of adolescents whose best friends either did or did not smoke marijuana and whose parents either did or did not use psychoactive drugs. Among those teenagers whose parents used drugs but whose friends did not, only 17% were marijuana users. When parents did not use drugs but best friends did, 56% of the adolescents were marijuana users. From these findings, we can conclude that the peer group is more influential than

parents in determining marijuana usage. However, the highest rate of marijuana smoking (67%) occurred among teenagers whose parents and peers *both* used psychoactive drugs, and a similar pattern emerges when we look at parental and peer influences on alcohol consumption and cigarette smoking (Feldman & Rosenkrantz, 1977; Krosnick & Judd, 1982). The implication of these findings is clear: Rather than thinking about childhood or adolescent socialization as an issue of parents *versus* peers, we must now determine how parental and peer influences combine to affect developing children.

Some theorists have argued that peers eventually become the primary reference group in situations in which the opinions of an individual's parents and peers are generally similar but varying in extremity (for example, ideas about an acceptable curfew, appropriate conduct on a date, or access to the family car). Although this conclusion is undoubtedly correct, it may underestimate the full impact of adult influence because the way peers feel about a particular behavior is often an expression of the *average level of parental support* for that behavior among the parents of *all* group members (Siman, 1977). For example, if a 17-year-old stays out with her friends until 11 P.M. when her parents want her in at 10, she may be returning home at a time that her friends' parents think is perfectly acceptable. She is rebellious by her parents' standards but not by those of other parents or the peer group. So parents have an effect on peer-group norms, and an adolescent's response to many issues may depend more on the group atmosphere (that is, the average parental opinion) than on the position of her own parents. The implication is that peer groups may act as a filter for the attitudes and opinions of individual parents, serving to reinterpret these standards as reasonable or unreasonable and thereby exerting a powerful influence on an adolescent's attitudes, values, and behavior.

The Role of the Peer Group in Other Societies

We have seen that the peer group plays a very important role in the social and emotional development of American children. However, the United States is often characterized as a rather atypical, youth-oriented culture whose younger constituents (and, indeed, many of their elders) seem obsessed with the notions that "young is beautiful" and that "people over 30 are not to be trusted." This perspective is very different from that of many Oriental cultures, in which children soon learn to respect their elders and to treat the ideas of the aged as "words of wisdom" (Benedict, 1946; DeVos & Hippler, 1969). In many nonindustrialized societies, young boys and girls are routinely assigned chores and responsibilities that restrict their opportunities for play (Leacock, 1971), and children from certain ethnic groups within Western societies may spend little time with peers because they are strongly encouraged to stay at home for family activities (DeVos & Hippler, 1969; Laosa, 1981). So there are reasons to believe that patterns of peer interaction and the nature of peer-group influences may vary considerably from culture to culture.

To date, the most extensive work on peer-group influences in other societies has been conducted by Urie Bronfenbrenner and his colleagues at Cornell University (Bronfenbrenner, 1967; Bronfenbrenner, Devereux, Suci, & Rodgers, 1965; Devereux, 1970). The subjects for these studies were 11–12-year-olds from England, Germany, the Soviet Union, and the United States. The children were asked to respond to a "dilemmas test" that consisted of 30 hypothetical situations, each of which pitted a norm endorsed by adults against peer pressure to deviate from that norm. Here is an example (Bronfenbrenner, 1967; p. 201):

> You and your friends accidentally find a sheet of paper which the teacher must have lost. On this sheet are the questions and answers for a quiz that you are going to have tomorrow. Some of the kids suggest that you not say anything to the teacher about it, so that all of you can get better marks. What would you really do? Suppose that your friends decide to go ahead. Would you go along with them or refuse?

Refuse to go along with my friends
Absolutely certain   Fairly certain   I guess so
or
Go along with my friends
Absolutely certain   Fairly certain   I guess so

Other dilemmas included situations such as neglecting homework to be with friends, wearing fashions approved by peers but not adults, and collaborating with friends to steal fruit from an orchard marked with "No Trespassing" signs.

Bronfenbrenner found that Russian children showed the greatest resistance to these deviant peer influences. U.S. and German children were more likely to go along with their peers than the Russians were, and English children showed the greatest willingness to take part in peer-sponsored misconduct. In all four cultures, boys showed less conformity to adult norms than girls.

Further analyses revealed that the U.S., English, and German children who spent the most time with their peers were the ones who were most likely to say that they would participate in the deviant activities of the peer group. Yet the amount of contact that a child had with peers was not the only factor that influenced his or her reactions to peer pressure. Both Soviet and American children have a great deal of contact with their peers during the first few years at school. However, these two groups react to examples of peer-sponsored misconduct in very different ways. Consider the following example.

Bronfenbrenner (1967) had Russian and American children take his "dilemmas test" under three different conditions: (1) a *neutral* condition in which they were told that their answers would be confidential, (2) an *adult exposure* condition in which they believed that their answers would be seen by parents and teachers, and (3) a *peer exposure* condition in which they were told that their answers would be shown to their classmates. In both cultures, children assigned to the adult-exposure condition were more likely than those in the neutral condition to conform to the socially desirable (adult) norms. However, the peer-exposure condition produced different reactions from the Soviet and the American samples. Soviet children responded as if their answers would be shown to adults—that is, their conformity to adult norms *increased* relative to their classmates in the neutral condition. In contrast, the American children became much more willing to conform to the *deviant peer norms* when they were led to believe that classmates would see their answers.

So here are two groups of children, both of whom have a substantial amount of contact with their peers. Yet members of one group (the Americans) often support peer-sponsored conduct, while members of the second group (the Russians) do not. The reasons for this cultural difference become clearer if we look carefully at how Soviet children are socialized. Bronfenbrenner (1970a) points out that Russian educators use the peer group as an instrument for teaching and continually reinforcing the important sociopolitical values of Soviet society—values such as cooperation, teamwork, and group *esprit*. Children in a

PHOTO 16-9. Russian children are taught to value teamwork and to subordinate individual interests to those of the group.

typical Russian classroom are divided into teams and encouraged to take part in cooperative, team-oriented activities. These teams frequently test their physical and academic skills against one another in regularly scheduled competitions, and group spirit is strengthened by administering rewards on the basis of *team*, rather than individual, accomplishments. Not surprisingly, Russian children learn to evaluate the individual in terms of his or her contributions to group goals, and indeed, they are instructed to keep tabs on their teammates, to assist them whenever possible, and to publicly censure those who are not inclined to "pull their weight." These lessons are apparently learned at an early age, as we see in the following conversations among third-graders from a Russian school:

> "Work more carefully" says Olga to her girlfriend. "See, on account of you our group got behind today. You come to me and we'll work together at home."

> Group leader to his classmates: "Today Valodya did the wrong problem. Marsha didn't write neatly and forgot to underline the right words in her lesson. Alyosha had a dirty shirt collar" [Bronfenbrenner, 1970a, p. 60].

In sum, the Soviet peer group is an extension of the adult sociopolitical system, whereas in the United States children are allowed greater freedom to evolve their own rules, norms, and customs—some of which will inevitably conflict with adult standards. Clearly, the peer group is an important socializing agent for both Russian and American children, and it would be inappropriate to conclude that Russians are less responsive than Americans to peer-group pressure. In fact, the Russian schoolchildren in Bronfenbrenner's (1967) study probably refused to endorse the misconduct of *hypothetical* peers because they expected little if any approval from their *real* classmates for doing so.

SUMMARY

In this chapter we have focused on three extrafamilial agents of socialization: television, schools, and children's peer groups. When television became widely available, children soon began to watch it and to spend less time in other leisure activities. Programming on American television is often violent, and there is evidence that a heavy diet of televised violence can instigate antisocial behavior and make children more tolerant of aggression. Television is also an important source of knowledge about people in the outside world. Unfortunately, the information that children receive is often inaccurate and misleading—frequently consisting of stereotyped portrayals of men, women, and various racial and ethnic groups. Children are also influenced by television commercials, and they may become angry or resentful if a parent refuses to buy a product that they have requested.

Yet the effects of television are not all bad. Children are likely to learn prosocial lessons and to put them into practice after watching acts of kindness on either commercial or educational programs. Parents can help by watching shows such as *Mister Rogers' Neighborhood* with their children and then encouraging them to verbalize or role-play the prosocial lessons they have observed. Educational programs such as *Sesame Street* and *The Electric Company* have been quite successful at fostering basic cognitive skills, particularly when children watch with an adult who discusses the material with them and helps them to apply what they have learned.

By age 6, children are spending several hours of each weekday at school. Schools seem to have two missions: to impart academic knowledge and to teach children how to become "good citizens."

Schooling also appears to facilitate cognitive development by teaching children general rules, or intellectual strategies, that help them to solve problems. However, the differences between educated and uneducated people are likely to be small on any intellectual task that does not depend on the use of cognitive strategies that are acquired at school.

Some schools are more "effective" than others at producing positive outcomes such as low absenteeism, an enthusiastic attitude about learning, academic achievement, occupational skills, and socially desirable patterns of behavior. Several factors, such as a school's resources, school and class size, the organization of the classroom, and the composition of the student body, have been proposed as possible contributors to effective schooling. It turns out that "effective" schools are those in which the staff works together to achieve well-defined educational objectives. Teachers are helpful and supportive rather than commanding and punitive. The emphasis is on pupil successes rather than failures, and students receive ample praise and recognition for good work. In short, the effective school environment is a comfortable but businesslike setting in which pupils are motivated to learn.

Traditionally, the task of motivating students has been assigned to classroom instructors. Teacher expectancies may create a self-fulfilling prophecy: students usually do well when teachers expect them to succeed, whereas they tend to fall short of their potential when teachers expect them to do poorly. Teaching style can also affect pupil outcomes. Generally speaking, it appears that an authoritative style is more likely than either authoritarian or permissive instruction to motivate students to do their best. Yet even the authoritative teacher may have to use different instructional techniques with different children in order to "get the most out of" all his or her pupils.

The middle-class bias of most schools may hinder the academic progress of disadvantaged children or those from minority subcultures. Textbooks and other materials tend to portray middle-class values and experiences that may seem irrelevant and uninteresting to these students. Parents of lower-class children are often less knowledgeable about the school system, less involved in school activities, and less likely to encourage their children to excel in the classroom.

Middle-class teachers are often more negative in their interactions with lower-class students and do not expect them to do well. All these factors may contribute to the low levels of academic achievement often seen among lower-class and minority populations. It was hoped that school desegregation would help to cure some of these ills. Although minority students often do achieve more in integrated schools, there is little evidence that desegregation has accomplished other important goals such as reducing racial prejudice or raising minority students' self-esteem.

Peer contacts represent a second world for children—a world of equal-status interactions that is very different from the nonegalitarian environment of the home. Contacts with peers increase dramatically with age, and during the preschool or early elementary school years, children are spending at least as much of their leisure time with peers as with adults. The "peer group" consists mainly of *same-sex* playmates of *different* ages. Indeed, developmentalists define peers as "those who interact at similar levels of behavioral complexity," because only a small percentage of the child's associates are actually age mates.

Research with monkeys and young children indicates that peer contacts are important in the development of competent and adaptive patterns of social behavior. Children who fail to establish and maintain adequate relations with their peers will run the risk of experiencing any number of severe emotional disturbances later in life. Among the factors that contribute to peer acceptance are secure emotional attachments to parents, physical attributes such as an attractive face, a mesomorphic physique, and early maturation, a popular name, good role-taking skills, and being a later-born child. Popular children are generally friendlier, more supportive, more cooperative, and less aggressive than unpopular children.

Peers influence one another in many of the same ways that parents do—by modeling, reinforcing, and discussing the behaviors and values that they condone. During middle childhood, children form peer groups, evolve norms, and begin to pressure group members to conform to these normative codes of conduct. In uncertain situations, children become more conforming with age. But adolescents are more likely than preadolescents to resist peer pressures in all but the most uncertain of situations if they believe

that the peer group is wrong. Children are more likely to accept influence from peers if the source of influence is competent or has high status, if they themselves have intermediate status in the group, or if the other members of the group strongly endorse the group norms.

Children's reactions to cross-pressures depend on their age and the issue in question. In situations involving status norms, friendship choices, or questions of personal and group identity, children become increasingly responsive to peers as they mature. But even older children and adolescents prefer the advice of parents to that of peers in situations involving scholastic matters or future aspirations. Cross-pressures are not a major problem for most children, because the values of the peer group are often consistent with those of parents and other adults.

The influence of peer groups may differ somewhat from culture to culture. For example, the Soviet peer group is a mechanism for teaching and maintaining the adult value system, and compliance with adult norms is rather uniform. In contrast, American children are allowed greater freedom to formulate their own rules, norms, and customs, some of which will inevitably conflict with adult standards.

REFERENCES

Adams, G. R., & Crane, P. (1980). An assessment of parents' and teachers' expectations of preschool children's social preference for attractive or unattractive children and adults. *Child Development, 51,* 224–231.

Adams, R. S., & Biddle, B. J. (1970). *Realities of teaching.* New York: Holt, Rinehart & Winston.

Alexander, B. K., & Harlow, H. F. (1965). Social behavior in juvenile rhesus monkeys subjected to different rearing conditions during the first 6 months of life. *Zoologische Jarbücher Physiologie, 60,* 167–174.

Allen, V. L., & Feldman, R. S. (1974). Learning through tutoring: Low achieving children as tutors. *Journal of Experimental Education, 42,* 1–5.

Allen, V. L., & Feldman, R. S. (1976). Studies on the role of tutor. In V. L. Allen (Ed.), *Children as teachers: Theory and research on tutoring.* New York: Academic Press.

Ames, L. B. (1981, March). Retention in grade can be a step forward. *Education Digest,* pp. 36–37.

Anderson, D. R., Lorch, E. P., Field, D. E., & Sanders, J. (1981). The effects of TV program comprehensibility on preschool children's visual attention to television. *Child Development, 52,* 151–157.

Atkin, C. (1978). Observation of parent-child interaction in supermarket decision-making. *Journal of Marketing, 42*, 41–45.

Ball, S., & Bogatz, G. (1973). *Reading with television: An evaluation of* The Electric Company. Princeton, NJ: Educational Testing Service.

Baran, S. J., Chase, L. J., & Courtright, J. A. (1979). Television drama as a facilitator of prosocial behavior: "The Waltons." *Journal of Broadcasting, 23*, 277–284.

Barker, R. G., & Gump, P. V. (1964). *Big school, small school.* Stanford, CA: Stanford University Press.

Barker, R. G., & Wright, H. F. (1955). *Midwest and its children.* New York: Harper & Row.

Baumrind, D. (1972). From each according to her ability. *School Review, 80*, 161–197.

Beez, W. V. (1968). Influences of biased psychological reports on teacher behavior and pupil performance. *Proceedings of the 76th Annual Convention of the American Psychological Association, 3*, 365–366.

Benedict, R. (1946). *The chrysanthemum and the sword.* Boston: Houghton Mifflin.

Berenda, R. W. (1950). *The influence of the group on the judgments of children.* New York: King's Crown Press.

Berndt, T. (1979). Developmental changes in conformity to peers and parents. *Developmental Psychology, 15*, 608–616.

Bixenstine, V. C., DeCorte, M. S., & Bixenstine, B. A. (1976). Conformity to peer-sponsored misconduct at four grade levels. *Developmental Psychology, 12*, 226–236.

Bogatz, G. A., & Ball, S. (1972). *The second year of* Sesame Street: *A continuing evaluation.* Princeton, NJ: Educational Testing Service.

Boocock, S. S. (1976). Children in contemporary society. In A. Skolnik (Ed.), *Rethinking childhood.* Boston: Little, Brown.

Brittain, C. V. (1963). Adolescent choices and parent-peer cross pressures. *American Sociological Review 28*, 358–391.

Brody, G. H., & Stoneman, Z. (1981). Selective imitation of same-age, older, and younger peer models. *Child Development, 52*, 717–720.

Bronfenbrenner, U. (1967). Response to pressures from peers versus adults in Soviet and American school children. *International Journal of Psychology, 2*, 199–207.

Bronfenbrenner, U. (1970a). *Two worlds of childhood.* New York: Russell Sage Foundation.

Bronfenbrenner, U. (1970b). *Who cares for America's children.* Invited address presented at the Conference of the National Association for the Education of Young Children, Washington, DC.

Bronfenbrenner, U., Devereux, E. C, Suci, G., & Rodgers, R. R. (1965). *Adults and peers as sources of conformity and autonomy.* Paper presented at the Conference for Socialization for Competence, San Juan, PR.

Brook, J. S., Whiteman, M., & Gordon, A. S. (1983). Stages of drug use in adolescence: Personality, peer, and family correlates. *Developmental Psychology, 19*, 269–277.

Brookover, W., Beady, C., Flood, P., Schweitzer, J., & Wisenbaker, J. (1979). *School social systems and student achievement: Schools can make a difference.* New York: Praeger.

Brophy, J. (1979). Teacher behavior and its effects. *Journal of Educational Psychology, 71*, 733–750.

Brophy, J. E., & Good, T. L. (1970). Teachers' communication of differential expectations for children's classroom performance: Some behavioral data. *Journal of Educational Psychology, 61*, 365–374.

Brown, J. R. (1976). *Children and television.* Beverly Hills, CA: Sage.

Bruner, J. S., Olver, R. R., & Greenfield, P. M. (1966). *Studies in cognitive growth.* New York: Wiley.

Chase, J. A. (1968). A study of the impact of grade retention on primary school children. *Journal of Psychology, 70*, 169–177.

Clark, K. B. (1965). *Dark ghetto.* New York: Harper & Row.

Coates, B., Pusser, H. E., & Goodman, I. (1976). The influence of "Sesame Street" and "Mister Rogers' Neighborhood" on children's social behavior in the preschool. *Child Development, 47*, 138–144.

Cohen, R., Bornstein, R., & Sherman, R. C. (1973). Conformity behavior of children as a function of group makeup and task ambiguity. *Developmental Psychology, 9*, 124–131.

Coie, J. D., Dodge, K. A., & Coppotelli, H. (1982). Dimensions and types of social status: A cross-age perspective. *Developmental Psychology, 18*, 557–570.

Coie, J. D., & Kupersmidt, J. B. (1983). A behavioral analysis of emerging social status in boys' groups. *Child Development, 54*, 1400–1416.

Cole, M. (1978, April). How education affects the mind. *Human Nature.*

Collins, W. A., & Getz, S. K. (1976). Children's social responses following modeled reactions to provocation: Prosocial effects of a television drama. *Journal of Personality, 44*, 488–500.

Collins, W. A., Sobol, B. L., & Westby, S. (1981). Effects of adult commentary on children's comprehension and inferences about a televised aggressive portrayal. *Child Development, 52*, 158–163.

Columbia Broadcasting System. (1974). *A study of messages received by children who viewed an episode of* Fat Albert and the Cosby Kids. New York: CBS Broadcast Group.

Cook, T. D., Appleton, H., Conner, R. F., Shaffer, A., Tabkin, G., & Weber, J. S. (1975). Sesame Street *revisited.* New York: Russell Sage Foundation.

Cooke, T., & Apolloni, T. (1976). Developing positive social-emotional behaviors: A study of training and generalization effects. *Journal of Applied Behavior Analysis, 9*, 65–78.

Cooling off the tube. (1976, September 6). *Newsweek*, pp. 46–47.

Copperman, P. (1978). *The literacy hoax.* New York: William Morrow.

Corder-Bolz, C. R., & O'Bryant, S. (1977, August). *Significant other modification of the impact of televised programming upon young children.* Paper presented at the annual meeting of the American Psychological Association, San Francisco.

Costanzo, P. R., & Shaw, M. E. (1966). Conformity as a function of age level. *Child Development, 37,* 967–975.

Cowen, E. L., Pederson, A., Babigan, H., Izzo, L. D., & Trost, M. A. (1973). Long-term follow-up of early detected vulnerable children. *Journal of Consulting and Clinical Psychology, 41,* 438–446.

Devereux, E. C. (1970). The role of peer group experience in moral development. In J. P. Hill (Ed.), *Minnesota Symposia on Child Psychology* (Vol. 4). Minneapolis: University of Minnesota Press.

DeVos, G. A., & Hippler, A. A. (1969). Cultural psychology: Comparative studies of human behavior. In G. Lindzey & E. Aronson (Eds.), *Handbook of social psychology* (Vol. 4). Reading, MA: Addison-Wesley.

Dion, K. K. (1972). Physical attractiveness and evaluations of children's transgressions. *Journal of Personality and Social Psychology, 24,* 207–213.

Dodge, K. A. (1983). Behavioral antecedents of peer social status. *Child Development, 54,* 1386–1399.

Dollinger, S. J., & Gasser, M. (1981). Imitation as social influence. *Journal of Genetic Psychology, 138,* 149–150.

Dorr, D., & Fey, S. (1974). Relative power of symbolic adult and peer models in the modification of children's moral choice behavior. *Journal of Personality and Social Psychology, 29,* 335–341.

Drabman, R. S., & Thomas, M. H. (1974). Does media violence increase children's toleration of real-life aggression? *Developmental Psychology, 10,* 418–421.

Educational Research Service. (1978). *Class size: A summary of research.* Arlington, VA: Author.

Elder, L. A. (1967). The use of students as tutors in after-school study centers. *Dissertation Abstracts International, 28* (1-A), 74.

Ellis, S., Rogoff, B., & Cromer, C. C. (1981). Age segregation in children's social interactions. *Developmental Psychology, 17,* 399–407.

Eron, L. D., Huesmann, L. R., Lefkowitz, M. M., & Walder, L. O. (1972). Does television violence cause aggression? *American Psychologist, 27,* 253–263.

Eron, L. D., Huesmann, L. R., Brice, P., Fischer, P., & Mermelstein, R. (1983). Age trends in the development of aggression, sex-typing, and related television habits. *Developmental Psychology, 19,* 71–77.

Feldman, B. H., & Rosenkrantz, A. L. (1977). Drug use by college students and their parents. *Addictive Diseases, 3,* 235–241.

Feldman, R. S., Devin-Sheehan, L., & Allen, V. L. (1976). Children tutoring children: A critical review of research. In V. L. Allen (Ed.), *Children as teachers: Theory and research on tutoring.* New York: Academic Press.

Finkelstein, N. W., & Haskins, R. (1983). Kindergarten children prefer same-color peers. *Child Development, 54,* 502–508.

Freud, A., & Dann, S. (1951). An experiment in group upbringing. In R. Eisler, A. Freud, H. Hartmann, & E. Kris (Eds.), *The psychoanalytic study of the child* (Vol. 6). New York: International Universities Press.

Friedrich, L. K., & Stein, A. H. (1973). Aggressive and prosocial television programs and the natural behavior of preschool children. *Monographs of the Society for Research in Child Development, 38* (4, Serial No. 51).

Friedrich, L. K., & Stein, A. H. (1975). Prosocial television and young children: The effects of verbal labeling and role-playing on learning and behavior. *Child Development, 46,* 27–38.

Friedrich-Cofer, L. K., Huston-Stein, A., Kipnis, D. M., Susman, E. J., & Clewett, A. S. (1979). Environmental enhancement of prosocial television content: Effects on interpersonal behavior. *Developmental Psychology, 15,* 637–646.

Frueh, T., & McGhee, P. H. (1975). Traditional sex-role development and the amount of time spent watching television. *Developmental Psychology, 11,* 109.

Fulkerson, K. F., Furr, S., & Brown, D. (1983). Expectations and achievement among third-, sixth-, and ninth-grade black and white males and females. *Developmental Psychology, 19,* 231–236.

Furman, W., & Masters, J. C. (1980). Peer interactions, sociometric status, and resistance to deviation in young children. *Developmental Psychology, 16,* 229–236.

Gelfand, D. M. (1962). The influence of self-esteem on rate of verbal conditioning and social matching behavior. *Journal of Abnormal and Social Psychology, 65,* 259–265.

Gerbner, G., Gross, L., Morgan, M., & Signorelli, N. (1980). The "mainstreaming" of America: Violence profile no. 11. *Journal of Communication, 30,* 10–29.

Good, T. L. (1979). Teacher effectiveness in the elementary school: What do we know about it now? *Journal of Teacher Education, 30,* 52–64.

Good, T. L., Biddle, B., & Brophy, J. E. (1975). *Teachers make a difference.* New York: Holt, Rinehart & Winston.

Gorn, G. J., Goldberg, M. E., & Kanungo, R. N. (1976). The role of educational television in changing the intergroup attitudes of children. *Child Development, 47,* 277–280.

Gottlieb, D. (1966). Teaching and students: The views of Negro and white teachers. *Sociology of Education, 37,* 344–353.

Gottlieb, J. (1978). Observing social adaptation in schools. In G. P. Sackett (Ed.), *Observing behavior.* Baltimore: University Park Press.

Graves, S. B. (1975, April). *How to encourage positive racial attitudes.* Paper presented at the biennial meeting of the Society for Research in Child Development, Denver.

Green, J. A., & Gerard, H. B. (1974). School desegregation and ethnic attitudes. In H. Franklin & J. Sherwood (Eds.), *Integrating the organization.* New York: Free Press.

Grimes, J. W., & Allinsmith, W. (1961). Compulsivity, anxiety, and school achievement. *Merrill-Palmer Quarterly, 7,* 247–269.

Grusec, J. E., & Abramovitch, R. (1982). Imitation of peers and adults in a natural setting: A functional analysis. *Child Development, 53*, 636–642.

Hamm, N. H., & Hoving, K. L. (1971). Conformity in children as a function of grade level, and real versus hypothetical adult and peer models. *Journal of Genetic Psychology, 118*, 253–263.

Hartup, W. W. (1970). Peer interaction and social organization. In P. H. Mussen (Ed.), *Carmichael's manual of child psychology* (Vol. 2). New York: Wiley.

Hartup, W. W. (1979). Children and their friends. In H. McGurk (Ed.), *Child social development*. London: Methuen.

Harvey, O. J., & Consalvi, C. (1960). Status and conformity to pressures in informal groups. *Journal of Abnormal and Social Psychology, 60*, 182–187.

Hetherington, E. M. (1981). Children and divorce. In R. M. Henderson (Ed.), *Parent-child interaction: Theory, research and prospects*. New York: Academic Press.

Hicks, D. J. (1965). Imitation and retention of film-mediated aggressive behavior of an adult model, a peer model, or no model. *Journal of Personality and Social Psychology, 2*, 97–100.

Horton, R., & Santogrossi, O. (1978, August). *Mitigating the impact of televised violence through concurrent adult commentary*. Paper presented at the annual meeting of the American Psychological Association, Toronto.

Hoving, K. L., Hamm, N., & Galvin, P. (1969). Social influence as a function of stimulus ambiguity at three age levels. *Developmental Psychology, 6*, 631–636.

Huston, A., & Wright, J. C. (1982). Effects of communications media on children. In C. B. Kopp & J. B. Krakow (Eds.), *The child: Development in a social context*. Reading, MA: Addison-Wesley.

Jersild, A. T. (1968). *Child psychology*. Englewood Cliffs, NJ: Prentice-Hall.

Johnson, D. (1981). Naturally acquired learned helplessness: The relationship of school failure to achievement behavior, attributions, and self-concept. *Journal of Educational Psychology, 73*, 174–180.

Johnson, N. (1967). *How to talk back to your television*. Boston: Little, Brown.

Johnston, J., Ettema, J., & Davidson, T. (1980). *An evaluation of "Freestyle": A television series designed to reduce sex-role stereotypes*. Ann Arbor, MI: Institute for Social Research.

Kagan, S., & Zahn, G. L. (1975). Field dependence and the school achievement gap between Anglo-American and Mexican-American children. *Journal of Educational Psychology, 67*, 643–650.

Kandel, D. (1973). Adolescent marijuana use: Role of parents and peers. *Science, 181*, 1067–1070.

Karnes, M. B., & Lee, R. C. (1979). Mainstreaming in the preschool. In L. G. Katz (Ed.), *Current topics in early childhood education* (Vol. 2). Norwood, NJ: Ablex.

Kerzner, R. L. (1982). *The effect of retention on achievement*. Unpublished master's thesis, Kean College.

Krosnick, J. A., & Judd, C. M. (1982). Transitions in social influence at adolescence: Who induces cigarette smoking. *Developmental Psychology, 18*, 359–368.

Lamb, M. E., Easterbrooks, M. A., & Holden, G. W. (1980). Reinforcement and punishment among preschoolers: Characteristics, effects, and correlates. *Child Development, 51*, 1230–1236.

Langlois, J. H., & Downs, A. C. (1979). Peer relations as a function of physical attractiveness: The eye of the beholder or behavioral reality? *Child Development, 50*, 409–418.

Langlois, J. H., & Styczynski, L. (1979). The effects of physical attractiveness on the behavioral attributions and peer preferences in acquainted children. *International Journal of Behavioral Development, 2*, 325–341.

Laosa, L. M. (1981). Maternal behavior: Sociocultural diversity in modes of family interaction. In R. W. Henderson (Ed.), *Parent-child interaction: Theory, research, and prospects*. New York: Academic Press.

Leacock, E. (1971, December). At play in African villages. *Natural History*, pp. 60–65.

Lerner, R. M., & Lerner, J. (1977). Effects of age, sex, and physical attractiveness on child-peer relations, academic performance, and elementary school adjustments. *Developmental Psychology, 13*, 585–590.

Lewin, K., Lippitt, R., & White, R. K. (1939). Patterns of aggressive behavior in experimentally created "social climates." *Journal of Social Psychology, 10*, 271–299.

Lewis, M., Feiring, C., McGuffog, C., & Jaskir, J. (1984). Predicting psychopathology in six-year-olds from early social relations. *Child Development, 55*, 123–136.

Lewis, M., & Rosenblum, M. A. (1975). *Friendship and peer relations*. New York: Wiley.

Liebert, R. M., & Baron, R. A. (1972). Some immediate effects of televised violence on children's behavior. *Developmental Psychology, 6*, 469–475.

Liebert, R. M., Sprafkin, J. N., & Davidson, E. S. (1982). *The early window: Effects of television on children and youth*. New York: Pergamon Press.

Lyle, J., & Hoffman, H. R. (1972). Children's use of television and other media. In E. H. Rubinstein, G. A. Comstock, & J. P. Murray (Eds.), *Television in day-to-day life: Patterns of use*. Washington, DC: U.S. Government Printing Office.

Mahan, A. M., & Mahan, T. W. (1970). Changes in cognitive style: An analysis of the impact of white suburban schools on inner city children. *Integrated Education, 8*, 58–61.

McDavid, J. W., & Harari, H. (1966). Stereotyping of names and popularity in grade school children. *Child Development, 37*, 453–459.

Miller, L. B., & Bizzell, R. P. (1983). Long-term effects of four preschool programs: Sixth, seventh, and eighth grades. *Child Development, 54*, 727–741.

Minuchin, P. P., & Shapiro, E. K. (1983). The school as a context for social development. In P. H. Mussen (Ed.), *Handbook of child psychology*. Vol. 4: *Socialization, personality, and social behavior*. New York: Wiley.

Mohan, M. (1972). *Peer tutoring as a technique for teaching the unmotivated: A research report.* Unpublished manuscript, Teacher Education Research Center, State University College, Fredonia, NY.

Montemayor, R. (1982). The relationship between parent-adolescent conflict and the amount of time adolescents spend alone and with parents and peers. *Child Development, 53,* 1512–1519.

Moore, S. G. (1967). Correlates of peer acceptance in nursery school children. In W. W. Hartup & N. L. Smothergill (Eds.), *The young child: Reviews of research.* Washington, DC: National Association for the Education of Young Children.

Morgan, M. (1982). Television and adolescents' sex-role stereotypes: A longitudinal study. *Journal of Personality and Social Psychology, 43,* 947–955.

Murray, J. P. (1980). *Television and youth: 25 years of research and controversy.* Boys Town, NE: Boys Town Center for the Study of Youth Development.

Papalia, D. E., & Olds, S. W. (1979). *A child's world.* New York: McGraw-Hill.

Patterson, G. R., Littman, R. A., & Bricker, W. (1967). Assertive behavior in children: A step toward a theory of aggression. *Monographs of the Society for Research in Child Development, 32* (5, Serial No. 113).

Paulson, F. L. (1974). Teaching cooperation on television: An evaluation of *Sesame Street's* social goals and programs. *AV Communication Review, 22,* 229–246.

Peterson, P. L. (1977). Interactive effects of student anxiety, teacher orientation, and teacher behavior on student achievement and attitude. *Journal of Educational Psychology, 69,* 779–792.

Plummer, D. L. (1982). *The impact of grade retention on the social development of elementary school children.* Unpublished master's thesis, University of Georgia.

Plummer, D. L., Hazzard-Lineberger, M., & Graziano, W. G. (1984). The academic and social consequences of grade retention: A convergent analysis. In L. Katz (Ed.), *Current topics in early childhood education* (Vol. 6). New York: Ablex.

Prather, M. (1969). Project Head Start teacher-pupil-parent interaction study. In E. Grotberg (Ed.), *Review of research 1965 to 1969.* Washington, DC: Project Head Start, Office of Economic Opportunity.

Putallaz, M. (1983). Predicting children's sociometric status from their behavior. *Child Development, 54,* 1417–1426.

Reynolds, D., Jones, D., St. Leger, S., & Murgatroyd, S. (1980). School factors and truancy. In L. Hersov & I. Berg (Eds.), *Out of school: Modern perspectives in truancy and school refusal.* Chichester: Wiley.

Rist, R. C. (1970). Student social class and teacher expectations: The self-fulfilling prophecy in ghetto education. *Harvard Educational Review, 40,* 411–451.

Roff, M. F. (1961). Childhood social interactions and adult bad conduct. *Journal of Abnormal and Social Psychology, 63,* 333–337.

Roff, M. F. (1974). Childhood antecedents of adult neurosis, severe bad conduct, and psychological health. In D. F. Ricks, A. Thomas, & M. Roff (Eds.), *Life history research in psychopathology* (Vol. 3). Minneapolis: University of Minnesota Press.

Roff, M. F., Sells, S. B., & Golden, M. M. (1972). *Social adjustment and personality development in children.* Minneapolis: University of Minnesota Press.

Rogoff, B. (1981). Schooling's influence on memory test performance. *Child Development, 52,* 260–267.

Rosenthal, R., & Jacobson, L. (1968). *Pygmalion in the classroom.* New York: Holt, Rinehart & Winston.

Rosenthal, T., Underwood, B., & Martin, M. (1969). Assessing classroom incentive practices. *Journal of Educational Psychology, 60,* 370–376.

Rothschild, N. (1979). *Group as a mediating factor in the cultivation process among young children.* Unpublished master's thesis, Annenberg School of Communications, University of Pennsylvania.

Ruble, D. N., Balaban, T., & Cooper, J. (1981). Gender constancy and the effects of sex-typed televised toy commercials. *Child Development, 52,* 667–673.

Rudolph, F. (1965). *Essays on early education in the republic.* Cambridge, MA: Harvard University Press.

Rutter, M. (1983). School effects on pupil progress: Research findings and policy implications. *Child Development, 54,* 1–29.

Rutter, M., Maughan, B., Mortimore, P., Ouston, J., & Smith, A. (1979). *Fifteen thousand hours: Secondary schools and their effects on children.* Cambridge, MA: Harvard University Press.

Sagotsky, G., & Lepper, M. R. (1982). Generalization of changes in children's preferences for easy or difficult goals induced through peer modeling. *Child Development, 53,* 372–375.

Sandoval, J., & Hughes, G. P. (1981). Success in non-promoted first grade children. *Resources in Education* (ERIC Document Reproduction Service No. ED 212 371), 1–204.

Schramm, W., Lyle, J., & Parker, E. B. (1961). *Television in the lives of our children.* Stanford, CA: Stanford University Press.

Seaver, W. B. (1973). Effects of naturally induced teacher expectancies. *Journal of Personality and Social Psychology, 28,* 333–342.

Sebald, H., & White, B. W. (1980). Teenagers' divided reference groups: Uneven alignment with parents and peers. *Adolescence, 15,* 980–984.

Sharp, D., Cole, M., & Lave, C. (1979). Education and cognitive development: The evidence from experimental research. *Monographs of the Society for Research in Child Development, 44* (1–2, Serial No. 178).

Siman, M. L. (1977). Application of a new model of peer group influence to naturally existing adolescent friendship groups. *Child Development, 48,* 270–274.

Sprafkin, J. N., Liebert, R. M., & Poulos, R. W. (1975). Effects of a prosocial televised example on children's helping. *Journal of Experimental Child Psychology, 20*, 119–126.

Sprafkin, J. N., & Rubinstein, E. A. (1979). A field correlational study of children's television viewing habits and prosocial behavior. *Journal of Broadcasting, 23*, 265–276.

Stein, A. H., & Friedrich, L. K. (1972). Television content and young children's behavior. In J. P. Murray, E. A. Rubinstein, & G. A. Comstock (Eds.), *Television and social behavior*. Vol. 2: *Television and social learning*. Washington, DC: U.S. Government Printing Office.

Steinberg, C. S. (1980). *TV facts*. New York: Facts on File.

Stephan, W. G. (1977). Cognitive differentiation and intergroup perception. *Sociometry, 40*, 50–58.

Stephan, W. G. (1978). School desegregation: An evaluation of the predictions made in *Brown* v. *Board of Education*. *Psychological Bulletin, 85*, 217–238.

Stevenson, H. W., Parker, T., Wilkinson, A., Bonnevaux, B., & Gonzalez, M. (1978). Schooling, environment, and cognitive development: A cross-cultural study. *Monographs of the Society for Research in Child Development, 43* (3, Serial No. 175).

St. John, N. H. (1975). *School desegregation: Outcomes for children*. New York: Wiley.

Study: Children with working mothers score lower on tests. (1983, June 26). *Atlanta Journal*, p. 4-A.

Stumphauzer, J. S. (1972). Increased delay of gratification in young inmates through imitation of high-delay peer models. *Journal of Personality and Social Psychology, 21*, 10–17.

Styczynski, L. E., & Langlois, J. H. (1977). The effects of familiarity on behavioral stereotypes associated with physical attractiveness in young children. *Child Development, 48*, 1137–1141.

Suomi, S. J., & Harlow, H. F. (1975). The role and reason of peer relationships in rhesus monkeys. In M. Lewis & L. A. Rosenblum (Eds.), *Friendship and peer relations*. New York: Wiley.

Suomi, S. J., & Harlow, H. F. (1978). Early experience and social development in rhesus monkeys. In M. E. Lamb (Ed.), *Social and personality development*. New York: Holt, Rinehart & Winston.

Thelen, M. H., & Kirkland, K. D. (1976). On status and being imitated: Effects on reciprocal imitation and attraction. *Journal of Personality and Social Psychology, 33*, 691–697.

Thelen, M. H., Miller, D. J., Fehrenbach, P. A., Frautschi, N. M., & Fishbein, M. D. (1980). Imitation during play as a means of social influence. *Child Development, 51*, 918–920.

Thomas, M. H., Horton, R. W., Lippincott, E. C., & Drabman, R. S. (1977). Desensitization to portrayals of real-life aggression as a function of exposure to television violence. *Journal of Personality and Social Psychology, 35*, 450–458.

Thomas, N. G., & Berk, L. E. (1981). Effects of school environments on the development of young children's creativity. *Child Development, 52*, 1153–1162.

Utech, D. A., & Hoving, K. L. (1969). Parent and peers as competing influences in the decisions of children of differing ages. *Journal of Social Psychology, 78*, 267–274.

Vaughn, B. E., & Langlois, J. H. (1983). Physical attractiveness as a correlate of peer status and social competence in preschool children. *Developmental Psychology, 19*, 561–567.

Wahler, R. G. (1967). Child-child interactions in five field settings: Some experimental analyses. *Journal of Experimental Child Psychology, 5*, 278–293.

Waters, H. F., & Malamud, P. (1975, March 10). Drop that gun, Captain Video. *Newsweek*, pp. 81–82.

Wright, J. C., & Huston, A. C. (1983). A matter of form: Potentials of television for young viewers. *American Psychologist, 38*, 835–843.

Yamamoto, J. Y., & Klentschy, M. P. (1972, November). *An examination of intergrade tutoring experience on attitudinal development of inner city children*. Paper presented at the annual meeting of the California Educational Research Association, San Jose, CA.

Zigler, E., & Muenchow, S. (1979). Mainstreaming: The proof is in the implementation. *American Psychologist, 34*, 993–996.

NAME INDEX

Abel, E. L., 130, 133, 136
Abelson, W. D., 408
Abraham, S., 192
Abramovitch, R., 267, 484, 624, 625, 680
Acebo, C., 432
Ackerman, B. P., 311
Acredolo, C., 351
Acredolo, L. P., 351
Adams, G. R., 477, 678
Adams, J. L., 164
Adams, R. E., 447
Adams, R. S., 663
Adelson, J., 543
Adkinson, C. D., 166
Adler, J., 119
Adler, T. F., 504, 522
Ainsworth, M. D. S., 68, 168, 429, 438, 439,
    443, 444, 445, 448, 449, 450, 482, 483,
    484, 611
Albert, J., 373
Alegria, J., 164
Alexander, B. K., 675
Allan, R. A., 360
Allen, L., 392
Allen, T. W., 219
Allen, V. L., 626, 682
Alley, T. R., 430, 439
Allinsmith, W., 664
Alwitt, L. F., 361
Amatruda, C. S., 391
Ambert, A., 630
Ambron, S. R., 561
Ambrose, J. A., 430
Ames, L. B., 179, 226, 670
Ammon, M. S., 315
Ammon, P. R., 315
Anastasi, A., 408
Anderson, B., 612
Anderson, C. W., 454, 455
Anderson, D. R., 269, 361, 646
Anderson, L. D., 391
Andres, R., 545, 632
Andrews, K., 164
Anglin, J., 343
Angrist, S. S., 525
Annis, R. C., 233
Anooshian, L. J., 352
Anthony, E. J., 146
Apgar, V., 89, 94, 95, 96, 119, 120, 121, 122,
    130, 134, 135, 138, 140, 141, 146, 158,
    195
Apolloni, T., 486, 679
Applebaum, M. I., 392
Arbuthnot, J., 568
Archer, S. L., 476, 477
Arend, R. A., 452, 503, 535
Aries, P., 9, 10, 11
Aristotle, 75, 76, 125, 357, 499
Arlin, P. K., 357, 358
Arling, G. L., 634

Arnold, S., 605
Aronfreed, J., 260, 261, 262, 571, 576
Aronson, E., 218, 219, 256
Aschenbrenner, B., 610
Ascher, E. J., 399
Ash, P., 122
Asher, S. R., 486, 487
Ashley, P. K., 577
Aslin, R. N., 210
Atkin, C., 652
Atkinson, J. W., 502
Atkinson, R. C., 367
Ault, R. L., 333
Azuma, H., 402

Babad, E. Y., 256
Babigan, H., 110, 676
Bachman, J. G., 475
Bacon, M. K., 235, 517, 603
Baggett, A. T., 543
Bakeman, R., 149
Baker, C. T., 403
Baker, D. P., 504
Baker, L., 184
Baker, N., 588
Baker, S. W., 529
Balaban, T., 535, 679
Baldwin, W. P., 610
Ball, S., 271, 656, 657
Ballantine, C., 629
Balow, B., 391
Baltes, P. B., 27
Bandura, A., 58, 59, 69, 263, 264, 265, 266,
    267, 268, 272, 273, 274, 314, 534, 535,
    571, 575, 584, 585
Bandura, M. M., 530
Banks, M. S., 163, 207
Baran, S. J., 654
Barclay, A., 543
Barcus, F. E., 271
Barenboim, C., 477, 478
Barglow, P. D., 149
Barker, R. G., 661, 674, 675
Barnett, M. A., 493
Baron, R. A., 494, 501, 648
Barr, H. M., 136
Barrera, M. E., 208, 209, 447
Barrett, C., 634
Barrett, D. E., 128
Barry, H., III, 235, 517, 603
Bar-Tal, D., 488
Baruch, G. K., 545
Basham, R. B., 149, 611, 612
Baskett, L. M., 623, 624
Bates, E., 288, 309
Bates, K. R., 314
Batson, C. D., 107
Battle, E. S., 403, 504
Baumrind, D., 485, 547, 570, 614, 615, 617,
    618, 667

Bausano, M., 210
Bayley, N., 186, 391, 485, 614
Beach, F. A., 528
Beady, C., 660
Beal, C. R., 314
Beck, J., 89, 94, 95, 96, 119, 120, 121, 122,
    130, 135, 138, 140, 141, 146
Becker, P. T., 432
Becker, W. C., 615
Beckwith, L., 611
Bee, H. L., 402
Beez, W. V., 666
Begley, S., 97
Beilin, H., 351
Bell, N. J., 632
Bell, R. Q., 59, 527
Bell, S. M., 168, 438
Bell, T. S., 367, 368
Bellugi, I., 302
Bellugi, U., 315
Belmont, L., 404, 405
Belsky, J., 160, 433, 434, 450, 455, 608, 610,
    611, 612, 613, 631, 634, 635
Belson, W. A., 270
Bem, S. L., 545, 546, 548
Benedict, H., 293
Benedict, R., 32, 107, 685
Bennett, S. M., 19, 470
Bentler, P. M., 522
Berbaum, M. L., 405
Berenda, R. W., 682
Berg, B., 629
Berg, K. M., 166
Berg, W. K., 166, 214
Bergman, A., 463
Bergman, T., 208
Berk, L. E., 664
Berko, J., 306
Berlin, C. M., 138
Berndt, T. J., 475, 479, 682
Bernstein, I. S., 529
Bernstein, R. M., 472
Bernstein, S., 267
Berry, J. W., 236, 622
Berscheid, E., 18, 184, 185
Bertenthal, B. I., 209
Best, D. L., 19, 470, 517, 523
Bhavnani, R., 346
Biaggio, A. M. B., 570
Biddle, B. J., 663, 664
Bierman, K. L., 479, 487
Bijou, S. W., 255
Biller, H. B., 541, 542
Binet, A., 61, 386, 387, 388, 394, 395
Birch, H. G., 104, 220
Birch, L. L., 273
Birnbaum, D. W., 269
Birns, B., 169, 406
Bixenstine, B. A., 683
Bixenstine, V. C., 683

Bizzell, R. P., 664
Bjorklund, D. F., 370
Blakemore, J. E. O., 519, 523, 524, 537
Blank, M., 169
Blasi, A., 570
Blehar, M., 429
Blewitt, P., 298
Blisk, D., 628
Bloom, L., 284, 300, 307, 308, 316
Blumberg, S. L., 430
Blurton-Jones, N., 67
Blyth, D. A., 475
Bochner, S., 585
Bogatz, G. A., 271, 656, 657
Bohannon, J. W., III, 317
Bohrnstedt, G., 184, 185
Boismier, J. D., 166
Bolin, L. J., 477
Bonnevaux, B., 658
Bonvillian, J. D., 302
Boocock, S. S., 658
Borland, M. D., 226
Bornstein, M. H., 163
Bornstein, R., 682
Borstelmann, L. J., 541
Borton, R. W., 219
Bower, T. G. R., 164, 165, 177, 178, 211,
    212, 213, 214, 216, 218, 219, 220, 343,
    430
Bowerman, M., 297, 298
Bowlby, J., 68, 161, 426, 429, 430, 438, 439,
    443, 445, 458
Boyd, E. F., 169
Brackbill, Y., 126, 146, 147, 169, 247, 406,
    431
Bradley, R. H., 400, 401, 402, 611
Braine, M. D. S., 300
Brainerd, C. J., 359, 360
Brazelton, T. B., 159, 160, 170, 195, 432,
    433, 603
Breland, H. M., 626
Brenner, J., 484
Bretherton, I., 441, 442, 445
Brice, P., 649
Bricker, W., 501, 677
Brickman, P., 490
Bridgeman, D. L., 481
Bridger, W. H. 169, 219, 406
Brierley, J., 174
Brill, S., 234
Brim, O. G., 626
Bringle, R. G., 406
Brinker, D. B., 267
Brion-Meisels, S., 481
Brittain, C. V., 683
Brody, E. B., 385, 394, 395, 396, 416, 417
Brody, G. H., 267, 271, 494, 535, 558, 605,
    608, 609, 616, 618, 625, 627, 680
Brody, L. R., 366
Brody, N., 385, 394, 395, 396, 416, 417
Brodzinsky, D. M., 374
Broman, S. H., 102, 147, 459
Bromley, D. B., 477
Bronfenbrenner, U., 23, 413, 414, 415, 458,
    555, 608, 647, 685, 686, 687
Bronson, W. C., 495
Brook, J. S., 683
Brookover, W., 660, 661, 668, 669
Brooks, J., 442, 470
Brooks, P. H., 343

Brooks-Gunn, J., 447, 469, 470, 536
Brophy, J. E., 664, 666, 668
Broughton, J. M., 213, 218
Broverman, D. M., 517, 545
Broverman, I. K., 517, 545
Brown, A. L., 363, 366
Brown, B., 522
Brown, B. G., 127, 136, 144, 147, 148, 150
Brown, C. J., 205
Brown, D., 669
Brown, D. G., 524, 525
Brown, J. R., 646
Brown, J. V., 149
Brown, M., 500
Brown, P., 500
Brown, R., 299, 301, 304, 315, 517
Brown, W. A., 138
Browne, J. C. M., 122, 124, 125, 126, 130,
    131, 133, 136, 139, 148, 150
Brucken, L., 523
Bruner, J. S., 234, 277, 658
Brunton, M., 91
Bryan, J. H., 17, 490, 491
Bryant, B. K., 501
Buchanan, N. R., 483
Burgess, R., 634
Buriel, R., 506
Burkhard, B., 243, 244, 253
Burns, G. W., 75, 76, 88, 89, 91, 93, 94
Burt, C., 383
Burtley, S. H., 235
Burton, R. V., 572, 573, 577
Bush, D. M., 475
Bushnell, W., 568
Buss, A. H., 494
Buss, D. M., 607, 618
Bussey, K., 501, 548
Butler, N. R., 137
Butterfield, E. C., 215, 289, 409
Byrne, D., 494

Cain, L., 610
Cain, R., 612
Cairns, R. B., 67
Caldwell, B. M., 400, 401, 402, 503, 611
Calvert, S. L., 270
Camara, K. A., 629
Campbell, D. T., 25, 393
Campbell, F. A., 404
Campbell, S., 581
Campbell, T., 271
Campos, J. J., 209, 211, 293, 428
Caputo, D. V., 150
Carey, J., 97, 119, 360, 361
Carey, S., 311
Carnevale, P. J. D., 547
Carroll, J. B., 323
Carter, C., 122
Carter, C. S., 529
Carter, D. B., 314, 523, 539
Carter-Saltzman, L., 103
Case, R., 305
Casey, W. M., 577
Casler, L., 458
Cassidy, H., 649
Catalano, R., 634
Cattell, R. B., 384, 386, 390
Cavanaugh, J. C., 370
Cazden, C., 315, 318
Cederquist, L. L., 97

Chall, J. S., 228
Chandler, M. J., 127, 146, 501
Chang, H. W., 215
Chang, P., 150, 429
Chapman, A. J., 312
Chapman, K., 315
Chapman, M., 631
Chapman, R. S., 297
Charlesworth, R., 18, 488
Charlesworth, W. R., 67
Chase, J. A., 670, 671
Chase, L. J., 654
Chavez, C. J., 138
Chemelski, B. E., 269
Chernovetz, M. E., 547
Chess, S., 104, 105, 106
Chihara, T., 475
Child, I. L., 235, 517, 603
Chomsky, C. S., 310
Chomsky, N., 288, 318, 322
Chow, K. L., 230
Christ, J., 9
Cicciarelli, A. W., 303
Cicirelli, V., 624
Clark, E. A., 459, 460
Clark, E. V., 296, 298, 307, 309, 311
Clark, H. H., 296, 298, 307, 309, 311
Clark, K., 669
Clark, L. V., 479, 535
Clark, R. A., 502
Clark, R. D., III, 69
Clarke, A. D. B., 459
Clarke, A. M., 459
Clarke-Stewart, K. A., 316, 435, 482, 483,
    602, 611
Clarkson, F. E., 517, 545
Clarkson, M. G., 214
Clausen, J. A., 185
Cleary, T. A., 408
Clemens, L., 529
Clewett, A. S., 272, 654
Coates, B., 26, 27, 267, 269, 277, 654
Coelen, C., 455
Cogan, R., 143
Cohen, D., 268, 344
Cohen, J. E., 150
Cohen, L. B., 209
Cohen, L. J., 426
Cohen, R., 682
Cohen, S., 375
Cohen, S. E., 611, 632
Cohn, J. F., 434
Coie, J. D., 679
Colby, A., 566, 568, 569
Cole, M., 658, 659
Cole, N., 408
Cole, P. M., 363
Coleman, J. S., 506
Collins, G., 192
Collins, J., 371
Collins, R. C., 413, 414
Collins, W. A., 270, 648, 651
Collmer, C. W., 263
Combs, M. L., 486
Commons, M. L., 358
Condon, W. S., 164, 214, 289
Condry, J., 520
Condry, S., 520
Conger, R., 634
Connolly, J., 346

Consalvi, C., 682
Cook, T. D., 25, 657
Cooke, T., 486, 679
Cookson, D., 626
Cooley, C. H., 467, 468, 474, 482
Cooper, H. M., 506
Cooper, J., 244, 535, 679
Coopersmith, S., 474, 616
Copperman, P., 657
Coppotelli, H., 679
Corah, N. L., 146
Corbin, C., 178
Corder-Bolz, C. R., 651
Cornoni-Huntley, J., 192
Corter, C., 445, 446, 484, 624, 625
Cosby, B., 656
Cosgrove, B. B., 136
Cosgrove, J. M., 313, 314
Costanzo, P. R., 682
Costomiris, S., 258
Courtright, J. A., 654
Cowan, G., 520
Cowan, P. A., 334, 335, 359
Cowen, E. L., 110, 676
Cox, M., 519, 543, 628
Cox, R., 519, 543, 628
Crandall, V. C., 403, 504, 506, 507
Crane, P., 678
Crano, W. D., 393
Crnic, K. A., 149, 611, 612
Crockenberg, S. B., 433, 452
Croft, K., 349
Cromer, C. C., 674
Crook, C. K., 164
Crook, T., 617
Crowley, C. G., 501
Crumrine, P. L., 626
Cummings, E. M., 454, 455
Cummins, M. S., 456
Cunningham, M. R., 524
Curtiss, S., 324
Cusumano, D. R., 543

Daglish, L., 523
Dale, P. S., 291, 298, 302, 306, 308, 310, 315
Dalton, K., 143, 144
Damon, W., 470, 472, 538, 539, 618
D'Andrade, R., 505, 517, 524
Daneman, M., 305
Danks, J. H., 300, 323
Dann, S., 675, 676
Danner, F. W., 257
Dansky, J., 346
Darlington, R., 413, 414
Darwin, C. A., 12, 13, 42, 69, 382
David, H. P., 610
David, K. H., 585
Davidson, E. S., 270, 536, 646
Davidson, T., 652
Davis, J. M., 366
Davis, W. L., 506
Day, D., 373
Day, R. H., 212
Deaux, K., 520, 547
de Baca, P. C., 258
de Benedictis, T., 271
DeCasper, A. J., 214, 289
DeCorte, M. S., 683
DeFries, J. C., 100, 101, 103, 104, 108, 398
Degerman, R., 582

De Lisi, R., 537
DeLoache, J. S., 209, 363
Delucci, K., 271
deMause, L., 9, 12
Dement, W. C., 166
Dempster, F. N., 364
Dennis, M., 310
Dennis, M. G., 194
Dennis, W., 194, 195, 459, 460
Denny, D., 108
Deregowski, J. B., 236
Desai, K. A., 502
Descartes, R., 204
Desimone-Luis, J., 629
Desor, J. A., 164
Despert, J. L., 9, 11, 12
Deur, J. L., 261
Devereux, E. C., 685
de Villiers, J. G., 286, 290, 291, 295, 296, 297, 298, 300, 301, 302, 303, 304, 308, 309, 310, 311, 312, 318, 322, 323, 324, 325
de Villiers, P. A., 286, 290, 291, 295, 296, 297, 298, 300, 301, 302, 303, 304, 308, 309, 310, 311, 312, 318, 322, 323, 324, 325
Devine, J. V., 258
Devin-Sheehan, L., 626, 682
DeVos, G. A., 685
DeVries, R., 537
Dice, C., 366
Dickens, C., 51
Dick-Read, G., 143
Dickson, W. P., 316, 402, 403
Dino, G. A., 493
Dion, K. K., 678
DiPietro, J. A., 519
Diskin, S. D., 611
Dittrichova, J., 430
DiVesta, F. J., 323
Dixon, G., 122, 124, 125, 126, 130, 131, 133, 136, 139, 148, 150
Dlugokinski, E. L., 494
Dodd, D. H., 297
Dodge, K. A., 497, 679
Dodsworth, R. O., 634
Dodwell, P., 164, 220
Doering, C. H., 126
Dolby, R. M., 147
Dollard, J., 56, 57
Dollinger, S. J., 681
Domjan, M., 243, 244, 253
Donahue, M., 519
Dooley, D., 634
Dornbusch, S. M., 187
Dorr, D., 679
Doty, R. L., 529
Douvan, E., 543
Dove, A., 408
Dowley, E. M., 582
Dowling, K., 163
Downs, A. C., 524, 534, 535, 679
Doxsey, P. A., 343
Doyle, D. C., 522
Drabman, R. S., 649, 650
Drake, C. T., 542
Drillien, C. M., 150
Dubnoff, S. J., 632
Dubois, L., 519
Dumais, S. T., 210

Dunkeld, J., 430
Dunn, J., 144, 623, 624
Dunst, C. J., 343
Durrett, M. E., 485
Dytrych, Z., 433, 617

Easterbrooks, M. A., 612, 613, 677
Eaton, W. O., 519, 523
Ebbesen, E. B., 587, 588
Eckerman, C. D., 441, 445
Edwards, C. P., 470, 476, 566, 567
Egeland, B. R., 432, 450, 451, 452, 455
Ehrhardt, A., 122, 529, 530, 531, 532, 538, 539
Eibl-Eibesfeldt, I., 99
Eichler, L. S., 141, 428, 610
Eichorn, D. H., 171, 187, 191, 192
Eimas, P. D., 214, 215, 290, 322
Einstein, A., 357
Eisen, M., 472
Eisenberg, N., 492, 524
Eisert, D. C., 353
Elardo, R., 611
Elder, L. A., 682
Eliot, J., 617
Elkind, D., 354
Elliot, R., 500
Ellis, S., 674, 675
Emde, R. N., 428, 430, 446
Emerson, P. E., 434, 435, 437, 438, 440, 443, 482
Emmerich, W., 496, 497, 524
Emmons, B. A., 590
Engen, T., 164
Entwisle, D. R., 504
Erikson, E. H., 43, 44, 50, 51, 52, 53, 70, 435, 448, 452, 470, 471, 474, 475, 476, 477, 555, 558, 613
Eron, L. D., 263, 270, 498, 649
Escalona, S., 392
Estes, D., 452
Etaugh, C., 454, 455, 522, 545
Ettema, J., 652
Everett, B. H., 349
Eyferth, K., 411
Eysenck, H. J., 382, 398, 400, 626

Fabricius, W. V., 370
Fagan, J. F., III, 206, 209, 244, 366
Fagot, B. I., 524, 534
Fairweather, D. V. I., 97
Fantz, R. L., 204, 205, 206
Farber, E. A., 450
Farran, D. C., 454, 621
Faust, M. S., 173, 183, 187
Fehrenbach, P. A., 680
Feig, E., 544, 545
Fein, G., 346
Feinman, S., 441
Feirig, C., 676
Feldman, B. H., 684
Feldman, R. S., 626, 682
Feldman, S., 483, 610
Feldman-Summers, S., 521
Ferguson, C. A., 291, 293
Ferguson, T. J., 496
Ferland, M. B., 219
Ferrarese, M., 110
Feshbach, N., 501
Feshbach, S., 501

Fey, S., 679
Fiedler, M., 459
Field, D., 351, 363
Field, D. E., 269, 646
Field, J., 164, 220
Field, T. M., 160, 268, 344, 611, 621
Fifer, W. P., 214, 289
Finch, F. H., 389
Fincher, J., 396, 397
Findley, M. J., 506
Fine, M. A., 628
Finkelstein, N. W., 459, 671, 672
Firestone, I. J., 494
Fisch, R. O., 150, 429
Fischer, P., 649
Fischer, W. F., 489, 575
Fishbein, M. D., 680
Fisher, D. M., 195
Fitch, S. A., 477
Fitzgerald, H. E., 247, 430
Flagg, P. W., 361
Flavell, E. R., 349
Flavell, J. H., 313, 314, 333, 334, 336, 338, 349, 351, 356, 359, 361, 364, 366, 367, 370, 371, 373, 470
Flood, P., 660
Foley, C., 490
Foltz, K., 360
Fontana, V. J., 637
Ford, L. H., Jr., 470
Ford, M. E., 535
Forehand, R. L., 605, 626
Forisha, B. L., 521
Forman, E. R., 481
Fox, N. A., 432
Fox, N. E., 452
Fox, R., 210
Fraiberg, S., 178
Frame, C. L., 497
Frankenberg, W. K., 503
Frankie, G., 534
Frautschi, N. M., 680
Freedle, R., 292
Freedman, D. A., 178
Freedman, D. G., 104, 170, 430, 483
Freeman, R. D., 231
Freitas, L., 254
Freud, A., 675, 676
Freud, S., 13, 14, 20, 32, 36, 42, 43, 44, 45, 46, 47, 48, 49, 50, 51, 52, 53, 56, 57, 65, 70, 144, 425, 435, 440, 447, 494, 499, 526, 532, 533, 534, 555, 556, 557, 558, 559, 570, 587, 591, 593
Frey, K. S., 523, 535, 537
Fried, P. A., 137
Friedrich, L. K., 23, 272, 649, 654
Friedrich-Cofer, L. K., 272, 654
Frodi, A. M., 168, 450, 633, 634
Frodi, M., 450
Frost, B., 233
Frueh, T., 536, 651
Fuchs, F. 97
Fuhrmann, W., 131
Fujimura, D., 215
Fulkerson, K. F., 669
Fuller, J. L., 99, 104, 108, 111
Furman, W., 460, 479, 487, 676
Furr, S., 669
Furth, H. G., 278
Fyans, L. J., Jr., 502

Gaensbauer, T. J., 430
Galbraith, R. C., 406
Galligan, R. F., 446
Gallimore, R., 624
Gallup, G. G., Jr., 469, 476
Galst, J. P., 271
Galton, F., 382, 386, 397
Galvin, P., 682
Garbarino, J., 433, 555, 634, 635
Garber, S. R., 303
Gardner, B. T., 320, 322
Gardner, L. J., 192, 193, 194
Gardner, R. A., 320, 322
Garmezy, N., 110
Garrow, H., 256
Garry, P. J., 191
Garvey, C., 303
Gasser, M., 681
Gath, A., 610
Gaulin-Kremer, E., 427
Gautier, T., 530
Gelabert, T., 366
Gelfand, D. M., 488, 682
Gelles, R. J., 34, 140
Gelman, R., 309, 312, 316, 350, 352
Gerard, H. B., 671
Gerbner, G., 270, 648, 651
Gershman, E., 477
Gesell, A., 166, 179, 194, 195, 391
Getz, S. K., 648
Gewirtz, H. B., 431
Gewirtz, J. L., 169, 251, 431, 437
Ghent, L., 225
Gibbs, J., 566, 569
Gibson, E. J., 210, 216, 226, 227
Gibson, J. J., 227
Gilbert, J. H. V., 290
Gill, T. V., 322
Gilligan, C., 568, 570, 571, 572, 573
Gilstrap, B., 612
Ginsberg, A., 632
Ginsburg, H. J., 519
Given, K., 611
Glantz, F., 455
Glass, D. C., 626
Gleitman, H., 317
Gleitman, L. R., 317
Glieberman, J., 371
Globerson, T., 406
Glorieux, J., 612
Glucksberg, S., 300, 312, 313, 323
Golbus, M. S., 97
Gold, D., 545, 632
Goldberg, M., 488
Goldberg, M. E., 652
Goldberg, P., 520
Goldberg, S., 428, 430
Goldberg, W. A., 612
Golden, M., 406, 485, 676
Goldfarb, W., 456, 457, 459, 460
Goldman, B. H., 521
Goldsmith, H. H., 104, 107, 483
Goldstein, H., 137
Gollin, E. S., 225, 275
Gonzalez, M., 658
Good, S., 507
Good, T., 664, 666
Goode, M. K., 611
Goodenough, D. R., 235, 236, 237
Goodenough, F. L., 495

Goodman, C. C., 234
Goodman, I., 654
Goodman, S. H., 276
Goodz, N. S., 309
Gordon, A. S., 683
Gordon, C., 467
Gordon, H., 399
Gordon, T. P., 529
Gorer, G., 498
Gorn, G. J., 652
Gottesman, I. I., 104, 108, 111
Gottfried, A. W., 219
Gottlieb, D., 669
Gottlieb, J., 662
Gouin-DeCarie, T., 232
Gouze, K. R., 523
Gove, F. L., 452, 455, 503
Goy, R. W., 528
Graves, S. B., 651
Gray, S. W., 413
Graziano, W. G., 267, 670
Green, F. P., 488
Green, J. A., 618, 671
Green, V., 611
Greenberg, M. T., 143, 149, 350, 440, 611, 612
Greenberg, R., 268, 344
Greene, D., 257
Greene, J. G., 432
Greenfield, P. M., 658
Greer, R. N. E., 368
Gregg, M., 131
Gregory, T. G., 636
Greif, E. B., 184
Grimes, J. W., 664
Grinder, R. E., 570, 572
Gross, L., 270, 648
Grossman, F. K., 141, 142, 428, 610
Grossmann, K., 427, 428
Grossmann, K. E., 427
Grotevant, H. D., 535, 536
Grusec, J. E., 263, 267, 491, 492, 494, 577, 607, 618, 680
Guilford, J. P., 385, 386
Gump, P. V., 501, 661
Gunnar, M. R., 259, 519
Gurucharri, C., 479
Gustafson, G. E., 618
Guttmacher, A. F., 148

Haaf, R. A., 205
Haan, N., 569
Haas, J., 139
Habicht, J., 128
Haegerstrom, G., 231
Hagen, J., 223, 582
Hainline, L., 544, 545
Haith, M. M., 206, 209
Halberstadt, A. G., 546
Hall, G. S., 13, 36, 425
Hall, J. A., 546
Haller, A. O., 620
Halverson, C. F., Jr., 520
Halverson, H. M., 177
Hamilton, J. S., 144
Hamm, A. C., 136
Hamm, N. H., 682, 683
Hammer, D., 626
Hancock, F. T., 626
Hanisee, J., 459, 460

Hanks, C., 611
Hanlon, C., 315
Hansen, G. D., 248
Hanson, R. A., 403
Hansson, R. O., 547
Harari, H., 678
Hardy-Brown, K., 353
Haring, N. G., 92
Harkness, S., 567, 568, 569
Harlan, W. R., 192
Harlow, H. F., 274, 275, 436, 437, 439, 448, 453, 454, 455, 456, 458, 460, 634, 675, 676
Harlow, M. K., 274, 453, 454, 634
Harmon, R. J., 430
Harrell, M. S., 395
Harrell, T. W., 395
Harris, C. S., 221
Harris, M. B., 264
Harrison, A., 582
Hart, D., 470, 472
Harter, S., 473, 474, 503
Hartman, S. R., 352
Hartmann, D. P., 488
Hartshorne, H., 488, 571, 572, 573
Hartup, W. W., 18, 26, 27, 267, 277, 460, 484, 488, 495, 496, 501, 672, 683
Harvey, O. J., 682
Haskins, R. A., 671, 672
Hatcher, R. P., 149
Haugh, S. S., 520, 522
Hay, D. F., 483, 486, 495
Hayden, A. H., 92
Hayes, C., 320
Hayes, D. S., 269, 477
Hazzard-Lineberger, M., 670
Hein, A., 231, 232
Heinicke, C. M., 611
Heinonin, O. P., 131, 135, 141
Held, R., 231, 232, 233, 234
Helmreich, R. L., 546, 547
Henderson, B. E., 136
Henderson, R. W., 626
Hendler, C. S., 485
Henneborn, W. L., 142
Herkowitz, J., 179
Herman, C. S., 136
Hertzog, C., 384
Hess, R. D., 316, 402, 620, 629
Heston, L., 108
Hetherington, E. M., 515, 519, 533, 534, 540, 541, 542, 543, 544, 545, 582, 602, 609, 627, 628, 629, 630, 676
Hicks, D. J., 680
Hildebrandt, K. A., 430
Hill, S. D., 469
Hilton, I., 626, 627
Hindley, C. B., 392
Hippler, A. A., 685
Hirsch, V. H. B., 230
Hiscock, M., 176
Hite, T., 524
Hobbes, T., 11, 12
Hodges, J., 457
Hodges, K. L., 504
Hodges, W. F., 629
Hodkin, B., 359
Hoffman, C. D., 520
Hoffman, H. R., 270, 647
Hoffman, L. W., 454, 541, 545, 631, 632

Hoffman, M. L., 69, 492, 494, 558, 561, 574, 578, 579, 580, 583, 593, 601
Hogarty, P. S., 392
Hoge, D. R., 475
Hohn, R. L., 433
Holden, G. W., 263, 607, 618, 677
Holstein, C., 568, 570
Holstein, R. B., 582
Homme, L. E., 258
Honzik, M. P., 391, 392, 393
Hood, L., 308, 316
Hooper, F. H., 350
Horn, J., 103, 107, 384, 390
Horton, R. W., 650, 651
Hoving, K. L., 497, 682, 683
Howard, J. A., 493
Hudson, L. M., 481
Hudson. W., 236, 237
Huesmann, L. R., 263, 270, 649
Hughes, G. P., 670
Hughes, R., Jr., 493
Hull, C., 56
Humphrey, K., 290
Humphries, L. G., 408
Hunt, D., 629
Hurley, J. R., 433
Huston, A., 270, 271, 647, 653, 655, 656
Huston-Stein, A., 272, 654
Hutchinson, C. A., 168
Hutt, C., 346, 527, 528
Hutt, S. J., 166
Hwang, C., 450
Hyde, J. S., 497

Ignatoff, E., 611
Ilg, F. L., 179
Ilgen, D. R., 521
Imperato-McKinley, J., 530
Ingram, D., 307
Inhelder, B., 336, 347, 352, 354, 356
Irwin, D. M., 561
Iwawaki, S., 475
Izzo, L. D., 110, 676

Jacklin, C. N., 126, 484, 497, 518, 519, 520, 523, 524, 529, 530, 535, 612
Jackson, S., 356
Jacobs, B. S., 626
Jacobs, P. A., 90, 91
Jacobson, C. B., 138
Jacobson, J. L., 442, 444
Jacobson. L., 666
Jagger, M., 365
Jakobson, R., 291
James, W., 157, 204, 214, 216, 232
Jarvik, L. F., 91
Jaskir, J., 676
Jenkins, J. J., 215
Jenkins, M. D., 411
Jensen, A. R., 40, 382, 399, 408, 409, 410, 413
Jensen, K., 164, 165
Jersild, A. T., 666
Johnson, C. J., 303
Johnson, C. N., 471
Johnson, D., 671
Johnson, H., 311
Johnson, L. B., 467
Johnson, N., 647
Johnson, R. D., 517

Johnson, S. M., 623, 624
Johnston, J., 652
Jones, D., 660
Jones, F. A., 611
Jones, K. L., 136
Jones, M. C., 186, 187, 248
Jones, W. H., 547
Judd, C. M., 684

Kaczala, C. M., 504, 522
Kagan, J., 207, 224, 373, 374, 375, 431, 442, 443, 444, 446, 455, 497, 525, 526, 543, 582
Kagan, S., 489, 668, 669
Kahle, L. R., 353
Kamin, L., 398, 400, 401
Kandel, D., 684
Kanfer, F. H., 586
Kant, I., 204
Kanungo, R. N., 652
Kappel, B. E., 545
Karnes, M. B., 662
Katcher, A., 50, 522, 534
Katkovsky, W., 507
Katz, S., 97
Kavanaugh, R., 269
Kaye, H., 247
Kaye, K., 340
Kean, A. W. G., 10
Kearsley, R. B., 442, 455
Keasey, B., 353
Keasey, C. B., 561, 569
Keating, D., 479
Keats, J. G., 519
Kee, D. W., 367, 368
Kefauver, E., 647
Kellaghan, T., 626
Keller, A., 470
Kellogg, L. A., 320
Kellogg, W. N., 320
Kelly, D., 610
Kelly, J. B., 628, 630
Kelly, R., 629
Kempe, C. H., 633, 634, 636, 637
Kempe, R. S., 633, 634, 636, 637
Kendall, P. C., 487
Kendler, H. H., 276, 277
Kendler, T. S., 276, 277
Kendrick, C., 144, 623, 624
Kendrick, S. A., 408
Keniston, A. H., 270
Kennedy, W. Z., 407
Kennell, J. H., 427, 428, 429
Kenny, J., 393
Kent, M. W., 110
Kerby, F. D., 486
Kerzner, R. L., 670
Kessen, W., 12, 458
Kessler, S., 108
Kessner, D. M., 124, 126, 148, 622
Key, C. B., 399
Kiesler, S., 521
King, R. A., 487
King, S., 519
Kinsbourne, M., 176
Kipnis, D. M., 272, 654
Kirkland, K. D., 681
Kister, M. C., 314
Klahr, D., 361
Klaus, H. M., 427, 428, 429

Klaus, R. A., 413
Klein, M., 633
Klein, R. E., 128, 438
Klentschy, M. P., 682
Klima, E. S., 302
Klineberg, O., 399
Kloosterman, G. J., 150
Klusman, L., 142
Kodin, V., 91
Koegel, R. L., 255
Kohen-Raz, R., 360
Kohlberg, L., 438, 470, 482, 526, 536, 537, 538, 555, 558, 563, 564, 565, 566, 567, 568, 569, 570, 571, 572, 573, 593, 618
Kohn, M. L., 526, 543, 604
Kokenes, B., 474, 475
Kolata, G. B., 147
Kolb, S., 195
Kolbe, R., 536
Konner, M. J., 356
Konop, M., 490
Koperski, J. A., 168
Kopp, C. B., 148, 150, 244
Koriat, A., 587
Korner, A. F., 168, 169, 433
Kotelchuck, M., 438
Kotsonis, M. E., 314
Kraemer, H., 126, 168
Kram, K. M., 191
Kramer, R., 569
Krauss, D. R., 611
Krauss, R. M., 312, 313
Krebs, D. L., 489
Kreitzberg, V. S., 484
Kremenitzer, J. P. 163
Kreutzer, M. A., 370
Kreye, M., 441
Kriger, A., 430
Krile, D., 481
Kron, R. E., 251
Krosnick, J. A., 684
Krowitz, A., 211
Kuczaj, S. A., II, 305
Kuczynski, L., 262, 263, 577, 582, 607, 618
Kuhn, D., 358, 523, 538, 569
Kulka, R. A., 632
Kupersmidt, J. B., 679
Kurdek, L. A., 479, 628, 630
Kurtz, S. T., 350
Kurtzberg, D., 163

Labouvie-Vief, G., 384
Ladd, G. W., 487, 488
LaForme, G. L., 497
Lahey, B. B., 626
Lamaze, F., 143
Lamb, M. E., 435, 450, 452, 484, 534, 612, 633, 634, 677
Lambert, R. D., 545
Lamke, L. K., 547
Lando, B., 484
Lange, G., 367, 488
Langer, A., 211
Langer, J., 569
Langlois, J. H., 430, 524, 535, 678, 679
Laosa, L. M., 621, 622, 685
Lapidus, D. R., 374
LaRue, A. A., 523
LaRussa, G. W., 517
Lave, C., 658

LaVine, L. O., 541
LaVoie, J. C., 536
Layzer, D., 410
Lazar, I., 413, 414
Leacock, E., 685
Leaverton, P. E., 192
Leboyer, F., 144
Lechelt, E. C., 235
Lectig, A., 128
Lee, E. S., 411
Lee, R. C., 662
Leehy, S. C., 234
Leeuwenhoek, A. van, 76
Lefford, A., 220
Lefkowitz, M. M., 137, 263, 270, 649
Leichty, M. M., 542
Leiman, A. L., 174
Leming, J., 570
Lempers, J. D., 303
Lenard, H. G., 166
Lenneberg, E. H., 176, 288, 290, 319, 322, 323
Leonard, B., 276
Leonard, C., 370
Leonard, L. B., 315
Lepper, M. R., 257, 679
Lerner, J., 678
Lerner, R. M., 185, 475, 678
Lessen-Firestone, J. K., 138
Lester, B. M., 438, 446
Leung, E. H. L., 302, 486
Levenstein, P., 414
Levenstein, S., 414
Leventhal, A. G., 230
Levin, H., 228, 260, 498, 575
Levin, J. R., 368
Levin, S. R., 270, 361
LeVine, R. A., 601, 602, 603, 604
Levinson, B., 274
Levitt, M. J., 259, 441, 442
Levy, N., 165
Levy, V. M., 370
Levy-Shiff, R., 458, 542, 543
Lewin, K., 39, 667
Lewin, R., 187, 189
Lewis, M., 244, 292, 432, 441, 442, 444, 447, 469, 470, 476, 484, 673, 676
Lewis, N. G., 633, 636
Lewkowicz, D. L., 218
Lewontin, R. C., 410
Liberman, A. M., 215
Liberty, C., 366, 367
Lickona, T., 561
Lieberman, M., 566
Lieberman, P., 291
Liebert, D. E., 356
Liebert, R. M., 22, 270, 356, 536, 646, 648, 651, 652, 653, 655, 656, 657
Liederman, P. H., 143, 612
Light, R. J., 634
Lightbown, P., 316
Lincoln, A., 86
Lindbergh, C., 609
Lindzey, G., 407
Linn, M. C., 271
Lippincott, E. C., 650
Lippitt, R., 667
Lipsitt, L. P., 164, 165, 167, 192, 247
Lipton, E. L., 169
Lipton, R. C., 456, 457, 458

Littenberg, R., 446
Littman, B., 244
Littman, R. A., 501, 677
Livesley, W. J., 477
Livson, N., 186, 187
Locke, J., 11, 12, 204
Lockman, J. J., 213
Loehlin, J. C., 407, 411
Londerville, S., 451, 484
London, P., 493
Longeway, K. P., 447
Longstreth, L. E., 404, 458
Lonky, E., 257
Lorch, E. P., 269, 361, 646
Lorenz, K. Z., 429, 438, 439, 494
Lovaas, O. I., 254, 255, 264
Loveland, K. K., 257
Low, H., 529
Lowe, C. R., 119, 122
Lowell, E. L., 502
Lower, J. E., 191
Lowery, G. H., 171, 179
Lubin, A. H., 191
Luria, A. R., 276, 582
Lyle, J., 270, 647, 648
Lynn, D. B., 541, 543
Lyons, A. E., 584
Lytton, H., 102

Maccoby, E. E., 126, 223, 260, 471, 483, 488, 492, 493, 497, 498, 515, 518, 519, 520, 523, 524, 527, 528, 529, 530, 535, 538, 539, 575, 582, 612, 616, 617, 618, 620, 622
MacDonald, A. P., 506
MacDonald, J., 220
MacFarlane, A., 117, 123, 144, 150, 165, 515
Macfarlane, J. W., 392
MacKain, K., 292
MacKinnon, C. E., 535, 540, 609, 625
MacKinnon, D. W., 578
MacNamara, J., 626
MacPhee, D., 404
Madden, J., 414
Maehr, M. L., 502, 619
Magenis, R. E., 93
Mahan, A. M., 672
Mahan, T. W., 672
Mahler, M. S., 468, 475
Maier, H. W., 51
Main, M., 445, 451, 484, 612
Major, B., 547, 548
Malamud, P., 648
Malina, R. M., 183
Maller, J. B., 488
Maller, O., 164
Mallick, S. K., 500
Mandell, W., 150
Mansfield, A. F., 545
Marantz, S. A., 545
Marcell, M., 219
Marcia, J. W., 476, 477
Marcus, D. E., 523, 537
Marcus, J., 340
Markus, G. B., 405, 626
Markus, H., 405, 626
Marolla, F. A., 128, 404, 405
Marquis, A. L., 317
Marshall, W. A., 172, 173
Martin, C. L., 520

Martin, D. C., 136
Martin, G. B., 69
Martin, J. A., 256, 261, 519
Martin, M., 668
Maruyama, G., 627
Marvin, R. S., 350, 440
Masden, M. C., 489
Masgud, M., 566
Massad, C. M., 547
Masten, A., 110
Masters, J. C., 535, 539, 676
Matas, L., 441, 452, 503
Matejcek, Z., 433, 617
Matheny, A. P., 104, 483
Matsuyama, S. S., 91
Matthews, K. A., 107
Matthews, W. S., 536
Mattsson, A., 529
Maughan, B., 659
Maurer, D., 208, 209, 447
May, M. A., 488, 571, 572, 573
Mayer, J., 192, 193
McArthur, L. Z., 536
McCall, R. B., 269, 392, 636
McCandless, B. R., 500
McCarthy, J. D., 475
McCartney, K., 112
McClearn, G. E., 100, 101, 104
McClelland, D. C., 397, 502, 505
McConaghy, M. J., 534
McDavid, J. W., 678
McDonald, R. L., 127
McDougall, D., 542
McDougall, W., 555, 556
McGhee, P. E., 312, 352, 505, 536, 632, 651
McGinnies, E., 234
McGlaughlin, J. E., 406
McGraw, M. B., 194, 195
McGuffog, C., 676
McGuire, K. D., 481
McGurk, H., 220, 221
McKenzie, B. E., 212
McLoyd, V. C., 257
McMillen, M. M., 83
McNally, J., 490
McNeill, D., 288, 316, 318
Meachum, J. A., 470
Mead, G. H., 467, 468, 482
Mead, M., 498, 530
Meadows, L., 609
Meese, J. L., 522
Mehl, L. E., 143, 612
Meilman, P. W., 476, 477
Melhuish, E. C., 214
Melton, E. M., 493
Meltzoff, A. N., 219, 344
Melville, M. M., 91
Mendel, G., 77, 84, 85, 86
Mendelson, M. J., 219
Mendes, H. A., 630
Menlove, F. L., 267, 272
Menyak, P., 290
Merkin, S., 307
Mermelstein, R., 649
Mervis, C. A., 297
Mervis, C. B., 297
Messer, S. B., 374, 375
Metraux, R. W., 226
Metzner, R., 584
Meyer, B., 523, 525

Mickelson, R., 525
Midlarsky, E., 17, 490, 491
Millar, W. S., 253
Miller, B. C., 610
Miller, D. J., 680
Miller, L. B., 664
Miller, N., 627
Miller, N. E., 56, 57
Miller, P. H., 362
Miller, S. M., 519
Miller, S. S., 131, 138, 139
Millodot, M., 231
Milton, J., 6
Milunsky, A. 95
Minnett, A. M., 624
Minton, H. L., 393, 394, 406, 407
Minuchin, P. P., 669
Minuchin, S., 184
Miranda, S. B., 206
Mischel, H. N., 591, 592
Mischel, W., 534, 584, 585, 587, 588, 591, 592
Mitchell, D. E., 230
Miyake, N., 402
Miyawaki, K., 215
Mohan, M., 682
Mohr, D. M., 472
Moir, J., 569
Molfese, D. L., 289, 322
Money, J., 122, 529, 530, 531, 532, 538, 539, 549
Montemayer, R., 473, 683
Moog, H., 215
Moore, B., 488, 492, 493, 588
Moore, L. P., 577, 590
Moore, M., 374
Moore, M. J., 208
Moore, M. K., 213, 218, 344
Moore, S. G., 673, 679
Moreland, J. R., 628
Moreland, R. L., 405
Morgan, G. A., 441, 443
Morgan, M., 270, 525, 648, 651
Morgan, T. S., 77
Morris, E. K., 261
Morris, M., 612
Morris, N., 143
Morris, S. J., 586
Mortimore, P., 659
Moskowitz-Cook, A., 234
Moss, A., 406
Moss, H. A., 170, 485, 497, 525, 526, 527, 626
Mossler, D. G., 350
Most, R. K., 611
Moynahan, E. D., 370
Mueller, E., 484
Muenchow, S., 662
Muir, D., 164, 220, 233
Mulhern, R. K., 263, 607
Mundy-Castle, A. C., 236, 343
Munro, G., 477
Munroe, R. H., 537
Munroe, R. L., 537
Murgatroyd, S., 660
Murphy, H., 366
Murphy, J. M., 568
Murray, A. D., 147
Murray, E., 524
Murray, J. P., 636, 646

Mussen, P. H., 186, 187, 489, 534, 616
Mutterer, M. L., 572
Muzio, J. W., 166
Myers, B., 160
Myers, N. A., 364
Myers, R. E., 148
Myers, S. E., 148

Nadelman, L., 523, 525, 582
Nagle, R. J., 454
Nash, A., 483
Nash, S. C., 523, 524
Nation, R. L., 147
Naus, M. J., 366
Neimark, E. D., 356, 374
Neisser, U., 381
Nelson, C. F., 373
Nelson, E. A., 570, 572
Nelson, K., 254, 294, 295, 296, 298, 302, 325
Nelson, K. E., 318
Nelson, S. A., 562
Nelson, T. M., 235
Nelson, V. L., 403
Netley, C., 90
Neulinger, J., 626
Newcomb, N., 363, 530
Newell, A., 360
Newport, E. L., 317
Neyzi, O., 192
Nichols, P. L., 102, 406
Nichols, R. C., 107
Nisan, M., 568, 587
Nisbett, R. E., 257
Nissen, H. W., 230
Noiret, E., 164
Nordsieck, M., 192
Nordstrom, L., 110
Norman-Jackson, J., 316, 626
Novack, L. L., 302
Novak, M. A., 456
Nowicki, S., 506
Nucci, L. P., 563
Nucci, M. S., 563

O'Brien, C. O., 314
O'Brien, R. G., 314
O'Bryant, S., 651
O'Connell, J. C., 454
Oden, M. H., 396
Oden, S., 487
Ogbu, J. U., 603, 606, 622
O'Hara, T., 490
Olds, S. W., 663
Olejnik, A. B., 523
Olley, J. G., 257
Oltman, P. K., 235
Olver, R. R., 658
Olweus, D., 497, 498, 529
O'Mahoney, K., 629
O'Malley, P. M., 475
Orlansky, M. D., 302
Orlick, T. D., 490
Orlofsky, J. L., 547
Ornstein, P. A., 366, 367
Ortony, A. 311
Osborne, J. G., 263
Osser, H. A., 227
Ostrea, E. M., 138
Ouston, J., 659
Overton, W. F., 523, 537

Oviatt, S. L., 293, 294
Owen, C. F., 392
Owen, G. M., 191

Painter, P., 146
Pallak, S. R., 258
Pancake, V. R., 452
Papalia, D. E., 663
Papousek, H., 252
Parikh, B., 566, 570
Parke, R. D., 260, 261, 262, 263, 269, 515,
    575, 577, 605, 618, 633, 636
Parker, E. B., 647
Parker, T., 658
Parmelee, A. H., 148, 150, 244
Parsons, J. E., 504, 522
Parsons, T., 516
Pascale-Leone, J., 374
Passman, R. H., 263, 447, 607
Pastor, D. L., 452, 484
Patterson, C. J., 313, 314, 523, 539, 588
Patterson, G. R., 498, 499, 500, 501, 628,
    677, 678
Paulhus, D., 626
Paulson, F. L., 654
Pavlov, I., 244, 245, 246
Pawlby, S., 621
Peck, M. B., 164
Pedersen, F., 612
Pedersen, J., 483
Pederson, A., 110, 676
Pederson, J. A., 482
Peeples, D. R., 163
Peery, J. C., 431
Peevers, B. H., 477
Penna, A. N., 525
Pennebaker, J. W., 485
Pennington, B. F., 90, 91
Pepler, D. J., 624, 625
Perlmutter, M., 364, 370
Perry, D. G., 256, 262, 501, 548, 575
Perry, L. C., 501
Peskin, H., 186, 187
Peterson, G. H., 143, 612
Peterson, P. L., 664
Peterson, R. E., 530
Petrella, F. W., 270
Petros, T. V., 270
Petterson, L., 213
Phares, E. J., 506, 620
Phillips, J. R., 317
Phillips, S., 519
Phillips, W., 373
Phoenix, C. H., 528
Piaget, J., 20, 21, 43, 60, 61, 62, 63, 64, 65,
    66, 67, 68, 71, 216, 219, 269, 277, 278,
    325, 333, 334, 335, 336, 337, 338, 339,
    340, 341, 342, 343, 344, 345, 346, 347,
    348, 349, 350, 351, 352, 353, 354, 355,
    356, 357, 358, 359, 360, 372, 373, 375,
    376, 381, 383, 438, 468, 478, 481, 482,
    495, 502, 555, 558, 559, 560, 561, 562,
    563, 564, 569, 592, 593
Pick, A. D., 227
Pick, H. L., 303
Pilon, R., 164, 220
Pine, F., 468
Pinneau, S. R., 458
Pittman, T. S., 258
Plomin, R., 100, 101, 103, 104, 106, 108, 398

Plummer, D. L., 669, 670, 671
Pollack, C. B., 433, 434, 634
Pollack, R. H., 237
Pollis, N. P., 522
Pope, B., 543
Postman, L., 234
Potts, R., 570, 577
Poulos, R. W., 22, 653
Powell, J. A., 628
Power, R. P., 221
Powers, A. B., 263
Prather, M., 668
Pratt, C. L., 458
Pratt, K. C., 163, 165
Pratt, M. W., 314
Prawat, R. S., 296
Prechtl, H. E. R., 166
Premack, A. J., 320, 321, 322
Premack, D., 256, 257, 320, 321, 322
Pressley, M., 365, 367, 368
Price, G. C., 316
Provence, S., 456, 457, 458
Przybycien, C. A., 375
Puck, M., 90
Pusser, H. E., 654
Putallaz, M., 679

Quay, L. C., 408

Rabban, M., 525
Rader, N., 210
Radke-Yarrow, M., 128, 487
Ragozin, A. S., 149, 454, 611, 612
Rahe, D. F., 460
Rajecki, D. W., 439
Ramey, C. T., 128, 129, 259, 404, 415, 454,
    459, 621
Ramsay, D. S., 293
Ramsey-Klee, D. M., 611
Rank, O., 144
Raskin, A., 617
Raviv, A., 488
Raynor, R., 246
Reagan, R. W., 414
Rebelsky, F., 611
Redd, W. H., 261
Redler, E., 492, 494
Reed, E. W., 92
Reeder, K., 309
Reese, H. W., 274
Regnemer, J. L., 568
Rembold, K. L., 303
Resko, B. G., 536
Rest, J., 568
Reynolds, A. G., 361
Reynolds, D., 660
Reynolds, R. E., 311
Rheingold, H. L., 164, 302, 441, 445, 486
Ribble, M., 456
Ricciuti, H. N., 441, 443
Rice, M., 271, 491
Rice, R. D., 149
Richards, D. D., 372
Richards, F. A., 358
Richards, J. E., 210
Richards, P., 485
Richardson, J. G., 524
Richert, E. J., 258
Richmond, J. B., 169
Riesen, A. H., 230

Rieser, J., 165
Rinkoff, R. F., 445, 446
Rist, R. C., 669
Ritchie, F. K., 590
Ritter, K., 361
Rivers, C., 657
Roberts, C. J., 119, 122
Roberts, W. A., 454
Robertson, T. S., 271
Robinson, A., 90
Robinson, N., 149, 611, 612
Roche, A. F., 183, 193
Rock, I., 221
Rode, S. S., 150, 429
Rodgers, R. R., 685
Roedell, J. L., 226
Roeper, A., 350
Roff, M. F., 485, 676
Roffwarg, H. P., 166
Rogoff, B., 658, 659, 674
Rohwer, W. D., Jr., 364, 368
Rolf, J. E., 110
Rommetveit, R., 310
Roopnarine, J. L., 535
Rorvik, D. M., 83
Rose, R. M., 529
Rose, S. A., 149, 219, 244, 366
Rosen, B. C., 505
Rosen, R., 629
Rosenberg, B. G., 536, 626
Rosenberg, F., 475
Rosenberg, M., 475
Rosenblatt, P. C., 524
Rosenbloom, S., 218, 219
Rosenblum, M. A., 673
Rosenhan, D. L., 16, 17, 19, 494
Rosenheim, M. K., 636
Rosenkoetter, L. I., 577
Rosenkrantz, A. L., 684
Rosenkrantz, P. S., 517, 545
Rosenman, R. H., 107
Rosenthal, M. K., 164, 289, 292
Rosenthal, R., 666
Rosenthal, T., 668
Rosenzweig, M. R., 174
Rosman, B. L., 184, 373
Ross, H. S., 495
Ross, J., 504
Ross, R. P., 271
Rosser, R. A., 373
Rossiter, J. R., 271
Rotenberg, K. J., 472
Rothbart, M. K., 405, 626, 627
Rothschild, N., 536, 651
Rousseau, J. J., 11, 12
Rovee-Collier, C. K., 366
Rovet, J., 90
Rovine, M., 450, 612
Rowan, L. E., 315
Rowe, D. C., 106
Rubin, K. H., 346, 347
Rubin, R., 391
Rubinstein, E. A., 654
Ruble, D. N., 504, 535, 537, 679, 680
Rudolph, F., 658
Rule, B. G., 496
Rumbaugh, D. M., 322
Ruopp, R., 455
Rushton, J. P., 491, 572, 577
Russell, C., 610

Rutherford, E., 489, 534, 616
Rutter, M., 106, 110, 417, 428, 433, 459, 460, 659, 660, 661, 662, 664, 665

Sacks, E. L., 409
Saco-Pollitt, C. S., 139
Saenger, G., 128
Sagi, A., 69
Sagotsky, G., 490, 679
Salapatek, P., 208
Salatas, H., 371
Salili, F., 502
Salkind, N. J., 373
Saltz, E., 581
Saltz, R., 311
Saltzstein, H. D., 569
Sameroff, A. J., 127, 146, 150
Sampson, E. E., 626
Samuels, H. R., 445, 625
Sander, L. W., 164, 214, 289
Sanders, J., 270, 646
Sandoval, J., 670
Sanford, F. H., 390
Santogrossi, O., 651
Santrock, J. W., 541, 543, 570, 609, 624, 630, 631
Sarason, S. B., 407
Sawin, D. B., 493, 618
Sawrey, W. L., 543
Scarr, S., 103, 107, 112, 398, 399, 412, 415, 417, 483
Scarrone, L. A., 192
Schachter, F. F., 631, 632
Schachter, S., 484, 626, 627
Schaefer, E. S., 485, 614
Schaefer, M., 149
Schaffer, H. R., 434, 435, 437, 438, 440, 443, 444, 482
Schaie, K. W., 384
Schalling, D., 529
Scharf, J. S., 352
Scheinfeld, A., 82
Schleimer, K., 184
Schneider, F. W., 393, 394, 406, 407, 488
Schneider, P. A., 168
Schrager, J. B., 584
Schramm, W., 647
Schreibman, L., 255
Schuller, V., 433, 617
Schwartz, P., 455
Schwartz, T. H., 491
Schwarz, J. C., 108, 584
Schwebel, A. I., 628
Schweitzer, J., 660
Scott, J. P., 104
Scott, P. M., 490
Sears, R. R., 260, 262, 263, 436, 442, 448, 498, 575
Seaver, W. B., 666
Sebald, H., 683
Secord, P. F., 477
Sedlak, A. J., 350
Seitz, V., 408
Seligman, M. E. P., 259
Sellers, M. J., 438
Sells, S. B., 485, 676
Selman, R. L., 472, 473, 478, 479, 480, 481, 561
Semmes, J., 230
Sewell, W. H., 620

Shaffer, D. R., 260, 346, 485, 494, 517, 543, 558, 605, 616, 618, 626
Shakespeare, W., 203, 233
Shannon, D., 167, 610
Shantz, D. W., 496
Shapiro, E. K., 669
Shapiro, S., 131
Sharp, D., 658, 659
Shatz, M., 309, 312, 316
Shaw, J. L., 427
Shaw, M. E., 682
Shea, J. D. C., 484, 485
Shea, S. L., 210
Shere, J. B., 662
Shereshefsky, P. M., 142
Sherk, H., 230
Sherman, D., 433, 634
Sherman, M., 399
Sherman, R. C., 682
Shettles, L. B., 83
Shields, J., 108
Shigetomi, C. C., 488
Shimmin, H. S., 537
Shinn, M., 406
Shirk, E. J., 275
Shirley, M. M., 174, 194
Shucard, D. W., 293
Shucard, J., 293
Shuey, A., 407
Shure, M. B., 487
Siegal, L. S., 392
Siegel, G. M., 303
Siegler, R. S., 356, 371, 372, 373
Siesky, A. E., Jr., 628
Sigel, I. E., 350
Sigman, M., 244
Signorelli, N., 270, 648
Simalek, Z., 138
Siman, M. L., 685
Simmons, R. G., 475
Simon, H., 360
Simon, T., 386, 387
Simpson, C. H., 524
Simutis, Z., 577
Sinclair, M., 164, 220
Singer, J., 346
Siperstein, G. N., 215, 289
Skeels, H. M., 399
Skinner, B. F., 40, 56, 57, 58, 59, 125, 247, 251, 252, 254, 314
Skodak, M., 399
Skotko, D., 581
Slaby, D. A., 486
Slaby, R. G., 501, 523, 535, 537
Slaughter, D. T., 414, 415
Slobin, D. I., 288, 300, 305, 306, 316, 319, 320, 323, 326
Slone, D., 131
Small, A. W., 504
Smetana, J. G., 563
Smith, A., 659
Smith, D. W., 136
Smith, F., 228
Smith, J. W., 454
Smith, L. B., 311
Smith, P. H., 205
Smith, P. K., 523
Smith, R. A., 588
Smith, S., 399
Smith, S. D., 91

Smitley, S., 205
Snow, C. E., 293, 318
Snow, M. E., 482, 484, 524, 534, 612
Sobesky, W., 570
Sobol, B. L., 651
Sollie, D. L., 610
Sontag, L. W., 127, 403
Sorce, J. F., 446
Sorell, G. T., 475
Spaulding, D. A., 438
Spearman, C., 383, 384
Spelke, E., 438
Spence, J. T., 546, 547
Spieker, S., 292
Spitz, H. H., 226
Spitz, R. A., 443, 456, 457, 458
Spivack, G., 487
Sprafkin, J. N., 22, 24, 270, 536, 646, 653, 654
Spuhler, J. N., 407
Sroka, S., 258
Sroufe, L. A., 150, 429, 440, 441, 445, 451, 452, 484, 503, 611
Staats, A. W., 246, 314
Staats, C. K., 314
Staffieri, J. R., 185, 186, 191
Starr, R. H., 138, 633
Staub, E., 585
Stayton, D. J., 168, 438, 445
Steele, B. F., 433, 434, 634
Stein, A. H., 23, 272, 545, 649, 654
Stein, Z. A., 128
Steinberg, C. S., 646
Steinberg, J., 450
Steinberg, L., 455, 631, 634
Steinhorst, R., 258
Steinmetz, S. K., 34
Steinschneider, A., 167, 169
Stephan, C. W., 430
Stephan, W. G., 665, 670, 671, 672
Stern, C. 83, 90, 109
Stern, D., 292, 431, 432
Stern, J. A., 146
Stern, L., 149, 633
Stern, W., 387, 388
Stevenson, H. W., 658
Stevenson, M., 435
Stewart, R. B., 625
Stifter, E., 586
St. John, N. H., 665, 672
St. Leger, S., 660
Stolberg, U., 441
Stolz, L. M., 542
Stone, B. P., 366
Stoneman, Z., 267, 271, 535, 608, 609, 625, 680
Strange, W., 215
Straus, M. A., 34, 620
Strauss, M. E., 138
Strauss, M. S., 209
Strayer, F. F., 523
Streissguth, A. P., 136
Streitfeld, P. P., 138, 139
Stremmel, A., 488
Stringer, S., 611
Strock, B. D., 166
Stryker, J. C., 138
Stryker, M. P., 230
Stuckey, M. F., 632
Stumphauzer, J. S., 679

Sturla, E., 530
Styczyski, L. E., 678, 679
Suci, G., 685
Sugar, J., 310
Sugarman, S., 341
Sullivan, H. S., 484
Sullivan, M. W., 366
Sumi, D., 124
Suomi, S. J., 455, 456, 634, 675, 676
Super, C. M., 567
Surber, C. F., 562
Susman, E. J., 272, 654
Susser, M. W., 128
Sutton-Smith, B., 536, 626
Svanum, S., 406
Svejda, M. J., 428
Swammerdam, J., 76
Symonds, L., 219

Tan, R. S., 536
Tanner, J. M., 172, 173, 174, 179, 180, 181,
    183, 187, 188, 189, 192, 194
Tauber, M. A., 524, 536
Taylor, D. G., 450
Tees, R. C., 290
Teeven, R. C., 505
Teller, D. Y., 163
Terborg, J. R., 521
Terman, L. M., 383, 388, 396, 397
Terrace, H. S., 322
Thane, K., 427
Thelen, E., 195
Thelen, M. H., 680, 681
Thoman, E. B., 427, 432
Thomas, A., 104, 105, 106
Thomas, D., 293
Thomas, D. B., 147
Thomas, M. H., 649, 650
Thomas, N. G., 664
Thompson, H., 194, 195
Thompson, J. R., 297
Thompson, R. A., 452, 453, 454, 484
Thompson, R. F., 86
Thompson, S. K., 470, 522, 525
Thompson, W. R., 99, 108
Thorndike, E. L., 247
Thurston, D., 146
Thurston, L. L., 384
Thurston, T. G., 384
Timney, H. H., 233
Tingle, B. A., 493
Tinklenberg, J. R., 138
Tinsley, V. S., 276
Tizard, B., 457
Tolar, C. J., 535
Tolar, H. C., 486
Tomikawa, S. A., 297
Tomlin, C., 469
Tomlinson-Keasey, C., 353, 359, 569
Toner, I. J., 570, 577, 582, 588, 589, 590
Torgesen, J., 366
Touhey, J. C., 522
Tracy, R. L., 450
Travers, J., 455
Trehub, S. E., 215
Treiber, F., 209
Trickett, P. K., 408
Tronick, E. Z., 434

Trost, M. A., 110, 676
Tryon, R. C., 99, 398
Tuchmann-Duplessis, H., 130
Tucker, P., 531
Tulkin, S. R., 356, 446
Turiel, E., 563, 566, 568
Turk, P., 271
Turkewitz, G., 218
Turnball, C. M., 498
Turner, E. W., 310
Tyack, D., 307
Tyler, L. E., 407

Ulleland, C. N., 136
Ullian, D. Z., 539
Ulman, K. J., 184
Umeh, B. J., 482
Underwood, B., 488, 492, 493, 668
Urbain, E. S., 487
Utech, D. A., 683

Van Cleave, E. F., 475
Vandell, D. L., 483, 484, 624
Vandenberg, B., 346
Vandenberg, S. G., 112
van de Reit, V., 407
van Doorninck, W. J., 503
Vaughn, B. E., 432, 452, 455, 679
Vaughn, H. G., Jr., 163
Vennart, J., 122
Verbrugge, R., 215
Verna, G. B., 261
Veroff, J., 632
Victoria (Queen of England), 94
Vincze, M., 482
Vlietstra, A. G., 361, 362
Vogel, F., 131
Vogel, S. R., 517, 545
Von Bargen, D., 523
Voos, D. K., 428
Voydanoff, D. R., 496
Vurpillot, E., 222
Vygotsky, L. S., 276, 277, 471

Waber, D. P., 530
Waddington, C. H., 111
Wahler, R. G., 431, 677
Walbek, N., 491
Walder, L. O., 263, 270, 649
Waldrip, M. F., 527
Walk, R. D., 164, 210, 213, 214, 215, 219,
    220, 230, 231, 232
Walker, A., 631
Walker, K., 219
Walker, L. J., 568, 569, 573
Walker, R. N., 226
Wall, S., 429
Wallace, J. C., 361
Wallace, J. R., 497
Wallerstein, J. S., 628, 630
Walster, E., 18, 184, 185
Walster, G. W., 18
Walters, R. H., 274, 500, 575, 577
Ward, W. D., 524
Warren, J. R., 626
Warshak, R. A., 541, 609, 630
Washborne, J. N., 584
Waterman, A. S., 475, 477

Waters, E., 429, 432, 441, 449, 450, 452, 484
Waters, H. F., 648
Waters, H. S., 276
Watkins, B. A., 270
Watson, J. B., 40, 53, 54, 56, 59, 65, 70, 246,
    248
Watson, J. S., 253, 259
Waxler, C. Z., 490
Weatherley, D., 186
Webber, P. L., 107
Webster, E. J., 303
Wechsler, D., 383, 389, 390
Wechsler, R. C., 629
Wehren, A., 537
Weinberg, R. A., 103, 107, 398, 399, 412,
    415
Weinraub, M., 444, 447
Weir, R. H., 291
Weisberg, P., 58, 302
Weisner, T. S., 624
Weiss, A. L., 315
Weiss, M. G., 362
Weisz, J. R., 481, 619
Weller, G. M., 527
Wellman, H. M., 270, 303, 361, 367, 370,
    371, 471
Werker, J. F., 290
Werner, H., 226
Werner, S., 163
Werner, P. D., 517
Wesman, A., 408
West, M. J., 618
Westby, S. D., 270, 651
Weston, D. R., 451, 484, 612
Whalen, C., 254
Whalen, W. T., 484
Wheeler, L. R., 399
Whitaker, H. A., 310
White, B. W., 683
White, C. B., 568
White, J. C., 407
White, R. K., 667
White, R. W., 502
White, S. H., 274, 276
Whiteman, M., 683
Whiting, B. B., 489
Whiting, J. W. M., 489
Whitley, B. E., Jr., 547
Wichern, F., 506
Widdowson, E. M., 194
Widmayer, S. M., 160, 611
Wiggam, A. E., 40
Wilcox, M. J., 303
Wilcox, S., 209
Wildfong, S., 296
Wilkinson, A., 658
Wilkinson, L. C., 303
Wilkner, K., 165
Willemsen, E., 167, 244
Willerman, L., 459
Williams, J., 228
Williams, J. E., 19, 470
Williams, T., 647
Wilson, K. S., 483, 484
Wilson, M., 87
Wilson, R. S., 102, 104, 187
Winick, M., 127, 190, 193
Winickoff, S. A., 141, 428, 610

Winterbottom, M., 505
Wippman, J., 452, 484
Wisenbaker, J., 660
Witkin, H. A., 91, 221, 235, 236, 237, 238
Wittig, M. A., 107
Witty, P. A., 411
Wolff, K. F., 76
Wolff, P. H., 165, 168, 290
Wood-Schneider, M., 490
Woodson, R., 268, 344
Wooten, B. R., 163
Wootten, J., 307
Worchel, S., 244
Worobey, J., 160
Wright, C., 503

Wright, H. F., 674, 675
Wright, J. C., 270, 271, 647, 653, 655, 656
Wrightsman, L. S., 390

Yalisove, D., 312
Yamamoto, J. Y., 682
Yando, R., 375
Yarbrough, C., 128
Yarrow, L. J., 142, 490, 491, 503
Yeates, K. O., 404
Yendovitskaya, T. V., 224
Yerkes, R. M., 390
Yonas, A., 165, 213
Young, W. C., 528
Yussen, S. R., 370, 577

Zack, P. M., 192
Zahn, G. L., 668, 669
Zahn-Waxler, C., 487, 493, 501
Zajonc, R. B., 405, 406, 626
Zegoib, L. E., 605
Zeiss, A. R., 588
Zelazo, N. A., 195
Zelazo, P. R., 195, 442, 455
Zeman, B. R., 370
Zeskind, P. S., 128, 129, 168, 454
Zigler, E., 408, 409, 662
Zimmerman, B. J., 264
Zimmerman, R. R., 436, 437
Zucker, K. J., 446
Zussman, J. U., 620, 622

Ability tracking, 416, 661–663
Aboriginal society, 585
Absurdity riddles, 312
Accommodation:
  cognitive growth and, 63–64, 337, 338
  defined, 63, 337
Achievement (*see also* Need for
    achievement):
  children's expectancies and, 504
  in desegregated schools, 672
  in effective and ineffective schools,
    659–660
  extrinsic orientation, 503
  family influences, 503–507
  grade retention and, 670–671
  of handicapped children, 662
  intrinsic orientation, 503
  and locus of control, 504–507
  in open and traditional classrooms,
    663–664
  peers as models of, 679
  teacher expectancies and, 522,
    666–667
  television and, 647
Achievement motivation (*see* Need for
    achievement)
Action for Children's Television, 650
Activity/passivity issue, defined, 41
Adaptation:
  cognitive growth and, 63–64, 337–338
  defined, 63, 337
Adjustment phase, in reactions to
    divorce, 628–629
Adolescent growth spurt:
  defined, 179
  hormonal influences on, 188–189
  timing of, 180–181
Adrenal gland, 188, 189
Age of viability, 124–125
Aggression:
  cultural influences, 497–498
  defined, 494–495
  developmental trends, 495–497
  family influences, 498–499, 500
  impulsivity and, 374
  methods of controlling, 499–502
  origins of, 495
  peer influences, 677–678, 680
  sex differences, 497, 519, 529
  stability of, 497, 526, 527
  television and, 270, 647–651, 653, 654
"Aging ova" hypothesis, 92–93
Alcohol, and prenatal development, 134,
    136–137
Allantosis, 120–121
Alleles:
  defined, 85
  dominant, 85–87
  and pleiotropism, 86
  recessive, 85–87

Altruism:
  cooperative games and, 490
  cultural influences, 489
  defined, 486, 487
  developmental trends, 486–488
  empathy and, 492–493
  family influences, 493–494
  moral reasoning and, 492
  observational learning of, 17, 491
  reinforcement and, 489–490
  sex differences, 488, 520
  television and, 22, 23–24, 272,
    652–654
Altruistic exhortations:
  and altruistic behavior, 491
  defined, 491
  and development of altruistic
    self-concept, 492
American Sign Language (ASL):
  characteristics of, 302
  children's acquisition of, 302–303
  chimpanzees' use of, 320, 322
Amish society, 498
Amniocentesis, 96–97
Amnion, 119–120
Anal stage, defined, 47
Androgenized females, 529–530
Androgyny, 545–548
Angry cry, 168, 290
Animism, 345
Anorexia nervosa, 184
Anoxia:
  altitude and, 139
  as a birth complication, 145–146
  defined, 139
  obstetric medication and, 146–148
Anxious/avoidant attachment:
  defined, 449
  development of, 450–451
Anxious/resistant attachment:
  defined, 449
  development of, 449–450
Anytime malformations, 131
Apgar test, 158–159
Aphasia:
  defined, 319
  and language development, 319,
    322–323
Apnea, 167
Apnea monitor, 168, 169
Arapesh society, 498, 530
Army Alpha Intelligence Test, 390
Assimilation:
  cognitive growth and, 63–64, 337–338
  defined, 63, 337
Attachment:
  caregiver-to-infant, 427–434
  defined, 426, 427
  father's role in, 450–451
  individual differences in, 448–450

Attachment (*contd*)
  infant-to-caregiver, 434–440
  long-term correlates of, 451–452,
    483–484, 503
  and separation anxiety, 444
  stability of, 452–453
  stages of, 434–435
  and stranger anxiety, 440
  theories of, 428, 435–440
Attachment object:
  defined, 426, 427
  fathers as, 435, 438, 441–442,
    450–451, 612
  mothers as, 434–436, 438–439,
    449–450
  as a secure base, 443, 445–446
  siblings as, 625
Attention, development of, 221–224,
    361–363
Attentional hypothesis, of delay of
    gratification, 587–588
Attention span, 223–225
Auditory perception, development of,
    214–215
Authoritarian parenting, 614–616
Authoritarian teacher, 667–668
Authoritative parenting, 614–616
Authoritative teacher, 667–668
Authority and social-order maintenance,
    stage of, 564–567
Autism, 254–255
Autonomous morality, 560–561
Autonomy vs. shame and doubt, 52, 470,
    471
Autostimulation theory, 166–167
Aversion therapy, 248

Babbling:
  as a contributor to attachments, 429,
    439
  development of, 290–291
  relation to meaningful speech, 291
Babinski reflex, 162, 165
Baby biography, 12–13
Balance-scale problems, 371–372
Basic gender identity, 537
Battered-child syndrome, 633–634 (*see
    also* Child abuse)
Behavioral comparisons phase, of
    impression formation, 477–478
Behavioral schema, defined, 335
Behavior genetics:
  defined, 99
  research methods in, 99–101
Behaviorism, 55 (*see also* Learning
    theory)
"Bill of rights" for children, 10
Biosocial theory, of sex typing, 531–532
Birthing room, 151

Birth order:
  and achievement, 626, 627
  and achievement training, 405
  and IQ, 403–406
  and obedience, 626, 627
  and popularity, 626–627, 678
  and sex typing, 626
  and sociability, 484, 626
Birth process:
  in birthing rooms, 151
  by Cesarean section, 146–147
  complications of, 145–150
  effects on baby, 144
  effects on older siblings, 144–145
  effects on parents, 142–144
  at home, 150–151
  stages of, 141–142
Birth trauma, 144
Blastocyst, 118–119
Blastula, 118–119, 120
Body build, and personality
    development, 185–186, 678
Bonding (*see* Emotional bonding)
Brain growth spurt, 174, 188
Brazelton Neonatal Behavioral
    Assessment Scale, 159–160, 432, 434
Brazelton training, 160, 170
Breech birth, 146, 147

Canalization, 111
Carpentered environment hypothesis,
    233–234
Case study method, 20–21
Castration anxiety, 48, 533–534
Catch-up growth, 189, 192
Categorical self, 470, 471
Catharsis hypothesis, 499
Cathartic technique, 500, 501
Centration:
  conservation and, 349
  defined, 279
  "5 to 7" shift and, 278, 279
Cephalocaudal development, 171–172,
    174, 176
Cerebral lateralization:
  defined, 175
  and language development, 176, 319,
    322–323
Cerebrum, 174–175
Cesarean section, 146–147
Child abuse:
  characteristics of abused children, 633,
    635
  characteristics of child abusers,
    633–634, 635
  environmental influences, 634–635
  incidence of, 632–633
  treatment and prevention of, 635–637
Children's Television Workshop (CTW),
    654–657
Chorion, 120–121
Chorionic villus biopsy, 97
Chromosomal abnormalities, 89–93
Chromosome, defined, 77
Cigarette smoking, and prenatal
    development, 134, 136–137, 140
Classical conditioning:
  and attitude formation, 246
  compared to operant conditioning, 247
  defined, 55, 244–245
  developmental trends in, 247

Classical conditioning (*contd*)
  and emotional development, 246
  as a therapeutic technique, 248
Class inclusion:
  defined, 347
  during middle childhood, 351
  during the preschool period, 347, 349,
    354
Classroom "zone of activity," 663
Clinical method, 20–21, 334, 336
Coaching technique, of social-skills
    training, 487
Codominance, 87
Coercive home environment:
  and children's aggression, 498–499
  defined, 499
  divorce and, 628–629
  modification of, 500
Cognition, defined, 333 (*see also*
    Cognitive development)
Cognitive contributors:
  to adjustment, health, and
    occupational status, 394–397
  to attachment, 438
  to the "5 to 7" shift, 277–278, 279
  to language development, 325–326
  to moral development, 558–571,
    575–577, 579–580
  to motor inhibition, 582
  to popularity, 8, 481, 678
  to role-taking skills, 479, 481
  to scholastic achievement, 393–394
  to self-concept, 469, 472, 475
  to self-control, 580–590, 591–592
  to separation anxiety, 446
  to sex typing, 536–538
  to stranger anxiety, 444
Cognitive development:
  in adolescence and beyond, 354–358,
    362, 367–369, 372
  defined, 61, 334
  and differences in cognitive style,
    373–375
  in infancy, 338–344, 365–366
  information-processing theory of, 334,
    360–373
  in middle childhood, 351–354, 362,
    363, 366–373
  and moral development, 558–571,
    575–577, 579–580
  Piaget's theory of, 62–65, 334–360
  play and, 346–347
  in the preschool period, 344–351, 361,
    362–363, 366
  schooling and, 658–659
  and sex typing, 536–538, 540
  stages of, 64–65, 338–358, 359–360
  television and, 271, 654–657
Cognitive model (of the "5 to 7" shift),
    277–278, 279
Cognitive operations:
  in the concrete-operational stage,
    351–352, 353, 359
  defined, 334, 335
  in the formal-operational stage,
    354–355, 356–357, 358
  in the preoperational stage, 345, 349,
    350–351
Cognitive rationales, for moral behavior,
    575–577
Cognitive social-learning theory, 58–60

Cognitive structure (*see* Schema)
Cognitive style, 373–375, 582
Color blindness, 87–88
Commercial messages:
  children's reactions to 270–271, 652
  effects on peer interaction, 652–653
Communication (*see also*
    Communication skills):
  defined, 285
  mother's intonation as a cue for, 292
Communication pressure hypothesis, 315
Communication skills (*see also*
    Pragmatics):
  cognitive determinants of, 313–314
  during the holophrastic stage, 298
  during middle childhood, 312–314
  during the prelinguistic stage, 292–294
  of preschool children, 309–310
  during the telegraphic stage, 301–304
Compensation, 349, 350–351
Compensatory education:
  Bronfenbrenner's prescription for, 415
  defined, 413
  and IQ, 413–414
  limitations of, 415–416
  and scholastic achievement, 413–414
Compensatory masculinity, 543
Conception, 78–79, 118
Concepts:
  defined, 273
  learning of, 273–278
Conceptual tempo (*see* Cognitive style)
Concordance rate, 108–109
Concrete-operations stage:
  characteristics of, 65, 351–352,
    356–357
  defined, 351
  education and, 353, 354
  linguistic humor and, 352–353
  and reactions to hypothetical
    propositions, 354, 356–357
"Conditioned anxiety" hypothesis,
    444–445
Conditioned response (CR), defined, 245
Conditioned stimulus (CS), defined, 245
Conformity (*see also* Cross-pressures):
  in peer groups, 681–683
  sex differences in, 521
Congenital defects:
  defined, 89
  prevention of, 140–141
Conservation, 348, 349–351, 353, 523,
    537
Constructivist, defined, 334, 335
Contact comfort, 436–438
Continuity/discontinuity issue, 41
Continuous reinforcement:
  defined, 253
  vs. partial reinforcement, 253–256
Contour:
  defined, 207
  and pattern perception, 206, 207, 224
Conventional morality:
  defined, 564–565
  developmental trends, 565–566
  examples of, 566–567
  relation to cognitive development, 569
Converging evidence, 16–17
Conversation, and language development,
    316–318, 319, 326
Cooing, 290–291

Correlation:
in behavior genetics research, 100–101
and causation, 25
Counterconditioning, 60, 247–248
Crib death (*see* Sudden infant death
syndrome)
Crisis phase, in reactions to divorce, 628,
629
Critical period:
defined, 439
for imprinting, 439
for language development, 322–323,
324
for sex typing, 530
for social development of humans,
459–460
for social development of monkeys,
455–456
Cross-cultural comparison, 31–33
Cross-generational problem, 28–29
Crossing-over phenomenon, 81
Cross-modal perception:
defined, 216, 217
development of, 219, 220
Cross-pressures:
cross-cultural studies of, 685–687
defined, 683
developmental trends, 683
importance in U.S. society, 683–685
situational influences on, 683
Cross-sectional comparison, 26–27
Cross-sectional/short-term longitudinal
comparison, 29–31
Crying:
developmental trends, 168–169
functions of, 168–169, 290, 429, 439
varieties of, 168, 290
Crystallized intelligence (g_c), 384, 385
Cultural influences:
on aggression, 497–498
on altruism, 489
on cognitive development, 338, 356,
359
on IQ, 407–409
on moral development, 567–568
on peer conformity, 685–687
on perceptual development, 233–235,
236–237
on self-control, 585–586
on separation anxiety, 444–445
on sex typing, 517, 530
on treatment of neonates, 160, 603
"Culture-fair" tests, 408–409
Cumulative-deficit hypothesis, 399
Curvature, and pattern perception, 206
Cystic fibrosis, 94–96, 98

Day care, 454–455
Deferred imitation, 269, 341, 344
Delay choice:
child's evaluation of, 587
defined, 583
determinants of, 584–586
developmental trends in, 584
Delay of gratification (*see also* Patience):
as altruism, 586
cultural influences on, 585–586
and development of patience, 587–592
individual differences in, 584, 585
observational learning of, 584–585
peers as models for, 679

Delay of gratification (*contd*)
situational determinants of, 584
Dependent variable, defined, 21
Depression, childhood antecedents of,
619
Deprivation dwarfism, 193–194
Depth perception:
cultural influences on, 236–237
development in infancy, 210–211
in monocular infants, 231
and the movement hypothesis,
232–233
DES (diethylstilbestrol), 134, 136–137,
140
Desegregated schools, effects of, 670–672
Desensitization hypothesis, 649–650
Development:
chronological overview of, 7
as a cumulative process, 6–7
defined, 6, 7
in historical perspective, 9–14
as a holistic process, 7–8
methods of studying, 14–36
theories of, 39–70
Developmental psychology, defined, 6, 7
Developmental quotient (*see* DQ)
Developmental schedules, 391–392
Developmental stage, 41–43
Developmental theories, 39–70
Diabetes:
defined, 94
and prenatal development, 132
treatment of, 98
Differentiation theory:
of intersensory perception, 216–220
of perceptual learning, 226–228
Directionality issue, in family research,
606–607
Discipline (*see also* Punishment):
and altruism, 494, 618
children's contributions to, 618–619
and moral development, 578–580, 618
patterns of, 494, 578–579, 618
and sociability, 618
social class differences in, 622
Discriminated smiling response (*see*
Social smiling)
Discrimination, 245, 273–274
Dishabituation, 244, 245
Distal stimulation, defined, 621
Distinctive features, 226–228
Distraction hypothesis, of delay-
of-gratification, 588–589
Divorce:
adjustment phase, 629, 630
crisis phase, 628, 629
incidence of, 609, 627
long-term reactions to, 630
sex differences in response to, 628
and sex-role development, 543–545
Dizygotic (DZ) twins:
defined, 82–83
as participants in family studies, 83,
101–109, 398, 400–401, 483
Doctrine of preformationism, 76
Doctrine of specificity:
defined, 571
evaluation of, 571–573, 578
Dominant allele, 84–85
Dove Counterbalance General
Intelligence Test, 408

Down's syndrome, 92–93
DQ:
defined, 391
relation to IQ, 391–392
Drive, 56–58
Drug use:
obstetric, and effects on infants,
146–148
parents as models for, 684
peers as models for, 684
and prenatal development, 133–138,
140
"Early experience" hypothesis, 448, 449
Echolalia, 290, 291
Eclampsia (*see* Toxemia)
Economic goal, of parenting 602–604
Ectoderm, 120
Ectomorphic physique:
defined, 185
and personality development, 185–186
Educational television:
and cognitive development, 271,
654–656
limitations of, 656–657
and prosocial behavior, 271–272, 654
and reduction of social stereotypes,
651–652
Effectance motivation, 502, 503
Effective schools:
and academic achievement, 660
defined, 659
determinants of, 659–665
Ego, defined, 45
Egocentrism:
cognitive development and, 346–347,
349–350, 351
defined, 345
and moral reasoning, 560–561
peer contacts and, 560–561
and sex-role stereotyping, 538–539
Ego-defense mechanisms, 49 (*see also*
Repression; Sublimation)
Elaboration:
defined, 365
development of, 367–368
as a retrieval process, 368–369
schooling and, 658–659
Electra complex:
defined, 49
and moral development, 49, 557–558
and sex typing, 533–534
Electric Company, 656
Embedded Figures Test, 225
Embryo, period of the, 118, 119–122
Emotional bonding, 427–429
Emotional stress:
of mother, and prenatal development,
126–127
and parent/child interactions, 612, 620,
628
and parent/infant attachments,
433–434
and physical development, 192–194
Empathic concern, 107
Empathy:
and aggression, 501
and altruism, 488, 492–493
biological bases, 69, 107
defined, 69, 489
Empiricist perspective (*see also*
Nature/nurture controversy):

Empiricist perspective (*contd*)
  on language development, 288
  on perceptual development, 204, 210
Endoderm, 120
Endomorphic physique:
  defined, 185
  and personality development,
    185–186, 191
Engrossment, 143, 428, 612
Enrichment theory, of intersensory
  perception, 216, 217, 219, 220
Enuresis, 248
Environmental determinism, 59
Environmental hypothesis, of group
  differences in IQ, 411–413
Environmental influences (*see also*
  Cultural influences; Family
  influences):
  on child abuse, 634–635
  on delay of gratification, 584–586
  on IQ, 398–406, 407, 410, 411–413
  on language development, 316–318,
    326
  on moral reasoning, 567–568, 569–570
  on parenting, 603–604, 606, 620
  on perceptual development, 229–237,
    238
  on physical development, 189–195
Equilibrium, 63–64
Eros, defined, 45
Erythroblastosis, 132–133
Estrogen, and sexual development, 188,
  189
Ethnocentrism, defined, 623
Ethological theory:
  of altruism, 68, 69
  of attachment, 438–440
  contributions and criticisms of, 67–70
  of separation anxiety, 445–446
  of stranger anxiety, 443
Ethology, defined, 67
Executive responses, 439
Expansions, 317–318
Experimental control, 22–23
Experimental method, 21–24
Expiatory punishment, 560, 561
Expressive communicators, 295
Expressive role, 517
Extended family, 602, 603
Externalizers, 505–506 (*see also* Locus of
  control)
Extinction, 246, 247, 253–256
Extrafamilial influences:
  defined, 645
  on developing children, 645–687
Extrinsic orientation, 503
Extrinsic reinforcement:
  vs. intrinsic reinforcement, 257
  and task performance, 257–258

Faceness schema, 208, 209
Facial attractiveness:
  and parent-to-infant attachments,
    429–430
  and popularity with peers, 678–679
Facial perception, 207–210
Factor analysis, 383–386
Failure to thrive, 192–193
Fake cries, 168, 169, 290, 291
Family(ies) (*see also* Family influences;
  Parenting; Siblings):

Family(ies) (*contd*)
  changing character of, 608–609
  and childrearing patterns, 613–619
  configuration of, and child
    development, 623–627
  cross-cultural studies of, 603–604, 606,
    622–623
  defined, 602
  divorce and, 627–631
  functions of, 602–605
  methods of studying, 604–605
  and parent/infant interactions, 609–613
  reconstituted, 609, 631
  as social systems, 608, 613
  television and, 647
Family influences (*see also* Parenting;
  Siblings):
  on achievement, 503–507
  on aggression, 496, 498–499, 500
  on altruism, 493–494
  on intellectual performance, 400–406
  on moral development, 561, 578–580
  on obesity, 192–193
  on perceptual development, 235–237
  on sex typing, 534–535, 536, 540–545
  on sociability, 485
Family social system, defined, 609
Family studies:
  defined, 100
  of intelligence, 101–104, 398, 400–401
  of mental illness, 108–109
  of personality, 106–108
  of sociability, 483
Famine, and infant mortality, 128
Father absence:
  incidence of, 540
  and sex typing, 542–545
Father/infant interactions, 435, 451–452,
  612–613
Fathers (*see also* Family influences;
  Parenting):
  as attachment objects, 435, 438,
    451–452, 612
  as custodial parents, 630
  as noncustodial parents, 629
  and sex typing, 533, 534–536, 612
"Fear of separation" hypothesis, 442–443
Feminine sex-typed individuals, 546
Fetal alcohol syndrome (FAS), 136–137
Fetus, period of the, 118, 119, 122–125
Field dependence/independence:
  cross-cultural variations, 236
  defined, 221
  development of, 235, 236
  and personality development,
    236–237, 238
  sex differences in, 236
Field experiment, 23–24
"5 to 7" shift:
  defined, 274, 275
  examples of, 274–276
  explanations of, 276–278
Fixation, 48
Fluid intelligence (g$_f$), 384, 385
Fontanelles, 173
"Forbidden toy" paradigm, 574, 575
Formal-operations stage:
  defined, 354, 355
  and higher stages, 357–358
  and hypothetical-deductive reasoning,
    354–355

Formal-operations stage (*contd*)
  and hypothetical propositions, 354,
    356–357
  incidence of, 356–357
  and moral development, 569
  and self-control, 592
  and sex-role stereotyping, 538
Form perception:
  in childhood, 224–229
  environmental influences on, 230,
    233–237
  in infancy, 209
Four-beaker problem, 354–355
Fraternal twins (*see* Dizygotic twins)
Freestyle, 652
Functional similarity hypothesis,
  296–297

g, 383, 384
Gametes, 80
Gender consistency:
  defined, 537
  role in sex typing, 537–538, 539–540
Gender constancy, 523 (*see also* Gender
  consistency)
Gender determination, 82–85
Gender identity:
  defined, 522, 523
  development of, 522–523, 532, 533,
    537, 538–540
Gender stability, 537
Generalizability, 20
Generalized reinforcer, 251, 256
Genes, defined, 77
Genetic counseling, 95–98, 140
Genetic dominance, 84–87
Genetic hypothesis:
  of group differences in IQ, 409–411
  of sociability, 483
Genetic transmission, principles of,
  78–89
Genital stage, 49
Genotype:
  defined, 82, 85
  relation to phenotype, 84–89, 109–112
Genotype/environment interactions,
  109–112
Gentle birthing, 144–145
Germ cells, 80
Germinal period, of prenatal
  development, 118–119
Glia, 173–174
"Good boy" or "good girl," stage of,
  564–567
Grade retention, effects of, 670–671
Grammatical morphemes:
  defined, 304, 305
  development of, 304–306
  errors in usage, 306, 319
Group tests, of intelligence, 390–391
Growth (*see* Physical development)
Growth hormone:
  defined, 189
  and physical development, 188, 189,
    194

Habit, 56–57
Habituation:
  defined, 165
  developmental trends, 244
  as a form of learning, 244–245

Habituation (*contd*)
  and perception, 164
Hallucinogenic drugs, and prenatal
    development, 134, 137–138
Head Start, 381, 413–414
Hemophilia, 94, 98
Hereditary defects, 89–98 (*see also*
    Chromosomal abnormalities)
Heredity:
  in historical perspective, 75–78
  and intelligence, 101–104, 382, 398,
    400–401, 409–411
  and language development, 288,
    318–319, 322–325
  and mental health, 108–109
  and perceptual development, 204
  and personality, 104–108
  and physical development, 187–188
  principles of, 77, 78–89
  and sex-role development, 527–528,
    529, 531–532
  and sociability, 483
Heritability:
  computational formula, 100–101
  defined, 99
  and group differences in IQ, 409–411
Heteronomous morality, 559–563
Heterozygous attribute, defined, 85
"High risk" neighborhood, 634–635
High SES, defined, 620, 621
Holistic development, 7–8, 9
Holophrase:
  defined, 294, 295
  toddlers' use of, 298
Holophrastic stage, of language
    development:
  defined, 294, 295
  and infants' choice of words, 294–296
  and production of holophrases, 298
  and semantic development, 296–298
Home-based interventions, 414–415
Home birthing, 150–151
HOME inventory:
  defined, 401
  as predictor of academic achievement,
    503–504
  as predictor of IQ, 402, 404
Homozygous attribute, defined, 85
Homunculus, 76–77
Horizontal decalage:
  in concrete operations, 353, 359
  defined, 353
  in formal operations, 355, 358
Hormonal influences:
  on aggression, 529–530
  on mothers' reactions to childbirth,
    144
  on physical development, 188–189,
    527–528, 531–532
  on prenatal development, 122, 127,
    134, 135–136, 531–532
  on sex typing, 529–530, 531–532
"Hormonal mediation" hypothesis, 428
Hostile aggression, 495, 496–497
Hunger cry, 168, 290
Huntington's chorea, 86, 89
Hutterite society, 498
Hyaline membrane disease, 148, 149
Hypothesis, defined, 15
Hypothetical-deductive reasoning,
    354–355

Id, defined, 45
Identical twins (*see* Monozygotic twins)
Identification 48, 533, 557–558
"Identification with the aggressor," 48
Identity achievement, 476–477
Identity crisis:
  defined, 475
  resolution of, 476–477
Identity diffusion, 476–477
Identity foreclosure, 476–477
Identity training, 351, 363
Ik society, 498
Illness, and physical development,
    191–192
Imaginary playmates, 345, 346
Imitation (*see also* Observational
    learning):
  development of, 268–269, 340, 344
  as an influence attempt, 680–681
  and language development, 288,
    315–318
Immanent justice, 560, 561
Implantation, 119
Impression formation:
  developmental trends, 476–478
  and role-taking skills, 479
Imprinting, 439
Impulsives, 584, 585
Impulsivity, 373–375
Incest, dangers of, 96
Incompatible-response technique, 264,
    265, 500–501
Incomplete dominance, 86–87
Independent variable, defined, 21
Indifferent gonad, 122, 123, 531
Indirect parental effects, 612–613
Indiscriminate attachment, 434
Induced labor, 150, 151
Inductive discipline:
  and altruism, 494, 618
  defined, 494, 495
  and moral development, 579–580,
    582–583, 618
Industry vs. inferiority:
  defined, 52, 474, 475
  and self-esteem, 474–475
Infant intelligence tests (*see*
    Developmental schedules)
Infant mortality:
  birth weight and, 124, 148
  chemicals and, 138–139
  disease and, 131–133, 140
  drugs and, 133–138, 140
  maternal age and, 126, 140
  nutrition and, 128, 140
  purity and, 126, 140
  radiation and, 138, 140
Informal curriculum, 658, 659
Information-processing theory, of
    intellectual development:
  assumptions of, 334, 360–361
  attentional processes, 361–363
  compared to Piaget's theory, 373
  memory processes, 363–371
  origins of, 360
  and problem solving, 371–373
Inhibitory controls:
  defined, 574, 575
  development of, 574–578
Initiative vs. guilt:
  defined, 52, 471

Initiative vs. guilt (*contd*)
  and development of self-concept, 470
Innate purity, 11, 40
Inner experimentation, 341
Insecure attachment (*see also*
    Anxious/avoidant attachment;
    Anxious/resistant attachment):
  development of, 449–451
  long-term correlates of, 451–452,
    483–484, 503
  stability of, 452, 454–455
  and stranger anxiety, 451
Instincts (*see also* Eros; Thanatos),
    44–45, 494
Institutionalized children, 456–459
Instrumental aggression, 495
Instrumental conditioning (*see* Operant
    conditioning)
Instrumental role, 517
Intellectual Achievement Responsibility
    Questionnaire, 506
Intellectual content, 62
Intellectual development (*see* Cognitive
    development)
Intellectual performance, 62, 393,
    416–417 (*see also* IQ)
Intelligence (*see also* Cognitive
    development; IQ):
  components of, 62–64, 335–337,
    383–386
  definitions of, 62, 334–335, 383–386,
    398
  environmental influences on, 103–104,
    398–399, 400–401
  and the nature/nurture controversy,
    101–104, 382–383, 398, 400–401
Intelligence quotient (*see* IQ)
Intelligence testing (*see also* Intelligence;
    IQ):
  distribution of scores, 389
  of infant intelligence, 391–392
  methodological considerations,
    394–395
  origins of, 386–388
  stability of scores, 392–393
  uses and abuses of, 416–417
Interactional synchrony, 430–432 (*see
    also* Synchronized routines)
Interactionist theory, of language
    development, 325–326
Intermittent reinforcement (*see* Partial
    reinforcement)
Internalization:
  and moral development, 556, 557–558,
    574, 576
  and sex typing, 48–49, 533
Internalizers 505–506 (*see also* Locus of
    control)
Intersensory perception, 215–221
Interview method, 19, 604
Intrinsic orientation, 503
Intrinsic reinforcement:
  vs. extrinsic reinforcement, 257
  and task performance, 257–258
Introversion/extraversion, 107
Intuitive period, of intellectual
    development, 347–349
In utero monitoring, 146
Invariant developmental sequence:
  of cognitive stages, 338, 359
  defined, 338, 339

Invariant developmental sequence (*contd*)
  of moral stages, 558, 561, 568–569
  of stages of gender identity, 537
IQ:
  compensatory education and, 413–415
  defined, 387
  environmental influences on, 398–399,
    400–401, 411–413
  family influences on, 400–406
  and health, adjustment, and life
    satisfaction, 396–397
  hereditary influences on, 398,
    400–401, 409–411
  infant schedules and, 391–392
  and intellectual ability, 393, 416–417
  and intellectual performance, 393,
    416–417
  and occupational status, 394–396
  race differences in, 406–413
  and scholastic achievement, 393–394,
    416–417
  social class and, 406–413
  stability of, 392–393
  tests of, 387–391
  uses and abuses of, 416–417
Irregular sleep, 165–166 (*see also* REM
  sleep)
Isolate monkeys, 453–457, 458, 460
Isolette, 147, 149
It scale, 541, 542

Karyotype, 82–83
Kewpie-doll effect, 429–430, 439
Kinesthetic sense, 220, 221
Kinship, 82–83, 100–101, 398
Klinefelter's syndrome, 90–91
Kohlberg's theory:
  of moral development, 563–571
  of sex typing, 536–538
Kwashiorkor, 190, 191

Labeling technique:
  and altruism, 492
  and delay of gratification, 590, 591
Labor:
  induced, 150, 151
  stages of, 141–142
Laissez-faire teacher, 667–668
Language:
  components of, 286–288
  defined, 285
  properties of, 285–286
Language acquisition device (LAD):
  defined, 288–289
  and language development, 289,
    318–319, 322, 323–326
Language development:
  biological influences on, 319, 322–323,
    325, 326
  in chimpanzees, 320–322
  cognitive development and, 325–326
  in deaf children, 291, 302–303
  environmental influences on, 316–318,
    326
  holophrastic stage of, 294–298
  interactionist theory of, 325–326
  learning theories of, 288, 314–318
  in mentally retarded children, 323
  in middle childhood, 310–314
  nativist theory of, 288–289, 318–319,
    322–325

Language development (*contd*)
  prelinguistic stage of, 289–294
Latency period, 49
Law of segregation, 77
Learned helplessness:
  defined, 259, 459
  in institutionalized infants, 459
Learning:
  of complex processes, 273–278
  defined, 55, 243
  development of, 244, 247, 251–252,
    268–269, 274–278
  Piaget's view of, 64–65
  theories of, 56–60
  types of, 54–55, 244–273
Learning/performance distinction,
  265–266
Learning theory:
  of attachment, 436–438, 440
  Bandura's cognitive approach, 59,
    264–269
  contributions of, 60
  criticisms of, 60
  of language development, 288,
    314–318
  of moral development, 571–578
  neo-Hullian approach, 56–57
  operant-learning approach, 57–58,
    247–260
  of separation anxiety, 444–445
  of sex typing, 534–536
  of stranger anxiety, 442–443
Learning to learn, 274–275
Lepcha society, 498
Level I abilities, 409
Level II abilities, 409
Libido, 46–50
Linguistic universals, 323
Locus of control:
  and academic achievement, 506
  defined, 505–506
  family influences on, 506–507, 620
  measurement of, 506
  social class and, 620
Longitudinal comparison, 27–28
Long-term memory (LTM)
  defined, 364, 365
  development of, 364, 365–371
Looking chamber, 204, 205
Looking-glass self:
  defined, 467
  in chimpanzees, 469
Love-oriented discipline:
  and altruism, 494
  defined, 494, 495
  and moral development, 578–580
Low birth weight:
  causes of, 148
  immediate complications, 124,
    148–149
  long-term complications, 149–150
Low SES, defined, 620, 621

Mad cry, 168, 290
Mainstreaming, 662
Malnutrition:
  and physical development, 189–191
  and prenatal development, 127–129
Manic depression, 108–109
Marasmus, 190, 191

Marfan's syndrome, 86, 97
Marital quality:
  and children's adjustment, 628, 630
  infant's effect on, 610
  and parent/infant interactions,
    433–434, 612
Masculine sex-typed individuals, 546
Masochist, defined, 615
Matching Familiar Figures Test, 373, 374
Maternal age:
  and hereditary abnormalities, 92–93
  and prenatal complications, 125–126
  and responsiveness to infants, 611
Maternal-deprivation hypothesis, 458
Maternal employment:
  and cognitive development, 632
  and emotional development, 454–455
  incidence of, 454, 541
  and sex typing, 631–632
  and sociability, 545, 631
Maturation:
  and cognitive development, 359, 360
  defined, 47
  and physical development, 170–187,
    194–195
  and social smiling, 430
Mean length of utterance (MLU), defined,
  299
Mediational model (of the "5 to 7" shift),
  276–277
Mediation deficiency:
  and concept learning, 277
  defined, 277, 367
  and recall memory, 366
Mediator, defined, 276, 277
Meiosis, 80–81
Memory:
  defined, 363
  development of, 364, 365–369
  information-processing theory of,
    363–365
  and metamemory, 369–371
Menarche:
  defined, 179
  secular trends, 183–184
Mennonite society, 498
Mental age (MA), 387–388
Mental illness:
  environmental influences, 110
  heritability of, 108–109
Mere exposure effect, 244, 245
Mesoderm, 120
Mesomorphic physique:
  defined, 185
  and personality development, 185–186
Metalinguistic awareness:
  cognitive development and, 278, 352
  defined, 279, 311
  and the "5 to 7" shift, 278
  and language development, 311
  and linguistic humor, 312, 352
Metamemory:
  defined, 369
  development of, 369–370
  relation to recall memory, 370–371
Metasystematic reasoning, 358, 359
Mexican society, 489
Middle-class bias, in family research,
  606, 622–623
Minimum distance principle (MDP), 310,
  311

Minority stereotyping:
  by teachers, 669
  television and, 651
Mitosis, 79–80
Modifier genes, 88–89
Monocular vision, and perceptual
  development, 231
Monozygotic (MZ) twins:
  defined, 82–83
  as participants in family studies, 83,
    101–109, 398, 400–401, 483
  and sexual reassignment, 531
Moral affect:
  defined, 557
  and inductive discipline, 579–580
  relation to moral behavior, 578
Moral behavior:
  cognitive rationales and, 575–577
  consistency of, 571–573
  defined, 557
  discipline and, 579–580, 582–583
  moral affect and, 578
  moral reasoning and, 570, 578
  observational learning of, 577
  punishment and, 575, 576
  reinforcement and, 574–575
  self-instructions and, 577–578
Moral development, 555–556, 557–580
  (see also Moral affect; Moral
  behavior; Moral reasoning)
Morality (see also Moral affect; Moral
  behavior; Moral reasoning):
  defined, 556, 557
  development of, 555–556, 557–580
  as a unitary attribute, 578
Morality of contract, individual rights,
  and democratically accepted
  principles, stage of, 565–567
Morality of individual principles of
  conscience, stage of, 565–567
Moral realism, 559–561, 562
Moral reasoning:
  cognitive development and, 560, 561,
    569
  consistency of, 570, 578
  cross-cultural studies of, 561, 566–568
  defined, 557
  discipline and, 579–580
  development of, 558–571
  invariance of stages, 559, 564, 568–569
  and moral behavior, 570, 578
  peer influences on, 561, 679
  sex differences, 570–571, 572–573
Moral relativism (see Autonomous
  morality)
Moral rules, 563
Moratorium status, 476–477
Moro reflex, 161, 163
Morphemes, defined, 286, 287
Mother dominance:
  and daughters' occupational
    aspirations, 541–542
  and sex typing, 541
Motherese, 316, 317
"Mother only" monkeys, 675
Motivational hypothesis, of group
  differences in IQ, 408–409
Motor development:
  in adolescence, 179
  in childhood, 177–178
  in infancy, 176–177

Motor development (contd)
  practice and, 194–195
  secular trends, 194
  visual/motor coordination and,
    177–178, 179
Motor inhibition, 581–582
Movement hypothesis, of perceptual
  development, 232–233
Mullerian inhibiting substance (MIS),
  531
Multiple sclerosis, 174
Mundugumor society, 498, 530
Muscular dystrophy (MD), 94
Mutations, 93–94
Myelinization, 174, 175, 225, 360

Naive hedonism, stage of, 564–566
Names, as contributors to popularity, 678
Narcotics, and prenatal development,
  134, 138
Nativist perspective:
  on intelligence, 382
  on language development, 288–289,
    318–325
  on perceptual development, 204, 210
Natural childbirth, 143
Naturalistic observation, 15–19, 604–605
Natural selection, 67
Nature/nurture controversy:
  defined, 41, 109
  and intelligence, 40, 101–104,
    382–383, 398, 400–401
  and language development, 288–289,
    314–326
  and perceptual development, 204–221
  and physical development, 187–195
Need for achievement (n Ach), 502–503,
  505
Need for social approval, 57
Negative reinforcement:
  in coercive home environments, 499
  compared with punishment, 250
Neo-Hullian theory, 56–57
Neonatal assessment, 158–160
Neonate:
  behavioral capabilities of, 161–163
  cognitive capabilities of, 62–63, 338,
    344
  defined, 127
  learning capabilities of, 247, 251–252,
    268–269
  methods of soothing, 169–170
  perceptual capabilities of, 205–208,
    213, 214–215, 217–219
  sensory capabilities of, 162–165
  states of consciousness, 165–166
  temperamental differences, 169–170
Neurons, 173–174
Neurotic disorders, 108–109
Nonimpulsives, 585
Nonrepresentative sample, 28–29
Nonreversal shift, 276, 277
Nonverbal gestures, and communication:
  in animals, 285, 320–322
  among deaf children, 302–303
  among infants and toddlers, 298, 302
Normal distribution, defined, 389
Norm of social responsibility, 489
Nuclear family, 602, 603
Nutrition:
  and intellectual development,

Nutrition (contd)
  128–129, 190
  and physical development, 189–191,
    192–193, 194
  and prenatal development, 127–129,
    140

Obesity, 191, 192–193
Object concept:
  and attachment, 438
  defined, 341
  development of, 341–343, 344
  and self-recognition, 469
Object permanence (see Object concept)
Oblique effect, 233–234
Observational learning:
  of achievement expectancies, 504
  of aggression, 265–266, 498, 680
  of altruism, 16–17, 491
  Bandura's theory of, 59–60, 264–269,
    273
  compared with trial-and-error learning,
    264
  defined, 55, 264, 265
  of delay of gratification, 584–585
  developmental trends, 268–269
  and language development, 264, 288,
    315–316
  and the learning/performance
    distinction, 265–266
  and moral behavior, 577
  and moral reasoning, 568
  peers as models for, 679–680
  of sex-typed attributes, 534–535, 536
  of social skills, 486
  television and, 22, 23–24, 25, 269–272,
    536, 646–657
  as a therapeutic technique, 272
Observer bias, 16–17
Observer reliability, 17, 604
Obstetrical forceps, 146
Obstetric medications, 146–148
Oddity learning:
  defined, 274, 275
  development of, 275
  theories of, 277, 278
Oedipal morality, 557–558, 559
Oedipus complex:
  defined, 49
  and moral development, 48, 557–558
  and sex typing, 48, 533–534
Open classroom, 663–664
Open-class words, 300
Operant conditioning:
  vs. classical conditioning, 247
  defined, 55, 247
  developmental trends, 251–252
  and language development, 288,
    314–315
  principles of, 249–259
Operant-learning theory, 57–58, 247–259
Operational schema, 336–337 (see also
  Cognitive operations)
Oral stage, 46–47, 435
Ordinal position, 626–627 (see also Birth
  order)
Ordinal-position hypothesis, of
  sociability, 484, 485
Organization:
  in information-processing theory,
    364–370

Organization (contd)
in Piaget's theory, 63–64, 337–338
Original sin, 11, 40
Overextension, 296, 297
Overregularization, 306, 307
Ovists, 77
Ovulation, 78–79

Parental control:
effects on children, 614–616
patterns of, 614
social-class differences in, 622
Parenting:
children's impressions of, 619
effects on preschool children, 613–619
goals of, 602–605
and indirect parental effects, 612–613
and infant development, 449–451,
610–613
infant's effect on, 608, 609–610
and perceptual development, 235
in reconstituted families, 631
in single-parent families, 628–630
social-class differences, 619–623
stress and, 620, 628–629, 634–635
transition to parenthood, 610
Parents Anonymous, 636, 637
Parity effect, in prenatal development,
127–128
Partial reinforcement:
vs. continuous reinforcement, 253
defined, 253
effect, 253–254, 255
inconsistent punishment and, 261
schedules of, 254–256
Patience:
defined, 584, 585
development of, 588–592
labeling and, 590
self-instructions and, 588–590
theories of, 587–588
Pattern perception, 205–207
Peer groups:
vs. adults as influence agents, 680,
683–687
characteristics of, 674–675
cross-cultural studies of, 685–687
defined, 681
formation of, 681
normative function of, 681–683
"Peer only" monkeys, 675
Peer relations (see Peers; Popularity,
determinants of)
Peers:
contacts with, and social competence,
675–677
defined, 673, 674
frequency of contacts with, 674
impact on moral reasoning, 561
popularity with, 678–679
as reinforcing agents, 677–679
as social models, 267, 271, 272,
679–681
as teachers, 682
Pendulum problem, 355
Perception:
defined, 203
development of, during childhood,
221–229
environmental influences on, 229–237
of faces 207–210

Perception (contd)
of forms, 209, 224–229
of patterns, 204–207
and reading, 228
of spatial relations, 210–213, 236–237
of speech and voices, 214–215
of music, 215
Perceptual learning:
defined, 227
Gibson's theory of, 226–228
Perceptual schema, 207, 209, 210, 225
"Perceptual sets," and spatial perception,
237
Permissiveness/restrictiveness, 613–614
(see also Parental control;
Warmth/hostility; Discipline)
Permissive parenting, 614–616
Permissive teacher (see Laissez-faire
teacher)
Perspective cues, 210, 211, 231
Phallic stage, 47–49
Phenotype:
defined, 85
relation to genotype, 84–89, 109–111
Phenylketonuria (PKU), 94, 98–99
Phocomelia, 135
Phonemes, 286, 287
Phonics method, of reading instruction,
228
Phonology:
defined, 286, 287
development of, 290–291, 323, 324
Physical development:
in adolescence, 179–187
biological contributors to, 187–189
of the brain and nervous system,
173–177
changes in body proportions, 171–172
changes in height and weight, 170–171
environmental influences on, 189–195
of the muscles, 172–173, 176, 179,
181, 195
psychological consequences of,
184–187
secular trends, 183–184
sex differences, 173, 179, 180, 181–182
of the skeleton, 172
Piaget's theory of intellectual
development:
basic assumptions, 62–64, 334–338
definition of intelligence, 62, 334, 335,
383
evaluation of, 358–360
vs. information-processing theory, 373
stages of, 65, 338–358
Piaget's theory of moral development:
evaluation of, 561–563
stages of, 559–561
Pincer grip, 177
Pituitary, and physical development,
188–189
Pivotal grammar, 300
Pivot-class words, 300
Placenta, 120–121, 131
Placental barrier, 120, 127, 131, 132
Play:
and cognitive development, 346–357
and social cognition, 481–482
Pleasure principle, 45
Pleiotropic allele, 86
Pointing, and language development, 302

Polygenic traits, 89
Poly-X syndrome, 90–91
Popularity, determinants of, 7–8,
185–187, 479–480, 678–679
Positive reinforcement, 250
Postconventional morality:
cognitive development and, 569–570
defined, 565
development of, 565–566, 567–568,
569
examples of, 566–567
Postmature babies, 150, 151
Postpartum depression, 143–144
Power-assertive discipline:
and altruism, 494
defined, 494, 495
and moral development, 579–580, 618
Practice, and motor development,
194–195
Pragmatics:
defined, 288, 289
development of, 292–293, 301–304,
309–310, 312–314
Preadapted characteristics, 438–439
Preconceptual period, of intellectual
development, 345–347
Preconventional morality:
defined, 564, 565
developmental trends, 565–566
examples of, 566–567
Preformationist theory (see Doctrine of
preformationism)
Prejudice:
defined, 247
development of, 246
school desegregation and, 671–672
Prelinguistic stage, of language
development:
and child's understanding of
meaningful speech, 292–294
defined, 289
and phonological development,
290–291
as preparation for meaningful speech,
292–294
Preliterate society, defined, 603
Premack principle, 256–257, 258
Premoral period, 559
Prenatal development:
altitude and, 139
defined, 117
germinal period, 118–119
maternal age and, 125–126
mother's emotional state and, 126–127
nutrition and, 127–129
parity and, 126
period of the embryo, 119–122
period of the fetus, 122–124
sexual intercourse and, 139–140
teratogens and, 129–139
Preoperational stage:
children's intellectual capabilities,
349–351
children's intellectual deficits,
345–349
defined, 65, 345
substages of, 345–349
Primary circular reactions:
defined, 339
and development of self-concept,
468–469

Primary mental abilities, 384
Primary reinforcer, 251
Private self:
    defined, 470, 471
    development of, 471–473
Problem-finding stage, 357
Production deficiency:
    in concept learning, 277
    defined, 277, 367
    recall memory and, 366, 367
Productive language, defined, 294, 295
Progesterone, 134, 136–137, 188, 189
Proprioception, 221
Prosocial behavior, defined, 23
Prosocial television:
    and children's aggression, 654
    defined, 649
    and prosocial behavior, 22, 23–24,
        271–272, 653–654
Protein/calorie deficiency, 190–191
Proximodistal development, 171–172,
    174, 176
Psychoanalytic theory:
    of achievement, 502
    of aggression, 494
    of attachment, 435–436, 440
    evaluation of, 49–50, 52–53
    of moral development, 557–558
    principles of, 13, 43–53
    research methods, 44
    and self-concept, 468, 470, 474, 475,
        476–477
    of separation anxiety, 444–445
    of sex typing, 532–534
    of stranger anxiety, 442–443
Psycholinguist, defined, 291
Psychological comparisons phase, of
    impression formation, 478
Psychological constructs phase, of
    impression formation, 478
Psychosexual development, stages of,
    46–49, 52–53
Psychosocial crises, (see Psychosocial
    development)
Psychosocial development, stages of,
    50–53, 470, 474, 475, 476–477
Puberty (see also Sexual maturation):
    defined, 179
    physical indications of, 180
Public self:
    defined, 470, 471
    vs. private self, 470–471, 472–473
Punishment:
    alternatives to, 263–264
    and child abuse, 263, 635
    child as determinant of, 263
    consistency of, and effectiveness, 261,
        576
    defined, 55, 250, 251
    intensity of, and effectiveness, 261, 576
    and moral behavior, 575–577
    vs. reinforcement, 250, 251, 261, 263
    timing of, and effectiveness, 261, 576
    undesirable effects of, 262–263
    verbal rationales for, and effectiveness,
        262, 575–577
    and warmth of punitive agent, 262, 576
Punishment and obedience, stage of,
    564–566
Pupillary reflex, 162–163
Pygmalion effect, 666, 667

Quasi-experiment, 24–25
Questionnaire technique, 13

Race:
    and choice of friends, 671–672
    and IQ, 460–463
    soothability and, 170
    stereotyping of, on television, 651
Radiation:
    and mutations, 94
    and prenatal development, 138, 140
Radical behaviorism (see
    Operant-learning theory)
Random assignment, 22–23
Range-of-reaction principle, 111
Rate of maturation:
    heritability of, 187
    and personality development, 186–187
Raven Progressive Matrices Test,
    408–409
Reading:
    cognitive development and, 353
    cognitive style and, 374
    methods of instruction, 228
    perceptual development and, 227, 228
Realism, and moral reasoning, 560, 561
Reality principle, 45
Recall memory:
    defined, 365
    development of, 366–369
Recasting, 318–319
Receptive language, defined, 294, 295
Recessive allele, 84–85
Reciprocal determinism, 59, 607
Reciprocal punishment, 560, 561
Recognition memory, 365–366
Reconstituted families, 609, 631
Referential communication accuracy, 403
Referential communicators, 295
Reflectivity, 373–374
Reflexes:
    adaptive significance of, 63, 161–163
    as contributors to attachment, 429, 430,
        439
    defined, 161
    innate, 63, 161–163
    and intellectual development, 63,
        339–340
    and neonatal status, 159–160
    and sudden infant death syndrome
        (SIDS), 167
Regression, defined, 48
Rehearsal, 364–366
Reinforcement:
    and achievement motivation, 505
    of aggression, 499–500, 677–678
    of altruism, 489–490
    and attachment, 436–438
    defined, 55, 249
    information value of, 256, 258, 259
    and language development, 288,
        314–315
    and locus of control, 507
    and moral development, 574–575
    and observational learning, 265–267
    and oddity learning, 275, 277, 279
    and peer popularity, 678
    primary, 57, 251
    vs. punishment, 250–251, 262, 263
    and reversal/nonreversal
        discriminations, 276

Reinforcement (contd)
    schedules of, 253–256
    secondary, 57, 251
    and sex typing, 534–535
    and shaping of complex responses,
        252–253
    use in social-skills training, 486, 487
    theories of, 256–260
    timing of, 253
    value of, 256
Reliability of IQ tests, 394 (see also
    Observer reliability)
REM sleep, 166–167
Representational stage, of perceptual
    development, 224–225
Repression, 46, 47
Research ethics, 32–36
Research methods:
    in behavior genetics, 99–101
    in cognitive-development research,
        336, 371–372
    in developmental psychology, 14–36
    in family research, 604–605
Respiratory distress syndrome (see
    Hyaline membrane disease)
Response-cost technique, 263
Reticular formation, 174, 224, 225
Retrieval processes, 368–369
Reversal shift (reversal learning),
    275–277
Reversibility, 336, 337, 349, 350–351
Rh disease, 131–133, 140
RH factor, 132–133
Rhogram, 132, 133
Role taking:
    and aggression 496, 501
    and altruism, 481, 493
    cognitive development and, 479, 481
    defined, 479
    and friendship formation, 481
    and moral reasoning, 561, 569
    and popularity, 479, 481, 678
    and social cognition, 479
    social experience and, 481–482, 561
    in social-skills training, 487
    stages of, 480
Rooting reflex, 161, 165, 252
Rouge test, 469
Rubber-band hypothesis, 109–110
Rubella, 131, 133, 140
Rule-assessment approach, to
    problem-solving research, 371–373

s, 384–385
Schema:
    defined, 63, 335
    development of, 337–338
    varieties of, 335–337
Schizophrenia, 108–109
Scholastic achievement (see also
    Schools; Teachers):
    ability tracking and, 661–662
    achievement expectancies and, 504
    class size and, 661
    compensatory education and, 413–415
    divorce and, 628
    in effective and ineffective schools,
        659–660, 665
    grade retention and, 670–671
    home environment and, 503–504
    IQ and, 393–394

Scholastic achievement (contd)
   locus of control and, 506
   mainstreaming and, 662
   monetary resources and, 660–661
   school desegregation and, 672
   teachers and, 666–668, 669
   textbooks and, 668–669
Schools (see also Teachers):
   and cognitive development, 658–659
   education of handicapped children,
      662
   effectiveness of, 660–665
   desegregation of, 670–672
   functions of, 658
   as a middle-class institution, 668–670
Scientific method, 14–15
Secondary circular reaction:
   defined, 339
   self-concept and, 468–469
Secondary reinforcer, 56–57, 251, 436
Secure attachment:
   defined, 449
   development of, 449, 454–455
   long-term correlates of, 451–452,
      483–484, 503
   stability of, 452
   and stranger anxiety, 451
Secure-base phenomenon:
   defined, 443
   father's part in, 450
   and separation anxiety, 445–446
   and stranger anxiety, 443
"Security of attachment" hypothesis,
   483–484
Selective attention:
   defined, 223
   development of, 222–223, 362
   training of, 362–363
Selective-breeding experiments, 99–100,
   398
Self (see also Self-concept; Self-esteem):
   defined, 467
   development of, 468–475
Self-actualization goal, of parenting,
   602–605
Self-concept:
   in adolescence, 472–473
   cognitive development and, 469, 472,
      475
   defined, 469
   during grade school, 472–473
   during infancy, 468–469
   during the preschool period, 469–471
Self-control (see also Delay of
      gratification):
   defined, 556, 557
   development of, 580–593
Self-esteem:
   androgyny and, 546–547
   defined, 473
   development of, 474–475
   facial attractiveness and, 679
   grade retention and, 671
   of pupils in desegregated schools, 672
Self-fulfilling prophecy, 185
Self-instructional technique:
   as an alternative to punishment, 264,
      265
   and delay of gratification, 588–590
   and moral behavior, 577–578
Self-recognition, development of, 469

Self-schemata, 469
Semantic-features hypothesis, 296–297
Semantic (functional) grammar, 300–301
Semantic integration, 311
Semantics:
   defined, 287
   development of, 296–298, 300–301,
      308–309, 311–313
Sensation:
   defined, 203
   in neonates, 162–165, 203
Sensitive period:
   for emotional bonding, 428–429
   for language development, 324
   for social development of monkeys,
      456
Sensorimotor schema (see Behavioral
      schema)
Sensorimotor stage:
   defined, 65, 338, 339
   and object permanence, 341–343
   overview of, 342, 344
   substages of, 338–341
Sensory dominance, 220–221
Sensory integration, 217–220
Sensory register, 363, 364
Separation anxiety:
   defined, 444, 445
   developmental trends, 444
   methods of reducing, 446–447
   theories of, 444–446
Seriation, 353, 354
Sesame Street, 25, 271, 652, 654–657
Sex differences (see also Sex-role
      stereotypes):
   in achievement expectancies, 504
   in aggression, 497, 519, 529–530
   in altruism, 488–489
   in cognitive performance, 519, 521,
      530
   in developmental disorders, 528
   in discipline received, 622
   in field dependence/independence, 235
   in moral reasoning, 570–571, 572–573
   in physical development, 173, 179,
      180, 181–182, 527, 531–532
   in reactions to custodial fathers, 630
   in reactions to divorce, 628
   in reactions to stepfathers, 631
   in sex typing, 518, 523–525
Sex hormones:
   and physical development, 188–189
   and prenatal development, 122, 134,
      135–136, 529, 530–531
Sex instincts, and psychosexual
      development, 46–50
Sex-linked characteristics, 87–88
"Sex-reversed" individuals, 546
Sex roles, development of, 515–548 (see
      also Sex differences; Sex typing)
Sex-role standards, 516–518
Sex-role stereotypes:
   accurate beliefs, 519–520
   development of, 19, 522, 523, 538–539
   and impression formation, 520–522
   overstated beliefs, 520
   parents' contributions to, 521–522
   and playmate selection, 675
   teachers' contributions to, 522
   on television, 536, 651–652
   unfounded beliefs, 521

Sex typing:
   and androgyny, 545–548
   cross-cultural studies of, 517–518, 519,
      523, 530
   defined, 516, 517
   developmental trends, 522–526
   in father-absent homes, 542–545
   maternal employment and, 545
   in mother-dominant homes, 541–542
   peer influences on, 535, 677, 678
   sex differences in, 518, 523–525
   social-class differences in, 525–526,
      543
   stability of, 526, 527
   theories of, 526–540
Sexual intercourse, and prenatal
      development, 139–140
Sexual maturation:
   in boys, 182
   in girls, 181–182
   hormonal influences, 188–189
   individual differences in, 182–183, 187
   psychological impact of, 184–187
   secular trends, 183–184
Shaping:
   defined, 251–252
   as a therapeutic technique, 254–255
Short-gestation (preterm) babies, 148–149
Short-term memory (STM):
   defined, 363
   development of, 364, 365–371
Sibling rivalry, 623–624
Siblings:
   as attachment objects, 625
   as caregivers, 624–625
   character of interactions, 623
   first-born, 626, 627
   and IQ, 404–406
   later-born, 626–627
   as rivals, 623–624
   and sex typing, 536, 626
   as social models, 625
   as teachers and tutees, 625–626
Sickle cell anemia, 87, 98
Signaling responses, 439
Single-parent family(ies):
   and children's IQs, 406
   children's reactions to, 627–630, 631
   defined, 602, 603
   with fathers as custodial parents, 630
   incidence of, 609
   and sex typing, 542–545
Size constancy, 211–213
Skeletal age, 172–173
Sleep:
   developmental changes in, 166–167
   functions of, 166
   and sudden infant death syndrome,
      166–168
   varieties of, 165–166
Small-for-date babies, 148–149
Smiling, and emotional development,
   429, 430–431, 439
Sociability:
   and adjustment in adulthood, 485, 676
   defined, 482, 483
   development in infancy, 482–483
   family contributions to, 484, 485
   as a heritable attribute, 483
   improvement of, 486–487
   nursery school and, 484–485

Sociability (contd)
 ordinal position and, 484, 626
 peer influences on, 675–677, 678–679
 among preschool children, 484–485
 security of attachment and, 483–484
 vs. social attachment, 482
 stability of, 485
Social-class differences:
 in attitudes about schooling, 620,
  668–669
 in IQ, 406–413
 in parenting, 620–623
 in sex typing, 525–526, 543
Social cognition:
 defined, 67, 477
 development of, 477–478
 role taking and, 479, 480, 481
 social interactions and, 481–482
Social-conventional rules, 563
Social deprivation, effects of:
 in human beings, 456–457
 in monkeys, 453–456
 recovery from, 455–456, 459–461
 theoretical explanations for, 457–459
Socialization, defined, 601
Social-learning theory:
 Bandura's model, 58–60, 264–269
 and moral development, 571–578
 neo-Hullian, 56–57
 operant-learning theory, 57–58,
  247–260
 and sex typing, 534–536
Social models (see also Imitation;
  Observational learning):
 child's choice of, 267, 269, 535, 537,
  539–540, 680
 imitator's influence on, 680–681
Social promotions, 669
Social-skills training, 486–487
Social smiling, development of, 430–431
Social-stimulation hypothesis, 458–459
Soviet society, 686–687
Spartan society, 9
Spatial perception:
 cultural influences on, 236–237
 defined, 205
 development of, in infancy, 210–213
 monocular vision and, 231
 movement and, 231–233
 visual deprivation and, 230–231
Stage (see Developmental stage)
Stanford-Binet intelligence tests,
 388–389, 390
States of consciousness, 165–168
Stepparent families (see Reconstituted
 families)
Stepping reflex, 163, 195
Stereopsis, 210, 211
Stereotyping:
 of ethnic minorities, 651, 669
 of males and females, 517, 518–522,
  651
 reduction of, on television, 651–652
Stimulus-deprivation hypothesis, 458
Stimulus generalization, 245, 273
Stranger anxiety:
 defined, 440, 441
 developmental trends, 440
 situational determinants of, 441–442
 theories of, 442–444
"Strange-situations" test, 448, 449

Structured interview, defined, 19
"Structure of intellect" model, 385
Subcortical reflexes, 161–163
Sublimation, 46, 47, 48
Sudden infant death syndrome (SIDS),
 138, 139, 167–168
Superego, defined, 45
"Superfemale" syndrome (see Poly-X
 syndrome)
"Supermale" syndrome, 91
Surrogate mothers, 436–437
Survival goal, of parenting, 602–604
Survival reflexes, 161–162
Swimming reflex, 163
Symbolic function, 345
Symbolic representations, in
 observational learning, 267, 269, 277
Symbolic schema, 335–336
Synchronized routines:
 caregivers' behavior and, 433, 444
 defined, 431
 development of, 430–432
Syntax:
 defined, 287
 development of, 300, 304–308,
  310–311
 use by chimpanzees, 321
Syphilis, 131, 132
Systematic reasoning, 358, 359

Tabula rasa, 11, 40, 54
Tachistoscope, defined, 234, 235
Tay-Sachs disease, 94, 96–97
Tchambuli society, 530
Teachers:
 as contributors to sex-role stereotypes,
  522
 expectancies, and children's
  achievements, 666–667
 impressions of disadvantaged students,
  669
 instructional style, and children's
  achievements, 667–668
 mothers as, 621–622
 peers as, 682
 siblings as, 625–626
Telegraphic speech:
 defining characteristics, 299–300
 semantic analysis of, 300–301
 syntactical properties of, 300
Telegraphic stage, 298–304
Televised violence:
 correlational studies of, 270, 649
 and desensitization, 649–650
 experimental studies of, 649–650
 incidence of, 270, 646–647
 parents' reactions to, 651
 strategies for reducing, 650
Television:
 and academic achievement, 647
 and aggression, 270, 647–651, 653, 654
 attention to and use of, 269, 270,
  646–647
 and changes in family life, 647
 and cognitive development, 271,
  654–705
 and peer interaction, 647, 652–653, 654
 and prosocial behavior, 22, 23–24,
  271–272, 653–654
 and reactions to advertising, 270–271,
  652–653

Television (contd)
 and sex typing, 536, 651, 652
 as a source of stereotypes, 651–652
Temne society, 622
Temperament:
 and attachment, 432–433, 449–450
 defined, 105
 environmental influences, 106–107
 heritability of, 104–105
 individual differences, 105, 169–170
Teratogens:
 defined, 122–123
 effects on prenatal development,
  129–139
Teratology, defined, 129
Tertiary circular reaction, 340, 341
"Test bias" hypothesis, 407–408
Testicular feminization syndrome, 122,
 529
Testosterone:
 and prenatal development, 531–532
 and sexual development in
  adolescents, 188–189
Thalidomide, 135
Thanatos, 45, 494
Theory, defined, 14, 39
Therapist monkeys, 455–456
Third-eye problem, 356–357
Thyroxine, and physical development,
 188, 189
Time-out technique, 263
"Timing of puberty" effect, 530, 531
Toxemia, 133
Toxoplasmosis, 133, 140
Toys, and children's aggression, 501
Traditional classroom, 663–664
Transductive reasoning, 345, 350
Transformational grammar, 306–308
Transitivity, 353, 354
Trinidad society, 585–586
Trophoblast, 118–119
Turner's syndrome, 90–91

Ulnar grasp, 177
Ultrasound, 97, 146
Umbilical cord, 120–121
Unconditioned response (UCR), defined,
 245
Unconditioned stimulus (UCS), defined,
 245
Unconscious motivation, 44, 45, 50
Underextension, 296, 297
"Undifferentiated" individuals, 546
Unitary morality, 578, 579
Unwanted children, 433, 617

Victim-centered discipline (see Inductive
 discipline)
Virtual object, 218, 219
Visual acuity, and perceptual
 development, 207
Visual astigmatism, 230–231
Visual cliff, 210–211, 212, 231, 232
Visual complexity:
 defined, 207
 and pattern perception, 206, 207, 224
Visual cortex, 230, 231
Visual deprivation, and perceptual
 development, 230–231
Visual looming, 212–213
Visual/motor coordination, 177–178, 179

Visual perception, development of:
in childhood, 221–229
in infancy, 204–213, 224
Visual search, development of:
in childhood, 222
in infancy, 208
Vitamin/mineral deficiency, 190–191
Vocables, 291
Vocabulary, development of:
in infancy, 294
in middle childhood, 311

Warmth/hostility:
as contributing to adult depression,
617

Warmth/hostility (*contd*)
defined, 614, 615
effects on children, 616–617
social-class differences in, 622
Wechsler intelligence tests, 389–390
White noise, 217
"Whole" vs. "part" perception, 226, 228
"Whole word" method, of reading
instruction, 228
"Win-stay, lose-shift," 274, 275
Working mothers (*see* Maternal
employment)

X chromosome, 83
XO (*see* Turner's syndrome)

XXX (*see* Poly-X syndrome)
XXY (*see* Klinefelter's syndrome)
XYY (*see* "Supermale" syndrome)

Y chromosome, 83
Yolk sac, 120–121
Younger-peer therapy:
defined, 456, 457
use with children, 460
use with monkeys, 455–456

Zygote, defined, 79

CREDITS

These pages constitute an extension of the copyright page.

CHAPTER ONE. 26, Figure 1-2 adapted from "Age and Verbalization in Observational Learning," by B. Boates and W. W. Hartup, 1969, *Developmental Psychology, 1,* pp. 556–562. Copyright 1969 by the American Psychological Association. Reprinted by permission. **33,** Table 1-3 from *Ethical Principles in the Conduct of Research with Human Participants,* 1973. Copyright 1973 by the American Psychological Association. Reprinted by permission.

CHAPTER TWO. 41, Figure 2-1 from *Perspectives on Social Psychology,* by D. R. Shaffer (Ed.). Copyright © 1977 by Lawrence Erlbaum Associates, Inc. Reprinted by permission of the publisher.

CHAPTER THREE. 93, Table 3-2 adapted from "Genetic Counseling," by S. M. Pueschel and A. Goldstein. In J. L. Matson and J. A. Mulick (Eds.), *Handbook of Mental Retardation,* 1983. Copyright 1983 by Pergamon Press, Inc. Reprinted by permission. **97,** Figure 3-7 based on a figure from "The Genetic Counselor," by S. Begley, J. Carey, and S. Katz, *Newsweek,* March 5, 1984. **100,** Figure 3-8 adapted from *Introduction to Behavioral Genetics,* by G. E. McClearn and J. C. DeFries. W. H. Freeman and Company. Copyright © 1973. **102,** Table 3-4 from "Genetics and Intelligence: A Review," by L. Erlenmeyer-Kimling and F. Jarvik, 1963, *Science,* Vol. 142, *13,* pp. 1477–1479, December, 1963. Copyright 1963 by the AAAS.

CHAPTER FOUR. 126, Figure 4-2 from "Infant Death: An Analysis by Maternal Risk and Health Care," by D. Kessner, 1973, p. 100. Copyright 1973 by the National Academy of Sciences, Washington, D.C. **129,** Figure 4-3 adapted from "Preventing Intellectual and Interactional Sequelae of Fetal Malnutrition: A Longitudinal, Transactional and Synergistic Approach to Development," by P. S. Zeskind and C. T. Ramey, 1981, *Child Development, 52.* © 1981 by The Society for Research in Child Development, Inc. Reprinted by permission. **130,** Figure 4-4 adapted from a figure in *The Developing Human,* by K. L. Moore, 1977, W. B. Saunders.

CHAPTER FIVE. 167, Figure 5-1 from "Ontogenetic Development of the Human Sleep-Dream Cycle," by J. N. Roffwarg and W. C. Muzio, 1966, *Science,* Vol. 152, *29,* pp. 604–619, Copyright 1966 by the AAAS. **173,** Figure 5-5 from "Somatic Development of Adolescent Girls," by M. S. Faust, 1977, *Monographs of the Society for Research in Child Development, 42* (Whole No. 169). © 1977 by The Society for Research in Child Development, Inc. Reprinted by permission. **177,** Table 5-4 adapted from "The Denver Development Screening Test," by W. K. Frankenberg and J. B. Dodds, 1967, *Journal of Pediatrics, 71,* pp. 181–191. **180,** Figure 5-7 from "Motor Development," by A. Espenschlade. In W. R. Johnson (Ed.), *Science and Medicine of Exercise and Sports,* 1960, Harper & Row, Publishers, Inc. **181,** Figure 5-8 based on a figure from *Archives of the Diseases of Child-*

hood, by J. M. Tanner, R. H. Whithouse, and A. Takaishi, 1966, *41,* 454–471. **182,** Figure 5-9 based on a figure from *Archives of the Diseases of Childhood,* by W. A. Marshall and J. M. Tanner, 1970, *45,* 13–23. **185,** Figure 5-10 from "Changes in the Stature and Body Weight of North American Boys during the Last 80 Years," by H. V. Meredith. In L. P. Spiker and C. C. Spiker (Eds.), *Advances in Child Development and Behavior* (Vol. 10). Copyright 1963 by Academic Press, Inc. Reprinted by permission. **190,** Figure 5-12 based on a figure from *Growth at Adolescence* by J. M. Tanner, 1963, Blackwell Scientific Publications, Ltd., London.

CHAPTER SIX. 205, Figure 6-1 from "The Origin of Form Perception," by R. L. Fantz, May 1961, *Scientific American, 204,* 66–72. Copyright © 1961 by Scientific American, Inc. All rights reserved. **206,** Figure 6-2 adapted from "Visual Attention to Size and Number of Pattern Details during the First Six Months," by R. L. Fantz and J. F. Fagan, 1975, *Child Development, 46,* 3–18. © 1975 by the Society for Research in Child Development, Inc. Reprinted by permission. **207,** Figure 6-3 from "Early Visual Selectivity," in R. L. Fantz, J. F. Fagan, and S. B. Miranda. In L. B. Cohen and P. Salapatek (Eds.), *Infant Perception: From Sensation to Cognition.* Copyright © 1975 by Academic Press, Inc. Reprinted by permission. **208,** Box 6-1 adapted from "Pattern Perception in Infancy," by P. Salapatek. In L. B. Cohen and P. Salapatek (Eds.), *Infant Cognition: From Sensation to Perception,* 1975. Copyright 1975 by Academic Press, Inc. Reprinted by permission. **209,** Box 6-2 adapted from "Perception of a Subjective Contour by Infants," by F. Treiber and S. Wilcox, 1980, *Child Development, 51,* 915–917. © 1980 by The Society for Research in Child Development. Reprinted by permission. **213,** Figure 6-5 adapted from "The Visual World of Infants," by T. G. R. Bower, December 1966, *Scientific American, 215,* 80–92. Copyright © 1966 by Scientific American, Inc. All rights reserved. **218,** Figure 6-7 adapted from "Intersensory Interaction in Newborns: Modification of Visual Preferences following Exposure to Sound," by D. J. Lewkowicz and G. Turkewitz, 1981, *Child Development, 52,* pp. 827–832. © 1981 by The Society for Research in Child Development. Reprinted by permission. **222,** Figure 6-9 adapted from a figure in "The Formation and Development of Perceptual Activity," by V. P. Zichenko, Van Chzhi-tsin, and V. Tarakanov, 1963, *Soviet Psychology and Psychiatry, 2,* pp. 3–12. **223,** Figure 6-10 adapted from a figure in "Selective Auditory Attention in Children," by E. E. Maccoby. In L. P. Lipsitt and C. C. Spiker (Eds.), *Advances in Child Development and Behavior.* Copyright 1967 by Academic Press. Reprinted by permission. **225,** Figure 6-11 from a figure in "Perception of Overlapping and Embedded Figures by Children of Different Ages," by L. Ghent, 1956, *American Journal of Psychology, 69,* pp. 575–587, University of Illinois Press. Figure 6-12 adapted from a figure in "Factors Affecting the Visual Recognition of Incomplete Objects: A Comparative Investigation of Children and Adults," by E. S. Gollin, 1962, *Perceptual and Motor Skills, 15,* pp. 583–590. **227,** Figure 6-14 adapted from "A Developmental Study of

V. van de Reit, and J. C. White, 1963, *Monographs of the Society for Research in Child Development, 28* (Serial No. 90). © 1963 by The Society for Research in Child Development. Reprinted by permission. **408,** Table 10-8 adapted from "The Chitling Test" by A. Dove, *Newsweek,* July 15, 1968. **412,** Table 10-9 adapted from "Negro Intelligence and Selective Migration: A Philadelphia Test of the Klineberg Hypothesis," by E. S. Lee, 1951, *American Sociological Review, 15,* pp. 227–233.

CHAPTER ELEVEN. 435, Figure 11-1 from "The Development of Social Attachments in Infancy," by H. R. Shaffer and P. E. Emerson, 1964, *Monographs of the Society for Research in Child Development, 20,* p. 3. © 1964 by The Society for Research in Child Development, Inc. Reprinted by permission. **437,** Figure 11-2 from "Affectional Responses in the Infant Monkey," by H. F. Harlow and R. R. Zimmerman, 1959, *Science, 130,* pp. 421–432. Copyright 1959 by the AAAS. **442,** Figure 11-3 adapted from "Contingent Feedback, Familiarization, and Infant Affect: How a Stranger Becomes a Friend," by M. J. Levitt, 1980, *Developmental Psychology, 16,* pp. 425–432. Copyright 1980 by the American Psychological Association. Reprinted by permission. **448,** Table 11-1 from *Patterns of Attachment,* by M. D. S. Ainsworth, M. Blehar, E. Waters, and S. Wall. Copyright © 1978 by Lawrence Erlbaum Associates, Inc. Reprinted by permission. **451,** Table in Box 11-2 adapted from "The Quality of the Toddler's Relationship to Mother and Father: Related to Conflict Behavior and the Readiness to Establish New Relationships," by A. Main and D. R. Weston, 1981, *Child Development, 52,* pp. 932–940. © 1981 by The Society for Research in Child Development, Inc. Reprinted by permission. **460,** Figure 11-4 adapted from "Rehabilitation of Socially Withdrawn Preschool Children through Mixed-Age and Same-Age Socialization," by D. F. Rahe and W. W. Hartup, 1979, *Child Development,* pp. 915–922. © 1979 by The Society for Research in Child Development, Inc. Reprinted by permission.

CHAPTER TWELVE. 477, Figure in Box 12-1 adapted from "Cross-Sectional Age Changes in Ego Identity Status during Adolescence," by P. W. Meilman, 1979, *Developmental Psychology, 15,* pp. 230–231. Copyright 1979 by the American Psychological Association. Reprinted by permission. **478,** Figure 12-2 adapted from "The Development of Person Perception in Childhood and Adolescence: From Behavioral Comparisons to Psychological Constructs, to Psychological Comparisons," by C. Barenboim, 1981, *Child Development, 52,* pp. 129–144. © 1981 by The Society for Research in Child Development, Inc. Reprinted by permission. **480,** Table 12-1 adapted from "Social-Cognitive Understanding: A Guide to Educational and Clinical Experience," by R. L. Selman. In T. Lickona (Ed.), *Moral Development and Behavior: Theory, Research, and Social Issues,* 1976, Holt, Rinehart & Winston. **481,** Table 12-2 adapted from "Development of Physical and Social Reasoning in Adolescence," by K. P. Keating and L. V. Clark, 1980, *Developmental Psychology, 16,* pp. 23–30. Copyright 1980 by the American Psychological Association. Reprinted by permission. **490,** Figure in Box 12-2 based on data described in "Positive Socialization via Cooperative Games," by T. Orlick, 1981, *Developmental Psychology, 17.* Copyright 1981 by the American Psychological Association. **493,** Figure 12-3 adapted from "Effect of Inducing Sadness about

Self or Other on Helping Behavior in High and Low Empathetic Children," by M. A. Barnett, J. A. Howard, E. M. Melton, and G. A. Dino, 1982, *Child Development, 53,* pp. 920–923. © 1982 by The Society for Research in Child Development. Reprinted by permission. **503,** Table 12-4 adapted from "The Relationship between Twelve-Month Home Stimulation and School Achievement," by W. J. van Doorninck, B. M. Caldwell, C. Wright, and W. K. Frankenberg, 1981, *Child Development, 52,* pp. 1080–1083. © 1981 by The Society for Research in Child Development. Reprinted by permission.

CHAPTER THIRTEEN. 518, Table 13-1 adapted from "Sex-Role Stereotypes: A Current Appraisal," by I. K. Broverman, S. R. Vogel, F. E. Clarkson, and P. S. Rosenkrantz, 1972, *Journal of Social Issues, 28,* pp. 59–78. Copyright 1972 by the Society for the Psychological Study of Social Issues. Used by permission. **519,** Table 13-2 adapted from "A Cross-Cultural Survey of Some Sex Differences in Socialization," by H. Barry III, M. K. Bacon, and I. L. Child, 1957, *Journal of Abnormal and Social Psychology, 55,* pp. 327–332. Copyright 1957 by the American Psychological Association. **521,** Table 13-3 adapted from *The Psychology of Sex Differences,* by Eleanor Emmons Maccoby and Carol Nagy Jacklin. Copyright © 1974 by Stanford University Press. Reprinted by permission of the Board of Trustees of the Leland Stanford Junior University. **524,** Figure 13-1 adapted from "Social Behavior at 33 Months in Same-Sex and Mixed-Sex Dyads," by C. N. Jacklin and E. E. Maccoby, 1978, *Child Development, 49,* pp. 557–569. © The Society for Research in Child Development, Inc. Reprinted by permission. **525,** Cartoon *Berry's World* reprinted by permission. © 1973 NEA, Inc. **527,** Figure 13-2 adapted from *Birth to Maturity* by K. Kagan and H. A. Moss, 1962, John Wiley & Sons. **532,** Figure 13-3 adapted from *Man and Woman, Boy and Girl,* 1972, Johns Hopkins University Press.

CHAPTER FOURTEEN. 562, Figures 14-1 and 14-2 adapted from "Factors Influencing Young Children's Use of Motives and Outcomes as Moral Criteria," by S. A. Nelson, 1980, *Child Development, 51,* pp. 823–829. © 1980 by The Society for Research in Child Development. Reprinted by permission. **566,** Figure 14-3 from "A Longitudinal Study of Moral Judgment," by A. Colby, L. Kohlbert, J. Gibbs, and M. Lieberman, 1983, *Monographs of the Society for Research in Child Development, 48.* © 1983 by The Society for Research in Child Development. Reprinted by permission. **566,** Figure 14-3 from "A Longitudinal Study of Moral Judgment," by A. Colby, L. Kohlbert, J. Gibbs, and M. Lieberman, 1983, *Monographs of the Society for Research in Child Development, 48.* © 1983 by The Society for Research in Child Development. Reprinted by permission. **579,** Table 14-2 adapted from "Contributions of Parents and Peers to Children's Moral Socialization," by G. H. Brody and D. R. Shaffer, 1982, *Developmental Review, 2,* pp. 31–75. **581,** Figure 14-4 adapted from "Verbal Control of Behavior: The Effects of Shouting," by E. Saltz, S. Campbell, and D. Skotko, 1983, *Developmental Psychology, 19,* pp. 461–464. Copyright 1983 by the American Psychological Association. Reprinted by permission. **583,** Figures in Box 14-3 adapted from "Reasoning, Prohibitions, and Motivations for Compliance," by L. Kuczynski, 1983, *Developmental Psychology, 19,* pp. 126–134. Copyright 1983 by the American Psychological Association. Reprinted by permission. **586,** Table in Box

PHOTO CREDITS

CHAPTER ONE. 2, (both) Frank Keillor; **3,** (both) Frank Keillor; **4,** Frank Keillor; **9,** Museum of Fine Arts, Boston; **15,** Constantine Manos, Magnum Photos, Inc.; **23,** Magnum Photos, Inc.; **29,** (left) Brown Brothers; (right) J. R. Hollard, Stock Boston, Inc.; **31,** Ken Heyman

CHAPTER TWO. 38, Frank Keillor; **44,** Historical Pictures; **47,** Elizabeth Crews; **57,** Harvard University News Office; **59,** Albert Bandura, Stanford University; **61,** Bill Anderson; **62,** Inge Morath, Magnum Photos, Inc.; **68,** Wayne Miller, Magnum Photos, Inc.

CHAPTER THREE. 72, (left) J. P. Revel, Caltech; (right) Frank Keillor; **73,** (both) Frank Keillor; **74,** Mary Ellen Mark, Archive Pictures, Inc.; **77,** Dr. G. F. Bahr, Armed Forces Institute of Pathology; **83,** (left) Elizabeth Crews; (right) Nancy Hays, Monkmeyer Press Photo Service; **84,** (both) Drs. U. Fraucke, N. Oliver, Phototake; **87,** R. M. Zucker, B. F. Cameron, and R. C. Leif/BPS; **90,** Dr. John Money, Sex Errors of the Body, The Johns Hopkins University Press; **92,** Elizabeth Crews, Stock Boston, Inc.; **105,** Hazel Hankin, Stock Boston, Inc.

CHAPTER FOUR. 116, Martin Rotker, Taurus Photos; **118,** J. P. Revel, Caltech; **120–125,** Dr. Landrum Shettles; **135,** Leonard McCombe, LIFE magazine, © 1968, Time, Inc.; **136,** James W. Hanson, M.D.; **137,** Jim Anderson, Stock Boston, Inc.; **145,** © Suzanne Arms, Jeroboam, Inc.; **149,** James Holland, Stock Boston, Inc.; **151,** Micky Pfleger

CHAPTER FIVE. 156, Frank Keillor; **159,** © Suzanne Arms, Jeroboam, Inc.; **161,** (left) Elizabeth Crews; (middle) Elizabeth Crews; (right) Ellis Herwig, Stock Boston, Inc.; **164,** George Malave, Stock Boston, Inc.; **169,** Anna Kaufman Moon, Stock Boston, Inc.; **179,** Elizabeth Crews; **183,** Donald Dietz, Stock Boston, Inc.; **191,** Chris Steele-Perkins, Magnum Photos, Inc.; **193,** © James Motlow, Jeroboam, Inc.

CHAPTER SIX. 200, (both) Frank Keillor; **201,** (both) Frank Keillor; **202,** Frank Keillor; **204,** David Linton from *Scientific American;* **212,** William Vandivert from *Scientific American;* **216,** George Malave, Stock Boston, Inc.; **217,** © Eileen Christelow, Jeroboam, Inc.; **229,** Linda Marcetti; **234,** © Don Ivers, Jeroboam, Inc.

CHAPTER SEVEN. 242, Frank Keillor; **245,** The Bettmann Archive, Inc.; **248,** ©Vince Companone, Jeroboam, Inc.; **255,** Roswell Angier, Archive Pictures, Inc.; **258,** © Eileen Christelow, Jeroboam, Inc.; **264,** Peter Menzel, Stock Boston, Inc.; **266,** "Imitation of Film-Mediated Aggressive Models," by A. Bandura, D. Ross and S. A. Ross, 1963, *Journal of Abnormal and Social Psychology, 66,* 3–11. Copyright 1981 by the American Psychological Association. Reprinted by permission.; **268,** Paul Conklin, Monkmeyer Press Photo Service

CHAPTER EIGHT. 284, Frank Keillor; **286,** Richard Wranghan, Anthro Photo; **287,** Elizabeth Hamlin, Stock Boston, Inc.; **294,** Elizabeth Crews; **301,** Elizabeth Crews; **310,** Christopher W. Morrow, Stock Boston, Inc,; **317,** © Irene Kane, Jeroboam, Inc.; **320,** Paul Fusco, Magnum Photos, Inc.

CHAPTER NINE. 332, Frank Keillor; **336,** Burt Glinn, Magnum Photos, Inc.; **339,** Grete Mannheim, DPI, Inc.; **342,** Peter Vandermark, Stock Boston, Inc.; **355,** Elizabeth Crews; **362,** Elizabeth Crews

CHAPTER TEN, 380, Frank Keillor; **382,** The Bettmann Archive, Inc.; **387,** The Bettmann Archive, Inc.; **403,** (left) Karen Rosenthal, Stock Boston, Inc.; (right) Bruce Davidson, Magnum Photos, Inc.; **404,** Judy Mason

CHAPTER ELEVEN. 422, (both) Frank Keillor; **423,** (both) Frank Keillor; **424,** Frank Keillor; **426,** Jean-Claude Lejune, Stock Boston, Inc.; **430,** Elizabeth Crews; **434,** © Michael Rothstein, Jeroboam, Inc.; **436,** University of Wisconsin Primate Laboratory; **440,** Chester Higgins, Photo Researchers, Inc.; **445,** Ken Heyman; **447,** Michael Kagan, Monkmeyer Press Photo Service; **450,** Elizabeth Crews; **453,** University of Wisconsin Primate Laboratory; **457,** © Suzanne Arms, Jeroboam, Inc.

CHAPTER TWELVE. 466, Frank Keillor; **469,** Inge Morath, Magnum Photos, Inc.; **471,** Owen Franken, Stock Boston, Inc.; **474,** Elizabeth Crews; **482,** David S. Strickler, Monkmeyer Press Photo Service; **487–491,** David Shaffer; **496,** Ulrike Welsch, Stock Boston, Inc.; **502–506,** David Shaffer

CHAPTER THIRTEEN. 514, Frank Keillor; **516,** Michael Weisbrot, Stock Boston, Inc.; **519,** Paul S. Conklin, Monkmeyer Press Photo Service; **528–535,** David Shaffer; **542,** Donald Dietz, Stock Boston, Inc.; **547,** (both) David Shaffer

CHAPTER FOURTEEN. 554, Frank Keillor; **556,** Christopher S. Johnson, Stock Boston, Inc.; **560,** David Shaffer; **574,** Paul Fusco, Magnum Photos, Inc.; **578,** © Eileen Christelow, Jeroboam, Inc.; **589,** David Shaffer

CHAPTER FIFTEEN. 598, (both) Frank Keillor; **599,** (both) Frank Keillor; **600,** Frank Keillor; **606,** Ken Heyman; **607,** Jean-Claude Lejune, Stock Boston, Inc.; **613,** Elizabeth Crews; **616,** Danny Lyon, Magnum Photos, Inc.; **624,** Elizabeth Crews; **625,** Robert V. Eckert, Jr., Stock Boston, Inc.; **629,** Mimi Forsyth, Monkmeyer Press Photo Service; **633,** Eugene Richards, Magnum Photos, Inc.; **636,** San Francisco Child Abuse Council, Inc.

CHAPTER SIXTEEN. 644, Frank Keillor; **648,** Mimi Forsyth, Monkmeyer Press Photo Service; **650,** Arthur Tress, Magnum Photos, Inc.; **654,** © 1984 Children's Television Workshop. Muppet characters, © 1984 Muppets, Inc. Courtesy of Children's Television Workshop; **664,** Kira Godbe; **669,** Nancy Hays, Monkmeyer Press Photo Service; **675,** University of Wisconsin Primary Laboratory; **677,** Elizabeth Crews; **684,** Charles Gatewood, Stock Boston, Inc.; **686,** Boris Erwitt, Photo Researchers, Inc.